The Law of
Higher Education

William A. Kaplin

Barbara A. Lee

The Law of Higher Education

A Comprehensive Guide to Legal Implications of Administrative Decision Making

VOLUME I

FOURTH EDITION

JOSSEY-BASS
A Wiley Imprint
www.josseybass.com

Published by Jossey-Bass
A Wiley Imprint
989 Market Street, San Francisco, CA 94103-1741   www.josseybass.com

Jossey-Bass books and products are available through most bookstores. To contact Jossey-Bass directly call our Customer Care Department within the U.S. at 800-956-7739, outside the U.S. at 317-572-3986, or fax 317-572-4002.

Jossey-Bass also publishes its books in a variety of electronic formats. Some content that appears in print may not be available in electronic books.

ISBN-10: 0-7879-7094-8
ISBN-13: 978-0-7879-7094-9

Library of Congress Cataloging-in-Publication Data

Kaplin, William A.
    The law of higher education / William A. Kaplin, Barbara A. Lee. — 4th ed.
        v. cm.
    Includes bibliographical references and index.
    Contents: Overview of higher education law—Legal planning and dispute resolution—The college and its trustees and officers—The college and its employees—Nondiscrimination and affirmative action in employment—Faculty employment issues—Faculty academic freedom and freedom of expression—Rights and responsibilities of individual students—Rights and responsibilities of student organizations and their members—Local governments and the local community—The college and the state government—The college and the federal government—The college and the education associations (on website)—The college and the business/industrial community (on website).
    ISBN-10: 0-7879-8659-3 (cloth)
    ISBN-13: 978-0-7879-8659-9 (cloth)
    1. Universities and colleges—Law and legislation—United States. 2. School management and organization—Law and legislation—United States. 3. Universities and colleges—United States—Administration. I. Lee, Barbara A. II. Title.
    KF4225.K36 2006
    344.73'074—dc22
                                    2006010076

Printed in the United States of America
FIRST EDITION
HB Printing   10 9 8 7 6 5 4 3 2 1

The Jossey-Bass
Higher and Adult Education Series

Notice to Instructors

A Student Edition of *The Law of Higher Education,* Fourth Edition, will be published shortly after this Fourth Edition is published, as will a compilation of teaching materials for classroom use by instructors and students. In addition, a Web site supporting the Fourth Edition and the Student Edition will be accessible to instructors and students and will include information on new legal developments, edited versions of new cases, and other materials. The Web site will be hosted by the National Association of College and University Attorneys (NACUA), and will be available at http://www.nacua.org. There will also be an Instructor's Manual available only to instructors, which will be available on the Web site of Jossey-Bass (http://www.Josseybass.com).

The Law of Higher Education, Student Edition, will be approximately one-half the length of the Fourth Edition and will contain material from the Fourth Edition that has been carefully selected by the authors for its particular relevance for classroom instruction. It will also include a new Preface and Introduction directed specifically to students and instructors. This Student Edition will be available from Jossey-Bass, Inc., Publishers in the spring or summer of 2007. Direct inquiries and orders to:

Jossey-Bass, A Wiley Imprint
Customer Service
10475 Crosspoint Blvd.
Indianapolis, IN 46256
800-956-7739

The compilation of teaching materials—*Cases, Problems, and Materials for Use with The Law of Higher Education, Fourth Edition*—is for instructors and students in courses on higher education law, as well as for leaders and participants in workshops that address higher education legal issues. This compilation contains court opinions carefully edited by the authors and keyed to the Student Edition, notes and questions about the cases, short problems designed to elicit discussion on particular issues, a series of "large-scale" problems suitable for role playing, and guidelines for analyzing and answering all the problems. The compilation will be available from the National Association of College and University Attorneys, which will also publish periodic supplements to the Fourth Edition and the Student Edition, and will host the Web site for these books. *Cases, Problems, and Materials* will be available in electronic format that can be downloaded from NACUA's Web site and in hard copies available for purchase at cost from NACUA (see below). Any instructor who has adopted the Student Edition or the full Fourth Edition as a required course text may download a copy of *Cases, Problems, and Materials,* or selected portions of it, free of charge and reproduce the materials for distribution to the students in the course. No other reproduction, distribution, or transmission is permitted. For hard copies, direct inquiries and orders to:

Manager of Publications
National Association of College and University Attorneys
Suite 620, One Dupont Circle, NW
Washington, DC 20036
(202) 833-8390; Fax (202) 296-8379

Further instructions for downloading or purchasing *Cases, Problems, and Materials* are on the NACUA Web site.

Notice of Web Site and Periodic Supplements for the Fourth Edition

The authors, in cooperation with the publisher, have made arrangements for two types of periodic updates for the Fourth Edition. First, the National Association of College and University Attorneys (NACUA) has generously agreed to host a Web site for *The Law of Higher Education,* Fourth Edition, whose purpose is to provide citations and brief updates on major new developments in a relatively informal format. This Web site may be accessed through the NACUA Web site at http://www.nacua.org. Second, the authors intend to prepare periodic supplements *to The Law of Higher Education,* Fourth Edition, as feasible. NACUA has also agreed to publish such supplements and to have them available for purchase in hard copy. Further directions for accessing the Fourth Edition Web site and for purchasing periodic supplements will appear on the NACUA Web site. Both of these updating services for users of the Fourth Edition are intended as a response to the law's dynamism—to the rapid and frequent change that occurs as courts, legislatures, government agencies, and private organizations develop new requirements, revise or eliminate old requirements, and devise new ways to regulate and influence institutions of higher education.

Contents

VOLUME II

9 Rights and Responsibilities of Individual Students   910

Preface

Overview of the Fourth Edition

Operating the colleges and universities of today presents a multitude of challenges for their leaders and personnel. Often the issues they face involve institutional policy, but with continually increasing frequency these issues have legal implications as well. For example, a staff member may decide to become a whistleblower and assert that another college employee is violating the law. If the complaining staff member's performance has been problematic, may the college discharge the staff member? A student religious organization may approach the dean of students seeking recognition or an allocation from the fund for student activities. If membership is limited to students of a particular faith, or if the student organization does not admit gays or lesbians, how should the administration respond? A faculty member may challenge a negative promotion or tenure decision. Will the college be required to disclose "confidential" letters and discussions of external evaluators or department faculty, and might the faculty member have any academic freedom rights to assert? A wealthy alumna may call the vice president for student affairs and offer to make a multimillion-dollar donation for scholarships on the condition that the scholarships be awarded only to African American students from disadvantaged families. Can and should the vice president accept the donation and follow the potential donor's wishes?

We have designed this book as a resource for college and university attorneys, officers and administrators, trustees, faculties, and staffs who may face issues such as these or innumerable others. The book provides foundational information, in-depth analysis, and practical suggestions on a wide array of legal issues faced by public and private institutions, and it recommends and describes numerous resources for further research and information. The discussions draw upon pertinent court opinions, constitutional provisions, statutes, administrative regulations, and related developments, and also cite selected journal articles, books, reports, Web sites, and other resources. In selecting topics and cases for discussion, we have primarily considered their significance for higher education policy making or legal risk management, their currency or timelessness, and their usefulness as illustrative examples of particular problems or as practical applications of particular legal principles.

Relationship Between the Fourth Edition and Earlier Editions

This Fourth Edition of *The Law of Higher Education* is the successor to the Third Edition published in 1995 and the periodic supplements published in 1997 and 2000. The Fourth Edition features a major reorganization of materials and a thoroughly revised, updated, and expanded text. This edition is current to approximately March 2006.

In the decade since publication of the Third Edition and then its supplements, many new and newly complex legal concerns have arisen on America's campuses—from the implications of the USA PATRIOT Act, to affirmative action in admissions and financial aid, to the allocation of mandatory student activities fees, to the clash between faculty and "institutional" academic freedom, to the rights of intercollegiate athletes. Indeed, it is difficult to identify any other entities—including large corporations and government agencies—that are subject to as great an array of legal requirements as are colleges and universities. To serve the needs occasioned by this continual growth of the law, the Fourth Edition retains all material of continuing legal currency from the Third Edition and the 1997 and 2000 supplements, reorganized and reedited (and often reanalyzed) to accommodate the deletion and addition of materials, and to maximize clarity and accessibility. We have added considerable new material to this base: well over one-third of the material in the Fourth Edition did not appear in earlier editions or supplements. Specifically, we have extended the discussion of matters that (in hindsight) were given insufficient attention in earlier editions or have since acquired greater significance; integrated pertinent new developments and insights regarding topics in the earlier editions; and introduced numerous new topics and issues not covered in earlier editions.

Although considerable material from earlier editions has lost its legal currency as a result of later developments, we have nevertheless retained some of this material for its continuing historical significance. What has been retained, however, is often presented in a more compressed format than in earlier editions. Thus, readers desiring additional historical context for particular issues may wish to consult the First, Second, and Third Editions. Moreover, we have sometimes deleted or compressed material that still has legal currency, because later cases or developments provide more instructive illustrations. Thus, readers seeking additional examples of particular legal issues may also wish to consult the First, Second, and Third Editions.

Like the earlier editions, the Fourth Edition covers all of *postsecondary* education—from the large state university to the small private liberal arts college, from the graduate and professional school to the community college and vocational and technical institution, and from the traditional campus-based program to the innovative off-campus or multistate program, and now to distance learning as well. The Fourth Edition also reflects the same perspective on the intersection of law and education as described in the Preface to the First Edition:

> The law has arrived on the campus. Sometimes it has been a beacon, at other times a blanket of ground fog. But even in its murkiness, the law has not come "on little cat feet," like Carl Sandburg's "Fog"; nor has it sat silently on its haunches; nor will it soon move on. It has come noisily and sometimes has stumbled. And even in its imperfections, the law has spoken forcefully and meaningfully to the higher education community and will continue to do so.

Audience

The Law of Higher Education was originally written for administrative officers, trustees, and legal counsel who dealt with the many challenges and complexities that arise from the law's presence on campus, and for students and observers of higher education and law who desired to explore the intersection of these two disciplines. Beginning with the Third Edition, and continuing in this Fourth Edition, we have expanded the book's materials and scope to serve additional groups that regularly encounter legal conflicts and challenges in their professional lives: for example, directors of student judicial affairs offices; directors of equal opportunity offices; staff who work with disabled students or foreign students, and other student affairs staff; deans and department chairs; risk managers; business managers and grants and contracts managers; technology transfer, intellectual property, and sponsored research administrators; athletics directors; and directors of campus security. In addition, others outside the colleges and universities may find this Fourth Edition useful: for example, officers and staff at higher education associations, executives and project officers of foundations serving academia, education policy makers in state and federal governments, and attorneys representing clients who enter into transactions with or have disputes with postsecondary institutions.

To be equally usable by administrators and legal counsel, the text avoids legal jargon and technicalities whenever possible and explains them when they are used. Footnotes throughout the book are designed primarily to provide additional technical analysis and research resources for legal counsel.

In seeking to serve its various audiences, this book organizes and conceptualizes the entire range of legal considerations pertinent to the operation of colleges and universities. It analyzes legal developments, identifies trends, and tracks their implications for academic institutions—often pointing out how particular legal developments may clash with, or support, important academic practices or values. The book also explores relationships between law and policy, suggests preventive law measures for institutions to consider, and includes other suggestions and perspectives that serve to facilitate effective working relationships between counsel and administrators who grapple with law's impact on their campuses.

Organization

We have organized this Fourth Edition into fifteen chapters, up from nine chapters in the Third Edition. These chapters are in turn organized into six parts: (1) Perspectives and Foundations; (2) The College and Its Governing Board, Personnel, and Agents; (3) The College and Its Faculty; (4) The College and Its Students; (5) The College and Local, State, and Federal Governments; and (6) The College and External Private Entities. Each of the fifteen chapters is divided into numerous Sections and subsections.

Chapter One provides a framework for understanding and integrating what is presented in subsequent chapters and a perspective for assimilating future legal developments. Chapter Two addresses foundational concepts concerning legal liability, preventive law, and the processes of litigation and alternative dispute resolution. Chapters Three through Ten discuss legal concepts and issues affecting the *internal* relationships among the various members of the campus community and address the law's impact on particular roles, functions, and responsibilities of trustees, administrators, faculty, and students. Chapters Eleven, Twelve, and Thirteen are concerned with the postsecondary institution's *external* relationships with government at the local, state, and federal levels. These chapters examine broad questions of governmental power and process that cut across all the *internal* relationships and administrative functions considered in Chapters Three through Ten; they also discuss particular legal issues arising from the institution's dealings with government and identify connections between these issues and those explored in the earlier chapters. Chapters Fourteen and Fifteen also deal with the institution's *external* relationships, but the relationships are those with the private sector rather than with government. Chapter Fourteen covers the various national and regional education associations with which the institution interacts; Chapter Fifteen covers the myriad relationships—many on the cutting edge—that institutions are increasingly forging with commercial and industrial enterprises.

What Is New in This Edition

In the light cast by recent developments, many new topics of concern have emerged on stage, and older topics that once were bit players have assumed major roles. To cover these topics, the Fourth Edition adds many entirely new Sections that did not appear in the 1997 or 2000 supplements or the earlier editions. These new Sections cover: the governance of higher education (Section 1.3); the relationship between law and policy (Section 1.7); the basics of legal liability (Section 2.1); judicial deference to institutional decision making (Section 2.2.5); alternative dispute resolution (Section 2.3); and various employment issues, such as employees versus independent contractors (Section 4.2.1), executive contracts (Section 4.3.3.7), civil service rules (Section 4.4), state-created dangers and Section 1983 liability (Section 4.7.4.2), and performance management strategies (Section 4.8)—these five Sections being part of a new chapter (Chapter 4) that focuses especially on employment of administrators and staff. Other new Sections cover: external versus internal restraints on academic freedom (Section 7.1.5); "institutional" academic freedom (Section 7.1.6); methods of analyzing academic freedom in teaching claims (Section 7.2.4); academic freedom in religious institutions (Section 7.8); student academic freedom (Section 8.1.4); students' legal relationships with other students (Section 8.1.5); discrimination by residence and immigration status in admissions (Sections 8.2.4.5 & 8.2.4.6); the use of government student aid funds at religious institutions (Section 8.3.7); student health services (Section 8.7.2); services for international students (Section 8.7.4); student speech via posters and fliers (Section 9.5.6); advertising in student publications (Section 10.3.4); and athletes' freedom of speech rights (Section 10.4.3). Yet other new Sections cover: research misconduct (Section 13.2.3.4); the USA PATRIOT Act and its impact on privacy and research (Section 13.2.4); the Health Insurance Portability and Accountability Act (HIPAA) and its impact on student health centers and university-affiliated hospitals (Section 13.2.14); federal taxation issues such as intermediate sanctions (Section 13.3.3), taxation of related entities (Section 13.3.7), and IRS audit guidelines (Section 13.3.8); retaliation claims under the federal civil rights spending statutes (Section 13.5.7.5); extraterritorial application of the federal civil rights spending statutes (Section 13.5.7.6); and the application of "federal common law" to accrediting agencies (Section 14.3.2.2).

Other Sections from the Third Edition have been reconceptualized and reorganized in our process of updating them: Section 1.6 on religion and the public-private dichotomy; Section 3.3 on institutional tort liability, including new subsections on liability for off-campus instruction, social activities, and student suicide; Section 3.6 on captive and affiliated organizations; Sections 5.4 and 6.5 on affirmative action in employment; Sections 7.1 and 7.2 on aspects of faculty academic freedom; Section 8.7 on support services for students; Section 9.3.4 on sexual harassment by faculty; Section 9.5 on student protest and freedom of speech; Section 9.6 on speech codes and hate speech; Sections 13.2.5 and 13.2.6 on copyright law and patent law (reorganized and updated by Georgia Harper); Section 13.3 on federal taxation (reorganized and updated by Randolph Goodman and Patrick Gutierrez); and Section 13.4.6 on disputes with federal funding agencies.

Yet other Sections from the Third Edition or its supplements have been extensively expanded to account for important recent developments. Examples of such Sections and the major new cases they address are Section 3.3.2.3 on liability for injuries to students on internship assignments or study-abroad programs; Section 7.2.2 on classroom academic freedom (the *Bonnell* and *Hardy* cases); Section 7.3 on faculty research (the *Urofsky* case); Sections 8.2.5 and 8.3.4 on affirmative action in admissions and financial aid (*Grutter v. Bollinger* and *Gratz v. Bollinger*); Section 9.5.3 on regulation of student protest (the free speech zone cases); Section 9.7.1 on Family Educational Rights and Privacy Act (FERPA)

(*Gonzaga University v. Doe*); Section 9.7.2 on the interplay between FERPA and state public meetings and records laws (*United States of America v. The Miami University and The Ohio State University*); Section 10.1.3 on the allocation of mandatory student activities fees (*Board of Regents of University of Wisconsin v. Southworth*); Section 10.1.4 on religious organizations and sexual orientation discrimination; Section 10.3.3 on regulating student newspapers (*Kincaid v. Gibson* and *Hosty v. Carter*); Section 13.2.5.2 on recent developments in copyright and fair use with respect to file sharing; and Section 13.4.4 on the tension between on-campus military recruitment and institutional nondiscrimination policies (*Rumsfeld v. FAIR*).

Citations and References

Each chapter ends with a Selected Annotated Bibliography. We suggest that readers use the listed books, articles, reports, Web sites, and other sources to extend the discussion of particular issues presented in the chapter, to explore related issues not treated in the chapter, to obtain additional practical guidance in dealing with the chapter's issues, to keep abreast of later developments, or to identify resources for research. Other such sources pertaining to narrower issues are cited in the text, and footnotes contain additional legal resources primarily for lawyers. Court decisions, constitutional provisions, statutes, and administrative regulations are also cited throughout the text. In addition, the footnotes contain copious citations to *American Law Reports* (A.L.R.) annotations that collect additional court decisions on particular subjects and periodically update each collection.

The citation form for the various legal sources cited in the fourth edition generally follows *The Bluebook: A Uniform System of Citation* (18th ed., Columbia Law Review Association, Harvard Law Review Association, University of Pennsylvania Law Review, and Yale Law Journal, 2005). The legal sources that these citations refer to are described in Chapter One, Section 1.4, of this Fourth Edition.

A Note on Nomenclature

The Fourth Edition, like previous editions, uses the terms "higher education" and "postsecondary education" to refer to education that follows a high school (or K–12) education. Often these terms are used interchangeably; at other times "postsecondary education" is used as the broader of the two terms, encompassing formal post-high school education programs whether or not they build on academic subjects studied in high school or are considered to be "advanced" studies of academic subjects. Similarly, this book uses the terms "higher education institution," "postsecondary institution," "college," and "university" to refer to the institutions and programs that provide post-high school (or post-K–12) education. These terms are also often used interchangeably; but occasionally "postsecondary institution" is used in the broader sense suggested above, and occasionally "college" is used to connote an academic unit within a university or an independent institution that emphasizes two-year or four-year undergraduate programs. The context generally makes clear when we intend a more specific meaning and are not using these terms interchangeably.

The term "public institution" generally means an educational institution operated under the auspices of a state, county, or occasionally a city government. The term "private institution" means a nongovernmental, nonprofit or proprietary, educational institution. The term "religious institution" encompasses a private educational institution that is operated by a church or other sectarian organization (a "sectarian institution"), or that is otherwise formally affiliated with a church or sectarian organization (a "religiously affiliated institution"), or that otherwise proclaims a religious mission and is guided by religious values.

Recommendations for Using the Book and Keeping Up to Date

There are some precautions to keep in mind when using this book, as noted in the Prefaces for the first three editions. We reemphasize them here for the Fourth Edition. The legal analyses throughout this book, and the numerous practical suggestions, are not adapted to the law of any particular state or to the circumstances prevailing at any particular postsecondary institution. The book is not a substitute for the advice of legal counsel, nor a substitute for further research into the particular legal authorities and factual circumstances that pertain to each legal problem that an institution, government agency, educational association, or person may face. Nor is the book necessarily the latest word on the law. There is a saying among lawyers that "the law must be stable and yet it cannot stand still" (Roscoe Pound, *Interpretations of Legal History* (1923), 1), and the law moves especially fast in its applications to postsecondary education. Thus, we urge administrators and counsel to keep abreast of ongoing developments concerning the legal sources and issues in this book. Various aids (described below) are available for this purpose.

Although new resources for staying up to date appear periodically, the total volume of law to keep track of continues to grow. Thus, keeping abreast of developments is as much a challenge now as it was when the previous editions were published. To assist readers in this task, we plan to maintain a Web site, hosted by the National Association of College and University Attorneys (NACUA), Washington, D.C. (available at http://www.nacua.org), on which we will announce or post pertinent new developments and key them to the Fourth Edition. In addition, there is a very helpful Web site, the Campus Legal Information Clearinghouse (CLIC) (available at http://counsel.cua.edu), operated by the General Counsel's Office at The Catholic University of America in conjunction with the American Council on Education, that includes information on recent developments, especially federal statutory and federal agency developments, and practical compliance suggestions. There is also a legal reporter that reprints new court opinions on higher education law and provides commentary on recent developments: *West's Education Law Reporter,* published biweekly by Thomson West Publishing Company, St. Paul, Minnesota. (Entries for this reporter and for CLIC are in the Selected Annotated Bibliography for Chapter One, Section 1.1.)

Also helpful are various periodicals that provide information on current legal developments. *Synthesis: Law and Policy in Higher Education,* published five times a year by College Administration Publications, Asheville, North Carolina, provides in-depth analysis and commentary on major contemporary issues. *Synfax Weekly Report,* a fax newsletter that is a division of College Administration Publications, digests and critiques current legal and policy developments. (Entries for these two resources are also in the Chapter One bibliography, respectively in Sections 1.2 and 1.1.) *Campus Legal Monthly,* published by Magna Publications (available at http://www.magnapubs.com), provides analysis of recent cases and campus issues, along with preventive law suggestions. *Lex Collegii,* a newsletter published quarterly by College Legal Information, Nashville, Tennessee (available at http://www.collegelegal.com/lexcolhp.htm), analyzes selected legal issues and provides preventive law suggestions, especially for private institutions. And *Business Officer,* a monthly magazine published for its members by the National Association of College and University Business Officers (available at http;//www.nacubo.org), emphasizes developments in Congress and the federal administrative agencies.

For news reporting of current events in higher education generally, but particularly for substantial coverage of legal developments, readers may wish to consult the *Chronicle of Higher Education,* published weekly in hard copy and daily online (available at http://www.chronicle.com) (see entry in Section 1.1 of the Chapter One bibliography); or *Education Daily,* published every weekday (available at http://www.educationdaily.net/ED/splash.jsp).

For keeping abreast of conference papers, journal articles, and pertinent government and association reports, *Higher Education Abstracts* is helpful; it is published quarterly by the Claremont Graduate School, Claremont, California (available at http://highereducationabstracts.org). The Educational Resources Information Center (ERIC) database (available at http://www.eric.ed.gov), sponsored by the U.S. Department of Education, performs a similar service encompassing books, monographs, research reports, conference papers and proceedings, bibliographies, legislative materials, dissertations, and journal articles on higher education. In addition, the IHELG monograph series published each year by the Institute for Higher Education Law and Governance, University of Houston Law Center, provides papers on a wide variety of research projects and timely topics.

For extended legal commentary on recent developments, we suggest these two journals: the *Journal of College and University Law,* published quarterly by NACUA and focusing exclusively on postsecondary education; and the *Journal of Law* and *Education,* which covers elementary and secondary as well as postsecondary education, published quarterly by Jefferson Lawbook Company, Cincinnati, Ohio.

A final resource may be of interest to those who wish to use the Fourth Edition as a classroom or workshop text. We have prepared, and will periodically update, a compilation of teaching materials that includes edited versions of leading court opinions, notes and discussion questions, large and small problems (some of which could be used as examination questions), outlines of suggested answers, and other materials. This compilation, titled *Cases, Problems, and Materials for Use with The Law of Higher Education, Fourth Edition*, is available on the Web site of the National Association of College and University Attorneys; for further information, see pages vi–vii of this book.

Endnote

Overall, the goal for this Fourth Edition remains much the same as the goal for the First Edition, set out in its Preface. The hope of this book is to provide a base for the debate concerning law's role on campus; for improved understanding between attorneys and academics; and for effective relationships between administrators and their counsel. The challenge of our age is not to remove the law from the campus or to marginalize it. The law is here to stay, and it will continue to play a major role in campus affairs. The challenge of our age, rather, is to make law more a beacon and less a fog. The challenge is for law and higher education to accommodate one another, preserving the best values of each for the mutual benefit of both. Just as academia benefits from the understanding and respect of the legal community, so law benefits from the understanding and respect of academia.

April 2006
William A. Kaplin
Washington, D.C.
Barbara A. Lee
New Brunswick, N.J.

Acknowledgments

Many persons graciously provided assistance to us in the preparation of this Fourth Edition. We are grateful for each person and each contribution listed below, and for all other support and encouragement that we received along the way.

For this edition, for the first time, we invited other colleagues to prepare several sections of the manuscript that we knew would particularly benefit from their special expertise. Georgia Harper, senior attorney and manager, Intellectual Property Section, Office of the General Counsel, University of Texas System, revised the copyright and patent law Sections. Randolph M. Goodman and Patrick T. Gutierrez, of Wilmer, Cutler, Pickering, Hale and Dorr, LLP, revised the Sections on federal tax law. Their work is identified by a footnote reference at the beginning of each section on which they worked.

Various colleagues reviewed sections of the Fourth Edition manuscript, providing helpful feedback on matters within their expertise and good wishes for the project: Donna Euben and Jordan Kurland at the national office of the American Association of University Professors (AAUP); Ann Franke, President, Wise Results, LLC; William Hoye, associate vice president and deputy general counsel, University of Notre Dame; Steven J. McDonald, general counsel, Rhode Island School of Design; Elizabeth Meers, of Hogan and Hartson, Washington, D.C.; Benjamin Mintz, The Catholic University of America; David Palfreyman, bursar and director of The Oxford Centre for Higher Education Policy Studies, New College, Oxford, U.K.; Craig Parker, general counsel, and Kathryn Bender, associate general counsel, The Catholic University of America; Gary Pavela, Editor, ASJA Law and Policy Report, and Synfax Weekly Report; Michael Olivas, director of the Institute for Higher Education Law and Governance, University of Houston; Robert O'Neil, director of The Thomas Jefferson Center for the Protection of Free Expression at the University of Virginia; Ted Sky, The Catholic University of America; Catherine Diamond Stone, Magill & Atkinson LLP; and Gerald Woods, at Kilpatrick Stockton, Augusta, Georgia.

Our research assistants provided valuable help with manuscript preparation: Andy Arculin, Sara Bromberg, Marie Callan, Eugene Hansen, Tracy Hartzler-Toon, Gordon Jimison, Catherine Lusk, Amy Mushahwar, and Michael Provost. Ms. Hartzler-Toon and Mr. Provost each served for two academic years, providing important continuity at critical stages of the manuscript's development, and also took on additional special assignments after graduating.

A number of persons skillfully performed important word processing and administrative services during the years in which this manuscript was in process: Rebecca Tinkham at Rutgers University; and at The Catholic University of America: Donna Snyder and Jean Connelly (primary preparers of the manuscript), Stephanie Michael and Linda Perez (overall supervisors of the project), Laurie Fraser, Sabrina Hilliard, Julie Kendrick, and Barbara McCoy. At Stetson University College of Law, the Faculty Support Services Office, under the direction of Connie Evans, assisted with the preparation of the front matter.

Library staff members at the Columbus School of Law, The Catholic University of America, provided important support functions: Yvette Brown, reference librarian, promptly responded to research requests and requests for materials throughout the project; Stephen Margeton, law library director, provided Bill Kaplin with a quiet study office in the library to facilitate research on this book; and Pat Petit, head reference librarian, devised an efficient system for cite checking the entire manuscript. At Stetson University College of Law, Sally Waters answered requests for materials.

We are also grateful for the excellent work of Liah Rose, who managed the copyediting process, Pam Suwinsky, the copy editor, and Bonnie Taylor, who created the indexes. Their attention to detail and their helpful suggestions played an important role in readying the manuscript for publication.

Bill Fox, then the law school dean at The Catholic University of America, greatly helped by awarding Bill Kaplin summer research grants for work on this book, approving two leaves of absence for work on this book, and consistently being sensitive to his research and writing commitments when approving teaching schedules and committee assignments.

The National Association of College and University Attorneys (NACUA) published the 1997 and 2000 supplements to the Third Edition of this book, as well as our supplementary teaching materials, *Cases, Problems, and Materials: An Instructional Supplement to The Law of Higher Education*. Linda Henderson at NACUA was primarily responsible for managing the smooth publication processes and designing the high-quality final products. Kathleen Curry Santora and Karl Brevitz at NACUA supported these publications, worked with Ms. Henderson to arrange for a Web site to support the Fourth Edition, and arranged a session on the Fourth Edition for NACUA's 2006 annual conference. NACUA publications also provided us with important information and guidance in the development of several sections of the Fourth Edition.

Robert Bickel, codirector of the Center for Excellence in Higher Education Law and Policy, Stetson University College of Law, encouraged our work by including us in the conference faculty for each of Stetson's Annual National Conferences on Law and Higher Education, from the Third Edition to the Fourth, and by devising a plenary session on the Fourth Edition for the 2006 Conference. Michael Olivas, director of the Institute for Higher Education Law and Governance, University of Houston, similarly supported this Fourth Edition by inviting Bill Kaplin to be a leader/mentor for the Institute's biannual Higher Education Law Roundtable, and by sharing information on new law and policy developments with us.

Barbara Kaplin accurately assisted with proofreading for the entire length of this project, and also typed manuscript inserts and assisted with verification of citations through the end of the project.

Bill Kaplin's mother, Joan Kaplin, wisely provided continual reminders (for us both) to "take a break" and "have some fun," even when the advice went unheeded.

Our spouses and families tolerated the years of intrusion that this Fourth Edition imposed on our personal lives; encouraged us when this project seemed too overwhelming to ever end; and looked forward with us (usually patiently) to the time when "the book" would finally be finished—at least for the time being.

The Authors

William A. Kaplin is professor of law at the Columbus School of Law, The Catholic University of America, Washington, D.C., where he is also special counsel to the university general counsel. He is also a Distinguished Professorial Lecturer at the Stetson University College of Law and a Fellow of Stetson's Center for Excellence in Higher Education Law and Policy. He has been a visiting professor at Cornell Law School, at Wake Forest University School of Law, and at Stetson; a distinguished visiting scholar at the Institute for Higher Education Law and Governance, University of Houston; and a visiting scholar at the Institute for Educational Leadership, George Washington University. He is the former editor of the *Journal of College and University Law,* on whose editorial board he currently sits, and a former member of the Education Appeal Board at the U.S. Department of Education. He is also a member of the U.S./U.K. Higher Education Law Roundtable that had its first meeting in summer 2004 at New College, Oxford University, and a mentor/leader for the biannual Higher Education Law Roundtable for emerging scholars at the University of Houston Law Center.

Professor Kaplin received the American Council on Education's Borden Award, in recognition of the First Edition of *The Law of Higher Education,* and the Association for Student Judicial Affairs' D. Parker Young Award for research contributions. He has also been named a Fellow of the National Association of College and University Attorneys.

In addition to the various editions and updates of *The Law of Higher Education,* and the derivative work *A Legal Guide for Student Affairs Professionals* (1997), Professor Kaplin also coauthored *State, School, and Family: Cases and Materials on Law and Education* (2d ed., 1979) and authored *The Concepts and Methods of Constitutional Law* (1992) and *American Constitutional Law: An Overview, Analysis, and Integration* (2004). He has also authored numerous articles, monographs, and reports on education law and policy and on constitutional law.

Bill Kaplin received his B.A. degree (1964) in political science from the University of Rochester and his J.D. degree *with distinction* (1967) from Cornell University, where he was editor-in-chief of the *Cornell Law Review.* He then worked with a Washington, D.C., law firm, served as a judicial clerk at the U.S. Court of Appeals for the District of Columbia Circuit, and was an attorney in the education division of the U.S. Department of Health, Education and Welfare, before joining the Catholic University law faculty.

Barbara A. Lee is professor of human resource management at the School of Management and Labor Relations, Rutgers University, in New Brunswick, New Jersey. She is also of counsel to the law firm of Edwards Angell Palmer & Dodge, LLP. She is a former dean of the School of Management and Labor Relations, and also served as associate provost, department chair, and director of the Center for Women and Work at Rutgers University. She chaired the editorial board of the *Journal of College and University Law,* served as a member of the Board of Directors of the National Association of College and University Attorneys, and was named a NACUA Fellow. She also serves on the Executive Committee of the New Jersey State Bar Association's Section on Labor and Employment Law, and formerly served on the executive committee of the Human Resource Management Division of the Academy of Management. She is also a member of the U.S./U.K. Higher Education Law Roundtable, as well as a member of the Advisory Board of the Center for Higher Education and Law Policy, Stetson University College of Law. She received a distinguished alumni award from the University of Vermont in 2003.

In addition to coauthoring the Third and Fourth Editions of *The Law of Higher Education* and its supplements and updates, as well as *A Legal Guide for Student Affairs Professionals* (1997), Professor Lee also coauthored *Academics in Court* (1987, with George LaNoue), as well as numerous articles, chapters, and monographs on legal aspects of academic employment. She serves as an expert witness in tenure, discharge, and discrimination cases, and is a frequent lecturer and trainer for academic and corporate audiences.

Barbara Lee received her B.A. degree *summa cum laude* (1971) in English and French from the University of Vermont. She received an M.A. degree (1972) in English and a Ph.D. (1977) in higher education administration from The Ohio State University. She earned a J.D. *cum laude* (1982) from the Georgetown University Law Center. Prior to joining Rutgers University in 1982, she held professional positions with the U.S. Department of Education and the Carnegie Foundation for the Advancement of Teaching.

Dedication

Much as it takes a village to raise a child, it takes an "academical village" (Thomas Jefferson's phrase) to raise a book—at least a book such as this that arises from and whose purpose is to serve a national (and now international) academic community. This book is dedicated to all those members of our academical village who in numerous and varied ways have helped to raise this book from its origins through this Fourth Edition, and to all those members who will face the great challenges of law and policy that will shape higher education's future.

The Law of
Higher Education

PART ONE

PERSPECTIVES
AND FOUNDATIONS

1

Overview of
Higher Education Law

Sec. 1.1. *How Far the Law Reaches and How Loud It Speaks*

Law's presence on the campus and its impact on the daily affairs of postsecondary institutions have grown continuously at least since the 1960s. From then until the present, the volume and complexity of litigation in our society generally, and involving higher education specifically, have increased dramatically. The growth of government regulations, especially at the federal level, has also been dramatic and pervasive. The potential for jury trials and large monetary damage awards, for court injunctions affecting institutions' internal affairs, for government agency compliance investigations, and even for criminal prosecutions against administrative officers, faculty members, and students, have all increased.

Many factors have contributed over the years to the development of this legalistic and litigious environment. The expectations of students and parents have increased, spurred in part by increases in tuition and fees, and in part by society's consumer orientation. The greater availability of data that measures and compares institutions, and greater political savvy among student and faculty populations, have led to more sophisticated demands on institutions. Advocacy groups have used litigation as the means to assert faculty and student claims against institutions—and applicant claims as well, in suits concerning affirmative action in admissions and employment. Satellite campuses, off-campus programs, and distance learning have extended the reach of the "campus," bringing into higher education's fold a diverse array of persons whose interests may conflict with those of more traditional populations. And an increasingly adversarial mindset, a decrease in civility, and a diminishing level of trust in societal institutions have made it more acceptable to assert legal claims at the drop of a hat.

Moreover, society has become more sensitized to civil rights; and Congress, state legislatures, and courts have focused more on their recognition and enforcement. Technological advances have raised a multitude of new legal issues regarding intellectual property, personal privacy, and freedom of speech. Study abroad programs, internships, and innovative field trips and off-campus assignments have created new exposures to legal risk. Federal, state, and local statutes and administrative regulations have raised difficult compliance challenges in many critical areas of campus life, such as confidentiality of records, worker safety, campus security, equal opportunity, computer network communications, and the status of foreign students. Since the beginning of the new century, terrorism and the "War on Terror" have enhanced many of these compliance challenges and created some new ones as well.

Financial pressures have led to competition for resources, which in turn has increased the likelihood of disputes about funding, salaries, and budgets. Financial pressures have also stimulated the growth of entrepreneurial activities as alternative sources of income. Faculty members' entrepreneurial activities have strained their traditional relationships with their institutions, while institutions' own entrepreneurial activities have drawn them increasingly into the commercial marketplace and exposed them to additional possibilities for legal disputes. In the face of all these pressures, institutions themselves have become better equipped to defend themselves vigorously when sued and are more willing to initiate lawsuits themselves when the institution's mission, reputation, or financial resources have been threatened.

Thus, whether one is responding to campus disputes, planning to avoid future disputes, or crafting an institution's policies and priorities, law is an indispensable consideration. Legal issues arising on campuses across America continue to be aired not only within the groves of academia but also in external forums. Students, faculty members, administrators and staff members, and their institutions have increasingly been litigants in the courts, for example, and outside parties (government agencies, corporations, and individuals) have increasingly been involved in such disputes. Institutions have responded by expanding their legal staffs and outside counsel relationships and by increasing the numbers of administrators in legally sensitive positions. As this trend has continued, more and more questions of educational policy have become converted into legal questions as well (see Section 1.7). Law and litigation have extended into every corner of campus activity.[1]

There are many striking examples of cutting-edge cases—or sometimes just wrong-headed cases—that have attracted considerable attention in, or had substantial impact on, higher education. Students, for example, have sued their institutions for damages after being accused of plagiarism; students have sued after being penalized for improper use of the campus computer network; objecting students have sued over mandatory student fee allocations; victims of

---

[1]Much of the introductory content of this section is adapted from Kathleen Curry Santora and William Kaplin, "Preventive Law: How Colleges Can Avoid Legal Problems," *Chron. Higher Educ.*, April 18, 2003, B20 (copyright © 2004 by Chronicles of Higher Education, Inc.).

harassment have sued their institutions and professors who are the alleged harassers; student athletes have sought injunctions ordering their institutions or athletic conferences to grant or reinstate eligibility for intercollegiate sports; disabled students have filed suits against their institutions or state rehabilitation agencies, seeking sign language interpreters or other auxiliary services to support their education; students who have been victims of violence have sued their institutions for alleged failures of campus security; hazing victims have sued fraternities, fraternity members, and institutions; parents have sued administrators and institutions after students have committed suicide; and former students involved in bankruptcy proceedings have sought judicial discharge of student loan debts owed to institutions. Disappointed students have sued over grades—and have even lodged challenges such as the remarkable 1980s lawsuit in which a student sued her institution for $125,000 after an instructor gave her a B+ grade, which she claimed should have been an A−. Women and minority students have challenged the heavy reliance by scholarship selection panels and medical schools on standardized tests, and "truth-in-testing" proponents have sued testing agencies to force disclosure of standardized test questions and answers. Students and others supporting animal rights have used lawsuits (and civil disobedience as well) to pressure research laboratories to reduce or eliminate the use of animals. And rejected female applicants have sued military colleges, seeking increased opportunities for women.

Faculty members have been similarly active. Professors have sought legal redress after their institutions have changed their laboratory or office space, their teaching assignments, or the size of their classes. One group of faculty members in the 1980s challenged their institution's plan to build a new basketball arena because they feared that construction costs would create a drain on funds available for academic programs; another group sued their institution and the state higher education commission, challenging a salary structure that allegedly benefited more recently hired faculty members; and another group challenged their institution's decision to terminate several women's studies courses, alleging sex discrimination and violation of free speech. Female faculty members have increasingly brought sexual harassment claims to the courts, and female coaches have sued over salaries and support for women's teams. Across the country, suits brought by faculty members who have been denied tenure— once one of the most closely guarded and sacrosanct of all institutional judgments—have become commonplace.

Outside parties also have been increasingly involved in postsecondary education litigation. Athletic conferences were sometimes defendants in the student athlete cases above. State rehabilitation agencies were sometimes defendants in the disabled student cases; fraternities were sometimes defendants in the hazing cases; and testing organizations were defendants in the truth-in-testing litigation. Sporting goods companies have been sued by universities for trademark infringement because they allegedly appropriated university insignia and emblems for use on their products. Broadcasting companies and athletic conferences have been in litigation over rights to control television broadcasts of intercollegiate athletic contests, and athletic conferences have been in dispute concerning teams leaving one conference to join another. Media organizations have brought suits and other complaints under open meetings and public records laws. Separate entities created by institutions, or with which institutions affiliate, have been involved in litigation with the institutions. Drug companies have sued and been sued in disputes over human subject research and patent rights to discoveries. And increasingly, other commercial and industrial entities of various types have engaged in litigation with institutions regarding purchases, sales, and research ventures. Community groups, environmental organizations, taxpayers, and other outsiders have also gotten into the act, suing institutions for a wide variety of reasons, from curriculum to land use. Recipients of university services have also resorted to the courts. In one late 1980s suit, a couple sued a state university veterinary hospital after their llama died while being examined by a veterinary student; and in another late 1980s suit, seed companies and potato farmers sued a state university for alleged negligence in certifying seed.

More recently, other societal developments have led to new types of lawsuits and new issues for legal planning. And, of course, myriad government agencies at federal, state, and local levels have frequently been involved in civil suits as well as criminal prosecutions concerning higher education. The spread of AIDS, for example, raised new legal issues from tort liability to privacy rights to nondiscrimination. Drug abuse problems have created other issues, especially those concerning mandatory drug testing of employees or student athletes and compliance with "drug-free campus" laws. Federal government regulation of Internet communications have led to new questions about liability for the spread of computer viruses, copyright infringement in cyberspace, transmission of sexually explicit materials, and defamation by cyberspeech. Outbreaks of racial, anti-Semitic, anti-Arabic, homophobic, and political/ideological tensions on campuses have led to speech codes, academic bills of rights, and a range of issues concerning student and faculty academic freedom. Alleged sexual inequities in intercollegiate athletics that prompted initiatives to strengthen women's teams have led to suits by male athletes and coaches whose teams have been eliminated or downsized. Sexual harassment concerns have expanded to student peer harassment and harassment based on sexual orientation, and has also focused on date rape and sexual assault. Hazing, alcohol use, and behavioral problems, implicating fraternities and men's athletic teams especially, have reemerged as major issues. New emphasis on conflicts between civil law and canon law, and between religious mission and governmental authority, has resulted in disputes concerning the legal rights of students and faculty at religiously affiliated institutions, and also concerning government funding for religious institutions and their students. In the realm of research, numerous issues concerning scientific misconduct, research on human subjects, bioterrorism research, patent rights, and conflicts of interest have emerged. New issues affecting student governments and extracurricular student activities arose in the wake of the U.S. Supreme Court's ruling on mandatory student activity fees in the *Rosenberger* case. The growth in relationships between research universities and private industry has led to increasing legal issues concerning technology transfer. Raised sensitivities to alleged sexual harassment and political bias in academia have prompted academic freedom disputes between faculty and students, manifested especially in student complaints about faculty members' classroom comments and course assignments. Increased attention to student learning disabilities, and the psychological and emotional conditions that may interfere with learning, have led to new types of disability discrimination claims and issues concerning the modification of academic standards. Renewed attention to affirmative action policies for admissions and financial aid have resulted in lawsuits, state legislation, and state referenda and initiative drives among voters. The contentious national debate on gay marriage has prompted renewed disputes on campus concerning gay rights student organizations, student religious organizations that exclude gay and lesbian students from membership or leadership, and domestic partnership benefits for employees.

As the numbers and types of disputes have expanded, along with litigation in the courts, the use of administrative agencies as alternative forums for airing disputes has also grown. In some circumstances, especially at the federal level, the courts (and particularly the U.S. Supreme Court) have imposed various technical limitations on access to courts, thus serving to channel various complainants to administrative agencies as an alternative to court. The increased presence of inspectors general for federal agencies and their state counterparts, and their use of investigatory powers, also appears to have helped stimulate an increased volume of disputes before administrative agencies. Administrative agency regulations at federal, state, and local levels may now routinely be enforced through agency compliance proceedings and private complaints filed with administrative agencies. Thus, postsecondary institutions may find themselves before the federal Equal Employment Opportunity Commission (EEOC) or an analogous state agency, the National Labor Relations Board (NLRB) or a state's public employee relations board, the administrative law judges of the U.S. Department of Education (ED), contract-dispute boards of federal and state contracting agencies, state workers' compensation and unemployment insurance boards, state licensing boards, state civil service commissions, the boards or officers of federal, state, and local taxing authorities, state or local human relations commissions, local zoning boards, or the mediators or arbitrators of various government agencies at all levels of government. Proceedings can be complex (with mediation usually being a notable exception), and the legal relief that agencies may provide to complainants or to institutions can be substantial.

Paralleling these administrative developments has been an increase in the internal forums created by postsecondary institutions for their own use in resolving disputes. Faculty and staff grievance committees, appeal processes for tenure denials, student judiciaries, honor boards, and grade appeals panels are common examples. In more recent years, mediation has also assumed a major role in some of these processes. In addition to such internal forums, private organizations and associations involved in postsecondary governance have given increased attention to their own dispute resolution mechanisms. Thus, besides appearing before courts and administrative agencies, postsecondary institutions may become involved in grievance procedures of faculty and staff unions, hearings of accrediting agencies on the accreditation status of institutional programs, probation hearings of athletic conferences, and censure proceedings of the American Association of University Professors (AAUP).

There are, of course, some counter-trends that have emerged over time and have served to ameliorate the more negative aspects of the growth in law and litigiousness in academia. The alternative dispute resolution (ADR) movement in society generally has led to the use of mediation and other constructive mechanisms for the internal resolution of campus disputes (see Section 2.3 of this book). Colleges and universities have increased their commitments to, and capabilities for, risk management and for preventive legal planning. On a broader scale, not only institutions but also their officers have increasingly banded together in associations through which they can maximize their influence on the development of legislation and agency regulations affecting postsecondary education. These associations also facilitate the sharing of strategies and resources for managing campus affairs in ways that minimize legal problems. Government agencies have developed processes for "notice" and "comment" prior to implementing regulations, for negotiated rulemaking, and for mediation of disputes. The trial courts have developed processes for pretrial mediation, and the appellate courts, including the U.S. Supreme Court, have developed a concept of "judicial deference" or "academic deference" that is used by both trial and appellate courts to limit judicial intrusion into the genuinely academic decisions of postsecondary institutions.

At the same time, administrators, counsel, public policy makers, and scholars have increasingly reflected on law's role on the campuses. Criticism of that role, while frequent, is becoming more perceptive and more balanced. It is still often asserted that the law reaches too far and speaks too loudly. Especially because of the courts' and federal government's involvement, it is said that legal proceedings and compliance with legal requirements are too costly, not only in monetary terms but also in terms of the talents and energies expended; that they divert higher education from its primary mission of teaching and scholarship; and that they erode the integrity of campus decision making by bending it to real or perceived legal technicalities that are not always in the academic community's best interests. It is increasingly recognized, however, that such criticisms—although highlighting pressing issues for higher education's future—do not reveal all sides of these issues. We cannot evaluate the role of law on campus by looking only at dollars expended, hours of time logged, pages of compliance reports completed, or numbers of legal proceedings participated in. We must also consider a number of less quantifiable questions: Are legal claims made against institutions, faculty, or staff usually frivolous or unimportant, or are they often justified? Are institutions providing effective mechanisms for dealing with claims and complaints internally, thus helping themselves avoid any negative effects of outside legal proceedings? Are courts and college counsel doing an adequate job of sorting out frivolous from justifiable claims, and of developing means for summary disposition of frivolous claims and settlement of justifiable ones? Have administrators and counsel ensured that their legal houses are in order by engaging in effective preventive planning? Are courts being sensitive to the mission of higher education when they apply legal rules to campuses and when they devise remedies in suits lost by institutions? Do government regulations for the campus implement worthy policy goals, and are they adequately sensitive to higher education's mission? In situations where law's message has appeared to conflict with the best interests of academia, how has academia responded: Has the inclination been to kill the messenger, or to develop more positive remedies; to hide behind rhetoric, or to forthrightly document and defend its interests?

We still do not know all we should about these questions. But we know that they are clearly a critical counterpoint to questions about dollars, time, and energies expended. We must have insight into *both* sets of questions before we can fully judge law's impact on the campus—before we can know, in particular situations, whether law is more a beacon or a blanket of ground fog.

Sec. 1.2. *Evolution of Higher Education Law*

Throughout the nineteenth and much of the twentieth centuries, the law's relationship to higher education was very different from what it is now. There were few legal requirements relating to the educational administrator's functions, and they were not a major factor in most administrative decisions. The higher education world, moreover, tended to think of itself as removed from and perhaps above the world of law and lawyers. The roots of this traditional separation between academia and law are several.

Higher education (particularly private education) was often viewed as a unique enterprise that could regulate itself through reliance on tradition and consensual agreement. It operated best by operating autonomously, and it thrived on the privacy afforded by autonomy. Academia, in short, was like a Victorian gentlemen's club whose sacred precincts were not to be profaned by the involvement of outside agents in its internal governance.

Not only was the academic environment perceived as private; it was also thought to be delicate and complex. An outsider would, almost by definition, be ignorant of the special arrangements and sensitivities underpinning this environment. And lawyers as a group, at least in the early days, were clearly outsiders. Law schools did not become an established part of American higher education until the early twentieth century, and the older tradition of "reading law" (studying and working in a practitioner's office) persisted for many years afterward. Lawyers, moreover, were often perceived as representatives of the crass aspects of business and industry, or as products of the political world, or as "hired guns" ready to take on any cause for a fee. Interference by such "outsiders" would destroy the understanding and mutual trust that must prevail in academia.

The special higher education environment was also thought to support a special virtue and ability in its personnel. The faculties and administrators (often themselves respected scholars) had knowledge and training far beyond that of the general populace, and they were charged with the guardianship of knowledge for future generations. Theirs was a special mission pursued with special expertise and often at a considerable financial sacrifice. The combination spawned the perception that ill will and personal bias were strangers to academia and that outside monitoring of its affairs was therefore largely unnecessary.

The law to a remarkable extent reflected and reinforced such attitudes. Federal and state governments generally avoided any substantial regulation of higher education. Legislatures and administrative agencies imposed few legal obligations on institutions and provided few official channels through which their activities could be legally challenged. What legal oversight existed was generally centered in the courts. But the judiciary was also highly deferential to higher education. In matters concerning students, courts found refuge in the *in loco parentis* doctrine borrowed from early English common law. By placing the educational institution in the parents' shoes, the doctrine permitted the institution to exert almost untrammeled authority over students' lives:

> College authorities stand *in loco parentis* concerning the physical and moral welfare and mental training of the pupils, and we are unable to see why, to that end, they may not make any rule or regulation for the government or betterment of their pupils that a parent could for the same purpose. Whether the rules or regulations are wise or their aims worthy is a matter left solely to the discretion of the authorities or parents, as the case may be, and, in the exercise of that discretion, the courts are not disposed to interfere, unless the rules and aims are unlawful or against public policy [*Gott v. Berea College*, 161 S.W. 204, 206 (Ky. 1913)].

Nor could students lay claim to constitutional rights in the higher education environment. In private education the U.S. Constitution had no application; and in the public realm—in cases such as *Hamilton v. Regents of the University of California*, 293 U.S. 245 (1934), which upheld an order that student conscientious objectors must take military training as a condition of attending the institution—courts accepted the proposition that attendance at a public postsecondary institution was a privilege and not a right. Being a "privilege," attendance could constitutionally be extended and was subject to termination on whatever conditions the institution determined were in its and the students' best interests. Occasionally courts did hold that students had some contract rights under an express or implied contractual relationship with the institution. But—as in *Anthony v. Syracuse University*, 231 N.Y.S. 435 (N.Y. App. Div. 1928), where the court upheld the university's dismissal of a student without assigning any reason other than that she was not "a typical Syracuse girl"—contract law provided little meaningful recourse for students. The institution was given virtually unlimited power to dictate the contract terms; and the contract, once made, was construed heavily in the institution's favor.

Similar judicial deference prevailed in the institution's relationship with faculty members. An employer-employee relationship substituted in this context for *in loco parentis,* but the relationship was based far more on judgments of senior faculty members and experienced administrators than on the formalities of written employment contracts. Courts considered academic judgments regarding appointment, promotion, and tenure to be expert judgments suitably governed by the complex traditions of the academic world. Judges did not possess the special skill needed to review such judgments, nor, without glaring evidence to the contrary, could they presume that nonacademic considerations might play a part in such processes. Furthermore, faculty members in private institutions, like their students, could assert no constitutional rights against the institution, since these rights did not apply to private activity. And in public institutions the judicial view was that employment, somewhat like student attendance, was a privilege and not a right. Thus, as far as the Constitution was concerned, employment could also be extended or terminated on whatever grounds the institution considered appropriate.

As further support for these judicial hands-off attitudes, higher education institutions also enjoyed immunity from a broad range of lawsuits alleging negligence or other torts. For public institutions, this protection arose from the governmental immunity doctrine, which shielded state and local governments and their instrumentalities from legal liability for their sovereign acts. For private institutions, a comparable result was reached under the charitable immunity doctrine, which shielded charitable organizations from legal liability that would divert their funds from the purposes for which they were intended.

Traditionally, then, the immunity doctrines substantially limited the range of suits maintainable against higher education institutions and, even when immunity did not apply, the judicial attitudes described above made the chances of victory slim in suits against either the institution or its officers and employees. Reinforcing these legal limitations was a practical limitation on litigation: in the days before legal services were available from education associations with litigation offices or from governmentally supported legal services offices, few of the likely plaintiffs—faculty members, administrators, and students—had enough money to sue.

In the latter half of the twentieth century, however, events and changing circumstances worked a revolution in the relationship between academia and the law. The federal government and state governments became heavily involved in postsecondary education, creating many new legal requirements and new forums for raising legal challenges. (See generally Carnegie Foundation for the Advancement of Teaching, *The Control of the Campus: A Report on the Governance of Higher Education* (Princeton University Press, 1982).) Students, faculty, other employees, and outsiders became more willing and more able to sue postsecondary institutions and their officials (see Section 1.1). Courts became more willing to entertain such suits on their merits and to offer relief from certain institutional actions. (See generally Robert O'Neil, *The Courts, Government, and Higher Education,* Supplementary Paper no. 37 (Committee for Economic Development, 1972).)

The most obvious and perhaps most significant change to occur was the dramatic increase in the number, size, and diversity of postsecondary institutions and programs. Beyond the obvious point that more people and institutions would produce more litigation is the crucial fact of the changed character of the academic population itself (see, for example, K. P. Cross, *Beyond the Open Door: New Students to Higher Education* (Jossey-Bass, 1971)). The GI Bill expansions of the late 1940s and early 1950s, and the "Baby Boomer" expansion of the 1960s and 1970s, brought large numbers of new students into higher education, which in turn required the addition of new faculty members and administrative personnel. Changes in immigration law and policy—in particular the passage in 1956 of the Immigration and Nationality Act—and a movement toward globalization in the aftermath of World War II, attracted increasing numbers of foreign students and scholars to the expanding opportunities for study and research in the United States. (See Gilbert Merkx, "The Two Waves of Internationalization in U.S. Higher Education," *International Educator,* Winter 2003, 13–21.) The stirrings of concern for equality of educational opportunity, and the advent of federal student aid programs, began to facilitate the increased presence of minority and low-income students on campus. Other new federal legislation (beginning with the Rehabilitation Act of 1973, Section 504) did the same for students with disabilities. In 1940 there were only about 1.5 million degree students enrolled in institutions of higher education; by 1955 the figure had grown to more than 2.5 million and by 1965 to nearly 6 million; and it has continued to rise, climbing to more than 15 million by 2001 (National Center for Education Statistics, *Digest of Education Statistics* (2003)). The expanding pool of persons seeking postsecondary education also prompted the establishment of new educational institutions and programs, and the development of new methods for delivering educational services. Great increases in federal aid for both students and institutions further stimulated these trends, and nondiscrimination requirements attached to these funds further broadened access to higher education.

As previously underrepresented social, economic, racial, and ethnic groups entered this wider world of postsecondary education, the traditional processes of selection, admission, and academic acculturation began to break down. Because of the pace of change occasioned by rapid growth, many of the new academics did not have sufficient time to internalize the old rules. Others were hostile to traditional attitudes and values because they perceived them as part of a process that had excluded their group or race or sex from educational opportunities in earlier days. For others in new settings—such as junior and community colleges, technical institutes, and experiential learning programs— the traditional trappings of academia simply did not fit. For many of the new students as well, older patterns of deference to tradition and authority became a relic of the past—perhaps an irrelevant or even consciously repudiated past.

Many factors combined to make the *in loco parentis* relationship between institution and student less and less tenable. The emergence of the student veteran, usually older and more experienced than the previous typical student, was one important factor; the loosening of the "lockstep" pattern of educational preparation that led students directly from high school to college to graduate work was another factor; and the lowered age of majority was a third (see Section 8.1.2 of this book). In addition, a students' rights movement took root in the courts and in national education associations, serving to empower students with their own individual rights apart from their parents (see Section 8.1.1, and see the 1967 "Joint Statement on Rights and Freedoms of Students," reprinted in *AAUP Documents and Reports* (9th ed., 2001), 261–67, drafted by five associations and endorsed by various others). The notion that, in such an environment, attendance was a privilege seemed an irrelevant nicety in an increasingly credentialized society. To many students, higher education became an economic or professional necessity; and some, such as the GI Bill veterans, had cause to view it as an earned right.

The post–World War II movement toward diversity of the postsecondary student population continued in important ways through the rest of the twentieth century. Women students had become a majority by 1980 (see R. Cowan, "Higher Education Has Obligations to a New Majority," *Chron. Higher Educ.,* June 23, 1980, A48), although they were still underrepresented in some programs. The proportion of minority students had also increased, with minority enrollment increasing more rapidly than white student enrollment in the 1970s, especially in community colleges (see generally G. Thomas (ed.), *Black Students in Higher Education: Conditions and Experiences in the 1970s* (Greenwood Press, 1981); Michael Olivas (ed.), *Latino College Students* (Teachers College Press, 1986); and compare B. Wright & W. G. Tierny, "American Indians in Higher Education: A History of Cultural Conflict," *Change,* March/April 1991, 11–18). Despite gains in some areas, diversity and access to education continued to be significant issues on most campuses.

The proportion of postsecondary students who were "adult learners," beyond the traditional college-age group of eighteen- to twenty-four-year-olds, also increased markedly through the latter part of the century (see, for example, K. P. Cross, *Adults as Learners: Increasing Participation and Facilitating Learning* (Jossey-Bass, 1982)), as did the proportion of part-time students (many of whom were also women and/or adult learners). The increase in part-time students resulted in a lengthening of the average number of years taken to earn the baccalaureate degree (see M. C. Cage, "Fewer Students Get Bachelor's Degrees in 4 Years, Study Finds," *Chron. Higher Educ.,* July 15, 1992, A29). Military personnel also became a significant component of the burgeoning adult learner and part-time populations, not only in civilian institutions but also in institutions established by the military services (see Section 1.3 of this book).

One further category of students, standing apart from the interlocking categories mentioned, also continued to grow substantially through the latter part of the century: foreign students. These students made a particularly important contribution to campus diversity and to the globalization of higher education, and also had a direct impact on the law. The application of immigration law to foreign students became a major concern for federal officials, who balanced shifting political and educational concerns as they devised and enforced regulations; and for postsecondary administrators, who applied these complex regulations to their own campuses (see, for example, Committee on Foreign Students and Institutional Policy, *Foreign Students and Institutional Policy: Toward an Agenda for Action* (American Council on Education, 1982)).

These changes in the student population were reflected, as expected, in changes in the universe of postsecondary institutions and programs. Community colleges and private institutions awarding associate's degrees became more prominent, as increases in their enrollments and in the numbers of institutions exceeded increases for baccalaureate and graduate institutions (see, for example, S. Brint & J. Karabel, *The Diverted Dream: Community Colleges and the*

Promise of Educational Opportunity in America, 1900–1985 (Oxford University Press, 1989)). Postsecondary education programs sponsored by private industry also increased, creating a new context for questions about state degree-granting authority, private accreditation, academic freedom, and other faculty/student rights and obligations (see, for example, Nell Eurich, *Corporate Classrooms: The Learning Business* (Princeton University Press, 1986); and Jack Bowsher, *Educating America: Lessons Learned in the Nation's Corporations* (Wiley, 1989)), as well as questions about academic credit and the transferability of industry-sponsored education (see Nancy Nash & Elizabeth Hawthorne, *Formal Recognition of Employer-Sponsored Instruction: Conflict and Collegiality in Postsecondary Education*, ASHE-ERIC Higher Education Report no. 3 (Association for the Study of Higher Education, 1987)). Work-study programs, internships, and other forms of experiential education also increased in numbers and importance (see, for example, M. T. Keeton & P. J. Tate (eds.), *Learning by Experience: What, Why, How*, New Directions for Experiential Learning no. 1 (Jossey-Bass, 1978), raising new questions about institutional liability for off-campus acts; the use of affiliation agreements with outside entities; and coverage of experiential learners under workers' compensation, unemployment compensation, and minimum wage laws. "Traditional" institutions of higher education, typically nonprofit entities, also faced competition from new forms of profit-making institutions that offered easily accessible classroom-based instruction. These offerings were particularly popular with adult learners who wished to earn a degree while working full time, alternative programs for professionals interested in developing "practical" expertise, and—later—distance learning. (See, for example, Kathleen Kelly, *Meeting Needs and Making Profits: The Rise of For-Profit Degree-Granting Institutions* (Education Commission of the States, 2001); Gordon C. Winston, "For-Profit Higher Education: Godzilla or Chicken Little?" *Change*, January/February 1999, 13–19.)

Other initiatives in the latter part of the century were fueled by the "lifelong learning" movement, which promoted diversity in delivery mechanisms and innovations in learning models and stimulated some of the corporate and experiential learning programs mentioned previously (see, for example, Chris Knapper & Arthur Cropley, *Lifelong Learning in Higher Education* (3d ed., Taylor & Francis Group, 1999)). First correspondence and television home-study courses, then off-campus and external degree programs, and later computer-based home-study courses and interactive distance learning programs all grew and significantly impacted postsecondary education (see, for example, Jonathan Alger & John Przypyszny (eds.), *Online Education: A Legal Compendium* (National Association of College and University Attorneys, 2002)).

Distance learning, in particular, has had substantial implications for colleges and universities, as public, private nonprofit, and profit-making institutions have developed Web-based degree programs and continuing education programs available online to students anywhere in the world. Many institutions scrambled to develop their own online programs out of concern that the market for traditional, campus-based programs would shrink as online degrees proliferated. Later, some institutions scaled back their involvement in the distance learning market as the market, or their views of its importance or profitability, changed. The rapid development in distance learning raised concerns for faculties about educational quality, oversight of distance instruction, faculty ownership of Web-based instructional materials, and faculty control over the creation, delivery, and updating of their own online courses. (See, for example, *The Chronicle of Higher Education's* archive of stories on distance learning and for-profit ventures at http://chronicle.com/weekly/indepth/forprofit.htm.)

As broader and larger cross-sections of the world passed through postsecondary education's gates in the latter part of the twentieth century, institutions became increasingly tied to the outside world. Government allocations and foundation support accounted for a larger share of institutional revenues. Competition for money, students, and outstanding faculty members focused institutional attentions outward. Institutions engaged increasingly in government research projects; state universities grew larger, as did annual state legislative appropriations for higher education; and federal and state governments increasingly paid tuition bills through grant and loan programs. Social and political movements—beginning with the civil rights movement and then the Vietnam antiwar movement in the 1960s—became a more integral part of campus life. And with all of these outside influences, the law came also.

In addition, student consumerism hit America's campuses (see, for example, D. Riesman, *On Higher Education: The Academic Enterprise in an Era of Rising Student Consumerism* (Jossey-Bass, 1980)). The competition for students, faculty members, and funds served to introduce marketing techniques and attitudes into postsecondary education. These developments helped turn institutional attentions toward competitor institutions, the business world and government agencies concerned about the education "marketplace." An increasing emphasis on students as consumers of education with attendant rights, to whom institutions owe corresponding responsibilities, further undermined the traditional concept of education as a privilege. Student litigation on matters such as tuition and financial aid, course offerings, awarding of degrees, campus security, and support services became more common, as did government consumer protection regulations, such as the required disclosure of graduation rates and campus crime statistics.

Institutional self-regulation, partly a response to student consumerism, was another important trend with continuing significance (see, for example, Carnegie Council on Policy Studies in Higher Education, *Fair Practices in Higher Education: Rights and Responsibilities of Students and Their Colleges in a Period of Intensified Competition for Enrollments* (Jossey-Bass, 1979)). This trend was not a movement back to the old days of "self-regulation," when institutions governed their cloistered worlds by tradition and consensus; but rather, a movement toward more and better institutional guidelines and regulations, and grievance processes, for students and faculty. On the one hand, by creating new rights and responsibilities or making existing ones explicit, institutions gave members of campus communities more claims to press against one another. But on the other hand, self-regulation facilitated the internal and more collegial resolution of claims and a greater capacity for full compliance with government regulations, thus reducing the likelihood that courts, legislatures, and administrative agencies would intervene in campus matters. (For analysis of ethical issues relating to self-regulation, see John Wilcox & Susan Ebbs, *The Leadership Compass: Values and Ethics in Higher Education*, ASHE-ERIC Report no. 1 (Association for the Study of Higher Education, 1992).) Despite such institutional efforts, the federal government and state governments continued to increase the scope and pervasiveness of their regulation of postsecondary education. At the state level, demands for assessment and accountability persisted, and new pressures were placed on research universities to demonstrate their devotion to teaching and service. At the federal level, new initiatives and regulations resulted from each reauthorization of the Higher Education Act.

As the twentieth century drew to its close, the development of higher education law continued to reflect, and be reflected in, social movements on the campuses and in the outside world. The civil rights movement continued to expand, covering not only racial and gender equality but also rights for persons with disabilities, as highlighted particularly by the Americans With Disabilities Act (ADA) of 1990; rights for religious adherents; and rights for gays and lesbians. (See, for example, Laura Rothstein, "Disability Law and Higher Education: A Road Map for Where We've Been and Where We May Be Heading," 63 *Maryland L. Rev.* 122 (2004).) Differences emerged regarding the extent of such rights, particularly for gays and lesbians. Abortion also remained an important issue, as pro-choice and pro-life movements continued to compete for predominance on many campuses.

Government financial support for higher education, having generally increased in the 1960s and 1970s, became problematic in the 1980s and 1990s. In the scramble for funds, postsecondary education was drawn even further into the political process. Issues emerged concerning equitable allocation of funds among institutions and among various categories of needy students. As the burden of diminishing support was perceived to fall on minority and low-income students, or on minority and women faculty newcomers who were most subject to layoffs prompted by budget cuts, new civil rights concerns arose. Moreover, as the resources available from government and traditional private sources failed to keep pace with institutional growth, and as economic conditions negatively affected institutions, financial belt tightening became a fact of life on most campuses. Legal questions arose concerning standards and procedures for faculty and staff layoffs, termination of tenured faculty, reduction and termination of programs, closures and mergers, and bankruptcies. (See, for example, James Martin, James Samels, & Associates, *Merging Colleges for Mutual Growth* (Johns Hopkins University Press, 2000).) Similarly, renewed attention was given to statewide planning for postsecondary education in financial hard times; and legal, political, and policy issues arose concerning program review and elimination in state systems, and concerning state authority to issue or refuse licenses for new programs of private (particularly out-of-state) institutions.

After mandatory retirement for faculty became unlawful in 1994, many institutions gave more attention to the performance of tenured faculty members. A trend toward post-tenure review developed haltingly, with the debate slowly shifting from whether to have such review to what procedures to use. Financial pressures on postsecondary institutions and legislatures' demands for accountability led institutional leaders to focus on faculty productivity. Institutions gave more attention to phased retirement programs, and age discrimination became a more important issue. In addition, in related developments, the dialogue on the continued propriety of faculty tenure intensified. Many state legislators, some college presidents, a small minority of faculty members, and some commentators asserted that tenure is unnecessary, since other systems that do not guarantee lifetime job security can still protect academic freedom. (See, for example, Richard Chait, "Thawing the Cold War over Tenure: Why Academe Needs More Employment Options," *Chron. Higher Educ.*, February 7, 1997, B4; and compare Matthew Finkin, *The Case for Tenure* (Cornell University Press, 1996).) Some institutions, such as Bennington College, eliminated tenure without suffering a loss of student enrollment (see Robin Wilson, "Bennington After Eliminating Tenure, Attracts New Faculty Members and Students," *Chron. Higher Educ.*, January 10, 1997, A10). Other institutions considered modifying their tenure systems but encountered substantial faculty resistance (see, for example, William H. Honan, "University of Minnesota Regents Drop Effort to Modify Tenure," *New York Times,* November 17, 1996, p. 21).

While the debate continued on whether tenure should continue to exist and, if so, in what form, the proportion of tenured faculty decreased on many campuses in the 1990s, and the proportion of part-time faculty continued to increase. A study by the U.S. Department of Education found that 42.5 percent of all faculty working in 1997 were employed part time, compared with 22 percent in 1970 (Courtney Leatherman, "Part-Timers Continue to Replace Full-Timers on College Faculties," *Chron. Higher Educ.*, January 28, 2000, A18). As their numbers increased, part-time faculty members sought improvements in their pay and benefits. Some formed unions, while others turned to litigation (see "Part-Time Faculty Members Sue for Better Pay and Benefits," *Chron. Higher Educ.*, October 15, 1999, A16). Graduate teaching assistants also clashed with faculty and administrators on many campuses over work assignments, the right to unionize, and the right to strike (Courtney Leatherman & Denise K. Magner, "Faculty and Graduate-Student Strife over Job Issues Flares on Many Campuses," *Chron. Higher Educ.*, November 29, 1996, A12). In addition, institutions have also increased their number of full-time, non-tenure track faculty positions (Courtney Leatherman, "Growth in Positions off the Tenure Track Is a Trend That's Here to Stay, Study Finds," *Chron. Higher Educ.*, April 9, 1999, A14). Although the proportion of women faculty increased slowly, women still lagged behind men at the tenured and full professor ranks, and even senior women faced inequitable working conditions at some institutions (see, for example, Robin Wilson, "An MIT Professor's Suspicion of Bias Leads to a New Movement for Academic Women," *Chron. Higher Educ.*, December 3, 1999, A16).

The latter years of the twentieth century also witnessed increasing conflict on campus relating to diversity of ideas, racial and ethnic identities, sexual orientation, gender concerns, and other matters concerning cultural diversity and lifestyle choices. These tensions were played out in clashes over "hate speech"; curriculum proposals placing greater emphasis on nonwhite, non-Western cultures and writers; issues regarding gender equity in the classroom and in college athletics; accommodation of students with disabilities; date rape, sexual assault, and sexual harassment; alcohol consumption and drug use; and issues regarding institutional ties with Greek organizations. Gays and lesbians became increasingly vocal as they sought parity with heterosexuals with respect to funding for student organizations, employment benefits, campus housing for same-sex couples, and equal access to careers in the military. Students with disabilities—particularly learning disabilities—challenged faculty and administrators' judgments with respect to course requirements, evaluation formats, and assignments.

The technological revolution on campus continued to surge ahead in the '90s, with critical ramifications for higher education. Biotechnological and biomedical research raised various sensitive issues (see below). Devising and enforcing specifications for the lease or purchase of technology for office support, laboratories, or innovative learning systems created complex problems involving contract and commercial law. The Internet and the World Wide Web opened virtually unlimited channels of communication and information for faculty, staff, and students. In turn, the mushrooming use of Web sites and e-mail by faculty and students for both pedagogical and personal purposes, and the continued growth of computer and telecommunications-assisted distance learning, spawned new challenges regarding intellectual property, free speech, harassment, invasion of privacy, defamation, plagiarism, and a multitude of other issues. These challenges have led institutions to review, and sometimes modify, campus policies on computer use, student conduct, academic integrity, and ownership of intellectual property, and have also led to changes in institutional methods, research methods, and dissemination of scholarly work.

Similarly, as a result of private industry's continual interest in university research, and universities' continual interest in private funding of research efforts, new alliances were forged between the campus and the corporate world. As new ties to the outside world were formed, questions arose concerning institutional autonomy, faculty academic freedom, and the specter of conflicts of interest (see, for example, Derek Bok, *Universities in the Marketplace: The Commercialization of Higher Education* (Princeton University Press, 2004); and Bernard Reams, Jr., *University-Industry Research Partnerships* (Quorum Books, 1986)). Federal government support for university-industrial cooperative research became an issue, as did federal regulation in sensitive areas such as genetic engineering.

Other new questions concerning research also arose. Research on both animals and human subjects became subject to control by institutional review boards. Stem cell research received considerable attention, and pertinent federal policies shifted with changes in the political party controlling federal research policy. Questions arose about the ownership of human tissue used in research, and about researchers' obligations to disclose the use to be made of the tissue and obtain informed consent. The patentability of living organisms and of human genes also raised complex legal and policy questions. And problems related to conflicts of interest and scientific misconduct plagued universities and the federal agencies that fund their research.

Universities' increasing ties to business and industry, and increasing pressures to become more efficient and cost-effective, led to demands from various quarters that universities be managed more like corporations. (See Ronald Ehrenberg (ed.), *Governing Academia* (Cornell University Press, 2004). In addition, outside the sphere of research, institutions increasingly engaged in entrepreneurial enterprises or outsourced entrepreneurial campus operations to commercial businesses. Big-time college athletics also increasingly became a profit-making "business" on some campuses. This "commercialization" of academia has had, and continues to have, enormous legal and policy implications for both public and private institutions. (See, for example, Stanley Aronowitz, *The Knowledge Factory: Dismantling the Corporate University and Creating True Higher Learning* (Beacon Press, 2001).)

The globalization of higher education also continued apace as the century moved to a close. The pervasive use of the Internet created the potential to involve institutions in legal problems on the other side of the globe, even if the institution had no physical presence there. U.S. institutions established branches and programs in other countries, and foreign entities established academic programs in the United States. The number of study abroad programs sponsored by U.S. universities continued to rise, as did the number of foreign students attending U.S. colleges and universities. These trends gave rise to issues concerning state coordination and control, and accrediting agency oversight, of programs in foreign countries; access to foreign-study programs for students with disabilities; the "extraterritorial" application of U.S. civil rights laws; compliance with foreign law requirements; and institutional liability for injuries to students and faculty participating in study abroad programs or overseas field trips. (See, for example, Note, "Foreign Educational Programs in Britain: Legal Issues Associated with the Establishment and Taxation of Programs Abroad," 16 *J. Coll. & Univ. Law* 521 (1990); and Richard Evans, Note, "'A Stranger in a Strange Land': Responsibility for Students Enrolled in Foreign-Study Programs," 18 *J. Coll. & Univ. Law* 299 (1991).) The numbers and types of questions concerning the immigration status of foreign students and scholars continued to grow.

Student and faculty demographics also continued to change in the late twentieth century, as did U.S. population demographics. The U.S. population was aging, and this change was reflected in college enrollments. The proportion of college students aged forty or older doubled between 1970 and 1993 (*Life After 40,* Institute for Higher Education Policy and Education Resources Institute, 1996). Faculties also reflected this aging of society. A 1999 survey found that nearly one-third of full-time faculty were age fifty-five or older (Denise K. Magner, "The Graying Professoriate," *Chron. of Higher Educ.,* September 3, 1999, A18). The U.S. population also became more diverse with respect to race and ethnicity. African Americans were 15 percent of the population under age eighteen in 1990, and Hispanics comprised 12.2 percent; these percentages continued to rise in the 1990s and into the twenty-first century (see Janice Hamilton Outtz, "Higher Education and the New Demographic Reality," 76 *Educational Record* 65 (1995)). These demographic realities exacerbated tensions over college admissions, hiring issues, and affirmative action, and supported continuing concerns about the proportion of minority students and faculty members in both undergraduate and post-baccalaureate programs. (See generally Caroline Turner, Mildred Garcia, Amaury Nora, & Laura Rendon, *Racial and Ethnic Diversity in Higher Education* (Association for the Study of Higher Education, 1996).) As institutions struggled to enhance the diversity of their student bodies, they confronted a new challenge: increasing the enrollment of a new minority: men. Women comprised approximately 55 percent of all college students in the 1990s. Women tended to earn better grades in high school than did men, and a larger proportion of women were graduating from high school.

In the first decade of the twenty-first century, as this book is written, there does not appear to be any lessening of the pace of change or the impact of new societal developments on higher education. Remnants, or new incarnations, of most of the 1980s and 1990s trends (and some of the earlier trends) continue to occupy the attentions of institutional officers, counsel, and faculty; and new trends and developments continue to emerge. The globalization, commercialization, "technologization," and diversification of higher education continue to be predominant overarching trends that affect higher education in numerous ways. These trends are now joined by the newest overarching development: global terrorism, and terrorist threats to the United States, in a post-9/11 world.

There are many specific issues and concerns that have arisen from these trends early in the new century and will likely continue in importance well into the future. The growth of the foreign student population in U.S. institutions slowed, and enrollment then dropped, at least temporarily, largely due to tightened federal restrictions of the issuance of visas in the wake of 9/11; and institutions have had to shoulder substantial new legal responsibilities in enrolling and monitoring foreign students. (See Burton Bollag, "Enrollment of Foreign Students Drops in U.S.," *Chron. Higher Educ.*, November 19, 2004, A1.) Similar effects for institutions are being encountered in recruiting foreign faculty candidates and researchers, and in inviting foreign speakers to campus. There are new federal restrictions on university research, largely due to concerns about the dissemination of research and research products pertinent to bioterrorism, and to the disclosure of research secrets. Increased federal investigatory powers, arising largely from the USA PATRIOT Act, have raised new issues concerning the privacy of computer communications and have stimulated broad debate on the appropriate balance between national security powers and individual rights.

The prelude to and aftermath of the U.S. Supreme Court's decisions in *Grutter v. Bollinger* and *Gratz v. Bollinger,* the University of Michigan affirmative action cases, have further stimulated the already extensive debate on university affirmative action policies. In addition, these developments have led to various state referendum and initiative drives aimed at prohibiting racial preferences; have spurred new research on alternatives to race-conscious affirmative action plans; and have reinvigorated legal issues concerning racial and ethnic preferences in financial aid, orientation programs, campus housing, and other institutional programming.

The hate speech phenomenon, the "political correctness" phenomenon, and concerns about ethnic, national origin, and religious discrimination have taken on new life, partly as a result of terrorism and its association with particular countries and religions. These developments, as well as recent court decisions, have prompted renewed attention to both faculty and student academic freedom, and to the relationship between these freedoms and institutional autonomy (sometimes called "institutional academic freedom").

Debate and research on the diversity of the higher education student population has taken on a new dimension, focusing on socioeconomic status. See generally William Bowen, Martin Kurzweil, & Eugene Tobin, *Equity and Excellence in American Higher Education* (U.Va. 2005). Some of the pertinent factors concern institutional and governmental financial aid programs. (See generally "The Quest for Students" (articles by various authors), *Chron. Higher Educ.,* April 30, 2004, Sec. B.) Rises in tuition costs continue to outpace increases in government programs of student aid, making it more difficult for low-income and middle-income students to afford the costs of four-year institutions. (See generally Edward St. John, *Refinancing the College Dream* (Johns Hopkins University Press, 2003).) A movement by institutions toward more merit-based aid and less need-based aid is exacerbating this problem. Other factors concern financial and competitive advantages that students from wealthier families may have in preparing for college. Besides apparent subtle effects of being in a family of low socioeconomic status (see Bowen, Kurzweil, & Tobin, above), there are more obvious considerations, such as the proliferation of private tutors, private admissions counselors, private test preparation courses, special summer academic programs, and "gap year" strategies providing competitive advantages generally available only to persons of means (see, for example, Ben Gose, "If at First They Don't Succeed . . . ," *Chron. Higher Educ.,* August 5, 2005, A30). Also, advanced placement (AP) courses and honors courses are generally more available to students in private high schools and wealthier public school districts.

Higher education governance is again becoming a major issue as many ideas have surfaced concerning the restructuring of state systems of higher education. Some state institutions, for instance, are seeking more autonomy from the state legislature and state agencies, and at the same time are building endowments and otherwise enhancing their capacities for fund-raising and innovation (see, for example, John Tagg, "Venture Colleges: Creating Charters for Change in Higher Education," *Change,* January/February 2005, 35–43). Other state institutions are becoming regionally oriented under state plans to serve better the particular needs of the state's various regions. As state institutions thus become more like private institutions, private institutions have become more like public institutions due to the ever-increasing federal regulations and federal aid conditions that generally treat private and public institutions the same. Within this mix of factors that is diminishing the distinction between public and private higher education, religious institutions seek to maintain their uniqueness and autonomy in light of increased government regulation and various financial and societal pressures.

In all, postsecondary education remains a dynamic enterprise in the new century, as it was in the old. Societal developments and technological breakthroughs continue to be mirrored in the issues, conflicts, and litigation that colleges and universities now face. The work of the university counsel has become even more challenging, the work of administrators even more demanding, and the work of scholars and students of higher education law even more fascinating, as recent trends and developments combine and are played out on the campuses of U.S. institutions. The challenge for the law is, as it has been, to keep pace with higher education by maintaining a dynamism of its own that is sensitive to institutions' evolving missions and the varying conflicts that institutions confront. And the challenge for higher education continues to be to understand and respond constructively to changes and growth in the law while maintaining its focus on its multiple purposes and constituencies.

Sec. 1.3. The Governance of Higher Education

1.3.1. Basic concepts and distinctions. It will be helpful for students, practitioners, and scholars of higher education law and policy to cultivate an understanding of higher education governance. "Governance" refers to the structures and processes by which higher education institutions and systems are governed in their day-to-day operations as well as their longer-range policy-making. (See generally William Tierney (ed.), *Competing Conceptions of Governance: The Paradox of Scope* (John Hopkins University Press, 2004); Edwin Duryea & Donald T. Williams (eds.), *The Academic Corporation* (Falmer, 2000).) Specifically, governance encompasses: (1) the organizational structures of individual institutions and (in the public sector) of statewide systems of higher education; (2) the delineation and allocation of decision-making authority within these organizational structures; (3) the processes by which decisions are made; and (4) the processes by which, and forums within which, decisions may be challenged.

Higher education governance can be divided into two categories: internal governance and external governance. "Internal governance" refers to the structures and processes by which an institution governs itself. "External governance" refers to the structures and processes by which outside entities (that is, entities external to the institution itself) play a role in the governance of institutional affairs. Internal governance usually involves "internal" sources of law (see Section 1.4.3); and external governance generally involves "external" sources of law (see Section 1.4.2). In turn, external governance can be further divided into two subcategories: public external governance and private external governance. "Public external governance" refers to the structures and processes by which the federal government (see Section 13.1), state governments (see Section 12.1), and local governments (see Section 11.1) participate in the governance of higher education. "Private external governance" refers to the structures and processes by which private associations and organizations participate in the governance of higher education. Major examples of such external private entities include accrediting agencies (see Section 14.3), athletic associations and conferences (see Section 14.4), the American Association of University Professors (see Section 14.5), and other higher education associations (see Section 14.1). Other examples include national employee unions with "locals" or chapters at individual institutions (see Sections 4.5 & 6.3); outside commercial, research, public service, or other entities with which institutions may affiliate (see Sections 3.6, 15.3.1, & 15.4.1); and public interest and lobbying organizations that support particular causes.

The governance structures and processes for higher education, both internal and external, differ markedly from those for elementary and secondary education. Similarly, the structures and processes for public higher education differ from those for private higher education. These variations between public and private institutions exist in part because they are created in different ways, have different missions, and draw their authority to operate from different sources (see generally Section 3.1); and in part because the federal Constitution's and state constitutions' rights clauses apply directly to public institutions and impose duties on them that these clauses do not impose on private institutions (see generally Section 1.5 below). Furthermore, the governance structures and processes for private secular institutions differ from those for private religious institutions. These variations exist in part because religious institutions have different origins and sponsorship, and different missions, than private secular institutions; and in part because the federal First Amendment, and comparable state constitutional provisions, afford religious institutions an extra measure of autonomy from government regulations, beyond that of private secular institutions, and also limit their eligibility to receive government support (see generally Section 1.6 below).

Governance structures and processes provide the legal and administrative framework within which higher education problems and disputes arise. They also provide the framework within which parties seek to resolve problems and disputes (see, for example, Section 2.3) and institutions seek to prevent or curtail problems and disputes by engaging in legal and policy planning (see Sections 1.7 & 2.4.2). In some circumstances, governance structures and processes may themselves create problems or become the focus of disputes. Internal disputes (often turf battles), for instance, may erupt between various constituencies within the institution—for example, a dispute over administrators' authority to change faculty members' grades. External governance disputes may erupt between an institution and an outside entity—for example, a dispute over a state board of education's authority to approve or terminate certain academic programs at a state institution, or a dispute over an athletic association's charges of irregularities in an institution's intercollegiate basketball program. Such disputes may spawn major legal issues about governance structures and processes that are played out in the courts. (See Sections 7.2.3 and 7.4.2 for examples concerning internal governance and Sections 12.2 and 14.4 for examples concerning external governance.) Whether a problem or dispute centers on governance, or governance only provides the framework, a full appreciation of the problem or dispute, and the institution's capacity for addressing it effectively, requires a firm grasp of the pertinent governance structures and processes.

Typically, when internal governance is the context, an institution's governing board or officers are pitted against one or more faculty members, staff members, or students; or members of these constituencies are pitted against one another. Chapters Three through Ten of this book focus primarily on such issues. When external governance is the context, typically a legislature, a government agency or board, a private association or other private organization, or sometimes an affiliated entity or outside contractor is pitted against a higher educational institution (or system) or against officers, faculty members, or students of an institution. Chapters Eleven through Fifteen of this book focus primarily on such issues.

The two categories of internal and external governance often overlap, especially in public institutions, and a problem in one category may often "cross over" to the other. An internal dispute about sexual harassment of a student by an employee, for instance, may be governed not only by the institution's internal policies on harassment but also by the external nondiscrimination requirements of the federal Title IX statute (see Section 9.3.4 of this book). Similarly, such a sexual harassment dispute may be heard and resolved not only through the institution's internal processes (such as a grievance mechanism), but also externally through the state or federal courts, the U.S. Department of Education, or a state civil rights agency. There are many examples of such crossovers throughout this book.

1.3.2. Internal governance.

As a keystone of their internal governance systems, colleges and universities create "internal law" (see Section 1.4.3 below) that delineates the authority of the institution and delegates portions of it to various institutional officers, managers, and directors, to departmental and school faculties, to the student body, and sometimes to captive or affiliated organizations (see Sections 3.6.1 & 3.6.2). Equally important, internal law establishes the rights and responsibilities of individual members of the campus community and the processes by which these rights and responsibilities are enforced. Circumscribing this internal law is the "external law" (see Section 1.4.2 below) created by the federal government, state governments, and local governments through their own governance processes. Since the external law takes precedence over internal law when the two are in conflict, institutions' internal law must be framed against the backdrop of applicable external law.

Internal governance structures and processes may differ among institutions depending on their status as public, private secular, or private religious (as indicated in subsection 1.3.1), and also depending on their size and the degree programs that they offer. The internal governance of a large research university, for instance, may differ from that of a small liberal arts college, which in turn may differ from that of a community college. Regardless of the type of institution, however, there is substantial commonality among the internal structures of American institutions of higher education. In general, every institution has, at its head, a governing board that is usually called a board of trustees or (for some public institutions) a board of regents. Below this board is a chief executive officer, usually called the president or (for some public institutions) the chancellor. Below the president or chancellor are various other executive officers, for example, a chief business officer, a chief information officer, and a general counsel. In addition, there are typically numerous academic officers, chief of whom is a provost or vice president for academic affairs.

Below the provost or vice president are the deans of the various schools, the department chairs, and the academic program directors (for instance, a director of distance learning, a director of internship programs, or a director of academic support programs). There are also managers and compliance officers, such as risk managers, facilities managers, affirmative action officers, and environmental or health and safety officers; and directors of particular functions, such as admissions, financial aid, and alumni affairs. These managers, officers, and directors may serve the entire institution or may serve only a particular school within the institution. In addition to these officers and administrators, there is usually a campuswide organization that represents the interests of faculty members (such as a faculty senate) and a campuswide organization that represents the interests of students (such as a student government association).

In addition to their involvement in a faculty senate or similar organization, faculty members are usually directly involved in the governance of individual departments and schools (see generally Section 7.4.1). Nationwide, faculty participation in governance has been sufficiently substantial that internal governance is often referred to as "shared governance" or "shared institutional governance" (see William Tierney & James Minor, *Challenges for Governance: A National Report* (Center for Higher Education Policy Analysis, University of Southern California (2003)). In recent times, as many institutions have been reconsidering their governance structures, usually under pressure to attain greater efficiency and cost-effectiveness, the concept and the actual operation of shared governance have become a subject of renewed attention.

1.3.3. External governance. The states are generally considered to be the primary external "governors" of higher education, at least in terms of legal theory. State governments are governments of general powers that typically have express authority over education built into their state constitutions. They have plenary authority to create, organize, support, and dissolve public higher educational institutions (see Section 12.2); and they have general police powers under which they charter and license private higher educational institutions and recognize their authority to grant degrees (see Section 12.3). The states also promulgate state administrative procedure acts, open meetings and open records laws, and ethics codes that guide the operations of most state institutions (see Sections 12.5.2–12.5.4 & 15.4.7). In addition, states have fiscal powers (especially taxation powers) and police powers regarding health and safety (including the power to create and enforce criminal law) that they apply to private institutions and that substantially affect their operations (see, for example, Sections 12.1, 12.5.1, & 12.5.5). And more generally, state courts establish and enforce the common law of contracts and torts that forms the foundation of the legal relationship between institutions and their faculty members, students, administrators, and staffs. (See Section 1.4.2.4 regarding common law and Section 1.4.4 regarding the role of the courts.)

The federal government, in contrast to the state governments, is a government of limited powers, and its constitutional powers, as enumerated in the federal Constitution, do not include any express power over education (Section 13.1.1 of this book). Through other express powers, however, such as its spending power (Section 13.1.2), and through its implied powers,[2] the federal government exercises substantial governance authority over both public and private higher education. Under its express powers to raise and spend money (see Sections 13.1.2 & 13.1.3), for example, Congress provides various types of federal aid to most public and private institutions in the United States, and under its implied powers Congress establishes conditions on how institutions spend and account for these funds. Also under its implied powers, Congress provides for federal recognition of private accrediting agencies—among the primary external private "governors" of education—whose accreditation judgments federal agencies rely on in determining institutions' eligibility for federal funds (see Section 14.3.3). The federal government also uses its spending power in other ways that directly affect the governance processes of public and private higher educational institutions. Examples include the federally required processes for accommodating students with disabilities (see Section 9.3.5.4); for keeping student records (see Section 9.7.1); for achieving racial and ethnic diversity through admissions and financial aid programs (see Sections 8.2.5 & 8.3.4); and for preventing and remedying sex discrimination and sexual harassment (see, for example, Sections 9.3.4 & 13.5.3).

Under other powers, and pursuing other priorities, the federal government also establishes processes for copyrighting works and patenting inventions of faculty members and others (see, for example, Section 13.2.5); for enrolling and monitoring foreign students (see Section 8.7.4); for resolving employment disputes involving unionized workers in private institutions (see Sections 4.5 & 6.3); and for resolving other employment disputes concerning health and safety, wages and hours, leaves of absence, unemployment compensation, retirement benefits, and discrimination (see, for example, Sections 4.6.1–4.6.4). In all these arenas, federal law is supreme over state and local law, and federal law will preempt state and local law that is incompatible with the federal law.

Furthermore, the federal courts are the primary forum for resolving disputes about the scope of federal powers over education (see, for example, Sections 13.1.4, 13.1.5, & 13.1.6), and for enforcing the federal constitutional rights of faculty members, students, and others (see, for example, Sections 7.4 & 9.5). Thus, federal court judgments upholding federal powers or individuals' constitutional rights serve to alter, channel, and check the governance activities of higher education institutions, especially public institutions, in many important ways.

In addition to all these aspects of federal governance, the federal government establishes and supports its own public higher education institutions that serve particular federal constitutional purposes. The military academies, such as the Naval Academy, are the most obvious examples but by no means the

---

[2]On implied powers, see William Kaplin, *American Constitutional Law: An Overview, Analysis, and Integration* (Carolina Academic Press, 2004), Chap. 6, Sec. B.3.

only ones. For example, the U.S. Department of Defense operates the Uniformed Services University of the Health Sciences under the direction of a board of regents. There is also the National Defense University (http://www.ndu.edu) and the Air University (http://www.au.af.mil)—both accredited, degree-granting institutions. The latter's various colleges include the Community College of the Air Force, which received its degree-granting authority directly from Congress (Pub. L. 94-361, July 14, 1976, 10 U.S.C. § 9315) and now offers more than sixty degree programs for enlisted personnel, billing itself on its Web site (http://www.au.af.mil/au/ccaf/) as "the largest multi-campus community college in the world." Together, the various colleges and universities of the military services serve not only commissioned officers and enlisted personnel, but also civilians who commit themselves to military careers, civilian officials of the U.S. government, and military personnel from other countries. In addition, the federal military services sponsor Reserve Officer Training Corps (ROTC) programs on the campuses of many civilian colleges and universities. And under the Senior Reserve Officers' Training Corps Act (10 U.S.C. §§ 2101 *et seq.*), Congress has also designated six civilian colleges with military-style training as "senior military colleges" entitled to certain special benefits provided by the military services (10 U.S.C. § 2111 a(a)–(c), (e), & (f)).

In another area of federal power and interest, the federal government, through the U.S. Department of the Interior, operates several accredited postsecondary institutions primarily serving American Indians—for example, Haskell Indian Nations University located in Lawrence, Kansas (http://www.haskell. edu).[3] The federal government also provides grants to approximately twenty-five tribally controlled colleges under the Tribally Controlled College or University Assistance Act, 25 U.S.C. §§ 1801 *et seq.* (For further information on these various colleges and universities, see the Web site of the American Indian Higher Education Consortium (http://www.aihec.org).)

The federal government also has a special interest in, and authority over, the governance of higher educational institutions in the District of Columbia. Since the District is not within the boundaries of any state, Congress for many years has provided for the chartering of D.C. institutions under its constitutional power to exercise exclusive legislative jurisdiction over the Nation's Capital (U.S. Const., Art. I, sec. 8, clause 17). In some cases, Congress itself has chartered D.C. institutions by enacting bills of incorporation (see, for example, Pub. L. 235, 70th Cong., Sess. 1 (1928)), confirming and expanding the Catholic University of America's 1887 charter under the D.C. incorporation statute). In addition, the federal government has historically provided additional support to two institutions in the District of Columbia, Howard University and Gallaudet University, due to their special national missions. (See, for example, Act to

---

[3]The other institutions operated by the Department of the Interior, as of this book's press deadline, are the Southwestern Indian Polytechnic Institute (http://www.sipi.bia.edu), the Saginaw Chippewa Tribal College, and the Tohoro O'odhem Community College.

Incorporate Howard University, 14 Stat. 428 (39th Cong. 2d Sess. 1866), and the act of June 16, 1882, for the relief of Howard University, 22 Stat. 104.)[4]

Local governments, in general, have much less involvement in the governance of higher education than either state governments or the federal government. The most important and pertinent aspect of local governance is the authority to establish, or to exercise control over, community colleges. But this local authority does not exist in all states, since state legislatures and state boards may have primary governance authority in some states. Local governments may also have some effect on institutions' internal governance—and may superimpose their own structures and processes upon institutions—in certain areas such as law enforcement, public health, zoning, and local taxation (see Sections 11.2, 11.3, & 11.5). But local governments' authority in such areas is usually delegated to it by the states, and is thus dependent on, and subject to being preempted by, state law (see Section 11.1).

External public governance structures and processes are more varied than those for internal governance—especially with regard to public institutions whose governance depends on the particular law of the state in which the institution is located (see Section 12.2). The statewide structures for higher education, public and private, also differ from state to state (see Section 12.1). What is common to most states is a state board (such as a state board of higher education) or state officer (such as a commissioner) that is responsible for public higher education statewide. This board or officer may also be responsible for private higher education statewide, or some other board or officer may have that responsibility. If a state has more than one statewide system of higher education, there may also be separate boards for each system (for example, the University of California system and the California State University system). In all of these variations, states are typically much more involved in external governance for public institutions than they are for private institutions.

At the federal level, there are also a variety of structures pertinent to the external governance of higher education, but they tend to encompass all postsecondary institutions, public or private, in much the same way. The most obvious and well known part of the federal structure is the U.S. Department of Education. In addition, there are numerous other cabinet-level departments and administrative agencies that have either spending authority or regulatory authority over higher education. The Department of Homeland Security (DHS), for instance, monitors foreign students while they are in the country to study (see Section 8.7.4); the Department of Health and Human Services (HHS) administers the Medicare program, which is important to institutions with medical

---

[4]At various points in U.S. history, presidents and congressional committees have proposed the creation of a national university in the District of Columbia under the auspices of the federal government. Although the idea was floated during the Constitutional Convention of 1787 and subsequently during George Washington's presidency, the high point of such considerations seems to have been during the late 1800s and early 1900s. See John W. Hoyt, "Memorial in Regard to a National University," Misc. Doc. No. 222, 52nd Cong., 1st Sess., August 3, 1892 (50 Cong. 1, vol. 5); and "University of the United States," Rpt. 945, 57th Cong., 1st Sess., April 1, 1902 (57 Cong. 1, vol. 6).

centers (see Section 13.2.13); the Department of Labor administers various laws concerning wages, hours, and working conditions (see Sections 4.5.1 & 4.6.2); the Occupational Safety and Health Administration (OSHA) administers workplace health and safety laws (see Section 4.6.1); several agencies have authority over certain research conducted by colleges and universities (see Section 13.2.3); and various other agencies, such as the National Institutes of Health (NIH) and the Department of Defense (DoD), provide research grants to institutions of higher education and grants or fellowships to faculty members and students (see generally Section 13.4.3).

At the local level, there is less public external governance than at the state and federal levels. The primary local structures are community college districts that have the status of local governments and community college boards of trustees that are appointed by or have some particular relationship with a county or city government. In some states, issues may arise concerning the respective authority of the community college board and the county legislative body (see Section 11.1). Some local administrative agencies, such as a human relations commission or an agency that issues permits for new construction, will also have influence over certain aspects of governance, as will local police forces (see Section 11.5).

Private external governance, like public external governance, also varies from institution to institution. Most postsecondary institutions, for example, are within the jurisdiction of several, often many, accrediting agencies. The agencies to which an institution is subject will depend on the region of the country in which the institution is located and the types of academic and professional programs that the institution offers (see Section 14.3.1). There are also various athletic conferences to which institutions may belong, depending on the level of competition, the status of athletics within the institution, and the region of the country; and there are several different national athletic associations that may govern an institution's intercollegiate competitions, as well as several different divisions with the primary association, the National Collegiate Athletic Association (NCAA) (see Section 14.4). Whether there is an outside sponsoring entity (especially a religious sponsor) with some role in governance will also depend on the particular institution, as will the existence and identity of labor unions that have established bargaining units. The influence that affiliated entities or grant-making foundations may have on institutional governance will also depend on the institution. One relative constant is the American Association of University Professors, which is concerned with all types of degree-granting postsecondary institutions nationwide (see Section 14.5).

Sec. 1.4. *Sources of Higher Education Law*

1.4.1. Overview. The modern law of postsecondary education is not simply a product of what the courts say, or refuse to say, about educational problems. The modern law comes from a variety of sources, some "external" to the postsecondary institution and some "internal." The internal law, as described in Section 1.4.3 below, is at the core of the institution's operations. It is the law the institution creates for itself in its own exercise of institutional governance. The external law, as described in Section 1.4.2 below, is created and enforced by bodies external to the institution. It circumscribes the internal law, thus limiting the institution's options in the creation of internal law.

1.4.2. External sources of law

1.4.2.1. Federal and state constitutions. Constitutions are the fundamental source for determining the nature and extent of governmental powers. Constitutions are also the fundamental source of the individual rights guarantees that limit the powers of governments and protect citizens generally, including members of the academic community. The federal Constitution is by far the most prominent and important source of individual liberties. The First Amendment protections for speech, press, and religion are often litigated in major court cases involving postsecondary institutions, as are the Fourteenth Amendment guarantees of due process and equal protection. As explained in Section 1.5, these federal constitutional provisions apply differently to public and to private institutions.

The federal Constitution has no provision that specifically refers to education. State constitutions, however, often have specific provisions establishing state colleges and universities or state college and university systems, and occasionally community college systems (see Section 12.2.3). State constitutions may also have provisions establishing a state department of education or other governing authority with some responsibility for postsecondary education.

The federal Constitution is the highest legal authority that exists. No other law, either state or federal, may conflict with its provisions. Thus, although a state constitution is the highest state law authority, and all state statutes and other state laws must be consistent with it, any of its provisions that conflict with the federal Constitution will be subject to invalidation by the courts. It is not considered a conflict, however, if state constitutions establish more expansive individual rights than those guaranteed by parallel provisions of the federal Constitution (see the discussion of state constitutions in Section 1.5.3.

1.4.2.2. Statutes. Statutes are enacted both by states and by the federal government. Ordinances, which are in effect local statutes, are enacted by local legislative bodies, such as county and city councils. While laws at all three levels may refer specifically to postsecondary education or postsecondary institutions, the greatest amount of such specific legislation is written by the states. Examples include laws establishing and regulating state postsecondary institutions or systems, laws creating statewide coordinating councils for postsecondary education, and laws providing for the licensure of postsecondary institutions (see Sections 12.3.1 & 12.4). At the federal level, the major examples of such specific legislation are the federal grant-in-aid statutes, such as the Higher Education Act of 1965 (see Section 13.4). At all three levels, there is also a considerable amount of legislation that applies to postsecondary institutions in common with other entities in the jurisdiction. Examples are the federal tax laws and civil rights laws (see Sections 13.3 & 13.5), state unemployment compensation and workers' compensation laws (see Sections 4.6.7 & 4.6.6), and local zoning and tax laws (see Sections 11.2 & 11.3). All of these state and federal statutes and local ordinances are subject to the higher constitutional authorities.

Federal statutes, for the most part, are collected and codified in the *United States Code* (U.S.C.) or *United States Code Annotated* (U.S.C.A.). State statutes are similarly gathered in state codifications, such as the *Minnesota Statutes Annotated* (Minn. Stat. Ann.) or the *Annotated Code of Maryland* (Md. Code Ann.). These codifications are available in many law libraries or online. Local ordinances are usually collected in local ordinance books, but those may be difficult to find and may not be organized as systematically as state and federal codifications are. Moreover, local ordinance books—and state codes as well— may be considerably out of date. In order to be sure that the statutory law on a particular point is up to date, one must check what are called the "session" or "slip" laws of the jurisdiction for the current year or sometimes the preceding year. These laws are usually issued by a designated state or local office in the order in which the laws are passed; many law libraries maintain current session laws of individual states in loose-leaf volumes and may maintain similar collections of current local ordinances for area jurisdictions.

1.4.2.3. Administrative rules and regulations. The most rapidly expanding sources of postsecondary education law are the directives of state and federal administrative agencies. The number and size of these bodies are increasing, and the number and complexity of their directives are easily keeping pace. In recent years the rules applicable to postsecondary institutions, especially those issued at the federal level, have often generated controversy in the education world, which must negotiate a substantial regulatory maze in order to receive federal grants or contracts or to comply with federal employment laws and other requirements in areas of federal concern (these regulations are discussed in Sections 13.2–13.5).

Administrative agency directives are often published as regulations that have the status of law and are as binding as a statute would be. But agency directives do not always have such status. Thus, in order to determine their exact status, administrators must check with legal counsel when problems arise. Every rule or regulation issued by an administrative agency, whether state or federal, must be within the scope of the authority delegated to that agency by its enabling statutes. Any rule or regulation that is not authorized by the relevant statutes is subject to invalidation by a court. And, like the statutes and ordinances referred to earlier, administrative rules and regulations must also comply with and be consistent with applicable state and federal constitutional provisions.

Federal administrative agencies publish both *proposed regulations,* which are issued to elicit public comment, and *final regulations,* which have the status of law. These agencies also publish other types of documents, such as policy interpretations of statutes or regulations, notices of meetings, and invitations to submit grant proposals. Such regulations and documents appear upon issuance in the *Federal Register* (Fed. Reg.), a daily government publication. Final regulations appearing in the *Federal Register* are eventually republished—without the agency's explanatory commentary, which sometimes accompanies the *Federal Register* version—in the *Code of Federal Regulations* (C.F.R.).

State administrative agencies have various ways of publicizing their rules and regulations, sometimes in government publications comparable to the *Federal Register* or the *Code of Federal Regulations*. Generally speaking, however, administrative rules and regulations are harder to find and are less likely to be codified at the state level than at the federal level.

Besides promulgating rules and regulations (called "rule making"), administrative agencies often also have the authority to enforce their rules by applying them to particular parties and issuing decisions regarding these parties' compliance with the rules (called "adjudication"). The extent of an administrative agency's adjudicatory authority, as well as its rule-making powers, depends on the relevant statutes that establish and empower the agency. An agency's adjudicatory decisions must be consistent with its own rules and regulations and with any applicable statutory or constitutional provisions. Legal questions concerning the validity of an adjudicatory decision are usually reviewable in the courts. Examples of such decisions at the federal level include a National Labor Relations Board decision on an unfair labor practice charge or, in another area, a Department of Education decision on whether to terminate funds to a federal grantee for noncompliance with statutory or administrative requirements. Examples at the state level include the determination of a state human relations commission on a complaint charging violation of individual rights, or the decision of a state workers' compensation board in a case involving workers' compensation benefits. Administrative agencies may or may not officially publish compilations of their adjudicatory decisions. Agencies without official compilations may informally compile and issue their opinions; other agencies may simply file opinions in their internal files or distribute them in a limited way. It can often be a difficult problem for counsel to determine what all the relevant adjudicatory precedents are within an agency. Examples of the interaction between administrative and judicial review are discussed in Section 6.7.1 of this book.

1.4.2.4. State common law. Sometimes courts issue opinions that interpret neither a statute, nor an administrative rule or regulation, nor a constitutional provision. In breach of contract disputes, for instance, the applicable precedents are typically those the courts have created themselves. These decisions create what is called American "common law." Common law, in short, is judge-made law rather than law that originates from constitutions or from legislatures or administrative agencies. Contract law (see, for example, Sections 6.2, 8.1.3, & 15.1) is a critical component of this common law. Tort law (Sections 3.3 & 4.7.2) and agency law (Sections 3.1 & 3.2) are comparably important. Such common law is developed primarily by the state courts and thus varies somewhat from state to state.

1.4.2.5. Foreign and international law. In addition to all the American or domestic sources of law noted, the laws of other countries (foreign laws) and international law have become increasingly important to postsecondary education. This source of law may come into play, for instance, when the institution sends faculty members or students on trips to foreign countries, or engages in business transactions with companies or institutions in foreign countries (see Section 15.4.2), or seeks to establish educational programs in other countries. (For a discussion of potential liability for issues that may arise in study abroad programs, see Section 3.3.2.)

Just as business is now global, so, in many respects, is higher education. For example, U.S. institutions of higher education are entering business partnerships with for-profit or nonprofit entities in other countries. If the institution enters into contracts with local suppliers, other educational institutions, or financial institutions, the law of the country in which the services are provided will very likely control unless the parties specify otherwise. Such partnerships may raise choice-of-law issues if a dispute arises. If the contract between the U.S. institution and its foreign business partner does not specify that the contract will be interpreted under U.S. law, the institution may find itself subject to litigation in another country, under the requirements of laws that may be very different from those in the United States. (For an example of such litigation taking place in the courts of Beijing, see Paul Mooney, "A Harvard Press and a Chinese Distributor Sue Each Other," *Chron. Higher Educ.*, September 10, 2004, A40.) Institutions planning business activities outside the borders of the United States should consult experienced counsel to ascertain what legal requirements will need to be met. This is particularly true for institutions that are founding or acquiring colleges in other countries (see, for example, Goldie Blumenstyk, "Spanning the Globe: Higher-Education Companies Take Their Turf Battles Overseas," *Chron. Higher Educ.*, June 27, 2003, A21).

If the institution operates an academic program in another country and hires local nationals to manage the program, or to provide other services, the institution must comply with the employment and other relevant laws of that country (as well as, in many cases, U.S. employment law). Employment laws of other nations may differ in important respects from U.S. law. For example, some European countries sharply limit an employer's ability to use independent contractors, and terminating an employee may be far more complicated than in the United States. Pension and other social security taxes are higher in many nations than in the United States, and penalties for noncompliance may be substantial. Tax treaties between the United States and foreign nations may exempt some compensation paid to faculty, students, or others from taxation. Definitions of fellowships or scholarships may differ outside the borders of the United States, which could affect their taxability. There is no substitute for competent local counsel to ensure that the institution is complying with all requirements pertaining to employees.

International agreements and treaties (between and among countries) are an increasingly important aspect of higher education law. Agreements on intellectual property protection and on sharing and regulating of technology are, and are likely to remain, leading examples. For example, the United States is a signatory to the World Trade Organization's Agreement on Trade-Related Aspects of

Intellectual Property Rights. Although this agreement prohibits the unauthorized copying of copyrighted material (such as textbooks), it can be difficult to enforce. (For an example of the problems in enforcing international copyright protections, see Martha Ann Overland, "Publishers Battle Pirates in India with Little Success," *Chron. Higher Educ.*, April 2, 2004, A40.) Other international copyright conventions to which the United States is a signatory are the Berne Convention and the Universal Copyright Convention.

Another important example of international agreements with implications for U.S. higher education is the Convention on the Recognition of Qualifications Concerning Higher Education in the European Region, signed by fifty countries, including the United States, in 1997. The agreement creates a unified system for evaluating and recognizing foreign academic credentials. The convention may be found at http://www.bologna-berlin2003.de/pdf/Lisbon_convention.pdf.

The European Union's (EU) Directive on the Protection of Individuals with Regard to the Processing of Personal Data and the Free Movement of Such Data has implications for institutions doing business with universities or businesses in the EU. The directive provides that data may be transferred to a non-EU country only if that country has subscribed to the standards of data privacy articulated in the directive. (For a discussion of this directive and its requirements, see Michael W. Heydrich, Note, "A Brave New World: Complying with the European Union Directive on Personal Privacy Through the Power of Contract," 25 *Brooklyn J. Int'l L.* 407 (1999).) Another EU directive may make U.S. institutions vulnerable to litigation in EU countries if they "pursue commercial or professional activities in a Member State" [of the EU]; it is unclear whether solely Internet-based activities would fall under the purview of this directive.

The General Agreement on Trade in Services (GATS), to which the United States is a signatory, may have important implications for institutions of higher education. The agreement, whose purpose is to expand free trade, requires the removal of barriers to access to markets and to competition. While the specific impact of GATS is not yet clear, it has the potential to increase federal regulation of higher education and, perhaps, international regulation of postsecondary education in those nations that participate in GATS. The American Council on Education maintains a Web site (http://www.acenet.edu/programs/international/gats/overview.cfm) on GATS and its activities with respect to the GATS negotiations. (For a review of the potential challenges and benefits of GATS from the perspective of a faculty union, see *Higher Education & International Trade Agreements: An Examination of the Threats and Promises of Globalization* (National Education Association, 2003), available at http://www2.nea.org/he/global/index.html.)

In addition to the possible application of international law to U.S. colleges and universities, U.S. institutions with programs, students, or employees living and working in other countries may still be required to follow U.S. law, particularly in the area of discrimination. (For a discussion of the extraterritorial application of U.S. law, see Section 5.2.1 (Title VII) and Section 13.5.7.6 (Titles VI and IX, Section 504, and the Age Discrimination Act).)

1.4.3. Internal sources of law

1.4.3.1. Institutional rules and regulations. The rules and regulations promulgated by individual institutions are also a source of postsecondary education law. These rules and regulations are subject to all the external sources of law listed in Section 1.4.2 and must be consistent with all the legal requirements of those sources that apply to the particular institution and to the subject matter of the internal rule or regulation. Courts may consider some institutional rules and regulations to be part of the faculty-institution contract or the student-institution contract (see Section 1.4.3.2), in which case these rules and regulations are enforceable by contract actions in the courts. Some rules and regulations of public institutions may also be legally enforceable as administrative regulations (see Section 1.4.2.3) of a government agency. Even where such rules are not legally enforceable by courts or outside agencies, a postsecondary institution will likely want to follow and enforce them internally, to achieve fairness and consistency in its dealings with the campus community.

Institutions may establish adjudicatory bodies with authority to interpret and enforce institutional rules and regulations (see, for example, Section 9.1). When such decision-making bodies operate within the scope of their authority under institutional rules and regulations, their decisions also become part of the governing law in the institution; and courts may regard these decisions as part of the faculty-institution or student-institution contract, at least in the sense that they become part of the applicable custom and usage (see Section 1.4.3.3) in the institution.

1.4.3.2. Institutional contracts. Postsecondary institutions have contractual relationships of various kinds with faculties (see Section 6.2); staff (see Section 4.3); students (see Section 8.1.3); government agencies (see Section 13.4.1); and outside parties such as construction firms, suppliers, research sponsors from private industry, and other institutions (see Section 15.1). These contracts create binding legal arrangements between the contracting parties, enforceable by either party in case of the other's breach. In this sense a contract is a source of law governing a particular subject matter and relationship. When a question arises concerning a subject matter or relationship covered by a contract, the first legal source to consult is usually the contract terms.

Contracts, especially with faculty members and students, may incorporate some institutional rules and regulations (see Section 1.4.3.1), so that they become part of the contract terms. Contracts are interpreted and enforced according to the common law of contracts (Section 1.4.2.4) and any applicable statute or administrative rule or regulation (Sections 1.4.2.2 & 1.4.2.3). They may also be interpreted with reference to academic custom and usage.

1.4.3.3. Academic custom and usage. By far the most amorphous source of postsecondary education law, academic custom and usage comprises the particular established practices and understandings within particular institutions. It differs from institutional rules and regulations (Section 1.4.3.1) in that it is not necessarily a written source of law and, even if written, is far more informal; custom and usage may be found, for instance, in policy statements from speeches, internal memoranda, and other such documentation within the institution.

This source of postsecondary education law, sometimes called "campus common law," is important in particular institutions because it helps define what the various members of the academic community expect of each other as well as of the institution itself. Whenever the institution has internal decision-making processes, such as a faculty grievance process or a student disciplinary procedure, campus common law can be an important guide for decision making. In this sense, campus common law does not displace formal institutional rules and regulations but supplements them, helping the decision maker and the parties in situations where rules and regulations are ambiguous or do not exist for the particular point at issue. Academic custom and usage is also important in another, and broader, sense: it can supplement contractual understandings between the institution and its faculty and between the institution and its students. Whenever the terms of such a contractual relationship are unclear, courts may look to academic custom and usage in order to interpret the terms of the contract. In *Perry v. Sindermann,* 408 U.S. 593 (1972), the U.S. Supreme Court placed its imprimatur on this concept of academic custom and usage when it analyzed a professor's claim that he was entitled to tenure at Odessa College:

> The law of contracts in most, if not all, jurisdictions long has employed a process by which agreements, though not formalized in writing, may be "implied" (3 *Corbin on Contracts,* §§ 561–672A). Explicit contractual provisions may be supplemented by other agreements implied from "the promisor's words and conduct in the light of the surrounding circumstances" (§ 562). And "the meaning of [the promisor's] words and acts is found by relating them to the usage of the past" (§ 562).
>
> A teacher, like the respondent, who has held his position for a number of years might be able to show from the circumstances of this service—and from other relevant facts—that he has a legitimate claim of entitlement to job tenure. Just as this Court has found there to be a "common law of a particular industry or of a particular plant" that may supplement a collective bargaining agreement (*United Steelworkers v. Warrior & Gulf Nav. Co.,* 363 U.S. 574, 579 . . . (1960)), so there may be an unwritten "common law" in a particular university that certain employees shall have the equivalent of tenure [408 U.S. at 602].

Sindermann was a constitutional due process case, and academic custom and usage was relevant to determining whether the professor had a "property interest" in continued employment that would entitle him to a hearing prior to nonrenewal (see Section 6.7.2). Academic custom and usage is also important in contract cases where courts, arbitrators, or grievance committees must interpret provisions of the faculty-institution contract (see Sections 6.2 & 6.3) or the student-institution contract (see Section 8.1). In *Strank v. Mercy Hospital of Johnstown,* 117 A.2d 697 (Pa. 1955), a student nurse who had been dismissed from nursing school sought to require the school to award her transfer credits for the two years' work she had successfully completed. The student alleged that she had "oral arrangements with the school at the time she entered, later confirmed in part by writing and carried out by both parties for a period of two years, . . . [and] that these arrangements and understandings imposed upon defendant the legal duty to give her proper credits for work completed." When the school argued that the court had no jurisdiction over such a claim, the court responded: "[Courts] have jurisdiction . . . for the enforcement of obligations whether arising under express contracts, written or oral, or implied contracts, including those in which a duty may have resulted from long recognized and established customs and usages, as in this case, perhaps, between an educational institution and its students" (117 A.2d at 698).

Faculty members may make similar contract claims relying on academic custom and usage. For example, in *Lewis v. Salem Academy and College,* 208 S.E.2d 404 (N.C. Ct. App. 1974), the court considered but rejected the plaintiff's claim that, by campus custom and usage, the college's retirement age of sixty-five had been raised to seventy, thus entitling him to teach to that age. And in *Krotkoff v. Goucher College,* 585 F.2d 675 (4th Cir. 1978) (discussed in Section 6.8.2 of this book), the court rejected another professor's claim that "national" academic custom and usage protected her from termination of tenure due to financial exigency. Custom and usage is also relevant in implementing faculty collective bargaining agreements (see the *Sindermann* quotation above), and such agreements may explicitly provide that they are not intended to override "past practices" of the institution.

Asserting that academic custom and usage is relevant to a faculty member's contract claim may help the faculty member survive a motion for summary judgment. In *Bason v. American University,* 414 A.2d 522 (D.C. 1980), a law professor denied tenure asserted that he had a contractual right to be informed of his progress toward tenure, which had not occurred. The court reversed a trial court's summary judgment ruling for the employer, stating that "resolution of the matter involves not only a consideration of the *Faculty Manual,* but of the University's 'customs and practices.' . . . The existence of an issue of custom and practice also precludes summary judgment" (414 A.2d at 525). The same court stated, in *Howard University v. Best,* 547 A.2d 144 (D.C. 1988), "[i]n order for a custom and practice to be binding on the parties to a transaction, it must be proved that the custom is definite, uniform, and well known, and it must be established by 'clear and satisfactory evidence.'" Plaintiffs are rarely successful, however, in attempting to argue that academic custom and usage supplants written institutional rules or reasonable or consistent interpretation of institutional policies (see, for example, *Brown v. George Washington University,* 802 A.2d 382 (D.C. App. 2002)).

1.4.4. The role of case law. Every year, the state and federal courts reach decisions in hundreds of cases involving postsecondary education. Opinions are issued and published for many of these decisions. Many more decisions are reached and opinions rendered each year in cases that do not involve postsecondary education but do elucidate important established legal principles with potential application to postsecondary education. Judicial opinions (case law) may interpret federal, state, or local statutes. They may also interpret the rules and regulations of administrative agencies. Therefore, in order to understand the meaning of statutes, rules, and regulations, one must understand the case law that has construed them. Judicial opinions may also interpret federal or state constitutional provisions, and may sometimes determine the constitutionality of particular statutes or rules and regulations. A statute, rule, or regulation that is found to be unconstitutional because it conflicts with a particular provision of the federal or a state constitution is void and no longer enforceable by the courts. In addition to these functions, judicial opinions also frequently develop and apply the "common law" of the jurisdiction in which the court sits. And judicial opinions may interpret postsecondary institutions' "internal law" (Section 1.4.3) and measure its validity against the backdrop of the constitutional provisions, statutes, and regulations (the "external law"; Section 1.4.2) that binds institutions.

Besides their opinions in postsecondary education cases, courts issue numerous opinions each year in cases concerning elementary and secondary education (see, for example, the *Wood v. Strickland* case in Section 4.7.4.1 and the *Goss v. Lopez* case in Section 9.4.2). Insights and principles from these cases are often transferable to postsecondary education. But elementary or secondary precedents cannot be applied routinely or uncritically to postsecondary education. Differences in the structures, missions, and clienteles of these levels of education may make precedents from one level inapplicable to the other or may require that the precedent's application be modified to account for the differences. In *Lansdale v. Tyler Junior College*, 470 F.2d 659 (5th Cir. 1972), for instance, the court considered the applicability to postsecondary education of a prior precedent permitting high schools to regulate the length of students' hair. The court refused to extend the precedent. As one judge explained:

> The college campus marks the appropriate boundary where the public institution can no longer assert that the regulation of . . . [hair length] is reasonably related to the fostering or encouraging of education. . . .
>
> There are a number of factors which support the proposition that the point between high school and college is the place where the line should be drawn. . . . That place is the point in the student's process of maturity where he usually comes within the ambit of the Twenty-Sixth Amendment and the Selective Service Act, where he often leaves home for dormitory life, and where the educational institution ceases to deal with him through parents and guardians. . . . The majority holds today that as a matter of law the college campus is the line of demarcation where the weight of the student's maturity, as compared with the institution's modified role in his education, tips the scales in favor of the individual and marks the boundary of the area within which a student's hirsute adornment becomes constitutionally irrelevant to the pursuit of educational activities [470 F.2d at 662–64].

More recently, courts in various cases have debated whether secondary education precedents permitting regulation of vulgar and offensive speech would apply to faculty or student speech in postsecondary institutions (see, for example,

Martin v. Parrish, 805 F.2d 583 at 585–86 (majority opin.) and 586–89 (concurring opin.) (5th Cir. 1986)). The U.S. Supreme Court's ruling in *Hazelwood School District v. Kuhlmeier,* 484 U.S. 260 (1988), a secondary education case involving the student press, has been a particular focus of attention. In this case, the Court affirmed a high school principal's editorial control over "school-sponsored speech" in the form of a student newspaper. The Court's opinion identified but did not address the question "whether the same degree of deference [to administrators' judgments] is appropriate with respect to school-sponsored expressive activities at the college and university level" (484 U.S. at 273 fn. 7). Lower courts in later cases have differed in their answers to this question. In *Kincaid v. Gibson,* 236 F.3d 342 (6th Cir. 2001) (*en banc*), for example, the Sixth Circuit declined to apply *Hazelwood* in a university setting. But in *Hosty v. Carter,* 412 F.3d 731 (7th Cir. 2005) (*en banc*), *reversing* 325 F.3d 945 (7th Cir. 2003), the court determined, by a vote of 7 to 4, that the *Hazelwood* framework "applies to subsidized student newspapers" in the university setting. (*Kincaid* and *Hosty* are discussed in Section 10.3.3.) In other cases, other U.S. Courts of Appeals have also adopted *Hazelwood* for use in higher education cases concerning student speech in the classroom (*Axson-Flynn v. Johnson,* 356 F.3d 1277 (10th Cir. 2004)), speech in course assignments (*Brown v. Li,* 308 F.3d 939 (9th Cir. 2002)), and even problems concerning faculty classroom speech (*Bishop v. Aronov,* 926 F.2d 1066 (11th Cir. 1991)). (*Axson-Flynn* and *Brown v. Li* are discussed in Section 8.1.4; *Bishop* is discussed in Section 7.2.2; compare Section 7.2.4 under "Pedagogical Concerns Analysis.")

Similar issues arise for lower courts when they seek to determine whether their own elementary/secondary precedents should apply to higher education cases as well (and vice versa).[5] In *Edwards v. California University of Pennsylvania,* 156 F.3d 488 (3d Cir. 1988) (discussed in Section 7.2.2), and in *Urofsky v. Gilmore,* 216 F.3d 401(4th Cir. 2000) (*en banc*) (discussed in Section 7.3), for example, the courts applied their own elementary/secondary education precedents to higher education in the course of rejecting faculty members' academic freedom claims. These courts, like some other courts that have applied elementary/secondary precedents to higher education, were somewhat uncritical in their transmutation of precedents from one level of education to the other. The courts' opinions in these cases generally do not meaningfully engage the questions concerning the differences in higher education's mission, structure, and clientele that must be confronted in any such transmutation, nor do they develop clear or helpful guidance for determining the extent to which precedents from one level of education should be applicable to the other.

A court's decision has the effect of binding precedent only within its own jurisdiction. Thus, at the state level, a particular decision may be binding either on the entire state or only on a subdivision of the state, depending on the court's

---

[5]For an example of a "vice versa" case, in which the court considers whether academic freedom precedents from postsecondary education are applicable to secondary education, see *Cary v. Adams Arapahoe School Board,* 427 F. Supp. 945 (D. Colo. 1977), *affirmed on other grounds,* 598 F.2d 535 (10th Cir. 1979).

jurisdiction. At the federal level, decisions by district courts and appellate courts are binding within a particular district or region of the country, while decisions of the U.S. Supreme Court are binding precedent throughout the country. Since the Supreme Court's decisions are the supreme law of the land, they bind all lower federal courts as well as all state courts, even the highest court of the state.

The important opinions of state and federal courts are published periodically and collected in bound volumes that are available in most law libraries. For state court decisions, besides each state's official reports, there is the National Reporter System, a series of regional case reports comprising the (1) *Atlantic Reporter* (cited A. or A.2d), (2) *Northeastern Reporter* (N.E. or N.E.2d), (3) *Northwestern Reporter* (N.W. or N.W.2d), (4) *Pacific Reporter* (P. or P.2d), (5) *Southeastern Reporter* (S.E. or S.E.2d), (6) *Southwestern Reporter* (S.W. or S.W.2d), and (7) *Southern Reporter* (So. or So.2d). Each regional reporter publishes opinions of the courts in that particular region. There are also special reporters in the National Reporter System for the states of New York (*New York Supplement,* cited N.Y.S. or N.Y.S.2d) and California (*California Reporter,* cited Cal. Rptr.).

In the federal system, U.S. Supreme Court opinions are published in the *United States Supreme Court Reports* (U.S.), the official reporter, as well as in two unofficial reporters, the *Supreme Court Reporter* (S. Ct.) and the *United States Supreme Court Reports—Lawyers' Edition* (L. Ed. or L. Ed. 2d). Supreme Court opinions are also available, shortly after issuance, in the loose-leaf format of *United States Law Week* (U.S.L.W.), which also contains digests of other recent selected opinions from federal and state courts. Opinions of the U.S. Courts of Appeals are published in the *Federal Reporter* (F., F.2d, or F.3d). U.S. District Court opinions are published in the *Federal Supplement* (F. Supp.) or, for decisions regarding federal rules of judicial procedure, in *Federal Rules Decisions* (F.R.D.). All of these sources, as well as those for state court decisions, are online in both the Westlaw and LEXIS legal research databases. Opinions are also available online, in most cases, from the courts themselves. For example, opinions of the U.S. Supreme Court are available from the Court's Web site at http://www.supremecourtus.gov/opinions/opinions.html.

Sec. 1.5. The Public-Private Dichotomy

1.5.1. Overview. Historically, higher education has roots in both the public and the private sectors, although the strength of each one's influence has varied over time (see generally F. Rudolph, *The American College and University: A History* (University of Georgia Press, 1990)). Sometimes following and sometimes leading this historical development, the law has tended to support and reflect the fundamental dichotomy between public and private education.

A forerunner of the present university was the Christian seminary. Yale was an early example. Dartmouth began as a school to teach Christianity to the Indians. Similar schools sprang up throughout the American colonies. Though often established through private charitable trusts, they were also chartered by the colony, received some financial support from the colony, and were subject to its regulation. Thus, colonial colleges were often a mixture of public and private activity. The nineteenth century witnessed a gradual decline in governmental involvement with sectarian schools. As states began to establish their own institutions, the public-private dichotomy emerged. (See D. Tewksbury, *The Founding of American Colleges and Universities Before the Civil War* (Anchor Books, 1965).) In recent years this dichotomy has again faded, as state and federal governments have provided larger amounts of financial support to private institutions, many of which are now secular.

Although private institutions have always been more expensive to attend than public institutions, private higher education has been a vital and influential force in American intellectual history. The private school can cater to special interests that a public one often cannot serve because of legal or political constraints. Private education thus draws strength from "the very possibility of doing something different than government can do, of creating an institution free to make choices government cannot—even seemingly arbitrary ones—without having to provide a justification that will be examined in a court of law" (H. Friendly, *The Dartmouth College Case and the Public-Private Penumbra* (Humanities Research Center, University of Texas, 1969), 30).

Though modern-day private institutions are not always free from examination "in a court of law," the law often does treat public and private institutions differently. These differences underlie much of the discussion in this book. They are critically important in assessing the law's impact on the roles of particular institutions and the duties of their administrators.

Whereas public institutions are usually subject to the plenary authority of the government that creates them, the law protects private institutions from such extensive governmental control. Government can usually alter, enlarge, or completely abolish its public institutions (see Section 12.2); private institutions, however, can obtain their own perpetual charters of incorporation, and, since the famous *Dartmouth College* case (*Trustees of Dartmouth College v. Woodward,* 17 U.S. 518 (1819)), government has been prohibited from impairing such charters. In that case, the U.S. Supreme Court turned back New Hampshire's attempt to assume control of Dartmouth by finding that such action would violate the Constitution's contracts clause (see B. Campbell, "*Dartmouth College* as a Civil Liberties Case: The Formation of Constitutional Policy," 70 *Ky. L.J.* 643 (1981–82)). Subsequently, in three other landmark cases—*Meyer v. Nebraska,* 262 U.S. 390 (1923); *Pierce v. Society of Sisters,* 268 U.S. 510 (1925); and *Farrington v. Tokushige,* 273 U.S. 284 (1927)—the Supreme Court used the due process clause to strike down unreasonable governmental interference with teaching and learning in private schools.

Nonetheless, government does retain substantial authority to regulate private education. But—whether for legal, political, or policy reasons—state governments usually regulate private institutions less than they regulate public institutions. The federal government, on the other hand, has tended to apply its regulations comparably to both public and private institutions, or, bowing to considerations of federalism, has regulated private institutions while leaving public institutions to the states.

In addition to these differences in regulatory patterns, the law makes a second and more pervasive distinction between public and private institutions: public institutions and their officers are fully subject to the constraints of the federal Constitution, whereas private institutions and their officers are not. Because the Constitution was designed to limit only the exercise of government power, it does not prohibit private individuals or corporations from impinging on such freedoms as free speech, equal protection, and due process. Thus, *insofar as the federal Constitution is concerned,* a private university can engage in private acts of discrimination, prohibit student protests, or expel a student without affording the procedural safeguards that a public university is constitutionally required to provide.

Indeed, this distinction can be crucial even within a single university. In *Powe v. Miles,* 407 F.2d 73 (2d Cir. 1968), seven Alfred University students had been suspended for engaging in protest activities that disrupted an ROTC ceremony. Four of the students attended Alfred's liberal arts college, while the remaining three were students at the ceramics college. The State of New York had contracted with Alfred to establish the ceramics college, and a New York statute specifically stated that the university's disciplinary acts with respect to students at the ceramics college were considered to be taken on behalf of the state. The court found that the dean's action in suspending the ceramics students was "state action," but the suspension of the liberal arts students was not. Thus, the court ruled that the dean was required to afford the ceramics students due process but was not required to follow any constitutional dictates in suspending the liberal arts students, even though both groups of students had engaged in the same course of conduct.

1.5.2. The state action doctrine. As *Powe v. Miles* in subsection 1.5.1 above illustrates, before a court will require that a postsecondary institution comply with the individual rights requirements in the federal Constitution, it must first determine that the institution's challenged action is "state action."[6] When suit is filed under the Section 1983 statute (see Sections 3.5 & 4.7.4 of this book), the question is rephrased as whether the challenged action was taken "under color of" state law, an inquiry that is the functional equivalent of the state action inquiry (see, for example, *West v. Atkins,* 487 U.S. 42 (1988)). Although the state action (or color of law) determination is essentially a matter of distinguishing public institutions from private institutions, and the public parts of an institution from the private parts—or more generally, distinguishing public "actors" from private "actors"—these distinctions do not necessarily depend on traditional notions of public or private. Due to varying patterns of government assistance and involvement, a continuum exists, ranging from the obvious public institution (such as a tax-supported state university) to the

[6]Although this inquiry has arisen mainly with regard to the federal Constitution, it may also arise in applying state constitutional guarantees. See, for example, *Stone by Stone v. Cornell University,* 510 N.Y.S.2d 313 (N.Y. 1987) (no state action).

obvious private institution (such as a religious seminary). The gray area between these poles is a subject of continuing debate about how much the government must be involved in the affairs of a "private" institution or one of its programs before it will be considered "public" for purposes of the "state action" doctrine. As the U.S. Supreme Court noted in the landmark case of *Burton v. Wilmington Parking Authority,* 365 U.S. 715, 722 (1961), "Only by sifting facts and weighing circumstances can the non-obvious involvement of the State in private conduct be attributed its true significance."

Since the early 1970s, the trend of the U.S. Supreme Court's opinions has been to trim back the state action concept, making it less likely that courts will find state action to exist in particular cases. The leading education case in this line of cases is *Rendell-Baker v. Kohn,* 457 U.S. 830 (1982). Another leading case, *Blum v. Yaretsky,* 457 U.S. 991 (1982), was decided the same day as *Rendell-Baker* and reinforces its narrowing effect on the law.[7]

Rendell-Baker was a suit brought by teachers at a private high school who had been discharged as a result of their opposition to school policies. They sued the school and its director, Kohn, alleging that the discharges violated their federal constitutional rights to free speech and due process. The issue before the Court was whether the private school's discharge of the teachers was "state action" and thus subject to the federal Constitution's individual rights requirements.

The defendant school specialized in education for students who had drug, alcohol, or behavioral problems or other special needs. Nearly all students were referred by local public schools or by the drug rehabilitation division of the state's department of health. The school received funds for student tuition from the local public school systems from which the student came and were reimbursed by the state department of health for services provided to students referred by the department. The school also received funds from other state and federal agencies. Virtually all the school's income, therefore, was derived from government funding. The school was also subject to state regulations on various matters, such as record keeping and student-teacher ratios, and requirements concerning services provided under its contracts with the local school boards and the state health department. Few of these regulations and requirements, however, related to personnel policy.

The teachers argued that the school had sufficient contacts with the state and local governments so that the school's discharge decision should be considered state action. The Court disagreed, holding that neither the government funding nor the government regulation was sufficient to make the school's discharge of the teachers state action. As to the funding, the Court analogized the school's situation to that of a private corporation whose business depends heavily on government contracts to build "roads, bridges, dams, ships, or submarines" for

---

[7]The beginning of this narrowing trend may be attributed to *Moose Lodge v. Irvis,* 407 U.S. 163 (1972).

the government thereby, but is not considered to be engaged in state action. And as to the regulation:

> Here the decisions to discharge the petitioners were not compelled or even influenced by any state regulation. Indeed, in contrast to the extensive regulation of the school generally, the various regulators showed relatively little interest in the school's personnel matters. The most intrusive personnel regulation promulgated by the various government agencies was the requirement that the Committee on Criminal Justice had the power to approve persons hired as vocational counselors. Such a regulation is not sufficient to make a decision to discharge made by private management, state action [*Blum*, 457 U.S. at 841–42].

The Court also rejected two other arguments of the teachers: that the school was engaged in state action because it performs a "public function" and that the school had a "symbiotic relationship" with—that is, was engaged in a "joint venture" with—government, which constitutes state action under the Court's earlier case of *Burton v. Wilmington Parking Authority*, 365 U.S. 715 (1961), (discussed above). As to the former argument, the Court reasoned in *Rendell-Baker*:

> [T]he relevant question is not simply whether a private group is serving a "public function." We have held that the question is whether the function performed has been "traditionally the *exclusive* prerogative of the state" (*Jackson v. Metropolitan Edison Co.*, 419 U.S. at 353). There can be no doubt that the education of maladjusted high school students is a public function, but that is only the beginning of the inquiry. [Massachusetts law] demonstrates that the State intends to provide services for such students at public expense. That legislative policy choice in no way makes these services the exclusive province of the State. Indeed, the Court of Appeals noted that until recently the State had not undertaken to provide education for students who could not be served by traditional public schools (*Rendell-Baker v. Kohn*, 641 F.2d at 26). That a private entity performs a function which serves the public does not make its acts state action [457 U.S. at 842].

As to the latter argument, the Court concluded simply that "the school's fiscal relationship with the state is not different from that of many contractors performing services for the government. No symbiotic relationship such as existed in *Burton* exists here."

Having rejected all the teachers' arguments, the Court, by a 7-to-2 vote, concluded that the school's discharge decisions did not constitute state action. It therefore affirmed the lower court's dismissal of the teachers' lawsuit.

As a key component of the narrowing trend evident in the Court's state action opinions since the early 1970s, *Rendell-Baker* well illustrates the trend's application to private education. The case serves to confirm the validity of various earlier cases in which lower courts had refused to find state action respecting the activities of postsecondary institutions (see, for example, *Greenya v. George Washington University*, 512 F.2d 556 (D.C. Cir. 1975); *Wahba v. New York University*, 492 F.2d 96 (2d Cir. 1974)). It also serves to cast doubt on some other earlier cases in which courts had found state action. (For an example, compare

Weise v. Syracuse University, 522 F.2d 397 (2d Cir. 1975), decided prior to *Rendell-Baker,* with 553 F. Supp. 675 (N.D.N.Y. 1982), the same case on remand just after the Supreme Court's ruling in *Rendell-Baker.*[8])

In the years preceding *Rendell-Baker,* courts and commentators had dissected the state action concept in various ways. At the core, however, three main approaches to making state action determinations had emerged: the "nexus" approach, the "symbiotic relationship" approach, and the "public function" approach.[9] The first approach, *nexus,* focuses on the state's involvement in the particular action being challenged, and whether there is a sufficient "nexus" between that action and the state. According to the foundational case for this approach, *Jackson v. Metropolitan Edison Co.,* 419 U.S. 345 (1974), "[T]he inquiry must be whether there is a sufficiently close nexus between the State and the challenged action of the [private] entity so that the action of the latter may be fairly treated as that of the State itself" (419 U.S. at 351 (1974)). Generally, courts will find such a nexus only when the state has compelled or directed, or fostered or encouraged, the challenged action. In *Jackson,* for example, the U.S. Supreme Court rejected the petitioner's state action argument because "there was no . . . [state] imprimatur placed on the practice of . . . [the private entity] about which petitioner complains," and the state "has not put its own weight on the side of the . . . practice by ordering it" (419 U.S. at 357).[10]

The second approach, usually called the "symbiotic relationship" or "joint venturer" approach, has a broader focus than the nexus approach, encompassing the full range of contacts between the state and the private entity. According to the foundational case for this approach, *Burton v. Wilmington Parking Authority,* 365 U.S. 715 (1961), the inquiry is whether "the State has so far insinuated itself into a position of interdependence with [the institution] that it must be recognized as a joint participant in the challenged activity" (365 U.S. at 725). When the state is so substantially involved in the whole of the private entity's activities, it is not necessary to prove that the state was specifically involved in (or had a "nexus" with) the particular activity challenged in the lawsuit.

The third approach, "public function," focuses on the particular function being performed by the private entity. The Court has very narrowly defined the type of function that will give rise to a state action finding. It is not sufficient that the private entity provide services to the public, or that the services are considered essential, or that government also provides such services. Rather, according to the *Jackson* case (preceding), the function must be one that is "traditionally exclusively reserved to the State . . . [and] traditionally associated with sovereignty" (419 U.S. at 352–53) in order to support a state action finding.

---

[8]The cases and authorities are collected in Annot., "Action of Private Institution of Higher Education as Constituting State Action, or Action Under Color of Law, for Purposes of Fourteenth Amendment and 42 U.S.C. § 1983," 37 A.L.R. Fed. 601.

[9]Subsequent to *Rendell-Baker,* in *Brentwood Academy v. Tennessee Secondary School Athletic Association,* discussed below, a fourth approach emerged: the "entwinement" approach.

[10]Such a showing of state involvement in the precise activity challenged may be eased, however, in some race discrimination cases (see *Norwood v. Harrison,* 413 U.S. 455 (1973), and *Williams v. Howard University,* 528 F.2d 658 (D.C. Cir. 1976)).

In *Rendell-Baker,* the Court considered all three of these approaches, specifically finding that the high school's termination of the teachers did not constitute state action under any of the approaches. In its analysis, as set out above, the Court first rejected a nexus argument; then rejected a public function argument; and finally rejected a symbiotic relationship argument. The Court narrowly defined all three approaches, consistent with other cases it had decided since the early 1970s. Lower courts following *Rendell-Baker* and other cases in this line have continued to recognize the same three approaches, but only two of them—the nexus approach and the symbiotic relationship approach—have had meaningful application to postsecondary education. The other approach, public function, has essentially dropped out of the picture in light of the Court's sweeping declaration that education programs cannot meet the restrictive definition of public function in the *Jackson* case.[11] Various lower court cases subsequent to *Rendell-Baker* illustrate the application of the nexus and symbiotic relationship approaches to higher education, and also illustrate how *Rendell-Baker, Blum v. Yaretsky* (*Rendell-Baker*'s companion case; (see above), and other Supreme Court cases such as *Jackson v. Metropolitan Edison* above) have served to insulate postsecondary institutions from state action findings and the resultant application of federal constitutional constraints to their activities. The following cases are instructive examples.

In *Albert v. Carovano,* 824 F.2d 1333, *modified on rehearing,* 839 F.2d 871 (2d Cir. 1987), *panel opin. vacated,* 851 F.2d 561 (2d Cir. 1988) (*en banc*), a federal appellate court, after protracted litigation, refused to extend the state action doctrine to the disciplinary actions of Hamilton College, a private institution. The suit was brought by students whom the college had disciplined under authority of its policy guide on freedom of expression and maintenance of public order. The college had promulgated this guide in compliance with the New York Education Law, Section 6450 (the Henderson Act), which requires colleges to adopt rules for maintaining public order on campus and file them with the state. The trial court dismissed the students' complaint on the grounds that they could not prove that the college's disciplinary action was state action. After an appellate court panel reversed, the full appellate court affirmed the pertinent part of the trial court's dismissal. The court (*en banc*) concluded that:

> [A]ppellants' theory of state action suffers from a fatal flaw. That theory assumes that either Section 6450 or the rules Hamilton filed pursuant to that statute constitute "a rule of conduct imposed by the state" [citing *Blum v. Yaretsky,* 457 U.S. at 1009]. Yet nothing in either the legislation or those rules required that these appellants be suspended for occupying Buttrick Hall. Moreover, it is undisputed that the state's role under the Henderson Act has

---

[11]This recognition that education, having a history of strong roots in the private sector, does not fit within the public function category, was evident well before *Rendell-Baker;* see, for example, *Greenya v. George Washington University,* 512 F.2d 556, 561 (D.C. Cir. 1975). For the most extensive work-up of this issue in the case law, see *State v. Schmid,* 423 A.2d 615, 622–24 (majority), 633–36 (Pashman, J., concurring and dissenting), 639-40 (Schreiber, J., concurring in result) (N.J. 1980). For another substantial and more recent work-up, see *Mentavlos v. Anderson,* 249 F.3d 301, 314–18 (4th Cir. 2001), discussed below in this subsection.

been merely to keep on file rules submitted by colleges and universities. The state has never sought to compel schools to enforce these rules and has never even inquired about such enforcement [851 F.2d at 568].

Finding that the state had not undertaken to regulate the disciplinary policies of private colleges in the state, and that the administrators of Hamilton College did not believe that the Henderson Act required them to take particular disciplinary actions, the court refused to find state action.

In *Smith v. Duquesne University,* 612 F. Supp. 72 (W.D. Pa. 1985), *affirmed without opin.,* 787 F.2d 583 (3d Cir. 1986), a graduate student challenged his expulsion on due process and equal protection grounds, asserting that Duquesne's action constituted state action. The court used both the symbiotic relationship and the nexus approaches to determine that Duquesne was not a state actor. Regarding the former, the court distinguished Duquesne's relationship with the state of Pennsylvania from that of Temple University and the University of Pittsburgh, which were determined to be state actors in *Krynicky v. University of Pittsburgh* and *Schier v. Temple University,* 742 F.2d 94 (3d Cir. 1984). There was no statutory relationship between the state and the university, the state did not review the university's expenditures, and the university was not required to submit the types of financial reports to the state that state-related institutions, such as Temple and Pitt, were required to submit. Thus the state's relationship with Duquesne was "so tenuous as to lead to no other conclusion but that Duquesne is a private institution and not a state actor" (612 F. Supp. at 77–78). Regarding the latter approach (the nexus test), the court determined that the state could not "be deemed responsible for the specific act" complained of by the plaintiff:

> [T]his case requires no protracted analysis to determine that Duquesne's decision to dismiss Smith cannot fairly be attributable to the Commonwealth. . . . The decision to expel Smith, like the decision to matriculate him, turned on an academic judgment made by a purely private institution according to its official university policy. If indirect involvement is insufficient to establish state action, then certainly the lack of any involvement cannot suffice [612 F. Supp. at 78].

In *Imperiale v. Hahnemann University,* 966 F.2d 125 (3d Cir. 1992), a federal appellate court held that the university had not engaged in state action when it revoked the plaintiff's medical degree. Considering both the joint venturer and the nexus tests, the court rejected the plaintiff's contention that the state action doctrine should apply because the university was "state-aided."

In *Logan v. Bennington College Corp.,* 72 F.3d 1017 (2d Cir. 1995), a tenured professor of drama at a private college was dismissed from his position after a college committee found that he had sexually harassed a student. The college had recently adopted a new sexual harassment policy and complaint procedure in response to a conciliation agreement resolving an earlier, unrelated sexual harassment complaint against the college. In that proceeding, the Vermont Human Rights Commission had found the previous version of the college's harassment policy to be ineffective. The new policy provided for a hearing before a committee comprised of faculty, staff, and one student. The professor asserted that, because of the Vermont Human Rights Commission's involvement in requiring the college to adopt the new policy and complaint process, the college's action in holding the hearing and dismissing him was "state action" subject to constitutional due process requirements. The court rejected the professor's argument, stating that the Human Rights Commission played no role in the proceedings against him, and that the new harassment policy did not require the college to dismiss him. The policy provided for a variety of sanctions, one of which was dismissal. Potential state action would have occurred only if the college had dismissed the professor because it believed that state law required it to do so. Even though the college had changed its policy to comply with state law, "its action in terminating [the professor] was in no way dictated by state law or state actors" (72 F.3d at 1028). The court therefore upheld the district court's grant of summary judgment for the college.

Rendell-Baker and later cases, however, do not create an impenetrable protective barrier for ostensibly private postsecondary institutions. In particular, there may be situations in which government is directly involved in the challenged activity—in contrast to the absence of government involvement in the actions challenged in *Rendell-Baker* and the four lower court cases above. Such involvement may supply the "nexus" that was missing in these cases. In *Doe v. Gonzaga University*, 24 P.3d 390 (Wash. 2001), for example, the court upheld a jury verdict that a private university and its teacher certification specialist were engaged in action "under color of state law" (that is, state action) when completing state certification forms for students applying to be certified as teachers. The private institution and the state certification office, said the court, were cooperating in "joint action" regarding the certification process.[12] Moreover, there may be situations, unlike *Rendell-Baker* and the four cases above, in which government officials by virtue of their offices sit on or nominate others for an institution's board of trustees. Such involvement, perhaps in combination with other "contacts" between the state and the institution, may create a "symbiotic relationship" that constitutes state action, as the court held in *Krynicky v. University of Pittsburgh* and *Schier v. Temple University*, above.

Craft v. Vanderbilt University, 940 F. Supp. 1185 (M.D. Tenn. 1996), provides another instructive example of how the symbiotic relationship approach might still be used to find state action. A federal district court ruled that Vanderbilt University's participation with the state government in experiments using radiation in the 1940s might constitute state action for purposes of a civil rights action against the university. The plaintiffs were individuals who, without their knowledge or consent, were involved in these experiments, which were conducted at a Vanderbilt clinic in conjunction with the Rockefeller Foundation and the Tennessee Department of Public Health. The plaintiffs alleged that the university and its codefendants infringed their due process liberty interests by withholding information regarding the experiment from them. Using the

---

[12]The Washington Supreme Court's decision was reversed, on other grounds, by the U.S. Supreme Court in *Gonzaga University v. Doe*, 536 U.S. 273 (2002). The Supreme Court's decision is discussed in Section 9.7.1.

symbiotic relationship approach, the court determined that the project was funded by the state, and that state officials were closely involved in approving research projects and making day-to-day management decisions. Since a jury could find on these facts that the university's participation with the state in these experiments created a symbiotic relationship, summary judgment for the university was inappropriate. Further proceedings were required to determine whether Vanderbilt and the state were sufficiently "intertwined" with respect to the research project to hold Vanderbilt to constitutional standards under the state action doctrine.

Because these and other such circumstances continue to pose complex issues, administrators in private institutions should keep the state action concept in mind in any major dealings with government. They should also rely heavily on legal counsel for guidance in this technical area. And, most important, administrators should confront the question that the state action cases leave squarely on their doorsteps: When the law does *not* impose constitutional constraints on your institution's actions, to what extent and in what manner will your institution nevertheless undertake on its own initiative to protect freedom of speech and press, equality of opportunity, due process, and other such values on your campus?

Over the years since *Rendell-Baker,* the U.S. Supreme Court has, of course, also considered various other state action cases. One of its major decisions was in another education case, *Brentwood Academy v. Tennessee Secondary School Athletic Association,* 531 U.S. 288 (2001). *Brentwood* is particularly important because the Court advanced a new test—a fourth approach—for determining when a private entity may be found to be a state actor. The defendant Association, a private nonprofit membership organization composed of public and private high schools, regulated interscholastic sports throughout the state. Brentwood Academy, a private parochial high school and a member of the Association, had mailed athletic information to the homes of prospective student athletes. The Association's board of control, comprised primarily of public school district officials and Tennessee State Board of Education officials, determined that the mailing violated the Association's recruitment rules; it therefore placed Brentwood on probation. Brentwood claimed that this action violated its equal protection and free speech rights under the federal Constitution. As a predicate to its constitutional claims, Brentwood argued that, because of the significant involvement of state officials and public school officials in the Association's operations, the Association was engaged in state action when it enforced its rules.

By a 5-to-4 vote, the U.S. Supreme Court agreed that the Association was engaged in state action. But the Court did not rely on *Rendell-Baker* or on any of the three analytical approaches sketched above. Instead Justice Souter, writing for the majority, articulated a "pervasive entwinement" test under which a private entity will be found to be engaged in state action when "the relevant facts show pervasive entwinement to the point of largely overlapping identity" between the state and the private entity (531 U.S. at 303). The majority grounded this entwinement theory in *Evans v. Newton,* 382 U.S. 296 (1966), where the Court had "treated a nominally private entity as a state actor . . . when it is 'entwined with governmental policies,' or when government is 'entwined in [its] management or control'" (531 U.S. at 296, quoting *Evans,* 382 U.S. at 299, 301). Following this approach, the Court held that "[t]he nominally private character of the Association is overborne by the pervasive entwinement of public institutions and public officials in its composition and workings . . ." (531 U.S. at 298).

The entwinement identified by the Court was of two types: "entwinement . . . from the bottom up" and "entwinement from the top down" (531 U.S. at 300). The former focused on the relationship between the public school members of the Association (the bottom) and the Association itself; the latter focused on the relationship between the State Board of Education (the top) and the Association. As for "entwinement . . . up," 84 percent of the Association's members are public schools, and the Association is "overwhelmingly composed of public school officials who select representatives . . . , who in turn adopt and enforce the rules that make the system work" (531 U.S. at 299). "There would be no recognizable Association, legal or tangible, without the public school officials, who do not merely control but overwhelmingly perform all but the purely ministerial acts by which the Association exists and functions in practical terms" (531 U.S. at 300). As for "entwinement . . . down," Tennessee State Board of Education members "are assigned ex officio to serve as members" of the Association's two governing boards (531 U.S. at 300). In addition, the Association's paid employees "are treated as state employees to the extent of being eligible for membership in the state retirement system" (531 U.S. at 300). The Court concluded that "[t]he entwinement down from the State Board is . . . unmistakable, just as the entwinement up from the member public schools is overwhelming." Entwinement "to the degree shown here" required that the Association be "charged with a public character" as a state actor, and that its adoption and enforcement of athletics rules be "judged by constitutional standards" (531 U.S. at 302).

The most obvious application of *Brentwood* is to situations where state action issues arise with respect to an association of postsecondary institutions rather than an individual institution. (For other examples of this type of state action case, all decided before *Brentwood,* see Section 14.3.2.3, regarding accrediting associations, and Section 14.4.1, regarding athletic associations.) But the *Brentwood* entwinement approach would also be pertinent in situations in which a state system of higher education is bringing a formerly private institution into the system, and an "entwinement up" analysis might be used to determine whether the private institution would become a state actor for purposes of the federal Constitution.[13] Similarly, the entwinement approach might be useful in circumstances in which a postsecondary institution has created a captive organization, or affiliated with another organization outside the university, and the question is whether the captive or the affiliate would be considered a state

---

[13]For pre-*Brentwood* examples of this problem and its analysis, see *Krynicky v. University of Pittsburgh* and *Schier v. Temple University,* above in this subsection.

actor. (The U.S. Supreme Court's decision in *Lebron v. National Railroad Passenger Corporation* (Amtrak), 513 U.S. 374 (1995), is also pertinent to this question; see Section 3.6.5 of this book.)

In addition to all the cases above, in which the question is whether a post-secondary *institution* was engaged in state action, there have also been cases on whether a particular *employee, student,* or *student organization*—at a private or a public institution—was engaged in state action; as well as cases on whether a *private individual or organization* that cooperates with a public institution for some particular purpose was engaged in state action. While the cases focusing on the institution, as discussed previously, are primarily of interest to ostensibly private institutions, the state action cases focusing on individuals and organizations are particularly pertinent to public institutions.

In a case involving students, *Leeds v. Meltz,* 898 F. Supp. 146 (E.D.N.Y. 1995), *affirmed,* 85 F.3d 51 (2d Cir. 1996), Leeds, a graduate of the City University of New York (CUNY) School of Law (a public law school) submitted an advertisement for printing in the law school's newspaper. The student editors rejected the advertisement because they believed it could subject them to a defamation lawsuit. Leeds sued the student editors and the acting dean of the law school, asserting that the rejection of his advertisement violated his free speech rights. The federal district court, relying on *Rendell-Baker v. Kohn,* held that neither the student editors nor the dean were state actors. Law school employees exercised little or no control over the publication or activities of the editors. Although the student paper was funded in part with mandatory student activity fees, this did not make the student editors' actions attributable to the CUNY administration or to the state. (For other student newspaper cases on this point, see Section 10.3.3.) The court granted the defendants' motion to dismiss, stating that the plaintiff's allegations failed to support any plausible inference of state action. The appellate court affirmed the district court's dismissal of the case, emphasizing that the CUNY administration had issued a memo prior to the litigation disclaiming any right to control student publications, even those financed through student activity fees.

In another case involving students, *Mentavlos v. Anderson,* 249 F.3d 301 (4th Cir. 2001), the court considered whether two cadets at the Citadel, a state military college, were engaged in state action when they disciplined a first-year (or "fourth-class") cadet. The first-year cadet, a female who subsequently withdrew from the college, alleged that the two male, upper-class cadets had sexually harassed, insulted, and assaulted her using their authority under the "fourth-class system," as described in the school's Cadet Regulations (the Blue Book), and thereby violated her right to equal protection under the Fourteenth Amendment. The regulations grant upper-class students limited authority to correct and report violations of school rules by first-year students. While hazing and discrimination based on gender as means of punishment for rules violations are expressly prohibited, punishments meted out by upper-class cadets may include mild verbal abuse or assignment to compete undesirable maintenance tasks. Ultimately, authority for observing the Citadel's rules rests with the college administration, not the upper-class cadets.

The appellate court affirmed the federal district court's decision that the upper-class students were not state actors and were not engaged in state action. Using the nexus approach,[14] the court emphasized that the upperclassmen enjoyed only limited disciplinary authority over students, authority that was not analogous to the broad discretionary powers of law enforcement officers. Moreover, the upperclassmen's actions were not authorized by the school and were in violation of the Blue Book rules, violations for which the cadets were disciplined. "Because the cadets' decision to engage in unauthorized harassment of [the plaintiff] was not coerced, compelled, or encouraged by any law, regulation or custom" of the state or the college, there was no "close nexus" between the cadets' action and the state, and the cadets were not state actors when they disciplined the plaintiff.[15]

Although the facts of the *Mentavlos* case are somewhat unique, involving a military-style discipline system at a military college, the court made clear that its analysis could have some application to honor code systems and other disciplinary systems at other public colleges:

> The Citadel may operate under a stricter form of student self-government, and one unique to military-style colleges, but the concept of student self-governance at public and private institutions of higher education, including the use of honor codes and the limited delegation of disciplinary authority to certain members of the student body, is hardly a novel concept. A public school or college student is not fairly transformed into a state official or state actor merely because the school has delegated to that student or otherwise allowed the student some limited authority to act [249 F.3d at 322].

Shapiro v. Columbia Union National Bank & Trust Co., 576 S.W.2d 310 (Mo. 1978), concerns a private entity's relationship with a public institution. The question was whether the public institution, the University of Missouri at Kansas City, was so entwined with the administration of a private scholarship trust fund that the fund's activities became state action. The plaintiff, a female student, sued the university and the bank that was the fund's trustee. The fund had been established as a trust by a private individual, who had stipulated that all scholarship recipients be male. The student alleged that, although the Columbia Union National Bank was named as trustee, the university in fact administered the scholarship fund; that she was ineligible for the scholarship solely because of her sex; and that the university's conduct in administering the trust therefore was unconstitutional. She further claimed that the trust constituted three-fourths of the scholarship money available at the university and that the school's entire scholarship program was thereby discriminatory.

---

[14]The court also used public function analysis (see 249 F.3d at 314–18), rejecting the plaintiff's arguments based on this approach because the Citadel was not analogous to the federal military academies, and the institution and the cadets therefore were not performing the traditional sovereign function of training men and women for service in the U.S. Armed Forces.

[15]As *Mentavlos* suggests, if the harassers had been employees of a public institution rather than students, the employees would likely have been found to be engaged in state action. For a case reaching this result, see *Hayut v. State University of New York*, 352 F.3d 733, 743–45 (2d Cir. 2003).

The trial court twice dismissed the complaint for failure to state a cause of action, reasoning that the trust was private and the plaintiff had not stated facts sufficient to demonstrate state action. On appeal, the Supreme Court of Missouri reviewed the university's involvement in the administration of the trust:

> [We] cannot conclude that by sifting all the facts and circumstances there was state action involved here. Mr. Victor Wilson established a private trust for the benefit of deserving Kansas City "boys." He was a private individual; he established a trust with his private funds; he appointed a bank as trustee; he established a procedure by which recipients of the trust fund would be selected. The trustee was to approve the selections. Under the terms of the will, no public agency or state action is involved. Discrimination on the basis of sex results from Mr. Wilson's personal predilection. That is clearly not unlawful. . . . The dissemination of information by the university in a catalogue and by other means, the accepting and processing of applications by the financial aid office, the determining of academic standards and financial needs, the making of a tentative award or nomination and forwarding the names of qualified male students to the private trustee . . . does not in our opinion rise to the level of state action [576 S.W.2d at 320].

Disagreeing with this conclusion, one member of the appellate court wrote a strong dissent:

> The University accepts the applications, makes a tentative award, and in effect "selects" the male applicants who are to receive the benefits of the scholarship fund. The acts of the University are more than ministerial. The trust as it has been administered has shed its purely private character and has become a public one. The involvement of the public University is . . . of such a prevailing nature that there is governmental entwinement constituting state action [576 S.W.2d at 323].

The appellate court's majority, however, having declined to find state action and thus denying the plaintiff a basis for asserting constitutional rights against the trust fund, affirmed the dismissal of the case. (For a discussion of the treatment of sex-restricted scholarships under the federal Title IX statute, see Section 13.5.3 of this book.)

DeBauche v. Trani, 191 F.3d 499 (4th Cir. 1999), concerns private actors who cooperated with officials of a public institution. The court considered whether the outside defendants were engaged in state action when they used the public university's facilities for a program that was assisted and promoted by the university. The plaintiff, a minor party gubernatorial candidate who had been excluded from a campaign debate held at, and broadcast from, the Virginia Commonwealth University (VCU), challenged the exclusion as a violation of her First Amendment rights. (See Section 11.6.2 for discussion of the free speech aspects of the case.) She sued not only the university and its president (Trani) but also the radio personality who had organized the debate (Wilder) and the two television stations that had broadcast the debate. The university and its president were clearly engaged in state action when they supported this debate, and the plaintiff argued that the other parties were as well, since they had solicited the university's funding and other assistance and had acted jointly with the university and its president in organizing and promoting the debate. The court rejected the plaintiff's argument and her reliance on the symbiotic relationship test as articulated in the U.S. Supreme Court's opinion in *Burton v. Wilmington Parking Authority* (above). The *Burton* case "certainly does not stand for the proposition that all public and private joint activity subjects the private actors to the requirements of the Fourteenth Amendment" and, since *Burton*, the U.S. Supreme Court has "articulate[d] numerous limits" to *Burton*'s "joint participation test." Moreover:

> As distinguished from *Burton*, DeBauche's . . . complaint does not describe facts that suggest interdependence such that VCU relied on the private defendants for its continued viability. While the state actors, VCU and Trani, worked with Wilder in the organization and promotion of the debate, their conduct cannot be thought to have controlled his conduct to such an extent that his conduct amounted to a surrogacy for state action. Moreover, they did not control the stations which only agreed to broadcast the debate [191 F.3d at 508].

1.5.3. Other bases for legal rights in private institutions. The inapplicability of the federal Constitution to private schools does not necessarily mean that students, faculty members, and other members of the private school community have no legal rights assertable against the school. There are other sources for individual rights, and these sources may sometimes resemble those found in the Constitution.

The federal government and, to a lesser extent, state governments have increasingly created statutory rights enforceable against private institutions, particularly in the discrimination area. The federal Title VII prohibition on employment discrimination (42 U.S.C. § 2000e *et seq.,* discussed in Section 5.2.1), applicable generally to public and private employment relationships, is a prominent example. Other major examples are the Title VI race discrimination law (42 U.S.C. § 2000d *et seq.*) and the Title IX sex discrimination law (20 U.S.C. § 1681 *et seq.*) (see Sections 13.5.2 & 13.5.3 of this book), applicable to institutions receiving federal aid. Such sources provide a large body of nondiscrimination law, which parallels and in some ways is more protective than the equal protection principles derived from the Fourteenth Amendment.

Beyond such statutory rights, several common law theories for protecting individual rights in private postsecondary institutions have been advanced. Most prominent by far is the contract theory, under which students and faculty members are said to have a contractual relationship with the private school. Express or implied contract terms establish legal rights that can be enforced in court if the contract is breached. Although the theory is a useful one that is often referred to in the cases (see Sections 6.2.1 & 8.1.3), most courts agree that the contract law of the commercial world cannot be imported wholesale into the academic environment. The theory must thus be applied with sensitivity to academic customs and usages. Moreover, the theory's usefulness is somewhat limited. The "terms" of the "contract" may be difficult to identify, particularly in the case of students. (To what extent, for instance, is the college catalog a source of contract terms?) Some of the terms, once identified, may be too vague or ambiguous to enforce. Or the contract may be so barren of content or so one-sided in favor of the institution that it is an insignificant source of individual rights.

Despite its shortcomings, the contract theory has gained in importance. As it has become clear that the bulk of private institutions can escape the tentacles of the state action doctrine, students, faculty, and staff have increasingly had to rely on alternative theories for protecting individual rights. (See, for example, *Gorman v. St. Raphael Academy,* 853 A.2d 28 (R.I. 2004).) Since the lowering of the age of majority, postsecondary students have had a capacity to contract under state law—a capacity that many previously did not have. In what has become the age of the consumer, students have been encouraged to import consumer rights into postsecondary education. And, in an age of collective negotiation, faculties and staff have often sought to rely on a contract model for ordering employment relationships on campus (see Section 4.5).

Such developments can affect both public and private institutions, although state law may place additional restrictions on contract authority in the public sphere. While contract concepts can of course limit the authority of the institution, they should not be seen only as a burr in the administrator's side. They can also be used creatively to provide order and fairness in institutional affairs and to create internal grievance procedures that encourage in-house rather than judicial resolution of problems. Administrators thus should be sensitive to both the problems and the potentials of contract concepts in the postsecondary environment.

State constitutions have also assumed critical importance as a source of legal rights for individuals to assert against private institutions. The key case is *Robins v. PruneYard Shopping Center,* 592 P.2d 341 (Cal. 1979), *affirmed, PruneYard Shopping Center v. Robins,* 447 U.S. 74 (1980). In this case a group of high school students who were distributing political material and soliciting petition signatures had been excluded from a private shopping center. The students sought an injunction in state court to prevent further exclusions. The California Supreme Court sided with the students, holding that they had a state constitutional right of access to the shopping center to engage in expressive activity. In the U.S. Supreme Court, the shopping center argued that the California court's ruling was inconsistent with an earlier U.S. Supreme Court precedent, *Lloyd v. Tanner,* 407 U.S. 551 (1972), which held that the First Amendment of the federal Constitution does not guarantee individuals a right to free expression on the premises of a private shopping center. The Court rejected the argument, emphasizing that the state had a "sovereign right to adopt in its own constitution individual liberties more expansive than those conferred by the federal Constitution."

The shopping center also argued that the California court's decision, in denying it the right to exclude others from its premises, violated its property rights under the Fifth and Fourteenth Amendments of the federal Constitution. The Supreme Court rejected this argument as well:

> It is true that one of the essential sticks in the bundle of property rights is the right to exclude others (*Kaiser Aetna v. United States,* 444 U.S. 164, 179–80 (1979)). And here there has literally been a "taking" of that right to the extent that the California Supreme Court has interpreted the state constitution to entitle its citizens to exercise free expression and petition rights on shopping center

property. But it is well established that "not every destruction or injury to property by governmental action has been held to be a 'taking' in the constitutional sense" (*Armstrong v. United States,* 364 U.S. 40, 48 (1960)). . . .

Here the requirement that appellants permit appellees to exercise state-protected rights of free expression and petition on shopping center property clearly does not amount to an unconstitutional infringement of appellants' property rights under the Taking Clause. There is nothing to suggest that preventing appellants from prohibiting this sort of activity will unreasonably impair the value or use of their property as a shopping center. The PruneYard is a large commercial complex that covers several city blocks, contains numerous separate business establishments, and is open to the public at large. The decision of the California Supreme Court makes it clear that the PruneYard may restrict expressive activity by adopting time, place, and manner regulations that will minimize any interference with its commercial functions. Appellees were orderly, and they limited their activity to the common areas of the shopping center. In these circumstances, the fact that they may have "physically invaded" appellants' property cannot be viewed as determinative [447 U.S. at 82–84].

PruneYard has gained significance in educational settings with the New Jersey Supreme Court's decision in *State v. Schmid,* 423 A.2d 615 (N.J. 1980) (this volume, Section 11.6.3). The defendant, who was not a student, had been charged with criminal trespass for distributing political material on the Princeton University campus in violation of Princeton regulations. The New Jersey court declined to rely on the federal First Amendment, instead deciding the case on state constitutional grounds. It held that, even without a finding of state action (a prerequisite to applying the federal First Amendment), Princeton had a state constitutional obligation to protect Schmid's expressional rights (N.J. Const. (1947), Art. I, para. 6 & para. 18). In justifying its authority to construe the state constitution in this expansive manner, the court relied on *PruneYard.* A subsequent case involving Muhlenberg College, *Pennsylvania v. Tate,* 432 A.2d 1382 (Pa. 1981), follows the *Schmid* reasoning in holding that the Pennsylvania state constitution protected the defendant's rights.

In contrast, a New York court refused to permit a student to rely on the state constitution in a challenge to her expulsion from a summer program for high school students at Cornell. In *Stone v. Cornell University,* 510 N.Y.S.2d 313 (N.Y. App. Div. 1987), the sixteen-year-old student was expelled after she admitted smoking marijuana and drinking alcohol while enrolled in the program and living on campus. No hearing was held. The student argued that the lack of a hearing violated her rights under New York's constitution (Art. I, § 6). Disagreeing, the court invoked a "state action" doctrine similar to that used for the federal Constitution (see Section 1.5.2 in this book) and concluded that there was insufficient state involvement in Cornell's summer program to warrant constitutional due process protections.

Additional problems may arise when rights are asserted against a private *religious* (rather than a private *secular*) institution (see generally Sections 1.6.1 & 1.6.2 below). Federal and state statutes may provide exemptions for certain actions of religious institutions (see, for example, Section 5.5 of this book).

Furthermore, courts may refuse to assert jurisdiction over certain statutory and common law claims against religious institutions, or may refuse to grant certain discovery requests of plaintiffs or to order certain remedies proposed by plaintiffs, due to concern for the institution's establishment and free exercise rights under the First Amendment or parallel state constitutional provisions (see, for example, Section 6.2.5). These types of defenses by religious institutions will not always succeed, however, even when the institution is a seminary. In *McKelvey v. Pierce*, 800 A.2d 840 (2002), for instance, the New Jersey Supreme Court reversed the lower courts' dismissal of various contract and tort claims brought by a former student and seminarian against his diocese and several priests, emphasizing that "[t]he First Amendment does not immunize every legal claim against a religious institution or its members." The plaintiff had taken a leave of absence from his seminary training shortly before ordination time, allegedly because he had been subjected to repetitive unwanted homosexual advances. After he did not return from his leave, the diocese billed him for the costs of his seminary education and terminated his candidacy for the priesthood. The appellate court determined that the trial court must "engage in [a] painstaking analysis" of each of the plaintiff's claims "to determine, on an issue-by-issue basis, whether any of [them] may be adjudicated consistent with First Amendment principles." The court also indicated that the plaintiff was not precluded from using "evidence . . . contained in documents with religious overtones . . . to establish the existence of a contractual relationship" with the diocese; that he "may argue that, like all similar secular contracts, his agreement with the Diocese carried with it a covenant of good faith and fair dealing"; that "it is also possible" that he could, "without implicating dogma, ecclesiastical policy or choice, . . . satisfy the elements of a breach of fiduciary duty"; and that "these claims, and others lurking in the margins of [the plaintiff's] complaint, could give rise to monetary damages . . ." (800 A.2d at 858–60). Moreover, the court suggested that, had the plaintiff filed a complaint under the federal Title VII statute (which he did not), "there would have been no First Amendment prohibition against [his] proving a Title VII case of sexual harassment."

Sec. 1.6. *Religion and the Public-Private Dichotomy*

1.6.1. Overview. Under the establishment clause of the First Amendment, public institutions must maintain a neutral stance regarding religious beliefs and activities; they must, in other words, maintain religious neutrality. Public institutions cannot favor or support one religion over another, and they cannot favor or support religion over nonreligion. Thus, for instance, public schools have been prohibited from using an official nondenominational prayer (*Engel v. Vitale*, 370 U.S. 421 (1962)) and from prescribing the reading of verses from the Bible at the opening of each school day (*School District of Abington Township v. Schempp*, 374 U.S. 203 (1963)).

The First Amendment contains two "religion" clauses. The first prohibits government from "establishing" religion; the second protects individuals' "free exercise" of religion from governmental interference. Although the two clauses have a common objective of ensuring governmental "neutrality," they pursue it in different ways. As the U.S. Supreme Court explained in *School District of Abington Township v. Schempp:*

> The wholesome "neutrality" of which this Court's cases speak thus stems from a recognition of the teaching of history that powerful sects or groups might bring about a fusion of governmental and religious functions or a concert or dependency of one upon the other to the end that official support of the state or federal government would be placed behind the tenets of one or of all orthodoxies. This the establishment clause prohibits. And a further reason for neutrality is found in the free exercise clause, which recognizes the value of religious training, teaching, and observance and, more particularly, the right of every person to freely choose his own course with reference thereto, free of any compulsion from the state. This the free exercise clause guarantees. . . . The distinction between the two clauses is apparent—a violation of the free exercise clause is predicated on coercion, whereas the establishment clause violation need not be so attended [374 U.S. at 222–23].

Neutrality, however, does not necessarily require a public institution to prohibit all religious activity on its campus or at off-campus events it sponsors. In some circumstances the institution may have discretion to permit noncoercive religious activities (see *Lee v. Weisman,* 505 U.S. 577 (1992) (finding indirect coercion in context of religious invocation at *high school* graduation)). Moreover, if a rigidly observed policy of neutrality would discriminate against campus organizations with religious purposes or impinge on an individual's right to freedom of speech or free exercise of religion, the institution may be required to allow some religion on campus.

In a case that has now become a landmark decision, *Widmar v. Vincent,* 454 U.S. 263 (1981) (see Section 10.1.5 of this book), the U.S. Supreme Court determined that student religious activities on public campuses are protected by the First Amendment's free speech clause. The Court indicated a preference for using this clause, rather than the free exercise of religion clause, whenever the institution has created a "public forum" generally open for student use. The Court also concluded that the First Amendment's establishment clause would not be violated by an "open-forum" or "equal-access" policy permitting student use of campus facilities for both nonreligious and religious purposes.[16]

---

[16]For later cases (involving elementary and secondary education) that affirm and extend these principles, see *Lamb's Chapel v. Center Moriches Union Free School District,* 508 U.S. 384 (1993), and *Good News Club v. Milford Central School,* 533 U.S. 98 (2001). A similar result could also be reached using the free exercise clause. In a pre-*Widmar* case, *Keegan v. University of Delaware,* 349 A.2d 14 (Del. 1975), for example, a public university had banned all religious worship services in campus facilities. The plaintiffs contended that this policy was unconstitutional as applied to students' religious services in the commons areas of campus dormitories. After determining that the university could permit religious worship in the commons area without violating the establishment clause, the court then held that the university was constitutionally required by the free exercise clause to make the commons area available for students' religious worship.

1.6.2. Religious autonomy rights of religious institutions and their personnel.

A private institution's position under the establishment and free exercise clauses differs markedly from that of a public institution. Private institutions have no obligation of neutrality under these clauses. Moreover, these clauses affirmatively protect the religious beliefs and practices of private religious institutions from government interference. For example, establishment and free exercise considerations may restrict the judiciary's capacity to entertain lawsuits against religious institutions.[17] Such litigation may involve the court in the interpretation of religious doctrine or in the process of church governance, thus creating a danger that the court—an arm of government—would entangle itself in religious affairs in violation of the establishment clause. Or such litigation may invite the court to enforce discovery requests (such as subpoenas) or award injunctive relief that would interfere with the religious practices of the institution or its sponsoring body, thus creating dangers that the court's orders would violate the institution's rights under the free exercise clause. Sometimes such litigation may present both types of federal constitutional problems or, alternatively, may present parallel problems under the state constitution. When the judicial involvement requested by the plaintiff(s) would cause the court to intrude upon establishment or free exercise values, the court must decline to enforce certain discovery requests, or must modify the terms of any remedy or relief it orders, or must decline to exercise any jurisdiction over the dispute, thus protecting the institution against governmental incursions into its religious beliefs and practices. These issues are addressed with respect to suits by faculty members in Section 6.2.5 of this book; for a parallel example regarding a suit by a student, see *McKelvey v. Pierce*, discussed in Section 1.5.3.

A private institution's constitutional protection under the establishment and free exercise clauses is by no means absolute. Its limits are illustrated by *Bob Jones University v. United States*, 461 U.S. 574 (1983) (see Section 13.3.2, footnote 38). Because the university maintained racially restrictive policies on dating and marriage, the Internal Revenue Service had denied it tax-exempt status under federal tax laws. The university argued that its racial practices were religiously based and that the denial abridged its right to free exercise of religion. The U.S. Supreme Court, rejecting this argument, emphasized that the federal government has a "compelling" interest in "eradicating racial discrimination in education" and that interest "substantially outweighs whatever burden denial of tax benefits places on [the university's] exercise of . . . religious beliefs" (461 U.S. at 575).

Although the institution did not prevail in *Bob Jones*, the "compelling interest" test that the Court used to evaluate free exercise claims does provide substantial protection for religiously affiliated institutions. The Court severely restricted the use of this "strict scrutiny" test, however, in *Employment Division*

---

[17]The federal constitutional principles are developed in *Jones v. Wolf*, 443 U.S. 595 (1979); *Serbian Orthodox Diocese v. Milivojevich*, 426 U.S. 696 (1976); *Presbyterian Church v. Hull Church*, 393 U.S. 440 (1969); *Kedroff v. Saint Nicholas Cathedral* 344 U.S. 94 (1952); and *Watson v. Jones*, 80 U.S. 679 (1871).

v. Smith, 494 U.S. 872 (1990), and thus severely limited the protection against governmental burdens on religious practice that are available under the free exercise clause. Congress sought to legislatively overrule *Employment Division v. Smith* and restore broad use of the compelling interest test in the Religious Freedom Restoration Act of 1993 (RFRA), 42 U.S.C. § 2000bb *et seq.*, but the U.S. Supreme Court invalidated this legislation. Congress had passed RFRA pursuant to its power under Section 5 of the Fourteenth Amendment (see Section 13.1.5 of this book), to enforce that amendment and the Bill of Rights against the states and their political subdivisions. In *City of Boerne v. Flores*, 521 U.S. 507 (1997), the Court held that RFRA is beyond the scope of Congress's Section 5 enforcement power. Although the Court addressed only RFRA's validity as it applies to the states, the statute by its express terms also applies to the federal government (§§ 2000bb-2(1), 2000bb-3(a)). RFRA thus may still be constitutional as to these latter applications. (See, for example, *Sutton v. Providence St. Joseph Medical Center*, 192 F.3d 826 (9th Cir. 1999), in which the court acknowledged that *City of Boerne* did not invalidate RFRA as to the federal government and assumed, without deciding, that RFRA is constitutional in this regard.) There is a contrary view, however. According to this view, the critical portions of the *Boerne* opinion that rely on *Marbury v. Madison* and the concept of judicial supremacy, and conclude that "RFRA contradicts vital principles necessary to maintain separation of powers" [between Congress and the Court] (521 U.S. at 508), apply just as fully to the federal government as to the states.[18]

The invalidation of RFRA has serious consequences for the free exercise rights of both religious institutions and the members of their academic communities. The earlier case of *Employment Division v. Smith* (above) is reinstituted as the controlling authority on the right to free exercise of religion. Whereas RFRA provided protection against generally applicable, religiously neutral laws that substantially burden religious practice, *Smith* provides no such protection. Thus, religiously affiliated institutions no longer have federal religious freedom rights that guard them from general and neutral government regulations interfering with their religious mission. Moreover, individual students, faculty, and staff—whether at religious institutions, private secular institutions, or public institutions—no longer have federal religious freedom rights to guard them from general and neutral government regulations that interfere with their personal religious practices. And individuals at *public* institutions no longer have federal religious freedom rights to guard them from general and neutral *institutional* regulations that interfere with their personal religious practices.

There are at least three avenues that an individual religious adherent or a religiously affiliated institution might now pursue to reclaim some of the protection taken away first by *Smith* and then by *Boerne*. The first avenue is to seek maximum advantage from an important post-*Smith* case, *Church of the Lukumi*

---

[18]A successor statute to RFRA, the Religious Land Use and Institutionalized Persons Act, 42 U.S.C. §§ 2000cc *et seq.* provides some additional protections for religious institutions regarding zoning and other land use issues. See, for example, *San Jose Christian College v. City of Morgan Hill*, 360 F.3d 1024 (9th Cir. 2004); but see *Elsinore Christian Center v. City of Lake Elsinore*, 291 F. Supp. 2d 1083 (C.D. Cal. 2003).

Babalu Aye v. City of Hialeah, 508 U.S. 520 (1993), that limits the impact of *Smith.* Under *Lukumi Babalu Aye,* challengers may look beyond the face of a regulation to discern its "object" from the background and context of its passage and enforcement. If this investigation reveals an object of "animosity" to religion or a particular religious practice, then the court will not view the regulation as religiously neutral and will, instead, subject the regulation to a strict "compelling interest" test. (For an example of a recent case addressing a student's First Amendment free exercise claim and utilizing *Lukumi Babalu Aye,* see *Axson-Flynn v. Johnson,* 356 F.3d 1277 (10th Cir. 2004), discussed in Section 8.1.4.)

The second avenue is to seek protection under some other clause of the federal Constitution. The best bet is probably the free speech and press clauses of the First Amendment, which cover religious activity that is expressive (communicative). The U.S. Supreme Court's decisions in *Widmar v. Vincent* (Section 10.1.5) and *Rosenberger v. Rectors and Visitors of the University of Virginia* (Sections 10.1.5 & 10.3.2) provide good examples of protecting religious activity under these clauses. Another possibility is the due process clauses of the Fifth and Fourteenth Amendments, which protect certain privacy interests regarding personal, intimate matters. The *Smith* case itself includes a discussion of this due process privacy protection for religious activity (494 U.S. at 881–82). Yet another possibility is the freedom of association that is implicit in the First Amendment and that the courts usually call the "freedom of expressive association" to distinguish it from a "freedom of intimate association" protected by the Fifth and Fourteenth Amendment due process clauses (see *Roberts v. United States Jaycees,* 468 U.S. 609, 617–18, 622–23 (1984)). The leading case is *Boy Scouts of America v. Dale,* 530 U.S. 640 (2000), in which the Court, by a 5-to-4 vote, upheld the Boy Scouts' action revoking the membership of a homosexual scoutmaster. In its reasoning, the Court indicated that the "freedom of expressive association" protects private organizations from government action that "affects in a significant way the [organization's] ability to advocate public or private viewpoints" (530 U.S. at 648).

The third avenue is to look beyond the U.S. Constitution for some other source of law (see Section 1.4 of this book) that protects religious freedom. Some state constitutions, for instance, may have protections that are stronger than what is now provided by the federal free exercise clause (see subsection 1.6.3 below). Similarly, federal and state statutes will sometimes protect religious freedom. The federal Title VII statute on employment discrimination, for example, protects religious institutions from federal government intrusions into some religiously based employment policies (see Section 5.5 of this book), and protects employees from intrusions by employers into some religious practices (see Section 5.3.6 of this book).

1.6.3. Government support for religious institutions. Although the establishment clause itself imposes no neutrality obligation on private institutions, this clause does have another kind of importance for private institutions that are religious. When government—federal, state, or local—undertakes to

provide financial or other support for private postsecondary education, the question arises whether this support, insofar as it benefits religious institutions, constitutes government support for religion. If it does, such support would violate the establishment clause because government would have departed from its position of neutrality.

Two 1971 cases decided by the Supreme Court provide the foundation for the modern law on government support for church-related schools. *Lemon v. Kurtzman,* 403 U.S. 602 (1971), invalidated two state programs providing aid for church-related elementary and secondary schools. *Tilton v. Richardson,* 403 U.S. 672 (1971), held constitutional a federal aid program providing construction grants to higher education institutions, including those that are church related. In deciding the cases, the Court developed a three-pronged test for determining when a government support program passes muster under the establishment clause:

> First, the statute must have a secular legislative purpose; second, its principal or primary effect must be one that neither advances nor inhibits religion . . .; finally, the statute must not foster "an excessive government entanglement with religion" [403 U.S. at 612–13, quoting *Walz v. Tax Commission,* 397 U.S. 664, 674 (1970)].

All three prongs have proved to be very difficult to apply in particular cases. The Court has provided guidance in *Lemon* and in later cases, however, that has been of some help. In *Lemon,* for instance, the Court explained the entanglement prong as follows:

> In order to determine whether the government entanglement with religion is excessive, we must examine (1) the character and purposes of the institutions which are benefitted, (2) the nature of the aid that the state provides, and (3) the resulting relationship between the government and the religious authority [403 U.S. at 615].

In *Hunt v. McNair,* 413 U.S. 734 (1973), the Court gave this explanation of the effect prong:

> Aid normally may be thought to have a primary effect of advancing religion when it flows to an institution in which religion is so pervasive that a substantial portion of its functions are subsumed in the religious mission or when it funds a specifically religious activity in an otherwise substantially secular setting [413 U.S. at 743].

But in *Agostini v. Felton,* 521 U.S. 203 (1997), the U.S. Supreme Court refined the three-prong *Lemon* test, specifically affirming that the first prong (purpose) has become a significant part of the test and determining that the second prong (effect) and third prong (entanglement) have, in essence, become combined into a single broad inquiry into effect. (See 521 U.S. at 222, 232–33.) And in *Mitchell v. Helms,* 530 U.S. 793 (2000), four Justices in a plurality opinion and two Justices in a concurring opinion criticized the "pervasively sectarian" test that had been developed in *Hunt v. McNair* (above) as part of the effects prong of *Lemon,* and overruled two earlier U.S. Supreme Court cases on elementary and secondary education that had relied on this test. These Justices also gave much stronger emphasis to the neutrality principle that is a foundation of establishment clause analysis.

Four U.S. Supreme Court cases have applied the complex *Lemon* test to religious postsecondary institutions. In each case the aid program passed the test. In *Tilton v. Richardson* (above), the Court approved the federal construction grant program, and the grants to the particular colleges involved in that case, by a narrow 5-to-4 vote. In *Hunt v. McNair* (above) the Court, by a 6-to-3 vote, sustained the issuance of revenue bonds on behalf of a religious college, under a South Carolina program designed to help private nonprofit colleges finance construction projects. Applying the primary effect test quoted previously, the court determined that the college receiving the bond proceeds was not "pervasively sectarian" (413 U.S. at 743) and would not use the financial facilities for specifically religious activities. In *Roemer v. Board of Public Works,* 426 U.S. 736 (1976), by a 5-to-4 vote, the Court upheld the award of annual support grants to four Catholic colleges under a Maryland grant program for private postsecondary institutions. As in *Hunt,* the Court majority (in a plurality opinion and concurring opinion) determined that the colleges at issue were not "pervasively sectarian" (426 U.S. at 752, 755), and that, had they been so, the establishment clause may have prohibited the state from awarding the grants. And in the fourth case, *Witters v. Washington Department of Services for the Blind,* 474 U.S. 481 (1986), the Court rejected an establishment clause challenge to a state vocational rehabilitation program for the blind that provided assistance directly to a student enrolled in a religious ministry program at a private Christian college. Distinguishing between *institution-based aid* and *student-based aid,* the unanimous Court concluded that the aid plan did not violate the second prong of the *Lemon* test, since any state payments that were ultimately channeled to the educational institution were based solely on the "genuinely independent and private choices of the aid recipients." (For a discussion of *Witters* against the backdrop of the earlier Supreme Court cases, and of the aftermath of *Witters* in the Washington Supreme Court, see Note, "The First Amendment and Public Funding of Religiously Controlled or Affiliated Higher Education," 17 *J. Coll. & Univ. Law* 381, 398–409 (1991).) Taken together, these U.S. Supreme Court cases suggest that a wide range of postsecondary support programs can be devised compatibly with the establishment clause and that a wide range of church-related institutions can be eligible to receive government support.

Of the four Supreme Court cases, only *Witters* focuses on student-based aid. Its distinction between institutional-based aid (as in the other three Supreme Court cases) and student-based aid has become a critical component of establishment clause analysis. In a later case, *Zelman v. Simmons-Harris,* 536 U.S. 639 (2002) (an elementary/secondary education case), the Court broadly affirmed the vitality of this distinction and its role in upholding government aid programs that benefit religious schools. Of the other three Supreme Court cases—*Tilton, Hunt, and Roemer—Roemer* is the most revealing. There the Court refused to find that the grants given a group of Catholic colleges constituted support for religion—even though the funds were granted annually and could be put to a wide range of uses, and even though the schools had church representatives on their governing boards, employed Roman Catholic chaplains, held Roman Catholic religious exercises, required students to take religion or theology classes taught primarily by Roman Catholic clerics, made some hiring decisions for theology departments partly on the basis of religious considerations, and began some classes with prayers.

The current status of the U.S. Supreme Court's 1976 decision in *Roemer v. Board of Public Works* was the focus of extensive litigation in the Fourth Circuit involving Columbia Union College, a small Seventh-Day Adventist college in Maryland. *Columbia Union College v. Clarke*, 159 F.3d 151 (4th Cir. 1998) (hereafter, *Columbia Union College I*), involved the same Maryland grant program that was at issue in *Roemer*. The questions for the court were whether, under then-current U.S. Supreme Court law on the establishment clause, a "pervasively sectarian" institution could ever be eligible for direct government funding of its core educational functions; and whether the institution seeking the funds here (Columbia Union College) was "pervasively sectarian." In a 2-to-1 decision, the court answered "No" to the first question, asserting that *Roemer* has not been implicitly overruled by subsequent Supreme Court cases (such as *Agostini*, above), and remanded the second question to the district court for further fact findings. The debate between the majority and dissent illustrates the two contending perspectives on the continuing validity of *Roemer* and that case's criteria and for determining if an institution is "pervasively sectarian." In addition, the court in *Columbia Union College I* considered a new issue that was not evident in *Roemer*, but was interjected into this area of law by the U.S. Supreme Court's 1995 decision in *Rosenberger v. Rector & Visitors of the University of Virginia* (see Section 10.1.5 of this book). The issue is whether a decision to deny funds to Columbia Union would violate its free speech rights under the First Amendment. The court answered "Yes" to this question because Maryland had denied the funding "solely because of [Columbia Union's] alleged pervasively partisan religious viewpoint" (159 F.3d at 156). That ruling did not dispose of the case, however, because the court determined that the need to avoid an establishment clause violation would provide a justification for this infringement of free speech.

On remand, and after extensive discovery and a lengthy trial, the federal district court ruled that Columbia Union was not pervasively sectarian and was therefore entitled to participate in the state grant program. Maryland then appealed, and the U.S. Fourth Circuit Court of Appeals reviewed the case for a second time in *Columbia Union College v. Oliver*, 254 F.3d 496 (4th Cir. 2001) (hereafter, *Columbia Union College II*). In its opinion in *Columbia Union College II*, the appellate court emphasized that, since its decision in *Columbia Union College I*, the U.S. Supreme Court had "significantly altered the Establishment Clause landscape" (254 F.3d at 501) by its decision in *Mitchell v. Helms*, 530 U.S. 793 (2000). In *Mitchell*, as the Fourth Circuit explained, the Supreme Court upheld an aid program for elementary and secondary schools in which the federal government distributed funds to local school districts, which then purchased educational materials and equipment, a portion of which were loaned to private, including religious, schools. In the school district whose lending program was challenged, "approximately 30% of the funds" went to forty-six private schools, forty-one of which were religiously affiliated (254 F.3d at 501).

Applying *Mitchell*, the Fourth Circuit noted that Justice O'Connor's concurring opinion, "which is the controlling opinion in *Mitchell*," replaced the pervasively sectarian test with a "neutrality-plus" test (254 F.3d at 504). The Fourth Circuit summarized this "neutrality-plus" test and its "three fundamental guideposts for Establishment Clause cases" as follows:

> First, the neutrality of aid criteria is an important factor, even if it is not the only factor, in assessing a public assistance program. Second, the actual diversion of government aid to religious purposes is prohibited. Third, and relatedly, "presumptions of religious indoctrination" inherent in the pervasively sectarian analysis "are normally inappropriate when evaluating neutral school-aid programs under the Establishment Clause" [254 F.3d at 505, quoting *Mitchell*, 530 U.S. at 858 (O'Connor, J., concurring)].

Using this "neutrality-plus" analysis derived from *Mitchell*, instead of *Roemer's* pervasively sectarian analysis, the Fourth Circuit found that Maryland's grant program had a secular purpose and used neutral criteria to dispense aid, that there was no evidence "of actual diversion of government aid for religious purposes," and that safeguards were in place to protect against future diversion of funds for sectarian purposes. The appellate court therefore affirmed the district court's ruling that the state's funding of Columbia Union College would not violate the establishment clause. Since a grant of funds would not violate the establishment clause, "the State cannot advance a compelling interest for refusing the college its [grant] funds." Such a refusal would therefore, as the appellate court had already held in *Columbia Union I*, violate the college's free speech rights. The court's opinion concluded with this observation:

> We recognize the sensitivity of this issue, and respect the constitutional imperative for government not to impermissibly advance religious interests. Nevertheless, by refusing to fund a religious institution solely because of religion, the government risks discriminating against a class of citizens solely because of faith. The First Amendment requires government neutrality, not hostility, to religious belief [254 F.3d at 510].

Alternatively, the Fourth Circuit concluded that the college would prevail even if the pervasively sectarian test were still the controlling law. Reviewing the district court's findings and the factors set out in the U.S. Supreme Court's decision in *Roemer*, the appellate court also affirmed the district court's ruling that the college is not pervasively sectarian and, on that ground as well, is eligible to receive the state grant funds.

Other post-*Roemer* cases in the lower courts have involved the state's issuance of revenue bonds[19] to finance the building projects of private religious

---

[19]Revenue bonds, in contrast to general obligation bonds, are not backed by the full faith and credit of the government issuing the bonds. The bond holders may look only to the entity receiving the bond proceeds for payment.

institutions. In *Virginia College Building Authority v. Lynn,* 538 S.E.2d 682 (Va. 2000), the Authority had issued tax-exempt revenue bonds on behalf of Regent University, a private religious institution, to finance several of its building projects. Virginia's highest court rejected challenges to the bond issue based both on the First Amendment's establishment clause and the Virginia Constitution's establishment clause. In *Steel v. Industrial Development Board of Metropolitan Government of Nashville,* 301 F.3d 401 (6th Cir. 2002), a local government's industrial development board issued tax-exempt industrial development bonds (a type of revenue bond) on behalf of David Lipscomb University, a private religious institution. The U.S. Court of Appeals for the Sixth Circuit rejected a First Amendment establishment clause challenge to the bond issue. In both cases the courts declined to rely on the "pervasively sectarian" test from *Hunt* (above) and *Roemer* (above), instead following *Agostini* (above) and *Mitchell v. Helms* (above) much as the Fourth Circuit did in *Columbia Union College II* (above). Under *Agostini* and (especially) *Mitchell,* the nature of the aid program, and its "neutrality," is a more important consideration than the nature of the institution receiving the aid. In the Virginia case, therefore, the court determined that the bond issue on behalf of Regent University was valid even if Regent is a "pervasively sectarian" institution; and in the *Steele* case the court declined to determine whether David Lipscomb University is "pervasively sectarian," saying it is an irrelevant question. Both courts did note, however, that the statute authorizing the bond program prohibited the bond proceeds from being used to finance facilities to be used for "sectarian instruction or as a place of religious worship" or to be used "primarily [for] the program of a school or department of divinity" (in the words of the Virginia statute); or to finance facilities to be used for "sectarian instruction," for "the program of a school or department of divinity," or for "the training of ministers, priests, rabbis, or other similar persons in the field of religion" (in the words of the Metro Nashville legislation); and both courts suggested that these statutory limitations on government assistance were required by the establishment clause. In *California Statewide Communities Development Authority v. All Persons Interested in Matter of Validity of Purchase Agreement* (Cal. App., 3d Dist. 2004, 92 P.3d 311 (Cal. 2004)), the court reached the opposite result from *Virginia Building Authority* and *Steele,* invalidating a bond issue for several religious institutions under the state constitution because the institutions were "pervasively sectarian" and the financing therefore would have "the direct and substantial effect of aiding religion." On further appeal, however, the California Supreme Court superseded this opinion and set the case for review (92 P.3d 311 (2004)); the appeal was pending as this book went to press.

When issues arise concerning governmental support for religious institutions, or their students or faculty members, the federal Constitution (as in the cases above) is not the only source of law that may apply. In some states, for instance, the state constitution will also play an important role independent of the federal Constitution. A line of cases concerning various student aid programs of the State of Washington provides an instructive example of the role of state constitutions and the complex interrelationships between the federal establishment and free exercise clauses and the parallel provisions in state constitutions. The first case in the line was the U.S. Supreme Court's decision in *Witters v. Washington Department of Services for the Blind,* above (hereinafter, *Witters I*), in which the Court remanded the case to the Supreme Court of Washington (whose decision the U.S. Supreme Court had reversed), observing that the state court was free to consider the "far stricter" church-state provision of the state constitution. On remand, the state court concluded that the state constitutional provision—prohibiting use of public moneys to pay for any religious instruction—precluded the grant of state funds to the student enrolled in the religious ministry program (*Witters v. State Commission for the Blind,* 771 P.2d 1119 (Wash. 1989) (hereinafter, *Witters II*)). First the court held that providing vocational rehabilitation funds to the student would violate the state constitution because the funds would pay for "a religious course of study at a religious school, with a religious career as [the student's] goal" (771 P.2d at 1121). Distinguishing the establishment clause of the U.S. Constitution from the state constitution's provision, the court noted that the latter provision "prohibits not only the *appropriation* of public money for religious instruction, but also the *application of* public funds to religious instruction" (771 P.2d at 1122). Then the court held that the student's federal constitutional right to free exercise of religion was not infringed by denial of the funds, because he is "not being asked to violate any tenet of his religious beliefs nor is he being denied benefits 'because of conduct mandated by religious belief'" (771 P.2d at 1123). Third, the court held that denial of the funds did not violate the student's equal protection rights under the Fourteenth Amendment, because the state has a "compelling interest in maintaining the strict separation of church and state set forth" in its constitution, and the student's "individual interest in receiving a religious education must . . . give way to the state's greater need to uphold its constitution" (771 P.2d at 1123).

Almost twenty years after *Witters I* and *II,* establishment clause issues arose again in the context of another State of Washington student aid program. This time, in *State ex rel. Mary Gallwey v. Grimm,* 48 P.3d 274 (Wash. 2002), the Supreme Court of Washington declared that the state program did not violate the state constitution's establishment clause, nor did it violate the federal establishment clause. At issue was the Educational Opportunity Grant (EOG) Program, which provided aid to "place-bound" students who lived in disadvantaged counties and were unable to travel to distant state universities and colleges. Qualifying students were awarded vouchers that they could use at a select number of participating public and private institutions in the state. Some of the private institutions were religiously affiliated, and a state taxpayer challenged their inclusion in the program as a violation of Article I, section 11 of the state constitution (the same provision that was at issue in *Witters II,* above, and *Locke v. Davey,* below), as well as the federal Constitution's establishment clause.

The Washington Supreme Court rejected the challenges, determining that it was permissible for the state to include religious colleges in the program. The court relied on a provision in the statute creating the EOG Program requiring that "no student will be enrolled in any program that includes religious worship, exercise, or instruction" (48 P.3d at 285, citing Rev. Code Wash. 28B.101.040). Under this provision, according to the court, a student could use an EOG voucher to pay educational costs at a "religious [college] with a religious mission," so long as the student is pursuing a "general, non-religious, four-year college degree." Such use of the vouchers, the court concluded, would not violate Article I, section 11.

Similarly, applying the three-pronged *Lemon* test (see above, this subsection), the Washington court determined that such inclusion of religiously affiliated schools in the EOG program did not violate the federal establishment clause. It was important, in this regard, that the EOG funds were awarded to the student directly, rather than to the school itself—a factor that the U.S. Supreme Court had emphasized in *Witters I.* The EOG Program was a "neutrally administered" program, said the Washington court, that represented an even more distant relationship between government and religion than the program upheld in *Witters I.*

The federal free exercise clause, which had been considered in the *Witters II* litigation, was not at issue in *Gallwey.* Had the State of Washington prohibited students from using EOG vouchers at religiously affiliated schools, even to pursue "non-religious" studies, then the prohibition could have been challenged as a violation of the excluded students' free exercise rights—much as the student in *Witters II* had challenged his exclusion from using state vocational rehabilitation funds. The specific issue would be different from that in *Witters II,* however, since *Witters II* concerned only a prohibition on using student aid funds for religious studies preparing the student for a religious vocation, and not a more general prohibition on using state funds for any studies at a religiously affiliated school. Students' challenges to such prohibitions, broad or narrow, in Washington or in other states, are now governed by a 2004 decision of the U.S. Supreme Court in *Locke v. Davey,* discussed below. In addition, challenges to such prohibitions may be brought by the religiously affiliated institutions that are excluded from the student aid program. An institution's challenge could also be based on *Locke v. Davey* (below), at least if the institution offered "nonreligious" studies; but could just as likely be based on an equal protection claim of discrimination against religious organizations or an establishment clause claim of hostility toward religion (see Section 1.6.2 above).

Locke v. Davey, 540 U.S. 712 (2004), involved a free exercise clause challenge to yet another student financial aid program of the State of Washington. In its opinion rejecting the challenge, the U.S. Supreme Court probed the relationship between the federal Constitution's two religion clauses and the relationship between these clauses and the religion clauses in state constitutions.

At issue was the State of Washington's Promise Scholarship Program, which provided scholarships to academically gifted students for use at either public or private institutions—including religiously affiliated institutions—in the state. Consistent with Article I, section 11 of the state constitution as interpreted by the Washington Supreme Court in *Witters II* (see above), however, the state stipulated that aid may not be awarded to "any student who is pursuing a degree in theology" (see Rev. Code Wash. § 28B.10.814). The plaintiff, Joshua Davey, had been awarded a Promise Scholarship and decided to attend a Christian college in the state to pursue a double major in pastoral ministries and business administration. When he subsequently learned that the pastoral ministries degree would be considered a degree in theology and that he could not use his Promise Scholarship for this purpose, Davey declined the scholarship. He then sued the state, alleging violations of his First Amendment speech, establishment, and free exercise rights as well as a violation of his equal protection rights under the Fourteenth Amendment.

In the federal district court, Davey lost on all counts. On appeal, however, the U.S. Court of Appeals for the Ninth Circuit upheld Davey's free exercise claim, concluding that the "State had singled out religion for unfavorable treatment" and that such facial discrimination "based on religious pursuit" was contrary to the U.S. Supreme Court's decision in *Church of Lukumi Babalu Aye, Inc. v. Hialeah,* 508 U.S. 520 (1993). Applying that decision, the Ninth Circuit determined that "the State's exclusion of theology majors" was subject to strict judicial scrutiny, and the exclusion failed this test because it was not "narrowly tailored to achieve a compelling state interest" (*Davey v. Locke,* 299 F.3d 748 (9th Cir. 2002)).

By a 7-to-2 vote, the U.S. Supreme Court reversed the Ninth Circuit and upheld the state's exclusion of theology degrees from the Promise Scholarship Program. In the majority opinion by Chief Justice Rehnquist, the Court declined to apply the strict scrutiny analysis of *Lukumi Babalu Aye.* Characterizing the dispute as one that implicated both the free exercise clause and the establishment clause of the federal Constitution, the Court recognized that "these two clauses . . . are frequently in tension" but that there is "play in the joints" (540 U.S. at 718, quoting *Walz v. Tax Comm'n of City of New York,* 397 U.S. 664, 669 (1970)) that provides states some discretion to work out the tensions between the two clauses. In particular, a state may sometimes give precedence to the antiestablishment values embedded in its own state constitution rather than the federal free exercise interests of particular individuals. To implement this "play-in-the-joints" principle, the Court applied a standard of review that was less strict than the standard it had usually applied to cases of religious discrimination.

Under the Court's prior decision in *Witters I* (above), "the State could . . . *permit* Promise Scholars to pursue a degree in devotional theology" (emphasis added). It did not necessarily follow, however, that the federal free exercise clause would *require* the state to cover students pursuing theology degrees. The question therefore was "whether Washington, pursuant to its own constitution, which has been authoritatively interpreted [by the state courts] as prohibiting even indirectly funding religious instruction that will prepare students for the ministry, . . . can deny them such funding without violating the [federal] Free Exercise Clause" (540 U.S. at 719).

The Court found that "[t]he State has merely chosen not to fund a distinct category of instruction"—an action that "places a relatively minor burden on Promise Scholars" (540 U.S. at 721, 725). Moreover, the state's different treatment of theology majors was not based on "hostility toward religion," nor did the "history or text of Article I, § 11 of the Washington Constitution . . . [suggest] animus towards religion." The difference instead reflects the state's "historic and substantial state interest," reflected in Article I, section 11, in declining to support religion by funding the religious training of the clergy. Based on these considerations, and applying its lesser scrutiny standard, the Court held that the State of Washington's exclusion of theology majors from the Promise Scholarship program did not violate the free exercise clause.

The Court has thus created, in *Locke v. Davey*, a kind of balancing test for certain free exercise cases in which a state's different treatment of religion does not evince "hostility" or "animus." Under the balancing test, the extent of the burden the state has placed on religious practice is weighed against the substantiality of the state's interest in promoting antiestablishment values. The lesser scrutiny, or intermediate scrutiny, that this balancing test produces stands in marked contrast to both the "strict scrutiny" required in cases like *Lukumi Babalu Aye* and the minimal scrutiny used in cases, like *Employment Division v. Smith* (subsection 1.6.2 above), that involve religiously neutral statutes of general applicability. Some of the Court's reasoning supporting this balancing test and its application to the Promise Scholarships seems questionable,[20] as Justice Scalia pointed out in a dissent (540 U.S. at 731–32). Moreover, the circumstances in which the balancing test should be used—beyond the specific circumstance of a government aid program such as that in *Davey*—are unclear. But the 7-to-2 vote upholding Washington's action nevertheless indicates strong support for a flexible and somewhat deferential approach to free exercise issues arising in programs of government support for higher education and, more specifically, strong support for the exclusion (if the state so chooses) of theological and ministerial education from state student aid programs—at least when the applicable state constitution has a strong antiestablishment clause.

Taken together, the *Locke v. Davey* case and the earlier *Witters I* case serve to accord a substantial range of discretion to the states (and presumably the federal government as well) to determine whether or not to include students pursuing religious studies in their student aid programs. The range of discretion may be less when a state is determining whether to include students studying secular subjects at a religiously affiliated institution, since the free exercise clause may have greater force in this context. And when a state determines whether to provide aid directly to religiously affiliated institutions rather than to students, the range of discretion will be slim because the federal establishment clause, and many state constitutional clauses, would apply with added force, as discussed earlier in this Section.

Though the federal cases have been quite hospitable to the inclusion of church-related institutions in government support programs for postsecondary education, administrators of religious institutions should still be most sensitive to establishment clause issues. As *Witters* indicates, state constitutions may contain clauses that restrict government support for church-related institutions more vigorously

---

[20]For instance, the Court emphasized that the state's scholarship program "does not require students to choose between their religious beliefs and receiving a government benefit" (540 U.S. at 721–22); and yet it later acknowledged that "majoring in devotional theology is akin to a religious calling" and that Davey's "religious beliefs" were the sole motivation for pursuing such studies (540 U.S. at 721). It thus seems that, for Davey, the state did indeed put him in the position of choosing between his religious calling and his Promise Scholarship.

than the federal establishment clause does.[21] The statutes creating funding programs may also contain provisions that restrict the programs' application to religious institutions or activities. Moreover, even the federal establishment clause cases have historically been decided by close votes, with considerable disagreement among the Justices and continuing questions about the current status of the *Lemon* test and spin-off tests such as the "pervasively sectarian" test. Thus, administrators should exercise great care in using government funds and should keep in mind that, at some point, religious influences within the institution can still jeopardize government funding, especially institution-based funding.

1.6.4. Religious autonomy rights of individuals in public post-secondary institutions. While subsections 1.6.2 and 1.6.3 focused on church-state problems involving private institutions, this subsection focuses on church-state problems in public institutions. As explained in subsection 1.6.1, public institutions are subject to the strictures of the First Amendment's establishment and free exercise clauses, and parallel clauses in state constitutions, which are the source of rights that faculty members, students, and staff members may assert against their institutions. The most visible and contentious of these disputes involve situations in which a public institution has incorporated prayer or some other religious activity into an institutional activity or event.

In *Tanford v. Brand*, 104 F.3d 982 (7th Cir. 1997), for example, the U.S. Court of Appeals for the Seventh Circuit addressed the issue of prayer as part of the commencement exercises at a state university. A law school professor, law students, and an undergraduate student brought suit, challenging Indiana University's 155-year-old tradition of nonsectarian invocations and benedictions during commencement. The plaintiffs claimed that such a use of prayer, nonsectarian or not, violated the First Amendment's establishment clause and was equivalent to state endorsement of religion. The court disagreed:

> [T]he University's practice of having an invocation and benediction at its commencements has prevailed for 155 years and is widespread throughout the nation. Rather than being a violation of the Establishment Clause, it is "simply a tolerable acknowledgment of beliefs widely held among the people of this country." *Marsh v. Chambers*, 463 U.S. 783, 792 (1983). As we held in *Sherman v. Community Consolidated School District* 21, 980 F.2d 437 (7th Cir. 1992), Illinois public schools may lead the Pledge of Allegiance, including its reference to God, without violating the Establishment Clause of the First Amendment. Similarly here, the invocation and benediction serve legitimate secular purposes of solemnizing public occasions rather than approving particular religious beliefs (*Lynch v. Donnelly*, 465 U.S. 668, 693 (1984) (O'Connor, J., concurring)). Finally, as the district court correctly determined, the University's inclusion of a brief nonsectarian invocation and benediction does not have a primary effect of endorsing or disapproving religion, and there is no excessive entanglement of church and state by virtue of the University's selection of a cleric or its instruction to

---

[21]Some of the cases are collected in Wayne F. Foster, Annot., "Validity, Under State Constitution and Laws, of Insurance by State or State Agency of Revenue Bonds to Finance or Refinance Construction Projects at Private Religiously Affiliated Colleges or Universities," 95 A.L.R.3d 1000.

the cleric that his or her remarks should be unifying and uplifting. Insofar as there is any advancement of religion or governmental entanglement, it is de minimis at best [104 F.3d at 986].

The plaintiffs also argued that the invocation and benediction violated the establishment clause because they were coercive (see *Lee v. Weisman*, 505 U.S. 577 (1992)). The court again disagreed. According to the court, nearly 2,500 of the 7,400 graduating students voluntarily elected not to attend commencement; those that did attend were free to exit before both the invocation and benediction, and return after each was completed; and those choosing not to exit were free to sit, as did most in attendance, during both ceremonies. These factors significantly undermined the suggestion that those attending graduation were coerced into participating in the nonsectarian invocation and benediction.

In *Chaudhuri v. Tennessee*, 130 F.3d 232 (6th Cir. 1997), the court endorsed and extended the holding in *Tanford*. The plaintiff, a practicing Hindu originally from India and a tenured professor at Tennessee State University (TSU), claimed that the use of prayers at university functions violated the First Amendment's establishment clause. The functions at issue were not only graduation ceremonies as in *Tanford*, but also "faculty meetings, dedication ceremonies, and guest lectures." After the suit was filed, TSU discontinued the prayers and instead adopted a "moment-of-silence" policy. The professor then challenged the moment of silence as well, alleging that the policy had been adopted in order to allow continued use of prayers. The appellate court determined that neither the prayers nor the moments of silence violated the establishment clause.

The *Chaudhuri* court used the three-part test from *Lemon v. Kurtzman*, 403 U.S. 602 (1971) (subsection 1.6.3), to resolve both the prayer claim and the moment-of-silence claim. Under the first prong of the *Lemon* test, the court found, as in *Tanford*, that a prayer may "serve to dignify or to memorialize a public occasion" and therefore has a legitimate secular purpose. Moreover, "if the verbal prayers had a legitimate secular purpose . . . it follows almost fortiori that the moments of silence have such a purpose." Under the second prong, the court found that the principal or primary effect of the nonsectarian prayers was not "to indoctrinate the audience," but rather "to solemnize the events and to encourage reflection." As to the moment of silence, it was "even clearer" that the practice did not significantly advance or inhibit religion:

A moment of silence is not inherently religious; a participant may use the time to pray, to stare absently ahead, or to think thoughts of a purely secular nature. The choice is left to the individual, and no one's beliefs are compromised by what may or may not be going through the mind of any other participant [130 F.3d at 238].

And, under the final prong of the *Lemon* test, the court found that "any entanglement resulting from the inclusion of nonsectarian prayers at public university functions is, at most, *de minimis*" and that the "entanglement created by a moment of silence is nil."

As in *Tanford,* the *Chaudhuri* court also concluded that the "coercion" test established in *Lee v. Weisman,* 505 U.S. 577 (1992), was not controlling. At Tennessee State University (in contrast to the secondary school in *Lee*), according to the court, there was no coercion to participate in the prayers. It was not mandatory for Professor Chaudhuri or any other faculty member to attend the TSU functions at issue, and there was no penalty for nonattendance. Moreover, there was no "peer pressure" to attend the functions or to participate in the prayers (as there had been in *Lee*), and there was "absolutely no risk" that any adult member present at a TSU function would be indoctrinated by the prayers.

The plaintiff also argued that the prayers and moments of silence at TSU functions constrained his practice of Hinduism and, therefore, violated the First Amendment's free exercise clause. The court disagreed: "Having found that Dr. Chaudhuri was not required to participate in any religious exercise he found objectionable, we conclude that his Free Exercise claim is without merit" (130 F.3d at 239).

Although both courts resolved the establishment clause issues in the same way, these issues may have been more difficult in *Chaudhuri* than in *Tanford*; and the *Chaudhuri* court may have given inadequate consideration to some pertinent factors that were present in that case but apparently not in *Tanford.* As a dissenting opinion in *Chaudhuri* points out, the court may have discounted "the strength of the prayer tradition" at TSU, the strength of the "community expectations" regarding prayer, and the significant Christian elements in the prayers that had been used. Moreover, the court lumped the graduation exercises together with other university functions as if the relevant facts and considerations were the same for all functions. Instead, each type of function deserves its own distinct analysis, because the context of a graduation ceremony, for instance, may be quite different from the context of a faculty meeting or a guest lecture.

The reasoning and the result in *Tanford* and *Chaudhuri* may be further subject to question in the wake of the U.S. Supreme Court's ruling in *Santa Fe Independent School District v. Doe,* 530 U.S. 290 (2000). In considering the validity, under the establishment clause, of a school district policy providing for student-led invocations before high school football games, the Court placed little reliance on factors emphasized by the *Tanford* and *Chaudhuri* courts, and instead focused on factors to which these courts gave little attention—for example, the "perceived" endorsement of religion implicit in the policy itself, the "history" of prayer practices in the district and the intention to "preserve" them, and the possible "sham secular purposes" underlying the student-led invocation policy. In effect, the arguments that worked in *Tanford* and *Chaudhuri* did not work in *Santa Fe,* and factors touched upon only lightly in *Tanford* and *Chaudhuri* were considered in depth in *Santa Fe,* thus leading to the Court's invalidation of the Santa Fe School District's invocation policy.

A later case, *Mellen v. Bunting,* 327 F.3d 355 (4th Cir. 2003), involved state-sponsored prayer before supper at Virginia Military Institute (VMI), a state institution. Two student cadets at VMI asserted that a daily prayer recited by cadets during supper violated the establishment clause of the First Amendment. At VMI, students lead very structured lives with minimal freedom or privacy. As part of the daily routine during the time that the plaintiffs were cadets, all first-year cadets attended the first seating of supper together and traveled to supper in formation. (A second seating for supper was held for those excused from the first seating for participation in sports and for other reasons.) After the first year, upper-class cadets had the option of "falling out" of formation and not attending the first seating of supper. At the start of each day's first-seating supper, the Post Chaplain recited a prayer beginning with "Almighty God," "O God," "Father God," "Heavenly Father," or "Sovereign God." According to the court, "[t]he Corps must remain standing and silent while the supper prayer is read, but cadets are not obligated to recite the prayer, close their eyes, or bow their heads."

The defendant, General Bunting, former Superintendent of VMI, instituted the daily supper prayer as a way to "bring a stronger sense of unity to the Corps." General Bunting argued that the prayer should be upheld because it is a "uniquely historical practice." This argument is similar to the one employed in *Marsh v. Chambers,* 463 U.S. 783 (1983), in which the U.S. Supreme Court upheld the Nebraska legislature's use of prayer opening its sessions because the practice of legislative prayers had a "unique history" stretching back to the early years of the country. The court rejected the argument based on *Marsh* stating that a supper prayer does not share the unique history of legislative prayers. General Bunting also asserted various reasons why the prayer should be considered constitutional under the establishment clause—for example, because it serves "an academic function by aiding VMI's mission of developing cadets into military and civilian leaders" and "provid[es] an occasion for American's tradition of expressing thanksgiving and requesting divine guidance."

To determine whether these justifications were sufficient under the establishment clause, the court used the "coercion" test from *Lee v. Weisman* and *Santa Fe Independent School District v. Doe* (see preceding) and the *Lemon* test (see preceding). The court held that the supper prayer failed both tests. As to the coercion, the court reasoned:

> Although VMI's cadets are not children, in VMI's educational system they are uniquely susceptible to coercion. VMI's adversative method of education emphasizes the detailed regulation of conduct and the indoctrination of a strict moral code. Entering students exposed to the "rat line," in which upperclassmen torment and berate new students, bonding "new cadets to their fellow sufferers and, when they have completed the 7-month experience, to their former tormentors." *United States v. Virginia,* 518 U.S. 515, 522 (1996). At VMI, even upper-classmen must submit to mandatory and ritualized activities, as obedience and conformity remain central tenets of the school's educational philosophy. In this atmosphere, General Bunting reinstituted the supper prayer in 1995 to build solidarity and bring the Corps together as a family. In this context, VMI's cadets are plainly coerced into participating in a religious exercise. Because of VMI's coercive atmosphere, the Establishment Clause precludes school officials from sponsoring an official prayer, even for mature adults [327 F.3d at 371–72].

As to the *Lemon* test, the court gave General Bunting the "benefit of all doubt" and "assume[d] the supper prayer to be motivated by secular goals."

Nevertheless, the court held that the supper prayer failed the second prong of the *Lemon* test because the "primary effect" of the prayer was to promote religion, "send[ing] the unequivocal message that VMI, as an institution, *endorses* the religious expressions embodied in the prayer" (327 F.3d at 374; emphasis added); and that the prayer failed the third prong of the *Lemon* test because the daily recitation of the prayer demonstrated that "VMI has taken a position on what constitutes appropriate religious worship—an entanglement with religious activity that is forbidden by the Establishment Clause" (327 F.3d at 375).

Sec. 1.7. *The Relationship Between Law and Policy*

There is an overarching distinction between law and policy, and thus between legal issues and policy issues, that informs the work of administrators and policymakers in higher education, as well as the work of lawyers.[22] In brief, legal issues are stated and analyzed using the norms and principles of the legal system, resulting in conclusions and advice on what the law *requires* or *permits* in a given circumstance. Policy issues, in comparison, are stated and analyzed using norms and principles of administration and management, the social sciences (including the psychology of teaching and learning), the physical sciences (especially the health sciences), ethics, and other relevant disciplines; the resulting conclusions and advice focus on the best policy options available in a particular circumstance. Or, to put it another way, law focuses primarily on the *legality* of a particular course of action, while policy focuses primarily on the *efficacy* of a particular course of action. Legality is determined using the various sources of law set out in Section 1.4; efficacy is determined by using sources drawn from the various disciplines just mentioned. The work of ascertaining legality is primarily for the attorneys, while the work of ascertaining efficacy is primarily for the policy makers and administrators.

Just as legal issues may arise from sources both internal and external to the institution (Section 1.4), policy issues may arise, and policy may be made, both within and outside the institution. Internally, the educators and administrators, including the trustees or regents, make policy decisions that create what we may think of as "institutional policy" or "internal policy." Externally, legislatures,

---

[22]The discussion in this section—especially the middle portions that differentiate particular policy makers' functions from those of attorneys, identify alternative policy-making processes, set out the steps of the policy-making process and the characteristics of good policy, and review structural arrangements for facilitating policy making—draws substantially upon these very helpful materials: Linda Langford & Miriam McKendall, "Assessing Legal Initiatives" (February 2004), a conference paper delivered at the 25th Annual Law and Higher Education Conference sponsored by Stetson University College of Law; Kathryn Bender, "Making and Modifying Policy on Campus: The 'When and Why' of Policymaking" (June 2004), a conference paper delivered at the 2004 Annual Conference of the National Association of College and University Attorneys; Tracy Smith, "Making and Modifying Policy on Campus" (June 2004), a conference paper delivered at the 2004 Annual Conference of the National Association of College and University Attorneys; and "Policy Development Process With Best Practices," a document of the Association of College and University Policy Administrators, and published on the Association's Web site (http://www.inform.umd.edu/acupa).

governors, and executive branch officials make policy decisions that create what we may think of as "public policy" or "external policy." In either case, policy must be made and policy issues must be resolved within the constraints of the law.

It is critically important for institutional administrators and counsel to focus on this vital interrelationship between law and policy whenever they are addressing particular problems, reviewing existing institutional policies, or creating new policies. In these settings, with most problems and policies, the two foundational questions to ask are, "What are the institutional policy or public policy issues presented?" and "What are the legal issues presented?" The two sets of issues often overlap and intertwine. Administrators and counsel may study both sets of issues; neither area is reserved exclusively for the cognitive processes of one profession to the exclusion of the other. Yet lawyers may appropriately think about and react to legal issues differently than administrators do; and administrators may appropriately think about and react to policy issues differently than do attorneys. These matters of role and expertise are central to the process of problem solving as well as the process of policy making. While policy aspects of a task are more the bailiwick of the administrator and the legal aspects more the bailiwick of the lawyer, the professional expertise of each comes together in the policy-making process. In this sense, policy making is a joint project, a teamwork effort. The policy choices suggested by the administrators may implicate legal issues, and different policy choices may implicate different legal issues; legal requirements, in turn, will affect the viability of various policy choices.[23]

The administrators' and attorneys' roles in policy making can be described and differentiated in the following way. Administrators identify actual and potential problems that are interfering or may interfere with the furtherance of institutional goals or the accomplishment of the institutional mission, or that are creating or may create threats to the health or safety of the campus community; they identify the causes of these problems; they identify other contributing factors pertinent to understanding each problem and its scope; they assess the likelihood and gravity of the risks that these problems create for the institution; they generate options for resolving the identified problems; and they accommodate, balance, and prioritize the interests of the various constituencies that would be affected by the various options proposed. In addition, administrators identify opportunities and challenges that may entail new policy-making initiatives; assess compliance with current institutional policies and identify needs for change; and assess the efficacy of existing policies (How well *do* they

---

[23]The focus on administrators and counsel, here and elsewhere in this Section, does not mean that faculties (the educators) are, or should be, cut out of the policy-making process. This Section is based on the assumptions that administrators are sometimes faculty members or educators themselves; that administrators will regularly provide for faculty participation in policy-making committees and task forces; that administrators who oversee academic functions will regularly consult with pertinent faculties of the institution, directly and/or through their deans; and that administrators will respect whatever policy-making and decision-making roles are assigned to faculties under the institution's internal governance documents.

work?) and of proposed policies (How well *will* they work?). Attorneys, on the other hand, identify existing problems that create, and potential problems that may create, legal risk exposure for the institution or raise legal compliance issues; they analyze the legal aspects of these problems using the applicable sources of law (Section 1.4); they generate legally sound options for resolving these problems and present them to the responsible administrators; they assess the legal risk exposure (if any) to which the institution would be subject (see Section 2.5) under policy options that the policy makers have proposed either in response to the attorneys' advice or on their own initiative; they participate in—and often take the lead in—drafting new policies and revising existing policies; and they suggest legally sound procedures for implementing and enforcing the policy choices of the policy makers. In addition, attorneys review existing institutional policies to ascertain whether they are in compliance with applicable legal requirements and whether there are any conflicts between or among existing policies; they make suggestions for enhancing the legal soundness of existing policies and reducing or eliminating any risk of legal liability that they may pose; and they identify other legal consequences or by-products of particular policy choices (for example, that a choice may invite a governmental investigation, subject the institution to some new governmental regulatory regime, expose institutional employees to potential liability, or necessitate changes in the institution's relationships with its contractors).

The processes by which institutional policy is made and changed should be carefully considered by key administrators and attorneys, as well as by the institution's governing board. It may be appropriate to have different types of policy-making processes for different types of policies. Institutional bylaws or other policies promulgated by the board, for example, may involve a different policy-making process than administrative regulations promulgated under the authority of the president or chancellor; and institution-wide administrative regulations may entail a different policy-making process than the regulations or policies of particular schools, departments, or programs within the institution. Similarly, academic policies may proceed through a different policy-making process than, say, facility use policies or student conduct policies.

Regardless of the type of policy that is being made or reviewed, there are various phases and steps that, as a matter of good practice, should be common to most policy-making processes.[24] These phases and steps, very briefly stated, should include:

1. An *identification* phase. This phase involves: (a) identifying the specifics of the problem or challenge that provides the impetus for the policy making; and (b) collecting data and research (including research

---

[24]One notable exception would be policy-making processes for use in crisis situations, which must usually be expedited and whose character may be shaped by the exigencies of the crisis. Policy making regarding technology may also involve some unique challenges; see Howard Bell & Nancy Tribbensee, "Technology Policy on Campus" (February 2005), a conference paper delivered at the 26th Annual Conference on Law and Higher Education sponsored by Stetson University College of Law.

into pertinent institutional records and policies) that is useful for understanding the character and scope of the problem or challenge and its consequences for the institution.

2. A *design* phase. This phase involves: (a) generating proposals for resolving the identified problem—for example, proposals for a new program, a new service, a new process, a new strategy or initiative, or a new policy statement; (b) assessing the viability of the various proposals and their relative merits; (c) involving pertinent constituencies, on campus—and sometimes off campus—that may be affected by the problem or the proposals or may otherwise have helpful expertise or perspective regarding them; (d) selecting (at least tentatively) a particular proposal or combination of proposals to pursue; (e) stating (at least tentatively) the goals to be achieved by the new proposal—short range and long range, academic and nonacademic; and (f) recommending means for administering, overseeing, or enforcing the new policy, as appropriate.

3. A *drafting* phase. This phase involves committing the new policy and other supporting documents to writing. The writing should incorporate all of the components of the policy, using language that is clear, pertinent, specific, and accessible. If the new policy would require amending or repealing other existing institutional policies, these amendments or repeals should be provided for as well.

4. An *approval* phase. This phase involves the consideration and approval of the new policy, or amendments to existing policies, and any supporting documents. Approval should usually be obtained from the drafters, other participants in the policy-making process, and institutional officials or bodies with review authority. Sometimes approval of the governing board will be required (or advisable) as well.

5. An *implementation* phase. This phase involves: (a) disseminating the written policy and other information that will help persons understand the policy, its purpose, and its justification; (b) pursuing initiatives to gain acceptance and support for the new policy, including leadership support; and (c) providing training, guidance, and resources, as appropriate, for the persons who will administer, monitor, and enforce the policy.

6. An *evaluation* phase. This phase involves the use of institutional personnel or outside consultants with expertise in evaluation, working with selected personnel who were involved in proposing or implementing the new policy, to evaluate the policy's success in resolving the identified problem (see phase 1) and achieving the goals established for the policy (see phases 2 and 3).

Depending on the policy being created and the policy makers involved in the process, these phases and steps may overlap one another at particular points, and some steps may be followed in a different order or repeated.

The policies that may result from following these phases and steps may differ markedly in their purposes, content, and format, but in general a good policy will share these characteristics: (1) it will clearly state who is covered under the policy, that is, who is protected or receives benefits and who is assigned responsibilities; (2) it will be carefully drafted so that it is clear, specific wherever it needs to be specific, and accessible to those who are affected by the policy; (3) it will describe the problem or need to which the policy is directed; (4) it will state the goals it is designed to achieve; (5) it will describe the activities to be undertaken, services to be provided, and/or processes to be effectuated in pursuit of the policy; (6) it will (or supporting documents will) provide for coordination with other institutional policies and policy makers as needed; (7) it will (or supporting documents will) explicitly provide for its implementation, perhaps including a timetable by which the steps in implementation will be completed; (8) it will (or supporting documents will) provide for training and funding as needed to implement and maintain the policy; (9) it will establish or provide for enforcement strategies and mechanisms where enforcement is needed as part of the policy; (10) it will specify who is responsible for implementation, who is responsible for enforcement, and who is the person to contact when anyone has questions about the policy, its implementation, or its enforcement; (11) it will provide for the maintenance of records that will be generated during the course of implementing and enforcing the policy, and provide for confidentiality of records where appropriate; (12) it will (or supporting documents will) provide for building awareness of its existence and for educating pertinent constituencies on the purpose and application of the policy; (13) it will (or supporting documents will) provide for dissemination of its content (at least the portions of the content that are pertinent to the constituencies that will be affected by the policy); and (14) it will (or supporting documents will) provide for codifying or organizing the policy within pertinent collections of institutional policies so that the policy will be easily identified and obtained by interested persons (perhaps preferably including online access to the pertinent policy).

There are various structural and organizational arrangements that colleges and universities may make to facilitate use of the policy-making phases and steps suggested and to enhance the likelihood that policies will contain the various characteristics suggested. For example, an institution can create an office of policy or policy management to oversee institutional efforts in preparing new policies and reviewing existing policies. An institution can adopt a program of periodic policy audits, similar or parallel to the legal audits that are suggested in Section 2.4.2. An institution can periodically review its job descriptions, delegations of authority, and contracts with employees or outside agents, to ensure that they are clear concerning individuals' and offices' authority to lead, participate in, and support particular policy-making initiatives. An institution can also develop what is sometimes called a "policy library" or a "policy codification" that organizes together all of the pertinent existing policies at each level of policy making—the governing board level, the president and officers level, and the levels of individual schools, departments, and programs of the institution. And, as has been suggested by the Association of College and University Policy

Administrators (see fn. 21 above) and others, an institution can create and peri-odically review a "policy on policies" that will inform the processes of policy making and assure that they adhere to particular criteria and procedures.

Yet other connections between law and policy are important for administra-tors and attorneys to understand, as well as faculty and student leaders. One of the most important points about the relationship between the two, concerning which there is a growing consensus, is that policy should transcend law. In other words, legal considerations should not drive policy making, and policy making should not be limited to that which is necessary to fulfill legal require-ments. Institutions that are serious about their institutional missions and the education of students, including their health and safety, will often choose to do more than the law would require that they do. As an example, under Title IX of the Education Amendments of 1972, the courts have created lenient liability standards for institutions with regard to faculty members' harassment of stu-dents (see Section 9.3.4). An institution will be liable to the victim only when it had "actual notice" of the faculty harassment, and only when its response is so insufficient that it amounts to "deliberate indifference." It is usually easy to avoid liability under these standards, and doing so would not come close to ensuring the safety and health of students on campus. Nor would it ensure that there would be no hostile learning environment on campus. Institutions, there-fore, would be unwise to limit their activities and policies regarding sexual harassment to only that which the courts require under Title IX.

Policy, moreover, can become law—a particularly important interrelationship between the two. In the external realm of public policy, legislatures customarily write their policy choices into law, as do administrative agencies responsible for implementing legislation. There are also instances where courts have leeway to analyze public policy and make policy choices in the course of deciding cases. They may do so, for instance, when considering duties of care under negligence law (see, for example, *Eiseman v. State of New York,* 511 N.E.2d 1128 (N.Y. 1987)); when determining whether certain contracts or contract provisions are contrary to public policy (see, for example, *Weaver v. University of Cincinnati,* 970 F.2d 1523 (6th Cir. 1992)); and when making decisions, in various fields of law, based on a general standard of "reasonableness." In the internal realm of institutional policy, institutions as well sometimes write their policy choices into law. They do so primarily by incorporating these choices into the institu-tion's contracts with faculty members; students, administrators, and staff; and agents of the institution. They may do so either by creating contract language that parallels the language in a particular policy or by "incorporating by refer-ence," that is, by identifying particular policies by name in the contract and indi-cating that the policy's terms are to be considered terms of the contract. In such situations, the policy choices become law because they then may be enforced under the common law of contract whenever it can be shown that the institu-tion has breached one or more of the policy's terms.

Finally, regarding the interrelationship between law and policy, it is impor-tant to emphasize that good policy should encourage "judicial deference" or "academic deference" by the courts in situations when the policy, or a particular application of it, is challenged in court. Under this doctrine of deference, courts often defer to particular decisions or judgments of the institution when they are genuinely based upon the academic expertise of the institution and its faculty (see Section 2.2.5). It is therefore both good policy and good law for institutions to follow suggestions such as those outlined here, relying to the fullest extent feasible upon the academic expertise of administrators and faculty members, so as to maximize the likelihood that institutional policies, on their face and in their application, will be upheld by the courts if these policies are challenged.

Selected Annotated Bibliography

Sec. 1.1 (How Far the Law Reaches and How Loud It Speaks)

Alger, Jonathan R., & Przypyszny, John R. *Online Education: A Legal Compendium* (National Association of College and University Attorneys, 2002). Collects statutes, regulations, policies, and forms involving online education. Includes discussion of employment issues, intellectual property rights and responsibilities, conflicts of interest and commitment, quality control, regulation and accreditation, discrimination and accessibility, and financial issues related to online learning.

American Association of University Professors. "Universities and the Law," 87 *Academe* 16 (November–December 2001). Special issue of the AAUP's journal, devoted to a variety of legal issues. Articles include David M. Rabban, "Academic Freedom, Individual or Institutional?"; Gary Pavela, "A Balancing Act: Competing Claims for Academic Freedom"; William R. Kaufman, Robert O'Neil, Robert Post, & Wendy White, "The University Counsel: A Roundtable Discussion"; Ann H. Franke, "Making Defensible Tenure Decisions"; Mary Ann Connell & Frederick G. Savage, "Does Collegiality Count?"; and Paul D. Grossman, "Making Accommodations: The Legal World of Students With Disabilities."

Brevitz, Karl, Snow, Brian A., & Thro, William A. *The NACUA Handbook for Lawyers New to Higher Education* (National Association of College and University Attorneys, 2003). Includes more than sixty outlines from NACUA annual conferences and continuing legal education workshops, as well as articles from the *Journal of College and University Law.* Topics discussed include taxation, athletics, student discipline, computer issues, intellectual property, federal regulatory laws such as the Family Educational Rights and Privacy Act (FERPA) and the Health Insurance Portability and Accountability Act (HIPAA), and discrimination.

Campus Legal Information Clearinghouse (CLIC). A joint project of The Catholic University of America (CUA) and the American Council on Education, available at http://counsel.cua.edu. A Web site featuring information, tools, and resources to assist institutions in complying with an array of federal legal requirements. Includes summaries of federal laws pertinent to higher education, lists of FAQs, examples of innovative compliance practices, compliance checklists and charts, issues of the *CUA Counsel Online* newsletter, and links to other useful sites.

The Chronicle of Higher Education. "Academe Today." A valuable online research service. Access to this Web site via http://www.chronicle.com is available only on request using access codes provided to subscribers. This site allows access to the *Chronicle*'s latest news stories concerning actions in Congress, the executive branch, and the courts, as well as other developments in higher education, along with background material, such as the full text of court opinions. The *Chronicle* has also archived its past publications, allowing for easy access to past articles, cases, and citations.

Edwards, Harry T. *Higher Education and the Unholy Crusade Against Governmental Regulation* (Institute for Educational Management, Harvard University, 1980). Reviews and evaluates the federal regulatory presence on the campus. Author concludes that much of the criticism directed by postsecondary administrators at federal regulation of higher education is either unwarranted or premature.

Folger, Joseph, & Shubert, J. Janelle. "Resolving Student-Initiated Grievances in Higher Education: Dispute Resolution Procedures in a Non-Adversarial Setting," 3 *NIDR Reports* (National Institute for Dispute Resolution, 1986). A short monograph exploring the various methods employed at twenty different institutions to resolve conflicts. Includes a flowchart entitled "Model of Possible Options for Pursuing Resolutions to Student-Initiated Grievances" and a set of criteria for evaluating the effectiveness of particular grievance procedures.

Gouldner, Helen. "The Social Impact of Campus Litigation," 51 *J. Higher Educ.* 328 (1980). Explores the detrimental effects on the postsecondary community of "the tidal wave of litigation . . . awash in the country"; identifies "increased secrecy on campus," "fragile friendships among colleagues," a "crisis in confidence" in decision making, and "domination by legal norms" as major effects to be dealt with.

Helms, Lelia B. "Litigation Patterns: Higher Education and the Courts in 1988," 57 *West's Educ. Law Rptr.* 1 (1990). Reviews and classifies litigation involving higher education during a one-year period. Uses the geographical area, the court, the parties, and the issue as classifying factors. Includes tables summarizing litigation patterns. Article provides "baseline data for later comparison" and a methodology for collecting later data. See also the Helms entry for Section 1.2.

Hobbs, Walter C. "The Courts," in Philip G. Altbach, Robert O. Berdahl, & Patricia J. Gumport (eds.), *Higher Education in American Society* (3d ed., Prometheus Books, 1994). Reviews the concept of judicial deference to academic expertise and analyzes the impact of courts on postsecondary institutions. Includes illustrative cases. Author concludes that, despite complaints to the contrary from academics, the tradition of judicial deference to academic judgments is still alive and well.

Kaplin, William A. *The Importance of Process in Campus Administrative Decision-Making*, IHELG Monograph 91-10 (Institute for Higher Education Law and Governance, University of Houston, 1992). Distinguishes between the *substance* and the *process* of internal decision making by campus administrators; develops a "process taxonomy" with six generic classifications (rule making, adjudication, mediation, implementation, investigation, and crisis management); examines the "process values" that demonstrate the importance of campus processes; and sets out criteria for identifying "good" processes.

Melear, Kerry B., Beckham, Joseph, & Bickel, Robert. *The College Administrator and the Courts* (College Administration Publications, 1988, plus periodic supps.). A basic casebook (by Bickel) written for administrators, supplemented by a second vol. of case briefs and quarterly supplements (by Melear & Beckham) each year. Briefs and explains leading court cases. Topics include the legal system, sources of law, the role of counsel, distinctions between public and private colleges, the state action concept, and issues regarding faculty.

Olivas, Michael A. *The Law and Higher Education: Cases and Materials on Colleges in Court* (3d ed., Carolina Academic Press, 2006, with periodic supps.). A casebook presenting both foundational and contemporary case law on major themes in higher education law and governance. Includes supportive commentary by the author, news accounts, and excerpts from and cites to writings of others.

O'Neil, Robert. *Free Speech in the College Community* (Indiana University Press, 1997). Provides an excellent analysis and overview of free speech issues that arise within academic communities. Explores a range of free speech problems from speech codes, to academic freedom in the classroom, to free inquiry in research, to the challenges to free expression presented by technological advances. The presentation of each problem is lively, current, and very practical. The author's analysis interrelates legal issues and policy issues. The book is reviewed at 24 *J. Coll. & Univ. Law* 699 (1998) (review by J. W. Torke).

Pavela, Gary (ed.). *Synfax Weekly Report* (Synfax, Inc.). Newsletter-style publication delivered by FAX technology to maintain optimum currency. Each issue digests and critiques one or more legal and policy developments as reflected in court opinions, news media accounts, and other sources.

Weeks, Kent M., & Davis, Derek (eds.). *A Legal Deskbook for Administrators of Independent Colleges and Universities* (2d ed., Center for Constitutional Studies, Baylor University/National Association of College and University Attorneys, 1993). A resource containing legal analysis, practical advice, and bibliographical sources on issues of particular import to administrators and counsel at private institutions.

West's Education Law Reporter (Thomson/West). A biweekly publication covering education-related case law on both elementary/secondary and postsecondary education. Includes complete texts of opinions, brief summaries written for the layperson, articles and case comments, and a cumulative table of cases and index of legal principles elucidated in the cases.

Zirkel, Perry A. "The Volume of Higher Education Litigation: An Update," 126 *West's Educ. Law. Rptr.* 21 (1998); and Zirkel, Perry A. "Higher Education Litigation: An Overview," 56 *West's Educ. Law Rptr.* 705 (1989). Charts the course, and quantifies the increases, of higher education litigation in state and federal courts from the 1940s through the 1990s.

Sec. 1.2 (Evolution of Higher Education Law)

Beach, John A. "The Management and Governance of Academic Institutions, 12 *J. Coll. & Univ. Law* 301 (1985). Reviews the history and development of institutional governance, broadly defined. Discusses the corporate character of postsecondary institutions, the contradictions of "managing" an academic organization, academic freedom, and the interplay among the institution's various constituencies.

Bok, Derek. "Universities: Their Temptations and Tensions," 18 *J. Coll. & Univ. Law* 1 (1991). Author addresses the need for universities to maintain independence with regard to research and public service. Discusses three sources of temptation: politicization, diversion of faculty time and interest from teaching and research to consulting, and the indiscriminate focus on commercial gain when one is seeking funding.

Clark, Burton R. *The Academic Life: Small Worlds, Different Worlds* (Carnegie Foundation for the Advancement of Teaching, 1987). Traces the evolution of postsecondary institutions, the development of academic disciplines, the nature of academic work, the culture of academe, and academic governance. The book emphasizes the rewards and challenges of the faculty role, addressing the significance of the "postmodern" academic role.

Finkelstein, Martin J., Seal, Robert K., & Schuster, Jack H. *The New Academic Generation: A Profession in Transformation* (Johns Hopkins University Press, 1998). Uses data from the 1993 National Study of Postsecondary Faculty; analyzes faculty demographic data, work and career patterns, and attitudes. Discusses the use of part-time and adjunct faculty and the increase in nonwhite and female faculty.

Finkin, Matthew. "On 'Institutional' Academic Freedom," 61 *Tex. L. Rev.* 817 (1983). Explores the history and theoretical basis of academic freedom and analyzes the constitutional basis for academic freedom claims. Throughout, author distinguishes between the freedom of private institutions from government interference (institutional autonomy) and the freedom of individual members of the academic community from interference by government or by the institution. Includes analysis of leading U.S. Supreme Court precedents from 1819 (the *Dartmouth College* case) through the 1970s, as well as copious citations to legal and nonlegal sources.

Fishbein, Estelle A. "New Strings on the Ivory Tower: The Growth of Accountability in Colleges and Universities," 12 *J. Coll. & Univ. Law* 381 (1985). Examines the impact of external forces on the management of colleges and universities. Focusing primarily on the effect of federal regulation (including that by federal courts), the author discusses the significance of internal accountability in responding to external regulation.

Gallin, Alice. *Negotiating Identity: Catholic Higher Education Since 1960* (University of Notre Dame Press, 2001). Examines how Catholic higher education institutions have been working to maintain and redefine their "Catholic identity" in the face of events such as Vatican Council II, changes in curricula during the 1960s and '70s, and the growing need for public funds.

Gooden, Norma A., & Blechman, Rachel S. *Higher Education Administration: A Guide to Legal, Ethical, and Practical Issues* (Greenwood, 1999). Provides legal background and practical advice for administrators on hiring, compensation, promotion and tenure, terminations, academic freedom, student disputes on academic matters, and transcript and degree issues. Appendices include a "values audit" process and several pertinent AAUP Statements.

Helms, Lelia B. "Patterns of Litigation in Postsecondary Education: A Case Law Study," 14 *J. Coll. & Univ. Law* 99 (1987). Analyzes reported cases in one state (Iowa) from 1850 to 1985. Categorizes cases in a variety of ways and develops findings that provide "perspective on patterns of litigation and possible trends."

Kaplin, William A. "Law on the Campus, 1960–1985: Years of Growth and Challenge," 12 *J. Coll. & Univ. Law* 269 (1985). Discusses the legal implications of social and political changes for colleges and universities. Issues addressed in historical context include the concepts of "public" and "private," the distinctions between secular and religious institutions, and preventive legal planning.

Kerr, Clark. *The Great Transformation in Higher Education, 1960–1980* (State University of New York Press, 1991). A collection of essays written over three decades by an eminent participant in and observer of American higher education's era of greatest expansion, development, and change. The essays are collected under four broad rubrics: "The American System in Perspective"; "The Unfolding of the Great

Transformation: 1960–1980"; "Governance and Leadership Under Pressure"; and "Academic Innovation and Reform: Much Innovation, Little Reform."

Kerr, Clark. *Troubled Times for American Higher Education: The 1990s and Beyond* (State University of New York Press, 1994). Also a collection of essays, this book addresses contemporary issues that face colleges and universities. Part I examines "possible contours of the future and . . . choices to be made by higher education"; Part II concerns the relationship between higher education and the American economy; Part III examines specific issues, such as quality in undergraduate education, teaching about ethics, the "racial crisis" in American higher education, and elitism in higher education.

Levine, Arthur (ed.). *Higher Learning in America, 1980–2000* (Johns Hopkins University Press, 1994). Examines the political, economic, and demographic shifts that are affecting higher education. A variety of issues critical to various sectors of postsecondary education (research universities, community colleges, and liberal arts colleges) are discussed.

Martin, Randy (ed.). *Chalk Lines: The Politics of Work in the Managed University* (Duke University Press, 1998). Includes twelve essays on the restructuring of higher education and the restructuring of faculty work and careers. The book emphasizes the shift from public to private support of higher education, even in "public" institutions, and argues that political action is necessary to counter the forces of capitalism in academe.

Metzger, Walter, et al. *Dimensions of Academic Freedom* (University of Illinois Press, 1969). A series of papers presenting historical, legal, and administrative perspectives on academic freedom. Considers how the concept has evolved in light of changes in the character of faculties and student bodies and in the university's internal and external commitments.

Pavela, Gary (ed.). *Synthesis: Law and Policy in Higher Education* (College Administration Publications). A five-times-yearly periodical primarily for administrators. Each issue focuses on a single topic or perspective of contemporary concern. Includes practical analysis, commentary from and interviews with experts, case studies, samples of documents, and bibliographies and case citations.

Reidhaar, Donald L. "The Assault on the Citadel: Reflections on a Quarter Century of Change in the Relationship Between the Student and the University," 12 *J. Coll. & Univ. Law* 343 (1985). Reviews changes in the legal relationships between students and institutions, with particular emphasis on student protest and equal opportunity challenges.

Stallworth, Stanley B. "Higher Education in America: Where Are Blacks Thirty-Five Years After *Brown?*" 1991 *Wis. Multi-Cultural Law J.* 36 (1991). Reviews the history of historically black colleges, discusses the effect of *Brown v. Board of Education,* analyzes the effect of federal attempts to desegregate public systems of higher education, and reviews the attitudes of alumni of black colleges toward the quality of their educational experience.

Stark, Joan S., et al. *The Many Faces of Education Consumerism* (Lexington Books, 1977). A collection of essays on the history and status of the educational consumerism movement. Discusses the roles of the federal government, state government, accrediting agencies, and the courts in protecting the consumers of education; the place of institutional self-regulation; and suggestions for the future. Provides a broad perspective on the impact of consumerism on postsecondary education.

Terrell, Melvin C. (ed.). *Diversity, Disunity, and Campus Community* (National Association of Student Personnel Administrators, 1992). Describes problems related to an increasingly diverse student body and recommends ways in which the campus climate can be improved. Discusses cultural diversity in residence halls, relationships with campus law enforcement staff, student and faculty perspectives on diversity and racism, and strategies for reducing or preventing hate crimes.

Van Alstyne, William. "The Demise of the Right-Privilege Distinction in Constitutional Law," 81 *Harvard L. Rev.* 1439 (1968). Provides a historical and analytical review of the rise and fall of the right-privilege distinction; includes discussion of several postsecondary education cases to demonstrate that the pursuit of educational opportunities and jobs at public colleges is no longer a "privilege" to which constitutional rights do not attach.

Wright, Thomas W. "Faculty and the Law Explosion: Assessing the Impact—A Twenty-Five-Year Perspective (1960–85) for College and University Lawyers," 12 *J. Coll. & Univ. Law* 363 (1985). Assesses developments in the law with regard to college faculty. Issues addressed include the impact of the law on teaching (for example, FERPA and student challenges to grading decisions), research (federal regulations, academic misconduct), and faculty-administration relationships (for example, in collective bargaining).

See the Bickel and Lake entry for Chapter Three, Section 3.3.

Sec. 1.3 *(The Governance of Higher Education)*

McGuinness, Aims C. (ed.). *State Postsecondary Education Structures Sourcebook* (National Center for Higher Education Management Systems, 1997, and periodic Web site updates). A reference guide that includes the history, current structure, and emerging trends in governance of public and private higher education. Provides information on the governance structures in each state, including contact information for each state's higher education executive officers.

See also the Bess entry for Chapter Three, Section 3.1.

Sec. 1.4 *(Sources of Higher Education Law)*

Bakken, Gordon M. "Campus Common Law," 5 *J. Law & Educ.* 201 (1976). A theoretical overview of custom and usage as a source of postsecondary education law. Emphasizes the impact of custom and usage on faculty rights and responsibilities.

Brennan, William J. "State Constitutions and the Protection of Individual Rights," 90 *Harvard L. Rev.* 489 (1977). Discusses the trend, in some states, toward expansive construction of state constitutional provisions protecting individual rights. The author, then an Associate Justice of the U.S. Supreme Court, finds that "the very premise of the [U.S. Supreme Court] cases that foreclose federal remedies constitutes a clear call to state courts to step into the breach." For a sequel, see William J. Brennan, "The Bill of Rights and the States: The Revival of State Constitutions as Guardians of Individual Rights," 61 *N.Y.U. L. Rev.* 535 (1986).

Edwards, Harry T., & Nordin, Virginia D. *An Introduction to the American Legal System: A Supplement to Higher Education and the Law* (Institute for Educational

Management, Harvard University, 1980). Provides "a brief description of the American legal system for scholars, students, and administrators in the field of higher education who have had little or no legal training." Chapters include summary overviews of "The United States Courts," "The Process of Judicial Review," "Reading and Understanding Judicial Opinions, State Court Systems," "Legislative and Statutory Sources of Law," and "Administrative Rules and Regulations as Sources of Law."

Evans, G. R., & Gill, Jaswinder. *Universities and Students* (Kogan Page, 2001). Discusses a variety of issues related to the rights of students in the United Kingdom, including the contractual rights of students, the rights of students with disabilities, student discipline and academic misconduct issues, and the treatment of "whistle-blowing" students.

Farnsworth, E. Allan. *An Introduction to the Legal System of the United States* (3d ed., Oceana, 1996). An introductory text emphasizing the fundamentals of the American legal system. Written for the layperson.

Farrington, Dennis J., & Palfreyman, David. *The Law of Higher Education* (2d ed., Oxford University Press, 2006). Reviews the structure and governance of higher education in the United Kingdom, discusses areas in which courts have jurisdiction over higher education disputes, reviews funding issues, student and faculty issues, technology problems, and future challenges to higher education in the United Kingdom.

Gifis, Steven. *Law Dictionary* (5th ed., Barron's Educational Series, 2003). A paperback study aid for students or laypersons who seek a basic understanding of unfamiliar legal words and phrases. Also includes a table of abbreviations used in legal citations, a map and chart of the federal judicial system, and the texts of the U.S. Constitution and the American Bar Association *Model Rules of Professional Conduct.*

Robinson, John H. "The Extraterritorial Application of American Law: Preliminary Reflections," 27 *J. Coll. & Univ. L.* 187 (2000). Explores the shift in judicial attitudes from a policy of rejecting the extraterritorial application of U.S. law to a great tendency to apply U.S. law to institutional activities beyond the U.S. borders, particularly with respect to study abroad programs.

Sorenson, Gail, & LaManque, Andrew S. "The Application of *Hazelwood v. Kuhlmeier* in College Litigation," 22 *J. Coll. & Univ. Law* 971 (1996). Addresses the effect of the "cross application of judicial standards" from secondary to postsecondary settings and the detrimental effect this practice may have in cases involving collegiate classrooms. Suggests that minimizing salient differences between K–12 and postsecondary education settings is potentially a threat to the delicate academic freedom concerns at the postsecondary level.

Sec. 1.5 *(The Public-Private Dichotomy)*

Lewis, Harold, Jr., & Norman, Elizabeth. *Civil Rights Law and Practice* (2nd ed., Thomson/West, 2004). Sections 2.11–2.15 of this text address the state action doctrine and the related "color-of-law" requirement, sorting out the approaches to analysis and collecting the major cases from the U.S. Supreme Court as well as lower courts.

Matasor, Richard. "Private Publics, Public Privates: An Essay on Convergence in Higher Education," 10 *J. of Law & Pub. Pol'y* 5 (1998). Identifies "the distinctions that remain between public and private higher education as the lines between the two blur and differences disappear" (p. 6). Author explores the "economic and social factors" that "characterize" public and private education, argues that these factors are "converging," and addresses "the remaining essential attributes of public education" that give it a special role "in a privatizing world."

Phillips, Michael J. "The Inevitable Incoherence of Modern State Action Doctrine," 28 *St. Louis U. L.J.* 683 (1984). Traces the historical development of the state action doctrine through the U.S. Supreme Court's 1982 decision in *Rendell-Baker v. Kohn* and analyzes the political and social forces that have contributed to the doctrine's current condition.

Sedler, Robert A. "The State Constitutions and the Supplemental Protection of Individual Rights," 16 *U. Toledo L. Rev.* 465 (1985). Analyzes the use of the "individual rights" clauses of state constitutions to protect individual rights.

Thigpen, Richard. "The Application of Fourteenth Amendment Norms to Private Colleges and Universities," 11 *J. Law & Educ.* 171 (1982). Reviews the development of various theories of state action, particularly the public function and government contacts theories, and their applications to private postsecondary institutions. Also examines theories other than traditional state action for subjecting private institutions to requirements comparable to those that the Constitution places on public institutions. Author concludes: "It seems desirable to have a public policy of protecting basic norms of fair and equal treatment in nonpublic institutions of higher learning."

See Finkin entry for Section 1.2.

Sec. 1.6 *(Religion and the Public-Private Dichotomy)*

Kaplin, William A. *American Constitutional Law: An Overview, Analysis, and Integration* (Carolina Academic Press, 2004). Chapter 13 covers the U.S. Constitution's establishment clause and free exercise clause, as well as religious speech and religious association under the free speech clause, and includes discussion of leading U.S. Supreme Court cases. Chapter 12, Section G covers the freedom of expressive association, including discussion of the *Roberts* and *Dale* cases. Chapter 14, Section E introduces state constitutional rights regarding religion and the relationship between state constitutional rights and federal constitutional rights.

Moots, Philip R., & Gaffney, Edward M. *Church and Campus: Legal Issues in Religiously Affiliated Higher Education* (University of Notre Dame Press, 1979). Directed primarily to administrators and other leaders of religiously affiliated colleges and universities. Chapters deal with the legal relationship between colleges and affiliated religious bodies, conditions under which liability might be imposed on an affiliated religious group, the effect that the relationship between a college and a religious group may have on the college's eligibility for governmental financial assistance, the "exercise of religious preference in employment policies," questions of academic freedom, the influence of religion on student admissions and discipline, the use of federally funded buildings by religiously affiliated colleges, and the determination of property relationships when a college and a religious body alter their affiliation. Ends with a set of conclusions and recommendations and three appendices discussing the relationships between three religious denominations and their affiliated colleges.

Sec. 1.7 (The Relationship Between Law and Policy)

Brown, Walter, & Gamber, Cayo. *Cost Containment in Higher Education: Issues and Recommendations* (Jossey-Bass/ERIC, 2002). Analyzes financial issues and strategies in various areas of institutional operations, for example, instruction, libraries, technology, facilities, research, and student services.

2

Legal Planning
and Dispute Resolution

Sec. 2.1. Legal Liability

2.1.1. Overview. Postsecondary institutions and their agents—the officers, administrators, faculty members, staff members, and others through whom the institution acts—may encounter various forms of legal liability. The type and extent of liability depends on the source of the legal responsibility that the institution or its agents have failed to meet, and also on the power of the tribunal that determines whether the institution or its agents have violated some legal responsibility.

The three sources of law that typically create legal liabilities are the federal Constitution and state constitutions, statutes and regulations (at federal, state and local levels), and state common law (see Section 1.4.2). Constitutions typically govern actions by public institutions and their agents, although state constitutions may also be applied, under certain circumstances, to the conduct of private institutions and individuals. Statutes typically address who is subject to the law, the conduct prohibited or required by the law, and the consequences of failing to comply with the law. For example, employment discrimination laws specify what entities (employers, labor unions, employment agencies) are subject to the law's requirements, specify the types of discrimination that are prohibited by the law (race discrimination, disability discrimination, and so on), and address the penalties for violating the law (back pay, injunctions, and so on). For many statutes, administrative agency regulations elaborate on the actions required or prohibited by the statute, the criteria for determining that an institution or individual has violated the statute or regulation, and the methods of enforcement. On the other hand, the common law, particularly contract and tort law, has developed standards of conduct (for example, tort law's concept of legal duty and its various "reasonable person" standards) that, if violated, lead to legal liability.

2.1.2. *Types of liability.* Liability may be institutional (corporate) liability on the one hand, or personal (individual) liability on the other. Depending on who is sued, both types of liability may be involved in the same case. Constitutional claims brought by faculty, students, or others against public institutions may create institutional liability (unless the institution enjoys sovereign immunity, as discussed in Section 3.5) as well as individual liability, if individuals are also sued and their acts constitute "state action" or action under "color of law" (see Section 4.7.4). Statutory claims often (especially under federal nondiscrimination statutes) create only institutional liability, but sometimes also provide for individual liability. Contract claims usually involve institutional liability, but occasionally may involve individual liability as well. Tort claims frequently involve both institutional and individual liability, except for situations in which the institution enjoys sovereign or charitable immunity. Institutional liability for tort, contract, and constitutional claims is discussed in Sections 3.3, 3.4, and 3.5; personal liability for these claims is discussed in Section 4.7.

2.1.3. *Agency law.* Since postsecondary institutions act through their officers, employees, and other agents, the law of agency plays an important role in assessing liability, particularly in the area of tort law. Agency law provides that the employer (called the "principal" or the "master") must assume legal responsibility for the actions of its employees (called "agents" or "servants") and other "agents" under certain circumstances. Under the general rules of the law of agency, as applied to tort claims, the master may be liable for torts committed by its employees while they are acting in the scope of their employment. But the employer will not be liable for its employees' torts if they are acting outside the scope of their employment, unless one of four exceptions can be proven: for example, (1) if the employer intended that the tort or its consequences be committed; (2) if the master was negligent or reckless; (3) if the master had delegated a duty to the employee that was not delegable and the tort was committed as a result; or (4) if the employee relied on "apparent authority" by purporting to act or speak on behalf of the master (*Restatement (Second) of Agency,* American Law Institute, 1956, sec. 219). Generally speaking, it is difficult for an employer (master) to avoid liability for the unlawful acts of an employee (servant) unless the allegedly unlawful act is taken to further a personal interest of the employee or is so distant from the employee's work-related responsibilities as to suggest that holding the employer legally responsible for the act would be unjust. The institution's liability for the acts of its agents is discussed in Section 3.1 of this book and in various places in Sections 3.3 through 3.5. Sections 5.2 and 9.3.4 discuss institutional liability for its agents' acts under federal civil rights statutes.

2.1.4. Enforcement mechanisms. Postsecondary institutions may incur legal liability in a variety of proceedings. Students, employees, or others who believe that the institution has wronged them may often be able to sue the institution in court. Section 2.2 discusses the various requirements that a plaintiff must meet to maintain a claim in state or federal court. Cases are usually (but not always) tried before a jury when the plaintiff claims monetary damages, but are tried before a judge when the plaintiff seeks only equitable remedies such as an injunction.

Some federal statutes permit an individual to sue for alleged statutory violations in federal court, but if the statute does not contain explicit language authorizing a private cause of action, an individual may be limited to seeking enforcement by a federal agency. (See, for example, the discussion in Section 13.5.9 concerning a plaintiff's ability to sue an institution under the federal civil rights laws, and Section 9.7.1 for a discussion of private lawsuits under the Family Educational Rights and Privacy Act (FERPA).)

Various federal laws are enforced through administrative mechanisms established by the administrative agency (or agencies) responsible for that law. For example, the U.S. Education Department enforces nondiscrimination requirements under federal spending statutes such as Title VI, Title IX, and Section 504 (see Sections 13.5.2–13.5.4 of this book). Similarly, the federal Occupational Safety and Health Administration (OSHA) enforces the Occupational Safety and Health Act (see Section 4.6.1), and the U.S. Department of Labor enforces the Fair Labor Standards Act and the Family and Medical Leave Act (see Sections 4.6.2 & 4.6.4). Administrative enforcement may involve a compliance review of institutional programs, facilities, and records; negotiations and conciliation agreements; hearings before an administrative law judge; and appeals through the agency prior to resort to the courts (see generally Sections 13.4.5 & 13.5.8). Many states have their own counterparts to the federal administrative agency enforcement system for similar state laws.

Several federal statutes provide for lawsuits to be brought by either an individual or a federal agency. In other cases, a federal agency may bring constitutional claims on behalf of one plaintiff or a class of plaintiffs. The U.S. Department of Justice, on occasion, acts as a plaintiff in civil cases against postsecondary institutions. For example, the Department of Justice sued Virginia Military Institute (VMI) under the U.S. Constitution's Fourteenth Amendment for VMI's refusal to admit women (see Section 8.2.4.2). It also sued the State of Mississippi under Title VI of the Civil Rights Act of 1964 and the Fourteenth Amendment, seeking to desegregate the state's dual system of higher education (see *United States v. Fordice,* discussed in Section 8.2.4.1), and acts as a plaintiff in antitrust cases as well (see, for example, *United States v. Brown University,* discussed in Section 13.2.8). The Justice Department also plays a role in cases brought under the False Claims Act (see Section 13.2.15). Other federal or state agencies may also sue postsecondary institutions in court. Such litigation may follow years of enforcement actions by the agency, and may result in fines or court orders to comply with the law.

Some institutions are turning to alternate methods of resolving disputes in order to avoid the time, expense, and public nature of litigation. Section 2.3

discusses the use of mediation, arbitration, and other methods of resolving disputes on campus.

2.1.5. *Remedies for legal violations.* The source of legal responsibility determines the type of remedy that may be ordered if an institution or its agent is judged liable. For example, violation of statutes and administrative agency regulations may lead to the termination of federal or state funding for institutional programs, debarment from future contracts or grants from the government agency, audit exceptions, or fines. Violation of statutes (and sometimes regulations) may also lead to an order that money damages be paid to the prevailing party. Equitable remedies may also be ordered, such as reinstatement of a terminated employee, cessation of the practice judged to be unlawful, or an injunction requiring the institution to perform particular acts (such as abating an environmental violation). Occasionally, criminal penalties may be imposed. For example, the Occupational Safety and Health Act provides for imprisonment for individuals who willfully violate the Act (see Section 4.6.1 of this book). Criminal penalties may also be imposed for violations of certain computer fraud and crime statutes (see Section 13.2.12).

2.1.6. *Avoiding legal liability.* Techniques for managing the risk of legal liability are discussed in Section 2.5. Although avoiding legal liability should always be a consideration when a postsecondary institution makes decisions or takes actions, it should usually not be the first or the only consideration. Legal compliance should be thought of as the minimum that the institution must do, and not as the maximum that it should do. Policy considerations may often lead institutional decision makers to do more than the law actually requires (see Section 1.7). The culture of the institution, its mission, the prevailing academic norms and customs, and particular institutional priorities, as well as the law, may help shape the institution's legal and policy responses to potential legal liability. To capture this dynamic, discussions of legal liability throughout this book are interwoven with discussions of policy concerns; administrators and counsel are often encouraged (explicitly and implicitly) to base decisions on this law/policy dynamic.

Sec. 2.2. Litigation in the Courts

2.2.1. *Overview.* Of all the forums available for the resolution of higher education disputes (see Sections 1.1 & 2.3), administrators are usually most concerned about court litigation. There is good reason for the concern. Courts are the most public and thus most visible of the various dispute resolution forums. Courts are also the most formal, involving numerous technical matters that require extensive involvement of attorneys. In addition, courts may order the strongest and the widest range of remedies, including both compensatory and punitive money damages and both prohibitive and mandatory (affirmative) injunctive relief. Court decrees and opinions also have the highest level of authoritativeness; not only do a court's judgments and orders bind the parties for the future regarding the issues litigated, subject to enforcement through judicial contempt powers and other mechanisms, but a court's written opinions may also create precedents binding other litigants in future disputes as well (see Section 1.4.4).

For these reasons and others, court litigation is the costliest means of dispute resolution that institutions engage in—costly in time and emotional effort as well as in money—and the most risky. Thus, although lawsuits have become a regular occurrence in the lives of postsecondary institutions, involving a broad array of parties and situations (see Section 1.1), administrators should never trivialize the prospect of litigation. Involvement in a lawsuit is serious and often complex business that can create internal campus friction, drain institutional resources, and affect an institution's public image, even if the institution eventually emerges as the "winner." The following history of a protracted university case illustrates the problem.

In *Hildebrand v. Board of Trustees of Michigan State University*, 607 F.2d 705 (6th Cir. 1979) and 662 F.2d 439 (6th Cir. 1981), the defendant had denied the plaintiff tenure in 1968 and officially ended his employment in 1969. Initiating the first of a series of intrauniversity appeals, Hildebrand addressed the full faculty and presented reasons why he should be tenured, but he did not persuade the faculty to change its mind. He then pled his case to the Departmental Advisory Committee (DAC), an elected committee to which he himself had recently been elected, and which contained a majority of nontenured members for the first time in its history; although the DAC issued a resolution that there was no basis for denying Professor Hildebrand tenure, this resolution was ineffectual. Finally, Hildebrand appealed to the University Faculty Tenure Committee, which denied his appeal.

Professor Hildebrand then began seeking forums outside the university. He complained to the American Association of University Professors (AAUP) (see Section 14.5). He filed two unfair labor practice charges (see generally Section 4.5) with the Michigan Employment Relations Commission, both of which failed. He petitioned the Michigan state courts, which denied him leave to appeal.

In 1971, Professor Hildebrand filed suit in federal court, requesting back pay and reinstatement. He claimed that the university had denied tenure in retaliation for his exercise of First Amendment rights (see Sections 6.6.1 & 7.1.1), and also that the university had violated his procedural due process rights (see Section 6.7.2.2). A five-day jury trial was held in 1974, but, literally moments before he was to instruct the jury, the judge belatedly decided that the plaintiff's claims were equitable in nature and should be decided by the judge rather than a jury. In 1977, the trial judge finally dismissed the professor's complaint. On appeal in 1979, the U.S. Court of Appeals held that the district judge had erred in taking the case from the jury and that "[t]he only fair solution to this tangled and protracted case is to reverse and remand for a prompt jury trial on all issues" (607 F.2d 705). The subsequent trial resulted in a jury verdict for the professor that included back pay, compensatory and punitive damages, and a directive that the university reinstate him as a professor. Ironically, however, the trial judge then entertained and granted the university's motion for a "judgment notwithstanding the verdict." This ruling, of course, precipitated yet another appeal by the professor. In 1981, the U.S. Court of Appeals upheld the trial court's decision in favor of the university (662 F.2d 439). At that point, thirteen years after the tenure denial, the case finally ended.

While the *Hildebrand* case is by no means the norm, even garden-variety litigation can become complex. It can involve extensive formal pretrial activities, such as depositions, interrogatories, subpoenas, pretrial conferences, and motion hearings, as well as various informal pretrial activities such as attorney-administrator conferences, witness interviews, document searches and document reviews, and negotiation sessions with opposing parties. If the case proceeds to trial, there are all the difficulties associated with presenting a case before a judge or jury: further preparatory meetings with the attorneys; preparation of trial exhibits; scheduling, travel, and preparation of witnesses; the actual trial time; and the possibility of appeals. In order for the institution to present its best case, administrators will need to be intimately involved with most stages of the process. Litigation, including the garden variety, is also monetarily expensive, since a large amount of employee time must be committed to it and various fees must be paid for outside attorneys, court reporters, perhaps expert witnesses, and so forth. Federal litigation is generally more costly than state litigation. (See generally D. M. Trubek et al., "The Cost of Ordinary Litigation," 31 *UCLA L. Rev.* 73 (1983).) Fortunately, lawsuits proceed to trial and judgment less often than most laypeople believe. The vast majority of disputes are resolved through settlement negotiations (see M. Galanter, "Reading the Landscape of Disputes: What We Know and Don't Know (and Think We Know) About Our Allegedly Contentious and Litigious Society," 31 *UCLA L. Rev.* 4 (1983)). Although administrators must also be involved in such negotiations, the process is less protracted, more informal, and more private than a trial.

Despite the potential costs and complexities, administrators should avoid overreacting to the threat of litigation and, instead, develop a balanced view of the litigation process. Lawsuits can usually be made manageable with careful litigation planning, resulting from good working relationships between the institution's lawyers and its administrators. Often lawsuits can be avoided entirely with careful preventive planning (see Sections 2.2.6 & 2.4). And preventive planning, even when it does not deflect the lawsuit, will likely strengthen the institution's litigation position, narrow the range of viable issues in the case, and help ensure that the institution retains control of its institutional resources and maintains focus on its institutional mission. Particularly for administrators, sound understanding of the litigation process is predicate to both constructive litigation planning and constructive preventive planning.

2.2.2. Access to court

2.2.2.1. Jurisdiction. Courts will not hear every dispute that litigants seek to bring before them. Rather, under the constitutional provisions and statutes that apply to it, a court must have jurisdiction over both the subject matter of the suit ("subject matter jurisdiction") and the persons who are parties to the suit (personal, or *in personam*, jurisdiction), and various other technical requirements must also be met. The jurisdictional and technical requirements for access to federal court differ from those for state courts, and variances exist among the state court systems as well. Skillful use of these requirements may enable institutions to stay out of court in certain circumstances when they are threatened with suit and also to gain access to courts when they seek to use them offensively.

The federal courts have only limited jurisdiction; they may hear only the types of cases listed in Article III of the federal Constitution, most especially cases that present issues of federal statutory or constitutional law ("federal question jurisdiction") or cases in which the plaintiff(s) and defendant(s) are citizens of different states ("diversity jurisdiction"). State courts, on the other hand, are courts of general jurisdiction and may, under the relevant state constitutional provisions, hear all or most types of disputes brought to them. (Often, however, there is more than one type of state trial-level court for the same geographical area—for example, a trial court for cases seeking damages below a certain amount and another for cases seeking damages above that amount.) State courts may also hear cases presenting federal law claims, except for certain federal statutory claims for which the statute gives the federal courts exclusive jurisdiction. It is the plaintiff's responsibility to meet these requirements of subject matter jurisdiction; if the plaintiff does not do so, the defendant may be able to escape from the suit altogether, especially in a federal court.

Jurisdiction must be established for both the subject matter of the dispute and for the individual parties to the dispute. Since the plaintiff initiates the lawsuit, it is assumed that the plaintiff voluntarily submits to the jurisdiction of the court. But the defendant does not, and the court may lack personal jurisdiction over the defendant if the defendant does not have ties to the state through business dealings, a physical presence, or committing unlawful acts in the state.

With respect to subject matter jurisdiction, the plaintiff must allege sufficient facts in his or her complaint to persuade the court that there is a dispute that is cognizable under federal or state law. For example, in *King v. Riverside Regional Medical Center*, 211 F. Supp. 2d 779 (E.D. Va. 2002), the court ruled that the plaintiff, a student who was dismissed from a nursing program, had not alleged the requisite facts to provide the court with jurisdiction under the law that the student was claiming had been violated.

Jurisdictional issues are further complicated when a lawsuit filed in federal court also presents state law claims, or when a lawsuit filed in state court also presents federal law claims. As a means of determining whether a federal court is a proper forum for the state law claim as well, the doctrines of "pendant" and "ancillary" jurisdiction are applied. The principles of "concurrent jurisdiction" and "removal" are invoked to support a claim that the state court is not a proper forum for the federal law claims.

A foundational case concerning suits filed in federal court but also containing state claims is *United Mine Workers v. Gibbs*, 383 U.S. 715 (1966). In this case the U.S. Supreme Court determined that a federal court may in its discretion exercise jurisdiction over an entire case, including its state law claims, whenever the federal and state law claims "derive from a common nucleus of operative fact and are such that a plaintiff would ordinarily be expected to try them all in one proceeding." In 1990, building on *Gibbs* and later cases interpreting the scope of pendant and ancillary jurisdiction, Congress enacted a statute that codified the two judicial doctrines and renamed them "supplemental jurisdiction" (28 U.S.C. § 1367). The statute establishes a uniform standard for determining whether a federal court has jurisdiction to hear a state claim attached to a federal claim and provides guidance to the trial court in determining whether to assert that jurisdiction or decline it. The court may decline jurisdiction over the state claim if it raises a novel or complex issue of state law; if it substantially predominates over the federal claim; if the federal claim has been dismissed; or if there are other compelling reasons for declining jurisdiction.

Where the plaintiff files an action in state court containing both federal and state claims, the state court generally may hear the federal claims as well as the state claims, because the state courts have concurrent jurisdiction with the federal courts over federal claims. Sometimes, however (as noted above), a state court will not have jurisdiction over the federal claim because the federal statute under which the claim arises gives the federal courts exclusive jurisdiction. Moreover, a state court may be deprived of jurisdiction if a defendant files a removal petition to remove the federal claim (and attached state claims) to federal court. The defendant has the option of removing most claims that would fall within the federal court's subject matter jurisdiction (28 U.S.C. § 1441). However, the decision by a public institution to remove a federal claim from state to federal court will act as a waiver of Eleventh Amendment immunity, according to the U.S. Supreme Court's decision in *Lapides v. Board of Regents of the University System of Georgia,* 535 U.S. 613 (2002).

To entertain a lawsuit, a court must have jurisdiction not only over the subject matter but also over the parties involved (personal or *in personam* jurisdiction). This type of jurisdictional question may arise, for instance, when an institution is a defendant in a lawsuit in a state other than its home state. Generally, a court has jurisdiction over defendants who consent to being sued in the state, are physically present in the state, reside in the state, or commit torts or conduct business within the state. Most challenges to jurisdiction arise in the last of these categories. Typically, a state's "long-arm" statute determines whether a court can exercise personal jurisdiction over an out-of-state defendant who commits a tort or conducts business within the state. In addition, the federal Constitution's Fourteenth Amendment, through its due process clause, has been found to limit the ability of state courts to exercise personal jurisdiction, since it prescribes the "minimum contacts" that a defendant must have with a state before that state's courts may exercise personal jurisdiction under a long-arm statute. If the contacts are both purposeful and substantial, so that maintenance of the suit would not offend traditional notions of fair play and substantial justice, the state may assert jurisdiction (see *Worldwide Volkswagen Corp. v. Woodson,* 444 U.S. 286 (1980)). In other words, an institution will not be compelled to bear the costs and inconvenience of a lawsuit out of state unless its activities in that state satisfy the state's long-arm statute *and* the statute is consistent with the Constitution's "minimum contacts" standard.

Jurisdictional issues also may arise when a lawsuit is filed in federal court. The popularity of the Internet as a recruiting tool for colleges and universities has led to attempts by out-of-state plaintiffs to argue that the institution may be sued in federal court in another state because the Web site may be accessed from that other state. For example, in *Scherer v. Curators of the University of Missouri,* 152 F. Supp. 2d 1278 (D. Kan. 2001), a rejected law school applicant attempted to sue the University of Missouri in federal district court in Kansas, arguing that the university recruited Kansas students through its Web site, and also had a large number of employees who were Kansas residents. The court ruled that neither of these facts was sufficient to justify personal jurisdiction over the university in Kansas. Similarly, a federal appellate court in *Revell v. Lidov,* 317 F.3d 467 (5th Cir. 2002) affirmed a Texas federal district court's refusal to assert jurisdiction over faculty members employed by Harvard University, despite the fact that Harvard hosted the Web site on which the defendants had posted an article that allegedly defamed the plaintiff.

Brainerd v. Governors of the University of Alberta, 873 F.2d 1257 (9th Cir. 1989), illustrates the assertion of jurisdiction based on the commission of a tort within the state. The court held that Arizona could exercise personal jurisdiction over the vice president of a Canadian university who received two telephone calls from and responded to one letter from a University of Arizona administrator. The calls and letter were employment inquiries concerning the plaintiff, a former professor at the Canadian university, who was applying for an appointment at the University of Arizona. The plaintiff claimed that the vice president's remarks defamed him. The court found that the vice president intentionally directed his communications to Arizona, that the alleged defamation (a tort) would have taken place in the state (the communications were themselves the defamation), and that Arizona had a strong interest in protecting its citizens from torts that cause injury within the state. The court therefore could assert personal jurisdiction over the vice president under the state's long-arm statute. In *Wagner v. Miskin,* 660 N.W.2d 593 (N.D. 2003), the Supreme Court of North Dakota rejected a defendant's claim that North Dakota courts lacked jurisdiction over a defamation claim brought against her by a professor. The defendant, a student who had used the Internet to post allegedly defamatory messages concerning the professor, claimed that North Dakota courts "have no jurisdiction over the Internet." The court disagreed, noting that her messages were targeted specifically at the state of North Dakota, thus giving the requisite contacts for North Dakota courts to assert jurisdiction.

Hahn v. Vermont Law School, 698 F.2d 48 (1st Cir. 1983), illustrates how personal jurisdiction may be obtained over a defendant who conducts business within the state. A Massachusetts resident sued his law school and one of his professors for breach of contract in a Massachusetts federal court. The student claimed that the law school breached its contract with him by hiring and not supervising the professor who gave Hahn an F on an examination. The court held that Massachusetts had personal jurisdiction over the law school because it had mailed application materials and an acceptance letter to the student in Massachusetts, and had done so as part of an overall effort "to serve the market for legal education in Massachusetts." According to the court, these were purposeful activities that satisfied the conducting-business requirement of the Massachusetts long-arm statute. The court could not exercise personal jurisdiction over the law professor, a citizen of Vermont, however, since the professor taught his courses in Vermont and did not participate in any recruiting activities in Massachusetts.

Despite the minimal nature of the contacts with the state that these cases require, it does not follow that all states and courts would be as permissive in accepting jurisdiction, or that any contact with the state will do. In *Gehling v. St. George's School of Medicine*, 773 F.2d 539 (3d Cir. 1985), for instance, parents sued in Pennsylvania for the wrongful death of their son, a Pennsylvania resident, who had attended the defendant school in the West Indies and had died after running in a school-sponsored race in Grenada. The court held that, even though the school placed recruiting information in New York newspapers that were circulated throughout Pennsylvania, sent officials to visit Pennsylvania and appear on talk shows there to gain exposure for the school, and was involved in a joint international program with a Pennsylvania university, it did not have sufficient contacts with the state to be subject to jurisdiction under the Pennsylvania long-arm statute for its alleged negligence and breach of contract in Grenada. None of the school's activities in Pennsylvania were continuous, or geared to recruiting students. Nor did the mere mailing of an acceptance letter and other information to the student in Pennsylvania constitute a contact sufficient to create jurisdiction. (However, the parents of the deceased student also claimed that, when school officials brought their son's body to Pennsylvania, they misrepresented the cause of his death. Since the misrepresentation constituted a tort actually committed within the state, the court did assert jurisdiction over the university for purposes of litigating the misrepresentation claim.)

In the state courts, there will sometimes be an added complexity when the claim is against a public institution. Such cases cannot always be brought in the state's court of general jurisdiction; sometimes a special state court, usually called the court of claims, will have exclusive subject matter jurisdiction. In *Miller v. Washington State Community College*, 698 N.E.2d 1058 (Ohio 1997), for instance, an appellate court affirmed the dismissal of a claim in the Common Pleas Court for Washington County, brought against a "state community college" by an employee whose appointment the college had not renewed. The state community college, said the court, was "an arm of the state of Ohio," like the Ohio state colleges and universities, and therefore was subject to suit only in the Ohio Court of Claims. If the defendant had been a "political subdivision" that is "autonomous from the state," however, as were certain other community colleges organized under Ohio law, it could have been sued in the Common Pleas Court.

The practical effect of a ruling like that in *Miller* is that all higher educational institutions that are "arms of the state" share in the state's sovereign immunity from suit in the state's own courts. The state, however, can waive this immunity and consent to certain suits, as Ohio had done in *Miller* by establishing the

Court of Claims. Courts in other states have relied more directly on this sovereign immunity concept than did the *Miller* court. In *Grine v. Board of Trustees, University of Arkansas,* 2 S.W.3d 54 (Ark. 1999), for example, a doctoral student had sued the University of Arkansas in a state trial court of general jurisdiction, alleging breach of contract, fraud, and other claims, after he did not receive his doctorate within the required seven-year period. The Supreme Court of Arkansas affirmed the trial court's dismissal of the case because it was barred by a provision of the Arkansas constitution establishing state sovereign immunity. According to the court, "sovereign immunity is jurisdictional immunity from suit, and where the pleadings show the action is one against the state, the trial court acquires no jurisdiction" (2 S.W.3d at 58). The court did note one difference, however, between sovereign immunity and subject matter jurisdiction: the former can usually be waived but the latter cannot. This difference was irrelevant in *Grine* because the state had not consented to such suits and, under the Arkansas constitution, "such consent is expressly withheld" (2 S.W.3d at 58, quoting *Pitcock v. State,* 121 S.W. 742 (1909)).

2.2.2.2. Other technical doctrines. Even when a court has subject matter jurisdiction, other technical access doctrines may keep the court from hearing the case. Such doctrines—primarily the doctrines of abstention, mootness, and standing—work together to ensure that the case involves proper parties, is brought at a proper time, and presents issues appropriate for resolution by the court in which the case is filed. These considerations tend to pose greater problems in federal than in state courts.

In *Ivy Club v. Edwards,* 943 F.2d 270 (3d Cir. 1991), for instance, "eating clubs" at Princeton had sued New Jersey officials in federal court after the state civil rights agency had asserted authority over the clubs. Determining that there were relevant, unresolved issues of *state* law regarding the civil rights agency's authority, and invoking one of the "abstention" doctrines, the federal district court abstained from hearing the case so that the New Jersey state courts could themselves resolve the state law issues (*Tiger Inn v. Edwards,* 636 F. Supp. 787 (D.N.J. 1986)).[1] After extended state court proceedings, resulting in an order that the eating clubs admit women as members (this book, Section 10.1.4), the clubs sought to revive their earlier federal court action, in order to assert that the order violated their federal constitutional rights. The federal appellate court ruled that the federal district court had improperly invoked *Pullman* abstention in the earlier federal action, that the clubs had explicitly reserved the right to return to federal court, and that the state courts had not litigated the federal constitutional issues. The clubs could therefore proceed in federal court with their federal claims.

In *People for the Ethical Treatment of Animals v. Institutional Animal Care and Use Committee of the University of Oregon,* 817 P.2d 1299 (Or. 1991), the

---

[1]The abstention doctrine invoked by the court was "*Pullman* abstention," named after the case of *Railroad Commission of Texas v. Pullman,* 312 U.S. 496 (1941), to be contrasted with "*Younger* abstention," a doctrine named after *Younger v. Harris,* 401 U.S. 37 (1971). See *Ivy Club v. Edwards,* 943 F.2d at 276–84.

question was whether the plaintiff (PETA) had "standing" to challenge (that is, was a proper party to challenge) the defendant's approval of a professor's proposal for research involving barn owls. The applicable requirements for obtaining state court standing were in a state statute governing challenges to state administrative agency actions (Or. Rev. Stat. § 183.480(1) (1993)). The court held that PETA was not "aggrieved," as required by this statute, because it had not suffered any injury to any substantial personal interest, did not seek to vindicate any interest that the state legislature had sought to protect, and did not have a "personal stake" in the outcome of the litigation. The court therefore dismissed the suit because PETA had no standing to bring it.

An association of wrestling coaches sued the U.S. Department of Education, asserting that its guidelines for compliance with Title IX by collegiate athletics programs were, in fact, a violation of Title IX because they motivated institutions to cut men's sports teams (such as wrestling) in order to comply with the guidelines' requirement of proportionality (see Section 10.4.6). In *National Wrestling Coaches Association v. Department of Education,* 366 F.3d 930 (D.C. Cir. 2004), *petition for en banc hearing denied,* 363 F.3d 239 (D.C. Cir. October 8, 2004), the panel reiterated its earlier holding that the coaches' association lacked standing to sue the Department of Education because the guidelines did not have the force of law. The proper defendant, said the panel, was the institutions who dropped men's sports in order to comply with Title IX. The U.S. Supreme Court declined to hear the appeal (125 S. Ct. 2537 (2005)). For further discussion of this case, see Section 10.4.6.

In *Cook v. Colgate University,* 992 F.2d 17 (2d Cir. 1993), the problem was "mootness," a problem concerning the timing of the lawsuit. Mootness doctrines generally require dismissal of a case if the controversy between the parties has expired as a result of the passage of time or changes in events. In the *Cook* case, this doctrine effectively negated a victory for the student plaintiffs, all of whom were members of the women's ice hockey club team of Colgate. They had sued in federal district court under Title IX, alleging that Colgate had failed to provide comparable programs for men's and women's ice hockey (see this book, Section 10.4.6). The court issued an order requiring Colgate to upgrade the women's club team to varsity status, starting with the 1993–94 season. However, three of the five plaintiffs had already graduated, and, by the time of the appeal, the other two had completed their college hockey careers and were scheduled to graduate in May 1993. The appellate court held that, because "none of the plaintiffs [could] benefit from an order requiring equal athletic opportunities for women ice hockey players," the case must be dismissed as moot. Although the appellate court noted that "situations 'capable of repetition, yet evading review'" (*Southern Pacific Terminal Co. v. Interstate Commerce Commission,* 219 U.S. 498, 515 (1911)), are an exception to the mootness doctrine, it reasoned that this exception applies only if the same plaintiffs might reasonably be expected to be involved again with the same type of suit. Because the plaintiffs here had graduated or were graduating, they did not fall within the exception. Moreover, the plaintiffs might have avoided the mootness doctrine had they sued "in a 'representational capacity' as the leader of a student organization" (see generally Section 2.2.3.1), but this argument was not open to them because they had sued "individually, not as representatives of the women's ice hockey club team or other 'similarly situated' individuals."

2.2.2.3. Statutes of limitations. Another type of timing problem arises from the application of statutes of limitations. In order to maintain a lawsuit, a plaintiff must file the claim within a restricted time period. This time period is defined by the "statute of limitations" applicable to the particular type of claim being asserted. If it is a state law claim, the court will apply a state statute of limitations; if it is a federal law claim, the court will apply a federal statute of limitations. Federal laws, however, sometimes do not stipulate a time period for bringing particular claims. In such circumstances the court may "borrow" a state statute of limitations applicable to state claims most similar to the federal claim at issue.

Postsecondary institutions may confront two types of issues when complying with or challenging a particular statute of limitations. The first issue concerns which state statute to borrow when a federal limitations statute does not exist. This problem frequently arises, for example, in Section 1983 litigation (see Section 3.5 in this book). In *Braden v. Texas A&M University System,* 636 F.2d 90 (5th Cir. 1981), a professor used Section 1983 to challenge his termination, claiming that the university had violated his property and reputational interests protected by the federal Constitution. Since the Section 1983 statute does not stipulate any period of limitation, the court had to borrow the state statute of limitations governing state claims most analogous to the federal claim at issue, as the U.S. Supreme Court had directed in *Board of Regents of the University of the State of New York v. Tomanio,* 446 U.S. 478 (1980) (see also *Wilson v. Garcia,* 471 U.S. 261 (1985)). In compliance with *Tomanio,* the court considered the essential nature of the plaintiff's claim and compared it to similar state law claims. The court rejected the professor's suggestion that state contract claims were most analogous to his claim and instead analogized his claims to tort actions for trespass, conversion of property, and injury done to the person of another. The court thus borrowed the state statute of limitations for tort actions, providing that such claims must be filed within two years of the date upon which the claim arose, rather than the statute of limitations for contract actions, which was three years. Since the professor's claim had arisen more than two (but less than three) years before he filed his case, the court dismissed the lawsuit, thus releasing the university from all liability, simply because the professor had filed the case too late. (For another example of a similar borrowing problem regarding a claim of disability discrimination under the federal Section 504 statute (this book, Section 13.5.4), see *Wolsky v. Medical College of Hampton Roads,* 1 F.3d 222 (4th Cir. 1993).)

The second type of issue concerns the determination of when the statute of limitations time period begins to "run." Generally that period begins when the plaintiff's claim first accrued, a technical question of some difficulty. *Pauk v. Board of Trustees of the City University of New York,* 654 F.2d 856 (2d Cir. 1981), another case in which the court dismissed a professor's Section 1983 claim against a university, is illustrative. The university had declined to reappoint the professor. The professor claimed that university officials had taken this action in retaliation for his active participation in the faculty union, thus violating his First Amendment rights. The federal court borrowed and applied a state statute of limitations of three years. The question before the court was whether that three-year time period commenced running in 1975, when the professor received final notification that he would not be reappointed, or in 1976, when his term appointment expired. Relying on the U.S. Supreme Court's decision in *Delaware State College v. Ricks,* 449 U.S. 250 (1980), the court determined that federal law defines when a claim accrues under Section 1983, and that the professor's claim had accrued when he received the notice in 1975. Because the professor had not filed his lawsuit within three years of the date he received notice, his claim was dismissed.

Other types of accrual issues arise in situations where a plaintiff attacks a general university policy, such as a retirement or seniority plan. In *Equal Employment Opportunity Commission v. City Colleges of Chicago,* 944 F.2d 339 (7th Cir. 1991), for example, the EEOC brought a claim based on the Age Discrimination in Employment Act (ADEA) of 1967 (this book, Section 5.2.6), which has a two-year statute of limitations. The EEOC challenged the colleges' retirement plan on grounds that it had been adopted with an intent to discriminate against older workers. The question was whether the EEOC's claim accrued when the colleges first adopted the early retirement plan rather than when the plan was later applied to harm particular older professors. Relying on the U.S. Supreme Court's decision in *Lorance v. AT&T Technologies, Inc.,* 490 U.S. 900 (1989), the court determined that "assessing when a statute of limitations begins to run" depends on a precise identification of the discriminatory act at issue and that, under the EEOC's complaint and the pertinent ADEA provisions and interpretive case law, "the relevant discriminatory act in this case . . . was the plan's adoption." The court thus held the claim to be time barred because it was not filed until 1988, six years after the plan's adoption in 1982. Had the court instead held that the EEOC's claim accrued anew each time a faculty member was injured by the application of the plan, the suit would not have been time-barred, since the claim then would have accrued within two years of filing the suit.

2.2.2.4. Exhaustion of remedies. A prospective plaintiff may sometimes be prevented (or at least delayed) from bringing a court suit by the "exhaustion-of-remedies" doctrine. Simply put, the doctrine requires that a court not hear a plaintiff's claim until the plaintiff has exhausted any and all administrative remedies that may be available—for example, a hearing before an administrative agency or a grievance board. The doctrine is particularly important to a postsecondary institution that is threatened with suit but has an internal process available for resolving the problem. Thus, in *Florida Board of Regents v. Armesto,* 563 So. 2d 1080 (Fla. 1990), the court refused to consider a student's request to enjoin Florida State University Law School from formally charging her with cheating on her final exams. The school had adopted internal procedures for challenging such charges, but the student had not exercised her right to use them (including the availability of a full hearing on the charges). Although the court recognized that an exception to the exhaustion-of-remedies doctrine exists in situations where the available procedures would not provide an adequate or timely remedy, it found no basis for applying the exception in this instance. Further, the court rejected the student's argument that she could bypass the administrative remedies because the school's investigation of the charges violated her due process rights. The exhaustion doctrine applies even when a suit is based on constitutional deficiencies in the application of the administrative process to the plaintiff. Quoting the trial judge's opinion, the Florida Supreme Court held that in such instances the doctrine ensures that "the responsible agency 'has had a full opportunity to reach a sensitive, mature, and considered decision upon a complete record appropriate to the issue'" (563 So. 2d at 1081).[2]

Similarly, in *Pfaff v. Columbia-Greene Community College,* 472 N.Y.S.2d 480 (N.Y. App. Div. 1984), the court dismissed the complaint of a student who had sued her college, contesting a C grade entered in a course, because the college had an internal appeal process and the student "failed to show that pursuit of the available administrative appeal would have been fruitless." And in *Beck v. Board of Trustees of State Colleges,* 344 A.2d 273 (Conn. 1975), where faculty members sought to enjoin the defendant board from implementing proposed new personnel policies that allegedly threatened tenured faculty rights, the court dismissed the suit under the exhaustion doctrine because the state's administrative procedure act "provides a comprehensive, potentially inexpensive, and completely adequate method of resolving the issues raised in the present . . . [suit]."

Failure to use an internal grievance process created by a collective bargaining agreement resulted in the dismissal of a wrongful discharge claim by two former faculty members at Montana State University's College of Technology. In *MacKay v. State,* 79 P.3d 236 (Mont. 2003), the state's supreme court, interpreting the language of the collective bargaining agreement, ruled that the grievance procedure was mandatory, and that exhaustion of that remedy was required by state legal precedent prior to litigation.

The case of *Long v. Samson,* 568 N.W.2d 602 (N.D. 1997), provides another good example of using the exhaustion-of-remedies doctrine to keep a case out of court. The plaintiff was a nontenured professor who brought tort and breach of contract claims after his appointment at the University of North Dakota (UND) was not renewed. The North Dakota Supreme Court affirmed the trial court's dismissal of the case because the plaintiff failed to exhaust the remedies available to him under the University of North Dakota's Faculty Handbook:

> Section II-8.1.3(C)(3) [of the Faculty Handbook] authorizes review of decisions based upon "inadequate consideration," which, by definition, is confined to procedural and not substantive issues. Section II-8.1.3(C)(4), however, authorizes substantive review of academic freedoms, constitutional rights, or contractual

---

[2]Plaintiffs filing civil rights claims under Section 1983, the federal civil rights statute, need not exhaust state administrative remedies; see *Patsy v. Board of Regents of the State of Florida,* 457 U.S. 496 (1982), discussed in Section 2.3.3.

rights. A remedy is not inadequate simply because it may not result in the exact relief requested. Administrative resolution of Long's nonrenewal may have eliminated or mitigated damages and developed a record to sharpen issues and avoid judicial proceedings. . . . We reject Long's argument that resort to UND's administrative procedures would have been futile, or the remedies at UND would have been inadequate [568 N.W.2d at 606].

In contrast, in *Brennan v. King,* 139 F.3d 258 (1st Cir. 1998), the court declined (with one exception) to require exhaustion. The plaintiff, a faculty member who had been denied tenure, brought various federal and state claims against the university and university officials—including federal and state discrimination claims, state tort claims, and a breach of contract claim. All of the claims arose from the plaintiff's central contention "that he was denied tenure because of his sexual orientation and his HIV-positive status."

Although the faculty member had bypassed all internal review processes, the court (with one exception) nevertheless permitted the case to proceed in court. As to the plaintiff's discrimination claims, the federal and state antidiscrimination laws that he invoked do not require exhaustion of a university's (or other employer's) internal remedies. Although these laws do require exhaustion of the federal and state government's own administrative remedies for discrimination (for example, filing a claim with the federal EEOC or comparable state agency), the plaintiff had "fully pursued" his claims in these arenas. As to the plaintiff's state tort claims, the court reached the same result, saying it found "nothing peculiar to these claims that would require exhaustion" of internal remedies provided by the employment contract.

The exception was the breach of contract claim. Here, as in *Long v. Samson,* above, the court required the faculty member to exhaust remedies provided by a contractual grievance process. The distinction between the contract claim and the other claims resulted from a particular principle of Massachusetts employment law: "[O]ne who alleges wrongful termination based upon a contract of employment which includes a grievance procedure cannot seek vindication of the claim in court without first invoking the contractual grievance procedure" (citing *O'Brien v. New England Telephone & Telegraph Co.,* 664 N.E.2d 843 (Mass. 1996)).

Key to all these cases, as administrators and counsel should carefully note, is the court's determination that available administrative remedies could provide adequate relief to the complaining party, in a timely fashion, and would thus not be fruitless to pursue.

2.2.3. Pretrial and trial issues

2.2.3.1. Class action suits. After access to court has clearly been established, attention shifts to the numerous technical and strategic matters regarding the pretrial phase and the trial itself. One of these matters arises when defendants are sued by a group or class of plaintiffs, using the mechanism of the "class action suit," rather than by a single person. Such suits may involve extensive financial costs, time-absorbing procedures, complex legal issues, and potentially vast liability for the defendants. The plaintiffs must obtain a judicial ruling certifying the class, however, before such a suit may proceed. For state courts, certification requirements are set out in state civil procedure statutes or rules, and for federal courts they are in Rule 23 of the Federal Rules of Civil Procedure (28 U.S.C. Appendix). Rule 23(a) sets out four prerequisites for certification:

1. *Numerosity.* There must be a large enough number of plaintiffs that individual suits are impracticable.
2. *Commonality.* The members of the class must have claims that include common questions of fact or law.
3. *Typicality.* The claims of the class representatives who are named plaintiffs must be typical of the claims of other class members.
4. *Adequacy of representation.* The class representatives must fairly and adequately protect the interests of the entire class.

Once the plaintiff has satisfied these four requirements, Rule 23(b) then imposes certain other requirements, under which the lawsuit is classified into one of three types of permissible class actions. The federal trial judge has discretion to grant or deny certification and to modify the class certification during the course of the proceedings.

Lamphere v. Brown, 553 F.2d 714 (1st Cir. 1977), illustrates the application of Federal Rule 23. The federal appellate court refused to review the trial judge's decision to certify a class of women for a class action suit against Brown University alleging gender discrimination (71 F.R.D. 641 (D.R.I. 1976)). The certified class consisted of

> [a]ll women who have been employed in faculty positions by Brown University at any time after March 24, 1972, or who have applied for but were denied employment by Brown in such positions after said date; all women who are now so employed; all women who may in the future be so employed or who may in the future apply for but be denied such employment"—a class that would cover an estimated 20,100 persons. The university argued that its academic decision making is decentralized into numerous departments and divisions, thus making a university-wide class and "broadside" approach to class actions inappropriate. Although the appellate court "decline[d] to intervene in what is essentially an exercise of discretion by the district court," it did caution the district court to "follow closely the developing evidence as to class-wide decision making" by the university, to consider "the implications of class-wide defense" on the university's pursuit of its institutional mission, and to "take seriously its power under [Federal Rule] 23(c)(1) to alter or amend its certification order before the decision on the merits."[3]

---

[3]There is an exception to Rule 23 applicable to the Equal Employment Opportunity Commission (EEOC). If the EEOC brings an employment discrimination suit on behalf of a group of employees, those employees need not be certified as a class under Rule 23. In *General Telephone Company of the Northwest v. EEOC,* 446 U.S. 318 (1980), the U.S. Supreme Court concluded that, under the powers conferred on the EEOC by Section 706 of Title VII (see this book, Section 5.2.1), the EEOC may bring a suit without satisfying Rule 23.

In contrast to *Lamphere,* in *Samuel v. University of Pittsburgh,* 538 F.2d 991 (3d Cir. 1976), the trial judge had refused to certify the plaintiff's proposed class (375 F. Supp. 1119 (W.D. Pa. 1974)), and the appellate court reviewed and reversed the trial judge's order. The class was defined as married female students at the university who were Pennsylvania residents but had been denied the lower tuition rate for state residents. The university had denied such rates because it assumed that the students' residences were the same as their husbands', and the husbands lived out of state. In reversing the trial court, the appellate court determined that the class's damages could be calculated easily and that the trial judge's decision had been based on sympathy for the university's financial constraints rather than on legal precedent.

Although both *Lamphere* and *Samuel* illustrate the institution's plight as defendant in a class action suit, institutions can also use the class action mechanism to their own benefit as prospective plaintiffs in litigation. In *Central Wesleyan College v. W. R. Grace & Co.,* 143 F.R.D. 628 (D.S.C. 1992), for example, a federal district judge certified a class of virtually all colleges and universities in the nation in a property damage suit against asbestos companies. In certifying the class under Federal Rule 23(b)(3), the court noted that (1) there was little interest among the nation's colleges in individually suing asbestos companies; (2) there was little preexisting litigation between colleges and the asbestos companies; (3) the South Carolina district court was a desirable forum and not unfair to the defendants; and (4) if the issues certified were limited to discrete, factual inquiries, the large size of the class would not pose undue problems. The appellate court affirmed (6 F.3d 177 (4th Cir. 1993)). Under this ruling, the individual colleges can save many thousands of dollars in legal fees and still have their claims adequately heard.

2.2.3.2. Pretrial discovery. One of the most important aspects of the pretrial process is "discovery." A prescribed period of discovery—which may include depositions, interrogatories, and requests for the production of documents, among other things—affords all parties the opportunity to request information to clarify the facts and legal issues in the case. Although the discovery process may be time-consuming, expensive, and sometimes anxiety-provoking, it is essential to the trial as well as to prospects for pretrial settlement. Many tactical issues will arise as the parties seek to confine the scope of discovery in order to protect confidential records or sensitive information, or to save money and time, or to broaden the scope of discovery in order to obtain more information from the opposing party.

The Federal Rules of Civil Procedure, generally Rules 26–37 (28 U.S.C. Appendix), define the permissible scope and methods of discovery in the federal courts. Most states have similar rules. The trial judge usually has broad discretion in applying such rules. In general, under the Federal Rules, the "[parties] may obtain discovery regarding any matter, not privileged, which is relevant to the subject matter in the pending action" (Rule 26(b)(1)). In making decisions concerning the propriety of particular discovery requests, the trial judge may consider whether the discovery is "unreasonably cumulative or duplicative, or is obtainable from some other source that is more convenient, less burdensome, or less expensive" and may also consider other matters, such as undue expense and burden of filling the request (Rule 26(b)(1)). A party seeking to confine the scope of discovery may make any of these objections or may contend that the information sought is irrelevant or privileged.

The opinion in *Zahorik v. Cornell University,* 98 F.R.D. 27 (N.D.N.Y. 1983), illustrates the federal courts' preference for full disclosure of information within the scope of Rule 26. The plaintiffs filed an employment discrimination suit against Cornell University. When the plaintiffs requested a class certification (see Section 2.2.3.1 above), the district court denied the request but suggested that the plaintiffs consider reapplying at a later date if they obtained proof that they fulfilled the class certification requirements under Rule 23(a) of the Federal Rules. In an effort to meet the numerosity requirement, the plaintiffs sought broad discovery of university records, requesting information on past internal complaints of sex discrimination and the results of investigations of those complaints, copies of university affirmative action plans, copies of university reports on various aspects of campus life, information about the capabilities of and data stored in university computers, and biographical and statistical data on tenure-track employees. The university opposed these discovery requests on grounds that they were oppressive, burdensome, and irrelevant to the lawsuit. Although the court disagreed, it did refine the scope and method of discovery. It determined that the discovery requests for reports on university campus life and for computer information were too broad and denied these requests subject to their reformulation and narrowing by the plaintiffs. It then approved all of the plaintiffs' other requests. As to the method of discovery, the court ruled that the university must either give the plaintiffs and their attorneys access to the records for review and copying, or produce the specific records requested on a college-by-college list that the plaintiffs would develop.[4]

2.2.3.3. Issues regarding evidence. During pretrial discovery as well as the trial itself, various issues concerning evidence are likely to arise. During discovery, for instance, each party may object to various discovery requests of the other party on grounds that the information sought is privileged or irrelevant (see Section 2.2.3.2 above); in pretrial motions, each party may seek to limit the evidence to be admitted at trial; and during presentation of each party's case at trial, one party may object on a variety of grounds to the introduction of information that the other party seeks to present.[5] In addition, parties may seek and courts may issue summonses and subpoenas directly to the other party or to witnesses. Such matters are governed by the rules of civil procedure, the rules of evidence, and the common law of the jurisdiction in which suit is brought.

Although the parties to the litigation are entitled to information that is relevant to the lawsuit, occasionally a party may object to disclosing otherwise

---

[4]At times a discovery request may include student educational records. Typically, an educational institution must receive consent from either a parent or a student prior to disclosing the records. According to FERPA, 34 C.F.R. § 99.31(9) (see this book, Section 9.7.1), an institution may disclose the information without consent if it does so in compliance with a judicial order or subpoena, but it must make a reasonable effort to notify the parent or student before disclosure.

[5]See, for example, Boyd J. Peterson, Annot., "Admissibility of School Records Under Hearsay Exceptions," 57 A.L.R.4th 1111.

relevant information on the grounds that it is privileged. A privilege is created by a court when the court views the maintenance of confidentiality to be a greater social good than disclosure of the information to the party. A privilege may be either absolute or qualified (sometimes called "conditional"). An absolute privilege is created by a court to protect a socially important relationship that requires confidentiality in order to foster trust in the relationship (attorney-client, doctor-patient, religious counselor-penitent, husband-wife). A qualified or conditional privilege is created only after the court balances the litigant's interest in obtaining relevant information with the social good of keeping the information confidential.

Questions about obtaining and using privileged information are among the most important and difficult of these pretrial and trial issues (see, for example, the attempts to create new privileges, discussed in Section 7.7.1). All jurisdictions apparently agree that a party cannot obtain privileged information through discovery. Rule 26(b)(1) of the Federal Rules of Civil Procedure, for instance, states that the scope of discovery is confined to information that is "not privileged" (28 U.S.C. Appendix). Privileged matter is information that is protected under the formal evidentiary privileges recognized under the rules of evidence of each particular jurisdiction. For federal courts, Section 501 of the Federal Rules of Evidence leaves the definition and implementation of privileges entirely to the "principles of common law." (See generally 8 *Wigmore on Evidence* § 2196 (McNaughton rev.) (4th ed., Little, Brown, 1961).) Section 501 also provides that, in federal court actions based on state law (diversity actions), state law will determine whether a privilege applies.

The privilege that postsecondary institutions are most likely to struggle with in litigation is the attorney-client privilege. Confidential communications between an attorney and the attorney's client may be both immune from discovery and inadmissible at trial (see *Wigmore,* above, at § 2290). As the U.S. Supreme Court explained in *Upjohn Co. v. United States,* 449 U.S. 383 (1981), the purpose of this attorney-client privilege is

> to encourage full and frank communication between attorneys and their clients and thereby promote broader public interests in the observance of law and administration of justice. The privilege recognizes that sound legal advice or advocacy serves public ends and that such advice or advocacy depends upon the lawyer's being fully informed by the client.
>
> . . . [T]he privilege exists to protect not only the giving of professional advice to those who can act on it but also the giving of information to the lawyer to enable him to give sound informed advice [449 U.S. at 389, 390].

In *Upjohn,* the Court reaffirmed that the attorney-client privilege applies to corporations as clients as well as to individuals, and may extend in certain situations to communications between a corporation's in-house general counsel and the corporation's employees. Corporate officers had sought legal advice from in-house counsel concerning the corporation's compliance with federal securities and tax laws. To gather information about compliance issues, counsel had interviewed corporate employees (not officers). In determining that counsel's communications with the employees were protected from disclosure, the Court considered that counsel had interviewed the employees about matters that were within their corporate duties and that the employees were aware that the interviews would assist the corporation in obtaining legal advice from its counsel. Under these circumstances, said the Court, the application of the privilege in this case would serve the purpose of the privilege. The result is thus broadly hospitable to the assertion of privilege by corporations (including private postsecondary institutions) for their attorneys' confidential communications with managers, staff, and other employees. Similar protection would apparently be available to public institutions as well.

An important corollary to the attorney-client privilege is the attorney work-product doctrine, established (at least for the federal courts) in *Hickman v. Taylor,* 329 U.S. 495 (1947), and subsequently codified in Rule 26(b)(3) of the Federal Rules of Civil Procedure. The doctrine protects from disclosure memos, notes, and other materials prepared by an attorney "in anticipation of litigation or for trial," subject to some exceptions where the other party can make a strong showing of need and unavailability of equivalent information from any other source (Rule 26(b)(3)). In *Upjohn,* the Court, relying on both *Hickman* and Rule 26, used the work-product doctrine as a supplement to the attorney-client privilege so that counsel's notes and memos, which "reveal[ed] the attorneys' mental processes in evaluating" their interviews with corporate employees, would be protected.

Higher education cases addressing the attorney-client privilege are increasing in frequency and importance. (See generally Robert Burgoyne, Stephen McNabb, & Frederick Robinson, *Understanding Attorney-Client Privilege Issues in the College and University Setting* (National Association of College and University Attorneys, 1998).) Courts generally have been supportive of the privilege. In *State ex. rel. Oregon Health Sciences University v. Haas,* 942 P.2d 261 (Ore. 1997), for instance, the Oregon Supreme Court held that a university department head and members of the departmental faculty were "representatives" of the university and that legal advice communicated to them was therefore covered by the attorney-client privilege. In *Osborne v. Johnson,* 954 S.W.2d 180 (Texas 1997), another court similarly held that a department chair was the university's representative, for purposes of an investigation into charges against a professor, so that the chair's communications with university counsel were covered by attorney-client privilege. And in *Kobluk v. University of Minnesota,* 574 N.W.2d 436 (Minn. 1998), the Supreme Court of Minnesota held that the privilege attached to two preliminary drafts that passed between the provost and the university counsel in the course of composing a tenure denial letter. The drafts were part of a process of requesting and rendering legal advice, reasoned the court, and the provost and the counsel had maintained the confidentiality of the drafts.

In contrast, in the important case of *Ross v. Medical University of South Carolina,* 453 S.E.2d 880 (S.C. 1994), the South Carolina Supreme Court addressed the scope of the attorney-client privilege as it applies in college and university grievance proceedings. The court's opinion rejecting the privilege claim, and holding the university in contempt, serves as fair warning that administrators and counsel should carefully define their roles and interrelationships in the grievance process context.

The plaintiff, Dr. Ross, had been terminated from his position as tenured professor and chairman of the radiology department at the Medical University of South Carolina (MUSC). He filed suit alleging various causes of action, including a claim under the state's administrative procedure act, that MUSC had denied him a fair hearing. The basis for this claim was several alleged procedural irregularities, especially: (1) that the vice president had acted as both prosecutor and judge during the grievance proceeding; and (2) that the vice president had had *ex parte* communications with MUSC's general counsel concerning the recommendation the faculty hearing committee had issued at the first step in the grievance process. The plaintiff sought information from MUSC about these alleged procedural irregularities, and the trial court found MUSC to be in contempt for not complying with the plaintiff's requests. The state Court of Appeals vacated the trial court's order and the state Supreme Court granted certiorari to determine if the information requested by the plaintiff was protected by the attorney-client privilege.

MUSC had a three-step faculty grievance process. At the first stage, the vice president referred the complaint to a Faculty Hearing Committee for a hearing and recommendation; at the second stage, the vice president reviewed the hearing record and made his own recommendation. No further action was taken on the matter if both recommendations were favorable to the faculty member. If the vice president's recommendation was unfavorable, the faculty member could, as a third step, appeal to the board of trustees. The plaintiff contended that, at step two, the vice president had conferred with the general counsel prior to his concurrence in the faculty committee's recommendation to terminate, and that the general counsel prepared the written concurrence for the vice president. In attempting to support these charges of procedural irregularity, the plaintiff served Requests for Admissions, which MUSC refused to answer, asserting that these alleged communications were covered by the attorney-client privilege and, thus, are not discoverable. In rejecting MUSC's privilege claim, the Court relied on Section 1-23-360 of the South Carolina Code, part of the state administrative procedure act:

> Unless required for the disposition of ex parte matters authorized by law, members or employees of an agency assigned to render a decision or to make findings of fact and conclusions of law in a contested case shall not communicate, directly or indirectly in connection with any issue of fact, with any person or party, nor in connection with any issue of law, with any party or his representative, except upon notice and opportunity for all parties to participate.

The court determined: (1) that the vice president had acted as "an intermediate judge" during step two of the grievance process and was therefore "'assigned to render a decision'" in the case at hand, and (2) that the general counsel had "represented MUSC in prosecuting the case before the Faculty committee," and thus acted as a "representative" of a "party" rather than as personal counsel to the vice president. The *ex parte* communications between the vice president and general counsel were therefore in violation of Section 1-23-360, and the court refused to extend the attorney-client privilege to communications that violated a state law under which (as was the case with Section 1-23-360) the violator could be subject to criminal sanctions.

The court's reasoning seems broad enough to jeopardize privilege claims even if the state had not had an administrative procedure statute such as Section 1-23-360, and even if the defendant had been a private institution and thus not subject to such statutes (which usually cover only public institutions). The crux of this broader reasoning is that the vice president, in the particular circumstances of this case, was not a "client" of the general counsel and the general counsel was not an "attorney" for the vice president, but rather for another "client" (the university itself). Thus, the necessary preconditions for assertion of the privilege did not exist. As the court stated at the conclusion of its opinion:

> [The] General Counsel was acting in a representative capacity for MUSC, and not as counsel for [the] Vice President. [The] Vice President, acting in a judicial capacity in the administrative process, was not entitled to confer with General Counsel, who was acting as a prosecutor against Ross [453 S.E.2d at 884–85].

A 1996 U.S. Supreme Court case addresses another evidentiary privilege of particular importance to postsecondary institutions. In the case of *Jaffee v. Redmond,* 518 U.S. 1 (1996), the issue was "whether it is appropriate for federal courts to recognize a 'psychotherapist privilege' under Rule 501 of the Federal Rules of Evidence" and, more specifically, "whether statements . . . made to [a licensed clinical social worker] during . . . counseling sessions are protected from compelled disclosure in a federal civil action. . . ." The court answered both questions in the affirmative. Regarding the psychotherapist's privilege in general, the court reasoned that "[l]ike the spousal and attorney-client privileges, the psychotherapist-patient privilege is 'rooted in the imperative need for confidence and trust'" (quoting *Trammel v. United States,* 445 U.S. 40, 51 (1980)). Such a privilege serves the important private interest of promoting development of the relationship between therapist and patient necessary for successful treatment, and the important public interest of "facilitating the provision of appropriate treatment for individuals suffering the effects of a mental or emotional problem." In addition, the court confirmed "that all 50 States and the District of Columbia have enacted into law some form of the psychotherapist privilege" and reasoned that "the existence of a consensus among the States . . . support[s] recognition of the privilege."

Regarding the second, more particular question, the Court determined that "[w]e have no hesitation in concluding in this case that the federal privilege should also extend to confidential communications made to licensed social workers in the course of psychotherapy." According to the Court:

> The reasons for recognizing a privilege for treatment by psychiatrists and psychologists apply with equal force to treatment by a clinical social worker. . . .
> Today, social workers provide a significant amount of mental health

treatment. . . . Their clients often include the poor and those of modest means
who could not afford the assistance of a psychiatrist or psychologist . . . , but
whose counseling sessions serve the same public goals [518 U.S. at 16].

While the Court's opinion in *Jaffee* gives strong support to a broad psychotherapist privilege, it is also important to note that this privilege, like others, is not absolute. In a concluding comment in *Jaffee,* the Court cautioned that
"there are situations in which the privilege must give way, for example, if a serious threat of harm to the patient or to others can be averted only by means of a
disclosure by the therapist" (518 U.S. at 18, n.19). (For a famous and graphic
illustration of this limit, see the *Tarasoff* case, discussed in Section 4.7.2.2. For
another helpful reminder of this limit, and an excellent overview of the implications of the *Jaffee* decision for postsecondary administrators, see Gary
Pavela (ed.), "The Benefits and Limits of Confidentiality," *Synfax Weekly Report,*
June 24, 1996, 500–501.)

Another type of privilege issue arose in *University of Pennsylvania v. EEOC,*
493 U.S. 182 (1990), in which the U.S. Supreme Court rejected the university's
claim that confidential evaluations of candidates for tenure were protected by
an "academic freedom privilege." The Court's opinion made it clear that any
"confidential" evaluations on which the university relied in a tenure decision
were relevant to a claim of sex discrimination in the denial of tenure and must
be disclosed. The case is discussed in Section 7.7.1.

2.2.3.4. Summary judgments and motions to dismiss. Both federal courts
and the state courts have procedures for streamlining litigation by summarily
disposing of lawsuits on the merits—that is, for a judicial determination prior
to trial as to whether the plaintiff's legal claim is valid and sustainable by the
facts. The most basic procedure is the defendant's motion to dismiss. Although
this type of motion is frequently used to raise jurisdictional and other access
issues (Section 2.2.2), it may also be used to dismiss a case on the merits if the
defendant can demonstrate that the facts pleaded in the plaintiff's complaint,
even if true, do not state a valid claim that would entitle the plaintiff to relief.
In the federal courts, this motion is provided for by Rule 12(b)(6) of the Federal
Rules of Civil Procedure.

Another procedure, potentially more important and usually utilized at a later
stage of the pretrial proceedings than the motion to dismiss, is the summary
judgment. In the federal courts, motions for summary judgment are governed
by Federal Rule 56. Under this rule and similar state laws, either the plaintiff or
the defendant may make such a motion. The moving party must demonstrate
that no genuine issue of material fact remains in the lawsuit and that the governing law, as applied to the undisputed facts, indicates that the moving party is
entitled to judgment as a matter of law. If the party makes such a showing, the
court will enter a judgment (a "summary judgment") in that party's favor. Successfully employed, then, this procedure can allow either party to avoid many
of the costs of litigation (see Section 2.2.1 above) while still obtaining the benefits of a judgment that is binding on the parties (see Section 2.2.3.6) and may
fully resolve the dispute.

2.2.3.5. Standards of judicial review and burdens of proof. Postsecondary institutions have numerous processes for making internal decisions regarding the status of faculty, students, and staff, and for internally resolving disputes among members of the campus community. Whenever a disappointed party seeks judicial review of an institution's internal decision, the reviewing court must determine what "standard of review" it will apply in deciding the case. This standard of review establishes the degree of scrutiny the court will give to the institution's decision, the reasons behind it, and the evidence supporting it. Put another way, the standard of review helps establish the extent to which the court will defer to the institution's decision and the value and fact judgments undergirding it. The more deference the court is willing to accord the decision (see subsection 2.2.5 below on deference), the less scrutiny it will give to the decision and the greater is the likelihood that the court will uphold it. Issues regarding standards of review are thus crucial in most litigation.

In turn, standards of review are related to the "burdens of proof" for the litigation. After a court determines which party is responsible for demonstrating that the institution's decision does or does not meet the standard of review, the court allocates the burden of proof to that party. This burden can shift during the course of the litigation (see, for example, Section 5.2.1). Burdens of proof also elucidate the elements or type of proof each party must submit to meet its burden on each claim or defense presented. Such issues are also critical to the outcome of litigation and can become very complicated (see, for example, Section 5.2.1).

There are many possible standards of judicial review (and likewise many variations of burdens of proof). The standard that applies in any particular litigation will depend on numerous factors: the type of institution subject to the review (whether public or private); the type of claim that the plaintiff makes; the institution's internal rules for reviewing decisions of the type being challenged; the character of the contractual relationship between the institution and the party seeking court review; and the common law and statutory administrative law of the particular state (see Section 1.4.2), insofar as it prescribes standards of review for particular situations. At a subtler level, the court's selection of a standard of review may also depend on comparative competence—the court's sense of its own competence, compared with that of the institution, to explore and resolve the types of issues presented by the case.

If a court is reviewing the *substance* of a decision (that is, whether the institution is right or wrong on the merits), it may be more deferential than it would be if it were reviewing the adequacy of the *procedures* the institution followed in making its decision—the difference being attributable to the court's expertise regarding procedural matters and relative lack of expertise regarding substantive judgments (for example, whether a faculty member's credentials are sufficient to warrant a grant of tenure).

There are three basic types of standards of judicial review. "Substantial evidence" standards are gauges of whether the institution's decision-making body carefully considered the evidence and had a substantial body of evidence on which to base its decision. A more demanding version of this type of standard is called the "clear and convincing evidence" standard. "Arbitrary and capricious" standards gauge whether the deciding body acted without reason or irrationally. "*De novo*" standards authorize the court to consider the case from scratch, giving virtually no deference to the decision-making body's decision, and requiring all evidence to be submitted and considered anew.

Of the three types, *de novo* standards provide for the highest level of judicial scrutiny of, and the least amount of deference to, the institution's decision; arbitrary and capricious standards call for the least scrutiny and the greatest deference; and substantial evidence standards are somewhere in between. In constitutional rights litigation, there is also sometimes a fourth type of standard, associated with *de novo* review, called "strict scrutiny" standards, which are the most stringent of all review standards.

The following two cases illustrate the operation of standards of review in the context of court challenges to institutional decisions to deny tenure and also illustrate the controversy that such issues may create.

In *Riggin v. Board of Trustees of Ball State University,* 489 N.E.2d 616 (Ind. 1986), the defendant, a public institution, had discharged a tenured professor, for cause. At an internal hearing, the university adduced evidence that the professor had attended virtually no faculty meetings, rescheduled and canceled a large number of classes, wasted a great deal of class time with irrelevant films and discussions, failed to cover the course material, and produced no research, among other things. The board of trustees affirmed the hearing committee's recommendation to terminate. In reviewing the professor's claim that the board of trustees' decision constituted a breach of contract, the trial court applied an "arbitrary and capricious" standard of review and upheld the board's decision. The appellate court affirmed both the trial court's decision and its selection of a standard of review. As a state institution, the university was considered to be an administrative agency under Indiana law and subject to the standard of review applicable to court review of agency decisions:

> [A] court of review will not interfere with the acts of an administrative agency which are within the agency's allowable scope of responsible discretion unless it found that the administrative act was arbitrary, capricious, an abuse of discretion or unsupported by substantial evidence. . . . The court may not substitute its own opinions for that of the Board of Trustees, but must give deference to its expertise. . . . A court may not reweigh the evidence or determine the credibility of witnesses. . . . The burden of proving that the administrative action was arbitrary and capricious or an abuse of discretion falls on the party attempting to vacate the administrative order. . . . An arbitrary and capricious act is one that is willful and unreasonable and done without regard to the facts and circumstances of the case; an act without some basis which would lead a reasonable and honest person to the same conclusion. . . .
>
> The court's review of the decisions of the committee and the Board of Trustees was not a hearing de novo. Rather, its sole function was to determine whether the action was illegal, or arbitrary and capricious. In doing so it must accept the evidence most favorable to support the administrative decision [489 N.E.2d at 625].

Because the court adopted this deferential standard of review, and because the university had foresight to present extensive evidence to the ad hoc hearing committee, the university easily prevailed in court.

An altogether different approach was taken by the court in *McConnell v. Howard University*, 818 F.2d 58 (D.C. Cir. 1987) (also discussed in Section 6.6.2). Again the defendant had discharged a tenured professor who thereupon sued for breach of contract. But in this case the university was a private institution, and the contract issues presented were different from those in *Riggin*. The professor refused to continue teaching one of his courses after a student had called him a racist and refused to apologize. The professor continued to teach his other courses and otherwise perform his professorial duties. After exhausting his internal university appeals, the professor went to federal court, and the court entered summary judgment for the university. The U.S. Court of Appeals then vacated the district court's ruling, noting that the district court had erred in using a lenient "arbitrary and capricious" standard to review the university's actions. The appellate court viewed the case as a standard contract claim and found no reason to accord the university any special deference in such a situation. Rejecting the trial court's choice of standard, the appellate court noted:

> In other words, according to the trial court, any Trustees' decision to fire a tenured faculty member is largely unreviewable, with judicial scrutiny limited to a modest inquiry as to whether the Trustees' decision was "arbitrary," "irrational" or infected by improper motivation. Such a reading of the contract renders tenure a virtual nullity. Faculty members like Dr. McConnell would have no real *substantive* right to continued employment, but only certain *procedural* rights that must be followed before their appointment may be terminated. We find this to be an astonishing concept, and one not compelled by a literal reading of the Faculty Handbook [818 F.2d at 67].

Thus, the court determined that "[o]n remand, the trial court must consider *de novo* the appellant's breach of contract claims; no special deference is due the Board of Trustees once the case is properly before the court for resolution of the contract dispute." The court also rejected an administrative agency model such as the *Riggin* court had used:

> [T]he theory of deference to administrative action flows from prudential concepts of separation of powers, as well as statutory proscriptions on the scope of judicial review. Obviously, none of those factors apply here. The notion of treating a private university as if it were a state or federal administrative agency is simply unsupported where a contract claim is involved [818 F.2d at 69; footnote omitted].

Further, the court explained:

> [W]e do not understand why university affairs are more deserving of judicial deference than the affairs of any other business or profession. Arguably, there might be matters unique to education on which courts are relatively ill equipped to pass judgment. However, this is true in many areas of the law, including, for example, technical, scientific and medical issues. Yet, this lack of expertise does not compel courts to defer to the view of one of the parties in such cases. The parties can supply such specialized knowledge through the

use of expert testimony. Moreover, even if there are issues on which courts are ill equipped to rule, the interpretation of a contract is not one of them [818 F.2d at 69].

One additional circumstance will influence a court's standard of review: if the institution's decision was subject to arbitration before the filing of the court suit, the court will accord great deference to the arbitrator's decision, because the parties have usually agreed ahead of time to abide by it. In *Samaan v. Trustees of California State University and Colleges*, 197 Cal. Rptr. 856 (Cal. 1983), the plaintiff, another terminated tenured professor, had lost his case in arbitration. When he proceeded to court, the court indicated that his only remedy was a motion to vacate the arbitrator's award. An applicable statute set out five narrow grounds—each essentially a standard of review—for vacating an arbitration award (Cal. Civ. Proc. Code § 1286.2). The professor had not alleged or demonstrated any of these grounds but instead sought a more stringent standard of review. In response, the court conducted an independent review of the record and determined that the professor could not prevail even if a more stringent standard of review were available. It therefore upheld the university's dismissal decision, and the appellate court affirmed.

Besides the standards of judicial review that courts use in cases challenging particular institutional decisions, there are other standards of review that institutions themselves use in internal dispute-resolution proceedings. Institutions may make their own determinations of what these "internal" standards of review (and accompanying burdens of proof) will be; or standards of review for particular types of disputes may be imposed upon institutions by courts or legislatures.

The court's opinion in *Reilly v. Daly*, 666 N.E.2d 439 (Ind. 1996), illustrates the distinction between internal standards of review and the standards of judicial review for court proceedings.

In *Reilly*, a medical student had been accused of cheating on a final examination and, after internal proceedings that included a hearing before the Student Promotions Committee, the student was dismissed. She then sued, alleging various violations of her due process rights under the Fourteenth Amendment. One of the plaintiff's claims was that due process required the university to judge her using a "clear and convincing" standard of review. The court rejected this claim, holding that due process required only that universities use a "substantial evidence" standard of review for suspension or expulsion decisions, and that the "record [in this case] amply supports the [Student Promotions] Committee's adherence to this burden." The student then argued that the university "lacked substantial evidence that she cheated" and that the court should overrule the university's decision for that reason. In response, the court asserted that the standard of review *in court* is different from the standard of review for a university tribunal: "Although due process requires schools and colleges to base their suspension and dismissal decisions on substantial evidence, the standard of review on appeal is whether there is some evidence to support the decision of the school or college. . . ." The court called this an "arbitrary or capricious" standard. Since there was "at least some evidence in support of the Committee's conclusion that [the student] had cheated," the court held that the student had not established that the university's decision was arbitrary and capricious.

The distinction that the court developed between internal and external (judicial) standards of review is a slippery one. If the court itself applies only an "arbitrary and capricious" standard of review, how can it know that the university actually adhered to a "substantial evidence" standard? The answer is that the court cannot know for sure. In effect, the court is saying that, as long as the record in the case reasonably supports a conclusion that the university followed a substantial evidence standard, the court will not itself reevaluate the substantiality of the evidence or otherwise make sure that the university "got it right" when it made its decision. Instead, the court will defer to the university and its internal processes.

2.2.3.6. Final judgments. If a court proceeds to the merits of a plaintiff's claim, and if the parties do not in the meantime enter a voluntary settlement or consent decree disposing of the litigation, the court will decide the dispute and enter judgment for one of the parties. Judgment may be entered either after trial; before (or during) trial, by way of a motion for summary judgment or a motion to dismiss (Section 2.2.3.4 above); or—if the defendant does not contest the plaintiff's claim—by "default judgment." When the losing party's rights to appeal have been exhausted, the court's judgment becomes final.

After entry of judgment, issues may still arise concerning the judgment's enforcement, the award of attorney's fees, and related matters, which are discussed in Section 2.2.4. Other issues may arise concerning the binding effect of the judgment in later litigation, as discussed below.

In general, the law forbids relitigation of claims disposed of in prior litigation, even if that litigation was in a different court system. The technical rules that preclude relitigation of claims are often cumulatively referred to as the doctrine of *res judicata* (a Latin term meaning "things which have been decided") or as "claim preclusion."[6] These rules become important when a party is involved in multiple lawsuits against the same party or related parties, either simultaneously or seriatim. A postsecondary institution, for example, may successfully defend itself against a lawsuit in state court, only to find itself sued again by the same plaintiff in federal court; or it may successfully defend itself against a suit seeking damages, only to find itself again in the same court in a second suit by the same plaintiff seeking a different remedy. In such circumstances the institution will generally be able to use *res judicata* to preclude the second suit if it challenges any part of the same institutional action that was challenged and fully litigated to final judgment in the first suit. The doctrine thus promotes defendants' interests in finality and society's interests in judicial economy while still according plaintiffs a full opportunity to press their claims.

Pauk v. Board of Trustees of the City University of New York, 488 N.Y.S.2d 685 (N.Y. App. Div. 1985), *affirmed,* 497 N.E.2d 675 (N.Y. 1986), illustrates the *res judicata* doctrine at work, in particular the manner in which a court analyzes the scope of the initial claim and determines whether the same transactions are challenged in the second claim and thus barred. The plaintiff, a professor at Queens College, challenged a denial of reappointment and tenure. He alleged

---

[6]Related rules, called "issue preclusion" or "collateral estoppel," also preclude relitigation of particular issues of fact or law. They are beyond the scope of this discussion.

that he had already acquired tenure de facto as an assistant professor because he had been employed for five years and reappointed for a sixth year. In 1976, in a state court proceeding, he had sought to compel the defendant to rescind the letter of termination and to declare him a tenured assistant professor. A dismissal of his claim on the merits was affirmed by the highest state court (401 N.E.2d 214 (N.Y. 1979)). The professor was persistent, however, and in 1981 brought another suit against the defendant, alleging three different claims. (In 1979, between this suit and the first suit, the professor had filed yet another lawsuit against the defendant in federal court. That suit was dismissed because it was filed after the statute of limitations had expired; see Section 2.2.2.3.) In the first claim in the 1981 suit, the professor alleged that the refusal to renew his employment contract violated the implied terms of that contract; in the second claim, he separately alleged that the defendant had violated his rights under an article of the state constitution and a section of the state education law; and in the third claim, he alleged that the defendant's policy of maintaining the secrecy of the personnel committee's votes was unconstitutional. The defendant argued that the court should dismiss the first two claims because they were based on transactions already challenged in the claim that was adjudicated and dismissed in the earlier state court proceeding. (The court dismissed the third claim on other unrelated grounds.) The trial court held that the second claim, but not the first, was barred under the *res judicata* doctrine. The appellate court affirmed as to the second claim and reversed as to the first, concluding that it, like the second claim, arose from the same transactions as the earlier claim adjudicated in the earlier state court proceeding. Although the second claim relied on a different legal theory of recovery than the earlier state court claim, the plaintiff could have used that legal theory in the earlier proceeding to obtain relief comparable to that sought in the later proceeding. *Res judicata* therefore applied.

The result in *Pauk* should be no different if the second action had been filed in a different jurisdiction—that is, in the courts of another state or in federal rather than state court. Generally, the Full Faith and Credit Clause of the federal Constitution (Art. IV, § 1) compels the courts in every state to give a judgment rendered in a different state the same full faith and credit as a judgment rendered in its own state; and a federal statute, 28 U.S.C. § 1738, compels the federal courts to give full faith and credit to the judgments of state courts in state matters. Additional complications arise, however, when the initial claim is not filed in a state court but rather with a state administrative agency. Neither the Full Faith and Credit Clause nor the federal statute applies to this situation, and the binding effect of an administrative determination will depend on the rules of the particular state or, in the federal courts, on federal common law. *University of Tennessee v. Elliott*, 478 U.S. 788 (1986), illustrates the problem in the federal courts, where the difficulties concern "issue preclusion" rather than *res judicata* as such (see footnote 6).

In *Elliott*, a black employee of the university's Agricultural Extension Service challenged his termination on grounds that it was racially motivated. He first petitioned for administrative review of his termination under the state administrative procedure act. While his administrative proceeding was pending, he filed suit in federal court, alleging employment discrimination violative of both Title VII (this book, Section 5.2.1) and Section 1983 (this book, Section 3.5). Subsequently, the state administrative law judge ruled that the employee's termination was not racially motivated. Instead of appealing this decision to the state courts, he persevered with the federal court suit. The federal courts then had to determine whether they were bound by the administrative law judge's *fact finding* that the termination was not racially motivated—that is, "whether this finding is entitled to preclusive effect in federal court." In a complicated analysis set against the backdrop of the federal common law of preclusion, the U.S. Supreme Court concluded that in passing Title VII, Congress expressed an intent to allow plaintiffs to relitigate the fact determinations of state agencies in federal court but that, in passing Section 1983, Congress expressed no such intent. Thus, the state administrative fact-findings had a preclusive effect as to the Section 1983 claim but not as to the Title VII claim.

A particularly interesting and important "preclusion" issue arose in *Smith v. Alabama Aviation and Technical College,* 683 So. 2d 431 (Ala. 1996). The problem was similar to that in *University of Tennessee v. Elliott,* except that the second claim was filed in state rather than federal court, and state law rules on preclusion therefore applied. The specific issue, according to the *Smith* court, was "the preclusive effect of an administrative determination of a constitutional claim when the aggrieved person does not seek judicial review of the administrative decision as authorized by law." The plaintiff was a tenured professor of avionics at the Alabama Aviation and Technical College who had been dismissed by the college. Contending that he was fired for criticizing the college's administration and curriculum, he charged the college with violating his free speech and due process rights. He presented these charges in a hearing before an employee review panel constituted pursuant to State Board of Education regulations. When the panel upheld his termination, the faculty member then filed a separate suit against the college in court.

In affirming the lower court's entry of summary judgment for the defendants, the Supreme Court of Alabama held that "an aggrieved person, such as Smith, who believes that the decision of a review panel did not adequately or correctly adjudicate his or her constitutional claim, can appeal that decision to the appropriate circuit court as provided for in the Alabama Code." But Smith had not done so; instead, he had sued the college in a separate suit independent of the administrative proceeding. "[T]o allow a plaintiff to raise the same issue in a subsequent lawsuit after having elected not to appeal from the administrative ruling would frustrate efforts to provide an orderly administration of justice, and could encourage one to relitigate issues rather than have those issues finally resolved." Therefore, since Smith had not pursued his statutory remedy by appealing the administrative ruling to the appropriate circuit court, which could have adequately reviewed his constitutional issues in such an appeal, he had forfeited his right to litigate those issues in an independent suit.

The U.S. Court of Appeals for the Tenth Circuit used claim preclusion (*res judicata*) to dismiss an Americans With Disabilities Act (ADA) and Section 504 (Rehabilitation Act) suit brought by a former medical student against a board of regents. *McGuinness v. Regents of the University of New Mexico,* 183 F.3d 1172 (10th Cir. 1999). The student had previously filed an ADA suit against the University of New Mexico (UNM) Medical School, and the court had entered judgment for the medical school. Since the causes of action and the parties were essentially the same in both suits, the final judgment in the first suit precluded litigation of the second suit.

2.2.4. *Judicial remedies*

2.2.4.1. Overview. If the defendant prevails in a lawsuit, the only needed remedy is dismissal of the action and perhaps an award of attorney's fees or court costs. If the plaintiff prevails, however, that party is entitled to one or more types of affirmative remedies, most prominent of which are money damages and injunctive relief, and may be entitled to attorney's fees and costs as well. If the defendant does not comply with the court's remedial orders, the court may also use its contempt powers to enforce compliance.

2.2.4.2. Money damages. Depending on the character of the plaintiff's claim and proof, a court may award compensatory damages and, less often, punitive damages as well (see, for example, Sections 3.5 and 4.7.4 regarding damages under Section 1983). Occasionally, even treble damages may be available (see, for example, Section 13.2.8 regarding federal antitrust laws). Money damages, however, are not necessarily a permissible remedy in all types of cases where the plaintiff sustains quantifiable injury. For example, in cases under the federal Age Discrimination Act, plaintiffs are entitled only to injunctive relief (see Section 13.5.9). But the trend appears to be to permit the award of money damages in an increasing range of cases. In Section 102 of the Civil Rights Act of 1991 (Pub. L. No. 102-166, 105 Stat. 1071, 1072 (1991)), for example, Congress amended Title VII so that it expressly authorizes the award of money damages in intentional discrimination actions under that statute (see this book, Section 5.2.1); and in *Franklin v. Gwinnett County Public Schools,* 503 U.S. 60 (1992), the U.S. Supreme Court construed Title IX to permit money damage awards in private causes of action under that statute (see Section 13.5.9).

When money damage awards are available, there may be caps on the amount of damages the court may award, or there may be questions about the measurement of the amount of damages. In *Memphis School District v. Stachura,* 477 U.S. 299 (1986), for example, the U.S. Supreme Court held that money damages based on the abstract "value" of the constitutional rights that had been infringed was not a proper component of compensatory damages in a Section 1983 suit. The plaintiff, a public school teacher, was fired because of certain teaching techniques he used for a course on human reproduction. The trial judge instructed the jury that, in addition to any other compensatory and punitive damages they might award to the plaintiff, they could also award damages based on the importance of the constitutional rights that were violated. The jury returned with a verdict for the plaintiff resulting in compensatory damages of $266,750 and punitive damages of $36,000, allocated among the school board and various individual defendants. The Supreme Court held that compensatory money damages are awarded on the basis of actual, provable injury, not on the basis of subjective valuation. If the jury were permitted to consider the "value" of the rights involved in determining the amount of compensatory damages, juries might "use their unbounded discretion to punish unpopular defendants." The court therefore remanded the case for a new trial on the issue of compensatory damages.

2.2.4.3. Injunctions. Injunctions are a type of specific nonmonetary, or equitable, relief. An injunction may be either permanent or temporary and may be either prohibitory (prohibiting the defendant from taking certain actions) or mandatory (requiring the defendant to take certain specified actions). A court may issue an injunction as a final remedy after adjudication of the merits of the lawsuit, or it may issue a "preliminary injunction" prior to trial in order to preserve the status quo or otherwise protect the plaintiff's rights during the pendency of the lawsuit.

Preliminary injunctions raise a host of important tactical questions for both plaintiffs and defendants. In determining whether to grant a motion for such an injunction, the court will commonly balance the plaintiff's likelihood of success on the merits of the lawsuit, the likelihood that the plaintiff will suffer irreparable harm absent the injunction, the injury that the defendant would sustain as a result of the injunction, and the general public interest in the matter. In *Jones v. University of North Carolina,* 704 F.2d 713 (4th Cir. 1983), the court applied such a balancing test and granted the plaintiff's request for a preliminary injunction. The plaintiff was a nursing student who had been accused of cheating on an examination, found guilty after somewhat contorted proceedings on campus, and barred from taking courses during the spring semester. She then filed a Section 1983 suit (this book, Section 3.5), alleging that the university's disciplinary action violated her procedural due process rights. She requested and the court granted a preliminary injunction ordering the university to reinstate her as a student in good standing pending resolution of the suit. The university appealed the court's order, claiming it was an abuse of the court's discretion. The appellate court considered the hardships to both parties and the seriousness of the issues the plaintiff had raised. Regarding hardships, the court noted that, without the injunction, the plaintiff would have been barred from taking courses and delayed from graduating, denied the opportunity to graduate with her classmates, and forced to explain this educational gap throughout her professional career. On the other hand, according to the court, issuance of the injunction would not significantly harm the university's asserted interests:

> While we recognize the University's institutional interest in speedy resolution of disciplinary charges and in maintaining public confidence in the integrity of its processes, Jones will suffer far more substantial, concrete injury if the injunction is dissolved and she is ultimately vindicated than will the University if the injunction stands and its position is finally upheld [704 F.2d at 716].

Similarly, in *Cohen v. Brown University*, 991 F.2d 888 (1st Cir. 1993), a U.S. Court of Appeals upheld a district court's preliminary injunction ordering Brown University to reinstate its women's gymnastics and women's volleyball programs to full varsity status pending the trial of a Title IX claim. Both programs had been reduced to club status as a result of budget constraints. Although men's programs were also cut back, the plaintiffs alleged that the cuts discriminated against women at the school. The appellate court approved the district judge's determination that the plaintiffs would most likely prevail on the merits when the case was finally resolved. Further, the court observed that if the volleyball and gymnastics teams continued in their demoted state for any length of time, they would suffer irreparably because they would lose recruitment opportunities and coaches. The court found that these harms outweighed the small financial loss the university would sustain in keeping the teams at a varsity level until final resolution of the suit. (The *Cohen* case is further discussed in Section 10.4.6.)

2.2.4.4. Attorney's fees. Either the plaintiff or the defendant may recover the reasonable costs of attorney's fees in certain situations where they are the prevailing party. For instance, under the Civil Rights Attorney's Fees Awards Act of 1976 (90 Stat. 2641 (1976), 42 U.S.C. § 1988), the federal courts may grant the prevailing parties in certain federal civil rights suits reasonable attorney's fees as part of the costs of litigation (see this book, Section 13.5.9). The U.S. Supreme Court has held that this Act applies to state governments and officials who are sued in their official capacities. In *Hutto v. Finney*, 437 U.S. 678 (1978), the Court held that Congress intended to set aside the states' Eleventh Amendment immunity in these cases in order to enforce the protection of individual rights under the Fourteenth Amendment of the Constitution, and that attorney's fees are therefore not barred. Attorney's fees are also sometimes available under the Equal Access to Justice Act, to parties who prevail in litigation involving the federal government (see this book, Section 13.6.1). More generally, Rule 11 of the Federal Rules of Civil Procedure (28 U.S.C. Appendix) permits federal courts to award attorney's fees in certain situations where a party files with the court a document that is not grounded in fact; is not based on existing law or a nonfrivolous argument for its modification; or is filed for an improper purpose, such as harassment or delay. In such circumstances the court may impose "a variety of sanctions, including attorney's fees and other expenses incurred as a direct result of the violation." Moreover, under Rule 38 of the Federal Rules for Appellate Procedure (28 U.S.C. Appendix), if a party's request for an appeal is frivolous, the court may award costs to the prevailing party, and such an award will typically include attorney's fees.

Weinstein v. University of Illinois, 811 F.2d 1091 (7th Cir. 1987), illustrates how a higher education institution may recover attorney's fees if forced to defend itself against a frivolous lawsuit. The appellate court relied on its authority under Rule 38 of the Federal Rules for Appellate Procedure to order the plaintiff professor to pay attorney's fees even though the university had not requested such an award. The professor, who was nontenured, challenged the refusal to renew his contract, claiming a violation of procedural due process. The court held that the claim was frivolous and may not have been brought in good faith, because it ignored the established rule that a nontenured faculty member has no property interest in continued employment (see Section 6.7.2.1). In fact, as the court emphasized, a prior case before the same court (*McElearney v. University of Illinois*, 612 F.2d 285, 289–91 (7th Cir. 1979)) "holds that a nontenured professor at the same university, employed under the same contract, lacked a property interest." Thus, according to the court, the plaintiff was "litigating a defunct claim. He hasn't a chance; he never did; but he has put the University to some expense. This is frivolous litigation."

Even when the court has authority to award attorney's fees and does so, the parties may challenge the reasonableness of the amount awarded. The case of *Craik v. Minnesota State University Board*, 738 F.2d 348 (8th Cir. 1984), illustrates several of the issues that may arise and suggests the various grounds on which a higher education institution may seek to diminish an award against it or enhance an award in its favor. The plaintiff in *Craik* prevailed in an employment discrimination suit against Minnesota State University and was awarded $126,127.40 in reasonable attorney's fees under 42 U.S.C. § 1988.

In order to reach this figure, and in reviewing the university's challenge to it, the court considered the nature and quality of the legal services rendered to the plaintiff for the appeal, the reasonableness of the rates charged by the plaintiff's out-of-state counsel, the inclusion of ten hours of travel time charged at the out-of-state counsel's normal office hourly rate, and the extent of the plaintiff's success on the appeal. The court rejected the university's arguments for reduction on the first three grounds but accepted its argument on the fourth ground. Because the plaintiff did not prevail on all issues raised on appeal, and because the relief awarded could be further narrowed on remand to the trial court, the appellate court reduced the attorney's fees award by 20 percent. In turn, however, in response to the plaintiff's argument, the court considered the degree of risk to their law practices that the plaintiff's attorneys assumed by taking the case and, on this ground, enhanced the fees of two of the four attorneys by 25 percent, thus leaving the amount awarded almost the same as it was before being challenged.

Tanner v. Oregon Health Sciences University, 980 P.2d 186 (Or. 1999), illustrates how attorney's fee awards may work in state (versus federal) courts. Three employees of the university who are lesbians, along with their domestic partners, had sued the university, claiming that they were denied health insurance benefits based on sexual orientation, in violation of the Oregon state constitution. At the appellate court level, in *Tanner v. Oregon Health Sciences University*, 971 P. 2d 435 (1998), the plaintiffs prevailed on this claim. They thereupon petitioned for an award of attorney's fees for their attorney, asserting that they were entitled to such an award both under Oregon statutes (Ore. Rev. Stat. 20. 107) and under Oregon case law (*Deras v. Myers*, 535 P.2d 541 (Ore. 1975)). The court did not address the statutory claim, but held for the plaintiffs under Oregon case law:

In *Deras*, the Oregon Supreme Court held:

[A]s a general rule American courts will not award attorney's fees to the prevailing party absent authorization of statute or contract. . . . [However,] courts of

equity have the inherent power to award attorney's fees. This power frequently
has been exercised in cases where the plaintiff brings suit in a representative
capacity and succeeds in protecting the rights of others as much as his own [980
P.2d at 188, citing 535 P.2d at 549].

Holding that the plaintiffs met all the requirements of *Deras,* the court determined that a rate of "$200 per hour reasonably reflects the complexity, contro-
versy, and novelty of the issues as well as the experience of counsel," and
awarded attorney's fees of $77,340. As to the requirement that the plaintiffs
must have protected rights beyond their own, the court reasoned that:

> In this case, plaintiffs complained about an unconstitutional violation of their
> civil rights as citizens of this state. The pecuniary benefits they obtained are not
> peculiar to themselves. The fact that, as defendants suggest, our decision on the
> merits of their claims will directly benefit "only a relatively small class of per-
> sons" is not controlling. How small or large the directly benefited class may be
> is not the point. . . . What controls is the extent to which the constitutional
> issue resolved is a matter of primary concern to the public at large. Vindicating
> the civil rights of a group of citizens who have been subject to disparate treat-
> ment in employment on the basis of a suspect classification in violation of
> the Oregon Constitution is a matter of primary concern to all Oregonians [980
> P.2d at 189].

This case is discussed further in Section 5.3.7.

(For a discussion of the appropriate process for determining attorney's fees
in the thirty-year litigation to desegregate the Tennessee system of public higher
education (discussed in Section 13.5.2), see *Geier v. Sundquist,* 372 F.3d 784
(6th Cir. 2004).)

2.2.4.5. Contempt of court. When a defendant does not comply with the
court's award of relief to the plaintiff, or when either party or their witnesses
do not comply with some other court order (for example, a subpoena to testify),
the court may enforce its own orders by various means. Primary and most powerful is the imposition of criminal or civil contempt. In *United States v. United
Mine Workers,* 330 U.S. 258 (1947), the U.S. Supreme Court distinguished the
two sanctions. A civil contempt judgment may be used to coerce the contemnor into compliance with a court order or to award compensation to the complaining party for incurred losses. On the other hand, a criminal contempt
judgment is used not simply to coerce but rather to punish the contemnor or
vindicate the authority of the court. Commonly, the court may impose a monetary fine or imprisonment for either type of judgment. In a civil contempt case,
the amount of the fine or term of the imprisonment may be indefinite, since the
purpose is to coerce the contemnor into compliance. Thus, a judge may imprison
someone until that person is willing to comply, or fine him a certain sum per day
until compliance. Further, once it becomes clear that no amount of coercion will
work, the fine or imprisonment must stop. Conversely, in criminal contempt,
there must be a definite fine or term of imprisonment set at the outset.

Dinnan v. Regents of the University System of Georgia, 625 F.2d 1146 (5th Cir.
1980), illustrates the reach of the contempt power as well as the potential

difficulty in determining whether a judge has imposed criminal or civil contempt. The plaintiff was a University of Georgia professor challenging a contempt order against him. He was a member of a committee that had denied a promotion to a female faculty applicant who subsequently sued the university for sex discrimination (see Section 5.3.3). When he refused to testify at the trial (see this book, Section 7.7.1), the court ordered him to pay $1,100 for every day (up to thirty days) he refused to testify. If he continued in contempt of the order after that time, he would be sentenced to ninety days' imprisonment subject to being released earlier any time he agreed to testify. Dinnan argued that the court's orders constituted criminal contempt and were unlawful because fines and imprisonment cannot be combined as punishment for criminal contempt. Both the trial court and the appellate court rejected his challenge, holding that these were coercive, not punitive, measures and that both sanctions were appropriate components of a civil order of contempt.

An opposite result obtained in *Martin v. Guillot,* 875 F.2d 839 (11th Cir. 1989). There, a university that had dismissed an administrator without affording him due process protections disobeyed a court order to afford the administrator (the plaintiff) an appropriate hearing and appeal. Although university officials (the defendants) eventually complied, the plaintiff requested that the court hold the university in contempt for its earlier delay in doing so. The trial court granted the request and, as a sanction, ordered the defendants to purge themselves of their contempt by giving the plaintiff back pay for the time from his unlawful dismissal to the eventual provision of full due process rights. The appellate court reversed the trial court's order, however, because the order was in the nature of a criminal contempt, and the trial court had not met the procedural requirements of the Federal Rules of Criminal Procedure (Rule 42) for imposing criminal contempt:

> [T]he sanction was not imposed either to coerce or compensate and therefore is not a civil contempt sanction. The defendants had already complied with the court orders and afforded Martin due process; there remained nothing to coerce them to do. The continued contempt could be construed as being compensatory in character because the sanction, approximately equal to back pay, was to be paid to the appellant rather than to the court. However, in its order specifying the amount of the sanction to be imposed, the district court explicitly stated its "object was and is to sanction defendants rather than to compensate Martin." Because the sanction levied by the district court was clearly designed predominately to punish defendants for their initial failings to comply with court orders, it is a criminal contempt sanction [875 F.2d at 845].

2.2.5. Judicial (academic) deference.
Another consideration that should play a role in the management of litigation, and in an institution's presentation of its case, is "judicial deference" or "academic deference." At trial as well as on appeal, issues may arise concerning the extent to which the court should defer to, or give "deference" to, the institution whose decision or other action is at issue. As one commentator has explained:

[A] concept of academic deference justifies treating many university processes
and decisions differently from off-campus matters. This formulation is hardly
novel. In fact, . . . many university cases recognize in this way the distinctive
nature of the academic environment. Illustrations come from many areas.
[Examples] that seem especially apt [include] university based research, personnel decisions, admissions of students, evaluation of student performance, and
use of university facilities. [Robert O'Neil, "Academic Freedom and the Constitution," 11 *J. Coll. & Univ. Law* 275, 283 (1984).]

This concept of academic deference is a branch of a more general concept of
judicial deference that encompasses a variety of circumstances in which, and
reasons for which, a court should defer to the expertise of some decision maker
other than itself.[7] Issues regarding academic deference can play a vital, sometimes even dispositive, role in litigation involving higher educational institutions. Institutions may therefore seek to claim deference at various points in the
litigation process. (See generally O'Neil, *supra,* at 283–89.) Deference issues
may arise, for example, with regard to whether a court should recognize an
implied private cause of action (see, for example, *Cannon v. University of
Chicago,* 441 U.S. 677, 709–10 (1979), discussed in Section 13.5.9 of this book);
with regard to the issuance of subpoenas and other aspects of the discovery
process (see, for example, *University of Pennsylvania v. EEOC,* 493 U.S. 182
(1990), discussed in Section 7.7); with regard to standards of review and
burdens of proof (see subsection 2.2.3.5 above);[8] and with regard to the remedies to be imposed against a losing defendant (see, for example, *Kunda v.
Muhlenberg College,* 621 F.2d 532, 547–51 (3d Cir. 1980)), discussed in Section 6.4.2). Sometimes requests for deference are framed as claims to institutional autonomy; sometimes as "institutional academic freedom" claims (see
Section 7.1.6) or faculty academic freedom claims (see Section 7.2); and
sometimes as "relative institutional competence" claims, asserting that the institution's or the faculty's competence over the matter at issue overshadows that
of the court. Sometimes institutions may contend that their claim to deference
is constitutionally based—especially when they rely on the academic freedom
rationale for deference and seek to ground academic freedom in the First
Amendment. At other times, in statutory cases, the deference claim may be
based on statutory interpretation; in effect, the institution contends that, under
the statute that is at issue, Congress was deferential to higher educational institutions and intended that courts should be deferential as well. And in yet other

---

[7]Another branch of judicial deference that is highly important to higher education arises when an
institution, or an association of institutions, challenges a rule or decision of a federal or state
administrative agency in court. Questions may then arise concerning the extent to which the
court should defer to the expertise or authority of the administrative agency. This type of deference issue is discussed in Sections 13.4.6 and 13.6.1.

[8]Standards of review and burdens of proof may also be important issues in hearings before colleges' and universities' own decision-making bodies (for example, a student disciplinary board).
For a case that illustrates the distinction between standards of review in court and standards of
review in internal proceedings, see *Reilly v. Daly,* 666 N.E.2d 439 (Ind. 1996), discussed in subsection 2.2.3.5 above.

situations, especially in common law contract or tort cases, the deference claim may be based on public policy or legal policy considerations—for instance, that any court intervention would unduly interfere with the institution's internal affairs, or that vigorous enforcement of legal principles against higher education institutions would not be an effective use of the court's limited resources (see, for example, the discussions of deference in Sections 8.1.3 and 9.3.1).

When plaintiffs assert constitutional claims against an institution of higher education, deference issues may work out differently than when statutory claims are asserted. In a statutory case—for example, a case asserting that the institution has violated a federal civil rights law—the court will first be concerned with interpreting and applying the law consistent with Congress's intentions, and in this regard will generally defer to Congress's own judgments about the law's application (see, for example, *Eldred v. Ashcroft*, 537 U.S. 186 (2003)). Thus the court will take its cue on deference from Congress rather than developing its own independent judgment on the matter. In *Cannon v. University of Chicago*, 441 U.S. 677 (1979) (discussed in Section 13.5.9 of this book), for example, the plaintiff sought to subject admissions decisions to the nondiscrimination requirements of Title IX of the Education Amendments of 1972. The defendant argued that it would be "unwise to subject admissions decisions of universities to judicial scrutiny at the behest of disappointed applicants" because "this kind of litigation is burdensome and inevitably will have an adverse effect on the independence of members of university committees." Responding, the Court asserted that "[t]his argument is not new to this litigation. It was forcefully advanced in both 1964 and 1972 by congressional opponents of Title VI and Title IX, and squarely rejected by the congressional majorities that passed the two statutes." The Court followed suit, rejecting the defendant's claim to deference. In other cases, involving other statutes, however, courts may discern that Congress intended to be deferential to postsecondary institutions in some circumstances and the courts should do the same. (See, for example, James Leonard, "Judicial Deference to Academic Standards Under Section 504 of the Rehabilitation Act and Titles II and III of the Americans With Disabilities Act," 75 *Nebraska L. Rev.* 27 (1996).)

In contrast, when plaintiffs assert constitutional claims, and institutions ask the court for deference, the court is on its own; its response is shaped by consideration of applicable prior precedents and the applicable standard of judicial review. *Grutter v. Bollinger*, 539 U.S. 306 (2003), a constitutional challenge to the University of Michigan Law School's race-conscious admission policy, is a leading example of this type of case. The plaintiffs, rejected applicants, sought a rigorous, nondeferential application of the equal protection clause; the university sought deference for the academic judgments it had made in designing and implementing its diversity plan for admissions. The Court applied strict scrutiny review, requiring the university to show that maintaining the diversity of its student body is a compelling state interest. But in applying this standard, the Court emphasized that:

> The Law School's educational judgment that such diversity is essential to its educational mission is one to which we defer. . . . Our scrutiny of the interest

asserted by the Law School is no less strict for taking into account complex educational judgments in an area that lies primarily within the expertise of the university. Our holding today is in keeping with our tradition of giving a degree of deference to a university's academic decisions, within constitutionally prescribed limits [539 U.S. at 328].

This deference was a critical aspect of the Court's reasoning that led it, in a landmark decision, to uphold the law school's admissions policy. (See generally Edward Stoner & J. Michael Showalter, "Judicial Deference to Educational Judgment: Justice O'Connor's Opinion in *Grutter* Reapplies Longstanding Principles, As Shown by Rulings Involving College Students in the Eighteen Months Before Grutter," 30 *J. Coll. & Univ. Law* 583 (2004).)

In other constitutional cases, courts may reach the opposite result. In the VMI case, *United States v. Virginia*, 518 U.S. 515 (1996) (discussed in Section 8.2.4.2), for instance, the U.S. Supreme Court bypassed the defendant institution's expert evidence and declined to defer to its judgment that maintaining VMI as an all-male institution was essential to the institution's educational mission. The Court's apparent reason for refusing to defer, and the apparent distinction between *Grutter* and *United States v. Virginia*, is that the Court did not view the state's judgments over the years about VMI's all-male character to be genuinely academic judgments, but rather viewed them as judgments based on other factors and later dressed up with educational research for purposes of the litigation. The state's proffered educational reasons for the all-male policy were "rationalizations for actions in fact differently grounded," said the Court, and were based on "overbroad generalizations" about the abilities and interests of the sexes.

The paradigmatic setting for institutions invoking academic deference, and courts granting it, is the setting of faculty tenure, promotion, and termination decisions. The deference issues arising in this setting, and the key cases, are discussed in Section 6.4.2, as is the evolving tendency of courts to subject these decisions to thorough scrutiny for fairness, while deferring to the academic standards used to evaluate the candidate for promotion or tenure.

When faculty members challenge adverse personnel decisions, they may assert statutory claims (such as a Title VII sex discrimination claim), or constitutional claims (such as a First Amendment free speech or academic freedom claim), or sometimes common law claims (such as a breach of contact claim). In response, institutions typically argue that courts should not involve themselves in institutional personnel judgments concerning faculty members, since these are expert and evaluative (often subjective) academic judgments to which courts should defer.[9] Institutions have had considerable success with

---

[9]Some personnel disputes will have gone to arbitration before landing in court. When an institution prevails in arbitration and the faculty member then files suit in court, the institution has an additional argument for deference: that the court should accord deference not only to the institution's judgment but also to the arbitrator's decision. See, for example, *Samoan v. Trustees of California State University and Colleges*, 197 Cal. Rptr. 856 (Cal. 1983).

such arguments in this setting. They have also achieved similar success in cases concerning their academic evaluations of students; indeed a student case, *Regents of the University of Michigan v. Ewing,* 474 U.S. 214 (1985) (discussed below), is one of the primary authorities on academic deference.

In a constitutional case, *Feldman v. Ho,* 171 F.3d 494 (7th Cir. 1999), for example, a professor claimed that Southern Illinois University did not renew his contract because he had accused a colleague of academic misconduct. The court rejected his First Amendment free speech claim by emphasizing the university's own academic freedom to make its own personnel decisions:

> A university seeks to accumulate and disseminate knowledge; for a university to function well, it must be able to decide which members of its faculty are productive scholars and which are not (or, worse, are distracting those who are). . . .
>
> If the University erred in telling [Professor] Feldman to seek employment elsewhere that is unfortunate, but the only way to preserve academic freedom is to keep claims of academic error out of the legal maw [171 F.3d at 495–97].

At the same time, the court in *Feldman* issued a strong statement on the need for courts to defer to the academic judgments of colleges and universities:

> [A]n unsubstantiated charge of academic misconduct not only squanders the time of other faculty members (who must analyze the charge, or defend against it) but also reflects poorly on the judgment of the accuser. A university is entitled to decide for itself whether the charge is sound; transferring that decision to the jury in the name of the first amendment would undermine the university's mission—not only by committing an academic decision to amateurs (is a jury really the best institution to determine who should receive credit for a paper in mathematics?) but also by creating the possibility of substantial damages when jurors disagree with the faculty's resolution, a possibility that could discourage universities from acting to improve their faculty. . . . If the kind of decision Southern Illinois University made about Feldman is mete for litigation, then we might as well commit all tenure decisions to juries, for all are equally based on speech [171 F.3d at 497].

Like the *Feldman* court, most contemporary courts will recognize that they should accord deference to the academic decisions of academic institutions with regard to faculty personnel matters. But seldom are courts as outspoken on this point as was the court in *Feldman.* Other courts, moreover, may (and should) give more attention than the *Feldman* court to whether the decision being challenged was a genuinely academic decision, based on expert review of professional qualifications and performance.

There are also many statutory employment discrimination cases in which courts defer substantially to the faculty personnel judgments of colleges and universities (see generally Section 6.4), sometimes with language as striking as that in the *Feldman* opinion (see, for example, *Kyriakopoulos v. George Washington University,* 657 F. Supp. 1525, 1529 (1987)). But this does not mean that courts will, or should, defer broadly in all or most cases challenging faculty personnel decisions. There have been and will continue to be cases where countervailing considerations counsel against deference—for example, cases where there is evidence that an institution has relied on race, ethnicity, or gender in making an adverse personnel judgment; or where an institution has relied on personal animosity or bias, internal politics, or other nonacademic factors; or where an institution has declined to afford the faculty member procedural safeguards; or where a decision for the plaintiff would not significantly intrude on university decision makers' ability to apply their expertise and discretion in making personnel decisions. The court in *Kunda v. Muhlenberg College,* above, strikes the right note about such situations:

> The fact that the discrimination in this case took place in an academic rather than commercial setting does not permit the court to abdicate its responsibility. . . . Congress did not intend that those institutions which employ persons who work primarily with their mental faculties should enjoy a different status under Title VII than those which employ persons who work primarily with their hands [621 F.2d at 550].

(See also Harry Tepker, "Title VII, Equal Employment Opportunity, and Academic Autonomy: Toward a Principled Deference," 16 *U. Cal. Davis L. Rev.* 1047 (1983).)

As the preceding discussion suggests, several interrelated factors are key in determining when a court should defer to the judgments of a postsecondary institution. First and foremost, the judgment must be a genuine academic judgment. In *Regents of the University of Michigan v. Ewing,* 474 U.S. 214 (1985), the Court stated this requirement well: "When judges are asked to review the substance of a *genuinely academic decision* . . . , they should show great respect for the faculty's professional judgment" (474 U.S. at 225 (emphasis added)). The demonstrated exercise of "professional judgment" is a hallmark of an academic decision. Generally, as *Ewing* indicates, such judgments must be made in large part by faculty members based on their expertise as scholars and teachers. Such judgments usually require "an expert evaluation of cumulative information" and, for that reason, are not readily amenable to being reviewed using "the procedural tools of judicial or administrative decisionmaking" (*Board of Curators, University of Missouri v. Horowitz,* 435 U.S. 78, 90 (1978)). Such judgments are also usually "discretionary" and "subjective," and thus even less amenable to reasoned review on their merits by the courts.

A second key factor, related to the first, concerns relative institutional competence. Courts are more likely to defer when the judgment or decision being reviewed, even if not academic in character, involves considerations regarding which the postsecondary institution's competence is superior to that of the courts. The *Kunda* court, for instance, spoke of inquiries whose substance is "beyond the competence of individual judges" (621 F.2d at 548). Another court has advised that "courts must be ever-mindful of relative institutional competencies" (*Powell v. Syracuse University,* 580 F.2d 1150, 1153 (2d Cir. 1978)).

Third, courts are more likely to defer to the institution when a judicial decision against it would create undue burdens that would unduly interfere with its ability to perform its educational functions—or when similar judgments to follow, against other institutions, would subject them to similar burdens. The *Kunda* court (above), for instance, suggested that deference may be appropriate when a court decision would "necessarily intrude upon the nature of the educational process itself" (621 F.2d at 547). The U.S. Supreme Court in the *Cannon* case (above) suggested that deference may be appropriate if litigating issues of the type before the court would be "so costly or voluminous that . . . the academic community [would be] unduly burdened" (441 U.S. at 710). And the court in *Feldman* warned of judicial decisions that would interfere with the institution's ability to fulfill its educational mission.

By developing the converse of the reasons for according deference, one can discern various reasons why a court would or should *not* defer to a college or university. Again, there are three overlapping categories of reasons. First, if the judgment to be reviewed by the court is not a "genuinely academic decision," courts are less likely to defer. As the Court in *Ewing* notes, if "the person or committee responsible did not actually exercise professional judgment" (474 U.S. at 225), there is little reason to defer. This is particularly so if the nonacademic reason for the decision may be an illegitimate reason, such as racial or gender bias (see *Gray v. Board of Higher Education*, 692 F.2d 901, 909 (2d Cir. 1982), and *Williams v. Lindenwood*, 288 F.3d 349, 356 (8th Cir. 2002)). Second, if the judgment being reviewed is a disciplinary rather than an academic judgment, the court's competence is relatively greater and the university's is relatively less; the factor of relative institutional competence may therefore become a wash or weigh more heavily in the court's (and thus the challenger's) favor. Similarly, when the challenge to the institution's decision concerns the procedures it used rather than the substance or merits of the decision itself, the court's competence is greater than the institution's, and there is usually little or no room for deference. The case of *Board of Curators v. Horowitz*, above, explores these two distinctions at length. Third, when reviewing and overturning an institutional decision would not intrude upon the institution's core functions, or would not likely burden other institutions with a flood of litigation, these reasons for deference diminish as well. The U.S. Supreme Court used this point in *University of Pennsylvania v. EEOC*, above, when it declined to defer to the university because upholding the plaintiff's request would have only an "extremely attenuated" effect on academic freedom.

2.2.6. *Managing litigation and the threat of litigation.*

Managing, settling, and conducting litigation, like planning to avoid it, requires at all stages the in-depth involvement of attorneys.[10] Institutions should place heavy

---

[10]The suggestions in this section apply not only to litigation against the institution but also to suits against officers or employees of the institution when the institution is providing them, or considering providing them, legal representation or related assistance. In suits in which both the institution and one or more named institutional officers or employees are defendants, questions may arise concerning possible conflicts of interest that could preclude the institution's legal staff from representing all or some of the officers or employees (see Section 2.4.3).

emphasis on this aspect of institutional operations. Both administrators and counsel should cultivate conditions in which they can work together as a team in a treatment law (see Section 2.4.2) mode. The administrator's basic understanding of the tactical and technical matters concerning jurisdiction, procedure, evidence, and remedies (see subsections 2.2.2–2.2.4 above), and counsel's mastery of these technicalities and the tactical options and difficulties they present, will greatly enhance the institution's capacity to engage in treatment law that successfully protects the institution's mission as well as its reputation and financial resources. Counsel's understanding of judicial deference (see subsection 2.2.5 above) and its tactical role in litigation is also of critical importance.

Litigation management is a two-way street. It may be employed either in a defensive posture when the institution or its employees are sued or threatened with suit, or in an offensive posture when the institution seeks access to the courts as the best means of protecting its interests with respect to a particular dispute. Administrators, like counsel, will thus do well to consider treatment law from both perspectives and to view courts and litigation as, in some circumstances, a potential benefit rather than only as a hindrance.

Although administrators and counsel must accord great attention and energy to lawsuits when they arise, and thus must emphasize the expert practice of treatment law, their primary and broader objective should be to avoid lawsuits or limit their scope whenever that can be accomplished consistent with the institutional mission. Once a lawsuit has been filed, administrators and counsel sometimes can achieve this objective by using summary judgment motions or (if the institution is a defendant) motions to dismiss, or by encouraging pretrial negotiation and settlement. Moreover, by agreement of the parties, the dispute may be diverted from the courts to a mediator or an arbitrator. Even better, administrators and counsel may be able to derail disputes from the litigation track before any suit is filed by providing for a suitable alternative mechanism for resolving the dispute. Mediation and arbitration are common and increasingly important examples of such alternative dispute resolution (ADR) mechanisms (see Section 2.3 below), which are usable whether the institution is a defendant or a plaintiff, and whether the dispute is an internal campus dispute or an external dispute with a commercial vendor, construction contractor, or other outside entity. For internal campus disputes, internal grievance processes and hearing panels (see, for example, Section 9.1) are also important ADR mechanisms and may frequently constitute remedies that, under the "exhaustion-of-remedies" doctrine (see subsection 2.2.2.4 above), disputants must utilize before resorting to court.

Even before disputes arise, administrators and counsel should be actively engaging in preventive law (Section 2.4.2) as the most comprehensive and forward-looking means of avoiding and limiting lawsuits. Preventive law also has a useful role to play in the wake of a lawsuit, especially a major one in which the institution is sued and loses. In such a circumstance, administrators may engage in a "post-litigation audit" of the institutional offices and functions involved in the lawsuit—using the audit as a lens through which to view institutional shortcomings of the type that led to the judgment against the institution, and to rectify such shortcomings in a way that serves to avoid future lawsuits in that area of concern.

Sec. 2.3. Alternate Dispute Resolution

2.3.1. Overview. The substantial cost of litigation, in terms of both time and money, and the law's limited capacity to fully resolve some types of disputes, have encouraged businesses, other organizations, and even courts to turn to alternate dispute resolution (ADR). ADR encompasses a variety of approaches to resolving disputes, from informal consultation with an ombuds who is vested with the authority to resolve some disputes and to seek resolution of others, to more formal processes such as grievance procedures, mediation, or arbitration. Commercial disputes and disputes in the financial services industry have been resolved through arbitration for decades. Academe has been slow to accept ADR, but it is becoming more common for certain kinds of disputes, and more institutions are turning to ADR in an attempt to reduce litigation costs and to resolve disputes, if possible, in a less adversarial manner.

Many employers embrace ADR because of its promise of quicker, less expensive resolution of disputes, and this is often the case. Discovery is not used in mediation, and is limited in arbitration as well. Arbitrators typically do not use judicial rules of evidence, may admit evidence that a court would not (such as hearsay evidence), and generally issue a ruling (called an "award") a month or two after the hearing, unless they issue an oral award on the spot. The parties select the mediator or arbitrator jointly, rather than being assigned a judge, which may give them more confidence in the process. Indeed, the parties design the process in order to meet their needs, and can change the process if it needs improvement.

ADR has some disadvantages, however. ADR is a private process, and there is typically no public record made of the outcome. This characteristic of ADR tends to benefit employers, who resist public inquiry into personnel decisions, and may make it difficult for an employee who must help to select a mediator or arbitrator to evaluate that individual's record or previous rulings. The lack of public accountability is viewed as problematic because many of these claims have a statutory basis, yet they are resolved without judicial or regulatory agency scrutiny. As discussed below, the decisions of arbitrators are difficult to appeal and are usually considered final. Furthermore, there may be a substantial difference in skill and knowledge between the employee who is challenging an employment decision and the individual who is representing the institution before the mediator or arbitrator. Many ADR systems prohibit attorneys for either party, and even if attorneys are permitted, the employee may not be able to afford to retain one.

Despite these concerns, ADR is becoming more popular on campus as a strategy for dispute resolution. (For an overview of the use of ADR in employment decisions, see Lawrence C. DiNardo, John A. Sherrill, & Anna R. Palmer, "Specialized ADR to Settle Faculty Employment Disputes," 28 *J. Coll. & Univ. Law* 129 (2001).)

2.3.2. Types of ADR. ADR may use internal processes, external third parties, or both. Internal processes include grievance procedures, in which a student or employee may challenge a decision by invoking a right, usually created by the employee's contract, state law, or a student code of conduct, to have the decision reviewed by an individual or small group who were not involved in the challenged decision. Grievance procedures, particularly those included in collective bargaining agreements, may have multiple steps, and may culminate either in a final decision by a high-level administrator or a neutral individual who is not an employee of the institution. (For a helpful discussion of how to draft grievance procedures that may serve as an alternative to litigation, see Ann H. Franke, "Grievance Procedures: Solving Campus Employment Problems Out of Court," *Employment Issues* (United Educators Insurance Risk Retention Group, Inc., February 1998).

Depending upon the language of any contracts with employees or relevant state law, the fact finding of a grievance panel may be viewed by a reviewing court as binding on the institution and the grievant. For example, in *Murphy v. Duquense University of the Holy Ghost,* 777 A.2d 418 (Pa. 2001), a tenure revocation case discussed in Section 6.7.3, the court ruled that a faculty panel's fact finding was binding on the plaintiff, and he could not relitigate the issue of whether the institution had demonstrated that the misconduct met the contractual grounds for termination. On the other hand, if a faculty grievance panel recommends a resolution to the dispute that involves compromise or other ADR mechanisms, a court may not allow the plaintiff to argue that this finding has preclusive effect in a breach of contract claim, as in *Breiner-Sanders v. Georgetown University,* 118 F. Supp. 2d 1 (D.D.C. 1999). In that case, the court ruled that the grievance panel had not applied contract law principles in its hearing of her grievance, and thus the panel's decision, which was favorable to the faculty member, did not have preclusive effect and did not support a motion for summary judgment on behalf of the faculty member.

The inclusion of a grievance procedure in a faculty or staff employee handbook may convince a court that a plaintiff who has not exhausted his internal remedies may not pursue contractual remedies in court. For example, in *Brennan v. King,* 139 F.3d 258 (1st Cir. 1998), an assistant professor who was denied tenure by Northeastern University brought breach of contract and discrimination claims against the university. With respect to Brennan's contract claims, the court ruled that Massachusetts law required him to exhaust his contractual remedies before bringing suit. However, the court allowed his discrimination claims to go forward because the handbook did not provide a remedy for the denial of tenure.

Even if there is no formal grievance process, in situations where faculty are challenging negative employment decisions (such as discipline or termination), a panel of peers may be convened to consider whether there are sufficient grounds for the challenged employment decision. (See, for example, the AAUP's "Recommended Institutional Regulations on Academic Freedom and Tenure," available at http://www.aaup.org.) The outcome of the peer panel's deliberations is usually considered a recommendation, which the administration may accept, modify, or reject. In addition, student judicial boards are a form of peer review of student charges of misconduct, although appeals are usually ultimately decided by a high-level administrator. Finally, ombudspersons, who are neutral employees of the institution who have the responsibility to try to resolve disputes informally and confidentially,[11] are appearing with more frequency on campus.[12]

ADR processes involving individuals external to the institution include mediation, in which a neutral third party is engaged to work with the parties to the dispute in an effort to resolve the conflict. The mediator may meet with the parties together to attempt to resolve the dispute, or may meet with each party separately, hearing their concerns and helping to craft a resolution. The mediator has no authority to decide the outcome, but may provide suggestions to the parties after listening to each party's concerns. All parties to the dispute must agree with the outcome in order for the process to be final.

Although mediation can be very successful in resolving disputes between employees or even between students (such as roommate disputes), there is one area in which mediation may not be a wise choice. The Office of Civil Rights (OCR), in its Title IX enforcement guidance for the sexual harassment of students, states that the Title IX regulations require schools and colleges to adopt grievance procedures. The Guidance goes on to say, however:

> Grievance procedures may include informal mechanisms for resolving sexual harassment complaints to be used if the parties agree to do so. OCR has frequently advised schools, however, that it is not appropriate for a student who is complaining of harassment to be required to work out the problem directly with the individual alleged to be harassing him or her, and certainly not without appropriate involvement by the school (e.g., participation by a counselor, trained mediator, or, if appropriate, a teacher or administrator). In addition, the complainant must be notified of the right to end the informal process at any time and begin the formal stage of the complaint process. In some cases, such as alleged sexual assaults, mediation will not be appropriate even on a voluntary basis . . . (*Sexual Harassment Guidance* 1977, revised in 1997, available at http://www.ed.gov/about/offices/list/ocr/docs/sexhar01.html).

In addition to concerns about the alleged victim's right to pursue a more formal grievance process, mediation of harassment or assault claims may mean that no formal record is made of the harassment or assault claim or its resolution, which could pose a problem if an alleged victim subsequently filed a

---

[11]For a case protecting confidential information given to a campus ombudsperson from discovery during related litigation, see *Garstang v. Superior Court of Los Angeles County,* 46 Cal. Rptr. 2d 84 (Cal. Ct. App. 1995), decided on state constitutional grounds. In *Kientzy v. McDonnell Douglas Corp.,* 133 F.R.D. 570 (E.D. Mo. 1991), the court created a privilege protecting communications in an informal mediation session held by an ombudsperson. See also Jeffrey Sun, "University Officials as Administrators and Mediators: The Dual Role Conflict and Confidentiality Problems," 1999 *B.Y.U. Educ. & L.J.* 19 (1999).

[12]For information about ombuds at colleges and universities, see the Web site of the University and College Ombuds Association (UCOA) at http://www.ucoa.org.

lawsuit against the college or its staff. (For a thorough discussion of the use of mediation at institutions of higher education, see Melinda W. Grier, "A Legal Perspective of Mediation," Annual Conference of the National Association of College and University Attorneys, available at http://www.nacua.org.)

Another form of ADR, used frequently at campuses where employees are represented by unions, is arbitration. An arbitrator, a third-party neutral with experience in employment issues, is brought in to act as a "private judge." The parties present their concerns to the arbitrator at a hearing, in which the employer has the burden of proving that the termination or discipline was justified. Arbitration is also used to resolve disputes over the meaning of contract language; in that case, the party disputing the application of the contract language to a problem (usually, but not always, the union), has the burden of demonstrating that the contract has been breached. Under a trio of U.S. Supreme Court cases called the "Steelworkers Trilogy,"[13] arbitration decisions are not reviewable by courts unless the arbitrator has exceeded the authority given to him or her by the contract, the arbitrator has engaged in misconduct, or the outcome of the arbitration violates some important principle of public policy.

ADR systems in collective bargaining agreements are subject to the negotiation process, and typically state that all claims arising under the contract will be subject to a grievance procedure that culminates in arbitration. Arbitration may be advisory to the parties, or they may agree to be bound by the decision of the arbitrator (called "binding arbitration"). At some colleges and universities, nonunionized employees may be asked to sign agreements to arbitrate all employment-related disputes, rather than filing lawsuits. These "mandatory arbitration agreements" have sustained vigorous court challenges, particularly by plaintiffs attempting to litigate employment discrimination claims. The legal standards for enforcing an arbitration agreement when employment discrimination claims are brought by unionized employees are discussed in Section 4.5.5 of this book.

If the employees are not unionized, however, the standards for enforcing arbitration clauses are somewhat less strict. Beginning with a decision by the U.S. Supreme Court in *Gilmer v. Interstate-Johnson Lane*, 500 U.S. 20 (1991), courts have agreed to enforce arbitration clauses in individual employment contracts. Gilmer, a registered securities representative, had signed a contract that required him to submit all employment disputes to compulsory arbitration. When he challenged his discharge by filing an age discrimination claim, his employer filed a motion to compel arbitration, which the trial court upheld. The appellate court reversed, but the U.S. Supreme Court sided with the trial court, ruling that the language of the contract must be enforced.

In several cases decided after *Gilmer*, trial courts have enforced arbitration clauses in situations where plaintiffs have filed employment discrimination claims with an administrative agency or in court. Although the Federal

---

[13]*Steelworkers v American Manufacturing Co.*, 363 U.S. 564 (1960); *Steelworkers v. Enterprise Wheel and Car Corp.*, 363 U.S. 593 (1960); and *Steelworkers v. Warrior and Gulf Navigation*, 363 U.S. 574 (1960).

Arbitration Act (9 U.S.C. § 1 *et seq.*) requires courts, in general, to enforce private arbitration agreements, language in the Act has been interpreted to preclude arbitration of employment contracts. Section I of the Act exempts "contracts of employment of seamen, railroad employees, or any other class of workers engaged in foreign or interstate commerce." The U.S. Supreme Court has not interpreted the meaning of "class of workers engaged in foreign or interstate commerce," and the conclusions of federal appellate courts regarding the reach of this language have been inconsistent. Some courts have interpreted the exclusion narrowly and applied it only to those workers actually engaged in the movement of goods in interstate commerce (see, for example, *Miller Brewing Co. v. Brewery Workers Local Union No. 9*, 739 F.2d 1159 (7th Cir. 1984), *cert. denied*, 469 U.S. 1160 (1985)); others have defined the exemption to include all employment contracts (see, for example, *Willis v. Dean Witter Reynolds, Inc.*, 948 F.2d 305 (6th Cir. 1991)).[14] While the Supreme Court in *Gilmer* did not expressly address this language, it did state that the Federal Arbitration Act favors arbitration agreements and that they should be upheld whenever appropriate.

Courts typically use contract law principles to determine whether an employee's agreement to use arbitration rather than to litigate is binding. In *Futrelle v. Duke University*, 488 S.E.2d 635 (N.C. App. 1997), a state appellate court dismissed a medical librarian's breach of contract, wrongful discharge, and defamation claims because she had used the university's internal grievance procedure, which culminated in arbitration. The plaintiff had prevailed at arbitration and Duke gave her a check for the damages the university had been ordered to pay by the arbitrator. The court ruled that, because the plaintiff had cashed the check, which was in satisfaction of the arbitration award, she was precluded from initiating litigation about the same issues that had been determined through arbitration.

2.3.3. *Applications to colleges and universities.* Litigation involving ADR in colleges and universities has focused primarily on arbitration and on these two issues: What issues may the arbitrator decide, and under what circumstances may the arbitration award be overturned by a court?

Although faculty at a number of unionized colleges and universities are covered by collective bargaining agreements that provide for arbitral review of most employment decisions, many agreements do not permit the arbitrator to grant or deny tenure, although they may allow the arbitrator to determine the procedural compliance or fairness of the tenure decision. If, for example, the agreement does not permit the arbitrator to substitute his or her judgment concerning the merits of the tenure decision, a court will overturn an award in which the arbitrator does his or her own review of the grievant's qualifications. For example, in *California Faculty Association v. Superior Court of Santa Clara County*, 75 Cal. Rptr. 2d 1 (Cal. Ct. App. 1998), a state appellate court affirmed a trial

---

[14]Cases related to the enforcement of arbitration clauses are collected in William G. Phelps, Annot., "Preemption by Federal Arbitration Act (9 U.S.C.S. § 1 *et seq.*) of State Laws Prohibiting or Restricting Formation or Enforcement of Arbitration Agreements," 108 A.L.R. Fed. 179.

court's decision vacating an arbitration award and remanding the case for another hearing before a different arbitrator. The arbitrator whose decision was challenged had conducted his own review of the scholarly achievements of a grievant who had been denied tenure, and had awarded her tenure. The trial court ruled that the arbitrator had exceeded his authority under the collective bargaining agreement, because the standard in the collective bargaining agreement for overturning a negative tenure decision required the arbitrator to find that the president could not have made a "reasoned judgment" in making the negative decision, and that the arbitrator could state with certainty that the grievant would have been granted tenure otherwise. In this case, the grievant had not gotten positive recommendations at various stages of the tenure decision process, and the arbitrator based his decision on testimony from witnesses who supported the grievant's quest for tenure, rather than on a review of the record that the president had used to reach his decision. Finding that the arbitrator had substituted his judgment for the president's, the court affirmed the trial court's remedy.

Grievants challenging a tenure denial may attempt to state claims of procedural noncompliance that actually attack the substance of the tenure decision. For example, in *AAUP, University of Toledo Chapter v. University of Toledo,* 797 N.E.2d 583 (Oh. Ct. Cmn. Pleas 2003), an assistant professor denied tenure challenged the negative decision as a procedural violation, stating that the determinations of the department chair and the dean that the professor had produced an insufficient number of publications violated the contract's procedural requirements. The arbitrator ruled that the agreement had not been violated and found for the university, and the plaintiff appealed the award to a state trial court. The court upheld the arbitrator's award, stating that the contract's procedural requirements afforded the chair and the dean the latitude to determine what weight to give a tenure candidate's publications compared with teaching and service, and that the arbitrator did not exceed his authority by interpreting the contract in the university's favor.

The decision of an institution to limit arbitration of employment decisions to procedural issues rather than to the merits of the decision may persuade a court to allow a plaintiff to litigate the merits of the decision in court—at least when discrimination is alleged. In *Brennan v. King,* cited above, a faculty handbook provided for arbitration of procedural issues in tenure disputes, but specifically provided that the arbitrator was without the power to grant or deny tenure. Because the arbitration procedure did not provide "a forum for the entire resolution" of the candidate's tenure dispute, said the court, the plaintiff did not have to exhaust his arbitral remedies prior to bring a lawsuit alleging discrimination.

With respect to judicial review of an arbitration award by a state court, Pennsylvania's highest court has established a two-part test for such review. First, the issues as defined by the parties and the arbitrator must be within the terms of the collective bargaining agreement. Second, the arbitrator's award must be rationally derived from the collective bargaining agreement (*State System of Higher Education v. State College and University Professional Association,* 743 A.2d 405 (Pa. 1999)).

If an arbitration award is challenged on public policy grounds, the party seeking to overturn the award must demonstrate that the award is contrary to law or some recognized source of public policy. For example, in *Illinois Nurses Association v. Board of Trustees of the University of Illinois*, 741 N.E.2d 1014 (Ct. App. Ill. 2000), an arbitrator had reinstated a nurse who had been fired for actions that endangered patient safety. An arbitrator reinstated her because he ruled that the hospital had not proven one of the charges, and that her long seniority and otherwise good work record mitigated the severity of her misconduct. The court refused to enforce the arbitrator's award, ruling that the nurse's actions had threatened patient safety and thus her reinstatement violated public policy with respect to patient care.

Faculty and administrators should carefully weigh the benefits and challenges of ADR systems when considering whether to implement such innovations as mediation, arbitration, or the creation of a campus ombuds. Entries in the Selected Annotated Bibliography for this section provide additional information and guidelines on ADR systems in general and their applications to institutions of higher education.

Sec. 2.4. Legal Services

2.4.1. Organizational arrangements for delivery of legal services.
There are numerous organizational arrangements by which postsecondary institutions can obtain legal counsel. (See generally F. B. Manley & Co., *Provision of Legal Services: A Survey of NACUA Primary Representatives* (National Association of College and University Attorneys, 1992).) Debate continues in the academic community concerning what arrangements are most effective and cost-efficient. The issues, which are especially visible in private institutions, range from escalating legal costs, to the appropriate balance between in-house and outside counsel, to new roles and fee schedules for outside counsel, to the use of legal consultants for staff training and other special projects. (See generally G. Blumentstyk, "Shake-Ups in Campus Law Offices," *Chron. Higher Educ.*, June 8, 1994, A27.)

The arrangements for public postsecondary institutions often differ from those for private institutions. The latter have a relatively free hand in deciding whom to employ or retain as counsel and how to utilize their services, and will frequently have in-house counsel and campus-based services. Public institutions, on the other hand, may be served by the state attorney general's office or, for some community colleges, by a county or city attorney's office, rather than or in addition to in-house counsel. Other public institutions that are part of a statewide system may be served by system attorneys appointed by the system's governing authority. In either case, working relationships may vary with the state and the campus, and legal counsel may be located at an off-campus site and may serve other campuses as well. In general, administrators in such situations should seek to have services centralized in one or a small number of assistant attorneys general or other government counsel who devote a considerable portion of their time to the particular campus and become thoroughly familiar with its operations.

A public postsecondary institution's authority to obtain other counsel to supplement or displace that furnished by the state attorney general's office may be limited by the state constitution or state statutes. Where such restrictions have existed by law or tradition, public institutions have sometimes challenged the existing arrangements by hiring their own counsel to represent the institution. Most courts that have ruled on such challenges acknowledged public institutions' authority to hire counsel, usually implying this authority from the express authority to manage and operate the institution.[15]

In *Board of Trustees of the University of Illinois v. Barrett,* 46 N.E.2d 951 (Ill. 1943), for example, the board of trustees and two employees it had hired as legal counsel (Hodges and Johnson) sued the state attorney general and the state auditor of public accounts. The plaintiffs sought a judicial affirmation of the board's authority to employ independent legal counsel, as well as an order precluding the attorney general from interfering with Hodges and Johnson and an order compelling the state to pay the compensation due them. In defense, the attorney general asserted that, by virtue of his office, he was sole legal counsel for the university and its board of trustees, and that the board must obtain the attorney general's approval before hiring additional counsel. Since he did not approve of the decision to hire Hodges or Johnson, he had sought their resignations and directed the auditor of public accounts to refrain from paying their salaries.

The Supreme Court of Illinois decided that the board, a "statutory" institution (see Section 12.2.2), had authority to employ independent legal counsel without the attorney general's approval as long as the arrangement complied with the provisions of the statute creating the university and with the legislature's appropriations for its operation and management. Regarding the attorney general's powers, the court concluded that neither the state constitution nor state statutes granted the attorney general express authority to represent public institutions. Thus, the university had

> the undoubted right to employ its own counsel or engage the services of any other employees it may deem necessary or proper. . . . This power is, however, always subject to the restriction that when such faculty members or other employees are to be paid from State funds, they must be within the classifications for which funds have been appropriated and are available [46 N.E.2d at 963].

Since the legislature had not appropriated funds for Hodges and Johnson, the court refused to compel the auditor to pay their salaries. Thus, although the court recognized the board's authority to hire legal counsel, the court also recognized that the legislature had not provided them the financial means to do so.

---

[15]Questions may also arise on occasion concerning the discharge of, rather than the initial employment of, institutional counsel. For illustrative cases on a private employer's discharge of in-house counsel, see Damien Edward Okasinski, Annot., "Attorneys—Wrongful Discharge of the In-House Counsel," 16 A.L.R.5th 239; and for a good example of limitations on the employer's authority to discharge an attorney employee, see *General Dynamics Corp. v. Superior Court,* 876 P.2d 487 (Cal. Supreme Ct. 1994).

Following the *Barrett* decision, three other state courts determined that other public institutions had authority to hire independent legal counsel. Cases from Oklahoma and New Jersey concerned statutory institutions; a case from South Dakota concerned a "constitutional" governing board (see Section 12.2.3). In the Oklahoma case, a public institution was granted authority to hire independent counsel to secure an injunction to prevent individuals from fishing on a college-owned lake (*Blair v. Board of Regents for the Oklahoma Agricultural and Mechanical Colleges*, 421 P.2d 228 (Okla. 1966)). In the New Jersey case, *Frank Briscoe Co., Inc. v. Rutgers, the State University*, 327 A.2d 687 (N.J. Super Ct. Law Div. 1974), a breach of contract case defended by the state attorney general, the court determined (despite the attorney general's suggestions to the contrary) that Rutgers had a right to sue and be sued. For purposes of this issue, the court permitted Rutgers's own counsel to participate in the litigation "because the interests of a public university may be different from those of a state and thus need separate representation from the Attorney General."

In the South Dakota case, concerning a constitutional board, *Board of Regents v. Carter*, 228 N.W.2d 621 (S.D. 1975), the court reached a similar result. It authorized the board to hire independent counsel to represent its interests in a lawsuit challenging its definition of a proper employee bargaining unit. The attorney general had challenged the board of regents' authority to do so. He contended that he was the sole legal counsel for the state and that the state constitution did not grant the regents power to institute its own lawsuits or hire its own counsel. Accordingly, he claimed that any legislative attempt to grant the regents this power violated the provisions of the state constitution creating the board and granting the attorney general executive powers. In disagreeing, the court relied on the language of the state constitution granting the regents authority to control South Dakota's public educational institutions, subject to rules and restrictions promulgated by the legislature. (This right of control and the legislature's power to pass rules and restrictions was reaffirmed and explicated in *South Dakota Board of Regents v. Meierhenry*, 351 N.W.2d 450 (S.D. 1984).) Here the legislature had promulgated a statute granting the regents power "to sue and to be sued." The court held that this statute was constitutional and that, in order for the regents to exercise their right "to sue and to be sued," the regents needed the authority to hire independent counsel free from the control of the attorney general.

A later case, *State of West Virginia ex rel. Darrell V. McGraw v. Burton*, 569 S.E.2d 99 (W. Va. 2002), addresses these issues about employing counsel on a broader scale, with a somewhat better result for the state's attorney general. In this case, West Virginia's attorney general challenged the authority of all executive branch agencies and related state entities to employ independent counsel without the attorney general's approval, and he asserted that all state statutes permitting such employment of counsel were unconstitutional infringements on the attorney general's constitutional powers. The state's institutions of higher education were included in this challenge. In opposition, the state legislature asserted its constitutional authority to prescribe duties for the executive branch and to allocate funds for executive agencies, including the attorney general's office. The executive agencies and related entities asserted their need for specialized counsel to assist them with their particular areas of concern.

The court acknowledged the attorney general's broad constitutional powers and sought to balance them against the legislature's powers and the executive agencies' need for diverse and specialized legal services. Interpreting the state constitution, the court determined that the attorney general, as chief legal officer of the state, was required to address legal issues facing the state and its agencies while overseeing and maintaining consistent legal policies across agencies and governing bodies. Under separation-of-powers principles, the legislature could not interfere with the "inherent duties" of the attorney general's office and was obligated to fund the office appropriately. However, "in light of long-established statutes, practice and precedent, and the evolving needs of modern state governments," the executive agencies and related entities—including the state's higher education institutions—could continue to employ their own attorneys on certain conditions. The attorney general must be the attorney-of-record whenever a state agency is in litigation in order to uphold the constitutional duties of the office. In addition, the attorney general must continue to have the authority to intervene in litigation on behalf of the state and state's interests in order to uphold state interests and maintain consistent legal positions statewide.

Many colleges and universities now employ their own in-house staff counsel. Such an arrangement has the advantage of providing daily coordinated services of resident counsel acclimated to the particular needs and problems of the institution. Though staff attorneys can become specialists in postsecondary education law, they normally will not have the time or exposure to become expert in all the specialty areas (such as labor law, tax law, patent law, or litigation) with which institutions must deal. Thus, these institutions may sometimes retain private law firms for special problems. Other institutions, large and small, may arrange for all their legal services to be provided by one or more private law firms. This arrangement has the advantage of increasing the number of attorneys with particular expertise available for the variety of problems that confront institutions. A potential disadvantage is that no one attorney will be conversant with the full range of the institution's needs and problems or be on call daily for early participation in administrative decision making. Administrators of institutions depending on private firms may thus want to ensure that at least one lawyer is generally familiar with and involved in the institution's affairs and regularly available for consultation even on routine matters.

Whatever the organizational arrangement, and regardless of whether the institution is public or private, counsel and administrators should have clear understandings of who is the "client" to whom counsel is responsible. Generally the client is the institution's board of trustees or, for some public institutions, the state system's board of trustees or regents—the entity in which operating authority is vested (see Section 3.2.1). Counsel generally advises or represents the president, chancellor, or other officers or administrators only insofar as they are exercising authority that derives from the board of trustees. If in certain circumstances institutional personnel or institutional committees have personal interests or legal needs that may be inconsistent with those of the institution, they may have to obtain their own separate legal assistance. Depending on the situation and on institutional policy, the institution and its counsel may or may not arrange for or help them obtain such separate legal representation.

2.4.2. Treatment law and preventive law.
With each of the organizational arrangements mentioned, serious consideration must be given to the particular functions that counsel will perform and to the relationships that will be fostered between counsel and administrators. Broadly stated, counsel's role is to identify and define actual or potential legal problems and provide options for resolving or preventing them. There are two basic, and different, ways to fulfill this role: through treatment law or through preventive law. To analogize to another profession, the goal of treatment law is to cure legal diseases, while the goal of preventive law is to maintain legal health. Under either approach, counsel will be guided not only by legal considerations and institutional goals and policies, but also by the ethical standards of the legal profession that shape the responsibilities of individual practitioners to their clients and the public (see subsection 2.4.3 below; and see generally G. Hazard, Jr., "Perspective: Ethical Dilemmas of Corporate Counsel," 46 *Emory L.J.* 1011 (1997); and S. Weaver, "Perspective: Ethical Dilemmas of Corporate Counsel: A Structural and Contextual Analysis," 46 *Emory L.J.* 1023 (1997).)

Treatment law is the more traditional of the two practice approaches. It focuses on actual challenges to institutional practices and on affirmative legal steps by the institution to protect its interests when they are threatened. When suit is filed against the institution or litigation is threatened; when a government agency cites the institution for noncompliance with its regulations; when the institution needs formal permission of a government agency to undertake a proposed course of action; when the institution wishes to sue some other party— then treatment law operates. Counsel seeks to resolve the specific legal problem at hand. Treatment law today is indispensable to the functioning of a postsecondary institution, and virtually all institutions have such legal service.

Preventive law, in contrast, focuses on initiatives that the institution can take before actual legal disputes arise. Preventive law involves administrators and counsel in a continual cooperative process of setting the legal and policy parameters within which the institution will operate to forestall or minimize legal disputes. Counsel identifies the legal consequences of proposed actions; pinpoints the range of alternatives for avoiding problems and the legal risks of each alternative; sensitizes administrators and the campus community to legal issues and the importance of recognizing them early; determines the impact of new or proposed laws and regulations, and new court decisions, on institutional operations; and helps devise internal processes that support constructive relationships among members of the campus community. Prior to the 1980s, preventive law was not a general practice of postsecondary institutions. But this approach became increasingly valuable as the presence of law on the campus increased, and acceptance of preventive law within postsecondary education grew substantially. Today preventive law is as indispensable as treatment law and provides the more constructive overall posture from which to conduct institutional legal affairs.

Institutions using or considering the use of preventive law face some difficult questions. To what extent will administrators and counsel give priority to
the practice of preventive law? Which institutional administrators will have
direct access to counsel? Will counsel advise only administrators, or will he or
she also be available to recognized faculty or student organizations or committees, or perhaps to other members of the university community on certain matters? What working arrangements will ensure that administrators are alert to
incipient legal problems and that counsel is involved in institutional decision
making at an early stage? What degree of autonomy will counsel have to influence institutional decision making, and what authority will counsel have to halt
legally unwise institutional action?

The following eight steps are suggested for administrators and counsel seeking to implement a preventive law system:[16]

1. *Review the institution's current organizational arrangements for obtaining legal counsel and implementing legal advice, seeking to maximize their
effectiveness.* Evaluate the legal needs of the various campus officers, administrators, and committees. Determine whether the needs are best met by in-
house counsel, outside counsel, or some combination of the two. If there is
in-house counsel, seek to assure that the office has adequate staff and
resources to practice effective treatment law, *as well as to initiate and maintain preventive law measures* such as those discussed following. Be sure that
counsel has access to key officers, administrators, and faculty leaders who
will serve as legal planning partners. Such a review can be effective, of
course, only if key institutional leaders understand the role and value of legal
counsel. A portion of the review process should therefore be devoted to
discussions designed to promote such understanding and a widely shared
commitment to provide suitable resources for legal planning.

For small institutions that may not now have an institutional legal counsel, the
focus should be on evaluating the institutional need for counsel and for preventive legal planning; and then on developing a strategy employing in-house counsel (at least part time) or executing a retainer agreement with a law firm.

2. *Encourage strong working relationships among the institution's attorneys,
administrators, and faculty, cultivating conditions within which they can cooperate with one another in preventive planning.* Preventive law will be effective
only if the leadership is committed to its practice, starting with the president or
chancellor and his or her top executive officers, including the general counsel.
The institution's leadership team thus should not only react to crisis situations
and other pressing concerns, but also should work cooperatively and creatively
on strategic and preventive planning. Shared responsibility and accountability

---

[16]These eight steps are adapted from Kathleen Curry Santora & William Kaplin, "Preventive Law:
How Colleges Can Avoid Legal Problems," *Chron. Higher Educ.,* April 18, 2003, B20 (copyright
©2004 by Chronicle of Higher Education, Inc.), which in turn was adapted in part from a set of
seven steps published in Section 1.7.2 of the 1995 third edition of this book.

among the members of the leadership team, as well as other institutional officers and committees, is essential to preventive planning.

Since the dividing line between the administrator's and the lawyer's functions is not always self-evident, roles should be developed through mutual interchange between the two sets of professionals. While considerable flexibility is possible, institutions should be careful to maintain a distinction between the two roles. The purpose of preventive law is not to make the administrator into a lawyer or the lawyer into an administrator. It is the lawyer's job to resolve doubts about the interpretation of statutes, regulations, and court decisions; to stay informed of legal developments and predict the directions in which law is evolving; and to suggest legal options and advise on their relative effectiveness in achieving the institution's goals. In contrast, it is the administrator's job (and that of the board of trustees) to stay informed of developments in the theory and practice of administration; to devise policy options within the constraints imposed by law and determine their relative effectiveness in achieving institutional goals; and ultimately, at the appropriate level of the institutional hierarchy, to make the policy decisions that give life to the institution.

Alleviating administrators' and faculty members' concerns about *personal* legal liability will also further cooperative and creative working relationships. Indemnity arrangements and suitable insurance coverages are key strategies here, requiring close cooperation between counsel and the institution's risk manager. Appropriate training (discussed in points 3 and 4 following) can also contribute substantially to alleviating concerns.

3. *Arrange training for administrators, staff, and faculty members that focuses on the legal aspects of their professional responsibilities and the legal implications of their actions; be prepared to commit adequate resources to support such training; and also provide similar training for student leaders.* Regular and consistent training is a critical aspect of preventive planning. Many counsel at prevention-oriented institutions now hold campus workshops for administrators, faculty, and staff on issues such as sexual harassment, disabilities, records management, public safety, or entrepreneurial activities. They also provide timely legal information through Web sites, newsletters, and memos to clients.

Management workshops for new deans and department chairs, or periodic workshops for middle managers, or counseling sessions for the staff of a particular office would be examples of such training. The institution's legal staff may conduct training sessions, or they may be provided on or off site by third parties. In conjunction with such training, the institution should ensure the availability of relevant and up-to-date legal information for administrators, through distribution of one or more of the newsletters and periodicals available from outside sources, or through legal counsel memos crafted to the particular circumstances of the institution.

Many institutions also provide training for student groups, such as student resident advisors in residence halls, student members of judicial boards, editors of student newspapers and journals, students who conduct freshman and parent orientation, and students who run summer conference programs and summer camps.

Remember that such training and information dissemination requires resources. These activities are not likely to occur if, due to inadequate resources, the institutional counsel is barely keeping pace with curing legal problems. An additional allocation of resources may therefore be necessary. In addition, seek to conserve resources by taking advantage of opportunities to disseminate information expeditiously through the use of technology. Also take advantage of the various continuing education programs in higher education law and policy that are held each year in locations throughout the nation.

4. *Provide additional training for the institution's various compliance officers, who are partners in identifying early warning signs of litigation, and empower them in their relationships with counsel.* Additional training should be available periodically for compliance officers, focusing on the legal aspects of their particular areas of responsibility. Counsel should also work closely with compliance officers to help them to identify early warning signs of litigation or compliance complaints from government agencies. The relationship between compliance officers and counsel should be one that encourages cooperation and coordination in the preventive law process.

Compliance officers have traditionally included those who ensure legal compliance in areas such as equal employment opportunity, environmental safety, employee health and safety standards, and human subjects research. But many other managers also have substantial responsibility for measuring compliance with federal, state, or local regulations—the disability services office, the campus security office, the registrar, the financial aid office, and human resources officers, among others. All should be included.

Training for compliance officers can help instill high levels of ethical commitment to compliance, assist compliance officers in understanding the technical and specialized legal aspects of their work, and help develop arrangements for obtaining specialized legal interpretations from outside counsel.

5. *Perform regular audits of the legal health of the institution and develop an early warning system to identify legal risks.* A legal audit is a legal "checkup" to determine the legal "health" of the institution. A complete audit would include a survey of every office and function in the institution. For each office and function, the lawyer-administrator team would develop the information and analysis necessary to determine whether that office or function is in compliance with the full range of legal constraints to which it is subject.

Attorneys should work closely with the institution's compliance officers, the institution's risk manager and risk management teams or committees (see Section 2.5.1 below), and other administrators and committees, to assess the institution's legal health by analyzing whether key campus offices are in compliance with legal requirements. While this can be a daunting task due to the myriad statutory, regulatory, and court-imposed requirements that now apply to higher education institutions, and the ever-increasing complexity of relationships with third parties, the exercise is an essential first step to preventive planning. For public institutions in states with strong open-records laws, this function must be undertaken with care, since such audits could be subject to disclosure to regulatory or law enforcement authorities.

To supplement legal audits, develop an early warning system that will apprise counsel and administrators of potential legal problems in their incipiency. The early warning system should be based on a list of situations that are likely to create significant legal risk for the institution. Such a list might include the following: an administrator is revising a standard form contract used by the institution or creating a new standard form contract to cover a type of transaction for which the institution has not previously used such a contract; administrators are reviewing the institution's code of student conduct, student bill of rights, or similar documents; a school or department is seeking to terminate a faculty member's tenure; a committee is drafting or modifying an affirmative action plan; administrators are preparing policies to implement a new set of federal administrative regulations; or administrators are proposing a new security system for the campus or temporary security measures for a particular emergency. Under an early warning system, all such circumstances, or others that the institution may specify, would trigger a consultative process between administrator and counsel aimed at resolving legal problems before they erupt into disputes.

Whenever the institution is sued, or administrators or faculty members are sued for matters concerning their institutional responsibilities, the institution should also perform a "post-litigation audit" after the lawsuit is resolved, seeking to determine how similar suits could be prevented in the future. Similarly, whenever there is a crisis or tragedy on campus, the institution should perform a "post-crisis audit" after the crisis ends, seeking to determine how such a crisis and its attendant legal risks could be prevented in the future.

6. *Use the information gathered through the legal compliance audits, the early warning system, and the post-litigation and post-crisis audits to engage the campus community in a continuing course of legal planning.* Legal planning is the process by which the institution determines the extent of legal risk exposure it is willing to assume in particular situations, and develops strategies for avoiding or resolving legal risks it is not willing to assume. In addition to legal considerations, legal planning encompasses ethical, administrative, and financial considerations, as well as the institution's policy preferences and priorities. Sometimes the law may be in tension with institutional policy; legal planners then may seek to devise alternative means for achieving a particular policy objective consistent with the law. Often, however, the law will be consistent with institutional policy; legal planners then may use the law to support and strengthen the institution's policy choices and may, indeed, implement initiatives more extensive than the law would require. Successful legal planning thus depends on a careful sorting out and interrelating of legal and policy issues, which in turn depends upon teamwork between administrators and counsel. (Regarding the relationship between law and policy, see Section 1.7.) Teamwork between administrator and lawyer is therefore a critical ingredient in legal planning. Sensitivity to the authority structure of the institution (see Section 3.1) and its established decision-making processes are also critical ingredients, so that legal planning decisions are made at the appropriate levels of authority and according to the prescribed processes.

7. *For the inevitable percentage of potential legal problems that do develop into actual disputes, establish internal grievance mechanisms, including nonadversarial processes such as mediation, to help forestall formal legal action.* The goal is to have accessible internal mechanisms for the collegial and constructive resolution of disputes among members of the campus community. Such mechanisms may also forestall resort to litigation and provide a potential alternative avenue for settlement even after litigation is under way. Such mechanisms—ranging from informal consultations to mediation to formal hearing panels—may be adapted to the particular characteristics and needs of academic institutions. In addition, institutions themselves must set a good example in the way they handle their own claims, and should seek alternative means of resolving disputes so as to avoid lawsuits when feasible and maintain rather than disrupt relationships when possible.

Whatever techniques are adopted should be generally available to students, faculty, and staff members who have complaints concerning actions taken against them by other members of the academic community. Some summary procedure should be devised for dismissing complaints that are frivolous or that contest general academic policy rather than a particular action that has harmed the complainant. Not every dispute, of course, is amenable to internal solution, since many disputes involve outside parties (such as business firms, government agencies, or professional associations). But for disputes among members of the campus community, grievance mechanisms provide an on-campus forum that can be attuned to the particular characteristics of academic institutions.

8. *Encourage campus leaders to work together to develop a campus culture that encourages, values, and takes particular satisfaction in the constructive resolution of conflict.* Such a campus culture is built on the basic values of fairness, respect, collegiality, inclusiveness, and civility. Promoting such values through community building is thus a critical element of any plan for constructive dispute resolution and a critical adjunct to preventive law planning. When we build community, we naturally have a less litigious and legalistic environment. We enable members of the campus community to resolve disputes in a manner that maintains rather than destroys relationships. The campus leadership team, including the institution's legal counsel, sets the tone and helps to create this type of environment. Everyone has a stake in the success of the community.

Legal disputes are expensive, not only in terms of dollars and cents, but also in terms of the amount of time spent and the emotional costs to all those involved. Lawsuits can divert higher education from its primary mission of teaching, research, and service. But by following the steps outlined above, institutions can avoid such negative consequences and achieve positive outcomes instead. The resources that college and university leaders invest in preventive legal planning and in community building will be well worth the price if the result is an institution that can focus constructively on fulfilling its mission and preserving its values.

2.4.3. Ethical issues. In their professional dealings with clients, attorneys are subject not only to legal but also to ethical standards. Ethical standards are embodied in the ethics (or "professional responsibility") codes and the rules of court of the various states. There are ethical rules, for instance, concerning attorney conflicts of interest. These rules have particular applicability in situations where counsel represents more than one party and these parties' legal claims or objectives may be opposed to one another. For example, a university and several of its administrators may be joined as defendants in the same lawsuit, or may all be likely defendants in a potential lawsuit, and the defenses that one administrator may seek to assert are in conflict with those of another. Counsel for the university then must decide whether the situation presents an actual or a potential conflict of interest, requiring that other attorneys not associated with the original counsel represent one or more of the individual defendants.

Another example of ethical standards concerns the confidentiality of communications between attorneys and their clients. (For a discussion of the attorney-client privilege, see Section 2.2.3.3.) But this privilege does not apply to all communications between university counsel and university employees. In *Ross v. Medical University of South Carolina*, 453 S.E.2d 880 (S.C. 1994), for example, the South Carolina Supreme Court refused to apply the privilege to certain *ex parte* communications between the university's general counsel and a university vice president in the context of an internal grievance proceeding. The court determined that the vice president, in the particular circumstances of the grievance proceeding, was not a "client" of the general counsel, and that the general counsel was not an "attorney" for the vice president but rather for another "client" (the university itself). Thus, the necessary preconditions for assertion of the privilege did not exist, and the university was required to divulge relevant information concerning the communications between the counsel and the vice president.

Sec. 2.5. Institutional Management of Liability Risk

2.5.1. Overview and suggestions. The risk of financial liability for injury to another party remains a major concern for postsecondary institutions as well as their officers, faculties, and other personnel. This section examines various methods for managing such risk exposure and thus minimizing the detrimental effects of liability on the institution and members of the campus community. Risk management may be advisable not only because it helps stabilize the institution's financial condition over time but also because it can improve the morale and performance of institutional personnel by alleviating their concerns about potential personal liability. In addition, risk management can implement the institution's humanistic concern for minimizing the potential

for injuries to innocent third parties resulting from its operations, and for compensating any such injuries that do occur.

The major methods of risk management may be called risk avoidance, risk control, risk transfer, and risk retention. (See generally J. Adams & J. Hall, "Legal Liabilities in Higher Education: Their Scope and Management" (Part II), 3 *J. Coll. & Univ. Law* 335, 360–69 (1976).) For risk transfer, there are three subcategories of methods: liability insurance, indemnity (or "hold-harmless") agreements, and releases (or waivers).

Institutions should find it helpful to develop these various methods of risk management, and strategies for their implementation, into a campus risk management plan. A key component of any such plan is a professional risk manager or an office of risk management that provides a focal point for the institution's risk management efforts. The institution's legal counsel should also be involved in all phases of risk management. Another helpful organizational device would be an institution-wide risk management team or committee, which may also include school-level or division-level coordinators or teams. Risk assessment should be an essential aspect of any risk management plan. For some institutions, external consultants may be an important source of assistance in undertaking a comprehensive assessment of institutional risks or periodically updating this assessment. Risk assessment teams from within various sectors of the institution may also be helpful. (For additional guidance and resources, see the Web site of the University Risk Management and Insurance Association, at http://www.URMIA.org.)

2.5.2. Risk avoidance and risk control. The most certain method for managing a known exposure to liability is risk avoidance—the elimination of conditions, activities, or programs that are the sources of the risks. This method is often not realistic, however, since it could require institutions to forgo activities important to their educational missions. It might also require greater knowledge of the details of myriad campus activities than administrators typically can acquire and greater certainty about the legal principles of liability (see Sections 3.3–3.5 & 4.7) than the law typically affords.

Risk control is less drastic than risk avoidance. The goal is to reduce, rather than eliminate entirely, the frequency or severity of potential exposures to liability—mainly by improving the physical environment or by modifying hazardous behavior or activities in ways that reduce the recognized risks. Although this method may have less impact on an institution's educational mission than would risk avoidance, it may similarly require considerable detailed knowledge of campus facilities and functions and of legal liability principles.

Risk assessments (see subsection 2.5.1 above) are critical to the implementation of risk avoidance and control strategies. Risk assessment teams would therefore be an important organizational device to use with these methods of risk management. Another important organizational device is a crisis management team to manage institution-wide crises, along with other smaller teams to deal with particular crises affecting an individual or a small number of individuals (for example, a mental health crisis).

2.5.3. Risk transfer

2.5.3.1. Liability insurance. Purchasing commercial liability insurance is the first way in which institutions can transfer the risk of liability to others. An institution can insure against liability for its own acts, as well as liability transferred to it by a "hold-harmless" agreement with its personnel (see Section 2.5.3.2). With the advice of insurance experts, the institution can determine the kinds and amounts of liability protection it needs and provide for the necessary premium expenditures in its budgeting process.

There are two basic types of insurance policies important to higher education institutions. The first and primary type is general liability insurance; it provides broad coverage of bodily injury and property damage claims, such as would arise in the case of a negligently caused injury to a student or staff member. The second type is directors and officers insurance ("D & O" coverage, or sometimes "errors and omissions" coverage). It typically covers claims for wrongful acts without bodily injury, such as employment claims, student discipline, and due process violations.

General liability insurance policies usually exclude from their coverage both intentionally or maliciously caused damage and damage caused by acts that violate penal laws. In *Brooklyn Law School v. Aetna Casualty and Surety Co.*, 849 F.2d 788 (2d Cir. 1988), for example, the school had incurred numerous costs in defending itself against a lawsuit in which a former professor alleged that the school, its trustees, and faculty members had intentionally conspired to violate his constitutional rights. The school sued its insurer—which insured the school under an umbrella policy—to recover its costs in defending against the professor's suit. The appellate court held that, under New York law, the insurer was not required to defend the insured against such a suit, which alleged intentional harm, when the policy terms expressly excluded from coverage injuries caused by the insured's intentional acts.

Liability arising from the violation of an individual's constitutional or civil rights is also commonly excluded from general liability insurance coverage—an exclusion that can pose considerable problems for administrators and institutions, whose exposure to such liability has escalated greatly since the 1960s. In specific cases, questions about this exclusion may become entwined with questions concerning intent or malice. In *Andover Newton Theological School, Inc. v. Continental Casualty Company*, 930 F.2d 89 (1st Cir. 1991), the defendant insurance company had refused to pay on the school's claim after a court had found that the school violated the Age Discrimination in Employment Act (ADEA) (this volume, Section 5.2.6) when it dismissed a tenured, sixty-two-year-old professor. The jury in the professor's case found that the school had impermissibly considered the professor's age in deciding to dismiss him, but the evidence did not clearly establish that the school's administrators had acted deliberately. Under the ADEA, behavior by the school that showed "reckless disregard" for the law was enough to sustain the verdict against it. When the school sought to have its insurance carrier pay the judgment, the insurer objected on grounds that it is against Massachusetts public policy (and that of most other states) to insure against intentional or deliberate conduct of the insured. The district court agreed and held the school's loss to be uninsurable.

On appeal, the appellate court reasoned that the school's suit against the insurer revolved around the following question:

> Does a finding of willfulness under the Age Discrimination in Employment Act (ADEA), if based on a finding of "reckless disregard as to whether [defendant's] conduct is prohibited by federal law," constitute "deliberate or intentional . . . wrongdoing" such as to preclude indemnification by an insurer under the public policy of Massachusetts as codified at Mass. Gen. L. ch. 175, section 47 Sixth (b)? [930 F.2d at 91.]

The appellate court certified this question to the Massachusetts Supreme Judicial Court, which answered in the negative. The federal appellate court then reversed the federal district court's decision and remanded the case to that court for further proceedings. The appellate court reasoned that, since the jury verdict did not necessitate a conclusion that the school had acted intentionally or deliberately, the losses incurred by the school were insurable and payment would not contravene public policy.[17]

Exclusions from coverage, as in the previous examples, may exist either because state law requires the exclusion (see subsection 2.5.5 below) or because the insurer has made its own business decision to exclude certain actions from its standard coverages. When the exclusion is of the latter type, institutions may nevertheless be able to cover such risks by combining a standard policy with one or more specialty endorsements or companion policies, such as a directors and officers policy. If this arrangement still does not provide all the coverage the institution desires, and if the institution can afford the substantial expense, it may request a "manuscript" policy tailored to its specific needs.

2.5.3.2. Hold-harmless and indemnification agreements. A second method of risk transfer is a "hold-harmless" or indemnification agreement, by which institutions can transfer their liability risks to other parties or transfer to themselves the liability risks of their officers or employees or other parties. In a broad sense, the term "indemnification" refers to any compensation for loss or damage. Insurance is thus one method of indemnifying someone. But in the narrower sense used here, indemnification refers to an arrangement whereby one party (for example, the institution) agrees to hold another party (for example, an individual officer or employee) harmless from financial liability for certain acts or omissions of that party that cause damage to another:

---

[17]On remand, the district court decided for the school, and the insurance company appealed (*Andover Newton Theological School, Inc. v. Continental Casualty Co.*, 964 F.2d 1237 (1st Cir. 1992)). The company challenged a number of the district court's actions: holding a hearing to determine whether the school had deliberately violated federal law in dismissing the professor; placing the burden of proving deliberateness on the insurance company; and finding that the officers of the school did not act with knowledge that their conduct was illegal. The appellate court rejected all these challenges and upheld the district court.

> In brief synopsis, the mechanism of a typical indemnification will shift to the institution the responsibility for defense and discharge of claims asserted against institutional personnel individually by reason of their acts or omissions on behalf of the institution, if the individual believed in good faith that his actions were lawful and within his institutional authority and responsibility. That standard of conduct is, of course, very broadly stated; and the question of whether or not it is satisfied must be determined on a case-by-case basis [R. Aiken, "Legal Liabilities in Higher Education: Their Scope and Management" (Part I), 3 *J. Coll. & Univ. Law* 121, 313 (1976)].

Institutions may also hold outside parties harmless from liability in certain circumstances, or be asked to do so. This matter is most likely to arise with parties that have some kind of professional affiliation (for example, for internship placements) or ongoing business relationship with the institution. Administrators and legal counsel should carefully review any indemnification clauses that outside parties place in proposed contracts with the institution. In particular, institutional personnel should be wary of signing vendor form contracts containing "boilerplate" clauses that would require the institution to indemnify the vendor.

Besides being an "indemnitor"—that is, the party with ultimate financial liability—the institution can sometimes also be an "indemnitee," the party protected from liability loss. The institution could negotiate for "hold-harmless" protection for itself, for instance, in contracts it enters with outside contractors or lessees. In an illustrative case, *Bridston v. Dover Corp. and University of North Dakota v. Young Men's Christian Association,* 352 N.W.2d 194 (N.D. 1984), the university had leased a campus auditorium to a dance group. One of the group's members was injured during practice, allegedly because of the negligence of a university employee, and sued the university for damages. The university invoked an indemnity clause in the lease agreement and successfully avoided liability by arguing that the clause required the lessee to hold the university harmless even for negligent acts of the university's own employees.

Like insurance policies, indemnification agreements often do not cover liability resulting from intentional or malicious action or from action violating the state's penal laws. Just as public policy may limit the types of acts or omissions that may be insured against, it may also limit those for which indemnification may be received.

Both public and private institutions may enter indemnification agreements. A public institution, however, may need specific authorizing legislation (see, for example, Mich. Comp. Laws § 691.1408), while private institutions usually can rely on the general laws of their states for sufficient authority. Some states also provide for indemnification of state employees for injuries caused by their acts or omissions on behalf of the state (see, for example, Cal. Govt. Code § 995 *et seq.*) or for torts committed within the scope of their employment (see, for example, Ill. Code, 5 ILCS 350(2)(d)).

In *Chasin v. Montclair State University,* 732 A.2d 457 (N.J. 1999), the New Jersey Supreme Court addressed the extent of the state's obligation to defend and indemnify state university professors (and other state employees) who have been sued. The dispute in this case began in fall 1990 at the onset of the United States' involvement in the Persian Gulf in Operation Desert Storm. In order to provide academic relief for college students called to active duty in that war, the New Jersey legislature enacted the "Desert Storm Law," 1991 N.J. Sess. Law Serv. Ch. 167 (3196) (W). The law entitled New Jersey students who were called to active duty "to receive a grade in each course for which the student has completed a minimum of 8 weeks' attendance and all other academic requirements during that period." These grades were "to be based on the work completed up to the time when the student was called to active service." At Montclair State University, a student called to active duty as a reservist sought to utilize the statute to receive a grade in Professor Chasin's course in "Sociology of Rich and Poor Nations." The student had achieved an A average at the point in the semester at which he was called away. Prior to the legislature's enactment of the statute, however, the student and the professor had entered into an "Incomplete Contract," by which the student agreed to complete the course through either a make-up final exam or an additional paper. When the student attempted to assert his right under the legislation, the professor refused to give the student a grade, despite advice from the deputy state attorney general and the provost of the university. When the student then took legal action against the professor, the attorney general refused to defend the professor. After the suit was settled, the professor demanded indemnification from the attorney general for her legal expenses.

The court first analyzed the professor's claim in relation to the attorney general's duty to defend an employee of the state, as set out in the New Jersey Tort Claims Act (NJTCA), N.J. Stat. Ann., tit. 59, Chap. 10A-1&2:

> Except as [otherwise] provided, the Attorney General shall, upon request of an employee or former employee of the State, provide for the defense of any action brought against such State employee or former State employee on account of an act or omission in the scope of his employment.
> The Attorney General may refuse to defend an employee, however, when:
>
> a. the act or omission was not within the scope of employment; or
>
> b. the act or failure to act was because of actual fraud, willful misconduct or actual malice; or
>
> c. the defense of the action or proceeding by the Attorney General would create a conflict of interest between the State and the employee or former employee.

Looking at the statute's history and purpose, the court determined that the statute only required the attorney general to defend suits seeking tort damages. Since the claim against the professor was one for injunctive relief, the court determined that the attorney general's obligation to defend the suit was discretionary rather than mandatory. The court further concluded that, because the professor was not entitled to legal assistance, she also was not entitled to indemnification. In the alternative, the court also held that the professor had disregarded advice of the attorney general when she refused to award the grade.

The NJTCA requires that the state employee "cooperate fully with the Attorney General's defense" (N.J. Stat. Ann., tit. 59, Chap. 10A-4). Since the provost and the attorney general had advised the professor to grant the student the grade in accordance with the Desert Storm Law and had provided her copies of the law, she had surrendered her right to indemnification. Two judges dissented.

State laws on defense and indemnification are often general, like the New Jersey law interpreted in the *Chasin* case, and may vary considerably from state to state. To have a sound and clear institutional policy, adapted to the academic environment, public institutions may need to expand upon applicable state law. (For one view of what such an institutional policy should provide, see the AAUP statement on "Institutional Responsibility for Legal Demands on Faculty," in *AAUP Policy Documents and Reports* (9th ed., 2001), 130.)

2.5.3.3. Releases and waivers. A third method of risk transfer is the release or waiver agreement. This type of arrangement releases one party from liability to another for injuries arising from some particular undertaking in which both parties are involved. In postsecondary education, this mechanism is most likely to be used for student activities and services, such as intercollegiate athletics, provision of medical services, study abroad programs, and student field trips, which involve acknowledged risks. In such circumstances, the institution may require the student to execute a release or waiver as a precondition to participation in the activity or receipt of the service. The *Porubiansky, Tunkl,* and *Wagenblast* cases, as well as *Kyriazis*—all discussed in Section 2.5.5—illustrate both the uses of releases and other substantial legal limitations on their use. For such a release to be valid, as the court emphasized in *Kyriazis v. West Virginia University,* 450 S.E.2d 649 (W. Va. 1994) (discussed further below), the student must have voluntarily exposed himself to the danger "with full knowledge and appreciation of its existence." The student in that case had signed a release as a condition of playing rugby. In the litigation, he asserted that he had no previous experience with the sport and had signed the release before "participating in a scrimmage" or observing a match, and that "the risks of injury were not explained to him." It was therefore unlikely that he "fully appreciated the attendant risks of club rugby," thus casting doubt on the validity of the release.

Postsecondary institutions may also use "consent forms" for certain activities or services, for example, a form securing a consent to a particular medical treatment, or consent for the institution to authorize medical treatment on the participant's or recipient's behalf. Consent forms are not the same as releases and will not have the legal effect of a release unless clear exculpatory language, like that used in releases, is added to the consent form. Absent such exculpatory clauses, use of a consent form may actually increase, rather than decrease, an institution's potential liability. In *Fay v. Thiel College,* 2001 WL 1910037 (Pa. 2001), for example, the college had had students sign medical consent forms before participating in a study abroad trip. The form authorized the college's representatives to secure medical treatment in case of emergency. The plaintiff, a student who became ill on the trip and was left behind for medical treatment at a medical clinic, alleged that she had received unnecessary surgery and been sexually assaulted at the clinic. The court held that the consent form created a "special relationship" between the college and the student and that, due to this relationship, the college owed the student a "special duty of care" regarding medical treatment while she was on the trip. The court therefore denied the college's motion for summary judgment and ordered a jury trial on whether the college had breached this duty.

2.5.4. Risk retention. The most practical option for the institution in some circumstances may be to retain the risk of financial liability. Risk retention may be appropriate, for instance, in situations where commercial insurance is unavailable or too costly, the expected losses are so small that they can be considered normal operating expenses, or the probability of loss is so remote that it does not justify any insurance expense (see Adams & Hall, "Legal Liabilities in Higher Education," subsection 2.5.1 above, at 361–63). Both insurance policy deductibles and methods of self-insurance are examples of risk retention. The deductible amounts in an insurance policy allocate the first dollar coverage of liability, up to the amount of the deductible, to the institution. The institution becomes a self-insurer by maintaining a separate bank account to pay appropriate claims. The institution's risk managers must determine the amount to be available in the account and the frequency and amount of regular payments to the account. This approach is distinguished from simple noninsurance by the planning and actuarial calculations that it involves.

2.5.5. Legal limits on authority to transfer risk. An institution's ability to transfer risk is generally limited under state law to situations that do not contravene "public policy." When financial liability is incurred as a result of willful wrongdoing, it is usually considered contrary to public policy to protect the institution or individual from responsibility for such behavior through insurance, indemnity agreements, or releases. Wrongdoing that is malicious, fraudulent, immoral, or criminal will generally fall within this category. Thus, insurance companies may decline to cover such behavior, and if they do cover it, courts may declare such coverage to be void and unenforceable. If protection against willful wrongdoing is provided by an indemnity agreement or release, courts may invalidate such provisions as well. Behaviors to which this public policy usually will apply include assault and battery, abuse of process, defamation, and invasion of privacy. This public policy may also apply to intentional deprivations of constitutional or civil rights; when the deprivation is unintentional, however, a transfer of risk may not violate public policy (see, for example, *Solo Cup Co. v. Federal Insurance Co.*, 619 F.2d 1178 (7th Cir. 1980)).

Public policy may also prohibit agreements insuring against financial loss from punitive damage awards. Jurisdictions differ on whether such insurance coverage is proscribed. Some courts have prohibited coverage because it would defeat the two purposes served by punitive damages: punishment for egregious wrongdoing and deterrence of future misconduct (see, for example, *Hartford Accident and Indemnity Co. v. Village of Hempstead*, 397 N.E.2d 737 (N.Y. 1979)). Other courts have permitted coverage at least when punitive damages are awarded as the result of gross negligence or wanton and reckless conduct rather than intentional wrongdoing (see, for example, *Hensley v. Erie Insurance Co.*, 283 S.E.2d 227 (W. Va. 1981)).[18]

Depending on their state's public policy, institutions may also be prohibited in some circumstances from using releases, waivers, or similar contractual agreements to transfer the risk of *ordinary negligence* (as opposed to willful wrongdoing) to the parties who would be harmed by the negligent acts. In *Emory University v. Porubiansky*, 282 S.E.2d 903 (Ga. 1981), for example, the Emory University School of Dentistry Clinic sought to insulate itself from negligence suits by inserting into its consent form a clause indicating that the patient waived all claims against the university or its agents. The Georgia Supreme Court voided the agreement as offensive to public policy because it purported to relieve state-licensed professional practitioners of a duty to exercise reasonable care in dealing with patients. Sometimes it may be difficult to determine what the state's public policy is and in what circumstances it will be deemed to be contravened by a risk transfer arrangement. The case of *Wagenblast v. Odessa School District*, 758 P.2d 968 (Wash. 1988), provides useful guidelines for making these determinations. In this case, the Supreme Court of Washington invalidated school district policies requiring that, as a condition of participating in interscholastic athletics, students and their parents sign standardized forms releasing the school district from liability for negligence. The court based its decision on the earlier case of *Tunkl v. Regents of University of California*, 383 P.2d 441 (Cal. 1963), thus suggesting that the legal principles from *Wagenblast* apply to higher education as well. *Tunkl* involved an action by a hospital patient against a charitable hospital operated by the defendant university. Upon his admission to the hospital, Tunkl signed a document releasing the regents and the hospital from any and all liability for negligent or wrongful acts or omissions of its employees. The California Supreme Court invalidated this release agreement, relying on a state statute that prohibited certain agreements exempting a person from his own fraud, willful injury to another, or violation of law. Such agreements were invalid if they were contrary to the public interest, which the *Tunkl* court determined by considering six factors that it had consolidated from previous cases: (1) whether the agreement concerned an endeavor suitable for public regulation; (2) whether the party seeking exculpation offered a service of public importance or necessity; (3) whether that party held itself out as willing to perform the service for any member of the public, or anyone who met predetermined standards; (4) whether that party possessed a bargaining advantage over members of the public desiring the service; (5) whether the release provision was in the nature of an adhesion contract (see Section 8.1.3, and see also *Fay v. Thiel College*, 2001 WL 1910037 (Pa. 2001)) that did not contain any option for the other party to obtain protection against negligence by paying an extra fee; and (6) whether the party seeking exculpation would be able to exert control over persons seeking its services, thus subjecting these persons to risk. The more these factors are implicated in a

---

[18]The cases are collected in Michael A. Rosenhouse, Annot., "Liability Insurance Coverage as Extending to Liability for Punitive or Exemplary Damages," 16 A.L.R.4th 11.

release agreement, the more likely it is that a court will declare the agreement invalid on public policy grounds.

Even though the Washington court in *Wagenblast* had no statute similar to California's to rely on, it nevertheless used a public policy approach similar to that of the California court and adopted the six *Tunkl* factors. Noting that all six factors applied to the releases being challenged, the court invalidated the releases.

The court in *Kyriazis v. West Virginia University,* 450 S.E.2d 649 (W. Va. 1994), also relied heavily on the *Tunkl* case (above), which the court called "the leading case on the issue whether an anticipatory release violates public policy under the 'public service' exception." In *Kyriazis,* the West Virginia Supreme Court of Appeals invalidated an "anticipatory release" that the university required students to sign before playing rugby, a club sport. The court's opinion provides useful explication of criteria 2, 4, and 5 from *Tunkl.* Applying criterion 2, the court determined that "[w]hen a state university provides recreational activities to its students, it fulfills its educational mission, and performs a public service. As an enterprise charged with a duty of public service here, the university owes a duty of due care to its students when it encourages them to participate in any sport" (450 S.E.2d at 654–55). Applying criteria 4 and 5 (450 S.E.2d at 655), the court examined whether the release was "an agreement that was freely and fairly made between parties who are in an equal bargaining position" and determined that it was not (450 S.E.2d at 655). The court therefore concluded that "[b]ecause . . . the university qualifies as a 'public service,' and [because] it possessed a decisive bargaining advantage over the [student] when he executed the Release, we find the anticipatory Release void as a matter of West Virginia public policy."[19]

This common law/public policy approach to releases, encapsulated in the six factors borrowed from *Tunkl,* as further refined in *Wagenblast* and *Kyriazis,* provides an analytical framework for determining whether and when higher education institutions may use releases or waivers of liability to transfer risk to the potential victims of the institution's negligence. Some states' public policy, however, will be more supportive of the use of releases than that of other states. (See, for example, *Sharon v. City of Newton,* 769 N.E.2d 738 (Mass. 2002).) The emphasis placed on various *Tunkl* factors, and the use of supplementary factors, may therefore vary from state to state, depending on the development of each state's statutory and common law. The specific results reached when the *Tunkl/Wagenblast* framework is applied may also vary with the particular circumstances, including the activity for which the release is to be used; the persons for whom the release is sought (students, institutional employees, or outside third parties); and perhaps the type of institution using the release (whether it is a public or a private institution).

---

[19]In another portion of its opinion (450 S.E.2d at 655–57), the court also held that the release "violates the equal protection guarantee under the West Virginia Constitution" because the university required club sports participants to sign the release but did not require intramural sports participants to do the same.

A different kind of legal problem may exist for postsecondary institutions that enjoy some degree of sovereign or charitable immunity from financial liability (see Section 3.3.1). Public institutions may not have authority to purchase liability insurance covering acts within the scope of their immunity. Where such authority does exist, however, and the institution does purchase insurance, its sovereign or charitable immunity may thereby be affected. Sometimes a statute authorizing insurance coverage may itself waive sovereign immunity to the extent of coverage. When such a waiver is lacking, in most states the purchase of insurance appears not to affect immunity, and the insurance protection is operable only for acts found to be outside the scope of immunity. In some states, however, courts appear to treat the authorized purchase of insurance as a waiver or narrowing of the institution's immunity, to the extent of the insurance coverage.[20]

Selected Annotated Bibliography

Sec. 2.1 *(Legal Liability)*

Hynes, J. Dennis. *Agency, Partnership, and the LLC in a Nutshell* (2d ed., West, 2001). Discusses principles of agency law, including principal-agent relationships, agency law as applied to boards of directors, duties of principals and agents to each other, vicarious tort liability, and the contractual powers of agents, among others.

O'Connell, John B. *Remedies in a Nutshell* (2d ed., West, 1984). A clearly written summary of the entire law of remedies. Explains the basics of the law without the use of case examples. Topics include contempt of court, basic contract remedies, injunctions, and methods of assessing damages.

Sec. 2.2 *(Litigation in the Courts)*

Burgoyne, Robert, McNabb, Stephen, & Robinson, Frederick. *Understanding Attorney-Client Privilege Issues in the College and University Setting* (National Association of College and University Attorneys, 1998). Discusses what types of communications are protected from disclosure and how university counsel can ensure that the privilege is protected and preserved. Provides suggestions for protecting communications and for avoiding waiver of the privilege.

Drinan, Robert F. "Lawyer-Client Confidentiality in the Campus Setting," 19 *J. Coll. & Univ. Law* 305 (1993). Traces traditional and current views of lawyer-client confidentiality and explores inherent conflicts of interest in representation of administration, faculty, students, and alumni. For use primarily by college and university attorneys.

Epstein, Edna S. *The Attorney-Client Privilege and the Work-Product Doctrine* (4th ed., American Bar Association, Section on Litigation, 2001). A comprehensive overview of the law that provides practical tips and guidance through numerous case illustrations and contextual examples. Topics include the scope and elements of the

---

[20]Relevant cases are collected in R. D. Hursh, Annot., "Liability or Indemnity Insurance Carried by Governmental Unit as Affecting Immunity from Tort Liability," 68 A.L.R.2d 1438; and Allan E. Korpela, Annot., "Immunity of Private Schools and Institutions of Higher Learning from Liability in Tort," 38 A.L.R.3d 480, 501–2.

attorney-client and work-product protections, waivers to and exceptions to these protections, choice of law issues, and ethical considerations. Primarily for attorneys.

Kane, Mary Kay. *Civil Procedure in a Nutshell* (5th ed., West, 2003). A book-length summary of the entire law of civil procedure, written in clear language; well organized and outlined. Explains the basics of the law and uses case examples for illustration. Includes a discussion of the structure of the court system and a step-by-step guide through a civil case from filing of the complaint to final disposition.

National Association of College and University Attorneys. *The Practical Litigation Series* (NACUA, appearing periodically). A series of pamphlets written for students, faculty, or administrators who may be involved in litigation. Topics include *I've Been Sued: What Happens Now?* by Nicholas Trott Long; *Helping Your Institution's Lawyer to Defend You,* by Nancy Tribbensee; *Giving a Deposition: A Witness Guide,* by Oren Griffin; and *Overview of a Lawsuit,* by David L. Harrison. Intended for use by university attorneys to help them counsel institutional clients involved in litigation.

Reynolds, William L. *Judicial Process in a Nutshell* (3d ed., West, 2002). Summarizes the operation of the American court system. Written clearly, the book uses case examples to illustrate such matters as the role of the Constitution, judicial precedent, and general court structure. Topics include the nature of common law, the use of precedent, the use of statutes, and the methods of constitutional interpretation.

Sec. 2.3 *(Alternative Dispute Resolution)*

Bales, Richard A. *Compulsory Arbitration: The Grand Experiment in Employment* (Cornell University Press, 1997). Traces the history of employment arbitration in the nonunionized sector; discusses arbitration programs in the securities industry. Summarizes the advantages and disadvantages of the use of arbitration as a substitute for litigation as a method of dispute resolution in the workplace.

Brand, Norman (ed.). *How ADR Works* (Bureau of National Affairs, 2002). Includes an overview of alternate dispute resolution, discusses how mediators and arbitrators operate, how advocates prepare for mediation and arbitration hearings, how ADR programs are developed, and other related issues. Chapters are written by ADR practitioners.

Campus Mediation Resources. Available at http://www.mtds.wayne.edu.campus.htm. Lists and provides links to several Web sites that provide information on mediation in higher education.

Colvin, Alexander J. S. "The Relationship Between Employment Arbitration and Workplace Dispute Resolution Procedures," 16 *Ohio St. J. on Disp. Resol.* 643 (2001). Discusses employment arbitration in the context of other dispute resolution practices in business organizations. Included are peer review panels, mediation, and ombuds.

DiNardo, Lawrence C., Sherrill, John A., & Palmer, Anna R. "Specialized ADR to Settle Faculty Employment Disputes," 28 *J. Coll. & Univ. Law* 129 (2001). Develops a system of alternate dispute resolution for challenges to tenure decisions. Proposes that the American Association of University Professors administer a program of arbitration of tenure disputes, and that all remedies available at law be available to prevailing faculty members, including the awarding of tenure by the arbitration panel.

Eaton, Adrienne E., & Keefe, Jeffrey H. (eds.). *Employment Dispute Resolution and Worker Rights in the Changing Workplace* (Industrial Relations Research Association, 1999). This edited volume discusses the use of mandatory arbitration clauses for nonunionized workers, the use of grievance systems in the organized and nonorganized workplaces, grievance mediation, and trends in dispute resolution in the public sector.

Franke, Ann H. *Grievance Procedures: Solving Campus Employment Problems Out of Court* (United Educators, 1998). Describes a variety of forms of grievance procedures and discusses their appropriateness for faculty, staff, and other employees. Outlines procedures and requirements for handling grievances. Includes a list of additional resources.

Lipsky, David B., Seeber, Ronald L., & Fincher, Richard D. *Emerging Systems for Managing Workplace Conflict* (Jossey-Bass, 2003). A thorough review of conflict management systems, including mediation, arbitration, grievance systems, mini-trials, and ombuds. Discusses legal, practical, and policy issues in creating and using these alternate systems for dispute resolution.

McCarthy, Jane (ed.). *Resolving Conflict in Higher Education,* New Directions for Higher Education no. 32 (Jossey-Bass, 1980). Describes and discusses mechanisms (such as mediation) that can be used by postsecondary institutions to resolve internal disputes without the necessity of lawsuits. Includes both legal and policy perspectives on alternative dispute resolution techniques.

McCarthy, Jane, Ladimer, Irving, & Sirefman, Josef. *Managing Faculty Disputes: A Guide to Issues, Procedures, and Practices* (Jossey-Bass, 1984). Addresses the problem of faculty disputes on campus and proposes processes for resolving them. Covers both disputes that occur regularly and can be subjected to a standard dispute resolution process, and special disputes that occur irregularly and may require a resolution process tailored to the circumstances. Includes model grievance procedures, case studies of actual disputes, and worksheets and checklists to assist administrators in implementing dispute resolution processes.

Menkel-Meadow, Carrie. "What Will We Do When Adjudication Ends? A Brief Intellectual History of ADR," 44 *UCLA L. Rev.* 1613 (1997). Reviews the history of alternate dispute resolution and describes issues and topics that remain controversial, such as discrimination in dispute resolution and the variations in the behavior of disputing parties with respect to the methods of dispute resolution that they select.

Mitchell, Michelle R. Note, "Arbitration Agreements: When Do Employees Waive Their Rights?" 14 *Brigham Young Univ. J. Public L.* 83 (1999). Reviews Supreme Court jurisprudence on enforceability of arbitration clauses in union and nonunion contracts. Identifies issues that have not been resolved by these cases, and provides suggestions for ensuring that the arbitration process does not unduly favor the employer.

Moffitt, Michael L., & Bordone, Robert C. (eds.). *The Handbook of Dispute Resolution* (Jossey-Bass, 2005). A collection of essays by experts in dispute resolution that synthesizes research on ADR and discusses a wide range of strategies for resolving disputes. Includes attention to the effect of personality factors, emotions, and perceptions on dispute resolution; discusses strategies for understanding disputes through differences in gender and culture.

Stone, Katherine VanWezel. "Dispute Resolution in the Boundaryless Workplace," 16 *Ohio St. J. on Disp. Resol.* 467 (2001). Discusses changes in the expectations of management and employees and ways to design arbitration systems to enhance workplace fairness.

Sec. 2.4 (Legal Services)

Bickel, Robert. "A Revisitation of the Role of College and University Legal Counsel," 85 *West's Educ. Law Rptr.* 989 (1993), updating the author's earlier article published at 3 *J. Law & Educ.* 73 (1974). Explores the various roles of an institution's legal counsel. Roles include representing the university in formal legal proceedings, giving administrators advice in order to prevent legal problems, and preventing unnecessary extensions of technical legal factors into institutional administration. Includes commentary on the viewpoints of others since the author's original publication in 1974 and concludes that the earlier observations are still valid.

Block, Dennis J., & Epstein, Michael A. *The Corporate Counsellor's Deskbook* (5th ed., Aspen Law & Business, 1999). A sourcebook in loose-leaf binder format. Provides practical information and analysis, checklists, and sample documents on selecting outside counsel, controlling costs of services, managing litigation and other work assignments, and protecting the attorney-client privilege. Designed for counsel of nonprofit institutions, including colleges and universities. Periodic supplements.

Daane, Roderick K. "The Role of University Counsel," 12 *J. Coll. & Univ. Law* 399 (1985). Addresses the ways in which social changes and differences among institutions have affected the role of attorneys that serve colleges and universities. Examines "the way law is now practiced on campuses," focusing especially on counsel's roles as "Advisor-Counsellor," "Educator-Mediator," "Manager-Administrator," "Draftsman," "Litigator," and "Spokesman."

Long, Nicholas Trott, & Weeks, Kent. *Strategic Legal Planning: The College and University Legal Audit* (College Legal Information, 1998). Provides guidelines and resources for conducting comprehensive audits of the institution's legal affairs and potential risk exposure. Covers sixty-five areas of institutional operations. Includes a forty-page instrument to use in conducting legal audits.

Ruger, Peter H. "The Practice and Profession of Higher Education Law," 27 *Stetson L. Rev.* 175 (1997). Traces the evolution of higher education law practice from the earliest times to the dawn of the twenty-first century. Includes discussion of the role of NACUA (the National Association of College and University Attorneys) in this evolution, and the importance of preventive law to the higher education attorney's role.

Semersheim, Michael D. *NACUA Contract Formbook: A Compilation of Sample Form Agreements and Other Selected Materials* (National Association of College and University Attorneys, 2003). Includes more than 475 sample documents—forms, agreements, checklists, and other documents—as well as a "clause bank" containing samples of commonly used contract clauses. CD-ROM. A practical resource for counsel and administrators at both public and private institutions.

Symposium, "Focus on Ethics and the University Attorney," 19 *J. Coll. & Univ. Law* 305 (1993). A collection of three articles examining the role and the ethical duties of the university attorney, especially with respect to other members of the campus community: Robert F. Drinan, "Lawyer-Client Confidentiality in the Campus Setting"; Stephen S. Dunham, "Case Studies on Wrongdoing on Campus: Ethics and the Lawyer's Role"; and Robert M. O'Neil, "The Lawyer and the Client in the Campus Setting: Who Is the Client, What Does the Client Expect and How May the Attorney Respond?"

Symposium, 2 *J. Coll. & Univ. Law* 1 (1974–75). A series of three papers discussing the role and functions of legal counsel: John Corbally, Jr., "University Counsel—Scope and Mission"; J. Rufus Beale, "Delivery of Legal Service to Institutions of Higher

Education"; and Richard Sensenbrenner, "University Counselor: Lore, Logic and Logistics." The first paper is written from the perspective of a university president; the other two are from the perspective of practicing university attorneys.

See also the Burgoyne, McNabb, & Robinson entry, and the Epstein entry, in Sec. 2.2 above.

Sec. 2.5 (Institutional Management of Liability Risk)

Aiken, Ray, Adams, John F., & Hall, John W. *Legal Liabilities in Higher Education: Their Scope and Management* (Association of American Colleges, 1976), printed simultaneously in 3 *J. Coll. & Univ. Law* 127 (1976). Provides an in-depth examination of legal and policy issues of institutional liability and the problems of protecting institutions and their personnel against liability through insurance and risk management.

Burling, Philip, & United Educators Risk Retention Group. "Managing Athletic Liability: An Assessment Guide," 72 *West's Educ. Law Rptr.* 503 (1993). A practical guide for developing and implementing risk management programs for athletics. Covers institutional duties to supervise; to provide safe facilities, adequate equipment, safe transportation, and medical treatment; and to protect spectators. Includes basic requirements and suggestions for risk management programs, "risk management action steps" for effectuating the institution's various duties, and a list of case citations.

Connell, Mary Ann, & Savage, Frederick G. "Releases: Is There Still a Place for Their Use by Colleges and Universities?" 29 *J. Coll. & Univ. Law* 525 (2003). Examines the factors that have led courts to uphold and enforce written releases obtained by universities from students participating in a variety of activities. Also provides advice for universities and lawyers for drafting and using releases.

Ende, Howard, Anderson, Eugene, & Crego, Susannah. "Liability Insurance: A Primer for College and University Counsel," 23 *J. Coll. & Univ. Law* 609 (1997). A comprehensive explanation and analysis of liability insurance and its role in college and university risk management.

Hollander, Patricia. *Computers in Education: Legal Liabilities and Ethical Issues Concerning Their Use and Misuse* (College Administration Publications, 1986). A monograph cataloging negligence, contract, criminal, and other problems in this area of potential liability. Provides practical guidance for identifying potential liabilities and avoiding or resolving the problems.

Moots, Philip R. *Ascending Liability: Planning Memorandum* (Center for Constitutional Studies, Mercer University (now at Baylor University), 1987). Discusses planning issues such as risk management, contract drafting, and restructuring of certain activities of the organization. Also discusses the role of the governing board and the institution's role vis-à-vis related organizations.

See also the Hoye entry for Chapter 3, Section 3.3.

PART TWO

THE COLLEGE AND ITS GOVERNING BOARD, PERSONNEL, AND AGENTS

3

The College and Its
Trustees and Officers

Sec. 3.1. The Question of Authority

Trustees, officers, and administrators of postsecondary institutions—public or private—may take only those actions and make only those decisions that they have authority to take or make. Acting or deciding without authority to do so can have legal consequences, both for the responsible individual and for the institution. It is thus critical, from a legal standpoint, for trustees, officers, and other administrators to understand and adhere to the scope and limits of their authority and that of other institutional functionaries with whom they deal. Such sensitivity to authority questions will also normally be good administrative practice, since it can contribute order and structure to institutional governance and make the internal governance system more understandable, accessible, and accountable to those who deal with it (see Section 1.3.2).

Authority generally originates from some fundamental legal source that establishes the institution as a legal entity. For public institutions, the source is usually a state constitution or state authorizing legislation (see Section 12.2); for private institutions, it is usually articles of incorporation, sometimes in combination with some form of state license (see Section 12.3). These sources, though fundamental, are only the starting point for legal analysis of authority questions. To be fully understood and utilized, an institution's authority must be construed and implemented in light of all the sources of law described in Section 1.4. For public institutions, state administrative law (administrative procedure acts and similar statutes, plus court decisions) and agency law (court decisions) provide the backdrop against which authority is construed and implemented; for private institutions, state corporation law or trust law (statutes and court decisions) plus agency law (court decisions) are the bases. Authority is particularized and

167

dispersed (delegated) to institutional officers, employees, committees and boards, and internal organizations such as a faculty senate or a student government. The vehicles for such delegations are usually the governing board bylaws, institutional rules and regulations, the institution's employment contracts, and, for public institutions, the administrative regulations of state education boards or agencies. Authority may also be delegated to outside entities such as an athletic booster club, a university research foundation, or a private business performing services for the institution. Vehicles for such delegations include separate corporate charters for "captive" organizations, memoranda of understanding with affiliated entities, and service contracts (for contracting out of services). Gaps in internal delegations may be filled by resort to the institution's customs and usages (see Section 1.4.3.3), and vagueness or ambiguity may be clarified in the same way. For some external delegations, the custom and usage of the business or trade involved may be used in such circumstances rather than that of the institution.

There are several generic types of authority. As explained in *Brown v. Wichita State University* (Section 3.4), authority may be express, implied, or apparent. "Express authority" is that which is found within the plain meaning of a written grant of authority. "Implied authority" is that which is necessary or appropriate for exercising express authority and can therefore be inferred from the express authority. "Apparent authority" is not actual authority at all; the term is used to describe the situation where someone acting for the institution induces a belief in other persons that authority exists when in fact it does not. Administrators should avoid this appearance of authority and should not rely on apparent authority as a basis for acting, because the institution may be held liable, under the doctrine of "estoppel," for resultant harm to persons who rely to their detriment on an appearance of authority (see Section 3.4). When an institutional officer or employee does mistakenly act without authority, the action can sometimes be corrected through "ratification" by the board of trustees or other officer or employee who does have authority to undertake the act in question (Section 3.4).

One other type of authority is occasionally referred to in the postsecondary context: inherent authority. In *Morris v. Nowotny,* 323 S.W.2d 301 (Tex. 1959), for instance, the court remarked that the statutes establishing the University of Texas "imply the power, and, if they do not so imply, then that power is inherent in University officials to maintain proper order and decorum on the premises of the University." In *Esteban v. Central Missouri State College,* 415 F.2d 1077 (8th Cir. 1969), the court held that the college had "inherent authority to maintain order and to discipline students." And in *Waliga v. Board of Trustees of Kent State University,* 488 N.E.2d 850 (Ohio 1986), it found inherent authority in the university's trustees to revoke an academic degree that had been obtained by fraud. (For the facts and reasoning of this case, see Section 9.3.3.) The inherent authority concept is often loosely used in judicial opinions and has no clear definition. Sometimes courts appear to apply the phrase to what is really a very broad construction of the institution's implied powers. In *Goldberg v. Regents of the University of California,* 57 Cal. Rptr. 463 (Cal. Ct. App. 1967), the court held that broad disciplinary authority over students was implicit in the state constitution's grant of power to the university, but then it called that authority "inherent." At other times the inherent authority concept is more clearly distinguished from implied authority; inherent authority then is said to exist not because of any written words but because it would not be sensible, as measured by the norms of postsecondary education, for an institution to be without authority over the particular matter at issue. In all, inherent authority is an elusive concept of uncertain stature and questionable value, and it is a slender reed to rely on to justify actions and decisions. If administrators need broader authority, they should, with counsel's help, seek to expand their express authority or to justify a broader construction of their implied authority.

The law is not clear on how broadly or narrowly authority should be construed in the postsecondary context. To some extent, the answer will vary from state to state and, within a state, may depend on whether the institution is established by the state constitution, by state statutes, or by articles of incorporation (see Sections 12.2 & 12.3). Although authority issues have been addressed in judicial opinions, such as those discussed in Section 3.2 below, the analysis is sometimes cursory. There has been debate among courts and commentators on whether postsecondary institutions should be subject to traditional legal principles for construing authority or whether such principles should be applied in a more flexible, less demanding way that takes into account the unique characteristics of postsecondary education. Given the uncertainty, administrators should rely when possible on express rather than implied or inherent authority and should seek clarity in statements of express authority, in order to avoid leaving authority questions to the vagaries of judicial interpretation. If institutional needs require greater flexibility and generality in statements of authority, administrators should consult legal counsel to determine how much breadth and flexibility the courts of the state would permit in construing the various types of authority.

Miscalculations of the institution's authority, or the authority of particular officers or employees, can have various adverse legal consequences. For public institutions, unauthorized acts may be invalidated by courts or administrative agencies under the *ultra vires* doctrine in the state's administrative law (a doctrine applied to acts that are beyond the delegated authority of a public body or official). For private institutions, a similar result occasionally can be reached under state corporation law.

When the unauthorized act is a failure to follow institutional regulations and the institution is public (see Section 1.5.2), courts will sometimes hold that the act violated procedural due process. In *Escobar v. State University of New York/College at Old Westbury,* 427 F. Supp. 850 (E.D.N.Y. 1977), a student sought to enjoin the college from suspending him or taking any further disciplinary action against him. The student had been disciplined by the judicial review committee, acting under the college's "Code of Community Conduct." After the college president learned of the disciplinary action, he rejected it and imposed more severe penalties on the student. The president purported to act under the "Rules of Public Order" adopted by the Board of Trustees of the State University of New York rather than under the college code. The court found that the president had violated the Rules, and it enjoined enforcement of his decision:

> [E]ven if we assume the President had power to belatedly invoke the Rules, it is clear that he did not properly exercise that power, since he did not follow the requirements of the Rules themselves. The charges he made against the plaintiff were included in the same document which set forth the plaintiff's suspension and the terms for his possible readmission. Contrary to the Rules, the President did not convene the Hearing Committee, did not give notice of any hearing, and received no report from the Hearing Committee. There is no authority in either the Rules or the Code for substituting the hearing before the Code's Judicial Review Committee for the one required to be held before the Rules' hearing committee. . . .
>
> Of course, not every deviation from a university's regulations constitutes a deprivation of due process. . . . But where, as here, an offending student has been formally charged under the college's disciplinary code, has been subjected to a hearing, has been officially sentenced, and has commenced compliance with that sentence, it is a denial of due process of law for the chief administrative officer to step in, conduct his own in camera review of the student's record, and impose a different punishment without complying with any of the procedures which have been formally established for the college. Here the President simply brushed aside the college's formal regulations and procedures and, without specific authority, imposed a punishment of greater severity than determined by the hearing panel, a result directly contrary to the Code's appeal provisions [427 F. Supp. at 858].

For both public and private institutions, an unauthorized act violating institutional regulations may also be invalidated as a breach of an express or implied contract with students or the faculty. *Lyons v. Salve Regina College*, 422 F. Supp. 1354 (D.R.I. 1976), *reversed*, 565 F.2d 200 (1st Cir. 1977), involved a student who had received an F grade in a required nursing course because she had been absent from several classes and clinical sessions. After the student appealed the grade under the college's published "Grade Appeal Process," the grade appeal committee voted that the student receive an Incomplete rather than an F. Characterizing the committee's action as a recommendation rather than a final decision, the associate dean overruled the committee, and the student was dismissed from the nursing program.

The parties agreed that the Grade Appeal Process was part of the terms of a contract between them. Though the grade appeal committee's determination was termed a "recommendation" in the college's publications, the lower court found that, as the parties understood the process, the recommendation was to be binding on the associate dean. The associate dean's overruling of the committee was therefore unauthorized and constituted a breach of contract. The lower court ordered the college to change the student's grade to an Incomplete and reinstate her in the nursing program. The appellate court reversed but did not disavow the contract theory of authority. Instead, it found that the committee's determination was not intended to be binding on the associate dean and that the dean therefore had not exceeded his authority in overruling the committee.

Authority questions are also central to a determination of various questions concerning liability for harm to third parties. The institution's tort liability may depend on whether the officer or employee committing the tort was acting within the scope of his or her authority (see Section 3.3). The institution's contract liability may depend on whether the officer or employee entering the contract was authorized to do so (Section 3.4). And, under the estoppel doctrine, both the institution and the individual may be liable where the institution or individual had apparent authority to act (Section 3.2.2).

Because of these various legal ramifications, a postsecondary institution should carefully organize and document its various delegations of authority. Delegations and subdelegations of authority among institutional officers, employees, and organizations should be considered, as well as delegations to outside captive or affiliated entities. Counsel should be involved in this process. Organizational statements or charts should be generally available to the campus community, so that persons with questions or grievances can know where to turn for assistance. Delegations should be reviewed periodically, to determine whether they accurately reflect actual practice within the institution and maintain an appropriate balance of specificity and flexibility. Where a gap in authority is found, or an unnecessary overlap or ambiguity, it should be corrected. Where questions concerning the permissible scope of authority are uncovered, they should be resolved.

Similarly, administrators should understand the scope of their own authority and that of the officers, employees, and organizations with whom they deal. They should understand where their authority comes from and which higher-level administrators may review or modify their acts and decisions. They should understand whether, and when and how, they have authority to act in the name of the institution. They should attempt to resolve unnecessary gaps or ambiguities in their authority. They should consider what part of their authority may and should be subdelegated to lower-level administrators or to faculty and what checks or limitations should be placed on those delegations. And they should attempt to ensure that their authority is adequately understood by the members of the campus community with whom they deal.

The discussion in the following subsections illustrates particular kinds of legal challenges that may be made to the authority of various functionaries in postsecondary institutions. Although the discussion reflects general concepts and issues critical to an understanding of authority in the postsecondary context, the specific legal principles that courts apply to particular challenges to authority may vary from state to state.

Sec. 3.2. Sources and Scope of Authority and Liability

3.2.1. Trustees

3.2.1.1. Overview. Questions of trustee authority may be resolved differently depending on whether the college is public or private. In public institutions, the authority of trustees is defined and limited by the state statutes, and sometimes by constitutional provisions, which create trustee boards for individual institutions. Such laws generally confer power on the board itself as an entity separate from its individual members. Individual trustees generally have authority to act only on behalf of the board, pursuant to some board bylaw, resolution, or other delegation of authority from the board. Other state laws, such as conflict-of-interest laws or ethics codes, may place obligations on individual board members as well as on the board itself. In private colleges, trustee authority typically emanates from the college's charter or articles of incorporation, but state regulatory or licensing laws may limit or dictate trustee action under certain circumstances.

3.2.1.2. Trustees of public colleges. For public colleges, disputes over the authority of trustees are resolved by the interpretation of state constitutions and state laws. For this reason, the resolution of any particular dispute may differ by state and may depend on the type of institution involved and on what other entities share authority with the institution's trustees. For example, decision-making authority for municipal or county community colleges may be shared among a municipal or county government, the college's board of trustees, and the state. *Warren County Community College v. Warren County Board of Chosen Freeholders,* 824 A.2d 1073 (N.J. 2003), for instance, concerned a conflict between a community college's trustees and the county board of freeholders regarding approval of a property tax assessment for capital projects at the college. The court held that the trustees could not compel the county board to approve the tax because the county's citizens had not agreed to subject themselves to such assessments. Similarly, the structure of state-level governance of higher education may lead to conflicts between boards of trustees of different sectors when, for example, the decisions of a university board of trustees have consequences for the viability of community colleges. (For an example of a conflict between two state boards, one for community colleges and one for public universities, see *Board of Trustees of State Institutions of Higher Learning v. Ray,* 809 So. 2d 627 (Miss. 2002).)

Despite the considerable influence of state law and governance structures, certain governance principles are standard. The college's trustees may not exercise authority beyond that which they have been delegated, either by the state (for a public college) or the college's charter (for a private college). In *First Equity Corp. of Florida v. Utah State University,* 544 P.2d 887 (Utah 1975), the plaintiff, a stock brokerage company, sued the university over its failure to pay for common stocks ordered by the university's assistant vice president of finance. The university defended itself by asserting that its board of trustees lacked the power to authorize the assistant vice president to invest in common stocks. The board had general control and supervision "of all appropriations made by the territory [state] for the support" of the school (Comp. Laws of Utah § 1855 (1888)), and the university had authority to handle its own financial affairs under the supervision of the board (Higher Education Act of 1969, Utah Code Ann. § 53–48–10(5)). After reviewing the provisions of the Utah constitution that specified the mechanisms for funding the university, the court held that these provisions did not give the university unlimited authority to encumber public funds. The court concluded:

> It is inconceivable that the framers of the constitution, in light of the provisions of Sections 1, 5, and 7 of Article X and the provisions as to debt limitations, intended to place the university above the only controls available for the people of this state as to the property, management, and government of the university. We are unable to reconcile respondent's position that the university has a blank check as to all its funds with no preaudit and no restraint under the provisions of the constitution requiring the state to safely invest and hold the dedicated funds and making the state guarantor of the public school funds against loss or diversion. To hold that respondent has free and uncontrolled custody and use of its property and funds while making the state guarantee said funds against loss or diversion is inconceivable. We believe the framers of the constitution intended no such result [544 P.2d at 890].

Because of this state constitutional limitation regarding finances, and the absence of any "specific authorizing grant" of investment power under the state statutes, the court held that the board did not have authority to purchase the particular type of stock involved. The board therefore could not authorize the assistant vice president or any other agent to make the purchases.

In *Feldman v. Regents of the University of New Mexico*, 540 P.2d 872 (N.M. 1975), the head football coach at the university sued the regents for discharging him during the term of his contract. According to New Mexico law, the regents have "power to remove any officer connected with the university when in their judgment the interests require it" (N.M. Stat. Ann. § 73-25-9). The regents relied on the statute as sufficient authority for dismissing the coach. In ruling on the regents' motion for summary judgment, the state courts refused to approve the dismissal under this statute. The courts reasoned that additional information was needed to determine whether the coach was an "officer" or an "employee" of the institution, since the statute would not authorize his discharge if he were an employee.

In *Baker v. Southern University*, 604 So. 2d 699 (La. Ct. App. 1992), a custodian who had civil service protections charged that the chancellor did not have the authority to dismiss him. The court was required to determine whether the Board of Supervisors of Southern University was legally authorized to delegate appointing and discharge authority to the university's chancellor. The court had to reconcile the provisions of the state's civil service statute as well as the statute that controls the organization of the state's colleges and universities. These statutes, said the court, give broad powers to the board of supervisors to "supervise and manage the university system . . . to exercise all power to direct, control, supervise and manage the university" (604 So. 2d at 701). This power, said the court, included the power to delegate appointing authority to the chancellor.

The outcome is different, however, if statutes provide that the board itself must act. In *Blanchard v. Lansing Community College*, 370 N.W.2d 23 (Mich. Ct. App. 1985), a faculty member challenged his discharge because the board of trustees had not voted on the matter. The board argued that it had delegated the power to hire and discharge to certain administrators. Turning to the relevant Michigan statute, the court noted that the statute specifies that the faculty employment contract is between the faculty member and the board, and ruled that the power to discharge was expressly committed to the discretion of the board and thus was not delegable.

Authority not delegated to a board by the state legislature, however, may not be assumed by that board. For example, in *Board of Regents v. Board of Trustees for State Colleges and Universities,* 491 So. 2d 399 (La. Ct. App. 1986), the court ruled that the board of trustees for the state's public colleges and universities did not have the authority to change the name of the state university; that was the prerogative of the legislature. Since neither the state constitution nor any statute gave the board of trustees the authority to change the university's name, the court ruled that the legislature had retained that authority.

Similarly, an attempt by a public university to affiliate with a private law school without state approval was quashed by a state supreme court. In *In re South Texas College of Law and Texas A&M University,* 4 S.W.3d 219 (Tex. 1999), the Supreme Court of Texas refused to suspend the trial court's injunction, pending resolution of the appeal on the merits. In an unpublished opinion, the trial court had ruled that Texas A&M lacked the authority to enter the affiliation agreement without the approval of the Texas Higher Education Coordinating Board, and that the agreement would violate the state constitution's prohibition against the use of public money for individuals or corporations. Despite the fact that the law school would remain private, said the trial court, officials of the Coordinating Board were concerned that the law school would eventually seek to be publicly funded (Katherine S. Mangan, "Texas Judge Rejects Campus Affiliation Plan," *Chron. Higher Educ.,* April 23, 1999, A48).

3.2.1.3. Trustees of private colleges. In private institutions the authority of institutional trustees is defined and limited by the institution's corporate charter (articles of incorporation) and the state corporation laws under which charters are issued. As in public institutions, the power generally lodges in the board of trustees as an entity separate from its individual members. But charter provisions, corporate bylaws, or board resolutions may delegate authority to individual trustees or trustee committees to act for the board in certain situations. Moreover, general state corporate law or trust law may place affirmative obligations on individual board members to act fairly and responsibly in protecting the institution's resources and interests.

The Missouri case of *Burnett v. Barnes,* 546 S.W.2d 744 (Mo. 1977), illustrates how the authority of a private institution's board of trustees may be limited by the institution's articles of incorporation. The institution in this case, the Kansas City College of Osteopathic Medicine, was a "membership" corporation; graduates of the college had the status of members of the corporation. When the college's board of trustees sought to amend the corporate bylaws to eliminate this membership status, the Missouri state courts determined that the trustees had no authority to make such a change. The Missouri General Not-for-Profit Corporation Law gave the trustees power "to make and alter bylaws not inconsistent with its articles of incorporation or with the laws of this state" (Mo. Rev.

Stat. § 355.090). The institution's original articles of agreement and its subsequent articles of acceptance each referred to the admission of new members to the corporation. On the basis of these two references, the courts concluded that the board's power to amend the bylaws was limited by the institution's articles of incorporation to matters that did not eliminate membership.

Even if a board acts within the parameters of its corporate charter, the authority of trustees of private colleges may be limited by the state if the state entity regulating (and licensing) private colleges believes that the board has abused its authority. New York's Education Law § 236(4) gives the state board of regents the authority to remove the trustees of any college or university in the state, whether it is a public or a private institution. After several years of litigation and publicity, a New York appellate court upheld the decision of the state's board of regents to initiate removal proceedings against most of Adelphi University's trustees and officers.

In *In re Adelphi University v. Board of Regents of the State of New York,* 652 N.Y.S.2d 837 (Sup. Ct., App. Div. 1997), the trustees sought to enjoin the proceeding, asserting that the board of regents could not initiate removal proceedings at the request of other parties (faculty, students, alumni, and former trustees of the University). The court ruled that the board of regents had the authority to establish its own procedures for initiating removal actions, that the petition seeking the trustees' removal was verified and sufficiently detailed, and that the board had reviewed the petition for legal sufficiency before accepting the petition. The board also had the authority to determine the process for prosecution of trustee removal petitions. According to the court, the only statutory provisions applicable to the board were adjudicatory; it had full authority to delegate both the investigatory and prosecutorial functions to third parties.

Trustees at both public and private colleges have a fiduciary duty to act in the best interest of the college. The scope of that fiduciary duty for private college trustees was examined and explicated in *Stern v. Lucy Webb Hayes National Training School for Deaconesses and Missionaries,* 381 F. Supp. 1003 (D.D.C. 1974) (the *Sibley Hospital* case), the first reported opinion to comprehensively review the obligations of the trustees of private charitable corporations and to set out guidelines for trustee involvement in financial dealings. Although the case concerns a hospital, the court's analysis is clearly transferable to private educational institutions. The court's decision to analyze the trustees' standard of duty in terms of corporate law, rather than trust law, apparently reflects the evolving trend in the law.

The plaintiffs represented patients of Sibley Hospital, a nonprofit charitable corporation in the District of Columbia and the principal concern of the Lucy Webb Hayes National Training School. Nine members of the hospital's board of trustees were among the named defendants. The plaintiffs charged that the defendant trustees had "conspired to enrich themselves and certain financial institutions with which they were affiliated [and which were also named as defendants] by favoring those institutions in financial dealings with the hospital" and that "they breached their fiduciary duties of care and loyalty in the management of Sibley's funds." The court examined evidence of the relationships between the defendant trustees and the defendant institutions. Although most of the hospital's funds were deposited in the defendant institutions, the funds were controlled and managed almost exclusively from the early 1950s until 1972 by a deceased trustee, without the active involvement of any of the defendant trustees.

The court concluded that the plaintiffs had not established a conspiracy but had established serious breaches of duty by the trustees. According to the court, the trustees owed a duty to the institution comparable to, and in some cases greater than, that owed by the directors of a business corporation.

1. Mismanagement

Both trustees and corporate directors are liable for losses occasioned by their negligent mismanagement of investments. However, the degree of care required appears to differ in many jurisdictions. A trustee is uniformly held to a high standard of care and will be held liable for simple negligence, while a director must often have committed "gross negligence" or otherwise be guilty of more than mere mistakes of judgment.

This distinction may amount to little more than a recognition of the fact that corporate directors have many areas of responsibility, while the traditional trustee is often charged only with the management of the trust funds and can therefore be expected to devote more time and expertise to that task. Since the board members of most large charitable corporations fall within the corporate rather than the trust model, being charged with the operation of ongoing businesses, it has been said that they should only be held to the less stringent corporate standard of care. More specifically, directors of charitable corporations are required to exercise ordinary and reasonable care in the performance of their duties, exhibiting honesty and good faith.

2. Nonmanagement

Plaintiffs allege that the individual defendants failed to supervise the management of hospital investments or even to attend meetings of the committees charged with such supervision. Trustees are particularly vulnerable to such a charge, because they not only have an affirmative duty to "maximize the trust income by prudent investment," but they may not delegate that duty, even to a committee of their fellow trustees. A corporate director, on the other hand, may delegate his investment responsibility to fellow directors, corporate officers, or even outsiders, but he must continue to exercise general supervision over the activities of his delegates. Once again, the rule for charitable corporations is closer to the traditional corporate rule: directors should at least be permitted to delegate investment decisions to a committee of board members, so long as all directors assume the responsibility for supervising such committees by periodically scrutinizing their work.

Total abdication of the supervisory role, however, is improper even under traditional corporate principles. A director who fails to acquire the information necessary to supervise investment policy or consistently fails even to attend the meetings at which such policies are considered has violated his fiduciary duty to the corporation. . . .

3. Self-Dealing

Under District of Columbia law, neither trustees nor corporate directors are absolutely barred from placing funds under their control into a bank having an interlocking directorship with their own institution. In both cases, however, such transactions will be subjected to the closest scrutiny to determine whether or not the duty of loyalty has been violated. A deliberate conspiracy among trustees or board members to enrich the interlocking bank at the expense of the trust or corporation would, for example, constitute such a breach and render the conspirators liable for any losses. In the absence of clear evidence of wrongdoing, however, the courts appear to have used different standards to determine whether or not relief is appropriate, depending again on the legal relationship involved. Trustees may be found guilty of a breach of trust even for mere negligence in the maintenance of accounts in banks with which they are associated, while corporate directors are generally only required to show "entire fairness" to the corporation and "full disclosure" of the potential conflict of interest to the board.

Most courts apply the less stringent corporate rule to charitable corporations in this area as well [381 F. Supp. at 1013–15; footnotes omitted].

On the basis of these principles, the court created explicit guidelines for the future conduct of trustees in financial matters:

The court holds that a director or so-called trustee of a charitable hospital organized under the Non-Profit Corporation Act of the District of Columbia (D.C. Code § 29-1001 et seq.) is in default of his fiduciary duty to manage the fiscal and investment affairs of the hospital if it has been shown by a preponderance of the evidence that:

(1) While assigned to a particular committee of the board having general financial or investment responsibility under the bylaws of the corporation, he has failed to use due diligence in supervising the actions of those officers, employees, or outside experts to whom the responsibility for making day-to-day financial or investment decisions has been delegated; or

(2) he knowingly permitted the hospital to enter into a business transaction with himself or with any corporation, partnership, or association in which he then had a substantial interest or held a position as trustee, director, general manager, or principal officer without having previously informed the persons charged with approving that transaction of his interest or position and of any significant reasons, unknown to or not fully appreciated by such persons, why the transaction might not be in the best interests of the hospital; or

(3) except as required by the preceding paragraph, he actively participated in or voted in favor of a decision by the board or any committee or subcommittee thereof to transact business with himself or with any corporation, partnership, or association in which he then had a substantial interest or held a position as trustee, director, general manager, or principal officer; or

(4) he otherwise failed to perform his duties honestly, in good faith, and with a reasonable amount of diligence and care [381 F. Supp. at 1015].

In *Corporation of Mercer University v. Smith,* 371 S.E.2d 858 (Ga. 1988), the Georgia Supreme Court echoed the D.C. court in the *Sibley Hospital* case when it considered whether trust law or corporate law would apply to trustees' merger and closure decisions; it also considered the scope of private institutional autonomy under state law. At issue was a challenge to a decision made by Mercer University's trustees to close Tift College in Atlanta, with which the university had recently merged. The merger agreement provided that Mercer would make a good-faith effort to continue operating Tift College at its original location. Plaintiffs—who included a district attorney, several alumni, and three former trustees—sued to set aside the merger and to keep the college open. The parties differed as to whether trust law or corporate law would apply to Mercer's actions. The plaintiffs wanted the court to apply the stricter fiduciary duty requirements of trust law; the college argued that trustees were bound only by the dictates of corporate law. Siding with the college, the court applied corporate law, rather than trust law, and concluded that under corporate law the trustees had the power to merge the college and then close it:

> [F]ormalities of trust law are inappropriate to the administration of colleges and universities which, in this era, operate as businesses. . . . [T]hose persons responsible for the operation of the universities need the administrative flexibility to make the many day-to-day decisions affecting the operation of the institution, including those decisions involving the acquisition of and sale of assets [371 S.E.2d at 860–61].

But the Supreme Court of New Hampshire appears to have used trust law to determine whether Dartmouth College had a fiduciary duty to its alumni who had made donations to the college's capital campaign. In *Brzica v. Trustees of Dartmouth College,* 791 A.2d 990 (N.H. 2002), several alumni were angered by Dartmouth's announcement that it would eliminate fraternities and sororities. The alumni sued Dartmouth under New Hampshire's Consumer Protection Act (N.H. Rev. Stat. Ann. § 358-A:2), and also sought a declaration that the trustees had breached their fiduciary duties. The court, referring to previous New Hampshire cases involving fiduciary duty under trust law, denied that the college had a fiduciary duty to alumni. It also found no evidence that the trustees had made misrepresentations to the alumni about how their donations would be used. The court affirmed the trial court's dismissal of the cause of action.

In re Antioch University, 418 A.2d 105 (D.C. 1980), illustrates the delineation of authority between the board of trustees and the institution's constituent units. The case arose as a dispute between the university, located in Ohio, and a law school that it operated in Washington, D.C. The dispute concerned the extent to which the law school could operate autonomously from the university, particularly with respect to oversight of its financial affairs. While the law school insisted that, for accreditation purposes, its finances should be managed locally and not commingled with the university's funds, the university officials argued that their fiduciary duty required them to have unilateral control of all institutional funds. The law deans countered that the university was contractually obligated to delegate financial authority to the law school and that its refusal to do so was a breach of its fiduciary duty to the law school and its students.

The law school officials sought a preliminary injunction that would enable the law school to administer its funds independently. When the trial court denied this relief, the officials appealed. The appellate court considered the officials' contract claim in the context of the law governing private boards of trustees, and affirmed the trial court's finding that the university trustees' resolution creating the law school did not limit the trustees' authority to control its operations and finances:

> The university is a not-for-profit corporation organized under the law of the state of Ohio. The university, [like] any corporation, is governed by the statutes of the state of its incorporation, its articles of incorporation, and its bylaws. The law school "is not organized as a corporation or other judicial entity." Concededly, it "was established pursuant to a resolution of the board of trustees of Antioch College (the predecessor in name to Antioch University) dated December 3 and 4, 1971." Resolutions adopted by the university in accordance with its articles of incorporation and bylaws effectuate the will of the corporation (see generally *Brown v. National Loan & Investment Co.,* 139 S.W.2d 364 (Tex. Civ. App. 1940)). However, the plain meaning of this resolution bespeaks a delegation of power for the establishment of an "interim governing structure" of the law school as it relates to the university. It cannot be concluded that such a delegation deprived the board of trustees of the power given to them in Article III of the university's Articles of Incorporation, to wit: "All of the rights and powers of the corporation and the entire control and management of its college, property, and affairs shall be vested in and exercised by a board of trustees composed of twenty-five (25) persons." In fact, a contract conveying such plenary power vested by corporation charter in the trustees would be void [418 A.2d at 111–12].

In thus affirming the denial of preliminary relief, the court determined that the board of trustees had acted in accordance with its fiduciary obligations under Ohio law and its charter and bylaws.[1] The court further cautioned that, had the board granted to the law school the administrative power it sought, the board's action would have been void. This conclusion is supported by the university's charter, which apparently precludes the trustees from delegating their management powers. It may also find support in the legal principle, recognized in varying degrees by the corporation laws of the states, that excessive delegation of management powers by a corporate board violates state law even if it is not precluded by the charter.

With a little muscle, a framework for analyzing the power relationship between private universities and their constituent units can be squeezed from the opinion in *In re: Antioch University.* First, the university is the legal entity that derives power from the state; the constituent unit usually has no separate

---

[1]A later case between the same parties, *Cahn v. Antioch University,* 482 A.2d 120 (D.C. 1984), dealt with the law school officials' fiduciary obligations to the university. See also *In re Antioch University,* 482 A.2d 133 (D.C. 1984), which rejected the law school officials' request that the university pay their attorney's fees for the litigation.

corporate status and thus derives its authority exclusively from the university. Second, the extent to which the board of trustees may delegate authority to a constituent unit is determined initially by the relevant provisions of the corporate charter; the trustees may delegate management powers only to the extent, and in the manner, authorized by the charter. Third, charter provisions, in turn, may authorize delegation of management powers only to the extent, and in the manner, that the state's corporation statutes and case law permit; charter provisions that conflict with state law on excessive delegation are invalid. Fourth, the extent to which the university has actually delegated authority to a constituent unit is determined by construing the trustees' resolutions, the university's bylaws, and other official acts of the university. Any claimed authority that is not found in these sources, construed consistently with the charter and state law, does not exist.

Even if trustees have the authority to make certain decisions, their decisions are subject to challenges that they were made arbitrarily or in bad faith. For example, in *In re Polishook v. City University of New York,* 651 N.Y.S.2d 459 (N.Y. App. Div. 1996), the faculty union at City University of New York (CUNY) challenged several decisions of the trustees when they declared the university to be facing a state of financial exigency. The court reviewed the trustees' actions to determine whether they were arbitrary and capricious, or whether they were made in good faith. The court determined that the declaration of financial exigency, and the decision to terminate tenured faculty as a result, were made in good faith. Because the CUNY bylaws did not require the trustees to consult with the faculty prior to implementing faculty layoffs, the failure to consult was not evidence of bad faith. But the court agreed with the plaintiffs that the trustees' decision to reduce the number of credits required for both the associate and baccalaureate degrees had no rational basis, was arbitrary and capricious, and lowered the value of a CUNY diploma. It vacated that decision, while upholding the rest of the challenged actions.

Another issue related to the authority of trustees involves their role in monitoring the management of assets over which they have no legal control, but which may benefit the institution in the future. In *Shriners Hospitals for Crippled Children v. First Security Bank of Utah,* 835 P.2d 350 (Wyo. 1992), the Wyoming Supreme Court addressed the concerns of two beneficiaries of a trust: the hospital and the University of Utah. A donor had established a "charitable remainder trust" in her will that provided income for her sister during the sister's lifetime and then reverted to the hospital and the university upon the sister's death. The trustee, a bank, had sold some land that was part of the trust's assets without notifying the contingent beneficiaries (the hospital and the university), and at a price allegedly below its market value. The Wyoming court rejected the challenge to the sale of the land, ruling that the trustee had no duty to notify the contingent beneficiaries of the sale of trust assets. The U.S. Supreme Court declined to review the case. The outcome of this case is troubling for colleges, because donors often use charitable remainder trusts to make gifts to colleges and universities. Although colleges may ask the trustee of the trust to notify them before selling assets, there may not be a legal obligation for the trustee to do so.

In a development that is somewhat similar to the outcome of the *Shriners Hospital* case, a pair of state court cases in Connecticut appears to have broadened the ability of colleges in that state to use donations for purposes other than those specified by the donor. In *Herzog Foundation v. University of Bridgeport*, 699 A.2d 995 (Conn. 1997), the state's highest court ruled that a state law did not confer standing on a donor to challenge the institution's use of donated funds. The plaintiff, a charitable foundation, had made gifts to the university to provide scholarships for nursing students. When the university decided to close its nursing school, the foundation sought a court order to require the university to either use the funds for their original purpose or return them to the foundation to be used for other charitable purposes. The university argued that the foundation lacked standing to sue under Connecticut law (the Connecticut Uniform Management of Institutional Funds Act, General Statutes §§ 45a-526 through 43a-534). The court ruled that, although the state law permitted the attorney general to bring an action against the recipient of a donation in order to enforce the donor's restrictions on the gift, the law did not authorize lawsuits by donors or other private parties. Nor did the foundation have standing to sue under common law, said the court, unless it had specifically reserved to itself the right to bring such an action as part of the terms of the gift.

Another Connecticut appellate court relied on the outcome in *Herzog Foundation* in a case brought against the trustees of Yale University. In *Russell v. Yale University*, 737 A.2d. 941 (Conn. App. 1999), heirs of the creator of a trust, alumni, and other donors challenged the decision of the trustees to reorganize the Yale Divinity School and to demolish portions of the buildings in which the school was housed. Funds from the trust had been used to construct the buildings. Using *Herzog* as authority, the court ruled that, because neither the trust instrument nor the other donations had specifically reserved to the donor the right to control the use of the donated funds, none of the donors, the donors' heirs, or the alumni had standing to challenge the decision of the trustees. Furthermore, the student plaintiffs lacked standing because they had alleged no injuries to themselves implicating fundamental rights.

Early in the new century, public disclosures of questionable business practices by large corporations have raised ethical and legal issues that are also pertinent to trustees of colleges and universities. These issues are thoughtfully and provocatively discussed by The Hon. Jose A. Cabranes in "University Trusteeship in the Enron Era" (2002), available at http://www.nacua.org.

3.2.2. Other officers and administrators.

The authority of the highest-ranking officers and administrators of postsecondary institutions may occasionally be set out in statutes or state board regulations (for public institutions) or in corporate charters (for private institutions). But more often even the highest-ranking officers and employees, and almost always the lower-ranking ones, derive their authority not directly from statute, state board regulation, or charter but rather from subdelegation by the institution's board of trustees. The lower the administrator in the administrative hierarchy, the greater the likelihood of sub-subdelegation— that is, subdelegation of authority from the board of trustees to an officer or administrator who in turn subdelegates part of this authority to some other administrator or employee.

Although delegation of authority to officers and administrators is necessary to allow the institution to function, there are limitations to the amount of authority, and the type of authority, that should be subdelegated. A review of cases and authorities on board delegations to administrators suggests five principles that boards should consider in balancing the need for administrators to make day-to-day operational decisions with the board's overall responsibility for setting policy and ensuring that the college operates properly:

1. The board's delegations must be consistent with the corporate articles and bylaws and other applicable law.

2. Proper guidelines should be provided to those who exercise delegated authority.

3. Power should only be delegated to competent persons or bodies.

4. Power should only be delegated to persons or bodies who will exercise the power properly and consistent with the governing board's intention.

5. The governing board should adopt appropriate procedures to review the actions taken under delegated authority (James F. Shekleton, "Delegation of Board Decision-Making Authority to Administrative Officers" (2002), available at http://www.nacua.org).

Silverman v. University of Colorado, 555 P.2d 1155 (Colo. 1976), illustrates the subdelegation of authority. A terminated assistant professor claimed that her termination constituted a breach of contract. In December 1972 the associate dean of the professor's school wrote the professor that she would be reappointed for 1973–74 if certain federal funding was renewed and if the professor's peers recommended reappointment. The professor claimed that, although both conditions were fulfilled, the school did not renew her contract, thus violating the terms of the December 1972 letter. The trial court held for the university, reasoning that the associate dean's letter could not create a contract because, by statute, only the board of regents had authority to appoint faculty members. The intermediate appellate court reversed, reasoning that the associate dean could have created a contract because he could have been acting under authority subdelegated to him by the board. The Supreme Court of Colorado then reversed the intermediate court and reinstated the trial court's decision, holding that hiring authority is not delegable unless "expressly authorized by the legislature."

In *People v. Ware*, 368 N.Y.S.2d 797 (N.Y. App. Div. 1975), however, an appellate court upheld a delegation of power from a systemwide board of trustees to the president of an individual institution and thence to campus police officers employed by that institution. The trial court had dismissed a prosecution against an illegal trespasser at the State University of New York (SUNY) at Buffalo because the officer making the arrest did not have authority to do so. According to this court, the New York Education Law (§ 355(2)(m)) designated the SUNY Board of Trustees to appoint peace officers, whereas the arresting officer had been appointed by the president of the university. In reversing, the appellate court reasoned that the board had authority under the Education Law to promulgate rules and regulations, and the rules and regulations promulgated by the board provided for the delegation of power to SUNY's executive and administrative officers. By resolution passed under these rules and regulations, the board had authorized administrative officers of each state institution to appoint peace officers for their campuses. Since the SUNY president had properly appointed the arresting officer pursuant to this resolution, the officer had authority to make the arrest.

The question of delegation from trustees to one or more administrators may arise in issues relating to contracts. In *FDIC v. Providence College*, 115 F.3d 136 (2d Cir. 1997), officials of the college had entered a contract with two construction companies as part of an asbestos abatement project for the campus. The companies applied for loans from a bank in order to obtain the capital necessary to begin work on the project. As a condition of making the loans, the bank required the companies to obtain from the college a written guaranty of the loans. The vice president for business affairs, who was a personal friend of the principal officer of both companies, signed the form, which obligated the college to repay the $621,000 loan if the borrowers could not. When the construction companies defaulted on the loans, the bank brought an action against the borrowers and the college. The college asserted that the vice president lacked the actual and the apparent authority to guaranty the loans. A trial judge granted summary judgment to the college on the issue of actual authority, but ruled that the issue of apparent authority must be determined at trial. Following a bench trial, the judge ruled that the vice president had apparent authority to guaranty the loan.

The appellate court reversed. The vice president was a personal friend of the borrowers, and his title did not appear on the loan document. There was no evidence to indicate that bank employees knew that the individual providing the guaranty was a college employee. Furthermore, a second loan obtained by the construction company had been guaranteed by the director of physical plant, and those amounts exceeded $1 million. In both cases, the bank had made no attempt to determine whether the individuals acting as guarantors had the authority to commit the college to liability that equaled the college's entire endowment and the value of its land and buildings. The court ruled that, in order for the bank to hold the college liable for the loan amount guaranteed by the vice president, it would have to prove that (1) the college itself was responsible for the appearance of authority in the vice president to sign the guaranty and (2) the bank's reliance on the appearance of authority in the vice president was reasonable. The court ruled for the bank on the first issue, but ruled that the bank should have inquired as to whether the trustees had delegated the authority to the vice president to guaranty a loan on the college's behalf. The bank's failure to do so was unreasonable, and therefore it could not hold the college responsible for repaying the loan.

(For a discussion of apparent authority and a university's liability when a department chair promises new faculty members that they will be tenured, see *The Johns Hopkins University v. Ritter* in Section 6.7.1.)

In some situations, a board is not permitted to delegate its authority to a president. In *Faculty of City University of New York Law School at Queens College v. Murphy*, 539 N.Y.S.2d 367 (N.Y. App. Div. 1989), the university chancellor had declined to forward to the board of trustees the applications of two candidates for tenure who had not received unanimous approval from a joint law school–college review committee. The court held that the chancellor did not have authority to withhold the applications and that the board of trustees had the exclusive, nondelegable power to award tenure.

Similarly, an Ohio appellate court ruled that the president of Central State University did not have the authority to promise at-will employees that their employment would be extended indefinitely. In *Marbury v. Central State University*, 2000 Ohio App. LEXIS 5815 (Ct. App. Ohio, December 14, 2000), the former registrar of Central State University sued for breach of contract after being terminated from her position. She asserted that the president had orally promised her and other employees that, despite the university's financial problems, they would eventually receive contracts and salary increases, despite their at-will status. The court, interpreting Ohio law (Ohio Rev. Code Ann. § 3343.06), ruled that the law gave all authority for hiring and termination to the board of trustees, and that the president lacked the authority to bind the university when he made the promises to at-will employees.

Other problems may occur when administrators assume authority that the board has not delegated. In *Mendez v. Reynolds*, 681 N.Y.S.2d 494 (N.Y. App. Div. 1998) students at Hostos Community College, one of six community colleges in the CUNY system, challenged the CUNY trustees' decision to require students to pass a test of written English in order to graduate. The written test, which had previously been required as a condition for graduation, had been suspended several months earlier by the dean of academic affairs without trustee action. The trustees' resolution reinstating it as a graduation requirement was passed five days prior to graduation. The appellate court overturned the trial court's issuance of a preliminary injunction requiring the trustees to allow the students to graduate without having taken the test. The CUNY Board of Trustees had the "sole and exclusive authority to impose graduation and course requirements for all CUNY colleges," and the administrators did not have the authority to revoke the test requirement. Because the administrators lacked this authority, said the court, their notice to the students that the examination was no longer required had no legal effect. Furthermore, it would be unfair to bind the trustees to misstatements made by the Hostos administrators, even though the students justifiably relied on those misstatements. Quoting from *Olsson v. Board of Higher Education of the City of New York* (discussed in Section 9.3.2), the court expressed strong deference to the academic judgments of those with the authority to make those judgments. Nor did the doctrine of equitable estoppel apply in these circumstances, according to the court, because the board was acting in a governmental capacity, not a ministerial one. Finally, the court noted that forcing a college to award degrees when the students had not demonstrated the requisite level of academic achievement would be a "disservice to society."

In some circumstances, boards of trustees may avoid problems arising when an institutional officer or administrator acts beyond the scope of his delegated power by "ratifying" the unauthorized act. That act must have been within the scope of the board's own authority. "Ratification" converts the initially unauthorized act into an authorized act. In *Silverman v. University of Colorado* (above), for instance, the intermediate appellate court held that, even if the associate dean did not have authority to reappoint the professor, the professor was entitled to prove that the offer of reappointment had been ratified by the board of regents (541 P.2d 93, 96 (1975)). Similarly, in *Tuskegee Institute v. May Refrigeration Co.,* 344 So. 2d 156 (Ala. 1977), two employees of a special program operated by Tuskegee had ordered an air conditioning unit from the May Company. May delivered and installed the unit but was not paid the agreed-upon price. An intermediate appellate court reversed a damages award for May on the theory that the Tuskegee employees who ordered the unit had no authority to do so. The highest state court then reversed the intermediate court. It reasoned that, even though the employees had no actual or apparent authority, Tuskegee had kept and used the unit that the employees ordered and therefore could have ratified their unauthorized acts.

Even when the board of trustees (or a higher level) officer or administrator with authority has not ratified the unauthorized act of an officer or administrator, a court will occasionally stop the institution from denying the validity of the act. Under this doctrine of estoppel, courts may—in order to prevent injustice to persons who had justifiably relied on an unauthorized act—treat the unauthorized act as if it had been authorized. In the *Silverman* case, the plaintiff professor argued that various officials of the school had "advised her that her position was secure for the coming academic year" and that she had "reasonably relied on these representations to her detriment in that she did not seek other employment." The intermediate appellate court ruled that, if the plaintiff's allegations regarding the assurances, the reasonableness of her reliance, and the detriment were true, then "the doctrine of estoppel may be invoked if necessary to prevent manifest injustice." The Colorado Supreme Court reversed, recognizing the estoppel doctrine but holding that the facts did not justify its application in this case. The court reasoned that, since the professor had received adequate notice of nonrenewal, there was no "manifest injustice" necessitating estoppel and that, since the faculty handbook clearly stated that the board of regents makes all faculty appointments, the professor's "reliance on statements made by university officials was misplaced."

Another illustration of estoppel is provided by *Blank v. Board of Higher Education of the City of New York,* 273 N.Y.S.2d 796 (N.Y. Sup. Ct. 1966). The plaintiff student sought to compel the defendant board to award him a Bachelor of Arts degree. The question about the student's degree developed after he was advised that he could take advantage of a Professional Option Plan allowing him to complete a certain minimum amount of coursework without attending any classes. This arrangement enabled him to begin law school in Syracuse before he had finished all his coursework at Brooklyn College. The student had been advised by faculty members, the head of the department of psychology, and a member of the counseling and guidance staff, and the arrangement had been approved by the professors of the psychology courses involved, each of whom gave him the necessary assignments. At the time of his expected graduation, however, the student was denied his degree because he had not completed the courses "in attendance."

In defending its refusal to grant the degree, the college argued that only the dean of the faculty had the authority to determine a student's eligibility for the Professional Option Plan and that the dean had not exercised such authority regarding the plaintiff. The college further argued that the dean had devised regulations concerning the Professional Option Plan and that these regulations contained residence requirements that the student had not met. While the court did not dispute these facts, it emphasized, as a contrary consideration, that the plaintiff had "acted in obvious reliance upon the counsel and advice of members of the staff of the college administration to whom he was referred and who were authorized to give him such counsel and advice." Thus, "all of the elements of an estoppel exist" and the "doctrine should be invoked" against the college. The court ordered the college to award the plaintiff the A.B. degree.

In cases involving apparent authority, plaintiffs must convince a court that reliance on that apparent authority was reasonable. In *Sipfle v. Board of Governors of the University of North Carolina,* 318 S.E.2d 256 (N.C. Ct. App. 1984), the plaintiff had signed up for a trip to China organized by a university faculty member and had paid him $52,000 for the cost of the trip. When the travel agency arranging the tour went bankrupt and did not provide the trip or return the plaintiff's money, she sued the university, claiming that the faculty member was its agent and thus the university was responsible for refunding her money. Although the faculty member had used university stationery to advertise the trip, the university escaped liability for his actions because the court ruled that the plaintiff's belief that the university was the sponsor was unreasonable.

Another institution also escaped contract liability on the theory that the defendant could not properly rely on the representations of a college employee. In *Student House, Inc. v. Board of Regents of Regency Universities,* 254 N.E.2d 496 (Ill. 1969), also discussed in Section 3.2.4, a corporation that owned and operated a private student housing facility at Northern Illinois University sued the university for building additional residence halls. The plaintiffs stated that several years earlier, the university's director of housing had told them that the university would not build additional residence halls; and in reliance on that representation, the plaintiffs formed the corporation and built a private residence hall. The court found that the board of regents had the authority to decide to build residence halls and that the board had not delegated such authority to the housing director. The plaintiffs had relied on the representations of the director without discussing the matter with the president or any board member, said the court; and such reliance on the statements of "lower echelon members of the University staff" (254 N.E.2d at 499) was not reasonable.

Given the complexities of authority and delegation issues, particularly for trustees and administrators of public colleges, it is important that administrators keep trustees informed of important decisions, such as those involving large expenditures, major changes in academic policy, or major investment decisions. Obtaining ratification by the board of administrative decisions will help protect the college against claims of unauthorized actions by administrators. And, as always, seeking the advice of experienced counsel with respect to the authority of either trustees or administrators to take certain actions is a wise litigation avoidance strategy.

3.2.3. *Campus organizations.* Authority in postsecondary institutions may be delegated not only to individual officers or administrators but also to various campus organizations that are accorded some role in governance. Common examples include academic senates, faculty assemblies, department faculties, and student or university judicial systems. (See Section 9.1.4 for a discussion of judicial systems.)

Searle v. Regents of the University of California, 100 Cal. Rptr. 194 (Cal. Ct. App. 1972), is a leading case. By a standing order of the regents, the academic senate was given authority to "authorize and supervise all courses and curricula." Pursuant to this authority, the senate approved a course in which 50 percent of the lectures would be taught by a nonfaculty member (Eldridge Cleaver). Subsequent to the senate's approval of the course, the regents adopted two pertinent resolutions. One resolution provided that a person without an appropriate faculty appointment could not lecture more than once during a university quarter in a course offering university credit; the other provided that the course to be taught by Cleaver could not be offered for credit if it could not be restructured.

The course was taught as originally planned. When the regents resolved that the course not be given academic credit, sixteen students who took the course and six faculty members sued to compel the regents to grant the credit and to rescind the two resolutions. The plaintiffs argued that the standing order granting the academic senate authority over courses and curricula deprived the regents of power to act. The court, however, found that the regents had specifically retained the power to appoint faculty members and concluded that this case involved an appointment to the faculty rather than just the supervisory power over courses provided by the standing order: "To designate a lecturer for a university course is to name the person to conduct the course, at least to the extent of the lectures to be given by him. When the designation is of one to conduct a full half of the course, it appears to be a matter of appointment to the faculty, which is clearly reserved to the regents." Moreover, the court indicated that the authority of the academic senate was subject to further diminishment by the regents:

In any event, the power granted to the senate is neither exclusive nor irrevocable. The bylaws specifically provide that neither they nor the standing orders "shall be construed, operate as, or have the effect of an abridgment or limitation of any rights, powers, or privileges of the regents." This limitation not only is authorized but seems required by the overriding constitutional mandate which vests the regents with "full powers of organization and government" of the university, and grants to them as a corporation "all the powers necessary or convenient for the effective administration of its trust" (Cal. Const. Art. IX, § 9). To accept appellants' argument would be to hold that a delegation of authority, even though specifically limited, amounts to a surrender of authority [100 Cal. Rptr. at 195–96].

The court therefore determined that the regents, and not the senate, had authority over the structuring of the course in question.

Another case illustrating delegation of authority to a campus organization—this time a student rather than a faculty group—is *Student Association of the University of Wisconsin-Milwaukee v. Baum*, 246 N.W.2d 622 (Wis. 1976). The Wisconsin legislature had passed a statute that accorded specific organizational and governance rights to students in the University of Wisconsin system, including the allocation of student fees to student organizations and the creation of student governance committees. The chancellor of the Milwaukee campus asserted that, despite the statute's passage, he retained the right to make student appointments to the Physical Environment Committee and the Segregated Fee Advisory Committee. The Student Association, the campuswide student government, argued that the chancellor no longer had this authority because the statute had delegated it to the association. Applying traditional techniques of statutory interpretation, the court agreed with the students. Concerning both disputed issues, the court held that the statute's enactment removed the chancellor's authority to make the appointments.

If campus organizations have the authority to recommend or to make decisions or appointments, questions have arisen as to whether such organizations at public colleges and universities are subject to state open meetings acts. (For a review of this issue, see the discussion in Section 12.5.2 of *Perez v. City University of New York* (finding that the community college senate and its executive committee were subject to New York's Open Meetings Law), and *Board of Regents of the Regency University System v. Reynard* (finding that the athletic council of Illinois State University was subject to the state's Open Meetings Act).)

3.2.4. Trustee liability.

3.2.4. Trustee liability. Even though trustees are not employed by the college or university, they may incur personal liability for tort, contract, or civil rights claims. The rationale for imposing individual liability on trustees is similar to that for imposing liability on individual employees: they were acting on behalf of the institution as its agent, and, unless some defense such as sovereign immunity or state law immunity applies, they may be found personally liable for violations of the law. (For a discussion of immunity theories that may shield trustees from individual liability, see Sections 4.7.2 & 4.7.4.)

A case brought against individual members of a community college board of trustees by a former president illustrates the potential liability that trustees may incur. In *Bakalis v. Board of Trustees of Community College District No. 504*, 886

F. Supp. 644 (N.D. Ill. 1995), a former president of Triton College sued several individual members of the board of trustees. For interfering with his employment contract. He claimed that he was ousted so that the board members could hire a president who would allow them to hire their political allies. In this case, the court characterized the "third party" as an "unbiased Board of Trustees," stating that "it can be argued that a Board of Trustees composed of individuals acting to further their personal interests and not the interests of the college could be found to have interfered with Dr. Bakalis's contract with Triton College" [886 F. Supp. at 645]. In other words, the clique of allegedly unethical board members interfered with the ability of an otherwise "unbiased" board of trustees to fulfill its contractual obligation to the former president.

"Quasi-contractual" theories, such as estoppel, may be used to assert personal liability against trustees. In *Student House, Inc. v. Board of Regents of Regency Universities,* 254 N.E.2d 496 (Ill. 1969), also discussed in Section 3.2.2, a private housing developer sought to enjoin the trustees of Northern Illinois University from building additional student housing. The developer claimed that several administrators, such as the director of student housing and the director of research, had promised that the university would not build housing if private housing met the university's needs. The Illinois Supreme Court ruled that, as a matter of law, the developer's reliance on these oral representations of lower-level administrators was unreasonable, and refused to apply the plaintiff's agency law and estoppel theories.

Trustees of public institutions may be protected by constitutional immunity theories, which are discussed in Section 4.7.4. Trustees of private institutions may be protected by charitable immunity in states that recognize such immunity (discussed in Section 3.3.1). Most institutions agree to indemnify their trustees, officers and employees if they are found personally liable, as long as these individuals are acting within the scope of their official responsibilities and have acted in good faith. For a discussion of indemnification agreements, see Section 2.5.3.2.

(For a discussion of potential personal liability of trustees and administrators for decisions with environmental consequences, see Comment, "Whistling Past the Waste Site: Directors' and Officers' Personal Liability for Environmental Decisions and the Role of Liability Insurance Coverage," 140 *U. Pa. L. Rev.* 241 (1991); see also Section 13.2.10.)

Sec. 3.3. *Institutional Tort Liability*

3.3.1. *Overview.* Several common law doctrines provide remedies to individuals who are injured through the action (or, on occasion, the inaction) of others. Colleges are subject to common law liability as well as to statutory liability. (See Section 2.1 for a general discussion of the sources of liability for colleges.) Although the college is usually named as a defendant when common law claims are brought, claims may also be brought against faculty and staff in their personal capacities; these theories of liability are discussed in Section 4.7.

The most frequent source of potential common law liability is tort law, which requires a college and its agents to refrain from injuring any individual to which the college owes a duty. Negligence or defamation claims may be brought against the institution itself or against faculty or staff (or, occasionally, against students). And contract law (discussed in Section 3.4) is increasingly being used by employees, students, and others to seek redress from the college for alleged wrongdoing.

Because these are common law claims, state law governs the legal analysis and the outcome. The cases discussed in this section provide a representative selection of issues and resolutions. Administrators and faculty should use caution, however, in assuming that the analysis or the outcome of any particular case in another state would be replicated in the state in which the college is located. As always, there is no substitute for experienced legal counsel in responding to actual or threatened litigation involving common law liability issues.

A tort is broadly defined as a civil wrong, other than a breach of contract, for which the courts will allow a remedy. A tort claim involves a claim that the institution, or its agents, owed a duty to one or more individuals to behave according to a defined standard of care, that the duty was breached, and that the breach of that duty was the cause of the injury.

While there is a broad range of actions that may expose an institution to tort liability, and any act fitting this definition may be considered a tort, there are certain classic torts for which the essential elements of the plaintiff's *prima facie* case and the defendant's acceptable defenses are already established. The two classic torts that most frequently arise in the setting of postsecondary education are negligence[2] and defamation, both of which are discussed in this section; but other tort theories, such as common law fraud, are also appearing in lawsuits against colleges and universities. Various techniques are available to colleges for managing the risks of tort liability, as discussed in Section 2.5.

A college is not subject to liability for every tortious act of its trustees, administrators, or other agents. But the institution will generally be liable, lacking immunity or some other recognized defense, for tortious acts committed within the scope of the actor's employment or otherwise authorized by the institution or subject to its control. For example, if a student, employee, or other "invitee"

[2]The relevant cases and authorities are collected at Tracey A. Bateman, Annot., "Tort Liability of Public Schools and Institutions of Higher Learning for Accidents Associated with Transportation of Students," 23 A.L.R.5th 1; Allan E. Korpela, Annot., "Tort Liability of Public Schools and Institutions of Higher Education for Accidents Occurring During School Athletic Event," 35 A.L.R.3d 725; Allan E. Korpela, Annot., "Tort Liability of Public Schools and Institutions of Higher Learning for Accidents Associated with Chemistry Experiments, Shopwork, and Manual or Vocational Training," 35 A.L.R.3d 758; Allan E. Korpela, Annot., "Tort Liability of Private Schools and Institutions of Higher Learning for Accidents Due to Condition of Buildings, Equipment, or Outside Premises," 35 A.L.R.3d 975; Allan E. Korpela, Annot., "Tort Liability of Public Schools and Institutions of Higher Learning for Injuries Caused by Acts of Fellow Students," 36 A.L.R.3d 330; Allan E. Korpela, Annot., "Tort Liability of Public Schools and Institutions of Higher Learning for Accidents Occurring During the Use of Premises and Equipment for Other Than School Purposes," 37 A.L.R.3d 712; Allan E. Korpela, Annot., "Tort Liability of Public Schools and Institutions of Higher Learning for Injuries Due to Condition of Grounds, Walks, and Playgrounds," 37 A.L.R.3d 738; Robin Cheryl Miller, Annot., "Tort Liability of Public Schools and Institutions of Higher Learning for Accidents Occurring in Physical Education Classes," 66 A.L.R.5th 1.

(an individual who is entitled or permitted to be on college property) is injured as a result of a careless or wrongful act of a college employee, the college may be liable for that injury, just as any landlord or business owner would be under similar circumstances (see, for example, *Lombard v. Fireman's Fund Insurance Co.*, 302 So. 2d 394 (La. Ct. App. 1974)) (university was liable to student injured when she fell in hallway of classroom building because janitors had applied excessive oil to floor, rendering it slippery. The duty to keep the premises in a safe condition was breached). A similar duty may exist in classroom, residence hall, athletics, or other settings—even, on occasion, if the activity is performed off-campus or abroad.

Whether or not a college may be held liable for torts committed by student organizations may depend upon whether a supervisory relationship exists between the college and the organization. Although dated, the case of *Mazart v. State*, 441 N.Y.S.2d 600 (N.Y. Ct. Cl. 1981) contains a valuable analysis of an institution's liability for the tortious acts of its student organizations. The case concerned a libelous letter to the editor, published by the student newspaper at SUNY-Binghamton. The court's opinion noted two possible theories for holding postsecondary institutions liable: (1) that the student organization was acting as an agent of the institution, and this institution, its principal, is vicariously liable for its agents' torts (the *respondeat superior* doctrine); and (2) that the institution had a legal duty to supervise the student organization, even if it was not acting as the institution's agent, because the institution supported or provided the environment for the organization's operation. In a lengthy analysis, the court refused to apply either theory against the institution, holding that (1) the institution did not exercise sufficient control over the newspaper to establish an agency relationship; and (2) given the relative maturity of college students and the rudimentary need and generally understood procedure for verifying information, the institution had no legal duty to supervise the newspaper's editorial process. (For more contemporary cases that followed *Mazart,* see *McEvaddy v. City University of New York*, 633 N.Y.S.2d 4 (Sup. Ct. N.Y., App. Div. 1995), and *Lewis v. St. Cloud State University*, 693 N.W.2d 466 (Minn. Ct. App. 2005).)

The second theory articulated in *Mazart,* the institution's purported "duty to control," became an issue in a case that, although it did not involve a tort claim, addressed issues similar to those addressed in tort actions against colleges. An attempt to hold a university responsible for acts of individual students and a faculty member was rejected by the Supreme Court of Vermont. In *Doria v. University of Vermont*, 589 A.2d 317 (Vt. 1991), an unsuccessful political candidate sued the University of Vermont under several sections of the state constitution, arguing that the university had a duty to supervise and control its students and faculty members in order to preserve his constitutional right to a fair election. The students had worked as telephone pollers for a faculty member and two newspapers; and, the plaintiff alleged, the questions and the ensuing poll results had given other candidates an unfair advantage.

The court rejected the plaintiff's "duty to control" theory, stating that "requiring defendant to strictly regulate and control the activity involved here, or any other student and faculty activity that might have an impact on the electoral process, would be basically inconsistent with the academic environment" (589 A.2d at 321). The result in *Doria* is deferential to the activities of faculty members and their students, particularly in matters related to curriculum or faculty research.

Colleges may be able to escape tort liability under various immunity theories. Public colleges may assert sovereign or governmental immunity, while in some states, the charitable immunity doctrine protects nonprofit educational organizations. Each is discussed below.

Sovereign immunity is a common law doctrine that protects the state as an entity, and its agencies, from litigation concerning common law or certain statutory claims. (Immunity of a state and its agencies from suit in federal courts is also guaranteed by the Eleventh Amendment to the U.S. Constitution, and is discussed in Section 3.5.) The availability of the sovereign immunity defense varies greatly from state to state. While the doctrine was generally recognized in early American common law, it has been abrogated or modified in many states by judicial decisions, state legislation, or a combination of the two.[3] When a public institution raises a defense of sovereign immunity, the court must first determine whether the institution is an arm of the state. Because the doctrine does not protect the state's political subdivisions, entities that are separate and distinct from the state are not protected by sovereign immunity. If the court finds that the institution is a state entity, then the court must determine whether the state has taken some action that would divest the institution of sovereign immunity, at least for purposes of the lawsuit. Some states, for example, have passed tort claims acts, which define the types of lawsuits that may be brought against the state and the procedures that must be followed (see, for example, Florida's Tort Claims Act, Fla. Stat. § 768.28 (2001)). Other exceptions have been created by decisions of state supreme courts.

In *Brown v. Wichita State University,* 540 P.2d 66 (Kan. 1975), *vacated in part,* 547 P.2d 1015 (Kan. 1976), the university faced both tort and contract claims for damages arising from the crash of an airplane carrying the university's football team. In Kansas, the university's home state, the common law doctrine of immunity had been partly abrogated by judicial decision in 1969, the court holding that the state and its agencies could be liable for negligence in the conduct of "proprietary" (as opposed to "governmental") activities. But in 1970 the Kansas legislature had passed a statute reinstituting the immunity abrogated by the court. The university in *Brown* relied on this statute to assert immunity to the tort claim. The court, after reconsidering the issue, vacated its prior judgment to the contrary and rejected plaintiffs' arguments that the statute was unconstitutional, thus allowing the university's immunity defense.

A case decided by a Texas appellate court illustrates the substantial protection afforded a public university—but not one of its employees—by a state tort claims act. In *Prairie View A&M University of Texas v. Mitchell,* 27 S.W.3d 323 (Ct. App. Tex., 1st Dist. 2000), a former student sued the university when it would not provide verification of his engineering degree. Despite the fact that

---

[3]The cases and authorities are collected in Allen E. Korpela, Annot., "Modern Status of Doctrine of Sovereign Immunity as Applied to Public Schools and Institutions of Higher Learning," 33 A.L.R.3d 703.

the student produced a valid transcript and a diploma issued to him earlier by the university, the university registrar's office would not confirm that he had earned a degree, and the former student's employer required him to take a leave of absence without pay because his degree could not be confirmed by the university. The university defended the negligence lawsuit by claiming that it was protected by sovereign immunity under the Texas Tort Claims Act (Tex. Civ. Prac. & Rem. Code Ann. § 101.021(2) (1997)).

Although the trial court rejected the university's defense, the appellate court sided with the university. The student cited an exception in the state's Tort Claims Act that abrogated immunity if a "personal injury" had resulted from "a condition or use of tangible personal or real property." Arguing that it was the university's misuse of its computers or other equipment that caused his injury, the student asserted that the university's actions should fall within this exception to immunity. The court disagreed. It was actions of university employees, rather than the "defective property," that caused the alleged injury to the plaintiff, according to the court. Although the university was immune from liability in this case, the court noted that the registrar, who had been sued individually, was not.

A public institution does not necessarily lose its immunity defense even if it subsumes—and then must answer for the actions of—an entity that, when independent, did not enjoy such immunity. In *Kroll v. Board of Trustees of the University of Illinois,* 934 F.2d 904 (7th Cir. 1991), a former employee of an athletics association sued the trustees for wrongful discharge. Although the athletics association had been a nonprofit corporation independent of the university, the state legislature had merged the association into the university through special legislation. The court ruled that the board had not waived its immunity when it absorbed the association, nor had the legislature so provided. Therefore, the university's immunity extended to acts of the former association, and the case was dismissed.

A college may not be able to take advantage of the sovereign immunity defense in a situation where the complained-of action is not a "governmental function," but is one that a private entity could perform. For example, in *Brown v. Florida State Board of Regents,* 513 So. 2d 184 (Fla. Dist. Ct. App. 1987), a student at the University of Florida drowned in a lake owned and maintained by the university. In response to the university's defense of sovereign immunity in the ensuing wrongful death claim, the appellate court ruled that since the type of activity was not a governmental one, the university could not assert the immunity defense; once the university decided to operate a lake, it then assumed the common law duty of care to those who used it.

But the definition of a "governmental function" is inconsistent across states. A New York appellate court determined that when a state university provides security at a university-sponsored concert, it is performing a governmental function and is thus immune from tort liability. In *Rashed v. State of New York,* 648 N.Y.S.2d 131 (Sup. Ct., App. Div. 1996), the plaintiff had been stabbed by another individual in the audience at a "rap" concert sponsored by City University. The plaintiff claimed that the university failed to provide adequate security, despite the fact that audience members were screened with a metal detector and a pat-down search. The court ruled that, unless the plaintiff could show that the university had assumed a "special duty of protection," a showing that the plaintiff had not made, no liability could arise for this government function.

Although private institutions can make no claim to sovereign immunity, nonprofit schools may sometimes be able to assert a limited "charitable" immunity defense to certain tort actions.[4] The availability of this defense varies from state to state. For example, a federal appellate court roundly criticized the charitable immunity doctrine in *President and Directors of Georgetown College v. Hughes,* 130 F.2d 810 (D.C. Cir. 1942), refusing to apply it to a tort suit brought by a special nurse injured on the premises of the college's hospital. And in *Mullins v. Pine Manor College,* 449 N.E.2d 331 (Mass. 1983), the Supreme Court of Massachusetts, noting that the state legislature had abrogated charitable immunity for torts committed in the course of activity that was primarily commercial (Mass. Gen. Laws Ch. 231, § 85K (2002)), rejected the college's charitable immunity defense. The court also refused the college president's request to apply a good-faith standard, rather than a negligence standard, to his actions. (A good-faith standard would absolve the president of liability even if he were found negligent, as long as he had acted in good faith.) The *Mullins* case is discussed further in Section 8.6.2.

Despite these attacks on the charitable immunity doctrine, the New Jersey Supreme Court has upheld the doctrine, and has applied it to public as well as private colleges. In *O'Connell v. State of New Jersey,* 795 A.2d 857 (N.J. 2002), the court interpreted the state's Charitable Immunity Act (N.J.S.A. § 2A:53A-7–11), which applies to any "nonprofit corporation, society or association organized exclusively for religious, charitable or educational purposes." The plaintiff, injured when he fell down a stairway on campus, had claimed that, as a recipient of public funds, Montclair State University should not be protected under this doctrine from its alleged negligence. The court disagreed, stating that the public university was a nonprofit entity organized exclusively for educational purposes, and found no legislative intent to exclude public colleges from the protections of the Charitable Immunity Act. Because the student was a beneficiary of the university's educational purposes, said the court, the plain meaning of the statute gave the university immunity from liability. An institution's charitable immunity may also protect it from liability if one of its students is injured as a result of a school-sponsored event in another state (*Gilbert v. Seton Hall University,* 332 F.3d 105 (2d Cir. 2003)).

Under Massachusetts law, a charitable organization, even if found liable for negligence, can be required to pay no more than $20,000 in damages if the tort was committed in an activity that is in furtherance of the organization's charitable purposes. In *Goldberg v. Northeastern University,* 805 N.E.2d 517 (Mass. App. Ct. 2004), the parents of a student who died after visiting the university's

---

[4]The cases and authorities are collected in Allan E. Korpela, Annot., "Immunity of Private Schools and Institutions of Higher Learning from Liability in Tort," 38 A.L.R.3d 480; and Janet Fairchild, Annot., "Tort Immunity of Nongovernmental Charities—Modern Status," 25 A.L.R.4th 517. See also Allan Manley, Annot., "Liability of Charitable Organization Under Respondeat Superior Doctrine for Tort of Unpaid Volunteer," 82 A.L.R.3rd 1213.

health center sued the university, arguing that the negligence of its staff caused their daughter's death. A state appellate court ruled that the operation of a student health center was not a commercial activity, and thus was within the charitable purposes of the university, so the statutory cap on damages applied to the lawsuit. The court went on to rule, however, that the university had not been negligent in operating the health center, and found for the university.

The remainder of this section discusses the most frequently occurring subjects of tort litigation faced by colleges. Although negligence claims outnumber other types of tort claims, defamation claims (discussed in Section 3.3.4 below) are increasing, as are claims of educational malpractice (a hybrid of tort and contract claims, discussed in Section 3.3.3 below). The complexity and variety of a college's activities are matched by the complexity and variety of the legal claims brought by individuals who claim to have been injured by the actions— or inaction—of a college or its agents.

3.3.2. *Negligence.* Higher education institutions are facing a growing array of negligence lawsuits, often related to students or others injured on campus or at off-campus functions. Although most college students have reached the age of majority and, theoretically, are responsible for their own behavior, injured students and their parents are increasingly asserting that the institution has a duty of supervision or a duty based on its "special relationship" with the student that goes beyond the institution's ordinary duty to invitees, tenants, or trespassers. Courts have rejected this "special relationship" argument for most tort claims, but they have imposed a duty on colleges of protecting students from foreseeable harm, such as in cases of hazing or the presence of dangerous persons on campus.

When the postsecondary institution is not immune from negligence suits under either sovereign or charitable immunity, liability depends, first, on whether the institution's actions fit the legal definition of the tort with which it is charged; and, second, on whether the institution's actions are covered by one of the recognized defenses that protect against liability for the tort with which it is charged. For the tort of negligence, the legal definition will be met if the institution owed a duty to the injured party but failed to exercise due care to avoid the injury. Whether or not a duty exists is a matter of state common law. Typical defenses to tort claims include the plaintiff's own negligence or the assumption of risk doctrine.

Negligence claims against colleges are typically a result of injury to a student or other invitee (an individual who is lawfully on campus or participating in a college activity) as a result of allegedly defective buildings or grounds (premises liability), accidents or other events occurring either on or off campus as a result of instructional activities, cocurricular activities, or outreach activities, or alleged educational malpractice. Cases involving claims in each of these areas are discussed below.

Although courts were historically reluctant to hold colleges to the same standard of care applied to business organizations, landlords, or other noneducational organizations, that attitude has changed markedly in the last decade.

While courts in the early and mid-twentieth century applied the doctrine of *in loco parentis* to shield colleges from liability in tort claims brought by students or their parents, that doctrine fell out of favor when the age of majority for students was lowered to eighteen, making virtually all college students "adults" in the eyes of the law. Following the demise of *in loco parentis,* a few courts issued influential rulings that characterized colleges as "bystanders" with respect to the activities of "adult" students.

The seminal case involving the college as "bystander" is *Bradshaw v. Rawlings,* 612 F.2d 135 (3d Cir. 1979), *cert. denied,* 446 U.S. 909 (1980), in which the court refused to impose liability on a college for injuries suffered by a student. The student, a sophomore at Delaware Valley College in Doylestown, Pennsylvania, was seriously injured in an automobile accident following the annual sophomore class picnic, which had been held off campus. The injured student was a passenger in a car driven by another student, who had become intoxicated at the picnic. Flyers announcing the picnic were mimeographed by the college duplicating facility. They featured drawings of beer mugs and were prominently displayed across the campus. The sophomore class's faculty adviser, who did not attend the picnic, cosigned the check that was used to purchase beer. The injured student brought his action against the college, as well as the beer distributor and the municipality, alleging that the college owed him a duty of care to protect him from harm resulting from the beer drinking at the picnic. The jury in the trial court awarded the student, who was rendered quadriplegic, damages in the amount of $1,108,067 against all defendants, and each appealed on separate grounds.

The college argued on appeal that the plaintiff had failed to establish that the college owed him a legal duty of care. The appellate court agreed with this argument. Its opinion began with a discussion of the custodial character of postsecondary institutions. The court noted that changes have taken place on college campuses in recent decades that lessen the duty of protection that institutions once owed to their students. Assertions by students of their legal rights as adults reduced the colleges' duty to protect them, according to the court.

The student had the burden of proving the existence of a legal duty by identifying specific interests that arose from his relationship with the college. Concentrating on the college's regulation prohibiting the possession or consumption of alcoholic beverages on campus or at off-campus college-sponsored functions, he argued that this regulation created a custodial relationship between the college and its students. A basic principle of law holds that one who voluntarily takes custody of another is under a duty to protect that person. The plaintiff reasoned that he was entitled to the protection voluntarily assumed by the college when it promulgated the regulation. The court dismissed this argument on the ground that the college regulation merely tracks state law, which prohibits persons under the age of twenty-one from drinking intoxicants.[5] By promulgating the regulation,

---

[5]In actuality the regulation went beyond the statute because it applied to every student regardless of age—a point that could have favored the plaintiff had the court been sensitive to it. Lawyers will thus want to exercise caution in relying on the court's analysis of this particular issue.

then, the college did not voluntarily assume a custodial relationship but only reaffirmed the necessity of student compliance with Pennsylvania law.

Bradshaw influenced the rulings of other courts throughout the 1980s, the most frequently cited of which are *Beach v. University of Utah,* 726 P.2d 413 (Utah 1986), and *Rabel v. Illinois Wesleyan University,* 514 N.E.2d 552 (Ct. App. Ill. 1987). The student in *Beach* was injured after falling off a cliff while participating in a university-sponsored field trip. The student, who was under the legal age for drinking alcohol, had consumed alcohol in full view of the faculty advisor shortly before wandering off and falling. Despite the fact that the university had promulgated regulations against drinking, and the faculty member had failed to enforce those regulations, the court refused to impose liability on the university. The student in *Rabel* was abducted from her residence hall by a fellow student engaged in a fraternity initiation; the court found no duty, even with respect to the university's role as landlord of the residence hall.

This "bystander" approach appears to be falling out of favor with courts, who, in cases decided over the past decade, are now imposing the same duty on colleges and universities that has traditionally been required of business organizations, landlords, and other nonacademic entities. (For a discussion of the movement from the *in loco parentis* standard through the "bystander" approach to the present trend to treat colleges like another business or landlord, see the Bickel & Lake entry in the Selected Annotated Bibliography for this section.)

Institutions may be liable for the negligence of their employees, and, under certain circumstances, may even be found liable for the negligence of nonemployees. For example, in *Foster v. Board of Trustees of Butler County Community College,* 771 F. Supp. 1122 (D. Kan. 1991), a basketball coach had asked a student to pick up a potential recruit at the airport and drive him to a nearby motel. On his return from the airport, the student ran a red light and hit a truck, resulting in his death and injuries to the recruit and the truck driver. Both injured parties sued the college.

A jury awarded the injured recruit $2.26 million against the college and the estate of the driver. On appeal, the college argued that it was not responsible for the actions of the student driver. The court, noting that the student's car was uninsured and unregistered and that the student had no valid driver's license, ruled that "the Butler Community College defendants could have discovered [the driver's] unfitness for the task had any investigation been conducted" (771 F. Supp. at 1128). The college had policies requiring students driving on the college's behalf to be licensed; the college's failure to follow its policies and its failure to ascertain whether the student was qualified to undertake the responsibility it assigned him resulted in the court's determination that, for purposes of *respondeat superior* liability, the student was a "gratuitous employee" of the college. (See Section 2.2 for a discussion of *respondeat superior* liability.)

Despite the outcome in the Butler Community College case, colleges are usually not responsible for the torts of students. For example, in *Gehling v. St. George's University School of Medicine,* 705 F. Supp. 761 (E.D.N.Y. 1989), *affirmed without opinion,* 891 F.2d 277 (2d Cir. 1989), medical students who treated a colleague after he collapsed in a road race did not expose the medical school to malpractice liability; the court ruled that they had not acted as agents of the school. The outcome might have been different, however, if the medical students had been involved in an athletic event sponsored by the medical school. (For a discussion of institutional tort liability related to athletic events, see Section 10.4.9.)

Even if the individual causing the injury is acting in a volunteer capacity rather than within the scope of employment, a college may be liable for injury caused by that person. In *Smith v. University of Texas,* 664 S.W.2d 180 (Tex. Ct. App. 1984), the court refused to award summary judgment to the university on its theory that the tortfeasor (the individual whose actions resulted in injury) was acting as a volunteer referee at a sporting event. Questions about the university's duty to supervise the event, the fact that these "volunteers" were also employees of the university, and unresolved questions of fact dictated that the matter go to trial.

An emerging area of potential negligence liability for colleges and their staffs is computer security. For example, in addition to potential liability for computer usages that violate federal statutes (see Sections 13.2.5 & 13.2.12 of this book) or the First Amendment (see Section 8.5.1), institutions may become liable for negligent loss or disclosure of confidential electronic records, negligent supervision of employees who use electronic information for unlawful purposes, negligent failures to keep networks secure from outsiders who gain access for unlawful purposes, or negligent transmission of data that intrudes upon privacy interests of students, faculty, staff, or outsiders. (For discussion of federal law immunity from some negligence liability related to campus computer systems, see Section 8.5.2.)

3.3.2.1. Premises liability. These claims involve injuries to students or other invitees who allege that a college breached its duty as a landlord or landowner to maintain reasonably safe buildings (classrooms, residence halls, sports facilities, performing arts centers) or land (parking lots, athletics field, pathway, sidewalks). If the "dangerous" condition is obvious, there is no duty to warn an invitee of potential danger. For example, in *Shimer v. Bowling Green State University,* 708 N.E.2d 305 (Ct. Cl. Ohio 1999), a student who fell into an open orchestra pit sued the college for the injuries she sustained. The court found for the college, stating that the plaintiff, who had been working on a theater production and was familiar with the stage and the orchestra pit's location, was negligent in not using care to avoid falling into the pit.

The majority rule that landowners are liable only for those injuries on their property that are foreseeable remains intact, but courts are differing sharply on what injuries they view as foreseeable. For example, in *Pitre v. Louisiana Tech University,* 655 So. 2d 659 (La. Ct. App. 1995), *reversed,* 673 So. 2d 585 (La. 1996), the intermediate appellate court had found the university liable for injuries to a student who was paralyzed during a sledding accident. When a rare snowstorm blanketed the university's campus, the administration issued a written warning to its students, placing it on each student's bed, urging them to use good judgment and to avoid sledding in dangerous areas. Pitre and two classmates used a trash can lid as a sled, rode down a long hill, and Pitre struck the base of a light pole in a university parking lot. The appellate court ruled that the university had a duty to prevent unreasonably unsafe student activities, and viewed the written warning as an encouragement to engage in sledding. Although the court acknowledged that Pitre's own behavior contributed to his injuries, it found the university 25 percent liable.

The Supreme Court of Louisiana reversed, reasoning that the danger encountered by Pitre and his friends was obvious to a reasonably careful invitee. The court stated that, since sledding is not inherently dangerous, the university could not foresee that Pitre would select a location unsuitable for sledding; furthermore, said the court, it was reasonable for the university to install light poles as a safety mechanism. The court ruled that the university bore no liability for the plaintiff's injuries.

Premises liability claims may also arise when an invitee misuses a college building or other college property, but that misuse is claimed to be foreseeable. For example, in *Robertson v. State of Louisiana,* 747 So. 2d 1276 (Ct. App. La. 1999), *writ denied,* 755 So. 2d 882 (La. 2000), the parents sued Louisiana Tech University for negligence after their son died from falling from the roof of a campus building. The university had built a roof over its swimming pool; the roof, whose apex was 56 feet high, extended to within several feet of the ground. The son, a twenty-three-year-old senior, had climbed onto the roof after spending the evening drinking with friends. There had been several earlier incidents of students climbing on the roof; in all cases the students were intoxicated, and in two cases the students had been seriously injured. The parents of the student who died claimed that, because of these earlier climbing incidents, the injury to their son was foreseeable, and the university should have erected some form of barrier to prevent students from climbing onto the roof. Despite the university's knowledge of the earlier climbing incidents, and testimony that a modest investment in shrubbery would likely have prevented future climbing expeditions, the court ruled that the roof was not unreasonably dangerous, that the danger of falling off the roof was obvious, and therefore that the university owed no duty to prevent the student from climbing onto the roof.

The outcome in *Robertson* has been echoed by courts in cases where a student's misconduct was judged to be the proximate cause of his or her injury. For example, in *Nicholson v. Northeast Louisiana University,* 729 So. 2d 733 (La. Ct. App.), *writ denied,* 744 So. 2d 633 (La. 1999), a student fell over the railing in a residence hall during horseplay. The court ruled that it was his own actions, rather than the design of the building or the failure of residence hall staff to supervise the student, that caused the injury. Again, the injury occurred after the student had been drinking.

Colleges in Florida have gained some protection from liability in cases such as *Nicholson.* The legislature of Florida has enacted a law creating a potential bar to recovery in a negligence lawsuit if the plaintiff is voluntarily intoxicated and the court determines that the plaintiff is the primary cause of his or her injuries (Fla. Stat. Ann. § 768.075 (2001)).

Invitees have attempted to impose tort liability on a college when some form of criminal activity on campus results in injury.[6] Again, the majority rule is that the criminal activity must have been foreseeable. For example, in *Nero v. Kansas State University*, 861 P.2d 768 (Kan. 1993) (discussed in Section 8.6.2), the Kansas Supreme Court reversed a summary judgment award for the university and ordered the case to be tried, ruling that a jury would need to decide whether the rape of a student by a fellow student in a residence hall was foreseeable because the alleged rapist had been accused of an earlier sexual assault on campus, and university officials were aware of that fact when they assigned him to live during summer session in a coed residence hall. But in *L.W. v. Western Golf Association*, 712 N.E.2d 983 (Ind. 1999), the Indiana Supreme Court ruled that the owners of a "scholarship house" at Purdue University were not liable to a student who became intoxicated and later was raped in her room by a fellow scholarship house resident. Finding that there was no record of similar incidents that would have made such a criminal act foreseeable, the court refused to impose liability.

The legal analysis is similar when plaintiffs allege that an injury occurring at a recreational event sponsored by the college was foreseeable. The Supreme Court of Kansas ruled that Wichita State University (WSU) was not liable for the death of an invitee who was shot by a gang member after a fireworks celebration on campus. In *Gragg v. Wichita State University*, 934 P.2d 121 (Kan. 1997), the children of Ms. Gragg claimed that the university and several corporate sponsors of the fireworks program failed to provide adequate security, that the lighting was inadequate, and that the defendants had failed to warn the victim that there had been criminal incidents near the WSU campus. The court ruled that the university and other defendants did not owe Gragg a legal duty to protect her from the criminal act of a third party. Since the WSU police did not know that the assailant was on campus, or that he intended to shoot a rival gang member, the shooting was not foreseeable. The court distinguished *Nero* because, in *Nero*, the university was aware of the assailant's previous criminal record. No such knowledge was present in this case. Furthermore, similar celebrations had been held on campus for the prior seventeen years; no shootings or other violent crime had taken place.

But in *Hayden v. University of Notre Dame*, 716 N.E.2d 603 (Ct. App. Ind. 1999), a state appellate court reversed a summary judgment award for the university. A football fan with season tickets was injured when a football was kicked into the stands and spectators lunged for it. The plaintiff argued that the university should have protected its spectators from being injured, and that lunging fans were a common occurrence at Notre Dame football games. The court ruled that, because there were many prior incidents of fans lunging for footballs, Notre Dame should have foreseen the type of injury sustained by the plaintiff. Given the foreseeability of this behavior, the court ruled that Notre Dame owed the plaintiff a duty to protect her from injury. (For a discussion of

[6]Cases and authorities are collected in Joel E. Smith, Annot., "Liability of University, College or Other School for Failure to Protect Student from Crime," 1 A.L.R.4th 1099.

risk management issues in campus sporting events, see William P. Hoye, "Legal Liability Arising out of Major Sporting and Other Events on Campus," Outline for Annual Conference of National Association of College and University Attorneys, 2004, available at http://www.nacua.org.)

3.3.2.2. Liability for injuries related to on-campus instruction. Students or other invitees injured while involved in on-campus instructional activities may file negligence claims against the institution and/or the instructor. For example, in *McDonald v. University of West Virginia Board of Trustees*, 444 S.E.2d 57 (W. Va. 1994), a student enrolled in a theater course sued the university for negligence, seeking damages for a broken leg and ankle. The professor was teaching a class in "stage movement" and had taken the class outdoors, where the students were asked to run across a lawn simulating fear. Several students performed the exercise before the plaintiff took her turn. As she was running, she encountered a small depression in the lawn, stumbled and fell, and was injured.

Although the jury had found for the plaintiff, the trial judge had entered judgment for the university, which the Supreme Court of West Virginia affirmed. The student had sought to demonstrate that the professor's supervision of the class was negligent, but the court disagreed. The professor had inspected the lawn area before the class and had not noticed the small depression. Furthermore, evidence showed that theater students at the university were given safety instructions, and that the professor had discussed safety issues in that class. The syllabus included information on safety, including what clothing to wear, layering of clothing, and body positioning. The faculty member required students to wear high-top tennis shoes as a further safety precaution. The faculty member was present at the time of the student's injury, and the court found that no amount of supervision or scrutiny would have discovered the "small depression" that caused the student to fall. Therefore, said the court, the faculty member's actions were not a proximate cause of the injury, and the university itself was not required to maintain a lawn completely free of "small depressions."

This case is notable because of the relatively high level of caution apparently displayed by the faculty member. Clearly, the safety instructions (which, since they were on the course syllabus, were easily proven) and the faculty member's statement that she inspected the lawn area prior to the class were important to the defense of this lawsuit. A similar degree of care could not be demonstrated in another case in New York, and this difference appears to have caused a very different result. In *Loder v. State of New York*, 607 N.Y.S.2d 151 (N.Y. App. Div. 1994), Alda Loder was enrolled in an equine studies course at the State University of New York at Cobleskill. It was her first such course. Each student was required to perform two weeks of "barn duty," which included grooming a horse assigned to the student. When Ms. Loder approached the stall of the mare to which she was assigned and attempted to enter the stall, the mare kicked her in the face, causing serious injuries. The student sued, alleging that the university was negligent both in the way that the horse was tethered in the stall and in its failure to properly instruct the student with respect to how to enter the stall of a fractious horse.

The trial court had found the university 60 percent liable for the student's injury. The university appealed, but the appellate court sided with the student. First, said the appellate court, there was sufficient evidence of the horse's propensity to kick to suggest that the university was negligent in its method of tethering the horse. Furthermore, there were no written instructions on how to enter the horse's stall. The university employee who had shown the student how to enter the stall had used the incorrect procedure, according to an expert witness called by the university. Therefore, the court concluded, although the owner of a domestic animal normally is not responsible for injuries caused by that animal, unless the animal is known to be "abnormally dangerous," in these circumstances, the university was negligent in both failing to instruct the student regarding safety and in its method of securing the horse.

The student in *Loder* was a beginning student, and her lack of familiarity or experience with horses was a significant factor. If the student is experienced, however, the court may be less sympathetic. In *Niles v. Board of Regents of the University System of Georgia,* 473 S.E.2d 173 (Ga. App. 1996), the plaintiff, a doctoral student in physics at Georgia Tech, was injured in a laboratory accident. The student had been working in the laboratory on a project related to a course in superconducting crystals, and had been cleaning some equipment with a mixture of acetone, ethanol, and nitric acid, a highly explosive combination. A more senior doctoral student had suggested that "recipe" as a cleaning solution. Following the accident, the student asserted that the university, through his professor, was negligent in its failure to instruct him that this combination of substances was volatile.

The court was not sympathetic to the student's claim that he needed instruction. He had graduated *summa cum laude* with a major in chemistry, and had obtained a master's degree in physics with a 4.0 average. He had spent "hundreds of hours" in laboratories, according to the court, and had previously worked with all three of the substances. Therefore, said the court, the professor had the right to assume that the student either would know of the dangers of these substances, or would "perform the research necessary to determine those dangers and take the necessary precautions" (473 S.E.2d at 175). Therefore, the faculty member had no duty to warn the student about the dangers of mixing "common chemicals," said the court. (For a similar case with the same result, see *Fu v. University of Nebraska,* 643 N.W.2d 659 (Neb. 2002).)

The defense of "assumption of risk" is routinely used in negligence claims in which the defendant argues that the plaintiff was fully aware of the risks of a particular course of action and thus the defendant had no duty to warn the plaintiff of those dangers. In cases involving classroom instruction, however, this defense may have limited success. For example, in *Drogaris v. Trustees of Columbia University,* 743 N.Y.S.2d 115 (N.Y. App. Div., 2d Dept., 2002) the court denied the university's motion for summary judgment. A student enrolled in a graduate course in kinesiology (the study of movement) was injured after the course instructor used her for a physical demonstration of a clinical test. The student alleged that the instructor hyperextended her leg, resulting in a muscle tear.

The court rejected the university's argument that the student assumed the risk of injury by participating in the class.

In physical injury claims related to classroom activities, courts seemingly will consider the student's knowledge level. If the student is a novice, as in *Loder* and *Drogaris,* there is likely to be a duty to instruct and supervise. If the student is experienced, however, and has knowledge that is similar to the knowledge of the professor, then the court may not find a duty to supervise or instruct. And, of course, the more the institution can demonstrate that safety precautions and safety training were carried out, the more likely the institution is to prevail.

3.3.2.3. Liability for injuries in off-campus courses. An increasing number of lawsuits seek to impose liability on the college and its staff for injuries occurring during off-campus courses. Many graduate, and an increasing number of undergraduate, programs require some form of off-campus internship experience for students. Student teaching is required for students seeking degrees or licenses in education; social work students are typically required to complete a practicum in a social service agency; and students enrolled in health care-related programs may also have off-campus educational requirements. These experiences provide valuable opportunities for student learning, but may create liability for the college or university, even if it has no real control over what the student encounters in the off-campus placement.

Liability for activities at the off-campus site can occur in several ways. For example, the institution may be responsible for maintaining the safety of premises it does not own if it schedules a course there. In *Delbridge v. Maricopa County Community College District,* 893 P.2d 55 (Ariz. App. 1994), the college offered a course in plant mechanics to the employees of the Salt River Project (SRP) on the site of that organization. Although SRP employees performed the instruction, they were considered adjunct faculty of the college, and they were paid by the college. Individuals participating in the course were considered students of the college. As part of the course, the students were required to learn to climb a utility pole. The plaintiff, a student in the class, climbed the pole, lost his grip, fell, and was seriously injured. His lawsuit alleged negligence on the part of the college in not providing him with a safe environment.

The trial court awarded summary judgment to the college, but the appellate court reversed, ruling that there was a special relationship between the college and the student. Despite the fact that the premises were also under the control of SRP, said the court, the college also had a duty not to expose its students to an unreasonable risk of harm. Furthermore, the student was acting under the supervision of a college instructor. The case was remanded for a trial court's determination as to whether the college breached its duty to the plaintiff.

A significant decision by a Florida appellate court addressed the liability of a college to a student injured at the site of an off-campus internship. In *Gross v. Family Services Agency and Nova Southeastern University, Inc.,* 716 So. 2d 337 (Fla. App. 1998), the plaintiff had enrolled in the doctoral program in psychology at Nova Southeastern University. The program required her to complete an eleven-month practicum at an off-campus organization. Nova gave each student a list of preapproved practicum sites, and students selected six possible sites.

Nova controlled the placement of students at the sites. Gross was placed at Family Services Agency, approximately 15 miles from the university. One evening, while leaving the agency, Gross was assaulted by a man in the agency's parking lot and was injured. Previous assaults had occurred in the parking lot, a fact of which the university was aware, but the student was not. The student sued the university for negligence in assigning her to an unreasonably dangerous internship site without adequate warning. She also sued the agency, which settled her claim.

Although the trial court awarded summary judgment to the university, stating that it had no duty to control the agency's parking lot, the appellate court reversed. The court rejected the trial court's determination that this was a premises liability case, characterizing the college's duty as one of exercising "reasonable care in assigning [the student] to an internship site, including the duty to warn her of foreseeable and unreasonable risks of injury" (716 So. 2d at 337). The court characterized the relationship between the student and the university as "an adult who pays a fee for services [the student] and the provider of those services [the university]." Therefore, said the court, the university had a duty to use ordinary care in providing educational services and programs.[7] If the student was injured by the acts of a third party, then the university would only be liable if a special relationship existed. The court ruled that a special relationship did exist in this situation, relying upon a case involving litigation by a British tourist who sued a car rental company for failure to warn customers about the risk of crime in certain areas of Miami. The car agency's knowledge of the risk of crime, and the fact that the tourist was not from the United States, created a special duty, said that court, to warn the foreign tourist of "foreseeable criminal conduct" (*Shurben v. Dollar Rent-A-Car*, 676 So. 2d 467 (Fla. App. 1996)). So, too, the university had a duty to warn the student of the risk of assault, given its knowledge that previous assaults had occurred in the vicinity.

The Supreme Court of Florida affirmed the appellate court's ruling on the issue of the university's duty to warn the student (*Nova Southeastern University v. Gross*, 758 So. 2d 86 (Fla. 2000)). In addition to agreeing with the appellate court's reasoning that the university had assumed a duty of "acting reasonably in making [those] assignments" to a specific location, the court declared: "There is no reason why a university may act without regard to the consequences of its

---

[7]The court cited the ruling of a Massachusetts trial court, which refused to grant summary judgment in a negligence claim by a student who was sexually assaulted by an employer to whom she had been referred by the college's placement office. In *Silvers v. Associated Technical Institute, Inc.*, 1994 Mass. Super. LEXIS 506 (Mass. Superior Ct. 1994), the court did not rule on the negligence claim, but merely rejected the college's attempt to have the case determined in its favor prior to trial. The court noted that the employer accused by the former student of assault had specifically asked the college's placement office to send him only résumés for female graduates. The placement staff did not inquire as to the reason for the gender restriction; the court viewed that omission as possible evidence of negligence. Although the court stated that the college only had a duty to exercise ordinary care in the placement of its students, it stated that the female-only request should have stimulated some sort of inquiry from the placement office. Its failure to do so, said the court, was fatal to its motion for summary judgment.

actions while every other legal entity is charged with acting as a reasonably prudent person would in like or similar circumstances" (758 So. 2d at 90). The court
stated that the college's duty was one of reasonableness in assigning students to
practicum locations, a duty that required the university to warn students of
potential dangers posed by that location.

For negligence liability purposes, then, whether the location at which a student or staff member is injured is on or off campus is not the controlling issue.
What is more important, according to these cases, is whether the college took
adequate precautions to ensure the safety of its students, even if it did not have
total physical control of the site. (For further information about potential tort
liability related to internship programs, see Lori Chamberlain, "The Perils of
Internship Programs," 26 *College Law Digest* 171–74 (1996). Guidelines for drafting agreements between colleges and students involved in off-campus internships can be found in "Internships and Service Learning Agreements: Issues
Checklist and Sample Language," by Leslie Myles-Sanders & Dan Sharphorn
(Outline for Annual Conference of National Association of College and University Attorneys, June 20–23, 2001).)

Simply because a student has an off-campus assignment, however, does not
mean that the college assumes a duty to ensure that the student arrives at the off-
campus location safely. In *Stockinger v. Feather River Community College,* 4 Cal.
Rptr. 3d 385 (Cal. Ct. App. 2003), a student who was injured when she was riding
to an off-campus assignment in the back of a classmate's pickup truck sued the
college and the course instructor for negligence in planning and supervising
the class assignment. The court rejected her claim, ruling that "a college must be
able to give its students off-campus assignments, without specifying the mode of
transportation, and without being saddled with liability for accidents that occur
in the process of transportation" (4 Cal. Rptr. at 401).

Study abroad programs may present liability issues for colleges as well. Since
the mid-1990s, several colleges have been sued by students, or their families,
for injuries or deaths to students participating in study abroad programs.
Although the courts have rejected claims that a college that sponsors a study
abroad program is the insurer of students' safety, the courts are imposing a duty
of reasonable care on colleges that requires them to take steps to protect students, faculty, and staff from reasonably foreseeable harm. Particularly if the
program takes place in a country, or in a portion of a country, that is deemed
unsafe or prone to criminal activity, considerable precautions will need to be
taken by the college.

For example, St. Mary's College (a public college in Maryland) settled a lawsuit filed by three students who were injured during a study abroad trip to
Guatemala. While a group of thirteen students, two faculty members, and the
study abroad director were returning by bus to Guatemala City from a trip to a
rural area, the bus was stopped by armed bandits and robbed. Five of the
students were raped. Three of the students sued the college, arguing that insufficient precautions were taken for their safety, and that additional precautions,
such as an armed guard, a convoy of several vehicles, and the selection of a
safer route would have prevented the injuries. The college argued that sufficient

precautions had been taken and that, because previous study abroad trips to Guatemala had been uneventful, the injuries were not foreseeable. However, the college settled with the plaintiffs in order to avoid prolonging the dispute (Beth McMurtrie, "College Settles Suit by 3 Students Over '98 Attack in Guatemala," *Chron. Higher Educ.*, July 5, 2002, available at http://chronicle.com/daily/2002/07/2002070502n.htm).

A student was unsuccessful in persuading a Minnesota court to impose liability on the University of Minnesota for an assault by a taxi driver in Cuernavaca, Mexico, where the student was participating in a study-abroad program. In *Bloss v. University of Minnesota*, 590 N.W.2d 661 (Ct. App. Minn. 1999), the student asserted that the university was negligent in not obtaining housing closer to the location of the classes, in not providing safe transportation to and from campus, and in not warning the students about the possibility of assault. The court ruled that governmental immunity protected the university from liability for its decision to use host families to house the students. But with respect to the student's allegations concerning safety issues, immunity would not protect the university if it had breached its duty in that regard. In this case, however, the court ruled that the university had behaved reasonably. There was no history of assaults on students or tourists in the eighteen years that the program had operated in Cuernavaca. Students had been given a mandatory orientation session on safety, and had been told not to hail a taxi on the street (which the student had done), but to call a taxi company. The assault occurred when the student took a taxi to meet friends—not to attend class. Given the university's efforts to warn students and the lack of foreseeability of the assault, the court refused to impose liability on the university.

Because of the potential for substantial liability, it is important that an audit of an international site be conducted prior to making a decision to commence a study abroad program. For those colleges with study abroad programs in place, a similar audit should be conducted to ascertain whether the studying and living accommodations are reasonably safe and what foreseeable risks, if any, students and employees will be exposed to. (Articles from a Symposium on International Programs provide useful guidance for administrators, faculty, and counsel in addressing risk analysis and developing policies and practices that will protect students and employees from harm and colleges from liability: John T. Hall & Rowan Ferguson, "Case Study: University of Anyplace: Strategic Legal Risk Review," 27 *J. Coll. & Univ. Law* 119 (2000); and William P. Hoye & Gary M. Rhodes, "An Ounce of Prevention Is Worth . . . the Life of a Student: Reducing Risk in International Programs," 27 *J. Coll. & Univ. Law* 151 (2000). For additional recommendations on reducing liability for international programs, see the NACUA conference outline by William P. Hoye and Rebecca Hovey, "Reducing Liability for International Programs Post September 11th," June 2002 (available at http://www.nacua.org).)

3.3.2.4. Liability for cocurricular and social activities. In addition to potential premises liability claims, discussed in Section 3.3.2.1 above, an individual injured as the result of a college-sponsored event, or as a result of activity that is allegedly related to college activities, may attempt to hold the college liable for negligence.

For example, in *Bishop v. Texas A&M University,* 35 S.W.3d 605 (Tex. 2000), a student participating in a university-sponsored play was stabbed accidentally during a performance of *Dracula.* The play was directed by a nonemployee, but two faculty members served as advisors to the student production. Although the state appellate court found the university immune from liability under the state's tort claims act because the faculty members were not acting within their job responsibilities of teaching, the Texas Supreme Court reversed. The court said that, although the faculty advisors were volunteers, their participation as advisors was considered when salary increase decisions were made, the drama club was required to have a faculty advisor as a condition of receiving university recognition, and university policies required the faculty advisors to enforce its rules and regulations. The high court ruled that a jury could potentially find that the faculty advisors were negligent, and thus that the university was liable to the injured student. On remand, the trial court found that the advisors were not protected by governmental immunity, and that they were negligent in supervising the students. A state appellate court affirmed in *Texas A&M University v. Bishop,* 105 S.W.3d 646 (Tex. App. 2002). However, the Texas Supreme Court reversed, ruling that the university had not waived its sovereign immunity because the conduct of the faculty advisors did not fall within a statutory exception to immunity, and the director was not an employee of the university (156 S.W.2d 580 (Tex. 2005)). In a case with very similar facts, however, a Kansas appellate court ruled that the state's tort claims act shielded Pittsburgh State University from liability for the student's injury (*Tullis v. Pittsburg State University,* 16 P.3d 971 (Ct. App. Kan. 2000)).

In several cases involving injuries to students who were participating in cocurricular events, the court imposed a "special duty" on the college beyond that owed to invitees or to the general public. For example, when the institution sponsors an activity such as intercollegiate sports, a court may find that the institution owes a duty to student athletes on the basis of a special relationship. In *Kleinknecht v. Gettysburg College,* 989 F.2d 1360 (3d Cir. 1993) (discussed in Section 10.4.9), a federal appellate court applying Pennsylvania law held that a special relationship existed between the college and a student who collapsed as a result of cardiac arrest and died during lacrosse practice, and that because of this special relationship the college had a duty to provide treatment to the student in the event of such a medical emergency. On the other hand, if the student is pursuing private social activities that the institution has not undertaken to supervise or control, a court may find that no duty exists. In *University of Denver v. Whitlock,* 744 P.2d 54 (Colo. 1987), for example, the Supreme Court of Colorado reversed a $5.26 million judgment against the University of Denver for a student rendered a quadriplegic in a trampoline accident.

The accident in *Whitlock* occurred in the front yard of a fraternity house on the university campus. The university had leased the land to the fraternity. Whitlock asserted that the university had a duty, based on a "special relationship," to make sure that the fraternity's trampoline was used only under supervised conditions. The special relationship, Whitlock asserted, arose either from his status as a student or the university's status as landowner and lessor to the fraternity. But the court held that the university's power to regulate student conduct on campus did not give rise to a duty to regulate student conduct or to monitor the conduct of every student on campus. Citing earlier cases in which no duty to supervise social activity was found (including *Bradshaw v. Rawlings*, discussed in Section 3.3.2 above), the court concluded that the university did not have a special relationship based merely on the fact that Whitlock was a student. Inspection of the lease between the university and the fraternity disclosed no right to direct or control the activities of the fraternity members, and the fire inspections and drills conducted by the university did not create a special relationship.

In determining whether a duty exists, the court will consider whether the harm that befell the individual was foreseeable. For example, in *Kleinknecht v. Gettysburg College*, discussed above, the court noted that the specific event need not be foreseeable, but that the risk of harm must be both foreseeable and unreasonable. In analyzing the standard of care required, the court noted that the potential for life-threatening injuries occurring during practice or an athletic event was clearly foreseeable, and thus the college's failure to provide facilities for emergency medical attention was unreasonable.

On the other hand, when the institution attempts to prohibit, or to control, inherently dangerous activities in which its students participate, a court may find that it has a duty to those students. In *Furek v. University of Delaware*, 594 A.2d 506 (Del. 1991), the Supreme Court of Delaware ruled that the university's pervasive regulation of hazing during fraternity rush created a duty to protect students from injuries suffered as a result of that hazing. Furek, who had pledged the local chapter of Sigma Phi Epsilon, was seriously burned and permanently scarred when a fraternity member poured a lye-based liquid oven cleaner over his back and neck as part of a hazing ritual. After he withdrew from the university and lost his football scholarship, he sued the university and was awarded $30,000 by a jury, 93 percent of which was to be paid by the university and the remainder by the student who poured the liquid on Furek.[8]

The university asserted on appeal that it had no duty to Furek. While agreeing that "the university's duty is a limited one," the court was "not persuaded that none exists" (594 A.2d at 517). Rejecting the rationales of *Bradshaw* (discussed in Section 3.3.2 above) and its progeny, the court used a public policy argument to find that the university did have a duty:

> It seems . . . reasonable to conclude that university supervision of potentially dangerous student activities is not fundamentally at odds with the nature of the parties' relationship, particularly if such supervision advances the health and safety of at least some students [594 A.2d at 518].

---

[8]Subsequent to the ruling of the trial court, the university moved for judgment notwithstanding the verdict, which the trial court awarded. While that ruling was on appeal, the student who had poured the substance on Furek agreed to pay all but $100 of the $30,000 compensatory damages award. Although the Delaware Supreme Court subsequently overturned the judgment for the university, and ordered a new trial on the apportionment of liability between the student and the university, it does not appear that Furek availed himself of the opportunity for a new trial, leaving the university responsible for only $100 of the damage award.

Although it refused to find a special duty based on the dangerous activities of fraternities and their members, the court held that:

> Certain established principles of tort law provide a sufficient basis for the imposition of a duty on the [u]niversity to use reasonable care to protect resident students against the dangerous acts of third parties. . . . [W]here there is direct university involvement in, and knowledge of, certain dangerous practices of its students, the university cannot abandon its residual duty of control [594 A.2d at 519–20].

The court determined that the university's own policy against hazing, and its repeated warnings to students against the hazards of hazing, "constituted an assumed duty" (594 A.2d at 520). Relying on Section 314A of the *Restatement (Second) of Torts,* the court determined that the "pervasive" regulation of hazing by the university amounted to an undertaking by the university to protect students from the dangers related to hazing and created a duty to do so.

Because the outcomes in cases involving injuries related to cocurricular or social events are particularly fact sensitive, it is difficult to formulate concrete suggestions for avoiding or limiting legal liability. The cases seem to turn on whether the court believes that the injury was foreseeable. For example, in *Knoll v. Board of Regents of the University of Nebraska* (discussed in Section 10.2.3), the court refused to award summary judgment to the university when the student attempted to hold the university responsible for the injuries he sustained during hazing in a fraternity house, which, under university policy, was considered student housing controlled by the university. The court ruled that the kidnapping and hazing of a student by a fraternity known to have engaged in prior acts of hazing could have been foreseen by the university. A Louisiana court reacted similarly in *Morrison v. Kappa Alpha Psi Fraternity* (also discussed in Section 10.2.3).

On the other hand, a federal district court refused to find institutional liability for the death of a first-year student who fell from a cliff during a social event sponsored by a student organization. In *Apfel v. Huddleston,* 50 F. Supp. 2d 1129 (D. Utah 1999), the court reaffirmed the teachings of *Beach,* and dismissed the complaint, stating that institutions generally will not be held liable for injuries that occur off campus and that are not part of the academic program. Particularly when the injury is alleged to have resulted, at least in part, from the intoxication of the injured student or other individual, the court will examine closely the degree to which the college supervised the social or cocurricular event (or had undertaken the responsibility to do so), the reasonableness of the injured individual's behavior, and the relationship between acts or omissions of the college and the subsequent injury. This is particularly true of litigation involving injuries that are a result of hazing related to fraternity or other social organizations, which is discussed in Sections 10.2.3 and 10.2.4.

A case decided by the U.S. Court of Appeals for the Eighth Circuit illustrates the continuing influence of *Bradshaw* and *Beach* (see Section 3.3.2), and some courts' continuing reluctance to find a special relationship that would create a duty on the college's part to protect students from their own risky behavior. In

Freeman v. Busch, 349 F.3d 582 (8th Cir. 2003), a female student was sexually assaulted after consuming alcohol at a private party in a college dorm room. She sought to hold the college and the resident advisor liable for negligence because the resident advisor, who had been told that she was intoxicated and unconscious, did nothing to assist her. The court refused to find that a college has a "custodial duty" to protect an adult college student, and affirmed the trial court's summary judgment ruling for the college and the resident advisor.

Additional sources of liability may arise in states where case or statutory law establishes civil liability for private hosts who furnish intoxicating beverages (see *Kelly v. Gwinnell*, 476 A.2d 1219 (N.J. 1984), and *Bauer v. Dann*, 428 N.W.2d 658 (Iowa 1988)) or for retail establishments that sell alcohol to minors. Sponsors of parties at which intoxicants are served, particularly to minors, could be found negligent under the social host doctrine. (See also G. Rinden, "Judicial Prohibition? Erosion of the Common Law Rule of Non-Liability for Those Who Dispense Alcohol," 34 *Drake L. Rev.* 937 (1985–86).) A court in such a jurisdiction could rely on this law to impose a legal duty on the institution when alcohol is served at college-sponsored activities. Many states also have Dram Shop Acts, which strictly regulate licensed establishments engaged in the sale of intoxicants and impose civil liability for dispensing intoxicants to an intoxicated patron. A college or university that holds a liquor license, or contracts with a concessionaire who holds one, may wish to enlist the aid of legal counsel to assess its legal obligations as a license holder.

3.3.2.5. Student suicide. According to the National Center for Health Statistics, suicide is the third-leading cause of death among college students between the ages of fifteen and twenty-four.[9] Several high-profile lawsuits, some of which have been resolved against the interests of institutions of higher education, make it clear that faculty and administrators must take this issue very seriously, become educated about the warning signs of a potential suicide, and ensure that proper actions are taken if a student exhibits those signs. Although courts historically have refused to create a duty to prevent suicide, holding that it was the act of the suicide victim that was the proximate cause of the death, more recently courts are beginning to find, under certain circumstances, a duty to prevent the suicide, or a duty to warn appropriate individuals that a student is a suicide risk.[10]

Plaintiffs in a series of lawsuits concerning the potential liability of a college for students who commit suicide have attempted to persuade courts to find a "duty to warn" parents or others of potential dangers to students. In *Jain v. State of Iowa*, 617 N.W.2d 293 (Iowa 2000), the state supreme court rejected the claims of the parents of a student who committed suicide that a "special relationship" between the university and the student required the university to notify the parents of a student's "self-destructive" behavior. Unlike the outcome of the

---

[9]Robert N. Anderson & Betty L. Smith, *Deaths: Leading Causes for 2001* (National Center for Health Statistics, 2002), available at http://www.cdc.gov/nchs/data/nvsr52/nvsr52_09.pdf.

[10]Cases and authorities are collected at Sonja Larsen, Annot., "Liability of School or School Personnel in Connection with Suicide of Student," 17 A.L.R.5th 179.

Tarasoff case (discussed in Section 4.7.2.2), the Iowa court ruled that the failure of university staff to warn the student's parents did not increase the risk of his committing suicide; university staff had encouraged him to seek counseling and had asked him for permission to contact his parents, which he had refused.

More recently, however, a court has found that, under certain circumstances, there may be a duty to take "affirmative action" to prevent a student from harming himself. In *Schieszler v. Ferrum College*, 236 F. Supp. 2d 602 (W.D. Va. 2002), the aunt of a college student, Michael Frentzel, sued the college, the dean of student affairs, and a resident assistant for wrongful death after the student committed suicide by hanging himself. Frentzel had a history of disciplinary problems during his freshman year, and the college had required him to enroll in anger management counseling. After completing the counseling, Frentzel had an argument with his girlfriend, and the campus police and Frentzel's resident assistant were called. At the same time, Frentzel sent the girlfriend a note indicating that he planned to hang himself. The campus police and resident assistant were shown the note. Frentzel wrote several notes over the next few days, but the police and residence hall advisor took no action, except to forbid the girlfriend to see Frentzel. Frentzel hanged himself three days after the initial altercation.

The plaintiff claimed that a special relationship existed between Frentzel and the college that created a duty to protect him from harm about which the college had knowledge. The defendants asked the court to dismiss the claim, stating that there was no duty to prevent Frentzel from harming himself. The court concluded that, because college employees knew of Frentzel's threats to kill himself, the self-inflicted injuries, and his history of emotional problems, the plaintiff had alleged sufficient facts to support a claim that a special relationship existed, which created a duty to protect Frentzel from "the foreseeable danger that he would hurt himself." The court also ruled that the plaintiff had alleged sufficient facts to support her claim that the defendants breached their duty to Frentzel. Although the court dismissed the claim against the resident assistant, it ruled that a wrongful death action could be maintained against the college and the dean. The college later settled the case (Eric Hoover, "Ferrum College Concedes 'Shared Responsibility' in a Student's Suicide," *Chron. Higher Educ.*, July 29, 2003, available at http://chronicle.com/daily/2003/07/2003072902n.htm).

The outcome in the Ferrum College case may have influenced a preliminary ruling in another lawsuit. The lawsuit asserted breach of contract and negligence claims against the Massachusetts Institute of Technology (MIT) for allegedly providing ineffective psychiatric care to a student who committed suicide in an MIT residence hall (*Shin v. MIT*). A state trial judge dismissed the claims of the student's parents against MIT itself, but allowed some of the claims against administrators and staff to go forward (Marcella Bombardieri, "Lawsuit Allowed in MIT Suicide," *Boston Globe*, July 30, 2005, available at http://www.boston.com/news/education/higher/articles/2005/07/30/lawsuit_allowed_in_mit-suicide/). The judge cited the Ferrum College case and its finding that administrators and staff had a "special relationship" with the student that created a duty to protect her from reasonably foreseeable harm to herself. In April of 2006, the parties settled the case, agreeing that the student's death was probably accidental, and not a suicide.

The visibility of the incident at MIT and the growing concern among student affairs and health professionals about student suicide has resulted in attempts to create programs to prevent student suicide. (See, for example, Paul Joffe, "An Empirically Supported Program to Prevent Suicide Among a College Population," presented at the 24th Annual National Conference on Law and Higher Education, Stetson University Law School, February 2003.)

A widespread misconception among college administrators is that the Family Educational Rights and Privacy Act (FERPA, discussed in Section 9.7.1) prevents college administrators from contacting parents or other relatives if a student is threatening suicide. FERPA contains an exception for emergencies, including those involving health and safety. Furthermore, there is no private right of action under FERPA since the decision of the U.S. Supreme Court in *Doe v. Gonzaga University* (discussed in Section 9.7.1). Therefore, a proactive stance could both save the lives of students and protect the institution against legal liability.

(For further discussion of law and policy issues, as well as suggestions for drafting institutional policies to respond to mental health emergencies, see Peter Lake & Nancy Tribbensee, "The Emerging Crisis of College Student Suicide: Law and Policy Responses to Serious Forms of Self-Inflicted Injury," 32 *Stetson L. Rev.* 125 (2003); and Ann H. Franke, "Before and After Student Suicide: Preventing Tragedies and Mitigating Liability," presented at the 25th Annual National Conference on Law and Higher Education, Stetson University Law School, February 2004.)

3.3.2.6. Liability for injuries related to outreach programs. Programs open to the community or to certain nonstudent groups may involve litigation over the college's supervision of its own students or of invitees to the campus (such as children or high school students enrolled in precollege programs). Children may be on campus for at least three reasons: they are enrolled in campus educational, athletic, or social programs (such as summer camps); they are attending an event or using a campus facility, such as a library or day care center; or they are trespassers. Potential claims may involve liability for injuries sustained in sporting events, assault or other crimes, vehicular accidents, or allegedly defective premises. The fact that children are below the age of majority makes it difficult for a college defendant to argue that a particular danger was "open and obvious," or that the child assumed the risk of the danger. A case against the State University of New York at Binghamton is instructive. In *Carol "WW" v. Stala*, 627 N.Y.S.2d 136 (N.Y. App. Div. 1995), a mother alleged that a university student, participating in a "Big Buddy" program sponsored by the student association, had sexually assaulted her children. These children were not participants in the program, but had encountered the student while he was in the neighborhood because of the Big Buddy program. Although the court ruled that the program sponsors had a duty to supervise program participants and to provide for the safety of the children participating in the program, that duty did not extend to other children who were not program participants.

Another case illustrative of the college's potential liability when minors are involved in campus programs is *Dismuke v. Quaynor*, 637 So. 2d 555 (La. App. 1994), *review denied*, 639 So.2d 1164 (La. 1994). Dismuke, a fifteen-year-old, was a participant in a summer camp sponsored by Grambling State University. The university hired college students as counselors. Dismuke alleged that Quaynor, a Grambling student and counselor, had sexually assaulted her in the student union building after the campers had been dismissed early because of inclement weather. She sued both Quaynor and the university. Quaynor did not respond, and the court entered a default judgment against him. In ruling against the university, the trial court found that Quaynor was acting within the scope of his employment when the alleged assault took place because he had gone to the student union to supervise boys attending the summer camp. This finding provided the basis for the court's ruling that the university was vicariously liable for the injury.

A college may also face liability for negligent supervision of children, even if the injury is not caused by the act of a staff member. For example, in *Traficenti v. Morre Catholic High School,* 724 N.Y.S.2d 24 (N.Y. App. Div. 2001), the appellate court rejected Fordham University's claim that a student spotter's failure to catch a high school cheerleader participating in a cheerleading competition was not foreseeable. The court ruled that the case must proceed to trial, stating that the university and the high school that the student attended may have had a duty to supervise the competition more closely.

(For analysis of potential risks and recommendations for reducing those risks when the college sponsors or provides the facilities for activities involving children, see Laura A. Kumin & Linda A. Sharp, *Camps on Campus* (United Educators Insurance Risk Retention Group, Inc., 1997, available at http://www.nacua. org). See also Angela Alkire & Ann Franke, "Children on Campus," Presentation at the 24th Annual National Conference on Law and Higher Education, Stetson University College of Law, February 2003.)

3.3.3. *Educational malpractice.*

Another potential source of negligence liability, albeit a generally unsuccessful one for plaintiffs, is the doctrine of "educational malpractice."[11] The claim (which may also be based on contract law, as discussed in Sections 3.4 and 8.1.3) arises from the duty assumed by a professional not to harm the individuals relying on the professional's expertise. An individual who performs "one of the professions, or a trade, calling or business, . . . [is] required to exercise that degree of skill (a special form of competence) and knowledge usually had by members of such profession or such trade in good standing" (S. Speiser, *The American Law of Torts* (Clark Boardman Callaghan, 1985), 319).

Although they often sympathize with students who claim that they have not learned what they should have learned, or that their professors were negligent in teaching or supervising them, courts have been reluctant to create a cause of action for educational malpractice. In *Ross v. Creighton University,* 740 F. Supp. 1319 (N.D. Ill. 1990), discussed in Section 10.4.5, a trial judge dismissed the

---

[11]Cases and authorities are collected in David P. Chapus, Annot., "Liability of School Authorities for Hiring or Retaining Incompetent or Otherwise Unsuitable Teacher," 60 A.L.R.4th 260; and Joel E. Smith, Annot., "Tort Liability of Public Schools and Institutions of Higher Learning for Educational Malpractice," 1 A.L.R.4th 1139.

claim by a former athlete that the university had negligently failed to educate him, although it did allow a contract claim to survive dismissal. Asserting that the university's curriculum was too difficult for him, the former basketball player argued that Creighton had a duty to educate him and not simply allow him to attend while maintaining his athletic eligibility. The judge disagreed, ruling that the student was ultimately responsible for his academic success. The appellate court affirmed (957 F.2d 410 (7th Cir. 1992)).

A similar result was reached in *Moore v. Vanderloo,* 386 N.W.2d 108 (Iowa 1986), although the plaintiff in this case was a patient injured by a chiropractor trained at Palmer College of Chiropractic. The patient sued the college, claiming that the injuries were a result of the chiropractor's inadequate training. After reviewing cases from other jurisdictions, the Iowa Supreme Court decided against permitting a cause of action for educational malpractice.

The court gave four reasons for its decision:

1. There is no satisfactory standard of care by which to measure an educator's conduct.

2. The cause of the student's failure to learn is inherently uncertain, as is the nature of damages.

3. Permitting such claims would flood the courts with litigation and would thus place a substantial burden on educational institutions.

4. The courts are not equipped to oversee the day-to-day operation of educational institutions.

The Supreme Court of Kansas reached a similar conclusion in *Finstand v. Washburn University of Topeka,* 845 P.2d 685 (Kan. 1993). Several students in the university's court-reporting program sued the university for consumer fraud (since, they alleged, it had falsely claimed that its program was accredited) and for malpractice (since, they alleged, the performance of students in the program on the state's certification test was worse than that of other students). Although the court found that the students' latter allegation was true, there was no evidence that the students' failure rate was caused by poor instruction. Citing *Ross* and a case in which New York's highest court rejected a malpractice claim against a school system (*Donohue v. Copiague Unified Free School District,* 391 N.E.2d 1352 (N.Y. 1979)), the Kansas Supreme Court refused to recognize such a claim for essentially the same reasons cited in *Moore.*

More recently, plaintiffs raising educational malpractice claims have found the same judicial hostility exhibited in *Ross v. Creighton University.* A Colorado appellate court relied on *Ross* to reject the educational malpractice claims of nineteen students in *Tolman v. CenCor Career Colleges, Inc.,* 851 P.2d 203 (Colo. App. Ct. 1992), *affirmed,* 868 P.2d 396 (Colo. 1994), stating that "there is no workable standard of care here and defendant would face an undue burden if forced to litigate its selection of curriculum and teaching methods" (851 P.2d at 205). As did the appellate court in *Ross,* however, the Colorado court refused to dismiss the plaintiffs' contract claims against the college, ruling that if plaintiffs could prove that the college breached an express warranty to the students, or that they relied on misrepresentations by college personnel, their contract claims might succeed. A similar result occurred in *Ansari v. New York University*, 1997 U.S. Dist. LEXIS 6863 (S.D.N.Y. 1997); the court dismissed the plaintiff's negligent misrepresentation claim, but refused to either dismiss or award summary judgment to the university on his contract claim.

Although a municipal court—the City Court of Yonkers, New York—afforded plaintiffs relief under an educational malpractice theory, that result was reversed on appeal. In *Andre v. Pace University*, 618 N.Y.S.2d 975 (City Ct. Yonkers 1994), *reversed*, 655 N.Y.S.2d 777 (N.Y. App. Div. 1996), the plaintiffs sought assistance from the Small Claims Court, asserting contract and tort claims stemming from their dissatisfaction with a computer programming course offered by Pace University. The plaintiffs asserted that the course instructor selected an unsuitable text (breach of contract), that the course description was false and misleading (contract rescission), that the wrong advice given to the plaintiffs by the department chair constituted a breach of fiduciary duty, that the selection of an unqualified instructor was educational malpractice, and several other claims. The court found the university liable on the breach of contract, breach of fiduciary duty, and educational malpractice (negligence) claims, as well as finding a violation of the New York law prohibiting deceptive business practices. With respect to the malpractice claim, the court found that the professor's selection of an inappropriate text and her refusal to teach the course at a beginning level (as both the catalog and the department chair had promised) constituted sufficient evidence of proximate cause for the students' inability to learn anything from the course. The court awarded compensatory damages in the amount of $1,000 for each of the two plaintiffs and, finding the university's behavior "morally culpable," awarded each plaintiff $1,000 in punitive damages as well.

On appeal, however, in *Andre v. Pace University*, 655 N.Y.S.2d 777 (Sup. Ct., App. Div. 1996), the state's intermediate appeals court reversed, rejecting every ruling of the municipal court. The appellate court noted that "the courts of this State have consistently declined to entertain actions sounding in 'educational malpractice,' although quite possibly cognizable under traditional notions of tort law, as a matter of public policy." Furthermore, said the appellate court, the breach of contract claim would require the court to insert itself into educational judgments about the quality of the texts, the effectiveness of the instructor's pedagogical method, and other matters "best left to the educational community." Similarly, another New York appellate court rejected the claim of a student that Columbia University had failed to provide the promised quality of educational environment and had made false representations concerning the university's disciplinary process (*Sirohi v. Lee*, 634 N.Y.S.2d 119 (Sup. Ct., App. Div. 1995)).

In addition to attempting to state claims of educational malpractice, students have turned to other tort theories in an attempt to recover for injuries allegedly incurred by relying on incorrect advice of academic advisors. In *Hendricks v. Clemson University*, 578 S.E. 2d 711 (S.C. 2003), the South Carolina Supreme

Court reversed the ruling of a state appellate court that would have allowed the plaintiff, a student-athlete who lost eligibility to play baseball because of the incorrect advice he received from an academic advisor, to state claims of negligence, breach of contract, and breach of fiduciary duty. The court rejected the student's argument that the university had affirmatively assumed a duty of care when it undertook to advise him on the courses necessary to obtain NCAA eligibility, finding no state law precedents that recognized such a duty. The court also refused to recognize a fiduciary relationship between the student and the advisor, and similarly rejected the breach of contract claim, finding no written promise by the university to ensure the student's athletic eligibility.

But another case demonstrates a court's willingness to entertain student negligence claims for specific acts of alleged misfeasance or nonfeasance. In *Johnson v. Schmitz*, 119 F. Supp. 2d 90 (D. Conn. 2000), a doctoral student sued Yale University and several faculty members, alleging that the chair of his dissertation committee had misappropriated the student's idea for his dissertation research and took credit for it himself. The student filed claims of negligence, breach of contract, breach of a fiduciary duty, and defamation. The breach of contract claim was premised on the argument that Yale had made both express and implied promises to "safeguard students from academic misconduct" (119 F. Supp. 2d at 96), and is discussed in Section 8.1.3. The court refused to dismiss the negligence claim, stating that because the student was alleging intentional misconduct by the faculty members, it was not an educational malpractice claim. The court ruled that the student should be given an opportunity to demonstrate that Yale had a duty to protect him against faculty misconduct, and that such misconduct was foreseeable. Similarly, the court refused to dismiss the claim that Yale had a fiduciary duty to the student, stating: "Given the collaborative nature of the relationship between a graduate student and a dissertation advisor who necessarily shares the same academic interests, the Court can envision a situation in which a graduate school, knowing the nature of this relationship, may assume a fiduciary duty to the student" (119 F. Supp. 2d at 97–98).

Another student claim related to educational malpractice is negligent misrepresentation or fraud. These claims tend to be brought by students claiming that the institution misled applicants or current students about the quality of its programs or its accreditation status. For example, in *Troknya v. Cleveland Chiropractic Clinic*, 280 F.3d 1200 (8th Cir. 2002), a federal appellate court upheld a jury verdict that the institution was liable to students for negligent misrepresentation. The plaintiffs, graduates of the chiropractic school, claimed that the school had failed to provide the quality and quantity of clinical training that it had promised; they filed claims of breach of contract, fraud, and negligent misrepresentation. The plaintiffs had graduated, passed the licensing exam, and had received licenses.

The jury found for the college on the breach of contract and fraud claims, but found for the plaintiffs on the negligent misrepresentation claims, awarding each plaintiff $1 in compensatory damages and $15,000 each in punitive damages. Although the court upheld the compensatory damages award, it reversed the punitive damages award, stating that there was no evidence that the school knew that the false information it provided would have injured the students.

In an earlier case, *Nigro v. Research College of Nursing,* 876 S.W.2d 681 (Ct. App. Mo. 1994), the court rejected students' claims that the college's failure to inform them that its accreditation had been delayed was grounds for a fraud claim. The court ruled that the students could not prove that they had relied on this representation in enrolling in the nursing program, and thus could not maintain a fraud claim. The court did not rule as to whether the college had a duty to disclose to applicants and students that the printed information concerning its accreditation status was incorrect.

The Alabama Supreme Court refused to dismiss a claim of promissory fraud against a dean and vice president of academic affairs brought by a student who alleged that he had been fraudulently advised about the music media curriculum at Alabama State University. In *Byrd v. Lamar,* 846 So. 2d 334 (Ala. 2003), the plaintiff alleged that, despite descriptions of such a program in institutional publications and the representations of the dean that he could complete the program within four years, no such program existed at the university. Finding that the student had sufficiently alleged facts to preclude summary judgment, the court ordered that the promissory fraud claim be tried.

A state appellate court refused to hear a former law student's claim that Loyola University of New Orleans had been unjustly enriched by accepting the student's tuition for a course whose instructor the law school later determined was incompetent. In *Miller v. Loyola University of New Orleans,* 829 So. 2d 1057 (La. App. 2002), the court ruled that, because the student had passed the course and received credit for it, and had retaken the course at his own expense voluntarily (despite the fact that the law school offered him the opportunity to audit the course at no charge), the university had not been unjustly enriched. The court also dismissed Miller's educational malpractice claim for the reasons discussed earlier in this section.

Lawsuits against accrediting associations for fraud or misrepresentation have typically been unsuccessful. These cases are discussed in Section 14.3.

3.3.4. Defamation.

Another tort asserted against postsecondary institutions, defamation, is committed by the oral or written publication of matter that tends to injure a person's reputation. The matter must have been published to some third person and must have been capable of defamatory meaning and understood as referring to the plaintiff in a defamatory sense.[12] (See Sections 10.3.6 and 10.3.7 for a further discussion of defamation.) Defamation claims are also asserted against officials of the institution, such as deans or department chairs. These claims are discussed in Section 4.7.2.3.

One of the most important defenses against a defamation action is the conditional or qualified privilege of fair comment and criticism. An application of

---

[12]Cases and authorities are collected at Theresa Ludwig Kruk, Annot., "Libel and Slander: Privileged Nature of Statements or Utterances by Members of Governing Body of Public Institution of Higher Learning in Course of Official Proceedings," 33 A.L.R.4th 632.

this privilege occurred in *Olsson v. Indiana University Board of Trustees*, 571 N.E.2d 585 (Ind. Ct. App. 1991). A prospective teacher, who had graduated from the university and had performed her student teaching under the supervision of one of its faculty, sued the university, claiming that a letter of reference written by a faculty member was libelous. The faculty member had described both the plaintiff's strengths and weaknesses with apparent candor.

The court ruled that the faculty member and the university were protected by a qualified privilege that may be asserted "if a need exists for full and unrestricted communication regarding matters on which the parties have a common interest or duty" (571 N.E.2d at 587). Such a privilege would cover any communication "if made in good faith on any subject matter in which the party making the communication has an interest or in reference to which he has a duty, either public or private, whether legal or moral, or social, if made to a person having a corresponding interest or duty" (571 N.E.2d at 587). Noting that the university had a responsibility to prepare teachers, the court ruled that this letter of recommendation was an appropriate occasion for the use of the qualified privilege.

The scope of the qualified privilege is a matter of state law, and may differ by state. A case decided by a federal trial court, applying District of Columbia law, examined that jurisdiction's case law regarding the qualified privilege in a defamation claim. In *Tacka v. Georgetown University*, 193 F. Supp. 2d 43 (D.D.C. 2001), a faculty member, Tacka, sued the university for breach of contract and defamation. His defamation claim was based on the use of an allegedly defamatory evaluation of Tacka's scholarly work by a faculty rank and tenure committee considering whether to recommend that Tacka receive tenure. The evaluation, written by an untenured professor at a university in another state, accused Tacka of plagiarizing portions of a journal article. Without determining whether the plagiarism claim was true, the rank and tenure committee recommended against tenure for Professor Tacka. Later, the University's Research Integrity Committee exonerated Tacka of plagiarism, and he was granted tenure the following year.

In its motion for summary judgment, the university claimed that the department chair's "publication" of the allegedly defamatory external evaluation to the rank and tenure committee was protected by a qualified privilege. The trial court ruled that the qualified privilege may be lost if the plaintiff can demonstrate that the publisher acts with malice, or published the evaluation beyond those who have a business reason for receiving the information. Tacka had alleged that the department chair's decision to solicit the sole external evaluation of his work from an individual who held a personal bias against him, and who was allegedly unqualified to perform the evaluation, demonstrated that the chair had acted with malice. The court ruled that Tacka should have the opportunity to have a jury decide whether the privilege was lost.

Another conditional privilege that is important for administrators in state institutions is the privilege afforded to executive and administrative officers of government. In *Shearer v. Lambert*, 547 P.2d 98 (Or. 1976), an assistant professor at Oregon State University brought a libel action against the head of her department. While admitting that the statement was defamatory, the defendant argued that the privilege of government officers should be extended to lesser executive or administrative officers, such as the head of a department. The court agreed, reasoning that, since "the privilege is designed to free public officials from intimidation in the discharge of their duties, we are unable to explain why this policy would not apply equally to inferior as well as to high-ranking officers." This qualified privilege is available, however, only where the defendant "publishes the defamatory matter in the performance of his official duties."

If a defamation lawsuit is brought against the institution by a prominent administrator, trustee, or faculty member, a constitutional privilege may come into play. If the plaintiff is a "public figure," he or she must prove that the defendant acted with "actual malice," and the privilege to defame is thus broader than it would be if the plaintiff were a "private figure." If a person is a public figure, another person may not be held liable for defaming him unless that other person's comment "was made with knowledge of its falsity or in reckless disregard of whether it was false or true" (*Garrison v. Louisiana,* 379 U.S. 64, 74 (1964)). Thus, to the extent that members of the academic community can be characterized as public figures, the institution's potential liability for defamation is reduced. It is unlikely on any given campus at any particular time, however, that many administrators, staff, or faculty would be considered public figures.

But athletics coaches, or even certain student athletes, may be considered to be public figures because of extensive press coverage or college-sponsored promotional activities. Furthermore, statements made concerning coaches or athletes are typically considered to be statements of opinion. For example, in two illustrative cases, coaches' defamation claims were unsuccessful because the courts ruled that the statements made about them were opinion, rather than fact, and thus did not meet the legal standard for defamation. In the first, *Moore v. University of Notre Dame,* 968 F. Supp. 1330 (N.D. Ind. 1997), a former offensive line football coach was terminated, according to the university, because he had behaved abusively toward the players. In the second, *Campanelli v. The Regents of the University of California,* 51 Cal. Rptr. 2d 891 (Cal. Ct. App. 1996), university officials stated that the coach was fired because parents felt that he was placing their children under so much pressure that the children were becoming ill. In both cases, the courts ruled that neither statement was a factual assertion and, therefore, could not form the basis for a defamation claim.

Charges of sexual misconduct against students have provided multiple opportunities for defamation litigation against colleges. One of the more famous cases is *Doe v. Gonzaga University,* 24 P.3d 390 (Wash. 2001), reversed on other grounds, *Gonzaga University v. Doe,* 536 U.S. 273 (2002). In *Doe,* a university administrator overheard a student office assistant tell another student that John Doe, an education student in his senior year, had raped a female student. At the time, John Doe was doing his student teaching. The administrator and a fellow staff member, both involved in placement for student teachers, met with the student whose conversation they had overheard, but the alleged victim had not reported any assault and refused to meet with the administrators to discuss the alleged incident. Despite the fact that the alleged victim would not provide information or corroborate the assault claim, the administrators decided not to recommend Doe for teacher certification because of these allegations. They gave Doe a letter to that effect; when Doe and his parents asked about his appeal rights, they were told there were none.

John Doe sued Gonzaga and several administrators for defamation, negligence, and breach of contract. At trial, Doe testified that his sexual relationship with the female student was consensual; in a videotaped deposition, the alleged student victim denied that Doe had assaulted her and denied that she had made any accusatory statements to university staff. A jury awarded Doe $500,000 for defamation and an additional $655,000 in compensatory and punitive damages for other claims, including a claim brought under FERPA that the Supreme Court dismissed (the FERPA claims in *Gonzaga v. Doe* are discussed in Section 9.7.1).

Although the appellate court reversed the jury's defamation verdict, the Washington Supreme Court reinstated it, but affirmed the appellate court's dismissal of the negligence claim, stating that the university had no duty to investigate the allegations of sexual assault. With respect to the defamation claim, the court ruled that the administrators were not protected by a qualified privilege because they were not acting "in the ordinary course of their work" when they involved themselves in the allegations of the student whose conversation they listed to secretly.

The result in *Doe* is instructive in many respects. First, the university's apparent refusal to provide Doe with an opportunity to tell his side of the story appears arbitrary and unfair, even though, as a private institution, Gonzaga was not required to provide due process protections to Doe. This refusal very likely influenced the jury's decision on the defamation claim and affected the size of the damage award. Second, the fact that the alleged victim was unwilling to make even an informal complaint is troubling. Although it is not unusual for victims of sexual assault to refuse to cooperate with either police or student affairs staff, proceeding to sanction a student without corroboration from the alleged victim or some other evidence (a witness, medical evidence, and so on) may create subsequent legal liability for the college.

(For a case with similar facts and ensuing liability for the institution, see *Mallory v. Ohio University,* 2001 Ohio App. LEXIS 5720 (Ct. App. Ohio, 10th Dist., 2001), *appeal denied,* 767 N.E.2d 272 (Ohio 2002). For suggestions on avoiding liability for defamation when investigating sexual harassment claims, see Ellen M. Babbitt & Zachary Silverstein, "Avoiding Defamation Claims Arising Out of Sexual Harassment Investigations," *Employment Action,* Vol. 4, no. 1 (Winter 2001), published by United Educators Risk Retention Group, Inc. (available at http://www.ue.org).)

Academic freedom may not protect a faculty member from potential defamation liability when research findings are communicated, or even during the research process. In *164 Mulberry Street Corp. v. Columbia University*, 771 N.Y.S. 2d 16 (N.Y. App. Div. 2004), a professor of business at Columbia University conducted a research project to study the responses of approximately fifteen restaurants when they received letters falsely accusing them of serving food that resulted in food poisoning of the letter writer's wife. The letters did not threaten to report the alleged food poisoning to the department of health. The restaurants responded by throwing away large quantities of food, subjecting their employees to scrutiny for mishandling food, attempting to send flowers to the fictitious address on the letter, and the New York City Department of Health became involved, subjecting the restaurants that received the letters to inspections. Some of the restaurant owners alleged that they suffered physical and psychiatric problems as a result of the "research." When the professor notified the restaurants that the letters were false, they responded by suing Columbia University and the professor for twenty-four counts of action involving libel, negligent and intentional infliction of emotional distress, and negligent misrepresentation. They sought compensatory and punitive damages.

The appellate court affirmed the trial court's refusal to dismiss the plaintiffs' claims of emotional distress, libel per se, and fraudulent and negligent misrepresentation claims, stating that the professor "recklessly disregarded the potential consequences of [his] conduct," and determining that there was a sufficient basis for allowing a jury to determine whether the professor's conduct met the standard of outrageousness necessary to find liability. The court dismissed the claim for punitive damages, however, stating that the professor did not act maliciously, even though his research project was "misguided." The court mentions in passing that there was apparently no system in the business school to review faculty research projects, which might have prevented such a project from taking place. (For a discussion of procedures for reviewing research involving human subjects, see Section 13.2.3.2.)

Institutions that operate computer networks may be sued for transmitted libelous statements that injure those mentioned in such statements. Service providers will often be immune from such liability, however, under 47 U.S.C. § 230 (see Section 8.5.1).

Institutions may incur liability to third parties who are injured because a letter of reference concerning a former employee does not disclose unsafe or illegal acts by that employee. The California Supreme Court ruled in *Randi W. v. Muroc Joint Unified School District*, 929 P.2d 582 (Cal. 1997), that school districts and their employees could be found liable for fraud and negligent misrepresentation. The case is discussed in Section 4.7.2.2.

3.3.5. Other sources of tort liability.
Colleges as employers may incur liability for the torts of their employees or agents. Liability for employee torts may be incurred under the *respondeat superior* doctrine, which makes the employer responsible for the tortious acts of its employees. If, however, the tortfeasor is acting outside the scope of his or her employment, the court may shield the employer from liability. Typical claims brought by plaintiffs include

negligent hiring, negligent supervision, and negligent retention of the offending employee or agent.[13]

In *Forester v. State of New York,* 645 N.Y.S.2d 971 (Ct. Cl. 1996), the court rejected the claim of an individual allegedly assaulted by a karate instructor employed by the State University of New York (SUNY). Despite the fact that the assault occurred while the plaintiff was a full-time student, on school property, and during school hours, the court ruled that the instructor's conduct did not further SUNY's business, SUNY did not authorize the violence, and the use of violence was not within the discretion afforded the instructor by the university.

A similar outcome occurred in *Smith v. Gardner and Board of Regents, San Jacinto College District,* 998 F. Supp. 708 (S.D. Miss. 1998). The plaintiff was involved in a two-car accident with Gardner, who was an assistant baseball coach employed by the college. The baseball team had traveled to Meridian, Mississippi, to participate in two baseball games; three college vans were used to make the trip. Gardner had the keys to one of the vans, and took it, without the knowledge or permission of the coach, to make two personal trips. One trip was to purchase beer for himself, which he then drank. The second trip was to purchase chewing tobacco and to engage in a sightseeing trip at 3:00 a.m. During this sightseeing trip, Gardner's van struck Smith. Gardner's blood alcohol content was well over the legal limit, and he was arrested for driving under the influence of alcohol.

The court rejected the plaintiff's claim that the College should bear responsibility for Gardner's actions. It noted that Gardner's supervisor had no knowledge of the trip, that Gardner was not engaging in activity that benefited the team, and that the excursion was for Gardner's personal benefit. To the plaintiff's argument that Gardner was on an officially sanctioned college trip, the court replied that simply being away "on business" did not mean that every action that Gardner took was related to his job. The court awarded summary judgment for the college.

In *Clement v. Delgado Community College,* 634 So. 2d 412 (La. App. 1994), nine members of the college's baseball team sued both the student coach, who had been driving a college van, and the college for injuries sustained when a tire blew out suddenly and a serious accident ensued. A jury had found the tire manufacturer 60 percent liable and the college 40 percent liable, primarily because

---

[13]Cases and authorities are collected in Reuben I. Friedman, Annot., "When Is Employer Chargeable with Negligence in Hiring Careless, Reckless, or Incompetent Independent Contractor," 78 A.L.R.3d 910; John H. Derrick, Annot., "Landlord's Tort Liability to Tenant for Personal Injury or Property Damage Resulting from Criminal Conduct of Employee," 38 A.L.R.4th 240; and Erwin S. Barbre, Annot., "Workmen's Compensation Provision as Precluding Employee's Action Against Employer for Fraud, False Imprisonment, Defamation, or the Like," 46 A.L.R.3d 1279; Allan E. Korpela, Annot., "Tort Liability of Public Schools and Institutions of Higher Learning for Injuries Resulting from Lack or Insufficiency of Supervision," 38 A.L.R.3d 830; Allan E. Korpela, Annot., "Liability of Private Schools and Institutions of Higher Learning for Negligence of, or Lack of Supervision by, Teachers and Other Employees or Agents," 38 A.L.R.3d 908; David P. Chapus, Annot., "Liability of School Authorities for Hiring or Retaining Incompetent or Otherwise Unsuitable Teacher," 60 A.L.R.4th 260.

it was established that the driver acted negligently in his reaction to the blowout by hitting the brakes and had not been trained. The court stated that the college had three duties to the baseball players: to properly maintain the vehicle, to select a qualified driver, and to train the driver properly. The appellate court affirmed the finding of the jury that the college had not properly maintained the vehicle, that the college was negligent in allowing a student to drive the van when its own policies required that all van drivers have a commercial driver's license (which the student did not possess), and that the college was negligent in not training the driver how to respond to a tire blowout, even though a similar incident had happened the previous year. It also reversed the liability finding against the tire manufacturer, resulting in a multimillion-dollar damage award to the nine plaintiffs to be paid in full by the college.

The outcome in the *Delgado Community College* case underscores the importance of serious attention to both vehicle maintenance and the training and supervision of drivers. The court noted that faculty and staff were never transported in these vans, and that the team's coaches used other forms of transportation and simply met the team wherever the games were held. These facts were very damaging to the college because they suggested a lack of concern on the college's part for student safety.

A state court has rejected a student's attempt to state a claim against a state university for "negligent investigation" of an alleged infraction of the student code of conduct. In *Weitz v. State* (discussed in Section 9.1.2), the student sued the college after being found not guilty of the infraction. The court stated that, because no cause of action exists under state law for negligent prosecution of a crime, such a theory could not be applied to investigation and "prosecution" of a disciplinary charge.

But the Supreme Court of Nebraska was more sympathetic to a student's claim that the University of Nebraska had failed to properly supervise a professor who uploaded two class papers written by the student on the Internet. The papers allegedly contained "intimate details" of the student's life, and she had not given the professor permission to post them on the Internet. In *Shlien v. Board of Regents of University of Nebraska,* 640 N.W.2d 643 (Neb. 2002), the student claimed that she did not discover that her papers had been posted to the Internet until her parents discovered them on a Web site two years after they had been posted by the professor. Although the university claimed that the lawsuit was time barred, the court refused to award summary judgment to the university, ruling that a trial was required to determine when the plaintiff could reasonably have been expected to discover that her papers had been posted to the Internet.

In addition to claims of negligent hiring or supervision, colleges may face invasion of privacy claims from students or staff. For example, in *Nemani v. St. Louis University,* 33 S.W.3d 184 (Mo. 2000), a faculty member filed an invasion of privacy claim against the university for using his name in a grant application without his express permission. The court rejected the claim, noting that the professor had executed an agreement with the university that required him to collaborate on research projects with other faculty members, thus impliedly consenting to the use of his name on grant applications. And in *Green v. Trinity International University*, 801 N.E.2d 1208 (Ill. App. Ct. 2003), a state appellate court found that the university had not invaded a professor's privacy by interviewing randomly selected students of his to collect information about his behavior in the classroom, or by releasing a statement that he had been relieved of his teaching duties. Because no reason had been given in the statement, said the court, the statement was not capable of being interpreted to imply that the plaintiff had been dismissed for reasons of moral turpitude.

Claims of negligent or intentional infliction of emotional distress are often added to other claims brought by former employees or students. Emotional distress claims do not challenge the outcome of the college's decision (although other claims in the lawsuit may make these charges), but the manner in which the decision was made or the information communicated. For example, in *Mason v. State ex rel. Board of Regents of the University of Oklahoma*, 23 P.3d 964 (Okla. Civ. App. Div. 1, 2001), a state appellate court ruled that a law student who had been expelled and was seeking readmission could not maintain a claim for negligent or intentional infliction of emotional distress. Citing Section 46 of the *Restatement (Second) of Torts*, the court ruled that the plaintiff had not proved that the university's decision not to readmit him was "so outrageous in character, and so extreme in degree, as to go beyond all possible bounds of decency, and to be regarded as atrocious, and utterly intolerable in a civilized community" (23 P.3d at 970).

Although many colleges have offices of risk management whose goal is to reduce potential institutional liability for premises liability or other tort claims related to the college's status as a landowner or landlord, it is obvious that the college's academic programs, its social, cocurricular and outreach activities, and its employment decisions are also sources of potential tort actions. For that reason, colleges should develop processes for risk managers to collaborate with academic and student affairs administrators and faculty when considering programs or activities that could lead to injuries. For example, including risk management staff and university counsel in planning for study abroad programs, internship programs, or summer camps for children may help the college avoid the type of problems discussed in this section. While a certain number of tort claims may be inevitable, responsible planning and assessment of risks, and efforts to reduce foreseeable risks, will be important components of the college's ability to defend against tort claims or to avoid them.

Sec. 3.4. *Institutional Contract Liability*

Institutions of higher education face potential breach of contract claims from employees (see Sections 4.3 & 6.2), students (see Sections 8.1.3, 8.2.3, & 9.4.4), and vendors, purchasers, or business partners (see Section 15.1). In this section, the institution's potential liability for contracts entered into by its employees or other agents is discussed.

The institution may be characterized as a "principal" and its trustees, administrators, and other employees as "agents" for purposes of discussing the potential liability of each on contracts transacted by an agent for, or on behalf of, the institution. The fact that an agent acts with the principal in mind does not necessarily excuse the agent from personal liability (see Section 4.7.3), nor does it automatically make the principal liable. The key to the institution's liability is authorization; that is, the institution may be held liable if it authorized the agent's action before it occurred or if it subsequently ratified the action. However, even when an agent's acts were properly authorized, an institution may be able to escape liability by raising a legally recognized defense, such as sovereign immunity. As mentioned in Section 3.3, this defense is available in some states to public institutions but not to private institutions.

The existence and scope of sovereign immunity from contract liability vary from state to state. In *Charles E. Brohawn & Bros., Inc. v. Board of Trustees of Chesapeake College*, 304 A.2d 819 (Md. 1973), the court recognized a very broad immunity defense. The plaintiffs had sued the trustees to compel them to pay the agreed-upon price for work and materials provided under the contract, including the construction of buildings for the college. In considering the college's defense, the court reasoned:

> The doctrine of sovereign immunity exists under the common law of Maryland. By this doctrine, a litigant is precluded from asserting an otherwise meritorious cause of action against this sovereign state or one of its agencies which has inherited its sovereign attributes, unless [sovereign immunity has been] expressly waived by statute or by a necessary inference from such a legislative enactment. . . . The doctrine of sovereign immunity or, as it is often alternatively referred to, governmental immunity was before this court in *University of Maryland v. Maas*, 173 Md. 554, 197 A. 123 (1938), where our predecessors reversed a judgment recovered against the university for breach of contract in connection with the construction of a dormitory at College Park. That opinion, after extensively reviewing the prior decisions of this court, succinctly summed up [our predecessors'] holdings: "So it is established that neither in contract nor tort can a suit be maintained against a governmental agency, first, where specific legislative authority has not been given, second, even though such authority is given, if there are no funds available for the satisfaction of the judgment, or no power reposed in the agency for the raising of funds necessary to satisfy a recovery against it" (173 Md. at 559, 197 A. at 125) [304 A.2d at 820; notes and citations omitted].

Finding that the cloak of the sovereign's immunity was inherited by the community college and had not been waived, the court rejected the plaintiff's contract claim.

A U.S. Supreme Court case demonstrates that sovereign immunity from contract liability will occasionally also be available to public institutions under federal (rather than state) law. In *Regents of the University of California v. Doe* (discussed in Section 3.5), the Court upheld the university's assertion of Eleventh Amendment immunity as a defense to a federal court breach of contract suit brought by a disappointed applicant for employment. Such a federal immunity claim applies only in those limited circumstances in which a federal district court could obtain jurisdiction over a breach of contract claim.

Regarding contract liability, there is little distinction to be made among trustees, administrators, employees, and other agents of the institution. Whether the actor is a member of the board of trustees or its equivalent—the president, the athletic director, the dean of arts and sciences, or some other functionary—the critical question is whether the action was authorized by the institution.

The issue of authorization can become very complex. In *Brown v. Wichita State University,* 540 P.2d 66 (Kan. 1975),[14] the court discussed the issue at length:

> To determine whether the record establishes an agency by agreement, it must be examined to ascertain if the party sought to be charged as principal had delegated authority to the alleged agent by words which expressly authorize the agent to do the delegated act. If there is evidence of that character, the authority of the agent is express. If no express authorization is found, then the evidence must be considered to determine whether the alleged agent possesses implied powers. The test utilized by this court to determine if the alleged agent possesses implied powers is whether, from the facts and circumstances of the particular case, it appears there was an implied intention to create an agency, in which event the relation may be held to exist, notwithstanding either a denial by the alleged principal, or whether the parties understood it to be an agency.
>
> "On the question of implied agency, it is the manifestation of the alleged principal and agent as between themselves that is decisive, and not the appearance to a third party or what the third party should have known. An agency will not be inferred because a third person assumed that it existed, or because the alleged agent assumed to act as such, or because the conditions and circumstances were such as to make such an agency seem natural and probable and to the advantage of the supposed principal, or from facts which show that the alleged agent was a mere instrumentality" [quoting *Corpus Juris Secundum,* a leading legal encyclopedia]. . . . The doctrine of apparent or ostensible authority is predicated upon the theory of estoppel. An ostensible or apparent agent is one whom the principal has intentionally or by want of ordinary care induced and permitted third persons to believe to be his agent even though no authority, either express or implied, has been conferred upon him.
>
> Ratification is the adoption or confirmation by a principal of an act performed on his behalf by an agent, which act was performed without authority. The doctrine of ratification is based upon the assumption there has been no prior authority, and ratification by the principal of the agent's unauthorized act is equivalent to an original grant of authority. Upon acquiring knowledge of his agent's unauthorized act, the principal should promptly repudiate the act; otherwise it will be presumed he has ratified and affirmed the act [540 P.2d at 74–75].

As mentioned in Section 3.3, the *Brown* case arose after the crash of a plane carrying the Wichita State football team. The survivors and personal representatives

---

[14]This decision reverses and remands a summary judgment in favor of the university by the trial court. In a second opinion in this case, 547 P.2d 1015 (1976), the court reaffirmed (without discussion) the portion of its first opinion dealing with authorization. The tort liability aspects of these two opinions are discussed in Section 3.3.

of the deceased passengers sued Wichita State University (WSU) and the Physical Education Corporation (PEC) at the school for breaching their Aviation Service Agreement by failing to provide passenger liability insurance for the football team and other passengers. The plaintiffs claimed that they were third-party beneficiaries of the service agreement entered into by WSU, the PEC, and the aviation company. The service agreement was signed by the athletic director of WSU and by an agent of the aviation company. The university asserted that it did not have the authority to enter the agreement without the board of regents' approval, which it did not have; that it did not grant the athletic director the authority to enter the agreement on its behalf; that the athletic director only had authority to act as the agent of the PEC; that WSU could not ratify the agreement because it lacked authority to enter it initially; and that, as a state agency, it could not be estopped from denying the validity of the agreement.

The court held that the PEC was the agent of the university and that the athletic director, "as an officer of the corporate agent [PEC], had the implied power and authority to bind the principal—Wichita State University." The court further held that failure to obtain the board of regents' approval did not invalidate the contract because the legislature had "delegated to the board of regents the authority to control, operate, manage, and supervise the universities and colleges of this state" (540 P.2d at 76),[15] and the board had created no policy, rule, or regulation that limited the authority of its agents to enter into contracts. The fact that the agreement had been partly performed was particularly persuasive to the court.

In a case involving both apparent authority and ratification doctrines, the Supreme Court of Massachusetts ruled that Boston University must pay a technical training company more than $5.7 million for its "willful and knowing" breach of contract (*Linkage Corporation v. Trustees of Boston University*, 679 N.E.2d 191 (Mass. 1997), *cert. denied*, 522 U.S. 1015 (1997). (The facts of the case are set out in Section 15.2.2.) One important issue in the case was whether an earlier contract between Boston University and Linkage for the provision of educational services by Linkage had been renewed; Linkage asserted that it had, but the university, on the other hand, stated that the contract had not been renewed, but had been lawfully terminated. A jury had found that the university's vice president for external programs had apparent authority to enter a renewal contract with Linkage, and also found that the university had ratified that agreement.

With respect to the apparent authority issue, the court noted that the vice president had "virtual autonomy" in supervising the relationship between Linkage and the university. He had been the university's representative in the negotiation of the earlier contract, and was named in the contractual documents as the university's primary representative for all legal notices. Boston University

---

[15]Not all courts will be so willing to find institutional authority in cases concerning public institutions. Other courts in other circumstances may assert that a person who deals with a public institution "does so at his peril," as in *First Equity Corp. of Florida v. Utah State University*, 544 P.2d 887 (Utah 1975), where the court upheld the university's refusal to pay for stocks ordered by one of its employees. (This case is discussed in Section 3.2.1.)

argued that the vice president lacked authority to enter the agreement because, at the same time that negotiations for the contract renewal were taking place, the university had issued a directive that required all payments greater than $5,000 to be authorized by the senior vice president. The court, however, ruled that, because the vice president for external programs had direct access to the president, and because the contractual relationship predated the directive, it was reasonable for Linkage's president to conclude that the directive would not be enforced with respect to its contract with the university.

With respect to the ratification issue, the court agreed with the jury that the conduct of university officials subsequent to the execution of the renewal contract supported the ratification argument. The vice president had asked his superiors, in writing, if additional review was necessary after he executed the renewal contract. Neither the senior vice president nor the president advised Linkage's president or their own vice president that they did not approve of the renewal contract. Characterizing the conduct of university officials as "informed acquiescence," the court endorsed the jury's finding that the university had ratified the agreement.

Although the behavior of university officials was sufficient to establish ratification, the court added that, because the university benefited financially from the execution of the renewal contract, this benefit was additional evidence of its ratification of the agreement.

A Texas appellate court addressed the question of whether ratification of a board of trustees' decision not to renew the contract of a college president could postdate the contractual date for notice of nonrenewal. In *Swain v. Wiley College,* 74 S.W.2d 143 (Ct. App. Tex. 2002), the plaintiff, the former president of Wiley College, challenged the decision by the board of trustees not to renew his contract. The contract provided that any nonrenewal decision must be made prior to May 30. The board of trustees met on May 13 and voted not to renew President Swain's contract. However, the meeting had been called in a manner that did not comply with the college's bylaws. The board next met in July (at a meeting that had been called properly), and ratified its earlier decision not to renew the president's contract. Swain argued that the ratification was too late, and thus his contract with the college was still in effect. The court disagreed. Ratification, said the court, refers back to the original transaction (the vote not to renew his contract), and is retroactive to the date of the transaction. Until the vote was ratified by the board, it could have been voided by the board. Once it was ratified, however, it was no longer voidable. The procedural irregularities in calling the May meeting, said the court, did not affect the validity of the decision, and Swain had received timely notice (prior to May 30) of the nonrenewal decision.

Colleges are increasingly being sued for breach of contract by current or former employees. These issues are discussed in Section 4.3. Even colleges controlled by religious organizations may be subject to breach of contract claims. For example, the Supreme Court of New Jersey ruled, in *McKelvy v. Diocese of Camden,* 800 A.2d 840 (N.J. 2002), that a former seminarian could sue the Diocese of Camden, New Jersey, for breach of contract. The plaintiff alleged that he had been sexually harassed while a student at the seminary, and sued for reimbursement of his tuition and loans, and for compensatory damages. Despite the argument by the diocese that such a lawsuit violated the First Amendment's free exercise clause, the state court ruled unanimously that the case could proceed. Jurisprudence on the liability of religiously affiliated colleges for discrimination lawsuits is discussed in Section 5.5.

Although students attempting to assert claims for educational malpractice are finding their tort claims dismissed (discussed in Section 3.3.3), their contract claims sometimes survive summary judgment or dismissal, as long as the contract claim is not an attempt to state a claim for educational malpractice. In *Swartley v. Hoffner*, 734 A.2d 915 (Pa. Super. 1999), *appeal denied*, 747 A.2d 902 (Pa. 1999), a doctoral student who was denied a degree brought a breach of contract claim against her dissertation committee members, claiming that they had failed to carry out their duties as required by university policies. The court ruled that "the relationship between a private educational institution and an enrolled student is contractual in nature; therefore, a student can bring a cause of action against said institution for breach of contract where the institution ignores or violates portions of the written contract" (734 A.2d at 919). But the court nevertheless affirmed the trial court's award of summary judgment to the defendants, finding no evidence that university policies required dissertation committee members to give the student a passing grade once her dissertation defense had been scheduled. But in *Gally v. Columbia University*, 22 F. Supp. 2d 199 (S.D.N.Y. 1998), a trial judge dismissed the student's contract claim, ruling that it was a disguised attempt to state a claim for educational malpractice.

Although most claims involving injury to students or other invitees are brought under negligence theories, one court allowed a contract claim to be brought against a public university as a result of injuries to a camper at a university-based program. In *Quinn v. Mississippi State University*, 720 So. 2d 843 (Miss. 1998), parents of a child injured at a baseball camp sponsored by the university filed both tort and contract claims against the university. The Supreme Court of Mississippi determined that their tort claim was barred by the university's sovereign immunity, but found that an implied contract existed between the plaintiffs and the defendants to provide baseball instruction safely at the baseball camp:

> The Quinns paid an "admission fee" to have their son, Brandon, attend the baseball camp at Mississippi State University. By doing so, they entered into an implied contract with the university. This contract carried with it the implied promise that the university would provide a safe instructional environment for the campers attending the baseball camp. This Court holds that when Brandon was hit in the mouth with the bat, the university breached its contract with the Quinns. Therefore, the suit against the university was not barred and was not ripe for summary judgment [720 So. 2d at 850].

The university argued that the plaintiffs had signed a waiver that released the university from liability. Because it was not clear from the language of the waiver whether the plaintiffs had waived liability for acts committed by the coach, the court remanded the matter for a jury's determination.

An institution sued for breach of contract can raise defenses arising from the contract itself or from some circumstance unique to the institution. Defenses that arise from the contract include the other party's fraud, the other party's breach of the contract, and the absence of one of the requisite elements (offer, acceptance, consideration) in the formation of a contract (see generally Section 15.1). Defenses unique to the institution may include a counterclaim against the other party, the other party's previous collection of damages from the agent, or, for public institutions, the sovereign immunity defense discussed earlier. Even if one of these defenses—for instance, that the agent or institution lacked authority or that a contract element was absent—is successfully asserted, a private institution may be held liable for any benefit it received as a result of the other party's performance. But public institutions may sometimes not even be required to pay for benefits received under such circumstances.

The variety of contract and agency law principles that may bear on contract liability makes the area a complex one, calling for frequent involvement of legal counsel. The postsecondary institution's main concern in managing liability should be the delineation of the contracting authority of each of its agents. By carefully defining such authority, and by repudiating any unauthorized contracts of which they become aware, postsecondary administrators can protect the institution from unwanted liability. While protection may also be found in other defenses to contract actions, such as sovereign immunity, advance planning of authority is the surest way to limit contract liability and the fairest to the parties with whom the institution's agents may deal.

Sec. 3.5. Institutional Liability for Violating Federal Constitutional Rights (Section 1983 Liability)

The tort and contract liabilities of postsecondary institutions (discussed in Sections 3.3 & 3.4) are based in state law and, for the most part, are relatively well settled. The institution's federal constitutional rights liability, in contrast, is primarily a matter of federal law, which has undergone a complex evolutionary development. The key statute governing the enforcement of constitutional rights,[16] commonly known as "Section 1983" and codified at 42 U.S.C. § 1983,[17] reads in pertinent part:

> Every person who, under color of any statute, ordinance, regulation, custom, or usage, of any State or Territory or the District of Columbia, subjects, or causes to

---

[16]In addition to federal constitutional rights, there are numerous federal statutes that create statutory civil rights, violation of which will also subject institutions to liability. (See, for example, Sections 5.2.1 through 5.2.4 and 13.5.2 through 13.5.5 of this book.) These statutory rights are enforced under the statutes that create them, rather than under Section 1983. Institutions may also be liable for violations of state constitutional rights, which are enforced under state law rather than Section 1983.

[17]Legal analyses of the various federal civil rights laws and extensive citations to important cases can be found in Sheldon Nahmod, Michael Wells, & Thomas Eaton, *Constitutional Torts* (2d ed., LexisNexis, 2004); and M. Schwartz & J. Kirklin, *Section 1983 Litigation: Claims, Defenses, and Fees* (Wiley Law Publications, 1986, and periodic supp.).

be subjected, any citizen of the United States or other person within the jurisdiction thereof to the deprivation of any rights, privileges, or immunities secured by the Constitution and laws, shall be liable to the party injured in an action at law, suit in equity, or other proper proceeding for redress. . . .

Section 1983's coverage is limited in two major ways. First, it imposes liability only for actions carried out "under color of" state law, custom, or usage. Under this language the statute applies only to actions attributable to the state, in much the same way that, under the state action doctrine (see Section 1.5.2), the U.S. Constitution applies only to actions attributable to the state. While public institutions clearly meet this statutory test, private postsecondary institutions cannot be subjected to Section 1983 liability unless the action complained of was so connected with the state that it can be said to have been done under color of state law, custom, or usage.

Second, Section 1983 imposes liability only on a "person"—a term not defined in the statute. Thus, Section 1983's application to postsecondary education also depends on whether the particular institution or system being sued is considered to be a person, as the courts construe that term.[18] Although private institutions would usually meet this test because they are corporations, which are considered to be legal persons under state law, most private institutions would be excluded from Section 1983 anyway under the color-of-law test. Thus, the crucial coverage issue under Section 1983 is one that primarily concerns public institutions: whether a public postsecondary institution is a person for purposes of Section 1983 and thus subject to civil rights liability under that statute.

A related issue, which also helps shape a public institution's liability for violations of federal constitutional rights, is the extent to which Article III and the Eleventh Amendment of the U.S. Constitution immunize public institutions from suit. While the "person" issue is a matter of statutory interpretation, the immunity issue is a matter of constitutional interpretation. In general, if the suit is against the state itself or against a state official or employee sued in his or her "official capacity," and the plaintiff seeks money damages that would come from the state treasury,[19] the immunity from federal court suit will apply. As discussed below, in Section 1983 litigation, the immunity issue usually parallels the person issue, and the courts have used Eleventh Amendment immunity law as a backdrop against which to fashion and apply a definition of "person" under Section 1983.

---

[18]Cases are collected in Kevin W. Brown, Annot., "Public Institutions of Higher Learning as 'Persons' Subject to Suit under 42 U.S.C.A. § 1983," 65 A.L.R. Fed. 490.

[19]State employees and officials may be sued in either their "official" capacities or their "personal" (or "individual") capacities under Section 1983. For a distinction between the two capacities, see *Hafer v. Melo,* 502 U.S. 21, 25–31 (1991). Since suits seeking money damages against employees or officers in their "official" capacities are generally considered to be covered by the state's Eleventh Amendment immunity, they are included in the discussion in this Section of the book. Suits against employees or officials in their "personal" capacities are discussed in Section 4.7.4 of this book.

In a series of cases beginning in 1978, the U.S. Supreme Court dramatically expanded the potential Section 1983 liability of various government entities. As a result of these cases, it is now clear that any political subdivision of a state may be sued under this statute; that such governmental defendants may not assert a "qualified immunity" from liability based on the reasonableness or good faith of their actions; that the officers and employers of political subdivisions, as well as officers and employers of state agencies, may sometimes be sued under Section 1983; and that Section 1983 plaintiffs may not be required to resort to state administrative forums before seeking redress in court.

The first, and key, case in this series is the U.S. Supreme Court's decision in *Monell v. Department of Social Services of the City of New York,* 436 U.S. 658 (1978). Overruling prior precedents that had held the contrary, the Court decided that local government units, such as school boards and municipal corporations, are "persons" under Section 1983 and thus subject to liability for violating civil rights protected by that statute. Since the definition of "person" is central to Section 1983's applicability, the question is whether the Court's definition in *Monell* is broad enough to encompass postsecondary institutions: Are some public postsecondary institutions sufficiently like local government units that they will be considered "persons" subject to Section 1983 liability?

The answer depends not only on a close analysis of *Monell* but also on an analysis of the particular institution's organization and structure under state law (see Section 12.2). Locally based institutions, such as community colleges established as an arm of a county or a community college district, are the most likely candidates for "person" status. At the other end of the spectrum, state universities established and operated by the state itself are apparently the least likely candidates. This distinction between local entities and state entities is appropriate because the Eleventh Amendment immunizes the states, but not local governments, from federal court suits on federal constitutional claims. Consequently, the Court in *Monell* limited its "person" definition "to local government units which are not considered part of the state for Eleventh Amendment purposes." And in a subsequent case, *Quern v. Jordan,* 440 U.S. 332 (1979), the Court emphasized this limitation in *Monell* and asserted that neither the language nor the history of Section 1983 evidences any congressional intention to abrogate the states' Eleventh Amendment immunity (440 U.S. at 341–45).

The clear implication, reading *Monell* and *Quern* together, is that local governments—such as school boards, cities, and counties—are persons suable under Section 1983 and are not immune from suit under the Eleventh Amendment, whereas state governments and state agencies controlled by the state are not persons under Section 1983 and are immune under the Eleventh Amendment. The issue in any particular case, then, as phrased by the Court in another case decided the same day as *Quern,* is whether the entity in question "is to be regarded as a political subdivision" of the state (and thus not immune) or as "an arm of the state subject to its control" (and thus immune) (*Lake County Estates v. Tahoe Regional Planning Agency,* 440 U.S. 391, 401–02 (1979)).

This case law added clarity to what had been the confusing and uncertain status of postsecondary institutions under Section 1983 and the Eleventh Amendment. But courts continued to have difficulty determining whether to place particular institutions on the person (not immune) or nonperson (immune) side of the liability line. A 1982 U.S. Court of Appeals case, *United Carolina Bank v. Board of Regents of Stephen F. Austin State University,* 665 F.2d 553 (5th Cir. 1982), provides an instructive illustration of the problem and surveys a range of considerations pertinent to its resolution. The plaintiff in this case was a professor who had been dismissed from his position. He brought a Section 1983 suit against the board of regents, the president of the university, and four university administrators, alleging violations of his First Amendment free speech and Fourteenth Amendment due process rights. (When the professor died during the course of the action, the bank, as administrator of his estate, became the plaintiff.) In approaching the threshold question of Eleventh Amendment immunity, the court sorted out the Section 1983 claims against the university itself from the claims against the president and administrators sued in their individual capacities (see Section 4.7.4 of this book). Regarding the institution's immunity, the court had to "decide whether the Board of Regents of SFA [Stephen F. Austin] is to be treated as an arm of the State, partaking of the State's eleventh amendment immunity, or is instead to be treated as a municipal corporation or other political subdivision to which the eleventh amendment does not extend."

The appellate court accepted the former characterization:

> Our analysis will first examine the status of the Board of Regents of SFA under Texas law. . . . Texas law provides: "'state agency' means a university system or an institution of higher education as defined in section 61.003 Texas Education Code, other than a public junior college." Tex. Rev. Civ. Stat. Ann. art. 62529b(8)(B) (Vernon). By contrast, Texas statutory definitions of "political subdivision" typically exclude universities in the category of SFA. . . .
>
> [W]e next examine the state's degree of control over SFA, and SFA's fiscal autonomy. SFA was created by the legislature in 1921, and in 1969 was placed under the control of its own Board of Regents. Texas' statutes . . . provide that members of the Board of Regents are to be appointed by the Governor with the advice and consent of the Senate. Tex. Educ. Code Ann. § 101.11. Texas also subjects SFA to some control by the Coordinating Board, Texas College and University System, which exercises broad managerial powers over all of the public institutions of higher learning in Texas. . . .
>
> SFA's Board has the power of eminent domain, but "the taking of the land is for the use of the state." Tex. Educ. Code Ann. § 95.30. The University's real property is state property, Tex. Rev. Civ. Stat. Ann. art. 601b § 1.02; . . . and the funds used to purchase it were appropriated by the legislature from the general revenues of the state. . . . State law is the source of the University's authority to purchase, sell, or lease real and personal property. *See* Tex. Rev. Civ. Stat. Ann. art. 601b. The University's operating expenses come largely through legislative appropriation. 1981 Tex. Sess. Law Serv. ch. 875 at 3695. Even those public funds which do not originate with the state are reappropriated to the University, *id.* ch. 875 at 3720, and become subject to rigid control by the state when

received. *Id.* ch. 875 at 3719–21. . . . [A]ll funds are subject to extensive reporting requirements and state audits. *E.g., id.* ch. 875 at 3721.

   In addition to the functions cited above, because SFA is a state agency it is
subject to state regulation in every other substantial aspect of its existence such
as employee conduct standards, promotions, disclosure of information, liability
for tort claims, [workers'] compensation, inventory reports, meetings, posting of
state job opportunities, private consultants, travel rules and legal proceedings.
See generally, 1981 Tex. Sess. Law Serv. ch. 875 at 3790–3824. . . . In short,
under Texas law SFA is more an arm of the state than a political subdivision
[665 F.2d at 557–58].

   The court carefully noted that its conclusion concerning Stephen F. Austin
University would not necessarily apply to state universities in other states, or
to all other postsecondary institutions in Texas: "Each situation must be
addressed individually because the states have adopted different schemes, both
intra and interstate, in constituting their institutions of higher learning." As an
example, the court noted the distinction between Texas institutions such as SFA,
on the one hand, and Texas junior colleges, on the other (see below).

   Eleventh Amendment and Section 1983 case law after the *Stephen F. Austin
State University* case developed along similar lines, with courts frequently equat-
ing the Eleventh Amendment immunity analysis with the "person" analysis
under Section 1983 (see, for example, *Thompson v. City of Los Angeles,* 885 F.2d
1439 (9th Cir. 1989), upholding dismissal of a claim against the board of regents
of the University of California at Los Angeles).[20] In the process, the law has
become clearer and more refined. In *Kashani v. Purdue University,* 813 F.2d 843
(7th Cir. 1987), for example, the court reaffirmed the proposition that the
Eleventh Amendment shields most state universities from damages liability in
Section 1983 actions.[21] The plaintiff, an Iranian graduate student, asserted that
his termination from a doctoral program during the Iranian hostage crisis was
based on his national origin. In dismissing his claim for monetary relief, the
court suggested that, although the states have structured their educational systems in many ways and courts review each case on its facts, "it would be an
unusual state university that would not receive immunity" (813 F.2d at 845).
The court also reaffirmed, however, that under the doctrine of *Ex parte Young,*
209 U.S. 123 (1908), the Eleventh Amendment does not bar claims against
university officers in their official capacities for the injunctive relief of reinstatement. In determining whether the defendant, Purdue University, was entitled to Eleventh Amendment immunity, the court placed primary importance

---

[20]State institutions that are immune under the Eleventh Amendment may waive their immunity,
as discussed in Section 13.1.5. But such a waiver may not be effective in Section 1983 litigation.
An institution entitled to Eleventh Amendment immunity is an "arm of the state" and is therefore
not a "person" under Section 1983. The statutory requirement that a government entity must be a
"person" in order to be sued under Section 1983 is apparently not waivable.

[21]For one example to the contrary, see the *Kovats* case concerning Rutgers University, discussed
below in this Section. For another such example, see *Honadle v. University of Vermont & State
Agricultural College,* 115 F. Supp. 2d 468 (D. Vt. 2000).

on the "extent of the entity's financial autonomy from the state," the relevant considerations being "the extent of state funding, the state's oversight and control of the university's fiscal affairs, the university's ability independently to raise funds, whether the state taxes the university, and whether a judgment against the university would result in the state increasing its appropriations to the university." Applying these considerations, the court concluded that Purdue was entitled to immunity because it "is dependent upon and functionally integrated with the state treasury."

Other courts have applied a more expansive set of nine factors to resolve Eleventh Amendment immunity questions. These factors, known variously as the "*Urbano* factors" or "*Blake* factors" to credit the cases from which they derived, gained increasing popularity in sovereign immunity cases. In the case that first articulated these factors, *Urbano v. Board of Managers of New Jersey State Prison*, 415 F.2d 247 (3d Cir. 1969), the court explained:

> (1) [L]ocal law and decisions defining the status and nature of the agency involved in its relation to the sovereign are factors to be considered, but only one of a number that are of significance. Among the other factors, no one of which is conclusive, perhaps that most important is (2) whether, in the event plaintiff prevails, the payment of the judgment will have to be made out of the state treasury; significant here also is (3) whether the agency has the funds or the power to satisfy the judgment. Other relevant factors are (4) whether the agency is performing a governmental or proprietary function; (5) whether it has been separately incorporated; (6) the degree of autonomy over its operations; (7) whether it has the power to sue and be sued and to enter into contracts; (8) whether its property is immune from state taxation; and (9) whether the sovereign has immunized itself from responsibility for the agency's operations [415 F.2d at 250–51; numbering added].

This nine-factor test was applied to higher education in *Hall v. Medical College of Ohio at Toledo*, 742 F.2d 299 (6th Cir. 1984), a case in which a student who had been dismissed from medical school alleged racial discrimination in violation of Section 1983. The district court, looking generally to the extent of the school's functional autonomy and fiscal independence, had held that the school was an "arm of the state" entitled to Eleventh Amendment immunity. Although the appellate court affirmed the district court's judgment, it emphasized that the nine-part *Urbano/Blake* test "is the better approach for examining the 'peculiar circumstances' of the different colleges and universities."

Similarly, the court in *Skehan v. State System of Higher Education*, 815 F.2d 244 (3d Cir. 1987), used the *Urbano/Blake* test to determine that the defendant State System "is, effectively, a state agency and therefore entitled to the protection of the eleventh amendment." In contrast, however, the court in *Kovats v. Rutgers, The State University*, 822 F.2d 1303 (3d Cir. 1987), determined that Rutgers is not an arm of the state of New Jersey and thus is not entitled to Eleventh Amendment immunity. The case involved Section 1983 claims of faculty members who had been dismissed. Focusing on

Urbano/Blake factors 2 and 3, the court considered whether a judgment against Rutgers would be paid by Rutgers or by the state and determined that Rutgers in its discretion could pay the judgment either with segregated non-state funds or with nonstate funds that were commingled with state funds. Rutgers argued that, if it paid the judgment, the state would have to increase its appropriations to the university, thus affecting the state treasury. The court held that such an appropriations increase following a judgment would be in the legislature's discretion, and that "[i]f the state structures an entity in such a way that the other relevant criteria indicate it to be an arm of the state, then immunity may be retained even where damage awards are funded by the state at the state's discretion." Then, considering the other *Urbano/Blake* factors, the court determined that, although Rutgers "is now, at least in part, a state-created entity which serves a state purpose with a large degree of state financing, it remains under state law an independent entity able to direct its own actions and responsible on its own for judgments resulting from those actions."

More recent cases on the Eleventh Amendment immunity of state universities continue to uphold the universities' immunity claims, relying on a variety of factors to reach this result.[22] In *Sherman v. Curators of the University of Missouri*, 16 F.3d 860 (8th Cir. 1994), *on remand*, 871 F. Supp. 344 (W.D. Mo. 1994), for instance, the appellate court focused on two factors: the university's degree of autonomy from the state, and the university's fiscal dependence on state funds as the source for payments of damage awards against the university. Applying these factors on remand, the district court ruled that the university was immune from suit under the Eleventh Amendment. Similarly, in *Rounds v. Oregon State Board of Higher Education*, 166 F.3d 1032 (9th Cir. 1999), the court focused on two primary factors in granting immunity to the University of Oregon. The factors differed somewhat, however, from those in *Sherman*. The *Rounds* court looked first to the university's "nature as created by state law," especially the extent to which the university is subject to the supervision of state officials or a state board of higher education; and second, the court looked to the university's functions, particularly whether the university "performs central governmental functions."

---

[22]A 1997 U.S. Supreme Court case also adds an important (though technical) clarification of Eleventh Amendment immunity analysis in situations where a third party has agreed to indemnify the state agency from liability. In *Regents of the University of California v. Doe*, 519 U.S. 425 (1997), the university's contract to operate the Livermore National Laboratory provided that the federal government (and not the state) would assume liability for any money damages judgment against the university arising from its performance of the contract. The Court rejected the plaintiff's argument that any judgment in his favor would not come from the state treasury and, therefore, the university was not immune from suit. The relevant inquiry, according to the Court, was whether the state was potentially liable for money judgments against the university, not whether the state would be able to shift its liability to a third party in the particular case at hand. Since the state did have potential liability for university money judgments, and since the university otherwise qualified as an "arm of the state," the university had an Eleventh Amendment immunity from the plaintiff's suit.

When the Eleventh Amendment immunity of a community college or junior college is at issue, the various factors that courts consider may suggest greater institutional autonomy from the state government, and courts are therefore less likely to grant immunity. In *Board of Regents of Stephen F. Austin State University* (above), for example, the court distinguished Texas junior colleges from the Texas state universities. Reaffirming its earlier decisions in *Hander v. San Jacinto Junior College,* 519 F.2d 273 (5th Cir. 1975), and *Goss v. San Jacinto Junior College,* 588 F.2d 96 (5th Cir. 1979), the court concluded that Texas junior colleges are not arms of the state and are thus suable under Section 1983:

> Junior colleges, rather than being established by the legislature, are created by local initiative. Tex. Educ. Code Ann. § 130.031. Their governing bodies are elected by local voters rather than being appointed by the Governor with the advice and consent of the Senate. *Id.* § 130.083(e). Most telling is the power of junior colleges to levy *ad valorem* taxes, *id.* § 130.122, a power which the Board of SFA lacks. Under Texas law, political subdivisions are sometimes defined as entities authorized to levy taxes. Tex. Rev. Civ. Stat. Ann. art. 2351b-3. *See generally, Hander,* 519 F.2d at 279 [665 F.2d at 558].

Similarly, the court denied immunity to a New Mexico junior college in *Leach v. New Mexico Jr. College,* 45 P.3d 46 (N.M. 2002), relying especially on the fact that the college had its own powers to levy taxes and to issue bonds, and its board members were not appointed by the governor.

On the other hand, in *Hadley v. North Arkansas Community Technical College,* 76 F.3d 1437 (8th Cir. 1996), by a 2-to-1 split vote, the court upheld the Eleventh Amendment immunity of a community college. The case also flags some unresolved issues concerning Eleventh Amendment immunity for community colleges (and for state institutions as well) and reemphasizes the important role played by fiscal factors in determining an institution's Eleventh Amendment status.

In *Hadley,* a vocational instructor filed a Section 1983 claim in federal court, alleging that the defendant's decision to terminate him violated his due process rights. The issue before the court was whether North Arkansas Community Technical College (NACTC) should be classified as an arm of the state, entitled to Eleventh Amendment immunity from damages, or a state political subdivision or municipal corporation which is not immune. According to the court:

> State universities and colleges almost always enjoy Eleventh Amendment immunity. On the other hand, community and technical colleges often have deep roots in a local community. When those roots include local political and financial involvement, the resulting Eleventh Amendment immunity questions tend to be difficult and very fact specific (citing cases) [76 F.3d at 1438–39].

Examining the structure and authority of NACTC under state law, the court determined "that NACTC is, both financially and institutionally, an arm of the State, and that any damage award to Hadley [the instructor] would inevitably be paid from the state treasury." Weighed against these factors, however, was the contrasting consideration that "Arkansas community colleges also have elements of local funding and control" suggestive of a political subdivision. The court considered the former factors to prevail over the latter because "exposure of the state treasury is a more important factor than whether the State controls the entity in question" (citing *Hess v. Port Authority Trans-Hudson Corp.*, 513 U.S. 30 (1994)). Thus, despite the fact that NACTC's daily operations were largely controlled by locally elected officials of a community college district, the district had residual authority to supplement NACTC's operating budget with local tax revenues, and it had the responsibility for funding capital improvements from local tax revenues, NACTC nevertheless remained financially dependent upon the state for its daily operations and, therefore, should be afforded immunity. In making this determination, the court dismissed the plaintiff's argument that the nominal sum he was seeking in damages could be entirely paid by NACTC's federal, tuition, and private revenues, or by future local tax increases, stating that "the nature of the entity, not the nature of the relief," was to be the determinative factor. (For another case in which the court, like the *Hadley* majority, granted Eleventh Amendment immunity to a community college, see *Cerrato v. San Francisco Community College District*, 26 F.3d 968 (9th Cir. 1994).)

Two other cases, *Pikulin v. City Univ. of NY*, 176 F.3d 598 (2d Cir. 1999), and *Clissuras v. City Univ. of NY*, 359 F.3d 79 (2d Cir. 2004), involved a *city* university rather than a state university or a community college. The court reached the same result as in the *Hadley* case, determining that the City University of New York (CUNY) was an "arm of the state" rather than a political subdivision of the state or an arm of the city of New York. Three factors were key to the court's determination. First, the state was responsible for paying money judgments against CUNY; second, the state had to approve CUNY's budget; and third, the governor of the state had appointed ten of the seventeen CUNY board members. Relying on these factors, the court in each case accepted CUNY's assertion of sovereign immunity and dismissed the claims against it.

More recent cases have also begun to make clear that a state university's Eleventh Amendment immunity may sometimes extend to other entities that the university has recognized or with whom it is otherwise affiliated. In the *Rounds* case (above), for example, the plaintiffs also sued the student government, the Associated Students of the University of Oregon. The court held that "[t]o the extent that the [plaintiffs] assert a Section 1983 claim against the Associated Students, this claim also is barred, as the Associated Students' status as the recognized student government at the University allows it to claim the same Eleventh Amendment immunity that shields the University itself" (166 F. 3d at 1035–36). (For further discussion of Eleventh Amendment defenses for affiliated entities, see Section 3.6.6.)

Since the Eleventh Amendment provides states and "arms of the state" with immunity only from *federal* court suits, it does not directly apply to Section 1983 suits in *state* courts. The definition of "person" may thus be the primary focus of the analysis in state court Section 1983 suits. In *Will v. Michigan Department of State Police*, 491 U.S. 58 (1989), the U.S. Supreme Court ruled that Section 1983 suits may be brought in state courts, but that neither the state nor state officials sued in their official capacities would be considered "persons" for purposes of such suits. In *Howlett v. Rose,* 496 U.S. 356 (1990), the Court reaffirmed that Section 1983 suits may be brought in state courts against other government entities (or against individuals) that are considered "persons" under Section 1983. In such cases, *state* law protections of sovereign immunity and other *state* procedural limitations on suits against the sovereign (see *Felder v. Casey,* 487 U.S. 131 (1988)) will not generally be available to the governmental (or individual) defendants.

In *Alden v. Maine,* 527 U.S. 706 (1999) (discussed in Section 13.1.5 of this book), however, the Court determined that, even though the Eleventh Amendment does not apply in state courts, the states do have an implied constitutional immunity from suits in state court. Thus states sued in the state court under Section 1983 may now invoke an implied sovereign immunity from state court suits that would protect them to the same extent as the Eleventh Amendment immunity protects them in federal court. States may assert this immunity defense in lieu of arguing, under *Will* and *Howlett,* that they are not "persons"; or may argue that, if they fall within the protection of *Alden's* implied sovereign immunity, they cannot be "persons" under Section 1983.

Even if an institution is characterized as a Section 1983 "person" with no Eleventh Amendment immunity, it may still be able in particular circumstances to avoid liability in both federal and state court. According to *Monell:*

> Local governing bodies . . . can be sued directly under [Section] 1983 . . . [where] the action that is alleged to be unconstitutional implements or executes a policy statement, ordinance, regulation, or decision officially adopted and promulgated by the body's officers. Moreover, although the touchstone of the Section 1983 action against a government body is an allegation that official policy is responsible for a deprivation of rights protected by the Constitution, local governments, like every other Section 1983 "person," by the very terms of the statute, may be sued for constitutional deprivations visited pursuant to governmental "custom" even though such a custom has not received formal approval through the body's official decision-making channels. . . .
>
> On the other hand, the language of Section 1983 . . . compels the conclusion that Congress did not intend municipalities to be held liable unless action pursuant to official municipal policy of some nature caused a constitutional tort. In particular, we conclude that a municipality cannot be held liable solely because it employs a tortfeasor—or, in other words, a municipality cannot be held liable under Section 1983 on a *respondeat superior* theory [436 U.S. at 690–91].

Thus, along with its expansion of the "persons" suable under Section 1983, *Monell* also clarifies and limits the types of government actions for which political subdivisions may be held liable.[23]

---

[23]The liability of political subdivisions under the *Monell* decision is not limited by the "qualified immunity" that officers and employees would have if sued personally (see this volume, Section 4.7.4). This type of immunity claim was rejected by the U.S. Supreme Court in *Owen v. City of Independence,* 445 U.S. 622 (1980), as being unsupported either by the text and history of Section 1983 or by public policy considerations.

In other cases, courts have considered what money damage awards may be imposed upon political subdivisions under Section 1983. In *City of Newport v. Fact Concerts, Inc.,* 453 U.S. 247 (1981), the Court held that punitive damages could not be assessed against political subdivisions, since the goal of deterrence would not be served by such awards. In another case, *Memphis Community School District v. Stachura,* 477 U.S. 299 (1986), the Court determined that, although compensatory damage awards may be assessed against political subdivisions, these awards may not be based on the "value" or "importance" of the constitutional right that has been violated. Citing *Carey v. Piphus,* 435 U.S. 247 (1978), the Court underscored that actual injuries are the only permissible bases for an award of compensatory damages caused by the denial of a constitutional right.

Various procedural issues of importance to colleges and universities have also arisen in the wake of *Monell.* For instance, in *Patsy v. Board of Regents of the State of Florida,* 457 U.S. 496 (1982), a suit by a staff employee of Florida International University alleging race and sex discrimination, the U.S. Supreme Court had to decide whether a Section 1983 plaintiff must "exhaust" available state administrative remedies before a court may consider her claim. For many years preceding *Patsy,* the Court had refused to impose an exhaustion requirement on Section 1983 suits. The Court in *Patsy* declined the Florida Board of Regents' invitation to overrule this line of decisions, because "Congress is vested with the power to prescribe the basic procedural scheme under which claims may be heard in federal courts," and "a court should not defer the exercise of jurisdiction under a federal statute unless it is consistent with . . . [Congress's] intent" (which it was not here).[24] And in *Burnett v. Grattan,* 468 U.S. 42 (1984), the Court rejected yet another procedural device for limiting the impact of Section 1983. The defendant, a state university, argued that the federal court should "borrow" and apply a six-month state statute of limitations to the case—the same time period as applied to the filing of discrimination complaints with the state human rights commission—and that the plaintiffs' complaint should be dismissed because it was not filed within six months of the harm (employment discrimination) that the plaintiffs alleged. The Court concluded that, in order to accomplish the goals of Section 1983, it was necessary to apply a longer, three-year, time period for bringing this particular suit—the same period generally allowed for civil actions under the law of the state whose statutes of limitations were being borrowed.

Given these substantial and complex legal developments, at least some public postsecondary institutions are now subject to Section 1983 liability, in both federal courts and state courts, for violations of federal constitutional rights. Those that are subject to suit may be exposed to extensive judicial remedies, which they are unlikely to escape by asserting procedural technicalities. Moreover, institutions and

---

[24]Even though exhaustion is not required under *Patsy,* the unreviewed findings of fact of a state administrative agency may nevertheless have a "preclusive" effect on subsequent federal litigation under Section 1983, as long as the parties in the administrative proceeding had an adequate opportunity to litigate disputed issues (*University of Tennessee v. Elliott,* 478 U.S. 788 (1986); see this volume, Section 1.4.4).

systems that can escape Section 1983 liability because they are not "persons," and are protected by sovereign immunity will find that they are subject in other ways to liability for violations of civil rights. They may be reachable under Section 1983 through "official capacity" suits against institutional officers that seek only injunctive relief (*Power v. Summers,* 226 F.3d 815, 819 (7th Cir. 2000))—relief that is directed to the particular officer or officers who are sued but that effectively would bind the institution. They may be reachable through "personal capacity" suits against the institution's officers or employees and seeking money damages from them individually, rather than from the institution or the state (see Section 4.7.4.1). They will be suable under other federal civil rights laws establishing statutory rights that parallel those protected by the Constitution, and that serve to abrogate or waive state sovereign immunity (see Section 13.1.5). (For examples, see the statutes discussed in Sections 5.2.1–5.2.3.) They may also be suable under similar state civil rights laws or under state statutes similar to Section 1983 that authorize state court suits for the vindication of state or federal constitutional rights.

In such a legal environment, administrators and counsel should foster full and fair enjoyment of federal civil rights on their campuses. Even when it is clear that a particular public institution is not subject to Section 1983 damage liability, administrators should seek to comply with the spirit of Section 1983, which urges that where officials "may harbor doubt about the lawfulness of their intended actions . . . [they should] err on the side of protecting citizens' . . . rights" (*Owen v. City of Independence,* 445 U.S. 622, 652 (1980)).

Sec. 3.6. *Captive and Affiliated Organizations*

3.6.1. *Overview.* The activities of higher education institutions are no longer conducted under the umbrella of a single corporate or governmental entity. In addition to the degree-granting entity itself, there may be numerous spin-off or related organizations, such as alumni and booster clubs, hospitals and clinics, entities that support research or market products, TV and radio stations, museums, foundations of various kinds, and auxiliary enterprises that provide services for the campus community (see generally Sections 15.3 & 15.4). Although often created by action of the institution itself, these organizations may have their own separate corporate existence and may be at least partially independent from the institution. In other situations, the related organization may have originated and developed completely apart from the institution but later entered an affiliation agreement with the institution—maintaining its separate corporate existence and autonomy but cooperating with the institution in some area of mutual interest. The creation of and affiliation with such organizations; their authority in relation to that of the institution itself; and the reorganization, dissolution, and termination of such relationships have all been the subject of policy debate and legal planning. The applicability of various tax and regulatory statutes to captive and affiliated organizations have also raised concerns, as have the potential legal liabilities of these organizations and the potential legal liabilities that postsecondary institutions might incur as a result of their relationships with them (see, for example, the *Brown* case in Section 3.4 above (contract liability) and *Jaar v. University of Miami*, 474 So. 2d 239 (Fla. Dist. Ct. App. 1985) (tort liability)).

To avoid such problems, as the cases below illustrate, an institution should carefully structure and document its relationships with each organization it creates or with which it affiliates. In so doing, it should focus on the purposes it seeks to fulfill, the degree of control it needs to attain or retain, and the consequences of particular structural relationships on the respective rights of the parties to act autonomously from one another (see subsection 3.6.2 below). The institution should also consider how particular structural arrangements would affect the applicability of tax and regulatory laws to the separate entity and to the institution (see subsections 3.6.3 & 3.6.4 below), or would subject the separate entity to "state action" determinations (see subsection 3.6.5 below). In addition, the institution should consider whether it may be liable for the actions of the separate entity and, if so, how the institution would control that risk (see subsection 3.6.6 below).

3.6.2. Structural problems.

Structural issues concerning captive and affiliated organizations may arise in various contexts. In one scenario an institution may wish to transfer part or all of a particular program or function to a separately incorporated entity. One objective of such a transfer may be to free that program or function from certain legal requirements that would apply if it remained within the institution's corporate or governmental structure. Issues may then arise concerning whether the institution has sufficiently relinquished its control over the separate entity that it operates independently from the institution and may be freed from legal restrictions that would apply to the institution itself. The case of *Colorado Association of Public Employees v. Board of Regents of the University of Colorado*, 804 P.2d 138 (Colo. 1990), provides an instructive example. The state had promulgated legislation that purported to reorganize the university's hospital into a private, nonprofit corporation. The legislation provided that the board of regents of the university would still control the hospital through regulations and that, "[s]hould the corporation dissolve, the assets of the corporation less amounts owed to creditors will revert to the Regents." In addition, the legislation required that the hospital must secure the approval of the state legislature before it could transfer the corporation to anyone other than the regents, and before it could exceed a $60 million debt level within the first two years of its creation. Under this reorganization scheme, more than two thousand state civil servants employed at the hospital had a choice of either continuing as regular members of the hospital staff, in which case they would lose their civil service status, or being assigned by the university to the hospital for a period of two years, after which they would have to relinquish their employment. The employees filed suit, claiming that the legislation violated the Colorado constitution. They asserted two alternative theories of unconstitutionality. If the legislation were construed to create an entity having the status of a *private* corporation, the employees claimed, it would violate Articles V and XI of the state constitution, which prohibit private corporations from receiving public funds or assets. If the legislation were construed to create an entity having the status of a *public* corporation, the plaintiffs claimed that it would violate Article XII, Section 13, the State Civil Service Amendment, and Article XI, Section 3, which forbids state indebtedness except in limited circumstances.

The Supreme Court of Colorado, with two dissents, held that the legislation reorganized the hospital into a public corporation subject to all laws that governed the University of Colorado itself. The court reasoned that "whether University Hospital may be considered private depends upon whether (1) it is founded and maintained by private individuals or a private corporation and (2) the state is involved in the management or control of its property or internal operations" (804 P.2d at 143). Analyzing the first of these factors, the court determined that "[u]nder the facts before us, the reorganized hospital clearly cannot be characterized as a private hospital [because] the Regents, who are elected officials, established the hospital pursuant to authority granted in Article VIII, Section 5 of the Colorado Constitution and in Colo. Rev. Stat. Section 23-21-403(1)(a)." Regarding the second factor, the court determined that the state maintained control of the hospital by granting the regents power to appoint and remove the hospital directors and to control certain aspects of the hospital's budgeting, spending, and indebtedness. Thus, despite language in the legislation that expressly precluded the hospital from being considered an agency of state government, "it is evident that the Regents have not sufficiently divested themselves of power over the hospital to enable the new corporation to operate independently as a private corporation. Thus, we find that the reorganized hospital is still a public entity." Since the hospital remained a state entity, and since the legislation would require more than two thousand of the hospital's employees to relinquish their civil service status, the court held that the legislation violated the State Civil Service Amendment (Article XII, Section 13) of the state constitution, "which protects state personnel from legislative measures designed to circumvent the constitutional amendment." The court also held that the financing provisions of the reorganizing legislation, allowing the hospital to become indebted, violated Article XI, which prohibits the state from incurring debts. (For another example of structural issues, see *Gulf Regional Education Television Affiliates v. University of Houston*, 746 S.W.2d 803 (Tex. 1988).)

A quite different set of problems arises when an organization that is not already part of the postsecondary institution's structure attempts to connect itself to the institution in some way. The general questions then are whether the institution has any obligation to allow particular outside entities to become affiliated with it, and whether and how an institution may restrict the rights of such an organization to claim or publicly assert an affiliation with the school. In *Ad-Hoc Committee of Baruch Black and Hispanic Alumni Association v. Bernard M. Baruch College*, 835 F.2d 980 (2d Cir. 1987), the plaintiff committee alleged that the college had improperly refused to recognize its proposed alumni association dedicated to the needs of minority students. This refusal, the committee argued, was a violation of the First Amendment and the equal protection clause of the Fourteenth Amendment. The college countered that an officially recognized alumni organization, which included minority alumni, already existed and that the creation of another alumni association could

overburden alumni with fund solicitations and thus dilute the current association's power to raise funds.

After a district court dismissed the committee's complaint, the U.S. Court of
Appeals reversed and remanded, holding:

> [I]t is possible that plaintiffs could demonstrate that the College's selective
> denial of official recognition to their alumni association was improperly moti-
> vated by discrimination based on political viewpoint or race. . . . In this case,
> the College has not yet offered any justification for its denial of recognition
> to the Black and Hispanic Alumni Association, and thus it is impossible to
> determine at this stage whether this action was motivated by a desire
> to "discourage one viewpoint and advance another" in violation of the First
> Amendment [835 F.2d at 982].

On remand, however, the district court held that the committee could show no
discrimination or other improper motive by the college in not recognizing the
proposed alumni association, and that the college was thus not required to
acknowledge or support the new association.[25]

3.6.3. Taxation issues.
The creation or reorganization of separate entities
may also give rise to taxation issues under state and federal law. The most
important of these issues usually involve tax exemption—in particular the issue
of how the relationship between the two entities affects their eligibility for tax-
exempt status. This subsection focuses on tax exemption issues under state law.
(For discussion of such issues (and other relevant tax issues) under federal
law, see Sections 13.3 & 15.3.4.1.) Resolution of such issues may depend on the
legal status of the separate entity in relation to the degree-granting entity, and
in particular on the degree of control the latter asserts over the former. In addition, the resolution may depend on the functions that the separate entity
performs and their relation to the functions of the institution itself.

In *Yale Club of Chicago v. Department of Revenue,* 574 N.E.2d 31 (Ill. App. Ct.
1991), for example, the court considered whether an alumni association that
recruited for Yale University qualified for a purchaser's exemption from the state
sales tax. The Yale Club of Chicago (YCC), a nonprofit corporation, dedicated its
efforts to promoting Yale University. One of its central purposes was to use its members to interview potential Yale students in the Chicago area. Although the club followed admissions guidelines prepared by Yale, it was not controlled in any way by
the university and did not receive any funding from the university. The club also
sponsored social events for its members: Yale alumni, parents of alumni, and
current Yale students.

The appellate court held that the YCC did not qualify for an educational or a
charitable tax exemption under Illinois law. Regarding the educational exemption,

---

[25]The parties resolved their dispute. By agreement, the Black and Hispanic Alumni Association
was allowed to use the college's name and some office space, and the committee expressed willingness to discuss a possible relationship with the Baruch Alumni Association ("College Settles
Lawsuit Filed by Minority Alumni," *Chron. Higher Educ.,* May 2, 1990, A2).

the club had argued that "because Yale University is a school to which the exemption would apply, and the YCC is performing the same functions that Yale could, the exemption should apply to those activities performed [to further] Yale's educational objectives." In rejecting this argument, the court reasoned that, under the statute and case law, the club could claim exemption based on its relationship with Yale only if the club's activities were "reasonably necessary" to Yale's "educational goals or administrative needs." The YCC's activities did not fit this characterization, according to the court. The *Yale Club* case thus demonstrates that an affiliated organization performing important beneficial functions for a postsecondary institution does not necessarily qualify for a tax exemption even though the institution itself could receive an exemption on the basis of the same activities.

Another illustrative case, *City of Morgantown v. West Virginia University Medical Corporation*, 457 S.E.2d 637 (W. Va. 1995), involved a health care entity rather than an alumni association and a business and occupation tax rather than a sales tax. The West Virginia University Medical Corporation is a faculty group-practice organization in which faculty members of the West Virginia University School of Medicine provide professional services to patients irrespective of their ability to pay. More than $13,000,000 in uncompensated medical care was provided by the corporation during fiscal year 1988–89. The corporation was already exempt from federal income taxes as a charitable organizations under Section 501(c)(3) of the Internal Revenue Code (see Section 13.3.1 of this book). West Virginia's tax code, like the federal tax code, contained an exemption for organizations "operated exclusively for religious or charitable purposes," but the state code did not include any definition of "religious or charitable." The West Virginia Supreme Court rejected the City of Morgantown's argument that the medical corporation does bill some patients for medical care and thus does not operate solely as a charitable organization. The actual billing practices of the organization were not determinative of charitable status in light of the substantial amount of uncompensated medical care that it provided yearly to the citizens of West Virginia:

> We see no reason why a non-profit medical faculty practice corporation that:
> (1) enhances educational opportunity for students at the West Virginia Medical School; (2) facilitates medical research; (3) provides medical care irrespective of ability to pay; (4) reasonably supplements clinical faculty salaries facilitating recruitment and retention of top physician faculty members; (5) operates to benefit the West Virginia University medical school; and (6) is exempt from federal tax under . . . Section 501(c)(3) as a charitable, education and scientific organization should not qualify for charitable exemption from the state business and occupation tax [457 S.E.2d at 641–42].

Resolution of tax exemption issues may also depend on technical interpretations of state statutory and constitutional provisions. In *University Medical Center Corporation v. The Department of Revenue of the State of Arizona*, 201 Ariz. 447, 36 P.3d 1217 (Ariz. Ct. App. 2001), for example, an Arizona court addressed the applicability of real property taxation laws to a full-service, acute care teaching hospital on the campus of the University of Arizona in Tuscon. Prior to 1984, the hospital was owned and operated by the Arizona Board of Regents, during which time the hospital incurred substantial losses, regularly burdening state funds. In 1984, the Arizona legislature adopted legislation that authorized the board of regents to "lease real property . . . owned by the Board to a nonprofit corporation . . . for purposes of operating a health care institution . . . ," subject to certain restrictions (Ariz. Rev. Stat. § 15–1637), and that extended a tax exemption to any such lessee (§ 15–1637 (D)). The board of regents then formed the University Medical Center Corporation (UMCC), leased the hospital to UMCC, and conveyed the hospital's assets to UMCC. After UMCC acquired several off-campus parcels of land, a dispute arose concerning the real property tax status of these properties. The appellate court closely examined the exemption provision, the entire legislation authorizing the lease of the hospital, and the state constitutional provision on tax exemptions before reversing the state tax court and upholding the tax exemption for the properties—so long as they were "not used or held for profit."

3.6.4. Application of regulatory laws.

Creation of or affiliation with another entity may also raise issues concerning the application of state regulatory statutes.[26] Various state statutes apply to state agencies or public bodies, for instance, but not to private entities. If a public postsecondary institution creates or affiliates with another entity, there may be questions regarding whether that entity will be subject to these laws. The answer usually depends on whether the separate entity is sufficiently controlled by or related to the public institution that the separate entity would be considered a state agency or public body.

In *Weston v. Carolina Research and Development Foundation*, 401 S.E.2d 161 (S.C. 1991), for example, the issue was whether South Carolina's Freedom of Information Act (S.C. Code Ann. §§ 30-4-10 to 30-4-110) applied to the Carolina Research and Development Foundation, a nonprofit corporation operating "exclusively for the benefit of the University of South Carolina" (401 S.E.2d at 162). The plaintiffs, media organizations, argued that the Act applied and gave them the right to inspect the foundation's records. The Act provides that it applies to "public bodies," defined in part as "any organization, corporation, or agency supported in whole or in part by public funds or expending public funds" (S.C. Code Ann. § 30-4-20(a)). The court determined that the foundation had received public funds on at least four separate occasions. It had accepted nearly 40 percent of the consideration the University of South Carolina received for selling one of the university's buildings; it had accepted more than $16 million in federal grant money on behalf of the university and managed the expenditure of these funds for construction of an engineering center for the university; it had accepted grants of money from the city of

---

[26]Such issues may also arise under federal regulatory statutes—for instance, whether a captive or affiliated entity is an "employer" for purposes of Title VII (42 U.S.C. §§ 2000e *et seq.*)—as well as under the federal civil rights spending statutes (see Sections 13.5.7.3 & 13.5.7.6 of this book).

Columbia and from Richland County, and a conveyance of real estate from the city, as part of the process of developing a real estate project for the university; and it had retained 15–25 percent of the total payments from private third parties under research and development contracts that the university had executed and channeled through the foundation. The court held that any one of these transactions qualified the foundation as a public body under the language of the Act. The foundation was thus required to permit the plaintiffs to inspect its records.

Similarly, in *State ex. rel. Guste v. Nicholls College Foundation*, 564 So. 2d 682 (La. 1990), the inspector general of Louisiana sought to view the records of the foundation pursuant to the state's Public Records Act (La. Rev. Stat. Ann. §§ 44:1 *et seq.*). The foundation, a nonprofit corporation organized to promote the welfare of Nicholls College, had received funds from the Nicholls State University Alumni Federation, another nonprofit organization promoting the college's interests. The federation received its funding through a mandatory fee charged to all Nicholls students registered for more than seven credit hours and transferred 10 percent of these funds to the foundation. Under the Public Records Act, the foundation's records would be "public records" subject to public inspection if either (a) the foundation were a "public body," or (b) the records concerned "the receipt or payment" of public funds. Using the second rationale, the Louisiana Supreme Court reasoned that the federation's close affiliation with Nicholls College (including its occupying a building on campus at only nominal rent, its use of state employees in its operations, and its inclusion in the college's yearly budget) made the federation a public body under the Act; that the student fees provided to the federation were public funds; and that the foundation's records of its receipt and use of these funds were thus public records subject to the Act. (Presumably, the federation's records were also subject to the Act.) The state's inspector general therefore had a right to view these records. (For further clarifications in later proceedings, see *State ex. rel. Guste v. Nicholls College Foundation*, 592 So. 2d 419 (La. 1991); and see generally Salin Geevarghese, "Looking Behind the Foundation Veil: University Foundations and Open Records Laws," 25 *J. Law & Educ.* 219 (1996).)

In *Encore College Bookstores, Inc. v. Auxiliary Services Corp. of State University of New York at Farmingdale*, 663 N.E.2d 302 (N.Y. 1995), however, the court reached a different result in a suit under the New York Freedom of Information Law (FOIL). The plaintiff was a private bookstore operating near the Farmingdale Campus of the State University of New York (SUNY). Using the FOIL (McKinney N.Y. Public Officers Law, § 87), the bookstore sought to require the Auxiliary Services Corporation (ASC) of SUNY-Farmingdale to disclose a booklist that its subcontractor had compiled in the course of its responsibilities for operating the campus bookstore and maintaining the inventory of textbooks necessary for the academic year. SUNY had created ASC to provide auxiliary services for the college community, and ASC had elected to contract out the responsibility for maintaining the campus bookstore to a private subcontractor. Like the courts in the *Weston* and *Nicholls* cases, the court determined that the booklist was a "record" within the ambit of the FOIL. Even though such records were kept by ASC, rather than SUNY, ASC nevertheless ran the bookstore and kept the records "on SUNY's behalf" and "for the benefit of SUNY." Moreover, to classify the booklist as something other than a record, simply because it was compiled by a subcontractor and held by an auxiliary corporation, would undermine the intent of the FOIL, and allow government agencies to insulate records from disclosure by delegating their creation and maintenance to nongovernmental entities (663 N.E.2d at 306). Unlike *Weston* and *Nicholls,* however, the court did not order release of the records, but held instead that they fell within one of the FOIL exemptions covering disclosures that would create a risk of "substantial competitive harm." According to the court, this "substantial competitive harm" could be inferred from the obvious commercial value of the booklist to the plaintiff and the likelihood of competitive disadvantage its disclosure would create for the subcontractor operating the campus bookstore.

(For examples of other cases concerning the applicability of open meetings laws, see *Smith v. City University of New York,* 708 N.E.2d. 983 (N.Y. 1999), and *Board of Regents of the Regency University System v. Reynard,* 686 N.E.2d 1222 (Ill. App. Ct. 1997).)

3.6.5. "State action" issues. When a public institution creates a separate entity, questions may also arise concerning whether the entity will be considered to be a state actor and thus bound, like the institution itself, to comply with the federal Constitution's individual rights guarantees (see generally Section 1.5.2). The U.S. Supreme Court's decision in *Lebron v. National Railroad Passenger Corp.,* 513 U.S. 374 (1995), provides guidance on this question. *Lebron* was a First Amendment challenge to Amtrak's refusal to permit an individual to post a political advertisement on a billboard owned by Amtrak. The Court ruled that Amtrak (the National Railroad Passenger Corporation), although nominally a private corporation, was created by Congress for the purpose of furthering governmental objectives. The U.S. President appoints six of the nine members of the board of directors, and the corporation is accountable to the federal government through reporting requirements. Given the purposes behind its creation and its accountability to the government, the Court ruled that Amtrak is "an agency or instrumentality of the United States for the purpose of individual rights guaranteed against the Government by the Constitution." By analogy from this case, it appears that public postsecondary institutions which have or seek to create separate organizations cannot escape their obligations to respect individuals' constitutional rights "by simply resorting to the corporate form" (513 U.S. at 397); and that whenever a public institution establishes a separate entity to pursue "governmental objectives under the direction and control of . . . governmental appointees" (513 U.S. at 398), the entity will be considered to be a state actor.

3.6.6. Liability issues. Postsecondary institutions may become liable for the acts of a captive or affiliated entity when it is engaged in joint action with the institution, when it is acting as the institution's agent (see Section 2.1.3), or when the institution has assumed the risk of such liability by way of a "hold-harmless" or indemnification agreement with the entity (see Section 2.5.3.2). In such circumstances the institution may then become liable for the separate entity's negligence or other tortious acts (see generally Section 3.3 above) or for the performance of contracts that the separate entity enters on the institution's behalf (see generally Section 3.4 above). In addition, public institutions or their officers could sometimes become liable for the separate entity's violation of constitutional rights; and private institutions could be subject to such liability in the narrower circumstance where the separate entity is a governmental entity or is otherwise engaged in state action (see subsection 3.6.5 above; and see generally Section 1.5.2).

State colleges and universities may sometimes escape such liability if the state's sovereign immunity, under state or federal law, extends to the captive or affiliated entity that has engaged in the allegedly unlawful action. In *Watson v. University of Utah Medical Center,* 75 F.3d 569 (10th Cir. 1996), for example, the court considered whether the university's Eleventh Amendment immunity (see Section 13.1.5) extended to the university medical center. The court determined that, although the medical center generated most of its own revenues, and could use them to pay judgments against it, it was nevertheless "an integral part" of the university. The court thus granted immunity to the medical center. But in another case involving a different type of entity, *Teichgraeber v. Memorial Union Corp. of Emporia State University,* 946 F. Supp. 900 (D. Kan. 1996), the court rejected the Eleventh Amendment's applicability to a state university's student union, a separately incorporated nonprofit corporation. According to the court, the student union had not demonstrated "that Kansas law characterizes [it] as an entity of the state subject to significant oversight and control by other state entities," or that "the judgment in this case would be satisfied out of the state treasury," and was therefore not entitled to immunity.

Because liability issues loom so large in many structural decisions, risk management should be a major part of the planning for creation of or affiliation with a separate entity. (See generally Section 2.5.)

Selected Annotated Bibliography

Sec. 3.1 *(The Question of Authority)*

Bess, James L. *Collegiality and Bureaucracy in the Modern University* (Teachers College Press, 1988). Examines governance in the contemporary university. Discusses the relationship among authority structures, power, and collegiality; and between organizational characteristics and faculty perceptions of administrators. A framework for analysis of university governance is provided.

Hornby, D. Brock. "Delegating Authority to the Community of Scholars," 1975 *Duke L.J.* 279 (1975). Provides excellent legal and policy analysis regarding delegations of authority in public systems of postsecondary education. Considers constitutional and statutory delegations to statewide governing boards and individual boards of trustees, and subdelegations of that authority to officials, employees, and other bodies in individual institutions. Contains many useful citations to legal and policy materials.

See also the Hynes entry in the Selected Annotated Bibliography for Chapter Two, Section 2.1.

Sec. 3.2 *(Sources and Scope of Authority)*

Chait, Richard, Holland, Thomas P., & Taylor, Barbara E. *Improving the Performance of Governing Boards* (ACE/Oryx, 1997). Presents the results of a study of how boards of trustees can raise their competence. Discusses effective ways to initiate board development efforts. Includes charts, exhibits, and practical advice for persuading trustees to engage in developmental processes.

Daugherty, Mary Schmid. "Uniform Management of Institutional Funds Act: The Implications for Private College Board of Regents," 57 *West's Educ. Law Rptr.* 319 (1990). Examines state laws based on the Uniform Act, which establishes guidelines for the management and use of the investments of nonprofit educational and charitable organizations. Discusses the standards to which regents are held, the issue of restitution, the types of investments that can be made under these laws, and issues that remain for the courts to clarify. Suggestions for monitoring the institution's investment plan are provided.

Evans, Eileen M., & Evans, William D., Jr. "'No Good Deed Goes Unpunished': Personal Liability of Trustees and Administrators of Private Colleges and Universities," 33 *Tort & Insurance L.J.* 1107 (1998).

Fishman, James J. "Standards of Conduct for Directors of Nonprofit Corporations," 7 *Pace L. Rev.* 389 (1987). Surveys the evolution in the law regarding nonprofit directors' duty of care, with emphasis on the *Sibley Hospital* case. Distinguishes between and critiques the "corporate" and the "trust" standards of care, and proposes a new "shifting standard of care," whose application would depend on "the type of nonprofit corporation and the nature of a director's conduct and interest in a particular transaction."

Frey, Jeannie Carmedelle, & Overton, George W. (eds.). *Guidebook for Directors of Nonprofit Corporations* (2d ed., ABA Section of Business Law, 2002). Discusses the duties and responsibilities of directors of nonprofits, such as college and university trustees.

Harpool, David. "Minimum Compliance with Minimum Standards: Managing Trustee Conflicts of Interest," 24 *J. Coll. & Univ. L.* 465 (1998). Supplements the author's article on *Sibley Hospital* (below) by surveying how 566 private colleges manage trustee conflicts of interest. Concludes that many colleges have not adopted adequate policies for avoiding trustee conflicts of interest; provides recommendations for the development of appropriate policies.

Harpool, David. "The *Sibley Hospital* Case: Trustees and Their Loyalty to the Institution," 23 *J. Coll. & Univ. L.* 255 (1996). Reviews the standards articulated in *Sibley Hospital* for trustee conduct, including conflict of interest problems.

Houle, Cyril O. *Governing Boards* (Jossey-Bass, 1997). Discusses the functions of a board of trustees, how to select and orient new board members, board policies and practices, board relationships with staff, and various laws (such as public meetings laws) that may affect board operations.

Ingram, Richard T., & Associates. *Governing Public Colleges and Universities: A Handbook for Trustees, Chief Executives, and Other Campus Leaders* (Jossey-Bass, 1993). A resource book for college trustees. Divided into three parts: "Understanding the

Environment of Public Higher Education," "Fulfilling Board Functions," and "Developing the Public Board." Each part is subdivided into chapters and topics, many of which address legal considerations. Appendices contain resources, including sample statements of board members' responsibilities and desirable qualifications for trustees; a survey of public governing boards' characteristics, policies, and practices; and self-study criteria for public multicampus and system boards. Also included is an extensive annotated list of recommended readings.

King, Harriet M. "The Voluntary Closing of a Private College: A Decision for the Board of Trustees?" 32 *S.C. L. Rev.* 547 (1981). Reviews the legal problems inherent in any decision of a board of trustees to close a private postsecondary institution. The article focuses on questions of trust law, especially the application of the doctrine of cy pres, an equitable doctrine permitting the assets of a charity to be used for a purpose other than that specified in the trust instrument when the original purpose can no longer be carried out.

Marsh, Gordon H. "Governance of Non-Profit Organizations: An Appropriate Standard of Conduct for Trustees and Directors of Museums and Other Cultural Institutions," 85 *Dickinson L. Rev.* 607 (1981). Compares the different standards of care applied by courts to the common law trustee and the corporate director, respectively, and considers the applicability of these standards to trustees of nonprofit organizations. Although the article will be of particular interest to institutions responsible for the management of museums or other cultural exhibits, its discussion of standards of care and the state of the case law defining a good-faith standard for trustees is of general interest for postsecondary institutions.

Waldo, Charles N. *A Working Guide for Directors of Not-for-Profit Organizations* (Greenwood, 1986). Provides an overview of the mission of an organization's board of directors in nontechnical terms. Also provided is a discussion of the responsibilities of directors and brief summaries of financial issues, planning, legal issues, and tax problems.

See also Connell & Savage entry for Chapter Two, Section 2.5.

Sec. 3.3 *(Institutional Tort Liability)*

Bazluke, Francine T., & Clother, Robert C. *Defamation Issues in Higher Education* (National Association of College and University Attorneys, 2004). A layperson's guide to defamation law. Authors review the legal framework for a defamation claim and the possible defenses, and then discuss specific employment issues and student disciplinary actions that may give rise to defamation claims. Discusses the institution's potential liability for defamatory student publications. Provides guidelines to minimize the institution's exposure to defamation claims.

Bickel, Robert D., & Lake, Peter F. *The Rights and Responsibilities of the Modern University: Who Assumes the Risk of College Life?* (Carolina Academic, 1999). Develops and describes the role of the college as a facilitator of student development and the significance of that model for the way that tort law is applied to colleges and universities. Focuses on balancing the rights and responsibilities of both students and the institution, while creating a climate in which academic and personal development are facilitated and risk is acknowledged but minimized.

Bowman, Cynthia Grant, & Lipp, MaryBeth. "Legal Limbo of the Student Intern: The Responsibility of Colleges and Universities to Protect Student Interns Against Sexual

Harassment," 23 *Harv. Women's L.J.* 95 (2000). Reviews the problem of sexual harassment of students in higher education and discusses three models of internships with varying degrees of institutional control and contractual relationships. Discusses the potential legal remedies for student interns who experience harassment and the university's potential liability under Title IX and contract law.

Burling, Philip. *Crime on Campus: Analyzing and Managing the Increasing Risk of Institutional Liability* (National Association of College and University Attorneys, 1990). Reviews the legal analyses that courts undertake in responding to claims that liability for injuries suffered on campus should be shifted from the victim to the institution. Includes a review of literature about reducing crime on campus and managing the risk of liability to victims whom the institution may have a duty to protect.

Evans, Richard B. Note, "'A Stranger in a Strange Land': Responsibility and Liability for Students Enrolled in Foreign-Study Programs," 18 *J. Coll. & Univ. L.* 299 (1991). Examines the doctrine of "special relationship" that has been applied to the student-institution relationship and discusses its significance to claims of students injured while participating in a study abroad program. Suggestions for limiting institutional liability are provided.

Feliu, Alfred G., & Johnson, Weyman T., Jr. *Negligence in Employment Law* (Bureau of National Affairs, 2002). Reviews a range of employment torts, including negligent hiring, liability for workplace violence, potential tort liability when dismissing employees, prevention and defense of employment tort claims, and insurance issues.

Gaffney, Edward M., & Sorensen, Philip M. *Ascending Liability in Religious and Other Non-Profit Organizations* (Center for Constitutional Studies, Mercer University (now at Baylor University), 1984). Provides an overview of liability case law related to nonprofit and religiously affiliated organizations, discusses constitutional issues, and provides suggestions for structuring the operations of such organizations to limit liability.

Gehring, Donald D., & Geraci, Christy P. *Alcohol on Campus: A Compendium of the Law and a Guide to Campus Policy* (College Administration Publications, 1989). Examines legal and policy issues related to alcohol on college campuses. Included are chapters reviewing research on student consumption of alcohol, including differences by students' race and gender; sources of legal liability for colleges if intoxicated students injure themselves or others; and procedural and substantive considerations in developing alcohol policies and risk management procedures. A state-by-state analysis of laws relevant to alcohol consumption, sale, and social host liability is included. The book is updated annually.

Green, Ronald M., & Reibstein, Richard J. *Employer's Guide to Workplace Torts* (Bureau of National Affairs, 1992). Reviews each of the areas of employment-related torts, explaining the general principles of law involved, summarizing case law precedent, and providing suggestions for avoiding liability.

Gregory, David L. "The Problematic Employment Dynamics of Student Internships," 12 *Notre Dame J.L. Ethics & Pub. Pol'y* 227 (1998). Views student interns as "exploited" and discusses various legal strategies for providing employment law protections to student interns.

Hoye, William P. "An Ounce of Prevention Is Worth . . . The Life of a Student: Reducing Risk in International Programs," 27 *J. Coll. & Univ. L.* 151 (2000). Reviews liability issues for college with study abroad programs; suggests measures for reducing risks to students and corresponding liability for institutions.

Lake, Peter F. "The Rise of Duty and the Fall of In Loco Parentis and Other Protective Tort Doctrines in Higher Education Law," 64 *Mo. L. Rev.* 1 (1999). Discusses the history of judicial deference to institutional actions under the *in loco parentis* doctrine, and the more recent tendency for courts to hold institutions of higher education to the same tort law standards as business organizations. Reviews the application of premises liability doctrines, judicial responses to injuries related to alcohol use, and concludes that tort law as applied to colleges is being "mainstreamed."

Lake, Peter F. "The Special Relationship(s) Between a College and a Student: Law and Policy Ramifications for the Post In Loco Parentis College," 37 *Idaho L. Rev.* 531 (2001). Discusses the further development of judicial rejection of the *in loco parentis* doctrine and the creation of the "special relationship" doctrine that may hold institutions of higher education responsible for injuries to students, particularly when their injuries arise from circumstances that are foreseeable.

National Association of College and University Attorneys. *Am I Liable? Faculty, Staff, and Institutional Liability in the College and University Setting* (NACUA, 1989). A collection of articles on selected liability issues. Included are analyses of general tort liability theories, liability for the acts of criminal intruders, student groups and alcohol-related liability, academic advising and defamation, and workers' compensation. Also discusses liability releases. A final chapter addresses risk management and insurance issues. Written by university counsel, these articles provide clear, useful information to counsel, administrators, and faculty.

Pavela, Gary. *Questions and Answers on College Student Suicide* (College Administration Publications, 2006). Discusses, in a question and answer format, the legal issues faced by college administrators and counselors, provides advice on parental involvement and notification, discipline of students who engage in self-destructive behavior, and responding to a student suicide, among others. Includes checklists and guidelines, OCR letter rulings, and training materials for residence life staff.

Prosser, William L., & Keeton, W. Page. *Handbook on the Law of Torts* (5th ed., West, 1984). A comprehensive survey of tort doctrines and concepts, with discussion of leading cases and relevant statutes. Includes discussion of sovereign and charitable immunity, defamation, negligence, and the contributory negligence and assumption-of-risk defenses.

Richmond, Douglas. "Institutional Liability for Student Activities and Organizations," 19 *J. Law & Educ.* 309 (1990). Provides an overview of a variety of tort theories, and judicial precedents related to these theories, in which the institution's liability for the allegedly wrongful acts of student organizations was at issue.

Stevens, George E. "Evaluation of Faculty Competence as a 'Privileged Occasion,'" 4 *J. Coll. & Univ. Law* 281 (1979). Discusses the law of defamation as it applies to institutional evaluations of professional competence.

Strohm, Leslie Chambers (ed.). *AIDS on Campus: A Legal Compendium* (National Association of College and University Attorneys, 1991). A collection of materials related to a range of legal, medical, and policy issues concerning AIDS. Included are Centers for Disease Control recommendations, guidelines, and updates regarding precautions to take if employees, patients, or students have AIDS; journal articles; occupational safety and health guidelines; institutional policy statements; and an extensive list of resources.

Whitten, Amy D., & Mosely, Deanne M. "Caught in the Crossfire: Employers' Liability for Workplace Violence," 70 *Miss. L.J.* 505 (2000). Reviews theories of employer liability for workplace violence, including *respondeat superior;* negligent hiring, retention, supervision, entrustment, and training; and failure to warn. Although the article focuses primarily on Mississippi cases, it is a useful summary of the various theories of liability involved when workplace violence occurs.

Sec. 3.4 (Institutional Contract Liability)

Bookman, Mark. *Contracting Collegiate Auxiliary Services* (Education and Nonprofit Consulting, 1989). Discusses legal and policy issues related to contracting for auxiliary services on campus. An overview chapter reviews legal terminology, the advantages and disadvantages of contracting, and the ways in which contracting decisions are made. Another chapter explains what should be negotiated when the contract is developed and how contracted services should be managed. Sample documents are included.

See also Cherry, LaTourette, and Meleaer entries for Chapter Eight, Section 8.1.

Sec. 3.5 (Institutional Liability for Violations of Federal Constitutional Rights)

Nahmod, Sheldon H. *Civil Rights and Civil Liberties Litigation: The Law of Section 1983* (3d ed., Shepard's/McGraw-Hill, 1991, with annual supp.). A guide to litigation brought under Section 1983. Primarily for legal counsel. Focuses on the positions the courts have taken on the procedural and technical questions common to all Section 1983 litigation.

Sec. 3.6 (Captive and Affiliated Organizations)

See Curry entry for Chapter 15, Section 15.4, which has several sections discussing research foundations.

See Matthews & Norgaard entry for Chapter 15, Section 15.1, which addresses alliances between higher educational institutions and private industry.

4

The College and Its Employees

Sec. 4.1. Overview of Employment Relationships

Employment laws and regulations pose some of the most complex legal issues faced by colleges and universities. Employees may be executive officers of the institution, staff members, or faculty members—some of whom may be in a dual appointment status as administrators and faculty members and others of whom may be in a dual employee-student status.

The discussion in this chapter, and in Chapter Five on employment discrimination law, applies to all individuals employed by a college or university, whether they are officers, faculty, or staff. Particular applications of employment law to faculty members, and concepts unique to faculty employment (such as academic freedom and tenure), are the subject of Chapters Six and Seven. Special issues of relevance to the employment status of the institution's executive officers are addressed in the first two Sections of Chapter Three and in subsection 4.3.3.7 below.

The institution's relationships with its employees are governed by a complex web of state and federal (and sometimes local) law. Contract law principles, based in state common law, provide the basic legal foundation for employment relationships (see Section 4.3 below). For employees who are covered by a collective bargaining agreement, however, federal or state statutory law and labor board rulings supplement, and to a substantial extent replace, common law contract principles (see Section 4.5 below). And for employees located in a foreign country, the civil law of that country will sometimes replace or supplement the contract law principles of the college's home state.

In addition to contract law and collective bargaining laws, public institutions' employment relationships are also governed by other federal and state statutes, federal and state agency regulations (including state civil service regulations), constitutional law (both federal and state), administrative law (both federal and state), and sometimes local civil rights and health and safety ordinances of cities and counties. For private institutions, the web of employment law includes (in addition to contract and collective bargaining law) various federal and state statutes and regulations, local ordinances, state constitutional provisions (in some states), and federal and state administrative law (in some circumstances). Whenever a public or private institution employs workers under a government procurement contract or grant, any contract or grant terms covering employment will also come into play, as will federal or state statutes and regulations on government contracts and grants; these sources of law may serve to modify common law contract principles (see generally Section 13.4.2). Moreover, for both public and private institutions, state tort law affects employment relationships because institutions and employees are both subject to a duty of care arising from common law tort principles (see Sections 3.3 & 4.7.2). Like common law contract principles, however, common law tort principles are sometimes modified by statute as, for example, is the case with worker's compensation laws (see Section 4.6.6).

Among the most complex of the federal and state laws on particular aspects of employment are the nondiscrimination statutes and regulations—the subject of Chapter Five. Other examples of complex and specialized laws include collective bargaining laws (Section 4.5 below), immigration laws (Section 4.6.5 below), tax laws (Sections 13.3.1 & 13.3.8), and employee benefits laws. In addition to the Employee Retirement Income Security Act (ERISA) (Section 4.6.3 below), employee benefits are subject to the Health Insurance Portability and Accountability Act of 1996 (HIPAA), discussed in Section 13.2.14, which has relevance not only for employee benefits but also for record keeping in hospitals and some student health centers; and the Consolidated Omnibus Budget Amendment Act of 1986 (COBRA), which requires employers to continue group health insurance benefits, at the employee's cost, after certain events, such as termination. (The Selected Annotated Bibliographies for this chapter, Chapter Five, and Chapter Thirteen contain basic references on the various specialized employment laws.)

A fundamental issue that each college or university must resolve for itself is whether all individuals working for the institution are its employees or whether some are independent contractors. These issues are discussed in Section 4.2.1 below. Similar issues may also arise concerning whether a particular worker is an employee or is working only in a student status. These issues are discussed in Section 4.6.2 below. Colleges and universities also need to address the issue of where their employees are working and what effect the location has on the applicable law. These issues, such as telecommuting, working at off-campus locations, and working in foreign countries, are discussed in Section 4.2.2.

Other legal concerns that may arise for colleges as employers include the free expression rights of employees, particularly in public colleges (see generally Section 7.1.1), privacy in the workplace (including "snail mail" and e-mail privacy), background checks on applicants for employment, drug and alcohol use by employees (see Section 4.3.3.6), and potential workplace violence. This chapter can only summarize briefly some of the more salient aspects of these issues or refer the reader to the resources in the Selected Annotated Bibliography.

The college may also face a variety of particularized legal issues, or particular risks of legal liability, regarding specific groups of employees. The faculty— the subject of Chapters Six and Seven—is the most common example of a group requiring some separate or special consideration. Another prominent example is the executive officers of the institution (see Chapter Three, Sections 3.1 and 3.2, as well as the discussion of executive contracts in Section 4.3.3.7 below). Other examples include security personnel, student judicial officers, health care personnel, and coaches of intercollegiate athletic teams.

Security personnel, particularly those who are "sworn officers" and carry firearms, may involve their institutions in claims regarding the use of force or off-campus law enforcement activities (see Section 8.6.1). Security personnel may also become the focus of negligence claims if crimes of violence occur on campus (see Section 8.6.2). Arrests and searches conducted by security personnel at public (and sometimes private) institutions may raise issues under the Fourth Amendment or comparable state constitutional provisions (see Sections 8.4.2 & 8.6.1). And the records kept by security personnel may raise special issues under the federal Campus Security Act (see Section 8.6.3) and under the Family Educational Rights and Privacy Act (FERPA) (see Section 9.7.1).

Student judicial officers may involve their institutions in due process claims that arise when students contest penalties imposed upon them for infractions of the college's code of conduct (see Sections 9.1, 9.2, & 9.4). Student judicial officers may also become involved in various issues concerning the confidentiality of their investigations and deliberations, including issues regarding a "mediation privilege" (see, for example, the *Garstang* case in Section 2.2.3.3).

Health care personnel, including physicians and mental health counselors, may involve their institutions in negligence claims when students under their care injure or kill themselves or others (see Sections 3.3.2.5 & 4.7.2), or in malpractice claims when something else goes wrong in the diagnosis or treatment process (see Section 12.5.5). Physicians and counselors who serve members of the campus community may also confront issues concerning the doctor-patient privilege and other confidentiality privileges (see Section 2.2.3.3).

Athletics coaches may file claims of sex discrimination against their institutions, either because they believe they have been discriminated against or because of a perceived inequity in resources allocated to women's teams (see, for example, Section 5.3.3.4). Or coaches may have lucrative contracts and fringe benefits that (in public institutions) prompt open-records law requests (see Section 12.5.3). Coaches may also become involved in disputes regarding NCAA rules (see the *Tarkanian* case in Section 14.4.2 and the *Law* case in Section 14.4.4).

The management of the institution's numerous and varying employment relationships requires the regular attention of professionally trained and experienced staff. In addition to human resources managers, the institution will need compliance officers to handle legal requirements in specialized areas such as nondiscrimination and affirmative action, immigration status, employee benefits, and health and safety; and a risk manager to handle liability matters concerning employees. The institution's legal counsel will also need to be involved in many compliance and risk management issues, as well as in the preparation of standard contracts and other employment forms, the preparation and modification of employee manuals and other written policies, the establishment and operation of employee grievance processes, and the preparation of negotiated (individual or collective) employment contracts. Sections 4.3.6 and 4.8 of this chapter, as well as Sections 2.4.2 and 2.5 above, provide some guidance on these matters.

Sec. 4.2. Defining the Employment Relationship

4.2.1. Employees versus independent contractors. An issue that colleges are likely to face with respect to their staff (more so than with respect to their faculty) is whether some of the individuals who work at the college are independent contractors rather than true employees. An independent contractor is an individual who sells his or her services to an organization but who is not considered an employee of that organization. For example, consultants, outside counsel, or other individuals with expertise that the college needs on a periodic basis are often considered independent contractors. The status of these individuals is important because many laws that protect employees do not necessarily protect independent contractors. On the other hand, an institution may incur liability under certain laws for independent contractors that it would not incur for employees. And in some cases, whether or not the individual is an employee or an independent contractor, liability may ensue.

Colleges and universities, like other employers, use a variety of forms of employment to maximize efficiency and minimize costs. Colleges may use independent contractors as consultants or trainers, or to work on short-term projects. Temporary employees may be used to fill in for regular employees who are on leave or to provide short-term help while the college seeks to fill a vacant position. Temporary employees may be the college's own employees, or they may be "leased employees" who are employed by a temporary agency but who may work for the college for extended periods of time. Although the "leased" employees are technically the employees of the providing agency, which pays them and provides them with benefits (if any), the college may be found to be a "joint employer" under certain laws, and may incur liability despite the fact that the individuals are not the college's employees.[1]

Certain laws, such as the Fair Labor Standards Act (Section 4.6.2), the state worker's compensation statutes (Section 4.6.6), federal and state equal employment opportunity laws (Chapter Five), and some provisions of the Internal Revenue Code (Section 13.1.3), apply to employees but not to individuals who are independent contractors. The definitions of "employee" in each of these laws

---

[1]For an example of coemployment in a case involving a temporary staffing agency and a "client" employer, see *Hunt v. State of Missouri, Dept. of Corrections*, 297 F.3d 735 (8th Cir. 2002).

differ from one another, so the employment status of the individual will need to be determined under the provisions of each law. On the other hand, there may be advantages to characterizing an individual as an employee; for example, the worker's compensation statutes limit an employer's liability for tort claims when an employee is injured; but an independent contractor is not precluded from suing for negligence if an injury occurs. And occasionally, individuals whom an employer believed to be independent contractors may be found by a federal or state agency to be employees, which may result in additional tax liability, wage and benefit costs, or other financial consequences.

Employee status is controlled by common law as well as by statute. The common law test for employee status derives from the law of agency and focuses on the degree of control the employer has over the work of the individual. The common law test includes the following factors, none of which, by itself, is dispositive:

- The skill required of the individual
- The source of the instrumentalities and tools used in the work
- The location of the work
- The duration of the relationship between the parties
- Whether the hiring party has the right to assign additional projects to the individual
- The extent of the individual's discretion of when and how long to work
- The method of payment
- Whether the individual can or does hire and pay assistants
- Whether the work is part of the regular business of the hiring organization
- Whether the hiring organization provides employee benefits to the individual
- The tax treatment of the individual

(*Aymes v. Bonelli,* 980 F.2d 857, 861 (2d Cir. 1992), cited in Stephen J. Hirschfeld, "Do You Know Who Your Employees Are?" Outline for Annual Conference of the National Association of College and University Attorneys, June 18–21, 1997, p. 3.) Depending upon which law or laws a claim is brought under, some or all of these factors may be relevant to statutory tests for employee status.

The issue of how independent contractor status is determined was highlighted in *Vizcaino v. Microsoft Corporation,* 120 F.3d 1006 (9th Cir. 1997) *(en banc).* The Internal Revenue Service (IRS) had determined that workers that Microsoft had categorized as independent contractors were actually employees, using the common law test. Rather than challenging that determination, Microsoft paid the employer's share of FICA taxes to the government and issued the workers W-2 forms. Eight former "independent contractors" who had been reclassified as employees then sued Microsoft, asserting that they were entitled to participate in the company's "savings plus" plan and the employee stock purchase plan.

The trial court granted summary judgment to the company, and an appellate panel reversed. After an *en banc* hearing, the full Ninth Circuit decided in the plaintiffs' favor. The court ruled that, because Microsoft offered these benefit plans to all of its employees, the individuals whom the IRS had determined to be employees were also entitled to participate in these benefit plans, and that Microsoft's failure to do so violated their contractual rights.

In addition to contract claims by "independent contractors," colleges using "leased" employees may face joint liability with the actual employers of these "leased" workers for discrimination under federal and state nondiscrimination laws. The Equal Employment Opportunity Commission (EEOC) has issued an Enforcement Guidance (dated December 3, 1997) detailing the application of the federal civil rights laws to "contingent workers," which the EEOC defines as "individuals placed in job assignments by temporary employment agencies, contract firms, and other firms that hire workers and place them in job assignments with the firms' clients." A subsequent Enforcement Guidance involving the Americans With Disabilities Act (ADA) (dated December 22, 2000) also covers contingent workers. This Guidance includes the assignment of workers to jobs or companies, unlawful harassment at the worksite, discriminatory wage practices, and other potentially discriminatory practices. The Guidance may be found at the EEOC's Web site, http://eeoc.gov.

Colleges using contingent workers may also face liability if a court determines that, because the individual is working at the college's worksite, coemployment principles apply. This principle was applied by the U.S. Court of Appeals in a finding that Wal-Mart Stores was liable to an independent contractor who was subjected to a racially hostile work environment (*Danco, Inc. v. Wal-Mart Stores, Inc.*, 178 F.3d 8 (1st Cir. 1999). Courts have also held that other laws, such as the Occupational Safety and Health Act (OSHA) (Section 4.6.1 of this book), the National Labor Relations Act (NLRA) (Section 4.5.1), and state worker's compensation laws (Section 4.6.6), may protect temporary workers or leased workers.

Colleges can take several steps to minimize the risk of having independent contractors "transformed" into employees, either by a court using the common law test or by a state or federal regulatory agency under the definition provided by the relevant law. A written document that spells out the relationship between the parties, the individual's right to control his or her own work, and the individual's obligations to pay income and self-employment taxes will help clarify the relationship. Paying for the individual's services on a project basis, rather than weekly or monthly, using independent contractors who have incorporated or who have other indicia of a business independent of the college (a bank account, letterhead, business cards, and so on), and reporting the payments to the individual on an IRS Form 1099 will help demonstrate that the individual is not an employee.

Colleges may also encounter situations where they need to determine whether a particular worker is an employee or a student. One example of this problem is demonstrated in Section 4.5.6, which discusses the status of graduate assistants, medical residents, and others under collective bargaining laws. Another example is discussed in Section 4.6.2, which discusses the status of residence hall staff as employees or students.

4.2.2. Where is the workplace? Advances in information technology, demands for greater work flexibility in order to balance work and family responsibilities, and limitations on office space have resulted in an increase in work that is performed somewhere other than the college campus. In addition, the idea of the "campus" as a fixed geographic location has changed, as institutions have implemented or expanded distance learning and multisite interactive video-based programs, study abroad programs, off-campus internships, and clinical rotations. Because of the recency of these phenomena, the boundaries of a college's liability for events that affect an employee off campus are not clear. In general, U.S. workers are protected by U.S. civil rights laws wherever they work in the world. (See Section 5.1 for a discussion of extraterritorial application of the federal civil rights laws.) Depending on the situation, the law of the state in which the college is located may apply to an alleged legal violation that occurs in another state or abroad.

Institutions who hire local nationals to work on study abroad or other college programs should draft contracts that comply with the law of the country in which the program is located as well as U.S. law. It may be necessary to engage the assistance of a local employment attorney in order to ensure that the contracts comply with national law. Administrators may also wish to consider the possibility of limiting the resolution of disputes that may arise under the contract, should national law permit such a limitation, such as through the use of arbitration clauses (see Section 4.5.5). However, the resolution of employment disputes in other nations may be limited to special labor courts or administrative tribunals; because of the differences between U.S. law and the law of other nations, there is no substitute for expert advice from an attorney who is familiar with the law of the country in which the program is operated.

Telework has raised many questions, most of which remain unanswered. For example, if an employee is injured in her own home while engaged in work for the college, is she protected by state worker's compensation laws? Application of the federal Occupational Safety and Health Act to teleworkers is also unresolved; an attempt by a prior U.S. Secretary of Labor in 1999 to apply OSHA's safety rules to telecommuters was reversed when the agency was criticized in the press (Dawn R. Swink, "Telecommuter Law: A New Frontier in Legal Liability," 38 *Am. Bus. L.J.* 857 (2001)). Because telework typically involves the use of computers, teleworkers may have concerns about privacy of e-mail correspondence and the possible electronic monitoring of their work if they are connected to a college's network (Donald H. Nichols, "Window Peeping in the Workplace: A Look into Employee Privacy in a Technological Era," 27 *Wm. Mitchell L. Rev.* 1587 (2001)). These issues remain to be resolved as telecommuting gains in popularity and as advances in digital technology permit more work to be done off site.

Sec. 4.3. Employment Contracts

4.3.1. Defining the contract. The basic relationship between an employee and the college is governed by contract. Contracts may be either written or oral; and even when there is no express contract, common law principles may allow

the courts to imply a contract between the parties. Contracts may be very basic; for example, an offer letter from the college stating a position title and a wage or salary may, upon acceptance, be construed to be a contract. In *Small v. Juniata College*, 682 A.2d 350 (Pa. Super. 1996), for example, the court ruled that an offer letter to the college's football coach created a one-year contract, and thus the employee handbook's provisions regarding grounds for termination did not apply. Absent any writing, oral promises by a manager or supervisor may nevertheless be binding on the college through the application of agency law (see Section 3.1). A court may also look to the written policies of a college, or to its consistent past practices, to imply a contract with certain employment guarantees. For these reasons, it is important that administrators and counsel ensure that communications to employees and applicants, whether written or oral, and the provisions in employee manuals or policies, clearly represent the institution's actual intent regarding the binding nature of its statements.

Sometimes a state statute will supercede common law contract principles as to a particular issue. This is the case, for instance, with state worker's compensation laws, which substitute for any contractual provisions the parties might otherwise have used to cover employee injuries on the job. Worker's compensation laws are discussed in Section 4.6.6; other statutes that play a similar role are discussed in other subsections of Section 4.6.

4.3.2. The at-will doctrine. Until the late 1970s, the common law doctrine of "employment at will" shielded employers from most common law contract claims unless an individual had a written contract spelling out job security protections. Employers had the right to discharge an individual for any reason, or no reason, unless the termination violated some state or federal statute. The at-will doctrine may apply to employees at both private and public colleges for those employees who are not otherwise protected by a state statute, civil service regulations, or contractual provisions according some right to continued employment. In fact, at-will employment in public colleges may defeat an employee's assertion of due process protections because no property interest is created in at-will employment (see, for example, *McCallum v. North Carolina Cooperative Extension Service*, 542 S.E.2d 227 (N.C. App. 2001), *appeal dismissed*, 548 S.E.2d 527 (N.C. 2001)).

Although the doctrine is still the prevailing view in many states, judges have developed exceptions to the doctrine in order to avoid its harsher consequences when individuals with long service and good work records were terminated without cause. Because these exceptions are created by state court rulings, the status of the employment-at-will doctrine varies by state. The two primary approaches to creating exceptions have been through the use of contract law and tort law. In some states, employee handbooks or other policy documents have been found to have contractual status, although courts in a minority of states have rejected this interpretation of contract law. In other cases, courts have allowed employees asserting that they were terminated for improper reasons to state tort claims for wrongful discharge. In *Wounaris v. West Virginia State College*, 588 S.E.2d 406 (W. Va. 2003), for example, the court held that it was against public policy for an employer to terminate a staff member for defending himself against an allegedly unfair termination.

Tort claims challenging a discharge as a violation of public policy are discussed in Section 4.6.8. (For a general discussion of the at-will doctrine and trends in the creation of judicial exceptions, see Mark A. Fahleson, "The Public Policy Exception to Employment at Will—When Should Courts Defer to the Legislature?" 72 *Neb. L. Rev.* 956 (1993); and Cornelius J. Peck, "Penetrating Doctrinal Camouflage: Understanding the Development of the Law of Wrongful Discharge," 66 *Wash. L. Rev.* 719 (1991).)

4.3.3. Sources, scope, and terms of the contract

4.3.3.1. Sources of the contract. Contracts may take various forms, even within the same institution. In public institutions, particularly if the college has a tenure system, contracts may be governed by state statute in public colleges, or even by state civil service or personnel regulations (see Section 4.4 below). They may also be governed by the state's common law of contract. In both public and private colleges, faculty contract provisions may be found in faculty handbooks, policy statements, or in the "academic custom and usage" doctrine through which courts seek to fill in gaps in written or implied contracts. These issues, as related to faculty contracts, are discussed in Section 6.2.

Contracts for staff and for nontenured or non-tenure-track faculty may range from a brief notice of appointment on a standard form, with blanks to be filled in for each employee, to a lengthy collective bargaining agreement negotiated under state or federal labor law. Or the contract may not be called by that name at all, but instead may be called an employee handbook or policy manual. As the discussion in Sections 4.3.3.2 and 4.3.3.3 explains, the formal writing does not necessarily include all the terms of the contract.

4.3.3.2. Contract interpretation. A contract's meaning is ascertained primarily by reference to its express terms. Where the contract language is unambiguous, it will govern any factual situation to which it clearly applies. *Billmyre v. Sacred Heart Hospital of Sisters of Charity*, 331 A.2d 313 (Md. 1975), illustrates this principle of contract interpretation. A nurse was employed as a coordinator-instructor at the hospital's nursing school under a contract specifying that either the employer or the employee could terminate the contract "at the end of the school year by giving notice in writing to the other not later than May 1 of such school year." On May 18 the nurse received a letter terminating her employment. The court held that the hospital had breached the contract, since the contract language unambiguously provided for notice to the employee by May 1 to effectuate a termination of the contract.

Careful drafting of contracts is important in order to avoid disagreements about their interpretation. For example, in *Washington v. Central State University*, 699 N.E.2d 1016 (Ct. Claims Ohio 1998), the vice president of academic affairs had served under a series of one-year contracts for five years. Each contract provided that the university could terminate the vice president's appointment at any time for cause, and could also terminate the contract prior to its expiration upon thirty days notice. Two months after executing another one-year contract, the university terminated the vice president from his academic position, returning him to the ranks of tenured faculty members. The court rejected the vice president's breach of contract claim, noting that the university had provided evidence of incompetence sufficient to support a finding of cause for terminating his administrative appointment.

On the other hand, if the contract does not provide for a specific term and does not specify that termination must be for cause, employment may be at-will (see Section 4.3.2 above). In *Knowles v. Ohio State University,* 2002 Ohio 6962 (Ohio Ct. App. 2002), the court interpreted a contract stating that a vice provost's continued employment was subject to "the results of an annual performance review and continued acceptable performance" as a contract for at-will employment. Although the court characterized the language as creating a "satisfaction contract"[2] under which the employee could be terminated if his supervisor, the provost, was not "satisfied" with his performance, the court noted that any determination that the employee's performance was unsatisfactory must be made in good faith. Because the trial court had excluded evidence of the performance review conducted by the provost and of allegedly defamatory remarks made by the provost, there was no evidence in the record of the provost's good faith in making the determination that the plaintiff's performance was unsatisfactory. The appellate court therefore reversed the trial court's dismissal of the vice provost's breach of contract and defamation claims. (For a contrasting case from the same state concluding that a researcher's termination for academic fraud was appropriate because he was an at-will employee, see *Matikas v. University of Dayton,* 788 N.E.2d 1108 (Ohio Ct. App. 2003), *appeal denied,* 792 N.E.2d 201 (Ohio 2003).)

Sometimes, particularly in public institutions, contravening statutes or other institutional policies will take precedence over the express language of the employment contract. In *Subryan v. Regents of the University of Colorado,* 698 P.2d 1383 (Colo. Ct. App. 1984), for example, the court determined that the one-year term specified in the plaintiff's contract was invalid because the regents had enacted a regulation that required appointments of all untenured faculty to be for three years. Although the regents argued that the one-year contract was justified because of a lack of funding for the plaintiff's position, the court declared that the regents could not ignore their own regulations, which they had the power to amend if financial problems so required.

Similarly, if a public college is subject to a state statute or administrative regulation regarding contract periods, for instance, or if the college's bylaws provide for notice provisions more generous than those in the contract, these other sources of law may supersede the terms of a contract. For example, in *Linkey v. Medical College of Ohio,* 695 N.E.2d 840 (Oh. Ct. Cl. 1997), the plaintiff had been employed under a series of one-year contracts from 1980 until his

---

[2]A "satisfaction contract" is considered to be a contract for at-will employment because the sole criterion for the employee's retention or termination is the subjective judgment of the supervisor that the employee's work is satisfactory.

termination in 1994. Although his contract did not provide for advance notice should the college determine not to renew him, it did specify that the contract was subject to the bylaws and other actions of the institution's board of trustees. The bylaws provided that an employee was entitled to ninety days notice prior to the expiration of an appointment. The college had provided the plaintiff with notice of its intent not to reappointment him to a subsequent one-year contract; but it had done so less than ninety days prior to the expiration of his one-year contract by paying him for the days beyond the contract's expiration date necessary to complete the ninety-day notice period.

The plaintiff filed a breach of contract claim, arguing that, because the college provided less than ninety days notice of its intent not to renew his appointment, he was entitled to another one-year contract. The court agreed, noting that the contract must be interpreted in light of the institution's bylaws. Furthermore, the court looked at the institution's past practice of consistently either notifying employees of nonrenewal at least ninety days in advance, or automatically renewing the employees' contract for another year. Because the plaintiff had not received timely notice, said the court, he had a reasonable expectation that his employment would continue for another year, and the institution had breached his contract.

4.3.3.3. Employee handbooks as contracts. Contracts are governed by common law, which may vary considerably by state. Some courts have refused to recognize employee handbooks as contracts under state law (see, for example, *Stanton v. Tulane University,* 777 So. 2d 1242 (La. App. 2001); see also *Raines v. Haverford College,* 849 F. Supp. 1009 (E.D. Pa. 1994)). The majority view, however, is that written employee handbooks, bylaws, or other similar policy documents may be construed to be express contracts (see, for example, *Woolley v. Hoffmann-La Roche, Inc.,* 491 A.2d 1257, *modified,* 499 A.2d 515 (N.J. 1985)). Moreover, an employer's consistent adherence to practices such as termination only for cause or progressive discipline, even if not expressed in writing, may give rise to an implied contract giving an employee rights beyond what an at-will employee would have. In *Pugh v. See's Candies, Inc.,* 171 Cal. Rptr. 917 (Cal. Ct. App. 1981), for instance, the court found an implied contract in periodic promotions and salary increases for an otherwise at-will employee.

In *Collins v. Colorado Mountain College,* 56 P.3d 1132 (Ct. App. Colo. 2002), a court ruled that the dispute resolution process contained in the employee handbook at Colorado Mountain College precluded judicial review of a breach of contract claim. The handbook provided that the decision rendered at the final step of the grievance process would be final. The plaintiff had used the internal grievance process specified in the handbook to challenge her termination for dishonesty. Her grievance was denied at every step of the internal process, including the final step. The court refused to exercise jurisdiction over the breach of contract claim, ruling that the terms of the employee handbook were clear and that the plaintiff had received all the rights to which she was entitled under the contract. The court interpreted the finality provision of the handbook as an expression of the parties' intent that the decision at the final step of the grievance procedure would be binding. (For a discussion of two Pennsylvania cases that took the same approach to professors' breach of contract claims, see Section 6.7.3.)

4.3.3.4. Other contract claims. In addition to using the doctrines of express and implied contract as mechanisms for avoiding the at-will doctrine, courts have applied other contractual or "quasi-contractual" doctrines to the employment relationship. For example, individuals who allege that an agent of the college has made false promises upon which the plaintiff has relied to his or her detriment may state a claim for promissory estoppel. The court in *Sonnichsen v. Baylor University*, 47 S.W. 3d 122 (Tex. Ct. App. 2001) considered but rejected such a claim, holding that a terminated coach could not assert promissory estoppel because the promise to execute a written contract did not meet the requirements of statute of frauds. See also *Heinritz v. Lawrence University*, 535 N.W.2d 81 (Ct. App. Wis. 1995) (employee cannot state claim for promissory estoppel because offer of employment was for at-will status). In addition, courts in some states have recognized an implied "covenant of good faith and fair dealing" that requires an employer to deal with an employee fairly and in good faith—an implicit "good cause" standard that substitutes for at-will status. (For a discussion of the use of the covenant of good faith and fair dealing as a contract interpretation device, see J. Wilson Parker, "At-Will Employment and the Common Law: A Modest Proposal to De-Marginalize Employment Law," 81 *Iowa L. Rev.* 347 (1995).) These exceptions and others underscore the importance of clarity in written documents and oral statements that could be construed as promises—in particular, clarity on whether the institution intends to be legally bound by the particular provisions or statements.

If the institution does not intend to give a handbook, set of bylaws, or other policy documents the status of a contract, the written document should make this point clearly and state what the purpose of the document is. Courts have ruled that a disclaimer making it clear that the document is not intended to have contractual status will defeat an employee's claim that the breach of any promises in the document should have legal consequences.[3] In *Galloway v. Roger Williams University*, 777 A.2d 148 (R.I. 2001), for example, language in the college's personnel policy manual disclaiming contractual status, and specific language stating that employment was at will, defeated the plaintiff's breach of contract claim for wrongful termination.

Although a clear disclaimer stating that the employee handbook is not a contract will defeat breach of contract claims that rely on handbook provisions, an incomplete or unclear disclaimer may not protect a college against breach of contract claims. For example, in *Dantley v. Howard University*, 801 A.2d 962 (D.C. 2002), the appellate court ruled that a disclaimer stating that "this document is not to be construed as a contract" was insufficient to justify the dismissal of the plaintiff's breach of contract claim. Although the trial court had dismissed the claim, relying on the disclaimer, the appellate court determined

---

[3]Cases and authorities are collected in George L. Blum, Annot., "Effectiveness of Employer's Disclaimer of Representations in Personnel Manual or Employee Handbook Alerting At-Will Employment Relationship," 17 A.L.R.5th 1.

that specific provisions in the handbook for the abolition of positions and reductions in force could be "rationally at odds" with the disclaimer, and thus a trial was necessary to determine whether the university was bound by the language of its handbook and, if so, whether it had breached the handbook's terms in its layoff of the plaintiff.

4.3.3.5. Contract rescission. Even if a contractual provision would ordinarily bind the college, fraud on the part of the employee may result in a contractual *rescission,* which means that the contract no longer exists. In *Sarvis v. Vermont State Colleges,* 772 A.2d 494 (Vt. 2001), for example, the Community College of Vermont hired Robert Sarvis as an adjunct professor of business law and business ethics, as well as a part-time administrator. Sarvis had not disclosed that he had recently been released from prison after serving a four-year sentence for bank fraud. When Sarvis's parole officer notified the college of his prison record, the college terminated his employment prior to the expiration of his contract. Sarvis sued for breach of contract. The court ruled that the college could rescind the contract because the plaintiff had procured that contract fraudulently.

Colleges and universities have also used contract rescission to protect themselves when they discover that a faculty member holds two full-time positions. In *Nash v. Trustees of Boston University,* 946 F.2d 960 (1st Cir. 1991), for example, the university had reversed its decision to award a professor an early retirement incentive when it learned that he had secured a full-time position at another institution without informing the university. The court held that, because the early retirement agreement was induced by the professor's fraud, the university's refusal to honor that agreement was not a breach but a rescission of the contract. And in *Morgan v. American University,* 534 A.2d 323 (D.C. 1987), the university terminated a tenured professor who had taught at the university for two years when it discovered that he held a full-time job concurrently at another institution. The court agreed with the university's argument that it was a contract rescission because the professor had withheld a material fact, and thus a pretermination hearing, as provided by the faculty handbook, was not required.

4.3.3.6. Drug testing and medical screening. Colleges and universities that are recipients of federal grants and contracts exceeding $100,000 are subject to the Drug-Free Workplace Act of 1988 (41 U.S.C. §§ 701–7) (see Section 13.4.4.1 of this book). And if a college or university hires employees to drive commercial vehicles, these employees may be subject to drug testing under the provisions of the Omnibus Transportation Employee Testing Act of 1991 (see below). Legislation such as this has encouraged many institutions to develop policies prohibiting employees from using controlled substances. Such policies may also provide for testing of employees suspected of using controlled substances. These policies may become part of the employment contract, both for unionized and nonunionized employees.

Whether or not a state or a higher educational institution may lawfully require its faculty or staff to submit to drug testing depends on many factors, including the nature of the individual's job, the type of institution (whether it is public or private), and the scope of the testing (whether it is done "for cause" or on a random basis). The authority of public institutions to require drug testing is limited by the Fourth Amendment, which protects public employees from unreasonable searches and seizures. (For more on the Fourth Amendment, see Sections 8.4.2 and 10.4.8.) But the U.S. Supreme Court has upheld the legality of drug testing for public employees holding certain types of jobs in *National Treasury Employees Union v. Von Raabe,* 489 U.S. 656 (1989). In this case, certain employees of the U.S. Customs Service were subject to drug testing, whether or not they were suspected of drug use. In a 5-to-4 opinion, the Court ruled that, because of the nature of their jobs (drug interdiction) and the agency's strong interest in ensuring that its employees were drug-free, the suspicionless drug testing did not violate the employees' Fourth Amendment rights. In a companion case, *Skinner v. Railway Labor Executives Association,* 489 U.S. 602 (1989), the Court ruled 7 to 2 that regulations of the Federal Railroad Administration, which required blood and urine testing for alcohol and drugs after accidents and when employees violated certain safety rules, did not violate the Fourth Amendment, and that individualized suspicion was not a necessary prerequisite for the testing.

Drug testing in response to other performance problems has also been upheld in the face of constitutional challenges. In *Pierce v. Smith,* 117 F.3d 866 (5th Cir. 1997), the court upheld the requirement that Pierce, a medical resident at Texas Tech University Health Sciences Center, submit to a drug test after she slapped a patient. Pierce had claimed that the test constituted an invasion of privacy and a violation of her Fourth Amendment rights. The court ruled that the "individualized suspicion" standard applicable to police searches did not apply in the educational context because, given the nature of a medical student's work, the university had a special need to ensure that these employees were not using drugs. The search was not intrusive on the basis of the facts alleged by Pierce, and because the test results were negative, no action had been taken against her. This case suggests that if a teaching hospital has written policies providing for drug testing when, in the judgment of an employee's supervisor, the employee's behavior is consistent with drug use, it can follow these policies without Fourth Amendment liability.

Fourth Amendment challenges to drug testing may be much stronger, however, if a public employer requires that all employees, or all applicants, agree to submit to drug tests. In *Georgia Association of Educators v. Harris,* 749 F. Supp. 1110 (N.D. Ga. 1990), for example, the State of Georgia enacted a law in 1990 that required all applicants for state jobs (including college faculty and staff) to submit to drug tests. The Georgia Association of Educators filed challenges under the Fourth Amendment as well as the equal protection and due process clauses. The federal district judge ruled that Georgia's general interest in maintaining a drug-free workplace was not sufficiently compelling to outweigh the applicants' Fourth Amendment protections against unreasonable searches and seizures. The judge also ruled that the plaintiffs had established equal protection and due process claims because the state had not identified any interest sufficiently compelling to outweigh the applicants' constitutional rights.

A court's attitude toward drug testing may also be very different if the employer implements random drug testing, particularly for employees in jobs that do not implicate safety. In these circumstances, employees may be protected not only by the Fourth Amendment but also by the Americans With Disabilities Act, which protects employees in private as well as public institutions. In *Roe v. Cheyenne Mountain Conference Resort,* 124 F.3d 1221 (10th Cir. 1997), the appellate court ordered the trial court to enjoin a private company's policy that provided for random testing of employees for drug or alcohol use. The plaintiff was an accounts manager who objected to the company's requirement that she disclose the use of all prescription medication (whether or not it was unlawfully obtained) in addition to submitting to random drug screening. The court ruled that the requirement to disclose all prescription medication violated Section 102 of the ADA (see Section 5.2.5 of this book), which prohibits medical examinations or inquiries about medical conditions unless they are job related and consistent with business necessity.

If the employee occupies a "safety-sensitive" position, however, some courts may be willing to allow random drug screening on the grounds that public safety needs outweigh individual privacy concerns (see, for example, *Hennessey v. Coastal Eagle Point Oil Company,* 609 A.2d 11 (N.J. 1992)). Federal law also provides for drug testing for certain employees in "safety-sensitive" positions. Drivers of commercial motor vehicles who are required to obtain a commercial driver's license are subject to the Omnibus Transportation Employee Testing Act of 1991, 49 U.S.C. § 31306, and the U.S. Department of Transportation's implementing regulations. These regulations, codified at 49 C.F.R. Part 382, provide for testing for alcohol and a variety of controlled substances at the pre-employment stage, and for testing of employees in various circumstances (49 C.F.R. §§ 382.303, 382.305, 382.309, 382.605, 382.311).

Medical screening tests also raise legal issues and may also violate employee rights unless they are closely related to job requirements. In *Norman-Bloodsaw v. Lawrence Berkeley Laboratory,* 135 F.3d 1260 (9th Cir. 1998), a federal appellate court ruled that the laboratory's practice of testing employees for syphilis, sickle cell anemia, and pregnancy violated their civil rights under Title VII (see Section 5.2.1 of this book) as well as their Fourth Amendment right to privacy. The laboratory, a unit of the University of California, had not notified applicants that they would be tested for these conditions and did not make a showing that the tests were job related. The appellate court reversed the trial court's award of summary judgment to the laboratory on the Title VII and privacy claims, ruling that the testing violated the plaintiff's Fourth Amendment rights because of the unconsented-to seizure of body fluids for purposes unknown to the plaintiffs. The court acknowledged that the plaintiffs had also stated a Fifth Amendment due process claim, but declined to undertake this analysis, since the plaintiffs had already prevailed on their Fourth Amendment claim. The court found a Title VII violation because non-job-related testing for sickle cell anemia singled out African Americans, and pregnancy testing singled out women. Although this case involved federal claims under the U.S. Constitution that could be brought only against public institutions, employees of private institutions could assert the Title VII claims against their employers, and could also assert both tort and contract actions claims to challenge the type of testing at issue in this case.

4.3.3.7. Executive contracts. As the leadership of postsecondary institutions has become more complex, boards of trustees have begun to offer more elaborate compensation packages and other perquisites to attract talented individuals to executive positions and to encourage them to stay. Where once a contract for a college president or vice president may have been one or two paragraphs, these executive contracts now address a broader range of issues and may include specific attention to the circumstances under which the board will terminate the executive's employment.

Contracts for executives of public institutions may be subject to state open records acts (see Section 12.5.3), or discussions of such contracts may be subject to open public meetings law (see Section 12.5.2). Particularly at institutions that are undergoing financial pressures, the contents of the president's contract may be of great interest to the student newspaper or to the media in general.

The following topics should be considered for explicit inclusion in executive contracts, particularly the president's contract:

1. Compensation, which may include salary, a "signing bonus," a housing allowance or the provision of a house, a car or a car allowance, and so forth. Some nonsalary perquisites, such as a house or car, may be taxable to the executive, so a tax expert should be consulted before the contract is executed. Deferred compensation, such as a retention payment, may also have tax consequences.

2. Benefits, including medical insurance, pension contributions and the pension plan, sick and vacation leave, memberships in clubs or other organizations, reimbursement of moving expenses, and others.

3. Travel and entertainment accounts.

4. A statement of the duration of the contract (if not at-will), and the circumstances under which the board of trustees may terminate the president. This statement may include notice provisions, as well as required mechanisms for resolving disputes that arise under the contract (such as restricting the executive to arbitration rather than litigation—see Section 4.3.6).

5. The expectations for the executive's spouse, if any, and any funding for spousal activities, entertaining, or other appropriate activities.

6. Standards of performance for the executive and the method by which the executive will be evaluated.

(For further discussion of executive contracts, see Daniel J. Bernard, "Presidential Contracts: Run, Don't Walk," outline of presentation at the NACUA Continuing Legal Education Conference, Fall 1999, available at http://www.nacua.org.)

4.3.4. Amendment of the contract.
The terms of the original employ-
ment contract need not remain static through the entire life of the contract.
Courts have accepted the proposition that employment contracts may be
amended under certain circumstances. In an early case that predated the prohibition on mandatory retirement for faculty, *Rehor v. Case Western Reserve University,* 331 N.E.2d 416 (Ohio 1975), the court found amendments to be valid
either where the right to amend was reserved in the original contract or where
there was mutual consent of the parties to amend and adequate consideration
was given in return for the changed terms. The plaintiff in *Rehor* was a tenured
professor employed under contract at Western Reserve University from 1942 to
1967. Throughout this period, the retirement age was always seventy. After Case
Institute of Technology joined with Western Reserve to form Case Western
Reserve University, Case Western, which took over the faculty contracts, adopted
a resolution requiring faculty members over sixty-eight to petition to be reappointed. The new university's bylaws provided that "the board of trustees shall
from time to time adopt such rules and regulations governing the appointment
and tenure of the members of the faculty as the board of trustees deems necessary." The court held that this bylaw language "includes a reservation of the
right to change the retirement age of the faculty" and thus defeats the plaintiff's
claim that the university was in breach of contract. Since the retirement policy is
part of tenure, "the reserved right to change rules of tenure includes the right to
change the retirement policy." The court also approved of the university's assertion that "an employment contract between a university and a tenured Faculty
member may be amended by the parties in writing when supported by adequate
consideration." These considerations were satisfied in *Rehor* by the professor's
execution of reappointment forms and acceptance of an increased salary after
the new retirement policy was put into effect. While current law prohibits retirement policies that use age as a criterion, the reasoning of *Rehor* is still applicable
to amendments of contracts between colleges and their faculty or staff.

The outcome in *Rehor* is based in large part upon the apparent renegotiation
of faculty members' terms and conditions of employment when they were
reappointed by the newly formed university. In contrast, in *Karr v. Board of
Trustees of Michigan State University,* 325 N.W.2d 605 (Mich. Ct. App. 1982),
the trustees of Michigan State University decided to respond to a budget crisis
by placing university employees on a two-and-a-half-day layoff, for which they
would receive no pay. Although employees were permitted to specify whether
they wanted the reduction in pay deducted in a lump sum or in six equal installments, there was no negotiation with the employees. Although the trial court
had granted summary judgment for the university, the appellate court reversed,
saying that, if the employees had contracts with the university for a fixed sum,
then the university's unilateral decision to withhold two and a half days of the
employees' pay was a breach of their employment contract. The existence of
such a contract was a question of fact, said the court, and was not amenable to
a summary judgment determination.

On the other hand, not all understandings between employees and a college
or university constitute a binding contract. In *Faur v. Jewish Theological*

Seminary of America, 536 N.Y.S.2d 516 (N.Y. App. Div. 1989), a male professor of rabbinics resigned when the seminary faculty voted to admit female rabbinical students, claiming that the change in admissions policy was incompatible with his personal religious beliefs. The professor argued that the new admissions policy breached his employment contract and also constituted religious discrimination. The court ruled that the seminary had no contractual duty to refrain from changing the admissions requirements in order to avoid offending the professor's religious beliefs. In addition, the court refused to examine whether the seminary's change in admission policy constituted religious discrimination on the grounds that it would require the court to impermissibly inquire into religious doctrine, a violation of the First Amendment (see Sections 1.6.2 & 6.2.5), and dismissed the professor's claim.

Under the common law of many states, a letter may be contractually binding on both parties. In *Levy v. University of Cincinnati,* 616 N.E.2d 1132 (Ohio Ct. App. 1992), a letter outlining the terms of a professor's employment was ruled a contract; a subsequent letter changing those contractual terms was also found to bind both parties. The court ruled that the professor had accepted the terms of the second letter, which established new employment rights and obligations, by continuing to teach at the university.

Occasionally contracts may also be amended unilaterally by subsequent state legislation. But the state's power to modify its own contracts legislatively or to regulate contracts between private parties is circumscribed by Article I, Section 10(1), of the U.S. Constitution, known as the contracts clause: "No state shall . . . pass any . . . law impairing the obligation of contracts." In *Indiana ex rel. Anderson v. Brand,* 303 U.S. 95 (1938) (discussed in Section 6.2.2 of this book), for instance, the U.S. Supreme Court held that an Indiana law that had the effect of canceling the tenure rights of certain public school teachers was an unconstitutional impairment of their employment contracts. Under this and subsequent contracts clause precedents, a state may not impair either its own or private contracts unless such impairment is both "reasonable and necessary to serve an important public purpose," with "necessary" meaning that the impairment is essential and no viable alternative for serving the state's purpose exists (*United States Trust Company of New York v. New Jersey,* 431 U.S. 1 (1977)).

4.3.5. Waiver of contract rights. Once a contract has been formed, the parties may sometimes waive their contract rights, either intentionally by a written agreement or unintentionally by their actions. *Chung v. Park,* 514 F.2d 382 (3d Cir. 1975), concerned a professor who after teaching at Mansfield State College for five years was notified that his contract would not be renewed. Through his counsel, the professor negotiated with the state attorney general and agreed to submit the issue of the nonrenewal's validity to an arbitration panel. When the panel upheld the nonrenewal, the professor brought suit, alleging that he was tenured and that the college did not follow the termination procedures set out in the tenure regulations and was therefore in breach of contract. The court, after pointing out that under the state law contract rights may be waived by subsequent agreement between the parties, upheld the district court's finding "that the parties had reached such a subsequent agreement when, after extensive negotiations, they specifically stipulated to the hearing procedures actually employed." Ruling that the hearing procedures were consistent with due process guidelines, the court upheld the trial court's ruling for the college.[4]

Public policy considerations may, however, preclude the waiver of certain contract terms. In *McLachlan v. Tacoma Community College District No. 22*, 541 P.2d 1010 (Wash. 1975), the court addressed this issue but found the rights in question to be properly waivable. The two plaintiffs were employed by the college district under contracts that specifically stated, "The employee waives all rights normally provided by the tenure laws of the state of Washington." The plaintiffs, who were aware that they were employed to replace people on one-year sabbaticals, contended that, for reasons of public policy, the contractual waivers should not be enforced. While avoiding the broad issue of whether a blanket waiver of tenure rights contravenes public policy, the court said:

> We envision no serious public policy considerations which would prohibit a
> teacher from waiving the statutory nonrenewal notice provisions in advance of
> the notice date, provided he knows the purpose of his employment is to replace the
> regular occupant of that position who is on a one-year sabbatical leave.

4.3.6. Legal planning with contracts. Given the wealth of legal theories that employees, including faculty members, may use to challenge employment decisions, careful drafting of employment contracts, employee handbooks, and institutional personnel policies is essential. State court opinions regarding the binding nature of such documents, while often favoring the employee, also suggest that the employee's rights vis-à-vis the institution should be carefully spelled out in these documents in order to reduce potential litigation.

Although careful drafting of contracts and policy documents is important, no amount of careful drafting can prevent litigation. Administrators and counsel may therefore wish to consider the use of individual employment contracts (for nonunionized employees) that contain a clause limiting the parties to arbitration for resolution of disputes arising under the contract. Arbitration and other alternate dispute resolution mechanisms (see Section 2.3) often provide quicker, less expensive, and less formal resolution of disputes than court litigation, and federal courts are beginning to dismiss lawsuits brought by employees who have signed contracts with arbitration clauses. Although the courts have been sharply criticized for enforcing "mandatory arbitration clauses" that deny employees the right to a judicial forum for their employment claims (see the Selected Annotated Bibliography for this Chapter for relevant resources), the U.S. Supreme Court has upheld the validity of such arbitration clauses, as long as they state specifically the types of disputes that are subject to the restriction and the statutory claims for which the employee is foregoing a judicial remedy.[5]

---

[4]This case was decided before the Supreme Court's ruling in *Loudermill* (discussed in Section 6.7.2.3). Thus, the court's discussion of the parameters of due process should be compared carefully with the rules set down in *Loudermill*.

[5]Cases are collected in Marjorie A. Shields, Annot., "Enforceability of Arbitration Clauses in Collective Bargaining Agreements as Regards Claims Under Federal Civil Rights Statutes," 152 A.L.R. Fed. 75.

In *Gilmer v. Interstate-Johnson Lane,* 500 U.S. 20 (1991), a registered securities representative had agreed to submit all disputes to compulsory arbitration, and the Court refused to permit him to litigate an age discrimination claim in court because he had entered the agreement to arbitrate. Distinguishing *Alexander v. Gardner-Denver* (a case involving a waiver in a collective bargaining agreement, discussed in Section 4.5.5), the Court noted three differences between *Gardner-Denver* and *Gilmer.* First, Gilmer had an individual contract in which he had agreed to arbitrate statutory claims, whereas the arbitration clause at issue in *Gardner-Denver* related to contract-based claims. Second, in *Gardner-Denver* the problem was that the Court did not believe the union should be permitted unilaterally to waive an individual employee's right to seek redress under nondiscrimination laws; in *Gilmer* no such problem existed because the individual employee had voluntarily entered the contract. And third, the Court noted that the Federal Arbitration Act (9 U.S.C. § 1, discussed in Section 15.1.5 of this book) favors arbitration agreements and that such agreements should be upheld whenever appropriate, a matter that had not been discussed in *Gardner-Denver.*

Gilmer unleashed a flood of litigation in the federal courts as employers in industries such as financial services and insurance required new and current employees to execute contracts containing mandatory arbitration clauses. Employees who then attempted to litigate discrimination claims found themselves defending an employer's motion to compel arbitration. Federal appellate courts were split on the propriety of enforcing mandatory arbitration clauses, particularly those that did not specify the laws to which the waiver applied. While the U.S. Court of Appeals for the Ninth Circuit ruled that these arbitration clauses violated Title VII (*Duffield v. Robertson Stephens & Company,* 144 F.3d 1182 (9th Cir. 1998)), others were willing to enforce them without close scrutiny of the language of the waiver (for example, *Seus v. John Nuveen & Co.,* 146 F.3d 175 (3d Cir. 1998)). Still others took the position that the clauses were enforceable if the waiver made it clear precisely which statutory claims were being waived (*Rosenberg v. Merrill Lynch, Pierce, Fenner & Smith, Inc.,* 170 F.3d 1 (1st Cir. 1999)).

The U.S. Supreme Court again addressed the enforceability of mandatory arbitration clauses in *Circuit City Stores, Inc. v. Adams,* 532 U.S. 105 (2001). In a 5-to-4 decision, the Court ruled that the Federal Arbitration Act permits parties to include enforceable arbitration clauses in employment contracts, rejecting the plaintiff's claim that enforcing such agreements requires employees to forego substantive rights afforded by the civil rights statutes. The majority characterized the effect of these agreements as merely a substitution of an arbitral for a judicial forum, and noted the advantages of arbitration in terms of efficiency, low cost, and informality. Subsequent to this case, the U.S. Supreme Court ruled that the Equal Employment Opportunity Commission was not bound by a mandatory arbitration clause entered into by an individual employee, and that the agency could seek injunctive and specific relief under the Americans With Disabilities Act and Title VII because the EEOC was not a party to the mandatory arbitration agreement (*EEOC v. Waffle House, Inc.,* 534 U.S. 279 (2002)).

Despite the Supreme Court's receptiveness to mandatory arbitration clauses, careful drafting is necessary to ensure that they will be enforceable. For example, federal appellate courts in some circuits will not enforce an arbitration clause that requires the employee to pay for the arbitrator's services (*Cole v. Burns International Security Services,* 105 F.3d 1465 (D.C. Cir. 1997)). Furthermore, the Equal Employment Opportunity Commission opposes the use of mandatory arbitration agreements entered prior to an actual dispute, despite the Supreme Court's rulings. The EEOC has issued a "Policy Statement on Mandatory Binding Arbitration of Employment Discrimination Disputes as a Condition of Employment" (July 10, 1997; see http://www.eeoc.gov/policy/docs/mandarb.html) rejecting these agreements unless they are completely voluntary and are entered into only after the dispute has arisen. A group of labor relations scholars has drafted a "Due Process Protocol for Mediation and Arbitration of Statutory Disputes Arising Out of the Employment Relationship." This protocol can be found on the "Protocols" section of the American Arbitration Association's Web site at http://www.adr.org.

Other forms of alternate dispute resolution, such as mediation or fact finding, may also be incorporated into employee contracts. Alternate dispute resolution strategies are discussed in Section 2.3 of this book.

Sec. 4.4. *Civil Service Rules*

In addition to statutory and common law protections, employees of some public colleges may be protected by civil service statutes and regulations (see, for example, W. Va. Code § 18-29-1 *et seq.*). The purpose behind the civil service system, initiated for employees of the federal government in 1883 by the Pendleton Act, is to ensure that government employees obtained their jobs through a system of "merit" rather than through political patronage. Although many of the top policymaking jobs in state and federal government are outside the civil service system (and thus may be filled for politically motivated reasons), the rank-and-file positions in federal and state governments are typically subject to civil service protections and restrictions. Faculty at some state colleges are also covered by civil service regulations.

Although the structure and design of these systems vary by state, the general approach is to classify jobs into categories (for example, clerical, custodial, administrative), develop career ladders within the categories (for example, Custodian I, Custodian II, and so on), to administer tests to determine which candidates are qualified for the position they seek, and to select from either a ranked list or from among a pool of individuals who passed the test. Many states have enacted preferences for military veterans, which may mean that if a veteran passes the test, he or she is ranked first on the hiring list. Hiring, promotions, and transfers are tightly regulated, and exceptions to the regulations are typically difficult to obtain. (See, for example, *Orange v. District of Columbia,* 59 F.3d 1267 (D.C. Cir. 1995), in which the court ruled that University of the District of Columbia's interim president lacked the authority to hire two staff members because he had bypassed the civil service requirements in hiring them; thus, their terminations were lawful.) In addition, discipline and termination are subject to due process requirements once the individual has successfully completed a probationary period. Prior to the completion of the probationary period, the employee typically has few due process or appeal rights. (See, for example, *Davis v. J. F. Drake State Technical College*, 854 So. 2d 1151 (Ct. Civ. App. Ala. 2002), in which the court affirmed an award of summary judgment to the college on the grounds that the terminated employee had not completed his probationary period and thus was not entitled to notice, a due process hearing, or a performance evaluation.)

The civil service system is usually administered by a state department of personnel or a civil service agency, which may also serve an adjudicatory role when an employee disputes a refusal to hire or promote, or a disciplinary or termination decision. Although state civil service systems originally followed the federal model, several states have initiated reforms in the past decade that have consolidated job classifications, introduced pay-for-performance systems, and elevated the significance of performance evaluations.

Although the rate of unionization in the private sector has declined over the past several decades, unionization of public sector employees has increased over this time period, particularly at the state and local level, where 82 percent of all unionized public employees work.[6] Disputes thus become complicated because such civil servants are protected by state and federal employment law, state labor law, and civil service regulations. State administrative procedure acts (see Sections 1.4.2.3 & 12.5.4) may regulate how a state college hires, evaluates, disciplines, rewards, and terminates its staff.

Differences in collective bargaining laws between the private and public sectors are discussed in Section 4.5.2. For example, many benefits that would be subjects of bargaining in the private sector, such as grievance procedures, health insurance, and holidays, are specified either by law or by civil service regulations in the public sector. A public agency may not be allowed to bargain on its own behalf, but may be represented in negotiations by a state-level commission or office of negotiations. In many states, strikes by public sector employees are illegal.

For colleges whose employees have civil service protections, issues involve whether the college followed the regulations, particularly those involving due process in discipline, layoff, or termination decisions (see, for example, *Christophel v. Kukulinsky*, 61 F.3d 479 (6th Cir. 1995) (termination)). Determining how much process is due an employee is particularly complicated in states, such as West Virginia, where tenured faculty may be protected by state administrative procedure acts or civil service laws as well as by institutional policies on the termination of tenured faculty (see, for example, *Barazi v. West Virginia State College and the Board of Directors of the State College System*, 498 S.E.2d 720 (W. Va. 1997)), and such issues become even more complicated at

---

[6]Evan M. Berman, James S. Bowman, Jonathan P. West, & Montgomery Van Wart, *Human Resource Management in Public Service* (Thousand Oaks, CA: Sage, 2001), 298, 300.

public colleges whose faculty have civil service or other state administrative law protections and are simultaneously covered by a collective bargaining agreement. Employees covered by civil service protections and/or collective bargaining agreements may have "bumping rights" when their positions are eliminated in a reduction in force that entitle them to a less senior employee's job. In *Passonno v. State University of New York at Albany,* 889 F. Supp. 602 (N.D.N.Y. 1995), however, one court held that there are no bumping rights for the least senior employee in a classification. Other issues involve whether a particular job should be afforded civil service status, and the guidelines the college must follow in making that determination (see, for example, *Civil Service Employees Association, Inc., Local 1000, AFSCME v. State University of New York,* 721 N.Y.S.2d 127 (Ct. App. N.Y., 3d Dept., 2001) (staff assistant in mail services department).

Civil service regulations or state administrative procedure laws may specify that a hearing board (such as a board of regents or a state personnel board) conducts fact finding and makes rulings on employee appeals of discipline or discharge, and that a covered employee must exhaust these remedies before seeking redress in court (see, for example, *Papadakis v. Iowa State University of Science and Technology,* 574 N.W.2d 258 (Iowa 1998)). In some states, this hearing board or panel may serve the function of a trial court, and appeals of the hearing board's rulings are made to the state court of appeals.

Sec. 4.5. *Collective Bargaining*

4.5.1. *Overview.* Collective bargaining has existed on many college campuses since the late 1960s, yet some institutions have recently faced the prospect of bargaining with their faculty or staff for the first time. Whether the union is a fixture or a recent arrival, it presents administrators with a complex mixture of the familiar and the foreign. Many demands, such as for shorter staff work weeks, lighter teaching loads and smaller class sizes, and larger salaries, may be familiar on many campuses; but other demands sometimes voiced, such as for standardized pay scales rather than individualized "merit" salary determinations, may present unfamiliar situations. Legal, policy, and political issues may arise concerning the extent to which collective bargaining and the bargained agreement preempt or circumscribe not merely traditional administrative "elbow room" but also the customary forms of shared governance. And potential tension for academia clearly exists when "outsiders" participate in campus affairs through their involvement in all the aspects of collective bargaining: certification of bargaining agents, negotiation of agreements, fact finding, mediation, conciliation, arbitration, and ultimate resolution of internal disputes through state or federal administrative agencies and courts.

Although the number of unionized faculty and staff has increased only slightly in the past few years, most of the organizing has occurred among graduate students and adjunct or part-time faculty. Graduate teaching and research assistants won and then lost the right to bargain at several elite private and public research universities (see Section 4.5.6). And bargaining is not limited to full-time employees of the college; adjunct and part-time faculty have won the right to bargain at institutions throughout the country (see Section 6.2.4).

Although state law regulates bargaining at public colleges, and federal law regulates bargaining at private colleges, many of these rights are similar. Employees typically have the right to organize and to select a representative to negotiate on their behalf with the employer over terms and conditions of employment. Once a representative is selected by a majority of the employees in a particular bargaining unit, the employer has a statutory duty to bargain with the employees' representative, and employees may not negotiate individually with the employer over issues that are mandatory subjects of bargaining. Either the union or the employer may file an "unfair labor practice" charge with a government agency alleging that the other party committed infractions of the bargaining laws. In the private sector, the National Labor Relations Board (NLRB) hears these claims, and in the public sector a state public employment relations board provides recourse for aggrieved unions or employers. Hearings before these agencies take the place of a civil trial; the rulings of these agencies are typically appealed to state or federal appellate courts.

In addition to claims of failure to bargain, a party may claim that the other has engaged in activity that breaches the collective bargaining agreement. Other contentious issues include the rights of covered individuals who choose not to join the union (but whom the union must represent anyway), and whether employees in the public sector may lawfully go out on strike. The mix of factors involved, the importance of the policy questions, and the complexity of the law make collective bargaining a potentially troublesome area for administrators. Heavy involvement of legal counsel is clearly called for. Use of professional negotiators, or of administrators experienced in the art of negotiation, is also usually appropriate, particularly when the faculty and staff have such professional expertise on their side of the bargaining table.

4.5.2. The public-private dichotomy in collective bargaining.

Theoretically, the legal aspects of collective bargaining divide into two distinct categories: public and private. However, these categories are not necessarily defined in the same way as they are for constitutional state action purposes (see Section 1.5.2). In relation to collective bargaining, "public" and "private" are defined by the collective bargaining legislation and interpretive precedents. Private institutions are subject to the federal law controlling collective bargaining, whereas collective bargaining in public institutions is regulated by state law. Privately chartered institutions (see Section 12.3) are likely to be considered private for collective bargaining purposes even if they receive substantial government support. Factors that may determine an institution's status under federal or state collective bargaining laws include actions by a state legislature to transform the institution to a public entity, and proportions of public versus private funds, among others. This issue was addressed in a lengthy case regarding the University of Vermont. In *University of Vermont and State Agricultural College,*

223 NLRB 423 (1976), the National Labor Relations Board, the agency that enforces the federal labor relations law, asserted jurisdiction over the university because it received only 25 percent of its support directly from the state and because it was chartered as private and nonprofit and was not a political subdivision of the state. However, in 1988 the state legislature passed a law bringing the university under the purview of state labor law. The state sought an advisory opinion from the NLRB on whether the university was still subject to federal law for collective bargaining purposes. In *University of Vermont and State Agricultural College,* 297 NLRB 42 (1989), the Board determined that the university was now a political subdivision of the state, reversing its earlier opinion.

4.5.2.1. Bargaining at private colleges. Private sector bargaining is governed by the National Labor Relations Act of 1935 (the Wagner Act) as amended by the Labor-Management Relations Act of 1947 (the Taft-Hartley Act), 29 U.S.C. § 141 *et seq.* The Act defines "employer" to exclude "any state or political subdivision thereof," thereby removing public employers, including public postsecondary institutions, from the Act's coverage (29 U.S.C. § 152(2)). The NLRA thus applies only to private postsecondary institutions and, under current National Labor Relations Board rules, only to those with gross annual unrestricted revenues of at least $1 million (29 C.F.R. § 103.1).

These laws provide that employees of an "industry affecting commerce" have the right "to form, join or assist labor organizations, to bargain collectively through representatives of their own choosing, and to engage in other concerted activities for the purpose of collective bargaining or other mutual aid and protection . . ." (29 U.S.C. § 157, commonly referred to as "Section 7"). The right to engage in "concerted activity" applies whether or not the employees are represented by a union.

The right of employees to engage in "concerted activity" has been interpreted to give an employee the right to be accompanied by a coworker when a manager or supervisor meets with that employee for an "investigatory interview" to discuss issues that could result in the employee being disciplined. Although these rights have been recognized for unionized employees since 1975 (*NLRB v. J. Weingarten Inc.,* 420 U.S. 251 (1975), the National Labor Relations Board extended these rights to unrepresented employees for a brief time. In *Epilepsy Foundation of Northeast Ohio,* 331 N.L.R.B. No. 92 (2000), the NLRB ruled that, because the source of "Weingarten rights" was Section 7 of the NLRA, which also covers nonunionized employees, whether or not an employee was represented by a union was irrelevant to his or her right to be accompanied by a co-worker at investigatory interviews. The U.S. Court of Appeals for the District of Columbia Circuit upheld the Board's decision (*Epilepsy Foundation of Northeast Ohio v. NLRB,* 268 F.3d 1095 (2001), *cert. denied,* 536 U.S. 904 (2002)). However, in 2004 the Board, reflecting the departure of some previous members and the arrival of new Board members, reversed itself by a 3-to-2 vote in *IBM Corp.,* 341 N.L.R.B. No. 148 (2004), ruling that Weingarten rights did not extend to unrepresented employees. The

Board based this most recent ruling on policy considerations involving the employer's need to conduct investigations in confidence.

The law prohibits the employer from interfering with or coercing employees in the exercise of their NLRA rights. It also prohibits domination of labor organizations, discrimination against union members or union activists, refusal to bargain with the union, and retaliation against employees who exercise their rights under the NLRA (29 U.S.C. § 158(a)). Similar prohibitions are placed on unions for refusal to bargain, for coercing employees in the exercise of their rights under the statute, or for coercing an employer to bargain with one union if another union is its employees' recognized representative (29 U.S.C. § 158(b)).

The Act defines "employee" to exclude "any individual employed as a supervisor" (29 U.S.C. § 152(3)); a "supervisor" is defined as

> any individual having authority, in the interest of the employer, to hire, transfer, suspend, lay off, recall, promote, discharge, assign, reward, or discipline other employees, or responsibly to direct them, or to adjust their grievances, or effectively to recommend such action, if in connection with the foregoing the exercise of such authority is not of a merely routine or clerical nature, but requires the use of independent judgment [§ 152(11)].

The National Labor Relations Board has also excluded confidential and managerial employees from the Act's protections.

In *National Labor Relations Board v. Quinnipiac College*, 256 F.3d 68 (2d Cir. 2001), a federal appellate court reversed a ruling by the NLRB that ordered the college to bargain with shift supervisors and acting shift supervisors for the college's security employees. Because the shift supervisors were held accountable for other security employees' performance, said the court, they exercised the power "responsibly to direct" the security employees, which fit the statutory definition of "supervisor" and thus excluded these individuals from the group of employees protected by the NLRA.

Universities with medical schools may have multiple bargaining units involving a variety of health care professionals. Prior to 1974, acute care hospitals had been exempt from coverage by the NLRA out of concern for the serious public health consequences of labor stoppages. But in 1974 Congress amended the law, in the "NLRA Amendments of 1974" (88 Stat. 395), and subjected all acute care hospitals to coverage by the NLRA. The Congressional Reports accompanying the amendments said that the National Labor Relations Board should give due consideration to "preventing proliferation of bargaining units in the health care industry" (S. Rep. No. 93-766, p. 5; H. R. Rep. No. 9301051, pp. 6-7 (1974), *reprinted in U.S. Code Cong. & Admin. News* 1974, pp. 3946, 3950). After years of public hearings and consultation, the Board, in 1989, issued a rule defining appropriate bargaining units in the health care industry. The rule, codified at 29 C.F.R. § 103.30, specifies that "except in extraordinary circumstances" or where there are existing nonconforming units, there will be no more than eight bargaining units at acute care hospitals. The rule dictates the type of employees (physicians, nurses, skilled maintenance) for each of these units. Although the hospitals' trade association challenged the rule as unconstitutional and in violation of Congressional intent regarding "undue proliferation," it was upheld by the U.S. Supreme Court in *American Hospital Association v. NLRB,* 499 U.S. 606 (1991). (For an example of the rule applied to a university hospital, see *Duke University,* 306 N.L.R.B. No. 101, 139 L.R.R.M. 1300 (1992).)

The NLRB has created an exception to the duty to bargain in situations where the employer has virtually no control over the terms and conditions of employment for its workers. This situation may occur when a college enters a contract with a private sector organization that will provide a service, such as food service or maintenance for the college. For example, in *ARA v. NLRB,* 71 F.3d 129 (4th Cir. 1995), the University of North Carolina at Greensboro, a public university, had contracted with ARA, a private entity, to provide food services on campus. ARA, as a private sector employer, is subject to the NLRA. However, the contract between the university and ARA dictated the terms and conditions of ARA's employees' employment, and the university retained veto authority over any modifications of the wages and fringe benefits of ARA's employees, as well as staffing levels under the contract. Given this relationship, the court ruled, the state of North Carolina controlled the terms and conditions of ARA's employees' employment, and the state was not subject to the jurisdiction of the NLRB. Therefore, ARA's employees were not protected by the NLRA.

Institutions that have attempted to use consultative decision-making practices for administrators and staff may wish to review the NLRB's decision in *Electromation Inc.,* 309 N.L.R.B. No. 163 (1992). In that case, a union charged that the company's joint employee-employer "action committees," created to develop company policy on attendance, pay policies, and other issues constituted an illegally "employer-dominated labor organization" under 29 U.S.C. §§ 152(5) and 158(a)(2). The NLRB agreed with the union, citing the fact that the employer created the committees unilaterally, specified their goals and responsibilities, appointed management representatives (employees volunteered for the committees), and permitted the committees to operate on paid time. The employer appealed the Board's ruling, but in *Electromation v. NLRB,* 35 F.3d 1148 (7th Cir. 1994), the appellate court agreed with the Board. In a subsequent decision in *Crown Cork & Seal Co.,* 334 N.L.R.B. No. 92 (2001), however, the Board ruled that employee participation committees that exercised authority delegated to them by the company were permissible under the NLRA because the committees were functioning similarly to supervisors, and thus were acting on behalf of management rather than on behalf of the workers themselves.

Although the coverage of staff under federal collective bargaining laws is relatively clear, it was not at all clear that faculty or other academic professionals could form unions under the protection of the NLRA. The NLRB first asserted jurisdiction over private nonprofit postsecondary institutions in *Cornell University,* 183 NLRB 329 (1970); and in *C. W. Post Center of Long Island University,* 189 NLRB 904 (1971), it specified that its jurisdiction extended to faculty members.[7] The Board's jurisdiction over higher education institutions was judicially confirmed in *NLRB v. Wentworth Institute*, 515 F.2d 550 (1st Cir. 1975), where the court enforced an NLRB order finding that Wentworth had engaged in an unfair labor practice in refusing to bargain with the certified faculty bargaining representative. Today all private postsecondary institutions, at least all those large enough to have a significant effect on interstate commerce, are included within the federal sphere, and faculty as well as staff are covered by the NLRA, unless the faculty are "managerial employees" (see Section 6.3.1 of this book). Disputes about collective bargaining in private institutions are thus subject to the limited body of statutory authority and the vast body of administrative and judicial precedent regarding the National Labor Relations Act.

Legal authority and precedent have provided few easy answers, however, for collective bargaining issues in postsecondary education. The uniqueness of academic institutions, procedures, and customs poses problems not previously encountered in the NLRB's administration of the national labor law in other employment contexts. There are, moreover, many ambiguities and unsettled areas in the national labor law even in nonacademic contexts. They derive in part from the intentionally broad language of the federal legislation and in part from the NLRB's historic insistence on proceeding case by case rather than under a policy of systematic rule making (see K. Kahn, "The NLRB and Higher Education: The Failure of Policy Making Through Adjudication," 21 *UCLA L. Rev.* 63 (1973); and A. P. Menard & N. DiGiovanni, Jr., "NLRB Jurisdiction over Colleges and Universities: A Plea for Rulemaking," 16 *William and Mary L. Rev.* 599 (1975)). Administrators and counsel will find working with the NLRB's body of piecemeal precedental authority to be a very different experience from working with the detailed regulations of other agencies, such as the U.S. Department of Education.

4.5.2.2. Collective bargaining in religiously affiliated institutions. Religiously affiliated or controlled private colleges are not statutorily exempt from coverage by the NLRA, but some colleges have argued successfully that the First Amendment's protections for religious organizations trump the provisions of the NLRA. For example, the U.S. Supreme Court's decision in *NLRB v. Catholic Bishop of Chicago*, 440 U.S. 490 (1979) paved the way for subsequent litigation by religiously affiliated colleges seeking to avoid coverage by the NLRA.

---

[7]The NLRA specifically includes "professional employees," defined as "any employee engaged in work (i) predominantly intellectual and varied in character as opposed to routine mental, manual, mechanical, or physical work; (ii) involving the consistent exercise of discretion and judgment in its performance; (iii) of such a character that the output produced or the result accomplished cannot be standardized in relation to a given period of time; (iv) requiring knowledge of an advanced type in a field of science or learning customarily acquired by a prolonged course of specialized intellectual instruction and study in an institution of higher learning or a hospital, as distinguished from a general academic education or from an apprenticeship or from training in the performance of routine mental, manual, or physical processes." Also included is anyone who has completed the specialized courses described above and is working under the supervision of the professional employee (29 U.S.C. § 152(12)). Cases regarding which types of employees fit this definition are collected in John F. Gillespie, Annot., "Who Are Professional Employees Within Meaning of National Labor Relations Act (29 U.S.C.S. § 152(12))?" 40 A.L.R. Fed. 25.

The *Catholic Bishop* case arose after teachers at two groups of Catholic high schools voted for union representation in NLRB-sponsored elections. Although the NLRB certified the unions as the teachers' collective bargaining representatives, the schools refused to negotiate, and the unions filed unfair labor practice charges against them. In response, the schools claimed that the First Amendment precluded the NLRB from exercising jurisdiction over them. After the Board upheld its authority to order the elections and ordered the schools to bargain with the unions, the U.S. Court of Appeals for the Seventh Circuit denied enforcement of the NLRB's order. By exercising jurisdiction over "church-operated" schools, the court said, the Board was interfering with the freedom of church officials to operate their schools in accord with their religious tenets, thus violating both the free exercise clause and the establishment clause of the First Amendment (see Section 1.6).

The U.S. Supreme Court affirmed the appellate court's decision, by a 5-to-4 vote, but it did so on somewhat different grounds. Rather than addressing the First Amendment issue directly, as had the appeals court, the Supreme Court focused on a question of statutory interpretation: whether Congress intended that the National Labor Relations Act would give the Board jurisdiction over church-operated schools. In deciding that issue, the Court considered the constitutional problem indirectly by positing that an Act of Congress should be construed, whenever possible, in such a way that serious constitutional problems are avoided. Emphasizing the key role played by teachers in religious primary and secondary schools, the Court found that grave First Amendment questions would result if the Act were construed to allow the Board jurisdiction over such teachers. The Court accepted the schools' argument that their employment policies were mandated, at least in part, by religious doctrine. The court found that simply making an inquiry into the good faith religious basis for certain employment policies would violate the First Amendment. Therefore, the Court reviewed the legislative history of the NLRA to ascertain whether Congress had addressed the issue of its jurisdiction over religious organizations.

A survey of the Act's legislative history convinced the Court that Congress had not manifested any "affirmative intention" that teachers in church-operated primary and secondary schools be covered by the Act. Since "Congress did not contemplate that the Board would require church-operated schools to grant recognition to unions," and since such a construction of the Act would require the Court "to resolve difficult and sensitive questions" under the First Amendment, the Court held that the Board's jurisdiction does not extend to teachers in church-operated schools.

The result in *Catholic Bishop* raised questions as to whether its reasoning would apply to church-operated institutions of higher education. The Supreme Court's opinion had given short shrift to the possible distinction between elementary/secondary and higher education. It asserted generally that, whenever extension of NLRB jurisdiction over teachers in "church-operated schools" would raise "serious constitutional questions," a court can uphold the NLRB only if it finds a "clear expression of Congress's intent" to authorize jurisdiction. Thus, the extension of *Catholic Bishop* to higher education hinged on two questions: (1) whether NLRB jurisdiction would raise "serious constitutional questions" in light of the First Amendment case law distinguishing between elementary/secondary and higher education; and (2) whether the legislative history of the NLRA and its amendments could be construed differently for higher education, so as to reveal a clearly expressed congressional intent to include higher education teachers within the Board's jurisdiction.

Before the courts had an opportunity to consider these questions, the NLRB asserted jurisdiction over three colleges and universities that had claimed to be exempt under *Catholic Bishop.* In these rulings, the Board held that *Catholic Bishop* did not apply because the college "is not church operated as contemplated by *Catholic Bishop.*" In *Lewis University,* 265 NLRB 1239 (1982), for example, the Board asserted jurisdiction over a historically church-related institution because operating authority had been transferred to a private board of trustees, and the local diocese "does not exercise administrative or other secular control" over, and does not perform any services for, the institution. This approach was contrary to an earlier ruling of a federal appellate court. In *NLRB v. Bishop Ford Central Catholic High School,* 623 F.2d 818 (2d Cir. 1980), the court had denied enforcement of an NLRB order asserting jurisdiction over lay teachers in a Catholic school severed from ownership and control of the local diocese and operated instead by a predominantly lay board of trustees. According to the court, the critical question in determining whether a school is "church operated" under *Catholic Bishop* is not whether a church holds legal title or controls management; it is whether the school has a "religious mission" that could give rise to "entanglement" problems under the establishment clause. Since the school's history and "present religious characteristics" indicated that its religious mission continued after separation from the diocese, the court held the school to be exempt from NLRB jurisdiction.

This "religious mission" test was used in the first application of *Catholic Bishop* to an institution of higher education when a federal appellate court, in an *en banc* opinion, split evenly on whether the NLRB could assert jurisdiction over a religiously affiliated university. In *Universidad Central de Bayamon v. NLRB,* 793 F.2d 383 (1st Cir. 1986), the divided *en banc* court did not enforce the NLRB's bargaining order; it thereby overturned the ruling of a three-judge panel that had ordered the university to bargain with its faculty. The question addressed by both groups of judges was whether a religiously affiliated university is sufficiently different from a parochial elementary or secondary school to justify a departure from *Catholic Bishop.*

The group holding that *Catholic Bishop* should apply cited the substantial religious mission of the university. It also noted that in *Catholic Bishop* the Court had not distinguished postsecondary education from elementary or secondary education and had rejected the NLRB's distinction between "completely religious schools" and "merely religiously associated schools" because of the potential for entanglement when the Board attempted to determine which of those categories an institution belonged in. The group believed that making such distinctions at the postsecondary level would be equally troublesome. The group favoring the application of the NLRA to the university held that the religious mission of the university was far less central than that of the high schools in *Catholic Bishop*. It further believed that most unfair labor practice charges would involve secular matters, and that the university still had the right to assert a First Amendment claim should entanglement be a potential problem in any particular Board action.

In subsequent cases, the NLRB and reviewing federal courts focused on the institution's mission and tried to determine whether employment policies derive from the religious sponsor's doctrines or whether they have been secularized (see Sections 6.2.5 & 5.5). For example, in *St. Joseph's College,* 282 NLRB 65 (1986), the Board ruled that it lacked jurisdiction over the college because the Sisters of Mercy exercised administrative and financial control and the college's mission was inextricably interwoven with the religious mission of the order. But in *Livingstone College,* 286 NLRB 1308 (1987), the Board found that the college's purpose was primarily secular, that it was not dependent upon the African Methodist Episcopal Zion Church, and that the church was not involved in the college's daily operations.

A ruling by the U.S. Court of Appeals for the District of Columbia Circuit provides a simpler, and arguably less intrusive, test for whether a religiously affiliated college is exempt from the NLRA. In *University of Great Falls,* 331 N.L.R.B. No. 188 (2000), the Board had found that the university's purpose and function were primarily secular, and exercised jurisdiction over the college, based on six factors. In particular, the curriculum lacked any emphasis on Catholicism, the university had a lay president and other lay leaders, neither faculty nor students were required to be Catholics or to support the teachings of the Catholic church, and the board of trustees was free to establish policy independent of the Catholic religion's teachings The appellate court refused to enforce the Board's bargaining order, stating that the Board had used the "wrong test." In *University of Great Falls v. NLRB,* 278 F.3d 1335 (D.C. Cir. 2002), the court adopted a three-part test derived from the *Bayamon* case, reasoning that any inquiry as to the centrality of a college's religious mission to its primary purpose posed an impermissible entanglement of church and state. Under this three-part test, an institution is exempt if it:

"holds itself out to students, faculty and community" as providing a religious educational environment;

is organized as a "nonprofit";

is affiliated with, or owned, operated, or controlled, directly or indirectly, by a recognized religious organization, or with an entity, membership of which is determined, at least in part, with reference to religion [278 F.3d at 1343, citing *Bayamon,* 793 F.2d at 400, 403, and 399–400].[8]

---

[8]The university had also argued that the Religious Freedom Restoration Act (RFRA) barred the NLRB from asserting jurisdiction. Although the U.S. Supreme Court invalidated RFRA in 1997 with respect to actions by states (see Section 1.6.2), the Board assumed that the law still applied to federal agencies but ruled that the exercise of jurisdiction over the university by the Board did not violate RFRA. The appellate court did not address the application of RFRA because it found for the university on constitutional grounds.

Should other appellate courts follow the reasoning of the appellate court in *University of Great Falls,* religiously affiliated colleges will find it much easier to avoid the application of the NLRA.

State courts have also been asked to determine whether state constitutions provide a constitutionally protected right to bargain for employees of a school controlled by a religious organization. In *South Jersey Catholic School Teachers Organization v. St. Teresa of the Infant Jesus Church Elementary School,* 696 A.2d 709 (N.J. 1997), the New Jersey Supreme Court was asked to determine whether lay teachers in a church-operated elementary school have an enforceable state constitutional right to unionize and to bargain without violating the First Amendment of the U.S. Constitution. The employer, the Diocese of Camden, had a longstanding bargaining relationship with its high school teachers, but objected to bargaining with its elementary school teachers, citing both establishment and free exercise clause defenses. In a unanimous opinion, the New Jersey court ruled for the teachers. The court distinguished *Catholic Bishop,* stating that the case had been decided on statutory interpretation rather than constitutional grounds. It also stated that the scope of negotiation under the state constitution, which requires private employers to bargain with their employees, was already limited by the First Amendment of the U.S. Constitution to secular issues: wages, benefit plans, and other secular terms and conditions of employment. With respect to the establishment clause claim, the court noted that the Diocese had retained its authority over religious matters despite its history of bargaining with high school teachers, and thus there was no impermissible entanglement between church and the state. The primary effect of the law, said the court, was not to inhibit religion, but to require a private employer to bargain with elected representatives of its employees. With respect to the free exercise claim, the court found that the state had a compelling interest in allowing private employees to unionize and bargain collectively over secular terms and conditions of employment, and thus any incidental burden on the free exercise of religion was outweighed by the state's interest in enhancing the economic welfare of employees in the private sector.

Faculty at Seton Hall University, who were barred from bargaining under the *Yeshiva* doctrine in 1983, attempted to use the ruling in the *South Jersey Catholic School Teachers Association* case to convince the state courts to allow them to bargain. A trial court judge dismissed the faculty members' claim, ruling that the NLRB's prior assertion of jurisdiction over Seton Hall University in the 1983 case preempted the use of a state constitutional provision to require the university to bargain. The state supreme court declined to hear the appeal (*Seton Hall University Faculty Association v. Seton Hall University,* 762 A.2d 657 (N.J. 2000)).

4.5.2.3. Bargaining at public colleges. Employees of public institutions, though not subject to the NLRA, may have similar protections. These protections are far from uniform, however, and have been characterized as "a crazy-quilt patchwork of state and local laws, regulations, executive orders, court decisions, and attorney general opinions" (John Lund & Cheryl Maranto, "Public Sector Labor Law: An Update," in Dale Belman, Morley Gunderson, & Douglas Hyatt, eds., *Public Sector Employment in a Time of Transition* (Industrial

Relations Research Association, 1996), 21). Thirty-five states either have legislation permitting some form of collective bargaining in public postsecondary education, or the state governing board has enacted a policy that permits employees in public institutions to bargain collectively.

Legislation that enables public employees to bargain collectively is often limited in coverage or in the extent to which it authorizes or mandates the full panoply of collective bargaining rights and services. A statute may grant employees' rights as narrow as the right to "meet and confer" with administration representatives. The permissibility of strikes is also a major variable among state statutes. Frequently, state legislation is designed to cover public employees generally and makes little, if any, special provision for the unique circumstances of postsecondary education. State labor law may be as unsettled as the federal labor law, providing few easy answers for postsecondary education, and may also have a smaller body of administrative and judicial precedents. State agencies and courts often fill in the gaps by relying on precedents in federal labor law.

Even where state collective bargaining legislation does not cover public postsecondary institutions, some "extralegal" bargaining may still take place. A public institution's employees, like other public employees, have a constitutional right, under First Amendment freedom of speech and association, "to organize collectively and select representatives to engage in collective bargaining" (*University of New Hampshire Chapter AAUP v. Haselton,* 397 F. Supp. 107 (D.N.H. 1975)). But employees do not have a constitutional right to require the public institution "to respond to . . . [employee] demands or to enter into a contract with them." The right to require the employer to bargain in good faith must be created by statute. Even if the public institution desires to bargain with representatives of its employees, it may not have the authority to do so under state law. Or state law may remove from the institution the right to set terms and conditions of employment and vest it instead in a state governing or regulatory board (see *Knight v. Minnesota Community College Faculty Association,* discussed in Section 6.3.2).

The employment powers of public institutions may be vested by law in the sole discretion of institutional governing boards; sharing such powers with collective bargaining representatives or arbitrators appointed under collective bargaining agreements may therefore be construed as an improper delegation of authority. In *Board of Trustees of Junior College District No. 508 v. Cook County College Teachers Union,* 343 N.E.2d 473 (Ill. 1976), for example, the court held that the board's powers to decide which faculty members to employ and promote were "nondelegable" and thus not subject to binding arbitration under the collective bargaining agreement.

A primary difference in the rights of public sector employees vis-à-vis their private sector counterparts is the scope of negotiation and permissible subjects of bargaining. These issues are explored in Section 4.5.4.

4.5.3. Organization, recognition, and certification.
Once the college's employees or a substantial portion of them decide that they want to bargain collectively with the institution, their representative can ask the administration

to recognize it for collective bargaining purposes. A private institution has two choices at this point. It can voluntarily recognize the employee representatives and commence negotiations, or it can withhold recognition and insist that the employee representatives seeking recognition petition the NLRB for a certification election (see *Linden Lumber Division v. NLRB*, 419 U.S. 817 (1974)). Public institutions that have authority to bargain under state law usually have the same two choices, although elections and certification would be handled by the state labor board.

Administrators should consider two related legal implications of choosing the first alternative. First, it is a violation of the National Labor Relations Act (and most state acts) for an employer voluntarily to recognize a minority union—that is, a union supported by fewer than 50 percent of the employees in the bargaining unit (see 29 U.S.C. § 158(a)(1) and (2), and *International Ladies Garment Workers Union v. NLRB*, 366 U.S. 731 (1961)). Second, it is also a violation of the NLRA (and most state acts) for an employer to recognize any union (even one with apparent majority support) when a rival union makes a "substantial claim of support," which the NLRB interprets to mean a claim "not . . . clearly unsupportable and lacking in substance" (*American Can Co.*, 218 NLRB 102, 103 (1975)). Thus, unless a union seeking recognition can prove the clear support of the majority of the members of the proposed bargaining unit (usually through "authorization cards" or a secret ballot poll), and the administration has no reason to believe that a rival union with a "substantial claim of support" is also seeking recognition, it is usually not wise to recognize any union without a certification election.

In the interim between the beginning of organizational activity and the actual certification of a union, administrators must be circumspect in their actions. In the private sector, the NLRA prohibits the employer from doing anything that would appear to favor any of the contenders for recognition (29 U.S.C. § 158(a)(2)) or that would "interfere with, restrain, or coerce employees in the exercise of their rights" to self-organize, form or join a union, or bargain collectively (29 U.S.C. § 158(a)(1)). This prohibition would apply to promises of benefits, threats of reprisals, coercive interrogation, or surveillance. Furthermore, the institution may not take any action that could be construed as discrimination against union organizers or supporters because of their exercise of rights under the Act (29 U.S.C. § 158(a)(3)). In the public sector, state laws generally contain comparable prohibitions on certain kinds of employer activities.

Another crucial aspect of the organizational phase is the definition of the "bargaining unit"—that is, the portion of the institution's employees that will be represented by the particular bargaining agent seeking certification. Again, most state laws parallel the federal law. Generally, the NLRB or its state equivalent has considerable discretion to determine the appropriate unit (see 29 U.S.C. § 159(b)). The traditional rule has been that there must be a basic "community of interest" among the individuals included in the unit, so that the union will represent the interests of everyone in the unit when it negotiates with the employer.[9] The question of the appropriate bargaining unit arises when a union represents both employees who may have different or even conflicting interests. For example, at several institutions the issue of whether a single bargaining unit may include both full-time and adjunct faculty has arisen. In *Vermont State Colleges Faculty Federation v. Vermont State Colleges,* 566 A.2d 955 (Vt. 1989), the state college system challenged the state labor board's ruling that both full-time and adjunct faculty should be combined in a single bargaining unit. The Vermont Supreme Court reversed the board's ruling, holding that the adjunct faculty did not share a community of interest with the full-time faculty because they were hired and paid differently, were ineligible for tenure, and had no advising responsibilities. Similar issues have arisen with respect to units of staff, particularly when police or firefighters seek to have separate units (see, for example, *Teamsters v. University of Vermont,* 19 VLRB 64 (1996) (approving separate unit of campus police)). Employers and their counsel typically seek broad campuswide units rather than occupational units, particularly in the public sector.

Under the NLRA (see 29 U.S.C. § 152(3) and (11)) and most state laws, supervisory personnel are excluded from any bargaining unit (see, for example, *National Labor Relations Board v. Quinnipiac College,* discussed in Section 4.5.2.1). Individual determinations must be made, in light of the applicable statutory definition, of whether particular personnel are excluded from the unit as supervisors.[10] Professionals, however, are explicitly included by the NLRA, and its definition clearly applies to college faculty and other professional staff (see footnote 7 in Section 4.5.2). (For a discussion of the placement of faculty in bargaining units, see Section 6.3.1.)

Once the bargaining unit is defined and the union recognized or certified, the union becomes the exclusive bargaining agent of all employees in the unit, whether or not they become union members and whether or not they are willing to be represented (see *J. I. Case Co. v. NLRB,* 321 U.S. 332 (1944)). Courts have generally upheld the constitutionality of such exclusive representation systems. The leading case for higher education, *Minnesota State Board for Community Colleges v. Knight,* 465 U.S. 271 (1984), discussed in Section 6.3.2, examines (but is not particularly sensitive to) the special concerns that exclusive systems may create for higher education governance. Although this case addresses a bargaining unit of faculty, it also has relevance for an institution whose staff have formed governance groups or self-managing work teams.

---

[9]Cases and authorities are collected in Francis M. Dougherty, Annot., "'Community of Interest' Test in NLRB Determination of Appropriateness of Employee Bargaining Unit," 90 A.L.R. Fed. 16; and Jean F. Rydstrom, Annot., "Who May Be Included in 'Unit Appropriate' for Collective Bargaining at School or College, Under Sec. 9(b) of National Labor Relations Act (29 U.S.C.S. § 159(b))," 46 A.L.R. Fed. 580.

[10]Cases and authorities are collected at C. R. McCorkle, Annot., "Who Are Supervisors Within Meaning of National Labor Relations Act, as Amended?" 11 A.L.R.2d 249; and at Russell J. Davis., Annot., "Who Are Supervisors Within Meaning of National Labor Relations Act (29 U.S.C.A. §§ 151 *et seq.*) in Education and Health Services," 52 A.L.R. Fed. 28.

In addition to limiting the independent actions of nonunion employees in matters of governance or institutional policy, the exclusivity doctrine has raised other legal issues. Supreme Court precedent interpreting federal labor law (*International Association of Machinists v. Street*, 367 U.S. 740 (1961)) and state labor law (*Abood v. Detroit Board of Education*, 431 U.S. 209 (1977)) permits unions to charge nonmembers an "agency fee" to underwrite the cost of services provided by the union. But if a union represents faculty at public institutions and uses nonmembers' fees to support political activity with which nonmembers do not agree, their First Amendment rights may have been violated by the forced payment (*Chicago Teachers' Union v. Hudson*, 475 U.S. 292 (1986)).

This doctrine has also been imputed to the National Labor Relations Act, which governs labor relations in private organizations. In *Communication Workers v. Beck*, 487 U.S. 735 (1988), the Supreme Court ruled that objecting bargaining unit members must pay for services provided to their bargaining unit by the union, such as the costs of negotiating contracts or processing grievances. But forced payment of agency fees to support other union activities to which the nonmembers objected, and which were not chargeable to the bargaining unit, violated Section 7 of the National Labor Relations Act.

In February 2001, President George W. Bush issued Executive Order No. 13,201, which required federal contractors receiving $100,000 or more to post notices informing employees of their right not to join a union or to pay the portion of union dues attributable to nonrepresentational activities. A group of labor organizations challenged the Executive Order, arguing that it was preempted by the NLRA. In *UAW-Labor Employment and Training Corp. v. Chao*, 325 F.3d 360 (D.C. Cir. 2003), the appellate court rejected this argument and upheld the Executive Order. Only those activities that are either protected or prohibited by the NLRA are preempted by that law, said the court, and the NLRB had not prohibited the posting of notices.

Questions concerning the degree to which objecting faculty must pay agency fees, whether and how the union must account for its use of nonmembers' fees, and the interplay among the NLRA, the First Amendment, and civil rights laws have all been examined in litigation between objecting faculty members and the unions representing faculty. In those states that permit collective bargaining contracts to specify nonpayment of union dues or agency fees as a permissible reason for discharging faculty, the issue has been particularly complex.[11]

In a case decided by the U.S. Supreme Court, *Lehnert v. Ferris Faculty Association*, 500 U.S. 507 (1991), nonmember faculty at Ferris State University sued the union representing them, an affiliate of the National Education Association, over the matter of agency fees. Michigan's Public Employment Relations Act permits a union and a public employer to negotiate an agency shop agreement,

[11]Cases related to this issue are collected in Wayne F. Foster, Annot., "Union Security Arrangements in State Public Employment," 95 A.L.R.3d 1102; and Tim A. Thomas, Annot., "Validity of Union Procedures for Fixing and Reviewing Agency Fees of Nonunion Employees Under Public Employees Representation Contract—Post-*Hudson* Cases," 92 A.L.R. Fed. 893.

and such an agreement was negotiated between the faculty union and the administration of Ferris State College. In their suit the plaintiffs claimed that being forced to support the state and national union's legislative lobbying activities, expenses for travel to conventions by union officers, preparation for a strike, and other activities violated their constitutional rights. The agency fee had been set at an amount equal to union members' dues. In a 5-to-4 decision, the Court ruled that agency fees were permissible for the purpose of supporting union activities directly related to services to bargaining unit members, and that activities by state or national affiliates that were related to collective bargaining, even if not of direct benefit to local union members, could be included in the calculation of the agency fee.

Several Justices wrote separate concurring opinions, and the majority joined only portions of the opinion written by Justice Blackmun. In analyzing the issues before the Court, Justice Blackmun, writing for himself and four other Justices, used a three-part test drawn from prior precedent. First, the chargeable activities must be "germane" to collective bargaining activity. Second, they must be justified by the "government's vital policy interest in labor peace and avoiding 'free riders.'" And third, the activities must "not significantly add to the burdening of free speech that is inherent in the allowance of an agency or union shop" (500 U.S. at 589).

The process developed by a union for employees challenging the calculation of nonmembers' dues was itself challenged by two University of Alaska faculty members in *Carlson v. United Academics,* 265 F.3d 778 (9th Cir. 2001). The professors objected to the union's practice of holding the dues of objecting employees who challenged the agency fee calculation. While employees who objected to paying full dues but accepted the union's calculation of the agency fee received immediate refunds, those who opted to have an impartial arbitrator determine whether the agency fee had been calculated accurately had to wait until the arbitration award had been issued to receive their refund. Furthermore, the arbitrator had the power to either increase or decrease the agency fee. The court ruled that the union's agency fee dispute resolution process satisfied the requirements of *Hudson* in all respects.[12] (For a contrasting case in which a federal district court held that the union's agency fee refund process violated *Hudson* in several respects, see *Swanson v. University of Hawaii Professional Assembly,* 269 F. Supp. 2d 1252 (D. Hawaii 2003).)

Another question concerning the use of nonmembers' agency fees is the potential for such use to violate an individual's First Amendment free exercise rights by compelling a nonmember to pay for union activities that conflict with the nonmember's religious beliefs. This matter is addressed in *EEOC v. University of Detroit,* Section 4.5.5 of this book.

---

[12]For a discussion of the implications of *Hudson* for faculty tenure, see S. Olswang, "Union Security Provisions, Academic Freedom and Tenure: The Implications of *Chicago Teachers Union v. Hudson,*" 15 *J. Coll. & Univ. Law* 539 (1988); the implications of *Beck* are discussed by R. Hartley, "Constitutional Values and the Adjudication of Taft-Hartley Act Dues Objector Cases," 41 *Hastings L.J.* 1 (1989). Although these cases involved faculty, the outcomes are equally relevant to staff employees.

Yet other legal issues may arise concerning the relationship between the union and the college or university as employer. For example, some colleges and universities have sought to insulate themselves against joint liability with the union if nonmembers challenge the amount and use of agency fee payments. In *Weaver v. University of Cincinnati,* 970 F.2d 1523 (6th Cir. 1992), nonmember staff challenged the amount of the agency fee (90 percent of dues) and its use by the union, suing both the union and the university because the university collected the fee through a "dues check-off" system. The university had negotiated an indemnification clause in the contract that disclaimed liability for any unconstitutional acts or practices by the union. The court refused to enforce the clause, stating that both the union and the employer had obligations under *Hudson,* and that relieving the employer of liability for failure to follow the law was a violation of public policy.

The use of a college's internal mail system by the faculty or staff union is a common practice on many campuses. The U.S. Supreme Court dealt a blow to unions in ruling that the University of California's refusal to permit a union to use the university's internal mail system was lawful. The California Public Employment Relations Board had ordered the university to permit the union to use its mail system under a provision of the California Higher Education Employer-Employee Relations Act that requires employers to grant unions access to their "means of communication" (Cal. Govt. Code Ann. §§ 3560–99). In *Regents of the University of California v. Public Employment Relations Board,* 485 U.S. 589 (1988), the Court ruled that under the Private Express Statutes (18 U.S.C. §§ 1693–99, 39 U.S.C. §§ 601–6) that protect the monopoly of the U.S. Postal Service, the university could not be compelled, over its objection, to carry the union's mail without postage. Justices Stevens and Marshall dissented from the majority opinion, arguing that the Court's prior ruling in *Perry Education Association v. Perry Local Educators' Association,* 460 U.S. 37 (1983) had established that internal mail systems were a type of public forum, and that any diminution of revenue to the Postal Service by the use of the university's internal mail system was minimal when weighed against the burden on the plaintiffs' First Amendment right to communicate through the internal mail system.

In addition to the numerous and complex issues related to the union's status as exclusive agent of the faculty, the question of when and whether the collective bargaining agreement supersedes or may be supplemented by other institutional policies and procedures can lead to thorny problems. These problems often arise when an employee's breach of contract claim concerns a matter that is covered by the collective bargaining agreement. In *White v. Winona State University,* 474 N.W.2d 410 (Minn. Ct. App. 1991), for example, the court was asked to determine whether a dean's decision to remove a department chair from office in the middle of a three-year term violated the faculty member's individual (rather than collective) contract rights. The faculty member cited a letter from the dean appointing him to a three-year term as the source of his contractual protection. The collective bargaining agreement that governed the faculty member's terms and conditions of employment contained a "zipper clause," stating that it was the complete agreement between the parties.

Furthermore, that agreement stated that removal of department chairs was not subject to the agreement's grievance procedure. Professor White argued that the contractual language excluded this issue from coverage by the agreement, and the letter thus became his contract. The court disagreed. Interpreting Minnesota law, the court ruled that if the collective agreement makes it clear that the grievance procedure is intended to be the exclusive remedy for employment disputes, then White could not bring action for common law breach of contract. A similar result was reached under the NLRA in *McGough v. University of San Francisco,* 263 Cal. Rptr. 404 (Cal. 1989), in which the court ruled that the NLRA preempted a faculty member's claim that his tenure denial breached an implied contract with the university. The NLRA did not, however, preempt the faculty member's common law tort claim of intentional infliction of emotional distress.

Although employees covered by a collective agreement have been unsuccessful in filing common law contract claims, they have won the right to file common law tort claims. This development gives employees a choice of the forum to use for dispute resolution. Prior to 1988, unionized employees had been limited to the grievance and arbitration procedures of their collective agreements under the doctrine of *Teamsters v. Lucas Flour Co.,* 369 U.S. 95 (1962), and *Allis-Chalmers Corp. v. Lueck,* 471 U.S. 202 (1985). But in *Lingle v. Norge Division of Magic Chef,* 486 U.S. 399 (1988), the U.S. Supreme Court ruled that an employee who asserts a state law tort claim of wrongful discharge may pursue this claim in court if its resolution does not depend on an interpretation of the collective agreement and even if the employee has already used the contractual grievance system. This ruling gives unionized employees two opportunities to challenge negative employment actions and diminishes some of the benefits afforded by binding arbitration: finality, speed, informality, and low cost. (For an analysis of this issue, see Note, "Steering Away from the Arbitration Process: Recognizing State Law Tort Actions for Unionized Employees," 24 *U. Richmond L. Rev.* 233 (1990).)

4.5.4. Bargainable subjects.

Once the unit has been defined and the agent certified, the parties must proceed to negotiations. In the private sector, under the NLRA, the parties may negotiate on any subject they wish, although other laws (such as federal employment discrimination laws) may make some subjects illegal. In the public sector, the parties may negotiate on any subject that is not specifically excluded from the state's collective bargaining statute or preempted by other state law, such as a tenure statute. Those subjects that may be raised by either party and that are negotiable with the consent of the other are referred to as "permissive" subjects for negotiation. Academic collective bargaining can range, and has ranged, over a wide variety of such permissive subjects (see M. Moskow, "The Scope of Collective Bargaining in Higher Education," 1971 *Wis. L. Rev.* 33 (1971)). A refusal to negotiate on a permissive subject of bargaining is not an unfair labor practice; on the contrary, it may be an unfair labor practice to insist that a permissive subject be covered by the bargaining agreement.

The heart of the collective bargaining process, however, is found in those terms over which the parties must negotiate. These "mandatory" subjects of bargaining are defined in the NLRA as "wages, hours, and other terms and conditions of employment" (29 U.S.C. § 158(d)). Most state laws use similar or identical language but often exclude particular subjects from the scope of bargaining or add particular subjects to it.[13] The parties must bargain in good faith over mandatory subjects of bargaining; failure to do so is an unfair labor practice under the NLRA (see 29 U.S.C. §§ 158(a)(5) and 158(b)(3)) and most state statutes.

The statutory language regarding the mandatory subjects is often vague (for example, "terms and conditions of employment") and subject to broad construction by labor boards and courts. Thus, the distinction between mandatory and permissive subjects is difficult to draw, particularly in postsecondary education, where employees have traditionally participated in shaping their jobs to a much greater degree than have employees in industry. Internal governance and policy issues that may never arise in industrial bargaining may thus be critical in postsecondary education. There are few court or labor board precedents in either federal or state law to help the parties determine whether educational governance and educational policy issues are mandatorily or permissibly bargainable. (For a thoughtful discussion of the scope of bargaining under federal law for professional employees, see D. Rabban, "Can American Labor Law Accommodate Collective Bargaining by Professional Employees?" 99 *Yale L.J.* 689 (1990).)

Under state law, where some subjects may be impermissible, there are few precedents to help administrators determine when particular subjects fall into that category. For example, courts in different states have reached opposing conclusions as to whether tenure or promotion criteria or procedures are negotiable, as discussed in Section 6.3.2 of this book. Although wages and salaries are mandatory subjects of negotiation, actions of state legislatures may interfere with or complicate the bargaining process at public colleges. For example, in *South Dakota Education Association v. South Dakota Board of Regents,* 582 N.W.2d 386 (S.D. 1998), the Supreme Court of South Dakota upheld a state appropriations bill providing that the distribution of salary increases to faculty members employed by state colleges and universities be made "at the sole discretion of the Board of Regents. . . ." The board of regents had been negotiating with the faculty union for several years after the expiration of the previous collective bargaining agreement, but no new agreement had been reached. The board had unilaterally implemented its last best offer after the previous agreement expired, and had reached a limited agreement with the union for the distribution of salary increases for one year. When no formal agreement was reached by the second year after the contract expired, and while the regents were still in negotiations with the faculty union, the legislature added language to the higher education appropriations bill to provide for faculty salary increases. The legislature took this action because public college leaders feared that they would lose highly qualified faculty if no salary increases were given. The court ruled that the legislature could direct the

---

[13]Cases on this issue are collected in Deborah Tussey, Annot., "Bargainable or Negotiable Issues in State Public Employment Labor Relations," 84 A.L.R.3d 242.

regents to distribute salary increases of a particular percentage amount, or could leave the distribution of the funds to the regents' discretion. The appropriations bill did not abrogate the requirement that the regents bargain with the faculty union, said the court, but merely reinforced the discretion the regents already had to distribute salary increases, subject to that body's obligation to negotiate over terms and conditions of employment.

A related issue was dealt with by the Supreme Court of Iowa in *Uni-United Faculty v. Iowa Public Employment Relations Board,* 545 N.W.2d 274 (Iowa 1996). Faculty at public colleges in Iowa are represented by a union, which had entered a collective bargaining agreement with the state concerning, among other issues, salary increases. The agreement provided for an across-the-board increase and for a portion of the salary funds to be awarded at the regents' discretion for individual salary adjustments, including merit pay. During the second year of the agreement, the Iowa legislature enacted an appropriations bill that allocated $275,000 for teaching excellence awards to faculty at the University of Northern Iowa. When the union demanded the right to negotiate the system for distributing the teaching excellence awards, the state refused, stating that the funds were part of the regular salary appropriation and, under the terms of the agreement, could be allocated at the regents' discretion. The union filed an unfair labor practice charge with the state Public Employment Relations Board (PERB), which ruled in favor of the state. The union appealed to the state district court, which upheld the PERB ruling. An appeal to the state supreme court followed.

The Iowa Supreme Court affirmed, ruling that the legislation actually limited the state's discretion to make salary awards under the contract, rather than unlawfully expanding its discretion. Under the terms of the collective bargaining agreement, the state had the right to allocate a portion of the salary appropriation at its discretion; the legislature had provided instructions to the state on the criterion (teaching excellence) upon which to make the allocations. There was no negative impact on collective bargaining in general, said the court, nor on the terms of the agreement between the union and the state.

When the parties are unable to reach agreement on an item subject to mandatory bargaining (called "impasse"), a number of resolution techniques may be available to them. In the private sector, the NLRA specifically recognizes that employees have the right to strike under certain circumstances (see 29 U.S.C. § 163). The basic premise of the Act is that, given the free play of economic forces, employer and union can and will bargain collectively and reach agreement, and the ultimate economic force available to a union is the strike. In the public sector, however, it is almost unanimously regarded as unlawful, either by state statute or state judicial decision, for an employee to strike. The rationale is that states have a vital interest in ensuring that government services remain available to the public without the interruption that would be created by a strike.[14]

---

[14]The statutes and cases are collected in James Duff, Jr., Annot., "Labor Law: Right of Public Employees to Strike or Engage in Work Stoppage," 37 A.L.R.3d 1147.

Consequently, almost all state statutes prescribe impasse resolution techniques to take the place of strikes. Depending on the statute, these techniques include mediation, fact finding, and interest arbitration. The most commonly prescribed impasse procedure is mediation, the appointment of a third party who may make recommendations to the disputing parties but who does not dictate any terms of settlement. Fact finding usually involves the appointment of an independent individual or panel to review the dispute and make findings regarding the critical facts underlying it. This process is sometimes mandatory if the parties fail to reach agreement within a specified time period; at other times a fact finder is appointed by order of a labor board or agreement of the parties (see J. Stern, "The Wisconsin Public Employee Fact-Finding Procedure," 20 *Indust. & Labor Rel. Rev.* 3 (1966)). Interest arbitration (as distinguished from grievance arbitration, discussed below) utilizes a third party to settle the contract terms on which the negotiating parties cannot agree. Interest arbitration can be either compulsory (in which case the statute requires the submission of unresolved issues to an arbitrator, who makes a final decision) or voluntary (in which case the parties decide for themselves whether to resort to binding arbitration).[15]

The same techniques used to resolve an impasse in bargaining may also be available in the public sector to resolve disputes concerning the application or interpretation of the bargaining agreement after it has gone into force. The most common technique for resolving such disputes is grievance arbitration.[16]

In the private sector, there are only two techniques for resolving an impasse in negotiating an agreement—mediation and interest arbitration—and the latter is rarely used. Mediation is available through the Federal Mediation and Conciliation Service, which may "proffer its services in any labor dispute . . . either upon its own motion or upon the request of one or more of the parties" (29 U.S.C. § 173(b)), as well as state mediation agencies and the American Arbitration Association. Interest arbitration may be used when the parties have a collective bargaining agreement that is about to expire, and they are willing to have the arbitrator decide any terms they cannot agree upon when negotiating their new agreement. Interest arbitration in the private sector has no statutory basis and is entirely the creature of an existing agreement between the parties.

Negotiated agreements usually provide for grievance arbitration to resolve disputes concerning the application or interpretation of the agreement. The arbitrator's power to entertain a grievance and to order a remedy comes from the language of the contract. In an illustrative case, *Trustees of Boston University v. Boston University Chapter, AAUP,* 746 F.2d 924 (1st Cir. 1984), the court upheld an arbitrator's interpretation of his powers under an arbitration clause of a

---

[15] Cases and authorities are collected in James D. Lawler, Annot., "Validity and Construction of Statutes or Ordinances Providing for Arbitration of Labor Disputes Involving Public Employees," 68 A.L.R.3d 885; and E. H. Schopler, Annot., "Matters Arbitrable Under Arbitration Provisions of Collective Labor Contract," 24 A.L.R.2d 752.

[16] Statutes and cases are collected in Judy E. Zelin, Annot., "Rights of State and Municipal Public Employees in Grievance Proceedings," 46 A.L.R.4th 912.

bargaining agreement and affirmed the arbitrator's award of equity and merit raises to three professors who had filed grievances.

The parties specify the degree of authority given to the arbitrator to hear a grievance initially and the remedy the arbitrator may award. In the public sector, some matters may be regulated by state law, and thus an arbitrator would lack the power to rule on those issues. Although most contracts provide that an arbitrator may hear grievances related to any alleged violation of the collective agreement, most contracts limit the arbitrator's authority when the grievance is related to a faculty employment decision, such as reappointment, promotion, or tenure. Although most contracts allow the arbitrator to determine whether a procedural violation has occurred in the decision-making process, the usual remedy is to order the decision to be made a second time, following the appropriate procedures. In the few cases where collective bargaining agreements between institutions of higher education and faculty unions have provided for binding arbitration of employment disputes, arbitrators have overturned a negative employment decision and awarded reappointment, promotion, or tenure in about half of the cases. (For analysis of the outcomes of binding arbitration of faculty employment disputes in the California state college system, see E. Purcell, "Binding Arbitration and Peer Review in Higher Education," 45 *Arbitration J.* 10 (December 1990); and for a more general discussion of alternative dispute resolution strategies, see Section 2.3 of this book.)

In the public sector, state law or regulation may require public employees to exhaust administrative remedies provided by collective bargaining agreements before resorting to the judicial system to resolve disputes. For example, in *Myles v. Regents of the University of California,* 2001 Cal. App. LEXIS 2374 (Ct. App. Cal., 2d App. Dist., 2001) (unpublished), the court ruled that it lacked jurisdiction to review a staff member's challenge to her termination by the university because, although she had filed a grievance (which had been denied), she had failed to exhaust her remedies under the collective bargaining agreement, which provided for arbitration, or under the state's Administrative Procedure Act, since her position was included within the state civil service.

Another method of dispute resolution is the filing of an unfair labor practice claim with the NLRB (for private colleges and universities) or the state public employment relations agency (for public institutions). Allegations of refusing to bargain over an issue that the union believes is a proper subject of bargaining and the administration does not, or allegations that one of the parties is in some way violating federal or state labor law, are often the subject of unfair labor practices. Remedies available to the federal or state agency include orders to bargain or to desist in the unlawful activity, reinstatement of individuals discharged in violation of the labor laws, and compensatory or equitable remedies.[17]

Not infrequently, an alleged violation of the collective bargaining agreement can also be characterized as an unfair labor practice under federal or state law.

---

[17]Statutes and cases are collected in Larry D. Scheafer, Annot., "What Constitutes Unfair Labor Practice Under State Public Employee Relations Acts," 9 A.L.R.4th 20.

A case decided by a Rhode Island court provides an illustration of the complexities that occur when parties attempt to use both contractual and statutory remedies for an alleged contract violation. In *University of Rhode Island v. University of Rhode Island Chapter of the American Association of University Professors*, 2001 R.I. Super. LEXIS 123 (Sup. Ct. R.I. 2001), the American Association of University Professors (AAUP), which represented faculty and librarians, objected to the university's decision to remove a library director's position from the bargaining unit without negotiating with the union. The AAUP proceeded under the contractual grievance process, which involved review of the grievance by the state Commissioner of Higher Education. The commissioner ruled in the university's favor, deciding that no contractual violation had occurred. Although the contract provided for arbitration as the next step of the grievance process, the AAUP instead filed an unfair labor practice with the Rhode Island Labor Board, which ruled that the university had committed an unfair labor practice by refusing to negotiate with the AAUP over the change in the position. The university turned to the court to resolve the contradiction between the two rulings.

Following federal law precedent interpreting the NLRA, the state court ruled that, when an action arises out of facts that would constitute both a contractual grievance and an unfair labor practice, the Labor Board should defer to the contractually created grievance process in order to effectuate the intent of the parties to the contract. The proper venue for the claim, said the court, was arbitration, which was the next step of the grievance process; the ruling of the Labor Board was an abuse of its discretion, according to the court, and was reversed.

4.5.5. Collective bargaining and antidiscrimination laws.

A body of case law is developing on the applicability of federal and state laws prohibiting discrimination in employment (see Section 5.2) to the collective bargaining process. Courts have interpreted federal labor relations law (Section 4.5.2) to impose on unions a duty to represent each employee fairly—without arbitrariness, discrimination, or bad faith (see *Vaca v. Sipes*, 386 U.S. 171 (1967)).[18] In addition, some antidiscrimination statutes, such as Title VII and the Age Discrimination in Employment Act (ADEA), apply directly to unions as well as employers. But these laws have left open several questions concerning the relationships between collective bargaining and antidiscrimination statutes. For instance, when employment discrimination problems are covered in the bargaining contract, can such coverage be construed to preclude employees from seeking other remedies under antidiscrimination statutes? If an employee resorts to a negotiated grievance procedure to resolve a discrimination dispute, can that employee then be precluded from using remedies provided under antidiscrimination statutes?

---

[18]Cases discussing the union's duty of fair representation are collected in Jerald J. Director, Annot., "Union's Liability in Damages for Refusal or Failure to Process Employee Grievance," 34 A.L.R.3d 884.

Most cases presenting such issues have arisen under Title VII of the Civil Rights Act of 1964 (see Section 5.2.1). The leading case is *Alexander v. Gardner-Denver Co.*, 415 U.S. 36 (1974). A discharged employee claimed that the discharge was motivated by racial discrimination, and he contested his discharge in a grievance proceeding provided under a collective bargaining contract. Having lost before an arbitrator in the grievance proceeding, and having had a complaint to the federal Equal Employment Opportunity Commission dismissed, the employee filed a Title VII action in federal district court. The district court, citing earlier Supreme Court precedent regarding the finality of arbitration awards, had held that the employee was bound by the arbitration decision and thus had no right to sue under Title VII. The U.S. Supreme Court reversed. The Court held that the employee could still sue under Title VII, which creates statutory rights "distinctly separate" from the contractual right to arbitration under the collective bargaining agreement. Such independent rights "are not waived either by inclusion of discrimination disputes within the collective bargaining agreement or by submitting the nondiscrimination claim to arbitration."

The fact that the grievance system is part of a collectively negotiated agreement, and not an individual employment contract, is important to the reasoning of *Gardner-Denver*. The Court noted in *Gardner-Denver* that it may be possible to waive a Title VII cause of action (and presumably actions under other statutes) "as part of a voluntary settlement" of a discrimination claim. The employee's consent to such a settlement would have to be "voluntary and knowing," however, and "mere resort to the arbitral forum to enforce contractual rights" could not constitute such a waiver (see 415 U.S. at 52). *Gardner-Denver* has also been applied to permit an employee covered by a contractual dispute resolution provision to litigate an alleged violation of Section 1983 (see Section 3.3.4) (*McDonald v. City of West Branch*, 466 U.S. 284 (1984)).

Subsequently, the U.S. Supreme Court addressed the waiver issue in *Gilmer v. Interstate-Johnson Lane*, 500 U.S. 20 (1991), a case involving the waiver of the right to a judicial forum in an individual employment contract rather than in a collective bargaining agreement, ruling that an express waiver in an individual employment contract was lawful. This case, and its progeny, are discussed in Section 4.3.6. The U.S. Supreme Court then revisited the issue of waivers in the collective bargaining context in *Wright v. Universal Maritime Service Corp.*, 525 U.S. 70 (1998). In *Wright*, the question was whether an arbitration clause in a collective bargaining agreement limited a bargaining unit member to an arbitral forum in seeking a remedy for an alleged violation of the Americans With Disabilities Act. In a unanimous opinion written by Justice Scalia, the Court determined that the arbitration clause in the agreement was too broad to constitute a "clear and unmistakable waiver" of the plaintiff's right to pursue a civil rights claim in court. Because the waiver was neither clear nor unmistakable with respect to the waiver of statutory rights, the Court found it unnecessary to reconcile *Gardner-Denver* and *Gilmer*.

Wright was applied to the higher education context in *Rogers v. New York University*, 220 F.3d 73 (2d Cir. 2000), in which the court ruled that the union did not waive plaintiff's right to bring an action for ADA and Family and

Medical Leave Act (FMLA) discrimination in federal court. (For a discussion of the arbitration of discrimination claims by unionized employees, see Susan A. Fitzgibbon, "After *Gardner-Denver, Gilmer,* and *Wright*: The Supreme Court's Next Arbitration Decision," 44 *St. Louis L.J.* 833 (2000).)

Given the holding of *Gardner-Denver,* some institutions have negotiated collective bargaining agreements with their faculty that contain a choice-of-forum provision. For example, the Board of Governors of the Illinois state colleges and universities negotiated with its faculty union a grievance procedure that gave the board the right to terminate grievance proceedings if a faculty member filed a discrimination claim with an administrative agency or in court. Raymond Lewis, a professor denied tenure, filed a grievance challenging the denial and, in order to preserve his rights under the federal Age Discrimination in Employment Act's (see Section 5.2.6) statute of limitations, filed a charge with the EEOC. The board terminated the grievance proceedings, citing the contractual provision. The EEOC filed an age discrimination lawsuit against the board, asserting that this provision constituted retaliation for exercising rights under the ADEA, which is forbidden by Section 4(d) of the Act (29 U.S.C. § 628(d)). After a series of lower court opinions resulting in victory for the board, the U.S. Court of Appeals for the Seventh Circuit reversed, agreeing with the EEOC's position. In *EEOC v. Board of Governors of State Colleges and Universities,* 957 F.2d 424 (7th Cir. 1992), the court, citing *Gardner-Denver,* reaffirmed the right of employees to overlapping contractual and statutory remedies and called the contractual provision "discriminatory on its face" (957 F.2d at 431).

Another situation where Title VII protections may conflict with the rights of the union as exclusive bargaining agent arises in the clash between Title VII's prohibition against religious discrimination and the union's right to collect an agency fee from nonmembers. Robert Roesser, an associate professor of electrical engineering at the University of Detroit, refused to pay his agency fee to the local union because, as a Catholic, he objected to the pro-choice position on abortion taken by the state union and the national union (the National Education Association). According to the university's contract with the union, nonpayment of the agency fee was grounds for termination, and Roesser was discharged.

Roesser filed a complaint with the EEOC, which sued both the union and the university on his behalf. The EEOC claimed that, under Title VII, the union was required to make a reasonable accommodation to Roesser's religious objections unless the accommodation posed an undue hardship (see Section 5.3.6). Roesser had offered to donate to a charity either the entire agency fee or the portion of the fee that was sent to the state and national unions. The union refused, but countered with the suggestion that the amount of the agency fee used for all social and political issues generally, including pro-choice and other issues, be deducted. Roesser refused because he did not want to be associated in any way with the state or national union (adding a First Amendment issue to the Title VII litigation).

The federal district court granted summary judgment to the union and the university, ruling that the union's accommodation was reasonable and that

Roesser's proposal imposed undue hardship on the union. That ruling was overturned by the U.S. Court of Appeals for the Sixth Circuit (*EEOC v. University of Detroit*, 701 F. Supp. 1326 (E.D. Mich. 1988), *reversed and remanded*, 904 F.2d 331 (6th Cir. 1990)). The appellate court stated that Roesser's objection to the agency fee had two prongs, only one of which the district court had recognized. Roesser had objected to both the contribution to and the association with the state and national unions because of their position on abortion; the district court had ruled only on the contribution issue and had not addressed the association issue.

In remanding the case, the appeals court asked the lower court to determine whether the associational prong of Roesser's objection could be reasonably accommodated without undue hardship to the union. In *dicta*, the appeals court suggested that Roesser might be required to pay the entire fee but that no portion of his fee would be sent to either the state or the national union, since he had stated no objection to the activities of the local union.

Thus, collective bargaining does not provide an occasion for postsecondary administrators to lessen their attention to the institution's Title VII responsibilities or its responsibilities under other antidiscrimination and civil rights laws. In many instances, faculty members can avail themselves of rights and remedies both under the bargaining agreement and under civil rights statutes.

4.5.6. Students and collective bargaining.

Although colleges and universities have traditionally regarded student-employees as students first who happen to work part or full time as institutional employees, state and federal labor law has been interpreted to include student-employees within the protections of the collective bargaining laws. Labor boards and courts have been asked to determine whether instructional, research, or clinical duties create an employment relationship or, instead, are part of an educational program that the student undertakes as student rather than employee.

Graduate assistants at public colleges and universities have enjoyed the protection of public sector bargaining laws for decades; graduate assistants at the University of Wisconsin-Madison have been unionized since 1969 (see Hurd, Foster, & Hillman, *Directory of Faculty Contracts* (National Center for the Study of Collective Bargaining in Higher Education and the Professions, 1997)). For example, in *Regents of the University of California v. Public Employment Relations Board*, 224 Cal. Rptr. 631 (Cal. 1986), the Supreme Court of California ruled that medical residents at University of California hospitals were employees and thus were permitted to bargain. After considering how much time the residents spent in direct patient care, how much supervision they received, and whether they had the "indicia" of employment, the court concluded that their educational goals were subordinate to the services they performed for the hospitals. A similar result was reached in *University Hospital, University of Cincinnati College of Medicine v. State Employment Relations Board*, 587 N.E.2d 835 (Ohio 1992). More recently, teaching assistants at Temple University were found to be employees entitled to bargaining rights by the Pennsylvania Labor Relations Board (*In the Matter of the Employees of Temple University*,

No. PERA-R-99–58-E (Pa. Labor Relations Bd. 2000)), which relied on the analysis of the NLRB in the *Boston Medical Center* case (discussed below). Graduate teaching assistants at the eight campuses of the University of California system voted to unionize after a favorable ruling by California's Public Employment Relations Board ("Footnotes," *Chron. Higher Educ.*, July 2, 1999, A12), and a union representing graduate assistants, tutors, and graders at the California State University system has been recognized by the California state labor board (Scott Smallwood, "Unions for Graduate Students Advance in California, New York, and Washington," *Chron. High. Educ.*, March 22, 2004, available at http://chronicle.com/daily/2004/03/2004032203n.htm). But in Illinois, where the state's Educational Labor Relations Act (115 ILCS 5/2(b)) specifically excludes students from the definition of "employee," only those graduate students whose tasks were not related to their education were permitted to organize, effectively excluding most teaching and research assistants (*Graduate Employees Organization v. Illinois Educational Labor Relations Board*, 733 N.E.2d 759 (Ct. App. Ill., 1st Dist.), *app. denied*, 738 N.E.2d 925 (Ill. 2000)).

In the private sector, however, the NLRB had at first refused to extend bargaining rights to student-employees. For example, in *Physicians National House Staff Ass'n. v. Fanning*, 642 F.2d 492 (D.C. Cir. 1980), the court held that interns, residents, and clinical fellows on staffs belonging to the association were "primarily students" and thus not covered by federal collective bargaining law. The Board reversed itself, however, in *Boston Medical Center Corp.*, 330 N.L.R.B. No. 30 (November 26, 1999), ruling that interns, residents, and holders of fellowships at the medical center met the NLRA's definition of employee because they worked for the employer, they were compensated for their services, and they provided direct patient care.

Subsequently, the Board ruled that graduate teaching assistants at Yale University were protected by the NLRA when they engaged in protected activity (*Yale University*, 330 N.L.R.B. No. 28 (November 29, 1999)), and that graduate teaching assistants at New York University met the definition of "employee" under the NLRA and thus were protected (*New York University*, 332 N.L.R.B. No. 111 (October 31, 2000)). The Board rejected the university's argument that giving bargaining rights to graduate students would infringe on the university's academic freedom, noting that faculty had been bargaining with their institutional employers since 1971 without limiting academic freedom.

Following the New York University precedent, a regional director of the NLRB ruled that teaching and research assistants could unionize at Brown University (*Brown University*, Case No. 1-RC-21368, October 16, 2001), and another regional director ruled that teaching and research assistants, including some undergraduate students, at Columbia University were employees protected by the NLRA (*Trustees of Columbia University in the City of New York*, Case No. 2-RC-22358, February 12, 2002). But in mid-2004, in *Brown University and International Union, United Automobile, Aerospace and Agricultural Implement Workers of* America, 342 N.L.R.B. No. 42 (July 13, 2004), the full National Labor Board, in a 3-to-2 ruling, overruled its earlier decision in *New York University* and determined that graduate assistants are students, not employees, and thus are not protected by the NLRA. The majority reasoned that the relationship between Brown and its graduate student assistants was primarily educational, as only students were given the opportunity to become teaching or research assistants, and most of Brown's academic departments required their doctoral students to teach as a condition of earning the Ph.D.

In another development, the first unit of undergraduate student residence hall advisors seeking to bargain with a college has been certified by the Massachusetts Labor Relations Commission. The commission noted that resident advisors at the University of Massachusetts-Amherst had signed an employment contract with the university, worked an average of twenty hours per week, and received W-2 forms and paychecks. The commission's ruling cleared the way for a unionization vote by the resident advisors (*Board of Trustees of the University of Massachusetts and United Auto, Aerospace and Agricultural Implement Workers*, Case No. SCR-01–2246, January 18, 2002). A majority of the resident assistants voted to unionize (Eric Hoover, "Resident Assistants at U. of Massachusetts at Amherst Vote to Unionize," *Chron. Higher Educ.*, March 2, 2002, available at http://chronicle.com/daily/2002/03/2002030603n.htm).

(For a review of graduate student organizing and a list of those institutions at which graduate teaching assistant unions have been recognized, see Scott Smallwood, "Success and New Hurdles for T.A. Unions," *Chron. Higher Educ.*, July 6, 2001, A10–A12. For an analysis of the legal issues, see Grant M. Hayden, "'The University Works Because We Do': Collective Bargaining Rights for Graduate Assistants," 69 *Fordham L. Rev.* 1233 (2001); and Joshua Rowland, Note, "'Forecasts of Doom': The Dubious Threat of Graduate Teaching Assistant Collective Bargaining to Academic Freedom," 42 *Boston College L. Rev.* 941 (2001).)

Sec. 4.6. Other Employee Protections

4.6.1. Occupational Safety and Health Act. Private postsecondary institutions must conform to the federal Occupational Safety and Health Act of 1970 (OSHA) (29 U.S.C. § 651 *et seq.*). Under this Act, a private institution must "furnish to each of [its] employees employment and a place of employment which are free from recognized hazards that are causing or are likely to cause death or serious physical harm" (29 U.S.C. § 654) (the "general duty clause"). Institutions must also comply with health and safety standards promulgated by the U.S. Secretary of Labor (§ 665). Violations may result in fines or imprisonment (§ 666). OSHA prohibits retaliation against an employee for filing a complaint with the Occupational Safety and Health Administration regarding a potentially unsafe workplace.[19]

Regulations of particular importance to higher education institutions include the Hazard Communication Standard (29 C.F.R. § 1910.1200), which requires employers to provide information and training to their workers about the hazards of the substances with which they are working. "Hazardous

---

[19]Cases and authorities are collected in Glenn A. Guarino, Annot., "Prohibition of Discrimination Against, or Discharge of, Employee Because of Exercise of Right Afforded by Occupational Safety and Health Act, Under § 11(c)(1) of the Act (29 U.S.C.S. § 660(c)(1))," 66 A.L.R. Fed. 650.

substances" are broadly defined. OSHA standards also regulate the handling of blood and other body fluids (29 C.F.R. § 1910.1030) as well as chemicals. Research laboratories are required to develop a "chemical hygiene plan" and to specify work procedures and policies in writing (29 C.F.R. § 1910.1450). Employers are also required to maintain records of all "lost-time" injuries, and are subject to fines if records are incomplete (29 U.S.C. § 657(c)). In the higher education context, science laboratories, art rooms, hospitals, and maintenance shops are particular targets for enforcement of OSHA regulations.

The original OSHA rule on record keeping was promulgated in 1971, and required all employers subject to OSHA to report any work-related accident resulting in either a fatality or the hospitalization of three or more workers. In 2001, OSHA issued a final rule designed to provide improved information about occupational illnesses and injuries, while simultaneously making the record-keeping system simpler and more accessible to workers. The revised final rule, which can be found at 66 Fed. Reg. 5916 (January 19, 2001), also provides for privacy protections for the documents used to record work-related injuries.

Violations of the record-keeping and reporting regulations can lead to citations, fines, and litigation. For example, in *Kaspar Wire Works, Inc. v. Sec'y of Labor*, 268 F.3d 1123 (D.C. Cir. 2001), the court upheld a finding by OSHA that the company's failure to record and report several hundred work-related injuries and illnesses was willful, and also upheld a fine of $224,000. Under OSHA, a violation may be shown to be "willful" if the employer intentionally disregarded the law's requirements; malice need not be proven.

An employee's repeated failure to follow safety procedures or to wear OSHA-required safety gear may provide grounds for discipline or termination. For example, in *Taylor v. St. Vincent's Medical Center*, 1998 U.S. App. LEXIS 7991 (6th Cir. 1998) (unpublished), an appellate court affirmed an award of summary judgment in favor of a hospital that had fired an X-ray technician for failing to wear the OSHA-required safety gear, rejecting the technician's discrimination, contract, and tort claims. To prevail in such cases, it is important that the employer document the employee's failures. Similarly, if an employee is injured because of his or her refusal to wear the required gear, it is important for the employer to document its discipline of the employee for refusing to follow OSHA standards, in order to avoid an OSHA citation.

The Act does not preempt an employee's right to pursue civil actions or other remedies under state laws (§ 653(b)(4)), but it does preempt some overlapping state laws. For example, many states have passed "right-to-know" laws that require employers to disclose the hazardous substances used at the workplace to employees, public safety agencies (such as the local fire department), and the general public. If these laws overlap or conflict with OSHA, however, they are subject to preemption challenges. For example, in *New Jersey Chamber of Commerce v. Hughey*, 774 F.2d 587 (3d Cir. 1985), the court held that New Jersey's Right-to-Know Law was preempted by OSHA, but only with regard to the regulation of safety in the workplace; provisions requiring disclosure to public safety agencies and the general public were not preempted.

OSHA provides that states with safety and enforcement plans approved by OSHA may assume responsibility for workplace safety and health (29 U.S.C.

§ 667). But approval must precede a state's attempt to fashion its own occupational safety and health laws. For example, the U.S. Supreme Court struck portions of two Illinois laws that established training and examination requirements for workers at certain hazardous waste facilities (*Gade v. National Solid Waste Management Ass'n.*, 505 U.S. 88 (1992)). Illinois did not have an OSHA-approved state plan, and the Court ruled that "a state law requirement that directly, substantially and specifically regulates occupational safety and health" is preempted by OSHA even if the state law has another nonoccupational purpose. Unless the state has an OSHA-approved state plan, the Court said, OSHA impliedly preempts any state regulation of an occupational safety and health issue where a federal standard has been established.

Public institutions of higher education are not subject to OSHA regulation, but they are subject to state occupational safety and health laws, many of which have used OSHA as a model.[20] For those states with OSHA-approved plans, state standards for both public and private employers must be at or above the level of federal OSHA protection. In states without OSHA-approved plans, the OSHA standard may be used to set tort standards of care in negligence suits against public employers.

Several of the federal environmental laws make "knowing endangerment" of a worker a felony (see Section 13.2.10). (For further information, see R. Schwartz, Comment, "Criminalizing Occupational Safety Violations: The Use of 'Knowing Endangerment' Statutes to Punish Employers Who Maintain Toxic Working Conditions," 14 *Harvard Environmental L. Rev.* 487 (1990).) In recent years, OSHA and the Environmental Protection Agency (EPA) have been coordinating enforcement and sharing information. (The Thompson entry in the Selected Annotated Bibliography for this Section discusses the coordination of effort between these two agencies.)

During the Clinton administration, OSHA attempted to promulgate an "ergonomic" standard that would require employers to organize work and purchase equipment that would minimize repetitive strain injuries for workers. The proposed regulation drew heavy criticism from employers, and it was withdrawn by the Bush administration. In early 2002, the Bush administration announced that OSHA would work with joint employer-employee groups to develop "voluntary" standards to reduce musculoskeletal disorders in industries in which such injuries are numerous, such as in health care organizations. Administrators and counsel should monitor developments in this area, particularly at institutions with medical schools and/or hospitals.

4.6.2. Fair Labor Standards Act. The Fair Labor Standards Act (FLSA), 29 U.S.C. § 201 *et seq.*, establishes the minimum hourly wage and the piecework rates as well as overtime pay requirements for certain nonsupervisory employees. In situations where an applicable state law establishes a minimum

---

[20]Whether a state-related institution (a formerly private institution that receives substantial public funding) is covered by OSHA may be difficult to determine. For cases related to this issue, see Kristine Cordier Karnezis, Annot., "Who Is 'Employer' for Purposes of Occupational Safety and Health Act (29 U.S.C. §§ 651 *et seq.*)," 153 A.L.R. Fed. 303.

wage rate that conflicts with the federal standard, the higher rate must prevail (29 U.S.C. § 218). The law does not apply to independent contractors.[21] The law also requires that records be kept of the hours worked by nonexempt employees and the compensation paid therefor.

The FLSA is enforced by the Wage and Hour Division of the U.S. Department of Labor. The Secretary of Labor has two years from the date of the violation to file an enforcement action, but the statute provides that if the violation is "willful," the limitations period is extended to three years (29 U.S.C. § 255(a)). A violation is "willful" if the employer "knew or showed reckless disregard for the matter of whether its conduct was prohibited by the FLSA" (*McLaughlin v. Richland Shoe Co.*, 486 U.S. 128 (1988)).

The FLSA specifically exempts employees employed as bona fide executive, administrative, professional, or outside sales employees from the minimum wage and maximum hour requirements (29 U.S.C. § 213(a)(1)). Another section, 29 U.S.C. § 213(a)(17), also exempts certain computer employees. The Department of Labor has revised the long-standing regulations implementing this provision (29 C.F.R. Part 541); the new regulations became effective on August 23, 2004. The regulations establish the conditions of employment that must exist before an employer may consider an employee to be an exempt "executive," "administrative," "professional," or an exempt sales employee and state clearly that an individual's job title does not determine exempt status. In addition to meeting one of these tests, the employee must be paid a salary of at least $455 per week.

Of particular interest to higher education, the term "administrative" includes persons "whose primary duty is performing administrative functions directly related to academic instruction or training in an educational establishment or department or subdivision thereof" (29 C.F.R. § 541.202(a)(2)) and who meet the other conditions set by the regulations. Furthermore, the employee's primary duty must involve the "exercise of discretion and independent judgment with respect to matters of significance" (29 C.F.R. § 541.202(a)). The term "professional" includes any person whose primary duty is the performance of work "requiring knowledge of an advanced type in a field of science or learning customarily acquired by a prolonged course of specialized intellectual instruction [the 'learned professional' exemption]; or requiring invention, imagination, originality or talent in a recognized field of artistic or creative endeavor [the 'creative professional' exemption]" (29 C.F.R. § 541.300(a)(2)). A teacher who meets the regulations' definition of "teaching, tutoring, instructing, or lecturing . . . and who [is] employed and engaged in this activity as a teacher in the . . . educational establishment or institution by which he is employed" (29 C.F.R. § 541.303(a)) is also considered an exempt professional. Professionals also must meet the regulations'

---

[21]For analysis of how an individual's status as independent contractor or employee is determined under the FLSA, see Debra T. Landis, Annot., "Determination of 'Independent Contractor' and 'Employee' Status for Purposes of § 3(e)(1) of the Fair Labor Standards Act (29 U.S.C.S. § 203(e)(1))," 51 A.L.R. Fed. 702.

other conditions, except that teachers need not meet the regulations' salary test (29 C.F.R. § 541.303(d)).

Employees who work in certain computer-related jobs may be exempt from the FLSA. The regulations specify that "computer systems analysts, computer programmers, software engineers or other similarly skilled workers in the computer field are eligible for exemption as professionals" (29 C.F.R. § 541.400(a)) as long as they perform one or more of a series of skilled duties that are detailed in § 541.400.

Under the revised regulations, certain athletic trainers are exempt professionals.

> Athletic trainers who have successfully completed four academic years of pre-professional and professional study in a specialized curriculum accredited by the Commission on Accreditation of Allied Health Education Programs and who are certified by the Board of Certification of the National Athletic Trainers Association Board of Certification generally meet the duties requirements for the learned professional exemption [29 C.F.R.§ 541.301(e)(8)].

Because the revised regulations have modified the previous tests for exemptions under the FLSA, care should be taken when determining whether any particular employee is exempt from the Act. The U.S. Department of Labor has posted on its Web site "Fair Pay Fact Sheets" that explain the revised regulations and provide examples of employees who meet and who do not meet the new tests (http://www.dol.gov/esa/regs/compliance/whd/fairpay/fs17a_overview.htm).

The FLSA has always applied to most private postsecondary institutions, but the Act's application to public postsecondary institutions has been the subject of historical turmoil. After several conflicting rulings by the U.S. Supreme Court, Congress amended the FLSA to limit the application of its overtime requirements. State and local government employers, including public postsecondary institutions, may provide compensatory leave in lieu of overtime compensation (Pub. L. No. 99-150, codified at 29 U.S.C. §§ 207(o) and (p)). The amendments also discuss the treatment of volunteers who perform services for a public agency. Regulations implementing these amendments are found at 29 C.F.R. Part 553. The rules include a special limited exemption for public employees in executive, administrative, or professional jobs: public employers will not risk having to pay overtime to these employees if they are occasionally paid on an hourly rather than on a salary basis. This rule was necessary to protect the exemption for public employees covered by public pay systems that reduce the pay of otherwise-exempt employees for partial day absences when paid leave is not used to cover such absences, and for deductions due to budget-required furloughs. The rule can be found at 29 C.F.R. § 541.710. (For a critique of the "salary basis" test, see Garrett Reid Krueger, "Straight-Time Overtime and Salary Basis: Reform of the Fair Labor Standards Act," 70 *Wash. L. Rev.* 1097 (1995).)

A public employer's policy of requiring that compensatory time off be taken in lieu of cash payment for overtime was upheld by the U.S. Supreme Court. In *Christensen v. Harris County,* 529 U.S. 576 (2000), the Court ruled that nothing in the law prohibited a public employer from requiring its employees to schedule time off in order to reduce the amount of accrued compensatory time and thus avoid having to compensate employees for unused compensatory time.

The FLSA has no exemption for religiously affiliated institutions, so they must also comply with this law. The U.S. Supreme Court ruled in *Alamo Foundation v. Secretary of Labor,* 471 U.S. 290 (1985), that religious organizations engaged in commercial activities (such as selling books)—if those activities met the Act's "enterprise" and "economic reality" tests—were subject to minimum wage and overtime requirements. The Court also ruled that neither the payment requirements nor the record-keeping provisions violated the First Amendment establishment clause or the free exercise clause; the record-keeping requirement applied only to the organization's business activities, not to its religious ones, and if individuals did not wish to receive wages, they could donate them back to the organization. The Fourth Circuit, following *Alamo,* ruled that a church-related elementary school was subject to the minimum wage and equal pay provisions of the FLSA (*Dole v. Shenandoah Baptist Church,* 899 F.2d 1389 (4th Cir. 1990)). Thus, the secular activities of a religiously affiliated college or university are subject to FLSA requirements.

Full-time faculty are typically exempt from the FLSA's overtime protections under the professional exemption. For example, in *Wong-Opasi v. Tennessee State University,* 2000 U.S. App. LEXIS 21242 (6th Cir. 2000) (unpublished), decided under the previous regulations, the court dismissed a faculty member's claim that she was entitled to overtime pay. Because she "falls within the advanced type of study specifically contemplated by the professional exemption," the court would not entertain her claim.

The revised regulations may change formerly exempt employees to nonexempt status, particularly if they do not exercise independent judgment. For example, the regulations are silent on whether assistant athletic coaches or admissions counselors are exempt or nonexempt. If admissions counselors exercise independent judgment, they may be exempt under the "general administrative employee exemption" (29 C.F.R. § 541.202). If, however, they do not exercise independent judgment, they may be covered by the law's overtime provisions. With respect to assistant coaches, unless they also teach for a substantial part of their responsibilities, they may not fall into the teacher exemption (29 C.F.R. § 541.303). The "academic administrative" exemption requires that the individual's work be "directly related to academic instruction or training," which would not apply to most assistant coaches unless they tutor students or provide other academic services, such as academic counseling. (For guidance on this complicated issue, see "Payment of Assistant Coaches Under Federal Overtime Laws," prepared by the law firm of Gibson, Dunn & Crutcher, August 2004, available at http://www.nacua.org.)

Even more basic than whether one is a professional, executive, or administrative employee is the question of whether one can be classified as an employee at all. In *Marshall v. Regis Educational Corp.,* 666 F.2d 1324 (10th Cir. 1981), the Secretary of Labor contended that the college's student residence hall assistants (RAs) were "employees" within the meaning of the Act and therefore must be paid the prescribed minimum wage. The college argued that its RAs were not employees and that, even if they were, application of the Act to these RAs would violate the college's academic freedom protected by the First Amendment. Affirming the district court, the appellate court accepted the college's first argument and declined to consider the second. The court focused on the unique circumstances of academic life, concluding that resident assistants performed an educational function as well as supervising students in residence halls.

Thus, said the court, the RAs were not employees because they were "legally indistinguishable from athletes and leaders in student government who received financial aid," categories of students who had previously been found not to be employees. The court warned that "[t]here are undoubtedly campus positions which can be filled by students and which require compliance with the FLSA. Students working in the bookstore selling books, working with maintenance, painting walls, etc., could arguably be 'employees'" (666 F.2d at 1326–28). But in *Alabama A&M University v. King,* 643 So. 2d 1366 (Ala. Ct. Civ. App. 1994), the court not only held that residence hall counselors were employees but refused to apply the administrative exemption to them, making them eligible for overtime payments if they worked more than forty hours per week.[22] Because the employees' duties involved making sure that rooms were clean, securing the building after the residence hall closed, and checking for repairs, the court ruled that their duties did not meet the test for the administrative exemption.

Private causes of action for employees to enforce FLSA are authorized by 29 U.S.C. § 216(b); see also 29 U.S.C. § 203(x). In recent years, controversy has arisen regarding use of this private cause of action to sue states and state agencies and institutions. In *Alden v. Maine* (discussed in Section 13.1.6), the U.S. Supreme Court held that states are immune from the FLSA suits of their employees whether brought in federal or in state court. As a result of this ruling, state colleges and universities may no longer be sued by their employees in state or federal court for FLSA violations unless they have expressly consented to such litigation. However, the U.S. Department of Labor can still sue public colleges and states for FLSA violations.

In another opinion that has significance for both public and private colleges, *Auer v. Robbins,* 519 U.S. 452 (1997), the U.S. Supreme Court addressed the claim of several police officers that they were owed overtime pay under the FLSA. The employer argued that the officers were exempt from the overtime pay requirements, in part because they were paid a salary. Under both the previous and the revised regulations implementing the FLSA, 29 C.F.R. § 541.602, an employee is considered to be salaried if "he regularly receives each pay period on a weekly, or less frequent basis, a predetermined amount constituting all or part of his compensation, which amount is not subject to reduction because

---

[22]In 1994 the Wage-Hour Administrator for the U.S. Department of Labor (DOL) issued an opinion letter stating that the DOL would not seek to apply the FLSA to graduate research assistants (as opposed to graduate teaching assistants or residence hall advisors). Given the NLRB's ruling in *Brown University,* discussed in Section 4.5.6 of this book, and the fact that the definition of "employee" has not changed either in the law or the revised regulations, it appears that the 1994 opinion letter remains valid.

of variations in the quality or quantity of the work performed" (29 C.F.R. § 541.602(a)). Because one police officer had been disciplined by having his salary reduced, the other police officers claimed that the "salary basis" test did not apply to them and they were eligible for overtime pay. Under the revised regulations, 29 C.F.R. § 541.603(c), employers who have imposed pay deductions on salaried employees may reimburse those employees and promise to comply with the regulation in the future, as long as the deductions were made inadvertently or for reasons other than lack of work. In a unanimous opinion by Justice Scalia, the Court upheld the regulations as reasonable and their application to public sector employees as appropriate. Of interest to colleges and universities is the portion of the opinion that discusses the implications of an employer practice or policy of making deductions from the pay of salaried employees for disciplinary reasons. If such a practice or policy exists, this may result in making all the employees subject to the policy qualified for overtime pay under the FLSA, as well as liquidated damages.

Although the "salary test" is still in effect, a federal circuit court has ruled that it is inapplicable when an otherwise exempt employee is paid on an hourly basis for working part time under the provisions of the Family and Medical Leave Act (see Section 4.6.4). In *Rowe v. Laidlaw Transit, Inc.,* 244 F.3d 1115 (9th Cir. 2001), the court ruled that an employer's compliance with the FMLA did not negatively affect an employee's exempt status, as provided in the FMLA regulations.

An issue that has received considerable judicial attention is whether employees who are "on call" and must be available to their employers within a specific period of time after being called in to work must be paid for the time they are "on call." Because these cases are very fact-specific, bright-line rules are difficult to determine. However, if the employee's time is spent predominantly for the benefit of the employer, the employee must be paid; if the employee can use the time for a variety of activities unrelated to the needs of the employer, then the employee will not be paid. (For a discussion of the on-call doctrine as applied to nurses employed by a hospital, see *Reimer v. Champion Healthcare,* 258 F.3d 720 (8th Cir. 2001).)

Ruling on a similar issue, a federal district court refused to grant Howard University's motion for summary judgment in a case involving an overtime claim by campus police officers. The police officers were paid for an eight-hour shift that did not include a paid meal break. The officers were permitted to leave campus for a thirty-minute meal break as long as they were available to respond to a campus emergency during that time and as long as they checked their weapons and equipment at the campus police station before leaving campus. The officers argued that the weapon and equipment checking requirements were so time consuming that it was virtually impossible for them to leave campus for their meal break, and asked to be paid for the additional thirty minutes that they were "required" to be on campus. The court ordered a trial on the matter (*Summers v. Howard University,* 127 F. Supp. 2d 27 (D.D.C. 2000)). The parties then entered a settlement agreement, but the university moved to vacate the settlement agreement, and refused to pay the damages and fees calculated by a special master appointed under the agreement, because the employees had filed a second lawsuit. The trial court refused to vacate the consent decree, and the appellate court affirmed (374 F.3d 1188 (D.C. Cir. 2004)), ruling that the university had not been prejudiced by the second lawsuit (which was subsequently dismissed). The court affirmed the lower court's order that the university pay the back wages and liquidated damages as calculated by the special master.

Although the FLSA requires employers to pay nonexempt workers for hours "worked," the Portal to Portal Act provides that employees need not be paid for activities that are "preliminary or postliminary" to actual work (29 U.S.C. § 254(a)(2)). For example, in *Bienkowski v. Northeastern University*, 285 F.3d 138 (1st Cir. 2002), a federal appellate court ruled that the time that police officers spent in emergency medical technician training was not work time, and rejected the plaintiffs' argument that they should have been paid overtime for attending these required sessions. The court stated that, during these mandatory training sessions, the plaintiffs were performing no "work" for the university. But in *IBP, Inc. v. Alvarez*, 126 S. Ct. 514 (2005), the U.S. Supreme Court ruled that time spent by workers "donning and doffing" protective clothing, as well as time spent walking from the changing area to the work area, was "integral and indispensable" to the employees' principal activity, and thus was compensable.

The FLSA includes a provision that prohibits retaliation against an employee who exercises rights provided for by the law (29 U.S.C. § 215). Individuals who engage in such retaliation may be held individually liable for FLSA violations. The Supreme Court of Colorado ruled that state employees do not enjoy sovereign immunity from individual liability under this FLSA provision (*Middleton v. Hartman*, 45 P.3d 721 (Colo. 2002)).

Class action litigation involving alleged violations of the FLSA has increased sharply over the past several years, and may be brought by either the Department of Labor or by private plaintiffs. In fact, the number of FLSA class actions exceeded the number of employment discrimination class actions in 2001 and 2002 (see Michael Orey, "Lawsuits Abound from Workers Seeking Overtime Pay," *Wall Street Journal*, May 30, 2002, p. B-1). In July 2004, after the Department of Labor filed a class action suit against the University of Phoenix for FLSA violations, the university entered an agreement with the agency to pay up to $3.5 million in claims for overtime pay by 1,700 current and former admissions counselors (*BNA Workplace Law Report*, Vol. 2, no. 31, July 30, 2004). (For advice on avoiding collective actions under the FLSA, see Terrence H. Murphy, "Special FLSA Issues for College and Universities," outline prepared for the 2004 Annual Conference of the National Association of College and University Attorneys, and available at http://www.nacua.org.)

4.6.3. *Employee Retirement Income Security Act.* The Employee
Retirement Income Security Act of 1974 (known as ERISA or the Pension Reform Act) establishes "standards of conduct, responsibility, and obligation for fiduciaries of employee benefit plans" (29 U.S.C. § 1001(b)). The terms "employee benefit plan" and "employee pension plan" are defined to encompass various health benefits, death benefits, disability benefits, unemployment benefits, retirement plans, and income deferral programs (29 U.S.C. § 1002(1) and (2)). The ERISA

requirements for the creation and management of these plans are codified partly in the federal tax law (26 U.S.C. § 401 *et seq.*) and partly in the federal labor law (29 U.S.C. § 1001 *et seq.*). These requirements apply only to private postsecondary institutions. The plans of public institutions are excluded from coverage as "governmental plan(s)" under 29 U.S.C. § 1002(32) and 26 U.S.C. § 414(d).[23]

The ERISA standards have been construed as minimum federal standards designed to curb the funding and disclosure abuses of employee pension and benefit plans (*Wadsworth v. Whaland,* 562 F.2d 70 (1st Cir. 1977)). Rules and regulations have been issued covering reporting and disclosure requirements, minimum standards of conduct, and fiduciary responsibilities (see 29 C.F.R. Parts 2510, 2520, 2530, & 2550). Interpretive bulletins explaining the Act have also been issued and reprinted at 29 C.F.R. Part 2509. Rules and regulations for group health plans are found at 29 C.F.R. Part 2590.

Some special rules apply to benefit plans for teachers and other employees of tax-exempt educational institutions. Under certain circumstances, for instance, such employees may delay their participation in a benefit plan until they reach the age of twenty-six (26 U.S.C. § 410(a)(1)(B)(ii); 29 U.S.C. § 1052(a)(1)(B)(ii)).

ERISA requirements are numerous and complex; a few are offered here for purposes of illustration only. For example, the Consolidated Omnibus Budget Reconciliation Act of 1986 (COBRA) (Title X, Pub. L. No. 99-272, 100 Stat. 222 (1986)) amended ERISA to require employers to permit employees who leave employment on good terms (for example, by retirement, voluntary resignations, or layoffs) to continue medical insurance coverage at their own expense at approximately the employer's group rate for eighteen months; their dependents have similar rights upon divorce or a child's emancipation. Regulations related to continuing health care coverage under COBRA are found at 29 C.F.R. § 2590.606 1–4; the final rule was published at 69 Fed. Reg. 30084 (May 26, 2004). Other amendments to ERISA in the Retirement Equity Act of 1984 (98 Stat. 1426 *et seq.*) protect employees' pension benefits during periods of maternity or paternity leave (§ 102(e)); establish requirements for the provision, by pension plans, of joint and survivor annuities and preretirement survivor annuities for surviving spouses of employees (§ 103); and establish rules for the assignment of rights to pension benefits in divorce proceedings (§ 104).

Another rule protects employers from lawsuits by workers who are dissatisfied with the return on their pension funds' investments. That rule, codified at 29 C.F.R. § 2550.404(c)(1), offers this protection if the employer fulfills the following conditions: the participant or beneficiary must have the opportunity under the plan to (1) choose from at least three investment alternatives; (2) give investment instruction to the plan administrator on a frequent basis; (3) diversify investments at least once every quarter; and (4) obtain information to make informed investment decisions.

---

[23]Only those public colleges that are an "agency or instrumentality" of a state or its political subdivisions are exempt from ERISA. Thus, a public college established by state law would meet this test, but a public college that was chartered as a nonprofit corporation might not. *Zarilla v. Reading Area Community College,* 1999 U.S. Dist. LEXIS 10448 (E.D. Pa. 1999) (unpublished).

With various listed exceptions, ERISA supersedes any and all state laws "insofar as they may now or hereinafter relate to any employee benefit plan" subject to the ERISA statute (29 U.S.C. § 1144(a)). The exceptions are for state laws regulating insurance, banking, or securities, and state criminal laws, none of which are superseded by ERISA (29 U.S.C. § 1144(b)). These provisions, and their relation to other provisions in the statute, have been the subject of varying interpretations by the courts, and it has often proved difficult in particular cases to determine when ERISA preempts state law. (See generally D. Gregory, "The Scope of ERISA Preemption of State Law: A Study in Effective Federalism," 48 *U. Pitt. L. Rev.* 427 (1987).) The U.S. Supreme Court has ruled that ERISA preempts common law contract or tort claims relating to employee benefits that are brought in state court, and that such claims may be removed to federal court and tried under ERISA (*Metropolitan Life Insurance v. Taylor,* 481 U.S. 58 (1987)). Remedies for ERISA violations, if not specified in the statute, have been developed under federal common law (see S. H. Thomsen & W. M. Smith, "Developments in Common-Law Remedies Under ERISA," 27 *Tort & Insurance L.J.* 750 (1992)).

The relationship between ERISA and state and federal disability discrimination laws has yet to be resolved. In *McGann v. H&H Music Co.,* 946 F.2d 401 (5th Cir. 1992), the court ruled that ERISA did not limit an employer's right to change or terminate a group health insurance plan to exclude coverage of certain diseases (in this case, AIDS). Another federal appellate court ruled that insurance caps for HIV-related diseases did not violate ERISA (*Owens v. Storehouse,* 984 F.2d 394 (11th Cir. 1993)). However, refusal to include certain diseases within medical insurance coverage may violate the Americans With Disabilities Act. The EEOC has published enforcement guidance on the circumstances under which employer-provided health insurance policy provisions may violate the ADA. Although the guidance is "interim," it had not been withdrawn or superseded as of late 2005. (See *Interim Enforcement Guidance on the Application of the Americans With Disabilities Act of 1990 to Disability-Based Distinctions in Employer Provided Health Insurance* (June 8, 1993) (available at http://eeoc.gov/ada/adadocs/html).)

As a result of the evolving nature of the relationship between ERISA and related state laws, as well as the overall complexity of this law and its regulations and the pace of ERISA developments, private institutions should obtain assistance from experienced ERISA counsel.

4.6.4. Family and Medical Leave Act.

The Family and Medical Leave Act (FMLA) of 1993 (Pub. L. No. 103-3, codified at 29 U.S.C. §§ 2601 *et seq.*) applies to all organizations that have employed fifty or more employees, within a radius of 75 miles, for each working day during each of twenty or more weeks in the preceding year. Employees who qualify may take up to twelve weeks of unpaid leave in any twelve-month period for the following:

1. The birth of a child and its care during the first year
2. The adoption of a child or placement in the employee's home of a foster child (not necessarily a newborn)

3. The care of the employee's spouse, child, or parent with a serious health condition

4. The serious health condition of the employee

Employees who take FMLA leave are entitled to reinstatement to an equivalent position upon their return to work, and the employer must maintain any health benefits to which the worker was entitled before taking FMLA leave.

The Department of Labor issued final rules interpreting the FMLA, which are codified at 29 C.F.R. Part 825. The regulations are lengthy and complicated; the following summary highlights only a few issues, and administrators should consult the full text of the regulations or employment counsel for assistance in applying the FMLA to the individual circumstances of employees.[24]

Most institutions of higher education will easily meet the fifty-employee requirement for coverage. If an institution has a small satellite location more than 75 miles away that employs fewer than fifty employees (and those employees work exclusively at that location), it is not clear that those employees would be protected by the FMLA. Institutions facing this situation, however, should consider the propriety of excluding such employees from coverage when the majority of their employees have FMLA protection.

Any employee who has worked for 1,250 hours during the previous twelve months (or, for a full-time salaried employee for whom records of hours worked are not kept, for twelve months in the past year) is entitled to twelve weeks of family and medical leave. The number of hours worked, according to the regulations, is to be calculated in conformance with Fair Labor Standards Act regulations (29 C.F.R. § 825.110(c)). Full-time faculty in institutions of higher education are deemed to have met the 1,250-hour test "in consideration of the time spent at home reviewing homework and tests" (29 C.F.R. § 825.110(c)).

The regulations specifically define the categories of "family member" (29 C.F.R. § 825.113). For example, "spouse" may include a common law spouse (if permitted by the law of the state in which the work site is located), but does not include an unmarried domestic partner. A "parent" is a biological parent or an individual who acted as the employee's parent when the employee was a child; this category does not include the parents of the employee's spouse. A "child" may be a biological, adopted, or foster child, stepchild, or a person for whom the employee is acting as a parent, if the child is either under age eighteen or is over eighteen but needs care because of a mental or physical disability.

The regulations expand upon the FMLA's definition of "serious health condition" and detail the employer's right to request medical certification of the employee's need for the leave, including consultation with second and third

---

[24]Cases and authorities are collected at Deborah F. Buckman, Annot., "Award of Damages Under Family and Medical Leave Act (29 U.S.C.A. §§ 2601 *et seq.*)," 176 A.L.R. Fed. 591; and Ann K. Wooster, Annot., "Individual Liability Under Family and Medical Leave Act (29 U.S.C.A. §§ 2601 *et seq.*)," 170 A.L.R. Fed. 561.

medical providers (29 C.F.R. §§ 825.114 & 825.305–307). The regulations also describe the employer's right to request certification of the employee's ability to return to work (29 C.F.R. § 825.310) and the meaning of an "equivalent position" (§ 825.215).

FMLA leave for medical reasons may be taken on an intermittent or part-time basis (called "reduced leave"), depending on the needs of the employee or the family member, but intermittent or reduced leave for the care of a newborn or an adopted child or a foster child may be taken only with the employer's agreement. If an employee takes intermittent or reduced leave, the employer may transfer that employee to a part-time position, as long as the pay and benefits remain equivalent (29 C.F.R. § 825.204).

The regulations also provide detailed information on the relationship between paid and unpaid leave, and the continuation of medical benefits. The law and regulations are silent on whether employers must continue or reinstate nonmedical benefits (such as tuition assistance or child care benefit plans).

The law and regulations permit the employer to deny reinstatement (but not FMLA leave) to a "key employee," defined as a salaried employee who is among the highest-paid 10 percent of all employees within 75 miles of the worksite. But the employer must show that "substantial and grievous economic injury" to its operations will ensue if reinstatement is required (the economic impact of the employee's absence is not part of the test for substantial and grievous economic injury). The specificity of the showing that employers must make to justify refusal to reinstate a key employee (29 C.F.R. §§ 825.216–18) suggests that the exception will rarely be used.

The FMLA requires employers to post a notice detailing its provisions and instructing employees on how complaints may be filed. Employee handbooks must incorporate FMLA information; in the absence of a handbook, employers must provide written information about the FMLA to any employee who asks for FMLA leave. The regulations specify the type of information that employers must give those individuals who request such a leave (29 C.F.R. § 825.301), as well as the law's record-keeping requirements (§ 825.500).

Employees have two avenues for redressing alleged violations of the FMLA. They may file a complaint with the Department of Labor or a lawsuit in federal court. Damages include lost earnings, interest, liquidated damages (lost earnings and interest), reinstatement, and attorney's fees (29 C.F.R. §§ 825.400–404). (For a description of the FMLA and a discussion of its application to colleges and universities, see T. Flygare, *The Family and Medical Leave Act of 1993: Applications in Higher Education* (National Association of College and University Attorneys, 1994). For a discussion of the FMLA's application to college faculty, see Donna Euben & Saranna Thornton, *The Application of the Family and Medical Leave Act to College and University Faculty: Some Questions and Answers* (American Association of University Professors, 2002).)

FMLA regulations promulgated by the U.S. Department of Labor have been challenged on a variety of grounds. The U.S. Supreme Court addressed the FMLA for the first time in *Ragsdale v. Wolverine Worldwide, Inc.*, 535 U.S. 81 (2002). *Ragsdale* involved 29 C.F.R. § 825.700(a), which provides that if the employer fails to notify an employee that a leave requested by the employee is FMLA leave, then the leave does not count against the employee's twelve-week entitlement. The plaintiff, Ragsdale, had been given thirty weeks of leave by her employer to seek treatment for cancer, and the company had held her job open and paid her health insurance benefits while she was on leave. When Ragsdale requested additional leave, it was denied, and she was terminated when she did not return to work. Ragsdale argued that she was entitled to an additional twelve weeks of leave because of her employer's failure to notify her that leave she had already taken would count against her FMLA entitlement. In a 5-to-4 opinion, the majority invalidated the regulation, stating that it required employers to provide more leave than the statute required, and that the regulation did not require the employee to demonstrate that the employer had interfered with, restrained, or denied the exercise of FMLA rights. The dissenters would have upheld the regulation as permissible, and because there had been no showing that the regulation was "arbitrary, capricious, or manifestly contrary to the statute" under the teaching of *Chevron U.S.A. Inc. v. Natural Resources Defense Council*, 467 U.S. 837 (1984).

Although *Ragsdale* invalidated the regulation at issue, it did not invalidate the requirement that employers notify employees that the leave will be counted toward their FMLA entitlement; only the automatic penalty portion of the regulation was invalid. Furthermore, the Court left the door open for claims by employees that they were harmed financially by an employer's failure to notify them that their leave would be charged to their FMLA entitlement. Therefore, in practical terms, it is still important for the employer to notify an employee in writing of this fact.

Although the FMLA entitles employees to twelve weeks of unpaid leave for a serious medical condition, some employees may need additional time. The Americans With Disabilities Act requires employers to provide "reasonable accommodation" for workers with disabilities (see Section 5.2.5 of this book). Such accommodations could include unpaid or paid leave (depending on the employer's policies) and part-time work. The FMLA and the ADA provide significant protections to employees with serious health conditions, and administrators should be aware that the ADA may be used to extend an employee's rights to leave for health-related reasons. (For an example of litigation against a college involving claims under both laws, see *Hatchett v. Philander Smith College*, 251 F.3d 670 (8th Cir. 2001), in which the court held that a business manager who could not perform the essential functions of her position was not entitled to intermittent leave under the FMLA or to protection under the ADA.)

Until the U.S. Supreme Court's ruling in *Nevada Department of Human Resources v. Hibbs*, 538 U.S. 721 (2003), many state employers invoked Eleventh Amendment sovereign immunity to defend themselves against FMLA claims brought by their employees. The federal appellate courts were split on whether the FMLA had validly abrogated sovereign immunity (see, for example, *Kazmier v. Widmann*, 225 F.3d 519 (5th Cir. 2000), *rejecting abrogation,* and *Hibbs v. Dept. of Human* Resources, 273 F.3d 844 (9th Cir. 2001), *affirming abrogation*).

The Supreme Court affirmed the Ninth Circuit's ruling in *Hibbs,* ruling that Congress had properly abrogated sovereign immunity because it had relied not only on its commerce power, but also on its Section 5 enforcement power under the Fourteenth Amendment. Congress had stated that the FMLA's purpose was to "balance the demands of the workplace with the needs of families" and "to promote the goal of equal employment opportunity for women and men" (29 U.S.C. § 2601(b)(1)). Relying on its earlier ruling in *City of Boerne v. Flores* (Section 13.1.5 of this book), the Court asserted that Congress had the power to enact "prophylactic legislation that proscribes facially constitutional conduct, in order to prevent and deter unconstitutional conduct" (538 U.S. at 727–28). The Court then distinguished the *Kimel* and *Garrett* cases, in which it had ruled that Congress had not validly abrogated sovereign immunity in enacting the ADA and the ADEA (see Sections 5.2.5 & 5.2.6 of this book), noting that the FMLA, unlike the ADA and ADEA, had been enacted to counter sex discrimination, which receives heightened scrutiny under the equal protection clause (538 U.S. at 735). (For more on sovereign immunity, abrogation, and Hibbs, see Section 13.1.6.)

Hibbs involved only the family care provisions of the FMLA; the high court has not yet ruled on whether the personal medical leave provisions of the law were a valid abrogation of sovereign immunity. (For an analysis of the results in federal circuit courts with respect to this issue, see *Brockman v. Wyoming Dept. of Family Services,* 342 F.3d 1159 (10th Cir. 2003).)

Similarly unresolved is the issue of individual liability of supervisors under the FMLA. For example, in the Tenth Circuit, a three-judge panel has ruled that supervisors may be held individually liable for FMLA violations because the Eleventh Amendment does not bar federal court jurisdiction over claims against a supervisor in his individual capacity (*Cornforth v. University of Oklahoma Board of Regents,* 263 F.3d 1129 (10th Cir. 2001)). And a three-judge panel in the Eighth Circuit has ruled that an employee of the Kansas City Police Department may sue police department officials and city managers individually because the FMLA allows an employee to sue public officials in their individual capacities (*Darby v. Bratch,* 287 F.3d 673 (8th Cir. 2002)). On the other hand, a panel from the Eleventh Circuit disagreed, saying that the FMLA's definition of "employer" was identical to that in the Fair Labor Standards Act (Section 4.6.2 of this book), which covered corporate officers but not public officials (*Wascura v. Carver,* 169 F.3d 683 (11th Cir. 1999)). Given the disagreement among the federal circuits, a final answer will only come from the Supreme Court.

4.6.5. Immigration laws.

U.S. immigration law, constantly in flux, is of particular interest to colleges because the college may wish to employ faculty, staff, or students who are not U.S. citizens. Laws enacted to regulate immigration also have consequences for all employees, including U.S. citizens. Administrators and counsel should ensure that they are aware of the latest developments in immigration law because the regulations and restrictions are numerous and complex. This Section discusses issues involving the employment of foreign nationals or permanent U.S. (noncitizen) residents. Section 13.2.2 of this book discusses issues involving noncitizen students and visitors who are not employees.

Under the Immigration Reform and Control Act of 1986 (IRCA) (Pub. L. No. 99-603, 100 Stat. 3359), codified at 8 U.S.C. § 1324a, employers must certify that employees are eligible to work in the United States.[25] They must also ensure that employees who are not citizens are either permanent residents or have unexpired visas that authorize them to work in the United States. IRCA applies to all newly hired employees, whether or not they are U.S. citizens, and requires that they present proof of identity and proof that they are entitled to work in the U.S. (8 U.S.C. § 1324a(a)). Employers must examine specific documents to make this determination before allowing the new employee to begin work (§ 1324a(b)). IRCA violations may be punished by civil fines or criminal prosecution penalties against either the employer or the employee, or both.

IRCA also prohibits employers from discriminating against applicants or employees simply because they may appear to be noncitizens; noncitizens who are authorized to work in the United States may not be discriminated against on the basis of citizenship (with certain exceptions for national security reasons). Individuals who believe they have been discriminated against on these bases may file discrimination claims under IRCA and also under Title VII of the Civil Rights Act of 1964 or state civil rights laws for national origin, race, or religious discrimination (see Section 5.2.1).

The U.S. Department of Labor plays an important role in labor certification for employees with H-1B visas or those seeking to establish permanent residence (http://www.doleta.gov). And the Department of State oversees the J-1 exchange program for foreign student visitors who may be employed under its "practical training" provisions. Spouses and children of noncitizen employees or visitors must also comply with a panoply of immigration regulations. Immigration law also circumscribes the postsecondary institution's decisions on employing aliens in faculty or staff positions and inviting aliens to campus to lecture or otherwise participate in campus life.

Aliens who are invited to work in the United States on a temporary basis must obtain a visa under the "H" category, which includes three subcategories of temporary alien workers: nurses, fashion models, and specialized workers (H-1's); other workers who will "perform temporary service or labor" when such services or labor are agricultural in nature or when "unemployed persons capable of performing such service or labor cannot be found in this country" (H-2's); and workers who will act as trainees (H-3's) (8 U.S.C. § 1101(a)(15)(H)(i)–(iii)). For each subcategory, the statute prescribes more limited rules for alien medical school graduates.

---

[25]In addition to IRCA, four federal laws form the core of employment-related immigration law: the Immigration Act of 1990 (IMMACT) (Pub. L. No. 101-649, 104 Stat. 4978); the Miscellaneous and Technical Immigration and Naturalization Amendments of 1991 (MTINA) (Pub. L. No. 102-232, 105 Stat. 1733); the Illegal Immigration Reform and Immigrant Responsibility Act of 1996 (IIRIRA) (Pub. L. No. 104-208, Div. C., 110 Stat. 3009-546); and the American Competitiveness and Workforce Improvement Act of 1998 (ACWIA) (Pub. L. No. 105-277, Title IV of Div. C, 112 Stat. 2861). Subsequent legislation has amended these laws and has increased the cap on H-1B visas, which are discussed below.

The most frequently used visa category for college or university employees is the H-1B visa. An individual holding an H-1B visa is limited to a stay of six years, but if the individual has applied for permanent resident status, this limitation may be extended. The employer must file a labor certification with the state workforce agency and must pay at least the prevailing wage for the position. The individual may not begin work until the petition for the H-1B visa has been approved, and the individual's authorization to work is specific to the employer, the geographic area, and the position. However, 8 U.S.C. § 1184(n) allows a holder of an H-1B visa to change employers as long as the new employer files a petition requesting permission for the change.

Congress has capped the number of H-1B visas that may be issued in any one year. Because of the demands of business for specialized workers from abroad, the cap has been reached early in each federal fiscal year (FY), which begins on the first of October. For example, the cap for FY 2005 was reached by October 1, 2004, the first day of the 2005 fiscal year. (Ed Frauenheim, "H-1B Visa Limit for 2005 Is Already Reached," *News.com,* available at http://news.com.com/ H-1B + visa + limit + for + 2005 + already + reached/2100-1022_3-5392917.html. For a recent history of amendments to immigration law and a discussion of the requirements of the H-1B visa, see Tracey Halliday, "The World of Offshoring: H-1B Visas Can Be Utilized to Curb the Business Trend of Offshoring," 25 *Hamline J. Pub. L. & Pol'y* 407 (2004).)

The Immigration Act of 1990 (IMMACT) created three additional categories that are important to higher education institutions. The "O" visa is for nonimmigrant visitors who have extraordinary ability in the areas of arts, sciences, education, business, or athletics and are to be employed for a specific project or event such as an academic year appointment or a lecture tour (8 U.S.C. § 1101(a)(15)(O); 8 C.F.R. § 214.2(o)). The "P" visa is for performing artists and athletes at an internationally recognized level of performance who seek to enter the United States as nonimmigrant visitors to perform, teach, or coach (8 U.S.C. § 1101(a)(15)(P); 8 C.F.R. § 214.2(p)). The "Q" visa is designated for

> coming temporarily (for a period not to exceed fifteen months) to the United States as a participant in an international cultural exchange program approved by the Attorney General for the purpose of providing practical training, employment, and the sharing of the history, culture, and traditions of the country of the alien's nationality [8 U.S.C. § 1101(a)(15)(Q); 8 C.F.R. § 214.2(q)].

The Web site of the U.S. Citizenship and Immigration Services has a special section for employers that explains the law and regulations regarding visitors and foreign workers, and directs employers to the correct forms (http://www. uscis.gov/graphics/services/employerinfo/index.htm).

The State Department also has authority over these employment and visitor categories as well as the foreign student categories. Pertinent State Department regulations are in 22 C.F.R. § 41.31 (temporary visitors) and 22 C.F.R. § 41.53 (temporary workers and trainees).

The U.S. Department of Labor issues "labor certifications" for aliens, indicating that their employment will not displace or adversely affect American workers (8 C.F.R. § 214.2(h)). Labor Department regulations on labor certification are codified at 20 C.F.R. § 656.2 and 29 C.F.R. Part 501. Regulations related to the labor certification process for individuals who will hold teaching positions at colleges or universities are found at 20 C.F.R. § 656.21a. This labor certification process need not be followed, however, if the individual can be classified as an individual of "extraordinary ability" under 8 C.F.R. § 204.5(h)(2).

4.6.6. Workers' compensation laws.
Every state requires employers to participate in a system that provides compensation to an employee or the employee's family in cases where the employee has been injured or killed in the course of employment. These laws are intended to limit employers' liability for negligence or other potential employee claims in exchange for the employer's agreement to pay for the employee's medical treatment and to provide a wage replacement while the employee cannot work. In some cases, employers purchase workers' compensation insurance, while in other states the state collects premiums from employers and pays the benefits out of a state fund.

Although the details of workers' compensation laws differ by state, several themes are common to this area of the law. Workers' compensation is the exclusive remedy for employees injured at work, which means that a court will dismiss tort claims filed against the employer. In order to be entitled to workers' compensation benefits, the individual must be an employee, must have been injured by accident, and the injury must either have occurred while the employee was working or be related to the individual's job responsibilities. Although most litigation concerns employees' (or other individuals') allegations that they were wrongfully denied workers' compensation benefits, workers in some cases seek to avoid the workers' compensation scheme and sue those responsible for their injuries; potential damage awards can greatly surpass the value of workers' compensation benefits.

Workers' compensation is a "no fault" system that awards benefits to workers who qualify whether or not the worker was negligent, and whether or not the employer was negligent. In certain situations, however, a worker may seek to avoid coverage in order to receive greater compensation. Several states have carved out an exception to the exclusivity doctrine if an injured worker can demonstrate that the employer intentionally acted in a manner that had a strong probability of resulting in injury. For example, the New Jersey Supreme Court in *Laidlow v. Hariton Machinery Co.*, 790 A.2d 884 (N.J. 2002) allowed a negligence lawsuit by an injured worker to proceed because the worker claimed that a supervisor removed a safety device from a machine, knowing that serious harm could result. Although it is difficult for plaintiffs to overcome the presumption of exclusivity that undergirds the workers' compensation system, intentional actions by a supervisor or manager that lead to serious and foreseeable consequences may convince a court to pierce the exclusivity shield, as in *Laidlow.*

An important benefit to employers is that, because workers' compensation is the exclusive remedy for workers injured in the course of employment, courts will typically dismiss employee tort claims such as negligence, negligent infliction of emotional distress, and so on. But state laws and judicial rulings differ as to whether intentional torts will fall under the workers' compensation law's exclusivity doctrine. In *Maas v. Cornell University*, 683 N.Y.S.2d 634 (N.Y. App. Div. 1999), for example, a faculty member sued Cornell University for negligence in its handling of a sexual harassment complaint against him. The court rejected the professor's claims of negligence and negligent infliction of emotional distress, ruling that he could not sue his employer in tort because of the exclusivity of workers' compensation as a remedy for unintentional employment-related injuries. On the other hand, a federal trial court ruled that Pennsylvania's workers' compensation law did not preclude claims for intentional infliction of emotional distress, and allowed a plaintiff to sue her employer for emotional injury arising from an alleged sexual harassment incident (*Brooks v. Mendoza,* 2002 U.S. Dist. LEXIS 4991 (E.D. Pa. 2002)). But in *Klan-Rastani v. Clark University,* 2001 Mass. Super. LEXIS 535 (Mass. Super. 2001), a Massachusetts trial court dismissed claims of negligent and intentional infliction of emotional distress brought by plaintiffs who were upset when they discovered alleged pay discrimination by the college. Because emotional distress is considered a personal injury, said the court, the state's workers' compensation statute was the exclusive remedy, and the plaintiff was limited to workers' compensation benefits. And a federal district court rejected a plaintiff's negligent hiring and retention claims against a college, ruling that workers' compensation benefits were the only remedy for injuries resulting from alleged negligence (*Gomez-Gil v. University of Hartford,* 63 F. Supp. 2d 191 (D. Conn. 1999)).

Most workers' compensation laws exempt employers from liability if a non-employee caused the employee's injury. For example, in *California State Polytechnic University-Pomona v. Workers' Compensation Appeals Board,* 179 Cal. Rptr. 605 (Cal. Ct. App. 1982), a claim had been filed on behalf of a former stenographer at the university who had been shot and killed while working at her desk. A great deal of circumstantial evidence implicated a former boyfriend as the likely suspect. The boyfriend was never prosecuted for the shooting because of what the court termed "evidentiary problems." The deceased's family argued that she was killed in the course of employment. The university argued that she was killed out of "personal motives," a defense that would shield it from the workers' compensation claim. The court decided the case in favor of the university.

With respect to those individuals who seek workers' compensation benefits, colleges and universities have faced claims from student interns that their injuries were employment-related and thus they were entitled to compensation. A student employee injured at an on-campus worksite would typically be covered by the workers' compensation law, although a federal trial court refused to make such a finding in *Grant v. Tulane University,* 2001 U.S. Dist. LEXIS 3041 (E.D. La. 2001) because the student plaintiff was paid by federal work-study funds (see Section 8.3.2) that could be characterized as financial aid rather than wages.

A more difficult issue is posed when students are required to participate in an internship at an off-campus site, supervised by both academic staff and nonemployees. Cases from two state courts suggest that, even if the students are not paid and are receiving college credit for their internship experience, the court will find them to be employees for workers' compensation purposes. For example, in *Ryles v. Durham County Hospital Corp.*, 420 S.E.2d 487 (N.C. Ct. App. 1992), *review denied*, 424 S.E.2d 406 (N.C. 1992), a student was injured when he slipped and fell in a puddle of water at the employer's site. He filed a negligence action against the hospital (the employer). The hospital argued that the negligence claim was barred by the state's workers' compensation law. The court held that the plaintiff was an "apprentice" of the employer, not a student, for workers' compensation purposes, since the employer received the same benefit from the student's work as it would have from a regular employee.

Similarly, in *Hallal v. RDV Sports, Inc.*, 682 So. 2d 1235 (Fla. Ct. App. 1996), a student was injured while he was participating in an internship with the marketing office of the Orlando Magic team. Hallal sued the Magic, and the defendant raised the defense of the exclusiveness of workers' compensation as a remedy for workplace injury. Hallal denied that he was an "employee" for workers' compensation purposes, but the court disagreed, citing *Ryles*. Although Hallal did not receive a salary, he did receive $250 from the Magic. Furthermore, said the court, even if he had not received any monetary compensation, his "participation in the internship program constituted valuable consideration in that such participation was necessary in order for him to satisfy the requirements of his degree" (682 So. 2d at 1237).

A Colorado appellate court ruled that an unpaid student intern at Colorado State University was entitled to workers' compensation benefits. In *Kinder v. The Industrial Claim Appeals Office of the State of Colorado*, 976 P.2d 295 (Colo. Ct. App. 1998), the student was injured during an internship and suffered permanent partial disability. The university had provided workers' compensation coverage for the student during her internship, and the student's medical costs had been paid. But because the student had not been paid a wage or salary, the state workers' compensation agency denied her permanent partial disability payments. The court ruled that the agency should have imputed an appropriate wage upon which to base her disability payments.

But the Supreme Court of Massachusetts rejected a student's claim that her institution owed her a duty to ensure that her internship-employer provided a safe workplace and covered her with workers' compensation insurance. In *Judson v. Essex Agricultural and Technical Institute*, 635 N.E.2d 1172 (Mass. 1994), the institute required students to find employment related to their course of study and to have the employer complete a placement agreement with the institute. The agreement stated that the employer would provide workers' compensation insurance coverage for the student, and also stated that the instructor would visit the workplace from time to time. After the plaintiff was injured falling from a barn loft, she was advised by her employer that it had not secured workers' compensation coverage for her. She sued the institute, claiming it had a duty to ensure that her employer had secured coverage for her, as well as a duty to ensure that she had a reasonably safe place to work. The court rejected both of these claims, noting that the placement agreement "merely provided notice to the plaintiff and [the employer] that it was the plaintiff's employer's responsibility to provide such insurance." The court similarly rejected the student's claim that the placement agreement's language concerning the visits of the instructor created a duty to inspect the place of employment for safety hazards.

Graduate students are particularly likely to have a mixed status as students and employees. In *Torres v. State,* 902 P.2d 999 (Mont. 1995), for example, a doctoral student pursuing a degree in chemistry at Montana State University was also employed there as a teaching and research assistant. Claiming that exposure to toxic substances in the chemistry lab had caused her injury, Torres filed a workers' compensation claim. The claim was eventually settled under the state's Occupational Disease Act. Torres then sued the university as a student (rather than an employee) for compensation for her injuries. The Montana Supreme Court affirmed summary judgment for the university, noting that workers' compensation is the exclusive remedy for injuries to employees, and that Torres had already received compensation for her injury. Three judges dissented, believing that, because Torres had dual status as an employee and student, her damages could be apportioned between exposure as a student and exposure as an employee.

A Wisconsin case illustrates the hazards of allowing a graduate student-employee to work at an off-campus site unrelated to the actual work. In *Begel v. Wisconsin Labor and Industry Review Commission,* 631 N.W.2d 220 (Ct. App. Wis., Dist. 4, 2001), a state appellate court reversed a denial of workers' compensation benefits to a student research assistant. The student was supervised by a professor who was building a house, had no telephone, and was seldom on campus. Therefore, the student had to travel to the professor's home in order to discuss his job responsibilities. When the student visited the construction site to discuss the research project he was working on for the professor, he agreed to help the professor with the house construction. While doing so, the student was injured, rendering him a quadriplegic. When he filed a workers' compensation claim against the university, the university argued that, although the student was its employee, he was not engaged in work for the university at the time he was injured. The court ruled that the student had traveled to the construction site for work-related purposes, and that under the circumstances it was both reasonable for him to be at the professor's home and to comply with the professor's request for help. The court therefore found the injury to be compensable.

In certain situations, the college would face less financial liability if it could characterize students as employees who were limited to workers' compensation benefits when injured. For example, the Vermont Supreme Court determined that student members of a volunteer fire department sponsored by Norwich University were not covered by the state's workers' compensation laws, leaving the university potentially exposed to negligence lawsuits as a result. In *Wolfe v. Yudichak,* 571 A.2d 592 (Vt. 1989), a student volunteer fire fighter sued the university for negligence after he was injured when a fire truck skidded off the road. The court ruled that, under Vermont law, the fire brigade had the choice of whether or not it wished to participate in the workers' compensation system, and since the brigade had not done so, the university could not unilaterally decide that its members were covered by workers' compensation. (See generally Bruce J. Berger & John R. Manthei, "Graduate Students' Injury Claims: Tort Liability or Workers Compensation and the Impact on Insurance Coverage," 26 *College L. Dig.* 9 (April 18, 1996).)

With respect to student athletes, several cases have raised the question whether a varsity scholarship athlete has an employment relationship with his institution and is therefore covered by workers' compensation when he loses the scholarship because he is injured and unable to play.[26] In *Rensing v. Indiana State University Board of Trustees,* 444 N.E.2d 1170 (Ind. 1983), the Supreme Court of Indiana upheld the Industrial Board of Indiana's denial of workers' compensation to a scholarship athlete who was permanently disabled by an injury received in football practice. Indiana's intermediate appellate court had overruled the board's decision (437 N.E.2d 78 (Ind. Ct. App. 1982)). In reversing the appeals court and reinstating the board's decision, the state supreme court held that "there was no intent to enter into an employer-employee relationship" when the student and the university entered into the scholarship agreement. Since the plaintiff athlete was therefore not considered an "employee" under the Indiana Workmen's Compensation Act (Ind. Code § 22-3-6-1(b)), he was not eligible for benefits under the Act. Other courts have issued similar rulings. In *Graczyk v. Workers' Compensation Appeals Board,* 229 Cal. Rptr. 494 (Cal. Ct. App. 1986), the court ruled that a student athlete who had received an athletic scholarship, and who was seriously injured during football practice, did not meet the statutory definition of "employee." In *Coleman v. Western Michigan University,* 336 N.W.2d 224 (Mich. Ct. App. 1983), the court ruled that, although an athletic scholarship was "wages," the student was not an "employee" for purposes of the state's workers' compensation act. A Texas appellate court reached a similar conclusion in *Waldrep v. Texas Employers Insurance Association,* 21 S.W.3d 692 (Ct. App. Tex., 3d Dist., 2000). (For critical commentary see A. Larson, *The Law of Workmen's Compensation,* Vol. IA, § 22.21(c) (Matthew Bender, 1993); Note, "Workers' Compensation and College Athletes: Should Universities Be Responsible for Athletes Who Incur Serious Injuries?" 10 *J. Coll. & Univ. Law* 197 (1983-84); Note, "Play for Pay: Should Scholarship Athletes Be Included Within State Workers' Compensation Systems?" 12 *Loyola L.A. Ent. L.J.* 441 (1992); and Jason Gurdus, Note, "Protection Off of the Playing Field: Student Athletes Should Be Considered University Employees for Purposes of Workers' Compensation," 29 *Hofstra L. Rev.* 907 (2001).)

The compensability of stress-related injuries has received considerable judicial attention. For example, in *Decker v. Oklahoma State Technical University,* 766 P.2d 1371 (Okla. 1988), an instructor whose relationship with his supervisor was difficult and stressful successfully argued that his heart attack should be compensated

---

[26]Cases and authorities are collected in Donald P. Duffala, Annot., "Workers' Compensation: Student Athlete as 'Employee' of College or University Providing Scholarship or Similar Financial Assistance," 58 A.L.R.4th 1259.

as a work-related injury. (For analysis of *Decker* and other workers' compensation issues related to college faculty, see K. N. Hasty, Note, "Workers' Compensation: Will College and University Professors Be Compensated for Mental Injuries Caused by Work-Related Stress?" 17 *J. Coll. & Univ. Law* 535 (1991).)

Under most state workers' compensation statutes, employees who are injured during the commute to work are not eligible for worker's compensation. If the employee has a home office and is injured while traveling between the worksite and the home office, the injuries may be compensable. On occasion, this "second job site" exception to the exclusion of injuries incurred on the way to or from one's place of work can result in workers' compensation benefits for faculty injured at home. This theory was not successful, however, in *Santa Rosa Junior College v. Workers' Compensation Appeals Board,* 708 P.2d 673 (Cal. 1985). The professor, who often graded papers and prepared for class at home because his office was noisy, was killed in an automobile accident on his way home from the college. The court denied benefits to his widow, ruling that the college did not require the professor to work at home and thus his home was not a second job site. Advances in technology that permit telecommuting have tested the boundaries of workers' compensation law. (For a review of litigation in this area, see Matthew B. Duckworth, Comment: "The Need for Workers' Compensation in the Age of Telecommuters," 5 *J. Small & Emerging Bus. L.* 403 (2001).) Other legal issues related to telecommuting are discussed in Section 4.2.2, above.

Although the employer is shielded from negligence claims, nonemployee visitors in the workplace, including the unborn children of employees, are not bound by the exclusivity rule. For example, if a pregnant employee is injured at work and the unborn child suffers physical or mental injuries as a result, the employer may not be immune from negligence claims because the child is not an employee and its injuries are distinct from those of the mother (*Meyer v. Burger King Corporation,* 26 P.3d 925 (Wash. 2001)). Thus, a college could face negligence liability for injuries to a fetus occasioned by a work-related injury to a pregnant employee, even though the college would be immune from litigation concerning the employee's injuries.

Employees with work-related injuries may also seek protections under the Americans With Disabilities Act (see Section 5.2.5). The Equal Employment Opportunity Commission has issued an Enforcement Guidance that discusses the interaction between the two systems of protection: *EEOC Enforcement Guidance: Workers' Compensation and the ADA* (September 1996) (available at http://eeoc.gov/docs/workcomp).

4.6.7. Unemployment compensation laws.

Federal law requires most postsecondary institutions, public or private, to make contributions to a state unemployment insurance program. Every state has a law, tailored to guidelines in the Federal Unemployment Tax Act (FUTA, 26 U.S.C. § 3301 *et seq.*), regulating the collection of unemployment taxes and the payment of unemployment benefits. The FUTA imposes a payroll tax on employers of 6.2 percent of the first $7,000 in wages of every covered employee; those employers operating in a state whose unemployment tax law tracks the requirements of FUTA receive a credit of up to 5.4 percent for any unemployment taxes they have paid to the state. Participating colleges are treated the same as other employers in the state. Even religiously affiliated colleges are typically required to participate in the unemployment compensation system (see, for example, *Salem College & Academy v. Employment Division,* 695 P.2d 25 (Ore. 1985), in which the Oregon Supreme Court rejected the college's claim that participation in the unemployment compensation system was a burden on the free exercise of religion).

State unemployment laws define the nature of "employment" and specify how long an individual must have been employed and how much the employee must have earned prior to becoming eligible for unemployment benefits. In most states, claimants must wait a week after losing their job prior to collecting unemployment benefits. Benefits typically extend for twenty-six weeks, although the payment period is occasionally extended in times of economic recession. Unemployment benefits are usually approximately 50 percent of the individual's prior weekly wage, with a statutory maximum.

Although a college's employees who work a full calendar year would typically be covered by the unemployment insurance system, it is less clear whether academic-year employees are eligible for unemployment compensation in the summer. The legal standard in most states is whether the claimant has a reasonable assurance of returning to his or her former position at the beginning of the next academic year.[27] This is a factual issue, and courts examine contracts, offer letters, handbooks, and an employer's past practice. In most cases, the courts have rejected the claims of academic year employees, even if their employment for the subsequent year is contingent on sufficient enrollments (see, for example, *Emery v. Boise State University and Embry Riddle Aeronautical,* 32 P.3d 1112 (Idaho 2001); see also *In re Claim of Doru Tsaganea,* 720 N.Y.S.2d 585 (Supreme Ct. N.Y., App. Div., 3d Dept., 2001)). On the other hand, a court in Washington ruled that, because a community college teacher had not been asked to teach during summer quarter, and had not been advised as to any employment for the fall quarter, she was entitled to unemployment insurance benefits after completing her teaching in the spring (*Evans v. Employment Security Dept.,* 866 P.2d 687 (Ct. App. Wash. 1994)). Since the intervening summer term was a regular term, rather than a break between terms, she was found eligible. In most states, academic year employees are not eligible for unemployment compensation during semester breaks if they have a reasonable assurance of returning to teaching after the break (see, for example, *Community College of Allegheny County v. Unemployment Compensation Board of Review,* 634 A.2d 845 (Pa. Commw. 1993), *app. denied,* 653 A.2d 1234 (Pa. 1994)).

The laws of most states deny unemployment benefits to individuals who are on strike. New York, however, allows striking employees to receive unemployment compensation if the strike lasts longer than seven weeks. In *In re*

---

[27]Cases and authorities are collected in Pataricia C. Kussman, Annot., "Right to Unemployment Compensation or Social Security Benefits of Teacher or Other School Employee," 33 A.L.R.5th 643.

Goodman and Barnard College, 709 N.Y.S.2d 884 (N.Y. 2000), the court ruled that, because the striking academic year employees had not received the usual rehire letter from the college during the strike, which had taken place during the summer, they were entitled to unemployment benefits.

The laws of each state list criteria for disqualifying an otherwise eligible employee from obtaining unemployment benefits. For example, individuals who leave work for personal reasons may be denied unemployment benefits in most states. In *Wimberly v. Labor and Industrial Commission of Missouri,* 479 U.S. 511 (1987), the U.S. Supreme Court upheld a provision of Missouri's unemployment law that included a resignation because of pregnancy in a list of reasons for disqualifying voluntary separation from employment. The Court rejected the plaintiff's argument that disqualification of persons who left because of pregnancy constituted sex discrimination. Although the state could not single out pregnancy for harsher treatment, the Court held, the state could characterize a resignation because of pregnancy as a "voluntary" separation. Similarly, individuals who refuse to perform certain required tasks may be denied benefits in most states. In *Stepp v. Review Board of the Indiana Employment Security Division,* 521 N.E.2d 350 (Ind. Ct. App. 1988), the court ruled that a laboratory technician who refused to perform tests on AIDS-infected fluids could be denied unemployment benefits. The technician had refused to perform the tests on the grounds that AIDS was a "plague on men" and thus the tests were against God's will. Challenging her discharge for insubordination, the technician claimed that she had the right to refuse to perform unsafe work. The court disagreed, ruling that the laboratory's safety procedures were appropriate and did not justify her insubordination. (She had not made a claim on the grounds of religious discrimination.) And employee misconduct, such as theft or dishonesty, may also be grounds for denial of unemployment benefits (see, for example, *Temple University v. Unemployment Compensation Board of Review,* 772 A.2d 416 (Pa. 2001) (falsification of time card); and *In Re Claim of Arlene Egelberg,* 664 N.Y.S.2d 186 (N.Y. Ct. App. 1997) (failure of instructor to report for class in violation of college policy)).

Many state laws exclude full-time college students from eligibility for unemployment compensation. In *Pima Community College v. Arizona Department of Economic Security,* 714 P.2d 472 (Ariz. Ct. App. 1986), for example, the court was asked to determine whether a former student who had been employed by the college under the federal work-study program was a student or an employee for eligibility purposes. The court ruled that the individual was a student and thus ineligible for unemployment compensation.

4.6.8. *Whistleblower protections.*

Employees who believe they have been subjected to negative employment action because they reported a workplace problem are protected by a variety of legal doctrines. Courts in most states allow certain employees to bring tort claims for wrongful discharge "in violation of public policy" if they have been terminated or penalized due to whistleblowing. In addition, all fifty states and the District of Columbia have some form of statutory protection for whistleblowers, although the scope of protection and the range of employees protected vary considerably by state. Several federal laws also provide protection for whistleblowers.

The federal protections are found in environmental, labor, and workplace health and safety laws that prohibit retaliation against workers who report suspected violations of these laws to appropriate federal regulatory agencies. For example, the Safe Drinking Water Act (42 U.S.C. § 9610) and the Toxic Substances Control Act (15 U.S.C. § 2622) contain such provisions. Labor relations laws, such as the Fair Labor Standards Act (see Section 4.6.2) and the National Labor Relations Act (see Section 4.5.2) also contain antiretaliation provisions. OSHA (see Section 4.6.1 of this book) provides protection for employees who report their employers' alleged health or safety violations.

In addition, the False Claims Act (31 U.S.C. § 3729–30), discussed in Section 13.2.15, allows individuals, including employees, to file claims against federal contractors for alleged misuse of federal funds. This law has been used frequently in recent years by college faculty and staff to challenge allegedly inappropriate use of federal research funds.

Most whistleblowers, however, will attempt to use either the common law "public policy" claim or will file claims under a state whistleblower law. Those individuals who choose to proceed under the common law tort claim (perhaps because the potential damage awards are higher than under state statutes) must be able to articulate a recognized source of public policy, such as a statute, constitutional provision, or professional code of ethics. For example, if an individual were discharged for complaining that an employer was violating the criminal law, such a complaint, if proven, would support a claim of wrongful discharge on the grounds of public policy (see *Shea v. Emmanuel College,* 682 N.E.2d 1348 (Mass. 1997)). On the other hand, an employee who simply disagreed with an employer's action could not avail herself of this theory if the employer's action was not unlawful or unsafe (see *Pierce v. Ortho Pharmaceutical,* 417 A.2d 505 (N.J. 1980)).

Although state whistleblower laws vary, individuals attempting to use these laws to challenge terminations or discipline will generally be required to demonstrate:

- that the employer has engaged in some behavior that is allegedly unsafe, unlawful, or a violation of public policy
- that the employee has notified a supervisor or other employer representative of the problem (although some laws waive this requirement if it is an emergency or the employee reasonably anticipates physical harm as a result of the report)
- that the employer has taken no action or inadequate action
- that the employee has notified the proper authority (for example, the police, the health department, a state or federal agency charged with the responsibility of preventing or curing the problem the employee has identified) (although some courts exempt employees from this requirement if the notification has been made to an appropriate individual inside the organization), and

- that the employer has taken some adverse employment action as a direct result of the employee's complaint (such as discipline, termination, involuntary transfer, failure to promote when a promotion is due, salary reduction or denial of a salary increase to which the employee is otherwise entitled)

For example, in *University of Houston v. Elthon,* 9 S.W.3d 351 (Ct. App. Tex. 1999), a professor and chair of the chemistry department complained to the dean of alleged ethical violations by his faculty colleagues. The dean took no action on the complaints. The professor complained to the provost and was later denied a salary increase on the recommendation of the dean and the provost. The professor filed a lawsuit under the Texas Whistleblower Act (Tex. Gov't. Code Ann. §§ 554.001–.009), and the university sought dismissal of the case, asserting that the professor should have used the institution's internal grievance procedure. Both the trial and appellate courts refused to dismiss the lawsuit, finding that the professor had used the university's ethical code and its procedures, which were sufficient to satisfy the Whistleblower Act's requirement that an individual must use an internal grievance or appeal procedure before suing under the law.

Similarly, in *Barrett v. University of Texas Medical Branch at Galveston,* 112 S.W.3d 815 (Tex. Ct. App. 2003), a physician whose appointments at the university and its affiliated hospital were not renewed challenged the nonrenewal under the Texas Whistleblower Act, alleging that complaints about colleagues' violations of hospital rules led to the nonrenewal. The appellate court reversed a trial court's award of summary judgment for the university and ordered that the whistleblower claim to be tried.

In contrast, in *Zinno v. Patenaude,* 770 A.2d 849 (R.I. 2001), Zinno, a staff employee at Brown University, reported an alleged work-related injury and was provided workers' compensation benefits for a year. Benefits were terminated when an orthopedic consultant retained by the university determined that Zinno's physical problems were not work related. Concurrently, Zinno had complained to his supervisors about alleged violations of the Occupational Safety and Health Act. Zinno claimed that he was forced into early retirement in retaliation for his OSHA complaints. The court found that Zinno had never complained, or threatened to complain, to OSHA, and therefore his conduct did not satisfy the requirements of the Rhode Island Whistleblowers' Protection Act.

Litigation by "whistleblowers" against public colleges or universities often includes allegations of First Amendment violations. These claims are generally analyzed under the *Pickering/Connick* line of cases and the *Mt. Healthy* line of cases, both concerning the free speech rights of public employees (see Sections 7.1.1 & 7.6). Unless the plaintiff can demonstrate that (1) the termination or discipline was a response to his or her speech activities and (2) that the speech was a matter of public concern, the plaintiff typically will not prevail. See, for example, *Nelson v. Pima Community College,* 83 F.3d 1075 (9th Cir. 1996), in which the court rejected both the free speech and whistleblowing complaints of a staff member whose contract was not renewed after her conflicts with several staff members "threw the whole college into turmoil," according to the court. But in *Jones v. Board of Regents of the University System of Georgia,* 585 S.E.2d 138 (Ga. App. 2003), although the court rejected the First Amendment claim of a former public safety director at Augusta State University, it allowed his claim that he had been dismissed for exposing police corruption to be tried under the state whistleblower act.

Closely related to whistleblower claims are claims that an employer retaliated against an employee for having exercised statutory rights, such as filing an employment discrimination claim. Plaintiffs are often more successful with retaliation claims than with the underlying discrimination claim. Retaliation claims and discrimination claims are both discussed in Sections 5.2.1 & 13.5.7.5.

Given the myriad protections available to employees who report real or imagined employer wrongdoing, colleges should train managers and supervisors to respond to whistleblower complaints appropriately and to document their responses. No response, or a response that indicates that the supervisor does not take the complaint seriously, can lead to litigation and to liability, even if the underlying "threat" was a product of the employee's imagination.

4.6.9. Uniformed Services Employment and Reemployment Rights Act.

Veterans of U.S. wars enjoy special protections under state civil service laws (Section 4.4) and under federal law as well. Congress has amended the laws providing employment and reemployment rights for veterans several times. In addition, individuals who are eligible for military duty, or whose reserve or national guard units are activated, are also protected by federal law.

The basic thrust of these laws is to prohibit discrimination against individuals on the basis of eligibility for military service and to provide reemployment rights for individuals who must leave their jobs to serve on active duty in the military. The Veterans Readjustment Benefits Act (Pub. L. No. 89-358 (1966)), amended by the Vietnam Era Veterans Readjustment Assistance Act of 1974 (Pub. L. No. 93-508, codified at 38 U.S.C. § 4212 *et seq.*), requires that employers who receive $100,000 or more in federal contracts "shall take affirmative action to employ and advance in employment qualified special disabled veterans and veterans of the Vietnam era" (39 U.S.C. § 4121(a)). Another law, first enacted in 1954 and modified, retitled, and recodified several times since then, is now entitled "Uniformed Services Employment and Reemployment Rights Act" (USERRA) (38 U.S.C. § 4301 *et seq.*). This law requires that all employers (defined as "any person, institution, organization, or other entity that pays salary or wages for work performed . . ." as well as the state and federal governments) (38 U.S.C. § 4304(4)(A)(I)) may not discriminate against any applicant or employee who has performed or who has an obligation to perform military service, and must restore individuals covered by these laws to their previous positions or similar ones, unless the employer can demonstrate that such restoration is impossible or unreasonable. Amendments added in 1991 (Pub. L. No. 102-25) require the employer to retrain returning veterans for their previous positions, if necessary; the amendments also regulate the provision of employer-offered health insurance for such individuals. In *King v. St. Vincent's Hospital,* 502 U.S. 215 (1991), the U.S. Supreme Court ruled unanimously that the Veterans' Reemployment Rights Act did not limit the amount of time individuals may serve on active duty before they lose the right to be restored to their former position. However, Congress amended this law in 1994 to limit the reinstatement protections to those veterans absent from their jobs for five years or less (38 U.S.C. § 4312, added by Pub. L. 103-353, 108 Stat. 3150 (1994)), and retitled the law the Uniformed Service Employment and Reemployment Rights Act.

USERRA provides that an employee returning from military leave with an honorable discharge is entitled to reemployment if:

1. The individual reports for work within ninety days of being relieved of his or her service obligations;

2. The individual has a certificate of completion of military service; and

3. The individual is qualified to perform his or her former job, or can become requalified without imposing undue hardship on the employer.

Exceptions to the reemployment requirement may be allowed if the employer's circumstances have so changed as to make reemployment impossible or unreasonable, or if the original employment was short term with no reasonable expectation of continued employment. These protections apply whether or not the employee's military service is voluntary or involuntary.

USERRA was further amended in 1998 to confer jurisdiction over lawsuits against a state employer only on state courts (Pub. L. No. 105-368, 112 Stat. 3315 (1998)). This provision is now unconstitutional due to the U.S. Supreme Court's ruling in *Alden v. Maine* (discussed in Section 13.1.6), which recognizes constitutional immunity for states against federal law claims filed in state court. Attempts by employees to file USERRA claims against state employers subsequent to *Alden* have been unsuccessful. (See, for example, *Larkins v. Dept. of Mental Health and Mental Retardation,* 806 So. 2d 358 (Ala. 2001).)

In response to *Alden*, Congress passed Section 211 of the Veterans Programs Enhancement Act (Pub. L. No. 105-368, 112 Stat. 3315, 3331, codified at 38 U.S.C. § 4323). This amendment allows the U.S. Department of Justice to sue a state employer on behalf of one or more state employees, which makes the United States the plaintiff and avoids the sovereign immunity problem. This strategy requires that the Justice Department first make a finding that the employee's case has legal merit. If the U.S. government prevails, it pays the damages it has received to the aggrieved employee. (For a discussion of employees' options if the Justice Department declines to act as plaintiff in a USERRA claim against a state employer, see "TJAGSA Practice Note: USERRA Note," 1999 *Army Lawyer* 52 (1999).)

The 1998 USERRA amendments also extended the reach of the act to U.S. citizens working in other countries for U.S.-owned companies and for foreign-owned companies that are "controlled" by a U.S. employer. Regulations related to this amendment are found at 5 C.F.R. § 353.103, "Restoration to Duty from Uniformed Service."

Final regulations interpreting the USERRA were published by the U.S. Department of Labor on December 19, 2005, and may be found at 29 C.F.R. Part 1002.

Information for employers and members of military reserve units on the protections of the USERRA can be found at the Web site of the National Committee for Employer Support of the Guard and Reserve (ESGR) at http://www.esgr.org. This Web site contains an "Employer Resource Guide" and describes its ombudsman service for the voluntary, informal resolution of disputes between returning veterans and their employers. The U.S. Department of Labor Web site also contains information about the USERRA at http://www.dol.gov/elaws/userra.htm.

Sec. 4.7. Personal Liability of Employees

4.7.1. Overview. Although most individuals seeking redress for alleged wrongs in academe sue their institutions, they may choose to add individuals as defendants, or they may sue only the person or persons who allegedly harmed them. Most colleges have indemnification policies that provide for defending a faculty or staff member who is sued for acts that occurred while performing his or her job. (For a discussion of indemnification, see Section 2.5.3.2.)

Individuals may face personal liability under various common law claims, such as negligence, defamation, intentional or negligent infliction of emotional distress, or fraud. And although courts have ruled that individuals typically are not liable for violations of federal nondiscrimination laws such as Title VII or the ADEA, since these laws impose obligations on the "employer," not on managers or individuals, some state courts have imposed individual liability under state nondiscrimination laws (see, for example, *Matthews v. Superior Court,* 40 Cal. Rptr. 2d 350 (Cal. App. 2 Dist. 1995), holding supervisors who participated in sexual harassment individually liable under California's Fair Employment and Housing Act). Other federal laws, such as Sections 1981 and 1983 of the Civil Rights Act (see Sections 3.5 & 5.2.4) do provide for individual liability. In addition, whistleblower laws in some states provide for individual liability of managers or supervisors.

Individuals may also face liability for intentional torts. For example, in *Minger v. Green,* 239 F.3d 793 (6th Cir. 2001), a federal appellate court applying Kentucky law ruled that the associate director of the housing office at Murray State University was not immune from personal liability in a wrongful death suit brought by the deceased student's mother. The associate director was accused of intentionally misrepresenting the seriousness of an earlier fire in the student's residence hall to his mother; the mother claimed that had she known that the first fire had been set by an arsonist, she would have removed her son from the residence hall, thus preventing his death when the arsonist returned and set a subsequent fire five days later.

Individuals may also face liability when they enter contracts on behalf of the college or university. Personal contract liability is discussed in Section 4.7.3 below.

4.7.2. Tort liability

4.7.2.1. Overview. An employee of a postsecondary institution who commits a tort may be liable even if the tort was committed while he or she was conducting the institution's affairs.[28] The individual must actually have committed the tortious act, directed it, or otherwise participated in its commission, however, before personal liability will attach. The individual will not be personally liable for torts of other institutional agents merely because he or she represents the institution for whom the other agents were acting. The elements of a tort and the defenses against a tort claim (see Section 3.3.2) in suits against the individual personally are generally the same as those in suits against the institution. An individual sued in his or her personal capacity, however, is usually not shielded by the sovereign immunity and charitable immunity defenses that sometimes protect the institution.

If an employee commits a tort while acting on behalf of the institution and within the scope of the authority delegated to him or her, both the individual and the institution may be liable for the harm caused by the tort. But the institution's potential liability does not relieve the individual of any measure of liability; the injured party could choose to collect a judgment solely from the individual, and the individual would have no claim against the institution for any part of the judgment he or she was required to pay. However, where individual and institution are both potentially liable, the individual may receive practical relief from liability if the injured party squeezes the entire judgment from the institution or the institution chooses to pay the entire amount.

If an employee commits a tort while acting outside the scope of delegated authority, he or she may be personally liable but the institution would not be liable (Section 3.3.1). Thus, the injured party could obtain a judgment only against the individual, and only the individual would be responsible for satisfying the judgment. The institution, however, may affirm the individual's unauthorized action ("affirmance" is similar to the "ratification" discussed in connection with contract liability in Section 3.4), in which case the individual will be deemed to have acted within his or her authority, and both institution and individual will be potentially liable.

Employees of public institutions can sometimes escape tort liability by proving the defense of "official immunity." For this defense to apply, the individual's act must have been within the scope of his or her authority and must have been a discretionary act involving policy judgment, as opposed to a "ministerial duty" (involving little or no discretion with regard to the choices to be made). Because it involves this element of discretion and policy judgment, official immunity is more likely to apply to a particular individual the higher in the authority hierarchy he or she is.

State tort claims acts may also define the degree to which public employees will be protected from individual liability. For example, the Georgia Tort Claims

---

[28]Cases and authorities are collected in Christopher Bello, Annot., "Personal Liability of Public School Teacher in Negligence Action for Personal Injury or Death of Student," 34 A.L.R.4th 228; Annot., "Personal Liability of Public School Executive or Administrative Officer in Negligence Action for Personal Injury or Death of Student," 35 A.L.R.4th 272; Annot., "Personal Liability in Negligence Action of Public School Employee, Other Than Teacher or Executive or Administrative Officer, for Personal Injury or Death of Student," 35 A.L.R.4th 328.

Act has been interpreted by that state's courts as extending immunity in two cases to the department chair and academic vice president at Gordon College who recommended that one professor be denied tenure (*Hardin v. Phillips,* 547 S.E.2d 565 (Ga. Ct. App. 2001)) and that an untenured professor be fired for neglect of duty and insubordination (*Wang v. Moore,* 544 S.E.2d 486 (Ga. Ct. App. 2001)).

4.7.2.2. Negligence. Although the institution is typically the defendant of choice in a negligence claim, faculty and staff are occasionally found liable for negligence if their failure to act, or their negligent act, contributed to the plaintiff's injury. The elements of a tort claim (discussed in Section 3.3.1) are the same for suits against institutions and suits against individuals. But employees of public institutions may enjoy immunity from liability, while employees of private institutions may not (unless they are shielded by charitable immunity, also discussed in Section 3.3.1). For example, in *Defoor v. Evesque,* 694 So. 2d 1302 (Ala. 1997), the Supreme Court of Alabama ruled that an employee of a public college was not immune from personal tort liability in relation to a slip-and-fall claim. The college had entered a contract with USX Corporation to provide testing services for individuals applying for certain jobs at USX. A college administrator hired Evesque to administer the tests. Although Evesque usually made certain that there was no spilled hydraulic fluid in the testing area, on the day that Defoor took his test, fluid was spilled on the floor, and Defoor fell, sustaining injuries. Although the college and USX were absolved from potential liability, Evesque was not, because the court characterized his duty to clean up the spill "ministerial" rather than "discretionary." The court explained that cleaning the site "involved no marshaling of State resources, no prioritizing of competing needs, no planning, and no exercise of policy-level discretion" (694 So. 2d at 1306).

Medical professionals and counselors may face individual liability for alleged negligence in treating student patients. In a widely reported case, *Tarasoff v. Regents of the University of California,* 551 P.2d 334 (Cal. 1976), the parents of a girl murdered by a psychiatric patient at the university hospital sued the university regents, four psychotherapists employed by the hospital, and the campus police. The patient had confided his intention to kill the daughter to a staff psychotherapist. Though the patient was briefly detained by the campus police at the psychotherapist's request, no further action was taken to protect the daughter. The parents alleged that the defendants should be held liable for a tortious failure to confine a dangerous patient and a tortious failure to warn them or their daughter of a dangerous patient. The psychotherapists and campus police claimed official immunity under a California statute freeing "public employee(s)" from liability for acts or omissions resulting from "the exercise of discretion vested in [them]" (Cal. Govt. Code § 820.2). The court accepted the official immunity defense in relation to the failure to confine, because that failure involved a "basic policy decision" sufficient to constitute discretion under the statute. But regarding the failure to warn, the court refused to accept the psychotherapists' official immunity claim, because the decision whether to warn was not a basic policy decision. The campus police needed no official immunity from their failure to warn, because, the court held, they had no legal duty to warn in light of the facts in the complaint. (For a discussion of the continuing viability of *Tarasoff*, despite rulings by other state courts that have rejected its outcome, see Peter F. Lake, "Virginia Is Not Safe for 'Lovers': The Virginia Supreme Court Rejects *Tarasoff* in *Nasser v. Parker,*" 61 *Brooklyn L. Rev.* 1285 (1995).)

The Supreme Court of Rhode Island, addressing a similar issue, ruled that a jury must determine whether a psychologist was individually liable. In *Klein v. Solomon,* 713 A.2d 764 (R.I. 1998), the mother of a Brown University student who had committed suicide filed a negligence suit against the university, the psychologist who had diagnosed her son as having suicidal tendencies, and another counselor to whom the psychologist had referred the son. She alleged that the psychologist was negligent in referring her son to a list of four therapists, none of whom specialized in suicide prevention, and none of whom could prescribe medication. The court affirmed a summary judgment for the university with respect to its own liability, but reversed the lower court's summary judgment award to the psychologist. The court stated that a jury could have concluded that the psychologist was negligent in failing to refer the student to someone who was qualified to treat him for suicidal tendencies. (For a discussion of a preliminary ruling in *Shin v. MIT,* in which the university was found not liable for a student's suicide but the judge allowed the case to proceed against individual defendants, see Section 3.3.2.5.)

Malpractice claims against doctors employed by hospitals affiliated with public institutions provide a potential opportunity for an immunity defense. The breadth of coverage is dependent upon state law. For example, in *Rivera v. Hospital Universitario,* 762 F. Supp. 15 (D.P.R. 1991), the court applied Puerto Rico law to determine that medical school professors who worked part time as attending physicians at the university hospital were employees, not independent contractors, and thus shared the university's governmental immunity.

On the other hand, the Supreme Court of Virginia in *James v. Jane,* 282 S.E.2d 864 (Va. 1980), rejected a defense of sovereign immunity asserted by physicians who were full-time faculty members at the state university medical center and members of the hospital staff. The defendants had argued that, as state employees, they were immune from a suit charging them with negligence in their treatment of certain patients at the university's hospital. The trial court accepted the physicians' defense. Although agreeing that under Virginia law certain state employees and agents could share the state's own sovereign immunity, the Virginia Supreme Court reversed the trial court and refused to extend this immunity to these particular employees.

In reaching its decision, the appellate court analyzed the immunity defense and the circumstances in which its assertion is appropriate, concluding that immunity was appropriate for officials such as the governor, state officials, and judges. Furthermore, said the court, if a state employee is acting on behalf of the state by "exercis[ing] broad discretionary powers, often involving both the determination and implementation of state policy," then immunity is appropriate. If, however, the state employee is engaged in an activity that is also performed in the private sector, immunity may not be appropriate. The court concluded that because the state exercised minimal control over the work of the doctors, they were not entitled to the state's immunity defense.

The "sovereign" or "state employee" immunity thus created by the Virginia court is potentially broader than the "official immunity" recognized in some other jurisdictions. In states recognizing "official immunity," the likelihood of successfully invoking the defense is, as mentioned, proportional to the officer's or employee's level in the authority hierarchy. This official immunity doctrine seeks to protect the discretionary and policy-making functions of higher-level decision makers, a goal that the *James v. Jane* opinion also recognized. The sovereign immunity defense articulated in *James*, however, encompasses an additional consideration: the degree of state control over the employee's job functions. In weighing this additional factor, the Virginia sovereign immunity doctrine also seeks to protect state employees who are so closely directed by the state that they should not bear individual responsibility for negligent acts committed within the scope of this controlled employment. Sovereign immunity Virginia-style may thus extend to lower-echelon employees not reached by official immunity. Although *James* held that this theory does not apply to physicians treating patients in a state university medical center, the theory could perhaps be applied to other postsecondary employees—such as middle- or low-level administrative personnel (*Messina v. Burden,* 321 S.E.2d 657 (Va. 1984), concerning the superintendent of buildings at a community college) or support staff.

Although *James* is binding law only in Virginia, it illustrates nuances in the doctrine of personal tort immunity that may also exist, or may now develop, in other states. When contrasted with the cases relying on the official immunity doctrine, *James* also illustrates the state-by-state variations that can exist in this area of the law. (For a contrasting view and a different result in a case with similar facts, see *Sullivan v. Washington,* 768 So. 2d 881 (Miss. 2000).)

Because state immunity is a matter of state law, the application and interpretation of this doctrine differ among the states. For example, a federal appellate court found several members of the athletic staff protected by a qualified immunity against liability for negligence in the death of a student. In *Sorey v. Kellett,* 849 F.2d 960 (5th Cir. 1988), a football player at the University of Southern Mississippi collapsed during practice and died shortly thereafter. The court applied Mississippi's qualified immunity for public officials performing discretionary, rather than ministerial, acts to the trainer, the team physician, and the football coach, finding that the first two were performing a discretionary act in administering medical treatment to the student. The coach was entitled to qualified immunity because of his general authority over the football program. Noting that "a public official charged only with general authority over a program or institution naturally is exercising discretionary functions" (849 F.2d at 964), the court denied recovery to the plaintiff.

Other potential sources of individual liability for alleged negligence include claims of negligent hiring, supervision, and retention. Employer liability for these claims is discussed in Section 3.3.5; individuals may also be found liable under these theories. (For a discussion of the standards applied to a claim of negligent supervision, see *Poe v. Leonard,* 282 F.3d 123 (2d Cir. 2002) (supervisor not personally liable for negligent supervision because he had neither actual nor constructive notice that subordinate would secretly videotape an individual while at work).)

4.7.2.3. Defamation. As discussed in Section 3.3.4, claims that an oral or written communication resulted in injury to an individual are a rapidly increasing area of litigation for colleges. College employees may face individual liability for defamation as well. Administrators and faculty have been sued for defamation by both faculty and students who allege that oral or written statements made by college employees have derailed academic careers or have interfered with employment opportunities.

Defamation claims brought by faculty and staff against college officials who have been critical of their work performance or their behavior have proliferated over the past few years, but few have been successful. Plaintiffs must meet a four-part test (discussed in Section 3.3.4) in order to make a claim of defamation. In some cases, courts have found that the communication was not defamatory, either because it did not harm the individual's reputation, or because the information in the communication was too general to cause harm to the plaintiff, or because the allegedly defamatory information was true. For example, in *Constantino v. University of Pittsburgh,* 766 A.2d 1265 (Pa. Super. 2001), a department chair who wrote a letter stating that there were "problems" with a faculty member's teaching was found not to have defamed the faculty member because the letter was sent to officials who were responsible for evaluating the plaintiff's performance, and the statements were general in nature. And in *Wynne v. Loyola University of Chicago,* 741 N.E.2d 669 (Ill. Ct. App. 1st Dist. 2000), an Illinois appellate court ruled that the faculty author of a letter discussing a department chair's alleged psychological problems and unpleasant behavior could not be found liable for defamation, even though the letter was circulated to departmental colleagues, because the plaintiff had admitted that the information in the letter was true, and the court characterized some of the author's statements as opinion.

Defendants who are employed by public colleges or universities may be shielded by state law official immunity. *Staheli v. Smith,* 548 So. 2d 1299 (Miss. 1989) provides an example of the application of state law official immunity. The Supreme Court of Mississippi was asked to determine whether the dean of the School of Engineering at the University of Mississippi was a public official for purposes of governmental immunity against a defamation lawsuit. A faculty member had sued the dean, stating that a letter from the dean recommending against tenure for the plaintiff was libelous. The court found that the dean was, indeed, a public figure and thus protected by qualified government immunity. Since the faculty handbook authorized administrators to make "appropriate" comments, and since making a subjective evaluation of a faculty member's performance is a discretionary, rather than a ministerial, duty, the court found that the dean had acted within the scope of his authority and had not lost the immunity by exceeding his authority.

Employees acting within the scope of their authority may also be protected by a common law privilege for communications between persons sharing a common duty or interest, such as communications between individuals within a business or an academic organization. In *Kraft v. William Alanson White Psychiatric Foundation*, 498 A.2d 1145 (D.C. 1985), the court applied an "absolute privilege" to communications among faculty members about the plaintiff's inadequate academic performance in a postgraduate certificate program. The court stated: "A person who seeks an academic credential and who is on notice that satisfactory performance is a prerequisite to his receipt of that credential consents to frank evaluation by those charged with the responsibility to supervise him" (498 A.2d at 1149). Despite the court's application of an "absolute" privilege in *Kraft,* the more typical approach is for a court to consider whether the communication should be protected by a "qualified" or "conditional" privilege, which may be lost if the confidential information is shared with one or more individuals who do not have a business-related reason to receive the information.

In *Gernander v. Winona State University,* 428 N.W.2d 473 (Minn. Ct. App. 1988), a female associate professor denied promotion sued her department chair, claiming that a memo he wrote to her and distributed to higher-level administrators was defamatory. The court rejected the claim on several grounds. First, the plaintiff had requested the promotion and thus "opened herself" to evaluation. Second, the memo had a limited audience and thus did not meet the "publication" requirement for defamation (see Section 3.3.4). And third, the memo expressed the chair's opinion, and thus was protected by the First Amendment.

Characterizing statements as opinion, however, may not provide complete protection against liability for defamation. A ruling by the U.S. Supreme Court in *Milkovich v. Lorain Journal* Co., 497 U.S. 1 (1990), suggests that this "opinion privilege" to defamation liability may not be legally sound when applied to a "public figure" (see Section 3.3.4). The plaintiff claimed that an article in which he was portrayed as a perjurer was defamatory. The defendant, a newspaper, asserted an "opinion privilege" as its entire defense to the defamation claim. In an opinion by Chief Justice Rehnquist, the Supreme Court denied that any constitutional "opinion privilege" existed, although it said that "statements on matters of public concern must be provable as false before liability attaches," at least in situations where "a media defendant is involved" (497 U.S. at 19). Although future nonmedia defendants may attempt to limit *Milkovich* to its narrow facts, the opinion's wholesale rejection of a constitutional "opinion privilege" appears to apply to all defendants, not just the media.

Certain university administrators or trustees may be viewed as "public figures" by a court; in such instances they would have to demonstrate that an employee who allegedly defamed them had acted with "actual malice" in publishing the defamatory information. The constitutional standard that a public figure must meet was established by the U.S. Supreme Court in *New York Times v. Sullivan,* 376 U.S. 254 (1964), in which the court defined "actual malice" to include knowledge of the falsity of the statement or reckless disregard for its truth or falsity. Athletics coaches, university trustees and administrators, and even prominent faculty have sometimes been determined to be public figures, in which case public comment on their activities or decisions must meet the "actual malice" standard in order to be actionable.

Faculty and staff at public colleges may also be provided a form of immunity from liability for defamation by provisions in state personnel laws. For example, in *Fieno v. State of Minnesota*, 567 N.W.2d 739 (Ct. App. Minn. 1997), an associate dean, Fieno, was terminated after her supervisor, the dean, gave her a very negative performance evaluation. Fieno sued the college and the dean for, among other claims, defamation. The court applied Minnesota statute, Section 13.43, subdivision 2, which affords absolute immunity from defamation actions to persons who disclose public personnel data that are not protected from disclosure by that law, such as complaints against a public employee. Characterizing the negative performance evaluation as a "complaint" against the employee, the court ruled that the dean was immune from liability.

Written or oral statements made in the course of litigation or settlement agreements may also be protected by an absolute judicial privilege. (For a discussion of the application of this privilege to a defamation claim concerning letters of apology made in a settlement of a sexual harassment lawsuit, see *Sodergren v. The Johns Hopkins University Applied Physics Laboratory*, 773 A.2d 592 (Ct. Spec. App. Md. 2001).)

But simply because an internal investigation is involved does not subject the allegedly defamatory statements to an absolute privilege. In *Arroyo v. Rosen*, 648 A.2d 1074 (Md. App. 1994), a faculty member sued his former postdoctoral fellow for defamation. Dr. Rosen chaired the Department of Pharmacology and Toxicology at the University of Maryland at Baltimore, where Dr. Arroyo was employed as a postdoctoral fellow and then as a research associate. The two scientists worked together on a project, and Arroyo drafted a paper, based on the research, listing herself as first author and Rosen as a coauthor. She submitted it to a journal; it was returned for revision. Although Rosen asked to see the reviewers' comments, Arroyo revised the paper and resubmitted it without showing it to Rosen. Rosen was concerned because he did not believe that their data supported the conclusions that Arroyo had drawn in the paper. Although the paper had been accepted for publication, Rosen asked Arroyo to withdraw it. She appealed to the pharmacy dean, who had the paper reviewed by external experts, who in turn agreed with Rosen's concerns. Arroyo then filed charges of scientific misconduct against Rosen with the U.S. Department of Health and Human Services; she also sent a letter to forty-three colleagues around the United States accusing Rosen of misconduct. Two investigations—one internal and one by his funding agency—cleared Rosen of all the charges. Arroyo continued her campaign against Rosen, and apparently provided a journalist with confidential material from the investigation. Rosen sued Arroyo for defamation and invasion of privacy. A jury found for him on both claims and also awarded him $25,000 in punitive damages.

On appeal, Arroyo claimed that her acts were privileged because they were related to the investigation. She attempted to use the absolute privilege afforded to witnesses when testifying in a judicial proceeding. The court rejected this argument, stating that a university hearing does not have the trappings of a judicial process (witnesses are not under oath or subject to cross-examination, the unavailability of discovery, and the lack of a record of the hearing). The appellate court affirmed the jury's finding that Arroyo had exhibited actual malice in her statements because she knew that they were false, or did not attempt to ascertain whether or not they were false. The court also found sufficient evidence of malice in Arroyo's act of providing confidential information from the hearing to a colleague and to a newspaper reporter. Distribution of the confidential information was also an invasion of privacy, said the court, since the report was not a public document.

But a scholarly article that criticized another scholar's scientific theory was found not to be defamatory in *Ezrailson v. Rohrich*, 65 S.W.3d 373 (Ct. App. Tex. 9th Dist. 2001). The court agreed with the defendants' argument that the article addressed a matter of public health and medicine, and was not actionable because the issue at hand was the subject of public debate and no reasonable person could perceive the article as defamatory. Furthermore, said the court, to rule that the article was defamatory would unduly restrict the free flow of ideas essential to medical science discourse.

Defendants in certain defamation cases may be protected by the concept of "invited libel" and thus found not to have been responsible for the "publication" element of a defamation claim. In *Sophianopoulous v. McCormick*, 385 S.E.2d 682 (Ga. Ct. App. 1989), for example, a state appellate court rejected a faculty member's defamation claim against his department chair. The professor had complained to the American Association of University Professors that his chair had mistreated him. When the AAUP contacted the chair to inquire about the professor's performance, the chair sent the AAUP copies of memoranda critical of the professor's performance. The judges ruled that, by involving the AAUP in the dispute with his chair, the plaintiff consented to having the offending information published to the AAUP.

The concept of privilege has also been applied to lawsuits brought by students against faculty and staff. For example, in *Ostasz v. Medical College of Ohio*, 691 N.E.2d 371 (Ct. Cl. Oh. 1997), Ostasz, a former medical resident seeking hospital privileges at the end of his residency, requested a letter of reference from the director of the Medical College of Ohio. The director, Dr. Horrigan, reviewed the former resident's file and noted that he had experienced academic problems during his residency, and that six other residents had provided letters expressing their reservations about Ostasz's competency. Horrigan's letter also expressed reservations about Ostasz's competency. When Ostasz was denied hospital privileges, he sued Horrigan and the Medical College of Ohio for defamation, intentional infliction of emotional distress, and negligent infliction of emotional distress. The court applied the doctrine of qualified privilege to the letter because its purpose was to assist the hospital in determining whether to grant Ostasz hospital privileges. Only if the writer of the letter had acted with actual malice would the privilege be lost. The court found no malice in Horrigan's letter and awarded judgment as a matter of law to the medical college and to Horrigan.

In *Hupp v. Sasser*, 490 S.E.2d 880 (W. Va. 1997), a graduate student was told that his teaching assistantship might not be renewed because several students had complained about his alleged unprofessional and intimidating behavior toward them. It was also alleged that an instructor had been exposed to abuse by the teaching assistant. After a meeting between the dean and the student, the student was told that his assistantship would be renewed on the condition that he did not repeat the abusive behavior, and that further complaints would result in immediate termination of his assistantship. The student rejected those conditions on his employment and filed a claim of defamation, as well as other nontort claims. The court examined each of the statements attributed to the dean that the student had alleged were defamatory, and concluded that each was either truthful and factual and, therefore, could not be defamatory, or was a subjective conclusion about the student's behavior protected by the First Amendment under the Supreme Court's *Milkovich* standard and, therefore, was not actionable. Because the court had determined that the statements had no defamatory content, it did not reach the issue of whether or not a qualified privilege existed.

Dean v. Wissmann, 996 S.W.2d 631 (Mo. Ct. App. 1999) provides an example of the successful use of the qualified privilege because the communication at issue was limited to individuals with a business need for the information. In this case, the professor had written a letter accusing the plaintiff, a nursing student, of stealing a test. The letter was read by the head of the nursing department, the college dean, and the vice president of student affairs. The court held that the professor had reported the alleged dishonesty to the appropriate people, and thus, the letter was not "published," an essential element of a defamation claim. Because the professor had communicated the allegedly defamatory information only to individuals within the organization with a legitimate organizational reason to be informed about the situation, the court ruled that internal "publication" of this information did not meet the "publication" element of the defamation claim.

The privilege may be lost, however, if an employee acts with malice or otherwise unprofessionally. In *Smith v. Atkins*, 622 So. 2d 795 (La. App. 1993), Theresa Smith, a first-year law student at Southern University, filed claims of defamation, invasion of privacy, and intentional infliction of emotional distress against one of her law professors, Curklin Atkins. Professor Atkins routinely discussed his social life in class and directed many sexually explicit comments to Smith and another female student. He called Smith a "slut" in front of the entire class on two occasions, and, also in front of the entire class, related a humiliating event experienced by Smith at a local bar. The trial court ruled in the plaintiff's favor on the defamation claim, but rejected her emotional distress claim. The appellate court affirmed the defamation ruling, but reversed the emotional distress ruling, and held in the student's favor, finding that "calling a female law student a 'slut' is defamatory per se" (622 So. 2d 799), and thus, she had sustained an intentional injury. A dissent suggests that the evidence supporting the emotional distress claim was very weak and that the majority wanted to "punish" the professor for his unprofessional conduct, despite the fact that punitive damages for defamation are not available in Louisiana. Although it is not possible to ascertain the majority's motivation from simply reading the published opinion, it is quite likely that the majority was incensed by the alleged behavior of the faculty member.

On occasion, faculty members have sued students for defamation. These claims tend to occur when sexual harassment is alleged by a student. For example, in *Chiavarelli v. Williams*, 681 N.Y.S.2d 276 (App. Div. 1998), the chair of the division of cardiothoracic surgery at the SUNY Health Science Center in Brooklyn sued the chief resident for defamation. The plaintiff claimed that the defendant wrote a libelous letter concerning sexual advances the plaintiff had allegedly made toward the defendant, and then circulated the letter to the plaintiff's supervisors. The letter claimed that the plaintiff had given the defendant negative evaluations because the defendant had spurned the plaintiff's sexual advances. Although the defendant sought to have the complaint dismissed (the plaintiff had not alleged or proven special damages), the court agreed that the claim should be characterized as a claim of libel per se, which does not require a plaintiff to allege special damages. Allegations suggesting that a professional is unfit for his or her professional role reflect adversely on that individual's integrity, and even if no claims are made that the professional is incompetent in his or her profession, defamation per se may be established without evidence of special damages.

Institutions should consider whether or not they wish to protect their personnel from the financial consequences of personal tort liability. Insurance coverage and indemnification agreements, discussed in Section 2.5.3.2, may be utilized for this purpose. (For an overview of liability insurance and related issues, see B. Higgins & E. Zulkey, "Liability Insurance Coverage: How to Avoid Unpleasant Surprises," 17 *J. Coll. & Univ. Law* 123 (1990).)

4.7.2.4. *Other tort claims.* Although negligence and defamation claims are the most frequent source of tort claims against individual employees, other tort theories are occasionally used by either employees or students. For example, several Rutgers University basketball players brought an invasion-of-privacy claim against their coach for forcing them to run laps in the nude after losing a game of free-throw shooting at the university's athletic center (Donna Leusner, "Ex-Players Can Sue Over Sprints in the Nude," *Newark Star Ledger*, July 5, 2001, p. 13). Employees who believe that managers or supervisors have deliberately provided them with false information to induce them to accept a job offer have prevailed in claims of fraudulent inducement. (For an example of a successful claim in a nonacademic context, see *Hyman v. International Business Machines Corp.*, 2000 U.S. Dist. LEXIS 15136 (S.D.N.Y. 2000).) But a former Northwestern University employee who alleged that her former supervisor's negative employment reference was responsible for her inability to obtain a job was unsuccessful in her suit against the supervisor. The plaintiff could not establish interference with prospective economic advantage because, the court ruled, she could not demonstrate that she had a reasonable expectation of obtaining that particular position (*Anderson v. Vanden Dorpel*, 667 N.E.2d 1296 (Ill. 1996)).

Closely related to the tort of interference with prospective economic advantage is the tort of interference with contractual advantage (or contractual relationship). Typically, the current or former employer of the plaintiff cannot be sued under this theory because the doctrine requires a plaintiff to demonstrate that a third party interfered with the contractual relationship between the plaintiff and his or her employer. While disappointed tenure candidates rarely convince a court to entertain a claim of intentional interference with contractual advantage, the court in *Witczak v. Gerald,* 793 A.2d 1193 (Ct. App. Ct. 2002), reversed a trial court's dismissal of a claim against three faculty members who had recommended that the plaintiff be denied tenure. According to the plaintiff, the defendants, who were members of the Dean's Advisory Council, destroyed a letter that supported the plaintiff's tenure candidacy, underreported the amount of external funding and the number of publications that the plaintiff had written, and rejected the plaintiff's request to correct these inaccuracies. Although Connecticut General Statute § 4-165 provides immunity for certain state employees acting within the scope of their employment unless their conduct is "wanton, reckless or malicious," the appellate court concluded that the actions alleged by the plaintiff could be sufficiently malicious so as to meet the terms of the exception to the immunity statute.

A perennial claim brought by individuals who are challenging the termination of employment or, for students, mistreatment by a faculty or staff member, is a claim of either intentional or negligent infliction of emotional distress. A student successfully raised this claim against several faculty and administrators in *Ross v. St. Augustine College,* 103 F.3d 338 (4th Cir. 1996). The plaintiff, an honors student who had testified on behalf of a professor who had successfully sued the college, claimed that faculty and administrators had retaliated against her by wrongfully awarding her low or failing grades, altering her transcript, and preventing her from graduating. The administration also tried to have her impeached as president of the senior class. The jury found the college and some of the individual defendants (including the academic vice president) liable for intentional infliction of emotional distress, and also awarded the student punitive damages. The appellate court upheld both awards.

A very significant case involving a middle school student is instructive for faculty and administrators who are asked to write letters of recommendation for current or previous students or employees. In *Randi W. v. Muroc Joint Unified School District,* 929 P.2d 582 (Cal. 1997), a middle school student and her parents sued several previous employers of Robert Gadams, the vice principal of the student's middle school, as well as individuals who had provided Gadams with letters of recommendation. The plaintiffs alleged that Gadams had sexually assaulted the student, and that he had been accused of similar conduct while serving in similar positions in other school districts. The plaintiffs stated claims of negligence, negligent hiring, negligent misrepresentation, fraud, and negligence per se, against the prior school districts where Gadams had worked as well as the individuals who had provided highly positive letters of reference written on Gadams's behalf. The court stated that:

> although policy considerations dictate that ordinarily a recommending employer should not be held accountable to third persons for failing to disclose negative information regarding a former employee, nonetheless liability may be imposed

if . . . the recommendation letter amounts to an affirmative misrepresentation presenting a foreseeable and substantial risk of physical harm to a third person [929 P.2d at 584].

The court rejected the plaintiffs' negligence, negligent hiring, negligence per se, and Title IX claims, but ruled in their favor on their negligent misrepresentation and fraud claims. The court ruled that, given the defendants' knowledge of the prior charges against Gadams, it was foreseeable that he would repeat the behavior in another school. And it was also reasonably foreseeable, said the court, that the hiring school district would read the letters of recommendation and would rely on them in making a hiring decision. The letters contained only positive information and omitted any mention of the charges that had been brought against Gadams. The employees of the former employers, said the court, had two choices in deciding how to write a letter of reference in this situation. First, they could write a "full disclosure" letter that discussed all the relevant facts known to the writer of the letter. Or second, they could have written a "no comment" letter or merely verified the dates of his employment. The court rejected the notion that an employer or an individual has a duty to disclose any relevant information to a prospective employer, absent some special relationship. No such special relationship had been alleged by the plaintiffs. Thus, the court held that "the writer of a letter of recommendation owes to third persons a duty not to misrepresent the facts in describing the qualifications and character of a former employee, if making these misrepresentations would present a substantial, foreseeable risk of physical injury to the third persons" (929 P.2d at 591). The letters, "essentially recommending Gadams for any position without reservation or qualification, constituted affirmative representations that strongly implied Gadams was fit to interact appropriately and safely with female students" (929 P.2d at 593). Furthermore, said the court, the injury to the student was the proximate result of the school district's decision to hire Gadams, in reliance on the letters of recommendation. (But the court rejected the plaintiffs' argument that the previous employer's failure to report the assault charges against Gadams to state authorities (as required by law) provided an independent basis for tort liability.)

As the cases discussed in this subsection demonstrate, courts are quite willing to impose personal liability on college faculty and staff if they fail to exercise care in carrying out their responsibilities. Particularly for staff whose responsibilities involve potentially dangerous activities or substances (for example, athletics staff, science laboratory staff, security officers, custodians, and drivers of vans and buses), training should be provided on appropriate performance of these responsibilities and how to handle emergency situations. In addition, faculty and administrators who are involved in making judgments about students or staff may need to limit the scope and content of their communications to avoid potential liability for defamation, misrepresentation, or fraud.

4.7.3. Contract liability. An employee who signs a contract on behalf of an institution may be personally liable for its performance if the institution breaches the contract. The extent of personal liability depends on whether the agent's participation on behalf of the institution was authorized—either by a grant of express authority or by an implied authority, an apparent authority, or a subsequent ratification by the institution. (See the discussion of authority in Sections 3.1 & 3.4.) If the individual's participation was properly authorized, and if that individual signed the contract only in the capacity of an institutional agent, he or she will not be personally liable for performance of the contract. If, however, the participation was not properly authorized, or if the individual signed in an individual capacity rather than as an institutional agent, he or she may be personally liable.

In some cases the other contracting party may be able to sue both the institution and the agent or to choose between them. This option is presented when the contracting party did not know at the time of contracting that the individual participated in an agency capacity, but later learned that was the case. The option is also presented when the contracting party knew that the individual was acting as an institutional agent, but the individual also gave a personal promise that the contract would be performed. In such situations, if the contracting party obtains a judgment against both the institution and the agent, the judgment may be satisfied against either or against both, but the contracting party may receive no more than the total amount of the judgment. Where the contracting party receives payment from only one of the two liable parties, the paying party may have a claim against the nonpayer for part of the judgment amount.

An agent who is a party to the contract in a personal capacity, and thus potentially liable on it, can assert the same defenses that are available to any contracting party. These defenses may arise from the contract (for instance, the absence of some formality necessary to complete the contract, or fraud, or inadequate performance by the other party), or they may be personal to the agent (for instance, a particular counterclaim against the other party).

Even if a contract does not exist, the doctrine of promissory estoppel may be used by a candidate for a position who is given an offer of employment that is subsequently withdrawn. This claim allows an individual to seek a remedy for detrimental reliance on a promise of employment, even where no contract existed (see *Restatement of Contracts,* § 90). In *Bicknese v. Sultana,* 635 N.W.2d 905 (Wis. Ct. App. 2001), the plaintiff had applied for a faculty position at the University of Wisconsin. The plaintiff claimed that the department chair, Sultana, had offered her the position, and that she resigned her faculty position at SUNY-Stony Brook and rejected a job offer from SUNY at Buffalo. A university committee rejected Sultana's recommendation that Bicknese be hired. She sued Sultana individually, and a jury ruled in her favor on her claim of promissory estoppel. Sultana appealed, claiming that he had been performing discretionary acts within the scope of his employment, and thus was immune from liability. The court agreed, rejecting the plaintiff's contentions that Sultana had acted maliciously or with the intent to deceive, and finding that Sultana's acts were discretionary rather than ministerial.

Department chairs, deans, and other individuals must be careful not to imply that they have the authority to hire, or to confer a promotion or tenure, when speaking with a prospective faculty member (unless, of course, they do have that authority). Clear statements on appointment letters and written contracts that only the Board of Trustees has the authority to confer promotion or tenure should help protect the college against later claims of oral contracts or promissory estoppel.

4.7.4. Constitutional liability (personal liability under Section 1983)

4.7.4.1. Qualified immunity. The liability of administrators and other employees of public postsecondary institutions (and also individual trustees) for constitutional rights violations is determined under the same body of law that determines the liability of the institutions themselves (see Section 3.5) and presents many of the same legal issues. As with institutional liability, an individual's action must usually be taken "under color of" state law, or must be characterizable as "state action," before personal liability will attach. But, as with tort and contract liability, the liability of individual administrators and other employees (and trustees) is not coterminous with that of the institution itself. Defenses that may be available to the institution (such as the sovereign immunity defense) may not be available to individuals sued in their personal capacities; conversely, defenses that may be available to individuals (such as the qualified immunity defense discussed later in this subsection) may not be available to the institution.

The federal statute referred to as Section 1983, quoted in Section 3.5 of this book, is again the key statute. Unlike the states themselves, state government (and also local government) officials and employees sued in their personal capacities are clearly "persons" under Section 1983 and thus subject to its provisions whenever they are acting under color of state law. Also unlike the states, officials and employees sued in their personal capacities are not protected from suit by a constitutional sovereign immunity. But courts have recognized a qualified immunity for public officials and employees from liability for monetary damages under Section 1983. (See K. Blum, "Qualified Immunity: A User's Manual," 26 *Ind. L. Rev.* 187 (1993).) This immunity applies to officials and employees sued in their *personal* (or *individual*) capacities rather than their *official* (or *representational*) capacities. *Mangaroo v. Nelson*, 864 F.2d 1202 (5th Cir. 1989), illustrates the distinction. The plaintiff had been demoted from a deanship to a tenured faculty position. She sued both Nelson, the acting president who demoted her, and Pierre, Nelson's successor, alleging that their actions violated her procedural due process rights. She sued the former in his *personal* (or *individual*) capacity, seeking monetary damages, and the latter in his *official* (or *representational*) capacity, seeking injunctive relief. The court held that Nelson was entitled to claim qualified immunity, since the plaintiff sought money damages from him in his personal capacity for the harm he had caused. In contrast, the court held that Pierre was not eligible for qualified immunity, because the plaintiff sued him only in his official capacity, seeking only an injunctive order compelling him, as president, to take action to remedy the violation of her due process rights. (For further explanation of the distinction between personal capacity suits and official capacity suits, see *Hafer v. Melo,* 502 U.S. 21, 25–31 (1991).)

In 1974 and again in 1975, the U.S. Supreme Court laid the foundation for qualified immunity as it applies to school officials. In *Scheuer v. Rhodes,* 416 U.S. 232 (1974), the Court considered a suit for damages brought on behalf of three students killed in the May 1970 Vietnam War protests at Kent State University. The Court rejected the contention that the president of Kent State and other state officials had an absolute "official immunity" protecting them from personal liability. The Court instead accorded the president and officials a "qualified immunity" under Section 1983: "[I]n varying scope, a qualified immunity is available to officers of the executive branch of government, the variation being dependent upon the scope of discretion and responsibilities of the office and all the circumstances as they reasonably appeared at the time of the action on which liability is sought to be based." Because the availability of this immunity depended on facts not yet in the record, the Supreme Court remanded the case to the trial court for further proceedings.[29]

In *Wood v. Strickland,* 420 U.S. 308 (1975), the Supreme Court extended, and added enigma to, the Section 1983 qualified immunity for school officials. After the school board in this case had expelled some students from high school for violating a school disciplinary regulation, several of the students sued the members of the school board for damages and injunctive and declaratory relief. In a 5-to-4 decision, the Court held that school board members, as public school officials, are entitled to a qualified immunity from such suits:

> We think there must be a degree of immunity if the work of the schools is to go forward; and, however worded, the immunity must be such that public school officials understand that . . . they need not exercise their discretion with undue timidity. . . .
>
> [B]ut an act violating a student's constitutional rights can be no more justified by *ignorance or disregard of settled, indisputable law* on the part of one entrusted with supervision of students' daily lives than by the presence of actual malice. To be entitled to a special exemption from the categorical remedial language of Section 1983 in a case in which his action violated a student's constitutional rights, a school board member . . . must be held to a standard of conduct based not only on permissible intentions, but also on *knowledge of the basic, unquestioned constitutional rights* of his charges. Such a standard imposes neither an unfair burden upon a person assuming a responsible public office . . . , nor an unwarranted burden in light of the value which civil rights have in our legal system. Any lesser standard would deny much of the promise of Section 1983. Therefore, in the specific context of school discipline, we hold that a school board member is not immune from liability for damages under Section 1983: (1) if he knew or reasonably should have known that the action he took

---

[29]On remand the case proceeded to trial against all defendants. No defendant was held immune from suit. The president of Kent State was eventually dismissed as a defendant, however, because the facts indicated that he had not personally violated any of the plaintiffs' rights (see *Krause v. Rhodes,* 570 F.2d 563 (6th Cir. 1977)). Eventually the case was settled, and an award of $600,000 plus attorney's fees was made to the plaintiffs (see *Krause v. Rhodes,* 640 F.2d 214 (6th Cir. 1981)).

within his sphere of official responsibility would violate the constitutional rights of the student affected, or (2) if he took the action with the malicious intention to cause a deprivation of constitutional rights or other injury to the student [420 U.S. at 321–22; emphasis and numbering added].

The Court's reliance on the *Scheuer* case at several points in its *Wood* opinion indicated that the *Wood* liability standard applied to public officials and executive officers in postsecondary education as well. While the immunity of lower-level administrators and faculty members was less clear under *Scheuer* and *Wood*, the Supreme Court and lower courts in later cases have generally applied the qualified immunity concept to all officers and employees named as defendants.

In *Harlow v. Fitzgerald*, 457 U.S. 800 (1982), the Court modified its *Wood* analysis in ruling on a suit brought against two senior aides to President Nixon. The immunity test developed in *Wood* had two parts (see quote above). The first part was objective, focusing on whether the defendant "knew or reasonably should have known that the action he took . . . would violate the constitutional rights" of the plaintiff (420 U.S. at 322). The second part was subjective, focusing on the defendant's "malicious intention to cause a deprivation of constitutional rights." The Court in *Harlow* deleted the subjective part of the test because it had inhibited courts from dismissing insubstantial lawsuits prior to trial:

> [W]e conclude today that bare allegations of malice should not suffice to subject government officials either to the costs of trial or to the burdens of broadreaching discovery. We therefore hold that government officials performing discretionary functions generally are shielded from liability for civil damages insofar as their conduct does not violate clearly established statutory or constitutional rights of which a reasonable person would have known (see *Procunier v. Navarette*, 434 U.S. 555, 565 (1978); *Wood v. Strickland*, 420 U.S. at 321).
>
> Reliance on the objective reasonableness of an official's conduct, as measured by reference to clearly established law, should avoid excessive disruption of government and permit the resolution of many insubstantial claims on summary judgment. . . . If the law at that time was not clearly established, an official could not reasonably be expected to anticipate subsequent legal developments, nor could he fairly be said to "know" that the law forbade conduct not previously identified as unlawful. . . . If the law was clearly established, the immunity defense ordinarily should fail, since a reasonably competent public official should know the law governing his conduct. Nevertheless, if the official pleading the defense claims extraordinary circumstances and can prove that he neither knew nor should have known of the relevant legal standard, the defense should be sustained [457 U.S. at 817–19].

In Section 1983 litigation, qualified immunity is an affirmative defense to be pleaded by the individual seeking to assert the immunity claim (*Gomez v. Toledo*, 446 U.S. 635 (1980)). Once the defendant has asserted the claim, the court must determine (1) whether the plaintiff's complaint alleges the violation of a right protected by Section 1983; and (2), if so, whether this right "was clearly established at the time of [the defendant's] actions" (*Siegert v. Gilley*, 500 U.S. 226, 232–33 (1991); *Saucier v. Katz*, 533 U.S. 194, 200 (2001)). If the court answers both of these inquiries affirmatively, it will reject the immunity claim unless the defendant can prove that, because of "extraordinary circumstances," he "neither knew nor should have known" the clearly established law applicable to the case (*Harlow,* above). The burden of proof here is clearly on the defendant, and it would be a rare case in which the defendant would sustain this burden.

As a result of this line of cases, personnel of public colleges and universities are charged with responsibility for knowing "clearly established law." Unless "extraordinary circumstances" prevent an individual from gaining such knowledge, the disregard of clearly established law is considered unreasonable and thus unprotected by the cloak of immunity. "The relevant, dispositive inquiry in determining whether a right is clearly established is whether it would be clear to a reasonable [person] that his conduct was unlawful in the situation he confronted" (*Saucier v. Katz,* 533 U.S. 194, 202 (2001)). This is a test of "objective legal reasonableness" (*Behrens v. Pelletier,* 516 U.S. 299, 306 (1996)), that is, a test that focuses on what an objective reasonable person would know rather than on what the actual defendant subjectively thought. Thus, a determination of qualified immunity "turns on the 'objective legal reasonableness' of the [challenged] action . . . assessed in light of the legal rules that were 'clearly established' at the time [the action] was taken" (*Anderson v. Creighton,* 483 U.S. 635, 639 (1987), quoting *Harlow,* 457 U.S. at 818–19).

It will often be debatable whether particular principles of law are sufficiently "clear" to fall within the Court's characterization. Moreover, the applicability of even the clearest principles may depend on a complex set of facts. In some qualified immunity cases, lower courts have sought to cope with this problem by considering whether there was a precedent in existence with facts and competing interests that are closely analogous to the situation in the current case. As one court explained, "[I]n the absence of case law that is very closely analogous," it would be "difficult for a government official to determine . . . whether the balance that he strikes is an appropriate accommodation of the competing individual and governmental interests" (*Gregorich v. Lund,* 54 F.3d 410, 414 (7th Cir. 1995)). But judges can and do disagree on whether the facts at issue are "closely analogous" to those in an earlier precedent. In *Crue v. Aiken,* 370 F.3d 668 (7th Cir. 2004), for example, the court rejected a university chancellor's qualified immunity defense to an employee's free speech claim that turned on a balancing of interests. According to the majority, there was a prior case in the Seventh Circuit that presented "a remarkably similar situation" (370 F.3d at 680). The dissent, however, distinguished the earlier case on two grounds and argued that "[t]he plaintiffs have not approached meeting their burden of showing "very closely analogous case law" (370 F.3d at 688 (Manion, J. dissenting)).[30]

---

[30]The *Crue* case also presents an interesting question of whether the law was clearly established when there were two lines of prior precedents that arguably applied to the current case, and one line used a more stringent test than the other. The majority argued that the plaintiff-faculty members' claim was governed by the balancing test from the U.S. Supreme Court's *National Treasury Employee Union* case, while the dissent argued that it was governed by the balancing test in the *Pickering/Connick* line of cases (370 F.3d at 678–80; compare 370 F.3d at 683–88). (The *National Treasury* case and the *Pickering/Connick* line are discussed and compared in Section 7.1.4 of this book.)

Other difficult issues have arisen concerning the "clearly established" standard. These issues have proven to be the most sensitive, and to create the greatest difficulties for plaintiffs, when the applicable law requires either a finding that the violation of the plaintiff's rights was intentional or some other finding regarding the defendant's motives. In such circumstances, subjective factors become a critical part of the plaintiff's claim that his or her rights have been violated, and it is unclear how these *subjective* factors are to be merged into a qualified immunity analysis that the U.S. Supreme Court has said is based on *objective* factors. In addition, qualified immunity issues are very sensitive and difficult when the determination of a rights violation requires a balancing of interests or a finding that the defendant acted "unreasonably." In such circumstances, the analysis becomes ad hoc and highly fact sensitive, making it difficult to determine whether the right claimed was "clear" or "clearly established." The following cases are illustrative.

In *Williams v. Alabama State University,* 102 F.3d 1179 (11th Cir. 1997), a former university professor alleged that she had been terminated in retaliation for her constitutionally protected criticism of a grammar textbook authored by several of her colleagues. The court determined that the issue she raised was governed by the balancing test laid out in *Pickering v. Board of Education,* 391 U.S. 563, 568 (1968) (see Section 7.1.1 of this book). Three administrators who were defendants asserted qualified immunity, claiming that the plaintiff had not alleged a "clearly established right" under the *Pickering* test.

The *Williams* court emphasized that the fact-sensitive analysis used to determine a violation of the professor's rights inevitably left some ambiguity in the extent of the rights themselves:

> Because the law in this area employs a balancing test rather than a bright-line rule to determine when a public employee's right to free speech is violated, "the employer is entitled to immunity except in the extraordinary case where *Pickering* balancing would lead to the inevitable conclusion that the discharge of the employee was unlawful" [102 F.3d at 1183, quoting *Dartland v. Metropolitan Dade County,* 866 F.2d 1321, 1323 (11th Cir. 1989)].

The court then proceeded to assess the university's action under the *Pickering* test, concluding that it was "not sufficiently clear" whether the plaintiff's speech activities "involved a matter of public concern," and that "the *Pickering* balancing test does not inevitably weigh in [the plaintiff's] favor." The defendants therefore had a qualified immunity from the plaintiff's damage claims under Section 1983.

Similarly, in *Arneson v. Jezwinski,* 592 N.W.2d 606 (Wis. 1999), Wisconsin's highest court accepted a qualified immunity defense to a university supervisor's claim that he had been denied procedural due process when he was found to have committed sexual harassment. The supervisor did have a clearly established property interest in his job, according to the court, but under the procedural due process balancing test that applies to deprivations of property interests (see Section 6.6.2), it was not clearly established that the supervisor was entitled to the presuspension hearing that he had requested.

In accepting the qualified immunity defense, the *Arneson* court also confirmed the difficulty (for plaintiffs) of cases requiring a balancing of interests:

> The federal circuit courts of appeals have observed that "allegations of constitutional violations that require courts to balance competing interests may make it more difficult to find the law 'clearly established.'" *Medina v. City and County of Denver*, 960 F. 2d 1493, 1498 (10th Cir. 1992) (citations omitted). And as the Seventh Circuit has explained:
>
> > [I]t would appear that there is one type of constitutional rule, namely that involving the balancing of competing interests, for which the standard may be clearly established, but its application is so fact-dependent that the "law" can rarely be considered "clearly established." In determining due-process requirements for discharging a government employee, for example, the courts must carefully balance the competing interests of the employee and the employer in each case. Thus, the Supreme Court has consistently stated that one can only proceed on a case-by-case basis and that no all-encompassing procedure may be set forth to cover all situations. It would appear that, whenever a balancing of interests is required, the facts of the existing caselaw must closely correspond to the contested action before the defendant official is subject to liability under . . . *Harlow*. . . . [Q]ualified immunity typically casts a wide net to protect government officials from damage liability whenever balancing is required. *Benson v. Allphin*, 786 F.2d 268, 276 (7th Cir. 1986) (internal citations and footnotes omitted) [592 N.W.2d at 621].

Edwards v. Wallace Community College, 49 F.3d 1517 (11th Cir. 1995), illustrates yet another difficult problem for plaintiffs seeking to avoid the qualified immunity defense: the problem that arises when the plaintiff's underlying claim is a disparate treatment claim requiring a showing of discriminatory intent.[31] In *Edwards*, an African American employee was terminated from her position as a word processing specialist after ten months in that position. The court addressed the qualified immunity claim of the vice president of the college, who had acted briefly as the plaintiff's supervisor. The court explained that "although intent is irrelevant for a qualified immunity inquiry per se, it is relevant if intent is an element of the underlying [claim]." The court cited a Sixth Circuit decision for the proposition that the "plaintiff must present direct evidence that the officials' actions were improperly motivated by racial discrimination when the officials have asserted qualified immunity as a defense" (quoting *Hull v. Cuyahoga Valley Joint Voc. Sch. Dist. Bd. of Educ.*, 926 F.2d 505, 512 (6th Cir. 1991)). The court did not continue this inquiry, however, because the plaintiff had "not presented any concrete evidence of discriminatory intent on the part of [the vice president]" and thus had not cleared the first obstacle in overcoming the qualified immunity defense: proof of a *prima facie* case of constitutional violation.

---

[31]In cases where subjective intent is an element of the plaintiff's *prima facie* case, there are many technical complexities about the parties' burdens of pleading the elements of qualified immunity, as well as about the scope of the plaintiff's discovery and the availability to defendants of partial summary judgment. See, for example, *Walker v. Schwalbe*, 112 F.3d 1127 (11th Cir. 1997). In 1998, in *Crawford-El v. Britton*, 523 U.S. 574 (1998), the U.S. Supreme Court addressed some of these complexities and provided some initial guidance on their resolution.

An Ohio case adds another twist to the complex body of law on Section 1983 qualified immunity. This twist concerns reliance on a state statute as a possible justification for violating clearly established law. In *F. Buddie Contracting Limited v. Cuyahoga Community College District*, 31 F. Supp. 2d 584 (N.D. Ohio 1998), the plaintiff used Section 1983 to challenge a community college district's minority business set-aside policy requiring prime contractors on public works projects of the college to award at least 10 percent of the contract's value to minority business subcontractors. The college had followed the policy when awarding a contract for the repair of planters located on a plaza. A nonminority contractor who was not selected for the project sued the college and also sued the members of the college's board of trustees, the college president, and two vice presidents.

The district court determined that the college's set-aside policy was inconsistent with the U.S. Supreme Court's requirements for governmental affirmative action programs, and thus violated the Fourteenth Amendment's equal protection clause. Furthermore, the court determined that the applicable legal principles on affirmative action were clearly established at the time the defendants applied their policy to the plaintiff. The individual defendants nevertheless contended that they were entitled to qualified immunity because, in devising and applying their policy, they had been following the mandate of an Ohio minority business enterprise statute. The court rejected this argument, relying in part on a U.S. Court of Appeals decision from the Ninth Circuit:

> "Courts have . . . held that the existence of a statute or ordinance authorizing particular conduct is a factor which militates in favor of the conclusion that a reasonable official would find that conduct constitutional." *Grossman v. City of Portland*, 33 F.3d 1200, 1209 (9th Cir. 1994). While an authorizing statute is evidence of objective good faith, it is not dispositive of the issue. "Where a statute authorizes official conduct which is patently violative of fundamental constitutional principles, an officer who enforces that statute is not entitled to qualified immunity." Id. . . .
>
> Thus, it is clear that the existence of an authorizing state law does not alter the qualified immunity analysis. A law which is clearly established by Supreme Court and/or Circuit court decisions does not become less clear by reason of conflicting state statutes [31 F. Supp. 2d at 589].

The court also noted two factors that provided additional justification for imposing this degree of responsibility on the individual defendants: (1) these trustees and officers "are endowed with independent policy-making authority [under state law] and have an obligation to make reasoned decisions with respect to programs and policies which they promulgate," and (2) the state statute that the trustees and officers were following "involves racial classifications and, therefore, enjoys no presumption of constitutionality" (31 F. Supp. 2d at 589, 590). Thus, had the defendants been lower-level administrators, or had the state statute presented a constitutional issue less obviously deserving of strict scrutiny, the good-faith adherence to the mandate of a state statute may have supported the defendants' claim to qualified immunity.

Officers, administrators, and other employees found personally liable under Section 1983 are subject to money damage awards in favor of the prevailing plaintiff(s). Unlike the institution itself, individual defendants may be held liable for punitive as well as compensatory damages. To collect compensatory damages, a plaintiff must prove "actual injury," tangible or intangible; courts usually will not presume that damage occurred from a violation of constitutional rights and will award compensatory damages only to the extent of proven injury (*Carey v. Piphus,* 435 U.S. 247 (1978)). To collect punitive damages, a plaintiff must show that the defendant's actions either manifested "reckless or callous disregard for the plaintiff's rights" or constituted "intentional violations of federal law" (*Smith v. Wade,* 461 U.S. 30, 51 (1983)).

The state of the law under Section 1983 and the Eleventh Amendment, taken together, gives administrators of public postsecondary institutions no cause to feel confident that either they or other institutional officers or employees are insulated from personal constitutional rights liability. Since it is extremely difficult to predict what unlawful actions would fall within the scope of qualified immunity, administrative efforts will be far better spent taking preventive measures to ensure that Section 1983 violations do not occur than in trusting that immunity will usually protect university officers and employees if violations do occur. To minimize the liability risk in this critical area of law and social responsibility, administrators should make legal counsel available to institutional personnel for consultation, encourage review by counsel of institutional policies that may affect constitutional rights, and provide personnel with information on, and training in, basic constitutional law. To absolve personnel of the emotional drain of potential liability, and the financial drain of any liability that actually does occur, administrators should consider the purchase of special insurance coverage or the development of indemnity plans. As discussed in Section 2.5.5, however, public policy in some states may limit the use of these techniques to cover intentional constitutional rights violations.

4.7.4.2. Issues on the merits: State-created dangers. In Section 1983 suits against individuals, difficult issues also arise concerning the merits of the plaintiffs' claims. (Such issues on the merits arise much less frequently in suits against institutions, since public institutions may usually assert sovereign immunity as a basis for dismissing the suit before reaching the merits (see Section 3.5).) Since Section 1983 provides remedies for "the deprivation of . . . rights . . . secured by the Constitution," analysis of the merits of a Section 1983 claim depends on the particular constitutional clause involved and the particular constitutional right asserted.

One particularly difficult and contentious set of issues on the merits has arisen concerning the "substantive" (as opposed to the procedural) content of the Fourteenth Amendment's due process clause. In *DeShaney v. Winnebago County Dept. of Social Services,* 489 U.S. 189 (1989), the U.S. Supreme Court held that the due process clause does not impose any general "affirmative obligation" on state officials to protect private individuals from danger. The Court did acknowledge, however, that such a duty may exist in "certain limited circumstances" where the state has a "special relationship" with the endangered person. As an example, the Court noted situations in which a state agency has an individual in its custody and "so restrains [the] individual's liberty that it renders him unable to care for himself" (489 U.S. at 200). In later cases, lower courts expanded this state duty to situations in which state officers or employers have themselves created the danger. (See, for example, *Kniepp v. Tedder,* 95 F.3d 1199 (3d Cir. 1996), recognizing an affirmative duty on the part of the state to protect individuals in such circumstances.) This approach to substantive due process liability under Section 1983 is now called "the state-created danger theory" (95 F.3d at 1205). While lower courts differ on the particulars of this state duty (and on the extent of their support for the theory), a state-created danger claim usually requires proof that state actors used their authority to create or increase a risk of danger to the plaintiff by making him or her "more vulnerable" to injury, and thus depriving the plaintiff of a "liberty interest in personal security" (95 F.3d at 1203). In addition, a plaintiff generally must show that, in acting or failing to act as they did, the state actors were deliberately indifferent to the plaintiff's safety.

The leading example of state-created danger claims in higher education is the litigation concerning the 1999 Texas A&M Bonfire collapse in which twelve students were killed and twenty-seven others were injured. In the aftermath, six civil suits were filed in federal court on behalf of eleven of the victims, alleging state claims as well as federal Section 1983 claims against the university and various university officials. The court dismissed the Section 1983 claims against the university because it had sovereign immunity (see Section 3.5 of this book), and the focus of the litigation became the plaintiff's substantive due process claims against university officials, based on the state-created danger theory.

The tradition of the Texas A&M Bonfire began in 1909. Over the years it became a symbol "not only of one school deeply rooted in tradition, but . . . representative of the entire Nation's passionate fascination with the most venerated aspects of collegiate football" (*Self v. Texas A&M University, et al.,* 2002 WL 32113753 (S.D. Tex. 2002)). Prior to the tragedy, the building of the bonfire had "occupied over five thousand students for an estimated 125,000 hours each fall." The students had developed a complex "wedding cake design" for the bonfire, weighing in at "over two million pounds" and standing "sixty to eighty feet tall" (*Self v. Texas A&M University*). The tower of logs collapsed on November 18, 1999, resulting in the twelve deaths and twenty-seven injuries. The university quickly appointed a special commission to investigate the bonfire collapse, which issued a final report in May 2000: Special Commission on the 1999 Texas A&M Bonfire, *Final Report,* May 2, 2000, available at http://www.tamu.edu/bonfire-commission/reports/Final.pdf. In the preliminary stages of the ensuing litigation, the parties accepted the Commission's *Final Report* as an authoritative account of the bonfire collapse.

In *Self v. Texas A&M University,* above, the district court combined the six lawsuits for a common ruling on the Section 1983 claims asserted in each case. As the court summarized these claims, the plaintiffs alleged that university officials "deprived the bonfire victims of their Fourteenth Amendment right to substantive due process by acting with deliberate indifference to the state-created danger that killed or injured them." In considering these claims the court acknowledged that an affirmative state duty arises in two situations: "when the state has a special relationship with the person or when the state exposes a person to a danger of its own creation" (*Self* at p. 6, citing *McClendon v. City of Columbia,* 258 F.3d 432, 436 (5th Cir. 2001)). Under the second approach, a plaintiff must prove that "(1) the state actors increased the danger to him or her; and (2) the state actors acted with deliberate indifference" (*Self* at p. 6, citing *Piotrowski v. City of Houston,* 51 F.3d 512 (5th Cir. 1995)). Applying these principles, the district court determined that "[t]he facts . . . clearly tend to suggest that the conduct of the University Officials may have contributed, at least in part, to the 1999 Bonfire collapse," but "it is quite clear that they did not do so with 'deliberate indifference'— the requisite culpability to make out a constitutional violation." Deliberate indifference, said the court, is "'a lesser form of intent' rather than a 'heightened form of negligence'" (*Self* at p. 7, quoting *Leffall v. Dallas Indep. Sch. Dist.,* 28 F.2d 521, 531 (5th Cir. 1994)). To establish deliberate indifference, "the environment created by the state actors must be dangerous; they must know it is dangerous; and . . . they must have used their authority to create an opportunity that would not have otherwise existed for the injury to occur" (*Self* at p. 7, quoting *Johnson v. Dallas Indep. School District,* 38 F.3d 198, 201 (5th Cir. 1994)). The "key . . . lies in the state actors' culpable knowledge and conduct in affirmatively placing an individual in a position of danger, effectively stripping a person of her ability to defend herself, or cutting off potential sources of private aid" (*Self* at p. 7, quoting *Johnson,* 38 F.3d at 201).

In resolving the plaintiffs' state-created danger claims, the district court adopted the Special Commission's *Final Report,* above, as the "definitive narrative of the relevant facts" and cited the *Report's* conclusion that the "absence of a proactive risk management model; the University community's cultural bias impeding risk identification; the lack of student leadership, knowledge and skills pertaining to structural integrity; and the lack of formal, written . . . design plans or construction methodology" were "the overarching factors that brought about the physical collapse." Thus, said the court, the "bonfire collapse was not caused by a specific event, error or omission in 1999, but, rather, by decisions and actions taken by both students and University officials over many, many years" (*Self* at p. 4). Relying on findings from the *Final Report,* the court reasoned that, although university officials "may have contributed" to the danger, they lacked the "requisite culpability" to meet the deliberate indifference prong. They "were aware of the dangers posed" and failed "to pro-actively avert or reduce those risks," but they "were unaware of the *precise* risk at hand—the risk that the entire bonfire would come tumbling down." Such ignorance "might appear naive," but "it cannot support a finding of deliberate indifference" in light of measures that were taken with respect to bonfire safety. The court then concluded that, because the officials' conduct was not sufficiently culpable to meet the deliberate indifference prong of the state-created danger test, plaintiffs' Section 1983 claims failed on the merits, and the defendants were therefore entitled to summary judgment.

On appeal, the U.S. Court of Appeals for the Fifth Circuit generally agreed with the legal principles stated by the district court, in particular that "plaintiff must show the defendants used their authority to create a dangerous environment for the plaintiff and that the defendants acted with deliberate indifference to the plight of the plaintiff" (*Scanlan v. Texas A&M University, et al.,* 343 F.3d 533, 537–38 (5th Cir 2003), citing *Johnson v. Dallas Indep. School District,* 38 F.3d 198, 201 (5th Cir. 1994)). But the appellate court held that the district court had erred in adopting the report of "a defendant-created commission rather than presenting the questions of material fact to a trier of fact" (*Scanlan v. Texas A&M University, et al.,* 343 F.3d at 539). Instead, construing allegations in the complaints in the light most favorable to the plaintiffs, the district court "should have determined the plaintiffs had pleaded sufficient factual allegations to show the bonfire construction environment was dangerous, the University Officials knew it was dangerous, and the University Officials used their authority to create an opportunity for the resulting harm to occur." The Court of Appeals therefore reversed the district court's judgment for the university officials and remanded the case to the district court for further proceedings.

On remand, the district court again dismissed the plaintiffs' Section 1983 claims, this time on "qualified immunity" grounds (see subsection 4.7.4.1 above) that had not been addressed in the district court's prior opinion. In its new opinion, in a case renamed *Davis v. Southerland,* 2004 WL 1230278 (S.D. Tex. 2004), the district court asserted that the Fifth Circuit had been noncommittal about the state-created danger theory in the decade preceding the bonfire collapse, and that the "validity of the state-created danger theory is uncertain in the Fifth Circuit." Thus the theory "was not clearly established at the time of Defendants' bonfire-related activities," and "a reasonable school official would not have been aware that the Fourteenth Amendment's Due Process Clause provided a constitutional right to be free from state-created danger, much less that an injury caused by a school administrator's failure to exercise control over an activity such as [the] bonfire would violate that right."

In addition, deferring to the circuit court's determination in *Scanlan* that the district court "should have concluded that the plaintiffs stated a section 1983 claim under the state-created danger theory," the district court analyzed the merits of the plaintiffs' claims "as if the theory is a valid one" and "the violations Plaintiffs claim are indeed constitutional ones." The court's conclusion was that resolution of the plaintiffs' rights "requires examination of literally hundreds of contested facts," and that the persistence of "multiple questions of fact . . . prevents the Court from deciding whether Defendants did or did not act with deliberate indifference as a matter of law."

Other contexts in which state-created-danger issues may arise include stalking, sexual assaults, and other crimes of violence that take place on campus and of which a student or employee is the victim. The institution, to be subject to suit, must be a public institution or otherwise be acting "under color of law" when it creates the alleged danger. It will be very difficult for plaintiffs to prevail in such suits, as the Texas A&M litigation suggests. It is not necessarily enough that institutional employees were aware of the stalking or impending violence, or that they were negligent in their response or lack thereof. In *Thomas v. City of Mount Vernon,* 215 F. Supp. 2d 329 (S.D.N.Y. 2002), for example, neither a professor who witnessed a student being confronted by her former boyfriend in the hallway of a classroom building, nor office personnel who declined to offer the student assistance when she ran into their office, were liable under Section 1983 for the severe injuries the student received when the boyfriend shot her shortly thereafter. The professor and staff members had not deprived the student of liberty or property "by virtue of their own actions"; and under *DeShaney* (above), "'a state's failure to protect an individual against private violence does not constitute a violation of the due process clause'" (215 F. Supp. 2d at 334, quoting 489 U.S. at 197).

Sec. 4.8. Performance Management Issues

4.8.1. Pre-hire issues. Although even the best-managed college may face litigation and potential liability for employment or academic decisions, a comprehensive system of performance management should reduce the number of potential lawsuits and should make it easier for the college to defend those lawsuits that are filed. This system should begin at the preemployment stage and continue throughout the life cycle of employment.

Whether the college is hiring a faculty member or a staff member, a written job description should provide information about what is expected of the employee. This is particularly important in light of the requirement of the Americans With Disabilities Act that an employee be capable of performing the "essential functions" of the position (see Section 5.2.5). Job descriptions may be considered to be contracts at some institutions, particularly if the employees are covered by a collectively negotiated agreement that incorporates them into the contract.

Employment interviews have the potential to create legal claims if promises made by managers or supervisors anxious to attract the candidate are not honored at a later time. Oral promises have contractual effect in some states. Furthermore, the nondiscrimination laws prohibit the use of irrelevant criteria such as gender, race, religion, national origin, or age from being used as criteria for determining whether to offer a candidate a position; questions that refer to any of these "protected" characteristics may expose the college to a civil rights lawsuit if the individual is not hired or is later terminated (see Section 5.2).

Administrators at various colleges have found, to their dismay, that reference or background checks should be done to ensure that the individual has not engaged in unlawful or violent behavior in a previous position, and that the individual actually holds the degrees and certificates claimed on the application. Failure to conduct reference or background checks could result in claims of negligent hiring (see Sections 3.3.5 & 4.7.2) if the employee engages in violent or dangerous behavior, and the college could have learned about previous similar actions had it checked the candidate's references.

The Fair Credit Reporting Act (FCRA), 15 U.S. § 1681 *et seq.,* regulates the collection and use of information by employers who use a third party to conduct background checks on employees. The law, designed to protect consumer privacy and to provide the opportunity to correct mistakes in credit reports, requires employers to notify applicants in writing that the employer may undertake an "investigative consumer report" as part of the application process, and to inform the applicant of the scope of the investigation. This notice must be in a document that is separate from other application materials. The law is not limited to reports on an applicant's credit rating; it applies to reports prepared by any consumer reporting agency that include information on reputation or personal characteristics. Examples of consumer reports covered by the law include records checks by the state's motor vehicle agency, criminal background checks, and, under some circumstances, drug test reports.

If the employer conducts its own background check without the use of an external agent, then the FCRA does not apply. If, however, the employer uses an outside credit reporting or investigative service to perform the background check, the FCRA requires that certain steps be taken.

1. The employer must notify the job candidate in writing, "in a document that consists solely of the disclosure," that a consumer report may be used to make a hiring decision.

2. The employer must obtain the candidate's written authorization to obtain a consumer report from an external agent.

3. If the employer relies on the consumer report to make a negative hiring or other employment decision, the employer must, prior to making the decision, give the candidate a "pre-adverse action disclosure," a copy of the consumer report, and a copy of "A Summary of Your Rights Under the Fair Credit Reporting Act," which the consumer reporting agency is required to provide along with the consumer report.

4. After the employer has made a negative employment decision, the employer must give the candidate notice of the negative action in oral, written, or electronic form. The notice must include the name, address, and telephone number of the consumer reporting agency that supplied the consumer report, a statement that the consumer reporting agency did not make the negative employment decision, and a notice of the candidate's right to dispute the accuracy or completeness of the information provided by the consumer reporting agency, as well as notice of the candidate's right to obtain a free consumer report from the agency within sixty days.

The employer will also be required to certify to the consumer reporting agency that the employer will not misuse any information in the report in a manner that would violate federal or state equal employment opportunity laws or regulations (15 U.S.C. § 1681(b)). The law excludes "investigative consumer reports," where information about the individual is collected by interviewing people who know the applicant, if they are made in connection with "suspected misconduct relating to employment" (§ 1681a(x)), such as an investigation of alleged sexual harassment or other workplace misconduct.

The Fair Credit Reporting Act is enforced by the Federal Trade Commission. The Commission's Web site, http://www.ftc.gov, provides additional information on the Act. The regulations, codified at 16 C.F.R. Part 600, include a "Notice to Users of Consumer Reports: Obligations of Users Under the FCRA," which is found at http://www.ftc.gov/statutes/2user.htm.

4.8.2. Evaluation. Evaluation of employee performance is important for both the college and the employee. Employees (including high-level administrators) should be evaluated on a regular basis so that any performance problems can be corrected early and discipline or termination can be avoided. The importance of evaluating probationary faculty on a regular basis is discussed in Section 6.7.1.

Employees should be provided with written performance criteria and evaluated against those criteria. It may be easier to develop written performance criteria for staff than for faculty, particularly at colleges where faculty are expected to produce high-quality research and scholarship. But clarifying what is expected of employees will reduce subsequent litigation over what the performance standards were and to what degree the employee met those standards.

It is important to train the individuals who will evaluate employee performance to ensure that they understand the performance criteria and how to apply them. Again, this training may be somewhat simpler for supervisors of staff than for department chairs or deans, but it is equally important for academic administrators to be trained to evaluate faculty. (For resources on training department chairs and deans, see the Selected Annotated Bibliography for this Chapter, under Section 4.8.)

The importance of training individuals who make employment recommendations or decisions was emphasized in *Mathis v. Phillips Chevrolet, Inc.,* 269 F.3d. 771 (7th Cir. 2001). In this case, an individual who was not hired was able to demonstrate that supervisors who interviewed candidates for sales positions routinely noted the candidates' age on the employment applications. The plaintiff sued the company for race and age discrimination Although not a case involving a college, this case sends an instructive message: "[L]eaving managers with hiring authority in ignorance of the basic features of the discrimination laws is an 'extraordinary mistake' for a company to make . . ." (269 F.3d at 778). The appellate court upheld a jury finding that the manager's treatment of the employee amounted to reckless indifference, a finding that, under the Age Discrimination in Employment Act (see Section 5.2.6 of this book) permitted the awarding of double damages to the plaintiff.

Performance evaluations should be committed to writing and should be discussed orally with the faculty or staff member. Individuals being evaluated should be allowed to provide a written response to the evaluation. This "rebuttal" provides two benefits: it allows the individual being evaluated to correct potential mistakes or misunderstandings by the supervisor, and it also demonstrates that the supervisor allowed the employee to respond to an evaluation in the event that a later lawsuit claims that the evaluation was unfair or inaccurate. (For potential legal claims involving performance evaluations, see Section 4.7.2.)

If a faculty or staff member's performance is judged to be inadequate, a performance improvement plan (PIP) should be developed between the supervisor and the individual. The written PIP should describe what steps the individual needs to take to improve his or her performance and to receive a satisfactory evaluation. The PIP should not promise that the employee will be retained or promoted if performance improves, but should indicate what performance improvements need to be made to raise the individual's performance to a satisfactory level.

4.8.3. Discipline. Employees who violate the employer's rules, policies, or state or federal laws, should be subject to discipline by the college. The college may have a handbook or written policies that address discipline or a collective bargaining agreement, and, for public institutions, state law or regulations (for employees with civil service protection, for example) may apply to faculty, staff, or both. It is important that these provisions be followed when the college imposes discipline, since procedural violations can lead to litigation and liability even if the misconduct leading to the discipline is acknowledged by the employee.

Although insubordination (failure to follow the order of a supervisor) is used routinely in nonacademic organizations as a reason for disciplining or even discharging an employee, it is less common in academic settings to punish a faculty or staff member for insubordination. Reasonable people may differ as to whether an employee's refusal to follow a supervisor's order that the employee believed to be unjust is insubordination. The case of *Butts v. Higher Education Interim Governing Board/Shepherd College*, 569 S.E.2d 456 (W. Va. 2002), provides some guidance on this issue. Butts, a tenured associate professor at Shepherd College, a public institution, refused to provide her supervisor with student grades because Butts interpreted Shepherd's student privacy policy as permitting only the registrar to release student grades to college employees. Butts's supervisor issued two reprimands, and Butts appealed this discipline. The college's hearing officer upheld the discipline, and the employee appealed to the state circuit court, which also upheld the discipline. She then appealed to the state's highest court, which reversed the ruling of the circuit court and ordered the discipline expunged.

The court in *Butts* ruled that, for an employee to be disciplined for insubordination, three elements must be present: (1) an employee must refuse to obey an order (or rule or regulation), (2) the refusal must be willful, and (3) the order (or rule or regulation) must be reasonable and valid. The court determined that the employee's conduct had met the first two conditions, but not the third, finding that the college's privacy policy was ambiguous and that the employee's refusal to follow her supervisor's order was done in good faith.

Public colleges are constitutionally required to provide due process to their employees when taking an action that can affect their terms and conditions of employment (such as suspension without pay or termination). Moreover, in order to avoid breach of contract claims, both public and private colleges should follow the procedures in their handbooks and policies, and in any written contracts they may have, whether they are collectively negotiated with a union or are individual employment contracts. Although private institutions are not required to provide the type of due process required of public institutions by the U.S. Constitution, procedural protections help assure a fair disciplinary process and should be followed by both public and private colleges.

Due process requires that the college provide notice to its faculty and staff of the rules, regulations, and performance standards that they must adhere to. It must also notify its employees that failure to comply with these requirements may lead to discipline or termination. Furthermore, due process requires that the college provide the employee with an opportunity to be heard before discipline that may impact a liberty or property interest is imposed, unless the alleged behavior has been so egregious that, for safety reasons, the employee must be removed from the college premises pending a hearing. (Due process requirements for faculty at public colleges are discussed in Section 6.7.2.)

Although not required by law, a grievance system provides a useful opportunity for colleges to reconsider employee discipline, and also provide an opportunity to demonstrate that the institution did not act arbitrarily in imposing discipline. Grievance systems are a standard component of collective bargaining agreements, and civil service regulations typically provide for a grievance process as well. At institutions that are not legally required to implement grievance systems, the system can be relatively simple, involving one or two levels of review beyond the supervisor who imposed the discipline. In some states, the institution's grievance system and hearing process may serve as the "trial" level for an employee challenging a negative employment decision (see Section 4.4). (For an example of an informal appeals process that passed constitutional muster, see *Gregory v. Hunt*, 24 F.3d 781 (6th Cir. 1994), in which an informal hearing by the chancellor of the University of Tennessee provided a discharged police officer with an opportunity to clear his name, thus satisfying constitutional requirements for protecting a liberty interest. See also *Ludwig v. Board of Trustees of Ferris State University*, 123 F.3d 404 (6th Cir. 1997), in which a head basketball coach terminated for making ethnic slurs against certain players received due process because he had three opportunities to tell his side of the story and had access to the information used by decision makers who made the termination decision.)

Another benefit of a formal discipline and grievance system is its usefulness if the employee challenges the discipline or termination in court. For example, in *Gaither v. Wake Forest University*, 129 F. Supp. 2d 863 (M.D.N.C. 2000), the university avoided a trial on a former employee's claim that his termination was motivated by racial discrimination. The court awarded summary judgment to the university after it produced fourteen written warnings given to the plaintiff over a six-year period for violating safety rules, sleeping on the job, and falsifying time records. (For a helpful resource on developing effective grievance procedures, see Ann H. Franke, *Grievance Procedures: Solving Campus Employment Problems Out of Court* (United Educators Insurance Risk Retention Group, Inc., 1998).)

4.8.4. Promotion.
For both faculty and staff, career ladders in colleges are relatively short. Particularly for faculty, a promotion decision may be made only twice in the individual's career—once when the faculty member is promoted from assistant to associate professor (often with a tenure decision at the same time), and a second time when the individual is promoted from associate to full professor. Staff may have the opportunity for more promotions, but the hierarchy in most colleges is flatter than in most business organizations. Their infrequency makes promotions very significant to faculty and staff, and the potential for conflict is increased because of this significance.

Criteria for promoting and tenuring faculty are discussed in Section 6.6, and procedures for promotion and tenure decisions are discussed in Section 6.7. Whether the candidate for promotion is a faculty or a staff member, however, similar principles apply. The criteria for promotion should be clear, the performance evaluations discussed in Section 4.8.2 above should have been performed regularly and accurately, and all applicable policies and procedures should be followed during the promotion process.

Challenges to negative promotion decisions tend to be based on allegations that the decision was infected with discrimination (see Sections 5.2 & 5.3), that a breach of contract occurred (see Section 4.3), that some employment tort occurred (see Section 4.7), or all of these. While documentation and careful adherence to policies and procedures are important to a defense to these claims, consistent treatment of similarly situated individuals is particularly important to defending discrimination claims. If the promotion criteria are interpreted differently for individuals of different genders or races, for example, these differences can suggest that discrimination occurred.

Because of the significance of promotion decisions to faculty and staff, the discussion of performance evaluation in Section 4.8.2 above is particularly relevant. If the college can demonstrate that an individual has been told regularly that his or her performance needs improvement, and can produce written confirmation of those communications, it will be difficult for the individual to prevail in litigation unless, of course, he or she can demonstrate that the evaluations were tainted as well. On the other hand, if an individual receives no feedback, or only positive feedback, on his or her performance and then is denied the promotion or tenure, it is not unreasonable for the individual to believe that the decision was not based on performance, but on some unlawful criterion.

A case involving the termination of a staff member after several years of inadequate performance is illustrative of the significance of written performance evaluations. In *Jones v. University of Pennsylvania*, 2003 U.S. Dist. LEXIS 6623 (E.D. Pa. March 20, 2003), the University of Pennsylvania was granted summary judgment by a federal trial court because the plaintiff, who claimed that her termination was motivated by racial discrimination, had been given numerous performance appraisals that warned her that her performance was unsatisfactory. The plaintiff, an administrative assistant, had a history of performance problems, and several students and faculty had complained about her behavior and her inability to provide them with information they needed. The plaintiff's supervisors had given her a performance improvement plan and had placed her on probation for ninety days. When her performance did not improve, they terminated her employment prior to the completion of the probationary period.

4.8.5. Termination. Although performance evaluations, progressive discipline, and grievance systems can help improve employee performance, they are not infallible, and termination decisions may be necessary. This Section discusses performance-based termination; terminations resulting from a reduction in force or financial exigency are discussed in Section 6.8.

If a progressive discipline system is used, termination would typically be the final step after an oral warning, written warning, and suspension have been used. If the employee is being discharged for especially severe or dangerous misconduct, the college may legitimately decide to bypass the earlier stages of discipline. Documentation of all previous discipline, and of the incidents or reasons for the termination, is important in the event that the employee challenges the termination decision through a grievance system, in an administrative agency proceeding, or in court.

Terminations are considered the "capital punishment" of employment relations, and administrators should prepare very carefully prior to making the termination decision. They should be able to answer these questions:

1. Is there sufficient documentation of performance problems to support the termination decision?

2. Have all relevant policies and procedures been followed, and can this be proven?

3. Have other individuals who have had similar performance problems also been terminated? If not, why not?

4. Has the termination decision been discussed with the college's counsel? With the supervisor's manager?

5. Is this employee capable of performing adequately in another position at the college that is available? If so, why has this not been considered?

6. Has some event that could be viewed as a reason for the termination happened recently (for example, the employee filed a workers' compensation claim, or announced that she was pregnant, or took a family or medical leave)?

Resources on "best practices" and guidelines for lawful termination are listed in the Selected Annotated Bibliography for this Chapter, under Section 4.8.

One strategy for avoiding litigation is to have the departing employee sign a waiver, or release, of liability. A waiver is a contract in which the employee promises not to sue the former employer for claims related to the employment in return for some form of severance payment. Although experts disagree as to the usefulness of waivers, and whether or not they actually encourage litigation, many colleges use them, particularly when employees terminate their employment (whether voluntarily or involuntarily). The Older Workers Benefit Protection Act (OWBPA), which is part of the Age Discrimination in Employment Act (see Section 5.2.6), provides guidelines for, among other issues, drafting waivers and giving the employee time to review and to rescind his or her agreement to the waiver. Waivers that follow the guidelines of the OWPBA are typically upheld by courts, unless there is evidence of coercion or fraud (see, for example, *Phillips v. Moore*, 164 F. Supp. 2d 1245 (D. Kan. 2001) (waiver upheld because it met OWBPA standard and the employee had retired voluntarily)).

Administrators should consider whether a pretermination hearing is necessary, as opposed to a hearing after the termination decision is made. If the college's policies or handbooks provide for such a hearing, then the college must provide one. (If the college is terminating a tenured faculty member, it will need to follow the AAUP guidelines for such a decision if the college has adopted those guidelines; the process is discussed in Section 6.7.2.3.) Even if there is no written requirement that a pretermination hearing be held, a public college should consider whether the individual being terminated could claim a "liberty interest" in his or her reputation (see Section 6.7.2.1), which would trigger the need for a name-clearing hearing. The wisdom of providing such a hearing is particularly strong if the allegations against the individual have been reported in the press or have otherwise been communicated beyond those with a business need to know, or if college officials have made public comments about the individual to be terminated. (See, for example, *Campanelli v. Bockrath*, 100 F.3d 1476 (9th Cir. 1996), holding that the head basketball coach at the University of California-Berkeley, who was terminated in mid-season, had a liberty interest and was entitled to a name-clearing hearing; failure to provide a hearing was a denial of due process.) As discussed in Section 4.8.3 above, the "hearing" need not be formal (unless the college's own written policies, collective bargaining agreement, or handbooks require a formal hearing). An opportunity to be heard by the individual or group making the decision should be sufficient in most circumstances (see, for example, the *McDaniels* case, discussed in Section 6.7.2.3), although following the guidance of *Loudermill*, discussed in Section 6.7.2.3, may be the wisest course of action.

A well-designed and carefully followed performance management system cannot insulate a college and its administrators from litigation. It can, however, provide the college with credible evidence that it followed its own rules and the law, should the college be sued by a current or former employee. Such a system will also demonstrate to employees, whether faculty or staff, that the college is committed to rewarding good performance and to correcting performance that falls short of the standard.

Selected Annotated Bibliography

Sec. 4.2 (Defining the Employment Relationship)

Carlson, Richard R. "Why the Law Still Can't Tell an Employee When It Sees One and How It Ought to Stop Trying," 22 *Berkeley J. Emp. & Lab. L.* 295 (2001). Criticizes both Congress and the courts for complicating employers' ability to distinguish between employees and independent contractors, examines the failure of the common law test to provide guidance to Congress and courts, and discusses the weaknesses of statutory definitions of employee. Proposes amending statutes to focus on the transactions between the parties rather than the status of the individual, which would eliminate the need to distinguish between employees and independent contractors, but would protect individuals from discrimination, unsafe workplaces, compensation irregularities, and workplace injury.

Sec. 4.3 (Employment Contracts)

Fritz, Ted P. *Employment Issues in Higher Education: A Legal Compendium* (2d ed., National Association of College and University Attorneys, 2003). Discusses training, dealing with difficult employees, retaliation, employee references, employee handbooks, leaves of absence, and downsizing.

Gross, Allen J. *Employee Dismissal Law: Forms and Procedures* (2d ed., Wiley, 1992, with 1997 Cumulative Supplement). Discusses suits alleging wrongful dismissal. Follows the litigation path from the time a decision to litigate is made through interrogatories, depositions, the trial, and its closing arguments. Useful for attorneys representing either party, the book focuses on the litigation process rather than the substance of the legal claims. Model forms and policies are included, as are suggestions for presenting wrongful discharge cases before a jury.

Holloway, William, & Leech, Michael. *Employment Termination: Rights and Remedies* (2d ed., Bureau of National Affairs, 1993, with 2003 supp.). Discusses legal issues surrounding employment termination under both federal and state law, as well as common law. Discusses discovery issues, settlement and release, insurance considerations, workplace investigations, workplace violence, and medical leave issues.

King, Kenneth. Note, "Mandating English Proficiency for College Instructors: States' Responses to 'the TA Problem,'" 31 *Vand. J. Transnat'l L.* 203 (1998). Reviews fifteen state statutes that mandate English proficiency for college instructors, discusses possible legal issues related to the enforcement of these statutes, and provides recommendations for avoiding legal liability related to these statutes.

Perritt, Henry H., Jr. *Employee Dismissal Law and Practice* (3d ed., Wiley, 1992, and periodic supp.). A guide to litigation for plaintiffs and defendants. Includes information on state statutory and common law of wrongful discharge, discusses common law actions in tort, implied contract, and the implied covenant of good faith. Also discusses the access to these theories by employees covered by collective bargaining agreements.

Berman, Evan M., Bowman, James S., West, Jonathan P., & Van Wart, Montgomery. *Human Resource Management in Public Service* (Sage, 2001). A textbook that reviews techniques for selection, evaluation, and discipline of public sector employees.

Condrey, Stephen E. *Handbook of Human Resource Management in Government* (Jossey-Bass, 2004). Discusses compensation, job analysis, sexual harassment, diversity, and performance appraisal for workers in the public sector. Also discusses total quality management, benchmarking, and budgeting.

"Developments in the Law—Public Employment," 97 *Harv. L. Rev.* 1611 (1984). A review of the law of public employment that includes a review of the development of civil service systems. It reviews collective bargaining in the public sector and its interaction with the civil service system; discusses limits placed on the free speech and association rights of public employees by civil service laws and regulations.

Light, Paul. *The Tides of Reform: Making Government Work 1945–1995* (Yale University Press, 1997). Reviews the history of the federal civil service system and discusses its implications for the functioning of the federal government. Discusses four theories of "reform" in the federal civil service, concluding that reform efforts overall have been ineffective.

Sec. 4.5 (Collective Bargaining)

American Federation of Teachers. *Recognition and Respect: Standards of Good Practice in the Employment of Graduate Employees* (AFT, 2004). Provides standards for compensating, hiring, and evaluating graduate students who serve as teaching or research assistants. Available at http://www.aft.org/pubs-reports/higher_ed/grad_ employee_standards.pdf.

Angell, George W., Kelly, Edward P., Jr., & Associates. *Handbook of Faculty Bargaining* (Jossey-Bass, 1977). A comprehensive guide to collective bargaining for administrators. Provides information and recommendations on preparing for collective bargaining, negotiating contracts, administering contracts, and exerting institutional leadership in the bargaining context. Includes a special chapter on statewide bargaining in state postsecondary systems.

Finkin, Matthew. "The NLRB in Higher Education," 5 *U. Tol. L. Rev.* 608 (1974). Probes the whole gamut of NLRB authority and activity in postsecondary education. Discusses and criticizes NLRB decisions dealing with jurisdiction over private institutions; faculty status as managers, supervisors, or employees; appropriate bargaining units; and employers' unfair labor practices.

Gregory, David L., & Russo, Charles J. "The First Amendment and the Labor Relations of Religiously-Affiliated Employers," 8 *B.U. Pub. Int. L.J.* 449 (1999). Provides a critical review of the *Catholic Bishops* case and suggests ways that religiously affiliated institutions can maintain their religious prerogatives while allowing their employees to unionize.

Hardin, Patrick, & Higgins, John E., Jr. (eds.). *Developing Labor Law: The Board, the Courts, and the National Labor Relations Act* (4th ed., Bureau of National Affairs, 2001, with 2004 Cumulative Supplement). The standard reference work for private sector labor relations law. Includes discussion of protected employee activity, the representation process, union recognition by the employer, strikes, and related issues.

Hutchins, Neal H., & Hutchens, Melissa B. "Catching the Union Bug: Graduate Student Employees and Unionization," 39 *Gonzaga L. Rev.* 105 (2003–04). Although written prior to the NLRB's decision in *Brown University,* reviews the rights of graduate assistants at public and private universities to unionize. Examines the potential conflict between the NLRA and FERPA with respect to the rights of union organizers to gain access to information about students in order to contact them. Reviews a variety of arguments for and against the unionization of graduate students.

Julius, Daniel J., & Gumport, Patricia J. "Graduate Student Unionization: Catalysts and Consequences," 26 *Rev. Higher Educ.* 187–216 (2002). Describes the "current land-scape" of graduate student unionization and draws conclusions about the reasons for graduate student organization and its effect on graduate education. Analyzes interview data from twenty institutions where graduate students are unionized and concludes that, although collective bargaining tends to rationalize the workloads and compensa-tion of graduate assistants across academic departments, it does not appear to have a negative effect on the pedagogical relationship between faculty and doctoral students.

Lee, Barbara A. "Faculty Role in Academic Governance and the Managerial Exclusion: Impact of the *Yeshiva University* Decision," 7 *J. Coll. & Univ. Law* 222 (1980–81). An in-depth analysis of the *Yeshiva* case. Discusses origins and definitions of the terms "supervisory," "managerial," and "professional" employees; the faculty's role in academic governance; and the implications of the *Yeshiva* decision for both unionized and nonunionized colleges and universities.

Lund, John, & Maranto, Cheryl L. "Public Sector Law: An Update." In Dale Belman, Morley Gunderson, & Douglas Hyatt, *Public Sector Employment in a Time of Transition* (Industrial Relations Research Association, 1996), 21–57. Reviews a vari-ety of developments in the collective bargaining law for public employees, includ-ing negotiable subjects, the interaction of state law and collective bargaining, and the use of interest arbitration.

Rabban, David. "Is Unionization Compatible with Professionalism?" 45 *Indus. & Lab. Rel. Rev.* 97 (1991). Analyzes the compatibility of unionization with professionalism by examining the provisions of more than one hundred collective bargaining agree-ments involving a variety of professions. Author discusses the effect of contractual provisions on professional standards, participation by professionals in organiza-tional decision making, and other issues of professional concern, and concludes that unionization and professionalism are not "inherently incompatible."

Sec. 4.6 *(Other Employee Protections)*

Burling, Philip, & Matthews, Kathryn A. *Responding to Whistleblowers: An Analysis of Whistleblower Protection Acts and Their Consequences* (National Association of College and University Attorneys, 1992). A practical guide to responding to employee complaints, with a discussion of federal and state statutory and state common law whistleblower protections.

Clemons, Jennifer. "FLSA Retaliation: A Continuum of Employee Protection," 53 *Baylor L. Rev.* 535 (2001). Discusses the degree of formality required to protect an employee who complains of FLSA violations under the law's anti-retaliation provisions. Reviews the concept of retaliation under the FLSA and comparable provisions in other employment laws (such as Title VII); recommends that employees who complain to employers about alleged FLSA violations be pro-tected by the anti-retaliation provisions.

Coleman, Barbara J. *Primer on ERISA* (4th ed., Bureau of National Affairs, 1993). A concise overview of the major provisions of the Employee Retirement Income Secu-rity Act, focusing on pension, health care, disability, and accident plans, and noting relevant sections of the Internal Revenue Code. Includes forms for disclosure, a calendar for reporting benefits, model statements of employee rights under ERISA, a checklist for summary plan descriptions, and other model statements.

Euben, Donna R., & Thornton, Saranna R. *The Family and Medical Leave Act: Questions and Answers for Faculty* (American Association of University Professors, 2002). Analyzes the rights of faculty to leave under the FMLA, discussing eligibility under the law, job protections and benefits, special issues for unionized faculty, and interaction among the FMLA, the ADA, and the Rehabilitation Act.

Fanning, Richard W. "Federal Standards and Enforcement: Introduction: The Federal-State Partnership of Unemployment Compensation," 29 *U. Mich. J.L. Reform* 475 (1996). This introduction to a symposium on unemployment compensation reviews the statutory and regulatory basis for the federal-state partnership that forms the unemployment compensation system. It discusses how the federal government works with states to administer the unemployment insurance (UI) system, and reviews how states interact when a UI claim involves more than one state.

Flygare, Thomas J. *The Family and Medical Leave Act of 1993: Applications in Higher Education* (National Association of College and University Attorneys, 1995). A comprehensive overview of the FMLA and its particular implications for higher education. Included are several hypothetical situations relevant to colleges and universities, and a discussion of how a college can determine whether the leave qualifies under the FMLA. A particularly helpful guide for supervisors, department chairs, and deans.

Flygare, Thomas J. *What to Do When the U.S. Department of Labor Comes to Campus: Wage and Hour Law in Higher Education* (National Association of College and University Attorneys, 1999). Designed to help colleges and universities respond to U.S. Department of Labor investigations of wage and hour issues as well as to provide guidance in complying generally with the Fair Labor Standards Act. Discusses exemptions, calculation of working time, and overtime issues. (Published prior to the revision of the FLSA exemptions in 2004.)

Hunter, Richard J., & Mason, Phyllis. "Law, Ethics and Public Policy in the Creation of an Environmental Imperative: The Hazard Communication Standard Insuring Workers' Rights," 18 *T. Jefferson L. Rev.* 1 (1996). Reviews the history and development of the Hazard Communication Standard, discusses significant appellate and Supreme Court cases, and discusses employers' responsibilities for communicating to employees the risks they face in the workplace.

Kearns, Ellen C. (ed.). *Fair Labor Standards Act* (Bureau of National Affairs, 1999, with 2004 Cumulative Supplement). Includes a discussion of the 2004 changes to regulations on exemptions for salaried workers, as well as recommendations for record keeping and other compliance issues.

Keller, J. J., & Associates. *OSHA Compliance Manual: Application of Key OSHA Topics* (J. J. Keller & Associates, 2000). This 600-page volume reviews OSHA's purpose and coverage, discusses the development and enforcement of workplace standards, the General Duty Clause, OSHA's record-keeping and reporting requirements, and workplace inspections. It discusses OSHA-approved state health and safety programs, employer and employee rights and responsibilities under OSHA, and lists the OSHA regional offices.

Kurzban's Immigration Law: A Comprehensive Outline and Reference Tool (American Immigration Law Foundation, published annually). Includes 1,200 pages, with appendices, of information concerning all areas of immigration law. Available from the American Immigration Lawyers Association at http://aila.org.

Malpert, Rodney A., & Peterson, Amanda. *Business Immigration Law: Strategies for Employing Foreign Nationals* (Law Journal Press, 2000, with periodic updates). A loose-leaf service that provides updated information on legal requirements for employing noncitizens. Includes an index and forms.

Phillips, Eric. Note: "On-Call Time Under the Fair Labor Standards Act," 95 *Mich. L. Rev.* 2633 (1997). Reviews litigation concerning whether an employee is working while on call, suggesting that neither the appellate courts nor the Supreme Court have provided clear guidance for determining when an employee is working. Proposes standards for determining whether an on-call worker is covered by the FLSA.

Rabinowitz, Randy S. (ed.). *Occupational Safety and Health Law* (2d ed., Bureau of National Affairs, 2002). Discusses the regulatory and enforcement authority of OSHA, the procedures used in an OSHA inspection, how to challenge an enforcement action, and significant developments in OSHA jurisprudence.

Song, Janet K., & Kushner, Michael G. (eds.). *ERISA: The Law and the Code* (Bureau of National Affairs, 2004). Includes the text of the statute and all amendments, with cross-references, as well as a cross-referenced index and a section-by-section finding list for ERISA and the Internal Revenue Code.

Thompson, Anthony J., et al. *OSHA Environmental Compliance Handbook* (West Group, Environmental Law Series, 1998). Discusses the interplay between occupational safety and health and environmental laws, and the collaborative enforcement activities of the two federal agencies charged with enforcing these laws. Provides a primer for OSHA's statutory and regulatory framework, discusses its record-keeping requirements and the agency's efforts to force ergonomic improvements in the workplace. Also reviews certain Environmental Protection Agency (EPA) regulations and provides references to other reference sources for both laws. Suggests strategies for dealing with OSHA inspections and conducting health and safety audits.

Welch, Edward M. *Employer's Guide to Workers' Compensation* (Bureau of National Affairs, 1999). Explains how to determine which injuries are covered, provides advice for working with workers' compensation insurance companies, describes the operation of state workers' compensation agencies, and provides checklists and suggestions for reducing the cost of workers' compensation programs.

Westman, Daniel P., & Modesitt, Nancy M. *Whistleblowing: The Law of Retaliatory Discharge* (2d ed., Bureau of National Affairs, 2004). Discusses state common law protections for employees as well as the protections of the Sarbanes-Oxley Act. Also reviews state statutes protecting whistleblowers. Includes an appendix listing relevant state and federal whistleblower laws.

Yamada, David C. "The Employment Law Rights of Student Interns," 35 *Conn. L. Rev.* 215 (2002). Discusses legal and policy issues related to student internships, including FLSA implications, protection by the nondiscrimination laws, and other potential legal protections if interns are considered to be employees.

Sec. 4.7 (Personal Liability of Employees)

Traynor, Michael. "Defamation Law: Shock Absorbers for Its Ride Into the Groves of Academe," 16 *J. Coll. & Univ. Law* 373 (1990). Reviews strategies for avoiding personal and institutional liability for defamation, with particular emphasis on research and publication by faculty.

See also Evans & Evans entry in Chapter Three, Section 3.2; NACUA entry in Section 3.3; and Nahmod entry in Section 3.5.

Sec. 4.8 (Performance Management Issues)

DelPo, Amy, & Guerin, Lisa. *Dealing with Problem Employees: A Legal Guide* (Nolo, 2001). Discusses the use of progressive discipline, how to investigate employee performance problems, and litigation avoidance. Includes sample forms and policies, checklists, and state statutes related to employment.

Mink, Oscar G., Owen, Keith Q., & Mink, Barbara P. *Developing High-Performance People: The Art of Coaching* (Perseus, 2001). Provides advice for managers and supervisors on working with employees to improve performance. Discusses performance improvement plans and provides suggestions for evaluating employee performance.

Seldin, Peter. *Evaluating and Developing Administrative Performance* (Jossey-Bass, 1988). Presents a comprehensive system for assessing administrative performance and helping administrators improve their performance. Chapters discuss the demand for accountability and its effect on evaluation, the use of evaluative information in personnel decisions, characteristics of a successful evaluation system, the process of creating an evaluation system, and legal pitfalls of evaluation.

5

Nondiscrimination and Affirmative Action in Employment

Sec. 5.1. The Interplay of Statutes, Regulations, and Constitutional Protections

The area of employment discrimination is probably more heavily blanketed with overlapping statutory, regulatory, and constitutional requirements than any other area of postsecondary education law. Several federal statutes and one major executive order prohibit discrimination by employers, including postsecondary institutions, and each has its own comprehensive set of administrative regulations or guidelines (see Section 5.2). Other federal laws prohibit retaliation for the exercise of the rights provided by the laws—also a form of discrimination. All states also have fair employment practices statutes, some of which provide greater protections to employees than federal nondiscrimination statutes.

Because of their national scope and comprehensive coverage of problems and remedies, and because in some cases they provide greater protection than the laws of many states, the federal antidiscrimination statutes have assumed great importance. The federal statutes, moreover, supplemented by those of the states, have outstripped the importance of the federal Constitution as a remedy for employment discrimination, particularly for employees of private colleges. The statutes cover most major categories of discrimination and tend to impose more affirmative and stringent requirements on employers than does the Constitution.

Race discrimination in employment is prohibited by Title VII of the Civil Rights Act of 1964 as amended, by 42 U.S.C. § 1981, and by Executive Order 11246 as amended. Sex discrimination is prohibited by Title VII, by Title IX of the Education Amendments of 1972, by the Equal Pay Act, and by Executive Order 11246. Age discrimination is outlawed by the Age Discrimination in

371

Employment Act (ADEA). Discrimination against employees with disabilities is prohibited by both the Americans With Disabilities Act (ADA) and the Rehabilitation Act of 1973. Discrimination on the basis of religion is outlawed by Title VII and Executive Order 11246. Discrimination on the basis of national origin is prohibited by Title VII and by Executive Order 11246. Discrimination against aliens is prohibited indirectly under Title VII and directly under the Immigration Reform and Control Act of 1986 (IRCA; discussed in Section 4.6.5). Discrimination against veterans is covered in part by 38 U.S.C. § 4301. Some courts have ruled that discrimination against transsexuals is sex discrimination, and thus violates Title VII (see, for example, *Smith v. City of Salem*, 378 F.3d 566 (6th Cir. 2004)). Other forms of discrimination are prohibited by the laws of some states.

The nondiscrimination aspects of the statutes and Executive Order 11246 are discussed in this Section, and they are contrasted with the requirements of the federal Constitution, as interpreted by the courts in the context of discrimination claims. The affirmative action aspects of the statutes and Executive Order 11246 are discussed in Section 5.4 (as applied to staff) and Section 6.5 (as applied to faculty).

The rationale for laws prohibiting discrimination in employment decisions is that characteristics such as race, sex, religion, or age (among others) are irrelevant for employment decisions. In debates prior to the passage of the Civil Rights Act of 1964, the first comprehensive federal law prohibiting employment discrimination, congressional leaders stressed the financial cost to both business and members of minority groups of employment decisions based not on individual qualifications or merit, but on "immutable" characteristics such as sex or race.

In cases where discrimination is alleged, the parties must follow a prescribed order of proof, which is described later in Section 5.2. In cases of intentional discrimination, for example, the plaintiff must present sufficient evidence to raise an inference of discrimination; the defense then is allowed to rebut that inference by presenting evidence of a legitimate, nondiscriminatory reason for the action the plaintiff alleges was discriminatory. The plaintiff then has an opportunity to demonstrate that the defendant's "legitimate nondiscriminatory reason" is a pretext, that it is unworthy of belief. The substantive and procedural requirements of each of the relevant laws are examined in Section 5.2, as are the nature of the remedies available to plaintiffs. Then each type of discrimination (race, sex, and so on) is examined in Section 5.3, with examples of how these claims typically arise, the types of issues that colleges defending these claims must generally address, and the implications of these cases for administrators and institutional counsel.

Although disputes arising under the nondiscrimination laws have tended to be litigated in federal court, some employers in the nonacademic sector are using "mandatory arbitration agreements" to require employees who raise allegations of employment discrimination to arbitrate their claims rather then submitting them to a judicial forum. The use and lawfulness of requiring employees to arbitrate discrimination claims is discussed in Section 2.3.

Beginning in the late 1990s, the U.S. Supreme Court handed down a series of rulings limiting congressional authority to abrogate the sovereign immunity of states with respect to their liability for violations of federal nondiscrimination laws. These cases are discussed in Section 13.1.6. They apply to claims asserted against state colleges and universities by their employees in federal court, but by extension may now also apply to such claims brought in state court (see *Alden v. Maine,* discussed in Section 13.1.6). These cases have addressed some, but not all, of the federal nondiscrimination laws discussed in this section. Application of the sovereign immunity doctrine to discrimination claims against state colleges is discussed for each law so affected.

Several of the federal nondiscrimination laws have extraterritorial application. This is significant for colleges that employ U.S. citizens outside the United States to staff study abroad programs or other college programs that occur outside of the United States. The Civil Rights Act of 1991, discussed in Section 5.2.1, amended Title VII and the Americans With Disabilities Act to provide for extraterritorial application, thus legislatively overruling a U.S. Supreme Court decision, in *EEOC v. Arabian American Oil Co.,* 498 U.S. 808 (1990), that Title VII did not have extraterritorial application. The Age Discrimination in Employment Act was amended in 1984 to extend extraterritorial jurisdiction to U.S. citizens working abroad for U.S. employers, or for a foreign company that is owned or controlled by a U.S. company (29 U.S.C. § 623(h)). The Equal Pay Act also provides for extraterritorial application; a 1984 amendment changed the definition of "employee" in the Fair Labor Standards Act (of which the Equal Pay Act is a part) to include "any individual who is a citizen of the United States employed by an employer in a workplace in a foreign country" (29 U.S.C. § 630(f)). Equal Employment Opportunity Commission (EEOC) Guidelines on the extraterritorial application of these three laws can be found on the EEOC's Web site, available at http://www.eeoc.gov.

Another issue of increasing importance is the number of retaliation claims that employees who allege discrimination are now filing. The nondiscrimination laws contain language that makes it unlawful to take an adverse employment action against an individual who opposes or otherwise complains about alleged employment discrimination. Language in Title VII is similar to that in other federal nondiscrimination laws:

> It shall be an unlawful employment practice for an employer to discriminate against any of his employees or applicants for employment . . . because he has opposed any practice made an unlawful employment practice by this title, or because he has made a charge, testified, assisted, or participated in any manner in an investigation, proceeding, or hearing under this title [42 U.S.C. § 2000e-3(a)].

Retaliation claims have more than doubled since the mid-1990s, and constituted 27 percent of all claims filed with the EEOC in 2002. Such claims are further discussed in Section 13.5.7.5.

Sec. 5.2. Sources of Law

5.2.1. Title VII.
Title VII of the Civil Rights Act of 1964, 42 U.S.C. § 2000e *et seq.*, is the most comprehensive and most frequently utilized of the federal employment discrimination laws. It was extended in 1972 to cover educational institutions both public and private. According to the statute's basic prohibition, 42 U.S.C. § 2000e-2(a):

> It shall be an unlawful employment practice for an employer—
>
> (1) to fail or refuse to hire or to discharge any individual, or otherwise to discriminate against any individual with respect to his compensation, terms, conditions, or privileges of employment, because of such individual's race, color, religion, sex, or national origin; or
>
> (2) to limit, segregate, or classify his employees or applicants for employment in any way which would deprive or tend to deprive any individual of employment opportunities or otherwise adversely affect his status as an employee, because of such individual's race, color, religion, sex, or national origin.

The law covers not only employers but labor unions and employment agencies as well. Liability under Title VII is corporate; supervisors cannot be held individually liable under Title VII, although they may under other legal theories (*Miller v. Maxwell's International*, 991 F.2d 583 (9th Cir. 1993)).

Students who are employees may be protected under Title VII, but whether a student is also an employee is a factual issue (see, for example, *Cuddeback v. Florida Board of Education*, 318 F.3d 1230 (11th Cir. 2004), ruling that a graduate student research assistant was an employee for Title VII purposes under the "economic realities test"). Fellowships may be considered wages, or they may be characterized as financial aid. (For a discussion of the guidelines for determining whether a fellowship recipient is an employee, see *Sizova v. National Institute of Standards and Technology*, 282 F.3d 1320 (10th Cir. 2002) (ruling that the National Institute of Standards and Technology (NIST), not the University of Colorado, was the plaintiff's employer because the plaintiff worked at the NIST site and was supervised by its employees, and thus dismissing the Title VII claim against the university).)

The major exception to the general prohibition against discrimination is the "BFOQ" exception, which permits hiring and employing based on "religion, sex, or national origin" when such a characteristic is a "bona fide occupational qualification necessary to the normal operation of that particular business or enterprise" (42 U.S.C. § 2000e-2(e)(1)). Religion as a BFOQ is examined in Section 5.5 in the context of employment decisions at religious institutions of higher education. Sex could be a permissible BFOQ for a locker room attendant or, perhaps, for certain staff of a single-sex residence hall. Race and national origin are not permissible BFOQs for positions at colleges and universities.

Title VII is enforced by the Equal Employment Opportunity Commission, which has issued a series of regulations and guidelines published at 29 C.F.R.

Parts 1600 through 1610. The EEOC may receive, investigate, and conciliate complaints of unlawful employment discrimination, and may initiate lawsuits against violators in court or issue right-to-sue letters to complainants (29 C.F.R. Part 1601).

Title VII was amended by the Civil Rights Act of 1991 (Pub. L. No. 102-166, 105 Stat. 1071, 1072 (1991)), in large part as a reaction by Congress to seven decisions of the U.S. Supreme Court in 1989 that sharply limited the procedural and substantive rights of plaintiffs under Title VII and several other nondiscrimination laws. These decisions are discussed briefly in this Section and in Section 5.4. In addition, the Civil Rights Act of 1991 provides for compensatory and punitive damages,[1] as well as jury trials, in cases of intentional discrimination.

Although Title VII broadly prohibits employment discrimination, it does not limit the right of postsecondary institutions to hire employees on the basis of job-related qualifications or to distinguish among employees on the basis of seniority or merit in pay, promotion, and tenure policies. Institutions retain the discretion to hire, promote, reward, and terminate employees, as long as the institutions do not make distinctions based on race, color, religion, sex, or national origin. If, however, an institution does distinguish among employees on one of these bases, courts have broad powers to remedy the Title VII violation by "making persons whole for injuries suffered through past discrimination" (*Albemarle Paper Co. v. Moody,* 422 U.S. 405 (1975)). Remedies may include back pay awards (*Albemarle*), awards of retroactive seniority (*Franks v. Bowman Transportation Co.,* 424 U.S. 747 (1976)), and various affirmative action measures to benefit the group whose members were the subject of the discrimination (see Section 5.4), as well as the right, in disparate treatment cases, to compensatory and punitive damages.

There are two basic types of Title VII claims: the "disparate treatment" claim and the "disparate impact" or "adverse impact" claim. In the former type of suit, an individual denied a job, promotion, or tenure, or subjected to a detrimental employment condition, claims to have been treated less favorably than other applicants or employees because of his or her race, sex, national origin, or religion (see, for example, *Lynn v. Regents of the University of California,* 656 F.2d 1337 (9th Cir. 1981) (alleged sex discrimination in denial of tenure)). In the "disparate impact" or "adverse impact" type of suit, the claim is that some ostensibly neutral policy of the employer has a discriminatory impact on the claimants or the class of persons they represent (see, for example, *Scott v. University of Delaware,* 455 F. Supp. 1102, 1123–32 (D. Del. 1978), *affirmed on other grounds,* 601 F.2d 76 (3d Cir. 1979) (alleging that requirement of Ph.D. for faculty

---

[1]Compensatory and punitive damages are capped on the basis of the size of the employer: organizations with 15–100 employees may be assessed up to $50,000; 101–201 employees, $100,000; 201–500 employees, $200,000; and more than 500 employees, $300,000. These damages may be assessed in addition to the "make-whole" remedies of back pay and attorney's fees. Other nondiscrimination statutes do not have these caps. Awards of "front pay" are not considered to be compensatory damages, and thus are not subject to the statutory cap (*Pollard v. E. I. duPont de Nemours & Co.,* 532 U.S. 843 (2001)).

positions discriminated against racial minorities)). Of the two types of suits, disparate treatment is the more common for postsecondary education. The disparate treatment and disparate impact theories are also sometimes used when claims are litigated under other nondiscrimination laws, such as the Equal Pay Act and Title IX of the Education Amendments of 1972.

Although the disparate treatment claim may involve either direct or circumstantial evidence of discrimination, most plaintiffs are unable to present direct evidence of discrimination (such as written statements that the institution will not hire or promote them because of their race, sex, and so on, or corroborated oral statements that provide direct evidence of discrimination). An example of direct evidence of discrimination occurred in *Clark v. Claremont University*, 6 Cal. App. 4th 639 (Ct. App. Cal. 1992), a case brought under California's Fair Housing and Employment Act (Cal. Gov't. Code § 12900 *et seq.*) but analyzed under the Title VII disparate treatment theory. The plaintiff, an assistant professor who was denied tenure, introduced evidence of numerous racist remarks made by faculty members involved in the tenure review process, and a jury found that racial discrimination had motivated the tenure denial. The appellate court upheld the jury verdict, finding that the number and the nature of the racist remarks made by the faculty members provided substantial evidence of race discrimination.

Most plaintiffs, however, must use circumstantial evidence to attempt to demonstrate that discrimination motivated some negative employment action. The U.S. Supreme Court developed a burden-shifting paradigm that allows the plaintiff to demonstrate his or her qualifications for the position, promotion, or other employment action, and then requires the employer to introduce evidence of the reason for the negative decision. In *McDonnell Douglas Corp. v. Green*, 411 U.S. 792 (1973). Under that decision:

> The complainant in a Title VII trial must carry the initial burden under the statute of establishing a prima facie case of racial discrimination. This may be done by showing (i) that he belongs to a [category protected by Title VII]; (ii) that he applied and was qualified for a job for which the employer was seeking applicants; (iii) that, despite his qualifications, he was rejected; and (iv) that, after his rejection, the position remained open and the employer continued to seek applicants from persons of complainant's qualifications. . . .
>
> The burden then must shift to the employer to articulate some legitimate, nondiscriminatory reason for the employee's rejection [411 U.S. at 802].

This burden-shifting approach requires the employer to provide a reasonable, job- or performance-related reason for the negative decision. It does not require the employer to prove that it did not discriminate. The *McDonnell Douglas* methodology has been applied to other types of discriminatory treatment prohibited by Title VII; likewise, though the case concerned only job applications, courts have adapted its methodology to hiring, termination, discipline, salary decisions, promotion, and tenure situations. This paradigm is used for the litigation of discrimination claims under other federal nondiscrimination laws as well. A subsequent Supreme Court case adds an important gloss to *McDonnell*

Douglas by noting that, in a disparate treatment (as opposed to disparate impact) case, "proof of discriminatory motive is critical [to complainant's case], although it can in some situations be inferred from the mere fact of difference in treatment" (*International Brotherhood of Teamsters v. United States,* 431 U.S. 324, 355 n.12 (1977)).

Courts had difficulty interpreting *McDonnell Douglas*'s requirements concerning the evidentiary burden of both the plaintiff and the defendant in Title VII cases. The Supreme Court clarified its "burden-of-proof" ruling in *Texas Department of Community Affairs v. Burdine,* 450 U.S. 248 (1981). The case was brought by a state agency employee whose position had been abolished in a staff reorganization. Justice Powell, writing for a unanimous Court, explained that the plaintiff's burden in the *prima facie* case was to create a presumption that discrimination motivated the employer's actions. The employer's burden, said Justice Powell, was to rebut that presumption, not by proving that the employer did not discriminate, but by articulating a "legitimate, nondiscriminatory reason" for its decision, which would then create an issue of fact as to the employer's motivation for the decision. Once the employer's reason is given, the burden shifts back to the plaintiff

> to demonstrate that the proffered reason was not the true reason for the employment decision. This burden now merges with the ultimate burden of persuading the court that she has been the victim of intentional discrimination. She may succeed in this either directly by persuading the court that a discriminatory reason more likely motivated the employer or indirectly by showing that the employer's proffered explanation is unworthy of credence [450 U.S. at 253–56; footnotes omitted].

Burdine clarifies the distinction between the burden of *production* (of producing evidence about a particular fact) and the burden of *persuasion* (of convincing the trier of fact that illegal discrimination occurred). The plaintiff always carries the ultimate burden of persuasion; it is only the burden of production that shifts from plaintiff to defendant and back to plaintiff again. The requirement that the defendant "articulate" rather than "prove" a nondiscriminatory reason does not relieve the defendant of the need to introduce probative evidence; it merely frees the defendant from any obligation to carry the ultimate burden of persuasion on that issue.

In *St. Mary's Honor Center v. Hicks,* 509 U.S. 502 (1993), the Supreme Court reemphasized that the plaintiff carries the ultimate burden of proving intentional discrimination (instead of merely demonstrating that the defendant's reasons for its action were false). In *Hicks,* the employer had offered two reasons for the plaintiff's discharge: a series of disciplinary violations and an incident of gross insubordination. In the "pretext" stage of the case, the plaintiff convinced the trial court that these were not the reasons for the discharge, because other employees with similar disciplinary problems had not been discharged. The trial court ruled against the plaintiff because the plaintiff was unable to show racial animus in the decision, but the U.S. Court of Appeals for the Eleventh Circuit reversed, saying that, under the *Burdine* language, if the plaintiff could demostrate that the employer's reasons were "unworthy of belief," the plaintiff should prevail.

The Supreme Court, in a 5-to-4 opinion written by Justice Scalia, disagreed, saying that Title VII did not afford a plaintiff a remedy simply because an employer gave untruthful reasons, but only if the employer's decision was based on the plaintiff's race. Justice Scalia wrote:

> We have no authority to impose liability upon an employer for alleged discriminatory employment practices unless an appropriate factfinder determines, according to proper procedures, *that the employer has unlawfully discriminated.* . . . [N]othing in law would permit us to substitute for the required finding that the employer's action was the product of unlawful discrimination, the much different (and much lesser) finding that the employer's explanation of its action was not believable [509 U.S. at 514–15; emphasis in original].

In other words, in order to prevail under Title VII, the plaintiff must show two things: that the employer's stated reasons for the challenged decision are untrue, and that the true reason is discrimination. Few plaintiffs have direct evidence of discrimination, and many plaintiffs who have prevailed in discrimination claims have done so by indirect proof of discrimination of the type that the majority appeared to reject in *Hicks.*

The U.S. Supreme Court clarified its *Hicks* ruling in *Reeves v. Sanderson Plumbing Products,* 530 U.S. 133 (2000). Although *Reeves* was brought under the Age Discrimination in Employment Act (discussed in Section 5.2.6), the Court reviewed the lower courts' evaluations of the plaintiff's evidentiary burdens under the teachings of *Hicks.* Reeves had alleged that his termination was a result of age discrimination rather than the employer's determination that he had falsified time cards. The Court ruled that because Reeves had established a *prima facie* case of age discrimination and had demonstrated that the employer's allegations regarding the falsification were untrue, he did not have to make a specific link between age-related comments by his supervisor and his termination. Said the Court:

> Whether judgment as a matter of law is appropriate in any particular case will depend on a number of factors. Those include the strength of the plaintiff's prima facie case, the probative value of the proof that the employer's explanation is false, and any other evidence that supports the employer's case and that properly may be considered on a motion for judgment as a matter of law [530 U.S. at 148–49].

Independent evidence of discrimination was not necessary under these circumstances, according to the Court.

Occasionally, a plaintiff will have direct evidence of discrimination and allege the problem of "mixed motives" in an employment decision. In such cases, the plaintiff demonstrates that one or more of the prohibited factors (sex, race, and so on) was a motivating factor in a negative employment decision. In *Price Waterhouse v. Hopkins,* 490 U.S. 228 (1989), the plaintiff had proved that a committee evaluating her for partnership in an accounting firm used gender stereotypes to reach its decision not to award her a partnership. Both the plaintiff's and the defendant's burden of proof were at issue in *Hopkins:* the plaintiff argued that, in order to hold the defendant liable for discrimination, she need only demonstrate that gender played a part in the decision; the defendant insisted that, before liability could be found, the plaintiff must prove that gender was the "decisive consideration" in the decision.

A plurality of the Court, in an opinion authored by Justice Brennan, ruled that the plaintiff need only show that gender was one of the considerations in the employment decision. With regard to the defendant's burden of proof, Justice Brennan wrote:

> [O]nce a plaintiff in a Title VII case shows that gender played a motivating part in an employment decision, the defendant may avoid a finding of liability only by proving that it would have made the same decision even if it had not allowed gender to play such a role [490 U.S. at 244].

In other words, in "mixed motive" cases, simply "articulating a legitimate nondiscriminatory reason" in the face of demonstrated bias would be insufficient for a defendant to rebut the plaintiff's evidence; instead, to be found not liable, an employer would have to demonstrate that it would have reached the same decision even if the impermissible factors were absent.

In the Civil Rights Act of 1991, Congress agreed with the plurality's determination regarding the plaintiff's burden, but it overturned its determination that a defendant could still prevail even if an impermissible factor contributed to an employment decision. The Act amended Title VII's Section 703 by adding subsection (m), which states that if the plaintiff shows that a prohibited factor motivated an employment decision, an unlawful employment practice is established. But if the plaintiff establishes a violation under subsection (m) and the employer successfully demonstrates that the same action would have been taken in absence of the prohibited factor, then a court may not award damages or make-whole remedies (such as reinstatement or promotion). This amendment permits plaintiffs who do not prevail on the merits to be awarded attorney's fees and declaratory relief.

Lower federal courts attempting to interpret the new language of Title VII in mixed motive cases differed on whether a plaintiff was required to present direct evidence of discrimination in such cases, or whether indirect evidence of discrimination was sufficient to obtain a mixed-motive jury instruction. The U.S. Supreme Court, in a unanimous opinion, ruled that indirect or circumstantial evidence was sufficient to entitle a plaintiff to a mixed motive jury instruction in such cases (*Desert Palace, Inc. v. Costa,* 539 U.S. 90 (2003)).

Disparate treatment cases may also be brought by a class of plaintiffs. In these cases, called "pattern and practice" cases, the plaintiffs must prove intentional discrimination by the employer in one or more employment conditions. For example, in *Penk v. Oregon State Board of Higher Education,* 816 F.2d 458 (9th Cir. 1987), female faculty alleged systemwide discrimination against women in salary, promotion, and tenure practices, because statistical analysis revealed that women, on the whole, were paid less than male faculty and tended to be at lower ranks. The appellate court affirmed the trial court's conclusion that the postsecondary system had provided legitimate nondiscriminatory reasons for the statistical differentials, such as the fact that most women faculty were less senior and that external economic factors had depressed the salaries of junior faculty compared with those of senior faculty, most of whom were male. The court's careful articulation of the burdens of proof in pattern and practice cases is instructive.

Although most Title VII litigation in academe involves allegations of disparate treatment, several class action complaints have been brought against colleges and universities using the disparate impact theory. For example, in *Scott v. University of Delaware*, 455 F. Supp. 1102 (D. Del. 1987), *affirmed on other grounds*, 601 F.2d 76 (3d Cir. 1979), a black professor alleged, on behalf of himself and other black faculty, that requiring applicants for faculty positions to hold a Ph.D. had a disparate impact on blacks because blacks are underrepresented among holders of Ph.D. degrees. The court agreed with the university's argument that training in research, symbolized by the doctoral degree, was necessary for universities because of their research mission.

The paradigm for disparate impact suits is *Griggs v. Duke Power Co.*, 401 U.S. 424 (1971). As the U.S. Supreme Court explained in that case: "Under [Title VII] practices, procedures, or tests neutral on their face, and even neutral in terms of intent, cannot be maintained if they operate to 'freeze' the status quo of prior discriminatory employment practices . . ." (401 U.S. at 429).

In its unanimous opinion in *Griggs*, the Court interpreted Title VII to prohibit employment practices that (1) operate to exclude or otherwise discriminate against employees or prospective employees on grounds of race, color, religion, sex, or national origin, and (2) are unrelated to job performance or not justified by business necessity. Both requirements must be met before Title VII is violated. Under the first requirement, it need not be shown that the employer intended to discriminate; the effect of the employment practice, not the intent behind it, controls. Under the second requirement, the employer, not the employee, has the burden of showing the job relatedness or business necessity of the employment practice in question.

The disparate impact test developed in *Griggs* was applied by the Supreme Court in *Watson v. Fort Worth Bank & Trust*, 487 U.S. 977 (1988). The Court added an element to the *Griggs* tests: where a practice with a disparate impact is justified by business necessity, the plaintiffs may still prevail if they can demonstrate that "other selection processes that have a lesser discriminatory effect could also suitably serve the employer's business needs" (487 U.S. at 1006, Blackmun concurrence). In addition, the Court ruled that plaintiffs could attack subjective decision-making practices under the disparate impact theory—a ruling that is particularly important to faculty plaintiffs, who have frequently alleged that subjective performance standards are susceptible to bias.

In 1989, the U.S. Supreme Court issued a ruling in *Wards Cove Packing Co. v. Atonio*, 490 U.S. 642 (1989), that changed *Griggs*'s requirement that the employer demonstrate the business necessity of the challenged practices and made the plaintiff's burden of production much more difficult. Congress responded in the Civil Rights Act of 1991 by codifying the *Griggs* standard, thus nullifying that portion of *Wards Cove.* The Act adds subsection (k) to Section 703. The subsection requires the employer to rebut a showing of disparate impact by demonstrating that "the challenged practice is job related for the position in question and consistent with business necessity" (42 U.S.C. § 2000e-2(k)(1)(a)(i)). The subsection also permits the plaintiff to challenge the combined effects of several employment practices if the plaintiff "can demonstrate to the court that the elements of a respondent's decision-making process are not capable of separation for analysis." The new law also codifies the Court's *Watson* holding by adding that unlawful disparate impact may also be established if the plaintiff can demonstrate that a less discriminatory and equally effective alternative practice is available to the employer but the employer refuses to use it.

Another issue litigated under Title VII has relevance for claims under other nondiscrimination laws. Under Title VII, an individual claiming discrimination must file a complaint with the EEOC within 180 days "after the alleged unlawful employment practice occurred" (42 U.S.C. § 2000e-5(e)), or within 300 days if a claim has first been filed with a state or local civil rights agency. The claim lapses if the individual does not comply with this time limit. Although this provision may appear straightforward, most colleges and universities use multiple decision levels on faculty status matters. In addition, many individuals may be involved in a staff employment decision. These practices make it difficult to determine exactly when an employment practice "occurred." Did it occur with the first negative recommendation, perhaps made by a department chair, or is the action by an institution's board of trustees the "occurrence"? And since many colleges give a faculty member a "terminal year" contract after denial of tenure, at what point has the alleged discrimination "occurred"?

In *Delaware State College v. Ricks,* 449 U.S. 250 (1980), the U.S. Supreme Court interpreted this time requirement as it applies to faculty members making claims against postsecondary institutions. Overruling the appellate court, the Supreme Court held that the time period commences when an institution officially announces its employment decision and not when the faculty member's employment relationship terminates.

In a 5-to-4 decision, the Court dismissed the claim of Ricks, a black Liberian professor who had been denied tenure, because he had not filed his claim of national origin discrimination within 180 days of the date the college notified him of its decision. Ricks had claimed that his terminal year of employment, after the tenure denial, constituted a "continuing violation" of Title VII, which allowed him to file his EEOC charge within 180 days of his last day of employment. The Court rejected this view, stating that the alleged discrimination occurred at a single point in time. The Court also rejected an intermediate position, adopted by three of the dissenters, that the limitations period should not have begun until after the final decision of the college grievance committee, which had held hearings on Ricks's complaint.

In *Chardon v. Fernandez,* 454 U.S. 6 (1981), a *per curiam* opinion from which three Justices dissented, the Court extended the reasoning of *Ricks* to cover non-renewal or termination of term appointments (as opposed to tenure denials). Unless there are allegations that discriminatory acts continued to occur after official notice of the decision, the 180-day time period for nonrenewal or termination claims also begins to run from the date the complainant is notified.

The U.S. Court of Appeals for the Seventh Circuit was asked to determine at what point the "official notice" of the decision occurs: when an administrator makes a decision to which higher-level administrators routinely defer, or when the chief academic officer confirms that decision? In *Lever v. Northwestern University,* 979 F.2d 552 (7th Cir. 1992), the appellate court ruled that the point at which the discriminatory act occurs is a question of fact, which must be determined by reference to the institution's policies and practices. In this case, language in the faculty handbook indicated that a dean's decision to deny tenure was final unless reversed by the provost on appeal, and that the provost did not review negative recommendations by deans unless asked to do so by the candidate. Citing *Ricks,* the court stated that appeal of a negative decision made by the dean does not toll the limitations period.

The Civil Rights Act of 1991 addresses the issue of timely filing, although it does not overturn *Ricks.* In a case decided in 1989, the U.S. Supreme Court ruled that the limitations period begins to run when a practice that later has a discriminatory effect on an individual or group is first enacted, rather than when the individual or group is harmed. In *Lorance v. AT&T Technologies,* 490 U.S. 900 (1989), a group of women were not permitted to challenge an allegedly discriminatory seniority provision that had been adopted several years earlier, because they waited until they were harmed by the provision's application rather than filing a claim within 180 days of the date the provision took effect. Congress reversed this ruling by adding a new paragraph (2) to Section 112 of Title VII. The law now provides that a seniority system that intentionally discriminates may be challenged when the system is adopted, when an individual becomes subject to it, or when an individual is actually harmed by it.

Remedies available to prevailing parties in Title VII litigation include reinstatement, back pay, compensatory and punitive damages (for disparate treatment discrimination), and attorney's fees. Front pay is also available to plaintiffs who can demonstrate that the discrimination diminished their future ability to earn an income at the level they would have enjoyed absent the discrimination. For example, in *Thornton v. Kaplan,* 958 F. Supp. 502 (D. Colo. 1996), a jury had found that the university had discriminated against the plaintiff when it denied him tenure, and had awarded him $250,000 in compensatory damages, plus attorney's fees and court costs. The university argued that the award was excessive and moved for remittur (a request that the judge reduce the damage award) to $50,000. The judge refused, citing evidence that the denial of tenure resulted in a "loss of enjoyment" that the plaintiff derived from teaching, a loss of income, diminished prospects for future employment, humiliation, stress, depression, and feelings of exclusion from the academic community. Calling these losses "significant," the judge refused to reduce the damage award.

Although punitive damage awards are unusual in employment discrimination cases (except for sexual harassment complaints, discussed in Section 5.3.3.3), plaintiffs often demand punitive as well as compensatory damages in discrimination lawsuits. The U.S. Supreme Court established the standard for awarding punitive damages in Title VII cases in *Kolstad v. American Dental Association*, 527 U.S. 526 (1999). The plaintiff must demonstrate that the individual found to have engaged in the discrimination is an agent of the employer, employed in a managerial capacity, acting within the scope of employment, and acting with malice or reckless indifference toward the plaintiff's federally protected rights (527 U.S. at 535–45). A finding that an employer has made a good-faith effort to comply with Title VII, despite the unlawful actions of one particular manager or supervisor, will prevent the award of punitive damages. (For a discussion of the *Kolstad* standard and its application to a sexual harassment lawsuit against Tulane University, see *Green v. Administrators of the Tulane Educational Fund*, 284 F.3d 642 (5th Cir. 2002).) As long as the plaintiff can establish the required "malice" or "reckless indifference" of the employer, she may receive punitive damages even if no compensatory damages are awarded (*Cush-Crawford v. Adchem Corp.*, 271 F.3d 352 (2d Cir. 2001)).

Institutions may be able to shield themselves from punitive damage awards, even if their conduct is found to violate the nondiscrimination laws, by implementing and following grievance or appeal procedures. For example, in *Elghamni v. Franklin College of Indiana*, 2000 U.S. Dist. LEXIS 16667 (S.D. Ind. October 2, 2000) (unpublished), a faculty member denied tenure sought both compensatory and punitive damages under Title VII. A federal trial court granted the college's motion for summary judgment with respect to the plaintiff's claim for punitive damages, stating that the plaintiff had availed himself of an "extensive grievance process" that reviewed his claim of alleged discrimination before the decision became final, and thus punitive damages were not warranted.

Although Title VII remains an important source of protection for faculty alleging discrimination, an increasing number of discrimination claims are being brought under state nondiscrimination laws. Many state laws have no caps on damages like those of Title VII, and thus allow more generous damage awards. Other states may have laws that make it easier for a plaintiff to establish a *prima facie* case of discrimination than is the case under Title VII. (For an example of the use of state law to challenge an allegedly discriminatory tenure decision in a case against Trinity College, see Section 6.4.)

The U.S. Supreme Court has not addressed the issue of whether states have immunity from federal court litigation under Title VII since its *Kimel* ruling (see Sections 13.1.5 & 13.1.6), but federal appellate courts have concluded that Congress expressly and validly abrogated sovereign immunity in crafting both Title VII and the Civil Rights Act of 1991. (See, for example, *Okruhlik v. The University of Arkansas*, 255 F.3d 615 (8th Cir. 2001).)

5.2.2. Equal Pay Act. Both the Equal Pay Act (part of the Fair Labor Standards Act (FSLA), 29 U.S.C. § 206(d)) and Title VII prohibit sex discrimination in compensation. Because of the similarity of the issues, pay discrimination claims under both laws are discussed in this subsection.

Congress's purpose in enacting this provision was to combat the "ancient but outmoded belief that a man, because of his role in society, should be paid more than a woman" and to establish, in its place, the principle that "'equal work will be rewarded by equal wages'" (quoting *Corning Glass Workers v. Brennan*, 417 U.S. 188 (1974)). The Equal Pay Act provides that:

> no employer [subject to the Fair Labor Standards Act] shall discriminate . . . between employees on the basis of sex . . . on jobs the performance of which requires equal skill, effort, and responsibility, and which are performed under similar working conditions, except where such payment is made pursuant to (i) a seniority system; (ii) a merit system; (iii) a system which measures earnings by quantity or quality of production; or (iv) a differential based on any other factor other than sex [29 U.S.C. § 206(d)(1)].

Thus, the determination of whether jobs are equal, and the judgment as to whether one of the four exceptions applies to a particular claim, is the essence of an equal pay claim under this law.

The plaintiff in an Equal Pay Act lawsuit must find an employee in the same job, of a different gender, who is paid more. Even if the titles and job descriptions are the same, the court examines the actual responsibilities of the plaintiff and the comparator. For example, in *Gustin v. West Virginia University*, 63 Fed. Appx. 695 (4th Cir. 2003), the court ruled that the job responsibilities of a female assistant dean for student affairs were not equal to the responsibilities of a male assistant dean who had responsibilities for physical facilities and budget, and thus her Equal Pay Act claim failed.

Nonwage benefits may also be subject to the provisions of the Equal Pay Act. For example, in *Stewart v. SUNY Maritime College*, 83 Fair Empl. Prac. Cases (BNA) 1610 (S.D.N.Y. 2000), a female public safety officer at the college was denied on-campus housing, although all male public safety officers doing the same work as the plaintiff were provided free on-campus housing. The trial court denied the college's motion for summary judgment, ruling that whether the on-campus housing provided to male public safety officers constituted "wages" for purposes of the Equal Pay Act was a question of fact that must be determined at trial.

As part of the FLSA, the Equal Pay Act provides for double back pay damages in cases of willful violations of the Act. A plaintiff must demonstrate an employer's knowing or reckless disregard for its responsibilities under this law to establish a willful violation. (For an example of a successful plaintiff in this regard, see *Pollis v. The New School for Social Research*, 132 F.3d 115 (2d Cir. 1997).)

Although several public colleges have attempted to argue that they are shielded from liability for Equal Pay Act violations by Eleventh Amendment immunity, the courts have disagreed. Because the Equal Pay Act prohibits discrimination on the basis of sex, courts have ruled that it was promulgated under the authority of the Fourteenth Amendment. (See, for example, *Cherry v.*

University of Wisconsin System Board of Regents, 265 F.3d 541 (7th Cir. 2001); see also *Varner v. Illinois State University,* 226 F.3d 927 (7th Cir. 2000), *cert. denied,* 533 U.S. 902 (2001).)

Equal Pay Act claims may be brought by an individual or by a class of individuals who allege that the college underpaid them relative to members of the opposite sex who were doing equal work. Most class action Equal Pay Act cases against colleges have been brought by women faculty, and are discussed in Section 6.4. The Equal Pay Act is enforced by the Equal Employment Opportunity Commission. The EEOC's procedural regulations for the Act are codified in 29 C.F.R. Parts 1620–21.

Salary discrimination claims under Title VII are not subject to the "equal work" requirement of the Equal Pay Act, and thus challenges can be brought to pay discrimination between jobs that are comparable rather than strictly equal. Several "comparable worth" claims have been brought by women faculty who have asserted that Title VII prohibits colleges and universities from setting the compensation of faculty in female-dominated disciplines at a level different from that of faculty in male-dominated disciplines. In each of these cases, plaintiffs have asserted that the Supreme Court's decision in *Gunther* permits a comparable worth claim under Title VII.

In the early 1980s, the U.S. Supreme Court appeared to open the door to comparable worth claims. In *County of Washington v. Gunther,* 452 U.S. 161 (1981), the Court sorted out the relationships between the Equal Pay Act and Title VII as they apply to claims of sex discrimination in pay. Although the *Gunther* decision broadened the avenues that aggrieved employees have for challenging sex-based pay discrimination, the Court's opinion did not adopt the "comparable worth" theory that some forecasters had hoped the case would establish. According to the majority:

> We emphasize at the outset the narrowness of the question before us in this case. Respondents' claim is not based on the controversial concept of "comparable worth," under which plaintiffs might claim increased compensation on the basis of a comparison of the intrinsic worth or difficulty of their job with that of other jobs in the same organization or community. Rather, respondents seek to prove, by direct evidence, that their wages were depressed because of intentional sex discrimination, consisting of setting the wage scale for female guards, but not for male guards, at a level lower than its own survey of outside markets and the worth of the jobs warranted. The narrow question in this case is whether such a claim is precluded by [Title VII] [452 U.S. at 166].

Although the *Gunther* opinion neither rejected nor accepted the comparable worth theory, the Court's application of Title VII to pay disparity claims provided impetus for further attempts to establish the theory. A number of lawsuits were filed in the wake of *Gunther.* In the first higher education case to reach the appellate courts, *Spaulding v. University of Washington,* 740 F.2d 686 (9th Cir. 1984), members of the university's nursing faculty raised both disparate treatment and disparate impact claims to challenge disparities in salary levels between their department and others on campus. The court rejected both claims. As to the former claim, the plaintiffs had not shown that the university acted with discriminatory intent in establishing the salary levels. According to the court, the direct evidence did not indicate such intent, and "we will not infer intent merely from the existence of wage differences between jobs that are only similar." As to the latter claim (which does not require a showing of intent), the court held that the law does not permit use of the disparate impact approach in cases, such as this one, that "involve wide-ranging allegations challenging general wage policies" for jobs that are "only comparable" rather than equal. In particular, said the court, an employer's mere reliance on market forces in setting wages cannot itself constitute a disparate impact violation.

Subsequent comparable worth litigation against nonacademic organizations has also been unsuccessful for plaintiffs. In *American Federation of State, County, and Municipal Employees v. State of Washington,* 770 F.2d 1401 (9th Cir. 1985), the federal appeals court overruled the finding of a trial judge that Washington's failure to implement a statutorily required comparable worth salary system was either intentional discrimination or satisfied the disparate impact theory under Title VII (see Section 5.3.2.1). The Supreme Court has not ruled on the comparable worth theory, either directly or indirectly, since its *Gunther* ruling. Several states have passed laws requiring comparable worth in the public sector, but there has been little activity related to college faculty, although women staff at some unionized colleges and universities have benefited from comparable worth adjustments in collective bargaining agreements.

A particularly troubling issue in salary discrimination claims is the determination of whether pay differentials are, in fact, caused by sex or race discrimination, or by legitimate factors such as performance differences, market factors, or educational background. These issues have been debated fiercely in the courts and in the literature. The use of "market factors" in salary discrimination claims brought by faculty is discussed in Section 6.4.

5.2.3. Title IX.

Title IX of the Education Amendments of 1972, 20 U.S.C. § 1681 *et seq.,* prohibits sex discrimination by public and private educational institutions receiving federal funds (see Section 13.5.3 of this book). The statute is administered by the Office for Civil Rights (OCR) of the Department of Education. The department's regulations contain provisions on employment (34 C.F.R. §§ 106.51–106.61) that are similar in many respects to the EEOC's sex discrimination guidelines under Title VII. The regulations may be found on the OCR Web site, available at http://www.ed.gov/offices/OCR/regs. Like Title VII, the Title IX regulations contain a provision permitting sex-based distinctions in employment where sex is a "bona fide occupational qualification" (34 C.F.R. § 106.61). Title IX also contains a provision exempting any "educational institution which is controlled by a religious organization" if Title IX's requirements "would not be consistent with the religious tenets of such organization" (20 U.S.C. § 1681(a)(3); 34 C.F.R. § 106.12).

The applicability of Title IX to employment discrimination was hotly contested in a series of cases beginning in the mid-1970s. The U.S. Supreme Court resolved the dispute, holding that Title IX does apply to and prohibit sex discrimination in employment (see *North Haven Board of Education v. Bell,* 456 U.S. 512 (1982) (discussed in Section 13.5.7.1)).

The decision of the U.S. Supreme Court in *Franklin v. Gwinnett County Public Schools,* 503 U.S. 60 (1992) (discussed in Sections 13.5.3 & 13.5.9), that plaintiffs alleging discrimination under Title IX may be awarded compensatory damages, has stimulated discrimination claims under Title IX that might otherwise have been brought under Title VII, given Title VII's cap on damages (see Section 5.2.1). Title IX does not require the exhaustion of administrative remedies, and it borrows its statute of limitations from state law, which may be more generous than the relatively short period under Title VII. Plaintiffs with dual status as employees and students (for example, graduate teaching assistants, work-study students, and residence hall counselors) may find Title IX appealing because they need not prove they are "employees" rather than students in order to seek relief.

Some courts have held, however, that plaintiffs are barred from filing employment discrimination claims seeking money damages under Title IX. For example, in *Cooper v. Gustavus Adolphus College,* 957 F. Supp. 191 (D. Minn. 1997), a male faculty member was found guilty of sexually harassing a student and was subsequently dismissed; he claimed that the dismissal procedure was flawed and that it violated Title IX, but he did not also bring a claim under Title VII. The court noted that, although students and prospective students may bring claims for damages under Title IX, an employee who asserts a sex discrimination claim must use Title VII because Title VII "provides a comprehensive and carefully balanced remedial mechanism for redressing employment discrimination, and since Title IX does not clearly imply a private cause of action for damages for employment discrimination, none should be created by the courts" (957 F. Supp. at 193). The court also rejected the plaintiff's claim that Title IX created an independent right to due process in the procedure used to determine whether an employee should be disciplined or terminated. Citing *Yusuf v. Vassar College* (Section 9.4.4), the court stated: "[T]here is no Title IX statutory due process right separate from a right to be free from discrimination, even for a student. This must be all the more true for an employee, whose action for damages for discrimination must be found in Title VII, not Title IX" (957 F. Supp. at 194).

The federal appellate courts are split on this issue. Appellate courts in the Fourth and Sixth Circuits have ruled that Title IX does permit a private right of action in employment cases (*Preston v. Virginia,* 31 F.3d 203 (4th Cir. 1994); and *Ivan v. Kent State Univ.,* 1996 U.S. App. LEXIS 22269 (6th Cir. 1996) (unpublished)).[2] (See also *Arceneaux v. Vanderbilt University,* 2001 U.S. App. LEXIS 27598 (6th Cir. 2001) (unpublished).) But appellate panels in the Fifth and Eleventh Circuits disagree. These courts view Title VII's remedial structure,

---

[2]The precedental value of these two cases is open to question; *Preston* has been criticized in subsequent trial and appellate court opinions, and *Ivan* is unpublished.

including its exhaustion of remedies requirement, as precluding a parallel right of action under Title IX. In *Morris v. Wallace Community College-Selma*, 125 F. Supp. 2d 1315 (S.D. Ala. 2001), *affirmed without opinion*, 34 Fed. Appx. 388 (11th Cir. 2002), the court stated that it had "discovered no appellate decision clearly and analytically holding that a plaintiff may maintain a Title IX action against her employer for a wrong prohibited, and a remedy provided, by Title VII" (125 F. Supp. 2d at 1343, n.38), citing *Lakoski v. James*, 66 F.3d 751 (5th Cir. 1997); and *Lowery v. Texas A&M University System*, 117 F.3d 242 (5th Cir. 1997). The *Lowery* court, however, did permit the plaintiff to state a claim under Title IX for retaliation, since the factual circumstances of her claim would not be covered by Title VII. Lowery asserted that she had been retaliated against for objecting to the university's alleged inequitable allocation of resources between male and female athletes; this assertion "stated a claim under Title IX but not under Title VII." The court therefore permitted her to claim retaliation, but not employment discrimination, under Title IX. The *Lowery* case is discussed in Section 5.3.3.4.

The decision of the U.S. Supreme Court in *Alexander v. Sandoval*, 532 U.S. 275 (2001), discussed in Section 13.5.9, persuaded some federal courts that even a claim of retaliation cannot be litigated in court under Title IX, since it relies upon the Title IX regulation on retaliation rather than any express retaliation provision in the Title IX statute itself. In *Atkinson v. Lafayette College*, 2002 U.S. Dist. LEXIS 1432 (E.D. Pa. 2002), a female athletics director alleged that she was terminated in retaliation for her complaints about the college's alleged infringements of Title IX. She also brought employment discrimination claims under Title VII and the state human rights law. The trial court dismissed her Title IX retaliation claim, which had been brought under Section 902 of Title IX, stating that the result in *Sandoval*, which involved Title VI of the Civil Rights Act of 1964, was directly applicable to Title IX because of the similarities in the interpretation and enforcement provisions of the two laws. A federal trial court in Virginia reached a similar conclusion, finding that Title IX's antiretaliation regulations were beyond the scope of the plain language of the statute (*Litman v. George Mason University*, 156 F. Supp. 2d 579 (E.D. Va. 2001)). That result, however, was vacated by the U.S. Court of Appeals for the Fourth Circuit (92 Fed. Appx. 41 (4th Cir. 2004)), based upon Fourth Circuit precedent in a case involving Title VI (*Peters v. Jenney*, 327 F.3d 307 (4th Cir. 2003)). In *Peters*, a case involving the dismissal of an elementary school administrator, the Fourth Circuit had ruled that Title VI confers a private right of action for challenging alleged retaliation. Thus, said the appellate court in *Litman*, the same rationale should apply to retaliation claims brought under Title IX.

The U.S. Supreme Court resolved this issue in a case involving the male coach of a high school girls' basketball team who claimed that he was terminated in retaliation for complaining about allegedly unequal facilities for boys' and girls' teams. In *Jackson v. Birmingham Board of Education*, 309 F.3d 1333 (11th Cir. 2002), *reversed*, 125 S. Ct. 1497 (2005), the appellate court had dismissed the case, stating that the plaintiff was not himself a victim of sex discrimination and thus could not sue under Title IX. The U.S. Supreme Court reversed, stating that retaliating against an individual for complaining about unlawful sex discrimination was itself intentional sex discrimination, a violation of Title IX. The Court rejected the lower courts' reliance on *Sandoval,* stating that the Title IX statute, not the retaliation regulation, provided the basis for Jackson's claim. This case is discussed in Section 13.5.7.5 of this book.

5.2.4. Section 1981. A post–Civil War civil rights statute, 42 U.S.C. § 1981, commonly known as "Section 1981," states:

> All persons within the jurisdiction of the United States shall have the same right in every state and territory to make and enforce contracts, to sue, be parties, give evidence, and to the full and equal benefit of all laws and proceedings for the security of persons and property as is enjoyed by white citizens, and shall be subject to like punishment, pains, penalties, taxes, licenses, and exactions of every kind, and to no other.

Section 1981 is enforced through court litigation by persons denied the equality that the statute guarantees.[3] It prohibits discrimination in both public and private employment, as the U.S. Supreme Court affirmed in *Johnson v. Railway Express Agency,* 421 U.S. 454 (1975).

Section 1981 covers racially based employment discrimination against white persons as well as racial minorities (*McDonald v. Santa Fe Trail Transportation Co.,* 427 U.S. 273 (1976)). Although in earlier cases Section 1981 had been held to apply to employment discrimination against aliens (*Guerra v. Manchester Terminal Corp.,* 498 F.2d 641 (5th Cir. 1974)), more recent federal appellate court rulings suggest that this broad reading of the law is inappropriate. In *Bhandari v. First National Bank of Commerce,* 829 F.2d 1343 (5th Cir. 1987), a federal appellate court overturned *Guerra* and, after a lengthy review of the 1866 Civil Rights Act, determined that Congress had not intended Section 1981 to cover private discrimination against aliens, although the court did not address the issue of such discrimination by a public entity. The U.S. Supreme Court vacated the *Bhandari* opinion because the appellate court had speculated that the Supreme Court would overturn *Runyon v. McCrary,* 427 U.S. 160 (1976), (which had applied Section 1981 to private discrimination) in its opinion in *Patterson v. McLean Credit Union,* 491 U.S. 164 (1989). On the contrary, the Supreme Court reaffirmed *Runyon* and, vacating *Bhandari,* instructed the Fifth Circuit to analyze this case in light of *Patterson.* On remand, the U.S. Court of Appeals,

---

[3]Cases interpreting Section 1981 are collected in Ann K. Wooster, Annot., "Actions Brought Under 42 USCA §§ 1981–1983 for Racial Discrimination—Supreme Court Cases," 164 A.L.R. Fed. 483; Donald T. Kramer, Annot., "What Constitutes Reverse or Majority Race or National Origin Discrimination Violative of Federal Constitution or Statutes—Public Employment Cases," 168 A.L.R. Fed. 1; Donald T. Kramer, Annot., "What Constitutes Reverse or Majority Race or National Origin Discrimination Violative of Federal Constitution or Statutes—Private Employment Cases," 150 A.L.R. Fed. 1.

sitting *en banc,* reinstated its holding in *Bhandari* at 887 F.2d 609 (1989), asserting that *Patterson* did not alter the rationale for its earlier ruling. The Supreme Court denied review (494 U.S. 1061 (1990)).[4]

Although Section 1981 does not specifically prohibit discrimination on the basis of national origin (*Ohemeng v. Delaware State College,* 676 F. Supp. 65 (D. Del. 1988), *affirmed,* 862 F.2d 309 (3d Cir. 1988)), some courts have permitted plaintiffs to pursue national origin discrimination claims under Section 1981 in cases where race and national origin were intertwined.[5] In two special cases, moreover, the U.S. Supreme Court has interpreted Section 1981 to apply to certain types of national origin and ethnicity discrimination. In *St. Francis College v. Al-Khazraji,* 481 U.S. 604 (1987), the Court permitted a professor of Arabian descent to challenge his tenure denial under Section 1981. And in *Shaare Tefila Congregation v. Cobb,* 481 U.S. 615 (1987), the Court extended similar protections to Jews. In both cases the Court looked to the dictionary definition of "race" in the 1860s, when Section 1981 was enacted by Congress; the definition included both Arabs and Jews as examples of races.

While Section 1981 overlaps Title VII (see Section 5.2.1) in its coverage of racial discrimination in employment, a back pay award is not restricted to two years of back pay under Section 1981, as it is under Title VII (see *Johnson v. Railway Express Agency,* 421 U.S. 454 (1975)). Furthermore, Section 1981 does not have the short statute of limitations that Title VII imposes. In *Jones v. R. R. Donnelley & Sons Co.,* 541 U.S. 369 (2004), the U.S. Supreme Court ruled that a four-year statute of limitations should apply to claims brought under the Civil Rights Act of 1866, of which Section 1981 is a part. Therefore, individuals alleging race discrimination in employment are likely to file claims under both Section 1981 and Title VII.

In *General Building Contractors Ass'n. v. Pennsylvania,* 458 U.S. 375 (1982), the U.S. Supreme Court engrafted an intent requirement onto the Section 1981 statute. To prevail in a Section 1981 claim, therefore, a plaintiff must prove that the defendant intentionally or purposefully engaged in discriminatory acts. This requirement is the same as the Court previously applied to discrimination claims brought under the equal protection clause (see Section 5.2.7).

Congress amended Section 1981 in the Civil Rights Act of 1991 by adding subsections (b) and (c), which read:

(b) For purposes of this section, the term "make and enforce contracts" includes the making, performance, modification, and termination of contracts, and the enjoyment of all benefits, privileges, terms, and conditions of the contractual relationship.

---

[4]Cases addressing whether aliens are protected by Section 1981 are collected in Tim A. Thomas, Annot., "Application of 42 U.S.C.S. Section 1981 to Private Discrimination Against Aliens," 99 A.L.R. Fed. 835.

[5]Cases related to national origin claims under Section 1981 are collected in Jean F. Rydstrom, Annot., "Applicability of 42 U.S.C.S. § 1981 to National Origin Employment Discrimination Cases," 43 A.L.R. Fed. 103.

(c) The rights protected by this section are protected against impairment by nongovernmental discrimination and impairment under color of State law.

(For a thoughtful analysis of race discrimination and its legal remedies, see L. Alexander, "What Makes Wrongful Discrimination Wrong? Biases, Preferences, Stereotypes, and Proxies," 141 *U. Pa. L. Rev.* 149 (1992).)

Although Section 1981 has been found to cover employment decisions of both private and public employers, colleges that are arms of the state are immune from Section 1981 damages liability under the Eleventh Amendment of the U.S. Constitution. (For an illustrative case holding that a federal trial court lacked jurisdiction to hear an employee's suit against the City University of New York, see *Bunch v. The City University of New York Queens College,* 2000 U.S. Dist. LEXIS 14227 (S.D.N.Y. 2000).)

5.2.5. Americans With Disabilities Act and Rehabilitation Act of 1973.
Two federal laws forbid employment discrimination against individuals with disabilities. The Americans With Disabilities Act (ADA), 42 U.S.C. § 12101 *et seq.,* prohibits employment discrimination by employers with fifteen or more employees, labor unions, and employment agencies. Section 504 of the Rehabilitation Act, 29 U.S.C. § 794 (also discussed in Section 13.5.4), also prohibits discrimination against individuals with disabilities, but unlike the ADA, there is no threshold number of employees required for coverage by Section 504 (*Schrader v. Fred A. Ray M.D.,* 296 F.3d 968 (10th Cir. 2002)). Section 504 is patterned after Title VI and Title IX (see Sections 13.5.2 & 13.5.3), which prohibit, respectively, race and sex discrimination in federally funded programs and activities. Each federal funding agency enforces the Rehabilitation Act with respect to its own funding programs.

Title I of the Americans With Disabilities Act of 1990 prohibits employment discrimination against "qualified" individuals who are disabled. (The other titles of the ADA are discussed in Section 13.2.11.) The prohibition of discrimination in the ADA uses language very similar to that of Title VII:

(a) No covered entity shall discriminate against a qualified individual with a disability because of the disability of such individual in regard to job application procedures, the hiring, advancement, or discharge of employees, employee compensation, job training, and other terms, conditions, and privileges of employment [42 U.S.C. §12102(a)].

The law defines "discrimination" very broadly, and prohibits the following practices: segregating or limiting the job opportunities of the individual with a disability; participating in a relationship with another entity, such as a labor union or employment agency, that engages in discrimination against an individual with a disability; using hiring or promotion standards that have a discriminatory effect or perpetuate the discrimination of others; denying employment or benefits to an individual who has a relationship with someone who is disabled; not making reasonable accommodation (unless an undue hardship exists); denying employment opportunities in order to avoid having to accommodate an individual; using selection tests or standards that screen out individuals with disabilities unless the tests or standards are job related and a business necessity; failing to use tests that identify an individual's skills rather than his or her impairments.[6]

The law defines a "qualified individual with a disability" as "an individual with a disability who, with or without reasonable accommodation, can perform the essential functions of the employment position that such individual holds or desires" (42 U.S.C. § 12111(8)). This definition, which would apply to an individual with a disability who could perform the job only if accommodated, rejects the U.S. Supreme Court's interpretation of the Rehabilitation Act's definition of "otherwise qualified" in *Southeastern Community College v. Davis*, 442 U.S. 397 (1979). Because the ADA's language is broader than that of the Rehabilitation Act, it is more likely that employees claiming disability discrimination will seek redress under the ADA rather than the Rehabilitation Act.

The law requires that, if an applicant or a current employee meets the definition of "qualified individual with a disability," the employer must provide a reasonable accommodation unless the accommodation presents an "undue hardship" for the employer. The terms are defined thusly in the statute:

> The term "reasonable accommodation" may include—
> (A) making existing facilities used by employees readily accessible to and usable by individuals with disabilities; and
> (B) job restructuring, part-time or modified work schedules, reassignment to a vacant position, acquisition or modification of equipment or devices, appropriate adjustment or modifications of examinations, training materials or policies, the provision of qualified readers or interpreters, and other similar accommodations for individuals with disabilities [42 U.S.C. §12111(9)].
>
> (10) (A) The term "undue hardship" means an action requiring significant difficulty or expense, when considered in light of the factors set forth in subparagraph (B).
> (B) In determining whether an accommodation would impose an undue hardship on a covered entity, factors to be considered include—
> (i) the nature and cost of the accommodation needed under this chapter;

---

[6]Cases and authorities related to the Americans With Disabilities Act are collected at William H. Danne, Jr., Annot., "Who Is 'Qualified Individual' Under Americans With Disabilities Act Provisions Defining, and Extending Protection Against Employment Discrimination to Qualified Individual with Disability (42 USCA §§ 12111(8), 12112(a))," 146 A.L.R. Fed. 1; Ann K. Wooster, Annot., "What Constitutes Employment Discrimination by Public Entity in Violation of Americans With Disabilities Act (ADA), 42 USCA §§ 12132," 164 A.L.R. Fed. 433; Laurel M. Cohn, Annot., "When Is Individual Regarded as Having, or Perceived to Have, Impairment Within Meaning of Americans With Disabilities Act (42 USCA §§ 12102(2))," 148 A.L.R. Fed. 305; Thomas J. Kapusta, Annot., "When Does Job Restructuring Constitute Reasonable Accommodation of Qualified Disabled Employee or Applicant," 142 A.L.R. Fed. 311; John F. Wagner, Annot., "What Constitutes Substantial Limitation on Major Life Activity of Working for Purposes of Americans With Disabilities Act (42 USCA §§ 12101–12213)," 141 A.L.R. Fed. 603.

    (ii) the overall financial resources of the facility or facilities involved in the provision of the reasonable accommodation; the number of persons employed at such facility; the effect on expenses and resources, or the impact otherwise of such accommodation upon the operation of the facility;

   (iii) the overall financial resources of the covered entity; the overall size of the business of a covered entity with respect to the number of its employees, the number, type, and location of its facilities; and

   (iv) the type of operation or operations of the covered entity, including the composition, structure, and functions of the workforce of such entity; the geographic separateness, administrative, or fiscal relationship of the facility or facilities in question to the covered entity [42 U.S.C. § 12111(10)].

The ADA also contains provisions regarding the use of preemployment medical examinations, the confidentiality of an individual's medical records, and the individuals who may have access to information about the individual's disability.[7]

The law specifically excludes current abusers of controlled substances from coverage, but it does protect recovering abusers, individuals who are incorrectly perceived to be abusers of controlled substances, and individuals who have completed or are participating in a supervised rehabilitation program and are no longer using controlled substances. Since the law does not exclude persons with alcoholism, they are protected by the ADA, even if their abuse is current. However, the law permits employers to prohibit the use of alcohol or drugs at the workplace, to outlaw intoxication on the job, and to conform with the Drug-Free Workplace Act of 1988 (41 U.S.C. § 701 *et seq.*) (discussed in this book, Section 13.4.3.1). Employers may also hold users of drugs or alcohol to the same performance standards as other employees, and the law neither requires nor prohibits drug testing.

The ADA's employment discrimination remedies are identical to those of Title VII, and the Act is enforced by the EEOC, as is Title VII. The same limitation on damages found in Title VII applies to actions brought under the ADA, except that language applicable to the ADA provides that if an employer makes a good-faith attempt at reasonable accommodation but is still found to have violated the ADA, neither compensatory nor punitive damages will be available to the plaintiff (42 U.S.C. § 1981A).[8] This provision also applies to the Rehabilitation Act. Regulations interpreting the ADA are published at 29 C.F.R. § 1630. In addition to

---

[7]Cases and authorities are collected in Deborah F. Buckman, Annot., "Construction and Application of § 102(d) of Americans With Disabilities Act (42 USCA § 12112(d)) Pertaining to Medical Examinations and Inquiries," 159 A.L.R. Fed. 89. See also the EEOC's "Enforcement Guidance on Disability-Related Inquiries and Medical Examinations of Employees Under the Americans With Disabilities Act," July 2000, at http://www.eeoc.gov.

[8]Cases and authorities regarding ADA remedies are collected in Mary L. Topliff, Annot., "Remedies Available Under Americans With Disabilities Act (42 USCA § 12101 *et seq.*)," 136 A.L.R. Fed. 63.

expanding on the concepts of "qualified," "reasonable accommodation," and "undue hardship," they include guidelines for determining whether hiring or retaining an employee with a disability would pose a safety hazard to coworkers or to the employee (29 C.F.R. § 1630.2(r)). The EEOC has also issued several Enforcement Guidance documents that state the agency's position on and interpretation of the ADA. These documents are available on the agency's Web site at http://www.eeoc.gov.

Title II of the ADA prohibits discrimination on the basis of disability by "public entities," which includes public colleges and universities. The language of Title II mirrors the language of Title VI and Section 504 of the Rehabilitation Act:

> [N]o qualified individual with a disability shall, by reason of such disability, be excluded from participation in or be denied the benefits of the services, programs, or activities of a public entity, or be subjected to discrimination by any such entity [42 U.S.C. § 12132].

The regulations interpreting Title II prohibit employment discrimination by a public entity (28 C.F.R. § 35.140). Title II adopts the remedies, rights, and procedures of Section 505 of the Rehabilitation Act, which has been interpreted to provide a private right of action for individuals alleging discrimination under the Rehabilitation Act (see Section 13.5.9 of this book). No exhaustion of administrative remedies is required by either Title II or Section 505.

In 1993, a federal district court examined the relationship between Titles I and II of the ADA—the first time such an examination had been made. An employee of the University of Wisconsin whose one-year contract was not renewed filed a lawsuit in federal court under Title II of the ADA. In *Petersen v. University of Wisconsin Board of Regents,* 818 F. Supp. 1276 (W.D. Wis. 1993), the university argued that the court lacked jurisdiction because Petersen did not exhaust his administrative remedies by first filing a charge with the EEOC, as required by Title I of the ADA. The court, noting the language of the statute, the regulations, and the legislative history, concluded that Title II includes employment discrimination as prohibited conduct and explicitly does not require exhaustion of administrative remedies. This ruling appears to create an exception for employees of public colleges and universities to the requirement that claims of employment discrimination under the ADA be first filed with the EEOC. (For a discussion of this issue, see Jason Powers, Note, "Employment Discrimination Claims Under ADA Title II: The Case for Uniform Administrative Exhaustion Requirements," 76 *Texas L. Rev.* 1457 (1998).)

Colleges and universities have been subject to the Rehabilitation Act since 1972, and a body of judicial precedent has developed interpreting that Act's requirements. The law was amended by the Rehabilitation Act Amendments of 1992 (Pub. L. 102-569, 106 Stat. 4344) to replace the word "handicap" with the word "disability" and to conform the language of the Rehabilitation Act in other ways with that of the ADA (see Section 13.5.4). Regulations interpreting the Rehabilitation Act's prohibitions against disability discrimination by federal contractors have been revised to conform to ADA provisions, and are found at 34 C.F.R. § 104.11 and 29 C.F.R. § 1641.[9]

The regulations implementing Section 504 of the Rehabilitation Act prohibit discrimination against qualified disabled persons with regard to any term or condition of employment, including selection for training or conference attendance and employers' social or recreational programs. Furthermore, the regulations state that the employer's obligations under the statute are not affected by any inconsistent term of any collective bargaining agreement to which the employer is a party (34 C.F.R. § 104.11).

In language similar to that of the ADA, the Section 504 regulations define a qualified person with a disability as one who "with reasonable accommodation can perform the essential functions" of the job in question (34 C.F.R. § 104.3(k)(1)). The regulations impose an affirmative obligation on the recipient to make "reasonable accommodation to the known physical or mental limitations of an otherwise qualified handicapped applicant or employee unless the recipient can demonstrate that the accommodation would impose an undue hardship on the operation of its program" (34 C.F.R. § 104.12(a)). Reasonable accommodations can take the form of modification of the job site, of equipment, or of a position itself. What hardship would relieve a recipient of the obligation to make reasonable accommodation depends on the facts of each case. As a related affirmative requirement, the recipient must adapt its employment tests to accommodate an applicant's sensory, manual, or speaking disability unless the tests are intended to measure those types of skills (34 C.F.R. § 104.13(b)).

The regulations include explicit prohibitions regarding employee selection procedures and preemployment questioning. As a general rule, the fund recipient cannot make any preemployment inquiry or require a preemployment medical examination to determine whether an applicant is disabled or to determine the nature or severity of a disability (34 C.F.R. § 104.14(a)). Nor can a recipient use any employment criterion, such as a test, that has the effect of eliminating qualified applicants with disabilities, unless the criterion is job related and there is no alternative job-related criterion that does not have the same effect (34 C.F.R. § 104.13(a)). These prohibitions are also found in the ADA and its regulations.

In *Southeastern Community College v. Davis*, 442 U.S. 397 (1979), discussed in Sections 8.2.4.3 and 13.5.4, the U.S. Supreme Court addressed for the first time the extent of the obligation that Section 504 imposes on colleges and universities. The case involved the admission of a disabled applicant to a clinical nursing program, but the Court's opinion also sheds light on the Rehabilitation Act's application to employment of disabled persons.

---

[9]Cases related to who is qualified under the Rehabilitation Act are collected in Colleen R. Courtade, Annot., "Who Is 'Qualified' Handicapped Person Protected from Employment Discrimination Under Rehabilitation Act of 1973 (29 U.S.C.S. §§ 701 *et seq.*) and Regulations Promulgated Thereunder," 80 A.L.R. Fed. 830. See also Francis M. Dougherty, Annot., "Who Is 'Individual with Handicaps' Under Rehabilitation Act of 1973 (29 U.S.C.S. § 701 *et seq.*)," 97 A.L.R. Fed. 40.

In *Davis*, the Court determined that an "otherwise qualified handicapped individual" protected by Section 504 is one who is qualified *in spite of* his or her disability, and thus ruled that the institution need not make major program modifications to accommodate the individual. Because the definition of "otherwise qualified" appears only in the Department of Education's regulations implementing Section 504, not in the statute, the Court did not consider itself bound by the language of the regulations, which defined a "qualified handicapped individual" for employment purposes as one who, "with reasonable accommodation," can perform the job's essential functions. However, statutory language in the ADA virtually repeats the language of Section 504's regulations; thus, the Court's opinion in *Davis* has limited relevance for employment challenges under the ADA.

The Court apparently equated accommodation of an individual with a disability with affirmative action rather than viewing the accommodation as the removal of barriers for an individual with a disability. The framers of the ADA have rejected the former interpretation; since the accommodation requirement is stated clearly in the ADA, and the term "affirmative action" appears nowhere in the statute, the continued vitality of *Southeastern Community College* in the context of employment is questionable.

The U.S. Supreme Court again interpreted the Rehabilitation Act in *School Board of Nassau County v. Arline*, 480 U.S. 273 (1987), in which the Court determined that persons suffering from a contagious disease (in this case, tuberculosis) were protected by the Act. The Court listed four factors that employers must take into consideration when determining whether an employee with a potentially contagious disease poses a danger to other employees or to clients, customers, or students:

1) the nature of the risk (how the disease is transmitted);

2) the duration of the risk (how long is the carrier infectious);

3) the severity of the risk (what is the potential harm to third parties); and

4) the probabilities the disease will be transmitted and will cause varying degrees of harm [480 U.S. at 288].

Congress adopted the Court's position in this case in an amendment to the Rehabilitation Act tacked onto the Civil Rights Restoration Act of 1987 (Pub. L. No. 100-259, 102 Stat. 28, § 9).

Section 503 of the Rehabilitation Act requires all institutions holding contracts with the federal government in excess of $10,000 to "take affirmative action to employ and advance in employment qualified handicapped individuals." While the Court in *Davis* emphatically rejected an affirmative action obligation under Section 504, its decision in no way affects the express obligation imposed on federal contractors by Section 503 of the Act (see Section 5.4 of this book).

Between 1998 and 2002, the U.S. Supreme Court issued eight decisions interpreting the employment provisions of the ADA. The first dealt with the issue of whether asymptomatic HIV qualified as a disability under the ADA's definition.

In *Bragdon v. Abbott,* 524 U.S. 624 (1998), the court ruled that HIV, whether or not the individual has symptoms of the disease, substantially limits an individual's ability to procreate (a major life function), and thus constitutes a disability for ADA purposes. Although *Bragdon* was brought under the public accommodation provisions of the ADA rather than the employment provisions, the definition of disability is common to all of the ADA's provisions.

The Court issued three opinions interpreting the ADA in 1999, all of which involved employment, and all of which dealt with the issue of "mitigating measures." Both the legislative history of the ADA and the EEOC's Interpretative Guidance state that the existence of a disability is to be determined without regard to any mitigating measures that the individual may have taken to ameliorate the condition (for example, medication to control the effects of a disease, or devices, such as corrective lenses, to improve poor eyesight) (29 C.F.R. § 1630.2(j) (Interpretive Guidance)). Several appellate courts had refused to follow the EEOC's guidance on this issue, stating that the statutory language made it clear that if the disorder did not "substantially limit" the individual in some major life activity, then the individual did not meet the statute's definition of disability. Other appellate courts followed the EEOC's guidance; the high court agreed to review three cases to resolve the dispute among the circuits.

In *Sutton v. United Air Lines, Inc.,* 527 U.S. 471 (1999), two plaintiffs challenged the airline's refusal to hire them as commercial pilots because they were nearsighted, even though their vision with corrective lenses was within airline guidelines. They sought to establish that myopia was a disorder that met the ADA's definition. In *Albertsons, Inc. v. Kirkingburg,* 527 U.S. 555 (1999), a truck driver with monocular vision challenged his discharge by a grocery store because he could not meet the basic vision standards of the U.S. Department of Transportation (DOT), despite the fact that he had received a waiver from the DOT and had been driving safely for many years. And in *Murphy v. United Parcel Service, Inc.,* 527 U.S. 516 (1999), a mechanic with high blood pressure challenged his termination, stating that, despite the fact that his blood pressure was controllable with medication, he was protected by the ADA because his disability should be assessed in its uncorrected state. In each of these cases, the Court ruled that, because the definition of "disability" states that the disorder must "substantially limit one or more major life activities," a corrected or correctable disorder would not necessarily limit the individual, and thus the definition would not be met. The Court expressly rejected the EEOC guidelines because the Court believed that the guidelines contradicted the clear wording of the statute. And because the Court determined that the ADA's language was clear, it did not consider the law's legislative history, which also stated that disorders were to be considered in their unmitigated state. The Court commented that an individual might be able to meet the definition even if the disorder were considered in its mitigated or corrected state if the disorder still limited the individual in a significant way.

The results in this trio of "mitigation" cases may reduce the number of ADA lawsuits brought by individuals whose disorders are controlled or controllable by medication or other devices. But a fifth Supreme Court opinion may have the opposite effect, for it may allow more individuals to maintain ADA lawsuits. In *Cleveland v. Policy Management Systems Corporation et al.*, 526 U.S. 795 (1999), the court ruled that an individual's representation that he or she is too disabled to work for purposes of receiving Social Security Disability Insurance (SSDI) does not necessarily prevent an individual from pursuing an ADA claim. Federal appellate courts were split on this issue; several had ruled that an individual's assertion that he or she could not work for SSDI purposes precluded an argument that the individual was a "qualified individual with a disability" who could perform the essential functions of a job if a reasonable accommodation were provided. Applying judicial estoppel to these claims, trial judges were dismissing plaintiffs' ADA claims based on their SSDI assertions. Because the ADA requires that the court determine whether an individual is qualified to perform a job with accommodation, an inquiry that is not part of the SSDI evaluation, the Court ruled that ADA plaintiffs should be given an opportunity to explain the discrepancy between their SSDI assertions and their ADA claims.

In 2002, the U.S. Supreme Court issued three more opinions: two involving the employer's duty to accommodate an otherwise qualified employee with a disability, and a third interpreting the Act's "direct threat" provisions. In *Toyota Motor Manufacturing, Kentucky, Inc. v. Williams*, 534 U.S. 184 (2002), the Court examined the Act's definition of disability, which requires that the individual demonstrate a substantial limitation of a "major life activity." The Court ruled unanimously that a "major life activity" must be one that is of "central importance to daily life." Thus, activities that are required for an employee's job, but which are not performed by most people as part of their daily lives, would not fit the definition of a "major life activity," and thus the individual would not meet the Act's definition of disability.

In *U.S. Airways v. Barnett*, 535 U.S. 391 (2002), the Court was asked to rule on whether altering a voluntarily adopted seniority system in order to provide an accommodation for a worker with a disability was an "undue hardship." In *Barnett*, a cargo handler (Barnett) for an airline injured his back and was transferred to a position in the mailroom. When a more senior employee bid on his mailroom position, Barnett was terminated. In a 5-to-4 decision written by Justice Breyer, the Court ruled that seniority systems—whether collectively negotiated or unilaterally imposed by the employer—provided "important employee benefits" in the form of job security and predictability of advancement. The Court refused to impose a rule that violating a seniority system in order to accommodate an otherwise qualified worker would always be an undue hardship. Instead, the Court created a rebuttable presumption in favor of seniority systems, stating that if a plaintiff could show "special circumstances," such as a history of exceptions to the seniority system, the accommodation might trump the seniority rights in that case.

In a concurring opinion, Justice O'Connor would have limited the determination of whether a reassignment that violated a seniority system was an undue hardship to whether the seniority system was legally enforceable. Voluntary systems, such as the system in question in *Barnett*, would not trump the accommodation requirement, in her opinion. Justice Scalia dissented because he viewed seniority systems as totally unrelated to disability, and thus never subject to violation in order to provide a reasonable accommodation for a disabled worker.

The third Supreme Court ruling on the ADA in 2002 involved the EEOC's interpretation of the term "direct threat." Among the reasons why employers may lawfully refuse to hire or to continue to employ a worker with a disability is the finding that the worker's disability poses a "direct threat" to the worker's own safety or to the safety of others (29 C.F.R. § 1630.15(b)(2)). In *Chevron v. Echazabal,* 536 U.S. 73 (2002), a worker with a history of hepatitis C who was denied employment by Chevron because the company feared that exposure to workplace chemicals would further damage the employee's liver challenged the EEOC regulation's use of "danger to self." In a unanimous opinion written by Justice Souter, the Court ruled that the EEOC's definition was a reasonable reading of the statute.

The U.S. Supreme Court has added Title I of the ADA to the list of federal non-discrimination laws that are unenforceable against state entities in federal court. In *Board of Trustees of the University of Alabama v. Garrett,* 531 U.S. 356 (2001), discussed in Sections 13.1.5 and 13.1.6, the Court ruled that Congress had not validly abrogated the states' Eleventh Amendment immunity when it enacted the ADA. Although the Court agreed that the statutory language makes it clear that Congress intended the ADA to apply to states as employers, the Court found that Congress was primarily concerned with employment discrimination against individuals with disabilities by private employers, and that Congress had not identified a history and pattern of disability-based discrimination by states sufficient to provide a constitutional foundation for outlawing such discrimination. Comparing the amount of state-created discrimination that engendered the Voting Rights Act to the legislative history of the ADA, the majority found insufficient justification to provide a rationale for abrogating the states' immunity to suit in federal courts. On remand, the U.S. Court of Appeals for the Eleventh Circuit ruled that the university had waived sovereign immunity by accepting federal funds, so it could be sued in federal court under Section 504 of the Rehabilitation Act (*Garrett v. University of Alabama at Birmingham Board of Trustees,* 344 F.3d 1288 (11th Cir. 1288)). The U.S. Court of Appeals for the Third Circuit reached a similar conclusion in *Koslow v. Pennsylvania,* 302 F.3d 161 (3d Cir. 2002). (For a discussion of ADA litigation by public employees post-*Garrett,* see Roger C. Hartley, "Enforcing Federal Civil Rights Against Public Entities After *Garrett,*" 28 *J. Coll. & Univ. Law* 41 (2001).)

5.2.6. Age Discrimination in Employment Act.

The Age Discrimination in Employment Act (ADEA), 29 U.S.C. § 621 *et seq.,* prohibits age discrimination only with respect to persons who are at least forty years of age. It is contained within the Fair Labor Standards Act (29 U.S.C. §§ 201–19) and is subject to the requirements of that Act (see Section 4.6.2).

Prior to the Act's amendment in 1978, the protection ended at age sixty-five (29 U.S.C. § 631). The 1978 amendments raised the end of protection to age seventy, effective January 1, 1979; and amendments added in 1986 removed the limit completely, except for persons in certain professions. Individuals in public safety positions (police officers, firefighters), "high-level policy makers,"[10] and tenured college faculty could be required to retire at certain ages (seventy for tenured faculty). The amendment provided that the exemption for individuals in public safety positions and tenured faculty would expire on December 31, 1993. Thus, as of January 1, 1994, mandatory retirement for most employees, whether tenured or not, became unlawful.

The Act, which is applicable to both public and private institutions, makes it unlawful for an employer:

(1) to fail or refuse to hire or to discharge any individual with respect to his compensation, terms, conditions, or privileges of employment, because of such individual's age;

(2) to limit, segregate, or classify his employees in any way which would deprive or tend to deprive any individual of employment opportunities or otherwise adversely affect his status as an employee, because of such individual's age; or

(3) to reduce the wage rate of any employee in order to comply with this chapter [29 U.S.C. § 623].[11]

The ADEA is enforced by the Equal Employment Opportunity Commission (EEOC), and implementing regulations appear at 29 C.F.R. Parts 1625–27. The law, regulations, and Enforcement Guidance may be found on the EEOC Web site at http://www.eeoc.gov. Among other matters, the interpretations specify the criteria an employer must meet to establish age as a bona fide job qualification.[12]

As under other statutes, the burden of proof has been an issue in litigation. Generally, the plaintiff must make a *prima facie* showing of age discrimination, at which point the burden shifts to the employer to show that "age is a bona fide occupational qualification reasonably necessary to the normal operation of the particular business" at issue (29 U.S.C. § 623(f)(1)); or that distinctions among employees or applicants were "based on reasonable factors other than

---

[10]"High-level policy makers" are considered to be those few individuals who are senior executives of the organization. For an example of a university that applied this exemption to a wide array of administrators and ran afoul of the ADEA as a result, see Alex P. Kellogg, "Under Federal Pressure, Indiana U. Will Scale Back Mandatory-Retirement Policy," *Chron. Higher Educ.*, January 30, 2002, at http://chronicle.com/daily/2002/01/2002013004n.htm.

[11]Relevant authorities construing the Act are collected in Brian L. Porto, Annot., "Who Is 'Employer' Within Meaning of Age Discrimination in Employment Act of 1967 (29 USCA §§ 621 *et seq.*)," 137 A.L.R. Fed. 551; Andrew M. Campbell, Annot., "What Constitutes 'Willful' Violation Under Age Discrimination in Employment Act, (29 USCA §§ 621 *et seq.*)," 165 A.L.R. Fed. 1; Elaine K. Zipp, Annot., "Proving That Discharge Was Because of Age, for Purposes of Age Discrimination in Employment Act, (29 USCA §§ 621 *et seq.*)," 58 A.L.R. Fed. 94.

[12]Cases regarding age as a BFOQ are collected in Teresa B. Jovanovic, Annot., "Age as Bona Fide Occupational Qualification 'Reasonably Necessary' for Normal Conduct of Business Under § 4(f)(1) of Age Discrimination in Employment Act (29 U.S.C.S. § 623 (f)(1)," 63 A.L.R. Fed. 610.

age" (29 U.S.C. § 623(f)(1)); or that, in the case of discipline or discharge, the action was taken "for good cause" (29 U.S.C. § 623(f)(3)). (See *Laugeson v. Anaconda Co.*, 510 F.2d 307 (6th Cir. 1975); and *Hodgson v. First Federal Savings and Loan*, 455 F.2d 818 (5th Cir. 1972).) Employment decisions that appear neutral on their face but that use criteria that are closely linked with age (such as length of service) and that tend to disadvantage over-forty employees disproportionately may run afoul of the ADEA. Litigation is particularly likely when colleges are merged or when there is a reduction in force of faculty and/or staff (program closures and mergers are discussed in Section 6.8).

Federal courts have routinely dismissed ADEA claims by plaintiffs who were over forty but who were ineligible for certain employment benefits (such as early retirement plans) because they were too young, under the theory that the law was intended to protect older workers from discriminatory employer actions. Although the U.S. Court of Appeals for the Sixth Circuit ruled that workers who were over forty but were too young for health benefit plans provided to older workers could state a claim under the ADEA, the U.S. Supreme Court reversed that ruling. In *Cline v. General Dynamics Land Systems, Inc.*, 296 F.3d 466 (6th Cir. 2002), *reversed*, 540 U.S. 581 (2004), the Court ruled that the ADEA does not prohibit favoring older workers at the expense of younger workers, and that the benefits plan in question was reasonable. The EEOC has issued final rules on retiree health benefits, which may be found at 29 C.F.R. Parts 1625 and 1627.

Federal courts were divided for many years as to whether a plaintiff may proceed under a disparate impact theory (see Section 5.2.1) to challenge alleged age discrimination. In *Smith v. City of Jackson*, 125 S. Ct. 1536 (2005), the U.S. Supreme Court ruled 6 to 3 that plaintiffs challenging alleged discrimination under the ADEA may use the disparate impact theory.

Individuals claiming age discrimination under the ADEA must first file a claim either with the federal EEOC (within 180 days) or with the appropriate state civil rights agency. Sixty days after such a claim is filed, the individual may bring a civil action in federal court (29 U.S.C. § 626(d)). A jury trial is provided for by the statute, and remedies include two years of back pay, liquidated damages (double back pay), front pay, and other make-whole remedies.

In *Oscar Mayer & Co. v. Evans*, 441 U.S. 750 (1979), the U.S. Supreme Court considered whether an employee or a former employee claiming age discrimination must seek relief from appropriate state agencies before bringing an ADEA suit in the federal courts. The Court held that such resort to state agencies is mandatory under Section 14(b) of the ADEA (29 U.S.C. § 633(b)) whenever there is a state agency authorized to grant relief against age discrimination in employment, but that the employee need not commence state proceedings within the time limit specified by state law. If the state agency rejects the employee's complaint as untimely or does not resolve the complaint within sixty days, the employee can then turn to the federal courts.

The ADEA was amended in 1990 by the Older Workers Benefit Protection Act (OWBPA), 104 Stat. 981, in part as a reaction to a decision by the U.S. Supreme Court in *Public Employees Retirement System of Ohio v. Betts*, 492 U.S. 158 (1989).

In that opinion, the Court had ruled that only employee benefit plans that could be shown to be a subterfuge for discrimination violated the Act, even if their terms had the effect of discriminating against older workers. OWBPA prohibited discriminatory employee benefit plans (29 U.S.C. § 623(k)) and codified the "equal benefits or equal cost" principle articulated in *Karlen v. City Colleges of Chicago,* 837 F.2d 314 (7th Cir. 1988). In *Karlen,* the appellate court had found discriminatory two provisions of a retirement plan that gave more generous benefits to faculty who were sixty-five years old and under. The court ruled that employers could provide benefits of equal *cost* to the employer, even if older workers received benefits of less *value* because of the higher cost of benefits to older workers. An employer, however, could not vary benefits (such as sick leave or severance pay) in ways that favored younger employees.

The law requires employers to give older workers benefits that are equal to or better than those given younger workers, unless the employer can demonstrate that benefits (such as term life insurance) carry a higher cost for older workers. The legislation also defines requirements for early retirement plans and regulates the conditions under which severance benefits may be offset by other benefits included in early retirement plans (29 U.S.C. § 623(1)). Furthermore, the law specifies how releases or waivers of an employee's right to sue under the ADEA must be formulated, and requires a twenty-one-day waiting period and a seven-day revocation period for releases (29 U.S.C. § 626(f)(1)). Employees who sign such waivers and then institute litigation, claiming that the waivers were not knowing or voluntary, are not required to return the additional payment they were given as an inducement to sign the waiver (29 C.F.R. § 1625.23). Institutions planning to offer early retirement incentives should confer with experienced counsel in order to comply with the numerous requirements of OWBPA.[13]

Congress included language in the Higher Education Amendments of 1998 (Pub. L. No. 105-244, October 7, 1998) that amends the Age Discrimination in Employment Act only for institutions of higher education. The Amendments allow colleges and universities to offer tenured faculty retirement incentive packages that include supplementary benefits that are reduced or eliminated on the basis of age, as long as there is compliance with certain provisions.

The language in 29 U.S.C. § 623(m) provides a "safe harbor" for colleges that offer tenured faculty members supplemental retirement incentives that either diminish or become unavailable as the faculty member's age increases. The law also provides that tenured faculty who would otherwise be too old for the incentive program at the time it is implemented must be allowed to participate.

The U.S. Supreme Court has ruled that states and their agencies cannot be sued under the ADEA in federal court by private individuals (*Kimel v. Florida Board of Regents,* 528 U.S. 62 (2000)). Relying on its earlier decision in *Seminole Tribe of Florida v. Florida* (discussed in Section 13.1.5), the Court stated that,

---

[13]For analysis of this issue, see James Lockhart, Annot., "'Bona Fide Employee Benefit Plan' Exception to General Prohibition of Age Discrimination in Employment Act (29 U.S.C.S. § 623(f) *et seq.*) as Applied to Early Retirement Incentive Plans," 176 A.L.R. Fed. 115.

although Congress had made its intent to abrogate states' Eleventh Amendment immunity "unmistakeably clear," the ADEA had been enacted under the authority of the commerce clause. And because age is not a suspect classification under the equal protection clause, said the Court, states could discriminate on the basis of age without violating the Fourteenth Amendment if the use of age was rationally related to a legitimate state interest.

5.2.7. Constitutional prohibitions against employment discrimination.

While the Fourteenth Amendment's equal protection clause applies to employment discrimination by public institutions (see Section 1.5.2), the constitutional standards for justifying discrimination are usually more lenient than the various federal statutory standards. (See the discussions of constitutional equal protection standards in Section 8.2.4.) Even where constitutional standards are very strong, as for race discrimination, the courts usually strike down only discrimination found to be intentional; the federal statutes, on the other hand, do not always require a showing of discriminatory intent. In *Washington v. Davis,* 426 U.S. 229 (1976), for instance, the U.S. Supreme Court distinguished between disparate impact cases brought under Title VII (see Section 5.2.1) and those brought under the equal protection clause, noting that the equal protection cases "have not embraced the proposition that a law or other official act, without regard to whether it reflects a racially discriminatory purpose, is unconstitutional solely because it has a racially disproportionate impact." Under Title VII, in contrast, "discriminatory purpose need not be proved." Title VII thus "involves a more probing judicial review of, and less deference to, the seemingly reasonable acts of administrators and executives than is appropriate under the Constitution where special racial impact, without discriminatory purpose, is claimed."

In *Personnel Administrator of Massachusetts v. Feeney,* 442 U.S. 256 (1979), the Court elaborated on the requirement of discriminatory intent, which must be met to establish a violation of the equal protection clause. *Feeney* concerned a female civil servant who challenged the constitutionality of a state law providing that all veterans who qualify for civil service positions must be considered ahead of any qualified nonveteran. The statute's language was gender neutral— its benefits extended to "any person" who had served in official U.S. military units or unofficial auxiliary units during wartime. The veterans' preference law had a disproportionate impact on women, however, because 98 percent of the veterans in Massachusetts were men. Consequently, nonveteran women who received high scores on competitive examinations were repeatedly displaced by lower-scoring male veterans. Feeney claimed that the preference law discriminated against women in violation of the Fourteenth Amendment.

The Court summarized the general approach it would take in ruling on such constitutional challenges of state statutes:

> In assessing an equal protection challenge, a court is called upon only to measure the basic validity of the . . . classification. When some other independent right is not at stake . . . and when there is no "reason to infer antipathy," it is presumed that "even improvident decisions will eventually be rectified by the democratic process" (*Vance v. Bradley,* 440 U.S. 93) [442 U.S. at 272; citations omitted].

The Supreme Court agreed with the district court's finding that the law was enacted not for the purpose of preferring males but, rather, to give a competitive advantage to veterans. Since the classification "nonveterans" includes both men and women, both sexes could be disadvantaged by the laws. The Court concluded that too many men were disadvantaged to permit the inference that the classification was a pretext for discrimination against women. Since neither the statute's language nor the facts concerning its passage demonstrated that the preference was designed to deny women opportunity for employment or advancement in the Massachusetts civil service, the Supreme Court, with two justices dissenting, upheld the statute.

Feeney extends the reasoning in *Washington v. Davis* by stating unequivocally that a statute that has a disproportionate impact on a particular group will withstand an equal protection challenge unless the plaintiff can show that it was enacted in order to affect that group adversely. Thus, a statute neutral on its face will be upheld unless the disparate impact of the law "could not plausibly be explained on neutral grounds," in which case "impact itself would signal that the classification made by the law was in fact not neutral." The effect of this reasoning—controversial especially among civil rights advocates—is to increase the difficulty of proving equal protection violations.

The Supreme Court applied its *Feeney* analysis in considering a challenge to an Alabama law that disenfranchised any individual who had been convicted of a crime "involving moral turpitude." Since these crimes included misdemeanors, two individuals who had been found guilty of passing bad checks, a misdemeanor in Alabama, were disenfranchised. The plaintiffs had demonstrated that the framers of the 1901 Alabama constitution, which contained the challenged provision, intended to discriminate against black voters, despite the fact that the law was applied to blacks and whites equally. Justice Rehnquist, writing for a unanimous court in *Hunter v. Underwood*, 471 U.S. 222 (1985), explained that if the intent of the law was discriminatory, then its effects are still discriminatory, and thus the Fourteenth Amendment was violated.

Besides its less vigorous standards, the equal protection clause also lacks the administrative implementation and enforcement mechanisms that exist for most federal nondiscrimination statutes. Consequently, postsecondary institutions will be subject to a narrower range of remedies for ensuring compliance under the Constitution, compared with the statutes, and also will not have the benefit of administrative agency guidance via regulations and interpretive bulletins.

In employment discrimination, the Constitution assumes its greatest importance in areas not covered by any federal statute. Age discrimination against persons less than forty years old is one such area, since the Age Discrimination in Employment Act does not cover individuals under age forty (although the laws of some states do). A second example is discrimination against aliens, which is no longer covered by Section 1981. Another important uncovered area is discrimination on the basis of sexual preference (such as discrimination against homosexuals), which is discussed in Section 5.3.7.[14] Discrimination on the basis of residence is a fourth important example.[15]

In *Ambach v. Norwick,* 441 U.S. 68 (1979), the U.S. Supreme Court considered the constitutionality of a New York statute that discriminated against aliens by prohibiting their employment as public school teachers. The Court determined that "the Constitution requires only that a citizenship requirement applicable to teaching in the public schools bear a rational relationship to a legitimate state interest." Applying this principle, the Court held that the state's citizenship requirement did not violate equal protection because it was a rational means of furthering the teaching of citizenship in public schools. The Court focused specifically on elementary and secondary education, however, and it is not clear that its reasoning would also permit states to refuse to employ aliens as teachers in postsecondary education, where the interest in citizenship education may be less.

5.2.8. Executive Orders 11246 and 11375. Executive Order 11246, 30 Fed. Reg. 12319, as amended by Executive Order 11375, 32 Fed. Reg. 14303 (adding sex to the list of prohibited discriminations), prohibits discrimination "because of race, color, religion, sex, or national origin," thus paralleling Title VII (Section 5.2.1). Unlike Title VII, the Executive Orders apply only to contractors and subcontractors who received $10,000 or more in federal government contracts and federally assisted construction contracts (41 C.F.R. § 60-1.5).[16] Agreements with each such contractor must include an equal opportunity clause (41 C.F.R. § 60-1.4), and contractors must file compliance reports after receiving the award and annual compliance reports thereafter (41 C.F.R. § 60-1.7(a)) with the federal contracting agency. In addition to their equal opportunity provisions, the Executive Orders and regulations place heavy emphasis on affirmative action by federal contractors, as discussed in Section 5.4.

The regulations implementing these Executive Orders exempt various contracts and contractors (41 C.F.R. § 60-1.5), including church-related educational

---

[14]Such discrimination is sometimes challenged on freedom-of-speech or freedom-of-association grounds rather than equal protection. See *Aumiller v. University of Delaware,* 434 F. Supp. 1273 (D. Del. 1977), where the court ordered reinstatement and $15,000 damages for a lecturer whose freedom of speech was violated when the university refused to renew his contract because of statements he had made on homosexuality.

[15]See, for example, *McCarthy v. Philadelphia Civil Service Commission,* 424 U.S. 645 (1976), upholding a continuing residency requirement for city employees; and *Cook County College Teachers Union v. Taylor,* 432 F. Supp. 270 (N.D. Ill. 1977), upholding a similar requirement for college faculty members. Compare *United Building and Construction Trades Council v. Camden,* 465 U.S. 208 (1984), suggesting that discrimination in employment on the basis of state or local residency may violate the privileges and immunities clause in Article IV, Section 2, of the Constitution. Also compare the student residency cases discussed in Section 8.3.5.

[16]The Executive Orders' affirmative action requirements apply to contractors who employ fifty or more employees and who receive $50,000 or more in federal contracts. These requirements are discussed in this book, Section 5.4.

institutions defined in Title VII (41 C.F.R. § 60-1.5(a)(5)). While the regulations contain a partial exemption for state and local government contractors, "educational institutions and medical facilities" are specifically excluded from this exemption (41 C.F.R. § 60-1.5(a)(4)). The enforcing agency may hold compliance reviews (41 C.F.R. § 60-1.20), receive and investigate complaints from employees and applicants (41 C.F.R. §§ 60-1.21 to 60-1.24), and initiate administrative or judicial enforcement proceedings (41 C.F.R. § 60-1.26(a)(1)). It may seek orders enjoining violations and providing other relief, as well as orders terminating, canceling, or suspending contracts (41 C.F.R. § 60-1.26(b)(2)). The enforcing agency may also seek to debar contractors from further contract awards (41 C.F.R. § 60-1.27(b)).

The requirements of the Executive Orders are enforced by the Office of Federal Contract Compliance Programs (OFCCP), located within the U.S. Department of Labor. The regulations require each federal contractor subject to the Executive Orders to develop a written affirmative action program (AAP) for each of its establishments. In November 2000, a provision was added at 41 C.F.R. § 60-2.1(d)(4) that permits federal contracts to develop AAPs organized by business or functional unit rather than by geographical location. A procedural directive for determining whether a college or university is eligible to submit a functional AAP can be found on the OFFCP Web site at http://www.dol.gov/esa.

The regulations interpreting the Executive Orders and explaining the enforcement process were revised, and a final rule was published at 165 Fed. Reg. No. 219 (November 13, 2000). The final rule can be accessed from the OFFCP Web site.

The primary remedy for violation of the Executive Orders is cutoff of federal funds and/or debarment from future contracts. Individuals alleging employment discrimination by federal contractors have sought to file discrimination claims in court, but have been rebuffed. For example, in *Weise v. Syracuse University*, 522 F.2d 397 (2d Cir. 1975), two women faculty members filed sex discrimination claims against the university under authority of the Executive Orders. Their claims were dismissed; the court found no private right of action in the Executive Orders. Similar outcomes occurred in *Braden v. University of Pittsburgh*, 343 F. Supp. 836 (W.D. Pa. 1972), *vacated on other grounds*, 477 F.2d 1 (3d Cir. 1973), and *Cap v. Lehigh University*, 433 F. Supp. 1275 (E.D. Pa. 1977).[17]

Sec. 5.3. The Protected Classes

5.3.1. Race. As noted above, race discrimination claims may be brought under Title VII (see Section 5.2.1 of this book), Section 1981 (Section 5.2.4), the U.S. Constitution (Section 5.2.7), or federal Executive Orders (Section 5.2.8). Race discrimination claims may also be brought under state nondiscrimination

---

[17]Cases related to private rights of action under the Executive Orders are collected in Phillip E. Hassman, Annot., "Right to Maintain Private Employment Discrimination Action Under Executive Order 11246, as Amended, Prohibiting Employment Discrimination by Government Contractors and Subcontractors," 31 A.L.R. Fed. 108.

laws.[18] In "disparate treatment" race discrimination claims (see Section 5.2.1 above), as in other employment discrimination claims, an employee must demonstrate that an adverse employment action was motivated by the individual's race rather than by some "neutral" reason unrelated to race. Because direct evidence of race discrimination (in the form of written or oral racist statements, for example) is very rare, most plaintiffs must use indirect methods of proving disparate treatment.

An individual alleging race discrimination may demonstrate that "similarly situated" employees of a different race were treated better than the plaintiff. If two employees are similar in skills, experience, job responsibilities, and job performance, but are of different races, race discrimination may be the reason that one employee experiences an adverse employment action while the similarly situated employee does not. However, if the plaintiff cannot identify a "comparator," proving race discrimination will be very difficult. For example, in *Jackson v. Northeastern Illinois University,* 2001 U.S. App. LEXIS 25339 (7th Cir. 2001) (unpublished), an African American building service worker fired for hitting his supervisor was unable to identify a Caucasian employee who had engaged in the same misconduct but was not terminated. In the absence of such a "similarly situated" employee, said the court, the plaintiff could not prevail.

As noted in the discussion of Title VII in Section 5.2.1, colleges typically defend against discrimination claims by asserting that there was a "legitimate nondiscriminatory reason" to support the adverse employment action. Documented poor performance of the plaintiff will typically allow the college to prevail unless there is direct evidence of race discrimination or a similarly situated coworker of a different race who is treated more favorably. (For cases involving successful defenses against alleged race discrimination by the use of documented poor performance, see *Fortson v. Embry-Riddle Aeronautical University,* 1998 U.S. Dist. LEXIS 20701 (N.D. Miss. 1998); and *Chambers v. McClenney,* 1999 U.S. App. LEXIS 329 (10th Cir. 1999) (unpublished).) Lack of funds may also provide a legitimate nondiscriminatory reason for a termination if there is no direct evidence of race discrimination (see *Lewis v. Chattahoochie Valley Community College,* 136 F. Supp. 2d 1232 (M.D. Ala. 2001)).

The plaintiff must identify a specific adverse employment action that has been taken, allegedly on the basis of the plaintiff's race. Typically, termination, discipline, demotion, or reducing an individual's pay are adverse employment actions. However, an involuntary lateral transfer that does not reduce an individual's salary may not be viewed as an adverse employment action (see, for example, *Adams and Moore v. Triton College,* 2002 U.S. App. LEXIS 8622 (7th Cir. 2002) (unpublished)).

---

[18]Cases involving race discrimination are collected in J. F. Ghent, Annot., "Racial Discrimination in Hiring, Retention, or Assignment of Teachers—Federal Cases," 3 A.L.R. Fed. 325. See also Donald T. Kramer, Annot., "What Constitutes Reverse or Majority Race or National Origin Discrimination Violative of Federal Constitution or Statutes—Public Employment Cases," 168 A.L.R. Fed. 1; and Donald T. Kramer, Annot., "What Constitutes Reverse or Majority Race or National Origin Discrimination Violative of Federal Constitution or Statutes—Private Employment Cases," 150 A.L.R. Fed. 1.

Harassment on the basis of race is a form of race discrimination, and federal courts have applied Supreme Court precedent from sexual harassment cases (see Section 5.3.3.3) to claims of racial harassment. Racial harassment claims may be brought under Title VII or Section 1981; the latter statute's lack of a cap on damages makes it likely that plaintiffs may file under both laws, as well as state nondiscrimination laws. A dramatic example of a plaintiff's success occurred in *Swinton v. Potomac Corp.,* 270 F.3d 794 (9th Cir. 2001), *cert. denied,* 535 U.S. 1018 (2002), in which the only African American employee of a small company quit after five months because of coworkers' daily racial jokes, which were observed and condoned by Swinton's supervisor. The court upheld a $1 million punitive damage award; his back pay award was less than $6,000. Conflicts between a supervisor and subordinate of different races, however, will typically not support a claim of racial harassment unless actual racist language is used. For example, in *Trujillo v. University of Colorado Health Sciences Center,* 157 F.3d 1211 (10th Cir. 1998), a Hispanic employee's claim of racial harassment by his African American supervisor was rejected by the court, which characterized the difficulties he faced as a "personality conflict" and upheld summary judgment for the college.

Tribal colleges are immune from race discrimination lawsuits, according to a federal appellate court. In *Hagen v. Sisseton-Wahpeton Community College,* 205 F.3d 1040 (8th Cir. 2000), the court ruled that because Indian tribes enjoy sovereign immunity, tribal colleges may not be sued in federal courts. The court reversed a jury award to two former employees of the college who alleged that their one-year employment contracts had not been renewed because of their race.

5.3.2. National origin and alienage. Claims of national origin discrimination may be brought under Title VII, the U.S. Constitution, or federal Executive Orders and, sometimes, under Section 1981. Title VII prohibits discrimination "because of [an] individual's . . . national origin" (42 U.S.C. § 2000e-2(a))—that is, discrimination based on the employee's nationality. In *Briseno v. Central Technical Community College Area,* 739 F.2d 344 (8th Cir. 1984), for example, the court held that the defendant had intentionally discriminated against the plaintiff, a Mexican American, because of his national origin. National origin claims are frequently combined with claims of race and/or religious discrimination (Sections 5.3.1 & 5.3.6).

The U.S. Supreme Court has ruled that the statutory term "national origin" does not cover discrimination on the basis of alienage—that is, discrimination against employees who are not citizens of the United States (*Espinoza v. Farah Manufacturing Co.,* 414 U.S. 86 (1973)). But the Court cautioned in *Espinoza* that a citizenship requirement may sometimes be part of a scheme of, or a pretext for, national origin discrimination and that "Title VII prohibits discrimination on the basis of citizenship [alienage] whenever it has the purpose or effect of discriminating on the basis of national origin." The Court also made clear that aliens, as individuals, are covered by Title VII if they have been discriminated against on the basis of race, color, religion, or sex, as well as national origin. To implement the statute and case law, the EEOC has issued guidelines barring discrimination on the basis of national origin (29 C.F.R. Part 1606).

Claims of alleged national origin discrimination brought under Title VII are evaluated under the *McDonnell Douglas* test described in Section 5.2.1. An illustrative case is *Castro v. Board of Trustees of the University of Illinois,* 1999 U.S. Dist. LEXIS 17303 (N.D. Ill. 1999), in which an individual of Puerto Rican descent applied for and was denied twenty-seven jobs at the University of Illinois at Chicago. The court ruled that Castro had established a *prima facie* case of national origin discrimination for three of the twenty-seven jobs because the individuals who were hired, who were not of Puerto Rican descent, had similar or lesser credentials than Castro. The court granted summary judgment to the university on Castro's discrimination claims for twenty-four of the twenty-seven positions, but denied summary judgment with respect to the three for which Castro had established a *prima facie* case.

Although *Espinoza* prevents plaintiffs from attacking citizenship (alienage) discrimination under Title VII, such plaintiffs may be more successful making constitutional claims. In *Chacko v. Texas A&M University,* 960 F. Supp. 1180 (S.D. Tex. 1997), *affirmed without opinion,* 149 F.3d 1175 (5th Cir. 1998), a Canadian citizen was terminated shortly after she was hired, allegedly because coworkers complained that the university was hiring "foreigners." With respect to her Title VII claim of national origin discrimination, the federal court awarded the university summary judgment, characterizing it as "citizenship" discrimination rather than national origin discrimination. But the court allowed the plaintiff's constitutional claims against individuals (but not against the institution) to proceed under Sections 1981 and 1983 (see Section 5.2.4 of this book). Her claims against the institution were dismissed on Eleventh Amendment immunity grounds.

Employers' requirements that employees speak only English while at work have stimulated claims of national origin discrimination. Although the EEOC guidelines state that English-only rules are a form of prohibited discrimination under Title VII (29 C.F.R. § 1606.7), most federal courts have upheld these rules if the employer has articulated a legitimate business reason (for example, customer service, safety) for the rules. (See, for example, *Garcia v. Gloor,* 618 F.2d 264 (5th Cir. 1980); and *Garcia v. Spun Steak,* 998 F.2d 1480 (9th Cir. 1993).) A federal trial court ruled that Cornell University could impose a requirement that employees speak English on the job because the interpersonal conflicts between the plaintiff and her coworkers made the requirement a business necessity (*Roman v. Cornell University,* 53 F. Supp. 2d 223 (N.D.N.Y. 1999)). However, if the court finds that the rule was applied in a manner indicating national origin discrimination rather than a legitimate business concern, the court may rule for an employee terminated for violating the rule. For example, the court in *Saucedo v. Brothers Wells Service,* 464 F. Supp. 919 (S.D. Tex. 1979), ruled that an employee terminated for speaking two words of Spanish on the job had been a victim of national origin discrimination.

The Arizona Supreme Court invalidated a state constitutional provision requiring state employees to speak only English on the job as a violation of the

First Amendment of the U.S. Constitution (*Ruiz v. Hull,* 957 P.2d 984 (Ariz. 1998), *cert. denied,* 525 U.S. 1093 (1999)). (The uncertain legality of English-only rules and a proposal to fully implement the EEOC guidelines are discussed in Mark Colon, Note, "Line Drawing, Code Switching, and Spanish as Second-Hand Smoke: English-Only Workplace Rules and Bilingual Employees," 20 *Yale L. & Pol'y Rev.* 227 (2002).)

State laws requiring colleges and universities to certify that non-native U.S. residents who are teaching assistants are proficient in English may be challenged as a violation of Title VII or Section 1981, in that no such standards are applied to individuals born in the United States. Testing the language proficiency of all teaching assistants should prevent discrimination claims. A statement in the institution's college catalog that instruction will be conducted in English would make English proficiency a bona fide occupational qualification, and as long as that requirement is applied to all instructors, it should not run afoul of the nondiscrimination laws.[19] Similarly, a requirement that unaccented English is required for a certain position would also be vulnerable to a national origin claim if the individual could be understood.[20] (For a discussion of bias against individuals with accents, see M. Matsuda, "Voices of America: Accent, Antidiscrimination Law, and a Jurisprudence for the Last Reconstruction," 100 *Yale L.J.* 1329 (1991).)

The terrorist attacks of September 11, 2001, have stimulated increased attention to potential national origin discrimination. The EEOC, the U.S. Department of Justice, and the U.S. Department of Labor have issued a "Joint Statement Against Employment Discrimination in the Aftermath of the September 11 Terrorist Attacks," as well as a set of questions and answers concerning the employee rights and employer responsibilities regarding Muslims, Arabs, South Asians, and Sikhs. These statements may be found at http://www.eeoc.gov.

In addition to Title VII and Section 1981, the Immigration Reform and Control Act of 1986 (Pub. L. No. 99-603, 100 Stat. 3359, codified in scattered sections of 8 U.S.C.) may pose potential liability for college and universities with regard to race and national origin. The Act prohibits employers from hiring workers who cannot document that (1) they are in the United States legally and (2) they are legally entitled to work. Employers must ask applicants for proof of both elements, and civil penalties may be assessed against the employer for each undocumented worker hired. The law also forbids discrimination against aliens who are lawfully entitled to work and describes the complaint procedures available through the U.S. Department of Justice (8 U.S.C. § 1324b). The law is discussed in more detail in Section 4.6.5.

---

[19]Cases related to requiring English proficiency are collected in Tim A. Thomas, Annot., "Requirement That Employees Speak English in Workplace as Discrimination in Employment Under Title VII of Civil Rights Act of 1964 (42 U.S.C.S. §§ 2000e *et seq.*)," 90 A.L.R. Fed. 806.

[20]Cases related to employment denials based on an individual's accent are collected in Timothy M. Hall, Annot., "When Does Adverse Employment Decision Based on Person's Foreign Accent Constitute National Origin Discrimination in Violation of Title VII of Civil Rights Act of 1964?" 104 A.L.R. Fed. 816.

With the advent of the Immigration Reform and Control Act, discrimination claims by individuals denied employment because the employer believes they may not be in the country lawfully have risen. (For discussion of this problem and a comparison of IRCA's antidiscrimination provisions with those of Title VII, see L. S. Johnson, "The Antidiscrimination Provisions of the Immigration Reform and Control Act," 62 *Tulane L. Rev.* 1059 (1988). See also Comment, "IRCA's Antidiscrimination Provisions: Protections Against Hiring Discrimination in Private Employment," 25 *San Diego L. Rev.* 405 (1988).)

5.3.3. Sex

5.3.3.1. Overview. Claims of sex discrimination may be brought under Title VII of the Civil Rights Act of 1964 (see Section 5.2.1 of this book), the Equal Pay Act (Section 5.2.2), the Constitution, the Executive Orders, or state civil rights laws.[21] In addition to claims that an individual was subject to an adverse employment action because of his or her sex, claims of sexual harassment may be brought under Title VII because sexual harassment is a form of discrimination on the basis of sex. Discrimination on the basis of pregnancy is also a form of sex discrimination, and is specifically prohibited by Title VII. In addition, differential treatment by sex in retirement plans has been found to violate Title VII. And there has been considerable litigation by coaches of women's sports alleging discrimination in salary and coaching assignments. Although Title VII does not outlaw discrimination on the basis of sexual orientation, several states have enacted laws prohibiting such discrimination (see Section 5.3.7).

Most sex discrimination claims against colleges have been brought by women faculty members. Illustrative cases are discussed in Section 6.4. However, several cases brought by nonfaculty employees illustrate significant principles in sex discrimination litigation.

Treating a similarly situated employee of one sex more favorably than a corresponding employee of the opposite sex may violate Title VII or state nondiscrimination laws. For example, in *Lawley v. Dept. of Higher Education,* 36 P.3d 1239 (Colo. 2001), the state supreme court ruled that the university had terminated a female director of parking in order to retain two male subordinates. The court ordered the university to reinstate the plaintiff to her former position. On the other hand, another federal appellate court reversed a trial court judgment in favor of a research assistant. In *Woodruff v. Ohman,* 2002 U.S. App. LEXIS 2087 (6th Cir. 2002) (unpublished), the plaintiff had claimed that her supervisor had mistreated her on the basis of her sex. The trial court had awarded punitive damages and injunctive relief in the form of an apology from the former

---

[21]Cases and authorities are collected at Thomas Fusco, Annot., "What Constitutes Sex Discrimination in Termination of Employee so as to Violate Title VII of Civil Rights Act of 1964 (42 U.S.C. §§ 2000e-2)," 115 A.L.R. Fed. 1; Wesley Kobylak, Annot., "Disparate Impact Test for Sex Discrimination in Employment Under Title VII of Civil Rights Act of 1964 (42 U.S.C. §§ 2000e-2)," 68 A.L.R. Fed. 19; Thomas Fusco, Annot., "What Constitutes Constructive Discharge of Employee Due to Sex Discrimination so as to Violate Title VII of Civil Rights Act of 1964 (42 U.S.C. §§ 2000e-2)," 116 A.L.R. Fed. 1.

supervisor. The appellate court noted that the trial court had not made specific findings concerning whether the plaintiff had been treated less favorably than similarly situated male research assistants, and thus liability had not been established.

Stereotyping an individual because of his or her gender may provide evidence of sex discrimination, as in *Price Waterhouse v. Hopkins,* the U.S. Supreme Court case discussed in Section 5.2.1. But in *Crone v. United Parcel Service,* 301 F.3d 942 (8th Cir. 2002), a federal appellate court sided with the company that had refused to promote a female employee who was not "confrontational enough" for promotion to a job supervising truck drivers; the court affirmed the dismissal of the plaintiff's sex discrimination claims. The court ruled that being "confrontational" was a bona fide occupational qualification for the position; it was the plaintiff's personality, not her gender, that disqualified her from the position.

5.3.3.2. Pregnancy and health benefits discrimination. The Pregnancy Discrimination Act of 1978 makes it a violation of Title VII for an employer to discriminate on the basis of pregnancy, childbirth, or related illnesses in employment opportunities, health or disability insurance programs, or sick leave plans.[22] Regulations issued by the Equal Employment Opportunity Commission pursuant to this law may be found at 29 C.F.R. § 1604.10 and Appendix, "Questions and Answers on the Pregnancy Discrimination Act." Pregnancy-related conditions must be treated the same as any other disabilities, and health insurance for pregnancy-related conditions must extend not only to female employees but also to wives of male employees (*Newport News Shipbuilding and Dry Dock Co. v. EEOC,* 462 U.S. 669 (1983)). Health benefit plans must also provide the same level of prescription coverage to women as to men. A federal trial court ruled that Title VII prohibits employers from excluding contraceptives used by women from a prescription drug plan if more comprehensive coverage is provided to men (*Erickson v. Bartell Drug Co.,* 141 F. Supp. 2d 1266 (W.D. Wash. 2001)).

Some states have enacted laws that attempt to "level the playing field" for women, who have the biological responsibility for bearing children, in order to ease their return to work. For example, a California law requires employers to give pregnant employees unpaid maternity leave and to reinstate them to the same or an equivalent position upon their return to work. That law was challenged in *California Federal Savings & Loan v. Guerra,* 479 U.S. 272 (1987), in which the employer claimed that Title VII did not permit more favorable treatment of an individual because of pregnancy, but merely mandated that pregnant women not be discriminated against. The Supreme Court ruled that the

---

[22]Cases and authorities are collected at Paul A. Fischer, Annot., "Pregnancy Leave or Maternity Leave Policy, or Lack Thereof, as Unlawful Employment Practice Violative of Title VII of the Civil Rights Act of 1964 (42 U.S.C. §§ 2000e *et seq.*)," 27 A.L.R. Fed. 537; Sheila A. Skojec, Annot., "Job Discrimination Against Unwed Mothers or Unwed Pregnant Women as Proscribed Under Pregnancy Discrimination Act (42 U.S.C.A. § 2000e(k))," 91 A.L.R. Fed. 178; J. A. Bryant, Jr., Annot., "Termination of Employment Because of Pregnancy as Affecting Right to Unemployment Compensation," 51 A.L.R.3d 254; Shauna Cully Wagner, Annot., "Discrimination Against Pregnant Employee as Violation of State Fair Employment Laws," 99 A.L.R.5th 1.

Pregnancy Discrimination Act provided a "floor" of protection for pregnant employees, but not a ceiling, and that Title VII did not preempt state laws that recognized the special circumstances of pregnant employees.[23]

However, in a challenge to Missouri's unemployment compensation law, which denies benefits to women who leave work because of the birth of a child, the Supreme Court ruled that Title VII does not prevent a state from categorizing a resignation on account of the birth of a child as a voluntary resignation, resulting in ineligibility for unemployment benefits (*Wimberly v. Labor & Industrial Relations Commission,* 479 U.S. 511 (1987)). (For discussion of state unemployment compensation laws, see Section 4.6.7.)

Another issue related to pregnancy, or potential pregnancy, is the lawfulness of employer policies that exclude pregnant or potentially pregnant employees from work sites where exposure to substances could cause birth defects. Lab assistants, postdoctoral fellows, faculty, or students may work with fetotoxins. And some nonacademic employers have excluded from such jobs all women who were capable of becoming pregnant.[24] They have done so in order to avoid liability for litigation by children seeking a remedy for birth defects allegedly traceable to their mothers' workplace exposure to fetotoxins.

These "fetal vulnerability" policies were challenged in *United Auto Workers v. Johnson Controls,* 499 U.S. 187 (1991). The company, which manufactures automobile batteries, argued that exposure to the lead used in the manufacturing process could cause birth defects, and that permitting women to work with the lead was unsafe. The company excluded all women capable of becoming pregnant—unless they could prove that they were unable to conceive a child—from the high-paying jobs involving lead exposure; but the company permitted men, even those who wished to father children, to work in these jobs.

A unanimous Supreme Court ruled that fetal vulnerability policies that excluded only women constituted intentional disparate treatment discrimination, and rejected the company's argument that, on the grounds of safety, inability to become pregnant was a bona fide occupational qualification for a position involving exposure to fetotoxins. The Court stated that the BFOQ is a narrow concept and is used only in "special situations" (499 U.S. at 201). The opinion clarifies the concept of BFOQ in the following manner:

> Our case law . . . makes it clear that the safety exception is limited to instances in which sex or pregnancy actually interferes with the employee's ability to perform the job. This approach is consistent with the language of the BFOQ provision itself, for it suggests that permissible distinctions based on sex must relate to ability to perform the duties of the job [499 U.S. at 204].

---

[23]The federal Family and Medical Leave Act of 1993 (Pub. L. No. 103-3) requires employers with fifty or more employees to grant up to twelve weeks of unpaid leave each year to an employee for the care of a sick, newborn, or recently adopted child, or a seriously ill family member, or for the employee's own serious health condition. This law is discussed in Section 4.6.4.

[24]Cases regarding fetal vulnerability policies are collected in Wesley Kobylak, Annot., "Exclusion of Women from Employment Involving Risk of Fetal Injury as Violative of Title VII of Civil Rights Act of 1964 (42 U.S.C.S. §§ 2000e *et seq.*)," 66 A.L.R. Fed. 968.

Given the language of *Johnson Controls,* it is unlikely that a college or university could successfully specify gender as a BFOQ for jobs involving exposure to fetotoxins, or for virtually any other job either.

5.3.3.3. Sexual harassment. Much attention has been given to the issue of sexual harassment in recent years. The number of sexual harassment claims by students, staff, and faculty is growing, as individuals become aware that such conduct is prohibited by law, whether the target is an employee or a student. Sexual harassment of staff and faculty is addressed in this Section; harassment of students is discussed in Sections 8.1.5 and 9.3.4.

Sexual harassment is a violation of Title VII of the Civil Rights Act of 1964 (discussed in Section 5.2.1) because it is workplace conduct experienced by an individual on the basis of his or her sex. It is also a violation of Title IX of the Education Amendments of 1972 (discussed in Section 5.2.3), although it may be difficult for an employee to state a sexual harassment claim under Title IX rather than under Title VII. Sexual harassment victims may be male or female, and harassers may be of either gender as well. Furthermore, same-sex sexual harassment is also a violation of Title VII and Title IX.

The EEOC's guidelines prohibiting sexual harassment expansively define sexual harassment and establish standards under which an employer can be liable for harassment occasioned by its own acts as well as the acts of its agents and supervisory employees. The guidelines define sexual harassment as:

> (a) . . . Unwelcome sexual advances, requests for sexual favors, and other verbal or physical conduct of a sexual nature constitute sexual harassment when (1) submission to such conduct is made either explicitly or implicitly a term or condition of an individual's employment, (2) submission to or rejection of such conduct by an individual is used as the basis for employment decisions affecting such individual, or (3) such conduct has the purpose or effect of unreasonably interfering with an individual's work performance or creating an intimidating, hostile, or offensive working environment . . . [29 C.F.R. § 1604.11].

Whether or not the alleged harasser is an employee, if the target of the harassment is an employee, the employer may be liable for the unlawful behavior. Because the EEOC guidelines focus on both speech and conduct, the question of the interplay between sexual harassment and academic freedom arises, particularly in the classroom context. This interplay is discussed in Sections 7.2.2 and 9.3.4.

Two forms of sexual harassment have been considered by the courts, and each has a different consequence with regard to employer liability and potential remedies. Harassment that involves the exchange of sexual favors for employment benefits, or the threat of negative action if sexual favors are not granted, is known as *"quid pro quo* harassment." The U.S. Supreme Court addressed this form of sexual harassment for the first time in *Meritor Savings Bank v. Vinson,* 477 U.S. 57 (1986), ruling that, if *quid pro quo* harassment were proven, employer liability under Title VII would ensue even if the victim had not reported the harassment. Using principles of agency law, the Court asserted that harassment involving an actual or threatened change in terms and conditions of employment would result in a form of strict liability for the employer.[25]

The Court did not elaborate on the showing that the plaintiff must make to demonstrate that the employer "knew or should have known," but it did mention two tests to assist courts in determining whether a plaintiff's decision not to report alleged sexual harassment was reasonable:

1) the employer should have a clearly-worded policy prohibiting sexual harassment in the workplace that is communicated to all employees;

2) the employer should have a system for reporting sexual harassment that provides an alternate channel so that the victim, if harassed by a supervisor, can avoid the traditional complaint procedure of discussing the problem with that supervisor [477 U.S. at 71–73].

The other form of harassment, the creation of a hostile or offensive environment, may involve virtually anyone that the target employee encounters because of the employment relationship. Supervisors, coworkers, clients, customers, and vendors have been accused of sexual harassment. (For an example of potential university liability for harassment of an employee by a homeless individual who frequented the law school library, see *Martin v. Howard University,* 1999 U.S. Dist. LEXIS 19516 (D.D.C. 1999).) If the allegations are proven, and if the employer cannot demonstrate that it responded appropriately when it learned of the harassment, the employer may be found to have violated Title VII or state law.

The U.S. Supreme Court has decided several cases involving hostile environment sexual harassment, beginning with *Harris v. Forklift Systems,* 510 U.S. 17 (1993). In *Harris,* the plaintiff had demonstrated that her supervisor had repeatedly engaged in verbal sexual harassment. The major issue in the case was not whether the behavior was harassment (the defense had conceded that it was), but whether the plaintiff must demonstrate serious psychological harm in order to convince a court that the harassment was sufficiently severe and pervasive to constitute a "hostile or offensive environment." In a unanimous opinion, the U.S. Supreme Court rejected the argument that serious harm must be demonstrated. The Court determined that the harassing conduct itself is unlawful, and whether it has a psychological, or even a financial, impact on the plaintiff is irrelevant.

Although the standard for *quid pro quo* harassment is clear in that the accused harasser must have the power to affect the target's terms and conditions of employment, the standard for establishing hostile or offensive environment is less clear, and is particularly fact sensitive. Name calling, sexual jokes, sexual touching, sexually explicit cartoons, and other sexual behavior by

---

[25]Cases and authorities are collected at Ethel R. Alston, Annot., "Sexual Advances by Employee's Superior as Sex Discrimination Within Title VII of Civil Rights Act of 1964 (42 U.S.C.A. § 2000e *et seq.*)," 46 A.L.R. Fed. 224; Linda A. Sharp, Annot., "Workers' Compensation as Precluding Employee's Suit Against Employer for Sexual Harassment in the Workplace," 51 A.L.R.5th 163.

supervisors or coworkers have been found to constitute sexual harassment (see, for example, *Alston v. North Carolina A&T State University,* 304 F. Supp. 2d 774 (M.D.N.C. 2004)). Furthermore, vandalism or harassing conduct of a nonsexual nature directed at a target because of his or her gender has also been found to violate Title VII, sometimes as sexual harassment and sometimes as sex discrimination (see, for example, *Hall v. Gus Construction Co.,* 842 F.2d 1010 (8th Cir. 1988)).

Words alone may be sufficient to constitute sexual harassment. In a case involving a female faculty member, *Jew v. University of Iowa,* 749 F. Supp. 946 (S.D. Iowa 1990), false rumors that the plaintiff had engaged in a sexual relationship with her department chair in order to obtain favorable treatment were found to constitute actionable sexual harassment, and the institution was ordered to promote the plaintiff and to give her back pay and attorney's fees. But a single remark, even if "crude," will probably not be sufficient to establish a claim of sexual harassment, according to the U.S. Supreme Court (*Clark County School District v. Breeden,* 532 U.S. 268 (2001)).

The U.S. Court of Appeals for the Ninth Circuit, in *Jordan v. Clark,* 847 F.2d 1368 (9th Cir. 1988), described the showing that the plaintiff must make in order to demonstrate a hostile environment. The plaintiff must prove:

1) that he or she was subjected to demands for sexual favors, or other verbal or physical conduct of a sexual nature;

2) that this conduct was unwelcome;

3) that the conduct was sufficiently severe or pervasive to alter the conditions of the victim's employment and create an abusive working environment [847 F.2d at 1373].

But the definition of an "abusive working environment" has not been uniformly interpreted. Establishing whether the conduct is sufficiently severe or pervasive, and whether the plaintiff's claim that the behavior was offensive meets the standard for liability, has been a problem for the courts.

The U.S. Court of Appeals for the Ninth Circuit created a special standard by which to determine whether the complained-of conduct constituted a hostile environment. In *Ellison v. Brady,* 924 F.2d 872 (9th Cir. 1991), the court created the "reasonable woman" standard, in which the court assumes the perspective of a reasonable person of the plaintiff's gender, since "conduct that many men consider unobjectionable may offend many women" (924 F.2d at 878).

EEOC guidelines use the "reasonable person" standard (*Policy Guidance on Sexual Harassment,* available at http://www.eeoc.gov), but several state courts have decided that the "reasonable woman" standard is appropriate (see, for example, *Lehman v. Toys 'R' Us,* 626 A.2d 445 (N.J. 1993)). While the U.S. Supreme Court did not discuss the question of standards in *Harris,* Justice O'Connor appeared to use the "reasonable person" rather than the "reasonable woman" standard. (For a brief discussion of interpretation problems related to the "reasonable woman" standard, see E. H. Marcus, "Sexual Harassment Claims: Who Is a Reasonable Woman?" 44 *Labor L.J.* 646 (1993).)

As sexual harassment jurisprudence developed in the federal courts, there was disagreement as to whether an employer could escape liability for harassment if it were unaware of the harassment or if no negative employment action had been taken. In 1998, the U.S. Supreme Court issued opinions in two cases that crafted guidelines for employer responses to harassment complaints, and also created an affirmative defense for employers who had acted in good faith. In *Faragher v. City of Boca Raton,* 524 U.S. 775 (1998), and in *Burlington Industries v. Ellerth,* 524 U.S. 742 (1998), the Court addressed the issue of an employer's liability for a supervisor's verbal sexual harassment when no negative employment action had been taken against the target of the harassment. In both cases, supervisors had made numerous offensive remarks based on the targets' gender and had threatened to deny them job benefits. Neither of the plaintiffs had filed an internal complaint with the employer; both had resigned and filed a sexual harassment claim under Title VII. The employers in both cases had argued that, because no negative employment actions were taken against the plaintiffs, and because the plaintiffs had not notified the employer of the alleged misconduct, the employers should not be liable under Title VII.

The Supreme Court rejected this argument, ruling that an employer can be vicariously liable for actionable discrimination caused by a supervisor. The employer, however, may assert an affirmative defense that examines the reasonableness of the employer's and the target's conduct. If the employer had not circulated a policy against sexual harassment, had not trained its employees concerning harassment, and had not communicated to employees how to file a harassment complaint, then the target's failure to use an internal complaint process might be completely reasonable, according to the Court. But if the employer had been proactive in preventing and responding to sexual harassment, then a plaintiff's failure to use an internal complaint process might not be reasonable.

The Court explained that the employer can establish an affirmative defense to a sexual harassment claim if it can demonstrate:

(a) that the employer exercised reasonable care to prevent and correct promptly any sexually harassing behavior and

(b) that the plaintiff employee unreasonably failed to take advantage of any preventive or corrective opportunities provided by the employer or to avoid harm otherwise [524 U.S. at 807].

The Court's rulings in *Ellerth* and *Faragher* blur the previous distinction between liability for *quid pro quo* harassment and liability for hostile environment harassment. But the cases also recognize an important defense for those "good employers" who have developed clear policies, advised employees of the complaint process, and conducted training about avoiding harassment. The approach taken by the Court has subsequently been applied to litigation concerning harassment on the basis of race (*Wright-Simmons v. The City of Oklahoma City,* 155 F.3d 1264 (10th Cir. 1998)).

An example of a college's successful use of the affirmative defense is *Gawley v. Indiana University,* 276 F.3d 301 (7th Cir. 2001). A female police officer alleged that she had endured verbal and physical sexual harassment by a supervisor for a period of seven months. At that point, the plaintiff filed a formal complaint under the university's harassment complaint process. The university investigated promptly, issued a report finding that harassment had occurred, and the harassment stopped as soon as the report was issued. The court ruled that the plaintiff's delay in reporting the harassment was unreasonable, and that, given the university's response when it learned of the harassment, filing a complaint promptly would have ended the harassment at a much earlier point in time. The appellate court affirmed the trial court's award of summary judgment to the university.

In order to take advantage of the *Faragher/Ellerth* affirmative defense, the employer must demonstrate that its policy effectively communicates to supervisors how they should handle harassment complaints and provides an effective mechanism for bypassing the supervisor should that individual be the alleged harasser. In *Wilson v. Tulsa Junior College,* 164 F.3d 534 (10th Cir. 1998), the Court ruled that the college had not established an affirmative defense because its complaint procedure was inadequate and it did not take timely and effective remedial action. The court criticized the college's harassment policy because it did not discuss the responsibilities of a supervisor who learned of alleged harassment through informal means. Furthermore, said the court, the unavailability of individuals to receive harassment complaints during the evening or on weekends, when the college was open and students and employees were present, was additional evidence of an ineffective harassment policy.

The U.S. Supreme Court addressed the question of whether a plaintiff who quit as a result of exposure to a sexually hostile work environment could establish a "constructive discharge" theory, and if so, whether the employer then lost the benefit of the *Faragher/Ellerth* affirmative defense. In *Pennsylvania State Police v. Nancy Drew Suders,* 542 U.S. 129 (2004), the Court, in an 8-to-1 ruling, determined that the plaintiff could establish constructive discharge by showing that the abusive work environment "became so intolerable that her resignation qualified as a fitting response." The Court stated that the employer would not be able to use the affirmative defense if a supervisor's "official act" (such as demotion or discipline) precipitated the constructive discharge, but that absent such a "tangible employment action," the affirmative defense would be available to employers if the employee resigned and then established a constructive discharge.

Consensual relationships that turn sour may result in sexual harassment claims and liability for the college. For example, in *Green v. Administrators of the Tulane Education Fund,* 284 F.3d 642 (5th Cir. 2002), a former office manager for a department chair alleged that the chair harassed her because their sexual relationship had ended and because the chair's new love interest insisted that the plaintiff be fired. Although the university provided evidence that it had attempted to transfer the plaintiff to another position and had attempted to ensure that the chair did not retaliate against her, a jury reached a verdict for the plaintiff and awarded her $300,000 in compensatory damages, in addition to back pay and front pay awards, and more than $300,000 in attorney's fees. The trial court had not allowed the jury to address the plaintiff's claim for punitive damages.

Although the appellate court upheld the jury award, it agreed with the university's argument that the standard for awarding punitive damages had not been met. Analyzing the facts under the standard established by the U.S. Supreme Court in *Kolstad v. American Dental Association,* 527 U.S. 526 (1999), the appellate court held that because the university had attempted in good faith to respond to the plaintiff's complaints about the chair's behavior, its behavior did not meet the "malice" or "reckless indifference" showing required by *Kolstad.*

Although most federal courts have ruled that liability for sexual harassment under Title VII is corporate rather than individual, some state laws provide for individual liability of supervisors for harassment (see, for example, *Matthews v. Superior Court,* 40 Cal. Rptr. 2d 350 (Cal. App. 2 Dist. 1995)). (For a discussion of individual liability under Title VII, see Scott J. Connolly, Note, "Individual Liability of Supervisors for Sexual Harassment Under Title VII: Courts' Reliance on the Rules of Statutory Construction," 42 *B.C. L. Rev.* 421 (2001).)

Although Title VII does not forbid harassment on the basis of sexual orientation, it does permit claims of same-sex sexual harassment if the target can demonstrate that the harassment was based on the sex of the target. The U.S. Supreme Court addressed this issue for the first time in *Oncale v. Sundowner Offshore Services,* 523 U.S. 75 (1997). The Court ruled that a claim of male-to-male harassment was cognizable under Title VII if the plaintiff could demonstrate that the offensive conduct occurred "because of" his gender. In a unanimous opinion, the Court, through Justice Scalia, stated that "[Title VII] does not reach genuine but innocuous differences in the ways men and women routinely interact with members of the same sex and of the opposite sex. [The law] forbids only behavior so objectively offensive as to alter the 'conditions' of the victim's employment" (523 U.S. at 81).

Same-sex sexual harassment claims have increased substantially since the Court's ruling in *Oncale* (see Reed Abelson, "Men, Increasingly, Are the Ones Claiming Sex Harassment by Men," *New York Times,* June 10, 2001, p. 1). Courts have allowed plaintiffs to state claims of same-sex sexual harassment if the alleged harasser is homosexual. For example, in *Mota v. University of Texas Houston Health Science Center,* 261 F.3d 512 (5th Cir. 2001), the appellate court affirmed an award of back pay, front pay, and compensatory damages and attorney's fees to a male professor harassed and retaliated against by a male superior whose sexual advances he had rejected. The trial judge had given the plaintiff a substantial award of front pay because, after the jury returned a verdict of retaliation against the plaintiff by the university, the university president sent an e-mail message to eight thousand university employees stating that the plaintiff had not been terminated but had failed to return from a leave of absence. Because of those comments, the trial judge added five years of front pay to the plaintiff's original front pay award, reasoning that such negative remarks would make it difficult for the plaintiff to find another position.

In other cases, plaintiffs who can demonstrate that they are harassed because of hatred or hostility toward them because of their gender may be allowed to state same-sex harassment claims. For example, a male employee who was verbally harassed by male coworkers because he was viewed as effeminate prevailed in his claim of sexual harassment in *Nichols v. Azteca Restaurant Enterprises,* 256 F.3d 864 (9th Cir. 2001). The court sided with the plaintiff's argument that the Supreme Court's theory developed in *Price Waterhouse v. Hopkins* (discussed in Section 5.2.1) should apply in this case, stating that the verbal abuse that the plaintiff endured was "closely linked to gender."

(For a discussion and analysis of same-sex sexual harassment claims in both academic and nonacademic settings, see Mary Ann Connell, "Evolving Law in Same-Sex Harassment and Sexual Orientation Discrimination," 23rd Annual National Conference on Law and Higher Education, Stetson University College of Law, 2002. See also Nailah A. Jaffree, Note, "Halfway Out of the Closet: *Oncale*'s Limitations in Protecting Homosexual Victims of Sex Discrimination," 54 *Fla. L. Rev.* 799 (2002).)

Subsection (f) of the EEOC guidelines emphasizes the advisability of implementing clear internal guidelines and sensitive grievance procedures for resolving sexual harassment complaints. The EEOC guidelines' emphasis on prevention suggests that the use of such internal processes may alleviate the postsecondary institution's liability under subsections (d) and (e) and diminish the likelihood of occurrences occasioning liability under subsections (c) and (g). Title IX requires grievance procedures.

In light of the social and legal developments, postsecondary institutions should give serious attention and sensitive treatment to sexual harassment issues. Sexual harassment on campus may be not only an employment issue but, for affected faculty and students, an academic freedom issue as well. Advance preventive planning is the key to successful management of these issues, as the EEOC guidelines indicate. Institutions should involve the academic community in developing specific written policies and information on what the community will consider to be sexual harassment.

5.3.3.4. Application to athletics coaches. Although there have been several federal appellate rulings on the application of Title IX of the Education Amendments of 1972 to participants in collegiate athletics activities (see Section 10.4.3), less attention has been paid to alleged discrimination against women coaches, or against coaches of either gender who coach women's teams. A survey of gender equity data collected under the Equity in Athletics Disclosure Act of 1994 (Pub. L. 103-382, 108 Stat. 3969, codified at 20 U.S.C. § 1092 (2002)) revealed that the average salary of women coaches was roughly two-thirds of the average salary of male coaches, and that pay disparities exist in all divisions (see Jennifer Jacobson, "Female Coaches Lag in Pay and Opportunities to Oversee Men's Teams," *Chron. Higher Educ.,* June 8, 2001, A38). Discrimination claims may be brought by coaches under Title VII of the Civil Rights Act of 1964 (see Section 5.2.1 of this book), the Equal Pay Act (Section 5.2.2), and Title IX (5.2.3).

Although the requirements of an Equal Pay Act claim differ somewhat from those of a Title VII or Title IX claim (in that a four-part test is required under the Equal Pay Act in order for a plaintiff to make a *prima facie* case of salary discrimination based on sex), in practice the courts have used the Equal Pay Act standards to evaluate these claims under all three statutes. In a few cases, male coaches have been the plaintiffs.

In 1997, the Equal Employment Opportunity Commission issued an "Enforcement Guidance on Sex Discrimination in the Compensation of Sports Coaches in Educational Institutions" (available at http://www.eeoc.gov/docs/coaches/). Cases decided prior to the issuance of the Guidance tended to reject the salary discrimination claims of women coaches. For example, plaintiffs who argued that the gender of the team members, rather than the gender of the coach, was responsible for the lower salary were not able to satisfy the *prima facie* case requirements of Title VII or the Equal Pay Act because team members are not employees (*Deli v. University of Minnesota*, 863 F. Supp. 958 (D. Min. 1994)). And plaintiffs who could not link institutional decisions regarding the status and value of women's sports to gender discrimination also did not prevail (*Bartges v. University of North Carolina at Charlotte*, 908 F. Supp. 1312 (W.D.N.C. 1995), *affirmed without opinion*, 94 F.3d 641 (4th Cir. 1996)).

The EEOC Guidance discusses the standards for evaluating claims of coaches alleging salary discrimination under the Equal Pay Act and Title VII. For Equal Pay Act claims, the Guidance states that plaintiffs must identify one or more comparators; "a plaintiff must show that a specific employee of the opposite sex earned higher wages for a substantially equal job," rather than using a hypothetical employee or the composite features of jobs of several employees. The Guidance notes that plaintiffs must demonstrate that they have equal skills, exert equal effort, have equal responsibility, and share the same working conditions as the individual with whom they wish to be compared. Therefore, if a plaintiff cannot prove that her skills or experience are equivalent to those of the comparator, she will not be able to make out a *prima facie* case.

With respect to employer defenses to Equal Pay Act claims, the most likely defense is that the salary differential was based on "any factor other than sex" (29 U.S.C. § 206(d)(1)). The Guidance states that, under the defense, the following justifications for differential pay are acceptable, if proven: additional responsibilities (for example, the size of the team, the number of assistants, the demands of event and media management, scheduling, and budgetary responsibilities); superior experience, ability, or skills as long as they are closely related to the coaching position; and "marketplace value of the particular individual's job-related characteristics." The Guidance rejects the following justifications for differential pay: that the salary is the "going rate" for a particular sport, the gender of the team members, and prior salary without examination of whether it was linked to prior discrimination. With respect to the argument that sports producing more revenue justify higher salaries for their coaches, the Guidance reserves judgment. Although recognizing that differentials in revenue might be a legitimate "factor other than sex," the Guidance states that "the Commission is also aware of the studies showing that women's athletic programs historically and currently receive considerably less resources than men's programs," and notes that the Commission will examine whether an institution has discriminatorily provided reduced support to a female coach to produce revenue for her team. (For a case in which the court rejected the Equal Pay Act claim of a male assistant coach on the grounds that his female counterpart had more numerous and significant responsibilities, see *Horn v. University of Minnesota,* 362 F.3d 1042 (8th Cir. 2004).)

The analysis for Title VII claims under the Guidance is similar to that for Equal Pay Act claims, insofar as the plaintiff asserts that the coaching positions are substantially equal. The Guidance notes that the sports need not be the same or similar; it is the functional duties of the coaches that are compared, not the nature of the sports. While an employment practice that violated Title VII would not necessarily violate the Equal Pay Act, a violation of the Equal Pay Act would also violate Title VII.

An illustrative case litigated under the Equal Pay Act, Title VII, and Title IX is *Weaver v. Ohio State University,* 71 F. Supp. 2d 789 (S.D. Ohio 1998), *affirmed* 194 F.3d 1315 (6th Cir. 1999). Weaver, the women's field hockey coach, brought claims of discriminatory termination, salary discrimination, and retaliation against the university. For her salary discrimination claims, she compared herself to the male ice hockey coach. The court rejected her claims, noting that there were sufficient differences between the responsibilities, skill, and effort required of the coaches. The ice hockey season was longer, and more games were played. Furthermore, there were more players to coach on the ice hockey team. The court also ruled that the male coach had additional responsibilities with respect to public relations and marketing, and that prevailing market rates for ice hockey coaches were higher than for field hockey coaches. The appellate court affirmed these rulings and declined the trial court's invitation to rule on whether Weaver's Title IX claim was preempted by Title VII.

Jan Lowery, the former women's basketball coach and women's athletics coordinator at Tarleton State University, asserted claims of salary discrimination under Title VII, the federal equal protection clause, and Title IX, as well as Title IX and First Amendment retaliation claims (for her opposition to allegedly discriminatory practices related to women's athletics at the university). Although Lowery resigned from Tarleton, she claimed constructive discharge, demotion, and failure to promote her to the position of overall athletic director.

In *Lowery v. Texas A&M University System,* 117 F.3d 242 (5th Cir. 1997), the court dismissed Lowery's Title IX salary discrimination claim, stating that there was no private right of action under Title IX for employment discrimination, but allowed her retaliation claims and other salary discrimination claims to proceed. The university then sought summary judgment on the remaining claims. The trial court denied the university's motion for summary judgment on these claims (11 F. Supp. 2d 895 (S.D. Tex. 1998)).

With respect to the Equal Pay Act claim, the university had conceded that Lowery and the male coach-athletic coordinator with whom she compared herself had comparable duties and responsibilities. The court ruled that Lowery had raised issues of fact that could not be resolved at the summary judgment stage about how the two individuals were paid, whether salary increases they received were for additional responsibilities or their current responsibilities, and other apparent inconsistencies in the way the two employees were treated. With respect to Lowery's Title VII claim, the court ruled that a demotion is an adverse employment action, and thus Lowery had established a *prima facie* case of retaliation under Title VII. With respect to the retaliation claims, the court held that Lowery could make out a *prima facie* case of retaliation under Title IX because the evidence showed that the university had reprimanded her for discussing her concerns about alleged Title IX violations with individuals outside the athletic department, and demoted her from the position of women's athletics coordinator shortly thereafter. Regarding Lowery's First Amendment retaliation claim, the court ruled that her stated concerns about potential Title IX violations were matters of public concern and thus were protected by the First Amendment's free speech clause (see Section 7.1.1).

But another women's basketball coach was less successful in her discrimination claims against the University of Southern California (USC). Marianne Stanley was hired by USC in 1989 and given a four-year contract at a salary substantially below that of the coach of the men's basketball team, George Raveling. The women's basketball team was very successful during Stanley's term as coach, and when it came time to negotiate a renewal of her contract, Stanley asked that she be paid a salary equivalent to Raveling's. The athletic director refused to pay her at that level, but offered her a new contract at a higher salary. Stanley held out for an equivalent salary, but the parties could not agree, and when Stanley's initial contract expired, it was not renewed. Stanley filed claims under the Equal Pay Act and Title IX, as well as state claims, including several under the California Fair Employment and Housing Act and the California constitution.

In 1995, the trial court awarded summary judgment to the university, and Stanley appealed. Four years later, the appellate court affirmed in *Stanley v. University of Southern California*, 178 F.3d 1069 (9th Cir. 1999). The university argued that the jobs held by Stanley and Raveling were different (primarily because the men's coach bears greater revenue-generating responsibilities and is under greater pressure from the media and fans to have a winning season, and because Raveling did generate more revenue than did Stanley), while Stanley argued that differences between the two jobs were primarily attributable to the university's prior gender-based decisions about resource allocation to men's and women's sports. The court assumed without ruling that the jobs were substantially equal for Equal Pay Act purposes, and then found that Raveling had qualifications superior to Stanley's. The court cited the following differences in their qualifications at the time each was hired: Raveling had thirty-one years of coaching experience (compared with Stanley's seventeen); Raveling had coached the men's Olympic basketball team, and had twice been named national coach of the year (Stanley had done neither); Raveling had nine years of marketing and promotional experience (Stanley had none); and Raveling had written several books on basketball, which Stanley had not. The court noted that the EEOC Guidance specifically permitted superior experience to justify pay differentials, and ruled that the university had successfully demonstrated that the salary differential was a result of a factor "other than sex." The court rejected Stanley's other discrimination claims on the same basis. Furthermore, the court ruled that the university had not retaliated against Stanley by refusing to enter a new contract, and that she was not constructively discharged simply because the parties could not agree on the terms of a new contract.

Claims of discrimination by athletics coaches are very fact sensitive, as the following case illustrates. The case also illustrates the effect of allowing a case to go to a jury, which most of the cases involving alleged discrimination against women coaches do not. A federal jury awarded the women's basketball coach and women's sports administrator at Brooklyn College, City University of New York (CUNY), $85,000 in compensatory damages plus back pay of $274,920 in her Equal Pay Act and Title VII claims. In *Perdue v. City University of New York,* 13 F. Supp. 2d 326 (E.D.N.Y. 1998), Molly Perdue established that she performed jobs that were substantially equal to the men's basketball coach and the men's sports administrator. She was paid less than half of the average salaries of the two male comparators, but asserted that she had the same responsibilities as each of these individuals. Furthermore, she had a smaller office, a smaller budget, fewer assistant coaches, and no locker room for her team; she also cleaned the gym and washed the players' uniforms, which the male coach did not. The court ruled that there was enough evidence for the jury to find that Perdue's job responsibilities, skill, and effort were comparable to each of the male comparators, despite the fact that each of the male comparators had more experience in these roles than did Perdue.

The laws prohibiting sex discrimination in employment protect male coaches as well as female coaches. The EEOC ruled in 1998, for instance, that the University of Pennsylvania had discriminated against the assistant coach of its men's rowing team by not permitting him to apply for the vacant position of head coach of the women's crew team (*Medcalf and University of Pennsylvania,* Charge No. 170980294, decided December 9, 1998). A federal trial court rejected the University's motion for summary judgment (*Medcalf v. Trustees of the University of Pennsylvania,* 2001 U.S. Dist. LEXIS 10155 (E.D. Pa. June 19, 2001)), and a federal jury found for the plaintiff, awarding him compensatory and punitive damages and lost wages. The university appealed, and a federal appellate court affirmed the jury's verdict (71 Fed. Appx. 924 (3d Cir. 2003)) (unpublished).

This area of the law is still developing, and it remains to be seen whether courts will follow the EEOC Enforcement Guidance's framework for analyzing claims of salary discrimination or will defer to the "business judgment" of the institution with respect to how it allocates resources for athletic programs. Coaches who believe that their pay is lower than that of similar coaches because of their gender (rather than the gender of the team members) may find some success under Title IX (at least for retaliation claims), the Equal Pay Act (if they can find a suitable comparator), or under Title VII. In fact, the EEOC's statement that the sports do not have to be the same suggests that coaches of women's teams, such as basketball or softball, might wish to compare themselves with coaches of different sports with similar-sized teams, responsibilities, and experience. The issue of whether revenue production is a neutral factor "other than sex" will have to be resolved on a case-by-case basis.

These cases suggest a strategy for avoiding litigation on, or defending against, claims of sex discrimination in coaches' salaries. First, the institution may find it useful to conduct an audit of coaches' salaries and to adjust the salaries of those coaches whose functions are similar to those of higher-paid coaches with similar experience, seniority, and coaching success. Written position descriptions for coaches should specify the duties, skills, and responsibilities necessary for satisfactory performance. New coaches should be recruited from a diverse pool that includes other-gender applicants and minorities. Drafting contracts that specify the duties of the coach, whether there will be bonuses and under what circumstances, and what other responsibilities are expected of each coach may also help an institution avoid liability. And the institution will need to clarify the basis for any negative employment action to defend against retaliation claims by coaches, which in some cases have been more successful than their underlying discrimination claims.

(For an analysis of how discrimination law is applied to pay disparities among coaches, see John Gaal, Michael S. Glazier, & Thomas S. Evans, "Gender-Based Pay Disparities in Intercollegiate Coaching: The Legal Issues," 28 *J. Coll. & Univ. Law* 519 (2002). For practical advice on this subject, see Janet Judge, David O'Brien, & Timothy O'Brien, "Pay Equity: A Legal and Practical Approach to the Compensation of College Coaches," 6 *Seton Hall J. Sports L.* 549 (1996).)

5.3.4. Disability.
Colleges have not escaped the flood of disability discrimination cases that resulted from the enactment of the Americans With Disabilities Act (ADA) of 1990. Like their counterparts in nonacademic organizations, college employees have usually been unsuccessful in establishing claims under this law.[26] Depending on the protections offered by state law, plaintiffs' counsel may prefer to bring these claims under state nondiscrimination law because of the narrowness of the ADA's definition of disability and the complications of establishing under the ADA that the plaintiff is "qualified."[27]

Employer defenses to ADA claims typically focus on the effect of the disorder on the employee's work performance, attendance, behavior, or some other relevant concern. In some cases, however, the employer's defense is that the disability was irrelevant to the negative employment action.

---

[26]A study of ADA employment cases litigated between the law's enactment and June 2000 concluded that plaintiffs succeeded on the merits only 4 percent of the time (Barbara A. Lee, "A Decade of the Americans With Disabilities Act: Judicial Outcomes and Unresolved Problems," 42 *Industrial Relations* 11 (2003)).

[27]For example, both California's and New Jersey's nondiscrimination laws have a more expansive definition of "disability" than the ADA, which greatly improves plaintiffs' ability to get their cases to a jury (California Fair Employment and Housing Act, Cal. Gov't. Code § 12940; New Jersey Law Against Discrimination, N.J.S.A. 10:5–5(q)).

Is the Employee Disabled for ADA Purposes?   As discussed in Section 5.2.5, an employee seeking a remedy for alleged disability discrimination must first demonstrate that he or she meets the Act's definition of disability. This has been a substantial hurdle for many plaintiffs. The law requires the plaintiff to demonstrate that the disorder "substantially limits" one or more "major life functions." The U.S. Supreme Court has determined that the effect of the disorder on the plaintiff must be evaluated taking into consideration any "mitigating measures," such as medication or physical aids (such as a prosthetic device). And if the disorder limits the plaintiff's ability to perform a particular job, but not a class of jobs, the courts have ruled that the individual is not "disabled" under the Act's definition (see discussion in Section 5.2.5).

The opinion in *Palotai v. University of Maryland at College Park,* 2002 U.S. App. LEXIS 12757 (4th Cir. 2002) (unpublished), provides an example of the application of ADA principles to a discrimination claim. The plaintiff, Thomas Palotai, was hired as a greenhouse technician. Because the greenhouse plants were used for research and teaching, Palotai was required to adhere to a specified schedule of care for the plants. On several occasions, Palotai was unable to complete his tasks within the time framework required by his supervisor. Seven months after he was hired, he informed his supervisor that he had a learning disability that made it impossible for him to meet the time frames. Several meetings were held with his supervisor to discuss his performance problems; he was disciplined after each meeting. In addition, Palotai disregarded safety rules, such as failing to wear protective glasses while spraying the plants with pesticides and wearing shorts in an area where the safety rules required that long pants be worn.

After several written warnings, the university suspended Palotai, who then requested sick leave because of an eye injury related to his pesticide spraying responsibilities. After returning from sick leave, his performance problems persisted, and he was terminated. Palotai filed a Fourteenth Amendment due process claim and an ADA claim. He claimed three "disabilities" under the ADA: a learning disorder, obsessive-compulsive disorder, and the eye injury sustained while working for the university. Noting that Palotai held a B.S. in biology and had completed thirty hours of graduate work, the court rejected the claim that Palotai's learning disability interfered with a major life function (learning). The court refused to characterize Palotai's obsessive-compulsive disorder as an ADA-protected disability because there was no evidence that it limited his ability to work. And because the visual impairment was quite moderate, the court concluded as well that Palotai was not disabled in this respect. The court concluded by ruling that, even assuming that Palotai's disorders met the ADA's definition of disability, the university's insistence that he perform his tasks within a specific time frame was reasonable, and an accommodation that disregarded those time frames would have been an undue hardship.

Similarly, a nurse with multiple sclerosis was found not to be disabled for ADA purposes in *Sorensen v. University of Utah Hospital,* 194 F.3d 1084 (10th Cir. 1999). Although her physician had cleared her to return to work after a five-day hospitalization related to her disorder, the physician in charge of the burn unit, where the plaintiff had worked, refused to allow her to return to work because he was concerned that she would encounter further problems related to her disorder. She was, however, allowed to work in the emergency room and in the surgical intensive care unit. Because of the hospital's continuing refusal to allow the plaintiff to return to the burn unit, she resigned and filed a claim of constructive discharge and disability discrimination. The court ruled that she was not disabled (she could perform all functions without accommodation), that she was not regarded as disabled, nor was she discriminated against because of a record of a disability, basing its ruling on the fact that the position in the burn unit was the only position from which the plaintiff had been excluded. Citing *Sutton* (Section 5.2.5), the court ruled that the inability to perform one job does not meet the ADA's definition of substantial limitation, and that the plaintiff was not excluded from a wide class of jobs. Similar reasoning led to a similar outcome for the parties in *Broussard v. University of California*, 192 F.3d 1252 (9th Cir. 1999), in which an animal care technician with carpal tunnel syndrome was found not be disabled under the ADA because her particular job was the only job she could not perform as a result of her disability.

Employees with mental disorders are also potentially protected by the ADA if the employee can meet the Act's definition of disability. But a mental disorder that is linked to a particular job or supervisor will probably not qualify as a disability for ADA purposes. For example, in *Schneiker v. Fortis Insurance Co.*, 200 F.3d 1055 (7th Cir. 2000), an employee diagnosed with major depression was unsuccessful in her discrimination claim because her work performance had been acceptable until she began working for a new supervisor. The court characterized her difficulties as a personality conflict rather than a disability.

IS THE EMPLOYEE QUALIFIED? If the plaintiff can convince the court that he or she has a disability that meets the ADA's narrow definition, the plaintiff's next task is to demonstrate that he or she is qualified for the position held or desired. The Act requires that the individual demonstrate that he or she can perform the "essential functions" of the position in question.

Hatchett v. Philander Smith College, 251 F.3d 670 (8th Cir. 2001) provides an analysis of whether an employee is qualified. Hatchett was the business manager for the college. When the position was upgraded to a dean of administrative services, Hatchett applied for, but was not offered, the position, and continued working as the business manager.

Approximately eight months after applying for the deanship, Hatchett was injured by falling debris while on college business. Although being treated by a neurologist and a psychologist for her injuries, Hatchett continued working, but could not perform all of the functions of the business manager. She then took medical leave, and the college eliminated the business manager position while she was on leave. A male employee whom Hatchett had trained, and who had performed the business manager responsibilities while she was on leave, was promoted to the deanship. The college president offered Hatchett three part-time positions, which she declined.

The court reviewed the recommendations of Hatchett's physician that she avoid conflict, only deal with individuals one on one, and not confer with students or attend meetings. The written job description for the deanship, in addition to Hatchett's own testimony, included these duties. The court determined that these duties, which Hatchett's physician stated that she could not perform, were essential functions of the position, and denied Hatchett's ADA claim.

Menes v. C.U.N.Y., 92 F. Supp. 2d 294 (S.D.N.Y. 2000) demonstrates how a college's adherence to the ADA's "interactive" process of attempting to accommodate a disabled employee provides protection against an ADA claim. The plaintiff had been diagnosed with depression, and his doctor had recommended a three-day work week as an accommodation. The college complied, but the plaintiff's performance was unsatisfactory even with the shorter work week. The court ruled that, although the plaintiff had established that he was disabled for ADA purposes, he could not perform the essential functions of his position, and thus was not qualified.

Another case demonstrates the interplay between the Family and Medical Leave Act (FMLA) (Section 4.6.4) and the ADA. A finding that an employer complied with the FMLA does not necessary lead to a finding of compliance with the ADA. A federal trial court rejected a college's motion for summary judgment in an ADA claim that involved the matter of the employee's qualifications. In *Rogers v. New York University,* 250 F. Supp. 2d 310 (S.D.N.Y. 2002), an administrative assistant had taken FMLA leave in order to cope with her mental disorders. Although the employee's FMLA claim was dismissed because the employee had received the twelve weeks of leave to which she was entitled and did not provide the proper written documentation of her fitness to return to work, the court ruled that her ADA claim must be tried to a jury. Her doctor had stated that an additional month's leave would have been sufficient to accommodate a return to work; the court ruled that the plaintiff was entitled to demonstrate that alternate positions had been available for which she was qualified. On the other hand, most courts concur that an indefinite leave of absence without a target date of return is not a reasonable accommodation under both state and federal law (see, for example, *Scott v. University of Toledo,* 739 N.E.2d 351 (Ct. App. Ohio 2000)).

An accommodation that requires other employees to perform essential functions of an individual's job is not required under the ADA. In *Piziali v. Grand View College,* 2000 U.S. App. LEXIS 1823 (8th Cir. 2000) (unpublished), a federal appellate court upheld a trial court's grant of summary judgment to the college on the grounds that the plaintiff was not qualified. The accommodations requested by the plaintiff would have required other faculty to perform some of her duties, which the court viewed as essential functions of her position.

IS THE REQUESTED ACCOMMODATION REASONABLE? The law states that an accommodation is not reasonable if it poses an undue hardship for the employer. Thus, indefinite leaves of absence, the creation of new light-duty positions, or the removal of a job's essential functions are typically viewed as undue hardships. In addition, the employer need not "bump" a nondisabled individual out of a position in order to accommodate an employee who is disabled (*Lucas v. W. Grainger, Inc.,* 257 F.3d 1249 (11th Cir. 2001)).

On the other hand, the law and its Interpretive Guidance require an employer to attempt to restructure the position, reassign the individual to a vacant position, or accommodate the employee in other ways that do not pose an undue hardship. Because so many plaintiffs cannot establish that they are disabled under the ADA, there are relatively few cases that examine the reasonableness of a requested accommodation, particularly those involving colleges or universities. One such case is *Norville v. Staten Island University Hospital*, 196 F.3d 89 (2d Cir. 1999). Norville, a nurse, sustained a spinal injury that prevented her from engaging in heavy lifting, stretching, or bending. The hospital offered her a transfer to other positions, but the positions were not equivalent in benefits. They involved the loss of seniority and the freezing of her pension benefits, and made her more vulnerable to layoffs. The plaintiff had claimed that vacant positions comparable to her former position were available, but were not offered to her. Although a jury had returned a verdict in favor of the hospital, the appellate court reversed, stating that the jury instructions were inadequate, and remanded for a new trial.

But in *Wright v. N.C. State University*, 169 F. Supp. 2d 485 (E.D.N.C. 2000), the trial court awarded summary judgment to the college, rejecting the plaintiff's claims that the employer had refused to provide a reasonable accommodation. The plaintiff, who was deaf and worked on the night shift in a building considered to be dangerous, requested either a different shift or a transfer to the library. The university had offered her an alternate accommodation: transfer to a new, safer building. The court ruled that the university's accommodation proposal was reasonable, noting that the employer is not required to provide the accommodation that the employee prefers if another accommodation is also reasonable.

THE "NONDISCRIMINATION" DEFENSE.   Although most ADA cases involve an employer's acknowledgment that the employee's disorder was related in some way to the negative employment action (but not unlawful), in some instances the employer's defense is that discrimination was unrelated to the employment decision. For example, in *King v. Hawkeye Community College*, 2000 U.S. Dist. LEXIS 1695 (N.D. Iowa 2000), a professor who was morbidly obese was not returned to his teaching job after taking medical leave for gastric bypass surgery. Although the court ruled that the college's failure to allow him to return was a breach of contract, it granted the college summary judgment on the employee's ADA claim. The court found that the individual who decided not to allow the employee to return to work was also morbidly obese, and thus found that disability discrimination was not a factor in the decision.

Although the federal circuits and state supreme courts differ on the issue, several courts have ruled that obesity is a disability under federal or state law. For example, in *Cook v. State of Rhode Island*, 10 F.3d 17 (1st Cir. 1993), a case brought under the Rehabilitation Act, the court ruled that a state agency's refusal to rehire a qualified former employee because of its concern that her weight (320 pounds) would interfere with her ability to evacuate patients in the event of an emergency, and its speculation that she had a higher probability of injury or illness than employees who were not obese, violated Section 504. The court did not say whether, in its view, obesity is a disability, but rather ruled that her obesity was perceived as a disability, which brought her under the law's protections. (The ADA has the same protections for nondisabled individuals who are perceived as disabled.) The EEOC has argued that obesity should be characterized as a disability protected under both Section 504 and the ADA.

Although the ADA is similar to the Rehabilitation Act in most respects (see Section 5.2.5), several differences suggest that employees will turn to the ADA first for relief when they believe discrimination has occurred. The ADA includes reassignment to a vacant position as a form of accommodation that the employer must consider (42 U.S.C. § 12111(9)(B)), a requirement absent from the language of the Rehabilitation Act, although it is included in its regulations. The ADA protects individuals with alcoholism, and it is not yet clear whether, or how often, a college or university would be required to offer an employee with alcoholism an opportunity for inpatient rehabilitation. The ADA has strict confidentiality requirements for medical information related to employees' disabilities (42 U.S.C. § 12112(d)(3)(B)); the interplay between these requirements and the right of a labor union to receive information related to an employment grievance is as yet unresolved.

5.3.5. Age.

With the elimination of the age-seventy cap from the ADEA, mandatory retirement for age is no longer legal, with the exception of certain law enforcement and public safety employees. This "uncapping" has required colleges that wish to terminate an older worker either to provide documentation of poor performance or financial reasons for the termination or to provide incentives for the employees to retire.

Although most lawsuits brought by college employees claiming age discrimination are unsuccessful for the plaintiffs, colleges can improve their chances of successfully defending such cases by careful documentation of performance problems, training of supervisors to refrain from ageist comments and actions, and consistent treatment of employees irrespective of age. A case illustrative of some of the problems that a college may encounter in defending an age discrimination claim is *Manning v. New York University,* 2000 U.S. Dist. LEXIS 19606 (S.D.N.Y. 2000). The court rejected the university's motion for summary judgment in an age discrimination case brought by the former director of security for the university. The director had been terminated at age sixty-seven, according to the university, for "poor communication skills," a contentious relationship with his supervisors, and inability to represent the university appropriately to outside agencies. The court, reviewing the plaintiff's claims, determined that the plaintiff had made a *prima facie* case of age discrimination based upon the following evidence: the supervisor had made negative comments about the plaintiff's age and noted the need for "new blood"; the supervisor had stated that the plaintiff would soon be "on the golf course" and need not be involved in contract negotiations; the supervisor insisted that the plaintiff bring his thirty-year-old assistant to meetings but did not require the same of other employees at the plaintiff's level; the supervisor's decision to promote all but the three oldest directors to assistant vice presidents; and the assignment of an important security responsibility to the plaintiff's young assistant rather than to the plaintiff. Furthermore, there were no written documents criticizing the plaintiff's performance, and he had received regular merit raises. The judge ruled that these allegations raised material factual issues that must be resolved at trial.

Similarly, remarks by trustees and a college president that could be interpreted as ageist were sufficient to persuade a court to deny summary judgment to a college accused of age discrimination in the termination of the former academic vice president. In *Lepanto v. Illinois Community College District #525,* 2000 U.S. Dist. LEXIS 46 (N.D. Ill. 2000), a new president told the academic vice president, who had served in that role for eleven years, that he wanted a "fresh start" and a "new mix" of leadership, and terminated the plaintiff at age sixty-one. Although the plaintiff was unable to persuade the court that these remarks, in addition to statements by trustees that there was a new majority on the board, "a younger group of people trying to break up this good old boy network who had their way for thirty years at the college," were direct evidence of age discrimination, the remarks were sufficient to support a *prima facie* case of discrimination. Given the lack of written criticism of the vice president's performance, the court ruled that a jury might conclude that the defendants' claim of poor performance was a pretext for discrimination.

On the other hand, if the college has investigated and documented an employee's performance problems, the college's motion for summary judgment may be successful. For example, in *Debs v. Northeastern Illinois University,* 153 F.3d 390 (7th Cir. 1998), a former chief engineer in the university's heating plant challenged his demotion at age fifty-five, alleging age discrimination. The university, after receiving complaints from several employees who had worked for the plaintiff, had engaged an outside consultant to investigate the employees' complaints, which included allegations of safety violations as well as dishonesty and abusive behavior toward subordinates. The investigator's report substantiated the employees' complaints and recommended that the plaintiff be relieved of supervisory responsibility. A state civil service Merit Board upheld the demotion, and the plaintiff filed a claim with the EEOC. This lawsuit followed.

The sole evidence of age discrimination provided by the plaintiff was an allegation that the plaintiff's supervisor had asked him when he was going to retire and a comment that the plaintiff was too old to work in the heating plant. These allegations were insufficient, according to the court, to rebut the university's legitimate nondiscriminatory reasons for demoting him. The court found the investigator's report credible because of her independence, and because she did not make the demotion decision.

In order to be helpful to the defendant college, the documentation must be contemporaneous and untainted by age-related language. In *EEOC v. Board of Regents of the University of Wisconsin System,* 288 F.3d 296 (7th Cir. 2002), a federal appellate court affirmed a jury verdict against the university for terminating four employees of the University of Wisconsin (UW) Press for age-related reasons. Although the plaintiffs could not have brought this claim against the university in federal court because of *Kimel*'s holding that state entities are protected from ADEA claims by sovereign immunity (see Section 5.2.6), the EEOC can bring claims on their behalf without constitutional limitations.

The UW Press was facing financial difficulties and decided to reduce its staff by four. The director of the Press selected the four oldest employees for layoff. When asked for a rationale for their selection (after determining who would be laid off), he created a written justification for selecting these four individuals, but he apparently did not conduct an overall evaluation of all the Press employees. The responsibilities of the laid-off workers were assumed by younger employees, some of whom were hired at the same time or shortly after the plaintiffs were laid off. According to the court, the justification document included language that could be viewed as age biased, and included several incorrect statements about the purportedly superior skills of younger staff. The court also upheld the jury's finding that the director's conduct was willful, a finding that allows a court to order that double damages be paid to prevailing plaintiffs.

Early retirement incentive programs are regulated by the ADEA, as amended by the Older Workers Benefit Protection Act (OWBPA), discussed in Section 5.2.6. The amendments to the ADEA that took effect January 1, 1988, require, among other things, that institutions continue pension contributions without regard to the individual's age. An opinion by the U.S. Court of Appeals for the Ninth Circuit applied the provisions of the OWBPA to a university's disability and retirement plans. In *Kalvinskas v. California Institute of Technology*, 96 F.3d 1305 (9th Cir. 1996), the plaintiff, a research scientist at CalTech's Jet Propulsion Laboratory, developed Parkinson's disease. He took a medical leave and began receiving long-term disability benefits. CalTech's disability plan provided that disability benefits could be reduced by pension payments or other disability benefits. The college's retirement plan did not allow the payment of pension benefits until an employee actually retired.

When the plaintiff reached age sixty-five, he was eligible to retire but chose not to. He was still receiving disability benefits. CalTech then offset his disability benefits by the amount of pension payments he would have received had he chosen to retire. Since the retirement benefits exceeded the disability benefits, the plaintiff received no payments after the age of sixty-five. He sued CalTech under the ADEA and California's nondiscrimination law, arguing that the offset policy forced him to retire at age sixty-five.

This was a case of first impression for the interpretation of provisions added to the ADEA by the OWBPA. The court was required to interpret two provisions of the ADEA: Section 4(f)(2), which forbids any action that would "require or permit the involuntary retirement of any individual," and Section 4(1)(3)(B), which permits the offset of benefits in order to prevent "double dipping"—circumstances in which a retiree would receive a windfall of both pension benefits and disability benefits. The appellate court ruled that reducing the plaintiff's disability benefits to zero effectively forced him to retire, a violation of Section 4(f)(2). Given the college's actions, said the court, a reasonable person would have believed he had no choice but to retire. With respect to the application of Section 4(1)(3)(B), the court examined the legislative history of the OWBPA. Since the plaintiff was not in a position to receive a windfall, this section did not protect CalTech's actions.

More recently, several retired employees sued the University of Rhode Island, asserting that the voluntary retirement incentive plan (VRIP) that they accepted violated both state and federal age discrimination laws. The plan provided that the university would pay a stipend for retiree health benefits that was based on the actual cost of these benefits. Employees who were under sixty-five when they retired received a $5,000-per-year health benefit stipend, while employees aged sixty-five or older received a stipend of $2,000 per year because they were eligible for Medicare. The court determined that, under the "safe harbor" provisions of the ADEA (29 U.S.C. § 623(f)(2)(B)(ii)) (discussed in Section 5.2.6), the VRIP was voluntary and the difference in stipends was linked directly to the differences in the actual cost of medical benefits.

The complexity of designing retirement incentive programs that do not run afoul of the ADEA may discourage some colleges from offering these programs. (For a discussion of these issues, see Christopher Condeluci, Comment, "Winning the Battle but Losing the War: Purported Age Discrimination May Discourage Employers from Providing Retiree Medical Benefits," 35 *J. Marshall L. Rev.* 709 (2002). See also Marianne C. DelPo, "Too Old to Die Young, Too Young to Die Now: Are Early Retirement Incentives in Higher Education Necessary, Legal, and Ethical?" 30 *Seton Hall L. Rev.* 827 (2000).)

5.3.6. Religion. Discrimination on the basis of religion is one of the prohibited forms of discrimination under Title VII (42 U.S.C. § 2000e-2(a)), subject to an exception for situations where a particular religious characteristic is a bona fide occupational qualification for the job (42 U.S.C. § 2000e-2(e)(1)). A related exception, applicable specifically to educational institutions, permits the employment of persons "of a particular religion" if the institution is "owned, supported, controlled, or managed" by that religion or if the institution's curriculum "is directed toward the propagation of a particular religion" (42 U.S.C. § 2000e-2(e)(2)). The application of nondiscrimination laws to religious colleges is discussed in Section 5.5.

Title VII defines "religion" to include "all aspects of religious observance and practice, as well as belief" (42 U.S.C. § 2000e(j)). The same section of the statute requires that an employer "reasonably accommodate to" an employee's religion unless the employer can demonstrate an inability to do so "without undue hardship."[28] In *Trans World Airlines v. Hardison*, 432 U.S. 63 (1977), the

---

[28]Cases and authorities are collected in Andrew M. Campbell, Annot., "What Constitutes Employer's Reasonable Accommodation of Employee's Religious Preferences Under Title VII of Civil Rights Act of 1964," 134 A.L.R. Fed. 1.

U.S. Supreme Court narrowly construed this provision, holding that it would be an undue hardship to require an employer to bear more than minimal costs in accommodating an employee's religious beliefs. To further explicate the statute and case law, the EEOC has issued revised guidelines on the employer's duty under Title VII to reasonably accommodate the religious practices of employees and applicants (29 C.F.R. Part 1605).

The Supreme Court addressed religious discrimination a second time in *Ansonia Board of Education v. Philbrook*, 479 U.S. 60 (1986). In *Ansonia* a schoolteacher had asked to use the paid "personal days" provided by the collective bargaining agreement for the observance of religious holidays. The collective bargaining agreement provided that religious holidays taken beyond those that were official school holidays would be taken as unpaid leave. Philbrook sued, alleging religious discrimination under Title VII and stating that the school board should have accommodated his religious needs by permitting him to use paid leave. In analyzing the scope of the "reasonable accommodation" requirement, the Court ruled that the employer need not accede to the employee's preferred accommodation, but could offer its own as long as that accommodation also met the "reasonableness" criterion articulated in *Hardison*. The employer did not have to prove that the employee's preferred accommodation would pose an undue hardship; it only had to prove that the accommodation it offered was a reasonable one.

Most litigation involving alleged religious discrimination against college staff involves scheduling disputes, as in the *Hardison* case, discussed above. For example, in *Gay v. SUNY Health Science Center of Brooklyn*, 1998 U.S. Dist. LEXIS 20885 (E.D.N.Y. 1998) (unpublished), a federal trial court rejected the claim of a hospital orderly that the hospital's decision to change his schedule was a form of religious discrimination. The hospital had accommodated the orderly, a Muslim, by allowing him to work a four-day week, with Friday off as a religious accommodation. When the hospital's staffing needs changed, the plaintiff was also required to work Friday mornings, but was allowed to leave in time to attend religious services on Friday.

Other conflicts involving alleged religious discrimination involve conflicts between an employee's religious beliefs and work assignments. For example, in *Shelton v. University of Medicine and Dentistry of New Jersey*, 223 F.3d 220 (3d Cir. 2000), a nurse working in the labor and delivery unit at the university's hospital refused because of her religious beliefs to accept assignments that involved the termination of pregnancies. After she refused to participate in emergency procedures determined necessary to save the life of the mother, the hospital offered her a transfer to the newborn intensive care unit as an accommodation to her religious beliefs. The nurse refused the transfer, however, because she had been told that newborn infants with serious medical problems were not treated but were allowed to die. Because there were no other positions for which the nurse was qualified, she was terminated. Although the trial court determined that the plaintiff had established a *prima facie* case of religious discrimination, the court found that the hospital had attempted to accommodate her. Because there was no corroboration for the claim that infants were untreated and allowed to die, the plaintiff could not rebut the employer's nondiscriminatory reason for her termination. The appellate court affirmed the trial court's summary judgment award.

The line between allowing an employee the right to exercise his or her religion freely and the employer's right to forbid proselytizing in the workplace may be difficult to draw, particularly for publicly supported colleges. For example, in *Knight v. Connecticut Department of Public Health*, 275 F.3d 156 (2d Cir. 2001), two employees of state agencies were disciplined for proselytizing clients of the agency during their work assignments. The court assumed without deciding that the speech involved a matter of public concern, but ruled that, because the proselytizing upset the clients in both instances, the speech was disruptive and thus was not entitled to First Amendment protection. The court ruled further that allowing these employees to proselytize at work was not a reasonable accommodation for their religious beliefs, because it hampered the state agency's ability to provide services on a religion-neutral basis.

But if the employee's religious beliefs or behavior do not interfere with work performance, and discipline is imposed solely because of those beliefs, a court may find that discrimination has occurred. In *EEOC v. University of Chicago Hospitals*, 276 F.3d 326 (7th Cir. 2002), a federal appellate court reversed an award of summary judgment for the defendant hospital, ruling that the hospital staff had engaged in religious discrimination. A supervisor had discharged a Southern Baptist staff recruiter because the recruiter used her own church as a source of hospital employees. The supervisor had called the plaintiff a "religious fanatic," had ordered her to remove a religious calendar and clock from her desk, and had fired another supervisor for refusing to terminate the plaintiff after criticizing her for "bringing religion into the workplace." The defendant hospital had not provided evidence of any disruption caused by the plaintiff's religious beliefs, and the evidence was sufficient, said the court, to reverse the summary judgment award and send the case to a jury.

According to the Supreme Court in *Hardison*, the employer's responsibility to provide a reasonable accommodation for an employee's religious beliefs is not a heavy one. When faced with a request for an accommodation, such as the reallocation of job responsibilities so that those that are offensive to the individual need not be performed, or revising work schedules so that an employee may attend religious services, the employer needs to determine whether these requests will pose an undue hardship. An undue hardship may be financial, or it may involve the employer's determination that the request will disrupt the efficiency or effectiveness of the workplace. Although the reasonable accommodation requirement under Title VII is easier to satisfy than the accommodation requirement under the Americans With Disabilities Act (see Section 5.2.5), the employer will need to document its attempt(s) to accommodate the religious needs of its workers in order to defend successfully a Title VII religious discrimination claim.

5.3.7. Sexual orientation.

Discrimination on the basis of sexual orientation is not prohibited by Title VII, nor is there any other federal law directed at such discrimination. However, seventeen states prohibit employment discrimination on the basis of sexual orientation in both the public and private sectors,[29] and numerous municipalities have enacted similar local laws prohibiting such discrimination. Laws prohibiting employment discrimination against gays were repealed in Iowa and Maine, and protections for gay employees in Ohio and Louisiana have been withdrawn.

Employment issues related to sexual orientation go beyond the issues—such as discipline, discharge, or salary discrimination—faced by other protected class members. Access to benefits for unmarried same-sex partners, access to campus housing reserved for heterosexual couples, and the effect of the military's refusal to recruit homosexuals add to the complexity of dealing with this issue.

The U.S. Supreme Court has not yet ruled in a case directly involving alleged employment discrimination on the basis of sexual orientation. The Court's opinion in *Oncale,* discussed in Section 5.3.3.3, involved same-sex sexual harassment, rather than sexual orientation discrimination, and was brought under Title VII. In March 2003, however, the Court overruled its earlier holding in *Bowers v. Hardwick,* 478 U.S. 186 (1986) that had upheld a Georgia law criminalizing sodomy. In *Lawrence v. Texas,* 539 U.S. 558 (2003), the Court struck down a Texas law that made sodomy a criminal offense on due process clause grounds. The Court stated that the individuals' "right to liberty under the Due Process Clause gives them the full right to engage in private conduct without government intervention. . . . The Texas statute furthers no legitimate state interest which can justify its intrusion into the individual's personal and private life."

On the other hand, the Court upheld the right of the Boy Scouts of America to exclude homosexuals from positions as volunteer leaders, ruling that the First Amendment's freedom of association protections prohibited New Jersey from using its nondiscrimination law, which includes sexual orientation as a protected class, to require that the Boy Scouts accept leaders who are homosexual. (*Boy Scouts of America v. Dale,* 530 U.S. 640 (2000)).

Although the EEOC has stated that Title VII does not extend to sexual orientation discrimination (EEOC Compliance Manual § 615.2(b)(3)), state and federal courts have been more responsive to sexual orientation discrimination claims brought under Section 1983 of the Civil Rights Act (see Section 3.5 of

---

[29]As of late 2005, the following states prohibited discrimination on the basis of sexual orientation in both private and public sector employment: California, Connecticut, Hawaii, Illinois, Maine, Maryland, Massachusetts, Minnesota, Nevada, New Hampshire, New Jersey, New Mexico, New York, Oregon, Rhode Island, Vermont, and Wisconsin. The District of Columbia also prohibits such discrimination in both private and public employment. In six states, sexual orientation discrimination is prohibited in public employment by law or Executive Order (Alaska, Arizona, Colorado, Delaware, Indiana, Kentucky, Louisiana, Montana, Pennsylvania, and Washington) (see http://www.lambdalegal.org).

this book), alleging violations of the Fourteenth Amendment's equal protection clause.[30] For example, in *Miguel v. Guess,* 51 P.3d 89 (Wash. Ct. App. 2002), a state appellate court rejected the employer's motion to dismiss a claim brought by a hospital employee under Section 1983 that her dismissal was a result of her sexual orientation, and that the dismissal violated the equal protection clause. Although the employee was allowed to proceed on her Section 1983 claim, the court rejected her claim that a dismissal based on one's sexual orientation violated the public policy of the State of Washington because the state legislature had not enacted a law prohibiting discrimination on the basis of sexual orientation (Washington's protection for gay employees is by Executive Order, not statute). Similarly, in *Lovell v. Comsewogue School District,* 214 F. Supp. 2d 319 (E.D.N.Y. 2002), a federal trial court denied the school district's motion to dismiss a teacher's claims that the school principal was less responsive to claims of sexual orientation harassment than he was to other types of harassment claims. The court stated that treating harassment complaints on the basis of sexual orientation differently than other types of harassment claims was, if proven, an equal protection clause violation, and actionable under Section 1983. On the other hand, a college that responded promptly to a staff member's complaints of sexual orientation harassment was successful in obtaining a summary judgment when the staff member resigned and then sued under Section 1983, asserting an equal protection clause violation (*Cracolice v. Metropolitan Community College,* 2002 U.S. Dist. LEXIS 22283 (D. Neb., November 15, 2002)).

Although not all same-sex harassment claims involve claims of sexual orientation discrimination, there is considerable overlap between the two. Same-sex harassment claims are potentially actionable under Title VII, while claims of sexual orientation discrimination and/or harassment are not. (The following discussion is adapted from Mary Ann Connell, "Evolving Law in Same-Sex Harassment and Sexual Orientation Discrimination," 23rd Annual National Conference on Law and Higher Education, Stetson University College of Law, February 18, 2002.)

The U.S. Supreme Court recognized a cause of action for same-sex sexual harassment in *Oncale v. Sundowner Offshore Services,* 523 U.S. 75 (1997), discussed in Section 5.3.3.3. Connell divides post-*Oncale* claims of same-sex harassment into three categories: (1) "desire" cases, in which there is evidence that the harasser sexually desires the target; (2) "hate" cases, in which there is evidence that the harasser is hostile to the presence of a particular sex in the

---

[30]Cases and authorities are collected in Elizabeth Williams, Annot., "Same-Sex Harassment Under Title VII (42 U.S.C. §§ 2000e *et seq.*) of Civil Rights Act," 135 A.L.R. Fed. 307; Norma Rotunno, Annot., "Same-Sex Sexual Harassment Under State Antidiscrimination Laws," 73 A.L.R.5th 1; Robin Cheryl Miller, Annot., "Validity, Construction, and Application of State Enactment, Order, or Regulation Expressly Prohibiting Sexual Orientation Discrimination," 82 A.L.R.5th 1; and Robin Cheryl Miller, Annot., "Federal and State Constitutional Provisions as Prohibiting Discrimination in Employment on Basis of Gay, Lesbian, or Bisexual Sexual Orientation or Conduct," 96 A.L.R.5th 391.

workplace; and (3) cases in which the court examines the alleged harasser's treatment of both sexes in the workplace.

An illustrative "desire" case is *Mota v. University of Texas Houston Health Science Center,* 261 F.3d 512 (5th Cir. 2001). The plaintiff claimed that he was harassed repeatedly by his male supervisor and department chair, who made unwanted and offensive sexual advances toward the plaintiff on several occasions at out-of-town conferences. The jury found for the plaintiff against the university (the alleged harasser had settled with the plaintiff prior to trial); the appellate court upheld the jury verdict, ruling that the university had failed to respond properly and to correct the harassment.

"Hatred" cases involve claims either that the plaintiff was harassed because he or she did not conform to gender stereotypes, or because the alleged harasser was motivated by contempt for the individual's sexual orientation. Plaintiffs bringing hatred cases based on sex stereotyping have been successful in a limited number of cases, but plaintiffs attempting to attack alleged harassment based on sexual orientation have been unsuccessful under Title VII. For example, the U.S. Court of Appeals for the Ninth Circuit found for a plaintiff who claimed that he was harassed because his behavior did not conform to the male stereotype. In *Nichols v. Azteca Restaurant Enterprises,* 256 F.3d 864 (9th Cir. 2001), the court ruled that a four-year pattern of verbal abuse by coworkers based on the plaintiff's effeminate behavior violated Title VII. But those courts that have characterized a same-sex harassment claim as grounding in sexual orientation discrimination rather than stereotyping have rejected plaintiffs' Title VII claims (see, for example, *Dandan v. Radisson Hotel Lisle,* 2000 U.S. Dist. LEXIS 5876 (N.D. Ill. March 28, 2000)), even if the harassment was instigated by individuals who disliked the plaintiff's nonconforming behavior.

An *en banc* ruling by the U.S. Court of Appeals for the Ninth Circuit, if followed by other circuits, may enable plaintiffs to establish sexual orientation harassment claims under Title VII. In *Rene v. MGM Grand Hotel, Inc.,* 243 F.3d 1206 (9th Cir. 2001), *reversed and remanded,* 305 F.3d 1061 (9th Cir. 2002) (*en banc*), the plaintiff asserted that he had endured severe and pervasive offensive physical conduct of a sexual nature, including numerous assaults, because of his perceived homosexuality. The trial court had granted the employer's motion for summary judgment, ruling that the plaintiff had not stated a claim under Title VII because the law did not prohibit discrimination on the basis of sexual orientation. A split three-judge panel of the Ninth Circuit agreed. That ruling was vacated, and the eleven-judge *en banc* court reversed. With four dissenting votes, the judges ruled that

> an employee's sexual orientation is irrelevant for purposes of Title VII. It neither provides nor precludes a cause of action for sexual harassment. That the harasser is, or may be, motivated by hostility based on sexual orientation is similarly irrelevant, and neither provides nor precludes a cause of action. It is enough that the harasser have [sic] engaged in severe or pervasive unwelcome physical conduct of a sexual nature. We therefore would hold that the plaintiff in this case has stated a cause of action under Title VII [305 F.3d at 1063–64].

The *en banc* court justified its reasoning by explaining that the conduct in *Rene* was similar to the offensive conduct in *Oncale,* which occurred in an all-male work environment, as did the harassment in *Rene.* But the ruling in this case appears to be a departure from the language of *Oncale,* which states that the offensive conduct must be directed at the target because of his or her sex; *Rene* appears to base its ruling on the sexual nature of the conduct, not the sex of the target. Two judges wrote opinions concurring in the result, but stating that they believed the proper theory of the case was sexual stereotyping, citing *Price Waterhouse v. Hopkins* (Section 5.2.1) and the Ninth Circuit's opinion in *Nichols,* discussed above. The dissenters disagreed with the majority's assertion that the sex or motive of the harasser was irrelevant as long as the conduct was sexual in nature.

The third category of post-*Oncale* cases involves claims that both men and women were subject to offensive sexualized treatment at work. In these cases, if the employer can demonstrate that both sexes were equally subject to the same type of offensive behavior, there is no Title VII violation (see, for example, *Holman v. Indiana,* 211 F.3d 399 (7th Cir. 2000)). But in some cases, the courts have ruled that the motives for the sexualized treatment of men were different than the motives of the offensive behavior toward women, and have allowed the claims to go forward (see, for example, *Steiner v. Showboat Operating Company,* 25 F.3d 1459 (9th Cir. 1994)).

Title IX prohibits discrimination on the basis of sex at colleges and universities receiving federal funds, and its enforcement guidelines specifically address the possibility of claims involving same-sex discrimination or harassment (OCR, *Revised Sexual Harassment Guidance: Harassment of Students by School Employees, Other Students, or Third Parties* (available at http://www.ed.gov/ocr/shguide/index.html)). Most federal courts, however, have ruled that claims of employment discrimination cannot be brought under Title IX because Title VII provides the federal remedy for sex discrimination (see Section 5.2.3).

In addition to employment discrimination or harassment claims, some colleges have faced litigation concerning the availability of medical and other benefits for the partners of gay employees. According to a survey conducted by the Lambda Legal Defense and Education Fund in mid-2001, more than eighty colleges offer domestic partner benefits to their employees (see http://www.lambdalegal.org/cgi-bin/iowa/documents/record?record-21).

Access to employment benefits for the partners of homosexual employees is a matter generally governed by state or local law.[31] One state, Vermont, has enacted a law that allows same-sex couples to enter into civil unions, a status that provides the couple with the same legal benefits and responsibilities enjoyed by married heterosexual couples (Vt. Stat. Ann. Tit. 32, 3001(c)). Other state legislatures may follow suit, although there is considerable opposition to these laws and their future is uncertain. Unless state law forbids it, a college may offer benefits to unmarried domestic partners, and may choose to limit this

---

[31]As of late 2005, twelve states offered domestic partnership benefits to public employees (see http://www.lambdalegal.org).

benefit to same-sex domestic partners on the grounds that they are not allowed to marry.

With respect to the availability of domestic partner benefits in states that have not enacted civil union laws, state courts have made opposing rulings in litigation concerning health insurance coverage for the domestic partners of gay employees. The state supreme court of Alaska ruled that the university's refusal to provide health insurance for the domestic partners of unmarried employees was a violation of the Alaska Human Rights Act (AS 18.80.220(a)(1)), which forbids employment discrimination on the basis of marital status. However, a New Jersey appellate court has ruled that Rutgers University did not violate state law when it refused to provide health benefits to the domestic partners of gay employees.

In the Alaska case, *University of Alaska v. Tumeo*, 933 P.2d 1147 (Alaska 1997), the court noted that the university had admitted that its position on health insurance constituted discrimination on the basis of marital status. But the university argued that the Human Rights Act's prohibition against such discrimination did not apply to these circumstances because the plaintiffs were not "similarly situated" to married couples in that they were not legally obligated to pay the debts of their domestic partners. The state's high court disagreed, saying that the university had three options, all of which complied with the Human Rights Act.

1. It could refuse to provide health insurance for spouses of its employees;
2. It could rewrite its plan to include within the category of "dependents" all individuals for whom its employees provide the majority of financial support;
3. It could rewrite the plan to specifically include coverage for domestic partners and could require employees and their partners to provide affidavits of spousal equivalency [933 P.2d at 1148].

Nor did the state laws governing health benefits for public employees supersede the Human Rights Act or prohibit the university from providing health insurance for unmarried domestic partners. Stating that the "clear language" of the law prohibits marital status discrimination, the court unanimously ruled for the plaintiff-employees. (In 1995, the university had changed its policy to provide benefits to those who provided "spousal equivalency" affidavits; in the *Tumeo* litigation, it had sought clarification of whether the law actually required such a program; see Lisa Guernsey, "State Courts Split on Benefits for Domestic Partners," *Chron. Higher Educ.*, March 28, 1997, A13.)

The New Jersey case, *Rutgers Council of AAUP Chapters v. Rutgers, The State University*, 689 A.2d 828 (N.J. Super. A.D. 1997), *certification denied*, 707 A.2d 151 (N.J. 1998), differs from the Alaska situation in several respects. First, although the state's Law Against Discrimination outlaws employment discrimination on the basis of both marital status and sexual orientation, the law contains an exemption for employee benefits plans. Therefore, the court was required to examine the wording of the state's statute on health benefits for state employees, which defines "dependents" as children of married spouses. Finding no language in the benefits statute that would compel the university to provide insurance for unmarried domestic partners, the trial judge noted that the impetus for providing such benefits should come from the legislature, not the courts; a first step would be to legalize marriage between gay or lesbian couples, according to the judge. Concurring judges noted that, although they could not disagree with the legal analysis, they found the decision "distasteful" and unfair, and urged the legislature to take action. The legislature did so, passing the Domestic Partnership Act (N.J. Stat. §§ 26:8A-1 *et seq.*) in 2004. The law requires the state to provide health benefits to dependent domestic partners of state employees.

In a third case, an Oregon appellate court ruled that the state constitution requires the Oregon Health Sciences University to provide life and health insurance benefits for the domestic partners of gay and lesbian employees. In *Tanner v. Oregon Health Sciences University,* 971 P.2d 435 (Ore. Ct. App. 1998), three lesbian nursing professionals challenged the university's refusal to provide medical and dental insurance benefits for their domestic partners. (Although the university had adopted an employee benefit plan during the pendency of this litigation that provided benefits for domestic partners of its employees, it maintained that it was not legally required to do so.)

The plaintiffs presented both statutory and constitutional claims. In regard to the former, the plaintiffs had argued that the university's policy of "treating all unmarried employees alike" with respect to the availability of benefits for domestic partners was a violation of the state's nondiscrimination law, which includes sexual orientation as a protected class, because homosexual couples could not marry. Although the court found that the university's "practice of denying insurance benefits to unmarried domestic partners of its homosexual employees had an otherwise unlawful disparate impact on a protected class," it also found that the university's benefits policy was not a subterfuge to discriminate against homosexuals, and thus, under Oregon statutory law, the university did not engage in an unlawful employment practice (971 P.2d at 444).

But the constitutional claim was a different matter. The court had to determine whether unmarried homosexual couples are members of a suspect class. The court determined that they were:

> [S]exual orientation, like gender, race, alienage, and religious affiliation is widely regarded as defining a distinct, socially recognized group of citizens, and certainly it is beyond dispute that homosexuals in our society have been and continue to be the subject of adverse social and political stereotyping and prejudice [971 P.2d at 447].

Although there was no showing that the university intended to discriminate against the plaintiffs on the basis of their sexual orientation, "its actions have the undeniable effect of doing just that. . . . What is relevant is the extent to which privileges or immunities are not made available to all citizens on equal terms" (971 P.2d at 447). Since homosexual couples were not permitted to marry, said the court, denying homosexual employees benefits for their domestic partners on the basis of marital status violated Article I, Section 20 of the Oregon constitution.

The issue of domestic partner benefits has been addressed in two opinions of the Vermont Labor Relations Board. In the first, *Grievance of B.M.S.S. et al.*, 16 VLRB 207 (1993), a case arising prior to the passage of the Vermont Civil Union law, the state labor board ruled that the university had committed an unfair labor practice under the State Employee Labor Relations Act (3 V.S.A. § 901 *et seq.*) by denying medical and dental benefits to the partners of gay and lesbian employees. Section 961(6) of the law prohibits discrimination on the basis of sexual orientation. The labor board concurred with the grievants' characterization of the denial of benefits as disparate impact discrimination, following the theory of *Griggs v. Duke Power Co.* (discussed in Section 5.2.1), and ordered the university to provide medical and dental benefits to the domestic partners of its gay and lesbian employees within sixty days.

In a second case involving the same university, *Willard Miller v. UVM*, 24 VLRB 1 (2001), an unmarried faculty member claimed that the university's refusal to provide medical and dental benefits to his female domestic partner violated the university's own policies against discrimination on the basis of sexual orientation. Shortly after the Vermont Civil Union law was passed, the university notified all of its employees that dependents (whose definition includes spouses or "same-sex spousal equivalents") would be entitled to medical and dental benefits only if the employee was either married to the spouse or had entered a civil union with a "same-sex spousal equivalent." The labor board reasoned that there was no disparate impact on unmarried heterosexual employees with domestic partners because there was no legal impediment to their marrying. Now that employees could qualify for health benefits for spouses by either marrying or entering a civil union, there was no disparate impact on the grounds of sexual orientation. The labor board denied Miller's claim.

The military services' ban on homosexuals has posed several problems for colleges whose employment and student life policies prohibit discrimination on the basis of sexual orientation. The military's policy has raised issues of whether the military may recruit students at campus locations, whether a campus is willing to host Reserve Officer Training Corps units, and eligibility for research funds from the U.S. Department of Defense. Under current federal law, institutions whose nondiscrimination policies include protections for sexual orientation or gender identity must, however, give the military access to their students for recruitment purposes. The "Solomon Amendment," discussed in Section 13.4.3, requires that colleges provide such access or risk the loss of federal funds.

Sec. 5.4. Affirmative Action

5.4.1. Overview. Affirmative action has been an intensely controversial concept in many areas of American life. While the ongoing debate on affirmative action in student admissions (Section 8.2.5) parallels in its intensity the affirmative action debate on employment, the latter has been even more controversial because it is more crowded with federal regulations and requirements. In addition, beneficiaries of affirmative action in employment may be more visible because they compete for often-scarce openings, particularly for faculty or other professional positions.

Affirmative action in employment is governed by federal Executive Orders (Section 5.2.8) and related federal contracting statutes, by Title VII of the Civil Rights Act of 1964 (Section 5.2.1), and by the equal protection clause of the Constitution's Fourteenth Amendment (Section 5.2.7). The affirmative action requirements of the Executive Orders apply to contractors with fifty or more employees who receive federal contracts of at least $50,000 (which covers most colleges and universities), while the equal protection clause applies only to public colleges and universities. Title VII applies to both private and public colleges. Each of these authorities poses somewhat different obligations for employers and involves different legal analyses.

Affirmative action became a major issue because the federal government's initiatives regarding discrimination have a dual aim: to "bar like discrimination in the future" and to "eliminate the discriminatory effects of the past" (*Albemarle Paper Co. v. Moody,* 422 U.S. 405 (1975)). Addressing this latter objective under Title VII, courts may "'order such affirmative action as may be appropriate'" (*Franks v. Bowman Transportation Co.,* 424 U.S. 747 (1976), quoting *Albemarle*). Affirmative action can be appropriate under *Franks* even though it may adversely affect other employees, since "a sharing of the burden of the past discrimination is presumptively necessary." Under statutes other than Title VII, and under Executive Orders 11246 and 11375, courts or administrative agencies may similarly require employers, including public and private postsecondary institutions, to engage in affirmative action to eliminate the effects of past discrimination.

Executive Orders 11246 and 11375 (see Section 5.2.8) have been the major focus of federal affirmative action initiatives. Aside from their basic prohibition of race, color, religion, sex, and national origin discrimination, these executive orders require federal contractors and subcontractors employing fifty or more employees and receiving at least $50,000 in federal contracts to develop affirmative action plans. The implementing regulations were revised in 2000 (65 Fed. Reg. No. 219, November 13, 2000) and are codified at 41 C.F.R. Parts 60-1 and 60-2. Section 60-1.40 of the regulations requires that a contractor have an affirmative action program. 41 C.F.R. Section 60-2.10 lists the required elements of an affirmative action program. One requirement is "placement goals" (41 C.F.R. § 60-2.16), which the contractor must establish in light of the availability of women and minorities for each job group. The regulation states that "placement goals may not be rigid and inflexible quotas which must be met, nor are they to be considered as either a ceiling or a floor for the employment of particular groups. Quotas are expressly forbidden" (41 C.F.R. § 60-2.16 (e)(1)).

An institution's compliance with affirmative action requirements is monitored and enforced by the Office of Federal Contract Compliance Programs (OFCCP), located in the U.S. Department of Labor. The OFCCP may also conduct an investigation of an institution's employment practices before a federal contract is awarded.

Postsecondary institutions contracting with the federal government are also subject to federal affirmative action requirements regarding persons with disabilities and veterans. "Qualified" persons with disabilities are covered by Section 503 of the Rehabilitation Act of 1973 (29 U.S.C. § 793), which requires affirmative action "to employ and advance in employment qualified individuals with disabilities" on contracts of $10,000 or more.

A variety of laws regarding the employment and training of veterans are codified at 38 U.S.C. Section 4212. The law specifies that organizations that enter a contract with the U.S. government worth $100,000 or more must "take affirmative action to employ and advance in employment qualified covered veterans" (§ 4212(a)(1)). Covered veterans include both disabled and nondisabled veterans who served on active duty "during a war or in a campaign or expedition for which a campaign badge has been authorized." The law regarding veterans thus has a broader scope than Section 503.

The Department of Labor has issued regulations to implement both Section 503 (41 C.F.R. Part 60-741) and the veterans' law (41 C.F.R. Part 60-250). Both sets of regulations provide that any job qualification that tends to screen out members of the covered groups must be job related and consistent with business necessity (41 C.F.R. § 60-741.21(g); 41 C.F.R. § 60-250.21(g)). The regulations also require contractors to accommodate the physical and mental limitations of employees and disabled veterans "unless the contractor can demonstrate that such an accommodation would impose an undue hardship on the operation of its business" (41 C.F.R. § 60-741.21(f); 41 C.F.R. § 60-250.21(f)).

Under the various affirmative action provisions in federal law, the most sensitive nerves are hit when affirmative action creates "reverse discrimination," that is, when the employer responds to a statistical "underrepresentation" of women or minorities by granting employment preferences to members of the underrepresented or previously victimized group, thus discriminating "in reverse" against other employees or applicants.[32] Besides creating policy issues of the highest order, such affirmative action measures create two sets of complex legal questions: (1) To what extent does the applicable statute, Executive Order, or implementing regulation require or permit the employer to utilize such employment preferences? (2) What limitations does the Constitution place on the federal government's authority to require or permit, or the employer's

---

[32]The relevant authorities are collected in Donald T. Kramer, Annot., "What Constitutes Reverse or Majority Gender Discrimination Against Males Violative of Federal Constitution or Statutes—Public Employment Cases," 153 A.L.R. Fed. 609; Donald T. Kramer, Annot., "What Constitutes Reverse or Majority Gender Discrimination Against Males Violative of Federal Constitution or Statutes—Private Employment Cases," 162 A.L.R. Fed. 273; Donald T. Kramer, Annot., "What Constitutes Reverse or Majority Race or National Origin Discrimination Violative of Federal Constitutional Statutes—Private Employment Cases," 150 A.L.R. Fed. 1; Donald T. Kramer, Annot., "What Constitutes Reverse or Majority Race or National Origin Discrimination Violative of Federal Constitution or Statutes—Public Employment Cases," 168 A.L.R. Fed. 1.

authority to utilize, such employment preferences, particularly in the absence of direct evidence of discrimination by the employer?

The response to the first question depends on a close analysis of the particular legal authority involved. The answer is not necessarily the same under each authority. In general, however, federal law is more likely to require or permit hiring preferences when necessary to overcome the effects of the employer's own past discrimination than it is when no such past discrimination is shown or when preferences are not necessary to eliminate its effects. Section 703(j) of Title VII, for instance, relieves employers of any obligation to give "preferential treatment" to an individual or group merely because of an "imbalance" in the number or percentage of employed persons from that group compared with the number or percentage of persons from that group in the "community, state, section, or other area" (42 U.S.C. § 2000e-2(j)). But where an imbalance does not arise innocently but, rather, arises because of the employer's discriminatory practices, courts in Title VII suits have sometimes required the use of hiring preferences or goals to remedy the effects of such discrimination (see, for example, *Local 28 of the Sheet Metal Workers' International Ass'n. v. EEOC,* 478 U.S. 421 (1986)).

Constitutional limitations on the use of employment preferences by public employers stem from the Fourteenth Amendment's equal protection clause. (See the discussion of that clause's application to admissions preferences in Section 8.2.5.) Even if the applicable statute, Executive Order, or regulation is construed to require or permit employment preferences, such preferences may still be invalid under the federal Constitution unless a court or an agency has found that the employer has discriminated in the past. Courts have usually held hiring preferences to be constitutional where necessary to eradicate the effects of the employer's past discrimination, as in *Carter v. Gallagher,* 452 F.2d 315 (8th Cir. 1971). Where there is no such showing of past discrimination, the constitutionality of employment preferences is more in doubt.

The U.S. Supreme Court has analyzed the legality of voluntary affirmative action plans and race- or gender-conscious employment decisions made under the authority of these plans. The cases have involved sharp divisions among the justices and are inconsistent in several ways. Furthermore, the Court's decision in *Grutter v. Bollinger,* 539 U.S. 306 (2003), discussed in Section 8.2.5 of this book, arose in the context of student admissions rather than employment, and its implications for employment are far from clear. Moreover, changes in the composition of the Court may alter its stance on the legality of voluntary affirmative action in employment. Therefore, the analysis of Supreme Court jurisprudence in the area of affirmative action is difficult, and predictions about future directions of the Court in this volatile area are nearly impossible.

5.4.2. Affirmative action under Title VII. The U.S. Supreme Court has addressed challenges to employment decisions in cases of both voluntary and court-ordered affirmative action plans. The Court has issued two rulings involving voluntary affirmative action plans in employment that were challenged under Title VII under a "reverse discrimination" theory. In its first examination of a voluntary affirmative action plan involving a private employer, the Court strongly endorsed the concept.

In *Weber v. Kaiser Aluminum Co.,* 443 U.S. 193 (1979), the Court considered a white steelworker's challenge to an affirmative action plan negotiated by his union and employer. The plan provided for a new craft-training program, with admission to be on the basis of one black worker for every white worker selected. The race-conscious admission practice was to cease when the proportion of black skilled craft workers at the plant reflected the proportion of blacks in the local labor force. During the first year the plan was in effect, the most junior black selected for the training program was less senior than several white workers whose requests to enter the training program were denied. One of those denied admission to the program filed a class action claim, alleging "reverse discrimination."

The federal district court ruled that the plan unlawfully discriminated against white employees and therefore violated Title VII of the Civil Rights Act (415 F. Supp. 761 (E.D. La. 1976)), and the appellate court affirmed (563 F.2d 216 (5th Cir. 1978)). In a 5-to-2 decision written by Justice Brennan, the Supreme Court reversed, ruling that employers and unions in the private sector may take race-conscious steps to eliminate "manifest racial imbalance" in "traditionally segregated job categories." Such action, the Court said, does not run afoul of Title VII's prohibition on racial discrimination (see Section 5.2.1).

The Court considered Weber's claim that, by giving preference to junior black employees over more senior whites, the training program discriminated against white employees in violation of the 1964 Civil Rights Act. Because the employment action did not involve state action, no constitutional issues were involved. The Court framed the issue as an inquiry into whether private parties could voluntarily agree to give racial preferences such as those in the collective bargaining agreement.

After reviewing the legislative history describing the concerns that led Congress to pass Title VII, the Court stated that, given Title VII's intent, voluntary efforts to achieve greater racial balance in the workforce did not violate the law. Thus concluding that the use of racial preferences in hiring is sometimes permissible, the Court went on to uphold the Kaiser plan in particular. In doing so, the Court found it unnecessary to set forth detailed guidelines for employers and unions. Instead, it identified several factors that courts in subsequent cases have used to measure the lawfulness of affirmative action programs.

First, there was a "manifest racial imbalance" in the job categories for which Kaiser had established the special training program. While the percentage of blacks in the area workforce was approximately 39 percent, fewer than 2 percent of the craft jobs at Kaiser were filled by blacks. Second, as the Court noted in a footnote to its opinion, these crafts had been "traditionally segregated"; rampant discrimination in the past had contributed to the present imbalance at Kaiser. Third, the Court emphasized that the plan in *Weber* did not "unnecessarily trammel" the interests of white employees; it did not operate as a total bar to whites, and it was temporary, designed to bring minority representation up to that of the area's workforce rather than to maintain racial balance permanently.

These factors cited by the Court left several questions open: How great a racial imbalance must there be before it will be considered "manifest"? What kind of showing must be made before a job category will be considered "traditionally segregated"? At what point will the effects of a plan on white workers be so great as to be considered "unnecessary trammeling"? These questions were raised in a subsequent challenge to a gender-conscious employment decision made under the authority of an affirmative action plan, this time by a public employer. To date, it is the only Supreme Court analysis of gender preferences in employment.

In *Johnson v. Transportation Agency, Santa Clara County*, 480 U.S. 616 (1987), Paul Johnson, who had applied for a promotion, alleged that the agency had promoted a less qualified woman, Diane Joyce, because of her gender, in violation of Title VII. In a 6-to-3 opinion, the Supreme Court, relying on its *Weber* precedent, held that neither the affirmative action plan nor Joyce's promotion violated Title VII.

As is the practice in many public agencies, the agency's promotion policies permitted the decision maker to select one of several individuals who were certified to be minimally qualified for the position in question—in this case, a road maintenance dispatcher. Both Joyce and Johnson, as well as several other men, had been rated "qualified," although Johnson's total score (based on experience, an interview, and other factors) was slightly higher than Joyce's.

The agency had developed an affirmative action plan that attempted to increase the number of women and racial minorities in jobs in which they were traditionally underrepresented. The agency had not submitted evidence of any prior discrimination on its part, but noted the statistical disparities between the proportion of potentially qualified women and their low representation in certain occupations.

The majority opinion, written by Justice Brennan, first addressed the burden-of-proof issue. It is up to the plaintiff, wrote Brennan, to establish that the affirmative action plan is invalid. In assessing the plan's validity, the Court applied the tests from *Weber*. First, the plan had to address a "manifest imbalance" that reflected underrepresentation of women in traditionally segregated job categories. Statistical comparisons between the proportion of qualified women in the labor market and those in segregated job categories would demonstrate the imbalance. Regarding the employer's responsibility for that imbalance, the majority rejected the notion that the employer must demonstrate prior discrimination, a requirement that would be imposed if the case had been brought under the equal protection clause of the Fourteenth Amendment.

Having determined that the affirmative action plan satisfied the first part of the *Weber* test, the majority then examined whether the plan "unnecessarily trammeled" the rights of male employees or created an absolute bar to their advancement. Finding that Johnson had no absolute entitlement to the promotion, and that he retained his position, salary, and seniority, the majority found that the plan met the second *Weber* test.

The majority then assessed whether the plan was a temporary measure, the third requirement of *Weber*. Although the plan was silent with regard to its duration, the Court found that the plan was intended to attain, rather than to maintain, a balanced workforce, thus satisfying the third *Weber* test. Justice Brennan wrote that "substantial evidence shows that the Agency has sought to take a moderate, gradual approach to eliminating the imbalance in its work force, one which establishes realistic guidance for employment decisions, and which visits minimal intrusion on the legitimate expectations of other employees" (480 U.S. at 640).

Both the *Weber* and the *Johnson* cases involved voluntary affirmative action plans that were challenged under Title VII. A year before *Johnson*, the Supreme Court had addressed the legality, under Title VII, of race-conscious hiring and promotion as part of court-ordered remedies after intentional discrimination had been proved. One issue in both cases centered on whether individuals who had not been actual victims of discrimination could benefit from race-conscious remedies applied to hiring and promotion. In both cases, the Supreme Court upheld those remedies in situations where lower courts had found the discrimination to be egregious. In *Local 93, International Association of Firefighters v. City of Cleveland*, 478 U.S. 501 (1986), a majority of six justices approved a consent decree that required race-conscious promotions for Cleveland firefighters as a means of remedying prior discrimination against blacks and Hispanics. In response to the assertion by the city that Title VII prohibited race-conscious remedies for individuals who had not themselves suffered discrimination, Justice Brennan, writing for the majority, said: "It is equally clear that the voluntary action available to employers and unions seeking to eradicate race discrimination may include reasonable race-conscious relief that benefits individuals who were not actual victims of discrimination" (478 U.S. at 516).

A majority of six justices also approved race-conscious selection and promotion requirements in *Local 28 of the Sheet Metal Workers' International Ass'n. v. EEOC*, 478 U.S. 421 (1986), as a remedy for long-standing and egregious race discrimination in access to union apprenticeship programs and admission to the union. (For a review and analysis of the affirmative action cases decided in 1986, see M. Clague, "The Affirmative Action Showdown of 1986: Implications for Higher Education," 14 *J. Coll. & Univ. Law* 171 (1987).)

Federal appellate courts reviewing affirmative action employment cases under Title VII have generally struck the plans unless there was substantial evidence that the plan was necessary to remedy the employer's past race or sex discrimination or a "manifest imbalance" in a segregated job title. For example, in *Taxman v. Board of Education of the Township of Piscataway*, 91 F.3d 1547 (3d Cir. 1996) (*en banc*), discussed in Section 6.4, a federal appellate court invalidated a race-conscious layoff whose purpose was to maintain racial diversity among teachers at a public high school rather than remedying any prior discrimination by the employer.[33] The same federal circuit invalidated the regulations of the

---

[33]Although the Supreme Court's opinion in *Grutter v. Bollinger*, 539 U.S. 306 (2003), may have invalidated part of the reasoning in *Taxman* (which had stated that diversity was not a compelling interest under Title VII), the outcome in *Taxman* is unaffected by *Grutter* because, in *Taxman*, race was used as the only criterion for making a layoff decision, a strategy outlawed in *Grutter*'s companion case of *Gratz v. Bollinger*, 539 U.S. 244 (2003).

New Jersey Casino Control Commission that established goals for hiring, promotion, demotion, layoff, and termination on the basis of gender, race, and ethnicity. In *Schurr v. Resorts International Hotels, Inc.,* 196 F.3d 486 (3d Cir. 1999), the court ruled that there had been no showing of prior or present discrimination either in the casino industry or in the job categories involved in the lawsuit. Similarly, in *Albright v. City of New Orleans,* 1999 U.S. Dist. LEXIS 2735 (E.D. La., March 9, 1999), a federal trial court invalidated a consent decree and related affirmative action plan because there was no evidence of a manifest racial imbalance and there was evidence that the rights of nonminorities were trammeled by the plan—a violation of two prongs of the *Weber* test.

On the other hand, when courts have found strong evidence of a manifest imbalance or overt discrimination in the past by the employer, they have been more willing to approve the affirmative action plan. For example, in *Dix v. United Air Lines, Inc.,* 2000 U.S. Dist. LEXIS 12464 (N.D. Ill., August 28, 2000), *affirmed,* 2001 U.S. App. LEXIS 3225 (7th Cir., February 23, 2001), *cert. denied,* 534 U.S. 892 (2001), a federal trial court rejected a "reverse discrimination" hiring claim by a white male, ruling that the airline had demonstrated that a historical imbalance existed and denying the plaintiff's motion for summary judgment. And in *Airth v. City of Pomona,* 2000 U.S. App. LEXIS 7270 (9th Cir., April 19, 2000), the court approved an affirmative action ranking plan that controlled the promotions of firefighters, but remanded for a determination as to whether the particular promotion decisions at issue had been made in a discriminatory fashion.

A challenge to an affirmative action hiring program at Illinois State University resulted in a ruling against the university. In *United States v. Board of Trustees of Illinois State University,* 944 F. Supp. 714 (C.D. Ill. 1996), the U.S. Department of Justice filed a Title VII lawsuit against the university, asserting that a program designed to circumvent veterans' preferences by filling custodial positions through a "learner's program" violated the statute. White males were not selected for the learner's program, as it was limited to women and to non-white males. The court ruled that the program failed all of the *Weber* tests in that it did not remedy a manifest imbalance, its purpose was to circumvent the veterans' preference rather than to remedy prior discrimination, and it trammeled the rights of white males who wished to be employed in these jobs.

Despite the difficulty of translating the outcome in *Grutter* to the employment context, it appears that employers who can demonstrate a "manifest imbalance" and whose voluntary affirmative action plans—and actions taken under their guidance—can pass the *Weber* test, may be able to practice affirmative action in hiring and promotion decisions. But the lessons of *Grutter* and its companion case, *Gratz,* discussed in Section 8.2.5, should be heeded, so that these programs are not practicing racial balancing or using quotas to accomplish the goal of diversity.

5.4.3. Affirmative action under the equal protection clause. The U.S. Supreme Court has also addressed the validity of affirmative action plans—both voluntary and involuntary—under the equal protection clause. In these cases, courts subject the plan to a "strict scrutiny" standard of review, requiring

proof that remedying the targeted discrimination is a "compelling government interest" and that the plan's race- or gender-conscious employment criteria are "narrowly tailored" to accomplish the goal of remedying the targeted discrimination.

In *United States v. Paradise,* 480 U.S. 149 (1987), an involuntary (or mandatory) affirmative action case, federal courts had ordered that 50 percent of the promotions to corporal for Alabama state troopers be awarded to qualified black candidates. The lower courts found that the state police department had systematically excluded blacks for more than four decades, and for another decade had resisted following court orders to increase the proportion of black troopers. The Supreme Court, in a 5-to-4 decision, found ample justification to uphold the one-black-for-one-white promotion requirement imposed by the lower federal courts.

The United States, acting as plaintiff in this case, argued that the remedy imposed by the court violated the equal protection clause. Justice Brennan, writing for the majority, noted that the Court had yet to agree on the appropriate standard of review for affirmative action cases brought under the equal protection clause. He refused to do so in *Paradise* because "we conclude that the relief ordered survives even strict scrutiny analysis: it is 'narrowly tailored' to serve a 'compelling [governmental] purpose'" (480 U.S. at 167). In reaching this conclusion, the majority determined that "the pervasive, systematic, and obstinate discriminatory conduct of the Department created a profound need and firm justification for the race-conscious relief ordered by the District Court" (480 U.S. at 167). The Court left for another day the delineation of more specific equal protection guidelines for remedial affirmative action plans.

The Supreme Court's opinion in *Paradise,* like its opinions in *Weber, Sheet Metal Workers, Cleveland Firefighters,* and *Johnson* (all Title VII cases analyzed in subsection 5.4.2. above), involved promotions or other advancement opportunities that did not result in job loss for majority individuals. When, affirmative action plans are used to justify racial preferences in layoffs, however, the response of the Supreme Court has been quite different. In *Firefighters v. Stotts,* 467 U.S. 561 (1984), for example, the Court invalidated a remedial consent decree that approved race-conscious layoff decisions in order to preserve the jobs of more recently hired minorities under the city's affirmative action plan.

In another case, *Wygant v. Jackson Board of Education,* 476 U.S. 267 (1986) (a case that had significance for the Third Circuit's later ruling in *Taxman;* see Section 6.4), the Supreme Court addressed the issue of voluntary racial preferences in reductions-in-force. The school board and the teachers' union had responded to a pending race discrimination claim by black teachers and applicants for teaching positions by adopting a race-conscious layoff provision in their collective bargaining agreement. The agreement specified that, if a layoff occurred, those teachers with the most seniority would be retained, except that at no time would there be a greater percentage of minority personnel laid off than the percentage of minority personnel employed at the time of the layoff. A layoff occurred, and the board, following the bargaining agreement, laid off some white teachers with more seniority than minority teachers who were retained in order to meet the proportionality requirement. The more senior white teachers challenged the constitutionality of the contractual provision. Both the federal district court and the U.S. Court of Appeals for the Sixth Circuit upheld the provision as permissible action taken to remedy prior societal discrimination and to provide role models for minority children. In a 5-to-4 decision, the Court reversed the lower courts, concluding that the race-conscious layoff provision violated the equal protection clause. In a plurality opinion by Justice Powell, four Justices agreed that the bargaining agreement provision should be subjected to the "strict scrutiny" test used for other racial classifications challenged under the equal protection clause (476 U.S. at 274, citing *Fullilove v. Klutznick,* 448 U.S. 448, 480). The fifth Justice concurring in the judgment, Justice White, did not address the strict scrutiny issue (476 U.S. at 294–95).

Rejecting the school board's argument that remedying societal discrimination provided a sufficient justification for the race-conscious layoffs, the plurality opinion stated:

> This Court never has held that societal discrimination alone is sufficient to justify a racial classification. Rather, the Court has insisted upon some showing of prior discrimination by the governmental unit involved before allowing limited use of racial classifications in order to remedy such discrimination [476 U.S. at 274].

The plurality then discussed the Court's ruling in *Hazelwood School District v. United States,* 433 U.S. 299 (1977), which established a method for demonstrating the employer's prior discrimination by comparing qualified minorities in the relevant labor market with their representation in the employer's workforce. The correct comparison was of teachers to qualified blacks in the labor market, not of minority teachers to minority children. Moreover, said the plurality:

> [B]ecause the role model theory does not necessarily bear a relationship to the harm caused by prior discriminatory hiring practices, it actually could be used to escape the obligation to remedy such practices by justifying the small percentage of black teachers by reference to the small percentage of black students [476 U.S. at 275–76].

Having rejected the "societal discrimination" and "role model" arguments, and having found no history of prior discrimination by the school board, the plurality concluded that the school board had not made the showing of a compelling interest required by the strict scrutiny test.

In a concurring opinion, Justice O'Connor considered whether it was necessary for a public employer to make specific findings of prior discrimination at the time it adopted an affirmative action plan. She concluded that requiring such a finding would be a powerful disincentive for a public employer to initiate a voluntary affirmative action plan, and stated that "a contemporaneous or antecedent finding of past discrimination by a court or other competent body is not a constitutional prerequisite to a public employer's voluntary agreement to an affirmative action plan" (476 U.S. at 289). But the employer should "act on the basis of information which gives [the public employer] a sufficient basis for concluding that remedial action is necessary" (476 U.S. at 291), so that findings by a court or an enforcement agency would be unnecessary. As long as the public employer had a "firm basis for believing that remedial action is required" (476 U.S. at 286), presumably through evidence demonstrating statistical disparity between the proportion of minorities in the qualified labor market and those in the workforce, a state's interest in affirmative action could be found to be "compelling." In addition, in a comment with potential significance for proponents of affirmative action as a tool to promote racial diversity, O'Connor noted: "Although its precise contours are uncertain, a state interest in the promotion of racial diversity has been found sufficiently 'compelling,' at least in the context of higher education, to support the use of racial considerations in furthering that interest" (476 U.S. at 286; citing *Bakke,* discussed in Section 8.2.5).

Justice Marshall, in a dissent joined by Justices Brennan and Blackmun, characterized the case quite differently from the plurality:

> The sole question posed by this case is whether the Constitution prohibits a union and a local school board from developing a collective-bargaining agreement that apportions layoffs between two racially determined groups as a means of preserving the effects of an affirmative hiring policy, the constitutionality of which is unchallenged [476 U.S. at 300].

Justice Marshall found that the school board's goal of preserving minority representation of teachers was a compelling interest under the factual record presented to the court. He concluded that the contractual provision was narrowly tailored because it neither burdened nor benefited one race but, instead, substituted a criterion other than absolute seniority for layoff decisions.

Two later Supreme Court cases, *Croson* and *Adarand* (below), confirm the applicability of the strict scrutiny test to affirmative action programs and provide additional guidance on use of the narrow tailoring test. In addition, although these cases did not involve employment, they suggest that public employers may need to demonstrate a history of race or sex discrimination in employment, rather than simply a statistical disparity between minority representation in the workforce and the labor market. In *City of Richmond v. J. A. Croson Co.,* 488 U.S. 469 (1989), the Court, again sharply divided, ruled 6 to 3 that a set-aside program of public construction contract funds for minority subcontractors violated the Constitution's equal protection clause. Applying the strict scrutiny test, a plurality of Justices (plus Justice Scalia, using different reasoning) ruled that the city's requirement that prime contractors awarded city construction contracts must subcontract at least 30 percent of the amount of each contract to minority-owned businesses was not justified by a compelling governmental interest, and that the set-aside requirement was not narrowly tailored to accomplish the purpose of remedying prior discrimination.

The Supreme Court extended its analysis of *Croson* in *Adarand Constructors v. Pena,* 515 U.S. 200 (1995), a case involving contracts awarded by the

U.S. Department of Transportation (DOT). Adarand, the low bidder on a sub-contract for guard rails for a highway project, mounted an equal protection challenge under the Fifth Amendment to the DOT's regulations concerning preferences for minority subcontractors. The regulations provided the prime contractor with a financial incentive to award subcontracts to small businesses certified as controlled by "socially and economically disadvantaged" individuals. Adarand was not so certified, and the contract was awarded to a certified subcontractor whose bid was higher than Adarand's.

In a 5-to-4 ruling, the Court held that "all racial classifications, imposed by whatever federal, state, or local governmental actor, must be analyzed by a reviewing court under strict scrutiny." The Court then remanded the case for a trial on the issue of whether the federal contracting program's subcontracting regulations met the strict scrutiny test.[34]

Since *Croson* and *Adarand*, litigation challenging race- or gender-conscious employment decisions, most of which involves challenges by white male police officers or firefighters to race- or gender-conscious hiring and promotion decisions, has focused squarely on the employer's ability to demonstrate its own prior discrimination. Affirmative action plans were invalidated in *Middleton v. City of Flint*, 92 F.3d 396 (6th Cir. 1996), *cert. denied*, 520 U.S. 1196 (1997); *Dallas Fire Fighters Association v. City of Dallas*, 150 F.3d 438 (5th Cir. 1998), *cert. denied*, 526 U.S. 1046 (1999); and *Alexander v. Estepp*, 95 F.3d 312 (4th Cir. 1996), *cert. denied*, 520 U.S. 1165 (1997). The courts in these cases determined either that there was insufficient data indicating the employer's discrimination or that the race-conscious provisions were not sufficiently narrowly tailored. However, in three other cases—*Majeske v. City of Chicago*, 218 F.3d 816 (7th Cir. 2000); *Danskine v. Miami Dade Fire Dept.*, 253 F.3d 1288 (11th Cir. 2001); and *Boston Police Superior Officers Federation*, 147 F.3d 13 (1st Cir. 1998)—affirmative action plans were upheld. The respective appellate courts cited substantial evidence of prior discrimination, and determined that the employers' race- or gender-conscious hiring and promotion criteria were narrowly tailored remedies for that discrimination.

In two other cases, the U.S. Court of Appeals for the D.C. Circuit invalidated the affirmative action regulations of the Federal Communications Commission (FCC). These courts ruled that the regulations were unconstitutional because they sought to promote diversity rather than to remedy documented discrimination. In the first case, *Lutheran Church—Missouri Synod v. Federal Communication Commission*, 141 F.3d 344 (D.C. Cir. 1998), the Lutheran Church challenged the regulations on both First Amendment free exercise and Fifth Amendment equal protection grounds. The church required employees of its

---

[34]On remand, the trial court ruled that the regulations, which the Department of Transportation had revised in response to the Supreme Court's ruling, still violated the equal protection clause. The U.S. Court of Appeals for the Tenth Circuit reversed, ruling that the government had met both the "compelling interest" test and the "narrow tailoring" test in the revised regulations (*Adarand Constructors, Inc. v. Slater*, 228 F.3d 1147 (10th Cir. 2000)). The plaintiffs appealed and, although the U.S. Supreme Court initially granted *certiorari*, it reversed itself and dismissed *certiorari* as improvidently granted (*Adarand Constructors, Inc. v. Mineta*, 534 U.S. 103 (2001)).

radio stations to have both knowledge of Lutheran doctrine and a background in classical music, since religion and classical music were the formats for the radio stations' programming. With respect to the church's claim that requiring the stations to use racial preferences in hiring violated the equal protection doctrine of the Fifth Amendment, the court, following *Adarand,* applied the strict scrutiny test and required the FCC to demonstrate that its regulations are narrowly tailored to serve a compelling governmental interest. The court rejected the FCC's contention that diversity—in both programming and employment—was a compelling interest. The court also rejected the FCC's argument that its regulations were narrowly tailored, since these regulations required the stations to use racial preferences for all positions, even those that had no influence over programming. Because the FCC had criticized the church for its religious preferences for employees in non-broadcast or programming positions, its insistence that racial preferences be used for all positions was irrational, according to the court. Because it had disposed of the church's appeal on equal protection grounds, the court did not address the church's free exercise claim.

In another challenge to FCC regulations, *MD/DC/DE Broadcasters Associations v. Federal Communications Commission,* 236 F.3d 13 (D.C. Cir. 2001), broadcasting associations brought equal protection claims. The regulations

> required stations to seek out sources likely to refer female and minority applicants for employment, to track the source of each referral, and to record the race and sex of each applicant and of each person hired. If these data indicated that a station employed a lower percentage of women and minorities than were employed in the local workforce, then the Commission would take that into account in determining whether to renew the station's license [236 F.3d at 16].

The appellate court found that the regulations were not narrowly tailored because the rule required the broadcasters to recruit women and minorities without a preliminary finding that the broadcaster had discriminated against these groups in the past. Having made this finding, the court did not rule on whether the FCC's interest in race-conscious recruitment policies was compelling.

The U.S. Supreme Court's decisions in *Gratz v. Bollinger* and *Grutter v. Bollinger,* both discussed in Section 8.2.5 of this book, concerned the diversity rationale for affirmative action rather than the remedying prior discrimination rationale, and neither case concerned employment. These cases therefore do not add to or change the analysis in *Croson* and *Adarand* or the lower court cases applying this analysis. But *Gratz* and *Grutter* do indirectly raise the important question of whether the diversity rationale, recognized in those cases for affirmative action in admissions, may have some applicability to employment affirmative action. The D.C. Circuit rejected that approach in the FCC cases discussed above, but in *Wygant* (above), Justice O'Connor's concurring opinion does suggest the possible applicability of diversity rationales to employment.

(For a thoughtful discussion of *Taxman,* the *Lutheran Church* case, and other cases related to affirmative action in employment published prior to the

Court's 2003 rulings in Grutter and Gratz, see Robert S. Whitman, "Affirmative Action on Campus: The Legal and Practical Challenges," 24 *J. Coll. & Univ. Law* 637 (1998).)

5.4.4. State regulation of affirmative action. In 1996, California voters approved Proposition 209, a state constitutional provision that prohibits public organizations from having affirmative action employment programs. The provision also applies to college admissions. This constitutional provision was used to invalidate a California state law (Education Code §§ 87100–107) that required each community college district to have an affirmative action plan. The purpose of the plans was to "hire and promote persons who are underrepresented in the work force compared to their number in the population," including disabled individuals, women, and racial and ethnic minorities (§ 87101, subdiv. (d)).

In *Connerly v. State Personnel Board,* 92 Cal. App. 4th 16 (Ct. App. Cal., 3d App. Dist. 2001), a group of plaintiffs challenged this law, and others involving affirmative action in the sale of state bonds, the state lottery, and the state civil service system. Although a state trial court had upheld the law, ruling that the community college law did not require the colleges to grant preferential treatment to any particular group, a state appellate court reversed, ruling that the law was incompatible with Proposition 209.

Voters in the state of Washington also approved a ballot question that outlawed the use of affirmative action in employment or admissions decisions (see Section 8.2.5 of this book). Neither the California nor the Washington law is directly affected by the U.S. Supreme Court's ruling in *Grutter.*

5.4.5. Conclusions. The collective implications of the complex decisions discussed in subsections 5.4.1 to 5.4.4 above, and especially the sharp differences of opinion by the Supreme Court justices regarding the lawfulness of race- or gender-conscious employment decisions, mean that employment decisions linked to affirmative action should be made with caution. It appears that private institutions that can document "manifest" underrepresentation of women or minority faculty or staff in certain positions, and that can show a substantial gap between the proportion of qualified women and minorities in the relevant labor market and their representation in the institution's faculty workforce, may be able to act in conformance with a carefully developed affirmative action plan.

Public colleges and universities located in states subject to *Adams* agreements (see Sections 13.5.2 & 13.5.8) will very likely have an easier time meeting the standards of the equal protection clause for voluntary affirmative action plans. Furthermore, for public institutions operating under the dictates of a judicially supervised consent decree regarding remedies for prior discrimination, the Civil Rights Act of 1991 has removed the threat of challenges to remedial employment decisions made under the aegis of the consent decree. In *Martin v. Wilks,* 490 U.S. 755 (1989), the Supreme Court had ruled that any nonparty to the litigation culminating in a consent decree could later challenge both the decree and employment decisions made in conformance with that decree. Congress overturned the result in *Martin v. Wilks* by adding a new subsection to Section 703 of Title VII of the Civil Rights Act of 1964 (42 U.S.C. § 2000e-2). The law now provides that a litigated or consent judgment may not be challenged by a person who had actual notice of the proposed judgment or order prior to its entry and an opportunity to object, or by a person whose interests were adequately represented by another person who had challenged the judgment or order.

For public colleges and universities that do not have a clearly documented history of prior discrimination, or that are unwilling to rely on such a rationale, it will apparently be necessary to rely on a diversity rationale in any attempt to justify the use of race or gender preferences in employment. In such a situation, to maximize its chance of success, the institution would need to demonstrate clearly how affirmative action-related hiring or promotion will promote the type of educational diversity that the Court found to be a compelling state interest in *Grutter* and *Gratz*. This showing may depend upon the specifics of each job or position covered by the affirmative action plan. For example, the race, gender, or national origin of a residence hall counselor or a teaching assistant might be linked to educational diversity, whereas it would be more difficult to demonstrate this linkage for a dining services worker, custodian, or groundskeeper.

Sec. 5.5. Application of Nondiscrimination Laws to Religious Institutions

A major coverage issue under federal and state employment discrimination statutes is their applicability to religious institutions, including religiously affiliated colleges and universities. The issue parallels those that have arisen under federal collective bargaining law (see the *Catholic Bishop* case in Section 4.5), unemployment compensation law (see *St. Martin Evangelical Lutheran Church v. South Dakota*, 451 U.S. 772 (1981)), and federal tax law (see the *Bob Jones* case in Section 13.3.2, footnote 38). Title VII (see Section 5.2.1 of this book), the primary federal employment discrimination statute, has been the focus of most litigation on religious institutions.[35]

Section 702(a) of Title VII, 42 U.S.C. § 2000e-1(a), specifically exempts "a religious corporation, association, educational institution, or society" from the statute's prohibition against religious discrimination "with respect to the employment of individuals of a particular religion" if they are hired to "perform work connected with the carrying on by such corporation, association,

---

[35]Issues about coverage of religious schools, however, can and do arise under other federal employment discrimination statutes. See, for example, *Dole v. Shenadoah Baptist Church*, 899 F.2d 1389 (4th Cir. 1990) (Equal Pay Act); and *DeMarco v. Holy Cross High School*, 4 F.3d 166 (2d Cir. 1993) (Age Discrimination in Employment Act). Such issues can and do also arise under state employment discrimination statutes. See, for example, *Schmoll v. Chapman University*, 83 Cal. Rptr. 2d 426 (Cal. App. 1999).

educational institution, or society of its activities."[36] The phrase "its activities" is not addressed in the statute, and it was unclear whether the organization's "activities" had to be closely related to its religious mission to be included within the exemption, or whether all of its activities would be exempt. The U.S. Supreme Court addressed this issue in *Corporation of the Presiding Bishop of the Church of Jesus Christ of Latter-Day Saints v. Amos*, 483 U.S. 327 (1987), a case concerning a challenge to the Mormon Church's decision that all employees working for a gymnasium owned by the church but open to the public must be members of the Mormon Church. The plaintiffs argued that, although Section 702(a) could properly be applied to the religious activities of a religious organization, the First Amendment's establishment clause did not permit the government to extend the exemption to jobs that had no relationship to religion. The Supreme Court held that Section 702 does not distinguish between secular and religious job activities, and that the Section 702 exemption could apply to all job positions of a religious organization without violating the establishment clause. The Court reasoned that Section 702's purpose is to minimize governmental interference with the decisions of religious organizations, and it would be "a significant burden on a religious organization to require it, on pain of substantial liability, to predict which of its activities a secular court will consider religious" (483 U.S. at 336).

Section 702(a) was also at issue in *Killinger v. Samford University*, 917 F. Supp. 773 (N.D. Ala. 1996), *affirmed*, 113 F.3d 196 (11th Cir. 1997), as was Section 703(e)(2) (42 U.S.C. § 2000e-2(e)(2)), another Title VII provision providing a similar exemption for some religiously affiliated schools. Section 703(e)(2) applies to any "school, college, university, or other educational institution" that is "owned, supported, controlled, or managed by a particular religion or religious corporation, association, or society. . . ." Institutions fitting this characterization are exempted from Title VII with respect to "hir[ing] and employ[ing] employees of a particular religion." In *Killinger*, the plaintiff was a faculty member at Samford University, a private institution affiliated with the Baptist faith. He alleged that administrators at Samford would not permit him to teach certain religion courses at its Beeson Divinity School because of the theological and philosophical positions that Killinger had taken. In defense, the university invoked the Section 702(a) and Section 703(e)(2) exemptions. The major issue was whether the university was a "religious" institution or was supported or controlled by a "religious" entity for purposes of the exemptions. The federal

---

[36]A college need not be affiliated with a particular denomination in order to receive the protection of the Section 702(a) exemption. In *Wirth v. College of the Ozarks*, 26 F. Supp. 2d 1185 (W.D. Mo. 1998), for example, a federal district court ruled that the College of the Ozarks was a religious organization that qualified for the exemption despite the fact that the college is a nondenominational Christian organization. Significant indicators of its religious nature were that the college's mission is to provide a "Christian education," that it belongs to the Coalition for Christian Colleges, and that it is a member of the Association of Presbyterian Colleges and Universities. The appellate court affirmed the trial court's ruling in an unpublished *per curiam* opinion (2000 U.S. App. LEXIS 3549 (8th Cir. 2000)).

district court, and then the appellate court, determined that the university is religious and is supported by a religious entity, and therefore applied both exemptions. The courts reasoned that the university was controlled by the Baptists, since all of its trustees were required to be practicing Baptists; that its students were required to attend religious convocations; and that university publications emphasized the religious nature of the education provided. Moreover, Samford received a substantial proportion of its budget (7 percent) from the Alabama Baptist State Convention, and the university required all faculty to subscribe to the Baptist Statement of Faith and Message. Both the Internal Revenue Service and the U.S. Department of Education recognized Samford as a religious institution. The appellate court noted that the substantial contribution from the Baptist Convention was sufficient, standing alone, to bring the university within the reach of Section 703(e)(2), since the university was "supported" in "substantial part" by a religious corporation.

In *Pime v. Loyola University of Chicago*, 803 F.2d 351 (7th Cir. 1986), the court used a different provision of Title VII to protect a religious institution's autonomy to engage in preferential hiring. Affirming a lower court ruling (585 F. Supp. 435 (N.D. Ill. 1984)), the appellate court held that membership in a religious order can be a "bona fide occupational qualification" (BFOQ) within the meaning of Section 703(e)(1) (42 U.S.C. §2000e-2(e)(1)) of Title VII. The plaintiff, who was Jewish, had been a part-time lecturer in the university's philosophy department when it adopted a resolution requiring that seven of the department's thirty-one tenure-track positions be reserved for Jesuit priests. The court, finding a historical relationship between members of the religious order and the university, concluded that the Jesuit "presence" was a significant aspect of the university's educational traditions and character, and important to its successful operation.

But in *EEOC v. Kamehameha Schools*, 990 F.2d 458 (9th Cir. 1993), the court distinguished *Pime* and ruled that two private schools could not restrict their hiring to Protestant Christians, even though the will that established the schools so required. The court examined the schools' ownership and affiliation, their purpose, the religious affiliations of the students, and the degree to which the education provided by the schools was religious in character, concluding that the schools did not fit within the Section 702(a) exemption. The court then also ruled that being Protestant was not a bona fide occupational qualification for employment at the schools. (For an analysis of the *Kamehameha Schools* decision, see Jon M. VanDyke, "The Kamehameha Schools/Bishop Estate and the Constitution," 17 *U. Hawaii L. Rev.* 413 (1995).)

Although Title VII, as construed in *Amos, Killinger, and Pime,* sanctions religious preferences in hiring for religious institutions that qualify for the pertinent exemptions, the statute does not exempt them from its other prohibitions on race, national origin, and sex discrimination. If a religious organization seeks to escape these other nondiscrimination requirements, it must rely on its rights under the federal Constitution's establishment and free exercise clauses (see generally Section 1.6 of this book). In two cases decided in 1980 and 1981, the U.S. Court of Appeals for the Fifth Circuit thoroughly analyzed the extent to which religious colleges and universities are subject to the race and sex discrimination prohibitions of Title VII. The cases also include useful analysis of how a religious institution may respond to investigatory subpoenas and other information requests served on it by the federal Equal Employment Opportunity Commission.

The first case, *EEOC v. Mississippi College,* 626 F.2d 477 (5th Cir. 1980), concerned a four-year coeducational school owned by the Mississippi Baptist Convention, an organization of Southern Baptist churches in Mississippi. The Baptist Convention's written policy stated a preference for employing active members of Baptist churches and also prohibited women from teaching courses concerning the Bible because no woman had been ordained as a minister in a Southern Baptist church. A female part-time faculty member, Dr. Summers, filed a charge with the EEOC when the college denied her application for a full-time faculty position. Summers alleged that the college's choice of a male constituted sex discrimination and that the college's employment policies discriminated against women and minorities as a class. When the EEOC attempted to investigate Summers's charge, the college refused to cooperate, and the EEOC sought court enforcement of a subpoena.

The college asserted that it had selected a male instead of Summers because he was a Baptist and she was not—thus arguing that religion, not sex, was the grounds for its decision and that its decision was therefore exempt from EEOC review under Section 702(a). The court agreed in principle with the college but indicated the need for additional evidence on whether the college had accurately characterized its failure to hire Summers:

> If the district court determines on remand that the College applied its policy of preferring Baptists over non-Baptists in granting the faculty position to Bailey rather than Summers, then Section 702 exempts that decision from the application of Title VII and would preclude any investigation by the EEOC to determine whether the College used the preference policy as a guise to hide some other form of discrimination. On the other hand, should the evidence disclose only that the College's preference policy could have been applied, but in fact it was not considered by the College in determining which applicant to hire, Section 702 does not bar the EEOC's investigation of Summers' individual sex discrimination claim [626 F.2d at 486].

The college also argued, in response to Summers's individual claim and her allegation of class discrimination against women and blacks, that (1) the employment relationship between a church-related school and its faculty is not covered by Title VII; and (2) if this relationship is within Title VII, its inclusion violates both the establishment clause and the free exercise clause of the First Amendment. The court easily rejected the first argument, reasoning that the relationship between a church-related school and its faculty is not comparable to the church-minister relationship that is beyond the scope of Title VII. The court spent more time on the second argument but rejected it as well.

Regarding the establishment clause, the court reasoned:

> The information requested by the EEOC's subpoena does not clearly implicate any religious practices of the College. . . . The only practice brought to the attention of the district court that is clearly predicated upon religious beliefs that

might not be protected by the exemption of Section 702 is the College's policy of hiring only men to teach courses in religion. The bare potential that Title VII would affect this practice does not warrant precluding the application of Title VII to the College.

* * * *

Although the College is a pervasively sectarian institution, the minimal burden imposed upon its religious practices by the application of Title VII and the limited nature of the resulting relationship between the federal government and the College cause us to find that application of the statute would not [violate the establishment clause] [626 F.2d at 487–88].

Regarding the free exercise clause, the court reasoned that:

the relevant inquiry is not the impact of the statute upon the institution, but the impact of the statute upon the institution's exercise of its sincerely held religious beliefs. The fact that those of the College's employment practices subject to Title VII do not embody religious beliefs or practices protects the College from any real threat of undermining its religious purpose of fulfilling the evangelical role of the Mississippi Baptist Convention, and allows us to conclude that the impact of Title VII on the free exercise of religious beliefs is minimal [626 F.2d at 488].

Even if the college had engaged in sex (or race) discrimination based on its religious beliefs, said the court,

creating an exemption from the statutory enactment greater than that provided by Section 702 would seriously undermine the means chosen by Congress to combat discrimination and is not constitutionally required. . . . If the environment in which [religious educational] institutions seek to achieve their religious and educational goals reflects unlawful discrimination, those discriminatory attitudes will be perpetuated with an influential segment of society, the detrimental effect of which cannot be estimated [626 F.2d at 488–89].

On this point, however, the court in *EEOC v. Mississippi College* was writing prior to the U.S. Supreme Court's decision in *Employment Division v. Smith,* 494 U.S. 872 (1990) (discussed in Section 1.6.2). That case introduced a new aspect to free exercise analysis: whether the statute at issue was "generally applicable" and neutral toward religion. It is possible that Title VII's prohibitions on race and sex discrimination would fit this characterization, in which case the courts would no longer need to engage in the type of "strict scrutiny" analysis highlighted by the court in the *Mississippi College* case.

In *EEOC v. Southwestern Baptist Theological Seminary,* 651 F.2d 277 (5th Cir. 1981), the same court refined its *Mississippi College* analysis in the special context of religious seminaries. The defendant seminary is a nonprofit corporation owned, operated, supported, and controlled by the Southern Baptist Convention. This seminary offers degrees only in theology, religious education, and church music, and its purposes and character were described by the court as "wholly sectarian." The EEOC had asked the seminary to complete form EEO-6, a routine information report. When the seminary refused, the EEOC sued to compel compliance under 42 U.S.C. § 2000e-8(c), Title VII's record-keeping and reporting provision.

The court determined that the general principles set out in *Mississippi College* applied to this case but that the differing factual setting of this case required a result partly different from that in *Mississippi College*. In particular, the court held that "Title VII does not apply to the employment relationship between this seminary and its faculty." Reasoning that the Southwestern Baptist Seminary, unlike Mississippi College, was "entitled to the status of 'church'" and that its faculty "fit the definition of 'ministers,'" the court determined that Congress did not intend to include this ecclesiastical relationship, which is a special concern of the First Amendment, within the scope of Title VII. Using the same reasoning, the court also excluded from Title VII administrative positions that are "traditionally ecclesiastical or ministerial," citing as likely examples the "President and Executive Vice-President of the Seminary, the chaplain, the dean of men and women, the academic deans, and those other personnel who equate to or supervise faculty." But the court refused to exclude other administrative and support staff from Title VII, even if the employees filling those positions were ordained ministers.

Having held "nonministerial" staff to be within Title VII, the court then considered whether the First Amendment would prohibit the EEOC from applying its reporting requirement to those employees. Again using the principles of *Mississippi College,* the court concluded that the First Amendment was not a bar and that the EEOC could require the seminary to provide the information requested in the EEO-6 form for its nonministerial employees. The court left open the question whether the First Amendment would prohibit the EEOC from obtaining further information on the seminary's nonministerial employees by use of the more intrusive investigatory subpoena, as was done in *Mississippi College.*

The "ministerial exception" recognized in *Southwestern Baptist Theological Seminary* was also at issue in *EEOC v. Catholic University,* 83 F.3d 455 (D.C. Cir. 1996). In that case, Sister McDonough, a Catholic nun in the Dominican Order, challenged a negative tenure decision at Catholic University. She had been hired as an assistant professor in the department of canon law, the first woman to hold a tenure-track position in the department. Five years later, she was promoted to associate professor and shortly afterward submitted an application for tenure. After a series of split votes and revotes at various levels of review, McDonough was ultimately denied tenure after a negative vote of the Academic Senate's Committee on Appointments and Promotions. McDonough, joined by the EEOC, filed a Title VII sex discrimination claim against the university. The district court determined that it could not review the university's tenure decision because McDonough's role in the department of canon law was the "functional equivalent of the task of a minister," and judicial review would therefore violate both the free exercise and the establishment clauses of the First Amendment (856 F. Supp. 1 (D.D.C. 1994)). In affirming, the U.S. Court of Appeals for the D.C. Circuit rejected the plaintiffs' argument that the "ministerial" exception should not apply to McDonough because she was neither an ordained priest nor did she perform religious duties. The appellate court determined, first, that ordination was irrelevant; the ministerial exception applies to individuals who perform religious duties, whether or not they have been ordained. Second, the court determined that McDonough's duties were indeed religious because the department's mission was to instruct students in "the fundamental body of ecclesiastical laws," and, as the only department in the United States empowered by the Vatican to confer ecclesiastical degrees in canon law, the mission of its faculty, including McDonough, was "to foster and teach sacred doctrine and the disciplines related to it" (quoting from the university's Canonical Statutes). Furthermore, said the court, it was irrelevant that the tenure denial had not been on religious grounds. The act of reviewing the employment decision of a religious body concerning someone with "ministerial" duties was offensive to the U.S. Constitution, regardless of the basis for the decision.

The above cases provide substantial clarification of Title VII's application to religious colleges and universities. What emerges is a balanced interpretation of the Section 702(a) and 703(e)(2) exemptions against the backdrop of First Amendment law. It is clear that these exemptions protect only employment decisions based on the religion of the applicant or employee. In most circumstances, the First Amendment does not appear to provide any additional special treatment for religious colleges; the two exemptions provide the full extent of protection that the First Amendment requires. There is one established exception to this position: the "ministerial exception" recognized by the *Southwestern Baptist Theological Seminary* and *Catholic University* cases, which provides additional protection by precluding the application of Title VII to "ministerial" employees. A second possible exception, mentioned briefly in the *Mississippi College* case, may be urged in other contexts: If an institution practices some form of discrimination prohibited by Title VII or other nondiscrimination laws, but can prove that its discrimination is based on religious belief, it may argue that the First Amendment protects such discrimination. The developing case law does not yet provide a definitive response to this argument. But the U.S. Supreme Court's opinion in the *Bob Jones* case (Section 13.3.2, footnote 38)—although addressing a tax benefit rather than a regulatory program such as Title VII—does suggest one way for courts to respond to the argument. As to the free exercise clause aspects of the argument, however, courts must now also take account of the Court's decision in *Employment Division v. Smith* (above), which suggests another approach that may involve only minimal scrutiny by the courts.

Selected Annotated Bibliography

Sec. 5.1 (The Interplay of Statutes, Regulations, and Constitutional Protections)

Franke, Ann H. (ed.). *Employment Discrimination Training for College and Universities: Resources for Developing Internal Programs for Faculty, Staff and Administrators* (National Association of College and University Attorneys, 2002). Provides resources to assist administrators in developing training programs concerning employment discrimination. Includes journal articles, conference outlines, institutional policies, training documents, and workshop evaluation forms.

Johnson, Laura Todd, & Schoonmaker, Linda C. *What to Do When the EEOC Comes Knocking on Your Campus Door* (National Association of College and University Attorneys, 2004). Discusses how an institution should respond to an EEOC charge, how to conduct internal investigations, what type of documentation should be collected and how to determine what should be shared with the EEOC. Also discusses the consequences of not participating in the EEOC investigation and the consequences of the failure of mediation. Includes tips for preparing for a visit by the EEOC.

Sec. 5.2 *(Sources of Law)*

Baldus, David C., & Cole, James L. *Statistical Proof of Discrimination* (Shepards/McGraw-Hill, 1980). A guide to the proper uses of statistics in discrimination litigation, with emphasis on employment discrimination. The book will be helpful to both plaintiffs' and defendants' counsel in such actions. Includes useful glossary and bibliography.

DiGiovanni, Nicholas. *Age Discrimination: An Administrator's Guide* (College and University Personnel Association, 1989). Written for campus administrators. Includes an overview of the ADEA, a discussion of how an age discrimination lawsuit is conducted and defended, and suggestions for minimizing the risk of liability. Additional chapters discuss planning for retirement (including the EEOC guidelines for retirement incentives), practical considerations in evaluating and counseling older workers, waivers and releases, and a table of state laws prohibiting age discrimination. (This book predates the passage of the Older Workers Benefit Protection Act, discussed in Section 5.2.6.)

Jewett, Cynthia L., & Rutherford, Lisa H. *What to Do When the U.S. Department of Education, Office for Civil Rights Comes to Campus* (National Association of College and University Attorneys, 2005). Discusses the actions colleges should take when they receive notice of an OCR investigation, including how to resolve a complaint, how to respond to a compliance review, and how to prepare for an on-site investigation. Includes a list of additional resources and websites.

Lindemann, Barbara, & Grossman, Paul (eds.). *Employment Discrimination Law* (3d ed., Bureau of National Affairs, 1996, with 2002 Cumulative Supplement). The standard treatise on employment discrimination law, updated regularly. Covers all federal equal employment laws, cites more than 7,000 cases, provides practical tips for defending employment discrimination litigation.

Lindemann, Barbara T., & Kadue, David D. *Age Discrimination in Employment Law* (Bureau of National Affairs, 2002). Reviews a variety of potential legal issues involving hiring, evaluation, promotion, and termination of older workers. Includes a section on special issues for unions and implications for collective bargaining agreements. Appendices include relevant cases, regulations, EEOC guidance, and sample policies and forms.

Perritt, Henry H., Jr. *Americans With Disabilities Act Handbook* (3d ed., Wiley, 1997, and periodic supp.). A comprehensive practice guide to Title I of the ADA. Chapters include a description of the statute, the legislative history, the various categories of protection, the employer's legal obligations, procedural and evidentiary issues, and suggestions for modifying employment policies and practices to comply with the ADA. The Rehabilitation Act of 1973 also is described, and an appendix provides a summary of the ADA's public accommodation provisions.

Sec. 5.3 (The Protected Classes)

Achtenberg, Roberta. *Sexual Orientation and the Law* (Clark Boardman Callaghan, 1985, and periodic supp.). A comprehensive treatise on many areas of the law related to homosexuality. Employment-related subjects include civil rights and discrimination, First Amendment issues, employment and AIDS, insurance and AIDS, and tax issues. Written for attorneys who represent gay clients, the book includes sample forms and contracts.

Barnard, Thomas H., & Downing, Timothy J. "Emerging Law on Sexual Orientation and Employment," 29 *U. Memphis L. Rev.* 555 (1999). Summarizes state and municipal legal prohibitions on discrimination on the basis of sexual orientation. Also discusses proposed federal legislation that would prohibit such discrimination, the military policy concerning gays, and same-sex benefits.

Clark, Matthew. "Stating a Title VII Claim for Sexual Orientation Discrimination in the Workplace: The Legal Theories Available After *Rene v. MGM Grand Hotel*," 51 *UCLA L. Rev.* 313 (2003). Discusses recent cases in which courts applied Title VII to discrimination on the basis of sexual orientation. Analyzes three legal theories that plaintiffs have used to challenge alleged discrimination on the basis of sexual orientation, and proposes an additional theory for use in these cases.

Clark, Robert L., & Hammond, P. Brett (eds.). *To Retire or Not? Retirement Policy and Practice in Higher Education* (University of Pennsylvania Press, 2001). Includes several studies of the impact on faculty retirement rates of the end of mandatory retirement for faculty. Discusses phased retirement programs, early retirement programs, and other incentives for retirement.

Cole, Elsa (ed.). *Sexual Harassment on Campus: A Legal Compendium* (4th ed., National Association of College and University Attorneys, 2003). Contains sample policies from various institutions as well as suggestions on how to develop a policy and how to handle complaints of harassment.

Cole, Elsa, & Hustoles, Thomas P. *How to Conduct a Sexual Harassment Investigation* (rev. ed., National Association of College and University Attorneys, 2002). Provides a checklist of suggestions for conducting an appropriate and timely sexual harassment investigation. Suggests questions to be asked at each step of the investigation, and offers alternatives for resolving harassment complaints.

Dziech, Billie Wright, & Hawkings, Michael W. *Sexual Harassment and Higher Education* (Garland, 1998). The authors, one a professor and one a practicing attorney, review the legal and regulatory environment and its application to higher education; discuss the importance of policy development that is sensitive to the institution's culture; examine the reactions of harassment targets; discuss the treatment of nonmeritorious cases; and review the effectiveness of banning consensual relationships.

Engle, Karen. "The Persistence of Neutrality: The Failure of the Religious Accommodation Provision to Redeem Title VII," 76 *Texas L. Rev.* 317 (1997). Compares judicial resolution of religious discrimination claims with other claims brought under Title VII; examines judicial interpretation of Title VII's reasonable accommodation requirement in comparison to the ADA's accommodation requirement.

Lindemann, Barbara, & Kadue, David D. *Sexual Harassment in Employment Law* (Bureau of National Affairs, 1992, with 1999 Cumulative Supplement). Discusses prevention and defense of sexual harassment claims; provides sample policies, EEOC guidelines, and relevant statutory text. Includes discussion of mandatory arbitration agreements, privilege issues, and wrongful termination claims by alleged harassers.

Paludi, Michele A. (ed.). *Ivory Power: Sexual Harassment on Campus* (State University of New York Press, 1991). A collection of articles and essays on sexual harassment. Includes discussions of the definition of harassment; the impact of sexual harassment on the cognitive, physical, and emotional well-being of victims; the characteristics of harassers; and procedures for dealing with sexual harassment complaints on campus. Sample materials for training faculty, draft forms for receiving harassment complaints, lists of organizations and other resources concerned with sexual harassment, and references to other written materials are also included.

Paludi, Michele A. (ed.). *Sexual Harassment on College Campuses: Abusing the Ivory Power* (State University of New York Press, 1996). A revised and updated edition of *Ivory Power.* Includes updates on case law and additional material on harassment training; expanded sections on consensual relationships and on dealing with targets of harassment; and additional information on training and resources on developing harassment policies and grievance procedures.

Rothstein, Laura F. "The Employer's Duty to Accommodate Performance and Conduct Deficiencies of Individuals with Mental Impairments Under Disability Discrimination Laws," 47 *Syracuse L. Rev.* 931 (1997). Reviews federal disability discrimination law and its impact on employer discipline or discharge of employees for misconduct.

Rubenstein, William B. "Do Gay Rights Laws Matter?: An Empirical Assessment," 75 *S. Cal. L. Rev.* 65 (2001). Analyzes discrimination complaints brought in states with protective legislation, concluding that a federal law protecting gays against employment discrimination would not result in a "deluge" of lawsuits.

Sandler, Bernice R., & Shoop, Robert J. (eds.). *Sexual Harassment on Campus: A Guide for Administrators, Faculty, and Students* (Allyn & Bacon, 1997). Includes chapters on peer sexual harassment of students, faculty harassment of other faculty, electronic sexual harassment, how to develop an effective policy, how to conduct an investigation, and numerous other issues. A thorough and well-organized resource for campus administrators and faculty.

Stoner, Edward N. II, & Ryan, Catherine S. "*Burlington, Faragher, Oncale,* and Beyond: Recent Developments in Title VII Jurisprudence," 26 *J. Coll. & Univ. Law* 645 (2000). Discusses three significant U.S. Supreme Court decisions related to sexual harassment in employment. Discusses subsequent lower court rulings that rely on these cases, and suggests ways that institutions of higher education can prevent and avoid liability for sexual harassment.

Weber, Mark C. "Disability Discrimination Litigation and Institutions of Higher Education," 25 *J. Coll. & Univ. Law* 53 (1998). Discusses administrative enforcement and litigation issues, settlement, and alternatives to litigation, for cases brought by employees or students.

See the Brandenberg entry for Section 13.5.

Sec. 5.4 (Affirmative Action)

Anderson, Terry H. *The Pursuit of Fairness: A History of Affirmative Action* (Oxford University Press, 2004). Provides a history of affirmative action, from the nondiscrimination policies of Presidents Roosevelt and Truman through the U.S. Supreme Court's University of Michigan cases. Discusses the multiple views of affirmative action and the central role of U.S. Presidents in the debate and the policy issues.

Foster, Sheila. "Difference and Equality: A Critical Assessment of the Concept of 'Diversity,'" 1993 *Wis. L. Rev.* 105 (1993). Explores and criticizes the concept of diversity as developed through equal protection jurisprudence, with special emphasis on *Bakke* and *Metro Broadcasting.* Examines the concept of "difference" and discusses that concept against the history of exclusion of various groups. Also discussed is the tension between equal treatment and equal outcomes.

Oppenheimer, David B. "Distinguishing Five Models of Affirmative Action," 4 *Berkeley Women's L.J.* 42 (1988). Discusses quotas, preference systems, the use of goals and timetables for selected occupations, expanded recruitment pools, and affirmative commitment not to discriminate as alternate models for increasing the proportion of underrepresented persons in the workforce. Selected discrimination lawsuits are also analyzed.

Tilles, Eric A. "Lessons From *Bakke*: The Effect of *Grutter* on Affirmative Action in Employment," 6 *U. Pa. J. Lab. & Emp. L.* 451 (2004). Reviews the effect of *Bakke* (discussed in Section 8.2.5) on subsequent litigation concerning affirmative action in employment. Concludes that *Grutter* may have some impact on employment-based affirmative action in public sector organizations, but that the current affirmative action jurisprudence in private sector employment may limit the impact of *Grutter.*

White, Rebecca Hanner. "Special Feature: The Future of Affirmative Action: *Gratz* and *Grutter* in Context: Affirmative Action in the Workplace: The Significance of *Grutter*?" 92 *Ky. L.J.* 263 (2003–2004). Reviews the judicial standards used to evaluate voluntary affirmative action plans under Title VII, including the Third Circuit's rejection of diversity as a permissible rationale for voluntary affirmative action. Suggests that, after *Grutter,* public employers may be able to demonstrate that diversity is a compelling public interest, but concludes that *Grutter*'s impact on voluntary affirmative action in employment, in either public or private organizations, is still an open question.

Sec. 5.5 (Application of Nondiscrimination Laws to Religious Institutions)

Sandin, Robert T. *Autonomy and Faith: Religious Preference in Employment Decisions in Religiously Affiliated Higher Education* (Omega Publications, 1990). Discusses the circumstances under which religiously affiliated colleges and universities may use religion as a selection criterion. Provides a taxonomy of religiously affiliated colleges and models of their preferential hiring policies, reviews state and federal nondiscrimination statutes, summarizes judicial precedent regarding secular and religious functions in establishment clause litigation, and discusses the interplay between religious preference and academic freedom.

PART THREE

THE COLLEGE AND ITS FACULTY

6

Faculty Employment Issues

Sec. 6.1. Overview

The legal relationship between a college and its faculty members is defined by an increasingly complex web of principles and authorities. In general, this relationship is governed by the common law doctrines, statutes, and constitutional provisions discussed in Chapter Four and Chapter Five. The particular applications of this law to faculty may differ from its applications to other employees, however, because courts and administrative agencies often take account of the unique characteristics of institutional customs and practices regarding faculty (such as tenure) and of academic freedom principles that protect faculty members but not all other employees. Therefore, special protections for faculty may emanate from contract law (see especially Section 6.2), labor relations law (Section 6.3), employment discrimination law (Sections 6.4 & 6.5), and, in public institutions, constitutional law (see especially Sections 6.6 & 6.7) and public employment statutes and regulations. Federal regulations also affect the faculty employment relationship (Section 13.2).

Sec. 6.2. Faculty Contracts

6.2.1. Overview. The special nature of the college's relationship with its faculty complicates the development and interpretation of faculty contracts. The college may enter formal written contracts with individual faculty members, or it may simply send an annual letter stating the faculty member's teaching and other obligations for the year. The college may have a faculty handbook that discusses faculty governance rights and responsibilities, or it may have a detailed, collectively negotiated agreement with an agent of the faculty (or both). Particularly for faculty at private colleges, contracts are a very important source of faculty and institutional rights and responsibilities. Faculty at public colleges may enjoy rights created by statute, but public colleges are making increasing use of contracts to define and delimit faculty—and institutional—rights and responsibilities.

One development of interest to administrators (and concern to faculty) is the suggestion that renewable term contracts replace lifetime tenure. While most of the shifts from tenure policies to long-term contracts have occurred within the private college sector (Robin Wilson, "Contracts Replace the Tenure Track for a Growing Number of Professors," *Chron. Higher Educ.*, June 12, 1998, A12), some states have considered this alternative as well ("Footnotes," *Chron. Higher Educ.*, May 14, 1999, A14). (For a survey of alternatives to tenure at a variety of institutions, see William T. Mallon, "Standard Deviations: Faculty Appointment Policies at Institutions Without Tenure," in Cathy A. Trower, ed., *Policies on Faculty Appointment: Standard Practices and Unusual Arrangements* (Anker, 2000).)

Contracts are governed by common law, which may vary considerably by state. As is the case for nonfaculty employees (see Section 4.3.2), faculty handbooks and oral promises to faculty have been ruled to create binding contracts in some states, while other state courts have rejected this theory. For example, in *Sola v. Lafayette College*, 804 F.2d 40 (3d Cir. 1986), a faculty member sought to maintain a cause of action for tenure denial by relying on the faculty handbook's language concerning affirmative action. The court ruled that such language had contractual status and provided the faculty member with a cause of action. Similarly, in *Arneson v. Board of Trustees, McKendree College*, 569 N.E.2d 252 (Ill. App. Ct. 1991), the court ruled that the faculty manual was a contract; however, a state appellate court in Louisiana reached the opposite result in *Marson v. Northwestern State University*, 607 So. 2d 1093 (La. Ct. App. 1992). In *Yates v. Board of Regents of Lamar University System*, 654 F. Supp. 979 (E.D. Tex. 1987), an untenured faculty member who had no written contract challenged a midyear discharge, asserting that oral representations made by the institution's officials constituted a contract not to be dismissed prior to the end of the academic year. The court, in denying summary judgment for the university, agreed that oral promises and policies could create an implied contract, citing *Perry v. Sindermann* (see Section 6.7.2.1). On the other hand, if the institution has a written tenure policy, a faculty member's claim that he had gained tenure through an unwritten, informal "understanding" will not succeed (*Jones v. University of Central Oklahoma*, 910 P.2d 987 (Okla. 1995)).

Unless a faculty handbook, individual contract, or other written policy document promises tenure, courts may be hesitant to infer that a tenure system exists. In *Tuomala v. Regent University*, 477 S.E.2d 501 (Va. 1996), for example, the Supreme Court of Virginia ruled that faculty at Regent University did not have tenure. Three professors at Regent had filed declaratory judgment suits asking the court to declare that they had tenure, and could only be dismissed if they were in breach of their contracts or unless their academic unit was disbanded. The university defended by stating that the individual contracts that the faculty had signed indicated that they were "three-year continuing contracts" that, under the terms of the faculty handbook, could be renewed annually. Determining that the language of both the contracts and the faculty handbook was ambiguous, the court reviewed testimony by members of the board of trustees concerning their intent vis-à-vis tenure. The board members denied that the university had a tenure system, stating that the three-year "continuing contracts" were a mechanism for cushioning the economic blow of job loss for a faculty member by ensuring two years of income after the faculty member's services were no longer desired. Although the university president had stated, during an accreditation team visit by the American Bar Association, that the law school faculty members were tenured, the court ruled that the president did not have the discretion to modify the trustees' determination that there would be no tenure system at Regent University.

Even if a university acknowledges that it has a tenure system, there may be a difference of opinion as to where the locus of tenure is. Is it in the position, the department, the school, or the institution as a whole? This issue is particularly significant when a reduction in force or program closure is initiated (see Section 6.8). In *Board of Regents of Kentucky State University v. Gale*, 898 S.W.2d 517 (Ky. Ct. App. 1995), the dispute involved whether Professor Gale's tenure was in the endowed chair he held or whether it was in the department or the university. The court examined the offer letter that Gale had accepted; it offered him the position of professor of humanities occupying Kentucky State University's Endowed Chair in the Humanities, and provided for tenure upon appointment to that position. When the university later attempted to remove Gale from the endowed chair, increase his teaching load, and reduce his salary, Gale sought a declaratory judgment and an injunction preventing the university from taking this action. Calling the university's argument a "bait and switch" approach, the court ruled that both the literal terms of the offer letter and academic custom with respect to attracting faculty stars to endowed chairs supported Gale's argument that his tenure was in the endowed chair. Had the university provided for a periodic review of Gale's performance in the endowed chair position, or had it specified that tenure was in the department and he would occupy the chair for a specific period of time, the result of the litigation would have been different.

Contracts may be used to limit the rights of faculty as well as to provide certain rights. For example, in *Kirschenbaum v. Northwestern University*, 728 N.E.2d 752 (Ct. App. Ill. 2000), the plaintiff, a tenured professor of psychiatry at Northwestern's medical school, brought a breach of contract claim against the university for failure to provide him with a salary. The court examined the language of the four documents that comprised the professor's contract. Two of the four documents specified that the professor's "base salary" was zero, and that total salary would be recommended annually by the department chair. The plaintiff had not received a salary from the university, but had from its affiliated hospital and a faculty practice plan. When the plaintiff's salary was reduced by the affiliated organizations because he had not generated sufficient clinical revenue, he sued the university.

Both the trial and appellate courts interpreted the contractual documents as providing for tenure but not for a salary. They found that the plaintiff was notified and understood that the relationship with the university involved tenure but no compensation, and that his compensation would be provided from other sources.

Even if written institutional policies are clear, administrators may make oral representations to faculty members or candidates for faculty positions that either contradict the written policies or that seem to create additional employment security that the institution may not have intended to provide. For example, in *The Johns Hopkins University v. Ritter* (discussed in Section 6.7.1), two faculty members with "visiting professor" titles failed to convince a state appellate court that they had tenured status on the basis of the department chair's assurances to that effect. The court rejected that argument, stating that the chair lacked both actual and apparent authority to abrogate the university's written tenure policies, which provided that only the board of trustees could grant tenure.

In *Geddes v. Northwest Missouri State University*, 49 F.3d 426 (8th Cir. 1995), a federal appellate court rejected a faculty member's claim that nonrenewal of her contract was impermissible because she was tenured. Geddes had been hired as dean, without tenure, of the School of Communications. When that school was merged with the School of Fine Arts three years later, Geddes was not offered the deanship of the combined school, but was offered the opportunity to continue as a professor in the speech department. She received annual contracts each year. At the time of the merger, the university's president had assured Geddes that she could teach at the university "for the rest of her life if she wanted to." The faculty handbook stated, however, that oral promises did not have contractual status, and that tenure could be awarded only after the formal tenure review process and only by the board of regents. The court rejected Geddes's tenure claim, stating that Geddes's reliance on the president's statement was not reasonable in light of the specificity of the annual contracts, the faculty handbook, and the university's tenure policies.

Some contracts clearly state that another document has been incorporated into the terms of employment. For a postsecondary institution, such documents as the faculty handbook, institutional bylaws, or guidelines of the American Association of University Professors (AAUP) may be referred to in the contract. The extent to which the terms of such outside writings become part of the faculty employment contract is discussed in *Brady v. Board of Trustees of Nebraska State Colleges*, 242 N.W.2d 616 (Neb. 1976), where the contract of a tenured professor at Wayne State College incorporated "the college bylaws, policies, and practices relating to academic tenure and faculty dismissal procedures." When the institution dismissed the professor, using procedures that violated a section of the bylaws, the court held that the termination was ineffective:

> There can be no serious question but that the bylaws of the governing body with respect to termination and conditions of the employment became a part of the employment contract between the college and [the professor]. At the time of the offer and acceptance of initial appointment . . . [the professor] was advised in writing that the offer and acceptance . . . constituted a contract honoring the policies and practices set forth in the faculty handbook, which was furnished to him at that time [242 N.W.2d at 230–31].

A case litigated under New York law demonstrates the significance of an institution's decision to adopt certain AAUP policy statements and not to adopt others. Fordham University had adopted the AAUP's "1940 Statement of Principles on Academic Freedom and Tenure" but not its 1973 statement "On the Imposition of Tenure Quotas," in which the AAUP opposed tenure quotas. (Both statements are included in *AAUP Policy Documents and Reports* (9th ed., AAUP, 2001), 3–10 and 47–49.) Fordham denied tenure to faculty whose departments would exceed 60 percent tenured faculty if they were awarded tenure. A professor of social service who had been denied tenure because of the quota policy sued the university, claiming that the tenure quota policy violated both of the AAUP statements. In *Waring v. Fordham University,* 640 F. Supp. 42 (S.D.N.Y. 1986), the court, noting that the university had not adopted the 1973 Statement, ruled that the university's action was appropriate and not a breach of contract.

But not all institutional policies are contractually binding. For example, in *Goodkind v. University of Minnesota,* 417 N.W.2d 636 (Minn. 1988), a dental school professor sued for breach of contract, stating that the institution's policy for searching for a department chair was part of his employment contract and that the university's failure to follow the dental school's written search policy violated his contractual rights. The Minnesota Supreme Court disagreed, asserting that the search policy was a general statement of policy and not sufficiently related to the faculty member's own terms and conditions of employment to be considered contractually binding on the university.

A breach of contract claim brought by a professor found to have engaged in sexual harassment of students posed the novel idea that the *student* code of conduct was incorporated into the faculty employment contract. In *Maas v. Cornell University,* 721 N.E.2d 966 (N.Y. 1999), the court rejected the plaintiff's claim that the university's student code of conduct, which included policies on how sexual harassment complaints would be investigated and adjudicated, could provide the basis for a breach of contract claim by a faculty member. The court stated:

> [T]he University nowhere reflected an intent that the provisions of its Code would become terms of a discrete, implied-in-fact agreement. . . . While the Code and its attendant regulations promulgate the University's sexual harassment policy and provide procedures for dealing with sexual harassment claims, Maas' essential employment duties and rights are only indirectly affected by these provisions [721 N.E.2d at 970].

This result differs from the willingness of the court in *McConnell v. Howard University,* discussed in Section 6.2.3 below, to entertain a claim that the student code of conduct created a duty on the part of the college to protect the professor's "professional authority" in a dispute over the professor's right to maintain discipline in his classroom.

On occasion a court is asked to fill in the "gaps" in a written or unwritten contract by determining what the intent of the parties was, even if that intent was not directly or indirectly expressed. The parties' intent may sometimes be ascertained from oral statements made at the time a hiring decision is made. In *Lewis v. Loyola University of Chicago,* 500 N.E.2d 47 (Ill. App. Ct. 1986), the plaintiff, a professor of medicine and chair of the pathology department at the university's medical school, argued that two letters from the dean of the medical school, in which the dean promised to recommend Dr. Lewis for early tenure consideration as soon as he obtained a license to practice medicine in Illinois, constituted a contract and that the institution's failure to grant him tenure breached that contract.

In 1980, the dean, as part of the process of recruiting Lewis as chair of the pathology department, wrote two letters in which he explicitly promised to recommend Lewis for tenure. Lewis accepted the university's offer, and his official appointment letter incorporated by reference the provisions of the faculty handbook. Lewis served as chair for three years on one-year contracts; just before the expiration of the third one-year contract, he received notice relieving him of his duties as department chair and advising him that his next one-year contract would be a terminal contract.

The dean did not submit Lewis's tenure candidacy at the time he had promised to, and several months later he resigned as dean and became a full-time faculty member. Before his resignation, the dean told Lewis orally that he had forgotten to submit his name for tenure and that he would do it the following year. The dean assured Lewis that the oversight would not be harmful.

Although the university argued that the letters and the dean's oral promises should not be considered part of Lewis's employment contract, the court disagreed. Noting that "the record discloses conversations, meetings and correspondence over a period of a year," the court asserted that "[it] cannot seriously be argued that a form contract for a teaching position . . . embodied the complete agreement and understanding of the parties" (500 N.E.2d at 50). Furthermore, said the court, objective—rather than subjective—criteria were used to make the tenure decision at the medical school, and Lewis was able to demonstrate that deans' tenure recommendations were rarely reversed. The court agreed with the trial judge's finding of "ample evidence" to indicate that Lewis would have been tenured absent the dean's oversight.

The opinion contains a useful discussion of remedies in academic breach of contract cases. The trial court had awarded Lewis the balance of his salary from the terminal contract (about $36,500) but had also awarded him $100,000 annually until he became disabled, died, or reached age sixty-five. The appellate court reversed this latter award, stating that it was based on speculation about the probable length of Lewis's employment had his contract not been breached. Thus, despite the finding of a contractual breach and the finding that Lewis should have been tenured, his damage award was relatively low. Furthermore, contractual remedies generally do not include reinstatement.

Challenges to tenure denials brought by faculty against private colleges are usually framed as breach of contract claims. Many of these cases involved alleged failure by the college or its faculty and administrators to follow written policies and procedures, such as in *Berkowitz v. President and Fellows of Harvard College,* 2001 Mass. Super. LEXIS 4 (Superior Ct. Mass., January 4, 2001). In *Berkowitz,* a professor denied tenure by Harvard brought a breach of contract claim, alleging that Harvard had failed to follow its written grievance procedures as set forth in the faculty handbook. The court denied the college's motion to dismiss the claim, stating that it was reasonable for the plaintiff to rely on the procedures in the handbook. The case is discussed in Section 6.7.3.

Although judicial review is often deferential in cases involving subjective judgments about faculty performance (see the discussions of judicial deference in Sections 2.2.5 & 6.4), the courts will apply standard tools of contractual interpretation if the terms of the contract are unambiguous. For example, in *Ferrer v. Trustees of the University of Pennsylvania,* 825 A.2d 591 (Pa. 2002), a jury found that the university had breached the plaintiff's employment contract by punishing him for alleged research misconduct when he had been found innocent by a faculty investigative committee. Under the university's policies, the finding of the committee was binding on the institution, but the dean and provost imposed sanctions on the plaintiff despite the finding of the committee. The jury awarded Ferrer $5 million in damages. The appellate court reversed, ruling that the standard of review for decisions by the leadership of a private university was deferential and that the punishment was reasonable. The Supreme Court of Pennsylvania reversed, rejecting the deferential standard of review. The high court reinstated the jury verdict, but reduced the damage award to $2.9 million. The court emphasized that ordinary principles of contract interpretation applied to its review of the institution's compliance with its own rules and procedures. Although the court noted that it was not appropriate to review the correctness of the decision, review of the institution's procedural compliance was within the competence of the court.

Breach of contract claims may be brought when a faculty member's assignment or routine teaching responsibilities are changed against his or her will. For example, in *Walker v. Board of Regents of the University System of Georgia,* 561 S.E.2d 178 (Ct. App. Ga. 2002), a dean accused of sexual harassment by a faculty member was removed from his administrative position, which provided for a twelve-month contract, and reassigned to a nine-month faculty position. The court rejected the former dean's breach of contract claim, stating that he was given a nine-month contract on terms that were similar to contracts given to other tenured faculty at the university, despite the fact that the rest of the faculty in the former dean's department were employed on twelve-month contracts.

On occasion, an institution may wish to include a noncompete clause in the contract of a faculty member, particularly if it wishes to limit the faculty member's ability to resign and establish a practice that competes with an institutional program. For example, in *Albany Medical College v. Lobel,* 745 N.Y.S.2d 250 (N.Y. App. Div. 2002), a state appellate court affirmed the finding of a trial court that a noncompete clause in a faculty member's employment contract was enforceable. The faculty member, a physician, had been employed as a professor and a member of the medical school's practice group. He had signed an agreement not to practice medicine within 30 miles of the city of Albany for five years if he left the medical school's employ. After a dispute with the medical school leadership, the faculty member left and set up a competing practice in Albany. The medical school sued, and the court enforced the noncompete clause because it was reasonably limited as to time and area, and the public was not denied access to medical care as a result of its enforcement.

Although tenured faculty are typically protected from termination without reasonable cause from their *faculty* positions, most faculty who also hold *administrative* positions do not have tenure in those administrative roles. Unless some written document provides for tenure in an administrative role, courts will reject breach of contract claims brought by tenured faculty who are ousted from administrative positions, as in *Murtaugh v. Emory University,* 152 F. Supp. 2d 1356 (N.D. Ga. 2001).

Even if a contractual provision would ordinarily bind the college or university, fraud on the part of the faculty member may result in a contractual *rescission,* which means that the contract no longer exists. Cases involving rescission of contracts, including faculty contracts, are discussed in Section 4.3.3.5.

Contracts may not only specify faculty's duties and rights but also may have additional requirements, such as acceptance of the tenets of a particular religion (if the institution is affiliated with a religious organization) or a code of conduct. For example, several colleges and universities have promulgated policies that forbid faculty from entering into sexual relationships with students who are in their classes or under their supervision.

Some states have enacted laws requiring that, as a condition of employment, faculty and graduate teaching assistants be competent in spoken English. In other states a statewide regulatory body or governing body has promulgated a similar requirement. Many of these laws or policies require that the institution certify the English proficiency only of nonnative speakers of English, a requirement that might be interpreted as discrimination on the basis of national origin (see Section 5.3.2). (For a discussion of these laws and policies, see P. Monoson & C. Thomas, "Oral English Proficiency Policies for Faculty in U.S. Higher Education," 16 *Rev. Higher Educ.* 127 (1993).)

Given the rapid changes in state common law of contract and the interest of state legislators in the conditions of faculty employment, administrators and faculty should continually be sensitive to the question of what institutional documents or practices are, or should be, part of the faculty contract. Where ambiguity exists, administrators and faculty should decide whether there is some good policy reason for maintaining the ambiguity. If not, the contracts should be clarified. And both faculty and administrators need to understand how the law of their state interprets handbooks, policy manuals, and oral promises. Careful drafting and the use, if desirable, of disclaimers in documents that are not intended to afford contractual rights may protect the institution against liability for claims that arise from oral promises or policy documents in some states, although substantial differences exist among states in judicial attitudes toward disclaimers.

6.2.2. Statutory versus contract rights in public institutions. A

public institution's legal relationship with faculty members may be defined by statute and administrative regulation as well as by written employment contract.[1] Tenure rights, for instance, may be created by a state tenure statute rather than by the terms of the employment contract; or pay scales may be established by a board of regents or state personnel rules rather than by the employment contract. The distinction between statutory rights and contract rights can be critical. A right created by statute or by administrative rule can be revoked or modified by a subsequent statute or rule, with the result that the public institution has no further obligation to recognize that right. A contract right, however, usually cannot be revoked or modified by subsequent statute or rule unless the parties have made provision for such changes in the contract itself, or unless the modification satisfies the requirements of the Constitution's contracts clause.

The Supreme Court's test for compliance with the contracts clause was created in *United States Trust Co. v. New Jersey*, 431 U.S. 1 (1977). In *Gardiner v. Tschechtelin*, 765 F. Supp. 279 (D. Md. 1991), a federal trial judge applied the *United States Trust* criteria to determine whether the state could abrogate tenure contracts with college faculty. In 1989, by act of the state legislature, the State of Maryland had assumed ownership of a municipal college, the Community College of Baltimore, because of the college's serious financial problems and a strong concern about the quality of the curriculum and the faculty. That legislation abolished faculty tenure and provided that faculty employed at the college would be employed only through the end of 1990. All faculty were sent termination notices. The faculty sued under Section 1983 of the Civil Rights Act (see Section 3.4 of this book), claiming that the legislation violated the Constitution's contracts clause (see Section 4.3.4 of this book) because their tenure was guaranteed by contract.

Under *United States Trust Co.*, the court was required to determine whether the legislation served a "legitimate public purpose" and whether the faculty contracts were private or public contracts. If the contracts were public, the court's standard of review would be higher, since the state's "self-interest" was at stake (765 F. Supp. at 288, citing 431 U.S. at 26). Because the faculty contracts were public, the court also was required to determine whether the legislation was "reasonable and necessary."

The judge determined that the legislature's concerns about the financial viability and quality of education at the college were legitimate, and that the state had chosen a less drastic means to try to improve the college than it could have by retaining all the faculty for one year and providing that those evaluated as above average or excellent teachers would receive additional annual contracts. Given the legislature's decision to continue supporting the college for only three

---

[1]Cases related to faculty rights under tenure statutes are collected in Annot., "Construction and Effect of Tenure Provisions of Contract or Statute Governing Employment of College or University Faculty Member," 66 A.L.R.3d 1018; James Timothy Payne, Annot., "Sufficiency of Notice of Intention to Discharge or Not to Rehire Teacher Under Statutes Requiring Such Notice," 52 A.L.R.4th 301; Dale A. Linden, Annot., "Who Is 'Teacher' for Purposes of Tenure Statute," 94 A.L.R.3d 141.

years, pending an evaluation of the appropriateness of continuing its existence, the court ruled that the abrogation of tenure and the dismissal of some of the faculty was "reasonable and necessary to serve an important public purpose" (765 F. Supp. at 290) and therefore did not violate the contracts clause.

Budgetary pressures have persuaded the legislatures of several states to implement "pay lags" or brief "furloughs" in which public employees either lose pay or sustain a delay in receiving their pay. With one exception, the courts have found these practices to conflict with the contracts clause if those employees' pay rights are protected by collective bargaining agreements. For example, in *University of Hawaii Professional Assembly v. Cayetano*, 183 F.3d 1096 (9th Cir. 1999), a federal appellate court upheld a preliminary injunction issued against the State of Hawaii, ruling that the state's "pay lag" law violated the contracts clause. The law provided that the employees would be paid several days later than provided for in their collective bargaining agreement (through consistent past practice over several decades), and also provided that the pay lag was not subject to negotiation. The court ruled that the "pay lag" law would impose a substantial hardship on employees. In its ruling, the court cited *Massachusetts Community College Council v. Commonwealth of Massachusetts*, 649 N.E.2d 708 (Mass. 1995), a state court opinion nullifying a state law creating an "employee furlough," which required employees to take unpaid days off in order to meet a budget crisis. Because the affected employees were covered by collective bargaining agreements, the court ruled that the furlough law violated the contracts clause. A contrary ruling by the U.S. Court of Appeals for the Fourth Circuit in *Baltimore Teachers Union v. Mayor of Baltimore*, 6 F.3d 1012 (4th Cir. 1993) was criticized by subsequent courts in similar cases, and in "Recent Case: Fourth Circuit Upholds City's Payroll Reduction Plan as a Reasonable and Necessary Impairment of Public Contract," 107 *Harv. L. Rev.* 949 (1994).

But if there is no contract protecting the employees (or former employees), the contracts clause is not at issue. The Supreme Court of Rhode Island was asked to rule on whether the state legislature had authority to change the terms under which retired faculty were reemployed by public institutions in the state. In *Retired Adjunct Professors of the State of Rhode Island v. Almond*, 690 A.2d 1342 (R.I. 1997), professors who had retired from state institutions argued that, at the time they retired, state law allowed them to be employed by the state for the equivalent of seventy-five days without losing their pension benefits. In 1994, the Rhode Island legislature changed the law to provide that pension benefits would be suspended for the period of time that the retired professors were paid by the state.

The law was later amended to permit them to earn up to $10,000 per year without suspending their pension benefits. The retired professors claimed that the action by the legislature violated the contract clauses of both the state and federal constitutions. A state trial court judge agreed and permanently enjoined the application of the new law to these plaintiffs.

The state supreme court reversed, ruling that there had been no contract between the state and the retired professors to reemploy them. Reemployment was discretionary on the part of the state institutions, and thus, the legislature could change the terms upon which state institutions made these discretionary employment decisions without implicating constitutional protections. The court added that a statutory public pension benefit plan such as the one at issue in this case is not a "bargained-for" exchange that characterizes a contract. Furthermore, the legislature needed the freedom to modify the state pension system when financial or other policy considerations dictated.

Even if particular rights emanate from statutes or regulations, they may become embodied in contracts and thus be enforceable as contract rights. The contract may provide that certain statutory rights become part of the contract. Or the statute or regulation may itself be so written or interpreted that the rights it creates become enforceable as contract rights. This latter approach has twice been dealt with by the U.S. Supreme Court in cases concerning tenure laws. *Phelps v. Board of Education of West New York*, 300 U.S. 319 (1937), concerned a New Jersey Act of 1909, which provided that teachers employed by local school boards could only be dismissed or subject to reduced salary for cause. By an Act of 1933, the state enabled the school boards to fix and determine salaries. When one board invoked this authority to reduce salaries without cause, teachers claimed that this action impaired their contracts in violation of the Constitution's contracts clause. The Court held that there was no constitutional impairment, since the Act of 1909 did not create a contract between the state and the teachers. The Court agreed with the New Jersey court that the statute established "a legislative status for teachers" but failed to establish "a contractual one that the legislature may not modify." Thus, "although the Act of 1909 prohibited the board, a creature of the state, from reducing the teacher's salary or discharging him without cause, . . . this was but a regulation of the conduct of the board and not a continuing contract of indefinite duration with the individual teacher" (300 U.S. at 323).

A year after *Phelps,* the Supreme Court came to a contrary conclusion in a similar impairment case. *Indiana ex rel. Anderson v. Brand*, 303 U.S. 95 (1938), dealt with Indiana's Teachers Tenure Act, adopted in 1927. The Act provided that, once a teacher had tenure, his or her contract "shall be deemed to be in effect for an indefinite period." Sometime after the Act was amended in 1933 to omit township school corporations, the job of the plaintiff, a tenured teacher, was terminated. The Court found that the Act of 1927 created a contract with the teacher because the title of the Act was "couched in terms of contract," the "tenor of the Act indicates that the word 'contract' was not used inadvertently or in other than its usual legal meaning," and the state courts had previously viewed the Act of 1927 as creating a contract. The Court then held that the 1933 amendment unconstitutionally impaired the contracts created by the Act of 1927.

Given the fundamental distinction between contract and statutory rights, and the sometimes subtle relationships between them, administrators of public institutions should pay particular attention to the source of faculty members' legal rights and should consult counsel whenever the administrators are attempting to define or change a faculty member's legal status.

6.2.3. Academic custom and usage. As a method of contractual interpretation, a court may look beyond the policies of the institution to the manner

in which faculty employment terms are shaped in higher education generally. In these cases the court may use "academic custom and usage" to determine what the parties would have agreed to had they addressed a particular issue. This interpretive device is only used, however, when the contract is ambiguous, or when a court believes that a significant element of the contract is missing. If the intent of the parties is clear, the court will not look beyond the words of the contract. (See, for example, *Kashif v. Central State University,* 729 N.E.2d 787 (Ct. App. Ohio 1999). For a general discussion of academic custom and usage as an "internal" source of law, see Section 1.4.3.3.)

If a contract's wording is alleged to be unclear, a court may be persuaded to look to external writings or statements for help in interpreting the parties' intent. For example, in *Katz v. Georgetown University,* 246 F.3d 685 (D.C. Cir. 2001), the appellate court referred to writings of experts and to policy statements of the American Association of University Professors to define the meaning of "tenure" in the university's faculty handbook. And in *Greene v. Howard University,* 412 F.2d 1128 (D.C. Cir. 1969), the court looked to outside writings to determine the customs and usual practices of the institution and interpret the contract in light of such custom and usage. The plaintiffs in *Greene* were five non-tenured professors who had been fired after a university investigation purported to find that they had been involved in disorders on campus. When the university terminated the professors as of the close of the academic year, the professors asserted that the university had breached a contractual obligation to give appropriate advance notice of nonrenewal or to provide a hearing prior to nonrenewal. The court concluded: "The contractual relationship existing here, when viewed against the regulations provided for, and the practices customarily followed in, their administration, required the university in the special circumstances here involved to afford the teachers an opportunity to be heard" (412 F.2d at 1131).

The court derived the institution's customary practices from the faculty handbook, buttressed by testimony in court, even though the handbook was not specifically incorporated by reference and even though it stated that the university did not have a contractual obligation to follow the notice-of-nonreappointment procedures. The professors were found to be relying "not only on personal assurances from university officials and on their recognition of the common practice of the university, but also on the written statements of university policy contained in the faculty handbook under whose terms they were employed." The court reasoned:

> Contracts are written, and are to be read, by reference to the norms of conduct and expectations founded upon them. This is especially true of contracts in and among a community of scholars, which is what a university is. The readings of the marketplace are not invariably apt in this noncommercial context. . . .
> The employment contracts of [the professors] here comprehend as essential parts of themselves the hiring policies and practices of the university as embodied in its employment regulations and customs [412 F.2d at 1135].

Courts may also look to an institution's customary practice for assistance in understanding the reasonable expectations of the parties to the contract. For example, in *Brown v. George Washington University*, 802 A.2d 382 (Ct. App. D.C. 2002), a faculty member denied tenure and promotion asserted that the university had breached her employment contract because the department's written policy provided that the candidate(s) for promotion would be invited to appear before the promotion committee "to provide additional information as may appear relevant." Departmental members testified that the department had a past practice of interpreting this language as discretionary, and had, in fact, excluded other candidates for promotion from the same meeting. The court ruled that the department faculty's interpretation of this policy was reasonable and not a breach of contract.

A court may look to the recommendations of an internal committee to aid in interpreting unclear or missing contractual provisions. In *Tacka v. Georgetown University*, 193 F. Supp. 2d 43 (D.D.C. 2001), a faculty member filed a breach of contract claim when the university refused to halt his tenure review process to deal with a claim of plagiarism against the tenure candidate. As part of the tenure review process, the department chair had solicited an evaluation of the candidate's research by an external expert. The external expert's evaluation accused Tacka of plagiarism in a paper he had published. The faculty handbook provided that any charges of academic misconduct were to be referred to the university's Research Integrity Committee. Before the department chair referred the plagiarism charge to that committee, however, the department voted to deny Tacka tenure. Tacka sued, saying that the department should have suspended the tenure review pending the outcome of the Research Integrity Committee's deliberations. (Several months after Tacka was denied tenure by the university, the Research Integrity Committee exonerated him; Tacka underwent a second tenure review the following year and was awarded tenure.)

Although the university argued that the faculty handbook did not require that the tenure process be suspended while an allegation of academic misconduct was reviewed, the court disagreed. The court was persuaded by the handbook's language requiring that such charges be reviewed and resolved promptly. The court also found relevant a memo from the chair of the Research Integrity Committee to the academic vice president, stating that the tenure review process should have been put on hold until the committee had completed its review of the allegations of academic misconduct. The views of these committee members, according to the court, are relevant "to construe the terms of the contract created by the Faculty Handbook in accordance with the University's understanding" (193 F. Supp. 2d at 48).

Another possible source of contractual protection for faculty could be the code of student conduct. In *McConnell v. Howard University*, 818 F.2d 58 (D.C. Cir. 1987), a professor refused to meet his class because the administration would not remove a disruptive student from the class. When the professor was discharged for failure to perform his professional duties, he sued for breach of contract, claiming that both the faculty handbook and the code of student conduct created a duty on the part of the university to protect his professional authority. The court ruled that he should have the opportunity to demonstrate that the university owed him this duty. A decade later, however, the highest court of New York rejected a similar theory in *Maas v. Cornell University,* discussed in Section 6.2.1.

Although academic custom and usage can fill in gaps in the employment contract, it cannot be used to contradict the contract's express terms. In *Lewis v. Salem Academy and College,* 208 S.E.2d 404 (N.C. 1974), a professor had been employed from 1950 to 1973 under a series of successive one-year contracts. The college had renewed the contract the last two years, even though the professor had reached age sixty-five, but did not renew the contract for the 1973–74 academic year. The professor argued that he had a right to continue teaching until age seventy because that was a usual and customary practice of the college and an implied benefit used to attract and retain faculty. The college's faculty guide, however, which was incorporated into all faculty contracts, had an explicit retirement policy providing for continued service beyond sixty-five to age seventy on a year-to-year basis at the discretion of the board of trustees.[2] The court held that custom and usage could not modify this clear contract provision.

Similarly, an attempt to convince a court to consider academic custom and usage in determining whether tenure survives the affiliation or merger of two colleges failed because the court found that the terms of the faculty handbook were clear. The case, *Gray v. Mundelein College,* 695 N.E.2d 1379, *appeal denied,* 705 N.E.2d 436 (Ill. 1998), is discussed in Section 6.8.2.

Selective incorporation of AAUP policies into handbooks or other policy documents will bind the college (and the faculty) only with respect to those policies that are clearly incorporated (*Jacobs v. Mundelein College* 628 N.E.2d 201 (Ill. Ct. App. 1993)). Furthermore, the college may decide to incorporate AAUP policies that regulate faculty conduct (such as its Statement on Professional Ethics), but not those that protect the faculty member's rights under other AAUP policy statements (*Barham v. University of Northern Colorado,* 964 P.2d 545 (Ct. App. Colo. 1997)).

While academic custom and usage as a device for interpreting contracts is useful under some circumstances, both the faculty and the college are better served by contracts that are specific and clear with respect to their protections for each party. If the parties wish AAUP statements or other recognized sources of academic custom and usage to be used as interpretation devices, incorporating these into faculty handbooks, policy documents, or other sources of contractual rights (see Section 6.2.1) will provide more predictability in their later interpretation by courts.

6.2.4. Part-time faculty.

6.2.4. Part-time faculty. Facing ever-increasing financial constraints, many colleges and universities have increasingly turned to part-time faculty to provide instruction at considerably lower cost than hiring a full-time faculty member. Part-time faculty often are paid on a per-course basis, and generally are not entitled to employee benefits such as medical insurance or pensions.

---

[2]Such a policy is now contrary to the dictates of the Age Discrimination in Employment Act (ADEA) (Section 5.2.6), which prohibits employment decisions made on the basis of an employee's age.

The status of part-time faculty members in postsecondary institutions has received attention within and outside the postsecondary community (see, for example, Judith Gappa & David Leslie, *The Invisible Faculty: Improving the Status of Part-Timers in Higher Education* (Jossey-Bass, 1993); Howard Bowen & Jack Schuster, *American Professors: A National Resource Imperiled* (Oxford University Press, 1986); David Leslie, ed., *The Use and Abuse of Adjunct Faculty* (New Directions in Higher Education no. 104, 1998)). The number and percentage of part-time faculty members in the academic workforce has increased substantially over the past decades. Data collected by the U.S. Education Department in 1999 reveal that part-time faculty accounted for 42 percent of all faculty across institutional types, but there are sharp differences by institutional type and control. In 1999, 65 percent of the faculty at public community colleges were employed part time, while 27.5 percent of the faculty at public four-year colleges taught part time. Percentages of part-time faculty at private four-year and two-year colleges in 1999 were 41 and 47.5 percent respectively. Women comprise nearly half (47 percent) of part-time faculty across institutional types, while they comprise only 37 percent of full-time faculty overall. Legal issues concerning this large and important faculty group are likely to demand special attention.

The questions being raised about part-time faculty involve such matters as pay scales, eligibility for fringe benefits (life insurance, health insurance, sick leave, sabbaticals, retirement contributions), access to tenure, rights upon dismissal or nonrenewal, and status for collective bargaining purposes. (For a description of a successful attempt by a union of part-time faculty to gain job security, higher wages, expanded benefits, and eligibility for academic leave, see John Gravois, "Both Sides Say Agreement at the New School Sets a Gold Standard for Adjunct-Faculty Contracts," *Chron. Higher Educ.,* November 2, 2005, available at http://chronicle.com/daily/2005/11/2005110207n.htm.) Each of these questions may be affected by two more general questions: (1) How is the distinction between a part-time and a full-time faculty member defined? (2) Are distinctions made between (or among) categories of part-time faculty members? The initial and primary source for answering these questions is the faculty contract (see Section 6.2.1). Also important are state and federal statutes and administrative rulings on such matters as defining bargaining units for collective bargaining (see *University of San Francisco and University of San Francisco Faculty Association,* 265 NLRB 1221 (1982), approving part-time faculty unit, and see also Section 6.3.1), retirement plans, civil service classifications, faculty tenure, wage-and-hour requirements, and unemployment compensation. These statutes and rulings may substantially affect what can and cannot be provided for in faculty contracts.

Two lawsuits brought by part-time faculty in the state of Washington highlight the difficult financial and policy issues related to the heavy reliance of colleges on part-time faculty. In the first, *Mader v. Health Care Authority,* 37 P.3d 1244 (Super. Ct. Wash. 2002), a group of part-time faculty members appealed the denial of their claim for paid health care coverage during the summer. The faculty plaintiffs acknowledged that they did not teach during the summer, but based their claim on language in state regulations that provided for paid health care during the summer to "seasonal" employees. The court rejected that argument because the language of the regulation explicitly excluded employees such as the plaintiffs. The plaintiffs' second claim was equally unsuccessful. A state regulation provides that employees who teach for two consecutive academic terms are entitled to paid health care benefits; it provides that the intervening summer between the spring and fall terms does not break the consecutive nature of the teaching. The court rejected the plaintiffs' claim that this language entitled them to paid health benefits during the summer if they had taught during the spring term.

The state supreme court reversed both rulings of the superior court, stating that the state's Health Care Authority was required to make an individualized determination, based upon the employee's actual work circumstances, as to whether the employee was eligible for employer contributions to their health care coverage (70 P.3d 931 (Wash. 2003)).

The same group of plaintiffs brought a second lawsuit against the state, this time claiming that the state had miscalculated the number of hours they had taught and thus had not contributed the appropriate amount to their retirement plans. They sought adjusted contributions back to 1977, and a ruling that future contributions would be made correctly. The parties settled this case for $12 million; $8.3 million for the underpayment of retirement benefits, and $3.6 million in attorney's fees (*Mader v. State of Washington*, King Co. Cause No. 98-2-30850 SEA settlement agreement, discussed in Daniel Underwood, "Adjunct Faculty and Emerging Legal Trends," Presentation to the 24th Annual National Conference on Law and Higher Education, Stetson University College of Law, February 16–18, 2003).

Another case brought in Washington state court involved an attempt by a group of part-time faculty to be paid overtime wages. In *Clawson v. Grays Harbor College District No. 2*, 61 P.3d 1130 (Wash. 2003), the state supreme court rejected that argument, stating that the college's practice of paying part-time faculty for the number of in-class instructional hours did not render the employees nonexempt for purposes of the state wage and hour law. The court ruled that the faculty were professionals, and that despite the fact that their compensation was calculated with reference to the number of hours they taught, it was a salary, not a wage.

Another issue relevant to the status of part-time faculty is whether full-time faculty at a community college engaged in a reduction in force can "bump" part-time faculty from the courses that faculty to be laid off are qualified to teach. In *Biggiam v. Board of Trustees of Community College District No. 516*, 506 N.E.2d 1011 (Ill. App. Ct. 1987), the court was required to determine whether the Illinois Community College Tenure Act and/or the collective bargaining agreement between the faculty and the board afforded tenured faculty the right to bump any instructor or just full-time faculty members. The court agreed with the board's argument that full-time faculty could bump nontenured or less senior faculty from "positions," but that part-time instructors were not "faculty" and did not have "positions," but only taught courses. Thus, faculty could not bump instructors from courses. Although this case rested on interpretation of a state law, it may have relevance to institutions in other states that need to reduce the number of full-time faculty.

As the proportion of part-time faculty continues to increase in relation to the proportion of full-time, tenure-track faculty, the scholarly debate continues about the propriety of using part-timers to avoid the long-term financial commitment of tenure. The January–February 1998 issue of *Academe,* the journal of the AAUP, includes several articles that discuss the use of part-time faculty (including graduate teaching assistants). The AAUP has developed statements and guidelines regarding the use of part-time faculty, such as "The Status of Non-Tenure-Track Faculty," *AAUP Policies and Documents* (2001), 77–87, which contains a discussion of the status of part-time and non-tenure-track faculty and offers recommendations for their employment. The AAUP has also developed "Guidelines for Good Practice: Part-Time and Non-Tenure-Track Faculty," available at http://www.aaup.org/Issues/part-time/Ptguide.htm. The American Federation of Teachers has also issued standards for the treatment of part-time faculty members, entitled "Standards of Good Practice in the Employment of Part-Time/Adjunct Faculty." The statement can be found at http://www.aft.org/higher_ed.

To respond effectively to issues involving part-time faculty, administrators should understand the differences in legal status of part-time and full-time faculty members at their institutions. In consultation with counsel, they should make sure that the existing differences in status and any future changes are adequately expressed in faculty contracts and institutional rules and regulations. Administrators should also consider the extent and clarity of their institution's legal authority to maintain the existing differences if they are challenged or to change the legal status of part-timers if changes are advisable to effectuate new educational policy.

6.2.5. Contracts in religious institutions.

In religious institutions, employment issues involving the interplay between religious doctrine and civil law have been litigated primarily in cases construing state and federal employment discrimination laws (see Section 5.5); however, when the faculty member is a member of a religious order or when the institution makes employment decisions on religious grounds, complex questions of contract law may also arise.

The contract made between a faculty member and a religious institution would normally be governed by state contract law unless the parties explicitly or implicitly intended that additional sources of law be used to interpret the contract. Some religiously affiliated institutions require their faculty to observe the code of conduct dictated by the doctrine of the religious sponsor; others incorporate church law or canon law into their contracts. Judicial interpretation of contracts is limited by the religion clauses of the First Amendment (see Section 1.6.2).

Several cases have addressed the nature of the contract between a religious institution and a faculty member. The religious institution typically argues that the U.S. Constitution's First Amendment prevents the court from reviewing the substance of the employment dispute. Both the free exercise and the establishment clauses have been invoked by religious colleges seeking to avoid judicial review of these employment disputes. In some of these cases, the courts have determined that the issues involved religious matters and that judicial intervention would be unconstitutional; in others, the court determined that only secular issues were involved and no constitutional violation was present.

In *Curran v. Catholic University of America,* Civ. No. 1562-87, 117 *Daily Wash. L.R.* 656 (D.C. Super. Ct., February 28, 1987), a tenured professor of Catholic theology filed a breach of contract claim when the university prohibited him from teaching courses involving Catholic theology. Curran had taken a public stand against several of the Catholic Church's teachings, and the Holy See had ruled him ineligible to teach Catholic theology. The university's board of trustees then withdrew Curran's ecclesiastical license, which is required of all faculty who teach in departments that confer ecclesiastical degrees. Although the university attempted to place Curran in another, nontheological teaching assignment, Curran argued that the university had constructively discharged him without a finding that he was not competent to teach Catholic theology. He also argued that the university had incorporated protections for academic freedom into his contract and that the treatment afforded him because of his scholarly beliefs constituted a violation of those protections.

The court was faced with three potential sources of contract law: District of Columbia common law, canon law, and explicit or implied contractual promises of academic freedom that were judicially enforceable (see Section 6.2.2). The court saw its duty not to interpret canon law, which it was forbidden to do by establishment clause principles, but to determine whether the parties had intended to be bound by canon law, a question of fact. The court found that, even though his contract did not explicitly mention canon law or its requirements, Curran knew that ecclesiastical faculties were different from nonecclesiastical faculties, that the Holy See could change the requirements for ecclesiastical faculties, and that the university was obligated to accede to those changes. In fact, the Apostolic Constitution of 1979 required ecclesiastical faculties to have a "canonical mission," meaning that such faculty were required to teach in the name of the Catholic Church and not to oppose its doctrine. The court noted:

> [I]f the court had come to the opposite conclusion on this issue [that Curran was contractually required to maintain a canonical mission], it would have been squarely presented with a substantial constitutional question [the Establishment Clause problem]. . . . In light of the court's conclusion that Professor Curran's contract required him to have a canonical mission as a condition of teaching in the Department of Theology, it is unnecessary to reach the University's "canon law defense" [the argument that the Constitution prohibited the court from interpreting canon law] [Civ. No. 1562-87, opinion, at 19].

The court ruled that the university had the right to require faculty who taught theology to meet the requirements of the Holy See, since that body could withdraw the university's authority to award ecclesiastical degrees if the university failed to comply with its requirements. Because the university had a special relationship with the Holy See, the court found implied in Curran's contract with the university an obligation to abide by the Holy See's requirements. The court also found that, whatever academic freedom Curran was due, his academic freedom could not limit the Holy See's authority to determine which ecclesiastical faculty were qualified to teach theology. (For a discussion of academic freedom in religious institutions, see Section 7.8.)

The New Jersey Supreme Court was faced with two cases involving the interplay between religious doctrine and civil contract law. In *Alicea v. New Brunswick Theological Seminary,* 608 A.2d 218 (N.J. 1992), an untenured assistant professor of theology who was an ordained minister claimed that the seminary's president offered him a non-tenure-track position with the promise of an eventual tenured position. When that promise was not acted upon, Alicea resigned, claiming constructive discharge and breach of contract. The ecclesiastical body that governed the seminary, the Reform Church's Board of Theological Education (BTE), had reserved to itself all final decision power regarding the hiring and retention of faculty. Alicea claimed that the BTE had impliedly ratified the promise made to him by the president, and that the president had the apparent authority to make such promises. The court ruled that it could not determine whether the seminary had breached an implied contract with an untenured professor because such an inquiry would constitute an inquiry into ecclesiastical polity or doctrine. Although the court refused to adopt a *per se* rule that courts may not hear employees' lawsuits against religious institutions, the court noted that "governmental interference with the polity, *i.e.,* church governance, of a religious institution could also violate the First Amendment by impermissibly limiting the institution's options in choosing those employees whose role is instrumental in charting the course for the faithful" (608 A.2d at 222). Explaining further, the court said:

> When State action would impose restrictions on a religious institution's decisions regarding employees who perform ministerial functions under the employment relationship at issue, courts may not interfere in the employment relationship unless the agreement between the parties indicates that they have waived their free-exercise rights and unless the incidents of litigation—depositions, subpoenas, document discovery and the like—would not unconstitutionally disrupt the administration of the religious institution [608 A.2d at 222].

The court noted that because Alicea taught theology and counseled prospective ministers, he performed a ministerial function. Therefore, although the case involved issues of church governance (rather than doctrine, as in the *Curran* case), the court was similarly required to abstain from exercising jurisdiction.

Although the faculty handbook contained a grievance provision, which the seminary had not honored, the court refused to order the parties to use the procedure, because it was "optional" in light of the BTE's reservation of full authority. The court stated: "Enforcement of the ministerial-employment agreement would have violated the Free Exercise Clause whether based on actual or apparent authority" (608 A.2d at 224). In other words, the court could suggest that the parties abide by the manual but could not enforce the manual because its provisions were "vague and clearly optional" (608 A.2d at 224).

The court outlined the analysis to be applied to such cases:

> [A] court should first ascertain whether, because of the ministerial role played by the employee, the doctrinal nature of the controversy, or the practical effect of applying neutral principles of law, the court should abstain from entertaining jurisdiction. . . . In assessing the extent to which the dispute implicates issues of doctrine or polity, factors such as the function of the employee under the relationship sought to be enforced, the clarity of contractual provisions relating to the employee's function, and the defendant's plausible justifications for its actions should influence the resolution of that threshold question. . . . If neither the threat of regulatory entanglement, the employee's ministerial function, nor the primarily-doctrinal nature of the underlying dispute mandates abstention, courts should effectuate the intent of the parties to the contract [608 A.2d at 223–224].

The court explained that, if compliance with the contract could be determined through the application of "neutral principles of law," then courts could enforce promises to comply with religious doctrine, or waivers of rights to act in compliance with religious beliefs. Examination of the text of the contract or handbook, on the type of employees supervised by the individual seeking judicial review, and the parties' positions as church officials would be relevant, as well as the apparent intent of the parties to seek judicial review of disputes arising under the contract.

The same court decided a case with similar issues on the same day as *Alicea*. In *Welter v. Seton Hall University*, 608 A.2d 206 (1992), two Ursuline nuns who had taught for three years at Seton Hall, a Catholic university, filed breach of contract claims when their contracts were not renewed. The university claimed that the sisters' order, the Ursuline Convent of the Sacred Heart, had refused permission for the sisters to continue teaching at the university, and that the court lacked jurisdiction to entertain the breach of contract claims.

The New Jersey Supreme Court ruled against the university on several grounds. First, the sisters did not perform a ministerial (pastoral) function— they taught computer science. Second, the dispute did not implicate either doctrinal issues or matters of church polity; the university simply refused to honor its contractual obligation to give the untenured sisters twelve months' notice (a one-year terminal contract) before discharging them. The contract included no mention of canon law, nor did it require the sisters to obtain the permission of their religious superiors before accepting employment. It was the same contract that the university used for lay faculty. Furthermore, when the Ursuline convent requested that the university forward the sisters' paychecks directly to it, the university refused and advised the sisters to open a checking account and deposit their paychecks.

There was substantial evidence that the university desired to terminate the sisters' employment because of dissatisfaction with their performance. Instead of issuing the terminal contracts, university administrators contacted the sisters' religious superiors and asked that they be recalled. The university then terminated the sisters' employment without the required notice. The university admitted that the issue would be a completely secular one if the sisters were not members of a religious order. In deciding this case, the court applied a two-part test. First, the court analyzed whether the sisters performed any ministerial functions for the university, and found that they did not. Second, the court assessed whether the sisters could have contemplated that canon law would have superseded the procedural safeguards of the contract, and found no such evidence:

> The purely secular nature of plaintiffs' employment obligations; the absence of a contractual provision imposing religious obligations on plaintiffs; Seton Hall's rejection of the Ursulines' prior request regarding plaintiffs' paychecks; and the absence of any religious connotations behind the hiring of, tenure of, or decision to terminate plaintiffs all plainly indicate the contrary [608 A.2d at 216].

Courts have also been asked to construe the authority religiously affiliated colleges to require lay faculty to adhere to religious doctrine in their teaching. In *McEnroy v. St. Meinrad School of Theology,* 713 N.E.2d 334 (Ct. App. Ind. 1999) (also discussed in Section 7.8), a professor of Catholic theology and doctrine at a seminary that trains candidates for the priesthood signed a statement opposing the pope's teachings on the ordination of women as priests. After learning that Professor McEnroy had signed this statement, the head of the seminary removed her as a professor. McEnroy sued for breach of contract and several related tort claims. The seminary sought dismissal of the case on First Amendment grounds, arguing that judicial review of the complaint would require the court to "decide religious issues regarding the Church's good faith motivation and doctrinal basis for removing [the plaintiff] under canon law" (713 N.E.2d at 336). The trial court agreed with the seminary's argument, and a state appellate court affirmed. Two years later, the U.S. Conference of Catholic Bishops issued "Guidelines Concerning the Academic *Mandatum* in Catholic Universities" (June 15, 2001), which specifies that all faculty who teach "theological disciplines" in a Catholic college or university must receive a *mandatum* (an acknowledgment by church authority that a Catholic professor of a theological discipline is teaching "within the full communion of the Catholic Church").

In another case, a lay faculty member was discharged by a Baptist seminary for failing to adhere to the "lifestyle and behavior" expected of a faculty member at the seminary. In *Patterson v. Southwestern Baptist Theological Seminary,* 858 S.W.2d 602 (Tex. Ct. App. 1993), the faculty member filed a wrongful discharge claim, alleging that his contractual rights had been violated. The faculty handbook required each faculty member to be an "active and faithful member of a Baptist church" and to "subscribe in writing to the Articles of Faith" of the Southern Baptist Convention. The court ruled that the explicit inclusion of these requirements in the faculty handbook made it evident that the seminary "makes employment decisions regarding faculty members largely upon religious criteria"

(858 S.W.2d at 1199), rendering judicial review of the discharge decision a violation of the Constitution's First and Fourteenth Amendments.

In a case involving a former priest, *Hartwig v. Albertus Magnus College*, 93 F. Supp. 2d 200 (D. Conn. 2000), a federal trial court rejected the college's motion for summary judgment on constitutional grounds. The ex-priest, who had been hired by the college as an associate professor in the department of religious studies and philosophy, was relieved of his teaching and administrative responsibilities when the college president was sent newspaper articles that identified the plaintiff as an ex-priest who was "married to another man." The plaintiff charged the college with breach of contract, defamation, and related tort claims.

Although the court ruled that the college was sufficiently affiliated with the Roman Catholic Church to be entitled to invoke the free exercise clause, it found insufficient evidence that the plaintiff's duties were primarily religious in nature in order to support summary judgment for the college. The court ruled that a trial on the merits of the breach of contract claim would not involve the court in matters of religious interpretation, but that the defamation claim would involve competing religious interpretations of whether an individual ordained as a priest remained a priest for life even after leaving the active priesthood. Therefore, the court awarded summary judgment to the college on the defamation claims, but ruled that the plaintiff could proceed with his contract claims.

The cases are consistent in deferring to religious institutions on matters that involve the interpretation of church doctrine (*Curran, Hartwig*) or matters of church governance. The decisions have clear implications for academic freedom disputes at religious institutions (Section 7.8), especially where issues of adherence to religious doctrine are intertwined with free speech issues. Counsel acting for religiously affiliated institutions whose leaders wish their faculty employment contracts to be interpreted under church law as well as civil contract law should specify in written contracts and other institutional documents that church law or religious doctrine will be binding on the parties to the contract, and that church law will prevail in any conflict between church and civil law.

Sec. 6.3. Faculty Collective Bargaining

6.3.1. Bargaining unit eligibility of faculty. Although the laws, cases, and doctrines discussed in Section 4.5 apply to faculty as well as to staff (and, in some cases, to students), the special nature of the faculty role has required labor boards and courts to interpret labor law in sometimes unique ways. Federal law, which regulates collective bargaining in the private sector, contains no special provisions (or exceptions) for college faculty. State law, which regulates collective bargaining in the public sector, may deal specifically with higher education (as in California), or may include college faculty with public school teachers or public employees in general (as in many other states). For this reason, faculty and administrators at public colleges need to pay special attention to their state's regulation of public sector bargaining, while the interpretation of federal labor relations law is somewhat more uniform across the country.

The National Labor Relations Board (NLRB) asserted jurisdiction over higher education in 1970 and determined in 1971 that college faculty in private institutions could organize under the protections of the National Labor Relations Act (NLRA) (see Section 4.5.2). Between 1971 and 1980, the NLRB routinely ruled that faculty were "employees" and thus were eligible to form unions under the NLRA, even if they participated in hiring, promotion, and tenure decisions and controlled the curriculum and their course content. The routine inclusion of faculty under the NLRA came to an abrupt halt, however, in 1980.

In *NLRB v. Yeshiva University*, 444 U.S. 672 (1980), the U.S. Supreme Court considered, for the first time, how federal collective bargaining principles developed to deal with industrial labor-management relations apply to private academic institutions. Adopting a view of academic employment relationships very different from that of the dissenting justices, a bare majority of the Court denied enforcement of an NLRB order requiring Yeshiva University to bargain collectively with a union certified as the representative of its faculty. The Court held that Yeshiva's full-time faculty members were "managerial" personnel and thus excluded from the coverage of the NLRA.

In 1975 a three-member panel of the NLRB had reviewed the Yeshiva University Faculty Association's petition seeking certification as bargaining agent for the full-time faculty members of certain of Yeshiva's schools. The university opposed the petition on the grounds that its faculty members were managerial or supervisory personnel and hence not covered by the Act. After accepting the petition and sponsoring an election, the Board certified the faculty association as the exclusive bargaining representative. The university refused to bargain, maintaining that its faculty members' extensive involvement in university governance excluded them from the Act. When the faculty association charged that the refusal was an unfair labor practice, the NLRB ordered the university to bargain and sought enforcement of its order in federal court. The U.S. Court of Appeals for the Second Circuit denied enforcement, holding that Yeshiva's faculty were endowed with "managerial status" sufficient to remove them from the coverage of the Act (*NLRB v. Yeshiva University*, 582 F.2d 686 (2d Cir. 1978)).

In affirming the appellate court's decision, Justice Powell's majority opinion discussed the application of the "managerial employee" exclusion to college faculty who were involved in governance decisions at a university. The Court looked to previous NLRB decisions and Supreme Court opinions to formulate a definition of managerial employee: those who "formulate and effectuate management policies by expressing and making operative the decisions of their employer . . . [or] exercise discretion within or even independently of established employer policy and [are] aligned with management" (444 U.S. at 682–83).

Applying this standard to the Yeshiva faculty, the Court concluded that the faculty exercised "managerial" authority because of their "absolute" authority over academic matters, such as which courses would be offered and when, the determination of teaching methods, grading policies, and admission standards, and admissions, retention, and graduation decisions. Said the court:

> When one considers the function of a university, it is difficult to imagine decisions more managerial than these. To the extent the industrial analogy applies, the faculty determines within each school the product to be produced, the terms upon which it will be offered, and the customers who will be served [444 U.S. at 686].

The NLRB had acknowledged this decision-making function of the Yeshiva faculty but argued that "alignment with management" was the proper criterion for assessing management status. Because the faculty were not evaluated on their compliance with university policy, nor on their effectiveness in carrying out university policy, according to the NLRB, their independence would not be compromised by allowing them to unionize and negotiate with the administration. Rather than being aligned with management, said the Board, the faculty pursued their own professional interests and should be allowed to organize as other professional employees do.

The Court explicitly rejected the Board's approach, noting that "the Board routinely has applied the managerial and supervisory exclusions to professionals in executive positions without inquiring whether their decisions were based on management policy rather than professional expertise." And furthermore, said the Court, the Board's determination that the "professional interests of the faculty and the interests of the institution are distinct, separable entities with which a faculty member could not simultaneously be aligned" was incorrect. According to the Court, "the faculty's professional interests—as applied to governance at a university like Yeshiva—cannot be separated from those of the institution" (444 U.S. at 686–88).

Four members of the Court dissented. On behalf of these dissenters, Justice Brennan argued that the NLRB's decision should be upheld. He argued that "mature" universities had dual authority systems: a hierarchical system of authority culminating in a governing board, and a professional network that enabled professional expertise to inform and advise the formal authority system. According to Brennan, the faculty has an independent interest that underlies its recommendations, but the university retains "the ultimate decision-making authority" and defers to faculty judgment, or not, as it "deems consistent with its own perception of the institution's needs and objectives." Brennan also argued that the faculty were not accountable to the administration for their governance functions, nor did the faculty act as "representatives of management" in performing their governance roles.

Just as the *Yeshiva* case sparked sharp debate within the Court, it generated much dialogue and disagreement among commentators. (See, for example, D. Rabban, "Distinguishing Excluded Managers from Covered Professionals under the NLRA," 89 *Columbia L. Rev.* 1775 (1989); see also G. Bodner, "The Implications of the *Yeshiva University* Decision for Collective Bargaining Rights of Faculty at Private and Public Institutions of Higher Education," 7 *J. Coll. & Univ. Law* 78 (1980–81); and the response in M. Finkin, "The *Yeshiva* Decision: A Somewhat Different View," 7 *J. Coll. & Univ. Law* 321 (1980–81).) The debate has developed on two levels. The first is whether the Court majority's view of academic governance and its adaptation of labor law principles to that context are justifiable—an issue well framed by Justice Brennan's dissenting opinion. The second level concerns the extent to which the "management exclusion" fashioned by the Court should be applied to university settings and faculty governance systems different from Yeshiva's.

The Court focused on the autonomy of the Yeshiva faculty to "effectively determine [the University's] curriculum, grading system, admission and matriculation standards, academic calendars, and course schedules." However, noted the Court, if faculty at other colleges seeking to bargain did not have the scope or amount of influence that the Court attributed to Yeshiva's faculty, they would not meet the test for "managerial employee" status and thus would be protected by the labor relations laws.

Thus, the *Yeshiva* decision appears to create a managerial exclusion only for faculty at "Yeshiva-like," or what the Court called "mature," private universities. Even at such institutions, it is unlikely that all faculty would be excluded from bargaining under federal law. Most part-time faculty, for instance, would not be considered managers and would thus remain eligible to bargain. Legitimate questions also exist concerning faculty with "soft money" research appointments, instructors and lecturers not on a tenure track, visiting professors, and even nontenured faculty generally, at mature universities.

At private institutions that are not "Yeshiva-like," the NLRB and reviewing appellate courts have refused to apply the managerial exclusion to faculty. For example, *NLRB v. Stephens Institute*, 620 F.2d 720 (9th Cir. 1980), concerned the faculty of an art academy on the opposite end of the spectrum from Yeshiva. The academy was a corporation whose principal shareholder was also chief executive officer. Faculty members, except department heads, were paid according to the number of courses they taught each semester. According to the court: "The instructors at the academy . . . have no input into policy decisions and do not engage in management-level decision making. They are simply employees. Also, the academy bears little resemblance to the nonprofit 'mature' university discussed in *Yeshiva*."

Another case, in which the court reached a similar conclusion, concerned the faculty of a liberal arts college that was closer to Yeshiva on the spectrum than was the art academy. In *Loretto Heights College v. NLRB*, 742 F.2d 1245 (10th Cir. 1984), the court determined that "faculty participation in college governance occurs largely through committees and other such groups" and that, outside such committees, faculty members' governance roles were limited to participation in decision making "within or concerning particular program areas" in matters such as hiring and curriculum development. Concluding that the faculty's authority in institutional governance was "severely circumscribed," the court concluded that they did not meet the "managerial employee" test and thus were permitted to organize.

Other cases in which the Board and courts refused to exclude faculty as managerial employees include *Bradford College and Milk Wagon Drivers and Creamery Workers Union, Local 380*, 261 NLRB 565 (1982); *Montefiore Hospital and Medical Center and New York State Federation of Physicians and Dentists*, 261 NLRB 569 (1982); *NLRB v. Cooper Union for Advancement of Science*, 783 F.2d 29 (2d Cir. 1986); *Marymount College of Virginia*, 280 NLRB 486 (1986); *NLRB v. Florida Memorial College*, 820 F.2d 1182 (11th Cir. 1987); *Kendall Memorial School v. NLRB*, 866 F.2d 157 (6th Cir. 1989); *Spencer v. St. John's University*, 1989 U.S. Dist. LEXIS 3421 (E.D.N.Y. 1989); *St. Thomas University*, 298 NLRB 280 (1990); and *Lemoyne-Owens College*, 338 N.L.R.B. No. 92 (2003).

But the Board and federal courts have applied the *Yeshiva* criteria to exclude faculty from coverage in several other cases. Faculty were found to be "managerial employees" excluded from bargaining in *Ithaca College and Ithaca College Faculty Ass'n.*, 261 NLRB 577 (1982); *Thiel College and Thiel College Chapter, AAUP*, 261 NLRB 580 (1982); *Duquesne University of the Holy Ghost and Duquesne University Law School Faculty Ass'n.*, 261 NLRB 587 (1982); *College of Osteopathic Medicine & Surgery*, 265 NLRB 295 (1982); *Fairleigh Dickinson University and Fairleigh Dickinson University Council of American Association of University Professors Chapters*, Case no. 22-RC-7198 (1986); *NLRB v. Lewis University*, 765 F.2d 616 (7th Cir. 1985); *University of New Haven*, 267 NLRB 939 (1986); *American International College*, 282 NLRB 189 (1986); *Livingstone College*, 286 NLRB 1308 (1987); *Boston University Chapter, AAUP v. NLRB*, 835 F.2d 399 (1st Cir. 1987); *University of Dubuque*, 289 NLRB 349 (1988); *Lewis and Clark College*, 300 NLRB 155 (1990); *Elmira College*, 309 NLRB 842 (1992); *Manhattan College*, 1999 NLRB LEXIS 903 (November 9, 2001); *Sacred Heart University*, Case No. 34-RC-1876, and *Sage Colleges*, Case No. 3-RC-11030 (July 31, 2001). (For a discussion of the *University of Great Falls* case, in which a federal appellate court ruled that the NLRB did not have jurisdiction over the university, which was owned by a religious order, see Section 4.5.2.2.)

Attempts have been made to apply *Yeshiva* by analogy to public sector institutions, but without success. The most notable example involved the University of Pittsburgh. Although a hearing examiner for the Pennsylvania Labor Relations Board ruled that the faculty were managerial, the full board reversed that finding and allowed an election to proceed (*University of Pittsburgh*, 21 Pa. Publ. Employee Rpts. 203 (1990)). The faculty elected "no agent," rejecting union representation (D. Blum, "After 7-Year Fight, Pitt Professors Vote Against Union," *Chron. Higher Educ.*, March 20, 1991, A2; see also J. Douglas, "The Impact of *NLRB v. Yeshiva University* on Faculty Unionism at Public Colleges," 19 *J. Coll. Negot. in the Pub. Sector* 1 (1990)).

At institutions that are not "Yeshiva-like," the managerial exclusion could apply to individual faculty members who have special governing responsibilities. Department heads, members of academic senates, or members of grievance committees or other institutional bodies with governance functions could be excluded as managerial employees, and have been at institutions where they have supervisory authority over faculty. But the numbers involved are not likely to be so large as to preclude formation and recognition of a substantial bargaining unit.

The NLRB and state employment relations agencies make decisions about which employees should be included in the same bargaining unit on the basis of the "community of interest" of the employees (see Section 4.5.3 of this book). Generally, several factors have traditionally been used to determine a "community of interest," including the history of past bargaining (if any), the extent of organization, the skills and duties of the employees, and common supervision. But these factors are difficult to apply in postsecondary education's complex world of collegially shared decision making. To define the proposed unit as "all faculty members" does not resolve the issue. For example, does the unit include all faculty of the institution, or only the faculty of a particular school, such as the law school? Part-time as well as full-time faculty members? Researchers and librarians as well as teachers? Graduate teaching assistants? Chairs of small departments whose administrative duties are incidental to their primary teaching and research functions? The problems are compounded in multicampus institutions, especially if the programs offered by the individual campuses vary significantly from one another.

The question of whether department chairs or coordinators are "employees" (who are protected by the NLRA) or "supervisors" (who are not) was addressed by the Board in *Detroit College of Business and Detroit College of Business Faculty Association,* 296 NLRB 318 (1989). Prior to this case, the Board had used the "50 percent" rule developed in *Adelphi University,* 195 NLRB 639 (1972), which stated that, unless an individual spent at least half of his or her time in supervisory functions, the supervisory exclusion did not apply. In *Detroit College of Business,* the Board rejected the "50 percent" rule, stating that even though the department coordinators spent the majority of their time teaching, their responsibilities to evaluate and hire part-time faculty brought them within the definition of "supervisor" and thus excluded them from the NLRA's protection.[3] Given the breadth of this definition of supervisor, it is possible that faculty members who supervise graduate student research or teaching assistants (who are employees also) could theoretically be excluded from the protections of the NLRA.

Part-time faculty have won the right to bargain, although they may be required to form a separate bargaining unit, rather than being included with full-time faculty, if a state labor board or NLRB panel finds that they do not share a "community of interest" (see Section 4.5.3) with full-time faculty. In most cases, part-time faculty are found not to share a community of interest with full-time faculty (see, for example, *New York University,* 205 NLRB 4 (1973); *NLRB v. Wentworth Institute,* 515 F.2d 550 (1st Cir. 1975); *University of San Francisco,* 207 NLRB 12 (1973); *Vermont State Colleges Faculty Federation v. Vermont State Colleges,* 152 Vt. 343 (1989); *Community College of Philadelphia,* 432 A.2d 637 (Pa. Commw. 1981)).

The nature of the employment relationship between part-time or adjunct faculty and their institutions has posed complex issues for labor relations agencies. For example, in *Appeal of the University System of New Hampshire Board of Trustees,* 795 A.2d 840 (N.H. 2002), the New Hampshire Supreme Court upheld the state labor board's decision to certifying a bargaining unit of adjunct faculty who had taught for the state university system, but remanded to the labor board the question of how to determine which adjuncts were "not temporary" and thus eligible for the unit. Furthermore, adjunct faculty at "mature" private universities have been given the right to unionize that has been denied to full-time faculty at those same universities under the *Yeshiva* doctrine (Scott Smallwood, "United We Stand?" *Chron. Higher Educ.,* February 21, 2003, A10–A11).

---

[3]Cases are collected in Russell J. Davis, Annot., "Who Are 'Supervisors' Within Meaning of NLRA (29 U.S.C.S. §§ 151 *et seq.*) in Education and Health Services," 52 A.L.R. Fed. 28.

Given the many possible variations from the circumstances in *Yeshiva*, faculty, administrators, and counsel can estimate the case's application to their campus only by comprehensively analyzing the institution's governance structure, the faculty's governance role in this structure, and the resulting decision-making experience.

On campuses with faculty members who would be considered "managers," bargaining does not become unlawful as a result of *Yeshiva*. The remaining faculty members not subject to exclusion may still form bargaining units under the protection of federal law. And even faculty members subject to the managerial exclusion may still agree among themselves to organize, and the institution may still voluntarily choose to bargain with them. But the administration may block the protection of federal law. Thus, for instance, faculty managers would have no federally enforceable right to be included in a certified bargaining unit or to demand good-faith bargaining over mandatory bargaining subjects (see Section 4.5.4). Conversely, the institution would have no federally enforceable right to file an unfair labor practice charge against a union representing only faculty managers for engaging in recognitional picketing, secondary boycotts, or other activity that would violate Section 8(b) of the NLRA (29 U.S.C. § 158(b)) if the federal law applied. A collective bargaining agreement entered through such a voluntary process could, however, be enforced in state court under the common law of contract.

In addition to raising questions about the legal status of faculties under *Yeshiva*, the decision has had a more subtle impact on relationships between faculty and administration (see generally J. V. Baldridge, F. Kemerer, & Associates, *Assessing the Impact of Faculty Collective Bargaining*, ERIC/Higher Education Research Report no. 8 (American Association for Higher Education, 1982)). It has given rise to numerous policy issues and sociological questions about faculty power on campus, and such matters merit reconsideration. Faculty at "mature" institutions have pressed for new mechanisms for exercising authority that the Supreme Court characterized as "managerial." At "nonmature" institutions, administrators have accorded greater authority to faculty in order to forestall their resort to the bargaining process highlighted by *Yeshiva*. And at all types of institutions—mature or not, public or private—all affected constituencies may wish to better define and implement faculty's role in academic governance, not as a legal matter but as an exercise of sound policy judgment.

6.3.2. Coexistence of collective bargaining and traditional academic practices.

A major concern of faculty and administrators alike when a union represents faculty is whether the union's right to negotiate over terms and conditions of employment will conflict with, or compete with, traditional academic governance practices. For example, curricular changes can have implications for faculty workload; if a committee or a faculty senate recommends curricular changes, the implications of those changes for faculty workload may need to be negotiated. To the degree possible, an agreement that allocates responsibility for representing faculty views on various aspects of institutional policy and practice to the union or to a nonunion committee or other structure will minimize conflict in the long run.

Collective bargaining contracts traditionally come in two kinds, those with a "zipper" clause and those with a "past practices" clause. A zipper clause usually states that the union agrees to forgo its rights to bargain about any employment term or condition not contained in the contract; prior relationships between the parties thus become irrelevant. A past practices clause incorporates previous customary relationships between the parties in the agreement, at least insofar as they are not already inconsistent with its specific terms. Administrators faced with collective bargaining should carefully weigh the relative merit of each clause. A contract without either clause will likely be interpreted consistently with past practice when there are gaps or ambiguities in the contract terms. (See Sections 1.4.3.3 & 6.2.3.)

The availability of the past practices clause, however, by no means ensures that such traditional academic practices will endure under collective bargaining. In the early days of faculty bargaining, several commentators argued that such academic practices would steadily and inevitably disappear (for example, see D. Feller, "General Theory of the Collective Bargaining Agreement," 61 *Cal. L. Rev.* 663, 718–856 (1973)). One view was that collective bargaining brings with it the economic warfare of the industrial bargaining model, forcing the two parties into much more clearly defined employee and management roles and diminishing the collegial characteristics of higher education. The opposing view was that collective bargaining can be domesticated in the postsecondary environment with minimal disruption of academic practices (see M. Finkin, "Collective Bargaining and University Government," 1971 *Wis. L. Rev.* 125 (1971); and M. Finkin, "Faculty Collective Bargaining in Higher Education: An Independent Perspective," 3 *J. Law & Educ.* 439 (1974)).

As with most opposing theories, the outcome seems to be somewhere between the predictions of those who believed faculty would negotiate away tenure for higher salaries and those who believed that faculty unions would have no effect on traditional governance mechanisms. Although faculty senates have either been abolished or atrophied at a few colleges and universities, relationships between faculty unions and senates have, for the most part, been cooperative and mutually supportive. In fact, on many campuses, faculty who are active in the union are also active in nonunion governance groups, such as a faculty senate. Thus, the issue for administrators is not whether traditional governance systems will be destroyed, but the extent to which faculty involvement in institutional governance should and can be maintained by incorporating such arrangements in the bargaining agreement, through either a past practices clause or a more detailed description of forms and functions. Given the result in *College of Osteopathic Medicine,* 265 NLRB 37 (1982), in which college faculty who attained a role in governance through their collective agreement were found to be managerial employees by the NLRB, faculty union leaders at private institutions may resist the incorporation of governance structures into the collective agreement.

On some campuses, however, traditional faculty governance structures have been replaced by the collective bargaining process. In *Minnesota State Board for Community Colleges v. Knight,* 465 U.S. 271 (1984), the Court upheld a

Minnesota law that requires public employers to "meet and negotiate" with exclusive bargaining representatives of public employees over mandatory subjects of bargaining and, when the employees are professionals, to "meet and confer" with their exclusive representatives regarding nonmandatory subjects. (Subjects of bargaining are discussed in Section 4.5.4.) Pursuant to this law, the Minnesota Community College Faculty Association was designated the exclusive bargaining agent for state community college faculty members. The association and the state board established statewide meet-and-confer committees as well as local committees on each campus. These committees discussed various policy matters, such as curriculum, fiscal planning, and student affairs. Only members of the association served on the committees.

This arrangement was challenged by a group of faculty members who were not members of the association and thus could not participate in the meet-and-negotiate or meet-and-confer processes. The faculty members argued that their exclusion deprived them of their First Amendment rights to express their views and also discriminated against them in violation of the Fourteenth Amendment's equal protection clause. The lower court (1) rejected these arguments as applied to the negotiation of mandatory bargaining subjects but (2) agreed with the faculty members that exclusion from the meet-and-confer committees violated the First Amendment (571 F. Supp. 1 (D. Minn. 1982)). On the faculty members' appeal from the first ruling, the U.S. Supreme Court summarily affirmed the lower court (*Knight v. Minnesota Community College Faculty Ass'n.*, 465 U.S. 271 (1984)). On the state board and the association's appeal from the second ruling, in an opinion joined by only five members, the U.S. Supreme Court overruled the lower court. According to the Court majority, the faculty members' free speech challenge to their exclusion from meet-and-confer committees was unavailing:

> Appellees have no constitutional right to force the government to listen to their views. . . . [T]his Court has never recognized a constitutional right of faculty to participate in policy making in academic institutions. . . . Even assuming that speech rights guaranteed by the First Amendment take on a special meaning in an academic setting, they do not require government to allow teachers employed by it to participate in institutional policy making. Faculty involvement in academic governance has much to recommend it as a matter of academic policy, but it finds no basis in the Constitution [465 U.S. at 287–88].

The equal protection claim similarly failed:

> The state has a legitimate interest in insuring that its public employers hear one, and only one, voice presenting the majority view of its professional employees on employment-related policy questions, whatever other advice they may receive on those questions. Permitting selection of the "meet-and-confer" representatives to be made by the exclusive representative, which has its unique status by virtue of majority support within the bargaining unit, is a rational means of serving that interest . . . [465 U.S. at 291–92].

When the faculty are represented by a union, some decisions traditionally made unilaterally by administrators may need to be negotiated with the union. For example, when the dean of arts and sciences at Rutgers University-Newark decided to move seven tenured faculty members from twelve-month to ten-month contracts because they were not performing work for the university during the summer, the union sued the university for breach of contract. In *Troy v. Rutgers, the State University of New Jersey,* 774 A.2d 476 (N.J. 2001), the state appellate court had ruled that the collective bargaining agreement superseded individual contracts between the faculty and the university, and the union appealed. The New Jersey Supreme Court reversed the appellate court, ruling that a trial was necessary to determine whether, in fact, the university had entered supplementary individual contracts with certain faculty members that enhanced the protections afforded by the collective bargaining agreement. In addition, the court ruled that decisions affecting the faculty members' salaries and working conditions were not a matter of managerial prerogative, but had to be negotiated.

But the decision of whether to transfer a faculty member whose position is eliminated in a reduction in force is a managerial prerogative, according to the Supreme Court of Massachusetts. In *Higher Education Coordinating Council/ Roxbury Community College v. Massachusetts Teachers' Association,* 666 N.E.2d 479 (Mass. 1996), the court vacated an arbitrator's award ordering the college to assign a laid-off professor trained as a civil engineer to a vacant position in the mathematics department. The court ruled that the college could not delegate the power to decide where to place a faculty member to the collective bargaining process because the assignment of work is a managerial prerogative.

Disputes have arisen over whether faculty have the right to bargain with the administration over tenure criteria or procedures. The issue turns on whether or not a court will view tenure criteria or procedures as a mandatory subject of bargaining rather than as a managerial prerogative. Courts have differed on this issue. For example, in *Ass'n. of New Jersey State College Faculties v. Dungan,* 316 A.2d 425 (N.J. 1974), a state statute gave public employees the right to bargain over the "terms and conditions of employment" and "working conditions." The court held that rules for granting tenure are not "mandatorily negotiable" under the statute because such rules "represent major educational policy pronouncements entrusted by the legislature [under the state's Education Law] to the board [of higher education's] educational expertise and objective judgment." Under such reasoning, tenure rules could also be beyond the scope of permissible bargaining, as "inherent managerial policy" (*University Education Association v. Regents of the University of Minnesota,* 353 N.W.2d 534 (Minn. 1984)) or as a nondelegable function of the board or as a function preempted by other state laws or administrative agency regulations (see *New Jersey State College Locals v. State Board of Higher Education,* 449 A.2d 1244 (N.J. 1982)).

Other courts or agencies, however, particularly when dealing with private institutions under the NLRA, may reason that tenure is a mandatory, or at least permissive, bargaining subject because it concerns job security (see A. Menard,

"May Tenure Rights of Faculty Be Bargained Away?" 2 *J. Coll. & Univ. Law* 256 (1975)). In *Hackel v. Vermont State Colleges*, 438 A.2d 1119 (Vt. 1981), for example, the court determined that faculty promotion and tenure are "properly bargainable" under that state's Employee Labor Relations Act and upheld a provision on tenure and promotion in a collective bargaining agreement. Given this variation in judicial results, it is impossible to generalize about whether tenure or promotion standards or procedures are negotiable in general.

In *Central State University v. American Association of University Professors*, 526 U.S. 124 (1999), a case concerning faculty workloads rather than tenure, the U.S. Supreme Court upheld the federal constitutionality of an Ohio law barring collective bargaining over faculty workloads. Public debate in Ohio in the early 1990s focused on a perceived decline in the amount of time faculty were spending teaching in relation to the time spent on research. In 1993, the Ohio legislature enacted a law that required a 10 percent increase in statewide undergraduate teaching activity. The law instructed public colleges to adopt a faculty workload policy and provided that workload policies were not appropriate subjects for collective bargaining. The law further provided that if collective bargaining agreements conflicted with the new workload policies, the policy would prevail over the agreement. The language concerning collective bargaining was inserted because the faculty at several large state universities are not unionized; it was feared that faculty on unionized campuses might be able to avoid the additional workload through negotiating, while faculty on nonunionized campuses would not.

The trustees of Central State University adopted a workload policy and notified the local AAUP chapter, the elected representative of the faculty, that it would not bargain over faculty workload. The union filed a complaint in state court for declaratory and injunctive relief, arguing that the law denied the faculty equal protection under both the U.S. and the Ohio constitutions because it created a class of public employees not entitled to bargain. In *American Association of University Professors v. Central State University*, 699 N.E.2d 463 (Ohio 1998), the Ohio Supreme Court struck the law under both the Ohio and the U.S. constitutions, ruling that, although the legislature's objective in enacting the statute was legitimate, there was no rational relationship between this objective (changing the balance between teaching and research) and collective bargaining because there was no evidence that collective bargaining had caused the decline in faculty teaching loads. The university appealed to the U.S. Supreme Court.

The Supreme Court issued a *per curiam* opinion reversing the Ohio Supreme Court's ruling concerning the U.S. Constitution and remanding the case for further proceedings. The Court held that the Ohio court had misapplied the "rational basis" test of the equal protection clause. The legislature's imposition of a faculty workload policy was "an entirely rational step. . . . The legislature could quite reasonably have concluded that the policy animating the law would have been undercut and likely varied if it were subject to collective bargaining" (526 U.S. at 128).

Justice Stevens dissented, arguing that the decision to bargain over the allocation of faculty time to research or teaching was a matter of academic freedom. Stevens concluded that the Court should have left this issue to the Ohio courts.

Because the federal and state laws governing collective bargaining are complex and involve substantial labor board and judicial interpretation, experienced labor counsel should be consulted when the faculty attempt to organize a union, or when the administration and faculty begin to negotiate a collective agreement. Particular attention should be paid to the structuring of dispute resolution processes under the agreement; administrators should consider the implications of including binding arbitration in the agreement for decisions such as promotion, tenure, and hiring of faculty.

Sec. 6.4. *Application of Nondiscrimination Laws to Faculty Employment Decisions*

6.4.1. *Overview.* Discrimination claims are particularly complex for faculty to prove and for colleges to defend against because of the subjective nature of employment decisions in academe. A successful discrimination claim generally depends on a plaintiff's ability to demonstrate unequal treatment of otherwise similar individuals. But identifying "similar" faculty members or demonstrating unequal treatment can be difficult. Particularly at institutions where faculty peers play a significant role in recommending candidates for hiring, promotion, or tenure, the locus of decision-making responsibility and the effect on upper levels of administration of potentially tainted recommendations at lower levels can be difficult to trace and to prove. Furthermore, opinions about what is "excellent" research or teaching may differ, even within the same academic department; and a plaintiff who attempts to compare herself or himself to colleagues in order to demonstrate unequal treatment may have difficulty doing so, especially in a small department.

Other issues facing academic institutions involve shifting performance standards, which may result in greater demands on recently hired faculty than those conducting the evaluation were required to meet—an outcome that can appear discriminatory whether or not there was a discriminatory intent. Comparisons of faculty productivity or quality across disciplines pose difficulties as well. And the practice at many colleges and universities of shielding the deliberations of committees or individuals from the scrutiny of the candidate or, in some cases, the courts (see Section 7.7) adds to the complexity of academic discrimination cases.

Discrimination claims have been brought by faculty challenging negative hiring, promotion, or tenure decisions or objecting to work assignments or other types of decisions (salary increases, office or lab space, and so on). A few cases illustrate the range of issues, and the judicial reaction, to these discrimination claims.

6.4.2. *Judicial deference and remedies for tenure denial.* Faculty challenging negative promotion or tenure decisions typically claim that the decision-making process was flawed or that the denial was a result of unlawful bias rather than some performance-related reason. Cases involving allegations of flawed decision-making processes are discussed in Section 6.7. Cases involving the rationale for the negative decision are discussed in this Section.

Despite the relatively large number of discrimination claims brought by faculty denied tenure or promotion, very few faculty have prevailed on the merits. A study of discrimination lawsuits brought between 1972 and 1986 by faculty denied tenure found that plaintiffs won on the merits only about 20 percent of the time (G. LaNoue & B. Lee, *Academics in Court: The Consequences of Faculty Discrimination Litigation* (University of Michigan Press, 1987)). Litigation results in subsequent years have been similar. In addition to the fact that the subjective nature of these decisions makes it difficult for a judge or jury to second-guess the determination of a university with regard to the quality of a faculty member's work, many courts have deferred to the judgment of faculty peers or other experts in these cases, finding for plaintiffs only if significant procedural errors had been made or if there was direct evidence that discrimination motivated the negative decision.

Early cases in which courts were asked to review denials of tenure or promotion made clear the judges' discomfort with the request. In situations where peer review committees had determined that a plaintiff's scholarship and/or teaching did not meet the proper standards, judges were reluctant to impose either their own judgments or their own performance standards on peer review committees, external evaluators, or college administrators. In an early case, *Faro v. New York University*, 502 F.2d 1229 (2d Cir. 1974), the U.S. Court of Appeals for the Second Circuit stated:

> [O]f all fields which the federal courts should hesitate to invade and take over, education and faculty appointments at a university level are probably the least suited for federal court supervision. Dr. Faro would remove any subjective judgments by her faculty colleagues in the decisionmaking process [502 F.2d at 1231–32].

The Fourth Circuit, echoing *Faro*, stated that "[c]ourts are not qualified to review and substitute their judgment for the subjective, discretionary judgments of professional experts on faculty promotions" (*Clark v. Whiting*, 607 F.2d 634, 640 (1979)).

Federal appellate courts in subsequent academic discrimination cases were more willing to review academic judgments. In *Powell v. Syracuse University*, 580 F.2d 1150 (2d Cir. 1978), the court rejected its earlier deference, stating that the courts' "anti-interventionist policy has rendered colleges and universities virtually immune to charges of employment bias," and that the court would not "rely on any such policy of self-abnegation where colleges are concerned" (580 F.2d at 1153). Despite this apparent rejection of the *Faro* deferential standard, courts have generally refused to overturn tenure decisions where there has been an internal determination that the candidate's performance does not meet the institution's standard for tenure. One state court declared flatly that the "arbitrary and capricious" standard should be used to evaluate the tenured faculty's recommendation against granting tenure is because it is a professional judgment, not an employment decision (*Daley v. Wesleyan University*. 772 A.2d 725 (Ct. App. Conn. 2000), *appeal denied*, 776 A.2d 1145 (Conn. 2001)). In most cases, however, the courts do examine the college's justification for the tenure denial to determine the credibility of the nondiscriminatory reason for the negative decision.

An illustrative case is *Fisher v. Vassar College*, 114 F.3d 1332 (2d Cir. 1997) (*en banc*), a case involving claims of age, marital status, and sex discrimination. The college had stated that Cynthia Fisher, a professor of biology, had been denied tenure in part because she "had been away from science" for too long. Fisher had interrupted her academic career for nine years to raise her children. The trial court had ruled in Fisher's favor, citing Fisher's strong publication record (finding it superior to that of several male faculty who were tenured just before and just after Fisher was denied tenure), her success at obtaining research grants, and the fact that no married woman had received tenure in the hard sciences at Vassar for the thirty years prior to Fisher's tenure review, as evidence that the college had engaged in age and "sex plus marital status" discrimination (852 F. Supp. 1193 (S.D.N.Y. 1994)). The court did not find that the college had engaged in sex discrimination, as such, because another female faculty member in that department had received tenure the same year that Fisher's tenure bid was denied. Instead, the trial court relied on a ruling by the U.S. Supreme Court in *Phillips v. Martin Marietta*, 400 U.S. 542 (1971) that a Title VII claim may arise if an employer discriminates against an employee because of sex plus another characteristic, such as marital status. The trial court also found that Fisher's salary was depressed as a result of sex discrimination, an Equal Pay Act violation.

On appeal, a panel of the U.S. Court of Appeals for the Second Circuit reversed. Although the panel upheld the trial court's rulings for the plaintiff in both the *prima facie* and pretext portions of the case (see Section 5.2.1), the panel reversed the trial court's ultimate finding that the college intentionally discriminated against Fisher, stating that there was insufficient direct evidence of such discrimination. That opinion was withdrawn when the full court determined to hear oral arguments *en banc*. The *en banc* court confined its review to whether it was permissible for an appellate court to affirm rulings for the plaintiff on the *prima facie* case and pretext issues, and yet reverse the ultimate finding of discrimination.

The *Fisher* case demonstrates the influence of *St. Mary's Honor Center v. Hicks* (Section 5.2.1). It also demonstrates that appellate judges are sharply divided on the meaning of *Hicks,* as well as on the standard of review to be used in a Title VII case. The dispute between the majority and dissenters concerned whether a trial court's finding for the plaintiff at both the *prima facie* stage and the pretext stage requires a ruling for the plaintiff on the merits. The majority insisted that some evidence of bias was needed; proving that the college was untruthful in the reasons it gave was insufficient to justify a verdict for Fisher. The minority argued that if the plaintiff prevailed at the pretext stage, the plaintiff should prevail in the lawsuit. Six judges joined the majority, one judge concurred in part and dissented in part, and four judges dissented from the majority opinion.

Simply because the plaintiff might have been able to demonstrate that the college's reason for the tenure denial was pretextual, said the majority, did not mean that a finding of discrimination was warranted. Showing some understanding of academic politics, the judge writing for the majority commented:

> In some cases, an employer's proffered reason is a mask for unlawful discrimination. But discrimination does not lurk behind every inaccurate statement. Individual decision-makers may intentionally dissemble in order to hide a reason that is non-discriminatory but unbecoming or small-minded, such as back-scratching, log-rolling, horse-trading, institutional politics, envy, nepotism, spite, or personal hostility. For example, a member of a tenure selection committee may support a protégé who will be eligible for tenure the following year. If only one tenure line is available, that committee member might be inclined to vote against tenure . . . thereby ensuring that the tenure line remains open. Any reason given by the committee member, other than the preference for his protégé, will be false. . . . [T]he fact that the proffered reason was false does not necessarily mean that the true motive was the illegal one argued by the plaintiff [114 F.3d at 1337].

The *en banc* majority left undisturbed the ruling by the appellate panel that, although Fisher had established a *prima facie* case of age and marital status discrimination, the college had supplied sufficient neutral reasons for the tenure denial (inability to meet the standards for tenure and qualifications inferior to those of other tenure candidates). Despite the trial court's finding that some of the college's reasons were inaccurate, the panel had held that the trial court's findings were insufficient to support a finding of actual discrimination against Fisher. The panel had thus overruled the trial court's findings of age and "sex plus marital status" discrimination in the tenure denial, as well as its ruling on sex-based wage discrimination. The *en banc* majority fully concurred with this reasoning and outcome of the panel discussion.

The dissenting judges criticized the *en banc* majority for substituting its judgment for that of the fact finder (the trial judge), and castigated the majority for protecting untruthful employers from a finding of discrimination, absent some clear evidence of discriminatory conduct. They also asserted that the *en banc* court should review every finding made by the trial court *de novo* rather than relying on the panel's review.

Faculty plaintiffs seeking to avoid the problems they face under the *Hicks* doctrine may not fare any better under state nondiscrimination laws. In a widely reported decision, a Connecticut jury awarded more than $12.6 million to a female chemistry professor who claimed sex discrimination in her tenure denial. In *Craine v. Trinity College,* 791 A.2d 518 (Conn. 2002), the state's high court affirmed the jury's finding that the college had breached Craine's employment contract and had negligently misrepresented the tenure criteria, but ruled that the plaintiff had not demonstrated a discriminatory motive on the part of the college. Because the plaintiff could not identify males with similar qualifications who had been granted tenure the same year she was denied tenure, she had to rely on procedural violations in order to make out a *prima facie* case of sex discrimination. The high court found that the breach of contract (the college's failure to advise Craine that she was not making adequate progress toward tenure) provided a rebuttable inference of discrimination. However, the court ruled that the procedural inconsistency and a single reference to a male tenure candidate as "old boy Jack" were insufficient to permit a reasonable jury to find that sex discrimination was the motive for the tenure denial. The college's defense that the plaintiff's scholarly productivity was too low was a legitimate nondiscriminatory reason for the tenure denial, according to the court, and it ruled that the plaintiff had not demonstrated that the college's reason was a pretext for discrimination.

Although the plaintiff claimed that two successful candidates for tenure were no better qualified than she, the court refused to perform a comparative analysis of the qualifications. First, said the court, the comparator faculty were in different departments (history and math). But more important, said the court:

> The first amendment guarantees that the defendant may pass its own judgment on the plaintiff's scholarship and accept or reject other evaluations in the process. . . . To compare these publication records would require an inadmissible substantive comparison between the candidates and an improper intrusion into the right of the defendant to decide for itself which candidates satisfied its publication requirements. In the absence of any independent evidence of discrimination, evidence that an academic institution appears to have been more critical of one candidate than of another is not sufficient to raise an inference of discrimination [791 A.2d at 537, 538].

In another tenure denial case involving a female chemistry professor, *Weinstock v. Columbia University,* 224 F.3d 33 (2d Cir. 2000), a federal appellate court, over a strong dissent by one panel member, affirmed a trial court's award of summary judgment to the university on the plaintiff's sex discrimination claim. Although the plaintiff, a faculty member at Barnard College, had been supported in her quest for tenure by the faculty in her department, by the dean and president of Barnard College, and by external reviewers of her scholarly work, the provost of Columbia University recommended against tenure, and the president concurred, on the basis that they considered her scholarship to be weak. Although Weinstock appealed the president's negative decision through an internal review process, the new president of Columbia upheld the negative decision. Despite Weinstock's assertion that numerous procedural irregularities infected the decision-making process, the court ruled that the university's reason for the tenure denial—inadequate quality of her scholarship—was a legitimate nondiscriminatory reason unrelated to her gender.

Even if the plaintiff has evidence that a tenure decision was affected by "academic politics," proving that discrimination was the reason for the tenure denial is very difficult. For example, a faculty member claiming that racial and national origin discrimination infected a denial of tenure was not able to persuade a federal appellate court to reverse a ruling in the university's favor. In *Fabunmi v. University of Maryland at College Park,* 1999 U. S. App. LEXIS 2726 (4th Cir. 1999) (unpublished), the court affirmed the trial court's ruling that the plaintiff had not provided evidence of either racial or national origin bias on the part of the individuals who recommended against tenure. Despite the fact that the department in which the plaintiff taught had "poor personnel management practices" (p. *6), the court remarked: "[A] professor who pursues a Title VII action in a tenure case cannot prevail merely by demonstrating that his tenure vote was animated by interpersonal conflict or petty academic politics" (p. *5).

An issue that has troubled courts analyzing academic Title VII cases is the appropriate remedy for a denial of tenure or promotion that is found to have been discriminatory. In nonacademic settings, reinstatement to the position along with retroactive promotion is a routine remedy. But the courts, citing their lack of expertise in evaluating the scholarly or teaching ability of college faculty, sometimes have been reluctant to award "make-whole" remedies to college faculty.

The issue of a remedy for a discriminatory denial of tenure was addressed squarely in *Kunda v. Muhlenberg College*, 621 F.2d 532 (3d Cir. 1980). The decision, written by Judge Dolores Sloviter, a former law professor, takes into account the need for academic freedom and the significance of peer evaluation while also recognizing that individuals who make academic judgments are still subject to Title VII's prohibitions on discrimination.

Connie Kunda, a physical education instructor, brought suit after the college had denied her applications for promotion and tenure. The trial court (463 F. Supp. 294 (E.D. Pa. 1978)), holding that the college had intentionally discriminated against Kunda because of her sex, awarded her (1) reinstatement to her position; (2) back pay from the date her employment terminated, less amounts earned in the interim; (3) promotion to the rank of assistant professor, backdated to the time her application was denied; and (4) the opportunity to complete the requirements for a master's degree within two full school years from the date of the court's decree, in which case she would be granted tenure.

In affirming the trial court's award of relief, the appellate court carefully analyzed the particular facts of the case. These facts, as set out below, played a vital role in supporting and limiting the precedent set by this opinion.

When Kunda was appointed an instructor in the Muhlenberg College physical education department in September 1966, she held a Bachelor of Arts degree in physical education. Although the department's terminal degree requirement, for tenure purposes, was the master's, Kunda was never informed that a master's was needed for advancement. Kunda was first recommended for promotion in the academic year 1971–72. Although her department supported the promotion, the Faculty Personnel and Policies Committee (FPPC) of the college rejected the recommendation after the dean of the college, who seldom attended FPPC deliberations on promotions, spoke against the recommendation. Subsequently, to determine the reasons for the denial, Kunda met individually with her department chairman, the dean, and the college's president. The court found that none of these persons told her that she had been denied promotion because she lacked a master's degree.

In the two subsequent years, Kunda's department colleagues and all relevant faculty committees recommended that she be promoted and, in the last year, granted tenure. Both times, the dean recommended against promotion and tenure, citing various institutional concerns rather than Kunda's lack of a master's degree, and affirming Kunda's worth to the college by recommending to the president that she be retained in a non-tenure-track status. Both years, the president recommended against promotion and tenure, and Kunda was given a terminal contract.

Kunda appealed the tenure denial to the Faculty Board of Appeals (FBA). The FBA recommended that Kunda be promoted and awarded tenure because (1) Kunda displayed the "scholarly equivalent" of a master's degree, (2) the policy of granting promotions only to faculty possessing the terminal degree had been bypassed frequently for the physical education department, and (3) no significant financial considerations mandated a denial of tenure. Despite the FBA recommendation, the board of trustees voted to deny tenure.

After reviewing these facts, the court of appeals examined other facts comparing Kunda's situation with that of similarly situated males at Muhlenberg. With respect to promotion, three male members of the physical education department had been promoted during the period of Kunda's employment, notwithstanding their lack of master's degrees. In another department of the college, a male instructor had been promoted without a terminal degree. There was also a difference between the counseling offered Kunda and that offered similarly situated males; while Kunda was not told that the master's would be a prerequisite for a grant of tenure, male members had been so advised.

Basing its conclusions on its analysis of these facts found by the trial court, and its approval of the trial court's allocation of burdens of proof, the appellate court agreed that Kunda had been discriminated against in both the denial of promotion and the denial of tenure. Concerning promotion, the appellate court affirmed the finding that the defendant's reason for denial articulated at trial, lack of the terminal degree, was a pretext for discrimination. Concerning tenure, the appellate court affirmed the trial court's determination that the articulated reason (lack of terminal degree) was not pretextual but that Kunda had been subjected to intentional disparate treatment with respect to counseling on the need for the degree.

Having held the college in violation of Title VII, the court turned to what it considered the most provocative issue raised on appeal: the propriety of the remedy fashioned by the trial court. Awards of back pay and reinstatement are not unusual in academic employment discrimination litigation; awards of promotion or conditional tenure are. The appellate court therefore treated the latter remedies extensively, emphasizing the special academic freedom context in which they arose.

The court discussed the tension between the freedom of a college to make employment decisions based upon institutional considerations and the academic judgment that is necessary to review a faculty member's qualifications for promotion or tenure. It also acknowledged the need for academics, rather than judges, to evaluate faculty performance. Said the court:

> Wherever the responsibility [for evaluating faculty performance] lies within the institution, it is clear that courts must be vigilant not to intrude into that determination, and should not substitute their judgment for that of the college

with respect to the qualifications of faculty members for promotion and tenure. Determinations about such matters as teaching ability, research scholarship, and professional stature are subjective, and unless they can be shown to have been used as the mechanism to obscure discrimination, they must be left for evaluation by the professionals, particularly since they often involve inquiry into aspects of arcane scholarship beyond the competence of individual judges [621 F.2d at 547–48].

The court noted that all faculty committees had judged Kunda to be qualified for promotion and tenure, and that the dean had recommended extending her a non-tenure-track appointment. Since the tenure denial was premised on the lack of a master's degree rather than upon the quality of her performance, the court found that its decision to award promotion and conditional tenure was consistent with the academic judgments made about Kunda.

The appellate court stated that the trial judge's award of "conditional tenure" placed Kunda in the position she would have been in had the dean and president informed her of the requirement of a master's degree. This ruling was consistent with remedies for discrimination in nonacademic settings, according to the court.

> The fact that the discrimination in this case took place in an academic rather than commercial setting does not permit the court to abdicate its responsibility to insure the award of a meaningful remedy. Congress did not intend that those institutions which employ persons who work primarily with their mental faculties should enjoy a different status under Title VII than those which employ persons who work primarily with their hands [621 F.2d at 550].

Kunda was a ground-breaking case because the court in effect awarded a promotion and conditional tenure as the remedy for the discrimination against the plaintiff. The case was also controversial because the remedy is subject to the charge that it interferes with institutional autonomy in areas (promotion and tenure) where autonomy is most important to postsecondary education. Yet, as a careful reading of the opinion indicates, the court's holding is actually narrow and its reasoning sensitive to the academic community's needs and the relative competencies of college and court. The court emphasizes that the case was unusual in that Kunda's performance had been found by all involved to be acceptable. Thus, the case's significance is tied tightly to its facts.

Another federal court of appeals addressed the thorny issue of remedies for academic discrimination in two cases, refusing in both to award tenure to plaintiffs who had prevailed on the merits. In *Gutzwiller v. University of Cincinnati*, 860 F.2d 1317 (6th Cir. 1988), the court, affirming the trial court's finding of discrimination, remanded the case to the trial court on the issue of a remedy, cautioning that court-awarded tenure should be "provided in only the most exceptional cases, [and] [o]nly when the court is convinced that a plaintiff reinstated to her former faculty position could not receive fair reconsideration . . . of her tenure application" (860 F.2d at 1333). The district court awarded Professor

Gutzwiller back pay, reinstated her without tenure for the 1989–90 academic year, and ordered that a new tenure review be conducted under the court's supervision within the following year. The university conducted a tenure review during the 1989–90 academic year and awarded Gutzwiller tenure.

In a second case before the same federal circuit court, *Ford v. Nicks,* 866 F.2d 865 (6th Cir. 1989), the appellate court reversed a trial court's award of reinstatement as a tenured full professor to Lanni Ford, who had been denied reappointment as an instructor in 1977 at Middle Tennessee State University. Although Ford had prevailed on the merits in 1984 (741 F.2d 858 (6th Cir. 1984)), the issue of the appropriate remedy had occupied the court for another five years. The plaintiff had argued that only reinstatement as a full professor would provide a "make-whole" remedy; the court disagreed, noting that Ford had taught for only two years and had never been evaluated for promotion or tenure. The court remanded the case to the trial court with instructions to fashion some remedy short of tenure that would compensate Ford for her losses.

The first time a federal appellate court examined and approved the outright award of tenure occurred in *Brown v. Trustees of Boston University,* 891 F.2d 337 (1st Cir. 1989).[4] Julia Brown, an assistant professor of English, had received the unanimous recommendation of her department and positive recommendations from outside evaluators, but was denied tenure by the university's president. After a jury trial, the university was found to have discriminated in its denial of tenure to Brown. The court, in reinstating Brown with tenure, noted that her peers had judged her to be qualified (a factor absent in *Gutzwiller* and *Ford,* but present in *Kunda*), and that the president's sexist remarks about the English department showed evidence of gender bias. The university had raised an academic freedom challenge to a court award of tenure, stating that it infringed upon its First Amendment right to determine "who may teach" (see *Sweezy v. New Hampshire,* discussed in Section 7.1). The appellate court rejected that argument, noting that the First Amendment could not insulate the university against civil rights violations.

The court also rejected the university's argument that the appropriate remedy be another three-year probationary period or a nondiscriminatory tenure review, such as was the remedy in *Gutzwiller.* The court said these remedies would not make the plaintiff whole. The court engaged in an extensive review of Brown's publications and teaching record, an unusual level of scrutiny for academic employment discrimination claims. Thus, the appellate court reviewed the substance of the decision as well as its procedural fairness, rather than the deferential review used by courts in previous cases. This willingness to review the substance of academic judgments is also evident in *Bennun v. Rutgers, The State University of New Jersey,* 737 F. Supp. 1393 (D.N.J. 1990), *affirmed,* 941

---

[4]Two federal trial courts had awarded tenure to plaintiffs, but in neither case was the remedy examined on appeal. See *Gladney v. Thomas,* 573 F. Supp. 1232 (D. Ala. 1983), and *Younus v. Shabat,* 336 F. Supp. 1137 (N.D. Ill. 1971), *affirmed mem.,* 6 Fair Empl. Prac. Cases 314 (7th Cir. 1973).

F.2d 154 (3d Cir. 1991) (discussed in Section 6.4.3.1), and in *Jew v. University of Iowa*, 749 F. Supp. 946 (S.D. Iowa 1990).[5]

Recent court opinions in academic discrimination cases make it clear that postsecondary institutions have no special dispensation from the requirements of federal antidiscrimination legislation. Courts will defer to institutions' expert judgments concerning scholarship, teaching, and other educational qualifications if they believe that those judgments are fairly reached, but courts will not subject institutions to a more deferential standard of review or a lesser obligation to repair the adverse effects of discrimination. And despite the fact that tenure is an unusual remedy in that it has the potential to give lifetime job security to a faculty member, the federal courts appear to have lost their reluctance to order tenure as a remedy when they believe that discrimination has occurred.

In addition to equitable remedies such as reinstatement or tenure, and damages, prevailing plaintiffs are entitled to attorney's fees under Title VII (42 U.S.C. § 2000e-5(k)). The Wisconsin Supreme Court was asked to determine whether a faculty member who prevailed in a sex discrimination claim in an internal university grievance procedure was entitled to attorney's fees under the rationale of Title VII. In *Duello v. Board of Regents, University of Wisconsin*, 501 N.W.2d 38 (Wis. 1993), the Wisconsin Supreme Court ruled that an internal university appeals committee's decision that the plaintiff had suffered sex discrimination was not a "proceeding" under the meaning of Title VII and thus the university was not liable to the plaintiff for her attorney's fees.

6.4.3. Challenges to employment decisions

6.4.3.1. Race and national origin discrimination claims. Faculty may bring claims of race and/or national origin discrimination under both Title VII and Section 1981 (see Sections 5.2.1 & 5.2.4 of this book). In *Bennun v. Rutgers, The State University of New Jersey*, 941 F.2d 154 (3d Cir. 1991), a Hispanic professor—stating both Title VII and Section 1981 claims—charged that the university's four refusals to promote him to full professor were based on his race and/or national origin. The trial court compared Professor Bennun's research and publication record with the record of a departmental colleague, a white female who had been promoted to full professor at the same time Bennun's promotion was denied. The trial court found nine instances in which different, and more demanding, standards were applied to Bennun than to the comparator faculty member. In light of these findings, the district court concluded that the university's reason for denying Bennun promotion—inadequate research production—was a pretext for discrimination. Although Bennun apparently had no direct evidence of discrimination, his ability to demonstrate pretext was sufficient to establish liability, the court ruled.

---

[5]Cases related to the issue of discrimination and the award of tenure are collected in Richard Neumeg, Annot., "Application to Tenured Positions in Educational Institutions of Provisions of Civil Rights Act of 1964, as Amended (42 U.S.C.S. § 2000e *et seq.*), Prohibiting Discrimination on Basis of Sex," 55 A.L.R. Fed. 842.

The comparison of Bennun with his departmental colleague was disputed at the appellate level. The university argued that, because the female professor had been rated "outstanding" in both teaching and service and Bennun had not, they were not "similarly situated" and thus the comparisons were inappropriate. The court rejected the university's argument, stating that the different standards applied to the professors' research quality and productivity were sufficient to establish disparate treatment, and that whether or not the two faculty were similar enough in other respects for comparison purposes was irrelevant.

The university petitioned the Third Circuit for a rehearing by the entire panel of judges, which was denied. Judge Sloviter, a former law school professor and the author of the *Kunda* decision (discussed in Section 6.4.2), believed that the rehearing should be granted, arguing that, unlike Kunda, Bennun's qualifications were in dispute, and that the trial judge had impermissibly inserted himself into the evaluation process.

A second race discrimination claim resulted in one of the largest damage awards in an academic discrimination lawsuit. It also demonstrates the inflammatory effect of racist comments upon a jury's decision concerning the amount of damages to award. Reginald Clark, an African American professor of education, asserting that the decision by Claremont Graduate School to deny him tenure was racially motivated, brought suit under California's Fair Employment and Housing Act (Govt. Code § 12900 *et seq.*), which permitted a jury trial. The jury found for Professor Clark, in part because Clark was able to demonstrate several examples of race-related remarks made by departmental colleagues, both before and during the time that they made the tenure recommendation (a split vote). The jury awarded Clark $1 million in compensatory damages and $16,327 in punitive damages. The trial judge awarded Clark attorney's fees of more than $400,000. The California Court of Appeal affirmed the jury verdict and damage awards (*Clark v. Claremont University Center,* 8 Cal. Rptr. 2d 151 (Cal. Ct. App. 1992)), stating:

> We must add we are not surprised by the jury's verdict. Many employment discrimination cases do not even survive to trial because evidence of the employer's improper motive is so difficult to obtain. This case is unusual, not because of Clark's claims, but because of Clark's strong evidence of improper motive. Our own computer-assisted research of tenure denial cases across the nation revealed none involving university professors who made such blatant remarks as in this case [8 Cal. Rptr. at 170].

White faculty have also used Section 1981 and Title VII to challenge negative employment decisions under a theory of "reverse discrimination." In *Craig v. Alabama State University,* 451 F. Supp. 1207 (M.D. Ala. 1978), a class action brought on behalf of white faculty and other white employees and former employees at a predominantly black institution, the court concluded on the basis of evidence presented at trial that "in the hiring of its administrative, teaching, and clerical and support staff and the promotion and tenure of its faculty, A.S.U. has . . . engaged in a pattern and practice of discrimination against whites." The U.S. Court of Appeals for the Fifth Circuit affirmed (614 F.2d 1295 (5th Cir. 1980)).

Shortly after *Craig*, the Fifth Circuit reached a similar result in a case brought by a single faculty member. In *Whiting v. Jackson State University*, 616 F.2d 116 (5th Cir. 1980), a white psychometry professor working at a predominantly black university claimed that his discharge was motivated by racial discrimination. The court outlined the burdens of proof applicable to the professor's claim, using the same standards applicable to other Title VII "disparate treatment" claims (see Section 5.2.1). Finding that the university's articulated reason for the discharge was a pretext and that the discharge had been motivated by racial considerations, the court affirmed the trial court's judgment for the professor: "Our traditional reluctance to intervene in university affairs cannot be allowed to undermine our statutory duty to remedy the wrong."

The *Whiting* standards were followed in *Fisher v. Dillard University*, 499 F. Supp. 525 (E.D. La. 1980), in which a predominantly black university had discharged a white Ph.D. psychologist and hired a black psychologist instead at a higher salary. The court entered judgment for the white professor. And in another similar case, *Lincoln v. Board of Regents of the University System of Georgia*, 697 F.2d 928 (11th Cir. 1983), the court affirmed the lower court's ruling that a white professor would have had her contract renewed but for her race.

In several cases that have arisen at traditionally black institutions, the defendants have argued that black faculty are needed to serve as role models for black students. However, in *Wygant v. Jackson Board of Education*, 476 U.S. 267 (1986) (see Section 5.4), the U.S. Supreme Court rejected the role model theory as a defense to race-conscious employment decisions. And in *Arenson v. Southern University*, 911 F.2d 1124 (5th Cir. 1990), a white professor seeking a tenure-track position at Southern University Law School argued that the dean's assertion that no tenure-track position existed was a pretext for race discrimination. The jury hearing Professor Arenson's Section 1981 claim found the school's defense to be pretextual, given the fact that a tenure-track position had been given to a less experienced black woman and the statement made by the chair of the law school's tenure and promotion committee that there were too many white professors on the faculty. After complicated procedural wranglings, an appellate court upheld the jury's award.[6]

---

[6]Although the jury found in Arenson's favor, the trial judge granted judgment to the university. Arenson appealed, a federal appellate court reversed the trial judge, and the trial judge then ordered a new trial. Arenson did not prevail at the second trial; the trial judge directed a verdict for all but one of the defendants at the close of the plaintiff's case. The jury found for the remaining defendant. Arenson appealed again, claiming that the district court should not have ordered the second trial because, at the time the trial court granted the judgment to the university, it did not rule on the university's motion for a new trial. Despite its discomfort with the fact that two juries reached different conclusions in this very close case, and that the trial judge had concluded that Arenson should not have prevailed, the federal appellate court ruled that the second trial should not have been granted. Judgment was granted for Arenson, and he was awarded attorney's fees as a prevailing party (*Arenson v. Southern University Law Center*, 43 F.3d 194 (5th Cir.), *decision clarified on rehearing*, 53 F.3d 80 (5th Cir. 1995)).

However, the fact that a black institution may attempt to recruit black faculty or emphasizes the role model theory is not necessarily dispositive. In *Dybczak v. Tuskegee Institute,* 737 F.2d 1524 (11th Cir. 1984), the only white academic administrator was returned to the faculty when the institute refused to agree to his demands for additional salary and a sabbatical leave. Although Professor Dybczak alleged that his return to the faculty was racially motivated, a jury found that the plaintiff's replacement, a black professor of aerospace science, was better qualified and that the plaintiff was neither discharged nor discriminated against. The appellate court found the jury's verdict supported by evidence and affirmed the verdict for the institute.

Some faculty challenging tenure or promotion denials under theories of race discrimination have claimed that bias on the part of *students,* rather than faculty or administrators, has infected the review process. This issue typically arises when a faculty member is denied promotion or tenure on the grounds of low student course evaluation scores. In these cases, the faculty member asserts that the course evaluation results are infected with students' racial bias, and thus should not be relied upon by either the college or the court. Absent some compelling evidence of student bias, however, these claims have been unsuccessful. (See, for example, *Bickerstaff v. Vassar College,* 992 F. Supp. 372 (S.D.N.Y. 1998).)

A federal trial court addressed the issue of whether a personality characteristic, alleged to be linked to an individual's national origin, can be a source of discrimination. In *Javetz v. Board of Control, Grand Valley State University,* 903 F. Supp. 1181 (W.D. Mich. 1995), a faculty member who was a native of Israel was notified that her contract would not be renewed and that she would not be evaluated for tenure. She sued the institution, alleging discrimination on the basis of national origin, religion, and gender. Among other claims, she asserted that she was discriminated against because of her personality. She argued that Israelis are "opinionated and direct," and that these are immutable characteristics and thus an inherent part of her national origin. To the extent that her colleagues and students perceived her as "confrontational, demanding, [and] difficult" (a few of the reasons given for her nonrenewal), she attributed this to her national origin and argued that negative reactions to her personality were national origin discrimination. The court refused to accept this characterization, adding that "the law does not prohibit discrimination in the workplace based on conduct that interferes with the performance of job responsibilities" (903 F. Supp. at 1190).

6.4.3.2. Sex discrimination. The largest number of discrimination lawsuits filed by faculty against colleges and universities have involved allegations of sex discrimination. Between 1972 and 1984, women filed more than half of all academic discrimination claims that resulted in decisions on the merits (George LaNoue & Barbara Lee, *Academics in Court: The Consequences of Faculty Discrimination Litigation* (University of Michigan Press, 1987), 35–36). Given the underrepresentation of women among college faculty in general (although not as severe as the underrepresentation of racial and ethnic minority faculty), and particularly at the tenured ranks, the perception that women have not been treated on equal terms with male faculty is not surprising (see

"Inequities Persist for Women and Non-Tenure-Track Faculty: The Annual Report on the Economic Status of the Profession 2004–05," *Academe,* March–April 2005, 19–98).[7]

Women faculty focused a spotlight on the problem of sex discrimination in academe with the release by the Massachusetts Institute of Technology (MIT) of a report stating that women professors in science disciplines were treated less favorably than their male counterparts (Carey Goldberg, "MIT Acknowledges Bias Against Female Professors," *New York Times,* March 23, 1999, pp. A1, A16). That report stimulated similar studies at other research universities around the country, and an examination of a wide variety of issues such as teaching assignments, workloads, office and laboratory space, and travel funds.

Sex discrimination claims have ranged from claims by individual women that a department or college applied higher standards to her than to comparable male faculty (*Namenwirth v. Regents of the University of Wisconsin,* 769 F.2d 1235 (7th Cir. 1985)) to class actions alleging that an entire institution's system of recruiting, hiring, and promoting faculty was infected with sex bias (*Lamphere v. Brown University,* 491 F. Supp. 232 (D.R.I. 1980), *affirmed,* 685 F.2d 743 (1st Cir. 1982)). In the *Lamphere* case, Brown University entered a consent decree containing guidelines on how faculty would be recruited and evaluated for hiring, promotion, and tenure. During the fourteen years that the consent decree was in effect, Brown increased the number of tenured women faculty from 12 to 67, and the number of female faculty members overall from 52 to 128 (A. De Palma, "Rare in Ivy League: Women Who Work as Full Professors," *New York Times,* January 24, 1993, at 1, 23). The University of Minnesota entered a similar consent decree after settling a class action sex discrimination case (*Rajender v. University of Minnesota,* 546 F. Supp. 158 (D. Minn. 1982), 563 F. Supp. 401 (D. Minn. 1983)).

Most sex discrimination lawsuits, however, involve a single plaintiff who argues that she was given less favorable treatment than comparable males. For example, in *Namenwirth v. Board of Regents of the University of Wisconsin,* 769 F.2d 1235 (7th Cir. 1985), an assistant professor of zoology, the first woman to be hired in a tenure-track position in the department in thirty-five years, challenged her tenure denial by arguing that her department colleagues had treated her less favorably than a male colleague with a very similar publication record. Despite the plaintiff's demonstration that more stringent standards were applied to her performance than to the comparable male faculty member, the court deferred to the department's judgment that Namenwirth showed "insufficient promise" to be granted tenure.

Women who have challenged the fairness of peer judgments have generally not been successful in court; between 1972 and 1984, only about one-fifth of individual women who claimed sex discrimination prevailed on the merits

---

[7]According to an AAUP survey conducted in academic year 2003–04, 23 percent of the full professors in U.S. colleges and universities, 38 percent of the associate professors, and 46 percent of the assistant professors were women. "Faculty Salary and Faculty Distribution Fact Sheet 2003–04," available at http://www.aaup.org/research/sal&distribution.htm.

(see LaNoue & Lee (cited above), 31). However, women who could demonstrate actual gender bias in employment decisions (such as the sexist language used in *Brown v. Trustees of Boston University,* discussed in Section 6.3.2) or a clearly different *objective* standard for men and women (such as in *Kunda v. Muhlenberg College,* also discussed in Section 6.4.2) have prevailed in their discrimination claims.

Cases involving claims of alleged sex discrimination in salary decisions are discussed in Section 6.4.4.

6.4.3.3. Disability discrimination. Most claims of disability discrimination by faculty involve allegations that the college has refused to accommodate the faculty member's physical or mental disorder. As with disability discrimination claims generally, most faculty claims of disability discrimination are unsuccessful because of the difficulty faced by all plaintiffs in meeting the Americans With Disabilities Act's (ADA) definition of disability (discussed in Section 5.2.5).

Very few ADA cases involving faculty have reached the federal appellate courts, but one such case is instructive. In *Newberry v. East Texas State University,* 161 F.3d 276 (5th Cir. 1998), the university terminated the tenure of a professor of photography, who then claimed that the termination was linked to a psychiatric disorder that he suffered. Although Newberry's behavior had been erratic and "noncollegial," and although his department peers recommended against it, the university had granted him tenure. After several incidents of problematic behavior over several years, the dean suggested that Newberry obtain counseling. The problematic behavior continued, and the dean warned Newberry that, if he did not behave more "professionally" toward his colleagues, he would be dismissed. When Newberry requested a year of disability leave, the university requested documentation of the disability, which Newberry then did not provide. The administration subsequently recommended his dismissal and, even though a faculty committee issued an advisory recommendation against this action, the president upheld Newberry's dismissal.

At trial, Newberry presented evidence that he suffered from obsessive-compulsive disorder and had been treated for that condition for several years. A jury found that Newberry was not a qualified individual with a disability for ADA purposes, and he subsequently appealed the verdict. Because there had been no testimony by any university employee that they regarded Newberry as disabled, the court affirmed the jury's verdict.

This ruling is important because it distinguishes between unprofessional behavior which, if serious enough, can sustain the termination of a tenured faculty member, and the perception that an individual who engages in problematic behavior suffers from a psychiatric disorder. The court made it clear that, particularly if the university is unaware that the individual has a psychiatric disorder, it may discipline or terminate the individual even if the misconduct is a product of the disorder.

If a faculty member's behavior interferes with the efficient operation of the institution, discharge may be upheld even if the behavior is a result of the disability. For example, in *Motzkin v. Trustees of Boston University,* 938 F. Supp. 983

(D. Mass. 1996), an untenured professor of philosophy was terminated after being found guilty by a faculty committee of sexually harassing several students and a faculty colleague. Motzkin challenged the termination, stating that he had a "depressive disorder" that caused the misconduct. The court ruled that, because teaching and interactions with students and faculty colleagues were an essential function of Motzkin's job as a professor, he was not qualified, and thus was not protected by the ADA. The court also noted that the university was not aware of Motzkin's disorder when it terminated him.

But in *Nedder v. Rivier College,* 908 F. Supp. 66 (D.N.H. 1995), 944 F. Supp. 111 (D.N.H. 1996), a federal trial court was more sympathetic to a faculty member's claim of disability discrimination. An untenured faculty member whose obesity made walking difficult was criticized by college officials and was denied reappointment. The court rejected the plaintiff's claim that her obesity constituted a disability because the court did not regard the difficulty she encountered in walking as a substantial limitation. But the court refused to grant summary judgment on the issue of whether college officials perceived Professor Nedder as disabled. A jury concluded that the college had regarded her as disabled, primarily because her supervisors had made critical comments characterizing her as a negative role model for students because of her obesity. The court ordered the college to reinstate Nedder to her faculty position, and awarded her $137,500 in compensatory damages.

In *Nedder,* unlike *Newberry* and *Motzkin,* there was testimony concerning critical remarks about the plaintiff's condition and negative stereotyping of the plaintiff. In cases in which a plaintiff attempts to demonstrate that he or she is regarded as disabled by an employer, the employer's own words and actions may be used to demonstrate an improper motive on the employer's part. The *Nedder* case provides an interesting and useful reminder of this fact.

For faculty and administrators who desire guidance on the type of issue presented in *Newberry*—employee disclosures of psychiatric disorders—the EEOC has issued "Enforcement Guidance on the Americans With Disabilities Act and Psychiatric Disabilities" (March 25, 1997), which is available on the EEOC's Web site at http://www.eeoc.gov. These guidelines describe the type of psychiatric disorders that may be protected by the ADA, discuss the circumstances under which an employer may seek information from an individual about a possible psychiatric disability, discuss the application of "reasonable accommodation" to psychiatric disabilities, examine the relationship between workplace misconduct and psychiatric disabilities, and review the "direct threat" standard in the context of psychiatric disabilities. (For a discussion of employers' obligations under the ADA to employees with psychiatric disorders, see Barbara A. Lee & Peter H. Ruger, *Accommodating Faculty and Staff with Psychiatric Disorders* (National Association of College and University Attorneys, 2003).)

6.4.3.4. Age discrimination. College faculty alleging age discrimination have directed their complaints at two major areas: discrimination with regard to pensions or other retirement benefits, and salary discrimination. An additional issue with both legal and policy ramifications for institutions of higher education is the "uncapping" of the mandatory age-seventy retirement provision in the Age Discrimination in Employment Act (ADEA) (see Section 5.2.6).

The elimination of mandatory retirement means that colleges and universities may divest themselves of older faculty in one of two ways: entice them to retire, usually by providing financial incentives, or dismiss them for cause. Legal issues related to dismissing tenured faculty for cause are discussed in Section 6.7.2; such action would require extensive documentation of performance or discipline problems. (For an analysis of this issue, see A. Morris, *Dismissal of Tenured Higher Education Faculty: Legal Implications of the Elimination of Mandatory Retirement* (National Organization on Legal Problems of Education, 1992). See also N. DiGiovanni, Jr., *Age Discrimination: An Administrator's Guide* (College and University Personnel Association, 1989).)

Others have questioned whether, in light of the elimination of mandatory retirement, colleges and universities should consider alternatives to tenure. (For discussion of potential alternatives to tenure for older faculty, see O. Ruebhausen, "The Age Discrimination in Employment Act Amendments of 1986: Implications for Tenure and Retirement," 14 *J. Coll. & Univ. Law* 561 (1988); and a rejoinder, M. Finkin, "Tenure After an Uncapped ADEA: A Different View," 15 *J. Coll. & Univ. Law* 43 (1988). For an analysis of the impact of uncapping on college staffing policies and practices, see Ronald G. Ehrenberg, "The Survey of Changes in Faculty Retirement Policies" (2001), conducted by Professor Ehrenberg for the American Association of University Professors, and available on its Web site at http://www.aaup.org/retrpt.htm.) A study comparing retirement patterns of faculty before and after the 1994 expiration of the faculty exemption concluded that retirement rates for faculty age seventy and over fell substantially after 1994 (Orley Ashenfelter & David Card, "Did the Elimination of Mandatory Retirement Affect Faculty Retirement?" 92 *American Economic Review* 957 (2002)).

6.4.4. Challenges to salary decisions.

The Equal Pay Act (see Section 5.2.2 of this book) forbids gender-based salary discrimination, and Title VII protects individuals from salary discrimination on the basis of gender, race, religion, national origin, and color. The Age Discrimination in Employment Act prohibits employers from treating older workers less favorably with respect to compensation. Most salary discrimination claims brought by faculty involve charges of either age or sex discrimination.

Individual faculty have challenged salary decisions under the ADEA, asserting that their institution favored younger faculty by paying newly hired faculty a higher salary than that of older faculty hired years earlier. In *MacPherson v. University of Montevallo*, 922 F.2d 766 (11th Cir. 1991), two business school professors who were the oldest and the lowest-paid faculty in the college alleged both disparate impact and disparate treatment discrimination in the university's salary practices. Their disparate impact claim was based on the business school's practice of basing the salary of incoming faculty on market factors and research productivity, since the school was seeking accreditation of its business school. The trial judge ordered a directed verdict for the university on the ground that, although the market-rate salary practice did exclude older faculty, the university made market-based salary adjustments for older faculty and each plaintiff had received one. The appellate court affirmed that portion of the ruling, holding that market-linked pay for new hires is a legitimate business reason for paying younger faculty more than older faculty.

With regard to the plaintiffs' claim of disparate treatment, the trial judge found that comparator faculty who were younger and more highly paid had more skills and different disciplines; furthermore, the plaintiffs had done little significant research and had few publications. There was some question, however, about the way in which salary decisions were made, so the appellate court affirmed the trial judge's order for a new trial.

The U.S. Court of Appeals for the Seventh Circuit was presented with a similar claim in *Davidson v. Board of Governors of State Colleges and Universities*, 920 F.2d 441 (7th Cir. 1990). A professor of business hired at age fifty-eight challenged a provision in the collective bargaining agreement that permitted the institution to give a salary adjustment to any faculty member who could present a bona fide offer of employment from another institution. Although Judge Posner, writing for a unanimous panel, agreed that salary practices that relied on market forces had a disparate impact on older faculty members, he noted that comparable worth is not required by the civil rights laws, and that the market is a neutral criterion on which to base salary determinations. Posner observed that the market alternatives of faculty who have been at an institution for a long time are "relatively poor and they fare relatively badly under any market-based compensation scheme, regardless of age" (920 F.2d at 446).

MacPherson and *Davidson* illustrate the difficult problem of salary compression faced by many institutions, and the potential for age discrimination allegations if salary decisions are not clearly based on factors unrelated to age. For example, merit pay systems have been challenged as discriminatory, and the criteria for decisions must relate closely to the institution's need for productive faculty. (For an example of a merit pay system that survived judicial scrutiny when sex discrimination was alleged, see *Willner v. University of Kansas*, 848 F.2d 1023 (10th Cir. 1988).)

A survey conducted during the 2004–05 academic year shows that nationally, women faculty at the same rank as male faculty earn less than their male peers. According to the survey results, women full professors earned 91 percent of what male full professors earned, women associate professors earned 94 percent of what their male counterparts earned, and women assistant professors earned 93 percent of male assistant professors' pay ("Inequities Persist for Women and Non-Tenure Track Faculty: The Annual Report on the Economic Status of the Profession," *Academe*, March–April 2005, 19–98). While some experts believe that rank and number of years since the doctorate are the strongest predictors of salary differences, others argue that rank may be a "tainted variable" if women or racial minorities are promoted more slowly than their male counterparts. And apart from these arguments, there is evidence that salaries are lower for faculty in predominantly female disciplines, such as nursing and social work (a potential equal pay issue).

An extreme example of the debate over the appropriate criteria to use in making salary equity comparisons occurred in *Sobel v. Yeshiva University*, 566 F. Supp. 1166 (S.D.N.Y. 1983), *reversed and remanded*, 797 F.2d 1478 (2d Cir. 1986), *on remand,* 656 F. Supp. 587 (S.D.N.Y. 1987), *reversed and remanded,* 839 F.2d 18 (2d Cir. 1988). In this class action, a female medical school professor alleged that salaries of women faculty were significantly lower than salaries of male faculty, using multiple regression analysis to isolate the effect of certain variables on salary levels. Although a trial judge twice found the plaintiff's statistical evidence to be inadequate, the appellate court remanded and ordered that the court apply the standard developed by the U.S. Supreme Court in *Bazemore v. Friday,* 478 U.S. 385 (1986). In *Bazemore,* the Court had ruled that plaintiffs could rely in their statistical analyses on pre–Title VII enactment salary data if they could show that such data influenced post–Title VII actions (or inaction) by the employer. (For analysis of the problems involved in demonstrating salary discrimination through the use of statistics, see J. McKeown, "Statistics for Wage Discrimination Cases: Why the Statistical Models Used Cannot Prove or Disprove Sex Discrimination," 67 *Ind. L.J.* 633 (1992); and T. Campbell, "Regression Analysis in Title VII Cases: Minimum Standards, Comparable Worth, and Other Issues Where Law and Statistics Meet," 36 *Stan. L. Rev.* 1299 (1984). For an analysis of the comparable worth doctrine in general, see "Symposium: Comparable Worth," 20 *J.L. Reform* 1 (1986).)

Classwide salary discrimination cases have been brought by faculty at the University of Washington, Virginia Commonwealth University, the University of Rhode Island, Kent State University, the University of Minnesota, and Illinois State University, among others (see Donna R. Euben, "Show Me the Money: Pay Equity in the Academy," *Academe,* July–August 2001, 30–36). Not all of the cases were brought by women faculty, however; the Virginia Commonwealth and Minnesota cases were brought by men who challenged salary adjustments given only to women whose salaries were found to be lower than those of comparable male faculty.

The cases differ in reasoning and outcome, since the defendant colleges have widely varying salary practices. For example, when women faculty sued the University of Rhode Island, claiming that its system of grouping similar disciplines in salary tiers discriminated against women, who were clustered in the lower-paid tiers, the court ruled for the university. In *Donnelley v. Rhode Island Board of Governors for Higher Education,* 110 F.3d 2 (1st Cir. 1997), the court found that "the professors' choice of academic field and the workings of the national market," not the university's salary structure, were the reasons for pay differences between men and women (110 F.3d at 5). And five women professors of dentistry suing the University of Washington were unable to persuade the court to grant them class certification because the women presented evidence of intentional salary discrimination only within the School of Dentistry, not the university as a whole (*Oda et al. v. State of Washington,* 44 P.3d 8 (Ct. App. Wash. 2002)). Women faculty at Kent State University and Eastern Michigan University, however, received classwide salary settlements as a result of salary discrimination litigation (both settlements are discussed in the Euben article, cited above).

Two cases of "reverse discrimination" resulted in victories for male faculty who challenged gender-based salary adjustments as violations of Title VII. In

Maitland v. University of Minnesota, 155 F.3d 1013 (8th Cir. 1998), a male professor, Ian Maitland, challenged the university's decision to distribute $3 million in salary increases to women faculty who could demonstrate that they were underpaid relative to men. (The special salary increases were a result of the *Rajender* settlement, discussed briefly in Section 6.4.2.2.) Although the trial court had ruled in the university's favor, the appellate court reversed, ruling that the statistical studies used by the women faculty and the university's own study were both flawed, and their conclusions concerning the seriousness of the salary gap did not agree.

In *Smith v. Virginia Commonwealth University,* 84 F.3d 672 (4th Cir. 1996), five male faculty members challenged the university's decision to distribute $440,000 in salary increases to women faculty whom a salary study had found were underpaid relative to similar male faculty. Although the trial court had ruled for the university, the appellate court reversed, criticizing the statistical study on which the decision had been based because it did not take into account the quality of the faculty members' performance or the fact that some of the male faculty had previously held administrative positions, which had inflated their subsequent faculty salaries. Although the appellate court remanded the case for trial, the university settled with the faculty plaintiffs.

Individual women faculty have achieved some success in equal pay claims. In *Siler-Khodr v. University of Texas Health Science Center San Antonio,* 261 F.3d 542 (5th Cir. 2002), a federal appellate court affirmed a jury verdict awarding nearly $100,000 in back pay to a female professor of obstetrics and gynecology whom a jury found was paid $20,000 per year less than a male colleague with the same academic qualifications and job responsibilities. The plaintiff had introduced two statistical reports that found that women faculty throughout the university were paid less than similar male faculty. The defendant university did not provide expert testimony to rebut the plaintiffs' reports. In addition to the back pay award, the judge ordered the university to raise the plaintiff's pay to the amount paid her male counterpart.

In *Lavin-McEleney v. Marist College,* 239 F.3d 476 (2d Cir. 2001), the plaintiff, a professor of criminal justice, sued the college under the Equal Pay Act. Her expert produced a statistical analysis demonstrating that the plaintiff was paid less than comparable male faculty in her division. Although the college provided evidence that the salary difference was linked to market factors (women faculty tended to cluster in lower-paying disciplines) rather than to gender, the jury returned a verdict for the plaintiff. The college appealed, criticizing the statistical analysis and arguing that it was based on a "composite" male comparator rather than an actual individual. The court disagreed, ruling that, although an actual comparator male faculty member used by the plaintiff was in a different department, he was in the same division, and the differences between the two disciplines were unrelated to salary.

In light of the attention generated by the MIT study of gender inequity, and the level of litigation activity with respect to gender equity in salary, colleges should carefully consider the implications of salary surveys and how they will respond to either individuals or to groups of faculty—of either gender—who believe that their compensation is below that of genuinely comparable faculty of the opposite gender. Regular evaluations of faculty performance linked to relevant criteria (such as the quality of teaching, publishing, and service), and salary decisions tied to those evaluations, should help institutions practice both good performance management and lawful salary-setting practices. Institutions that allow administrators to make salary increase decisions without clear criteria and without explicit links to performance risk the outcome of *Harrington v. Harris*, 118 F.3d 359 (5th Cir. 1997), in which a federal appellate court considered whether the law school's associate dean at Texas Southern University, an historically black institution, had discriminated against three white law professors in determining their salaries over a period of several years. Using African American faculty of the same seniority and rank as comparators, the plaintiff professors had claimed that the approximately $3,000 average gap between the salaries of white faculty and African American faculty was due to race discrimination. The court upheld the jury verdict and trial court judgment that the associate dean's actions violated Section 1981 (see Section 5.2.4).

6.4.5. Other workplace issues.
The end of mandatory retirement for college faculty appears to have stimulated litigation over changes in work assignments for older faculty. For example, in *Boise v. Boufford*, 127 F. Supp. 2d 467 (S.D.N.Y. 2001), *affirmed in part and vacated in part*, 42 Fed. Appx. 496 (2d Cir. 2002) (unpublished), a seventy-two-year-old professor of public administration claimed that actions by the dean of the School of Public Service to reduce his teaching assignments and to assign him to develop new courses under the direction of a less experienced professor of lower rank constituted discrimination. He also claimed that these actions constituted "endentured [sic] servitude, involuntary service, maladministration, administrative malpractice, and hostile work environment." The appellate court affirmed the trial court's dismissal of the latter claims, but refused to dismiss the age, disability, gender, and race discrimination claims, finding that the allegations were sufficient to establish a *prima facie* case of discrimination. (The complaint was later dismissed at 2003 U.S. Dist. LEXIS 18639 (S.D.N.Y. October 21, 2003).)

However, the outcome was different for a sixty-two-year-old professor of psychology. The plaintiff had not published for several years nor supervised a dissertation for nearly a decade, and was reassigned from graduate teaching to undergraduate courses by the graduate director. The plaintiff filed an age discrimination claim. In *Curley v. St. John's University*, 19 F. Supp. 2d 181 (S.D.N.Y. 1998), the graduate director and dean had received complaints from graduate students about the poor quality of the plaintiff's teaching. The graduate director had made negative age-related comments about the plaintiff in the past, and the court ruled that these were sufficient to allow the case to proceed to trial; the university's motion for summary judgment was denied.

In a case with facts similar to those in *Curley*, but no evidence of age-related remarks by administrators, the plaintiff did not withstand the college's motion for summary judgment. In *Tuttle v. Brandeis University*, 2002 Mass. Super. LEXIS 7 (Mass. Super. 2002), a chemistry professor of thirty-four years' tenure at the university who had received poor student course evaluations was given no salary increase that year, and was assigned to develop new interdisciplinary courses. When the plaintiff responded by refusing to participate in administering Ph.D. examinations, his salary was reduced by $500 the following year. When the plaintiff refused to develop the new interdisciplinary course, the university reduced his salary by 30 percent. A faculty committee reviewed the administration's decision to invoke the salary reduction, but split into majority and minority groups. The salary reduction was done, and the plaintiff sued under state law for age discrimination, retaliation, and breach of contract. The court entered summary judgment for the university, ruling that there was no evidence that either the new work assignment or the salary reduction were based upon his age.

Sec. 6.5. *Affirmative Action in Faculty Employment Decisions*

As discussed in Section 5.4, affirmative action in employment has had a volatile history, and that history is still being written. The principles of affirmative action, the legal justifications and criticisms, and judicial reaction to affirmative action in employment are discussed in Section 5.4. The rulings of the U.S. Supreme Court in two college admissions cases involving affirmative action, *Gratz v. Bollinger* and *Grutter v. Bollinger,* are discussed in Section 8.2.5.

Race- or gender-conscious faculty hiring or promotion decisions are equally controversial, if not more so, because of the relative scarcity of faculty positions and the intense competition for them. Challenges to such hiring or promotion decisions tend to be brought under federal or state employment discrimination laws by a white plaintiff who alleges "reverse discrimination," a claim that the college improperly used race, gender, or some other protected characteristic to make the employment decision. (For a discussion of nondiscrimination law as applied to faculty, see Section 6.4.)

Affirmative action for remedial purposes requires the college to prove a history of racial segregation or other racial discrimination. Even for those colleges in states where segregation was practiced prior to the Civil Rights Act of 1964, showing the present effects of past discrimination may be difficult (see, for example, the *Podberesky* case, discussed in Section 8.3.4). For public institutions in states where a history of *de jure* segregation of public higher education has not been documented or addressed, however, establishing prior discrimination in the employment of faculty may be even more difficult. Similar difficulties may arise in attempting to ascertain the present effects of prior gender discrimination.

Given the outcomes in *Weber, Wygant,* and related cases (discussed in Section 5.4), both public and private institutions should analyze carefully the effect of their affirmative action plans on existing and prospective majority faculty members to ensure that racial or gender preferences are not implemented in a way that would "unnecessarily trammel" their interests (under Title VII) or fail the strict scrutiny test (under the federal equal protection clause). Two of the factors relied on in *Weber*—that the plan did not require the discharge of any white workers and that the plan was temporary—appear to be easily transferable to and easily met in the context of postsecondary faculty hiring. But the third factor—that the plan did not "create an absolute bar to the advancement of white employees"—bears careful watching in postsecondary education. The special training programs at issue in *Weber* benefited both black and white employees. Thirteen workers were selected, seven black and six white. At postsecondary institutions, however, faculty vacancies or special opportunities such as department chairmanships generally occur one at a time and on an irregular basis. A decision that a particular opening will be filled by a minority (or a woman) may, in effect, serve as a complete bar to whites (or men), especially in a small department where there is little turnover and where the date of the next opening cannot be predicted. Institutions that use race or gender only as a "plus" factor, rather than targeting specific positions for a particular race or gender, may be able to satisfy the *Weber* test more successfully (see the *Johnson* case in Section 5.4.2). Public institutions, however, must still satisfy the requirements of the equal protection clause. The rulings of the U.S Supreme Court in *Gratz v. Bollinger* and *Grutter v. Bollinger* (2003) suggest that using race or gender as one nondecisive criterion among others used to make a hiring or promotion decision may pass equal protection clause scrutiny (and Title VII scrutiny as well). The success of such arguments will depend on whether the courts accept a diversity rationale as a basis for affirmative action in employment (see Section 5.4.3).

The U.S. Supreme Court has not yet ruled on a case in which a college or university used race-conscious provisions in an affirmative action plan to make a faculty employment decision. A federal appellate court, however, addressed this issue. In *Valentine v. Smith*, 654 F.2d 503 (8th Cir. 1981), Valentine, a disappointed white job applicant, challenged an affirmative action plan in place at Arkansas State University (ASU) under the equal protection clause. ASU had an affirmative action program for faculty hiring that was implemented as part of a court-ordered desegregation plan for the Arkansas state college and university system. The court found the affirmative action plan to have relied upon appropriate governmental findings of prior *de jure* segregation, and ruled that the use of race as a hiring criterion was lawful.

Although *Valentine*, unlike *Weber*, is an equal protection case, the court's equal protection analysis of affirmative action plans is similar to the *Weber* and *Johnson* Title VII analyses, and does not apply the strict scrutiny test later mandated by *Croson*. The court's opinion focuses, for example, on the existence of racial imbalance in the relevant job categories, on the temporary character of the affirmative action plan, and on the absence of "unnecessary trammeling" on white employees' interests—the same factors emphasized in *Weber*. The court's failure to apply the strict scrutiny test, used subsequently by the Supreme Court in *Wygant, Croson, Adarand, Gratz*, and *Grutter*, suggests that it is unlikely that the analysis used in *Valentine* meets equal protection clause standards, although the outcome of the case might have been the same because of the remedial nature of the affirmative action plan.

Once findings of the institution's historical discrimination and its present effects are made, a public college or university apparently has much the same authority as a private institution to implement a remedial affirmative action plan.[8] One difference is that *Weber* allows private employers to use explicit quotas under Title VII, while the equal protection clause, applicable to public employers, prohibits the use of explicit quotas (see *Bakke, Croson, Adarand, Grutter,* and *Gratz*).

An unusual lawsuit against the City University of New York (CUNY) suggests that administrators should consider carefully the implications of including certain ethnic groups (beyond the traditional categories of African American, Asian, Hispanic, and Native American) in affirmative action plans. In *Scelsa v. City University of New York*, 806 F. Supp. 1126 (S.D.N.Y. 1992), *affirmed* 76 F.3d 37 (2d Cir. 1996), an Italian American professor challenged a decision by CUNY to transfer the Calendra Italian American Institute from Manhattan to Staten Island and to reassign its director of nearly twenty years to other administrative responsibilities. Scelsa, the director, sued the university under Title VI of the Civil Rights Act (see Section 13.5.2) as well as under Title VII and the equal protection clause. He asserted that the university's affirmative action plan, developed nearly two decades earlier, had designated Italian Americans an underrepresented group among its faculty and staff, but the university had done little to correct that underrepresentation. The plaintiffs sought a preliminary injunction to halt the transfer of the institute and its director, which the judge granted, citing evidence of underrepresentation of Italian Americans among CUNY's faculty and staff and the evident failure of the university to follow its voluntarily adopted affirmative action plan.

Three other "reverse discrimination" cases demonstrate the continuing struggles of courts to reconcile the equal opportunity laws with universities' concern for diversity. The most thoughtful discussion of the issue occurs in *Hill v. Ross*, 183 F.3d 586 (7th Cir. 1999). In *Hill*, the psychology department at the University of Wisconsin at Whitewater had selected a male candidate for a tenure-track position. The dean rejected the department's recommendation, stating that the department was required to hire a woman because there were fewer women faculty in the department than their proportion among holders of doctoral degrees in psychology. Hill, the male candidate who was not hired, filed a sex discrimination claim against the dean and the university under both Title VII and the equal protection clause. The university defended its actions on the basis of its affirmative action plan, and the trial court awarded summary judgment to the university. The appellate court reversed.

The appellate court reviewed U.S. Supreme Court affirmative action cases, including *Wygant* and *Johnson*. Those cases, the court said, concluded that race or gender could be used "only as factors in a more complex calculus, not as independently dispositive criteria" (183 F.3d at 588). The dean had used gender as the "sole basis" for the hiring decision, and did not discuss Hill's qualifications

---

[8]See, for example, *Palmer v. District Board of Trustees of St. Petersburg Junior College*, 748 F.2d 595 (11th Cir. 1984) (judicial and federal agency findings of prior *de jure* segregation justified race-conscious hiring by the university). See also *Enright v. California State University*, 57 Fair Empl. Prac. Cases 56 (E.D. Cal. 1989) (university's actions complied with *Weber* test). Both cases were brought under Title VII.

nor the department's recommendation in his memo rejecting Hill's candidacy. Nor did the dean use the department's apparent failure to follow the recruitment process required by the university's affirmative action plan as justification for rejecting Hill. A jury could conclude, said the court, that the dean had created a quota system for hiring in the psychology department.

Citing the U.S. Supreme Court's opinion in *United States v. Commonwealth of Virginia* (see Section 8.2.4.2 of this book), the court said that any preference for a particular sex must be "exceedingly persuasive." And even if the plaintiff had the burden to demonstrate that the affirmative action plan was unconstitutional (as *Wygant* and *Johnson* had established), the court suggested that this burden may no longer exist after *Adarand*. Moreover, Hill had proven that the dean's reliance on the plan was pretextual. The plan's own terms did not support the dean's decision, said the court, and because the university denied having engaged in prior discrimination, it could not justify the plan as a remedial strategy. The court then embarked on a lengthy discussion of how women (or some other group) could be "underrepresented" in a small department as a result of chance rather than as a result of discrimination. Furthermore, said the court, the university had not provided institution-wide data, so it could not demonstrate systemic exclusion of women from faculty positions (a showing that might have justified gender-conscious hiring as a remedy, such as in *Johnson*). The court concluded that "a plan to have every department duplicate the pool from which it is drawn cannot be sustained as a valid affirmative action plan" (183 F.3d at 592), and remanded the case for trial.[9]

In *Stern v. Trustees of Columbia University,* 131 F.3d 305 (2d Cir. 1997), the court vacated the trial court's grant of summary judgment for the university in a "reverse" national origin discrimination case. Professor Stern, a white male, had served as acting director of the Spanish Language program. The university decided to appoint a full-time director. Following the requirements of its affirmative action plan, and despite the department's strong preference that Stern be given the full-time position, the university initiated a national search for applicants. The vice president for arts and sciences appointed an interdepartmental search committee, most of whom did not speak, read, or write Spanish. Stern was among three finalists for the position. The other candidates were a white woman and a Latino male, Augustus Puelo. After conducting interviews and observing each of the candidates teaching a "model" class, the search committee recommended that Puelo be given the position on the strength of his superior teaching. Stern was the only candidate who held a doctorate, the only candidate who had extensive publications and teaching experience, and the only candidate who could teach Portuguese, a language that the department needed additional faculty to teach. Stern then sued the university for national origin discrimination under Title VII.

---

[9]The reasoning of this case, and the Supreme Court's opinions in *Gratz* and *Grutter,* suggest that the analysis used in *Enright v. California State University,* 57 Fair Empl. Prac. Cases 56 (E.D. Cal. 1989) may be insufficient to satisfy equal protection clause requirements (manifest imbalance between the proportion of women in the population and the proportion of women with Ph.D.s in sociology rendered the sociology profession a "traditionally segregated" field, justifying gender-conscious hiring by a public university).

The trial court granted the university's motion for summary judgment, stating that Stern had not provided sufficient evidence to rebut the university's contention that Puelo had administrative and teaching skills that were superior to Stern's. The appellate court vacated that judgment, ruling that the trial court had given insufficient weight to Stern's assertions that the vice president had predetermined the outcome of the search, and that members of the search committee had stated that Stern would not be given serious consideration for the job. Stern had also offered evidence of the preference of several search committee members for a Latino director. The court ruled that Stern's case should go to trial.

A dissenting judge objected to the majority's "improper" substitution of its own judgment for that of the university, citing *Fisher v. Vassar College* (Section 6.4.2). Despite Stern's allegedly superior qualifications, said the dissenting judge, the university had the right to make the hiring decision based on the faculty's reaction to the candidates' teaching prowess; the determination of which qualifications were more important rested with the university, said the judge, not with the court.

In contrast to *Stern* and *Hill*, the Nevada Supreme Court was more deferential to the judgment of a university with respect to an allegation of "reverse discrimination." The reasoning used by that court was closer to the reasoning of *Grutter*, particularly in its reliance on *Bakke*, than the decisions discussed above. In *University and Community College System of Nevada v. Farmer*, 930 P.2d 730 (Nev. 1997), the state's highest court reversed a state trial court's ruling that the University of Nevada, Reno impermissibly used racial criteria to hire a black male for a faculty position in the sociology department. The university had instituted a "minority bonus policy" because of its concern that only 1 percent of its faculty were black and 25 percent were women. The policy allowed a department to hire an additional faculty member if it first hired a candidate from a racial minority group.

The department of sociology had a vacant faculty position in 1990 and instituted a national search. Farmer, a white female, and Makoba, a black male, were two of the three finalists. The department sought permission to interview only Makoba, the candidate ranked most qualified by the department. The university agreed, and Makoba was hired at a salary of $35,000, which would increase to $40,000 when he completed his dissertation. This salary exceeded the published salary range in the position description. One year later, Farmer was hired by the same department at a starting salary of $31,000, and a $2,000 increase upon completion of her dissertation.

Farmer subsequently sued the university, challenging its affirmative action plan and its "minority bonus policy" as both unconstitutional and as contrary to Title VII's proscription of race and gender discrimination. The trial court entered judgment for Farmer in the amount of $40,000. On appeal, the Nevada Supreme Court reversed the trial court. Citing *Bakke* (see Section 8.2.5), the court noted that Makoba had been selected not only because of his race, but because he was well qualified for the position by virtue of his publications, teaching experience, and his area of specialization. The court said: "We also view the desirability of a racially diverse faculty as sufficiently analogous to the constitutionally permissible attainment of a racially diverse student body countenanced by the *Bakke* Court" (930 P.2d at 735). The university's affirmative action plan complied with the *Weber* factors, said the court, and even passed the strict scrutiny test:

> The University demonstrated that it has a compelling interest in fostering a culturally and ethnically diverse faculty. A failure to attract minority faculty perpetuates the University's white enclave and further limits student exposure to multicultural diversity. Moreover, the minority bonus policy is narrowly tailored to accelerate racial and gender diversity [930 P.2d at 735].

Thus the plan passed constitutional muster, and, since the court determined the qualifications of the candidates to be equivalent (although the university had concluded that Makoba was slightly better qualified), "the University must be given the latitude to make its own employment decisions provided that they are not discriminatory" (930 P.2d at 735).

Farmer had also asserted an Equal Pay Act claim. The court rejected it as well, since the higher salary was necessary to attract Makoba who, as a scarce resource in the labor market, could command a higher salary. The university had paid higher salaries to women in disciplines in which they were underrepresented (such as chemistry), so it was able to persuade the court that the salary differential was a result of market forces, not discrimination.

The Supreme Court's ruling in *Grutter* established that student body diversity is a compelling interest for public colleges and universities. Although it remains to be seen how directly subsequent courts will apply *Grutter* to affirmative action in employment (rather than in admissions), it appears that colleges could make the argument that diversity of faculty is as important to "educational diversity" as the diversity of the student body. The opinion in *Farmer* suggests that such an argument could comply with *Grutter* if the protected characteristic (race, gender) were not the sole reason for the hiring or promotion decision, but only one factor among others used after determining that the individual was well qualified for the position and that there was a "manifest imbalance" that needed to be addressed. Although the Court in *Grutter* did not explicitly apply the *Weber* test to the admissions decisions at the University of Michigan Law School, it stated that narrow tailoring (a required element of strict scrutiny under the equal protection clause) requires that there be no "undue harm" to nonminorities, and that the affirmative action plan be limited in time—two of the *Weber* criteria. *Grutter* also exhibits deference to the decisions of academic institutions, citing *Sweezy* (see Section 7.1.4) regarding the academic freedom of institutions to select their own students. That case also discusses the selection of "who may teach" as an element of an institution's academic freedom, suggesting that the rationale of *Grutter* could also be applied to academic employment decisions.

Although *Grutter* did not address employment at all, its declaration that diversity in an educational institution is a compelling state interest, and its reaffirmance of the vitality of Justice Powell's opinion in *Bakke,* provides some guidance for colleges with respect to academic employment. For private colleges, *Grutter* does not limit, and in some ways enhances, the colleges' ability to implement carefully developed voluntary affirmative action programs for faculty hiring that meet the *Weber* test and that involve hiring and promotions rather than dismissals or layoffs. For public colleges, *Grutter* suggests that affirmative action plans that are closely linked to the institution's educational mission, and that can demonstrate a strong relationship between the institution's educational mission and the diversity of its faculty, may survive constitutional challenge. Of course, the plan would need to use goals rather than quotas, and would need to ensure that the protected characteristic (race, gender) was not the sole criterion, but one of a constellation of relevant factors, in the hiring decision.

Sec. 6.6. Standards and Criteria for Faculty Personnel Decisions

6.6.1. General principles. Postsecondary institutions commonly have written and published standards or criteria to guide decisions regarding faculty appointments, contract renewals, promotions, and the granting and termination of tenure. Since they will often constitute part of the contract between the institution and the faculty member (see Section 6.2) and thus bind the institution, such evaluative standards and criteria should receive the careful attention of administrators and faculty members alike. If particular standards are not intended to be legally binding or are not intended to apply to certain kinds of personnel decisions, those limitations should be made clear in the standards themselves.

While courts will enforce standards or criteria found to be part of the faculty contract, the law accords postsecondary institutions wide discretion in determining the content and specificity of those standards and criteria. And although the traditional criteria of teaching, scholarship (or creative activity), and service have been applied for decades to faculty employment decisions, additional criteria (and challenges to the use of those criteria) have developed in the past decade. Additional performance criteria addressing the interpersonal relationships of the tenure or promotion candidate ("collegiality") have been applied—and challenged—on many campuses. Cases alleging that the interpretation of tenure criteria has changed between a faculty member's hiring and eventual tenure review have also been brought—and generally rejected by courts. And criteria unrelated to a faculty member's performance, such as the proportion of tenured faculty already present in a department, have been used, and challenged, as well. Judicial responses to these challenges are discussed in Section 6.6.3.

Courts are less likely to become involved in disputes concerning the substance of standards and criteria than in disputes over procedures for applying standards and criteria. (Courts draw the same distinction in cases concerning students; see the discussion in Sections 9.2 through 9.4.) In rejecting the claims of a community college faculty member, for example, the court in *Brouillette v. Board of Directors of Merged Area IX*, 519 F.2d 126 (8th Cir. 1975), quoted an earlier case to note that "such matters as the competence of teachers and the standards of its measurement are not, without more, matters of constitutional dimensions. They are peculiarly appropriate to state and local administration." And in *Riggin v. Board of Trustees of Ball State University*, 489 N.E.2d 616 (Ind. Ct. App. 1986), the court indicated that it "must give deference to [the board of trustees'] expertise" and that it "may not reweigh the evidence or determine the credibility of witnesses," since "peer groups make the judgment on the performance of a faculty member." And in *Dorsett v. Board of Trustees for State Colleges and Universities*, 940 F.2d 121, 123 (5th Cir. 1991) (quoting earlier cases), the court warned that "[o]f all fields that the federal courts 'should hesitate to invade and take over, education and faculty appointments at the university level are probably the least suited for federal court supervision.'"

Despite this generally deferential judicial attitude, there are several bases on which an institution's standards and criteria may be legally scrutinized. For both public and private institutions, questions regarding consistency with AAUP policies may be raised in AAUP investigations (Section 14.5) or in court (Section 6.2.3). When standards or criteria are part of the faculty contract, both public and private institutions' disputes over interpretation may wind up in court or in the institution's internal grievance process. Cases on attaining tenure and on dismissal from tenured positions for "just cause" are prominent examples. For public institutions, standards or criteria may also be embodied in state statutes or administrative regulations that are subject to interpretation by courts, state administrative agencies (such as boards of regents or civil service commissions), or decision makers within the institution's internal grievance process. The tenure denial and termination cases are again excellent examples.[10] And under the various federal nondiscrimination statutes discussed in Section 5.3, courts or federal administrative agencies may scrutinize the standards and criteria of public and private institutions for their potential discriminatory applications (see, for example, *Bennun v. Rutgers, The State University of New Jersey*, 941 F.2d 154 (3d Cir. 1991)); these standards and criteria also may be examined in the course of an internal grievance process when one is required by federal regulations or otherwise provided by the institution.

In public institutions, standards and criteria may also be subjected to constitutional scrutiny under the First and Fourteenth Amendments. Under the First Amendment, a standard or criterion can be challenged as "overbroad" if it is so broadly worded that it can be used to penalize faculty members for having exercised constitutionally protected rights of free expression. Under the Fourteenth Amendment, a standard or criterion can be challenged as "vague" if it is so unclear that institutional personnel cannot understand its meaning in concrete circumstances. (The overbreadth and vagueness doctrines are discussed further

---

[10]The cases and authorities for both statutes and contract clauses are collected in Annot., "Construction and Effect of Tenure Provisions of Contract or Statute Governing Employment of College or University Faculty Member," 66 A.L.R.3d 1018.

in Sections 9.1.3, 9.2.2, and 9.5.3.) The leading U.S. Supreme Court case on overbreadth and vagueness in public employment standards is *Arnett v. Kennedy,* 416 U.S. 134 (1974). A federal civil servant had been dismissed under a statute authorizing dismissal "for such cause as will promote the efficiency of the service." A majority of the Court held that this standard, as applied in the federal service, was neither overbroad nor vague.

While the result in *Arnett* suggests that the overbreadth and vagueness doctrines do not substantially restrict the standard-setting process, it does not necessarily mean that public postsecondary institutions can use the same "cause" standard approved in *Arnett.* Employment standards should be adapted to the characteristics and functions of the group to which the standards apply. A standard acceptable for a large heterogeneous group such as the federal civil service may not be acceptable for a smaller, more homogeneous group such as a college faculty. (See, for example, *Bence v. Breier,* 501 F.2d 1185 (7th Cir. 1974), which held that the discharge standard of a local police force must be more stringently scrutinized for overbreadth and vagueness than was the federal discharge standard in *Arnett.*) Courts may thus be somewhat stricter with a postsecondary institution's standards than with the federal government's—particularly when the standards are applied to what is arguably expressive activity, in which case the overbreadth and vagueness doctrines would combine with academic freedom principles (see Section 7.1) to create important limits on institutional discretion in devising employment standards.

Under the Fourteenth Amendment, a public institution's standards and criteria for personnel decisions may also be challenged using substantive due process principles. Such challenges are only occasionally successful. In *Harrington v. Harris,* 118 F.3d 359 (5th Cir. 1997), for instance, a federal appellate court affirmed a jury's verdict that the manner in which merit pay decisions were made at the Thurgood Marshall School of Law of Texas Southern University was arbitrary and capricious, and constituted a violation of professors' substantive due process rights. The parties had agreed that the professors had a property interest in a "rational application" of the university's merit pay policy. The court assumed, without deciding, that such a property interest existed, and held that the jury could reasonably conclude, based on the evidence, that the dean and associate dean had "acted in an arbitrary and capricious manner" in making their recommendations for merit pay increases. The most important evidence, apparently, concerned the possible manipulation of the evaluation system so that black faculty members would receive higher increases than white faculty members with similar records of scholarship and teaching achievements. Other courts will not be as hospitable to substantive due process claims as the *Harrington* court. (See, for example, *Boyett v. Troy State Univ. at Montgomery,* 971 F. Supp. 1403, 1414 (M.D. Ala. 1997), *affirmed without opin*ion, 142 F.3d 1284 (11th Cir. 1998).)

(For a discussion of tenure definitions and criteria for tenure across a variety of institutional types, see Thomas P. Hustoles, "Auditing a Tenure Policy from the Perspective of the University Administration," National Association of College and University Attorneys Conference Outline, June 26, 2000, available from http//www.nacua.org.)

The continued justification for tenure systems has been the subject of much recent scholarly and popular writing, legislative action, and litigation. The Selected Annotated Bibliography for this Section and for Section 7.1 contains various resources on the meaning of tenure, alternatives to tenure, efforts to preserve tenure, and the relationship between tenure and academic freedom.

6.6.2. Terminations of tenure for cause.

Perhaps the most sensitive issues concerning standards arise in situations where institutions attempt to dismiss a tenured faculty member "for cause" (see T. Lovain, "Grounds for Dismissing Tenured Postsecondary Faculty for Cause," 10 *J. Coll. & Univ. Law* 419 (1983–84)). Such dismissals should be distinguished from dismissals due to financial exigency or program discontinuance, discussed in Section 6.8. For-cause dismissals—being more personal, potentially more subjective, and more debilitating to the individual concerned—may be even more troublesome and agonizing for administrators than dismissals for reasons of financial exigency or program discontinuance. Similarly, they may give rise to even more complex legal issues concerning adequate procedures for effecting dismissal (see Section 6.7); the adequacy of standards for defining and determining "cause"; and the types and amount of evidence needed to sustain a termination decision under a particular standard of cause.

The American Association of University Professors' 1976 "Recommended Institutional Regulations on Academic Freedom and Tenure" (in *AAUP Policy Documents and Reports* (AAUP, 2001), 21–30) acknowledges "adequate cause" as an appropriate standard for dismissal of tenured faculty. These guidelines caution, however, that "adequate cause for a dismissal will be related, directly and substantially, to the fitness of faculty members in their professional capacities as teachers or researchers." Since the guidelines do not further define the concept, institutions are left to devise cause standards on their own or, occasionally for public institutions, to find standards in state statutes or agency regulations.

A straightforward example of a dismissal for cause—incompetence—occurred in *Weist v. State of Kansas*, Dkt. # 00 C 3 09 (Dist. Ct., Riley Co. Kan., October 17, 2002). The university had adopted a post-tenure review program that provided that if a tenured faculty member's performance had been found to be unsatisfactory for two consecutive years, the faculty member could be terminated after a hearing before a faculty committee. The university's procedure provided that there must be clear and convincing evidence that the faculty member was performing below the "minimum level of productivity." Furthermore, the department had provided the faculty member with an "improvement plan" that he failed to follow. The court upheld the termination.

Performance failures may also be characterized as "neglect of duty," as in *In re Bigler v. Cornell University*, 698 N.Y.S.2d 472 (N.Y. App. Div. 1999); or as misconduct, as in *Wells v. Tennessee Board of Regents*, 9 S.W.3d 779 (Tenn. 1999) (sexual harassment of student by tenured professor), and *Holm v. Ithaca College*, 682 N.Y.S.2d 295 (N.Y. App. Div. 1998) (sexual harassment of multiple students by tenured professor). Dishonesty as a justification for dismissal of a tenured faculty member has also been sanctioned by the courts (see, for example, *Lamvermeyer v. Denison University,* 2000 Ohio App. LEXIS 861 (Ct. App. Ohio, 5th Dist. 2000) ("moral delinquency"—falsification of expense vouchers)).

For-cause dismissals may raise numerous questions about contract interpretation. In *McConnell v. Howard University,* 818 F.2d 58 (D.C. Cir. 1987), for example, a mathematics professor had been verbally abused during class by a student and refused to resume teaching his course until "the proper teaching atmosphere was restored" (818 F.2d at 61). The university did not take any disciplinary action against the student, did not take other initiatives to resolve the situation, and rejected a grievance committee's recommendation in favor of the professor. It then dismissed the professor for "neglect of professional responsibilities"—an enumerated "cause" stated in the faculty handbook. The professor sued the institution for breach of contract. Construing the pertinent contract provisions in light of custom and usage (see Section 1.4.3.3), the court held that the institution, in a for-cause dismissal, must consider not only the literal meaning of the term "cause" but also all surrounding and mitigating circumstances; in addition, the institution must evaluate the professor's actions "according to the standards of the profession." Since the institution had not done so, the court remanded the case to the district court for further proceedings.

Courts also might question the clarity or specificity of an institution's dismissal standards. In *Garrett v. Matthews,* 625 F.2d 658 (5th Cir. 1980), the University of Alabama had dismissed the plaintiff, a tenured professor, for "insubordination and dereliction of duty." The charges had been brought pursuant to a faculty handbook provision permitting dismissal for "adequate cause" as found after a hearing. The plaintiff argued that the handbook's adequate-cause standard was so vague that it violated constitutional due process. Although due process precedents suggest that this argument is one to be taken seriously,[11] the court rejected it in one terse sentence that contains no analysis and relies on a prior opinion in *Bowling v. Scott,* 587 F.2d 229 (5th Cir. 1979) (this book, Section 6.7.2.3), which does not even address the argument. Thus, although *Garrett* is authority for the constitutionality of a bare adequate-cause standard, it is anemic authority indeed.

In a more instructive case, *Korf v. Ball State University,* 726 F.2d 1222 (7th Cir. 1984), the university had adopted the AAUP's 1987 "Statement on Professional Ethics" (in *AAUP Policy Documents and Reports* (AAUP, 1990), 75–76) and published it in the faculty handbook. Subsequently, the university applied the statement's ethical standards to a tenured professor who, according to the findings of a university hearing committee, had made sexual advances toward and exploited male students. Specifically, the university relied on the portions of the AAUP statement that prohibit "exploitation of students . . . for private advantage" and require that a professor "demonstrates respect for the student as an

---

[11]See, for example, *H & V Engineering, Inc. v. Board of Professional Engineers and Land Surveyors,* 747 P.2d 55 (Idaho 1987) (invalidating disciplinary action taken under "misconduct" and "gross negligence" standard); *Tuma v. Board of Nursing,* 593 P.2d 711 (Idaho 1979) (invalidating suspension under standard of "unprofessional conduct"); and *Davis v. Williams,* 598 F.2d 916 (5th Cir. 1979) (invalidating regulation prohibiting "conduct prejudicial to good order").

individual and adheres to his proper role as intellectual guide and counselor." When the university dismissed the professor for violating these standards, the professor sued, claiming that the dismissal violated due process because the statement did not specifically mention sexual conduct and therefore did not provide him adequate notice of the standard to which he was held. The court rejected this claim (which was essentially a claim of unconstitutional vagueness), stating that a code of conduct need not "specifically delineate each and every type of conduct . . . constituting a violation" (726 F.2d at 1227–28).

In a later case, *San Filippo v. Bongiovanni*, 961 F.2d 1125 (3d Cir. 1992), Rutgers University had adopted the AAUP's "Statement on Professional Ethics" (University Regulation 3.91). In separate regulations, however, it had also adopted an adequate-cause standard to govern dismissals of tenured faculty (University Regulation 3.93) and had defined "adequate cause" as "failure to maintain standards of sound scholarship and competent teaching, or gross neglect of established University obligations appropriate to the appointment, or incompetence, or incapacitation, or conviction of a crime of moral turpitude" (University Regulation 3.94). Relying on both the AAUP Statement and the adequate-cause regulations, the university dismissed the plaintiff, a tenured chemistry professor. The charges stemmed from the professor's "conduct towards visiting Chinese scholars brought to the University to work with him on research projects." A university hearing panel found that the professor had "'exploited, threatened and been abusive'" to these student scholars and had "'demonstrated a serious lack of integrity in his professional dealings'" (961 F.2d at 1132; quoting the panel report).

The professor challenged his dismissal in federal court, arguing (among other things) that the university's dismissal regulations were unconstitutionally vague because they did not give him fair notice that he could be dismissed for the conduct with which he was charged. The university argued that the adequate-cause regulations (Regulations 3.93 & 3.94) "incorporated" the AAUP "Statement on Professional Ethics" (3.91), which applied to the professor's conduct and gave him sufficient notice. The appellate court (like the district court) rejected the university's "incorporation" argument and determined that the grounds for dismissal must be found in the adequate-cause regulations themselves, apart from the AAUP statement. But the appellate court (unlike the district court) nevertheless rejected the professor's vagueness argument because the portion of the adequate-cause regulation on "failure to maintain standards of sound scholarship and competent teaching" (3.94) was itself sufficient to provide fair notice:

> A reasonable, ordinary person using his common sense and general knowledge of employer-employee relationships would have fair notice that the conduct the University charged Dr. San Filippo with put him at risk of dismissal under a regulation stating he could be dismissed for "failure to maintain standards of sound scholarship and competent teaching." Regulation 3.94. He would know that the standard did not encompass only actual teaching or research skills. . . . It is not unfair or foreseeable for a tenured professor to be expected to behave decently towards students and coworkers, to comply with a superior's directive, and to be truthful and forthcoming in dealing with payroll, federal research

funds or applications for academic positions. Such behavior is required for the purpose of maintaining sound scholarship and competent teaching [961 F.2d at 1137].

An Ohio court overturned the termination of a tenured professor in *Ohio Dominican College v. Krone,* 560 N.E.2d 1340 (Ohio Ct. App. 1990) because the faculty member's alleged misconduct had not met the contractual standard for dismissal. The court interpreted the faculty handbook's specification of "grave cause" for tenure termination as limiting the college's ability to discharge a faculty member with whom it had a contractual dispute. Joan Krone was a tenured assistant professor and chair of the mathematics department at Ohio Dominican College (ODC). After the college received federal funds to initiate a computer science department, Krone was granted a one-year paid leave for academic year 1982–83 to obtain a master's degree in computer science, in return for her agreement to return and to teach for at least two years. Leaving ODC prior to her two-year teaching obligation would require her to reimburse ODC for the costs of her education.

Krone completed her master's degree in 1983 but continued her graduate work in computer science under a series of agreements with ODC, including a one-semester unpaid leave during which she had agreed to perform several tasks for the college. Her obligation was now to teach for three years upon returning to the college. In contemplating Krone's return to work in the fall of 1984, the academic vice president offered her a half-time contract for the fall semester for $5,500 in salary. Krone signed the contract after changing the salary to $10,000.

ODC rejected the change made by Krone and offered her a full-time teaching contract at an annual salary of $22,000. The letter making this offer stated that failure to sign and return it within ten days would be interpreted as a resignation and forfeiture of tenure. The day before the contract was due, Krone requested a meeting with the ODC president. The meeting was held, and ODC officials refused to change the most recent offer. At the same time, the college was negotiating with a male professor, who accepted the college's offer eleven days after Krone's signed contract was due. A week after that, ODC sent a letter to Krone, informing her that she had forfeited her tenured faculty position and must begin reimbursing the college for her educational expenses within a month.

When Krone refused to reimburse the college, stating that the terms of its offer were unacceptable, the college sued her for reimbursement; Krone countersued for wrongful termination. A trial judge granted judgment for the college based on the written contracts.

Krone appealed, asserting that the college had breached its contract (contained in the faculty handbook), and also arguing that under the Ohio constitution and the U.S. Constitution's Fourteenth Amendment she was entitled to a pretermination hearing. The ODC faculty handbook contained the following provision: "An appointment with continuous tenure is terminable by the institution only for grave cause or on account of extraordinary financial emergencies. Grave cause shall include demonstrated incompetence, crime, or similar matters" (560 N.E.2d at 1343). Krone also noted that the faculty handbook defined a full-time teaching load as three courses per semester; the college's last offer to Krone was to teach five courses and to serve as department chair. This portion of the contract was the basis for Krone's refusal to sign it.

The court concluded that the contract negotiations between ODC and Krone were separate from her status as a tenured professor, and that her inability to reach an agreement with the college was not a form of misconduct. The court ruled that ODC breached Krone's contract for tenure "by unilaterally setting forth a condition for continued employment" (560 N.E.2d at 1345). The court refused to address Krone's constitutional claims, but upheld Krone's claim of wrongful discharge and concluded that she was entitled to reinstatement in order to meet her three-year teaching obligation to ODC.

Freedom-of-expression issues may also become implicated in the institution's application of its dismissal standards. In *Adamian v. Jacobson*, 523 F.2d 929 (9th Cir. 1975), a professor from the University of Nevada at Reno had allegedly led a disruptive demonstration on campus. Charges were brought against him under a university code provision requiring faculty members "to exercise appropriate restraint [and] to show respect for the opinions of others," and the board of regents determined that violation of this provision was adequate cause for dismissal. In court the professor argued that this standard was not only unconstitutionally vague but also unconstitutionally "overbroad" in violation of the First Amendment (see Sections 9.1.3, 9.2.2, & 9.5.3 regarding overbreadth). The appellate court held that the standard would violate the First Amendment if interpreted broadly but could be constitutional if interpreted narrowly, as prescribed by AAUP academic freedom guidelines, so as not to refer to the content of the professor's remarks. The court therefore remanded the case to the trial court for further findings on how the university interpreted its code provision. On a second appeal, the court confined itself to the narrow issue of the construction of the code provision. Determining that the university's construction was consistent with the AAUP guidelines and reflected a limitation on the manner, rather than the content, of expression, the court held that the code provision was sufficiently narrow to avoid an overbreadth (as well as a vagueness) challenge (608 F.2d 1224 (9th Cir. 1979)).

Despite the summary approval in *Garrett*, institutions should not comfortably settle for a bald adequate-cause standard. Good policy and (especially for public institutions) good law should demand more. Since incompetency, insubordination, immorality, unethical conduct, and medical disability are the most commonly asserted grounds for dismissals for cause, institutions may wish to specifically include them in their dismissal policies.[12] If unethical conduct is a stated ground for dismissal, the institution should consider adopting the AAUP "Statement on Professional Ethics," as did the institution in the *Korf* case. If it adopts the AAUP statement or its own version of ethical standards, the

---

[12]Another ground for dismissal or other discipline is the ground of "scientific misconduct." The ground refers to particular types of ethical problems that arise in the context of scientific research. See also this book, Sections 13.2.3 and 13.4.2.

institution should make clear how and when violations of the statement or standards may be considered grounds for dismissal—thus avoiding the problem in *San Filippo*. If medical disability (either physical or mental) is a stated ground for dismissal, the institution should comply with the requirements of Section 504 and the Americans With Disabilities Act (this book, Section 5.2.5). The AAUP's recommended regulation on termination for medical reasons (Regulation 4(e), in *AAUP Policy Documents and Reports* (AAUP, 2001), 25) may also be helpful.

For each ground (or "cause") included in its dismissal policy, the institution should also include a definition of that ground, along with the criteria or standards for applying the definition to particular cases. (The AAUP Statement may serve this purpose for the "unethical conduct" ground.) Since such definitions and criteria may become part of the institution's contract with faculty members, they should be drafted clearly and specifically enough, and applied sensitively enough, to avoid contract interpretation problems such as those faced by the institution in the *McConnell* case. Such definitions and criteria should also be sufficiently clear to guide the decision makers who will apply them and to forewarn the faculty members who will be subject to them, thus avoiding vagueness problems; and (as in *Adamian*) they should be sufficiently specific to preclude dismissal of faculty members because of the content of their expression. In addition, such definitions and criteria should conform to the AAUP's caution that cause standards must have a direct and substantial relationship to the faculty member's professional fitness. Hand in hand with such standards, if it chooses to adopt them, the institution will want to develop record-keeping policies, and perhaps periodic faculty review policies (see S. Olswang & J. Fantel, "Tenure and Periodic Performance Review: Compatible Legal and Administrative Principles," 7 *J. Coll. & Univ. Law* 1 (1980–81)) that will provide the facts necessary to make reliable termination decisions. The case of *King v. University of Minnesota*, 774 F.2d 224 (8th Cir. 1985), provides an instructive example of a university's success in this regard.

Administrators will also want to keep in mind that involuntary terminations of tenured faculty, because of their coercive and stigmatizing effect on the individuals involved, usually create a far greater number of legal problems than voluntary means for dissolving a tenured faculty member's employment relationship with the institution. Thus, another way to minimize legal vulnerability is to rely on voluntary alternatives to dismissals for cause. For example, the institution might provide increased incentives for retirement, or opportunities for phased or partial retirement, or retraining for midcareer shifts to underpopulated teaching or research. Or it might maintain flexibility in faculty development by increased use of fixed-term contracts, visiting professorships, part-time appointments, and other non-tenure-track appointments. All these alternatives have one thing in common with involuntary termination: their success depends on thorough review of personnel policies, coordinated planning for future contingencies, and careful articulation into written institutional policies.

6.6.3. Denial of tenure. Although the typical criteria for evaluating a faculty member for tenure are the quality of the individual's performance in teaching, scholarship (at research-oriented institutions), and service, additional criteria are sometimes used. Religiously affiliated colleges and universities may require faculty members to adhere to the religion's tenets or the institution's religious mission, or may even require that the faculty member profess that particular religion. At research institutions, tenure candidates in certain disciplines may be evaluated on the basis of their ability to obtain external funding for research or other activities. Collegiality, or institutional "citizenship," is increasingly being used, either openly or covertly, to make tenure decisions. And considerations of student enrollment trends or institutional/departmental financial health may also figure (either openly or covertly) into tenure decisions.

A line of cases has examined whether departments are permitted to interpret criteria for promotion or tenure more strictly than the way they were interpreted for previous tenure decisions. For example, plaintiffs denied tenure have argued that requirements for numbers or quality of publications had risen between the time they were hired and the time they were evaluated for tenure. The courts have been unsympathetic to these claims. In *Lawrence v. Curators of the University of Missouri,* 204 F.3d 807 (8th Cir. 2000), a federal appellate court affirmed a trial court's summary judgment ruling in favor of the university. Lawrence, an assistant professor of accounting, had been denied tenure primarily on the basis of a weak record of scholarly publication. She was criticized by senior faculty in her department for not placing her articles in top-tier journals. Although the plaintiff introduced evidence that the standards for what a top-tier journal was considered to be changed during the years she was at the university, and that male faculty who published in the same journals that she did were awarded tenure two years before she was denied tenure, the trial court had ruled that this evidence was insufficient to establish a discriminatory motive for the tenure denial. A vigorous dissent by Judge McMillan points out the effect of the shifting standards on the plaintiff's tenure review and states that summary judgment should have been denied in order to resolve the factual dispute.

A federal appellate court ruled that a university could apply higher standards when evaluating an internal applicant for a newly created faculty position than it had used to hire her for a temporary lecturer position. In *Kobrin v. University of Minnesota,* 121 F.3d 408 (8th Cir. 1997), the university had hired Kobrin, one of its own graduates, to fill a lecturer position. When the department was permitted to create two tenure-track faculty positions, Kobrin applied for the junior position but was not selected. A male was judged to be better qualified because he possessed two areas of expertise while Kobrin possessed only one. Kobrin's argument that the university changed its criteria did not impress the court, which ruled that even if inconsistent reasons had been given at various times during the hiring process, Kobrin was not as well qualified as the male who was selected, nor as well qualified as several of the female candidates.

In *Weinstock v. Columbia University,* 224 F.3d 33 (2d Cir. 2000), the plaintiff, a professor at Barnard College, a unit of Columbia University, argued that the standards applied to her tenure review were inappropriately high, because Barnard professors were traditionally held to a lower standard of scholarly productivity than were their counterparts at Columbia because the teaching loads at Barnard were heavier. The court rejected that argument, stating that it was the quality, not the quantity, of her research and publications that was the concern, and that it was undisputed that the same standards of quality were required for both Barnard and Columbia faculty.

In *Lim v. Trustees of Indiana University,* 297 F.3d 575 (7th Cir. 2002), a federal appellate court affirmed a trial court's award of summary judgment to the university. Professor Lim, who was denied tenure at Indiana University, alleged that the denial was caused by sex discrimination. The same year that Lim was hired as an assistant professor, the department chair, who recruited and hired Lim, instituted higher standards for research and publication for untenured faculty than had been expected in the past. Lim was denied tenure, in large part, for her failure to meet these higher standards.

The court noted that Lim had been warned on a regular basis during her six-year probationary period that she was not meeting the department's publication standards. The court rejected Lim's attempt to compare her publication record to that of male faculty who were tenured prior to the implementation of the new standards. The court ruled that these faculty were not similarly situated and could not serve as comparators for purposes of Lim's sex discrimination claim.

Disputes over the propriety of using collegiality as a criterion for tenure decisions have flared for more than two decades. In an early case, *Mayberry v. Dees,* 663 F.2d 502 (4th Cir. 1981), a federal appellate court ruled that collegiality was an appropriate criterion for evaluating faculty members for tenure. Federal trial courts have also upheld tenure denials on the grounds of poor relationships between the candidate and faculty colleagues (*Stein v. Kent State Univ. Bd. of Trustees,* 994 F. Supp. 898 (N.D. Ohio 1998); *Bresnick v. Manhattanville College,* 864 F. Supp. 327 (S.D.N.Y. 1994)). The plaintiffs in these cases argued that college documents did not list collegiality as a criterion for tenure and it was therefore improper to judge them on this basis. The courts replied that, even if institutional documents do not specifically mention collegiality, this criterion is implicit in the other express criteria or otherwise appropriate for consideration.

This issue was prominent in *University of Baltimore v. Peri Iz,* 716 A.2d 1107 (Md. Ct. Special App. 1998). Professor Iz, a specialist in decision science, was hired in 1990 as an assistant professor in the university's business school. She was reviewed for tenure in 1993. Although her departmental colleagues and department chair rated Iz's teaching as good to excellent and her research and service as very good, and the business school's tenure and promotion committee rated her highly on all three criteria, the dean recommended against tenure because of Iz's uncollegial relationships with her departmental colleagues. The provost concurred with the dean, and Iz filed an internal appeal. A university-wide faculty appeals committee received testimony from Iz and several other witnesses, but the committee could not agree on whether to uphold the provost's tenure denial recommendation. The committee members who voted to reverse the provost's recommendation did so on the grounds that university documents did not specify lack of collegiality as a reason for denying tenure. When the president accepted the provost's recommendation against tenure, Iz sued the university for sex and national origin discrimination under Title VII, violation of equal protection, and breach of contract.

The breach of contract claim was based upon Iz's assertion that the university could use only criteria listed in university policy documents to make tenure decisions. Rejecting all claims except the contract claim, the jury determined that the university had breached the professor's contract and awarded $425,000 in compensatory damages. The sole issue before the appellate court was whether the university had the discretion to use collegiality as a criterion for tenure. The court ruled that it did. Because the award of tenure was a discretionary decision delegated to the president, said the court, a breach of contract claim would lie only if the president had exercised his discretion in bad faith or in a discriminatory fashion. "We are persuaded that collegiality is a valid consideration for tenure review. . . . Without question, collegiality plays an essential role in the categories of both teaching and service" (716 A.2d at 1122). The court held that the trial court should have ruled, as a matter of law, that the university could use collegiality as a tenure criterion.

The propriety of using collegiality as a criterion for tenure was also at issue in *McGill v. The Regents of the University of California,* 52 Cal. Rptr. 2d 466 (Ct. App. Cal. 4th Dist. 1996). The University of California at Irvine (UCI) hired McGill as an untenured assistant professor of mathematics. McGill's area of specialization was probability studies, and he was hired because his early scholarly work was considered very influential. Four years after being hired, he was evaluated for tenure.

Although all but one outside reviewer praised McGill's scholarship, a departmental tenure committee recommended denial of tenure for several reasons. The committee members believed that McGill's recent scholarly work was not significant, that he interacted poorly with graduate students, and that his teaching as "adequate at best." The full department voted 23 to 2 to recommend against tenure. The department chair concurred on the basis of the limited impact of McGill's scholarship, his difficulty interacting with faculty, his lack of success as a teacher, and his minimal service to the university. The chair also found McGill to be deficient in collegiality, noting that McGill had criticized departmental colleagues to candidates for faculty positions. The dean also recommended that McGill be denied tenure. A university-wide Committee on Academic Personnel (CAP) then recommended that the tenure decision be deferred for two years because the tenure file was "confusing" (and that in the meantime McGill be given a salary increase). Furthermore, said the CAP, collegiality was not a proper criterion for a tenure decision. But the vice chancellor and chancellor recommended against tenure, primarily on the basis of lack of scholarly achievement while at UCI.

McGill appealed the decision to the CAP, which granted him a remand. The entire tenure process was repeated, starting with the department level. McGill was permitted to submit additional materials, including teaching evaluations and articles. He was also permitted to submit a statement describing alleged animosity against him by certain departmental faculty. The department considered all of the material submitted by McGill, but reaffirmed its earlier vote. All succeeding levels repeated their earlier recommendations, including the CAP, which recommended tenure. The chancellor ruled against tenure, and McGill filed for a writ of administrative mandamus (attempting to persuade the court to reverse the tenure denial) under state law, as well as claims of fraud, due process violations, and age discrimination.

Although the trial court granted the writ and directed the chancellor to set aside the tenure denial and repeat the tenure process the following year, the appellate court disagreed. Focusing on the writ of mandamus, the appellate court held that the court could overrule the university's action only if it were "arbitrary, capricious, or entirely lacking in evidentiary support." The court then examined the actions of the faculty and administrators under this more deferential standard of review.

In a well-reasoned opinion, the appellate court discussed the subjective nature of tenure decisions, even when criteria are stated objectively. It held that collegiality was an appropriate criterion because the AAUP "Statement on Professional Ethics," which the university had adopted as policy, requires professors to respect the opinions of others and to accept "a share of faculty responsibilities for the governance of the institution" (52 Cal. Rptr. at 470, quoting AAUP Statement). Furthermore, collegiality was only one of several reasons for the tenure denial. Concerns about the quality of McGill's scholarship and teaching, and his limited university and public service, buttressed the university's defense. The court also warned of the inappropriateness of judicial determination of the merits of a tenure case, stating that "the University may even have shown poor judgment in not granting McGill tenure. But nothing in the record suggests its decision was made for illegal or improper reasons" (52 Cal. Rptr. at 473).

In *Bresnick v. Manhattanville College,* 864 F. Supp. 327 (S.D.N.Y. 1994), another court rejected the claim of a faculty member that the college's use of "cooperation" as a criterion for a tenure decision breached his employment contract. The plaintiff, a professor of dance and theater, was denied tenure because he had difficulty working with other faculty in a collaborative manner. Even though the written tenure criteria included only teaching excellence, scholarship, and service to the college, the court rejected the breach of contract claim, stating: "It is predictable and appropriate that in evaluating service to an institution, ability to cooperate would be deemed particularly relevant where a permanent difficult-to-revoke long-term job commitment is being made to the applicant for tenure" (864 F. Supp. at 329). In other words, the court viewed "cooperation" as a component of the service criterion.

(For an analysis of judicial reaction to challenges to the use of collegiality in tenure decisions, see Mary Ann Connell & Frederick G. Savage, "The Role of Collegiality in Higher Education Tenure, Promotion, and Termination Decisions," 27 *J. Coll. & Univ. Law* 833 (2001). See also Piper Fogg, "Do You Have to Be a Nice Person to Win Tenure?" *Chron. Higher Educ.,* February 1, 2002, A8.)

Another controversial criterion for tenure that has been reviewed in court is "academic politics," which is closely related to "collegiality." In *Kumbhojkar v. University of Miami,* 727 So. 2d 275 (Ct. App. Fla. 1999), a state appellate court rejected the plaintiff's claim that his tenure denial was inappropriately based on personal animosity between himself and his department head because the department head was not the ultimate decision maker in the case. The plaintiff had also claimed that the negative decision was inappropriately based on "prior internal disputes within his department." Characterizing these disputes as "academic politics," the court rejected the plaintiff's claim that "academic politics" was an inappropriate grounds for tenure denial, noting that academic politics was a fact of life on campus.

A similar result was reached in *Slatkin v. University of Redlands*, 88 Cal. App. 4th 1147 (Ct. App. Cal. 4th Dist. 2001), where the court ruled that academic politics could be viewed as a legitimate nondiscriminatory reason for denying a professor tenure. The professor had made negative comments about a departmental colleague; the court ruled that the "inability of colleagues to forgive her" for making these comments was the motive for the negative tenure recommendation, and that such a motive was not discriminatory.

Other colleges have faced challenges to tenure denials made on the basis of declining enrollments or concerns about the financial health of the institution. There is strong judicial support for the removal of tenured faculty due to documented financial difficulties of the institution (Section 6.8), and unless an institution has somehow limited its authority to use financial reasons or enrollment declines as a criterion for denying tenure, courts usually will affirm its discretion to do so. (See, for example, *Hudson v. Wesley College*, 1998 Del. Ch. LEXIS 235 (Ct. Chancery, Del., December 23, 1998) (unpublished); see also *Roklina v. Skidmore College*, 702 N.Y.S.2d 161 (N.Y. App. Div. 2000), *appeal denied*, 95 N.Y.2d 758 (N.Y. 2000) (unpublished).) In *Spuler v. Pickar*, 958 F.2d 103 (5th Cir. 1992), a federal appellate court upheld the authority of the University of Houston to deny tenure to a faculty member for financial reasons, even though the university hired a new faculty member in the same department shortly after Spuler was denied tenure. The court found that Spuler was not qualified to teach upper-level courses that the department needed, and that legitimate financial considerations motivated the tenure denial.

But if the institution has promised not to use enrollment stability as a criterion for determining tenure, it cannot do so, even in a time of enrollment downturn, without first changing its written policy. In *In Re Bennett v. Wells College*, 641 N.Y.S.2d 929 (N.Y. App. Div. 1996), the college's faculty manual stated that if the college determined that a tenure-track position was necessary at the time of hiring a faculty member, the status of enrollment would not be used at the time of the tenure decision. Because the dean and president used a criterion that the college's own policies forbid them to use, the court ruled that the tenure decision had to be repeated without consideration of enrollment issues.

Some institutions have implemented "tenure caps" that limit the proportion of tenured faculty in a particular department. In *Roufaiel v. Ithaca College*, 660 N.Y.S.2d 595 (N.Y. App. Div. 1997), Ithaca College had a tenure cap of 75 percent, a figure that was included in offer letters to faculty and in the faculty handbook. When Professor Roufaiel was hired as an accounting instructor, she was advised of the tenure cap in writing. But at the time that Roufaiel was evaluated for tenure, the provost told the dean of the business school that the tenure cap would not be applied to the accounting department, assuming that enrollment remained stable. Roufaiel was recommended for tenure, but the provost rejected the recommendation, stating that enrollment considerations precluded a favorable decision. Roufaiel filed breach of contract, estoppel, and fraudulent misrepresentation claims.

The court denied the college's summary judgment motion because the parties disagreed about the enrollment numbers, an issue that was central to the college's defense. But the court dismissed the estoppel and fraudulent misrepresentation claims because the plaintiff could not provide evidence that she had been promised tenure.

These cases suggest that, if an institution can articulate a reasonable justification for a particular tenure criterion, and if it has not explicitly prevented itself from using that criterion, the courts will typically defer to the institution even if it has not expressly stated the criterion in its tenure policies. Of course, the institution will still have to demonstrate that it applies the criterion evenhandedly and reasonably, and that the criterion furthers the institutional interest in providing high-quality teaching, research, or service to its students or the wider community. The better practice, however, will be to expressly and clearly articulate each tenure criterion in the institution's written policies, and to maintain mechanisms for systematically evaluating tenure candidates against these criteria. To the extent the institution does so, litigation should be either reduced or, at a minimum, more easily defended against.

6.6.4. Post-tenure review. Many institutions have decided to establish regular evaluations of tenured faculty through a system of post-tenure review. Although the American Association of University Professors initially adopted a policy on post-tenure review that was sharply critical of the concept ("On Post-Tenure Review," November 1983), quoted in "Post Tenure Review: An AAUP Response," the AAUP issued a second report in 1999 ("Post-Tenure Review: An AAUP Response," *AAUP Policy Documents and Reports* (2001), 50). The more recent AAUP report suggests guidelines that should be followed in order to protect faculty members' academic freedom and to ensure that the process is fair.

Post-tenure review programs may be created by collective bargaining agreements or faculty handbooks (the contractual approach), by state statute or administrative regulation (such as Ark. Code Ann. § 6-63-104(a) (2001) and S.C. Code Ann. § 59-103-30 (2001), both of which explicitly include post-tenure review in statutory language regarding review of faculty performance generally), by regulations or policies of state systems of higher education (such as those of Arizona, Wisconsin, and Oregon), or by institutional policies. (A review of various approaches to post-tenure review programs is in Cheryl A Cameron, Steven G. Olswang, & Edmund Kamai, "Tenure, Compensation and Productivity: A Select Review of Post-Tenure Personnel Issues," National Association of College and University Attorneys Conference Outline, 2002, available at http://nacua.org.)

Challenges to post-tenure review programs have been unsuccessful. A faculty member at Colorado State University challenged the authority of the state board of agriculture to implement a post-tenure review system as an unconstitutional retrospective change to the tenure contract. In *Johnson v. Colorado State Board of Agriculture*, 15 P.3d 309 (Colo. Ct. App. 2000), the court rejected the request for a declaratory judgment against the board, stating that the faculty were already subject to periodic review and the new policy did not "remove or impair vested rights" nor "create a new obligation." The court characterized the policy as procedural, for it merely changed the process by which a faculty member would be subject to discipline for poor performance.

Individual faculty challenging dismissals have attempted to assert the post-tenure review process to *protect them* from termination. For example, in *Barham v. University of Northern Colorado*, 964 P.2d 545 (Colo. Ct. App. 1997), a tenured faculty member who had taught at the university for twenty-nine years was accused of "harassment, misuse and/or misappropriation of government property, conduct detrimental to the efficient and productive operation of the school, unacceptable job performance, and violations of the standards of professional conduct," according to the court. The dean had received numerous complaints from students, faculty, and staff. Just before the plaintiff was due for a regularly scheduled post-tenure review, the dean suspended him and initiated termination proceedings. Although the plaintiff argued that he was entitled to the post-tenure review prior to any determination with respect to his termination, the court disagreed, saying that the faculty dismissal proceedings operated separately from the post-tenure review policies, and that the university was justified in proceeding through the de-tenuring process.

Similarly, another state appellate court rejected the claim of a tenured professor terminated for incompetence that he was entitled to the remedial benefits of the post-tenure review process prior to termination. In *Wurth v. Oklahoma City University*, 907 P.2d 1095 (Okla. Ct. App. 1995), the court distinguished between "failure to maintain the level of competence necessary for tenure" and unsatisfactory performance. For the former, said the court, the termination process was sufficient. For a termination based on unsatisfactory performance, however, said the court, the university would have been required to provide the faculty member with an evaluation and an opportunity to improve his performance prior to termination. The court did not elaborate on the differences between these two concepts.

According to a variety of sources (collected in Gabriella Montell, "The Fallout From Post-Tenure Review," *Chron. Higher Educ.*, October 17, 2002, available at http://chronicle.com/jobs/2002/10/2002101701c.htm), the number of faculty who have received unsatisfactory evaluations is very small. This result may explain the low number of legal challenges to terminations made subsequent to post-tenure reviews, and the unusual legal strategy of attempting to use post-tenure review to protect a faculty member against termination. Despite the infrequent use of post-tenure review to identify tenured faculty for termination, institutions should be careful to specify how the information from the review will be used and which individuals or groups will conduct the evaluation. If post-tenure review results are used to discipline or dismiss faculty, then the procedural safeguards discussed in Section 6.6 should be followed.

(For further information on post-tenure review, see Christine Licata & Joseph Morreale, *Post-Tenure Review: Policies, Practices, Precautions,* New Pathways Inquiry no. 2 (American Association for Higher Education, 1997).)

Sec. 6.7. Procedures for Faculty Employment Decisions

6.7.1. General principles.
Postsecondary educational institutions have established varying procedural requirements for making and internally reviewing faculty personnel decisions. Administrators should look first at these requirements when they are attempting to resolve procedural issues concerning appointment, retention, promotion, and tenure. Whenever such requirements can reasonably be construed as part of the faculty member's contract with the institution (see Section 6.2), the law will usually expect both public and private institutions to comply with them. In *Skehan v. Board of Trustees of Bloomsburg State College,* 501 F.2d 31 (3d Cir. 1976), for instance, a nonrenewed professor alleged that the institution had not complied with a college policy statement providing for hearings in academic freedom cases. The appellate court held that the college would have to follow the policy statement if, on remand, the lower court found that the statement granted a contractual right under state law and that the professor's case involved academic freedom within the meaning of the statement. Upon remand and a second appeal, the court held that the professor did have a contractual right to the procedures specified in the statement and that the college had violated this right (590 F.2d 470 (3d Cir. 1978)). Similarly, in *Zuelsdorf v. University of Alaska, Fairbanks,* 794 P.2d 932 (Alaska 1990), the court held that a notice requirement in the university's personnel regulations was part of the faculty contract, and that the university had breached the contract by not giving the plaintiffs timely notice of nonrenewal.

Public institutions will also often be subject to state statutes or administrative regulations that establish procedures applicable to faculty personnel decisions. In *Brouillette v. Board of Directors of Merged Area IX,* 519 F.2d 126 (8th Cir. 1975), for example, the court determined that a state statute requiring a public pretermination hearing for public school teachers applied to the termination of a community college faculty member as well. The institution had, however, complied with the statutory requirements. In a "turnabout" case, *Rutcosky v. Board of Trustees of Community College District No. 18,* 545 P.2d 567 (1976), the court found that the plaintiff faculty member had not complied with a state procedural requirement applicable to termination-of-employment hearings and therefore refused to grant him any relief.

Institutional procedures and/or state laws also control the conditions under which a faculty member acquires tenured status. Many institutions have adopted policies that state that only the trustees can grant tenure, and courts have denied an award of *de facto* tenure in those cases. For example, in *Hill v. Talladega College,* 502 So. 2d 735 (Ala. 1987), the court refused to award *de facto* tenure to a faculty member employed at the college for ten years because the faculty handbook specifically stated that only the trustees could grant tenure and that tenure could not be acquired automatically at the college. And in *Gray v. Board of Regents of University System of Georgia,* 150 F.3d 1347 (11th Cir. 1999), the court ruled that, absent evidence of either a custom of awarding *de facto* tenure or some established institutional understanding that *de facto* tenure existed, an assistant professor employed under annual contracts for nine years did not acquire tenure simply by being so employed for more than the seven-year probationary period.

In other cases, however, faculty members have claimed that, by virtue of longevity, they had acquired tenure *de facto,* even though no official action was taken to grant tenure. For example, in *Dugan v. Stockton State College,* 586 A.2d 322 (N.J. Super. Ct. App. Div. 1991), a faculty member who had been employed at a state college for thirteen years, during several of which she was in a nonfaculty status, claimed that her years of service entitled her to tenure. The court examined the state law in effect at the time of her hiring, which stated that any individual consecutively employed for five years in a state college was tenured. Although the state board of higher education had issued regulations providing that only the board could confer tenure, the court noted that the regulations were contrary to the clear language of the statute, and thus beyond the power of the board to promulgate.

The procedures used by a state institution or other institution whose personnel decision is considered state action (see Section 1.5.2) are also subject to constitutional requirements of procedural due process. These requirements are discussed in Section 6.7.2.

Since private institutions are not subject to these constitutional requirements, or to state procedural statutes and regulations, contract law may be the primary or sole basis for establishing and testing the scope of their procedural obligation to faculty members. In *Johnson v. Christian Brothers College,* 565 S.W.2d 872 (Tenn. 1978), for example, an associate professor instituted suit for breach of his employment contract when the college did not grant him tenure. The college, a religiously affiliated institution in Memphis, had a formal tenure program detailed in its faculty handbook. The program included a seven-year probationary period, during which the faculty member worked under a series of one-year contracts. After seven years, on the prior recommendation of the tenure committee and approval of the president, the faculty member either received tenure along with the award of the eighth contract or was dismissed. The plaintiff claimed that, once he had reached the final probationary year and was being considered for tenure, he was entitled to the formal notice and hearing procedures utilized by the college in terminating tenured faculty. The Supreme Court of Tennessee held that nothing in the terms of the one-year contracts, the published tenure program, or the commonly used procedure of the college evidenced an agreement or practice of treating teachers in their final probationary year as equivalent to tenured faculty. The college therefore had no express or implied contractual obligation to afford the professor notice and an opportunity to be heard.

As discussed in Section 6.2, institutional policies and other documents may become part of the faculty member's contract of employment. Interesting legal questions may arise when the institution attempts to enforce its policy against sexual harassment and uses that policy to discipline or terminate a faculty member when other institutional policies on discipline or termination exist that may provide greater procedural or substantive protections to faculty.

In *Chan v. Miami University*, 652 N.E.2d 644 (Ohio 1995), Professor Chan asserted that the university had breached his contract by terminating him under the rule prohibiting sexual harassment rather than under the rule that governed the termination of tenured faculty members. Although Miami University is a public institution, the plaintiff did not bring constitutional claims, but rather focused on the due process rights provided by the university's rule concerning the termination of tenured faculty. Chan did not dispute the university's right to determine the validity of the sexual harassment charge against him using its harassment policy and procedure; his argument was that after this determination was made, he was entitled to the benefits of the university's procedure for the termination of tenured faculty members prior to his separation from the university. Although the university argued that the sexual harassment complaint process provided sufficient procedural safeguards for respondents, nothing in that policy superseded the more general termination regulations. Furthermore, while the more general regulations provided for representation by counsel, the harassment policy did not. The court held that terminating Chan under the harassment policy and procedures, without using the more general regulations, constituted a breach of contract that denied him due process.

A Maryland appellate court rejected the claims of two professors that Johns Hopkins University hired them with tenure in *The Johns Hopkins University v. Ritter*, 689 A.2d 91 (Ct. App. Md. 1996). Professors Ritter and Snider were recruited from tenured positions at Cornell and Duke universities, respectively, to join the department of pediatrics at Johns Hopkins. The department chair, Professor Oski, assured them that they would be hired at the full professor rank; consequently, both resigned tenured professorships at their respective institutions and joined the faculty at Johns Hopkins. Oski had told them, both orally and in writing, that their rank and salary had to be formally approved by a faculty committee and by the dean. The professors began work at Johns Hopkins in January 1994 as visiting professors, but their rank and tenure review had not been completed by the end of spring semester, and, thus, was held over until the fall of 1994. During the spring and summer of 1994, many disagreements arose between Ritter and Snider and their new colleagues, and many faculty and staff complained about the new professors to the dean of the medical school. The dean decided to terminate the appointments of the pair before the medical school's advisory board, the dean, or the university's board of trustees had acted on their appointments.

Ritter and Snider brought a contract claim against the university, asserting that Oski had promised them tenure, and that they had resigned their tenured positions at other institutions in reliance on his representations in letters and oral communications to the pair. A jury found for the plaintiffs, but the appellate court overturned those verdicts.

The appellate court addressed the nature of the contract and Oski's authority to alter the university's written tenure procedures. Although the court agreed with the plaintiffs that both the letters and the conversations with Oski were included in the contract, it found that Oski had no authority to abrogate the university's written tenure procedures. He did not have actual authority to do so because there was no evidence that the board of trustees or the advisory board of the medical school (both of which had to approve a faculty personnel decision) had authorized Oski to make a commitment on their behalf. Nor did Oski have apparent authority to bind the university, for no one at a higher level than Oski met with or told the plaintiffs that Oski was authorized to promise tenure. The court also rejected the plaintiffs' estoppel claim, noting that no one, including Oski, had ever represented that he had the authority to bypass the written tenure procedure.

This case is important for private institutions that are subject primarily to common law contract challenges, particularly in *de facto* tenure claims such as that against Johns Hopkins. It also suggests that deans or other officials should oversee contractual negotiations and be the ones to offer letters in order to avoid the misunderstandings that led to this litigation.

6.7.2. The public faculty member's right to constitutional due process.

In two landmark cases, *Board of Regents v. Roth*, 408 U.S. 564 (1972), and *Perry v. Sindermann*, 408 U.S. 593 (1972), the U.S. Supreme Court established that faculty members have a right to a fair hearing whenever a personnel decision deprives them of a "property interest" or a "liberty interest" under the Fourteenth Amendment's due process clause. The "property" and "liberty" terminology is derived from the wording of the Fourteenth Amendment itself, which provides that states shall not "deprive any person of life, liberty, or property, without due process of law." (The identification of property and liberty interests is also important to many procedural due process questions concerning students; see Sections 8.3.1, 8.3.8.1, 8.6.1, and 9.4.2.)

In identifying these property and liberty interests, one must make the critical distinction between faculty members who are under continuing contracts and those whose contracts have expired. It is clear, as *Roth* notes, that "a public college professor dismissed from an office held under tenure provisions . . . and college professors and staff members dismissed during the terms of their contracts . . . have interests in continued employment that are safeguarded by due process" (408 U.S. at 576–77). But the situation is not clear with respect to faculty members whose contracts are expiring and are up for renewal or a tenure review. Moreover, when a personnel decision would infringe a property or liberty interest, as in tenure termination, other questions then arise concerning the particular procedures that the institution must follow.

6.7.2.1. Nonrenewal of contracts. *Roth* and *Perry* (above) are the leading cases on the nonrenewal of faculty contracts. The respondent in *Roth* had been hired as an assistant professor at Wisconsin State University for a fixed term of one year. A state statute provided that all state university teachers would be employed for one-year terms and would be eligible for tenure only after four years of continuous service. The professor was notified before February 1 that he would not be rehired. No reason for the decision was given, nor was there an opportunity for a hearing or an appeal.

The question considered by the Supreme Court was "whether the [professor] had a constitutional right to a statement of reasons and a hearing on the university's decision not to rehire him for another year." The Court ruled that he had no such right because neither a "liberty" nor a "property" interest had been violated by the nonrenewal. Concerning liberty interests, the Court reasoned:

> The state, in declining to rehire the respondent, did not make any charge against him that might seriously damage his standing and associations in his community. It did not base the nonrenewal of his contract on a charge, for example, that he had been guilty of dishonesty or immorality. Had it done so, this would be a different case. For "where a person's good name, reputation, honor, or integrity is at stake because of what the government is doing to him, notice and an opportunity to be heard is essential" (*Wisconsin v. Constantineau*, 400 U.S. 433, 437 (1971)) [other citations omitted]. In such a case, due process would accord an opportunity to refute the charge before university officials. In the present case, however, there is no suggestion whatever that the respondent's "good name, reputation, honor, or integrity" is at stake.
>
> Similarly, there is no suggestion that the state, in declining to reemploy the respondent, imposed on him a stigma or other disability that foreclosed his freedom to take advantage of other employment opportunities. The state, for example, did not invoke any regulations to bar the respondent from all other public employment in state universities. Had it done so, this, again, would be a different case. . . .
>
> Hence, on the record before us, all that clearly appears is that the respondent was not rehired for one year at one university. It stretches the concept too far to suggest that a person is deprived of "liberty" when he simply is not rehired in one job but remains as free as before to seek another [408 U.S. at 573–74, 575].

The Court also held that the respondent had not been deprived of any property interest in future employment:

> To have a property interest in a benefit, a person clearly must have more than an abstract need or desire for it. He must have more than a unilateral expectation of it. He must, instead, have a legitimate claim of entitlement to it. . . . Property interests, of course, are not created by the Constitution. Rather, they are created and their dimensions are defined by existing rules or understandings that stem from an independent source such as state law—rules or understandings that secure certain benefits and that support claims of entitlement to those benefits. . . . Respondent's "property" interest in employment at Wisconsin State University-Oshkosh was created and defined by the terms of his appointment, [which] specifically provided that the respondent's employment was to terminate on June 30. They did not provide for contract renewal absent "sufficient cause." Indeed, they made no provision for renewal whatsoever. . . . In these circumstances, the respondent surely had an abstract concern in being rehired, but he did not have a property interest sufficient to require the university authorities to give him a hearing when they declined to renew his contract of employment [408 U.S. at 578].

Since the professor had no protected liberty or property interest, his Fourteenth Amendment rights had not been violated, and the university was not required to provide a reason for its nonrenewal of the contract or to afford the professor a hearing on the nonrenewal.

In the *Perry* case, the respondent had been employed as a professor by the Texas state college system for ten consecutive years. While employed, he was actively involved in public disagreements with the board of regents. He was employed on a series of one-year contracts, and at the end of his tenth year the board elected not to rehire him. The professor was given neither an official reason nor the opportunity for a hearing. Like Roth, Perry argued that the board's action violated his Fourteenth Amendment right to procedural due process.

But in the *Perry* case, unlike the *Roth* case, the Supreme Court ruled that the professor had raised a genuine claim to *de facto* tenure, which would create a constitutionally protected property interest in continued employment. The professor relied on tenure guidelines promulgated by the coordinating board of the Texas College and University System and on an official faculty guide's statement that:

> Odessa College has no tenure system. The administration of the college wishes the faculty member to feel that he has permanent tenure as long as his teaching services are satisfactory and as long as he displays a cooperative attitude toward his coworkers and his superiors, and as long as he is happy in his work [408 U.S. at 600].

According to the Court:

> We have made clear in *Roth* . . . that "property" interests subject to procedural due process protection are not limited by a few rigid technical forms. Rather, "property" denotes a broad range of interests that are secured by "existing rules or understandings." A person's interest in a benefit is a "property" interest for due process purposes if there are such rules or mutually explicit understandings that support his claim of entitlement to the benefit and that he may invoke at a hearing. . . . In this case, the respondent has alleged the existence of rules and understandings, promulgated and fostered by state officials, that may justify his legitimate claim of entitlement to continued employment absent "sufficient cause." . . . [W]e agree that the respondent must be given an opportunity to prove the legitimacy of his claim of such entitlement in light of "the policies and practices of the institution." . . . [S]uch proof would obligate officials to grant a hearing at his request, where he could be informed of the grounds for his nonretention and challenge their sufficiency [408 U.S. at 603].

One other Supreme Court case should be read together with *Roth* and *Perry* for a fuller understanding of the Court's due process analysis. *Bishop v. Wood,* 426 U.S. 341 (1976), concerned a policeman who had been discharged, allegedly on the basis of incorrect information, and orally informed of the reasons in a private conference. With four Justices strongly dissenting, the Court held that the discharge infringed neither property nor liberty interests of the policeman. Regarding property, the Court, adopting a stilted lower-court interpretation of the ordinance governing employment of policemen, held that the ordinance created no expectation of continued employment but only required the employer to provide certain procedural protections, all of which had been provided in this case. Regarding liberty, the Court held that the charges against an employee cannot form the basis for a deprivation of liberty claim if they are privately communicated to the employee and not made public. The Court also held that the truth or falsity of the charges is irrelevant to the question of whether a liberty interest has been infringed.

Under *Roth, Perry,* and *Bishop,* there are three basic situations in which courts will require that a nonrenewal decision be accompanied by appropriate procedural safeguards:

1. The existing rules, policies, or practices of the institution, or "mutually explicit understandings" between the faculty member and the institution, support the faculty member's claim of entitlement to continued employment. Such circumstances would create a property interest. In *Soni v. Board of Trustees of University of Tennessee,* 513 F.2d 347 (6th Cir. 1975), for example, the court held that a nonrenewed, nontenured mathematics professor had such a property interest because voting and retirement plan privileges had been extended to him and he had been told that he could expect his contract to be renewed.

2. The institution, in the course of nonrenewal, makes charges against the faculty member that could seriously damage his or her reputation, standing, or associations in the community. Such circumstances would create a liberty interest.[13] *Roth,* for instance, suggests that charges of dishonesty or immorality accompanying nonrenewal could infringe a faculty member's liberty interest. And in *Wellner v. Minnesota State Junior College Board,* 487 F.2d 153 (8th Cir. 1973), the court held that charges of racism deprived the faculty member of a liberty interest.

The *Bishop* case makes clear that charges or accusations against a faculty member must in some way be made public before they can form the basis of a liberty claim. Although *Bishop* did not involve faculty members, a pre-*Bishop* case, *Ortwein v. Mackey,* 511 F.2d 696 (5th Cir. 1975), applies essentially the same principle in the university setting. Under *Ortwein* the institution must have made, or be likely to make, the stigmatizing charges "public 'in any official or intentional manner, other than in connection with the defense of [related legal] action'" (511 F.2d at 699; quoting *Kaprelian v. Texas Woman's University,* 509 F.2d 133, 139 (5th Cir. 1975)). Thus, there are still questions to be resolved concerning when a charge has become sufficiently "public" to fall within *Ortwein* and *Bishop.*

---

[13]In *Paul v. Davis,* 424 U.S. 693 (1976), the U.S. Supreme Court held that "defamation, standing alone" does not infringe a liberty interest. But defamation can still create a liberty infringement when combined with some "alteration of legal status" under state law, and termination or nonrenewal of public employment is such a change in status. Defamation "in the course of declining to rehire" would therefore infringe a faculty member's liberty interest even under *Paul v. Davis.*

3. The nonrenewal imposes a "stigma or other disability" on the faculty member that "foreclose[s] his freedom to take advantage of other employment opportunities." Such circumstances would create a liberty interest. *Roth,* for instance, suggests that a nonrenewal that bars the faculty member from other employment in the state higher education system would infringe a liberty interest. Presumably, charges impugning the faculty member's professional competence or integrity could also infringe a liberty interest if the institution keeps records of the charges and if the contents of these records could be divulged to potential future employers of the faculty member. But if the faculty member's contract is merely not renewed, the fact that it may be difficult for an individual to locate another teaching position does not mean that the nonrenewal creates a liberty interest. In *Putnam v. Keller,* 332 F.3d 541 (8th Cir. 2003), the court ruled that a nonrenewed faculty member accused of misappropriating funds and planning musical events with "inappropriate sexual overtones" had a liberty interest and was entitled to a hearing on his nonrenewal decision. The court determined that these charges stigmatized the plaintiff, and had been made known to other faculty and staff members at the college, thus entitling him to a hearing to clear his name.

A liberty or property interest might also be infringed when the nonrenewal is based on, and thus would penalize, the faculty member's exercise of freedom of expression. The Supreme Court dealt with this issue briefly in a footnote in the *Roth* case (408 U.S. at 575 n.14), appearing to suggest that a hearing may be required in some circumstances where the nonrenewal "would directly impinge upon interests in free speech or free press." In the *Putnam* case, discussed above, the college had banned Professor Putnam from the campus, an act that resulted in a free speech and freedom of association claim by the plaintiff in addition to his liberty interest claim. Again, the court ruled in Putnam's favor, stating that the campus is a public forum, thus giving Putnam the same right of access to the campus as any other citizen enjoys.

A case in which a public university prevailed in a constitutional challenge to a nonrenewal decision is instructive because of the care taken by various administrators to provide procedural due process to the accused professor. In *Trejo v. Shoben,* 319 F.3d 878 (7th Cir. 2003), the University of Illinois refused to reappoint Trejo, an assistant professor of psychology, after investigating the complaints of several students about Trejo's behavior at an out-of-state scholarly conference that Trejo and the students had attended. Several female graduate students complained that at a dinner they attended with Trejo and other faculty, Trejo made lengthy comments of a sexual nature, some of which were directed at the students and included vulgar hand gestures. According to the court, "every other man and woman seated at the table that evening was offended by Trejo's speech, concluding that he was 'out of control' and that his remarks were little more than thinly veiled sexual solicitations directed at the female graduate students in the group." Apparently the sexual innuendo and solicitations toward the graduate students continued when the group returned to campus. The students complained to the department chair, who investigated their complaints and obtained corroborating information from others who had attended the dinner. The investigation also revealed the Trejo had behaved inappropriately toward other female graduate students from the beginning of his employment at Illinois, and also that similar problems had taken place at Trejo's previous place of employment.

The chair provided the dean with a written report, which recommended that Trejo not be reappointed. The dean provided the report to Trejo and met with him, as well as providing Trejo with the opportunity to provide a written response to the report. The dean met with a faculty advisory committee, conducted an independent review of the department chair's findings, and recommended that Trejo not be reappointed.

Trejo sued, claiming due process violations and also arguing that his discussion at the conference was protected speech under the First Amendment. The trial court disagreed, and the appellate court affirmed that ruling. Said the court: "[T]he statements were simply parts of a calculated type of speech designed to further Trejo's private interests in attempting to solicit female companionship . . ." (319 F.3d at 887) rather than matters of public concern (see further discussion of the case in Sections 7.4.3, 7.5.2, & 9.3.4). Furthermore, ruled the court, the university complied with due process requirements because the chair, dean, and provost all met with Trejo to seek his side of the story, and allowed him to provide a written response to the chair's report.

Whenever a nonrenewed faculty member has a basis for making a liberty or property interest claim (see Sections 7.2–7.5), administrators should consider providing a hearing. Properly conducted, a hearing may not only vitiate any subsequent procedural due process litigation by the faculty member but may also resolve or defuse First Amendment claims that otherwise might be taken to court. And as seen in *Trejo,* the hearing may be informal, as long as the institution follows its own procedures and provides the accused faculty member with notice of the charges and an opportunity to respond to them.

In 1971, the American Association of University Professors adopted a "Statement on Procedural Standards in the Renewal or Nonrenewal of Faculty Appointments" (in *AAUP Policy Documents and Reports* (AAUP, 2001), 15–20). The procedures include notice of criteria for reappointment, periodic review of the performance of probationary faculty, notice of reasons for nonreappointment, and an appeal process for decisions that allegedly involved academic freedom violations or gave inadequate consideration to the department's recommendation.

6.7.2.2. Denial of tenure. Denials of tenure, like contract nonrenewals, must be distinguished analytically from terminations of tenure. Whereas a tenure termination always infringes the faculty member's property interests, a tenure denial may or may not infringe a property or liberty interest, triggering due process protections. The answer in any particular case will depend on application of the teachings from *Roth* and *Perry* (Section 6.7.2.1) and their progeny. Denials of promotions, for due process purposes, are generally analogous to denials of tenure and thus are subject to the general principles developed in the tenure denial cases below. For a leading illustration, see *Clark v. Whiting,* 607 F.2d 634 (4th Cir. 1979), where the court held that an associate professor had no right to an evidentiary hearing upon denial of promotion to full professor.

In 1978, a West Virginia court determined that a faculty member denied tenure had been deprived of a property interest (*McLendon v. Morton*, 249 S.E.2d 919 (W. Va. 1978)). Parkersburg Community College published eligibility criteria for tenure, which included six years as a teaching member of the full-time faculty and attainment of the rank of assistant professor. Having fulfilled both requirements, McLendon applied for tenure. After her tenure application was rejected on grounds of incompetence, McLendon filed suit, claiming that the institution's failure to provide her a hearing abridged her due process rights. The court held that (1) satisfying "objective eligibility standards gave McLendon a sufficient entitlement, so that she could not be denied tenure on the basis of her competence without some procedural due process"; and (2) minimal due process necessitates notice of the reasons for denial and a hearing before an unbiased tribunal, at which the professor can refute the issues raised in the notice. This decision thus extends the *Roth* doctrine to include, among persons who have a property interest in continued employment, faculty members who teach at public institutions and have met specified objective criteria for tenure eligibility (assuming that the institution uses objective criteria). In West Virginia and any other jurisdiction that may accept the *McLendon* reasoning, institutions must give such faculty members notice and an opportunity for a hearing before any final decision to deny tenure. Most institutions, however, use subjective criteria, or a combination of objective and subjective criteria, for making tenure decisions, and thus would not be bound by *McLendon.*

In contrast to *McLendon,* the court in *Beitzel v. Jeffrey,* 643 F.2d 870 (1st Cir. 1981), held that a professor hired as a "probationary employee" did not have a sufficient property interest at stake under *Roth* to challenge his denial of tenure on due process grounds. The standards for the granting or denial of tenure were outlined in the university handbook; but, unlike those in *McLendon,* these standards were subjective. The court determined that the professor had no basis for the expectation that he would be granted tenure automatically. Similarly, in *Goodisman v. Lytle,* 724 F.2d 818 (9th Cir. 1984), the court rejected a professor's claim that he had a property interest in the university's procedures and guidelines for making tenure decisions. The court concluded that the procedures and guidelines "do not significantly limit university officials' discretion in making tenure decisions. They provide only an outline of relevant considerations. They do not enhance a candidate's expectation of obtaining tenure enough to establish a constitutionally protected interest" (724 F.2d at 821).

In *Davis v. Oregon State University,* 591 F.2d 493 (9th Cir. 1978), the same court that later decided *Goodisman* rejected a different type of professorial claim to a hearing prior to tenure denial. The plaintiff had been an associate professor in the university's department of physics. He alleged that the department chairman had assured him at the time of his appointment that he would be granted tenure "as a matter of course." In 1972 and again in 1973, under the university's published tenure policy, the university tenure committee reviewed Davis's case and on both occasions obtained insufficient votes to either grant or deny tenure. Davis was thereafter terminated at the end of the 1973–74 academic year and brought suit, contending that he had *de facto* tenure arising from an oral contract with the department chairman. The court ruled that the university's written tenure policy defeated any claim to a contractual tenure agreement, since the policy vested no authority to grant tenure in department chairmen, and Davis was fully aware of this fact. The court thus held that Davis had no property interest that would support his claim to a hearing.

Institutional procedures for making a tenure decision do not themselves create a property interest, according to *Siu v. Johnson,* 748 F.2d 238 (4th Cir. 1984). Siu was denied tenure by George Mason University, a public institution, despite the positive recommendation of her departmental colleagues. Citing language in the faculty handbook that "the faculty is primarily responsible for recommendations involving appointments, reappointments, promotions, [and] the granting of tenure" (748 F.2d at 241) (although the final decision was explicitly afforded to the board or president), Siu asserted that the university's written procedures for making tenure decisions created a constitutionally protected property interest, and that the institution's failure to defer to the peer evaluation violated that property interest. The court stated that most untenured faculty were at-will employees and thus had no legitimate expectation of reemployment.

The court then turned to Siu's contention that detailed procedures for making tenure decisions created a property interest in having those procedures followed. The court responded:

> Put this way the claim is a circular one: the state's detailed procedures provide the due process guarantees which create the very property interest protected by those guarantees. This is conceptually unacceptable. Its logical effect would be to "constitutionalize" all state contractual provisions respecting the continuation of public employment [748 F.2d at 244].

The court then provided guidance regarding the analysis of whether a property interest exists, noting that the decision-making procedures used are not coextensive with the property right, which, in this case, was created by state law.

> The special relevance of the procedures to this limited inquiry is their indication of the general nature of the decisional process by which it is contemplated that the "interest" may be terminated. In particular, the procedures will likely indicate whether the decisional process is intended to be essentially an objective one designed to find facts establishing fault, or cause, or justification or the like, or instead to be essentially a subjective, evaluative one committed by the sources to the professional judgment of persons presumed to possess special competence in making the evaluation [748 F.2d at 244].

Concluding that the process in tenure decisions was subjective rather than objective, the court held that:

> the process due one subject to this highly subjective evaluative decision can only be the exercise of professional judgment by those empowered to make the final decision in a way not so manifestly arbitrary and capricious that a

reviewing court could confidently say of it that it did not in the end involve the exercise of professional judgment [748 F.2d at 245].

The court then turned to Siu's claim that the institution's refusal to defer to the faculty's judgment violated its tenure procedures, an alleged violation of substantive, rather than procedural, due process:

> Required deference to "working" faculty judgments in evaluating the professional qualifications of their peers may . . . be a proper subject for vigorous faculty associational efforts, for negotiated contractual ordering, or for voluntary conferral by sufficiently enlightened and secure academic institutions. But we are not prepared to hold that it is an essential element of constitutionally guaranteed due process, whether or not it is contractually ordered or otherwise observed as a matter of custom in a particular institution [748 F.2d at 245].

In another case a federal district court concluded that the tenure decision-making criteria and policies at Rutgers University created neither a property nor a liberty interest. The faculty union and a class of individuals denied tenure by Rutgers had asserted that probationary faculty had a legitimate expectation of being evaluated under the same standards that were in effect when currently tenured faculty were evaluated (in other words, that raising the standards for achieving tenure infringed the probationary faculty members' property interests). In an unpublished opinion, *Varma v. Bloustein,* Civ. No. 84-2332 (D.N.J. 1988), the trial judge granted summary judgment for the university, ruling that the tenure criteria and procedures did not "provide the significant substantive restrictions on University discretion in tenure appointments required to create a protected property interest." Furthermore, she wrote, previous patterns of tenure decisions did not bind the university to similar outcomes in the future, particularly in light of the very general nature of the tenure criteria and their reliance on subjective assessments of faculty performance.

As evidence of the existence of a liberty interest, the plaintiffs cited prisoners' rights cases in which the U.S. Supreme Court analyzed the factors that establish a liberty interest in state regulations or procedures. In *Olin v. Wakinekona,* 461 U.S. 238 (1983), the Court noted that "a state creates a protected liberty interest by placing substantive limitations on official discretion." When a state's regulations contain such substantive limitations, the plaintiff may have a protected liberty interest (*Hewitt v. Helms,* 459 U.S. 460 (1983)). The judge rejected the application of *Olin* and *Hewitt* to tenure decisions at Rutgers, stating that a liberty interest arises only when there are "particularized standards or criteria." The university's tenure standards did not restrict its discretion to award or deny tenure, and thus no liberty interest was created.

The court in *Kilcoyne v. Morgan,* 664 F.2d 940 (4th Cir. 1981), rejected yet another argument for procedural protections prior to denial of tenure. The plaintiff, a nontenured faculty member at East Carolina University, argued that his employment contract incorporated a provision of the faculty manual requiring department chairmen to apprise nontenured faculty—both by personal conference and written evaluation—of their progress toward tenure. Although Kilcoyne received a letter from the department chairman and had a follow-up conference toward the end of each of his first two years at the university, he argued that these procedures did not conform to the faculty manual. University guidelines also mandated a tenure decision following a three-year probationary period. At the beginning of his third year, Kilcoyne was notified that he would be rehired for a fourth year; later in the third year, however, he was informed that he would not be granted tenure or employed beyond the fourth year. After his claim of "de facto tenure" was summarily dismissed by the courts (405 F. Supp. 828 (E.D.N.C. 1975), *affirmed,* 530 F.2d 968 (4th Cir. 1975)), Kilcoyne argued that the alleged failure of the university to conform precisely to the faculty manual procedures incorporated into his contract deprived him of procedural due process. The court held that Kilcoyne lacked any *Roth* property interest in further employment at the university; denial of tenure would thus have been constitutionally permissible even if accompanied by no procedural safeguards. According to the court, if a state university gratuitously provides procedural safeguards that are not constitutionally mandated, deviations from such procedures will not violate due process even if the procedures are enumerated in the faculty contract. Although the contract may provide a basis for a breach of contract action, the mere fact that the state is a contracting party does not raise the contract problem to the status of a constitutional issue.

Other potential sources of property interests relevant to tenure denials (as well as to terminations of tenured faculty, discussed in Section 6.6.2.3) are the fair employment laws enacted by the states. In *Logan v. Zimmerman Brush Co.,* 455 U.S. 422 (1982), the U.S. Supreme Court ruled that a former employee challenging his dismissal had a property interest in the adjudicatory processes of the Illinois Fair Employment Practices Commission. The commission had failed to schedule a hearing on Logan's timely complaint of discriminatory dismissal, and the Illinois courts had ruled that the commission's procedural error deprived the commission of jurisdiction and thus extinguished Logan's cause of action. The court, in an opinion written by Justice Blackmun, disagreed. Justice Blackmun wrote: "[Logan's] right to use the [state law] adjudicatory procedures is a species of property protected by the Due Process Clause. . . . The hallmark of property is an individual entitlement grounded in state law, which cannot be removed except for cause" (455 U.S. at 431). The statute created a property interest because it gave Logan an entitlement to use the state's enforcement process; the state's own error deprived Logan of this protected property interest, and no due process protections had been afforded him.

Although a few courts have ordered a college to grant tenure to a faculty member who has prevailed in a constitutional or civil rights challenge to a tenure denial (see the discussion in Section 6.4.1), it is much more common for a court to remand the decision to the university for a new tenure review that avoids the procedural violations found by the court to have prejudiced the review process. For example, in *Sugano v. University of Washington,* 2000 Wash. App. LEXIS 504 (Ct. App. Wash., March 27, 2000) (unpublished), a state appellate court determined that an untenured professor of romance languages had not been properly mentored, and also ruled that the university had not followed the appropriate process in the plaintiff's tenure review. Although the plaintiff was subsequently denied tenure after a second review, the court awarded her back pay and ordered the university to pay her attorney's fees.

In *Skorin-Kapov v. State University of New York at Stony Brook,* 722 N.Y.S.2d 576 (N.Y. App. Div. 2001), *appeal denied,* 96 N.Y.2d 720 (N.Y. 2001), a state appellate court reversed the order of a trial court to grant the plaintiff tenure after a finding that the tenure denial was arbitrary, capricious, and "without a sound basis in reason." Although the appellate court agreed with the trial court's findings of fact, it rejected its remedy and remanded the matter to the university to conduct a new tenure evaluation. (For a case with similar facts and the same remedy, see *Aievoli v. State University of New York,* 694 N.Y.S.2d 156 (N.Y. App. Div. 1999).)

Procedural protections for public college faculty may also be found in faculty handbooks or other college policies that have contractual significance. For example, the faculty handbook at Washington State University requires that tenured faculty members conduct annual evaluations of untenured faculty. In *Trimble v. Washington State University,* 993 P.2d 259 (Wash. 2000), a faculty member denied tenure filed a breach of contract claim, stating that the failure of the mentoring process caused his tenure denial. The state's supreme court affirmed a summary judgment ruling for the university, stating that the tenured faculty members' failure to provide written evaluations of an untenured faculty member during his probationary period did not constitute a breach of contract. One justice dissented, stating that the failure to provide feedback to the untenured faculty member from tenured faculty in his department prevented him from making the kind of changes in his research program that could have led to a positive tenure decision.

Carefully drafted contract language can help colleges deflect contractual claims to tenure as a result of defective procedures. For example, in *University of Nevada v. Stacey,* 997 P.2d 812 (Nev. 2000), the state's highest court rejected a breach of contract claim brought by a professor who had received excellent evaluations during his employment at the university. The court interpreted the language of the professor's contract as stating that a decision to grant tenure was discretionary; therefore, denial of tenure was not a breach of contract.

With the exception of *McLendon,* which addressed issues not usually present in challenges to tenure denials, the courts have clearly stated that denial of tenure is not a "termination" per se, and affords no constitutional due process guarantees (although state statutes or regulations may provide procedural guarantees, which, if violated, could form the basis for a claim under state law). As is the case with nonreappointment, however, if the faculty member alleges that the tenure denial was grounded in unconstitutional reasons (retaliation for constitutionally protected speech, for example), then liberty interests would arguably have been infringed and procedural due process protections would therefore apply.

6.7.2.3. Termination of tenure. Whenever an institution's personnel decision would infringe a property or liberty interest, constitutional due process requires that the institution offer the faculty member procedural safeguards before the decision becomes final. The crux of these safeguards is notice and opportunity for a hearing. In other words, the institution must notify the faculty member of the reasons for the decision and provide a fair opportunity for him or her to challenge these reasons in a hearing before an impartial body.

Decisions to terminate tenured faculty members must always be accompanied by notice and opportunity for a hearing, since such decisions always infringe property interests. The cases in this Section provide specific illustrations of the procedural due process requirements applicable to tenure termination cases. Decisions to terminate a nontenured faculty member during the contract term are generally analogous to tenure terminations and thus are subject to principles similar to those in the cases below; the same is true for nonrenewal and denial-of-tenure decisions when they would infringe property or liberty interests.

Because of the significance of the property interest, a pretermination hearing is required. The standards for the pretermination hearing that must be provided to a discharged faculty member were developed by the U.S. Supreme Court in *Cleveland Board of Education v. Loudermill,* 470 U.S. 532 (1985). Prior to making the final termination decision, the institution should hold a pretermination hearing, according to the *Loudermill* opinion. "The tenured public employee is entitled to oral or written notice of the charges against him, an explanation of the employer's evidence, and an opportunity to present his side of the story" (470 U.S. at 546). If the pretermination hearing is as informal as the *Loudermill* criteria suggest is permissible, then a post-termination hearing is necessary to permit the individual to challenge the decision in a manner designed to protect his or her rights to due process. The nature of the hearing and the degree of formality of the procedures have been the subjects of much litigation by tenured faculty who were discharged.

Although there is no requirement that the termination hearing have all the elements of a judicial hearing (*Toney v. Reagan,* 467 F.2d 953 (9th Cir. 1972)), such hearings must meet minimal constitutional standards. A federal appeals court set forth such standards in *Levitt v. University of Texas,* 759 F.2d 1224 (5th Cir. 1985):

1. The employee must be given notice of the cause for dismissal.
2. The employee must be given notice of the names of witnesses and told what each will testify to.
3. The employee must be given a meaningful opportunity to be heard.
4. The hearing must be held within a reasonable time.
5. The hearing must be conducted before an impartial panel with appropriate academic expertise.

Many institutions, however, have adopted the procedures recommended by the American Association of University Professors. Formal adoption of the AAUP's 1958 "Statement on Procedural Standards in Faculty Dismissal Proceedings" (in *AAUP Policy Documents and Reports* (AAUP, 2001), 15–20) will require the institution to follow them.

A federal trial court developed a set of carefully reasoned and articulated due process standards in *Potemra v. Ping,* 462 F. Supp. 328 (E.D. Ohio 1978). In that case, a tenured member of the economics department at Ohio University claimed that he was denied due process when the university dismissed him for failure to perform his faculty duties and inability to communicate with students. The court ruled that the teacher's minimum due process safeguards included (1) a written statement of the reasons for the proposed termination prior to final action, (2) adequate notice of a hearing, (3) a hearing at which the teacher has an opportunity to submit evidence to controvert the grounds for dismissal, (4) a final statement of the grounds for dismissal if it does occur. The court held that the university had complied with these requirements and had not infringed the faculty member's due process rights.

In a similar case, *Bowling v. Scott,* 587 F.2d 229 (5th Cir. 1979), a tenured English professor at the University of Alabama filed suit after the university terminated his tenure. The court enunciated a minimum due process standard similar to that used in *Potemra* and ruled that no deprivation of procedural due process had occurred, since the university had served Bowling with a list of charges; informed him that formal proceedings would commence; given advance notice of each of fourteen hearing sessions, all of which the faculty member had attended with his lawyer; and subsequently issued a twelve-page report stating the grounds for dismissal.

In another case, *King v. University of Minnesota,* 774 F.2d 224 (8th Cir. 1985), the court upheld the university's dismissal of a tenured faculty member for neglect of his teaching responsibilities and lack of scholarship. The university had provided the following due process protections:

1. Frequent communications with King concerning his poor teaching, his unexcused absences, and his refusal to cooperate with the department.

2. A departmental vote, with King present, to remove him from the department because of his history of poor performance.

3. Notice to King of the charges against him and the university's intent to initiate removal proceedings.

4. A hearing panel of tenured faculty and the right to object to any of the individual members (which King did for one member, who was replaced).

5. Representation by counsel and substantial documentary discovery, including depositions of administrators.

6. A prehearing conference in which the parties exchanged issue lists, witness lists, and exhibit lists.

7. A hearing occurring over a two-week period, during which King was represented by counsel, who cross-examined witnesses, presented witnesses and documentary evidence, and made oral and written arguments.

8. Review of the entire record by the university president.

9. Review by the regents of the panel's findings, the president's recommendation, and briefs from each of the parties.

10. An opportunity for King to appear before the regents before they made the termination decision.

The appellate court characterized the procedural protections that King received as "exhaustive" and determined that they satisfied constitutional requirements (774 F.2d at 228).

In *Frumkin v. Board of Trustees, Kent State,* 626 F.2d 19 (6th Cir. 1980), the court focused particularly on the type of hearing an institution must provide prior to a decision to terminate tenure. The university had slated the professor for dismissal after federal funding for his position was cut. In support of the recommendation for dismissal, the university charged the professor with "unsatisfactory performance as grant director, recurring unproven charges against faculty members, unprofessional conduct, false charges against the department, and violation of university policy." When the professor chose to contest his dismissal, the university scheduled a hearing. The professor was permitted to have a lawyer present at the hearing, but the lawyer's role was limited. He was permitted to consult and advise his client and to make closing arguments in his client's behalf. But he was prohibited from conducting any cross-examination or direct examination of witnesses or from raising objections.

Reasoning that this limited hearing was well suited to the type of decision to be made, the court held that the university had not violated the professor's due process rights. The court examined the ruling in *Mathews v. Eldridge,* 424 U.S. 319 (1976), in which the U.S. Supreme Court had established guidelines for procedural due process. In *Mathews,* the Court had identified three factors which must be considered:

> [F]irst, the private interest that will be affected by the official action; second, the risk of an erroneous deprivation of such interest through the procedures used, and the probable value, if any, of additional or substitute procedural safeguards; and finally, the government's interest, including the function involved and the fiscal and administrative burdens that the additional or substitute procedural requirement would entail [626 F.2d at 21].

Using these criteria, the court rejected Frumkin's contention that his counsel's inability to cross-examine witnesses was a violation of procedural due process. Despite the fact that the administrative burden on the university would have been "comparatively slight" should Frumkin's attorney have been permitted to examine witnesses, said the court, the institution's interest in avoiding a "full-fledged adversary trial" was reasonable and there was no showing that Frumkin had been prejudiced by the limited role played by his attorney.

As long as reviewing courts believe that the fundamental protections articulated in *Loudermill* have been provided, the procedures for making the termination decision need not be elaborate. In *McDaniels v. Flick,* 59 F.3d 446 (3d Cir. 1995), the court reversed a jury finding on behalf of the professor, ruling that the college should have been awarded summary judgment. McDaniels, a tenured professor at Delaware County Community College, had been warned, after two male students complained that McDaniels had sexually harassed them, that he would be disciplined or terminated if he repeated the behavior. The following year, another student filed a harassment complaint against McDaniels. After investigating the charges, the college decided to discharge him. He was told to attend a meeting with the college's personnel director and the dean to "discuss a student problem." He was not advised that the "problem" was a charge of sexual harassment until he arrived at the meeting, at which time he was also advised that the college would begin termination proceedings. Later, the personnel director confirmed this information in writing.

The college's policies provided for a pretermination appeal to the president, of which McDaniels took advantage. The president, after investigating the allegations, recommended to the board of trustees that they proceed with the termination. The trustees voted unanimously to terminate McDaniels. The college's collective bargaining agreement also provided for post-termination arbitration. Although McDaniels began arbitration proceedings, he also filed an action under 42 U.S.C. Section 1983 (see Section 3.5 of this book), claiming that the college had violated his Fourteenth Amendment due process rights. The arbitration was stayed pending the results of the litigation.

The college filed a motion for summary judgment, but the trial judge denied the motion and held a trial. Although the jury found that the college had adequately informed McDaniels of the charges against him, it determined that the college had not given him an opportunity to respond fully to the charges before it made the termination decision. The judge ordered McDaniels reinstated with back pay.

The appellate court reversed the trial court's ruling. Evaluating the college's actions in light of *Loudermill*, the appellate court made short work of McDaniels's claim that, because he was a tenured professor of twenty years' standing, he was due more procedural protection than that provided by *Loudermill*:

> It is true that McDaniels has a property interest in his continued employment and perhaps a liberty interest in clearing his reputation of sexual harassment charges. But McDaniels appears to argue that because he is a professor and has been at the college for 20 years, his property interest in continued employment is constitutionally greater than those held by the employees in *Loudermill*. Yet he has not offered any basis on which we could or should distinguish reasonably between the interest of a tenured employee who has worked 20 years and the interest of one who has worked only one year for the same employer and we can conceive of no principled way to distinguish between the two. Arguably, the interest in continued employment may be greater for younger employees who have started only recently because they have potentially more years of employment ahead [59 F.3d at 455].

The court also rejected McDaniels's assertion that he should have received the procedural safeguards approved by that same appellate court in *Skehan v. Board of Trustees of Bloomsburg State College* and *Chung v. Park* (discussed in Section 6.7.4 below). Although that court in those opinions had approved a six-step pretermination procedure as consistent with due process requirements, the *McDaniels* court stated that in neither case had it ruled that all of these steps were required prior to the termination, and that some of the steps could be provided after termination.

The court rejected the jury's finding that McDaniels had not been afforded an opportunity to respond to the charges. He had denied the charges at the initial meeting with the personnel director, had provided additional written information, and was given nearly a month to prepare for his appeal to the president. The president read and responded to McDaniels's submissions, said the court, and that was a sufficient opportunity for the college to consider his side of the story.

The court rejected McDaniels's claim that his due process rights were denied because he was never given a copy of the allegations against him. "[P]retermination notice of the charges and evidence against an employee need not be in great detail as long as it allows the employee 'the opportunity to determine what facts, if any, within his knowledge might be presented in mitigation of or in denial of the charges'" (59 F.3d at 457, citations omitted). The fact that, at the initial meeting, McDaniels was asked specific questions about the allegations gave him an opportunity to respond meaningfully to the charges, said the court.

McDaniels also argued that the pretermination procedure was a sham because the administrators were biased against him, knew that the harassment allegations were false, and were simply trying to rid the college of a highly paid tenured professor. The court stated: "In the case of an employment termination case, 'due process [does not] require the state to provide an impartial decision maker at the pre-termination hearing. The state is obligated only to make available "the means by which [the employee] can receive redress for the deprivations"'" (59 F.3d at 459, quoting *Schaper v. City of Huntsville*, 813 F.2d 709, 715–16 (5th Cir. 1987)). Because the board of trustees provided McDaniels with a neutral decision maker at the post-termination stage, the due process protections were sufficient.

One judge dissented, agreeing with McDaniels's assertion that the lack of notice of the charges prior to the pretermination meeting violated his due process rights. But the majority responded that McDaniels was not terminated at the end of the meeting; the board of trustees terminated him three weeks later after an appeal to the president, which the majority believed gave McDaniels sufficient time and opportunity to respond to the charges.

McDaniels probably represents the minimum due process that institutions must afford tenured professors or other employees who have a property right in continued employment. Despite the favorable outcome for the college in this case, most public institutions will very likely continue to follow a version of the termination procedure described in *Chung v. Park*, 514 F.2d 382 (3d Cir. 1975) (discussed in Section 6.7.4), or a similar procedure.

Clarke v. West Virginia Board of Regents, 279 S.E.2d 169 (W. Va. 1981) provides particularly useful guidance to administrators and counsel in developing a written decision based on the record upon which a reviewing court may rely. In this case, the court considered the reasons and evidence an institution must provide to support a decision terminating tenure. Clarke, a tenured professor at

Fairmont State College, had been dismissed following a hearing before a hearing examiner. The hearing examiner made a written report, which merely cited the testimony of witnesses who supported dismissal and did not state any specific reasons or factual basis for affirming the dismissal. The professor argued in court that this report did not comply with due process requirements. Although the court's analysis is based on the state constitution, the opinion relied on federal constitutional precedents and is indicative of federal constitutional analysis as well.

As a starting point for determining what a hearing examiner's report must contain, the court consulted a policy bulletin of the West Virginia Board of Regents. The policy bulletin did not require the hearing examiner to make findings of fact and conclusions of law, but did require the hearing examiner "enter such recommendations as the facts justify and the circumstances may require" and to "state the reasons for his determination and indicate the evidence he relied on" (279 S.E.2d at 177). The court stressed the importance of an adequate report to give a reviewing court a basis for review and to give the affected individual a basis for identifying grounds for review:

> The need for an adequate statement of the hearing examiner's reasons for his determination and the evidence supporting them is obvious. Our function as a reviewing court is to review the record to determine if the evidence adduced at the hearing supports the findings of the hearing examiner and whether his conclusions follow from those findings. We must rely on the facts and logic upon which the hearing examiner ruled . . . and determine whether he erroneously applied them in reaching his final determination. If the record of the administrative proceeding does not reveal those facts which were determinative of the ruling or the logic behind the ruling, we are powerless to review the administrative action. We are thrust into the position of a trier of fact and are asked to substitute our judgment for that of the hearing examiner. That we cannot do [279 S.E.2d at 178].

The court also noted that the party appealing a hearing examiner's ruling needed a statement of findings and the evidence which the examiner relied upon in making those findings in order to develop an appropriate appeal.

On the basis of its review of the regents' bulletin and applicable constitutional principles, the court held that the hearing examiner's report did not meet due process standards:

> In the report of findings and recommendations, a hearing examiner should list the specific charges found to be supported by the evidence adduced at the hearing and provide some reference to the evidence supporting those findings. In view of our discussion above, we conclude that the failure of the hearing examiner to state on the record the charges against Dr. Clarke which were found to be supported by the evidence constitutes reversible error [279 S.E.2d at 178].

In termination proceedings, questions may arise as to whether defects in one segment of the proceeding constitute a sufficient violation of due process to invalidate the entire proceeding. In *Fong v. Purdue University*, 692 F. Supp. 930 (N.D. Ind. 1988), for example, Professor Fong had asked for several delays in the scheduling of the hearing on his dismissal. The faculty hearing committee granted one delay, but decided to proceed on the rescheduled date. Although Fong was available on that date, he refused to attend the hearing because his attorney was not present. The hearing panel recorded and had transcribed the proceedings; and Fong later appeared with his attorney and presented his own witnesses and cross-examined the university's witnesses. In appealing the university's decision to dismiss him, Fong asserted that his absence from part of the hearing was a denial of due process. The court found that Fong had been given, and had taken advantage of, ample opportunity to present his side of the case and that no due process denial had occurred.

> Any problems that might have arisen in this regard from the fact that the university panel proceeded without Dr. Fong and without his counsel at the early stages, were adequately obviated by permitting him to call witnesses at a time when counsel was present. He was afforded an opportunity to cross-examine witnesses and to present his own witnesses. He was provided full and complete notice of the charges against him, and had an opportunity to confront and challenge those charges. Considering the record in its totality, and not in isolated segments, it is difficult to imagine what other procedural due process the officials at Purdue University could have provided to Dr. Fong [692 F. Supp. at 957].

In addition to claims of procedural due process violations, a substantive due process claim may be brought by a faculty plaintiff who claims that the termination decision was made for arbitrary, irrational, or improper reasons. In a claim of substantive due process violation, the plaintiff must demonstrate that the interest at stake is "fundamental" under the U.S. Constitution. Federal courts have been reluctant to create a substantive due process right in continued public employment, following the reasoning of Justice Powell's concurring opinion in *Regents of Univ. of Michigan v. Ewing,* 474 U.S. 214 (1985) (discussed in Section 9.3.1). See, for example, *Nicholas v. Pennsylvania State University,* 227 F.3d 133 (3d Cir. 2000), in which a federal appellate court upheld a jury finding of procedural due process violations but rejected the plaintiff's substantive due process claims, stating that a property right in public employment was not a fundamental constitutional right.

In *Dismissal Proceedings Against Huang,* 431 S.E.2d 541 (N.C. Ct. App. 1993), a tenured faculty member was dismissed as a result of several assaults. Because the assaults had occurred as long as fifteen years earlier, the professor claimed that the use of "old" misconduct violated his substantive due process rights. Although the appellate court agreed, characterizing the university's actions as arbitrary and capricious, the state's supreme court reversed (441 S.E.2d 696 (1994)), finding ample evidence that the professor had engaged in conduct that constituted just cause for dismissal. Although the university ultimately prevailed, the case underscores the importance of prompt administrative response to faculty misconduct.

A federal appellate court ruled that substantial procedural compliance, rather than full compliance, with an institution's de-tenuring procedures was sufficient to pass constitutional muster. In *de Llano v. Berglund,* 282 F.3d 1031

(8th Cir. 2002), the appellate court upheld a trial court's award of summary judgment to North Dakota State University. De Llano, a tenured professor of physics, had a troubled history at the university. He had been hired to chair the department, but was removed five years later at the request of the departmental faculty to improve departmental morale. After being removed as chair, de Llano began a letter-writing campaign, critical of faculty colleagues and discussing various intradepartmental conflicts. Some of these letters were sent to the press. Students disliked de Llano as well—one semester more than 90 percent of the students in his introductory physics class requested a transfer to a different section. The university decided to terminate de Llano on six grounds: (1) lack of collegiality, (2) harassment of departmental staff, (3) refusal to process complaints through proper channels, (4) making false accusations about the department chair and dean, (5) failure to correct problem behavior after several reprimands, and (6) excessive filing of frivolous grievances.

A faculty review committee concluded that the charges were insufficient to support his termination. After the president rejected the findings of that committee, at de Llano's request a second faculty committee held a hearing and concluded that there was adequate cause for his dismissal. The president accepted the findings of this committee and terminated de Llano. De Llano appealed to the state board of higher education, which upheld the dismissal. The lawsuit followed, claiming due process violations (for not following university procedures) and First Amendment violations (for punishing him for his oral and written statements of criticism).

The court looked to *Cleveland Board of Education v. Loudermill*, cited above, for the type of due process protections to which an individual with a property interest in his job is entitled. The court concluded that the university had afforded de Llano notice of the charges against him (the multiple reprimands as well as the final notice of charges), an explanation of those charges, and an opportunity to respond to those charges (two hearings). Despite the fact that de Llano claimed that there were several violations of university procedure, the court concluded that "federal law, not state law or NDSU policy, determines what constitutes adequate procedural due process" (282 F.3d at 1035).

With respect to de Llano's claim that his First Amendment rights had been violated, the court determined that the subject of his letters was his personal grievances against his colleagues and the administration. The court concluded that the subjects of these letters were not matters of public concern and thus were unprotected by the First Amendment.

If a long-tenured professor is dismissed for a single incident, the failure to use progressive discipline may be construed as an unconstitutional procedural violation. In *Trimble v. West Virginia Board of Directors, Southern West Virginia Community & Technical College*, 549 S.E.2d 294 (Ct. App. W. Va. 2001), the court reversed the termination of a tenured assistant professor of English on the grounds of alleged insubordination. Trimble had claimed that the termination violated his First Amendment rights, and that his property right to continued employment required the college administration to provide progressive discipline before terminating him.

Trimble's performance had been acceptable for nearly twenty years. When a new president took office at the college, Trimble helped organize a faculty labor union and became its president. Trimble and several faculty colleagues objected to the new president's insistence that all faculty use a particular type of software to generate course syllabi and to evaluate student achievement. Trimble refused to attend four "mandatory" meetings about the software, and was terminated for insubordination.

The court found that, given Trimble's nineteen years of satisfactory service to the college, and the lack of any criticism of his teaching or relationships with students, the dismissal was arbitrary and capricious. "Because of Mr. Trimble's property interest in continued employment with the College and his previously unblemished record, due process required the College to utilize progressive disciplinary measures against Mr. Trimble" (549 S.E.2d at 305). The court ordered Trimble reinstated with back pay and retroactive benefits. One judge dissented, commenting that the majority was "micro managing" the college's employment decisions and applying its "own subjective notions of justice."

Procedural due process may also be required for a faculty member whose employment contract has been rescinded. In *Garner v. Michigan State University*, 462 N.W.2d 832 (Mich. Ct. App. 1990), the university, without holding a hearing, rescinded the contract of a tenured professor who allegedly lied to the dean about allegations of unprofessional conduct in his prior faculty position. When the dean discovered that serious charges had been made against the professor at his former place of employment, the university rescinded the professor's tenured contract of employment. The professor denied that he had lied about the charges. Although the university asserted its right to rescind an employment contract because of the employee's misrepresentations, citing *Morgan v. American University*, 534 A.2d 323 (D.C. 1987) (see Section 4.3.2), the court disagreed, distinguishing *Morgan* on two grounds. First, the plaintiff in *Morgan* had admitted the misrepresentation, meaning that there was no factual dispute. Second, *Morgan* involved a private institution. The court noted that the plaintiff, as a tenured professor, had a property interest in continued employment and must be afforded the same due process protections that he would be entitled to if the university had terminated him.

Due process protections are not necessary, however, if a tenured professor abandons his position and permits several years to elapse before reclaiming it. In *Osborne v. Stone*, 536 So. 2d 473 (La. Ct. App. 1988), a state court applied the doctrine of laches (a doctrine that says the individual has abandoned his or her rights by failing to assert those rights in a timely manner) in determining that a tenured law professor at Southern University who failed to report for class for an entire academic year had abandoned his position and thus was deemed to have resigned. Since Southern University did not discharge Professor Osborne, the university owed him no hearing or other due process protections.

Taken together, these cases provide a helpful picture of how courts will craft procedural requirements for tenure termination decisions. When reviewing such decisions, courts will generally look for compliance with basic elements of due process, as set out in *Potemra*. When an institution fails to accord the faculty member one or more of these basic elements, *Clarke, Garner,* and *Trimble* indicate that courts will invalidate the institution's decision. But *Bowling* and *Frumkin* illustrate judicial reluctance to provide more specific checklists of procedures mandated by due process. Beyond the minimum requirements, such as those in *Potemra,* courts will usually defer to institutional procedures that appear suited to the needs and expectations of the faculty member and the institution.

6.7.2.4. Other personnel decisions. Courts interpreting *Roth* and *Sindermann* have made it clear that in only a narrow range of employment decisions will the claim that the faculty member has a property interest in the decision apply. For example, in *Swartz v. Scruton,* 964 F.2d 607 (7th Cir. 1992), a professor sued Ball State University, alleging a constitutionally defective failure to follow the proper procedures in determining the recipients of merit salary raises. The court ruled that there was no constitutionally protected property interest in the process of determining merit raises that would support a substantive due process claim, and that the faculty member's procedural interests were not themselves property rights (in other words, the purpose of due process was to protect a property interest, had one existed, but the process itself was not a property interest). Furthermore, the professor had no property interest in a specific pay increase, and even if the professor could have demonstrated a contractual right to the use of proper procedures, this right would not equal a property interest.

Although courts have found that tenured faculty have a property right in continued employment, they do not have such a right in either promotion or other employment decisions. For example, in *Herold v. University of South Florida,* 806 So. 2d 638 (Ct. App. Fla. 2d Dist. 2002), the court rejected the plaintiff's contention that the university's failure to promote him to full professor did not implicate either procedural or substantive due process protections, and thus no hearing regarding the denial of promotion was required.

On the other hand, if institutional policies or contracts provide protections beyond those implicated by the Constitution, additional protections may be required for demotion decisions. For example, in *Moosa v. State Personnel Board,* 102 Cal. App. 4th 1379 (Ct. App. Cal. 3d Dist. 2002), a tenured full professor was demoted to associate professor because of his alleged unprofessional conduct. The dean, concerned about what he believed to be Moosa's poor teaching performance, had directed Moosa to submit a plan for improving his teaching performance. Instead, Moosa submitted a peer evaluation report stating that his performance was acceptable. The dean then demoted Moosa for five years on the basis of "unprofessional conduct." The court ruled that under the collective bargaining agreement that dealt with faculty employment, the dean could request, but not require, that Moosa submit a performance improvement plan. Thus, Moosa's insubordination did not rise to the level of unprofessional conduct, and thus the dean lacked the authority to demote Moosa.

Courts have similarly refused to find a protected property interest in other decisions related to faculty employment—for instance, decisions to transfer faculty members to other departments or to less desirable office space within a department. In *Maples v. Martin,* 858 F.2d 1546 (11th Cir. 1988), the plaintiffs, all of whom were tenured professors, were transferred from the mechanical engineering department to other engineering departments at Auburn University. (The professors also asserted academic freedom claims, discussed in Section 7.4.2.) The plaintiffs claimed that they were denied due process in the transfer decision, but the court concluded that their claim was unfounded.

Considering first whether the property interests that they asserted were sufficient to satisfy the Fourteenth Amendment's due process clause, the court determined that "[t]ransfers and reassignments have generally not been held to implicate a property interest" (858 F.2d at 1550). It indicated that, in this case, neither the faculty handbook nor state law contained any provision protecting a professor from transfer to another department without his or her consent, and such decisions apparently were left to the discretion of university administrators. Thus rejecting the professors' property interest claim, the court also summarily rejected their liberty interest claim, because they had not suffered any loss of rank or salary, could still teach in their areas of specialization, and could not show any stigma resulting from the transfers that would damage their professional reputations or foreclose them from other employment opportunities (858 F.2d at 1550–51, n.5 and accompanying text).

The court held further that, even if the transfer had infringed a property or liberty interest, the professors still would not have been denied procedural due process. The professors had been given notice of the transfers, and the grievance procedures in the faculty handbook were available to them to challenge the transfers (an opportunity that the professors did not pursue).

Another federal court, asked to determine whether a tenured professor had a property interest in a particular position, ruled that no property interest existed in the position itself and that the faculty member's only property interest was in receiving his full compensation (*Huang v. Board of Governors of the University of North Carolina,* 902 F.2d 1134 (4th Cir. 1990)). Furthermore, the court ruled that the university had afforded the plaintiff ample due process because he had had an opportunity to present his grievances to a faculty committee during a nine-day hearing. The procedures used were sufficient, the court ruled, to ensure that the transfer decision was not arbitrary and that it was reached impartially.

In a departure from what appears to be the majority view, another federal appellate court found that a tenured professor had a property right in his tenured position in the accounting department, based upon "contract, confirmed by [the institution's] customs and practices." But the court rejected the professor's claim that his involuntary transfer to a different department did not comply with due process requirements. In *Hulen v. Yates,* 322 F.3d 1229 (10th Cir. 2003), the court ruled that the extensive correspondence between the professor and the dean concerning the transfer, the professor's utilization of the grievance procedure, and the lack of evidence of significant financial or career harm satisfied procedural due process requirements. The court commented: "We reject the suggestion that Dr. Hulen was entitled to a formal . . . evidentiary hearing before being laterally transferred. It would be remarkable if such a hearing were constitutionally required, since the Constitution does not even require such a hearing before an employee is *fired*" (322 F.3d at 1247, citing *Loudermill*).

Another faculty member unsuccessfully attempted to assert a property interest in the number of credits assigned to his course and to his entitlement to serve on a search committee. He filed a variety of claims against his departmental colleagues, including alleged constitutional deprivation of his due process rights. In *Hollister v. Tuttle,* 210 F.3d 1033 (9th Cir. 2000), the court rejected these claims. The professor claimed that he had been retaliated against for criticizing curriculum decisions and the research of his fellow departmental faculty because his colleagues reduced the number of credits assigned to his course from nine to eight and left him off a search committee. The court stated that the number of credits assigned to a course is "an academic decision," and furthermore, that "a place on a college search committee is not property."

Unless an administrative position is explicitly identified as a tenured position, incumbents have no property interest in retaining their administrative positions. In *Garvie v. Jackson,* 845 F.2d 647 (6th Cir. 1988), the former head of the speech and theater department at the University of Tennessee argued that his removal from that position (to a position as a tenured faculty member) without a hearing violated his rights to due process. The court disagreed. The faculty handbook stated clearly that positions as department heads were not tenured; furthermore, a letter appointing the plaintiff as head stated that he would serve at the pleasure of the chancellor. To the plaintiff's claim that removal as department head violated his liberty interests because "rumors" accompanied the removal, the court determined that, since the plaintiff returned to a tenured faculty position, he could not demonstrate the kind of interference with career opportunities that would normally give rise to a liberty interest.

The U.S. Supreme Court has issued a ruling that establishes the due process rights of a tenured public employee who is suspended without pay. In *Gilbert v. Homar,* 520 U.S. 924 (1997), Richard Homar, a police officer at East Stroudsburg University, was arrested by the state police in a drug raid. He was charged with possession of marijuana and other drug-related crimes that constitute felonies under Pennsylvania law. When the state police notified Homar's supervisor of the arrest, the supervisor notified the director of human resources, who had been delegated authority by the president to discipline employees. The director immediately suspended Homar without pay, and sent him a letter advising him of the suspension and the university's intention to investigate the charges.

The criminal charges were dropped approximately one week later; two weeks after that, the director of human resources and Homar's supervisor met with him to give him the chance to explain his side of the story. Homar was not told that university officials had the police report, which contained a confession that he had allegedly made. Six days later, Homar received a copy of the police report and a letter from the director of human resources, advising him that he had been demoted to a groundskeeper, and that he would receive back pay at the groundskeeper rate from the date of his suspension. (He eventually received full back pay at the rate of a police officer.) Homar requested a meeting with the university president. After giving Homar an opportunity to respond to the charges made by the university officials, the president sustained the demotion.

Homar filed a Section 1983 claim (see Section 4.7.4 of this book), contending that his suspension without pay prior to meeting with university officials violated his due process rights. Although the U.S. Court of Appeals for the Third Circuit had ruled that the university's failure to provide Homar with a presuspension hearing violated due process guidelines, the Supreme Court reversed in a unanimous opinion written by Justice Scalia. Noting that the extent of due process clause protections for discipline short of termination was an issue of first impression for the Court, the opinion emphasized the flexible nature of due process, particularly in situations such as Homar's, where the employer believed it needed to act quickly to protect the public's confidence in the integrity of law enforcement personnel. Evaluating the university's actions against the standard of *Mathews v. Eldridge*, the Court distinguished between an employee's interest in remaining employed and his interest in the temporary loss of pay, characterizing the loss in this case as "insubstantial." On the other hand, said the Court, the university had a strong interest in acting quickly, given that felony charges had been filed against Homar. Furthermore, there was little need for a presuspension hearing, since the felony charges that had been filed against Homar provided a reasonable basis for suspending him.

The lower courts had not addressed the issue of whether the university violated Homar's due process rights because of the lapse of time between the dropping of the felony charges and his meeting to explain his side of the story (sixteen days). As a consequence, the Court remanded the case to the appellate court for consideration of this issue.

The Court's focus on the university's need to act quickly suggests that this case may not have general applicability to the suspension of tenured faculty members. Unless a college could demonstrate that it needed to remove a tenured faculty member quickly because he or she was a potential threat to the health or safety of others, or because the faculty member had committed some act that rendered him or her unfit to continue teaching pending a disciplinary hearing, it would probably be difficult for a public college to justify suspension without the panoply of presuspension due process protections. On the other hand, in *Simonson v. Iowa State University*, 603 N.W.2d 557 (Iowa 1999), the Iowa Supreme Court ruled that placing a tenured professor on paid administrative leave pending the completion of an investigation of sexual harassment claims against him did not violate constitutional protections. The court ruled that the professor suffered no economic loss, and thus no deprivation of property interest, and similarly rejected his liberty interest claim. Because no university official had publicly discussed the reason for placing the professor on paid leave, said the court, no liberty interest was at risk.

Some medical centers affiliated with universities are implementing new salary policies for their tenured faculty, in many cases as a result of the changes brought by managed health care. In *Williams v. Texas Tech University Health Sciences Center*, 6 F.3d 290 (5th Cir. 1993), a tenured professor at the medical school challenged his reduction in salary as a violation of his due process rights, alleging that he should have been provided a hearing before the decision was made. His salary had been reduced because, according to his department chair, Williams had not generated the expected amount of grant income. Williams was given six months' notice of the salary reduction, which was from $68,000 to $46,500.

Although the court did not explicitly find that Williams had a property interest in the former salary amount, it determined that he received sufficient due process protections. Citing the U.S. Supreme Court decision in *Mathews v. Eldridge* (Section 6.7.2.3), the court noted that *Mathews* provided that the individual must be given notice of the reasons for the proposed deprivation of a property right and an opportunity to respond to the decision maker. In this situation, said the court, the letter provided Williams with notice and with the opportunity to seek grant funding to supplement his salary. Williams responded to the letter. Nothing more was required to be done, according to the court, noting that state institutions needed substantial discretion to administer their educational programs and to make budgetary decisions. Furthermore, said the court, Williams's interest in attaining a specific income does not outweigh the state's interest. The court affirmed the trial court's summary judgment for the university.

A federal appellate court has rejected the claim of department chairs at the University of the District of Columbia that because the university had given them summer contracts for the previous ten years, they had a property interest in their summer pay. A decision had been made near the end of spring semester to withhold summer contracts because of budget limitations; the chairs asserted that they were denied due process. The court rejected the property interest claim outright. In addition, the court ruled that, because the chairs had not used the university grievance system, any lack of due process protections was the result of their own inaction. The court affirmed the trial court's award of summary judgment for the university (*UDC Chairs Chapter, American Association of University Professors v. Board of Trustees of the University of the District of Columbia*, 56 F.3d 1469 (D.C. Cir. 1995)).

6.7.3. The private faculty member's procedural rights. The rights of faculty employed by private colleges and universities are governed primarily by state contract law and, where applicable, by state constitutions. Although the lack of constitutional protections for faculty at private institutions gives the institution more flexibility in fashioning its decision-making procedures and in determining what procedural protections it will afford faculty, written policies, faculty handbooks, and other policy documents are interpreted as binding contracts in many states (see Section 6.2), and "academic custom and usage" (see Section 1.4.3.3) may also be used by judges to evaluate whether a private institution afforded a faculty member the appropriate protections. Because challenges to negative employment decisions brought by faculty against private institutions are interpreted under state law, the outcomes and reasoning of any particular case must be applied with care to institutions in states other than the state in which the litigation occurred.

Many private institutions have adopted, either in whole or in part, policy statements promulgated by the American Association of University Professors with regard to reappointment and dismissal of tenured faculty. Formal adoption of these policy statements, or consistent adherence to their terms (which could create an implied contract, as discussed in Section 6.2.1), will require the private institution to follow them. Failure to follow these policies can result in breach of contract claims.

The term of the contract, the conditions under which it may be renewed, and the individual's right to certain procedures in the renewal decision are all matters of contract law. If the contract states a specific term (one year, three years), then language to the contrary in other documents may not afford the faculty member greater protection. For example, in *Upadhya v. Langenburg,* 834 F.2d 661 (7th Cir. 1987), a faculty member was employed under several one-year contracts, which stated that the tenure evaluation would take place during the fifth year of employment. The faculty member was notified that he would not be given a fourth one-year contract. Asserting that language in the contracts guaranteed him five years of employment, the faculty member sued for breach of contract. The court disagreed with the plaintiff's interpretation, stating that the language regarding a fifth-year tenure review was not contractually binding on the college and that the contract was clearly intended to be issued for only a one-year period. Furthermore, the faculty handbook stated that there was no guaranteed right to renewal for probationary faculty members.

The written terms of the contract will generally prevail, even if the faculty member can demonstrate that oral representations were made that modified the written contract. In *Baker v. Lafayette College,* 504 A.2d 247 (Pa. Super. Ct. 1986), the plaintiff argued that the head of his department had promised him a full four-year probationary period. When Baker's two-year contract was not renewed, he sued for breach of contract. Pointing to language in the faculty handbook that gave the faculty member a right to *consideration* for reappointment, rather than an absolute right to reappointment, the court denied the claim.

Even handbook language that appears to afford probationary faculty members rights to reappointment may not bind the institution. In *Brumbach v. Rensselaer Polytechnic Institute,* 510 N.Y.S.2d 762 (N.Y. App. Div. 1987), the plaintiff, an assistant professor of public archaeology, was given a three-year contract. Her work was evaluated formally each year and was found to be satisfactory. Just before the contract's expiration, the department faculty decided to change the plaintiff's position to one in computer archaeology, a position for which the plaintiff was not qualified. The department offered the plaintiff a one-year terminal contract. At its expiration, the plaintiff instituted an action for breach of contract, asserting that the faculty handbook's statement, "If the result of the evaluation is satisfactory, it is normal for an assistant professor to be re-employed for a second three-year period," obligated the institution to reappoint her.

The court disagreed, stating that, upon expiration of the contract, the plaintiff became an employee at will. The handbook's language regarding evaluation did not amount to a promise to dismiss a probationary faculty member only for just cause, and there was no showing that the decision to modify the plaintiff's position was arbitrary or capricious. For those reasons, the trial court's grant of summary judgment to the institution was affirmed.

An often-litigated issue in nonreappointment decisions is the timeliness of notice. Depending on the wording of the contract, faculty handbook, or policy document, failure to notify a faculty member of a nonrenewal decision in a timely manner may give rise to contractual damages and, in some cases, to tenure. In *Howard University v. Best,* 547 A.2d 144 (D.C. 1988), a trial court and an appellate court considered the issue of timeliness of notice—specifically, whether a faculty member was entitled to "indefinite tenure" if timely notice of nonreappointment was not given—and the meaning of the term "prior appointment."

Marie Best had initially held a three-month nonfaculty appointment at Howard University. She was then given a three-year faculty appointment but was not given the one-year notice of nonrenewal of that appointment in a timely manner. Best sued for breach of contract, arguing that the university's failure to notify her of the nonrenewal entitled her to tenure. Alternatively, she argued that the three-year faculty appointment was really a reappointment, since she had previously held a position at Howard, and that the faculty handbook's provision that faculty received tenure upon reappointment after a previous appointment entitled her to tenure.

The court attempted to determine whether it was Howard University's "custom and practice" to grant tenure to a faculty member who had served in a part-time, nonfaculty position. Finding no evidence of a pattern of such tenure awards, the court ruled against Best's theory of tenure on reappointment. With regard to Best's theory that late notice of nonreappointment entitled her to tenure, or at least to an additional three-year appointment without tenure, the court found evidence that the university had given other faculty additional appointments in situations where reappointment notices were late. For that reason, the appellate court affirmed the jury verdict for a second three-year appointment without tenure, and $155,000 in damages.

Faculty contesting denial of tenure at private colleges have asserted that procedural violations materially altered the outcome of the tenure decision. In most cases, courts have ruled that substantial compliance with the college's policies is sufficient to defend against such claims. For example, a state supreme court ruled that, although the dean violated the faculty handbook provisions by not providing a formal written annual evaluation of an untenured faculty member prior to the tenure evaluation, the informal annual evaluation provided the faculty member gave her notice that her performance did not meet the requirements for tenure, and thus there was no procedural violation (*Karle v. Board of Trustees/Marshall University,* 2002 W. Va. LEXIS 212 (W. Va., December 2, 2002)).

Similarly, informal means of complying with the procedures may be sufficient. For example, a state appellate court ruled that, although the university did not follow its written procedures that required notification of the plaintiff in writing that he was being considered for tenure, the professor knew about the meetings at which his tenure candidacy was discussed, he was invited to several meetings to respond to questions about his performance, and he was informed in writing about the department's concerns. The court ruled that the lack of procedural compliance did not prejudice his application for tenure (*Galiatsatos v. University of Akron*, 2001 Ohio App. LEXIS 4051 (Ct. App. Ohio 10th Dist., September 13, 2001), *appeal denied*, 761 N.E.2d 47 (Ohio 2002)).

A state appellate court ruled that New York University substantially complied with its rules and procedures in a remanded tenure review of the plaintiff. The dean's failure to include the department chair on the ad hoc review committee and the university's determination not to follow the advice of the grievance committee concerning the conduct of the remanded evaluation did not render the dean's or the university's actions arbitrary or capricious. Simply because some faculty disagreed with the dean's conclusions and recommendations did not make them arbitrary, according to the court (*In re Loebl v. New York University*, 680 N.Y.S.2d 495 (N.Y. App. Div. 1998)).

On the other hand, providing misleading information to an untenured faculty member concerning his or her progress toward tenure has been found to be a major procedural violation that will sustain a breach of contract claim. For example, a state supreme court ruled that a college's deviation from its tenure standards was a breach of contract, and the misleading assurances of the candidate's department chair that she was performing adequately supported her claim for negligent misrepresentation, although she did not prevail in her discrimination claims (*Craine v. Trinity College*, 791 A.2d 518 (Conn. 2002), discussed in Section 6.4.2).

In addition to procedural claims, faculty denied tenure may assert that the criteria used, or the basis for the decision, were arbitrary and capricious (a substantive rather than a procedural violation of the contract). Courts are most reluctant to entertain these claims, as they require the court to substitute its judgment for the decisions of faculty and administrators. For example, in *Daley v. Wesleyan University*, 772 A.2d 725 (Ct. App. Ct. 2001), *appeal denied*, 776 A.2d 1145 (Ct. 2001), a professor denied tenure claimed that the department's report to the vice president mischaracterized the evaluations of his scholarly work by external evaluators. The court rejected the breach of contract claim, ruling that the plaintiff was required to prove by a preponderance of the evidence that the tenure denial decision was made arbitrarily, capriciously, or in bad faith, and upheld the jury's verdict for the college.

The importance of carefully drafting tenure revocation policies is highlighted in cases involving breach of contract claims. The case of *Murphy v. Duquesne University of the Holy Ghost*, 777 A.2d 418 (Pa. 2001) is instructive. Murphy, a tenured professor of law, was terminated after the university determined that he had violated its sexual harassment policy. Murphy challenged his dismissal, asserting, among other claims, that his conduct did not meet the standard for "serious misconduct" as articulated in the faculty handbook, and that the university had not followed its tenure revocation processes, also contained in the faculty handbook.

The state supreme court upheld the judgment of the state appellate court that the university had not breached the terms of the faculty handbook, but chastised the appellate court for using a "substantial evidence" standard rather than traditional principles of contract interpretation. The court then explained the extent of its role when reviewing the decisions of private parties under contract law.

> [P]rivate parties, including religious or educational institutions, may draft employment contracts which restrict review of professional employees' qualifications to an internal process that, if conducted in good faith, is final within the institution and precludes or prohibits review in a court of law. . . . When a contract so specifies, generally applicable principles of contract law will suffice to insulate the institution's internal, private decisions from judicial review [777 A.2d at 428].

The court then turned to the language of the faculty handbook, and determined that it reserved to the faculty and the university the determination of whether a faculty member's conduct met the definition of "serious misconduct" such that it justified a decision to dismiss a tenured faculty member. The handbook required the university to demonstrate to the faculty hearing body by clear and convincing evidence that the individual had engaged in serious misconduct. It provided that the president could disagree with the faculty hearing body, and that if that occurred, the individual could appeal that decision to the board of trustees. Given the specificity of the process and the clear allocation of the decision-making authority to the president and the trustees, the court ruled, Murphy was not entitled to have a jury "re-consider the merits of his termination."

Faculty and administrators can help ensure that judges and juries do not second-guess the judgments of academics by ensuring that written policies are clear, that the criteria applicable to faculty employment decisions are stated clearly, that the procedures for making these decisions are followed carefully, and that written justifications are given for recommendations or decisions made under the faculty handbook or other policies. Because these documents are the source of employment rights at private colleges, they should reflect the consensus of the academic community with respect to both the criteria and procedures that will be used to make these critical employment decisions.

6.7.4. Implementing procedural requirements. An institution's procedures for making and internally reviewing faculty personnel decisions should be put in writing and made generally available. Public institutions must, at a minimum, comply with the constitutional due process requirements in Section 6.7.2 of this book and may choose to provide additional procedures beyond those required by the Constitution. Private institutions are not required to comply with constitutional requirements but may wish to use these requirements as a guide in establishing their own procedures.

Though personnel procedures can be administratively burdensome, that is not the whole story. They can also help the institution avoid or rectify mistaken assessments, protect the academic freedom of the faculty, foster faculty confidence in the institution, and encourage the resolution of nonrenewal and termination disputes in-house rather than in the courts. When effective personnel procedures do exist, courts may require, under the "exhaustion-of-remedies" doctrine (see Section 2.2.2.4), that the faculty member "exhaust" those procedures before filing suit. This may be the case for either private or public colleges. For example, in *Rieder v. State University of New York*, 366 N.Y.S.2d 37 (N.Y. App. Div. 1975), *affirmed*, 351 N.E.2d 747 (N.Y. 1976), employees at a state institution were covered by a collective bargaining agreement containing a four-step grievance procedure. When some employees filed suit while awaiting a determination at step 2, the appellate courts ordered the suit dismissed for failure to exhaust administrative remedies.[14]

In cases such as *Rieder* (and see also *Beck v. Board of Trustees of State Colleges*, Section 2.2.2.4), where public institutions are involved, the administrative law of the state provides the source of the exhaustion doctrine. Such administrative law principles do not apply to private institutions, since they are not agencies of the state. Private institutions may be subject to a comparable exhaustion doctrine, however, stemming from the common law of "private associations" (see Section 9.4.4). Or the contract may require exhaustion of remedies by its own terms. Depending on the wording of the faculty handbook or other institutional policy, the courts may apply contract law in cases involving either a public or a private institution, and may refuse to review a tenure denial if the plaintiff has not followed the grievance processes prescribed within the handbook or policy. For example, in *Neiman v. Yale University*, 851 A.2d 1165 (Conn. 2004), the Connecticut Supreme Court, interpreting Yale University's faculty handbook, granted the university's motion to dismiss a faculty member's breach of contract claim because she had not used the internal grievance process to challenge her denial of tenure. The court ruled that the handbook's language, stating that an aggrieved faculty member "may" file a grievance (rather than "shall"), meant that use of the grievance process was mandatory. The court ruled that the handbook gave the plaintiff a choice between filing a grievance or accepting the university's decision without complaint.

In some states, such as California and New York, state law provides that challenges to the final decisions of certain private entities not involving claims of discrimination may be brought only under state administrative code procedures, rather than in civil court as breach of contract claims. Such procedures provide for a narrower scope of review than common law breach of contract claims in that the judge is limited to evaluating whether the college followed its policies and procedures and, if there were deviations, whether those deviations influenced the outcome of the tenure decision. The typical standard used in such proceedings is whether the decision of the college was arbitrary and capricious, and whether discretion was properly exercised (*Sackman v. Alfred University*, 717 N.Y.S.2d 461 (Sup. Ct. N.Y. 2000)). (See generally Section 2.2.3.5.)

---

[14]Plaintiffs filing civil rights claims under Section 1983, the federal civil rights statute, need not exhaust state administrative remedies (see *Patsy v. Board of Regents of the State of Florida*, 457 U.S. 496 (1982), discussed in Section 2.2.2.4).

For example, in *Pomona College v. The Superior Court of Los Angeles County,* 45 Cal. App. 4th 1716 (Ct. App. Cal. 2d Dist. 1996), a professor denied tenure by Pomona College filed a breach of contract claim in a state trial court. The trial court rejected the college's assertion that the professor's sole remedy was through an administrative proceeding. The college appealed, seeking a writ of mandate from the appellate court to direct the trial court to set aside its rejection of the college's motion.

The court first addressed whether the state law, Section 1094.5 of the California Code of Civil Procedure,[15] applied to the final decisions of a private university. Previous state court decisions had applied this law to the final decisions of a private hospital, a private dental insurance plan, and a private manufacturer. Although the faculty member argued that Section 1094.5 did not apply to Pomona College because the college was not "required by law" to hold a hearing prior to its final decision (a requirement of the statute), the court disagreed. Noting that the faculty handbook provided for a grievance procedure involving a hearing and the consideration of evidence provided by the grievant, the court ruled that because the handbook was a contract, and its provisions required a hearing, the preconditions for Section 1094.5 had been met. Said the court: "Because the Handbook governed [the grievant's] employment relationship with Pomona, the college was required by law to provide the hearing described therein" (45 Cal. App. 4th at 1727, n.10), and a mandamus action under the statute was thus the proper remedy to pursue.

In the state of New York, Article 78 of the state's civil practice code provides the opportunity for an individual aggrieved by the action (or inaction) of a government body or a private corporation chartered by the state to have that decision reviewed in the state courts. If the institution has an internal grievance process, an employee may be required to use that process (to exhaust his or her remedies, as discussed in Section 2.2.2.4) prior to seeking judicial review of the negative decision. However, if this grievance process is voluntary rather than mandatory, the statute of limitations for filing a claim in court may not be tolled. For example, in *Bargstedt v. Cornell University,* 757 N.Y.S.2d 646 (N.Y. App. Div. 2003), an employee terminated for dishonesty attempted to use the state's C.P.L.R. Article 78 to challenge her termination. Under New York's C.P.L.R. law, an aggrieved party has only four months from the time of the final decision to file a claim in state court. The court ruled that the grievance process in question at Cornell University was voluntary, not mandatory, and thus the lawsuit, which was brought more than four months after the termination, was time barred.

A contrary result was reached in *Sackman v. Alfred University,* 717 N.Y.S.2d 461 (Sup. Ct. N.Y. 2000). A professor of music challenged his denial of tenure, which was based primarily on a determination by his department chair that

---

[15]Section 1094.5 provides that challenges to "any final administrative order or decision made as the result of a proceeding in which by law a hearing is required to be given, evidence is required to be taken, and discretion in the determination of facts is vested in the inferior tribunal, corporation, board, or officer" must be made through a mandamus action rather than through a common law contract claim.

his teaching performance was inadequate. The professor appealed the university's denial of tenure, and a faculty appeals committee concluded that his rights had been violated because the department chair had observed his teaching only once, and had not observed Sackman's teaching of two ensembles, a responsibility that made up two-thirds of his teaching load.

Sackman filed a complaint under New York C.P.L.R. Article 78 seeking to set aside the negative tenure decision. The court concluded that the department chair's failure to observe more than one of Sackman's classes violated the faculty handbook and constituted arbitrary and capricious behavior. The court remanded the case to the university for a new tenure review of Sackman. The court rejected Sackman's breach of contract claim, however, stating that the handbook did not create a tenure contract, but created the criteria and procedures for obtaining tenure. Sackman's contract with the university, said the court, was for a tenure-track appointment, not for tenure.

Other states have laws that limit public employees, such as faculty of public colleges and universities, to administrative law challenges rather than breach of contract claims when contesting employment decisions. See, for example, *Gaskill v. Ft. Hays State University,* discussed in Section 12.5.4.

In devising or reviewing procedures, administrators should carefully consider what procedural safeguards they should provide *before* making a personnel decision or suspending or terminating job benefits, as opposed to *after.* In public institutions, for example, a full-scale hearing need not be provided before the personnel decision is tentatively made. Some courts, however, require a hearing before an institution actually implements the decision by terminating the faculty member's pay or other substantial employment benefits. In *Skehan v. Board of Trustees of Bloomsburg State College,* 501 F.2d 31 (3d Cir. 1974), for instance, the plaintiff had been relieved of his duties, dismissed, and removed from the payroll for almost three months before he was afforded a hearing. The court held that the hearing, because of its timing, did not meet due process requirements. In *Peacock v. Board of Regents of University and State Colleges of Arizona,* 510 F.2d 1324 (9th Cir. 1975), however, the court upheld a post-termination hearing where the faculty member had been removed only from a nonpaying position as department head; and in *Chung v. Park,* 514 F.2d 382 (3d Cir. 1975), the court ruled for the institution because the hearing had been provided after the decision to terminate was made but before job benefits were actually terminated.

The question of when and in what detail statements of reasons for personnel decisions are to be given must also be carefully considered. The question of who shall preside over hearings is likewise important, with impartiality being the key consideration. Other critical issues are the confidentiality of the statements of reasons—and of any proceedings in which the faculty member challenges these reasons—and the question of what permanent records should be kept of adverse personnel decisions and who should have access to them. While the legal principles in Sections 6.7.1 and 6.7.2 create some limits on administrative discretion in these areas, considerable flexibility remains for administrators to make wise policy choices.

Sec. 6.8. Closure, Merger, and Reduction in Force

6.8.1. Overview. The financial difficulties that began for postsecondary education in the late 1960s created a new and particularly sensitive faculty personnel issue, an issue with equal salience today.[16] In an era of inflation and shrinking resources, what are the legal responsibilities of an institution that must terminate an academic program or otherwise initiate a reduction in force? What are its obligations to faculty and students? And is there a difference between the institution's legal obligations during financial exigency and its obligations when it decides to close or reduce an academic program? On these questions, which should continue to stalk postsecondary education for the foreseeable future, the law is still developing. But enough judicial ink has been spilled to give administrators a fair idea of how to prepare for the unwelcome necessity of terminating faculty jobs in a financial crunch.

6.8.2. Contractual considerations. The faculty contract (Section 6.2) is the starting point for determining both a public and a private institution's responsibilities regarding staff reductions. Administrators should consider several questions concerning the faculty contract. Does it, and should it, provide for termination due to financial exigency or program discontinuance? Does it, and should it, specify the conditions that will constitute a financial exigency or justify discontinuance of a program and stipulate how the institution will determine when such conditions exist? Does it, and should it, set forth criteria for determining which faculty members will be released? Does it, and should it, require that alternatives be explored (such as transfer to another department) before termination becomes permissible? Does it, and should it, provide a hearing or other recourse for a faculty member chosen for dismissal? Does it, and should it, provide the released faculty member with any priority right to be rehired when other openings arise or the financial situation eases?

Whenever the faculty contract has any provision on financial exigency or program discontinuance, the institution should follow it; failure to do so will likely be a breach of contract. Whether such contractual provisions exist may depend on whether the AAUP guidelines[17] have been incorporated into the faculty contract. In *Browzin v. Catholic University of America*, 527 F.2d 843 (D.C. Cir.

---

[16]This Section is limited to financial exigency and program discontinuance problems concerning faculty. But such problems also affect students, and an institution's response may occasionally give students a basis on which to sue. See *Eden v. Board of Trustees of State University; Beukas v. Board of Trustees of Fairleigh Dickinson University;* and *Unger v. National Residents Matching Program,* discussed in Section 8.2.3; see also *Aase v. South Dakota Board of Regents,* 400 N.W.2d 269 (S.D. 1987). See generally Section 8.2.3, concerning an institution's contractual obligation to students.

[17]See "Recommended Institutional Regulations on Academic Freedom and Tenure," Regulation 4 (in *AAUP Policy Documents and Reports* (AAUP, 2001), 21), and "On Institutional Problems Resulting from Financial Exigency: Some Operating Guidelines" (in *AAUP Policy Documents and Reports,* 230). An earlier (1968) version of the "Recommended Institutional Regulations"—specifically the 1968 version of Regulation 4(c)—was interpreted in the *Browzin* case, discussed in the text in this Section. The court concluded that the defendant university had not violated the requirement that it "make every effort" to place terminated faculty members "in other suitable positions."

1975), for instance, the parties stipulated that the AAUP guidelines had been adopted as part of the faculty contract, and the court noted that such adoption was "entirely consistent with the statutes of the university and the university's previous responses to AAUP actions." As in *Browzin,* it is important for administrators to understand the legal status of AAUP guidelines within their institutions; any doubt should be resolved by consulting counsel.

The contract provisions for tenured and nontenured faculty members may differ, and administrators should note any differences. Nontenured faculty members generally pose far fewer legal problems, since administrators may simply not renew their contracts at the end of the contract term (see Section 6.7.2.1). If the faculty contract is silent regarding financial exigency or program discontinuance, in relation to either tenured or nontenured faculty members, the institution still may have the power to terminate. Under the common law doctrine of "impossibility," the institution may be able to extricate itself from contractual obligations if unforeseen events have made it impossible to perform those obligations (see J. D. Calamari & J. M. Perillo, *Contracts* (4th ed., West, 1998), § 13-1).

The first major contract case on financial exigency was *AAUP v. Bloomfield College,* 322 A.2d 846 (N.J. Super. Ct. Ch. Div. 1974), *affirmed,* 346 A.2d 615 (App. Div. 1975). On June 29, 1973, Bloomfield College, a private school, notified thirteen tenured faculty members that their services would not be needed as of June 30, 1973. The college gave financial exigency as the reason for this action. The college also notified the remaining faculty members, tenured and nontenured, that they would be put on one-year terminal contracts for 1973–74, after which they would have to negotiate new contracts with the school.

The thirteen fired faculty members brought suit based on their contracts of employment. Paragraph C(3) of the "policies" enumerated in the contract provided that "a teacher will have tenure and his services may be terminated only for adequate cause, except in case of retirement for age, or under extraordinary circumstances because of financial exigency of the institution." Paragraph C(6) provided that "termination of continuous appointment because of financial exigency of the institution must be demonstrably bona fide. A situation which makes drastic retrenchment of this sort necessary precludes expansion of the staff at other points at the same time, except in extraordinary circumstances."

The faculty members alleged that no bona fide financial exigency existed and that the hiring of twelve new staff members three months after the plaintiffs were dismissed violated the requirement that during a financial exigency new staff persons would be hired only "in extraordinary circumstances." Thus, the court had to determine whether there was a "demonstrably bona fide" financial exigency and whether there were such extraordinary circumstances as would justify the hiring of new faculty members.

The trial court analyzed the college's finances and determined that no bona fide financial exigency existed because the college owned a large piece of valuable property that it could have sold to meet its needs. The appellate court, however, disagreed, finding that there was ample evidence that the college was facing financial exigency in terms of its operating budget and endowment.

> [I]t was improper for the judge to rest his conclusion in whole or in part upon the failure of the college to sell the knoll property which had been acquired several years before in anticipation of the creation of a new campus at a different locale. . . . Whether such a plan of action to secure financial stability on a short-term basis is preferable to the long-term planning of the college administration is a policy decision for the institution. Its choice of alternative is beyond the scope of judicial oversight in the context of this litigation [346 A.2d at 617].

Though the appellate court thus held that the college was in a state of financial exigency, it was unwilling to find that the faculty members were fired because of the college's financial condition. The trial court had determined that the reason for the terminations was the college's desire to abolish tenure, and the appellate court found ample evidence to support this finding.

On the question of whether extraordinary circumstances existed sufficient to justify the hiring of twelve new faculty members, the trial court also held in favor of the plaintiffs. The college had argued that its actions were justified because it was developing a new type of curriculum, but the court noted that the evidence put forth by the college was vague and did not suggest that any financial benefit would result from the new curriculum. The appellate court did not disturb this part of the trial court's decision, nor did it even discuss the issue.

A major overarching issue of the case concerned the burden of proof. Did the college have the burden of proving that it had fulfilled the contract conditions justifying termination? Or did the faculty members have the burden of proving that the contractual conditions had not been met? The issue has critical practical importance; because the evidentiary problems can be so difficult, the outcome of financial exigency litigation may often depend on who has the burden of proof. The trial court assigned the burden to the college, and the appellate court agreed:

> It is manifest that under the controlling agreement among the parties the affected members of the faculty had attained the protection of tenure after completing a seven-year probationary service. This was their vested right which could be legally divested only if the defined conditions occurred. The proof of existence of those conditions as a justifiable reason for terminating the status of the plaintiffs plainly was the burden of the defendants [346 A.2d at 616].

Since the college had not proven that it had met the contract conditions justifying termination, the courts ordered the reinstatement of the terminated faculty members.

A similar result occurred in *Pace v. Hymas*, 726 P.2d 693 (Idaho 1986). The University of Idaho's faculty handbook stated that a tenured faculty member's service could be terminated for cause or for financial exigency. The handbook defined financial exigency as "a demonstrably bona fide, imminent financial crisis which threatens the viability of an agency, institution, office or department as a whole or one or more of its programs . . . and which cannot be adequately alleviated by means other than a reduction in the employment force" (726 P.2d at 695).

Pace, a professor of home economics, was laid off after the State Board of Education issued a declaration of financial exigency. Relying on *Bloomfield College,* as well as on more recent cases, the Idaho Supreme Court ruled that the university had the burden of proof regarding the existence of financial exigency, and that it had not carried that burden.

Although the university had sustained a budget shortfall in the Agricultural Extension Service, the unit to which Pace was appointed, the university had received an increased appropriation from the state, it had received funds for a 7 percent salary increase for faculty, and it had a surplus of uncommitted funds at the end of its fiscal year. No alternatives to laying off faculty—including salary freezes, reduction in travel and other expenses, or other cost-saving practices— had been considered prior to Pace's layoff. Because the university had not determined if the financial crisis could be alleviated by less drastic means than firing tenured faculty, the court ruled that the university had not met the faculty handbook's definition of a bona fide financial exigency.

In *Pace,* the faculty handbook explicitly mentioned financial exigency as a permissible reason for termination of a tenured faculty member. Two U.S. Court of Appeals cases upheld institutional authority to terminate tenured faculty members even in the absence of any express contractual provision granting such authority. The first case, *Krotkoff v. Goucher College,* 585 F.2d 675 (4th Cir. 1978), concerned a termination due to bona fide financial exigency; the second case, *Jimenez v. Almodovar,* 650 F.2d 363 (1st Cir. 1981), concerned a termination due to discontinuance of an academic program. Both cases resort to academic custom and usage (Sections 1.4.3.3 & 6.2.3) to imply terms into the faculty contract. Both cases also identify implicit rights of tenured faculty members that limit the institution's termination authority. The opinion in *Krotkoff* is discussed at some length as an illustration of the type of showing that, in this court's opinion, attested to the good faith of the college's actions.

Krotkoff was a tenured professor of German at Goucher College, a private liberal arts college for women. After having taught at the college for thirteen years, she was notified in June 1975 that she would be terminated on the grounds of financial exigency. Her performance had been at all times acceptable. Since her contract was silent on the question of financial exigency, the professor argued that the termination was a breach of contract. The college argued that it had implied authority to terminate in order to combat a bona fide financial exigency.

The college had sustained budget deficits each year from 1968 through 1975, and the trustees decided not to renew the contracts of eleven untenured faculty members and to terminate four tenured faculty members. A faculty committee had made recommendations concerning curricular changes, one of which was to eliminate all but introductory courses in German. Krotkoff had taught advanced German literature courses, while another tenured faculty member had taught introductory German. The department chair and dean recommended that the other faculty member be retained because she was experienced in teaching introductory German and because she could also teach French. The president concurred and notified Krotkoff that she would be laid off.

Although a faculty committee reviewing Krotkoff's ensuing grievance recommended her retention, it did not recommend that the other faculty member be discharged, nor did it consider how the college could retain both professors. The president rejected the committee's recommendation, and the trustees concurred. The committee had made an alternate recommendation that Krotkoff teach German courses and the other professor replace an assistant dean, who would be dismissed. This suggestion was also rejected by the president.

The college provided Krotkoff with a list of all positions available for the next year, and Krotkoff suggested that she assume a position in the economics department at her present faculty rank and salary and with tenure. The college refused her suggestion because she had no academic training in economics and terminated her appointment.

In a four-part opinion, the appellate court analyzed the facts regarding the college's overall retrenchment program and the particular termination at issue. It concluded that the faculty contract, read in light of "the national academic community's understanding of the concept of tenure," permitted termination due to financial exigency; that a bona fide financial exigency existed; and that the college had used reasonable standards in selecting which faculty to terminate and had taken reasonable measures to afford the plaintiff alternative employment. The well-reasoned and organized opinion not only discusses the difficult legal issues but also touches on practical considerations, such as the complexities of relying on faculty committees to recommend candidates for termination.

Since the college's policy statements and bylaws did not specify financial exigency as a reason for the discharge of a tenured professor, the court first turned to "academic custom and usage" to determine whether such a reason for discharge was subsumed within the concept of tenure. The court, with the help of an expert witness, examined the AAUP's 1940 "Statement of Principles on Academic Freedom and Tenure," which included financial exigency as a permissible reason for terminating tenured faculty.[18] The court also reviewed previous cases involving the termination of tenured faculty for financial exigency, concluding that none had established "a right to exemption from dismissal for financial reasons." Furthermore, the court concluded that, given the college's financial problems, academic freedom was not threatened by Krotkoff's dismissal because she was not being dismissed for her ideas or speech, nor would she be replaced by a newly hired faculty member with views more compatible with those of the administration.

After the court determined that the contract between Krotkoff and Goucher permitted termination on the basis of financial exigency, it then considered Krotkoff's claim that a jury should have determined whether the college had breached its

---

[18]The statement (in *AAUP Policy Documents and Reports* (AAUP, 2001), 3, 4) reads, in pertinent part: "After the expiration of a probationary period, teachers or investigators should have permanent or continuous tenure, and their services should be terminated only for adequate cause, except in the case of retirement for age, or under extraordinary circumstances because of financial exigencies.

"In the interpretation of this principle, it is understood that the following represents acceptable academic practice:

. . .

"(5) Termination of a continuous appointment because of financial exigency should be demonstrably bona fide."

contract. In particular, Krotkoff argued that the court should submit for the jury's determination the question of whether the trustees' belief that financial exigency existed was reasonable. The court disagreed, stating that Krotkoff had not asserted that the trustees had acted in bad faith, and that the existence of financial exigency should be determined based upon "the adequacy of a college's operating funds rather than its capital assets" (585 F.2d at 681).

Finally, the court considered whether Goucher had used reasonable standards to determine that Krotkoff's appointment should be terminated, and whether the college had made reasonable efforts to find her another position. Although Goucher had argued that neither of these subjects was appropriate for judicial review, the court disagreed. The court ruled that she was "contractually enti- tled to insist (a) that the college use reasonable standards in selecting which faculty appointments to terminate and (b) that it take reasonable measures to afford her alternative employment" (585 F.2d at 682). First, said the court, there was no contractual requirement that the college retain Krotkoff and discharge another professor of German. And, given the evidence that the only vacancy was one for which Krotkoff was not qualified, the court ruled that the college had complied with its contractual obligations.

Krotkoff provides an instructive analysis of postsecondary institutions' author- ity and obligations when terminating tenured faculty because of financial exigency. The case also provides an outstanding example of judicial reliance on academic custom and usage to resolve postsecondary education contractual disputes.

Somewhat different issues arise when the reduction is caused by a program closure, which may be done either on "educational" grounds or because of finan- cial exigency. The plaintiffs in *Jimenez v. Almodovar*, cited above, were two pro- fessors who had been appointed to a pilot program in physical education and recreation at a regional college of the University of Puerto Rico. Their teaching positions were eliminated as a result of low enrollment and an unfavorable eval- uation of the program. The court had to resolve some contractual questions in ruling on the plaintiffs' claim of deprivation of property without procedural due process (see Section 6.7.2). The parties stipulated that the plaintiffs had prop- erty interests established by their letters of appointment, but the letters did not detail the extent of these interests. Therefore, in order to determine the scope of procedures required by due process, the court had to determine the extent of the plaintiffs' contractual rights.

According to the court:

> American courts and secondary authorities uniformly recognize that, unless
> otherwise provided in the agreement of the parties, or in the regulations of the
> institution, or in a statute, an institution of higher education has an implied con-
> tractual right to make in good faith an unavoidable termination of right to the
> employment of a tenured member of the faculty when his position is being elim-
> inated as part of a change in academic program. . . . That the [institution's]
> implied right of bona fide unavoidable termination due to changes in academic
> program is wholly different from its right to termination for cause or on other
> personal grounds is plainly recognized in the following definition of tenure of
> the [AAUP/AAC] Commission on Academic Tenure in Higher Education [in]
> *Faculty Tenure: A Report and Recommendations* [Jossey-Bass, 1973]:

> An arrangement under which faculty appointments in an institution of higher education are continued until retirement for age or disability, subject to dismissal for adequate cause or unavoidable termination on account of financial exigency or change of institutional program (emphasis in original omitted).

> The foregoing authorities lead to the conclusion that, unless a Puerto Rican statute or a university regulation otherwise provides, the instant contracts should be interpreted as giving the University of Puerto Rico an implied right of bona fide unavoidable termination on the ground of change of academic program [650 F.2d at 368; footnotes omitted].

Finding no Puerto Rican statute or university regulation to the contrary, the court confirmed the university's implied contractual right to terminate tenured faculty. The court then analyzed the procedures available to the plaintiffs to challenge their terminations and concluded that they met procedural due process requirements.

The *Jimenez* decision is consistent with earlier precedents and AAUP policy in recognizing, first, a distinction between dismissals for causes personal to the individual and dismissals for impersonal institutional reasons and, second, a distinction between institutional reasons of financial exigency and reasons of program discontinuance. AAUP policy on the latter distinction, however, is found not in the 1940 Statement cited by the court but in the 1976 "Recommended Institutional Regulations on Academic Freedom and Tenure" (*AAUP Policy Documents and Reports* (AAUP, 2001), 21), which authorize program discontinuances "not mandated by financial exigency" when "based essentially upon educational considerations" and implemented according to AAUP specifications. Under this policy, if the institution adheres to it, or under the precedent now established by *Jimenez*, postsecondary institutions may, if they follow prescribed standards and procedures for doing so, terminate tenured faculty because of a bona fide academic program change.

The merger of two institutions may create complicated contractual issues that require courts to determine which contractual rights remain after the two institutions become one. Litigation related to the merger of Loyola University and Mundelein College provides an instructive example of legal issues that may accompany mergers.

Although faculty handbooks may deal clearly with the reasons for terminating a tenured faculty member while the institution is still operating, they may be either silent or ambiguous on the issue of whether tenure rights survive a merger or assimilation by another institution. In *Gray v. Mundelein College*, 695 N.E.2d 1379, *appeal denied*, 705 N.E.2d 436 (Ill. 1998), the court was asked to address the obligations to tenured faculty at Mundelein College when it entered an affiliation agreement with Loyola University. Mundelein was facing severe financial difficulties, and entered an agreement with Loyola in which Loyola acquired Mundelein's assets and assumed some of Mundelein's financial obligations. The agreement provided that Mundelein would remain in existence as a separate college governed and administered by Loyola. Loyola offered tenured positions to twenty-six of Mundelein's tenured faculty members; it offered another eleven tenured faculty five-year appointments without tenure; and it offered three tenured faculty two years of salary as severance. Three of the faculty who were not offered tenured positions sued both institutions, claiming that their contract rights had been breached.

The trial and appellate courts adopted the view that the faculty handbook was contractually binding on the parties. The handbook listed four reasons for termination of tenured faculty: (1) financial exigency, (2) program discontinuance, (3) health, or (4) cause. There was no provision for the termination of tenured faculty in the event of a merger or affiliation. The trial court ruled that because the board of trustees had never declared the existence of financial exigency, the termination of the tenured faculty was unlawful. Furthermore, ruled the trial court, because the college still had valuable assets, a bona fide financial exigency did not exist. It ruled that Mundelein had breached the plaintiffs' contract, and ordered damages to be paid to the two plaintiffs who had been given severance. The third, who had accepted a five-year contract, was denied damages because the trial court viewed her acceptance of the contract as a waiver of tenure.

On appeal, the college argued that academic custom and usage should control the outcome of the case, and that AAUP policies and guidelines provide that tenure does not survive an affiliation or merger unless the parties have specifically agreed that it would. The court did not rule on whether tenure survives affiliation or merger; a custom and usage analysis is only necessary, said the court, when a court must interpret uncertain or ambiguous contract terms. In this situation, the court believed that the terms of the faculty handbook were clear. "Mundelein could have taken whatever course was necessary to remedy its financial difficulties without continued obligation to tenured faculty if it had followed the procedures set out in its manual" (695 N.E.2d at 1387).

The court affirmed the rulings for the terminated plaintiffs and reversed the trial court's ruling against the plaintiff who had accepted a five-year contract, ruling that this act was not a waiver of tenure, but an appropriate attempt to mitigate damages. Furthermore, said the court, if Loyola had intended to terminate the plaintiff's tenure claim against Mundelein by offering her a five-year contract, it could have included that provision in the terms of the contract. The Illinois Supreme Court denied review.

The effect of an institution's failure to declare financial exigency was also at issue in *Board of Community College Trustees for Baltimore County—Essex Community College v. Adams*, 701 A.2d 1113 (Ct. App. Md.), *cert. denied*, 702 A.2d 290 (Md. 1997). In the early 1990s, both the state and the county reduced their appropriations to Essex Community College. College officials developed a process for determining which programs would be reduced or terminated. Faculty were represented on the committee that made recommendations about program termination. Seven programs were selected for termination, one of which was the Office Technology program. The plaintiffs were tenured faculty in that program who were dismissed when the program was terminated. They pursued a grievance through the internal system that culminated in the trustees denying their grievance.

The terminated faculty filed a motion for mandamus relief, in which they asked the court to order the college to reinstate them because, under the terms of the faculty handbook, they could only be terminated for "immorality, dishonesty, misconduct in office, incompetency [sic], insubordination, or willful neglect of duty." There was no language in the contract about program reduction or closure, or the rights of the faculty should that occur. There had been no finding that the faculty were terminated for any of these reasons; the stated reason for the termination was program closure. This reason, said the faculty, was not provided for in the contract and therefore their terminations were unlawful.

The court reviewed legal authority in Maryland and other states, and determined that "the great weight of authority supports a holding that tenured professors may be terminated for reasons unrelated to them personally" (701 A.2d at 1117). To the plaintiffs' claim that the financial crisis was a pretext for a breach of contract, the court responded that the clear weight of the evidence indicated that the financial crisis was real. And although the trial judge had ruled in the plaintiffs' favor because the trustees had never declared a state of financial exigency, the appellate court reversed, stating that "the actions taken by the College were designed to avoid the necessity of declaring an 'exigency.' They were, nonetheless, indicative of attempts to resolve the present and anticipated financial shortfall in order to solve the financial problems without the necessity of taking the last step" (701 A.2d at 1140). The court remanded, however, on the plaintiffs' due process claim, in which they claimed that the process of selecting tenured members for termination was flawed.

Significant to the outcome of this case was the court's review of other litigation against the State of Maryland concerning budget cuts and the state's authority to reduce personnel. The fact that the defendant college was public rather than private may provide part of the reason for the difference between this case and *Mundelein.*

If faculty handbooks, collective bargaining agreements, or other institutional policy documents specify a faculty role in determining how program reductions or closures, or the criteria for selecting faculty, will be accomplished, then excluding faculty from this process will invite breach of contract claims. But in some instances, despite the fact that handbooks and policy documents did not specify a faculty role in the process, breach of contract claims have been brought. For example, when Mercer University closed its Atlanta College of Arts and Sciences, the faculty asserted that excluding them from participating in the closure decision breached their contract because in the academic community the term "bona fide discontinuance of a program," used in the faculty handbook, meant that faculty must be involved in the decision (Corinne Houpt, "The Age of Austerity: Downsizing for the 90s," in *Academic Program Closures: A Legal Compendium,* Ellen M. Babbitt, ed. (2d ed., National Association of College and University Attorneys, 2002)).

Students have also asserted contract claims against a college or university for reducing or eliminating an academic program. These cases are discussed in Section 8.1.3.

6.8.3. Constitutional considerations. Public institutions must be concerned not only with contract considerations relating to financial exigency and

program termination but also with constitutional considerations under the First and Fourteenth Amendments. Even if a termination (or other personnel decision) does not violate the faculty contract or any applicable state statutes or administrative regulations, it will be subject to invalidation by the courts if it infringes the faculty member's constitutional rights.

Under the First Amendment, a faculty member may argue that financial exigency was only a pretext for termination and that termination was actually a retaliation for the faculty member's exercise of First Amendment rights (see Note, "Economically Necessitated Faculty Dismissal as a Limit on Academic Freedom," 52 *Denver L.J.* 911 (1975); and see generally Chapter 7). The burden of proof on this issue is primarily on the faculty member (see the *Mt. Healthy* case discussed in Section 7.6). *Mabey v. Reagan*, 537 F.2d 1036 (9th Cir. 1976), is illustrative. The defendant college had not renewed the appointment of a nontenured philosophy instructor. The instructor argued that the nonrenewal was due to an argument he had had with other faculty members in an academic senate meeting and that his argument was a protected First Amendment activity. The college argued that this activity was not protected under the First Amendment and that, at any rate, the nonrenewal was also due to overstaffing in the philosophy department. In remanding the case to the trial court for further fact finding, the appellate court noted:

> We emphasize that the trier [of fact] must be alert to retaliatory terminations. . . . Whenever the state terminates employment to quell legitimate dissent or punishes protected expressive behavior, the termination is unlawful. . . .
>
> We stress that this holding does not shield those who are legitimately not reappointed. Where the complainant . . . does not meet his burden of proof that the state acted to suppress free expression, . . . the termination will stand [537 F.2d at 1045].

Under the Fourteenth Amendment, a faculty member whose job is terminated by a public institution may argue that the termination violated the due process clause. To proceed with this argument, the faculty member must show that the termination infringed a "property" or "liberty" interest, as discussed in Section 6.7.2.1. If such a showing can be made, the questions then are (1) What procedural protections is the faculty member entitled to?, and (2) What kinds of arguments can the faculty member raise in his or her "defense"? A case that addresses both issues is *Johnson v. Board of Regents of University of Wisconsin System*, 377 F. Supp. 227 (W.D. Wis. 1974), *affirmed without opinion*, 510 F.2d 975 (7th Cir. 1975).

In this case the Wisconsin legislature had mandated budget reductions for the university system. To accommodate this reduction, as well as a further reduction caused by lower enrollments on several campuses, the university officials devised a program for laying off tenured faculty. The chancellor of each campus determined who would be laid off, after which each affected faculty member could petition a faculty committee for "reconsideration" of the proposed layoff. The faculty committee could consider only two questions: whether the layoff decision was supported by sufficient evidence, and whether the chancellor had followed the procedures established for identifying the campus's fiscal and programmatic needs and determining who should be laid off. Thirty-eight tenured professors selected for layoff sued the university system.

The court determined that the due process clause required the following minimum procedures in a financial exigency layoff:

> [F]urnishing each plaintiff with a reasonably adequate written statement of the basis for the initial decision to lay off; furnishing each plaintiff with a reasonably adequate description of the manner in which the initial decision had been arrived at; making a reasonably adequate disclosure to each plaintiff of the information and data on which the decision makers had relied; and providing each plaintiff the opportunity to respond [377 F. Supp. at 240].

Measuring the procedures actually used against these requirements, the court held that the university system had not violated procedural due process. The most difficult issue was the adequacy of information disclosure (the third requirement above), about which the court said:

> Plaintiffs have shown in this court that the information disclosed to them was bulky and some of it amorphous. They have shown that it was not presented to the reconsideration committees in a manner resembling the presentation of evidence in court. They have shown that in some situations . . . they encountered difficulty in obtaining a coherent explanation of the basis for the initial layoff decisions, and that, as explained in some situations, the basis included judgments about personalities. But as I have observed, the Fourteenth Amendment does not forbid judgments about personalities in this situation, nor does it require adversary proceedings. The information disclosed was reasonably adequate to provide each plaintiff the opportunity to make a showing that reduced student enrollments and fiscal exigency were not in fact the precipitating causes for the decisions to lay off tenured teachers in this department and that; and it was also reasonably adequate to provide each plaintiff the opportunity to make a showing that the ultimate decision to lay off each of them, as compared with another tenured member of their respective departments, was arbitrary and unreasonable. I emphasize the latter point. On this record, plaintiffs' allegations about the inadequacy and imprecision of the disclosure related principally to those stages of the decision making which preceded the ultimate stage at which the specific teachers, department by department, were selected.
>
> Had the disclosure as it was made not been "reasonably adequate," it is possible that it could have been made adequate by permitting plaintiffs some opportunity to confront and even to cross-examine some of the decision makers. But I hold that the opportunity to confront or to cross-examine these decision makers is not constitutionally required when the disclosure is reasonably adequate, as it was here [377 F. Supp. at 242].

The court also determined that the university system could limit the issues which the faculty members could address in challenging a termination under the above procedures:

> I am not persuaded that, after the initial decisions had been made, the Fourteenth Amendment required that plaintiffs be provided an opportunity to

persuade the decision makers that departments within their respective colleges, other than theirs, should have borne a heavier fiscal sacrifice; that non-credit-producing, nonacademic areas within their respective campus structures should have borne a heavier fiscal sacrifice; that campuses, other than their respective campuses, should have borne a heavier fiscal sacrifice; or that more funds should have been appropriated to the university system. However, I believe that *each plaintiff was constitutionally entitled to a fair opportunity to show: (1) that the true reason for his or her layoff was a constitutionally impermissible reason; or (2) that, given the chain of decisions which preceded the ultimate decision designating him or her by name for layoff, that ultimate decision was nevertheless wholly arbitrary and unreasonable.* I believe that each plaintiff was constitutionally entitled to a fair opportunity to make such a showing in a proceeding within the institution, in order to permit prompt reconsideration and correction in a proper case. Also, if necessary, each plaintiff was and is constitutionally entitled to a fair opportunity to make such a showing thereafter in a court [377 F. Supp. at 239–40; emphasis added].

Although the Constitution requires that institutions avoid terminations for a "constitutionally impermissible reason" and "wholly arbitrary" terminations, the court made clear that the Constitution does not prescribe any particular bases for selection of the faculty members to be terminated. The court stated that there was no constitutional requirement that the selection criteria be related to seniority or performance, and that the institution retained the discretion to develop appropriate criteria for selecting those to be laid off.

A federal appellate court found constitutional violations in the treatment of two professors who were laid off without being granted a hearing on the criteria for selecting faculty for layoff. In *Johnson-Taylor v. Gannon*, 907 F.2d 1577 (6th Cir. 1990), the trustees of Lansing Community College determined that financial exigency required the layoff of several faculty members. Under the collective bargaining agreement with the faculty, the trustees had the right to make the ultimate decision about how many faculty were to be laid off, but the union had the right to recommend criteria for selecting faculty and the procedure to be used.

Two faculty who were laid off argued that they were denied due process because no hearing had been held regarding their selection for layoff. Both asserted that they had been chosen to be laid off because of their criticisms of the institution and their union activity. Although both had filed grievances under the collective bargaining agreement, an arbitrator had concluded that they had been afforded all the protections that the contract required.

The court first examined whether the professors had a property or liberty interest at stake. Finding that the collective bargaining agreement provided for continued employment, the court concluded that the professors, indeed, had a property interest, which required the college to afford them due process. Furthermore, one of the professors was tenured, and thus had a second basis for a protected property interest.

The court concluded that the professors' due process rights had been violated because neither had been afforded a hearing at which they were informed why they were selected for layoff, nor had they had an opportunity to challenge the existence of financial exigency. The court remanded the matter to the trial court for an evidentiary hearing on both of these issues.

In *Milbouer v. Keppler*, 644 F. Supp. 201 (D. Idaho 1986), the plaintiff, a tenured professor of German, was laid off because of financial exigency and charged Boise State University with constitutional violations of her substantive and due process rights under the Fourteenth Amendment. A federal district court sketched out the basic due process rights to which a tenured faculty member is entitled when financial exigency requires termination.

First, said the court, the institution must demonstrate that a genuine financial exigency exists. It can do so by submitting evidence of budget shortfalls, legislative or executive branch reductions in funding, or other financial data indicating that funds are limited or may not be used to retain the faculty member.

With regard to the substantive due process claim, the court stated, the institution must demonstrate that uniform procedures were used to determine how the reduction would be effected and which faculty members would be terminated. In this case the institution had used enrollment trends, faculty/student ratios, and historical data on the number of majors in the foreign language department. The elimination of the department was justified, the judge ruled, by the small number of majors and low enrollments.

The plaintiff had been offered a part-time position teaching in the English department, which she had refused. She had also been offered retraining as a linguistic specialist in the business education department, but did not avail herself of that opportunity either. Although the plaintiff argued that a one-month notice prior to her termination was insufficient, the court ruled that that period of time was long enough to permit the plaintiff to write a detailed letter of appeal and to have her appeal heard by a hearing committee, which had been done.

Despite the fact that the university hired fifteen new faculty members for other "viable" programs at the same time that it closed its foreign language department, the judge ruled that the institution had demonstrated that a genuine financial exigency existed, and that its procedures afforded the plaintiff both substantive and procedural due process.

If faculty members have property interests in their jobs, the cases make it clear that the institution must provide a hearing for those selected for layoff, so that they can be told the reasons for their selection and given an opportunity to challenge the sufficiency of those reasons. But must faculty members be given a hearing when the institution decides to reduce or eliminate an academic program?

This question was considered in *Texas Faculty Association v. University of Texas at Dallas*, 946 F.2d 379 (5th Cir. 1991). The deans of the Education School and the School of Natural Sciences and Mathematics at University of Texas at Dallas (UTD) decided to eliminate two academic programs because of low enrollment and the desire to reallocate the resources devoted to those programs. The university was not facing a situation of financial exigency. The faculty teaching in those programs were told that their employment would be terminated.

The tenured faculty asserted that they had a right to a hearing on the merits of the decision to eliminate the two programs. They also asserted a right to a hearing to determine whether their employment should be terminated. No hearings were held, although the university counsel sent the faculty a letter stating that they could meet with the deans informally to discuss the reasons for the program elimination. The faculty responded by filing a lawsuit claiming denial of procedural due process with respect to both the closure decision and their terminations.

The court refused to require the university to hold adversarial hearings on the decision to eliminate academic programs. The court stated that such a requirement would "seriously impair the university's significant interest in administering its educational programs in the manner it deems best" (946 F.2d at 385). Noting that courts are typically deferential to decisions based on academic judgments (citing *Board of Curators v. Horowitz*, 435 U.S. 78 (1978), discussed in Section 9.4.3), the court concluded that the judicial system was poorly equipped to review the substance of academic decisions, stating that "only the barest procedural protections of notice and an opportunity to be heard need be afforded the individual faculty member" (946 F.2d at 387). Because the faculty had been given nearly two years' notice and had been invited on several occasions to discuss the matter with their dean, the institution had met this portion of its due process obligation.

With regard to the propriety of decisions to terminate individual faculty, however, the court's attitude differed:

> [W]e perceive the risk that a particular faculty member will be terminated erroneously to be somewhat greater [than the risk of incorrectly deciding to eliminate a program] under the rather unusual facts of this case. Unlike many, if not most, institutions of higher learning, faculty in the University of Texas system are tenured to their particular component *institution* rather than to a particular school or program within that institution [citing regulations of the board of regents]. . . . Consequently, UTD faculty had a right of continuing appointment to the University of Texas at Dallas as a *whole*, and not merely to their particular schools or academic programs [946 F.2d at 386; emphasis in original].

The court noted that many of the faculty were qualified to teach in other programs within the university. "Unless the procedures afforded appellants meaningfully considered whether each appellant should be retained at UTD in *some* teaching capacity, then the risk that a given faculty member could be terminated erroneously seems to us patent" (946 F.2d at 386; emphasis in original).

The court concluded that the university had failed to provide due process with regard to the termination decisions:

> Because UTD faculty are tenured to the *institution*, each appellant was entitled to a meaningful opportunity to demonstrate that, even if his or her program was to be discontinued and the number of faculty positions associated with that program eliminated, he or she should nevertheless be retained to teach in a field in which he or she is qualified.
>
> We do not believe affording faculty such an opportunity would unduly interfere with the university's interest in academic freedom. A procedure ensuring

that (1) an instructor was not terminated for constitutionally impermissible reasons, (2) the administration's actions were taken in good faith, and (3) objective criteria were employed and fairly applied in determining whom, from *among the faculty at large,* to terminate, is all that the Fourteenth Amendment requires [946 F.2d at 387; emphasis in original].

The court elaborated on the practical consequences of its ruling, saying that not all faculty would need to be afforded adversarial hearings:

> Initially, the administration probably need only consider, in good faith, a written submission from each affected faculty member setting out why he or she deserves to be retained. Only if a particular faculty member makes a colorable showing that, under the objective criteria the university employs, he or she deserves to be retained in another academic program, must any sort of "hearing" be offered. Otherwise, a brief written statement from the decision maker of the reasons why the faculty member does not deserve to be retained would suffice. The "hearing" offered need only be an opportunity for the aggrieved faculty member to meet with the ultimate decision maker, to present his or her case orally, and to explore with the decision maker the possible alternatives to termination. If the decision maker nevertheless decides not to retain the faculty member, a written statement of reasons is required. Of course, if the retention of one faculty member results in the displacement of another, the displaced faculty member is equally entitled to due process [946 F.2d at 388].

The court discussed the faculty members' contention that they were entitled to a full-blown adversarial hearing, with counsel, before an official other than the one who made the initial termination decision; the right to cross-examination; and a written record. Absent clear evidence of bias on the part of the decision maker, said the court, the official responsible for the termination decision may conduct the hearing. Because the termination was not for performance reasons, the presence of counsel, the right to cross-examine, and a written record were not necessary. But the court agreed that the plaintiffs did have a right to present documentary evidence and to receive a written statement of the hearing officer's conclusions. Because the faculty had not been afforded the type of due process outlined by the court, the court remanded the case for further proceedings.

In some cases, faculty also allege that the termination is related to statements they have made or to expressive conduct, a free speech claim. In *Brine v. University of Iowa,* 90 F.3d 271 (8th Cir. 1996), the university's decision to eliminate its dental hygiene program was challenged on constitutional and civil rights grounds. Three tenured associate professors in the Dental Hygiene program were reassigned to faculty positions in the College of Dentistry. They filed sex discrimination, First and Fourteenth Amendment claims, and state statutory and constitutional claims, asserting that because all of the faculty and students in the Dental Hygiene program were women, the university's decision to terminate the program was both intentionally discriminatory and also had a disparate effect on women (Section 5.2.1). They also alleged that the university retaliated against them for objecting to the program closure. In a mixed bench and jury trial, the jury and judge rejected most of the plaintiffs' claims, but the judge allowed the jury's verdict for the plaintiffs on the retaliation claim to stand, and the plaintiffs were awarded damages and attorney's fees.

The appellate court affirmed all of the lower court's rulings in favor of the university, and reversed the ruling on the retaliation claim (and attorney's fees award). The plaintiffs had claimed that they had been excluded from the committees that reviewed the recommendations for program closure, that the department of dental hygiene had been abolished a year before the program actually ended, and that the former chair of the dental hygiene department had been retaliated against by being demoted to a program director position with less autonomy. The court found that the plaintiffs had no right to participate in the process, that the university had the discretion to abolish the department at the time of its choice, and that the department chair's demotion was an "inevitable consequence" of the decision to close the department. Furthermore, said the university, the program closure decision was made in concert with the university's strategic plan, and despite the fact that the university gave different reasons at different times for selecting the Dental Hygiene program (cost, lack of centrality to the university's mission), the reasons were not a pretext for sex discrimination. And finally, because the plaintiffs produced insufficient evidence of salary discrimination, they could not demonstrate that they had suffered an adverse employment action.

The UTD and *Brine* cases are very helpful to administrators at public institutions seeking guidance about program reduction or closure. Unless the institution has adopted procedures that require additional due process protections, or unless state statutes or regulations require more, the due process protections described in the UTD case should satisfy the institution's constitutional obligations to tenured faculty.

6.8.4. Statutory considerations.

A public institution's legal responsibilities during financial exigency or program discontinuance may be defined not only by contract and by constitutional considerations but also by state statutes or their implementing administrative regulations. The case of *Hartman v. Merged Area VI Community College*, 270 N.W.2d 822 (Iowa 1978), illustrates how important statutory analysis can be.

In *Hartman*, a community college had dismissed a faculty member as part of a staff reduction occasioned by declining enrollment and a worsening financial condition. For authority for its action, the institution relied on a state statute authorizing it to discharge faculty "for incompetency, inattention to duty, partiality, or any good cause" (Iowa Code of 1973 § 279.24). The institution's position was that the phrase "good cause" supported its action because it is a broad grant of authority encompassing any rational reason for dismissal asserted by the board of directors in good faith. The appellate court disagreed and invalidated the dismissal. It reasoned that "good cause," interpreted in light of the statute's legislative history and in conjunction with other related Iowa statutes, "refer[s] only to factors personal to the teacher"; that is, factors that can be considered the teacher's own "personal fault" (see Section 6.7.2.3 for a consideration of such personal factors).

While *Hartman* deals only with substantive standards for staff reduction, state statutes or administrative regulations may also establish procedures with which institutions must comply. In *Mabey v. Reagan,* 537 F.2d 1036 (9th Cir. 1976), for instance, a college did not renew an instructor's contract, in part because his department was overstaffed. The instructor challenged the nonrenewal, arguing that the college had followed the wrong procedures in reaching its decision. The court rejected the challenge, agreeing with the college that the applicable procedures were found in the statutes dealing with tenure and non-reappointment rather than in the statutes dealing with separation for "lack of work or lack of funds."

Statutory analysis was important to the outcome of a claim by tenured faculty members terminated during a reduction in force (RIF) that the college should have applied its RIF policy to part-time as well as full-time faculty. In *Ackerman v. Metropolitan Community College Area,* 575 N.W.2d 181 (Neb. 1998), nine tenured faculty were dismissed when the college reorganized its Office Skills and Technology program. According to the RIF policy that the board had adopted, faculty were selected for dismissal on the basis of their previous evaluations, their level of placement, diversity issues, and their length of service. The faculty selected for dismissal were given the opportunity to participate in a hearing concerning the method for selecting faculty to be dismissed.

The court examined the Nebraska statutes applicable to the employment and termination of public employees. It concluded that these statutes were intended to apply to full-time employees who had employment contracts with a public employer. Part-time faculty were employed on a semester basis, said the court, and these laws did not apply to them. The court affirmed the ruling of the trial court, which had upheld the board's decision in all respects.

Public institutions considering staff reductions must identify not only the applicable substantive standards but also the applicable procedures specified by state law. The procedures may be contained in a legal source different from that setting out the standards (see, for example, *Council of New Jersey State College Locals v. State Board of Higher Education,* 449 A.2d 1244 (N.J. 1982) (substantive criteria from state board policy on financial exigency applicable despite collective bargaining agreement, but some procedures derived from board policy bargainable); *Board of Trustees of Ohio State University v. Department of Administrative Services,* 429 N.E.2d 428 (Ohio 1981) (state administrative procedure act applicable to termination of nonfaculty personnel)).

6.8.5. Preparing for closures and reductions in force.

Everyone agrees that institutions, both public and private, should plan ahead to avoid the legal difficulties that can arise if financial or programmatic pressures necessitate staff reductions. Much can be done to plan ahead. Faculty contracts should be reviewed in light of the questions raised in Section 6.8.1. Where the contract does not clearly reflect the institution's desired position concerning staff reductions, its provisions should be revised to the extent possible without breaching existing contracts.

For institutional planning purposes, administrators should carefully distinguish between the two alternative approaches to faculty termination—financial exigency and program discontinuance:

1. When drafting or amending contracts for nontenured, tenure-track faculty, the institution should consider specific provisions on both alternatives. Public institutions should consult state law (Section 6.8.3 above) to determine whether it permits use of both alternatives. If the institution chooses, the AAUP's recommended regulations on either alternative (see Section 6.8.2, n.18) may be incorporated by reference into its faculty contracts. The institution may also draft provisions altogether different from the AAUP's, although it will want to give close attention to the competing policy considerations.

2. When interpreting existing tenure contracts, the institution should determine whether it has already, either expressly or by institutional custom, adopted AAUP policy for either alternative; or whether, in the face of institutional silence, courts would likely fill the gap with AAUP policy (see Section 6.8.2 above). In such circumstances the institution should consider itself bound to follow AAUP requirements and thus not free under existing contracts to strike out unilaterally on a different course.

3. When faced with circumstances mandating consideration of tenured faculty terminations, and when authorized to follow either alternative approach, the institution should carefully consider its choice. Which alternative—institution-wide financial exigency or discontinuance of specific programs—can better be substantiated by existing circumstances? Which would better serve the institution's overall mission? If the institution decides to pursue one of the alternatives, it should be careful to identify and follow the particular decision-making requirements and protections for faculty specified for that alternative.

When the institution does have authority for staff reductions necessitated by financial exigency, it should have a policy and standards for determining when a financial exigency exists and which faculty members' positions will be terminated. It should also specify the procedures by which the faculty member can challenge the propriety of his or her selection for termination. Before administrators make a termination decision, they should be certain (1) that a financial exigency does actually exist under the institution's policy, (2) that the terminations will alleviate the exigency, and (3) that no other motivation for a particular termination may exist. After dismissing faculty members, administrators should be extremely careful in hiring new ones, to avoid the impression, as in the *Bloomfield* case (see Section 6.8.2), that the financial exigency was a pretext for abolishing tenure or otherwise replacing old faculty members with new. Similar considerations would apply in implementing program discontinuations.

Finally, administrators should remember that, in this sensitive area, some of their decisions may wind up in court despite careful planning. Administrators should thus keep complete records and documentation of their staff reduction policies, decisions, and internal review processes for possible use in court and should work closely with counsel both in planning ahead and in making the actual termination decisions.

Selected Annotated Bibliography
Sec. 6.1 (Overview)

American Association of University Professors. *AAUP Policy Documents and Reports* (the "Redbook") (9th ed., AAUP, 2001). A collection of the AAUP's major policy statements on academic freedom, tenure, collective bargaining, professional ethics, institutional governance, sexual harassment, part-time faculty, and other topics. Includes a discussion of the role and usefulness of AAUP policy statements and an appendix with selected judicial decisions and articles referring to AAUP statements.

American Association of University Professors/Association of American Colleges, Commission on Academic Tenure in Higher Education. *Faculty Tenure: A Report and Recommendations* (Jossey-Bass, 1973). An evaluation of the status and limitations of tenure. Includes special essays on "Legal Dimensions of Tenure" by Victor Rosenblum and "Faculty Unionism and Tenure" by W. McHugh.

Brown, Ralph S., & Kurland, Jordan E. "Academic Tenure and Academic Freedom," 53 *Law & Contemp. Probs.* 325 (1990). Discusses the role of tenure in reinforcing academic freedom; the costs of tenure; benefits of tenure, in addition to its role in protecting academic freedom; and various alternatives to tenure. Also discusses various perceived weaknesses in tenure and several methods of protecting the academic freedom of faculty who are not tenured.

Chait, Richard P., & Ford, Andrew T. *Beyond Traditional Tenure: A Guide to Sound Policies and Practices* (Jossey-Bass, 1982). Includes chapters on "Tenure in Context," "Institutions Without Tenure," "Life Without Tenure," "Tenure and Nontenure Tracks," "Extended Probationary Periods and Suspension of 'Up-or-Out' Rule," "Tenure Quotas," "Sound Tenure Policy," "Evaluating Tenured Faculty," "Distributing Rewards and Applying Sanctions," and "Auditing and Improving Faculty Personnel Systems." Based on authors' survey and analysis of tenure options in existence at various institutions around the country. Provides case studies of leading examples. For extended reviews of the book, see 10 *J. Coll. & Univ. Law* 93–112 (1983–84).

Finkin, Matthew W. "Regulation by Agreement: The Case for Private Higher Education," 65 *Iowa L. Rev.* 1119 (1980), reprinted in 67 *AAUP Bulletin* no. 1 (Parts I and II of the article), no. 2 (Part III), and no. 3 (Part IV) (1981). Provides a multifaceted review of various problems unique to employment relations in higher education. Part I of the article serves as a general introduction; Part II discusses the nature of the contract of academic employment and various questions that arise in contract litigation; Part III discusses the continued relevance of academic organization by collective agreement, notwithstanding *NLRB v. Yeshiva University;* Part IV sets out a proposal for an alternative system of self-regulation of employment matters.

Furniss, W. Todd. "The Status of AAUP Policy," 59 *Educ. Record* 7 (1978). Reviews the role that AAUP policy statements play in the university employment scheme. Notes the increasing use of such statements in employment litigation and urges institutions of higher education to clarify the extent to which they accept AAUP policy statements as their own institutional policy. The arguments raised in this article are challenged in a companion article: Ralph S. Brown, Jr., & Matthew W. Finkin, "The Usefulness of AAUP Policy Statements," 59 *Educ. Record* 30 (1978).

McCarthy, Jane, Ladimer, Irving, & Sirefman, Josef. *Managing Faculty Disputes: A Guide to Issues, Procedures, and Practices* (Jossey-Bass, 1984). Addresses the problem of faculty disputes on campus and proposes processes for resolving them. Covers both disputes that occur regularly and can be subjected to a standard dispute resolution process, and special disputes that occur irregularly and may require a resolution process tailored to the circumstances. Includes model grievance procedures, case studies of actual disputes, and worksheets and checklists to assist administrators in implementing dispute-resolution processes.

Sec. 6.2 *(Faculty Contracts)*

Biles, George E., & Tuckman, Howard P. *Part-Time Faculty Personnel Management Policies* (ACE/Macmillan, 1986). Chapters include discussions on how to define a part-time faculty member, equal employment opportunity and affirmative action issues, appointment and reappointment practices, salaries and benefits for part-timers, tenure eligibility, the professional obligations of part-time faculty, evaluation of part-time faculty, and due process and collective bargaining issues. Also included are suggestions for a handbook for part-time faculty.

McKee, Patrick W. "Tenure by Default: The Non-Formal Acquisition of Academic Tenure," 7 *J. Coll. & Univ. Law* 31 (1980–81). Analyzes the impact of *Board of Regents v. Roth* and *Perry v. Sindermann* on the concept of nonformal tenure. Distinguishes among "automatic tenure," "tenure by grant," "nonformal or *de facto* tenure," and "tenure by default." To resolve confusion in lower court opinions applying *Roth* and *Perry* to nonformal tenure claims, the article develops a common law analysis covering employment relationships in both private and public institutions.

Sec. 6.3 *(Faculty Collective Bargaining)*

Hustoles, Thomas P., & DiGiovanni, Nicholas, Jr. *Negotiating a Faculty Collective Bargaining Agreement* (National Association of College and University Attorneys, 2005). Provides a framework for negotiating a faculty collective bargaining agreement. Includes suggestions for negotiation strategies and sample contractual provisions and clauses. Focuses on strategies for preserving institutional flexibility.

Sec. 6.4 *(Application of Nondiscrimination Laws to Faculty Employment Decisions)*

"The Academy in the Courts: A Symposium on Academic Freedom," 16 *U. Cal. Davis L. Rev.* 831 (1983). A two-part article. The second part is titled "Discrimination in the Academy" (for a description of the first part, see "Academy in the Courts" entry in bibliography for Section 7.1). This part contains three articles: Christine Cooper, "Title VII in the Academy: Barriers to Equality for Faculty Women"; John D. Gregory, "Secrecy in University and College Tenure Deliberations: Placing Appropriate Limits on Academic Freedom"; and Harry F. Tepker, "Title VII, Equal Employment Opportunity, and Academic Autonomy: Toward a Principled Deference."

Achtenberg, Roberta. *Sexual Orientation and the Law* (Clark Boardman Callaghan, 1985, and periodic supp.). A comprehensive treatise on many areas of the law related to homosexuality. Employment-related subjects include civil rights and discrimination, First Amendment issues, employment and AIDS, insurance and AIDS, and tax issues. Written for attorneys who represent gay clients, the book includes sample forms and contracts.

Baldus, David C., & Cole, James L. *Statistical Proof of Discrimination* (Shepards/ McGraw-Hill, 1980). A guide to the proper uses of statistics in discrimination litigation, with emphasis on employment discrimination. The book will be helpful to both plaintiffs' and defendants' counsel in such actions. Includes useful glossary and bibliography.

Barnard, Thomas H., & Downing, Timothy J. "Emerging Law on Sexual Orientation and Employment," 29 *U. Memphis L. Rev.* 555 (1999). Reviews state and municipal laws prohibiting employment discrimination on the basis of sexual orientation, as well as legal challenges to such laws. Also reviews litigation and other developments related to domestic partner benefits, as well as litigation strategies in states where no protective legislation exists.

Bompey, Stuart H., & Witten, Richard E. "Settlement of Title VII Disputes: Shifting Patterns in a Changing World," 6 *J. Coll. & Univ. Law* 317 (1980). Reviews the types of settlements available to plaintiffs and defendants and the various means of reaching such settlements. Examines the settlement process from the commencement of an action (when a plaintiff files charges with the EEOC) to the culmination of litigation through the entry of consent decrees.

Centra, John A. *Reflective Faculty Evaluation* (Jossey-Bass, 1993). Provides new approaches for fostering and evaluating good faculty performance.

Cole, Elsa Kircher (ed.). *Sexual Harassment on Campus: A Legal Compendium* (4th ed., National Association of College and University Attorneys, 2003). A collection of resources on sexual harassment: law review articles; EEOC policy guidelines; and sexual harassment policy statements from five universities, the AAUP, and the American Council on Education. Includes how to conduct an investigation (also available separately, see below), and a list of additional resources and suggestions for developing a sexual harassment policy.

Cole, Elsa Kircher, & Hustoles, Thomas P. *How to Conduct a Sexual Harassment Investigation* (National Association of College and University Attorneys, 1997). Provides a checklist of suggestions for conducting an appropriate and timely sexual harassment investigation. Suggests questions to be asked at each step of the investigation, and offers alternatives for resolving harassment complaints.

DiGiovanni, Nicholas. *Age Discrimination: An Administrator's Guide* (College and University Personnel Association, 1989). Written for campus administrators. Includes an overview of the ADEA, a discussion of how an age discrimination lawsuit is conducted and defended, and suggestions for minimizing the risk of liability. Additional chapters discuss planning for retirement (including the EEOC guidelines for retirement incentives), practical considerations in evaluating and counseling older workers, waivers and releases, and a table of state laws prohibiting age discrimination. (This book predates the passage of the Older Workers Benefit Protection Act, discussed in Section 5.2.6, this volume.)

Dziech, Billie Wright, & Hawkins, Michael W. *Sexual Harassment and Higher Education* (Garland, 1998). The authors, one a professor and one a practicing attorney, review the legal and regulatory environment and its application to higher education; discuss the importance of policy development that is sensitive to the institution's culture; examine the reactions of harassment targets; discuss the treatment of nonmeritorious cases; and review the effectiveness of banning consensual relationships.

Fitzgerald, Louise F. *Sexual Harassment in Higher Education: Concepts and Issues* (National Education Association [NEA], 1992). A brief, practical guide to the major issues facing faculty and administrators with regard to sexual harassment. Includes definitions of harassment, an estimate of its prevalence, and a brief summary of the legal issues. Also includes suggestions for developing institutional sexual harassment policies and complaint procedures; a discussion of whether institutions should extend their prohibitions to include consensual amorous relationships between faculty and students; a comprehensive bibliography; a typology of sexual harassment; a sexual harassment experiences questionnaire; sample campus policies on sexual harassment; and the NEA's Sexual Harassment Statement.

Gamble, Barbara S. (ed.). *Sex Discrimination Handbook* (Bureau of National Affairs, 1992). A concise guidebook to sex discrimination claims, their defense, and their avoidance. Case summaries and the text of federal nondiscrimination laws and regulations are included, as well as sample forms and policies. A directory of EEOC offices and the states' fair employment agencies is also provided.

Gutek, Barbara. "Understanding Sexual Harassment at Work," 6 *Notre Dame J.L. Ethics & Pub. Pol'y.* 335 (1992). A review of social science research related to sexual behavior in the workplace. Discusses the definition of sexual harassment, the frequency of sexual behavior in the workplace, the impacts of such behavior, and the concept of "sex role spillover" and its implications for workplace behavior.

Kesselman, Marc L. "Putting the Professor to Bed: Mandatory Retirement of Tenured University Faculty in the United States and Canada," 17 *Comp. Lab. L.J.* 206 (1995). Argues that the ADEA can be interpreted to permit the mandatory retirement of tenured faculty by using the decisions of Canadian courts that have upheld mandatory retirement of tenured faculty as a judicially created exception to the prohibition against age discrimination.

LaNoue, George, & Lee, Barbara A. *Academics in Court: The Consequences of Faculty Discrimination Litigation* (University of Michigan Press, 1987). A comprehensive study of all academic discrimination lawsuits between 1972 and 1986. Chapter 2 describes the sources of protection against employment discrimination and discusses their application in the academic context. Five academic discrimination cases are discussed, and interview data from the parties involved are presented. The final chapter provides a series of recommendations for faculty members considering filing discrimination claims and for administrators who must determine how and whether to defend these claims in court.

Lee, Barbara A. "Balancing Confidentiality and Disclosure in Faculty Peer Review: Impact of Title VII Litigation," 9 *J. Coll. & Univ. Law* 279 (1982–83). Analyzes Title VII litigation brought by faculty of higher education institutions. Includes a section on "Burdens of Proof and Persuasion," which elucidates the three stages of a Title VII case—the "*prima facie* case," "the institution's rebuttal," and plaintiff's proof of "pretextual behavior"—using illustrations from higher education cases. Also reviews issues concerning "evidence admitted by courts in challenges to peer review decisions" and "standards applied by courts to the peer review process."

Lindemann, Barbara, & Kadue, David D. *Primer on Sexual Harassment* (Bureau of National Affairs, 1992). A concise overview of the legal, social, and policy issues related to sexual harassment in the workplace. Written for a nonlegal audience, the primer discusses the definition of sexual harassment; appropriate employer responses to reports of alleged harassment; significant court opinions; discipline and discharge issues; and other issues, such as workers' compensation for harassment claims.

National Association of College and University Business Officers. *Federal Regulations and the Employment Practices of Colleges and Universities* (NACUBO, 1977, and periodic supp.). A loose-leaf service that provides information and guidance on applying federal regulations affecting personnel administration in postsecondary institutions.

Paludi, Michele A. (ed.). *Sexual Harassment on College Campuses: Abusing the Ivory Power* (State University of New York Press, 1996). A collection of articles and essays on sexual harassment. Include discussions of the definition of harassment; the impact of sexual harassment on the cognitive, physical, and emotional well-being of victims; the characteristics of harassers; and procedures for dealing with sexual harassment complaints on campus. Sample materials for training faculty, draft forms for receiving harassment complaints, lists of organizations and other resources concerned with sexual harassment, and references to other written materials are also included.

Perritt, Henry H., Jr. *Americans With Disabilities Act Handbook* (2d ed., Wiley, 1991, and periodic supp.). A comprehensive practice guide to Title I of the ADA. Chapters include a description of the statute, the legislative history, the various categories of protection, the employer's legal obligations, procedural and evidentiary issues, and suggestions for modifying employment policies and practices to comply with the ADA. The Rehabilitation Act of 1973 also is described, and an appendix provides a summary of the ADA's public accommodation provisions.

Rothstein, Laura F. "The Employer's Duty to Accommodate Performance and Conduct Deficiencies of Individuals with Mental Impairments Under Disability Discrimination Laws," 47 *Syracuse L. Rev.* 931 (1997). Reviews federal disability discrimination law and its impact on employer discipline or discharge of employees for misconduct.

Sandin, Robert T. *Autonomy and Faith: Religious Preference in Employment Decisions in Religiously Affiliated Higher Education* (Omega Publications, 1990). Discusses the circumstances under which religiously affiliated colleges and universities may use religion as a selection criterion. Provides a taxonomy of religiously affiliated colleges and models of their preferential hiring policies, reviews state and federal nondiscrimination statutes, summarizes judicial precedent regarding secular and religious functions in establishment clause litigation, and discusses the interplay between religious preference and academic freedom.

Sandler, Bernice R., & Shoop, Robert J. (eds.). *Sexual Harassment on Campus: A Guide for Administrators, Faculty, and Students* (Allyn & Bacon, 1997). Includes chapters on peer sexual harassment of students, faculty harassment of other faculty, electronic sexual harassment, how to develop an effective policy, how to conduct an investigation, and numerous other issues. A thorough and well-organized resource for campus administrators and faculty.

Sullivan, Charles A., Zimmer, Michael J., & Richards, Richard F. *Federal Statutory Law of Employment Discrimination* (Michie/Bobbs-Merrill, 1980). A one-volume basic text on the federal law of employment discrimination, supplemented annually. Includes discussions of Title VII, the Equal Pay Act, the Age Discrimination in Employment Act, and 42 U.S.C. § 1981. Examines both the substantive and the procedural law developed under these statutes and integrates this law with other areas of law, such as the National Labor Relations Act. Includes extensive case citations and table of cases.

Van Tol, Joan E. "Eros Gone Awry: Liability Under Title VII for Workplace Sexual Favoritism," 13 *Indust. Rel. L.J.* 153 (1991). Examines the difficult issue of workplace romance and its potential legal implications for the employer. Although the article does not focus specifically on academic organizations, the issues addressed are relevant for academic workplaces as well as others.

Weber, Mark C. "Disability Discrimination Litigation and Institutions of Higher Education," 25 *J. Coll. & Univ. Law* 53 (1998). Discusses administrative enforcement and litigation issues, settlement, and alternatives to litigation, for cases brought by employees or students.

West, Martha S. "Gender Bias in Academic Robes: The Law's Failure to Protect Women Faculty," 67 *Temple L. Rev.* 67 (1994). Reviews data on the employment of women in tenured and tenure-track positions, analyzes the evolution of employment discrimination law and its effect on academic discrimination litigation, and suggests an agenda for changing academic employment policies to enhance equity.

Sec. 6.5 (*Affirmative Action in Faculty Employment Decisions*)

Bureau of National Affairs. *Affirmative Action Compliance Manual for Federal Contractors* (BNA, published and updated periodically). A comprehensive loose-leaf guide. Provides detailed and continually updated information on the federal government's affirmative action program and the compliance responsibilities and procedures of the Departments of Labor, Education, Defense, and other federal agencies.

Clague, Monique Weston. "Affirmative Action Employment Discrimination: The Higher Education Fragment," in John B. Smart (ed.), *Higher Education: Handbook of Theory and Research,* Vol. 2 (Agathon, 1986), 109–62. Discusses significant decisions by the U.S. Supreme Court, including *Weber* and *Wygant.* Although the article predates more recent Supreme Court decisions in this area, it provides a thorough and thoughtful analysis of the legal and historical context for affirmative action in the 1970s and early 1980s.

Foster, Sheila. "Difference and Equality: A Critical Assessment of the Concept of 'Diversity,'" 1993 *Wis. L. Rev.* 105 (1993). Explores and criticizes the concept of diversity as developed through equal protection jurisprudence, with special emphasis on *Bakke* and *Metro Broadcasting.* Examines the concept of "difference" and discusses that concept against the history of exclusion of various groups. Also discussed is the tension between equal treatment and equal outcomes.

Oppenheimer, David B. "Distinguishing Five Models of Affirmative Action," 4 *Berkeley Women's L.J.* 42 (1988). Discusses quotas, preference systems, the use of goals and timetables for selected occupations, expanded recruitment pools, and affirmative commitment not to discriminate as alternate models for increasing the proportion of underrepresented persons in the workforce. Selected discrimination lawsuits are also analyzed.

Taylor, Bron Raymond. *Affirmative Action at Work: Law, Politics and Ethics* (University of Pittsburgh Press, 1991). Reports the result of a survey of state agency employees'

attitudes toward affirmative action and provides suggestions for organizations that
wish to strengthen their affirmative action programs. Includes a brief legal history
of affirmative action, as well as philosophical and ethical perspectives on affirmative action.

Sec. 6.6 (Standards and Criteria for Faculty Employment Decisions)

American Association of University Professors. *Post-Tenure Review: An AAUP Response*
(AAUP, 1999). Offers "practical recommendations for faculty at institutions where
post-tenure review is being considered or put into effect"; argues that the purpose
of post-tenure review should be developmental, not for accountability or dismissal
purposes; provides guidelines for faculty in deciding whether or not to support the
development of a post-tenure review process; and lists "minimum standards for
good practice" for post-tenure review systems. Available at http://www.aaup.org/
postten.htm.

Copeland, John D., & Murray, John W Jr. "Getting Tossed from the Ivory Tower: The
Legal Implications of Evaluating Faculty Performance," 61 *Missouri L. Rev.* 233
(1996). Discusses legal issues related to faculty performance evaluation, including
post-tenure review.

Finkin, Matthew W. (ed.). *The Case for Tenure* (Cornell University Press, 1996). A collection of writings by several eminent scholars on academic freedom and tenure.
Also includes selected court opinions and commentary on reductions in force,
faculty retirement, and post-tenure review.

Olswang, Steven G., & Fantel, Jane I. "Tenure and Periodic Performance Review: Compatible Legal and Administrative Principles," 7 *J. Coll. & Univ. Law* 1 (1980–81).
Examines the "separate concepts of tenure and academic freedom and their relation
to one form of accountability measure: systematic reviews of the performance of
tenured faculty." Identifies the "differences between tenure and academic freedom"
and the purposes and uses of periodic performance reviews "in an overall system of
faculty personnel management." Includes discussion of tenure terminations for
cause based on incompetence, immorality, insubordination, and other such factors.

See the Centra entry for Section 6.4.

Sec. 6.8 (Closure, Merger, and Reduction in Force)

Babbitt, Ellen M. (ed.). *Academic Program Closures: A Legal Compendium* (2d ed.,
National Association of College and University Attorneys, 2002). A comprehensive resource for administrators, faculty, and legal counsel. Included are six
chapters and law review articles discussing legal issues and planning issues,
such as the roles of trustees, administrators, faculty, students, and other constituencies in planning for and implementing program closures. Also included
are AAUP guidelines, policies from five institutions on faculty reductions and
program termination, and documents on related issues, as well as a list of
relevant books and articles.

Johnson, Annette B. "The Problems of Contraction: Legal Considerations in University
Retrenchment," 10 *J. Law & Educ.* 269 (1981). Examines the financial circumstances that justify retrenchment, how and by whom retrenchment decisions
should be made, and the procedures to follow after the decision in order to preserve the legal rights of individuals affected by the retrenchment.

Ludolph, Robert Charles. "Termination of Faculty Tenure Rights Due to Financial Exigency and Program Discontinuance," 63 *U. Detroit L. Rev.* 609 (1986). Reviews faculty property rights (for both tenured and untenured faculty), discusses constitutional requirements for reductions in force and program closures, and analyzes contractual issues related to faculty terminations. Author proposes an analytical model that helps counsel develop an appropriate defense to challenges to program closures, reductions based on financial exigency, and the closing of a campus or an institution.

Martin, James, Samels, James E., & Associates. *Merging Colleges for Mutual Growth* (Johns Hopkins University Press, 1993). Provides practical and theoretical advice, by college administrators and legal counsel experienced in these matters, about merging colleges to avoid bankruptcy. Discusses a typology of models of mergers, the role of trustees and governing boards, the role of administrators and faculty, and financial planning. Attention is also given to planning for the effects of mergers on students and alumni, as well as academic support concerns, such as the merging of libraries.

Mingle, James R., & Associates. *Challenges of Retrenchment: Strategies for Consolidating Programs, Cutting Costs, and Reallocating Resources* (Jossey-Bass, 1981). Describes the actual retrenchment efforts of public and private institutions through an extensive set of case studies. Analyzes the complex organizational, legal, and political issues that arise when colleges and universities lay off faculty and cut back programs and departments because of rising inflation, declining enrollments, or both.

Olswang, Steven G. "Planning the Unthinkable: Issues in Institutional Reorganization and Faculty Reductions," 9 *J. Coll. & Univ. Law* 431 (1982–83). Examines the legal and policy issues inherent in institutional reorganization and faculty reduction. Analyzes the "three primary alternatives"—"financial exigency declarations, program eliminations, and program reductions"—for achieving reorganization and reduction. Also provides policy guidelines for determining which faculty to lay off and discusses faculty members' rights and prerogatives when they are designated for removal.

7

Faculty Academic Freedom and Freedom of Expression

Sec. 7.1. General Concepts and Principles

7.1.1. Faculty freedom of expression in general. Whether they are employed by public or by private institutions of higher education, faculty members as citizens are protected by the First Amendment from governmental censorship and other governmental actions that infringe their freedoms of speech, press, and association. When the restraint on such freedoms originates from a governmental body external to the institution (see subsection 7.1.5 below), the First Amendment protects faculty members in both public and private institutions. When the restraint is internal, however (for example, when a provost or dean allegedly infringes a faculty member's free speech), the First Amendment generally protects only faculty members in public institutions. Absent a finding of state action (see Section 1.5.2), an internal restraint in a private institution does not implicate government, and the First Amendment therefore does not apply. The protection accorded to faculty expression and association in private institutions is thus usually a matter of contract law (see Section 1.5.3).

While faculty contracts may distinguish between tenured and nontenured faculty, as may state statutes and regulations applicable to public institutions, tenure is immaterial to most freedom of expression claims. Other aspects of job status, such as tenure track versus non-tenure track and full time versus part time, are also generally immaterial to freedom of expression claims. In *Perry v. Sindermann,* 408 U.S. 593 (1972), discussed in Section 6.6.2.1, the U.S. Supreme Court held that a nonrenewed faculty member's "lack of a contractual or tenure right to reemployment . . . is immaterial to his free speech claim" and that "regardless of the . . . [teacher's] contractual or other claim to a job," government cannot "deny a benefit to a person because of his constitutionally protected speech or associations."[1]

When faculty members at public institutions assert First Amendment free speech claims, these claims are usually subject to a line of U.S. Supreme Court cases applicable to all public employees: the *"Pickering/Connick"* line. The foundational case in this line, *Pickering v. Board of Education*, 391 U.S. 563 (1968), concerned a public high school teacher who had been dismissed for writing the local newspaper a letter in which he criticized the board of education's financial plans for the high schools. Pickering brought suit, alleging that the dismissal violated his First Amendment freedom of speech. The school board argued that the dismissal was justified because the letter "damaged the professional reputations of . . . [the school board] members and of the school administrators, would be disruptive of faculty discipline, and would tend to foment 'controversy, conflict, and dissension' among teachers, administrators, the board of education, and the residents of the district."

The U.S. Supreme Court determined that the teacher's letter addressed "a matter of legitimate public concern," thus implicating his free speech rights as a citizen. The Court then balanced the teacher's free speech interests against the state's interest in maintaining an efficient educational system, using the following considerations: (1) Was there a close working relationship between the teacher and those he criticized? (2) Is the substance of the letter a matter of legitimate public concern? (3) Did the letter have a detrimental impact on the administration of the educational system? (4) Was the teacher's performance of his daily duties impeded? (5) Was the teacher writing in his professional capacity or as a private citizen? The Court found that Pickering had no working relationship with the board, that the letter dealt with a matter of public concern, that Pickering's letter was greeted with public apathy and therefore had no detrimental effect on the schools, that Pickering's performance as a teacher was not hindered by the letter, and that he wrote as a citizen, not as a teacher. Based on these considerations and facts, the Court concluded that the school administration's interest in limiting teachers' opportunities to contribute to public debate was not significantly greater than its interest in limiting a similar contribution by any member of the general public, and that "in a case such as this, absent proof of false statements knowingly or recklessly made by him, a teacher's exercise of his right to speak on issues of public importance may not furnish the basis for his dismissal from public employment."

The *Pickering* balancing test was further explicated in later Supreme Court cases. The most important of these cases are *Givhan v. Western Line Consolidated School District*, 439 U.S. 410 (1979); *Connick v. Myers*, 461 U.S. 138 (1983); and *Waters v. Churchill*, 511 U.S. 661 (1994). They are discussed *seriatim* below.

---

[1]The *Perry* Court also held, in contrast, that the professor's job status, "though irrelevant to his free speech claim, is highly relevant to his procedural due process claim" (408 U.S. at 599). The Fourteenth Amendment due process clause is the one constitutional basis for an academic freedom claim (see subsection 7.1.4 below) that distinguishes among faculty members on the basis of job status.

In *Givhan,* the issue was whether *Pickering* protects public school teachers who communicate their views in private rather than in public. In a series of private meetings with her school principal, the plaintiff teacher in *Givhan* had made complaints and expressed opinions about school employment practices that she considered racially discriminatory. When the school district did not renew her contract, the teacher filed suit, claiming an infringement of her First Amendment rights. The trial court found that the school district had not renewed the teacher's contract primarily because of her criticisms of school employment practices, and it held that such action violated the First Amendment. The U.S. Court of Appeals reversed, reasoning that the teacher's expression was not protected by the First Amendment because she had expressed her views privately. The U.S. Supreme Court, in a unanimous opinion, disagreed with the appeals court and remanded the case to the trial court for further proceedings. According to the Supreme Court, "[N]either the [First] Amendment itself nor our decisions indicate that . . . freedom [of speech] is lost to the public employee who arranges to communicate privately with his employer rather than to spread his views before the public" (439 U.S. at 415–16). Rather, private expression, like public expression, is subject to the same balancing of factors that the Court utilized in *Pickering.* The Court did suggest in a footnote, however, that private expression may involve some different considerations:

> Although the First Amendment's protection of government employees extends to private as well as public expression, striking the *Pickering* balance in each context may involve different considerations. When a teacher speaks publicly, it is generally the content of his statements that must be assessed to determine whether they "in any way either impeded the teacher's proper performance of his daily duties in the classroom or . . . interfered with the regular operation of the schools generally" (*Pickering v. Board of Education,* 391 U.S. at 572–73). Private expression, however, may in some situations bring additional factors to the *Pickering* calculus. When a government employee personally confronts his immediate superior, the employing agency's institutional efficiency may be threatened not only by the content of the employee's message but also by the manner, time, and place in which it is delivered [439 U.S. at 415 n.4].

In *Connick v. Myers,* the issue was whether *Pickering* protects public employees who communicate views to office staff about office personnel matters. The plaintiff, Myers, was an assistant district attorney who had been scheduled for transfer to another division of the office. In opposing the transfer, she circulated a questionnaire on office operations to other assistant district attorneys. Later on the same day, she was discharged. In a 5-to-4 decision, the Court declined to apply *Givhan,* arguing that Givhan's statements about employment practices had "involved a matter of public concern." In contrast, the various questions in Myers's questionnaire about office transfer policy and other office practices, with one exception, "[did] not fall under the rubric of matters of 'public concern.'" The exception, a question on whether office personnel ever felt pressured to work in political campaigns, did "touch upon a matter of public concern." In the overall context of the questionnaire, which otherwise concerned only internal office matters, this one question provided only a "limited First Amendment interest" for Myers. Therefore, applying *Pickering* factors, the Court determined that Myers had spoken "not as a citizen upon matters of public concern, but instead as an employee upon matters only of personal interest"; and that circulation of the questionnaire interfered with "close working relationships" within the office. The discharge thus did not violate the plaintiff's freedom of speech.

Givhan and *Connick* emphasize the need to distinguish between communications on matters of public concern and communications on matters of private or personal concern—a distinction that, under *Givhan*, does not depend on whether the communication is itself made in public or in private. The dispute between the majority and dissenters in *Connick* reveals how slippery this distinction can be. The majority did, however, provide a helpful methodological guideline for drawing the distinction. "Whether an employee's speech addresses a matter of public concern," said the Court, "must be determined by the *content, form, and context* of a given statement, as revealed by the whole record" (461 U.S. at 147–48; emphasis added). Because the "content, form, and context" will depend on the specific circumstances of each case, courts must remain attentive to the "enormous variety of fact situations" that these cases may present. In a more recent case, *City of San Diego v. Roe*, 543 U.S. 77 (2004), the Court reiterated this aspect of *Connick* and added that "public concern is something that is a subject of legitimate news interest; that is, a subject of general interest and of value and concern to the public at the time of publication" (543 U.S. at 83–84).

In *Waters v. Churchill*, 511 U.S. 661 (1994), the third key case explicating *Pickering*, a public hospital had terminated a nurse because of statements concerning the hospital that she had made to a coworker. In remanding the case to the trial court for further proceedings, the Justices filed four opinions displaying different perspectives on the First Amendment issues. Although there was no majority opinion, the plurality opinion by Justice O'Connor and two concurring opinions (by Justice Souter and Justice Scalia) stressed the need for courts to be deferential to employers when applying the *Pickering/Connick* factors. In particular, according to these Justices, it appears that (1) in evaluating the impact of the employee's speech, the public employer may rely on its own reasonable belief regarding the content of the speech, even if that belief later proves to be inaccurate;[2] and (2) in evaluating the disruptiveness of the employee's speech, a public employer does not need to determine that the speech actually disrupted operations, but only that the speech was potentially disruptive.

Under the first of these points from *Waters*—the "reasonable belief" requirement—the employer's belief concerning the content of the employee's

---

[2]As with other cases in the *Pickering/Connick* line, there is potentially a related question whether the employer terminated the employee because of unprotected (disruptive) speech or conduct, or because of other, protected, speech. See Section 7.6 below. In *Waters*, the Court raised this issue but did not resolve it, instead remanding the case to the lower courts for further fact determinations (511 U.S. at 682 (opinion of O'Connor, J.)).

speech apparently must be an actual or real belief arrived at in good faith. Justice O'Connor's plurality opinion, for instance, indicates that the employer must "really . . . believe" (511 U.S. at 679) the version of the facts on which it relies. In addition, the employer's belief must also be objectively reasonable in the sense that it is based on "an objectively reasonable investigation" of the facts (511 U.S. at 683; opinion of Souter, J.) or based on a standard of care that "a reasonable manager" would use under the circumstances (511 U.S. at 678; plurality opinion of O'Connor, J.). This aspect of *Waters* is discussed further in Section 7.6 below.

Under the second point from *Waters*—the potential disruption requirement—the employer may prevail by showing that it made a "reasonable prediction of disruption, to the effect" that "the [employee's] speech is, in fact, likely to be disruptive" (511 U.S. at 674; O'Connor J.). The reasonableness of the prediction would likely be evaluated under an objective standard much like that which Justice O'Connor would use to determine the reasonableness of the employer's belief about the facts. Even if the predicted harm "is mostly speculative," the Court apparently will be deferential to the employer's interests and give the employer's finding substantial weight (511 U.S. at 673; opinion of O'Connor, J.). In *Waters* itself, for instance, "the potential disruptiveness of the [nurse's] speech as reported was enough to outweigh whatever First Amendment value it might have had" (511 U.S. at 680; opinion of O'Connor, J.). This aspect of *Waters* was discussed and relied on in *Jeffries v. Harleston*, a U.S. Court of Appeals case examined in Section 7.5 below.

In various cases, lower courts have questioned whether there are circumstances in which they should not apply the *Pickering/Connick/Waters* analysis to public employees' free speech claims. In *Harrington v. Harris*, 118 F.3d 359 (5th Cir. 1997), for instance, the issue was whether there must be an "adverse employment action" by the employer before the *Pickering/Connick* line will apply. The plaintiffs were tenured law school professors at Texas Southern University who challenged the amount of the salary increases the dean had awarded them. The professors did not claim censorship, but rather claimed retaliation—that the dean had lowered the amount of their salary increases in retaliation for critical statements they had made concerning the dean. The appellate court declined to apply the *Pickering/Connick* public concern analysis and rejected the professors' free speech retaliation claim because they had "failed to show that they suffered an adverse employment action."

The professors in *Harrington* had alleged two possible adverse actions: first, that the dean had evaluated one of the plaintiffs as "counterproductive"; and second, that the dean had perennially discriminated against the plaintiffs in awarding salary increases. As to the first, the court held that "an employer's criticism of an employee, without more, [does not constitute] an actionable adverse employment action. . . . [M]ere criticisms do not give rise to a constitutional deprivation for purposes of the First Amendment." As to the second alleged adverse action, the court emphasized that each of the professors had received salary increases each year and that the professors' complaint "amounted to nothing more than a dispute over the quantum of pay increases." The court then limited its holding to these facts: "If Plaintiffs had received no merit pay increase at all or if the amount of such increase were so small as to be simply a token increase which was out of proportion to the merit pay increases granted to others, we might reach a different conclusion."

The appellate court in *Power v. Summers,* 226 F.3d 815 (7th Cir. 2000), however, disagreed with the *Harrington* analysis and ruled that proof of an adverse employment action is not a prerequisite for a faculty member's free speech claim against the institution. The case concerned a claim by three professors that they had received reduced bonuses in retaliation for their criticisms of institutional policies. The district court dismissed the case on grounds that the award of smaller bonuses was not an adverse employment action; the appellate court, in an opinion by Judge Posner, reversed. The court's opinion explained that proof of an adverse employment action is an appropriate component of a Title VII employment discrimination claim but not of a First Amendment free speech claim; employees asserting free speech claims need only show that some institutional action had inhibited their exercise of free expression: "Any deprivation under color of law that is likely to deter the exercise of free speech, whether by an employee or anyone else, is actionable . . . if the circumstances are such as to make a refusal an effective deterrent to the exercise of a fragile liberty"(226 F.3d at 820). This "deterrence" test is apparently objective in that it depends on whether, in the particular circumstances of the case, the average reasonable person would be deterred by the challenged action—not on whether the person asserting First Amendment rights was or would have been deterred in the particular circumstances (see, for example, *Davis v. Goord,* 320 F.3d 346, 352–54 (2d Cir. 2003)).

In *United States v. National Treasury Employees Union,* 513 U.S. 454 (1995) (the *NTEU* case), the U.S. Supreme Court itself carved out a category of public employee speech cases to which *Pickering/Connick* does not apply. In the course of invalidating a federal statute that prohibited federal employees from receiving honoraria for writing and speaking activities undertaken on their own time, the Court developed an important distinction between: (1) cases involving "a *post hoc* analysis of one employee's speech and its impact on that employee's professional responsibilities," and (2) cases involving a "sweeping statutory impediment to speech that potentially involves many employees." In the first type of case, the employee challenges an employer's "adverse action taken in response to actual speech," while in the second type of case the employee challenges a statute or administrative regulation that "chills potential speech before it happens" (513 U.S. at 459–60). The *Pickering/Connick* balancing test applies to the first type of case but not to the second. This is because the second type of case "gives rise to far more serious concerns" than does the first. Thus, "the Government's burden is greater with respect to [a] statutory restriction on expression" (the second type of case), than it is "with respect to an isolated disciplinary action" (the first type of case). To meet this greater burden of justification, the Government must take into account the interests of "present and future employees in a broad range of present and future expression," as well as the interests of "potential audiences" that have a "right to read and hear what the employees would otherwise have written and said" (513 U.S. at 468, 470); and must demonstrate that those interests "are outweighed by that expression's 'necessary impact on the actual operation' of the Government" (513 U.S. at 468, quoting *Pickering,* 391 U.S. at 571).

The critical distinction that the Court made in the *NTEU* case—the distinction between a "single supervisory decision" and a "statutory impediment to speech"—seems compatible with the Court's earlier analysis in *Keyishian v. Board of Regents,* 385 U.S. 589 (1967) (discussed in subsection 7.1.4 below). Both *NTEU* and *Keyishian* are concerned with statutes or administrative regulations that limit the speech of a broad range of government employees, rather than with a particular disciplinary decision of a particular administrator. Both cases also focus on the meaning and application of the statute or regulation itself, rather than on the motives and concerns of a particular employer at a particular workplace. And both cases focus on the special problems that arise under the First Amendment when a statute or regulation "chills potential speech before it happens" (513 U.S. at 468). Given these clear parallels, the *NTEU* case has apparently laid the foundation for a merger of the *Keyishian* case and the *Pickering/Connick* line of cases as they apply to large-scale faculty free expression disputes, particularly academic freedom disputes. The two cases, in tandem, would apply particularly to external conflicts arising under a state or federal statute or administrative regulation that is alleged to impinge upon the free expression, or academic freedom, of many faculty members at various institutions (see subsection 7.1.5 below). But they would also appear to apply to internal conflicts involving a college's or university's written policy that applies broadly to all or most faculty members of the institution. The case of *Crue v. Aiken,* 370 F.3d 668 (7th Cir. 2004), provides an example of the latter type of application of *NTEU.* There the court majority applied *NTEU* analysis to invalidate a chancellor's "preclearance directive" applicable to all faculty and staff of the institution (370 F.3d at 678–80); while a dissenting judge argued that the *Pickering/Connick* line, and not *NTEU,* provided the applicable test (370 F.3d at 682–88). (For discussion of *Crue v. Aiken,* see Section 10.4.3.)

In addition to the *Pickering/Connick* line of cases and *NTEU,* the cases on the "public forum" doctrine might also be invoked as a basis for some faculty free speech claims. While the public forum doctrine is often applied to free speech problems concerning students (see Section 9.5.2), however, it will only occasionally apply to the analysis of faculty free speech rights on campus. The mere fact that campus facilities are open to employees as workspace does not make the space a designated public forum or limited designated forum. In *Tucker v. State of California Department of Education,* 97 F.3d 1204, 1209, 1214–15, the court held that employer offices and workspaces are not public forums. Similarly, in *Bishop v. Aronov,* 926 F.2d 1066, 1071 (11th Cir. 1991), and *Linnemeir v. Board of Trustees, Indiana University-Purdue University,* 260 F.3d 757, 759–60 (7th Cir. 2001), the courts declined to consider classrooms to be public forums during class time; and in *Piarowski v. Illinois Community College District,* 759 F.2d 625 (7th Cir. 1985), the court declined to apply public forum analysis to a campus art gallery used for displaying the works of faculty members. On the other hand, for certain other types of property, the institution may have opened the property for faculty members, the academic community, or the general public to use for their own personal expressive purposes. In such circumstances, the institution will have created a designated forum, and faculty members will have the same First Amendment rights of access as other persons to whom the property is open. In *Giebel v. Sylvester*, 244 F.3d 1182 (9th Cir. 2001), for example, the court considered certain bulletin boards on a state university's campus to be designated public forums open to the public.

In addition to their free expression rights, faculty members at public institutions also have a right to freedom of association under the First Amendment. Public employees, for example, are free to join (or not join) a political party and to adopt whatever political views and beliefs they choose (*Branti v. Finkel*, 445 U.S. 507 (1980)). They cannot be denied employment, terminated, or denied a promotion or raise due to their political affiliations or beliefs (*Rutan v. Republican Party of Illinois*, 497 U.S. 62 (1990)). Nor are these associational rights limited to political organizations and viewpoints; public employees may also join (or not join), subscribe to the beliefs of, and participate in social, economic, and other organizations (see *NAACP v. Button*, 371 U.S. 415 (1963)). Since these rights extend fully to faculty members (see *Jirau-Bernal v. Agrait*, 37 F.3d. 1 (1st Cir. 1994)), they may—like other public employees—join organizations of their choice and participate as private citizens in their activities. Moreover, public employers, including institutions of higher education, may not require employees to affirm by oath that they will not join or participate in the activities of particular organizations. (See generally, William Van Alstyne, "The Constitutional Rights of Teachers and Professors," 1970 *Duke L.J.* 841.) In *Cole v. Richardson*, 405 U.S. 676 (1972), however, the U.S. Supreme Court did uphold an oath that included a general commitment to "uphold and defend" the U.S. Constitution and a commitment to "oppose the overthrow of the government . . . by force, violence, or by any illegal or unconstitutional method." The Court upheld the second commitment's constitutionality only by reading it narrowly as merely "a commitment not to use illegal and constitutionally unprotected force to change the constitutional system." So interpreted, the second commitment "does not expand the obligation of the first [commitment]."

Public employees and faculty members also have other constitutional rights that are related to and supportive of their free expression and free association rights under the First Amendment. The petition clause of the First Amendment,[3] for example, may protect faculty members from retaliation if they file grievances or lawsuits against the institution or its administrators. (See *San Filippo v. Bongiovanni*, 30 F.3d 424 (3rd Cir. 1994).) And the Fourth Amendment search and seizure clause provides faculty members some protection for teaching and research materials, and other files, that they keep in their offices. In *O'Connor v. Ortega*, 480 U.S. 709 (1987), for example, the Court used the Fourth Amendment to protect an employee who was in charge of training physicians in the

---

[3]The petition clause prohibits government from "abridging . . . the right of the people . . . to petition the Government for a redress of grievances."

psychiatric residency program at a state hospital. Hospital officials had searched his office. The Court determined that public employees may have reasonable expectations of privacy in their offices, desks, and files; and that these expectations may, in certain circumstances, be protected by the Fourth Amendment. A plurality of the Justices, however, asserted that an employer's warrantless search of such property would nevertheless be permissible if it is done for "noninvestigatory, work-related purposes" or for "investigations of work-related misconduct," and if it meets "the standard of reasonableness under all the circumstances."[4]

7.1.2. Academic freedom: Basic concepts and distinctions. Faculty

academic freedom claims are often First Amendment freedom of expression claims; they thus may draw upon the same free expression principles as are set out in subsection 7.1.1 above. Academic freedom claims may also be based, however, on unique applications of First Amendment free expression principles, on constitutional rights other than freedom of expression, or on principles of contract law. The distinction between public and private institutions applicable to free expression claims (subsection 7.1.1 above) applies equally to academic freedom claims. Similarly, as is also the case for First Amendment freedom of expression claims, neither tenure, nor a particular faculty rank, nor even full-time status, is a legal prerequisite for faculty academic freedom claims. (See generally Ralph Brown & Jordan Kurland, "Academic Tenure and Academic Freedom," 53 *Law & Contemp. Probs.* 325 (1993); J. Peter Byrne, "Academic Freedom of Part-Time Faculty," 27 *J. Coll. & Univ. Law* 583 (2001).)

Academic freedom traditionally has been considered to be an essential aspect of American higher education. (See generally Walter Metzger, *The American Concept of Academic Freedom in Formation* (Arno, 1977).) It has been a major determinant of the missions of higher educational institutions, both public and private, and a major factor in shaping the roles of faculty members as well as students. Yet the concept of academic freedom eludes precise definition. It draws meaning from both the world of education and the world of law. In the education, or professional, version of academic freedom, educators usually use the term with reference to the custom and practice, and the aspirations, by which faculties may best flourish in their work as teachers and researchers (see, for example, the "1940 Statement of Principles on Academic Freedom and Tenure" of the American Association of University Professors (AAUP), discussed below in this section and found in *AAUP Policy Documents and Reports* (9th ed., 2001), 3–10). In the law, or legal version, lawyers and judges usually use "academic freedom" as a catchall term to describe the legal rights and responsibilities of the teaching profession, and courts usually attempt to define these rights by reconciling basic constitutional law or contract law principles with prevailing views of academic freedom's intellectual and social role in American life.

---

[4]Related cases are collected in Ralph V. Seep, Annot., "Warrantless Search by Government Employer of Employee's Workplace, Locker, Desk, or the Like as Violation of Fourth Amendment Privacy Rights—Federal Cases," 91 A.L.R. Fed. 226.

(See generally Walter P. Metzger, "Profession and Constitution: Two Definitions of Academic Freedom in America," 66 *Texas L. Rev.* 1265 (1988).)

More broadly, academic freedom refers not only to the prerogatives and rights of faculty members but also to the prerogatives and rights of students. Student academic freedom is explored in Section 8.1.4 of this book.[5] In addition, especially for the legal version of academic freedom, the term increasingly is used to refer to the rights and interests of institutions themselves, as in "institutional academic freedom" or "institutional autonomy." This third facet of academic freedom is explored in subsection 7.1.6 below.[6]

In the realm of law and courts (the primary focus of this chapter), yet another distinction regarding academic freedom must be made: the distinction between constitutional law and contract law. Though courts usually discuss academic freedom in cases concerning the constitutional rights of faculty members, the legal boundaries of academic freedom are initially defined by contract law. (See generally Jim Jackson, "Express and Implied Contractual Rights to Academic Freedom in the United States," 22 *Hamline L. Rev.* 467 (1999).) Faculty members possess whatever academic freedom is guaranteed them under the faculty contract (see Section 6.1)—either an individual contract or (in some cases) a collective bargaining agreement. The "1940 Statement of Principles on Academic Freedom and Tenure," AAUP's 1970 "Interpretive Comments" on this Statement, and AAUP's 1982 "Recommended Institutional Regulations on Academic Freedom and Tenure" (all included in *AAUP Policy Documents and Reports,* 3–10, 21–30) are sometimes incorporated-by-reference into faculty contracts, and it is crucial for administrators to determine whether this has been done—or should be done—with respect to all or any of these documents. For any document that has been incorporated, courts will interpret and enforce its terms by reference to contract law principles. Even when these documents have not been incorporated into the contract, they may be an important source of the "academic custom and usage" that courts will consider in interpreting unclear contract terms (see generally Section 6.2.3).

Contract law limits both public and private institutions' authority over their faculty members. Public institutions' authority is also limited by constitutional concepts of academic freedom, as discussed below, and sometimes also by state statutes or administrative regulations on academic freedom. But in private institutions, the faculty contract, perhaps supplemented by academic custom and usage, may be the only legal restriction on administrators' authority to limit faculty academic freedom. In private religious institutions, the institution's special religious mission may add additional complexities to contract law's application to academic freedom problems (see, for example, the *Curran* case discussed in Section 6.1.5 and the *McEnroy* case discussed in Section 7.8 below). For instance, the establishment and free exercise clauses of the First Amendment

---

[5]For students, as for faculty members, there is both an education version of academic freedom and a law, or legal, version.

[6]As discussed in subsection 7.1.6, "institutional academic freedom" is in some circumstances a misnomer and an inappropriate usage.

may limit the capacity of the courts to entertain lawsuits against religious institutions brought by faculty members alleging breach of contract (see, for example, the *Welter* and *Alicea* cases discussed in Section 6.1.5).

Constitutional principles of academic freedom have developed in two stages, each occupying a distinct time period and including distinct types of cases. The earlier stage, in the 1950s and 1960s, included the cases on faculty and institutional freedom from interference by external (extramural) governmental bodies. These earlier cases pitted faculties and their institutions against a state legislature or state agency—the external conflict paradigm of academic freedom (see subsection 7.1.5 below). In the later stage, covering the 1970s and 1980s, the cases focused primarily on faculty freedom from institutional intrusion—the internal conflict paradigm. (See generally William Van Alstyne, "Academic Freedom and the First Amendment in the Supreme Court of the United States: An Unhurried Historical Review," 53 *Law & Contemp. Probs.* 79 (1990).) These later cases pitted faculty members against their institutions—thus illustrating the clash between faculty academic freedom and institutional prerogatives often referred to as "institutional academic freedom" or "institutional autonomy." Both lines of cases have continued to the present, and both retain high importance, but the more recent academic freedom cases based on the second stage of developments (internal conflicts) have been much more numerous than those based on the first stage of developments (external conflicts). Developments in the first years of the twenty-first century suggest, however, that the external conflicts cases are becoming more numerous and are attracting much more attention than they have since the 1950s and 1960s (see subsection 7.1.5 below).

7.1.3. Professional versus legal concepts of academic freedom.
The education, or professional, version of academic freedom is based on "professional" concepts, as distinguished from the "legal" concepts discussed later in this subsection. The professional concept of academic freedom finds its expression in the professional norms of the academy, which are in turn grounded in academic custom and usage. The most recognized and most generally applicable professional norms are those promulgated by the American Association of University Professors. Most of these norms appear in AAUP standards, statements, and reports that are collected in *AAUP Policy Documents and Reports* (2001). This publication, called "The Redbook," is available in a print version and also online on the AAUP's Web site, at http://www.aaup.org/statements/Redbook/.

The national academic community's commitment to academic freedom as a core value was formally documented in the "1915 Declaration of Principles on Academic Freedom and Academic Tenure," promulgated by the AAUP and currently reprinted in *AAUP Policy Documents and Reports,* pages 292–301. (See generally Neil Hamilton, "Academic Tradition and the Principles of Professional Conduct," 27 *J. Coll & Univ. Law* 609, 625–28 (2001).) The 1915 Declaration emphasized the importance of academic freedom to higher education and recognized two components of academic freedom: the teachers' freedom to teach and the students' freedom to learn. Twenty-five years later, the concept of academic freedom was further explicated, and its critical importance reaffirmed, in the "1940 Statement of Principles on Academic Freedom and Tenure" (*AAUP Policy Documents and Reports,* 3–10), developed by the AAUP in conjunction with the Association of American Colleges and Universities and subsequently endorsed by more than 185 educational and professional associations. (See generally Walter P. Metzger, "The 1940 Statement of Principles on Academic Freedom and Tenure," 53 *Law & Contemp. Probs.* 3 (1990).) The 1940 Statement emphasizes that "[i]nstitutions of higher education are conducted for the common good. . . . The common good depends upon the free search for the truth and its free exposition. Academic freedom is essential to these purposes . . ." (*AAUP Policy Documents and Reports,* 3).

The 1940 Statement then identifies three key aspects of faculty academic freedom: the teacher's "freedom in research and in the publication of the results"; the teacher's "freedom in the classroom in discussing [the subject matter of the course]"; and the teacher's freedom to speak or write "as a citizen," as "a member of a learned profession," and as "an officer of an educational institution." These freedoms are subject to various "duties correlative with rights" and "special obligations" imposed on the faculty member (*AAUP Policy Documents and Reports,* 3, 4; see generally Hamilton, above, at 634–52).

In 1970, following extensive debate within the American higher education community, the AAUP reaffirmed the 1940 Statement and augmented it with a series of interpretive comments (1970 "Interpretive Comments," *AAUP Policy Documents and Reports,* 4–9). In addition, in 1957 the AAUP promulgated and adopted the first version of its "Recommended Institutional Regulations on Academic Freedom and Tenure," subsequently revised at various times, most recently in 1999 (*AAUP Policy Documents and Reports,* 21–30). Regulation No. 9, on academic freedom, provides that "[a]ll members of the faculty, whether tenured or not, are entitled to academic freedom as set forth in the *1940 Statement of Principles on Academic Freedom and Tenure* . . ." (*AAUP Policy Documents and Reports,* 28).

The AAUP documents articulate academic national norms that evidence *national* custom and usage on academic freedom. Professional norms, however, are also embodied in the regulations, policies, and custom and usage of individual institutions. These institutional norms may overlap or coincide with national norms, especially if they incorporate or track AAUP statements. But institutional norms may also be local norms adapted to the particular institution's character and mission or that of some particular organization with which the institution is affiliated. Whether national or local, professional academic freedom norms are enforced through the internal procedures of individual institutions. In more egregious or intractable cases, or cases of broad professional interest that implicate national norms, AAUP investigations and censure actions (see generally Section 14.5 of this book) may also become part of the enforcement process.

The legal version of academic freedom, in contrast to the professional version, is based on legal concepts that find their expression in legal norms enunciated by the courts. These legal norms, by definition, have the force of law and thus are binding on institutions and faculty members in a way that professional norms are not.[7] In this sense, the distinction between legal norms of academic freedom and professional norms is similar to the broader distinction between law and policy (see Section 1.7). The primary source of legal norms of academic freedom is the decisions of the federal and state courts. These decisions are based primarily on federal constitutional law and on the common law of contract of the various states. (The foundational constitutional law principles are outlined in subsection 7.1.4 below.) Legal norms are enforced through litigation and court orders, as well as through negotiations that the parties undertake to avoid the filing of a lawsuit or to settle a lawsuit before the court has rendered any decision.

Trends from the 1970s to the present suggest that, overall, there has been relatively too little emphasis on the professional norms of academic freedom within individual institutions and relatively too much emphasis on the legal norms. The time may be ripe for faculty members and their institutions to reclaim the classical heritage of professional academic freedom and recommit themselves to elucidating and supporting the professional norms within their campus communities. (See Neil Hamilton, "Buttressing the Neglected Traditions of Academic Freedom," 22 *Wm. Mitchell L. Rev.* 549 (1996).) Such developments would increase the likelihood that litigation could be reserved for more extreme cases where there has been recalcitrance and adamant refusals to respect academic customs and usages, national or institutional; and for cases where there is deep conflict between faculty academic freedom and "institutional" academic freedom, or between faculty academic freedom and student academic freedom. (See Robert O'Neil, ". . . But Litigation Is the Wrong Response," *Chron. Higher Educ.*, August 1, 2003, B9; and Robert O'Neil, "Academic Freedom and the Constitution," 11 *J. Coll. & Univ. Law* 275, 289–90 (1984).) The law and the courts could then draw the outer boundaries of academic freedom, providing correctives in extreme cases (see, for example, Section 7.1.4 below); while institutions and the professoriate would do the day-by-day and year-by-year work of creating and maintaining an environment supportive of academic freedom on their own campuses.

7.1.4. The foundational constitutional law cases.

In a series of cases in the 1950s and 1960s, the U.S. Supreme Court gave academic freedom constitutional status under the First Amendment freedoms of speech and association, and to a lesser extent under the Fourteenth Amendment guarantee of procedural due process. The opinions in these cases include a number of ringing declarations on the importance of academic freedom. In *Sweezy v. New Hampshire*, 354 U.S. 234 (1957), both Chief Justice Warren's plurality opinion and Justice Frankfurter's concurring opinion lauded academic freedom in the course of reversing a contempt judgment against a professor who had refused to answer the state attorney general's questions concerning a lecture delivered

---

[7]As suggested above in this subsection, professional norms may sometimes be converted into legal norms by being incorporated into a faculty contract or by being used as academic custom and usage that fills in gaps in a faculty contract.

at the state university. The Chief Justice, writing for a plurality of four Justices, stated that:

> to summon a witness and compel him, against his will, to disclose the nature of his past expressions and associations is a measure of governmental interference in these matters. These are rights which are safeguarded by the Bill of Rights and the Fourteenth Amendment. We believe that there unquestionably was an invasion of petitioner's liberties in the area of academic freedom and political expression— areas in which the government should be extremely reticent to tread.
>
> The essentiality of freedom in the community of American universities is almost self-evident. . . . Teachers and students must always remain free to inquire, to study and to evaluate, to gain new maturity and understanding; otherwise our civilization will stagnate and die [354 U.S. at 250].

Justice Frankfurter, writing for himself and Justice Harlan, made what has now become the classical statement on "the four essential freedoms" of the university:

> It is the business of a university to provide that atmosphere which is most conducive to speculation, experiment and creation. It is an atmosphere in which there prevail "the four essential freedoms" of a university—to determine for itself on academic grounds who may teach, what may be taught, how it shall be taught, and who may be admitted to study [354 U.S. at 263, quoting a conference statement issued by scholars from the Union of South Africa].

In *Shelton v. Tucker*, 364 U.S. 479 (1960), the Court invalidated a state statute that compelled public school and college teachers to reveal all organizational affiliations or contributions for the previous five years. In its reasoning, the Court emphasized:

> The vigilant protection of constitutional freedoms is nowhere more vital than in the community of American schools. "By limiting the power of the states to interfere with freedom of speech and freedom of inquiry and freedom of association, the Fourteenth Amendment protects all persons, no matter what their calling. But, in view of the nature of the teacher's relation to the effective exercise of the rights which are safeguarded by the Bill of Rights and by the Fourteenth Amendment, inhibition of freedom of thought, and of action upon thought, in the case of teachers brings the safeguards of those amendments vividly into operation. Such unwarranted inhibition upon the free spirit of teachers . . . has an unmistakable tendency to chill that free play of the spirit which all teachers ought especially to cultivate and practice; it makes for caution and timidity in their associations by potential teachers" [364 U.S. at 487, quoting *Wieman v. Updegraff*, 344 U.S. 183, 195 (1952) (Frankfurter, J., concurring)].

In *Griswold v. Connecticut*, 381 U.S. 479 (1965), the Court majority of six, in an opinion by Justice Douglas, stated that:

> the State may not, consistently with the spirit of the First Amendment, contract the spectrum of available knowledge. The right of freedom of speech and press includes not only the right to utter or to print, but the right to

distribute, the right to receive, the right to read and freedom of inquiry, freedom
of thought, and freedom to teach—indeed the freedom of the entire university
community. Without those *peripheral rights* the specific rights would be less
secure [381 U.S. at 482–83; emphasis added].

This statement is particularly important, not only for its comprehensive-
ness, but also because it focuses on "peripheral rights" under the First
Amendment. These rights—better termed "correlative rights" or "ancillary
rights"—are based on the principle that the express or core rights in the First
Amendment are also the source of other included rights that correlate with or
are ancillary to the express or core rights, and without which the core rights
could not be fully protected. This principle is an important theoretical underpinning for the concept of academic freedom under the First Amendment. Academic freedom correlates to the express rights of free speech and press in the
specific context of academia. The rights of speech and press, in other words,
cannot be effectively protected in the college and university environment
unless academic freedom, as a corollary of free speech and press, is also recognized. This correlative rights argument is closely related to the argument
for implied rights under the First Amendment and other constitutional guarantees. Since it is generally accepted that the First Amendment is the source
of an implied right of freedom of association (see, for example, *NAACP v.
Alabama ex rel. Patterson*, 357 U.S. 449 (1958)), and since implied rights are
recognized under other constitutional guarantees (see, for example, *Zablocki
v. Redhail*, 434 U.S. 374 (1978), recognizing the right to marry as an implied
right under the due process clause), there is considerable support, beyond
Griswold, for a correlative or implied right to academic freedom under the First
Amendment.

And in *Keyishian v. Board of Regents*, 385 U.S. 589 (1967), the Court quoted
both *Sweezy* and *Shelton*, and added:

Our nation is deeply committed to safeguarding academic freedom, which
is of transcendent value to all of us and not merely to the teachers concerned.
That freedom is therefore *a special concern of the First Amendment,* which
does not tolerate laws that cast a pall of orthodoxy over the classroom. . . .
The classroom is peculiarly the "marketplace of ideas." The Nation's future
depends upon leaders trained through wide exposure to that robust exchange
of ideas which discovers truth "out of a multitude of tongues, [rather] than
through any kind of authoritative selection" . . . [385 U.S. at 603; emphasis
added].[8]

Keyishian is the centerpiece of the formative 1950s and 1960s cases. The
appellants were State University of New York faculty members who refused to

---

[8]These strong statements of support for academic freedom did not stop with *Keyishian,* and they
are not merely relics of the past. In *Rosenberger v. Rector & Visitors of University of Virginia*, 515
U.S. 819 (1995), for example, and again in *Grutter v. Bollinger*, 539 U.S. 306 (2003), the Court
issued glowing statements on the importance of academic freedom to American higher education.
See 515 U.S. at 835–36; 539 U.S. at 329.

sign a certificate (the "Feinberg Certificate") stating that they were not and never had been Communists. This certificate was required under a set of laws and regulations designed to prevent "subversives" from obtaining employment in the state's educational system. The faculty members brought a First Amendment challenge against the certificate requirements and the underlying law barring employment to members of subversive organizations, as well as other provisions authorizing dismissal for the "utterance of any treasonable or seditious word or words or the doing of any treasonable or seditious act," and for "by word of mouth or writing wilfully and deliberately advocating, advising, or teaching the doctrine of forceful overthrow of the government."

The Court held that the faculty members' First Amendment freedom of association had been violated by the existence and application of this series of laws and rules that were both vague and overbroad (see Section 6.6.1 regarding the vagueness and overbreadth doctrines). The word "seditious" was held to be unconstitutionally vague, even when defined as advocacy of criminal anarchy:

> [T]he possible scope of "seditious utterances or acts" has virtually no limit. For under Penal Law § 161, one commits the felony of advocating criminal anarchy if he "publicly displays any book . . . containing or advocating, advising or teaching the doctrine that organized government should be overthrown by force, violence, or other unlawful means." Does the teacher who carries a copy of the Communist Manifesto on a public street thereby advocate criminal anarchy? . . . The teacher cannot know the extent, if any, to which a "seditious" utterance must transcend mere statement about abstract doctrine, the extent to which it must be intended to and tend to indoctrinate or incite to action in furtherance of the defined doctrine. The crucial consideration is that no teacher can know just where the line is drawn between "seditious" and nonseditious utterances and acts [385 U.S. at 598–99].

The Court also found that the state's entire system of "intricate administrative machinery" was

> a highly efficient *in terrorem* mechanism. . . . It would be a bold teacher who would not stay as far as possible from utterances or acts which might jeopardize his living by enmeshing him in this intricate machinery. . . . The result may be to stifle "that free play of the spirit which all teachers ought especially to cultivate and practice" [385 U.S. at 601, quoting *Wieman v. Updegraff,* 344 U.S. 183, 195 (Frankfurter, J., concurring)].

Noting that "the stifling effect on the academic mind from curtailing freedom of association in such a manner is manifest," the Court rejected the older case of *Adler v. Board of Education,* 342 U.S. 485 (1951), which permitted New York to bar employment to teachers who were members of listed subversive organizations. In its place, the Court adopted this rule:

> Mere knowing membership without a specific intent to further the unlawful aims of an organization is not a constitutionally adequate basis for exclusion from such positions as those held by appellants. . . . Legislation which sanctions

membership unaccompanied by specific intent to further the unlawful goals of the organization or which is not active membership violates constitutional limitations [385 U.S. at 606, 608].

One year after *Keyishian,* the Supreme Court decided *Pickering v. Board of Education,* 391 U.S. 563 (1968), and thus stepped gingerly into a new line of cases that would become the basis for the second stage of academic freedom's development in the courts. This line of cases, now called "the *Pickering/ Connick* line," centers on the free speech rights of all public employees, not merely faculty members, and is therefore addressed in subsection 7.1.1 above.

In addition to its reliance on free speech and press, and procedural due process, the U.S. Supreme Court has also tapped into the First Amendment's religion clauses to develop supplementary protection for academic freedom. In *Epperson v. Arkansas,* 393 U.S. 97 (1968), and again in *Edwards v. Aguillard,* 482 U.S. 578 (1987), the Court used the establishment clause (see Section 1.6 of this book) to strike down state statutes that interfered with public school teachers' teaching of evolution. (See A. Morris, "Fundamentalism, Creationism, and the First Amendment," 41 *West's Educ. Law Rptr.* 1 (1987).) And in *O'Connor v. Ortega,* discussed in subsection 7.1.1 above, the U.S. Supreme Court used the Fourth Amendment's search and seizure clause in protecting an academic employee's office and his papers from warrantless searches. Similar Fourth Amendment issues are increasingly arising concerning electronic and digital records (see Martha McCaughey, "Windows Without Curtains: Computer Privacy and Academic Freedom," *Academe,* September–October 2003, 39–42). If faculty members' academic writings, research results, or other research materials are stored in their offices or laboratories on their own computer disks or on the hard drive of a computer they own, there may be an expectation of privacy, and thus a level of Fourth Amendment protection, similar to that in *O'Connor v. Ortega.* But if the writings or materials are stored on the hard drive of a computer that the institution (or the state) owns, or stored on the institution's network, the expectation of privacy and the Fourth Amendment protection will likely depend on the terms of the institution's computer use policies. (See, for example, Robert O'Neil, "Who Owns Professors' E-Mail Messages?" *Chron. Higher Educ.,* June 25, 2004, B9 (special legal issues supp.).)[9]

The lower federal and state courts have had many occasions to apply U.S. Supreme Court precedents to a variety of academic freedom disputes pitting faculty members against their institutions. The source of law most frequently invoked in these cases is the First Amendment's free speech clause, as interpreted in the *Pickering/Connick* line of cases. Some cases have also relied on *Keyishian* and its forerunners, either in lieu of or as a supplement to the *Pickering/Connick* line. The legal principles that the courts have developed based on these two lines of

---

[9]The Web site of the Electronic Privacy Information Center, available at http://www.epic.org/ privacy/workplace, contains current information on electronic privacy in the workplace and numerous sources to consult for further information.

cases, however, are not as protective of faculty academic freedom as the Supreme Court's declarations in the 1950s and 1960s cases might have suggested. As could be expected, the courts have focused on the specific facts of each case and have reached varying conclusions based on the facts, the particular court's disposition on liberal versus strict construction of First Amendment protections, and its sensitivities to the nuances of academic freedom. Sections 7.2 through 7.5 below provide analysis and case examples in four broad areas of concern, and Sections 7.6 through 7.8 address some additional special problems.

7.1.5. *External versus internal restraints on academic freedom.*

As indicated in subsection 7.1.2 above, there are two paradigms for academic freedom conflicts: they may be either external ("extramural") or internal ("intramural"). The first type of conflict occurs when a government body *external* to the institution has allegedly impinged upon the institution's academic freedom or that of its faculty or students (see Robert O'Neil, "Academic Freedom and the Constitution," 11 *J. Coll. & Univ. Law* 275, 276–83 (1984)). The second type of conflict occurs when the institution or its administrators have allegedly impinged upon the academic freedom of one or more of the institution's faculty members or students.[10] The means of infringement, the competing interests, and, to some extent, the applicable law may differ from one type of conflict to the other. The first type of conflict, or case, is usually controlled by the *Keyishian* line of cases (see subsection 7.1.4 above) or by the *NTEU* case that is an offshoot of *Pickering/Connick* analysis (see subsection 7.1.1 above); the second type of conflict is usually controlled by the *Pickering/Connick* line of cases.

The primary source of law involved in external conflicts is likely to be the First Amendment—not only free speech and free press, but also freedom of association and freedom of religion. If the conflict were between a government body and a private institution, the institution would have its own First Amendment rights to assert against the government, as would its faculty members (and its students, as the case may be). If the conflict were between a government body and a public institution, the institution's faculty members (and students, as the case may be) could assert their First Amendment rights against the government; but the public institution itself would not have its own constitutional rights to assert, since it is an arm of government. (It could, however, assert and support the rights of its faculty members and/or students.)

The government body that allegedly interferes with academic freedom could be: (1) a state legislature, as in the *Keyishian* case and the *Epperson* and *Edwards* cases (see subsection 7.1.4 above) and *Urofsky v. Gilmore* (discussed in Section 7.3 below); (2) a state legislative committee; (3) a state attorney general, as in the

---

[10]Such infringement can occur in overt and formal ways, as in most of the cases in Sections 7.2 to 7.5 below, or in covert and informal ways that may be too amorphous to be legally redressable. For examples of the latter type of impingement, see Alison Schneider, "The Academic Path to Pariah Status: Personal Disputes and Controversial Research Lead Some Scholars to Be Shunned by Colleagues," *Chron. Higher Educ.*, July 2, 1999, A12.

Sweezy case (see subsection 7.1.4 above); (4) a grant-making agency, such as the National Institutes of Health in *Board of Trustees of Stanford University v. Sullivan* (see Section 7.7.2 below) or the National Endowment for the Arts in the *Finley* case (see Section 13.4.6; and see generally Christopher Myers, "Many Colleges Deplore Anti-obscenity Pledge, but Most Accept U.S. Arts Grants Anyway," *Chron. Higher Educ.*, July 11, 1990, A1); (5) a regulatory agency, such as the federal Equal Employment Opportunity Commission (EEOC) in *University of Pennsylvania v. EEOC* (see Section 7.7.1 below); (6) a grand jury, as in *Hammond v. Brown*, 323 F. Supp 326 (N.D. Ohio 1971), *affirmed* 450 F.2d 480 (6th Cir. 1971); (7) a city police department, as in *White v. Davis*, 533 P.2d 222 (Cal. 1975) (see Section 11.5); or (8) a court, as in some of the cases discussed in Section 7.7 below (see also *Kay v. Board of Higher Education*, 18 N.Y.S.2d 821 (N.Y. 1940) (the Bertrand Russell case)).

External or extramural academic freedom conflicts may also involve *private* bodies external to the institution that allegedly interfere with the academic freedom of the institution or its faculty members (or students). The external private body may be a foundation or other funding organization (see, for example, Erin Strout, "Provosts Object to Language Added to Foundations' Grant Agreements," *Chron. Higher Educ.*, May 14, 2004, A29); a religious organization or informal group of religious persons, as in the *Linnemeir* case discussed below; a political interest group, as in some of the "political correctness" examples discussed below; or a group of taxpayers as in the *Yacovelli* case discussed below. If it is a private body that infringes upon academic freedom, neither the institution nor its faculty members may assert constitutional claims against that body, except in the unusual case where the private body is engaged in state actions (see Section 1.5.2).

From the 1970s through the end of the twentieth century, internal academic freedom conflicts arose much more frequently than did external conflicts, at least in terms of litigation that resulted in published opinions of the courts. This ascendance of internal conflicts, at least in public institutions, was probably fueled by the U.S. Supreme Court's decision in the *Pickering* case (see subsection 7.1.1), which provided a conceptual base upon which faculty members could assert free expression claims against their institutions. In the early years of the twenty-first century, however, external conflicts became more frequent and more visible, and commanded considerably more attention from practitioners, scholars, courts, and the media. (See, for example, Mary Burgan, "Academic Freedom in a World of Moral Crises," *Chron. Higher Educ.*, September 6, 2002, B20.) The impetus for this reemergence apparently came primarily from two developments. One was the escalating terrorism marked by the disasters of September 11, 2001, which led to the USA PATRIOT Act, 115 Stat. 272 (2001), and other federal statutes and regulations that substantially impact America's campuses. (See generally "Academic Freedom and National Security in a Time of Crisis: A Report of the AAUP's Special Committee," *Academe*, November–December 2003, 34–59.) The other development was a resurgence of the "political correctness" phenomenon,[11] in particular emphasizing allegations of political, ethnic, and religious bias or favoritism, on America's campuses.

---

[11]For background, see generally Paul Berman (ed.), *Debating P.C.: The Controversy over Political Correctness on College Campuses* (Dell, 1992).

Regarding the first development, the PATRIOT Act has been a focal point of concern. (See Section 13.2.4 of this book for a general discussion of the PATRIOT Act.) The Act permits federal investigators to access various private communications, including those of faculty members, undertaken by way of telephones or computer networks; and permits access into certain library records kept by libraries, including those on America's campuses. (For this aspect of the Act, see Section 13.2.12.2 of this book and "Academic Freedom and National Security," above, 38–41.) The Act also places certain restrictions on foreign students wishing to study at American colleges and universities and foreign scholars seeking to visit American colleges and universities. It has frequently been argued that some uses of these federal powers on American campuses would, by interfering with the privacy of academic communications, interfere with faculty academic freedom and institutional autonomy. (See, for example, Jonathan Cole, "The Patriot Act on Campus: Defending the University Post–9/11," *Boston Review,* Summer 2003; available at http://bostonreview.net/BR.3/cole.html.)

Another concern post–9/11 has been various federal government initiatives that restrict or potentially restrict scientific research undertaken at American colleges and universities. Some of these restrictions are in the PATRIOT Act itself; others are in regulations promulgated by various government agencies. (See Jamie Keith, "The War on Terrorism Affects the Academy: Principal Post–September 11, 2001 Federal Anti-Terrorism Statutes, Regulations, and Policies That Apply to Colleges and Universities," 30 *J. College & Univ. Law* 239 (2004).) It has frequently been argued that several of these restrictions on university research, including restrictions imposed upon the granting of federal research funds, can limit research and publication in ways that interfere with faculty academic freedom and institutional autonomy. (See, for example, Julie Norris, *Restrictions on Research Awards: Troublesome Clauses, A Report of the AAU/COGR Task Force* (March 2004), available at http://www.cogr.edu and at http://www.aau.edu; and see also "Academic Freedom and National Security," above, 34–59.)

Regarding the second development mentioned above, claims regarding racial and religious bias, there have been various challenges to college programs, events, or decisions that are said to reflect such bias. In *Linnemeir v. Board of Trustees, Indiana University-Purdue University, Fort Wayne,* 260 F.3d 757 (7th Cir. 2001), for example, state taxpayers and individual state legislators challenged the planned performance of a play that a student had selected for his senior thesis and his departmental faculty had approved. The plaintiffs argued that the play, which presented a critique of Christianity, would violate the First Amendment's establishment clause and would be offensive to many Christians. The federal district court denied the plaintiffs' motion for a preliminary injunction (155 F. Supp. 2d 1034 (N.D. Ind. 2001)), and the appellate court affirmed the denial (260 F.3d 757 (7th Cir. 2001)). Similarly, in *Yacovelli v. Moeser,* taxpayers and students challenged an orientation reading program planned for incoming students at the University of North Carolina/Chapel Hill. The plaintiffs claimed that use of the assigned book, which concerned the early history of the Islamic faith, would violate the federal establishment clause and would also be an exercise in "political correctness." At around the same time, a legislative appropriations committee of the North Carolina legislature sought to block the use of public funds for the planned orientation program. In the lawsuit, the U.S. District Court for the Middle District of North Carolina rejected the plaintiffs' challenge (August 15, 2002), and the U.S. Court of Appeals for the Fourth Circuit affirmed (August 19, 2002). (See Donna Euben, "Curriculum Matters," *Academe,* November–December 2002, 86, for discussion of this case.) Subsequently, the district court also rejected the plaintiffs' alternative argument that the program violated students' free exercise rights under the First Amendment (2004 WL 1144183 (M.D.N.C. 2004) and 324 F. Supp. 2d 760 (M.D.N.C. 2004)).

There have also been various challenges to professors' or departmental faculties' decisions regarding courses, course materials, classroom discussions, and grades. The challengers typically cite particular decisions that they claim foster indoctrination or otherwise reflect a political (usually liberal) bias. The challengers often claim that such decisions violate student academic freedom, thus adding an additional dimension of conflict to the situation—a dimension that is illustrated by the *Yacovelli* case above. For additional examples of student academic freedom claims, and challenges to faculty academic freedom, in the context of political bias disputes, see the discussion of the proposed "Academic Bill of Rights" in Section 8.1.4.

7.1.6. "Institutional" academic freedom.

As academic freedom developed, originally in Europe and then later in the United States, it had two branches: faculty academic freedom and student academic freedom. (See generally Richard Hofstader & Walter Metzger, *The Development of Academic Freedom in the United States* (Columbia University, 1955), 386–91.) But in modern parlance, articulated primarily in court decisions beginning in the early 1980s, a third type of academic freedom has joined the first two: that of the colleges and universities themselves, or "institutional academic freedom." (See, for example, *Feldman v. Ho* and *Edwards v. California University of Pennsylvania* in Section 7.2.2; *Urofsky v. Gilmore* in Section 7.3; and *University of Pennsylvania v. EEOC* in Section 7.7.) Consequently, there are now three sets of beneficiaries of academic freedom protections: faculty members, students, and individual higher educational institutions. Obviously the interests of these three groups are not always compatible with one another, therefore assuring that conflicts will arise among the various claimants of academic freedom. As the court stated in *Piarowski v. Illinois Community College,* 759 F.2d 625 (7th Cir. 1985):

> [T]he term [academic freedom] is equivocal. It is used to denote both the freedom of the academy to pursue its ends without interference from the government . . . and the freedom of the individual teacher (or in some versions—indeed in most cases—the student) to pursue his ends without interference from the academy; and these two freedoms are in conflict . . . [759 F.2d at 629].

(See generally David Rabban, "A Functional Analysis of 'Individual' and 'Institutional' Academic Freedom Under the First Amendment," 53 *Law & Contemp. Probs.* 227 (1990); and David Rabban, "Academic Freedom, Individual or Institutional?" *Academe,* November–December 2001, 16.)

Institutional academic freedom (or institutional autonomy) entails the freedom to determine who may teach, the freedom to determine what may be taught, the freedom to determine how the subject matter will be taught, and the freedom to determine who may be admitted to study. In American law and custom, these four freedoms are usually traced to Justice Felix Frankfurter's concurring opinion in *Sweezy v. New Hampshire,* 354 U.S. 234, 263 (1957) (discussed in subsection 7.1.4 above). But it was not until the case of *Regents of University of Michigan v. Ewing,* 474 U.S. 214 (1985) (further discussed in Section 9.3.2), that the U.S. Supreme Court explicitly distinguished between an institution's academic freedom and that of its faculty and students.[12] "Academic freedom," said the Court, "thrives not only on the independent and uninhibited exchange of ideas among teachers and students . . . but also, and somewhat inconsistently, on autonomous decisionmaking by the academy itself" (474 U.S. at 226 n.12). This statement on institutional academic freedom, however, is not free from ambiguity. Although the Court did recognize the "academic freedom" of "state and local educational institutions," in the very same paragraph it also focused on "the multitude of academic decisions that are made daily by faculty members of public educational institutions . . ." (474 U.S. at 226). Thus the Court may not have intended to juxtapose the interests of the institution against those of its faculty, and was apparently assuming that the defendant university was either acting through its faculty members or acting in their interest.[13] The Court's distinction between institutional academic freedom and faculty (or student) academic freedom thus does not entail a separation of the institution's interests from those of its faculty members, nor does it suggest that institutional interests must prevail over faculty interests if the two are in conflict. (See Richard Hiers, "Institutional Academic Freedom vs. Faculty Academic Freedom in Public Colleges and Universities: A Dubious Dichotomy," 29 *J. Coll. & Univ. Law* 35, 56–57, 81–82 (2002).)

The same might be said of the Court's later statement on institutional academic freedom in *Grutter v. Bollinger,* 539 U.S. 306 (2003), the University of Michigan affirmative action case (see Section 8.2.5). As in *Ewing,* the Court in *Grutter* spoke of the academic freedom or autonomy interests of the institution (539 U.S. at 324, 329).[14] But, as in *Ewing,* the Court did not separate those interests from the

---

[12]Prior to *Ewing,* Justice Powell had drawn a similar distinction in his opinion in *Regents of the University of California v. Bakke,* 438 U.S. 265, 312 (1978), but he was speaking only for himself, not for the Court.

[13]Indeed, in academic matters, institutions do not operate separately from their faculties. It is "the traditional role of deans, provosts, department heads, and faculty [to make] academic decisions," and they make "discretionary choices . . . in the contexts of hiring, tenure, curriculum selection, grants, and salaries" (*Urofsky v. Gilmore,* 216 F.3d 401, 432–33 (Wilkinson, Ch. J., concurring in result)).

[14]Interestingly, the defendant in both *Ewing* and *Grutter,* the University of Michigan, happens to be a "constitutionally based institution" (see Section 12.2.3) with the constitutional status under Michigan's state constitution. This status provides the university considerable institutional autonomy (perhaps one might also say institutional academic freedom) *as a matter of state law.* It was apparently *not* this type of autonomy that the Court had in mind in *Ewing* and *Grutter;* and there is no indication that the Court would distinguish between constitutionally based and statutorily based state institutions in applying its rulings in *Ewing* and *Grutter/Gratz.*

interests of the faculty, or pit the two sets of interests against one another, or suggest that the institutional academic freedom claims would necessarily prevail over faculty academic freedom claims. (See Richard Hiers, "Institutional Academic Freedom—A Constitutional Misconception: Did *Grutter v. Bollinger* Perpetuate the Confusion?" 30 *J. Coll.& Univ. Law* 531, 568–77 (2004).)

Had the Court in *Ewing* or *Grutter* recognized institutional academic freedom as a First Amendment right separate from that of faculty members, additional conceptual difficulties would have arisen. The institution in these cases is a public institution that, like many other public colleges and universities, is an arm of the state government. States and state governmental entities do not have federal constitutional rights (see, for example, *Native American Heritage Commission v. Board of Trustees of the California State University*, 59 Cal. Rptr.2d. 402 (1996)). According to constitutional theory, persons (that is, private individuals and private corporations)—not governments—have rights; and rights are limits on governmental power to be asserted against government, rather than extensions of government power to be asserted on the government's own behalf. (See William Kaplin, *American Constitutional Law: An Overview, Analysis, and Integration* (Carolina Academic Press, 2004), 38–40, 42–44.) Public institutions' claims of institutional academic freedom therefore cannot be federal constitutional rights claims as such. These claims are better understood as claims based on interests—"governmental interests"—that can be asserted by public institutions to defend themselves against faculty members' or students' claims that the institution has violated their individual constitutional rights. This is the actual setting in which institutional academic freedom is discussed in both *Ewing* and *Grutter*. In this context, "institutional autonomy" is a more apt descriptor of the institution's interests than is "institutional academic freedom," since the former does not have the "rights" connotation that the latter phrase has.

Public colleges and universities may assert these institutional autonomy interests not only in internal or intramural academic freedom disputes with their faculties (or students) but also in external or extramural disputes with other governmental bodies or private entities that seek to interfere with the institution's internal affairs. In the context of an external dispute, there may be no conflict between the institution's interests and those of its faculty (or its students), in which case the institution may assert its faculty's (or student body's) academic interests as well as its own autonomy interests. If the institution is a private institution, however, and it is in conflict with an agency of government, it may also assert its own First Amendment constitutional right to academic freedom (see subsection 7.1.5 above). A rights claim fits this context because a private college or university is a corporate person within the meaning of the federal Constitution and therefore may assert the same constitutional rights as a private individual may assert. This is the only context in which institutional academic freedom makes sense as a constitutional rights claim.

Sec. 7.2. Academic Freedom in Teaching

7.2.1. In general. Courts are generally reticent to become involved in academic freedom disputes concerning course content, teaching methods, grading practices, classroom demeanor, and the assignment of instructors to particular courses, viewing these matters as best left to the competence of the educators themselves and the administrators who have primary responsibility over academic affairs. Academic custom also frequently leaves such matters primarily to faculty members and their deans and department chairs (see "1940 Statement of Principles on Academic Freedom and Tenure," in *AAUP Policy Documents and Reports* (9th ed., 2001), 3–7; and "Statement on Government of Colleges and Universities," in *AAUP Policy Documents and Reports,* 217). Subsections 7.2.2 and 7.2.3 below explore the circumstances in which courts may intervene in such disputes, particularly in public institutions. Subsection 7.2.4 identifies and critiques the various types of analysis that courts may use in academic freedom cases concerning teaching. The concluding subsection (7.2.5) considers the sources and extent of protections for the freedom to teach in private institutions.

7.2.2. The classroom. Two classical cases from the early 1970s illustrate the traditional posture of judicial deference concerning classroom matters. *Hetrick v. Martin,* 480 F.2d 705 (6th Cir. 1973), concerned a state university's refusal to renew a nontenured faculty member's contract. The faculty member's troubles with the university administration apparently began when unnamed students and the parents of one student complained about certain of her in-class activities. To illustrate the "irony" and "connotative qualities" of the English language, for example, the faculty member once told her freshman students, "I am an unwed mother." At that time she was a divorced mother of two, but she did not reveal that fact to her class. On occasion she also apparently discussed the war in Vietnam and the military draft with one of her freshman classes.

The faculty member sued the university, alleging an infringement of her First Amendment rights. The court ruled that the university had not based the nonrenewal on any statements the faculty member had made but rather on her "pedagogical attitude." The faculty member believed that her students should be free to organize assignments in accordance with their own interests, while the university expected her to "go by the book." Thus, viewing the case as a dispute over teaching methods, the court refused to equate the teaching methods of professors with constitutionally protected speech:

> We do not accept plaintiff's assertion that the school administration abridged her First Amendment rights when it refused to rehire her because it considered her teaching philosophy to be incompatible with the pedagogical aims of the University. Whatever may be the ultimate scope of the amorphous "academic freedom" guaranteed to our Nation's teachers and students . . . it does not encompass the right of a nontenured teacher to have her teaching style insulated from review by her superiors . . . just because her methods and philosophy are considered acceptable somewhere in the teaching profession [480 F.2d at 709].

Clark v. Holmes, 474 F.2d 928 (7th Cir. 1972), also involved a state university's refusal to rehire a nontenured instructor due to his teaching methods and classroom behavior. Clark had been told that he could be rehired if he was willing to remedy certain deficiencies—namely, that he "counseled an excessive number of students instead of referring them to [the university's] professional counselors; he overemphasized sex in his health survey course; he counseled students with his office door closed; and he belittled other staff members in discussions with students." After discussions with his superiors, in which he defended his conduct, Clark was rehired; but in the middle of the year he was told that he would not teach in the spring semester because of these same problems.

Clark brought suit, claiming that, under the *Pickering* case (see Section 7.1 above), the university had violated his First Amendment rights by not rehiring him because of his speech activities. The court, disagreeing, refused to apply *Pickering* to this situation: (1) Clark's disputes with his colleagues about course content were not matters of public concern, as were the matters involved in *Pickering*; and (2) Clark's disputes involved him as a teacher, not as a private citizen, whereas the situation in *Pickering* was just the opposite. The court then held that the institution's interest as employer overcame any academic freedom interests the teacher may have had:

> But we do not conceive academic freedom to be a license for uncontrolled expression at variance with established curricular contents and internally destructive of the proper functioning of the institution. First Amendment rights must be applied in light of the special characteristics of the environment in the particular case (*Tinker v. Des Moines Indep. Community School Dist.*, 393 U.S. 503, 506 (1969); *Healy v. James*, 408 U.S. 169 (1972)). The plaintiff here irresponsibly made captious remarks to a captive audience, one, moreover, that was composed of students who were dependent upon him for grades and recommendations. . . .
>
> Furthermore, *Pickering* suggests that certain legitimate interests of the state may limit a teacher's right to say what he pleases: for example, (1) the need to maintain discipline or harmony among coworkers; (2) the need for confidentiality; (3) the need to curtail conduct which impedes the teacher's proper and competent performance of his daily duties; and (4) the need to encourage a close and personal relationship between the employer and his superiors, where that relationship calls for loyalty and confidence [474 F.2d at 931].

Most of the more recent cases are consistent with *Hetrick* and *Clark*. In *Wirsing v. Board of Regents of the University of Colorado*, 739 F. Supp. 551 (D. Colo. 1990), *affirmed without opinion*, 945 F.2d 412 (10th Cir. 1991), for example, a tenured professor of education taught her students "that teaching and learning cannot be evaluated by any standardized test." Consistent with these beliefs, the professor refused to administer the university's standardized course evaluation forms for her classes. The dean denied her a pay increase because of her refusal. The professor sought a court injunction ordering the regents to award her the pay increase and to desist from requiring her to use the form. She argued that standardized forms were "contrary to her theory of education" and that by forcing her to administer the forms, the university was "interfering arbitrarily with her classroom method, compelling her speech, and violating her right to academic freedom." The court rejected her argument:

> Here, the record is clear that Dr. Wirsing was not denied her merit salary increase because of her teaching methods, presentation of opinions contrary to those of the university, or otherwise presenting controversial ideas to her students. Rather, she was denied her merit increase for her refusal to comply with the University's teacher evaluation requirements. . . . [A]lthough Dr. Wirsing may have a constitutionally protected right under the First Amendment to disagree with the University's policies, she has no right to evidence her disagreement by failing to perform the duty imposed upon her as a condition of employment. *Shaw v. Board of Trustees,* 396 F. Supp. 872, 886 (D.C. Md. 1975), *aff'd,* 549 F.2d 929 (4th Cir. 1976) [739 F. Supp. at 553].

Since the professor remained free to "use the form as an example of what not to do . . . [and to] criticize openly both the [standardized] form and the University's evaluation form policy," the university's requirement was "unrelated to course content [and] in no way interferes with . . . academic freedom." Moreover, according to the court, adoption of a method of teacher evaluation "is part of the University's own right to academic freedom." Thus, in effect, the court reasoned that the university's actions did not interfere with *faculty* academic freedom and that, at any rate, the university's actions were protected by *institutional* academic freedom.[15] (See Section 7.1.6 above for more on institutional academic freedom.)

In *Martin v. Parrish,* 805 F.2d 583 (5th Cir. 1986), the court upheld the dismissal of an economics instructor at Midland College in Texas, ruling that the instructor's use of profane language in a college classroom did not fall within the scope of First Amendment protection. Applying *Connick v. Myers* (Section 7.1 above), the court held that the instructor's language did not constitute speech on "matters of public concern." The court also acknowledged the professor's claim that, apart from *Connick,* he had "a first amendment right to 'academic freedom' that permits use of the language in question," but the court summarily rejected this claim because "such language was not germane to the subject matter in his class and had no educational function" (805 F.2d at 584 n.2). In addition, the court used an alternative basis for upholding the dismissal. Applying elementary/secondary education precedents (see *Bethel School District v. Fraser,* 478 U.S. 675 (1986)), it held that the instructor's use of the language was unprotected because "it was a deliberate, superfluous attack on a 'captive audience' with no academic purpose or justification."

---

[15]In other situations, rather than challenging a requirement that he or she administer the student evaluation forms, a faculty member may challenge the institution's use of student evaluations as a means of reviewing the faculty member's classroom teaching. Assuming that the evaluations are adequately constructed and administered, and the results are accurately tabulated, a claim that use of student evaluation data infringes the faculty member's academic freedom is likely to fail. (See *Yarcheski v. Reiner,* 669 N.W.2d 487 (S.D. 2003), in which the court rejected such a claim; and see generally Section 6.6 of this book.)

In a separate opinion, a concurring judge agreed with the court majority's *Connick v. Myers* analysis but disagreed with its alternative "captive audience" analysis, on the grounds that the elementary/secondary precedents the court had invoked should not apply to higher education. The concurring judge also agreed with the majority's rejection of the professor's argument based on an independent "first amendment right to 'academic freedom.'" Like the majority, the concurring judge acknowledged the possibility of a First Amendment academic freedom argument independent of the *Pickering/Connick* line of cases (Section 7.1 above) but rejected the notion that the professor's language was within the bounds of academic freedom.[16] According to the concurring judge: "While some of [the professor's] comments arguably bear on economics and could be viewed as relevant to Martin's role as a teacher in motivating the interest of his students, his remarks *as a whole* are unrelated to economics and devoid of any educational function."

Bishop v. Aronov, 926 F.2d 1066 (11th Cir. 1991), continued the trend toward upholding institutional authority over faculty members' classroom conduct while raising new issues concerning religion and religious speech in the classroom. An exercise physiology professor, as the court explained, "occasionally referred to his religious beliefs during instructional time. . . . Some of his references concerned his understanding of the creative force behind human physiology. Other statements involved brief explanations of a philosophical approach to problems and advice to students on coping with academic stresses." He also organized an optional after-class meeting, held shortly before the final examination, to discuss "Evidences of God in Human Physiology." But "[h]e never engaged in prayer, read passages from the Bible, handed out religious tracts, or arranged for guest speakers to lecture on a religious topic during instructional time." Some students nevertheless complained about the in-class comments and the optional meeting. The university responded by sending the professor a memo requiring that he discontinue "(1) the interjection of religious beliefs and/or preferences during instructional time periods and (2) the optional classes where a 'Christian Perspective' of an academic topic is delivered." The professor challenged the university's action as violating both his freedom of speech and his freedom of religion (see generally Section 1.6.2) under the First Amendment. The district court emphasized that "the university has created a forum for students and their professors to engage in a free interchange of ideas" and granted summary judgment for the professor (732 F. Supp. 1562 (N.D. Ala. 1990)). The U.S. Court of Appeals disagreed and upheld the university's actions.

With respect to the professor's free speech claims, the appellate court, like the majority in *Martin* (above), applied recent elementary/secondary education

---

[16]For earlier appearances of this academic freedom or "germaneness" analysis, see *State Board for Community Colleges v. Olson*, 687 P.2d 429, 437 (Colo. 1984), and two classic elementary/secondary cases: *Pred v. Board of Instruction of Dade County, Florida*, 415 F.2d 851, 857 n.17 (5th Cir. 1969); and *Mailloux v. Kiley*, 323 F. Supp. 1387 (D. Mass. 1971), *affirmed on other grounds*, 448 F.2d 1242 (1st Cir. 1971). For related analysis, focusing on the problem of hate speech in the classroom, and also distinguishing between germane and nongermane comments, see J. Weinstein, "A Constitutional Roadmap to the Regulation of Campus Hate Speech," 38 *Wayne L. Rev.* 163, 192–214 (1991).

precedents that display considerable deference to educators—relying especially on *Hazelwood School District v. Kuhlmeier,* 484 U.S. 260 (1988), a secondary education case involving student rights.[17] Without satisfactorily justifying *Hazelwood*'s extension either to higher education in general or to faculty members, the court asserted that "educators do not offend the First Amendment by exercising editorial control over the style and content of student [or professor] speech in school-sponsored expressive activities so long as their actions are reasonably related to legitimate pedagogical concerns" (926 F.2d at 1074, citing *Hazelwood,* 484 U.S. at 272–73). Addressing the academic freedom implications of its position, the court concluded:

> Though we are mindful of the invaluable role academic freedom plays in our public schools, particularly at the post-secondary level, we do not find support to conclude that academic freedom is an independent First Amendment right. And, in any event, we cannot supplant our discretion for that of the University. Federal judges should not be ersatz deans or educators. In this regard, we trust that the University will serve its own interests as well as those of its professors in pursuit of academic freedom [926 F.2d at 1075].

In upholding the university's authority in matters of course content as superior to that of the professor, the court accepted the validity and applicability of two particular institutional concerns underlying the university's decision to limit the professor's instructional activities. First was the university's "concern . . . that its courses be taught without personal religious bias unnecessarily infecting the teacher or the students." Second was the concern that optional classes not be conducted under circumstances that give "the impression of official sanction, which might [unduly pressure] students into attending and, at least for purposes of examination, into adopting the beliefs expressed" by the professor. Relying on these two concerns, against the backdrop of its general deference to the institution in curricular matters, the court concluded:

> In short, Dr. Bishop and the University disagree about a matter of content in the course he teaches. The University must have the final say in such a dispute. Though Dr. Bishop's sincerity cannot be doubted, his educational judgment can be questioned and redirected by the University when he is acting under its auspices as a course instructor, but not when he acts as an independent educator or researcher. The University's conclusions about course content must be allowed to hold sway over an individual professor's judgments. By its memo to Dr. Bishop, the University seeks to prevent him from presenting his religious viewpoint during instructional time, even to the extent that it represents his professional opinion about his subject matter. We have simply concluded that

---

[17]*Hazelwood* was also relied on in the *Silva* case, discussed below in this section. For other applications of *Hazelwood* to higher education, see *Brown v. Li,* 308 F.3d 939 (9th Cir. 2002), and *Axson-Flynn v. Johnson,* 356 F.3d 1277 (10th Cir. 2004), both discussed in Section 8.1.4. For a more general discussion on applying lower education precedents to higher education, see Section 1.4.4.

the University as an employer and educator can direct Dr. Bishop to refrain from expression of religious viewpoints in the classroom and like settings [926 F.2d at 1076–77].

Though the appellate court's opinion may seem overly deferential to the institution's prerogatives as employer, and insufficiently sensitive to the particular role of faculty academic freedom in higher education (see generally Robert O'Neil, "*Bishop v. Aronov:* A Comment," 18 *J. Coll. & Univ. Law* 381 (1992)), the court did nevertheless demarcate limits on its holding. These limits are very important. Regarding the professor's classroom activities, the court clearly stated that the university's authority applies only "to the classroom speech of [the professor]—wherever he purports to conduct a class for the University." Even in that context, the court conceded that "[o]f course, if a student asks about [the professor's] religious views, he may fairly answer the question." Moreover, the court emphasized that "the university has not suggested that Dr. Bishop cannot hold his particular views; express them, on his own time, far and wide and to whomever will listen; or write and publish, no doubt authoritatively, on them; nor could it so prohibit him." Similarly, regarding the optional meetings, the court noted that "[t]he University has not suggested that [the professor] cannot organize such meetings, make notice of them on campus, or request University space to conduct them; nor could it so prohibit him." As long as the professor "makes it plain to his students that such meetings are not mandatory, not considered part of the coursework, and not related to grading, the university cannot prevent him from conducting such meetings."

With respect to the professor's freedom of religion claims, the court's analysis was much briefer than its free speech analysis but just as favorable for the university. The professor had claimed that the university's restrictions on his expression of religious views violated his rights under the free exercise clause and also violated the establishment clause, because only Christian viewpoints, but not other religious viewpoints, were restricted.

The court rejected the professor's free exercise claim because he "has made no true suggestion, much less demonstration, that any proscribed conduct of his impedes the practice of religion. . . . [T]he university's restrictions of him are not directed at his efforts to practice religion, per se, but rather are directed at his practice of teaching." In similar summary fashion, the court rejected the establishment clause claim because "the University has simply attempted to maintain a neutral, secular classroom by its restrictions on Dr. Bishop's expressions."[18] Moreover, the university's restrictions affected only Christian speech

---

[18]For another classroom case in which the court rejected a professor's freedom of religion claims, see *Lynch v. Indiana State University Board of Trustees,* 378 N.E.2d 900 (Ind. 1978). For cases involving the establishment clause, see *Linnemeir v. Board of Trustees, Indiana University-Purdue University, Fort Wayne,* 260 F.3d 757 (7th Cir. 2001), discussed in Donna Euben, "The Play's the Thing," *Academe,* November–December 2001 (rejecting an establishment clause challenge to a student-selected and faculty-approved play challenging conventional Christianity); and *Calvary Bible Presbyterian Church of Seattle v. University of Washington,* 436 P.2nd 189 (Wash. S. Ct. 1967) (rejecting an establishment clause challenge to teaching the Bible as literature).

because that was the only speech at issue in the situation the university was addressing; "[s]hould another professor express [other] religious beliefs in the classroom," presumably the university would impose similar restrictions.[19] (For a suggested framework for analyzing the religion claims in *Bishop* and related cases, see O'Neil, above.)

More recent cases have served to enhance institutional authority to determine the content of particular courses and assign instructors to particular courses. For example, in *Webb v. Board of Trustees of Ball State University*, 167 F.3d 1146 (7th Cir. 1999) (further discussed in Section 7.2.2), the court relied on the distinction between institutional academic freedom and faculty academic freedom (see Section 7.1.6 above) to reject a professor's claimed right to teach certain classes. Quoting from Justice Frankfurter's concurrence in *Sweezy* (Section 7.1.4 above), the court asserted that recognizing such a claim would "impose costs . . . on the University, whose ability to set a curriculum is as much an element of academic freedom as any scholar's right to express a point of view" (167 F.3d at 1149). Moreover, said the court, "when deciding who to appoint as a leader or teacher of a particular class, every university considers speech (that's what teaching and scholarship consists in) without violating the Constitution."

Similarly, in *Edwards v. California University of Pennsylvania*, 156 F.3d 488 (3d Cir. 1998), perhaps the most far-reaching and deferential case to date, the court rejected the free speech claims of a tenured professor who was disciplined for failing to conform his course content to the syllabus provided by the departmental chair and faculty. The court held flatly that "the First Amendment does not place restrictions on a public university's ability to control its curriculum," and therefore "a public university professor does not have a First Amendment right to decide what will be taught in the classroom" (156 F.3d at 491). In its result, and in its reliance on the university's own academic freedom to decide what shall be taught, the *Edwards* case is consistent with the *Hetrick* and *Clark* cases above. But *Edwards* also introduces new and potentially far-reaching reasoning based on the U.S. Supreme Court decision in *Rosenberger v. Rector & Visitors of University of Virginia* (Sections 10.1.4 & 10.3.2 of this book). Relying on the *Rosenberger* concept of the public university or the state as a "speaker," the *Edwards* court concluded that a university acts as a "speaker" when it enlists faculty members to convey the university's own message or preferred course content to its students, and that the university was thus "entitled to make content-based choices in restricting Edwards' syllabus." (For criticism of *Edwards*, see the discussion of *Brown v. Armenti* in Section 7.2.3 below.)

A third case, *Scallet v. Rosenblum*, 911 F. Supp. 999 (W.D. Va. 1996), *affirmed on other grounds*, 1997 WL 33077 (4th Cir. 1997) (unpublished), differs from *Webb* and *Edwards* in that the district court determined that an instructor's

---

[19]There was also an establishment clause issue concerning whether the professor's religious speech was proselytizing or support for religion that could be attributed to the university and would violate the establishment clause. The court declined to resolve this issue because "[t]he university can restrict speech that falls short of an establishment violation, and we have already disposed of the university's restrictions of [the professor] under the free speech clause."

choices of course content could be considered speech on matters of public concern. The issue was whether a business school instructor's classroom materials and discussions on increasing racial and gender diversity in the business community were protected speech. Using the *Pickering/Connick* analysis, the court first determined that this speech did involve matters of public concern:

> [I]t appears unassailable that [the instructor's] advocacy of diversity, through the materials he taught in class, relate to matters of public concern. Debate is incessant over the role of diversity in higher education, employment and government contracting, just to name a few spheres. Indeed, political debate over issues such as affirmative action is inescapable [911 F. Supp. at 1014].

In reaching this conclusion, the court rejected the university's argument that the instructor "was simply discharging his duties as an employee [of the business school] when he made his classroom remarks." Rather, said the court, a classroom instructor "routinely and necessarily discusses issues of public concern when *speaking as an employee.* Indeed, it is part of his educational mandate" (911 F. Supp. at 1013).

Nevertheless, the court ultimately sided with the university by concluding that the instructor's free speech interest was overridden by the business school's "powerful interest in the content of the [departmental] curriculum and its coordination with the content of other required courses." The school could restrict the classroom materials and discussions of its instructors when this speech "disrupt[ed], or sufficiently threaten[ed] to disrupt, [the school's] educational mandate in a significant way." The instructor's speech did so in this case because it "hamper[ed] the school's ability effectively to deliver the [required writing and speech] course to its students . . . ; created divisions within the [departmental] faculty"; and raised concerns among faculty members outside the department about the instructor's class "trenching upon their own." (Interestingly, the instructor had raised diversity issues in faculty meetings that were comparable to the issues he had addressed in class. In that different context, the court held that the speech was protected "because the defendants offer no competing interest served by stifling that speech" (see Section 7.4 below)).

Another later case, *Bonnell v. Lorenzo,* 241 F.3d 800 (6th Cir. 2001), like *Martin* (above), arose from student complaints about a professor's vulgar and profane classroom speech. The appellate court sought to pattern its decision after *Martin v. Parrish* and, like *Martin,* the *Bonnell* case resulted in a victory for the college. After a female student in Professor Bonnell's English class had filed a sexual harassment complaint against him, the college disciplined him for using language in class that created a "hostile learning environment." The language, according to the court, included profanity such as "shit," "damn," and "fuck," and various sexual allusions such as "blow job," used to describe the relationship between a U.S. President (now former President) and a female Washington intern. The college determined that these statements were "vulgar and obscene," were "not germane to course content," and were used "without reference to assigned readings."

The professor disagreed and claimed that disciplining him for this reason violated his First Amendment free speech rights.[20]

The appellate court accepted the college's characterization of the professor's statements and rejected the professor's free speech claims:

> Plaintiff may have a constitutional right to use words such as . . . "fuck," but he does not have a constitutional right to use them in a classroom setting where they are not germane to the subject matter, in contravention of the College's sexual harassment policy. . . . This is particularly so when one considers the unique context in which the speech is conveyed—a classroom where a college professor is speaking to a captive audience of students (see *Martin [v. Parrish]*, 805 F.2d at 586) who cannot "effectively avoid further bombardment of their sensibilities simply by averting their [ears]" [241 F.3d at 820–821, quoting *Hill v. Colorado*, 530 U.S. 703, 753 n.3 (2000)].

The court's result seems correct, and its "germaneness" and captive audience rationales seem relevant to the analysis, but in other respects the court's reasoning is shaky in ways that other courts and advocates should avoid. *First,* although the court grounded its analysis on the crucial characterization of the professor's speech as "not germane to course content," the court neither made its own findings on this issue nor reviewed (or even described) whether and how the college made and supported its findings. *Second,* the court relied on the college's sexual harassment policy without quoting it or considering whether it provided fair warning to the professor and a comprehensible guideline by which to gauge his classroom speech (see the *Cohen* and *Silva* cases below). *Third,* the court relied heavily on the captive audience rationale for restricting speech without asking the questions pertinent to making a well-founded captive audience determination. Such questions would include whether the course was a required or an elective course; whether there were multiple sections with different instructors that the students could choose from; whether the students could withdraw from the course or transfer to another section without penalty; and whether the professor had given full and fair advance notice of the content and style of his class sessions. *Fourth,* the court began its discussion with lengthy references to the public concern/private concern distinction drawn in the *Pickering/Connick* line of cases but did not apply this distinction specifically to the classroom speech. It is therefore unclear whether the court assumed that the professor's speech was not on a matter of public concern, or whether the court assumed that the public/private concern distinction was not relevant to its analysis. And *fifth,* the court asserted that the college's case was strengthened because "it was not the content of Plaintiff's speech itself which led to the disciplinary action. . . ." This statement apparently ignores the U.S. Supreme Court's opinion in *Cohen v. California,* 403 U.S. 15 (1971), in which

---

[20]The *Bonnell* case is quite similar to the *Cohen v. San Bernardino Valley College* case, which is discussed below in this subsection. The court's reasoning in *Bonnell* can usefully be compared with the district court's reasoning in the *Cohen* case.

the Court determined that a punishment for using profanity was based on the content of the speech, and also made clear that courts must protect the "emotive" as well as the "cognitive" content of speech (see Section 9.6 of this book).

Although the above cases strongly support institutional authority over professors' instructional activities, it does not follow that institutions invariably prevail in instructional disputes. The courts in *Wirsing, Martin, Bishop, Scallet,* and *Bonnell,* in limiting their holdings, all suggest situations in which faculty members could prevail. Other cases also include strong language supportive of faculty rights. In *Dube v. State University of New York,* 900 F.2d 587 (2d Cir. 1990), for instance, the court acknowledged the legal sufficiency, under the First Amendment, of a former assistant professor's allegations that the university had denied him tenure due to a public controversy that had arisen concerning his course in "The Politics of Race" and the views on Zionism that he had expressed in the course. Relying on the *Sweezy, Shelton v. Tucker,* and *Keyishian* cases, and quoting key academic freedom language from these opinions (see Section 7.1.4 above), the court emphasized that "for decades it has been [clear] that the First Amendment tolerates neither laws nor other means of coercion, persuasion or intimidation 'that cast a pall of orthodoxy' over the free exchange of ideas in the classroom"; and "that, assuming the defendants retaliated against [the professor] based on the content of his classroom discourse," such facts would support a claim that the defendants had violated the professor's free speech rights.

Moreover, in other cases, faculty members—and thus faculty academic freedom—have prevailed over institutional authority. In *DiBona v. Matthews,* 269 Cal. Rptr. 882 (Cal. Ct. App. 1990), for example, the court provided a measure of protection for a professor's artistic and literary expression as it relates to the choice of class content and materials. Specifically, the court held that San Diego Community College District administrators violated a teacher's free speech rights when they canceled a controversial play production and a drama class in which the play was to have been performed. The play that the instructor had selected, entitled *Split Second,* was about a black police officer who, in the course of an arrest, shot a white suspect after the suspect had subjected him to racial slurs and epithets. The play's theme closely paralleled the facts of a criminal case that was then being tried in San Diego. The court determined that the college administrators had canceled the class because of the content of the play. While the First Amendment free speech clause did not completely prevent the college from considering the play's content in deciding to cancel the drama class, the court held that the college's particular reasons—that the religious community opposed the play and that the subject was controversial and sensitive—were not valid reasons under the First Amendment. Moreover, distinguishing the present case from those involving minors in elementary and secondary schools, the court held that the college could not cancel the drama class solely because of the vulgar language included in the play.

In two other cases later in the 1990s, *Cohen v. San Bernardino Valley College* and *Silva v. University of New Hampshire,* courts also sided with the faculty member rather than the institution in disputes regarding teaching methods and classroom demeanor. Both cases, like *Bonnell,* above, arose in the context of alleged sexual harassment in the classroom, thus presenting potential clashes among the faculty's interest in academic freedom, the institution's interest in enforcing sexual harassment policies, and the students' interest in being protected against harassment.

In the *Cohen* case, 92 F.3d 968 (9th Cir. 1996), *reversing* 883 F. Supp. 1407 (C.D. Cal. 1995), the appellate court used the constitutional "void for vagueness" doctrine to invalidate a college's attempt to discipline a teacher for classroom speech. The plaintiff, Professor Dean Cohen, was a tenured professor at San Bernardino Valley College who was the subject of a sexual harassment complaint made by a student in his remedial English class. According to the court:

> One student in the class . . . became offended by Cohen's repeated focus on topics of a sexual nature, his use of profanity and vulgarities, and by his comments which she believed were directed intentionally at her and other female students in a humiliating and harassing manner. During [one] class Cohen began a class discussion on the issue of pornography and played the "devil's advocate" by asserting controversial viewpoints. Cohen has for many years typically assigned provocative essays such as Jonathan Swift's "A Modest Proposal" and discussed subjects such as obscenity, cannibalism, and consensual sex with children in a "devil's advocate" style. During classroom discussion on pornography in the remedial English class . . . Cohen stated in class that he wrote for *Hustler* and *Playboy* magazines and he read some articles out loud in class. Cohen concluded the class discussion by requiring his students to write essays defining pornography. When Cohen assigned the "Define Pornography" paper, [the student] asked for an alternative assignment but Cohen refused to give her one. [The student] stopped attending Cohen's class and received a failing grade for the semester [92 F.3d at 970].

The student filed a grievance against Cohen, alleging that his behavior violated the college's new sexual harassment policy, which provided that:

> [s]exual harassment is defined as unwelcome sexual advances, requests for sexual favors, and other verbal, written, or physical conduct of a sexual nature. It includes, but is not limited to, circumstances in which:
>
> . . .
>
> (2) Such conduct has the purpose or effect of unreasonably interfering with an individual's academic performance or creating an intimidating, hostile, or offensive learning environment . . . [92 F.3d at 971].

After a hearing and appeal, the college found that Cohen had violated part (2) of the policy and ordered him to:

> (1) Provide a syllabus concerning his teaching style, purpose, content, and method to his students at the beginning of class and to the department chair . . . ; (2) Attend a sexual harassment seminar . . . ; (3) Undergo a formal evaluation procedure . . . ; and (4) Become sensitive to the particular needs and backgrounds of his students, and to modify his teaching strategy when it

becomes apparent that his techniques create a climate which impedes the students' ability to learn [92 F.3d at 971].

The district court rejected Cohen's claim that application of the sexual harassment policy violated his right to academic freedom:

> The concept of academic freedom . . . is more clearly established in academic literature than it is in the courts . . . [and] judicial application of this doctrine is far from clear. [Furthermore], a review of the case law shows that, despite eloquent rhetoric on "academic freedom," the courts have declined to cede all classroom control to teachers [883 F. Supp. at 1412, 1414].

The district court also rejected Cohen's claim that, under *Connick v. Myers,* the college had violated his free speech rights as a public employee. The court divided Cohen's speech into two categories: (1) vulgarities and obscenities, and (2) comments related to the curriculum and focusing on pornography and other sexual topics. It concluded that the speech in the first category was not on matters of public concern, but that the speech in the second category was, because Cohen did not speak merely to advance some purely private interest. Thus, under *Connick,* the college could regulate the first type of speech but could regulate the second only if it could justify a restriction in terms of the professor's job duties and the efficient operation of the college. The court agreed that the college had demonstrated sufficient justification:

> [A]lthough there is evidence in the record that Cohen's teaching style is effective for at least some students [and that] Cohen's colleagues have stated that he is a gifted and enthusiastic teacher . . . [whose] teaching style is within the range of acceptable academic practice . . . the learning process for a number of students was hampered by the hostile learning environment created by Cohen. According to one peer evaluator who observed a class in which Cohen discussed . . . the topic of consensual sex with children, Cohen's "specific focus impedes academic success for some students" [883 F. Supp. at 1419].

In an important qualification, however, the district court addressed the problem of the "thin-skinned" student:

> In applying a "hostile environment" prohibition, there is the danger that the most sensitive and the most easily offended students will be given veto power over class content and methodology. Good teaching should challenge students and at times may intimidate students or make them uncomfortable. . . . Colleges and universities . . . must avoid a tyranny of mediocrity, in which all discourse is made bland enough to suit the tastes of all the students. However, colleges and universities must have the power to require professors to effectively educate all segments of the student population, including those students unused to the rough and tumble of intellectual discussion. If colleges and universities lack this power, each classroom becomes a separate fiefdom in which the educational process is subject to professorial whim. Universities must be able to ensure that the more vulnerable as well as the more sophisticated students receive a suitable

education. . . . Within the educational context, the university's mission is to effectively educate students, keeping in mind students' varying backgrounds and sensitivities. Furthermore, the university has the right to preclude disruption of this educational mission through the creation of a hostile learning environment. . . . The college's substantial interest in educating all students, not just the thick-skinned ones, warrants . . . requiring Cohen to put potential students on notice of his teaching methods [883 F. Supp. at 1419–21].

Thus, although the court ruled in the college's favor, at the same time it sought to uphold the proposition that the college "must avoid restricting creative and engaging teaching, even if some over-sensitive students object to it" (883 F. Supp. at 1422). Moreover, the court cautioned that "this ruling goes only to the narrow and reasonable discipline which the College seeks to impose. A case in which a professor is terminated or directly censored presents a far different balancing question."

On appeal, the U.S. Court of Appeals for the Ninth Circuit unanimously overruled the district court's decision, but did so on different grounds than those explored by the lower court. The appellate court emphasized that neither it nor the U.S. Supreme Court had yet determined the scope of First Amendment protection for a professor's classroom speech. Rather than engage in this analysis, the court focused its opinion and analysis on the vagueness of the college's sexual harassment policy and held that "the Policy's terms [are] unconstitutionally vague as applied to Cohen in this case." The court did not address whether or not the "College could punish speech of this nature if the policy were more precisely construed by authoritative interpretive guidelines or if the College were to adopt a clearer and more precise policy."

In its analysis, the appellate court noted three objections to vague college policies:

> First, they trap the innocent by not providing fair warning. Second, they impermissibly delegate basic policy matters to low level officials for resolution on an ad hoc and subjective basis, with the attendant dangers of arbitrary and discriminatory application. Third, a vague policy discourages the exercise of first amendment freedoms [92 F.3d at 972].

Guided by these concerns, the court reasoned that:

> Cohen's speech did not fall within the core region of sexual harassment as defined by the Policy. Instead, officials of the College, on an entirely ad hoc basis, applied the Policy's nebulous outer reaches to punish teaching methods that Cohen had used for many years. Regardless of what the intentions of the officials of the College may have been, the consequences of their actions can best be described as a legalistic ambush. Cohen was simply without any notice that the Policy would be applied in such a way as to punish his longstanding teaching style—a style which, until the College imposed punishment upon Cohen under the Policy, had apparently been considered pedagogically sound and within the bounds of teaching methodology permitted at the College [92 F.3d at 972].

(See generally Sonja Smith, *"Cohen v. San Bernadino Valley College*: The Scope of Academic Freedom Within the Context of Sexual Harassment Claims and In-Class Speech," 25 *J. Coll. & Univ. Law* 1 (1998).)

Since the appellate court's reasoning is different from the district court's, and since the appellate court does not disagree with or address the issues that were dispositive for the district court, the latter's analysis remains a useful illustration of how other courts may handle such issues when they arise under policies that are not unconstitutionally vague.

In the second case, *Silva v. University of New Hampshire*, 888 F. Supp. 293 (D.N.H. 1994), a tenured faculty member at the University of New Hampshire (UNH) challenged the university's determination that he had created a hostile or offensive academic environment in his classroom and therefore violated the university's sexual harassment policy. Seven women students had filed formal complaints against Silva. These complaints alleged that, in a technical writing class, he had compared the concept of focus to sexual intercourse: "Focus is like sex. You seek a target. You zero in on your subject. You move from side to side. You close in on the subject. You bracket the subject and center on it. Focus connects the experience and language. You and the subject become one" (888 F. Supp. at 299). The complaints also alleged that two days later in the same class, Silva made the statement "[b]elly dancing is like jello on a plate with a vibrator under the plate" to illustrate the use of metaphor. In addition, several female students reported that Silva had made sexually suggestive remarks to them, both in and out of the classroom. For example, there were allegations that Silva told a female student, whom he saw in the library kneeling down to look through a card catalog, that "it looks like you've had a lot of experience down there"; that he gave a spelling test to another student in which every third word had a "sexual slant"; that he had asked two of his female students how long they had been together, implying a lesbian relationship; that he had asked another female student, "How would you like to get an A?"; and that he had physically blockaded a student from exiting a vending machine room and complained to her about students' actions against him (888 F. Supp. at 310–11).

These complaints were presented to Silva in two "informal" meetings with university administrators, after which he was formally reprimanded. Silva then challenged the reprimand through the university's "formal" grievance process, culminating in hearings before a hearing panel and an appeals board. (The court reviewed these procedures and some potential flaws in them in its opinion (888 F. Supp. At 319–26).) Finding that Silva's language and innuendos violated the university's sexual harassment policy, the hearing panel emphasized that a reasonable female student would find Silva's comments and behavior to be offensive; that this was the second time in a two-year period that Silva had been formally notified "about his use of inappropriate and sexually explicit remarks in the classroom"; and that Silva had given the panel "no reason to believe that he understood the seriousness of his behavior" or its impact on the students he taught. The university thereupon suspended Silva without pay for at least one year, required him to undergo counseling at his own expense, and prohibited him from attempting to contact or retaliate against the complainants.

In court, prior to trial, Silva argued that the university's actions violated his First Amendment free speech rights. The court agreed that he was "likely to succeed on the merits of his First Amendment claims" and entered a preliminary injunction against the university. In its opinion, the court pursued three lines of analysis to support its ruling. First, relying on the U.S. Supreme Court's decision in the *Keyishian* case (Section 7.1.4), the court reasoned that the belly dancing comment was "not of a sexual nature," and the sexual harassment policy therefore did not give Silva adequate notice that this statement was prohibited—thus violating the First Amendment requirement that teachers be "clearly inform[ed]" of the proscribed conduct in order to guard against a "chilling effect" on their exercise of free speech rights. Second, relying in part on *Hazelwood v. Kuhlmeier* (see above), the court determined that the sexual harassment policy was invalid under the First Amendment, as applied to Silva's speech, because it "fails to take into account the nation's interest in academic freedom" and therefore is not "*reasonably* related to the legitimate pedagogical purpose of providing a congenial academic environment . . ." (888 F. Supp. at 314). In reaching this conclusion, the court reasoned that (1) the students were "exclusively adult college students . . . presumed to have possessed the sophistication of adults"; (2) "Silva's classroom statements advanced his valid educational objective of conveying certain principles related to the subject matter of his course"; and (3) "Silva's classroom statements were made in a professionally appropriate manner . . ." (888 F. Supp. at 313).

For its third line of analysis, the court resorted to the *Pickering* and *Connick* cases. Purporting to apply the public concern/private concern dichotomy, the court determined that "Silva's classroom statements . . . were made for the legitimate pedagogical, *public* purpose of conveying certain principles related to the subject matter of his course." Thus, these statements "were related to matters of public concern" and, on balance, "Silva's First Amendment interest in the speech at issue is overwhelmingly superior to UNH's interest in proscribing [the] speech" (888 F. Supp. at 316).[21]

Yet another, and more recent case, in which the faculty member (and faculty academic freedom) prevailed over institutional authority is the important case of *Hardy v. Jefferson Community College*, 260 F.3d 671 (6th Cir. 2001). In this case, the U.S. Court of Appeals for the Sixth Circuit held that an adjunct instructor's classroom speech was protected because it was on a matter of public concern and was germane to the subject matter of the course. The instructor had claimed that the community college's refusal to rehire him violated his "rights of free speech and academic freedom," and the appellate court agreed.

The instructor, Hardy, was teaching a summer course on Introduction to Interpersonal Communication when the incident prompting his nonrenewal occurred. He gave a lecture on "how language is used to marginalize minorities." Along with his lecture, he conducted a group exercise in which he asked students to suggest examples of words that had "historically served the interests

---

[21]For another interesting example of a case in which the court used the *Pickering/Connick* line of cases to protect a faculty member's in-class speech, see *Blum v. Schlegel*, 18 F.3d 1005 (2d Cir. 1994).

of the dominant culture." Their suggestions included "the words 'girl,' 'lady,' 'faggot,' 'nigger,' and 'bitch.'" A student in the class who was offended by the latter two words raised her concerns with the instructor and college administrators, and the instructor apologized to the student. But the student took her complaint to a vocal religious leader in the community, who subsequently met with college administrators to discuss the incident. The administrators then met with the instructor to discuss the classroom exercise and, in the course of the discussion, informed him "that a 'prominent citizen' representing the interests of the African-American community had . . . threatened to affect the school's already declining enrollment if corrective action was not taken." After this meeting, Hardy completed his summer course without further incident and received positive student evaluations from all students except the one who had complained about the class exercise. Nevertheless, Hardy was informed that he would not be teaching the following semester; he then filed suit against the college, the president, the former acting dean, and the state community college system.

The appellate court used a *Pickering/Connick* analysis to determine whether the instructor's speech was on a matter of public concern and, if so, whether the employee's interest in speaking outweighed the college's interest in serving the public. Applying the first prong of the *Pickering/Connick* test, the court found that the instructor's speech "was germane to the subject matter of his lecture on the power and effect of language" and "was limited to an academic discussion of the words in question." The court also distinguished Hardy's speech from the unprotected speech at issue in its previous ruling in *Bonnell v. Lorenzo* (above); Bonnell's speech, unlike Hardy's, was "gratuitous" and "not germane to the subject matter of his course." Thus, in considering "the content, form, and context" of Hardy's speech, as the *Connick* case requires, the court emphasized the academic "content" and "form" of the speech and its higher education classroom "context." This same emphasis was apparent in the court's conclusion that Hardy's speech was on a matter of public concern:

> Because the essence of a teacher's role is to prepare students for their place in society as responsible citizens, classroom instruction will often fall within the Supreme Court's broad conception of "public concern." . . . Hardy's lecture on social deconstructivism and language, which explored the social and political impact of certain words, clearly meets this criterion. Although Hardy's in-class speech does not itself constitute pure public debate, it does relate to matters of overwhelming public concern—race, gender, and power conflicts in our society. . . .
>
> Hardy has thus satisfied the first prong of the two-part test set forth in *Pickering* [260 F.3d at 679].

A similar emphasis on the academic context of the dispute also marked the court's application of the second prong of the *Pickering/Connick* test, in which it balanced Hardy's interest in speaking on a matter of public concern against the college's interest in efficiently providing services to its students and the community. Citing *Keyishian* and *Sweezy,* the court in *Hardy* asserted that "[i]n balancing the competing interests involved, we must take into account the robust tradition of academic freedom in our nation's post-secondary schools" (260 F.3d at 680). The college had presented no evidence that Hardy's speech had "undermined [his] working relationship within his department, interfered with his duties, or impaired discipline." In fact, Hardy had successfully completed his summer course and received favorable student course evaluations (see above). Nor did the concerns about the religious leader's threat to affect the college's enrollment weigh in the college's favor. Such concerns represented no more than the college administrators' "undifferentiated fear of disturbance" that, under the *Tinker* case (see Section 7.1.1 above), cannot "overcome the right to freedom of expression." The instructor's interests, supported by the tradition of academic freedom, therefore outweighed the interests of the college.

The court's analysis in *Hardy* draws upon both the *Pickering/Connick* line of cases and the germaneness approach to faculty academic freedom. The germaneness analysis follows the pathway that the court had previously sketched in *Bonnell. Hardy,* however, unlike *Bonnell,* places the germaneness analysis within the *Pickering/Connick* analysis, using it as a crucial component of its consideration of the content, form, and context of the speech, rather than as a separate analysis providing an alternative to *Pickering/Connick.* In doing so, the Sixth Circuit seems to have corrected much of the weaknesses of its reasoning in *Bonnell* (see above) and to have crafted an approach to faculty academic freedom claims that merges the better aspects of *Pickering/Connick* with the better aspects of the germaneness test.

Most of the cases discussed in this subsection concern the "classroom" as a physical, on-campus, location where the faculty member instructs students. In contemporary settings, however, instruction may often take place in varying locations that are not as fixed, and not as tied to the campus, as the traditional classroom, and some instructional activities may be optional rather than required. Such new settings may create new academic freedom issues. In the case of *Bishop v. Aranov* (above), for example, the court addressed the extent to which faculty members are free to have optional instructional meetings with students that they are currently teaching in a formal course. In *DiBona v. Matthews* (above), the court considered an issue involving a drama course that centered on the public performance of a play. A more recent case, *Hudson v. Craven,* 403 F.3d 691 (9th Cir. 2005), considers the scope of a faculty member's right to arrange optional field trips for her students. The court found that such activities implicate both freedom of association and freedom of speech but ruled, applying the *Pickering* balancing test (see Section 7.1.1), that the institution's interests prevailed over the instructor's on the particular facts of the case.

7.2.3. Grading.

Grading is an extension of the teaching methods that faculty members use in the classroom and is an essential component of faculty members' evaluative functions. Just as courts are reluctant to intervene in disputes regarding the classroom (subsection 7.2.2 above), they are hesitant to intervene in grading disputes among professors, students, and the administration. While the administration (representing the institution) usually prevails when the court rules on such disputes, there are circumstances in which faculty members may occasionally prevail.

In a case concerning grading policies in general, *Lovelace v. Southeastern Massachusetts University*, 793 F.2d 419 (1st Cir. 1986), the court upheld institutional authority over grading in much the same way that other courts had done in classroom cases. The university had declined to renew a faculty member's contract after he had rejected administration requests to lower the academic standards he used in grading his students. The faculty member claimed that the university's action violated his free speech rights. Citing *Hetrick* and *Clark* (subsection 7.2.2 above), the court rejected the professor's claim because the university itself had the freedom to set its own grading standards, and "the first amendment does not require that each nontenured professor be made a sovereign unto himself." According to the court:

> Whether a school sets itself up to attract and serve only the best and the brightest students or whether it instead gears its standard to a broader, more average population is a policy decision which, we think, universities must be allowed to set. And matters such as course content, homework load, and grading policy are core university concerns, integral to implementation of this policy decision [793 F.2d at 425–26].

(For a more recent case to the same effect, see *Wozniak v. Conry*, 236 F.3d 888, 890 (7th Cir. 2001).)

When the dispute concerns an individual grade rather than general grading policies, however, different considerations are involved that may lead some courts to provide limited protection for the faculty member who has assigned the grade. The case of *Parate v. Isibor*, 868 F.2d 821 (6th Cir. 1989), provides an example. The defendant, dean of the school in which the plaintiff was a nontenured professor, ordered the plaintiff, over his objections, to execute a grade-change form raising the final grade of one of his students. The plaintiff argued that this incident, and several later incidents alleged to be in retaliation for his lack of cooperation regarding the grade change, violated his First Amendment academic freedom. Relying on the free speech clause, the court agreed that "[b]ecause the assignment of a letter grade is symbolic communication intended to send a specific message to the student, the individual professor's communicative act is entitled to some measure of First Amendment protection" (868 F.2d at 827). The court reasoned (without reliance on the *Pickering/Connick* methodology) that:

> the professor's evaluation of her students and assignment of their grades is central to the professor's teaching method. . . . Although the individual professor does not escape the reasonable review of university officials in the assignment of grades, she should remain free to decide, according to her own professional judgment, what grades to assign and what grades not to assign. . . . Thus, the individual professor may not be compelled, by university officials, to change a grade that the professor previously assigned to her student. Because the individual professor's assignment of a letter grade is protected speech, the university

officials' action to compel the professor to alter that grade would severely
burden a protected activity [868 F.2d at 828].

Thus, the defendant's act of ordering the plaintiff to change the grade, contrary to the plaintiff's professional judgment, violated the First Amendment. The
court indicated, however, that had university administrators changed the student's grade themselves, this action would not have violated the plaintiff's First
Amendment rights. The protection that *Parate* accords to faculty grading and
teaching methods is therefore quite narrow—more symbolic than real, perhaps,
but nonetheless an important step away from the deference normally paid institutions in these matters. (For a more extended critique and criticism of *Parate,*
see D. Sacken, "Making No Sense of Academic Freedom: *Parate v. Isibor,*" 56
West's Educ. Law Rptr. 1107 (January 4, 1990).)

The narrow protection accorded faculty members in *Parate* does not necessarily mean that administrators in public institutions can never direct a faculty
member to change a grade, or that faculty members can always refuse to do so.
As in other free speech cases, the right is not absolute and must be balanced
against the interests of the institution. The professor's free speech rights in
Parate prevailed, apparently, because the subsequent administrative change
could fulfill whatever interests the administration had in the professor's grading of the student whose grade was at issue. If, however, the administration or
a faculty or faculty-student hearing panel were to find a professor's grade to be
discriminatory or arbitrary, the institution's interests would be stronger, and perhaps a directive that the professor change the grade would not violate the professor's free speech rights. In *Keen v. Penson,* 970 F.2d 252 (7th Cir. 1992), for
example, the court upheld the demotion of a professor due to unprofessional
conduct regarding his grading of a student. The professor had argued that "the
grade he gave [the student is] protected by the First Amendment under the concept of academic freedom." In rejecting the argument, the court explained:

> As this case reveals, the asserted academic freedom of a professor can con-
> flict with the academic freedom of the university to make decisions affecting
> that professor. . . . Even if we were to assume that the First Amendment applies
> [to the professor's grading of the student], it would not be dispositive, because
> we would then balance Keen's First Amendment right against the University's
> interest in ensuring that its students receive a fair grade and are not subject to
> demeaning, insulting, and inappropriate comments [970 F.2d at 257–58].

On the other hand, once a court accepts the propriety of balancing interests
in grading cases, it is also possible that some *post hoc* administrative changes
of grades could violate a faculty member's academic freedom rights. Such might
be the case, for instance, if the faculty member could show that an administrator's change of a grade was itself discriminatory or arbitrary (see generally Section 9.3.1).

Some courts will avoid such a balancing of interests, and refuse to engage in
reasoning such as that in the Sixth Circuit's *Parate* opinion, by emphasizing
institutional academic freedom in grading (see the *Lovelace* case above) or by

positing that the faculty member grades students as an "agent" of, and thus a "speaker" for, the institution. *Brown v. Armenti,* 247 F.3d 69 (3rd Cir. 2001), is the leading example of this judicial viewpoint. The professor (Brown) alleged that he had assigned an F to a student who had attended only three of the fifteen class sessions for his practicum course; that the university president (Armenti) had instructed him to change this student's grade from an F to an Incomplete; that he had refused to comply; and that he was therefore suspended from teaching the course. The professor claimed that the university had retaliated against him for refusing to change the student's grade, thus violating his right to "academic free expression." In an appeal from the district court's denial of the defendants' motion for summary judgment, the U.S. Court of Appeals for the Third Circuit sought to determine whether the facts alleged amounted to a violation of the professor's First Amendment rights.

The *Armenti* court declined to follow *Parate* and instead applied its own prior case of *Edwards v. California University of Pennsylvania,* 156 F.3d 488 (3d Cir. 1998), discussed in Section 7.2.2 above. The court drew from *Edwards* the proposition that "in the classroom, the university was the speaker and the professor was the agent of the university for First Amendment purposes" (*Armenti,* 247 F.3d at 74). Using this "university-as-speaker" theory, the *Edwards* court had asserted that, as the university's agent or "proxy," the professor in the classroom fulfills one of the university's "four essential freedoms" set out in Justice Frankfurter's concurring opinion in *Sweezy v. New Hampshire,* 354 U.S. at 263 (Section 7.1.4 above). Thus, relying on *Edwards,* the court in *Armenti* reasoned that "[b]ecause grading is pedagogic, the assignment of the grade is subsumed under [one of the four essential freedoms], the university's freedom to determine how a course is to be taught." Since this freedom is the university's and not the professor's, the professor "does not have a First Amendment right to expression via the school's grade assignment procedures." The change of a grade from an F to an Incomplete, according to the court, is thus not a matter that warrants "'intrusive oversight by the judiciary in the name of the First Amendment'" (247 F.3d at 75, quoting *Connick v. Myers,* 461 U.S. 138, 146 (1983)).

Even though its opinion is in direct conflict with the Sixth Circuit's earlier opinion in *Parate,* the court in *Brown v. Armenti* does not explain or document why its reasoning based on *Edwards* is superior to the *Parate* reasoning. It makes the conclusory statement that the "*Edwards* framework . . . offers a more realistic view of the university-professor relationship" but provides neither empirical data nor expert opinion to support this conclusion. Nor does the *Armenti* court consider the broader implications of its global reasoning and conclusion. If the professor in the classroom—or its technological extensions—were merely the university's agent subject to the university's micromanagement, there would be no room at all for faculty academic freedom, and the full range of professors' academic judgment and professional discretion would be subject to check at the mere whim of university officials. These potential broader implications of *Armenti* (and the earlier *Edwards* case) seem discordant with the past seventy-five years' development of academic freedom in the United States, as well as with the spirit of the *Sweezy* and *Rosenberger* cases on which the *Armenti* court (and the *Edwards* court) rely.

7.2.4. Methods of analyzing academic freedom in teaching claims.

Taken together, the cases in subsections 7.2.2 and 7.2.3 illustrate and confirm five alternatives for analyzing First Amendment faculty academic freedom claims involving teaching: (1) "institution-as-speaker" analysis and the related institutional academic freedom analysis; (2) *Pickering/Connick* analysis; (3) vagueness analysis; (4) "pedagogical concerns" analysis; and (5) germaneness analysis.[22] These alternatives are discussed under numbers 1–5 below, followed by a discussion of other miscellaneous alternatives under number 6. As will be seen, more than one of the alternatives may be applicable to a particular problem; judges may disagree on which alternative fits best or may combine two or more of the various alternatives together to enhance the power of the analysis.

1. *"Speaker" analysis and institutional academic freedom analysis.* Speaker analysis—the newest alternative—is exemplified by *Edwards v. California University of Pennsylvania* (Section 7.2.2) and *Brown v. Armenti* (Section 7.2.3). The key point of this analysis is to determine whether, in the circumstances, the institution is itself acting as a speaker seeking to convey its own message through the instructors and materials it selects. If so, and if the institution's message conflicts with that of the faculty member, the institution's prerogatives as speaker will take precedence over the faculty member's academic freedom. As noted in Section 7.2.2 above, the concept of the institution as a speaker—rather than a facilitator or regulator of the speech of others—arises from the U.S. Supreme Court's decision in the *Rosenberger* case. The Court's later decision in *Finley v. National Endowment for the Arts* (Section 13.4.5) also develops this concept, and it is referenced as well in *Board of Regents of the University of Wisconsin System v. Southworth*, 529 U.S. 217, 234–35 (2000)

Reliance on institution-as-speaker analysis would generally yield the same result, for much the same reason, as would heavy reliance on the concept of institutional academic freedom. The *Webb* case (Section 7.2.2 above), in which the court ruled strongly in the university's favor based on its institutional academic freedom, illustrates this parallelism. That case's distinction between the institution's and the faculty member's academic freedom parallels the distinction between the institution as speaker and the faculty member as speaker; in effect, institutional academic freedom trumps faculty academic freedom when the institution, in the circumstances, is acting as a speaker seeking to convey a message inconsistent with that of the faculty member. The *Wirshing* case, in Section 7.2.2 above, also uses institutional academic freedom analysis in this

---

[22]The second and third of these analytical approaches, *Pickering/Connick* and vagueness, and the institutional academic freedom branch of the first approach, may also be used to resolve the types of academic freedom claims that arise under Sections 7.3, 7.4, and 7.5 below. The other three approaches seem adaptable primarily to academic freedom claims concerning teaching functions.

manner, although its reasoning is not as strongly stated or as developed as that in *Webb*.

Of the five modes of analysis, the institution-as-speaker and institutional academic freedom mode provides the greatest protection for institutions and the least protection for faculty members. Indeed, this approach tilts so much in favor of the institution that it leaves almost no room in the teaching context for faculty academic freedom or for accommodation of faculty members' interests with those of the institution. (For further criticism of the institution-as-speaker analysis, see the discussion of *Brown v. Armenti* in Section 7.2.3 above.)

2. Pickering/Connick *analysis.* This analysis is addressed at length in the *Scallet v. Rosenblum* opinion, as well as in the *Cohen* district court opinion and the *Silva* opinion (all in Section 7.2.2 above). The earlier opinion in *Martin v. Parrish* (Section 7.2.2) also uses this analysis, as does the court in *Blum v. Schlegel* (Section 7.2.2, fn.21). The central issue in this analysis is whether the faculty member's classroom statements were on "matters of public concern" or on "matters of private concern" (see Section 7.1.1 above; and see also Chris Hoofnagle, "Matters of Public Concern and the Public University Professor," 27 *J. Coll. & Univ. Law* 669 (2001)). This distinction is difficult to draw in many contexts, but perhaps especially so in the context of classroom speech. The district court in *Scallet* does a creditable job with this distinction when it relates the classroom speech to societal issues currently the subject of broad public debate. The *Cohen* district court also does a creditable job discerning the nuances of this distinction, particularly when it sorts out the various types of comments made by the professor. The *Silva* opinion, on the other hand, does not reflect these nuances and appears to expand the public concern category beyond the U.S. Supreme Court's boundaries (see Todd De Mitchell & Richard Fossey, "At the Margin of Academic Freedom and Sexual Harassment: An Analysis of *Silva v. University of New Hampshire*," 111 *West's Educ. Law Rptr.* 13 (September 19, 1996)). *Silva,* therefore, is not a helpful example of this type of analysis.

3. *Vagueness analysis.* This analysis is exemplified by the appellate court's opinion in *Cohen.* The argument that the court accepted is that the college's policy was unconstitutionally vague *as applied to* Cohen under the particular facts of that case. The court in *Silva* accepted a similar argument. The court in *Bishop,* however, rejected a vagueness argument (926 F.2d at 1071–72). Another, broader, version of the vagueness argument would be that a policy is unconstitutionally vague *on its face,* that is, in all or most of its possible applications rather than only as applied to the particular plaintiff's circumstances.

Vagueness analysis as in *Cohen* and *Silva* is derived not from the speech clause alone but from that clause in conjunction with the Fourteenth Amendment's due process clause. Vague policies are invalidated by the courts in part because they "trap the innocent by not providing fair warning" (*Cohen,* 92 F.3d at 972) to the speaker subjected to the policy or clear guidelines for the decision makers applying the policy, and can therefore result in a "legalistic ambush" (*Cohen,* 92 F.3d at 972); that is the problem to which the due process clause speaks. Vague policies are also invalidated in part because they "discourage" speakers from exercising their rights (*Cohen,* 92 F.3d at 972) or, in other words, because they have a "chilling effect" on the exercise of free speech rights (*Silva,* 888 F. Supp. at 312); that is the problem to which the free speech clause speaks. The *Keyishian* case (see Section 7.1 above), which the *Silva* court relied upon, is the classic U.S. Supreme Court precedent upon which to base a vagueness argument and, in particular, a chilling effect argument. In *Keyishian,* and in various other higher education cases, vagueness analysis is yoked with "overbreadth" analysis to emphasize the additional "chill" that may result from a policy so broadly worded that it covers a substantial amount of activity protected by the free speech clause. (For more on overbreadth and vagueness as applied to regulations of faculty conduct, see Section 6.6.1.)[23]

4. *"Pedagogical concerns" analysis.* This type of analysis derives from the case of *Hazelwood School District v. Kuhlmeier,* 484 U.S. 260 (1988), in which the U.S. Supreme Court upheld the validity of a high school's regulation of a student newspaper because the regulation was "reasonably related to legitimate pedagogical concerns" (484 U.S. at 273). The Court has never applied this standard to higher education (as opposed to elementary/secondary education) or to faculty members (as opposed to students), but some lower courts have done so. The court in *Bishop v. Aronov* used this standard (or a modified version of it), as did the court in *Silva.*[24] The standard, as applied in *Hazelwood,* is a highly deferential standard that affords elementary and secondary school administrators broad discretion regarding the "school-sponsored" speech activities of their students. Because this deference appears to be justified in large part by the immaturity of elementary and secondary education students, and because the deference is so extensive that it does not leave room for higher education's traditions of faculty and student academic freedom (see Sections 7.1, 7.2.2, & 8.1.4), the *Hazelwood* standard should not be applied unmodified to higher education (see generally *Scallett v. Rosenblum,* 911 F. Supp., 999, 1010–11 (W.D. Va. 1996)). The *Bishop* court and the *Silva* court both adopted modest modifications of the standard (*Bishop* at 1074–76; *Silva* at 313). With any such modification, the extent of deference should be less for higher education than what the U.S. Supreme Court provides for elementary/secondary education. This would necessitate that the "reasonably related" requirement and the "legitimate" requirement take on a different meaning in the higher education context, such that more weight is given to the faculty member's own pedagogical interests and a greater burden is imposed on the institution to produce proof of its "pedagogical concerns" and the threat to its interests that the professor's speech poses.

---

[23]The *Silva* court used a version of vagueness analysis in accepting the argument that, since Silva's statement about a vibrator did not violate the university's policy, Silva could not have been on notice that his statement was impermissible, and he therefore could not be penalized for it. Thus, as *Silva* illustrates, this type of analysis, focusing on the lack of notice to the professor, can be used not only in situations where the policy is vague and the court cannot determine whether it covers the particular behavior at issue, but also in situations where the court determines that the particular behavior is not covered by the policy.

[24]For another example, where the court applied the *Hazelwood* standard in a higher education faculty case but did not "definitively" decide whether the standard is appropriate for this context, see *Vanderbilt v. Colorado Mountain College District,* 208 F.3d 908, 913–15 (10th Cir. 2000).

5. *Germaneness analysis.* This analysis is used prominently in *Silva,* providing the first extended example of a court implementing germaneness analysis in a higher education academic freedom case. Germaneness was also used, briefly, by both the majority and the concurrence in *Martin v. Parrish* (Section 7.2.2 above). The best example to date of germaneness analysis, however, is provided by two cases decided by the Sixth Circuit U.S. Court of Appeals in 2001, *Bonnell* and *Hardy,* both discussed in Section 7.2.2 above. In *Bonnell,* in determining that a professor's classroom speech was not protected, the court emphasized that the speech was "not germane to the subject matter." In *Hardy,* in the course of protecting the professor's classroom speech, the court emphasized that it "was germane to the subject matter and advance[d] an academic message." In both cases, the court also recognized "the robust tradition of academic freedom in our nation's post-secondary schools" (*Hardy,* 260 F.3d at 680; see also *Bonnell,* 241 F.3d at 823) and used the germaneness test as an adjunct to this tradition of academic freedom. So used, germaneness analysis differs from pedagogical concerns analysis (number 4 above) because it focuses first on the *faculty member's* rather than the *institution's* pedagogical interests. Both sets of interests are pertinent to germaneness analysis, as well as to pedagogical concerns analysis; but germaneness analysis gives more immediate and direct attention, and greater weight, to the faculty interests.[25]

The germaneness approach does not provide that faculty members will always prevail if their classroom speech is germane to the subject matter, since this analysis must take account of institutional pedagogical interests as well as faculty pedagogical interests. It is therefore necessary to supplement the germaneness analysis by borrowing from one of the other approaches that consider both institutional and faculty interests. The two approaches that could fit this bill are the *Pickering/Connick* approach (number 2 above) and the pedagogical concerns approach (number 4 above). The *Silva* court's opinion provides a modest example of a merger of pedagogical concerns analysis and germaneness analysis. More important, the Sixth Circuit's opinion in the *Hardy* case provides a highly instructive example of a merger of germaneness analysis and *Pickering/Connick* analysis. (See Section 7.2.2 above for further discussion of this "merger.")

---

[25]A germaneness or "germane speech" test was also at issue in *Board of Regents of the Univ. of Wisconsin System v. Southworth,* 529 U.S. 217 (2000) (see Sections 10.1.3 & 8.1.4)—a case raising questions pertinent to student academic freedom and institutional autonomy. Although the Court had used this test in other contexts (see 529 U.S. at 227, 230–32), including a faculty rights case, it rejected the test as "unworkable" and "unmanageable in the public university setting" (*Id.* at 231–32) when applied to extracurricular student speech such as that in *Southworth.* The circumstances of *Southworth,* however, are clearly distinguishable from those in the academic freedom in teaching cases discussed in this Section. In *Southworth,* the Court would have had to address numerous abstract questions of whether particular types of speech content were germane to the university's mission and "the whole universe of speech and ideas" (*Id.* at 232). It was this "vast extent of permitted expression" that made "the test of germane speech inappropriate . . ." (*Id.*). In contrast, in the faculty academic freedom cases, there are "discernable limits" (see 529 U.S. at 232) to the speech pertinent to a particular course or class session. Moreover, the germaneness issues arising in the classroom cases are amenable to testimony by deans, department chairs, faculty colleagues, and outside academic experts in ways that the issues in *Southworth* were not.

The germaneness approach, supplemented by *Pickering/Connick* analysis or a modified pedagogical concerns analysis, is the approach most likely to take suitable account of the unique circumstances of academic life. The professor's "freedom of germane speech" would be based directly on a "freedom to teach" that can be considered a correlative or implied right emanating from the free speech clause (see *Griswold v. Connecticut*, 381 U.S. 479, 483 (1965), as discussed in Section 7.1 above). The freedom of germane speech would also be compatible with AAUP policies on academic freedom (see Section 7.1 above)—in particular the 1940 Statement, which declares that faculty members have a freedom to teach in the classroom but cautions that this freedom does not extend to "teaching controversial matter which has no relation to [the] subject"; the 1970 Interpretive Comments, which add that "the intent of [the 1940 Statement] is not to discourage what is 'controversial' [but] to underscore the need for teachers to avoid persistently intruding material which has no relation to their subject"; and the 1995 statement on "Sexual Harassment: Suggested Policy and Procedures for Handling Complaints," which provides that speech or conduct is not considered sexual harassment "in the teaching context" unless it is "persistent, pervasive, and not germane to the subject matter" (*AAUP Policy Documents and Reports*, 3, 6, 172; see also Robin Wilson, "Wisconsin Scales Back Its Faculty Speech Code: Professors Will Now Have Blanket Protection for All Comments That Are 'Germane' to a Course," *Chron. Higher Educ.*, March 12, 1999, A10.) This fifth approach, then, bears careful watching and could become the preferred approach in most circumstances (see, for example, *Rubin v. Ikenberry*, 933 F. Supp. 1425 (C.D. Ill. 1996)). While this would be a welcome development, it would be imperative that the germaneness analysis be applied with considerable reliance on internal peer review of teaching and, in especially difficult cases, on outside expert opinion regarding learning theory, teaching methodology, and the academic parameters of particular subjects.

6. *Other (miscellaneous) types of analysis. Clark v. Holmes, Martin v. Parrish,* and *Bonnell v. Lorenzo* (Section 7.2.2 above) all include abbreviated versions of "captive audience" analysis. (See the analysis of *Bonnell* for examples of factors to consider in determining whether students in a particular course may be considered a "captive audience.") While this approach may be useful in some situations concerning classroom speech, it is better viewed as an adjunct to the other approaches rather than as a separate and independent alternative. In particular, under the *Pickering/Connick* approach, "captive audience" considerations could be relevant to the "form" and "context" of the speech under the first prong of the test; and protecting a "captive audience" from discomfort and embarrassment could be a relevant interest on the institution's side of the scale under the second prong of the test. Also, under the germaneness approach, "captive audience" considerations could be relevant in determining how much leeway a court should provide for "nongermane" speech in the classroom; a court may be less tolerant of arguably nongermane speech, and less willing to protect the faculty member, when the faculty member has a "captive audience" for his classes. If captive audience analysis is used, however, serious attention

must be given to whether the class is actually "captive." The pertinent questions to ask are set out in the *Bonnell* discussion (Section 7.2.2 above).

Parate v. Isibor (Section 7.2.3 above) includes an example of "compelled speech" analysis. This analysis may apply when a faculty member is penalized for what he or she *would not say,* or said only under protest, rather than for what he or she did say or did not object to saying. The basic argument is that the free speech clause protects individuals from being compelled by government to express ideas or opinions with which they disagree. As such, this type of analysis could be pertinent to grading disputes like that in *Parate,* as well as to classroom situations in which an instructor is directed to express others' ideas or opinions as if they were his or her own, or to support ideas and opinions to which he or she is conscientiously opposed. Like germaneness analysis (number 5 above), however, compelled speech analysis should not be applied in a manner that ignores the institution's legitimate academic interests. When government is regulating its citizens in general, there are usually no governmental interests that would justify compelled speech (*Wooley v. Maynard,* 430 U.S. 705 (1977)); and this is also usually the case when government is regulating members of the academic community (*West Virginia State Board of Education v. Barnette,* 319 U.S. 624 (1943)). But in the specific context of the classroom and teaching, if the institution's academic interests are genuinely at stake, there may be an occasional situation in which courts will find an institution's interests to be sufficiently strong to justify a regulation of speech that includes an element of compulsion. (For an example of such a case, and a court opinion that provides an extended example of compelled speech analysis, see *Axson-Flynn v. Johnson,* 356 F.3d 1277 (10th Cir. 2004), discussed in Section 8.1.4.)

Another possibility is the "material and substantial disruption" and the "undifferentiated fear of disturbance" analysis that comes from the *Tinker* case (see Section 9.5.1 of this book) (or a similar standard that can be implied from the *Pickering* case's consideration of whether the teacher's speech had a disruptive effect on the operation of the public schools (see Section 7.1.1 of this book)). In *Bishop v. Aronov* (Section 7.2.2), the appellate court declined to apply the *Tinker* case or the material and substantial disruption standard to the classroom speech at issue there. In the *Hardy* case, however, the court did use the "undifferentiated fear" part of the *Tinker* analysis in a secondary, supporting role: to determine whether the college's interests were based on "undifferentiated fear of disturbance" and thus insufficient to overcome the faculty member's free speech interests. Used in this way, the *Tinker* analysis becomes an addendum to the second prong of the *Pickering/Connick* test rather than an independent line of analysis.

Finally, in *Bishop,* the federal district court used public forum analysis (see Section 9.5.2 of this book) to decide the case in the professor's favor. The appellate court disagreed and, appropriately, declined to treat the classroom as a public forum (926 F.2d at 1071; and see also Section 7.1.1 of this book).

7.2.5. Private institutions. Since First Amendment rights and other federal constitutional rights generally do not apply to or limit private institutions, as

explained in Section 1.5.2 of this book, legal arguments concerning the freedom to teach in private institutions are usually based on contract law. The sources, scope, and terms of faculty contracts are discussed in Section 6.1 of this book, and the contractual academic freedom rights of faculty members are discussed more specifically in Section 7.1.3. When the "1940 Statement of Principles on Academic Freedom" is incorporated into the faculty contract or relied upon as a source of custom and usage (see Section 7.1.3 above), it will usually provide the starting point for analyzing the faculty member's freedom in teaching. The 1940 Statement provides that "[t]eachers are entitled to freedom in the classroom in discussing their subject," but also contains this limitation: "[Teachers] should be careful not to introduce into their teaching controversial matter which has no relationship to their subject . . ." (*AAUP Policy Documents and Reports*, 3).

The case of *McConnell v. Howard University*, 818 F.2d 58 (D.C. Cir. 1987) (discussed further in Sections 2.2.5 & 6.6.2) is an instructive example of a dispute in a private institution about contractual protections for the freedom to teach. In *McConnell*, a professor had been discharged after challenging his university's handling of an in-class conflict that arose between him and a student in one of his classes. The professor brought a breach of contract action, and the appellate court was sympathetic to the professor's argument that the university's actions breached the contract between the professor and the university. In reversing a summary judgment for the university, and remanding the case for a trial *de novo*, the appellate court declined to adopt traditional contract principles so as to accord deference to the judgments of the university's administrators. The court's reasoning indicates that, in some circumstances, contract law will protect the teaching freedom of faculty members in private institutions and that contract claims may sometimes be more promising vehicles for faculty members than federal constitutional claims.

Contractual freedom to teach issues may arise in private religious institutions as well as private secular institutions (as in *McConnell*), in which case additional complexities may be present (see Section 7.8 below). The unusual case of *Curran v. Catholic University of America* (discussed in Section 6.2.5) is an instructive example of this type of case.

Sec. 7.3. Academic Freedom in Research and Publication

Academic freedom protections clearly extend to the research and publication activities of faculty members.[26] Such activities are apparently the most ardently protected of all faculty activities. In the "1940 Statement of Principles on Academic Freedom and Tenure" (see Section 7.1.3 above), "full freedom in research and in the publication of the results" is presented as the first of three essential

---

[26]Research and publication also includes artistic creation, and the performance and display of artistic works. See generally Robert O'Neil, "Artistic Freedom and Academic Freedom," 53 *Law & Contemp. Probs.* 177 (1993). The freedom to research and publish would also apparently include a freedom to seek and obtain funds to support such efforts. For an example, see Julie Nicklin, "Arbitrator Tells U. of Delaware to Allow Grant Requests to 'Racist' Fund," *Chron. Higher Educ.*, September 4, 1991.

aspects of faculty academic freedom, and this "full freedom" does not include any limitation regarding subject matter, as does the freedom in the classroom that is listed second (*AAUP Policy Documents and Reports* (9th ed., 2001), 3). The courts, moreover, tend to distinguish between research and teaching and to provide stronger protection for the former. In *Bishop v. Aronov,* 926 F.2d 1066 (11th Cir. 1991) (discussed in Section 7.2.2 above), for example, the court upheld university limitations on the content of a professor's classroom speech. At the same time, however, the court emphasized that "[t]he University has not suggested that [the professor] cannot hold his particular views; express them, on his own time, far and wide and to whomever will listen; *or write and publish, no doubt authoritatively,* on them, *nor could it so prohibit him*"; and that the professor's "educational judgment can be questioned and redirected by the University when he is acting under its auspices as a course instructor, but not when he acts as an independent . . . researcher" (926 F.2d at 1076–77, emphasis added). The case of *Levin v. Harleston,* discussed below, illustrates this broad protection for faculty research and publication.

As colleges and universities have moved further into the age of information technology—and faculty members employ new means of researching, storing research, and disseminating their views—new questions have arisen about the freedom of research and publication. One example concerns research that faculty members do on computers supplied by the institution and the extent to which the institution or (in the case of public institutions) the state might impose limitations on faculty members' research using such equipment. The case of *Urofsky v. Gilmore,* discussed at length below, illustrates the issues that may arise if the state or a public institution restricts the content of the materials that faculty members may access or store on state-owned computers. In other situations, issues could arise if an institution seeks access to research or communications faculty members have stored on their office computers (see Martha McCaughey, "Windows Without Curtains: Computer Privacy and Academic Freedom," *Academe,* September–October 2003, 39–42). Another example concerns faculty members' use of the institution's Web page and server to display research or communicate personal viewpoints, and the extent to which the institution might impose limits on such use. Issues might arise, for instance, if an institution orders a faculty member to remove controversial or offensive content from a Web log that he or she maintains on the university's Web site (see Robert O'Neil, "Controversial Weblogs and Academic Freedom," *Chron. Higher Educ.,* January 16, 2004, B16). In most cases, such issues—though tinged with new technological implications—can nevertheless be resolved by careful application of traditional legal principles and sensitive consideration of the traditional attributes of the college and university environment, as addressed in the discussion below.

Levin v. Harleston, 770 F. Supp. 895 (S.D.N.Y. 1991), *affirmed in part and vacated in part,* 966 F.2d 85 (2d Cir. 1992), involves traditional media, not new technology, for faculty members' publication of views and features the application of classical First Amendment and academic freedom principles. A philosophy professor at City College of the City University of New York had opined in certain writings and publications that blacks are less intelligent on average than whites. In addition, he had opposed all use of affirmative action quotas. As a result of these writings, he became controversial on campus.[27] Student groups staged demonstrations; documents affixed to his door were burned; and students distributed pamphlets outside his classroom. On several occasions, groups of students made so much noise outside his classroom that he could not conduct the class. The college's written regulations prohibited student demonstrations that have the effect of disrupting or obstructing teaching and research activities. Despite this regulation and the professor's repeated reports about the disruptions, the university took no action against the student demonstrators. The college did, however, take two affirmative steps to deal with the controversy regarding the professor. First, the college dean (one defendant) created "shadow sections" (alternative sections) for the professor's required introductory philosophy course. Second, the college president (another defendant) appointed an ad hoc faculty committee "to review the question of when speech both in and outside the classroom may go beyond the protection of academic freedom or become conduct unbecoming a member of the faculty."

To implement the shadow sections, the college dean sent letters to the professor's students, informing them of the option to enroll in these sections. The dean stated in the letter, however, that he was "aware of no evidence suggesting that Professor Levin's views on controversial matters have compromised his performance as an able teacher of Philosophy who is fair in his treatment of students." After implementation of the shadow sections, enrollment in the professor's classes decreased by one-half. The college had never before used such sections to allow students to avoid a particular professor because of his views.

To implement the ad hoc committee, the president charged the members "to specifically review information concerning Professor Michael Levin . . . and to include in its report its recommendations concerning what the response of the College should be." The language of the charge tracked certain language in college bylaws and professional contracts concerning the discipline of faculty members and the revocation of tenure. Three of the seven committee members had previously signed a faculty petition condemning the professor. Moreover, although the committee met more than ten times, it never extended the professor an opportunity to address it. The committee's report, as summarized by the district court, stated "that Professor Levin's writings constitute unprofessional and inappropriate conduct that harms the educational process at the college, and that the college has properly intervened to protect his students from his views by creating the shadow sections."

The professor sought declaratory and injunctive relief, claiming that the defendants' failure to enforce the student demonstration regulations, the creation of the shadow sections, and the operation of the ad hoc committee violated his rights under the federal Constitution's free speech and due process clauses. After trial, the district court issued a lengthy opinion agreeing with the

---

[27]The *Levin* case is often compared with the later case of *Jeffries v. Harleston*—not only because the two cases involve the same university but also because both cases involve derogatory speech regarding particular minority groups. *Jeffries* is discussed in Section 7.5.2 below.

professor. Relying on *Keyishian* (see Section 7.1.4), the court noted the chilling and stigmatizing effect of the ad hoc committee's activities, as demonstrated by the fact that, during the time the committee was meeting, the professor had declined more than twenty invitations to speak or write about his controversial views. The court held that the professor had "objectively reasonable bases" to fear losing his position, and that the effects on him were "exactly that predicted in *Keyishian*. . . . Professor Levin was forced to 'stay as far away as possible from utterances or acts which might jeopardize his living.'" To determine whether this infringement on the professor's speech was nonetheless legitimate, the court then undertook a *Pickering/Connick* analysis. It held that there was "no question" that the professor's speech was "protected expression," since his writings and statements addressed matters that were "quintessentially 'issues of public importance.'" The only justification advanced by the defendants for the ad hoc committee and shadow sections was the need to protect the professor's students from harm that could accrue "if they thought, because of the expression of his views, that he might expect less of them or grade them unfairly." The court, however, rejected this justification because City College had presented no evidence at trial to support it. Consequently, the trial court granted injunctive relief, compelling the defendants to investigate the alleged violations of the college's student demonstration regulations and prohibiting the defendants from any further use of the shadow sections or the ad hoc committee.

The appellate court generally agreed with the district court's reasoning regarding the shadow sections and the ad hoc committee. The court noted that the "formation of the alternative sections would not be unlawful if done to further a legitimate educational purpose that outweighed the infringement on Professor Levin's First Amendment rights." But the defendants had presented no evidence to support their contention that the professor's expression of his ideas outside the classroom harmed the educational process within the classroom. In fact, "none of Professor Levin's students had ever complained of unfair treatment on the basis of race." The court concluded that the defendants' "encouragement of the continued erosion in the size of Professor Levin's class if he does not mend his extracurricular ways is the antithesis of freedom of expression." The appellate court also agreed that the operation of the ad hoc committee had a "chilling effect" on the professor's speech and thus violated his First Amendment rights. Affirming that "governmental action which falls short of direct prohibition on speech may violate the First Amendment by chilling the free exercise of speech," the court determined that, when the president "deliberately formed the committee's inquiry into Levin's conduct to mirror the contractual standard for disciplinary action, he conveyed the threat that Levin would be dismissed if he continued voicing his racial theories."

The appellate court disagreed, however, with the district court's conclusion regarding the college's failure to enforce its student demonstration regulations. Since the college generally had not enforced these regulations, and there was no evidence that "the college treated student demonstrations directed at Professor Levin any differently than other student demonstrations," the defendants' inaction could not be considered a violation of the professor's constitutional rights.

To implement its conclusions, the appellate court affirmed the portion of the trial court's injunction prohibiting the defendants from using the shadow sections. Regarding the ad hoc committee, the appellate court modified the relief ordered by the trial court. Since the ad hoc committee had recommended no disciplinary action and had no further investigations or disciplinary proceedings pending, the injunction was unnecessary. It was sufficient to issue an order that merely declared the unconstitutionality of the defendants' use of the committee, since such declaratory relief would make clear that "disciplinary proceedings, or the threat thereof, predicated solely upon Levin's continued expression of his views outside of the classroom" would violate his free speech rights. Regarding the student demonstration regulations, the appellate court vacated the portion of the trial court's injunction ordering the defendants to investigate the alleged violations of the regulations.

Levin is an important case for several reasons. It painstakingly chronicles a major academic freedom dispute centering on faculty publication activities; it demonstrates a relationship between academic freedom and the phenomenon of "political correctness";[28] and it strongly supports faculty academic freedom in research by using the federal Constitution as a basic source of protection. The courts' opinions do not break new legal ground, however, since they use established principles and precedents applicable to public employees generally and do not emphasize the unique circumstances of academic freedom on the college campus. But these opinions do provide a very useful response to the particular facts before the court. The case dealt with traditionally protected faculty speech—writing and outside publication expressing opinions on matters of public concern—and not with opinions expressed in classroom lectures or in course materials. Not only is such publication given the highest protection, but the defendants produced no evidence that the professor's writings and views had any adverse impact on his classroom performance or his treatment of students. The college had never before created shadow sections and had advanced no "legitimate educational interest" in using them in this circumstance. Finally, the numerous procedural flaws in the establishment and operation of the ad hoc committee strongly supported, if only circumstantially, the professor's claims that his constitutional rights were being chilled.

In *Urofsky v. Gilmore*, 216 F.3d 401 (4th Cir. 2000) (*en banc*), the full twelve-member bench of the Fourth Circuit issued a ruling that contrasts starkly with *Levin* and is deeply inhospitable to faculty academic freedom in research. The case concerned a Virginia statute, codified as "Restrictions on State Employee Access to Information Infrastructure," that restricts the Internet-based research

---

[28]According to the trial court, "[t]his case raises serious constitutional questions that go to the heart of the current national debate on what has come to be denominated as 'political correctness' in speech and thought on the campuses of the nation's colleges and universities" (footnote omitted). See generally Paul Berman (ed.), *Debating P.C.: The Controversy over Political Correctness on College Campuses* (Dell, 1992).

of state employees, including faculty members at the state's higher educational institutions. The relevant codified language states:

> Except to the extent required in conjunction with a bona fide, agency-approved research project or other agency-approved undertaking, no agency employee shall utilize agency-owned or agency-leased computer equipment to access, download, print or store any information infrastructure files or services having sexually explicit content [Va. Code Ann. § 2.2-2827(B)(2001); an earlier version of this statute, in force during the *Urofsky* litigation, was cited as Va. Code Ann. §§ 2.1-804 to 806 (1996), as amended in 1999)].

The statute defines "informational infrastructure" as including the various types of computer files and the modes of accessing and securing these files (that is, computer networks and the Internet). "Computer equipment" is not defined.

The statute prohibits state employees from using state-owned or state-leased computers to access information with "sexually explicit content" without prior approval from the head of the agency for which the employee works. The plaintiffs, who were professors at various Virginia state colleges and universities, argued that the statute interfered with their ability to do research concerning sexuality and the human body in various fields such as art, literature, psychology, history, and medicine. Specifically, the professors made two claims: (1) that the statute was unconstitutional on its face, since it restricted the content of the speech of public employees speaking on matters of public concern; and (2) that the statute was unconstitutional as applied to "academic employees," since it burdened their First Amendment "right to academic freedom" in research. The state responded that the statute restricted only employee speech, not the speech of citizens addressing matters of public concern, and that this restriction served state interests in "maintain[ing] operational efficiency in the workplace" and "prevent[ing] the creation of a sexually hostile work environment" (995 F. Supp. at 639).

The district court, using the *Pickering/Connick* standards (see Section 7.1.1), invalidated the statute as an impermissible restriction on speech on matters of public concern (*Urofsky v. Allen*, 995 F. Supp. 634 (E.D. Va. 1998)). In applying *Pickering/Connick*, the court emphasized various factors regarding the statute that served to increase the state's burden of justifying the statute's restrictions on speech. *First,* the statute is broad in scope, deterring a large number of potential speakers and covering a broad category of speech. *Second,* the statute has a substantial capacity to "chill" speakers in advance because of their concern that their speech activities may violate the statute. *Third,* the statute has a substantial adverse impact on the general public's right to receive information, an impact exacerbated by the fact that the information suppressed is that of state employees who have special expertise of particular benefit to the public. *Fourth,* the statutory restriction on speech is explicitly content based, targeting sexual speech, but not any other speech that could impinge on state interests in the workplace. *Fifth,* the statute restricts the use of the Internet, "arguably the most powerful tool for sharing information ever developed," thus enhancing the burden the statute places on speech (see generally *Reno v.*

American Civil Liberties Union, 521 U.S. 844, 849–53 (1997), discussed in Section 13.2.12.2).

On appeal, a three-judge panel of the Fourth Circuit reversed the district court, reasoning that the professors were speaking (and were restricted by the statute) only in their capacities as state employees, not as citizens commenting upon matters of public interest, and therefore had no First Amendment protection (*Urofsky v. Gilmore,* 167 F.3d 191 (4th Cir. 1999)). The full appellate court (all twelve judges) then reviewed the case *en banc.* The majority agreed with the panel's decision but issued a majority opinion that is much more expansive than the panel's and even more inhospitable to faculty academic freedom. The full Fourth Circuit thus upheld the panel decision, ruling that the Virginia statute did not violate the First Amendment. Seven judges joined in the majority opinion (two of whom also wrote concurring opinions); one judge (Chief Justice Wilkinson) wrote an opinion concurring only in the judgment, and four judges joined in a dissenting opinion.

The *en banc* majority relied on an abbreviated *Pickering/Connick* analysis based on the reasoning of the three-judge panel to conclude that the statute did not violate the free speech rights of public employees (that is, it was facially constitutional). The majority then undertook a lengthy review of the theory and practice of academic freedom to conclude that the statute did not violate faculty members' First Amendment rights regarding their research projects (that is, the statute was constitutional as applied to the plaintiffs). Under the majority's reasoning, therefore, faculty members, like all public employees, do have free speech rights, and these rights protect them in the same way and to the same extent as other public employees; they do not have any additional or different free speech rights, beyond those of other public employees, that accrue to them because they work in academia.

In the *Pickering/Connick* part of its analysis (addressing the statute's facial constitutionality), the *en banc* court in *Urofsky* first reviewed the scope and application of the Virginia statute. The critical threshold question, according to the court, is whether the statute regulates employees "primarily in [their] role as citizen[s] or primarily in [their] role as employee[s]." Only in the former circumstance, according to the majority, do public employees enjoy the First Amendment protections articulated in the *Pickering/Connick* line of cases. The *Urofsky* court therefore focused only on the status or "role" of the person speaking—whether he or she is speaking as a citizen or as an employee—and did not consider the type of speech being regulated—whether the speech addresses a matter of public concern or a matter of private concern:

> This focus on the capacity of the speaker recognizes the basic truth that speech by public employees undertaken in the course of their job duties will frequently involve matters of vital concern to the public, without giving those employees a First Amendment right to dictate to the state how they will do their jobs. . . .
> [T]he government is entitled to control the content of the speech because it has, in a meaningful sense, "purchased the speech at issue" through . . . payment of a salary [216 F.3d at 407 and 408 n.6].

Having declared its preference for using the role or status of the speaker as the litmus test for employee speech protections, the court then determined that the professors were speaking only as employees and not as citizens. As a result, the court did not analyze whether the speech at issue—access to and dissemination of sexually explicit materials for particular professional research projects—could rise to the level of public concern speech. Nor did the majority balance the professors' free speech interests against the state's interest in maintaining an efficient and nonhostile workplace. Instead, the majority simply determined that:

> The speech at issue here—access to certain materials using computers owned or leased by the state for the purpose of carrying out employment duties—is clearly made in the employee's role as employee. [T]he challenged aspect of the Act does not regulate the speech of the citizenry in general, but rather the speech of state employees in their capacity as employees. . . . Because . . . the challenged aspect of the Act does not affect speech by [faculty members] in their capacity as private citizens speaking on matters of public concern, it does not infringe the First Amendment rights of state employees [216 F.3d at 408–9].

By adopting this strained view of the public concern test and thereby avoiding the *Pickering/Connick* balancing test, the *en banc* court also conveniently avoided the impact of *United States v. National Treasury Employees Union,* 513 U.S. 454 (1995) (discussed in Section 7.1 of this book). This case requires a different and stronger showing of government interest when the speech of a large group of employees is limited by statute or administrative regulation. The case also warns of the burdens placed on employee speech by a "ban" that "deters an enormous quantity of speech before it is uttered, based only on speculation that the speech might threaten the Government's interests" (513 U.S. at 467 n.11). The dissenting opinion in *Urofsky* provides an example of how the *NTEU* case's balancing analysis would apply to the Virginia statute (216 F.3d at 439–41 (Murnaghan, J. dissenting)). In addition, by taking the position it did on the public concern test, the court majority avoided the "overbreadth" and "vagueness" analysis often applied to statutes regulating speech and thus also avoided any application of the *Keyishian* case (see Section 7.1), which employed such analysis and warned against statutes that exert a "chilling effect" on free speech.

In his concurring opinion, Chief Judge Wilkinson criticized the *en banc* majority's use of the *Pickering/Connick* line of cases[29] because:

> [B]y placing exclusive emphasis on the fact that the statute covers speech of "state employees in their capacity as employees . . ." the majority rests its conclusions solely on the "form" of the speech. The public concern inquiry, however, does not cease with form. The majority fails to examine the "content" of the speech, which surely touches on matters of political and social importance.

---

[29]The Wilkinson opinion, in turn, was criticized by another judge writing a concurring opinion (216 F.3d at 416–25 (Luttig, J., concurring)).

It also fails to examine the "context" of the speech, which can occur in a variety of settings, including the public university. As this case was brought by public university professors, I consider the statute's application to academic inquiry as a useful illustration of how the statute restricts material of public concern [216 F.3d at 426–27].

Regarding "context," for instance, Chief Judge Wilkinson made these points that, in his view, are central to the first prong of the *Pickering/Connick* analysis but are ignored by the majority:

[T]he context of the affected speech is unique. In the university setting "the State acts against a background and tradition of thought and experiment that is at the center of our intellectual and philosophic tradition." *Rosenberger v. Rector & Visitors of Univ. of Va.*, 515 U.S. 819, 835 (1995). Internet research, novel though it be, lies at the core of that tradition. These plaintiffs are state employees, it is true. But these particular employees are hired for the very purpose of inquiring into, reflecting upon, and speaking out on matters of public concern. A faculty is employed professionally to test ideas and to propose solutions, to deepen knowledge and refresh perspectives. See William W. Van Alstyne, "Academic Freedom and the First Amendment in the Supreme Court of the United States: An Unhurried Historical Review," 53 *Law & Contemp. Probs.* 79, 87 (1990). Provocative comment is endemic to the work of a university faculty whose "function is primarily one of critical review." Id.

Furthermore, state university professors work in the context of considerable academic independence. The statute limits professors' ability to use the Internet to research and to write. But in their research and writing university professors are not state mouthpieces—they speak mainly for themselves. See generally David M. Rabban, "Functional Analysis of 'Individual' and 'Institutional' Academic Freedom Under the First Amendment," 53 *Law & Contemp. Probs.* 227, 242–44 (1990). It is not enough to declare, as the majority does, "The speech at issue here . . . is clearly made in the employee's role as employee." No one assumes when reading a professor's work that it bears the imprimatur of the government or that it carries the approval of his or her academic institution [216 F.3d at 428–29].

By failing to consider the "content" and "context" of the prohibited speech, the Chief Judge said, the majority has reached a result under which:

even the grossest statutory restrictions on public employee speech will be evaluated by a simple calculus: if speech involves one's position as a public employee, it will enjoy no First Amendment protection whatsoever. My colleagues in the majority would thus permit any statutory restriction on academic speech and research, even one that baldly discriminated on the basis of social perspective or political point of view [216 F.3d at 434].

The dissenting opinion (joined by four judges) also criticizes the majority's use of *Pickering/Connick*, arguing that "the majority has adopted an unduly restrictive interpretation of the 'public concern' doctrine" and that its "formalistic focus on the 'role of the speaker' in employee speech cases . . . runs directly contrary to Supreme Court precedent" (216 F.3d at 435–39). Even one of the judges joining in the majority opinion wrote a separate concurrence indicating that he had joined the majority because he felt bound by a prior Fourth Circuit case in which he had dissented, and that were he "left to [his] own devices," he "would hold that the [professors'] speech in this case is entitled to some measure of First Amendment protection, thus triggering application of the *Connick/Pickering* balancing test" (216 F.3d at 425–26 (Hamilton, J., dissenting)).[30]

In the academic freedom part of its analysis (addressing the Virginia statute's application to "academic employees' right to academic freedom"), the *Urofsky* majority acknowledged that the U.S. Supreme Court, in various cases, has addressed and supported a constitutional concept of academic freedom. The Supreme Court's focus, however—according to the *Urofsky* majority—was always on the institution's own academic freedom, and not on the academic freedom of individual faculty members: "the Supreme Court, to the extent it has constitutionalized a right of academic freedom at all, appears to have recognized only an institutional right to self-governance in academic affairs" (216 F.3d at 412). (See Section 7.1.6 above for discussion of "institutional academic freedom.") The *Urofsky* majority then determined that faculty members do not have any constitutional right to academic freedom, under the First Amendment, whether in regard to research or to other faculty functions. The majority therefore rejected the professors' academic freedom claim because its "review of the law" led it "to conclude that to the extent the Constitution recognizes any right of 'academic freedom' above and beyond the First Amendment rights to which every citizen is entitled, the right inheres in the University, not in individual professors . . ." (216 F.3d at 410).[31]

Although it rejected the professors' free speech and academic freedom claims, the *Urofksy* majority did acknowledge that other claims might validly arise when the Virginia statute's provision on prior approval for research with sexually explicit content (Va. Code Ann. § 2.2-2827(B)) is applied to individual cases: "[A] denial of an application under the Act based upon a refusal to approve a particular research project might raise genuine questions—perhaps even constitutional ones—concerning the extent of the authority of a university to control the work of its faculty. . . ." But, said the majority, "such questions

---

[30]The majority, having rejected the professors' claim under the first prong of the *Pickering/Connick* analysis (the public concern test), did not consider the second prong (the balancing test) mentioned in Judge Hamilton's concurring opinion. Both the Wilkinson concurring opinion and the dissent, however, did reach the second prong of the analysis. The Wilkinson opinion concluded that the state's interests, on balance, outweighed the professors' speech interests (216 F.3d at 431–34 (Wilkinson, Ch. J., concurring in judgment)); the dissent reached the opposite conclusion. The Chief Judge relied extensively on the unique circumstances of higher education and academic freedom; the dissenters relied on more general factors that would be common to most public employee speech. Both opinions provide useful (though divergent) illustrations of how to do the balancing analysis in faculty speech cases.

[31]Neither the Wilkinson opinion, the Hamilton opinion, nor the dissent directly addresses the majority's broad rejection of the plaintiffs' second claim. The Wilkinson opinion does contain extended and supportive discussion of academic freedom (see 216 F.3d at 428, 431–35) that seems to acknowledge both faculty and institutional academic freedom, and also applies the *Pickering/Connick* test with particular reference to faculty members' freedom of inquiry.

are not presented here" (216 F.3d at 415 n.17). Thus the majority did recognize that other legal issues may arise if a faculty member who seeks prior approval is refused permission; but at the same time the majority determined that this possibility of future violations was not sufficient to invalidate the statute either on its face or as applied to the plaintiffs (who had not sought prior approvals).

The dissenters, on the other hand, echoed the district court's opinion in arguing that the Virginia statute is unconstitutional because it gives institutions broad, virtually unfettered, discretion as the sole arbiters for approving prior requests for accessing and disseminating sexually explicit materials used for professional purposes.[32] In rejecting the statute as both overinclusive and under-inclusive in restricting broad categories of speech used for beneficial public purposes, the *Urofsky* dissent determined that the statute's prior approval requirement could lead to arbitrary decisions that could "chill" faculty members' speech:

> The danger of arbitrary censorship is particularly relevant in the instant case, given the differing views on the merits of research and discussion into sexually-related topics. . . . [T]he mere existence of the licensor's unfettered discretion, coupled with the power of prior restraint, intimidates parties into censoring their own speech, even if the discretion and power are never actually abused [216 F.3d at 441].

Faculty members subject to the Virginia statute, or a similar statute or regulation in another state, apparently have two options for avoiding such strictures on computer-based research. First, a faculty member may conduct the research using personally owned computer equipment; and second, the faculty member may seek the institution's prior approval for a professional research project that will utilize the restricted materials. The first option is available because the statute addresses only a professor's use of "agency-owned or agency-leased computer equipment"; thus, as the majority acknowledged, "state employees remain free to access sexually explicit materials from their personal or other computers not owned or leased by the state." Presumably, faculty members could use personal computers in their faculty offices to access or store sexually explicit research material. But the statute may prohibit the use of personal computers to access the university's Internet connections or search engines, or to store sexually explicit materials on the university's network, since they may be considered to be "computer equipment" within the meaning of Section 2-2.2827.

The second option is available under the statute's prior approval clause just discussed. This option requires that faculty members be aware of how their institutions have interpreted and implemented this clause. The option will be more meaningful if faculty members, collectively and individually, become involved in their institution's policy making and decision making on prior approvals. The institution could, apparently, adopt a blanket approval policy or

---

[32]Judge Wilkinson, in his concurrence, takes a quite different tack. He viewed the prior approval requirement as a feature of the statute that preserved academic freedom and helped secure the Virginia statute's constitutionality (216 F.3d at 432–34 (Wilkinson, Ch. J., concurring in result)).

an "advance permission" policy for faculty members in particular disciplines or departments—or perhaps all faculty members—thus minimizing the statute's restraint on faculty research. (See the district court's discussion of this point; 995 F. Supp. at 642–43.) If an institution establishes more rigorous criteria for gaining prior approval to access the restricted materials, then it would be important to assure that the criteria are clear, that there is a tight time frame for making decisions on approval requests, and that any faculty member whose request is denied will receive a full statement of the reasons for the denial. In the case of a denial, the decision may apparently be challenged in court, the *Urofsky* court having left the door open for such challenges (216 F.3d at 415 n.17; see also 216 F.3d at 441 (Murnaghan, J., dissenting)).

When the *en banc* majority opinion in *Urofsky* is viewed together with the concurrences and dissents, and with the district's court's opinion, the case provides a highly instructive debate on faculty academic freedom, especially (but not only) with respect to academic research. While the majority opinion is the controlling law in the Fourth Circuit, there is good reason to question whether its abrupt rejection of public employee speech rights and faculty academic freedom rights will, or should, become the prevailing legal view. The seven judges in the *Urofsky* majority were strongly criticized by the remaining five judges: Chief Judge Wilkinson concurring in the result (216 F.3d at 426–35) and Judge Murnaghan and the other three judges joining in his dissenting opinion (216 F.3d at 435–41)). The Wilkinson opinion and the dissent both make important points worth serious consideration, as does the district court's opinion in the same case (995 F. Supp. 634). The majority's reasoning has also been strongly criticized in the legal literature (see, for example, Richard Hiers, "Institutional Academic Freedom vs. Faculty Academic Freedom in Public Colleges and Universities: A Dubious Dichotomy," 29 *J. Coll. & Univ. Law* 35 (2002); J. Peter Byrne, "Constitutional Academic Freedom in Scholarship and in Court," *Chron. Higher Educ.*, January 5, 2001, B13). Moreover, the *Urofsky en banc* majority opinion for the Fourth Circuit appears to be inconsistent with the Second Circuit's opinion in the *Levin* case, discussed above, and with many other faculty academic freedom cases (see Sections 7.2 above & 7.4 below). The *Levin* opinion, the district court opinion in *Urofsky*, the Wilkinson concurrence in *Urofsky*, and the Murnaghan dissent in *Urofsky* all differ from one another in their reasoning in certain respects, and present four somewhat different views of the law, but all are united in their insistence that faculty members at public institutions do have First Amendment protections that extend to their research and writing activities. That is the better view of the law and is a view that can be well supported by a combination of the points made in these four sources.

Sec. 7.4. *Academic Freedom in Institutional Affairs*

7.4.1. In general. Faculty members are not only teachers and scholars; they are also participants in the governance of their academic programs, departments, and schools, and of the institution itself (see generally William G. Tierney & James T. Minor, *Challenges for Governance: A National Report* (Center for Higher Education Policy Analysis, 2003), available at http://www.usc.edu/ dept/chepa/gov/survey.shtml). Just as a faculty member's duties extend beyond instruction and research to governance, so do the possibilities for academic freedom disputes.

Although faculty members do not have any federal constitutional right to participate in the governance of their institutions (*Minnesota State Board for Community Colleges v. Knight,* 465 U.S. 271 (1984), discussed in Section 6.2.2), "[f]aculty involvement in academic governance has much to recommend it as a matter of academic policy," (465 U.S. at 288) and academic policy considerations have supported "a strong, if not universal or uniform, tradition of faculty participation in school governance" (465 U.S. at 287). In many institutions, moreover, faculty members' governance responsibilities and rights have been set out, at least in part, in institutional bylaws, faculty handbooks, or other documents that are part of the faculty member's contract with the institution. In addition to such formal or official participation in governance—at the institutional, school, department, and program levels—faculty members may also involve themselves informally in institutional affairs at any of these levels.

In both circumstances—formal participation in governance and informal involvement in institutional affairs—freedom of expression issues may arise, particularly issues concerning the faculty member's freedom to criticize the institution, or its trustees or officers, without fear of reprisal. In both public and private institutions, such issues may be dealt with using AAUP policy statements (in particular the "Statement on Government of Colleges and Universities," in *AAUP Policy Documents and Reports* (9th ed., 2001), 217), the statements of other associations,[33] or the policies and customs of the institution where the dispute arises. Principles of contract law may also be pertinent (see Section 7.1.3 above). In public institutions, issues about faculty expression may also be, and often are, dealt with using the federal Constitution's First Amendment. As the cases below illustrate, disputes about governance and institutional affairs that implicate the First Amendment are usually the most controversial and the most likely to result in litigation.

Many, but not all, faculty freedom of expression claims concerning governance and institutional affairs may also be considered academic freedom claims. The claim may properly be characterized as an academic freedom claim, and the dispute as an academic freedom dispute, if the opinions and ideas that the faculty member expresses implicate the *academic* operations of a program, department, or school; or if the faculty member's expression results in some administrative penalty that adversely affects his or her teaching or research opportunities or "chills" the expression of other faculty members on academic matters. When such connections to academic affairs are not apparent, the dispute may only concern free speech in general; in this situation, the faculty member's rights are essentially the same as those of any other public employee. If

---

[33]See, for example, the "AGB Statement on Institutional Governance" (Association of Governing Boards of Universities and Colleges, 1998); and see Neil Hamilton, "Are We Speaking the Same Language? Comparing AAUP and AGB," *Liberal Education,* Fall 1999, 24–31.

the dispute is genuinely an academic freedom dispute, however, questions may arise concerning whether the faculty member's constitutional rights to speak out regarding institutional affairs differ in kind or degree from those of other public employees. (See generally, Matthew Finkin, "'A Higher Order of Liberty in the Workplace': Academic Freedom and Tenure in the Vortex of Employment Practices and Law," 53 *Law & Contemp. Probs.* 357 (1990).)

In either situation, the interests that faculty members seek to protect, and those that institutions seek to protect, are different from interests relating to instruction or research. The institution may be concerned primarily with maintaining faculty members' focus on their contractual duties, promoting harmonious working relationships among faculty and administration, or maintaining the public's confidence in the institution. In contrast, the faculty member may be concerned about meaningful participation in governance, the freedom to criticize administrators, officers, and trustees as warranted, and more generally, the freedom to express views or personality on campus without fear of reprisal.

7.4.2. Speech on governance matters. In the cases discussed in this subsection, the First Amendment free speech clause is the primary focus of analysis, and courts have increasingly resorted to the *Pickering/Connick* line of cases (see Section 7.1.1) as the governing authority. From that line the lower courts have extracted a three-stage decision-making methodology. At the first stage, as explained in *Connick*, the question is whether the faculty member's speech is on a "matter of public concern." If it is not, the inquiry ends, and the faculty member is afforded no First Amendment protection. If the speech is on a matter of public concern, the court moves to the second stage and applies the *Pickering/Connick* balancing test. If the balance of interests weighs in favor of the institution, the inquiry ends, and the faculty member again obtains no First Amendment protection. If the balance of interests weighs in favor of the faculty member, however, the court will either protect the faculty member or proceed to a third stage of analysis, where questions of motivation and causation are considered. At this stage, if the faculty member cannot show that his protected statements were a "motivating factor" in the institution's decision to penalize him, or if the institution can show that, even though it may have considered the protected speech it would have nevertheless taken adverse action against the faculty member for reasons independent of the speech, the court will afford no First Amendment protection to the faculty member even if the speech was on a matter of public concern and the balance of interests weighed in the faculty member's favor. This potential third stage of the analysis is the focus of Section 7.6 below.

With some notable exceptions, the trend in the cases concerning institutional affairs has been to deny First Amendment protection to faculty speech. In many cases, courts accomplish this result by finding that the speech activities at issue were not "matters of public concern" (stage 1); in other cases, courts acknowledge that the speech addressed matters of public concern but then deny protection by applying the balancing analysis in a manner that favors the institution (stage 2); and occasionally a court will find no causation (stage 3). The following cases are illustrative.

Ayoub v. Texas A&M University, 927 F.2d 834 (5th Cir. 1991), involved an Egyptian-born professor, originally hired in 1968, who made repeated complaints that his starting salary was low and that, as a result, his salary in each succeeding year remained too low. In 1985, the professor's interim department head reviewed the salary and recommended no raise for the professor (as well as for four other professors who were white U.S. citizens), and the college dean also determined that the salary was appropriate. Later in 1985, the new department head attempted to move the professor's office to a different building, allegedly because of complaints other department members had made about his disruptiveness. The professor then initiated legal action, "alleging that his civil rights had been violated when his office was relocated in retaliation against his complaints about the University's past discriminatory pay scale."

The court recognized the difficulty in distinguishing between public and private concerns, as required by *Connick* (Section 7.1.1), "because almost anything that occurs within a public agency could be of concern to the public." The court's role

> [is] "not [to] focus on the inherent interest or importance of the matters discussed by the employee [but instead] to decide whether the speech at issue in a particular case was made *primarily* in the plaintiff's role as a citizen or *primarily* in his role as employee. In making this distinction, the mere fact that the topic of the employee's speech was one in which the public might or would have had a great interest is of little moment" [927 F.2d at 837; emphasis added, quoting *Terrell v. University of Texas System Police*, 792 F.2d 1360, 1362 (5th Cir. 1986)].

Applying this test, the court determined that the professor had spoken primarily as an employee, because his speech "involved only his personal situation." Only after the professor filed suit did he "characterize his complaint in terms of a 'two-tier' system perpetuated by the University, whereby foreign-born professors were paid less than white, native-born professors." Nor was there any evidence that the professor "ever uttered such a protest at any time before the alleged retaliatory acts by the defendants." Thus, even if his comments were viewed "in terms of a disparate, 'two-tier' pay system, the record is absolutely clear that he only complained about its application to him." Consequently, the court concluded that the professor

> consistently spoke not as a citizen upon matters of public concern, but rather as an employee upon matters of only personal interest. . . . [T]here is no evidence that [he] expressed concern about anything other than his own salary. Although pay discrimination based on national origin can be a matter of public concern, in the context in which it was presented in this case by [the professor] it was a purely personal and private matter [927 F.2d at 837–38].

In *Dorsett v. Board of Trustees for State Colleges and Universities*, 940 F.2d 121 (5th Cir. 1991), a tenured mathematics professor at a state university claimed that he had been retaliated against because he had "challenged several departmental decisions and [had] publicly supported another professor who had been attacked by the administration for refusing to lower academic standards." The departmental decisions he challenged concerned teaching assignments, pay increases, and other administrative and procedural matters. The appellate court held that "the alleged harms suffered by Dorsett [did] not rise to the level of a constitutional deprivation" and that, even if they did, nothing in the content, form, or context of the speech indicated an intent to address an issue of public concern, as required by *Connick*. The court specifically noted that the professor's complaints had been directed to persons within the university and had not arisen in the context of a public debate about academic standards or about the administration of the university or the mathematics department. The court did not reach the *Pickering/Connick* balancing test because the speech in question was a matter of personal rather than public concern.

Colburn v. Trustees of Indiana University, 973 F.2d 581 (7th Cir. 1992), involved two nontenured sociology professors employed under one-year renewable contracts. Their department had for several years been split into two contending factions. The majority faction controlled the department's primary committee, which constituted the first level of review for all promotion and tenure decisions. The two professors, members of the minority faction, each wrote a letter to university officials asserting that the "department was so divided that individual careers, and the effective functioning of the department, were being threatened," and requesting an external review of the sociology department's internal peer review system for professional advancement. University officials responded to the letters by urging the department to resolve its conflict internally. The primary committee continued to be controlled by the majority faction, however, and the two professors, along with the other members of the minority faction, wrote to the department chair describing "the deplorable and intolerable [situation], especially for junior members of the department who face discrimination by the now unchallenged dominant group." Each professor subsequently nominated himself for promotion, but the primary committee recommended against promotion. The committee also recommended that one of the plaintiffs not be reappointed, noting that his "written and verbal comments to people outside the department have hurt the image of the Sociology faculty and undermined the integrity of the peer review process." The second professor was also considered for tenure; although he received a favorable recommendation from the committee, the recommendation of the department chair was negative, and he was ultimately denied not only tenure but reappointment as well.

The two professors challenged these actions in court, charging that the university had retaliated against them for engaging in expression protected by the First Amendment. The trial court granted summary judgment for the university, finding that the professors' speech was not on matters of public concern. On appeal, the professors advanced four arguments for classifying their speech as a matter of public concern. The appellate court rejected each argument and affirmed the trial court's judgment.

First, the professors argued that "their letters were not simply an internal matter, but revealed that the integrity of the university was being threatened."

The court recognized that "[e]xposing wrongdoing within a public entity may be a matter of public concern," and that there is "[n]o doubt [that] the public would be displeased to learn that faculty members at a public university were evaluating their colleagues on personal biases." The court asserted, however, that "the fact the issue could be 'interesting' to the community does not make it an issue of public concern." The court viewed the plaintiffs' letters as "principally an attempt to seek intervention in a clash of hostile personalities" rather than an "attempt to expose some malfeasance that would directly affect the community at large."

Second, the professors argued that the "division in the department fell along the lines of membership and non-membership in the faculty union, and that pressures to join a union make the faculty clashes of deep public concern." Again, the court recognized that "[s]peech which is related to collective activity may be a matter of public concern." In this case, however,

> [a]lthough union affiliation may have been a factor in determining membership in one of the two competing groups, pressure to join the union was not the central reason for the request for review of the department, nor were [the plaintiffs] attempting to inform the public that faculty members were being pushed into union membership. . . . [T]he point of their speech . . . was to highlight how the department's in-fighting had affected them and would affect their futures at the university [973 F.2d at 587].

Third, the professors argued that "simply because they had some personal interest in calming the tensions in the department does not prevent their requests for review from being matters of public concern." The court recognized that:

> [s]peech is not unprotected simply because it raises complaints or other issues personal to the speaker. . . . However, where the overriding reason for the speech is the concern of a few individuals whose careers may be on the line, the speech looks much more like an internal personal dispute than an effort to make the public aware of wrongdoing [973 F.2d at 587].

Although the plaintiffs "emphasize[d] that they did not speak simply to further their own career interests but everyone in the department's interest," the court believed that the department's "deterioration was principally of importance to the few faculty members who had to tolerate the bickering."

Fourth, the professors argued that "the forum in which [they] raised their concerns is relevant to whether their statements should be characterized as a matter of public concern." The court recognized that "[e]mployee speech does not go unprotected simply because the chosen forum is private and addressed solely to others in the workplace. . . . But statements made privately in the workplace themselves must be of some public concern in order to be protected." The fact that the plaintiffs had communicated their concerns to only a few university officials "underscores the internal nature of the dispute."

Thus, the court concluded, consistent with the trial court, that the professors' letters and statements "are most reasonably characterized as relating to matters of personal interest. Plaintiffs were not speaking primarily as citizens, but as faculty members concerned about the private matter of the processes by which they were evaluated."

Taken together, these cases illustrate how lower courts have adapted the U.S. Supreme Court's directives in *Pickering* and *Connick* to the particular circumstances of higher education. Most important, these cases establish a framework for determining whether the speech at issue was on a matter of public concern. As discussed below, this framework, and much of the courts' reasoning under *Pickering* and *Connick,* is insensitive to the shared governance context of higher education and may be criticized on numerous grounds.

First, these cases accord relatively little weight to the particular "context" of the speech. According to *Connick,* "Whether an employee's speech addresses a matter of public concern must be determined by the content, form, *and context* of a given statement, as revealed by the whole record" (461 U.S. at 147–48) (emphasis added). The courts have generally used the same analysis in faculty cases that they use in cases involving other types of public employees, thereby attaching no significance to the special context of higher education. While there are many similarities between college and university employees and other public employees, there are also important differences. Primary among them are the special governance structure of higher education and the special status of academic freedom. When courts are inattentive to such matters, the strictness of the "public concern" test and the fact sensitivity and malleability of the balancing test may combine to chill the faculty member's willingness to participate forthrightly in departmental and institutional debate.

Similarly, these cases employ a cramped version of the *Connick* distinction between speaking out as a "private citizen" and as a "public employee." This distinction is useful in the general employment context, as in *Connick,* but in the higher education context it ignores the fact that shared governance requires professors to speak out as professionals on matters of institutional concern. Those who do so may enhance rather than threaten the operation of the institution. When a court ends its inquiry because the speech is not a matter of public concern, as strictly conceived in *Ayoub, Colburn,* and *Dorsett,* it never considers the vital participatory role professors may play in shared-governance systems or the constructive impact that speech about "institutional concerns" may have on institutional operations over the long run.

Perhaps most problematic, these cases assign excessive weight to whether the speech was communicated to the general public. The *Ayoub* opinion relied on a previous case (*Terrell v. University of Texas System Police,* 792 F.2d 1360 (5th Cir. 1982)), in which the court, holding that First Amendment protections did not apply to a diary, "emphasized that [the claimant] made no effort to communicate its contents to the public." Applying this reasoning to the professor's claims, the *Ayoub* court noted that "[c]ertainly, [he] never attempted to air his complaints in a manner that would call the public's attention to the alleged wrong." Similarly, the *Colburn* court considered the fact that the professors had brought their concerns only to the attention of university officials and viewed this fact as underscoring the private, internal character of the speech.

This heavy emphasis on the audience of the speech, along with precious little emphasis on the subject matter, appears to conflict with the U.S. Supreme Court's holding in *Givhan* (Section 3.7.1). There, the Court made clear that the determination of whether speech is a matter of public concern does not depend on whether the communication itself was made in public or private. As an appeals court explained in *Kurtz v. Vickrey,* 855 F.2d 723 (11th Cir. 1988):

> Although an employee's efforts to communicate his or her concerns to the public are relevant to a determination of whether or not the employee's speech relates to a matter of public concern, focusing solely on such behavior, or on the employee's motivation, does not fully reflect the Supreme Court's directive that the content, form, and context of the speech must all be considered. The content of the speech is notably overlooked in such an analysis. . . . Moreover, such a focus overlooks the Court's holding in *Givhan* . . . [855 F.2d at 727].

When courts ignore the nature of the higher education context while focusing on the "private citizen/public employee" distinction and the public/private context of the speech, they undercut the concepts of shared governance and collegiality. In the cases described above, the professors who followed administrative channels and did not communicate their criticisms to persons outside the institution did not receive First Amendment protection. Those professors who did communicate outside the institution, specifically to accrediting agencies, were afforded at least threshold First Amendment protections. These results seem to suggest that, to guarantee themselves protection under the First Amendment, faculty members should bypass internal administrative procedures and go directly to persons or agencies outside the institution. A First Amendment rule that would encourage, if not require, such behavior would conflict with the best interests and the customs of institutions that protect shared governance and collegiality.

In contrast to cases like *Ayoub, Dorsett,* and *Colburn,* other courts have occasionally applied the *Pickering/Connick* analysis in a manner that is more sensitive to the uniqueness of higher education and more hospitable to faculty members' academic freedom and free speech claims. One highly instructive example is *Johnson v. Lincoln University,* 776 F.2d 443 (3d Cir. 1985)—a case that avoids the problems characteristic of the cases above, and could serve as a model for later judicial developments. In declining to side with the university, the court found that the faculty member's speech was on matters of public concern; and although it then remanded the case to the trial court to apply the *Pickering/Connick* balancing test, the appellate court clearly signaled its inclination to give great weight to the faculty member's free speech interests.

The *Johnson* plaintiff was a chemistry professor challenging the termination of his tenure. The lawsuit grew out of a dispute within the university that began in 1977. At that time the university decided to make substantial reductions in its faculty. Led in part by the professor, the faculty responded with sharp criticism of both the university and its president. An initial lawsuit ensued, in which the faculty asserted that "various disciplinary actions had been taken in order to suppress faculty criticism of university policy." That case eventually was settled out of court. Four months later, the chemistry department chair initiated dismissal proceedings against the professor. The charges were based primarily on events related to the "rancorous, longstanding dispute within the chemistry department." After a hearing, the presiding committee recommended the termination of the professor's tenure. The university president accepted the committee's recommendation, and the board of trustees upheld his decision. The professor thereupon sued in federal court, challenging the termination of his tenure on several grounds, including the ground that the termination was in retaliation for his statements about university policies and academic standards. The trial court focused both on the professor's speech regarding disputes within the chemistry department and on letters he had written to the Middle States Association of Colleges and Schools regarding the university's academic standards in general. Reasoning that disputes within the chemistry department were of interest only to those within the department and that the professor's letters were "merely an outgrowth of his personal dispute with the university," the trial court held that each of these speech activities concerned matters of "purely private concern" and therefore were not protected.

The appellate court vacated the trial court's judgment, holding that it had erred as a matter of law in determining that the professor's speech activities did not involve matters of public concern. First the court emphasized "that the mere fact that an employee's statement is an 'outgrowth of his personal dispute' does not prevent some aspect of it from touching upon matters of public concern." While the controversies within the department may have some personal aspects, other aspects are "concerned [with] questions of educational standards and academic policy of a scope broader than their application within the department." As an example, the court quoted from a memorandum written by the professor regarding departmental standards: "'I believe such grade inflation is a kind of crime against students, Lincoln University, and Black people. Standards of Black Colleges are always suspect and it took 50–60 years for Lincoln to earn a high reputation for quality education and high standards. . . . What [the department chair] has done is to encourage non-quality education and non-quality character. . . . A good reputation for academic quality was the only thing of value Lincoln ever had or ever will have'" (776 F.2d at 452).

Commenting on this passage, the court asserted that "[i]t is difficult to imagine a theme that touches more upon matters of public concern." The court then noted that the same theme was present in the professor's letters to the Middle States Association, in which he criticized the standards of a master's degree program at Lincoln because it did not require a bachelor's degree. In these letters the professor "proceeded to connect the decline of academic standards at Lincoln with the demoralization caused by the suppression of academic freedom during the [prior] controversy, and encouraged the Middle States Association to investigate Lincoln." The professor specifically emphasized "the vital importance of high educational standards to the future of mankind—and the special circumstances that make it a kind of crime to allow lower standards at Black institutions" (776 F.2d at 452).

Tracking the language of *Connick,* the court declared that "questions of academic standards are of 'apparent . . . interest to the community upon which it is essential that public employees be able to speak out freely without fear of retaliatory dismissal.'" As to the letters, the court stated that "it is difficult to see any distinguishing features between these letters and the one which the *Pickering* court held to be protected activity."

The appellate court also found that the trial court erred in limiting its inquiry to the two types of speech activities identified above. The professor's claims also included "his role in [the prior] litigation [against the university], his role in the underlying activities leading up to that litigation, his longstanding criticisms of [the current] administration's academic policy, his newspaper articles proposing that Lincoln eliminate the F grade, his attempts to have other faculty members censured for allowing students to take advanced courses without passing the prerequisites, and his criticisms of his department chairman over academic standards." The court observed that whether these items "touch[ed] upon matters of public concern seems hardly open to question."

In remanding the case to the trial court so that it could undertake the *Pickering* balancing analysis, the appellate court provided considerable guidance. Quoting one of its own prior decisions, it noted that "'even if there were some evidence of disruption caused by plaintiff's speech, such a finding is not controlling. . . . *Pickering* is truly a balancing test, with office disruption or breached confidences being only weights on the scales.'" The appellate court further cautioned that "a stronger showing [of the employer's justification] may be necessary if the employee's speech more substantially involved matters of public concern."

Of special interest, and in marked contrast to *Ayoub, Colburn,* and *Dorsett,* the *Johnson* court placed significant importance on the circumstances of the academic environment. It began by declaring that "[d]espite the inappropriateness of this forum for resolving issues of academic policy and academic freedom, we find ourselves reviewing charges [of wrongful] termination of tenure." Then, after asserting the importance of context, and tracking the language of *Tinker v. Des Moines School District* (see Section 9.5.1 of this book), the court stated:

> [It] is particularly important that in cases dealing with academia, the standard applied in evaluating the employer's justification should be the one applicable to the rights of teachers and students "in light of the special characteristics of the school environment." . . . In an academic environment, suppression of speech or opinion cannot be justified by an "undifferentiated fear or apprehension of disturbance," . . . nor by "a mere desire to avoid the discomfort and unpleasantness that always accompany an unpopular viewpoint" [776 F.2d at 453–54, quoting *Tinker*; other citations omitted].

Some other courts after *Johnson* have similarly adopted a more sensitive approach to institutional affairs cases and have classified particular faculty speech within the "public concern" category. In *Maples v. Martin,* 858 F.2d 1546 (11th Cir. 1988), for example, five disgruntled tenured professors in the mechanical engineering department at Auburn University had continually opposed the personnel and administrative decisions of their department head. In anticipation of an accreditation review by the American Board of Education Technology, the professors distributed a survey to departmental faculty and students, to some alumni and administrators, and to the accreditation board. The professors compiled the data from these surveys into a report that discussed departmental problems, especially a morale problem, and was highly critical of the department head. Largely as a result of this report and related events that preceded and followed it, the university reassigned the five professors to other engineering departments, without loss of pay or rank.

The professors argued that reassigning them for having published the report violated their rights to freedom of speech. The district and appellate courts disagreed, upholding the reassignment. Applying *Connick,* the appellate court concluded that a portion of the professors' report was speech on matters of public concern because it would influence the public's perception of the quality of education at the university. The court then used the *Pickering* balancing test to weigh the professors' free speech interests in publishing the report against the report's "disruptive impact on the workplace." The report had "distracted both students and faculty from the primary academic tasks of education and research"; it was "produced in an atmosphere of tension created by the authors' longstanding grievance" against the department's administration; and the report's publication "contributed to a lack of harmony among the faculty and . . . severely hampered communication between the members of the faculty and the Department Head." The court therefore concluded that the report's "interference with the efficient operation of the [Mechanical Engineering] Department at Auburn was sufficient to justify the transfer[s]" and outweighed the professors' need to speak on matters of public concern.

In *Mumford v. Godfried,* 52 F.3d 756 (8th Cir. 1995), the appellate court relied on the U.S. Supreme Court's opinions in *Connick* and *Givhan* (Section 7.1.1 above) to reverse a trial court determination that a professor's speech was not on a matter of public concern. The professor had criticized his own department, the Department of Architecture at the University of Iowa. Speaking at various times with his colleagues, he had openly expressed his opinion that the department maintained a potentially unethical link with the Des Moines architectural professional community. In remanding the case to the trial court, the appellate court emphasized that the professor's statements did not lose their First Amendment protection merely because they were "only expressed to his colleagues," and that a speaker need not reach or intend to reach a "public audience" in order to be "acting as a concerned public citizen speaking on a matter of public interest."

In *Scallet v. Rosenblum,* 911 F. Supp. 999 (W.D. Va. 1996), *affirmed on other grounds,* 1997 WL 33077 (4th Cir. 1997), the court relied on *Mumford* to conclude that an instructor's faculty meeting comments on the importance of addressing "diversity" in the classroom were "related to matters of public concern." The speech, "although curricular in nature, cannot be said to relate to matters solely of institutional or personal concern since it also speaks to the general debate on multiculturalism that currently thrives in all quarters of American society" (911 F. Supp. at 1017).

Similarly, in *Bloch v. Temple University,* 939 F. Supp. 387 (E.D. Pa. 1996), the court held that a professor's complaints about the condition of his physics laboratory "embodied matters of public concern." The professor had made statements about "improper storage of toxic and unidentified materials" in the laboratory. The university argued that the speech was not protected because the professor was speaking as an employee and was not seeking to inform the public. In rejecting the university's contention, the court emphasized that the professor's statements could be public concern speech even though he "undeniably had a personal stake in the cleanup" of the laboratory and even though the statements "may have been the outgrowth of personal disputes within the department."

Even when courts determine that a faculty member's speech is not on a matter of public concern, they can do a better job of elucidating the distinction between public concern and private concern than courts have done in cases like *Ayoub, Dorsett,* and *Colburn. Clinger v. New Mexico Highlands University, Board of Regents,* 215 F.3d 1162 (10th Cir. 2000), is an instructive example. The plaintiff, an assistant professor, claimed she was denied tenure partly in retaliation for four exercises of free speech: first, her "advocacy before the Faculty Senate of a 'no confidence' vote with respect to four members of the Board of Regents in light of their purported failure to comply with an internal policy on the appointment of a new president"; second, her "comments before the Faculty Senate criticizing [a] Regent. . . as untrustworthy based on the presidential appointment process"; third, her "criticism of Selimo Rael for accepting the position of University President"; and fourth, her "criticism of a proposed academic reorganization purportedly in conflict with the Faculty Handbook and the Board of Regents policy manual."

The appellate court agreed with the trial court that the professor's speech was not on matters of public concern. According to the appellate court: "Speech concerning individual personnel disputes or internal policies will typically not involve public concern. However, speech that exposes improper operations of the government or questions the integrity of government officials clearly concerns vital public interests" (215 F.3d at 1166 (internal citations omitted)). Using these guidelines, the court found that the professor's speech did not challenge "the integrity, qualifications, [or] alleged misrepresentations of a public official." Rather, "plaintiff simply differed with the Board of Trustees on the internal process they followed in selecting a president and reorganizing the University. Rather than challenging the president's actual credentials, the professor "merely faulted him for taking part in an allegedly unsatisfactory process." The statements relating to the Regent's integrity did not concern vital public interests because they were based solely on his role in the internal decision-making process. The court therefore held that the professor's statements only challenged internal structures and governance and did not "transcend the internal workings of the university to affect the political or social life of the community" (quoting the court's previous decision in *Bunger v. University of Okla. Bd. of Regents,* 95 F.3d 987, 992 (10th Cir. 1996)) and that "[t]he First Amendment does not require public universities to subject internal structural arrangements and administrative procedures to public scrutiny and debate."

More recent cases have raised cutting-edge issues concerning free speech claims arising in the context of heated or prolonged internal disputes. These cases follow upon and build upon the earlier *Johnson v. Lincoln University* and *Maples v. Martin* cases, both of which also involved protracted internal disputes. In *Webb v. Board of Trustees of Ball State University,* 167 F.3d 1146 (7th Cir. 1999), for example, a professor and former department chair was involved in ongoing disputes within his department. The court described the disputes as "internecine warfare" and the department as one "suffer[ing] a collapse of cooperation and decorum." The professor claimed that the university had retaliated against him by stripping him of his departmental chairship, in violation of the First Amendment, for views he had expressed in the context of the departmental disputes. The appellate court affirmed the trial court's denial of a preliminary injunction for the professor. Accepting both the trial court's refusal to "disentangle the public and private aspects of the speech" and the trial court's conclusion that the plaintiff's speech had become "disruptive," the appellate court announced this guideline for cases involving internal disputes:

> Universities are entitled to insist that members of the faculty (and their administrative aides) devote their energies to promoting goals such as research and teaching. When the bulk of a professor's time goes over to fraternal warfare, students and the scholarly community alike suffer, and the university may intervene to restore decorum and ease tensions. . . . Under the circumstances, the University's right as employer to achieve the organization's goals must prevail . . . [167 F.3d at 1150].

In another case decided by the same Circuit shortly after *Webb, Feldman v. Ho,* 171 F.3d 494 (7th Cir. 1999), the court rejected the free speech claim of a former professor whose contract was not renewed after he had precipitated an internal dispute by making accusatory statements about a departmental colleague. Like the court in *Webb,* and somewhat like the court in the earlier *Maples v. Martin* case, the court in *Feldman* held that the professor's free speech interests were overcome by the university's interests in protecting other faculty members from the distractions of an internal dispute. But the court added a significant, and potentially far-reaching, new twist to its analysis by asserting that the professor's claims did not even deserve to be submitted to a jury:

> [I]t does not follow that a jury rather than the faculty determines whether Feldman's accusation was correct. . . . [T]he Constitution does not commit to decision by a jury every speech-related dispute. If it did, that would be the end of a university's ability to choose its faculty—for it is speech that lies at the core of scholarship, and every academic decision is in the end a decision about speech.

* * * *

If the kind of decision Southern Illinois University made about Feldman is mete for litigation, then we might as well commit all tenure decisions to juries, for all are equally based on speech [171 F.3d at 495, 496, 497].

The court did take care to note, however, that its deference to the university's judgments "is limited to the kind of speech that is part of the [university's] mission":

> Feldman's speech was neither unrelated to his job . . . nor unrelated to mathematics. . . . Feldman objected to the way the Mathematics Department handled its core business of choosing and promoting scholars. That task is both inevitably concerned with speech and so central to a university's mission that the university's role as employer dominates [171 F.3d at 497–498].

In contrast, in *de Llano v. Berglund,* 282 F.3d 1031 (8th Cir. 2002), the court sorted out various statements that a professor had made after he was removed as chair of the physics department at North Dakota State University (NDSU). The statements appeared in numerous letters that the professor wrote to the local newspaper, to the school newspaper, and to officers of the university, criticizing the university administration and various faculty members. These letters "expressed [the professor's] dissatisfaction with a variety of ongoing conflicts he was having with the department." Prior to his removal as chair, there had been, in the court's words, "several years of acrimonious relations between de Llano, the NDSU administration and his Physics Department colleagues." After the professor sent the letters, further events transpired, including a censure of the professor by his department, followed by his dismissal from the faculty. Challenging this dismissal in court, he argued that six of his letters constituted public concern speech protected under the *Pickering/Connick* line of cases. The court found that most of the statements in these letters were not on matters of public concern and therefore were not protected by the First Amendment:

> [A]lthough couched in general terms, [these comments] related specifically to the ongoing feuds he was having with the defendants. His letters essentially amounted to publicly airing his dissatisfaction with his removal as chair of the physics department and the department's undervaluation of his strong commitment to research. . . . These are just a few examples of de Llano's pattern of publicly complaining about private disputes that were unique to him and not a matter of public concern [282 F.3d at 1036–37].

On the other hand, some of the statements in the letters "are properly characterized as issues of public concern." Examples included statements "criticiz[ing] the growing percentage of non-academic staff at NDSU" and statements "citing the rising salaries of NDSU administrators as evidence that money was being poorly spent." These statements qualified for protection, said the court, because "[w]e generally have held that speech about the use of public funds touches upon a matter of public concern" (282 F.3d at 1037). Despite this finding in his favor, however, the professor did not prevail in his lawsuit because he had not proven that the public concern statements were "a substantial factor in the decision to terminate him." (For discussion of this part of the case, see Section 7.6 below.)

Subsequently, another Circuit weighed in on the application of the *Pickering/Connick* line to speech issues arising from acrimonious internal disputes. *Hulen v. Yates*, 322 F.3d 1229 (10th Cir. 2003), was actually the fourth in a line of helpful Tenth Circuit cases concerning the *Pickering/Connick* line's application to intramural faculty speech.[34] Hulen was a tenured faculty member in the accounting and tax department at Colorado State University (CSU). According to the dean's characterization, there had been "more than six years of divisiveness and dysfunction" within this department. In this context, Professor Hulen and other faculty members had sought to bring charges against another tenured faculty member in the department ("Dr. M."), had pressed for an investigation of the charges, and had called for termination of Dr. M.'s tenure. The charges included "plagiarism and copyright violations, emotional abuse of students, abuse and harassment of staff, [and] misuse of state funds" (322 F.3d at 1233). Hulen made statements supportive of an investigation and of the termination of Dr. M.'s tenure to various members of the university administration, in particular to his department chair and the university provost. When an investigation did take place, Hulen made statements criticizing its inadequacy. When Hulen and his colleagues allegedly received threats delivered to them by the "then-Accounting Department Chair, . . . who advised that his message was from the CSU Administration"(322 F.3d at 1233), Hulen wrote memos to the university president requesting an investigation of the alleged threats. Subsequently, Hulen was transferred to another department against his wishes. In his lawsuit, Hulen claimed that this transfer was in retaliation for various statements he had made in the context of the dispute concerning Dr. M., and that such retaliation for an exercise of free speech violated the First Amendment.

Beginning its analysis, the appellate court set forth this guideline: "'Speech which discloses any evidence of corruption, impropriety, or other malfeasance on the part of [state] officials, in terms of content, clearly concerns matters of

---

[34]The first of these cases is *Bunger v. University of Oklahoma Board of Regents*, 95 F.3d 987, 991–92 (10th Cir. 1996), in which the court determined that two untenured professors' complaint about the exclusion of untenured faculty members from the graduate school's administrative council was not public concern speech. The second case is *Gardetto v. Mason (Eastern Wyoming College)*, 100 F.3d 803 (10th Cir. 1996), in which the court held that a female professor's speech regarding a no-confidence vote against the institution's president and speech criticizing the president's plan for reduction in force were matters of public concern. The third case is *Clinger v. New Mexico Highlands University Board of Regents*, 215 F.3d 1162 (10th Cir. 2000), in which the court distinguished *Gardetto* and determined that the faculty speech at issue was not on matters of public concern. (*Clinger* is discussed more fully earlier in this section.) A fifth case, decided after *Hulen*, is *Schrier v. University of Colorado*, 427 F.3d 1253 (10th Cir. 2005), in which the court determined that a department chair's comments on a proposed relocation of the university's health sciences center were on matters of public concern (427 F.3d at 1262–63). A careful comparison of these five cases and their facts should yield very useful insights concerning the difficult lines to be drawn between public and private concern speech in the arena of institutional affairs.

public import'" (322 F.3d at 1237, quoting *Conaway v. Smith*, 853 F.2d 789, 796 (10th Cir. 1998)). Applying this guideline to the facts in the record, the court determined that:

> The speech in this case fairly relates to charges at a public university that plainly would be of interest to the public, e.g., plagiarism and copyright violations, emotional abuse of students, abuse and harassment of staff, misuse of state funds, receipt of kickbacks from a publisher in return for adopting textbooks, and a claimed inadequate investigation of the allegations and alleged retaliation against those who made the allegations [322 F.3d at 1238, citing *Maples v. Martin*, 858 F.2d 1546, 1553 (11th Cir. 1988)].

The court thus ruled, at the first stage of the *Pickering/Connick* analysis, that Hulen's speech was on matter of public concern. Furthermore, the court explained: "The fact that Dr. Hulen might receive an incidental benefit of what he perceived as improved working conditions does not transform his speech into purely personal grievances. Moreover, speech which touches on matters of public concern does not lose protection merely because some personal concerns are included" (322 F.3d at 1238).

At the second stage of the *Pickering/Connick* analysis, the court was unable to complete its analysis because the facts in the record were not yet sufficiently developed. The court did acknowledge, however, in a statement favorable to the professor, that "at this point in the proceedings, the evidence is far too general to link the actual disruption of the accounting department to Dr. Hulen's protected speech." The court also instructed that, in considering the university's claims regarding disruption of the efficient operation of the department, the trial court should take into account "the inherent autonomy of tenured professors and the academic freedom that they enjoy" (citing Chief Justice Warren's opinion and Justice Frankfurter's concurrence in the *Sweezy* case, discussed in Section 7.1.4 above, as well as the "1940 Statement of Principles on Academic Freedom and Tenure," discussed in Section 7.1.3 above).

All four of these cases—*Webb, Feldman, de Llano,* and *Hulen*—add to an understanding of *Pickering/Connick*'s application to free speech in the context of prolonged faculty-administration disputes. The *Webb* case provides a good general guideline on the threat to institutional interests that arises when a faculty member's time is spent more on "fraternal warfare" than on teaching and scholarship duties. This guideline is useful only as a *general* guideline, however. In particular cases, postsecondary administrators, as well as the courts, must be on the alert not only for genuinely disruptive circumstances, but also for situations where discipline is selectively imposed upon some of the faculty members involved in a dispute but not others, based on the sides taken or the viewpoints expressed in the dispute. In such circumstances, the institution's rationale of alleviating disruption may not be weighty enough to prevail in the *Pickering/Connick* balance.

The *Feldman* case, like *Webb*, provides a useful reminder of the important interests of the institution that may be at stake in divisive disputes. In *Feldman*, however, unlike *Webb*, the institution's interest was not focused on the faculty member's diversion of his own time and energy to the dispute at the expense of other faculty duties, but rather to the need to protect other faculty members from the distraction of a prolonged dispute. *Feldman* seems to overstate the case in this regard by its dictum that many faculty free speech claims arising from internal disputes do not even deserve to go to a jury. Surely there are faculty free speech claims, even in the Seventh Circuit, that deserve to go to a jury for various reasons—the primary one probably being that there are entrenched factual disputes about the causes, extent, and effects of the disruption; but the dictum in the *Feldman* case provides no basis for determining which claims deserve to go to a jury and which do not. Moreover, the *Feldman* court, in its second dictum set out above, suggests that the more related the professor's speech is to his or her professional job functions and expertise, the less protection his or her statements will have. This seems to turn an academic freedom claim on its head; it is usually when there is a close connection to the professor's professional duties and professional expertise that the academic freedom claim has the most credibility. Given these two difficulties with the court's reasoning, it is likely that the *Feldman* decision is best understood only as a decision that, in total, suggests that "institutional" academic freedom (or autonomy) will trump faculty academic freedom most, if not all, of the time in the area of institutional affairs.

The guidelines in the *Hulen* case are probably the most useful of any in the more recent cases about divisive internal disputes. The *Hulen* case is particularly helpful when compared with the earlier *Clinger* case, decided by the same circuit (*Clinger* is discussed above). In comparing the facts of those two cases, the court had to make fine judgments about the line between public concern and private concern speech in the context of internal faculty-administration disputes. The two cases together, therefore, provide an instructive illustration of how and where to draw that line in the difficult situations that typically arise in cases about prolonged disputes.

In all three of these cases, there appeared to be statements of private concern mixed in with the public concern statements that provided the basis for the faculty member's free speech claim. The three courts dealt with this problem in different ways. The *Webb* court, for instance, refused to "disentangle" the public and private concern aspects of the statements at issue in that case, apparently determining that the speech was sufficiently disruptive that the university would prevail at any rate in the second stage of the *Pickering/Connick* analysis. In contrast, the *de Llano* court carefully sorted through the various statements, but then asked whether the public concern statements were a cause of the university's action against the professor. The *Hulen* court, in a more nuanced opinion, also sorted the statements, determining that the public concern statements were the primary statements that the professor had made and were representative of the professor's primary motivation. Thus, the public concern statements would prevail, and the faculty member's claim would not fail simply because there would be some private benefit, or there had occasionally been some private motivation, for the faculty member's various statements made in the context of the heated dispute.

The case of *Sholvin v. Univ. of Medicine and Dentistry of New Jersey*, 50 F.Supp.2d 297 (D.N.J. 1998), provides another useful illustration consistent with *Hulen*. In this case, a tenured professor in the dental school had engaged in disputes with the school's administration that extended over several years and focused on various issues. Characterizing the case as one "where a faculty member during continuing disagreement with his department's administration and administrators addressed matters both of public and private concern," the court undertook to review and sort "the different categories of statements at issue here." The court also made clear that statements of public concern do not lose their protected character because they are made in the context of heated disputes or motivated in part by self-interest:

> Plaintiff's apparent enmity for Buchanan, Catalanotto and other members of the NJDS [New Jersey Dental School] administration does not preclude a finding that some of this evidence was of public concern. Nor is it determinative that plaintiff was politically and/or otherwise allied with the Slomiany group. Many of his statements and expressions are in the realm of public concern and therefore may be entitled to First Amendment protection notwithstanding the personal disputes and interests which in part motivated plaintiff [50 F. Supp. 2d at 313, citing *Johnson*, 776 F.2d at 452].

On balance, nevertheless, the court determined that the disruptiveness of the plaintiff's expressive activities outweighed his interest in free speech.

Other cutting-edge issues about faculty intramural speech were raised in *Bonnell v. Lorenzo*, 241 F.3d 800 (6th Cir. 2001). This case was different from most of the others above because it did not involve a faculty member's grievance about wages, benefits, or working conditions (as did cases like *Ayoub* and *Bloch* above) or a protracted internal dispute (as did cases like *Webb*, *Feldman*, *de Llano*, and *Hulen* above); instead it involved a faculty member's intramural speech in the context of one of the institution's official governance functions—the processing of student grievances. The only other cases above to focus on a particular governance process or particular structure of governance are the *Clinger* case, which focused on debates in the faculty senate, and the *Scallett* case, which involved a faculty member's statements during faculty meetings.[35] Different institutional interests may be implicated in such cases, compared to the interests articulated in most of the other cases above.

In *Bonnell*, a female student alleged that a male professor had used language in his English class that constituted sexual harassment. (See Section 7.2.2 above for this aspect of the case.) The student filed a letter of complaint with college officials, who then scheduled a meeting with the professor and provided him a copy of the complaint. According to the court, the professor "made copies of the Complaint and passed them out to the students in all six of his classes after redacting the complaining student's name, and also posted a copy of the Complaint on the bulletin board outside of his classroom." In addition, the

---

[35]For another example of a case involving a faculty member's statements at a faculty meeting, see *Hall v. Kutztown University*, 1998 WL 10233, 75 Fair Empl. Prac. Cases 1440 (E.D. Pa. 1998).

professor "distributed copies of the Complaint to the more than two hundred College faculty members" along with his response to the charges in the form of "an eight-page essay entitled 'An Apology: Yes Virginia, There is a Sanity Clause.'" (The "sanity clause" was a reference to the First Amendment's free speech clause.)

After the college had disciplined the professor for distributing these materials, the professor filed suit, claiming that his distribution of the materials was protected by the First Amendment. The court first addressed the distribution of the complaint and then addressed the distribution of the "Apology," in each instance agreeing that the distributions were "acts of expression" and then applying the *Pickering/Connick* analysis (see Section 7.1.1 above). Both the complaint and the apology, according to the court, covered matters of public concern. Regarding the complaint, "it is well-settled that allegations of sexual harassment, like allegations of racial harassment, are matters of public concern." As to the apology:

> [S]peech which sets forth the type of remarks that served as the catalyst to a sexual harassment complaint lodged against a college professor, and the professor's reaction thereto, is speech which can "fairly be considered as relating to any matter of political, social, or other concern to the community." *Connick*, 461 U.S. at 146 & 147–48. Said differently, the subject of profane classroom language which precipitates a sexual harassment complaint lodged against the instructor for his use of this language in relation to the First Amendment, as well as the sanctity of the First Amendment in preserving an individual's right to speak, involves a matter of public import. . . . Stated more broadly, there is a public interest concern involved in the issue of the extent of a professor's independence and unfettered freedom to speak in an academic setting [241 F.3d at 816–17].

Since the professor's speech was on matters of public concern, the court proceeded to apply the *Pickering/Connick* "balancing" test. The court acknowledged that the professor's interests in free speech and academic freedom on campus are "paramount," but are nevertheless limited by the institution's own academic autonomy (see Section 7.1.6 above). The college's interests at stake were also strong and varied; the most important apparently were (1) "maintaining the confidentiality of student sexual harassment complaints," (2) "prohibiting retaliation against students who file sexual harassment complaints," and (3) "preserving a learning environment free of sexual harassment" and a "hostile-free learning environment." Undertaking this "delicate" balance, the court determined that the college's interests prevailed in the particular fact circumstances of this case.

7.4.3. Intramural speech on extramural public affairs. Whereas all the cases above concerned "intramural" speech, *Starsky v. Williams*, 353 F. Supp. 900 (D. Ariz. 1972), *affirmed in pertinent part*, 512 F.2d 109 (9th Cir. 1975), presents a different type of academic freedom problem. The case involved institutional affairs not in the sense that the speech concerned campus issues but rather in the sense that the professor's on-campus speech

activities allegedly conflicted with his institutional responsibilities. Although the speech at issue did take place on campus, it concerned external public affairs rather than internal institutional operations. The case illustrates that, when campus speech regarding external affairs is at issue, the "public concern" test is easily met (compare *Jeffries v. Harleston* in Section 7.5.2 below) and the analysis will focus either on the *Pickering/Connick* balancing test (see Section 7.1.1 above) or on the *Keyishian* case's concepts of "chilling effect" and "pall of orthodoxy" (see Section 7.1.4).

The plaintiff in *Starsky* was a philosophy professor who had taught at Arizona State for six years before the university dismissed him on a series of charges, some involving on-campus activity and others involving off-campus activity. (The charges in the latter category are discussed in Section 7.5 below.) After several incidents, generally involving the professor's dissemination on campus of information about socialism, the board of regents directed the president to institute proceedings against him. The Committee on Academic Freedom and Tenure then held hearings and filed a report that concluded that the charges and evidence did not provide an adequate basis for dismissal. The board nevertheless terminated the professor's employment, and the professor sought redress in the courts.

The federal district court held that the dismissal violated the professor's constitutional right to free speech. One of the charges against the professor concerned his peaceful distribution of leaflets to other faculty members at the entrance to a faculty meeting. The leaflet was an "open letter" by a Columbia University student containing a philosophical and political discussion of activity taking place at Columbia. The university charged that the professor, in distributing the leaflet, had "failed to exercise appropriate restraint or to exercise critical self-discipline and judgment in using, extending, and transmitting knowledge" (353 F. Supp. at 907). The court, quoting the academic freedom declaration from the *Keyishian* case, stated:

> There is a serious constitutional question as to whether speech can be stifled because the ideas or wording expressed upset the "austere" faculty atmosphere [as one faculty member had complained]; certainly the board has no legitimate interest in keeping a university in some kind of intellectual austerity by an absence of shocking ideas. Insofar as the plaintiff's words upset the legislature or faculty because of the contents of his views, and particularly the depth of his social criticism, this is not the kind of detriment for which plaintiff can constitutionally be penalized [353 F. Supp. at 920].[36]

A case from the Seventh Circuit, *Trejo v. Shoben*, 319 F.3d 878 (7th Cir. 2003), illustrates the limits on judicial protection for intramural speech on external issues. The professor's statements were made at an off-campus function involving the professor's official duties rather than on the campus itself; but the

---

[36]For a more recent problem concerning faculty speech on extramural affairs, arising in the aftermath of 9/11, see Robin Wilson, "CUNY Leaders Question Faculty Comments of Terror Attacks," *Chron. Higher Educ.*, October 19, 2001, A11.

court's analysis would apparently have been the same if the statements had been made in a similar context on campus. The university had declined to renew the contract of the professor, a probationary assistant professor of psychology. The nonrenewal was due in part to certain complaints about the professor's behavior at an academic conference that he attended with several of his graduate students. Of primary concern were statements the professor had made at a late-night dinner while in the company of his graduate students and other conference attendees. According to the court, the professor "attempted to regale his dinner companions with a discussion of a documentary recently aired on a local television station concerning the sexual behavior of primates. [He] vociferously opined that there is a relationship between pregnancy, orgasms, and extramarital affairs and went on to advocate sex outside marriage and extramarital affairs" (319 F.3d at 881). The court declined to provide First Amendment protection for these statements under either the *Keyishian* case or the *Pickering/Connick* line of cases. Regarding the latter, the professor claimed that "his intent was to foster an academic debate over socio-biological theories of mating," and that his statements were therefore protected as matters of public concern. The court disagreed:

> These statements were simply parts of a calculated type of speech designed to further [the professor's] private interests in attempting to solicit female companionship and, at the same time, possibly to irritate the other graduate students to whom he was speaking. . . . [T]he individuals seated at the table all agreed that [the professor's] off-color remarks were delivered in a flirtatious manner peppered with double entendres and ribald references [319 F.3d at 887].

Thus, the professor's statements regarding the sexual behavior of primates "failed to address an issue of public concern."

Sec. 7.5. *Academic Freedom in Private Life*

7.5.1. In general. Faculty members would seem most insulated from institutional interference when they are engaging in private activities or practices. These activities and practices may be purely personal, or may be of a professional nature but not part of or related to the faculty member's responsibilities as an employee of the institution. In such circumstances, especially the former, the faculty member may be acting as an ordinary citizen, protected by rights that an ordinary citizen may claim or that any public employee may claim. Disputes concerning a faculty member's private life may thus often be viewed more as "personal freedom" than "academic freedom" disputes. "Personal freedom" disputes may have ramifications for academic freedom, however, if the faculty member's private activity has a negative effect on the fulfillment of his or her teaching or research responsibilities, or if the institution imposes a penalty on the faculty member that infringes upon his academic freedom or "chills" the academic freedom of other faculty members. A 1987 AAUP report on the case of Jeannette Quilichini Paz, a tenured professor who had been dismissed from the Pontifical Catholic University of Puerto Rico (CUPR), is illustrative.

In this case, the university administration had dismissed Quilichini when it learned that she had remarried, even though her previous Catholic marriage had ended in civil divorce and had not been ecclesiastically annulled ("Academic Freedom and Tenure: The Catholic University of Puerto Rico," *Academe,* May–June 1987, 33–38). Relying on church law, under which the remarriage was considered sinful, the university administration insisted that their Catholic faculty members must adhere to the laws of the church in both their academic and their private lives. In disapproving the dismissal, the AAUP investigating committee emphasized that "[t]he issue of direct concern in Professor Quilichini's case, however, is not academic freedom but personal freedom. It was her private conduct rather than her conduct as a teacher and researcher or any intramural or extramural statements she may have made that was the administration's ground for dismissal." Yet the university administration's action affected the academic freedom of all the university's faculty members:

> The administration of CUPR, in basing the dismissal of Professor Quilichini from her tenured position on vaguely stated religious standards not demonstrably related to professional performance, has placed in question the academic freedom of all faculty members at CUPR. The statement in the faculty manual that a faculty member is expected to "conduct himself in accordance with the values and ethical principles of the Catholic Church (both within and without the University) . . ." is subject to such broad interpretation that it would allow the administration to dismiss almost any faulty member at will [*Academe,* May–June 1987, 38].[37]

Because a faculty member's private life may involve activities not traditionally thought of as academic freedom concerns, rights other than free speech rights may be implicated in this type of dispute. In *Hander v. San Jacinto Junior College,* 519 F.2d 273 (5th Cir. 1975), for instance, the court considered a state college's authority to enforce faculty grooming regulations. The college had dismissed the plaintiff, a professor, when he refused to shave his beard. Relying on the due process clause and the equal protection clause, the court ruled in favor of the professor. In its analysis, the court first distinguished faculty members from certain other government employees with respect to grooming regulations: "Teachers even at public institutions such as San Jacinto Junior College simply do not have the exposure or community-wide impact of policemen and other employees who deal directly with the public. Nor is the need for discipline as acute in the educational environment as in other types of public service."

The court then enunciated this rule for institutions seeking to impose grooming regulations on their teachers:

> School authorities may regulate teachers' appearance and activities only when the regulation has some relevance to legitimate administrative or educational functions. . . .

---

[37]The professor subsequently sued the university, but the Puerto Rico courts ruled in the university's favor (Docket No. RE-90-578, Supreme Court of Puerto Rico, June 27, 1997). The appellate court declined to rule on the professor's claim concerning personal privacy, since it involved religious matters in which the court could not intervene.

The mere subjective belief in a particular idea by public employers is, however, an undeniably insufficient justification for the infringement of a constitutionally guaranteed right. . . . [It] is illogical to conclude that a teacher's bearded appearance would jeopardize his reputation or pedagogical effectiveness with college students [519 F.2d at 277].

Another aspect of faculty freedom in private life, and another application of the equal protection clause, is illustrated by *Trister v. University of Mississippi,* 420 F.2d 499 (5th Cir. 1969).[38] The plaintiffs were part-time faculty members who also worked at a legal services office of the federal Office of Economic Opportunity (OEO). University administrators warned them that they would lose their jobs at the university if they continued to work at OEO. There was no evidence that the OEO jobs consumed any more time than the part-time jobs of other faculty members. The court ruled that it was unconstitutional for a state law school to prohibit some part-time faculty members from working part-time at outside legal jobs while allowing other faculty members to do so. In upholding the plaintiffs' right to work at the OEO office, the court used the equal protection clause in this way:

We are not willing to take the position that plaintiffs have a constitutional right to participate in the legal services program of the OEO, or in any other program. Nor do they have a constitutional right to engage in part-time employment while teaching part time at the Law School. No such right exists in isolation. Plaintiffs, however, do have the constitutional right to be treated by a state agency in no significantly different manner from others who are members of the same class, i.e., members of the faculty of the University of Mississippi School of Law [420 F.2d at 502].

While this narrow reasoning was sufficient to uphold the plaintiffs' claim, other courts may be more willing to find a limited constitutional right to certain types of outside employment, as an aspect of First Amendment freedom of association or Fourteenth Amendment due process privacy rights, where such employment does not interfere with any substantial interest of the institution.

Other issues may arise concerning a faculty member's private behavior that offends the academic community's or broader community's conceptions of morality or propriety. The *Quilichini* case, discussed above, provides an example of this type of dispute. Other examples might involve allegations of extramarital sexual relationships, sexual "perversions," displays of racial or ethnic prejudices, sexual harassment not involving the campus community, or lying or misrepresentations in personal affairs—especially when such allegations, if proven, may constitute crimes. Such disputes about private behavior are more likely to arise in private institutions, especially religious institutions (as in the *Quilichini* case), than in public institutions. This is because private, and especially religious, institutions are more likely to have institutional missions that

---

[38]For an AAUP report on this matter, see "Academic Freedom and Tenure: The University of Mississippi," *AAUP Bulletin* (now *Academe*), Spring 1970, 75–86.

arguably implicate matters of private conduct; and because private institutions have more legal leeway to regulate the private conduct of their faculties and staffs. Private institutions are not bound by the federal constitutional rights clauses that substantially limit public institutions' authority to regulate such matters. The Fourteenth Amendment's due process clause, for example, limits a public (but not a private) institution's authority to use moral judgments as a basis for regulating a person's "liberty" to live a private personal life (see generally *Lawrence v. Texas,* 539 U.S. 558 (2003)). Similarly, the First Amendment's establishment and free exercise clauses limit a public (but not a private) institution's authority to regulate a person's private religious practices or to regulate other aspects of a faculty member's private life in the name of religion (see generally Michael Perry, "Religion, Politics, and the Constitution," 7 *J. Contemp. Legal Issues* 407, 412–17 (1996).[39] For such disputes in private institutions, then, any legal issues that arise are likely to be cast in terms of contract law (see Section 7.1.3 above and Section 7.8 below). AAUP policies will also be relevant, either as part of the faculty contract or (as in the *Quilichini* case) as the basis for an AAUP investigation.

7.5.2. *Extramural speech.* When a faculty member at a public institution engages in "extramural" speech in his or her private life and is penalized by the institution for this speech, the dispute is likely to implicate the First Amendment's free speech clause. The applicable legal principles will therefore be more like those used in Sections 7.2 through 7.4 than those immediately above in subsection 7.5.1; but the rights at stake may often be generic free speech rights rather than academic freedom rights. In *Starsky v. Williams,* for example (also discussed in Section 7.4.3 above), a faculty member at Arizona State University had made a television appearance in which he criticized the board of regents, calling its actions hypocritical, and had also issued a press release in which he criticized the board. These acts provided part of the basis for dismissing him from the university.[40] The district court, finding for the professor, stated:

> In each of these communications, plaintiff spoke or wrote as a private citizen on a public issue, and in a place and context apart from his role as faculty member. In none of these public utterances did he appear as a spokesman for the University, or claim any kind of expertise related to his profession. He spoke as any citizen might speak, and the Board was, therefore, subject to its own avowed standard that when a faculty member "speaks or writes as a citizen, he should be free from institutional censorship or discipline" [353 F. Supp. at 920].

---

[39]A private institution's authority would be limited to some extent, however, by the Title VII employment discrimination statute (see Section 5.2.1 of this book). But religious private institutions would be exempted from some of these Title VII requirements (see Section 5.5 of this book).

[40]The professor had also been charged with deliberately cutting a class in order to speak at a campus rally at another university. The court determined that he had broken no specific regulation by canceling the class and that such matters were usually handled informally within the department. The court chastised the board for selectively enforcing its general attendance policy against the professor in this particular instance and dismissed the charge.

The results may be different from those in *Starsky,* however, if the faculty member's extramural speech is not on a matter of public concern. In *Trejo v. Shoben,* 319 F.3d 878 (7th Cir. 2003) (also discussed in Section 7.4.3), for example, a university had denied reappointment to a professor and, in making this decision, had considered "all the facts and circumstances dealing with [the professor's] conduct during his three years as a non-tenured probationary employee at the University. . . ." Among these facts and circumstances were various charges and complaints about "boorish" and "unprofessional" behavior, often including statements or comments as a primary part of the behavior (319 F.3d at 883). One set of concerns, as the court described it, involved "off-color comments [the professor] made while he was attending parties, playing cards, or frequenting taverns around the University—such as his comment that he wanted to 'get his hands' on one graduate student and 'get naked' or 'drink some good beer' with another . . ." (319 F.3d at 887). The professor claimed that these comments were protected freedom of speech. The court disagreed, asserting that such comments were "casual, idle, and flirtatious chit-chat that may not form the basis of a First Amendment claim."

Moreover, under more recent precedents, the results in extramural speech cases may also differ from that in *Starsky* when the institution can make a connection between the extramural speech and an identifiable harm to the institution. The protracted litigation in *Jeffries v. Harleston* provides a leading example. A tenured professor and chair of the Black Studies Department at the City University of New York (CUNY) had made a controversial off-campus speech in the capacity of "an appointed consultant of the State Education Commissioner." While addressing the topic of reforming the educational system to promote diversity, the professor "made strident attacks against particular individuals, and made derogatory comments about specific ethnic groups" (828 F. Supp. at 1073). When CUNY subsequently removed the professor from his position as department chair, he claimed a violation of the First Amendment. The district court upheld a jury verdict in the professor's favor (820 F. Supp. 741 (S.D.N.Y. 1993), *motion to set aside jury verdict granted in part and denied in part, and permanent injunction granted,* 828 F. Supp. 1066 (S.D.N.Y. 1993)). Relying on *Pickering* and *Connick* (see Section 7.1.1), the court held that the speech was on a matter of public concern and that "Professor Jeffries's statements, when spoken outside the classroom, remain under the umbrella of constitutional protection, as long as those statements do not impede the efficient and effective operation of the College or University." Relying on the *Mt. Healthy* case (see Section 7.6 below), the court determined that the speech was "a substantial or motivating factor" in the university's decision to remove him as department chair. The court thus concluded that "[w]hile there may have been compelling and legitimate grounds upon which to discipline Professor Jeffries, the University chose to act upon illegitimate and unconstitutional grounds, specifically upon [the off-campus speech] and the publicity surrounding it." The appellate court affirmed the district court in all pertinent respects, remanding the case, however, for further proceedings regarding punitive damages (21 F.3d 1238 (2d Cir. 1994)).

The U.S. Supreme Court then granted the university's petition for review of the appellate court's opinion and, upon review (513 U.S. 996 (1994)), remanded the case to the lower courts for reconsideration in light of the Court's 1994 decision in *Waters v. Churchill* (see Section 7.1.1). After reconsideration, and relying on the Supreme Court's ruling in *Waters,* the appellate court reversed its earlier decision and ordered the district court to enter judgment for the defendants (*Jeffries v. Harleston,* 52 F.3d 9 (2d Cir. 1995)). (For contrasting critiques of the case, see Richard Hiers, "New Restrictions on Academic Free Speech: *Jeffries v. Harleston II,*" 22 *J. Coll. & Univ. Law* 217 (1995); and Stephen Newman, "At Work in the Marketplace of Ideas: Academic Freedom, the First Amendment, and *Jeffries v. Harleston,*" 22 *J. Coll. & Univ. Law* 281 (1995); and see also Michael Sherman, "The Leonard Jeffries Problem: Public University Professor/Administrators, Controversial Speech, and Constitutional Protection for Public Employees," 30 *Loyola U. Chi. L.J.* 651 (1999).)

In reversing its earlier decision, the appellate court in *Jeffries* did not revise its determination that the professor's speech was on a matter of public concern. Instead the court focused on the *Pickering/Connick* balancing test, determined that *Waters* had clarified this test in a way favorable to employers, and then reworked its balance of factors. According to the appellate court:

> Even when the speech is squarely on public issues—and thus earns the greatest constitutional protection—*Waters* indicates that the government's burden is to make a substantial showing of *likely* interference and not an *actual* disruption. [W]hittled to its core, *Waters* permits a government employer to fire an employee for speaking on a matter of public concern if: (1) the employer's prediction of disruption is reasonable; (2) the potential disruptiveness is enough to outweigh the value of the speech; and (3) the employer took action against the employee based on this disruption and not in retaliation for the speech. By stressing that *actual* disruption is not required, *Waters* pulls a crucial support column out from under our earlier *Jeffries* opinion [52 F.3d at 13 (emphasis in original)].

Guided by this reading of *Waters,* the appellate court reviewed the jury's findings in the trial record and concluded that a majority of the defendants had "a reasonable expectation that the [off-campus] speech would harm CUNY"; and that a majority of the defendants were motivated by this "reasonable prediction of disruption," and not by a "retaliatory animus," when they demoted Jeffries. The court struck the balance in favor of the university by concluding (without any elaboration) that the university's concern about the potential disruptiveness of the speech was sufficient to outweigh Jeffries's interest in free speech.

The court did not mention academic freedom until the conclusion of its analysis. In a cryptic and enigmatic paragraph, the court noted that Jeffries's position as department chair was "ministerial" and "provided no greater public contact than an ordinary professorship," and that the university has not tried to silence "or otherwise limit [Jeffries's] access to the 'marketplace of ideas' in the classroom." Jeffries therefore did not have a viable "academic freedom" claim (52 F.3d at 14–15).

The *Jeffries* court's reasoning provides precious little guidance on how to make the various sensitive determinations required by its analysis. To reach its ultimate conclusion, the court had to determine that university officials' beliefs or predictions about the impact of Jeffries's speech were reasonable (rather than unreasonable), that university officials took action against Jeffries because of the potential impact his speech would have on university operations (rather than because of their dislike of the content of the speech), and that the potential disruptiveness of the speech outweighed its First Amendment value (rather than the speech outweighing the potential disruptiveness). The opinion sets forth neither a methodology for making these determinations nor a substantive justification for the court's conclusions—other than statements on the need to defer to the university.

It is especially difficult to determine how the *Jeffries* court distinguished between reasonable concerns about disruption and improper retaliatory motives. The problem seems to be with the court's formulation of the issues: the university could not constitutionally discipline Jeffries for the content of his speech, yet it would not have had reason to discipline him without the speech. It was the speech that created the potential disruption. At most large universities, it would be hard to imagine "public concern" speech that would not stir any concerns regarding potential disruption of some university interest. The point at which mere offense at a particular message moves to a reasonable concern for university operations is not altogether clear. It is also not clear what types of impacts would be considered disruptions. Certainly the more extreme cases are imaginable—for example, the loss of substantial financial support directly attributable to the speech could be a disruption—but what of smaller financial losses, or losses attributable to a mix of factors? Or a small potential decline in student applications to a particular department? Or a student demonstration in reaction to the speech?

As used in *Jeffries,* the *Waters* concept of "potential" disruption seems to give colleges and universities wide discretion in controlling faculty members' extramural speech. Even if the university concluded that Professor Jeffries had engaged in hate speech off campus, why was it reasonable to believe that this speech would disrupt university operations? And, if it was reasonable to conclude that Jeffries's speech would disrupt university operations, then would it be reasonable to believe that all unpopular speech has a similar potential to disrupt? Neither *Waters* nor *Jeffries* provides any sound guidance on where and how to draw these lines, suggesting only the cursory standard of "reasonable belief."

Some structure could be added to the analysis if the issues regarding retaliatory motives were treated as analogous to the causation issues addressed in the *Mt. Healthy* line of cases (see Section 7.6 below). When the case concerns a single speech or a related pattern of speeches on matters of public concern, and the faculty member has been terminated for this speech, the court must determine whether the speech can be separated into disruptive (unprotected) and nondisruptive (protected) portions. If the nondisruptive portions of the speech are the cause of—or motivation for—the termination, then the termination is invalid. If the court can identify portions of the speech that were disruptive, however, the university should have to show a causal link between these particular statements and some particular (potential) disruption. Absent any such link, it would be reasonable to conclude that the university was motivated by its disagreement with, or its taking offense at, the speech, and that the termination was an act of retaliation rather than a well-considered attempt to protect university interests from disruption.

In *Waters,* Justice O'Connor, citing *Mt. Healthy,* used a similar analysis that provides helpful guidance for recognizing and resolving retaliation issues in cases like *Waters* and *Jeffries.* According to Justice O'Connor:

> Churchill has produced enough evidence to create a material issue of disputed fact about petitioners' actual motivation. Churchill had criticized the [hospital's] cross-training policy in the past; management had exhibited some sensitivity about the criticisms; Churchill pointed to some other conduct by hospital management that, if viewed in the light most favorable to her, would show that they were hostile to her because of her criticisms. A reasonable factfinder might therefore, on this record, conclude that petitioners actually fired Churchill not because of the disruptive things she said to Perkins-Graham, but because of nondisruptive statements about cross-training that they thought she may have made in the same conversation, or because of other statements she may have made earlier. If this is so, then the court will have to determine whether those statements were protected speech, a different matter than the one before us now [511 U.S. at 681–82].

The opinions in *Scallet v. Rosenblum,* discussed in Section 7.6 below, also develop a helpful relationship between retaliation analysis and the *Mt. Healthy* analysis.

Not all courts will be as deferential to a university's predictions of disruption as was the court in *Jeffries.* For instance, in *Burnham v. Ianni,* 119 F.3d 668 (8th Cir. 1997) (*en banc*), the court issued this warning:

> The government employer must make a substantial showing that the speech is, in fact, disruptive before the speech may be punished. *Waters* [*v. Churchill*], 511 U.S. 661, at 674 (1994). We recognize that the government, as an employer, has broader powers in suppressing free speech than the government as a sovereign. Indeed, we have given some deference to an employer's predictions of workplace disruption. *Id.* However, we have never granted any deference to a government supervisor's bald assertions of harm based on conclusory hearsay and rank speculation.
>
> Even if we were to attempt [in this case] to balance the plaintiffs' free speech rights against the purported disruption of the pedagogical tasks of [the university], it is clear that the impact of the speech on [the university's] mission is totally unproven and unaddressed except in the most conclusory fashion. There is simply no evidence that establishes a nexus between the [speech] and an exacerbated climate of fear on the campus or, more importantly, that establishes a relationship between the [speech] and a decrease in the efficiency and effectiveness of [the university's] educational mission [119 F.3d at 680].

Sec. 7.6. Administrators' Authority Regarding Faculty Academic Freedom and Freedom of Expression

The discussions in Sections 7.1 through 7.5 above make clear that academic freedom and freedom of expression are areas in which the law provides few firm guidelines for college and university administrators—particularly those in private institutions, since the decided cases are mostly constitutional decisions applicable only to public institutions. The constitutional cases themselves are sometimes incompletely reasoned or difficult to reconcile with one another. Moreover, because these cases often depend heavily on a balancing of faculty and institutional interests in light of the peculiar facts of the case, it may be difficult to generalize from one case to another. Thus, institutions need to develop their own regulations on academic freedom and free expression, and their own internal systems for protecting academic freedom and free expression in accordance with institutional policy and the applicable law. The AAUP's guidelines (see Sections 7.1.3 & 14.5 of this book) often can be of assistance in this endeavor.

As the discussions in Sections 7.1.4 and 7.2.4 above suggest, administrators and counsel at public institutions must ensure that the institution's academic freedom policy and its faculty conduct regulations avoid the constitutional dangers of "overbreadth" and "vagueness" (see generally Section 6.6.1). Institutional policies and regulations should also protect faculty members from penalties imposed on the basis of their viewpoints (that is, viewpoint discrimination). In addition, policies and regulations must provide for procedural due process protections in situations where their application would deprive a faculty member of a "liberty" or "property" interest (see Section 6.7.2). Although these constitutional requirements bind only public institutions, they may provide useful guidance for private institutions as well.

For both public and private institutions, faculty handbooks and related documents may provide some guidance for administrators, and contract law will likely impose some limitations on administrators' authority to regulate academic freedom (see Section 7.1.3 above). The importance and usefulness of those limits, however, will depend on the particular terms of the institution's contract with its faculty members (see Section 6.1). Express academic freedom clauses, or clauses incorporating AAUP guidelines, may create substantial limits on administrative authority—and also substantial guidance for resolving disputes. So may contract clauses establishing procedural safeguards that must precede adverse personnel actions (see Sections 6.7.1, 6.7.3, & 6.7.4) and clauses establishing "for-cause" standards that limit administrative discretion to terminate the contract (see Sections 6.6.1 & 6.6.2).

For public institutions, the constitutional law cases, for all their difficulties, do provide other guidance and also further restrict administrators' authority to limit faculty academic freedom. Despite continuing disagreements among courts, there are cases that protect faculty academic freedom and that recognize limits on that freedom in all three internal arenas of concern: teaching (Section 7.2 above), research and publication (Section 7.3), and institutional affairs

(Section 7.4 above). Beyond these three internal arenas, faculty members have considerable freedom in external arenas to express themselves on public issues as private citizens, to associate with whom they please, and to engage in outside activities of their choice on their own time. In general, whether in an internal or external arena, administrative authority over faculty members' behavior or activities increases as their job-relatedness increases and as their negative impact on the educational process or other institutional functions increases.

Using all these contractual and constitutional, internal and external, sources of guidance, administrators should carefully avoid any reliance on an activity or behavior protected by academic freedom whenever they are deciding to terminate or discipline a faculty member or to deny tenure, promotion, or a contract renewal. Sticky problems can arise when the faculty member has engaged in possibly protected activities but has also engaged in unprotected activities that might justify an adverse personnel decision. Suppose, for instance, that a faculty member up for renewal has made public statements critical of state policy on higher education (probably protected) and has also often failed to hold his classes as scheduled (unprotected). What must an administrator do to avoid later judicial reversal of a decision not to renew?

The U.S. Supreme Court addressed this problem in *Mt. Healthy City School District Board of Education v. Doyle,* 429 U.S. 274 (1977), a constitutional case binding on public institutions but providing guidance for private institutions as well. The plaintiff schoolteacher had made statements regarding school policy to a radio broadcaster, who promptly broadcast the information as a news item. A month later the school board informed the teacher that he would not be rehired and gave the radio broadcast as one reason. It also gave several other reasons, however, including an incident in which the teacher made an obscene gesture to two students in the school cafeteria. The Supreme Court determined that the radio communication was protected by the First Amendment and had played a substantial part in the nonrenewal decision, but that the nonrenewal was nevertheless valid if the school board could prove that it would have declined to rehire the teacher even if the radio incident had never occurred:

> Initially, in this case, the burden was properly placed upon . . . [the teacher] to show that his conduct was constitutionally protected, and that this conduct was a "substantial factor" or, to put it in other words, that it was a "motivating factor" in the Board's decision not to rehire him. [The teacher] having carried that burden, however, the District Court should have gone on to determine whether the Board had shown by preponderance of the evidence that it would have reached the same decision as to . . . [the teacher's] reemployment even in the absence of the protected conduct [429 U.S. at 287].

Numerous court decisions have applied the *Mt. Healthy* test to public postsecondary education in situations where both proper and improper considerations are alleged to have contributed to a particular personnel decision. In an early case, *Goss v. San Jacinto Junior College,* 588 F.2d 96 (5th Cir. 1979), the plaintiff, a junior college instructor, claimed that her contract had not been renewed because of her political and union activities, which were protected activities under the First Amendment. The college responded that the instructor had not been rehired because of declining enrollment and poor evaluation of her work. After a jury trial, the jury agreed with the instructor and awarded her $23,400 in back pay. In affirming the jury verdict, the federal appeals court issued an opinion illustrating what administrators should *not* do if they wish to avoid judicial invalidation of their personnel decisions:

> There was ample evidence to support the jury finding that Mrs. Goss had not been rehired "because of her political and/or professional activities." Dr. Spencer [the president of the college] testified that, when Mrs. Goss sought to organize a local chapter of the National Faculty Association, he distributed by campus mail a faculty newsletter expressing his concern about the organization, while denying proponents of the National Faculty Association the privilege of distributing literature by campus mail. Mrs. Goss testified that, after her husband had filed a petition to run for a seat on the Board of Regents, Dr. Carl Burney, chairman of the Division of Social and Behavioral Sciences, advised her to have her husband withdraw from the election. In deposition testimony, Dr. O. W. Marcom, Academic Dean, stated that, when Mrs. Goss presided at an organizational meeting of a local chapter of the Texas Junior College Teachers Association in the spring of 1971, he attended and voiced his objection to the group. Dr. Spencer himself testified by deposition that he had recommended the nonrenewal of Mrs. Goss's contract to discipline her for "creating or trying to create ill will or lack of cooperation . . . with the administration."
>
> There was sufficient evidence to support the jury finding that "matters other than Mrs. Goss's political and/or professional activities" were not responsible for the Board of Regents' action. Appellants justified the nonrenewal of Mrs. Goss's contract on the grounds that declining enrollment necessitated a staff reduction and that Mrs. Goss received a poor evaluation from Dr. Edwin Lehr, Chairman of the History Department, and Dr. Burney. Although Dr. Spencer had recommended a reduction of three faculty members in the History Department, Mrs. Goss was one of four faculty members in the History Department in 1971–72 who did not teach at San Jacinto Junior College in 1972–73.
>
> Furthermore, Dr. Lehr's evaluation of Mrs. Goss, upon which Dr. Spencer allegedly relied in making his recommendation to the Board of Regents, was inconsistent with the objective criteria established for the rating. The criteria by which the teachers were rated include the number of years of teaching at San Jacinto Junior College, enrollment in a doctoral program, the number of doctoral-level courses completed, the percentage of the teacher's students earning credits, and other factors. Mrs. Goss was not awarded five points to which she was entitled on the objective scale for academic courses she had taken while employed as an instructor. Thus, she was assigned eighty points, rather than eighty-five. If she had been awarded the points to which she was entitled, she would have ranked in the middle of the seventeen history instructors rather than in the bottom three [588 F.2d at 99–100].

Evidence of an intrusion into academic freedom is not always as clear as it was to the court in *Goss,* however, and postsecondary institutions have often emerged victorious in court. In *Allaire v. Rogers,* 658 F.2d 1055 (5th Cir. 1981), for example, the court considered whether a university president had denied merit raises to a group of tenured professors because they had lobbied for increased salary appropriations at the state legislature (protected) or because of their lack of merit (unprotected). Only one of the eight original plaintiffs ultimately prevailed on appeal. In *Hillis v. Stephen F. Austin State University*, 665 F.2d 547 (5th Cir. 1982), the court considered whether the contract of a non-tenured faculty member had not been renewed because of his private criticism of his superiors (apparently protected) or his insubordination and uncooperativeness (unprotected). After losing at trial, the university prevailed on appeal. In *Hildebrand v. Board of Trustees of Michigan State University*, 607 F.2d 705 (6th Cir. 1979), *appeal after remand*, 662 F.2d 439 (6th Cir. 1981) (further discussed in Section 2.2.1), the court considered whether a faculty member had been denied tenure because of his criticism of the department's curriculum (protected), his election to the departmental advisory committee (protected), or his unsuitability for the multidisciplinary emphasis of the department (unprotected). After extended litigation, the university eventually emerged victorious. In *Ollman v. Toll*, 518 F. Supp. 1196 (D. Md. 1981), *affirmed*, 704 F.2d 139 (4th Cir. 1983), the court considered whether the University of Maryland refused to appoint the plaintiff as department chair, after his selection by a search committee, because he held Marxist political views (protected) or because he lacked the necessary qualifications to develop the department according to the university's plans (unprotected). The university prevailed at trial and on appeal. (Compare *Cooper v. Ross*, 472 F. Supp. 802 (D. Ark. 1979).) In *Harden v. Adams*, 841 F.2d 1091 (11th Cir. 1988), the court considered whether a professor's tenure had been terminated because he helped maintain discrimination charges against the university and helped organize a chapter of a state education association (protected) or because he quarreled with supervising faculty members and sought to draw students into the disputes, caused dissension within the faculty, neglected faculty duties, and violated minor institutional rules (unprotected). The court concluded that the latter reasons had been the basis for the termination. And in *Nicholas v. Pennsylvania State University*, 227 F.3d 133 (3d Cir. 2000), the court considered whether a tenured faculty member had been terminated because of his criticisms of his supervisor (possibly protected) or because of his excessive outside consulting work (unprotected). The appellate court upheld a jury verdict in favor of the university.[41]

As these cases illustrate, and as *Mt. Healthy* provides, there are two ways in which public postsecondary institutions can win their cases even if the faculty member has engaged in speech on a matter of public concern. First, the institution

---

[41]The *Nicholas* case, like the *Goss* case discussed above, illustrates the important role that juries may play in litigation raising issues of "causation" (the "cause" of the institution's adverse action against the faculty member) or "motive" (the institution's "motive" for its adverse action). Causation and motive are largely fact determinations and thus with the province of the jury. The respective burdens of proof imposed upon the parties by *Mt. Healthy* (above) is therefore a critical consideration, as is the means available to the parties to prove or disprove causation or motive. The trial judge's instructions to the jury are also a critical consideration. On appeal in the *Nicholas* case, the professor challenged the accuracy of the jury instructions, but the appellate court rejected the challenge and upheld the instructions.

will prevail if the faculty member fails to meet his or her burden of proving that the public concern speech was "a substantial factor" or "motivating factor" in the institution's decision; and second, the institution will prevail if it carries its burden of proving "that it would have reached the same decision [regarding the faculty member] even in the absence of the protected [speech]" (*Mt. Healthy,* above). The first alternative is illustrated by *de Llano v. Berglund,* and the second alternative is illustrated by *Scallet v. Rosenblum,* both of which are discussed below.

In *de Llano v. Berglund,* 282 F.3d 1031 (8th Cir. 2002), the professor demonstrated that some of the comments in letters he wrote were on matters of public concern (see Section 7.4, above, for this aspect of the case), but he nevertheless lost because "there is no evidence in the record that these few comments on matters of public concern were a substantial or motivating factor in the decision to terminate him." According to the court:

> We are unable to ascertain any evidence that [de Llano] was terminated because of the letters he wrote to the various venues. The dismissal notice given to de Llano outlines a number of reasons for his termination, and those reasons were substantiated in two separate hearings. Not one of the reasons stated for his termination related to de Llano's letters. . . . We conclude that as a matter of law, even when viewed in the light most favorable to the plaintiff, the record establishes that de Llano failed to meet his burden of showing that his letters were a substantial factor in the decision to terminate him [283 F.3d at 1037].

In *Scallet v. Rosenblum,* 911 F. Supp. 999 (W.D. Va. 1996), *affirmed,* 197 WL 33077 (4th Cir. 1997) (unpublished), an instructor at the University of Virginia's Darden Graduate School of Business (Darden) claimed that the university refused to renew his contract in retaliation for speaking out on matters of public concern. Three categories of speech were at issue: (1) the professor's classroom discussions on the importance of "diversity" in education programs and in the corporate world; (2) the professor's advocacy in faculty meetings regarding diversity issues and concerns; and (3) articles and cartoons the professor had placed on his office door. The district court determined that only the latter two categories were protected speech (see Sections 7.2.2 & 7.4). The instructor then had to demonstrate, as required by the *Mt. Healthy* case above, that the speech in these two categories was a "motivating factor or played a substantial role" in the contract nonrenewal; the court apparently accepted that the instructor's evidence did show "some . . . illegal motivation." Nevertheless, the defendants had demonstrated that the speech at issue "was not the 'but for' cause of his nonrenewal." Rather, the reasons for the nonrenewal were the instructor's "[f]ailure to observe and follow [the] institutional determination of which courses should embrace which matters within the particular course curriculum," which led to "disaffections of the other [departmental] instructors" and "strong complaints about [the instructor's] personal interrelations with those instructors."

On appeal, the U.S. Court of Appeals for the Fourth Circuit affirmed the district court's decision. The appellate court noted that there had been various complaints to the effect that the instructor had "a confrontational style that made the other writing teachers feel physically and emotionally threatened, and that did, as the district court said, border on sexual harassment." This, the appellate court determined, was the reason for the discharge, and not the desire to retaliate against the instructor for the protected speech.

By placing burdens on faculty members who assert violations of academic freedom or freedom of expression, *Mt. Healthy* and its progeny give administrators at public institutions breathing space to make sound personnel decisions in situations where faculty members may have engaged in protected activity. Administrators in private institutions already have such breathing space, and more, since they are not limited by the First Amendment; but they may nevertheless wish to use their breathing space in the way that is suggested below.

The goal for administrators, of course, is to make personnel decisions untainted by any consideration of protected expression or other illegitimate factors implicating academic freedom. But in the real world, that goal is not always attainable, either because under current legal standards it is difficult to determine whether particular expression is protected or because events involving conduct protected by academic freedom are so widely known that administrators cannot claim to have been unaware of them at the time they made their decision. In situations where both protected and unprotected conduct has occurred, administrators can still avoid judicial invalidation if they make sure that strong and dispositive grounds, independent of any grounds impinging academic freedom, exist for every adverse decision, and that such independent grounds are considered in the decision-making process and are documented in the institution's records.

Administrators should also consider what procedures they will use in investigating situations that could give rise, or have given rise, to a claim of an academic freedom violation. The need to investigate in order to resolve factual disputes, and to clarify the nuances of what may be subtle and complex circumstances, may be especially great when the institution is contemplating disciplinary action against a faculty member because of activities that he or she may claim are protected by academic freedom. The U.S. Supreme Court's decision in *Waters v. Churchill*, 511 U.S. 661 (1994) (discussed in Section 7.1.1 above), underscores the need for caution in such situations and provides some (although murky) guidance to public employers regarding investigations in cases with First Amendment overtones. In *Waters*, a hospital had discharged a nurse based on a third-party report that she had made disruptive statements concerning the hospital to a coworker. There was a fact dispute about the content of these statements; in the nurse's version, the statements were on matters of public concern protected under the *Connick* case (Section 7.1.1 above). Although the Justices were splintered, a majority apparently did agree that, in these circumstances, the employer had a duty to conduct a "reasonable" investigation of the facts and could not dismiss the employee unless it had a "reasonable" belief that the third party's or the employer's version of the facts was accurate (see 511 U.S. at 682–86 (concurring opinion of Justice Souter)).

While the *Mt. Healthy* case and the *Waters* case, as First Amendment precedents, bind only public institutions, they can guide private institutions in establishing review standards for their own internal investigations of personnel disputes; and they may, by analogy, assist courts in reviewing academic freedom claims based on a contract theory (see Section 7.1.3).

In addition to fair and probative investigatory processes, both public and private institutions will want to have well-conceived and well-drafted dispute resolution processes, such as grievance mechanisms and mediation, for resolving conflicts concerning academic freedom (see generally Section 2.3). Such dispute resolution mechanisms must be accompanied and supported by sound written policy statements and regulations on academic freedom—that is, policies that are both respectful of national and local custom and usage on academic freedom and sensitive to the particular needs of the institution. A key to the success of dispute resolution mechanisms and accompanying policies is the ability to accommodate the mix of legitimate interests that are likely to be at stake in academic freedom disputes. Interests of faculty members, students, and the institution, for instance, may all be involved in the same dispute; similarly, both the rights and the responsibilities of these stakeholders are likely to be involved. Successful dispute resolution and successful accommodation, in short, require recognition that all interests at stake must to some extent be limited to allow some room for the other legitimate interests; and that freedom entails both rights and responsibilities, each of which must be accounted for in resolving disputes. Thus institutions should strive for policies and processes that provide vigorous protection of the faculty's (and students') academic freedom as well as acceptance of the "duties correlative with rights" that accompany academic freedom (see the "1940 Statement of Principles on Academic Freedom and Tenure," in *AAUP Policy Documents and Reports* (9th ed., 2001), 3–4, 5 (under comment 1)).

Sec. 7.7. Protection of Confidential Academic Information: The "Academic Freedom Privilege"

7.7.1 Overview. A difficult and divisive academic freedom problem for postsecondary faculty members and administrators is whether courts or administrative agencies may compel faculty members or their institutions to disclose confidential academic information if such information is relevant to issues in litigation. Faculty members may confront this problem if they are asked to provide a deposition, to answer interrogatories, or to be a witness in ongoing litigation, or if they are served with a subpoena or a contempt citation or are otherwise ordered by a court or administrative agency to surrender information within their control.

Administrators may become entwined in the problem if the institution seeks to assist a faculty member with such matters or, more generally, if the institution seeks to monitor institutional affairs so as to avoid litigation. Although faculty members and administrators may disagree on how best to respond to demands for confidential information, the primary clash is not between members of the academic community—as in the cases in Sections 7.2 through 7.6— but between the academic community, on the one hand, and the courts, administrative agencies, and opposing litigants on the other.

Issues related to the protection of confidential information tend to arise in two contexts: (1) requests to disclose the views of individual evaluators of faculty performance at the time that reappointment, promotion, or tenure decisions are made; and (2) the demand that unpublished data or research findings be released against the will of the researcher. These issues are examined in Sections 7.7.2 and 7.7.3.

7.7.2. Personnel issues. Many colleges and universities rely on the judgments of a faculty member's peers—either colleagues within the institution or experts in the faculty member's discipline from other institutions—to assess the quality of that individual's scholarship, teaching, and service and to recommend whether reappointment, promotion, or tenure should be conferred. Historically, candidates have not been given access to peer evaluations at many institutions; in fact, many external reviewers have been willing to provide candid judgments about a faculty member only if the institution provided assurances that the candidate would not have access to the evaluation. Institutions, their faculty, and external evaluators have argued that confidentiality is essential to encourage candor. On the other hand, candidates denied reappointment, promotion, or tenure have argued that refusing to give them access to the confidential evaluations upon which a negative decision may have been based is unfair and restricts their ability to challenge what may be an unlawful decision in court. Although this latter view prevailed in a decision of the U.S. Supreme Court, which required a university to disclose "confidential" evaluations to the Equal Employment Opportunity Commission (EEOC) (*University of Pennsylvania v. EEOC*, 493 U.S. 182 (1990)), it took ten years of litigation and a sharp division among the federal appellate courts to obtain an answer to this dilemma.[42]

The official beginning of judicial attention to this issue occurred when a trial court had ordered a University of Georgia professor serving on a faculty review committee to reveal and explain his vote on a promotion and tenure application that the committee had rejected. The professor refused, citing an "academic freedom privilege." The appellate court (in *In re Dinnan*, 661 F.2d 426 (11th Cir. 1981)) rejected the professor's claim to an academic freedom privilege, stating that no constitutional issues were involved, and that Professor Dinnan was claiming a privilege that had never been recognized by any court.

While recognizing the significance of academic freedom, the court characterized Dinnan's claim as seeking to suppress information, and stressed the potential for frustrating the plaintiff's attempt to ascertain the reasons for her tenure denial. "This possibility is a much greater threat to our liberty and academic freedom than the compulsion of discovery in the instant case" (661 F.2d at 431).

The opinion demonstrates apparent irritation with Dinnan's claim that forcing disclosure of votes and evaluations will harm colleges and universities:

> We fail to see how if a tenure committee is acting in good faith, our decision today will adversely affect its decision-making process. Indeed, this opinion should work to reinforce responsible decision-making in tenure questions as it

---

[42]Cases are collected in Martin J. McMahon, Annot., "Academic Peer Review Privilege in Federal Court," 85 A.L.R. Fed. 691.

sends out a clear signal to would-be wrongdoers that they may not hide behind "academic freedom" to avoid responsibility for their actions. . . . Society has no strong interest in encouraging timid faculty members to serve on tenure committees [661 F.2d at 431–32].

The court therefore affirmed the trial court's orders that Dinnan answer deposition questions about his committee vote and that he be fined and jailed for contempt if he continued to refuse. Dinnan again refused, and the court ordered him jailed. He arrived at the jail dressed in full academic regalia.

Although the point of view expressed in *Dinnan* foreshadowed the unanimous opinion of the U.S. Supreme Court in the *University of Pennsylvania* decision, nine years would elapse and several more appellate decisions would consider this issue before the high court resolved it.

The following year, another court, in *Gray v. Board of Higher Education*, 692 F.2d 901 (2d Cir. 1982), reached the same result as *Dinnan*, but on much narrower grounds, and left the door open for the creation of such a privilege under appropriate circumstances. Because the plaintiff, Gray, had not been given a reason for his tenure denial, the court ruled that he must be provided the "confidential" documents he sought; had he been given a reason, the court suggested, the university might have been able to withhold them. By leaving room for recognition of an academic freedom privilege in other cases, the court in effect adopted a middle-ground position earlier espoused by the AAUP (see "A Preliminary Statement on Judicially Compelled Disclosure in the Nonrenewal of Faculty Appointments," *Academe*, February–March 1981, 27).

The U.S. Court of Appeals for the Seventh Circuit created and applied an academic freedom privilege in *EEOC v. University of Notre Dame*, 715 F.2d 331 (7th Cir. 1983), ordering the EEOC to accept redacted documents from which information identifying the writer had been removed, and asserting that the identity of the evaluators was protected by an "academic freedom privilege." The court also accepted the university's argument that the EEOC should be required to sign a nondisclosure agreement before it obtained the files of faculty who were not parties to the lawsuit. But the U.S. Court of Appeals for the Third Circuit rejected the attempt of Franklin and Marshall College to assert an academic freedom privilege when the EEOC requested "confidential" evaluative information in order to investigate a professor's claim that his denial of tenure was a result of national origin discrimination. In *EEOC v. Franklin and Marshall College*, 775 F.2d 110 (3d Cir. 1985), the court, while recognizing the importance of confidentiality in obtaining candid evaluations, nevertheless ruled that the plaintiff's need for information relevant to his discrimination claim outweighed the college's interests in confidentiality.

Given the sharp differences among the four federal appellate courts that had addressed this issue, the U.S. Supreme Court granted review of a case in which Rosalie Tung, a professor in the University of Pennsylvania's business school, sued the university for race, sex, and national origin discrimination in denying her tenure. The EEOC had subpoenaed the confidential peer evaluations on which the university had relied to make its negative decision. Although the university complied with much of the EEOC's request, it refused to submit confidential letters written by Tung's evaluators, letters from the department chair, and accounts of a faculty committee's deliberations. It also refused to submit similar materials for five male faculty in the business school who were granted tenure during that year, which the EEOC wanted to review for comparison purposes. The EEOC filed an action to enforce the subpoena; both the district court and the U.S. Court of Appeals for the Third Circuit ordered the university to produce the documents, relying on *Franklin and Marshall.* Still refusing to produce the materials, the university appealed the ruling to the U.S. Supreme Court. The university argued that quality tenure decisions require candid peer evaluations, which in turn require confidentiality. It asserted that requiring such disclosure would "destroy collegiality" and that either a common law privilege or a constitutionally based privilege should be created. The Court agreed to determine whether a qualified "academic freedom privilege" should be created or whether a balancing test should be used that would require the EEOC to show "particularized need" for the information before it was disclosed.

Writing for a unanimous court, Justice Harry Blackmun upheld the EEOC's need for peer evaluations and refused either to create a privilege or to require the EEOC to show "particularized need" (*University of Pennsylvania v. EEOC,* 493 U.S. 182 (1990)). Justice Blackmun first noted that Title VII contains no language excluding peer evaluations from discovery and that the EEOC's need for relevant information was not diminished simply because the defendant in this case was a university.

The Court gave the following reasons for its refusal to create a common law privilege:

1. Congress, in amending Title VII in 1972 to extend its protections to employees of colleges and universities, had not included such a privilege.

2. Title VII confers upon the EEOC a broad right of access to relevant evidence, and peer evaluations were clearly relevant.

3. Title VII includes sanctions for the disclosure of confidential information by EEOC staff.

4. Evidence of discrimination is particularly likely to be "tucked away in peer review files" (493 U.S. at 193).

5. Requiring the EEOC to show particularized need for the information could frustrate the purpose of Title VII by making the EEOC's investigatory responsibilities more difficult.

The Court also rejected the university's request that a constitutionally based academic freedom privilege be created. While acknowledging academe's strong interest in protecting academic freedom, the Court viewed the EEOC's request as an "extremely attenuated" infringement on academic freedom, characterizing it as a "content-neutral" government action to enforce a federal law rather than a government attempt to suppress free speech (493 U.S. at 198–99).

It was clear that the Court regarded the potential injury to academic freedom as speculative, and the argument that academe deserved special treatment as inappropriate:

> We are not so ready as petitioner seems to be to assume the worst about those in the academic community. Although it is possible that some evaluators may become less candid as the possibility of disclosure increases, others may simply ground their evaluations in specific examples and illustrations in order to deflect potential claims of bias or unfairness. Not all academics will hesitate to stand up and be counted when they evaluate their peers [493 U.S. at 200].

The result in this case appears to require an institution, when confronted with an EEOC subpoena, to produce relevant information, whether or not the institution has promised to keep it confidential. Although the Supreme Court did not address the issue of whether an institution could provide peer review materials with identifying information redacted, the Court's very broad language upholding the need of the EEOC for relevant information suggests that, should the EEOC assert that identifying information is relevant to a particular claim, the information would have to be provided. And although this case involves access to information by the EEOC, rather than by a private plaintiff, it is likely that the case will be interpreted to permit faculty plaintiffs in discrimination cases to see letters from outside evaluators, written recommendations of department or other committees, and other information relevant to a negative employment decision. (For analysis of the *University of Pennsylvania* case's implications for faculty personnel decisions, see B. Lee, *Peer Review Confidentiality: Is It Still Possible?* (National Association of College and University Attorneys, 1990).)

Discovery requests in litigation challenging tenure denials since the *University of Pennsylvania* case have returned to the principles of relevance and burdensomeness that courts apply in nonacademic settings. For example, in *Kern v. University of Notre Dame du Lac*, 1997 U.S. Dist. LEXIS 21158 (N.D. Ind., August 12, 1997), a female professor denied tenure in the School of Business sought to obtain the promotion file of a male colleague who had been promoted to full professor the same year that she was denied tenure. Although the university objected on the grounds that the standards for promotion to associate professor with tenure were different from the standards for promotion to full professor, the court ordered the university to produce the dossier. There was no discussion of an academic freedom privilege. (For an unusual ruling barring a plaintiff from discovering the individual votes of faculty on a university-wide promotion and tenure committee, see *Staton v. Miami University*, 2001 Ohio App. LEXIS 1421 (Ct. App. Ohio, 10th App. Dist., March 27, 2001).[43])

For public institutions (and some private ones as well) in states with open records laws, the result in *University of Pennsylvania* may have little significance,

---

[43]The court ruled that, because the institution's tenure policies specified that members of the university-wide promotion and tenure committee were not allowed to divulge the committee's decision-making process, that was a contractual requirement binding on both the committee members and all candidates for tenure.

because several of these laws have been interpreted to apply to faculty personnel decisions. For example, in *Pennsylvania State University v. Commissioner, Department of Labor and Industry,* 536 A.2d 852 (Pa. Commw. Ct. 1988), a state court interpreted the open records law as permitting faculty to see peer evaluations solicited for promotion or tenure decisions, calling them "performance evaluations" (for which the state law requires disclosure) rather than "letters of reference" (which are exempted from the law's disclosure requirements). The state law was applied in the same manner when a faculty member at a private college sought access to peer evaluations after he was denied tenure (*Lafayette College v. Commissioner, Department of Labor and Industry,* 546 A.2d 126 (Pa. Commw. Ct. 1988)). Similarly, the Supreme Court of Alaska ruled that promotion and tenure decisions are subject to the state's "sunshine law" (*University of Alaska v. Geistauts,* 666 P.2d 424 (Alaska 1983)).

But a Michigan court exempted some peer evaluations from disclosure in *Muskovitz v. Lubbers,* 452 N.W.2d 854 (Mich. Ct. App. 1990), ruling that a letter from a dean to the provost regarding a faculty member's performance was exempt from the Michigan Employee Right-to-Know Act (Mich. Comp. Laws § 423.501 *et seq.*). The court characterized the letter as a "staff planning document" (one of the law's exemptions). It also ruled that the names of persons who prepared the evaluations, and specific words used in them (if those words would reveal the identity of the writer), were exempt under the law as "employee references supplied to an employer" and could be removed from documents submitted to a plaintiff. The court noted the Supreme Court's ruling in *University of Pennsylvania* but stated that it did not control interpretation of the Michigan law. Similarly, a state appellate court in Florida, in interpreting that state's open-records law, ruled that tenure committee votes are exempt from disclosure (*Cantanese v. Ceros-Livingston,* 599 So. 2d 1021 (Fla. Dist. Ct. App. 1992)).

But the Supreme Court of Ohio read its own state open records law differently and refused to create a privilege for "confidential" materials in a tenure file. In *State ex. rel. James v. Ohio State University,* 637 N.E.2d 911 (Ohio 1994), an assistant professor of geology requested copies of records in his tenure and promotion file and the files of other faculty, as well. Although the dean informed James that he would give him a redacted version of the information in his tenure file, he rejected James's request for the contents of other faculty members' promotion and tenure files. He also refused to give James the letter from his department chair regarding the chair's evaluation of James's performance, and withheld the identity of individuals who had evaluated James's work. James brought a mandamus action in the Supreme Court of Ohio, seeking a court order to force the university to disclose the information.

The university asserted that the tenure file documents were protected by a confidentiality exception in the Ohio Public Records Act, and also claimed that disclosure would violate the university's academic freedom. The court rejected both defenses. To the first defense, the court noted that the confidentiality exemption in the public records law was limited to law enforcement investigatory records, and did not cover tenure files. Furthermore, said the court, the university had admitted in its tenure guidelines that internal and external letters of evaluation were not exempted from the public records act. Regarding the second defense, the court cited *University of Pennsylvania v. EEOC* as authority for rejecting the university's argument. The court held that "promotion and tenure records maintained by a state-supported institution of higher education are 'public records'" under Ohio law, and ordered the university to provide the records sought by James.

Faculty in California attempted to use that state's education laws to seek access to their confidential peer evaluations, but without success. Section 92612 of the state's Education Code guarantees a faculty member access to material in his or her personnel files (although the name and affiliation of the writer may be redacted). In *Scharf v. Regents of the University of California,* 286 Cal. Rptr. 227 (Cal. Ct. App. 1991), the plaintiffs—six faculty members who had been denied tenure and the American Federation of Teachers—asserted that the state's Education Code gave them the right to review letters from outside reviewers and other confidential material in their personnel files. The university had given the faculty members summaries of the material but refused to provide the actual letters. The appellate court, citing Article IX, Section 9 of the California constitution, noted that the University of California has constitutional autonomy and that the provision in the state Education Code giving faculty access to confidential evaluations was, in its application to the university, unconstitutional. Distinguishing the *University of Pennsylvania* decision, the court noted that the faculty were not involved in litigation regarding their promotion or tenure decisions and that the reasoning of that case did not bind the California court in this case.

In light of the *University of Pennsylvania* decision and the proliferation of open records laws at the state level, the American Association of University Professors developed a policy on access to faculty personnel files. The report provides a thoughtful discussion of the two conflicting interests—preserving confidentiality in order to ensure complete candor, and ensuring access to evaluative material in order to encourage responsible and careful evaluation and to ascertain whether inappropriate grounds for a negative employment decision exist. The report, "Access to Faculty Personnel Files," is published in *AAUP Policy Documents and Reports* (9th ed., 2001), pages 41–46. It is a joint report of Committee A on Academic Freedom and Tenure and Committee W on the Status of Women in the Academic Profession, and reaches the following conclusions:

1. Faculty members should, at all times, have access to their own files, including unredacted letters, both internal and external.

2. A faculty member should be afforded access upon request to general information about other faculty members such as is normally contained in a *curriculum vitae.* . . .

3. Files of a faculty complainant and of other faculty members, for purposes of comparison, should be available in unredacted form to faculty appeals committees to the extent such committees deem the information relevant and necessary to the fair disposition of the case before them.

706 Faculty Academic Freedom and Freedom of Expression

4. A faculty appeals committee should make available to the aggrieved faculty member, in unredacted form and without prejudging the merits of the case, all materials it deems relevant to the complaint, including personnel files of other faculty members, having due regard for the privacy of those who are not parties to the complaint [pp. 44–45].

The report acknowledges that these recommendations "go beyond the practices regarding access to personnel files that are common in many colleges and universities" (p. 46).

Given the broadened access of candidates for reappointment, promotion, and tenure to formerly confidential evaluative information, college and university administrators and faculty should assess their policies and practices regarding peer evaluation and access of candidates to such information. Particularly in those states where access is afforded by state law, faculty evaluators should be well informed about the institution's criteria for such decisions and should be trained to provide appropriate documentation to support their recommendations. Given the heightened judicial scrutiny of institutions' denials of tenure to faculty (see Sections 5.2, 6.7.2.2, & 6.7.3), time spent ensuring that peer evaluations and the ensuing employment decisions are amply supported by evidence is an excellent investment.

7.7.3. Research findings.
Researchers are asked from time to time to provide their findings for a variety of lawsuits, the most common of which are products liability and regulatory actions. In some of these cases, the data have not been fully analyzed and the researcher is unwilling to make them public at that time. In other cases, the type of disclosure required would violate the confidentiality of research subjects. The legal question presented in these cases is whether, under evidence law or under the First Amendment, the information can be said to be privileged—protected from disclosure by a "researcher's privilege."

Judges, lawyers, and legal scholars disagree on the propriety of creating a "researcher's privilege." According to Robert O'Neil, compelling the disclosure of research has four "devastating effects":

1. The researcher loses control over how and to whom the data are reported;

2. The process of responding to a subpoena and compiling the data requested "may severely hamper the research process" by either delaying or terminating the project;

3. Compelled discovery may lead to the use or publication of unverified information;

4. If the researcher has promised confidentiality to the research subjects, this confidentiality may be compromised (Robert M. O'Neil, "A Researcher's Privilege: Does Any Hope Remain?" 59 *Law & Contemp. Probs.* 35, 36 (1996)).

On the other hand, "judges operate within a system that places a high priority upon obtaining relevant evidence that will aid in the truth-finding process" (Barbara B. Crabb, "Judicially Compelled Disclosure of Researchers' Data: A Judge's View," 59 *Law & Contemp. Probs.* 9 (1996)). Because of these tensions, the cases are fact sensitive and the outcomes are inconsistent.

In *Dow Chemical Co. v. Allen,* 672 F.2d 1262 (7th Cir. 1982), the court looked to the First Amendment rather than creating an absolute privilege, and balanced the interests of the researchers in confidentiality of the data and in freedom from intrusion into their research against the needs of the parties for the sought-after data. The court refused to enforce subpoenas issued by an administrative law judge presiding over a hearing convened by the Environmental Protection Agency to consider canceling the registration of certain herbicides manufactured by Dow:

> [The researchers had] stated, without contradiction by Dow [the company seeking the information], that public access to the research data would make the studies an unacceptable basis for scientific papers or other research; that peer review and publication of the studies was crucial to the researchers' credibility and careers and would be precluded by whole or partial public disclosure of the information; that loss of the opportunity to publish would severely decrease the researchers' professional opportunities in the future; and that even inadvertent disclosure of the information would risk total destruction of months or years of research. . . .
>
> We think it clear that whatever constitutional protection is afforded by the First Amendment extends as readily to the scholar in the laboratory as to the teacher in the classroom. . . . Of course, academic freedom, like other constitutional rights, is not absolute and must on occasion be balanced against important competing interests. . . . [W]hat precedent there is at the Supreme Court level suggests that to prevail over academic freedom the interests of government must be strong and the extent of intrusion carefully limited. . . .
>
> In the present case, the . . . . subpoenas by their terms would compel the researchers to turn over to Dow virtually every scrap of paper and every mechanical or electronic recording made . . . [and] to continually update Dow on "additional useful data" which became available during the course of the proceedings. These requirements threaten substantial intrusion into the enterprise of university research, and there are several reasons to think they are capable of chilling the exercise of academic freedom. To begin with, the burden of compliance certainly would not be insubstantial. More important, enforcement of the subpoenas would leave the researchers with the knowledge throughout continuation of their studies that the fruits of their labors had been appropriated by and were being scrutinized by a not-unbiased third party whose interests were arguably antithetical to theirs. . . . In addition, the researchers could reasonably fear that additional demands for disclosure would be made in the future. If a private corporation can subpoena the entire work product of months of study, what is to say further down the line the company will not seek other subpoenas to determine how the research is coming along? To these factors must be added the knowledge of the researchers that even inadvertent disclosure of the subpoenaed data could jeopardize both the studies and their careers.

Clearly, enforcement of the subpoenas carries the potential for chilling the exercise of First Amendment rights.

We do not suggest that facts could not arise sufficient to overcome respondents' academic freedom interests in the . . . studies. . . . If, for example, Dr. Allen, Mr. Van Miller, or other researchers were likely to testify about the . . . studies at the [Environmental Protection Agency] hearing, there might well be justification for granting at least partial or conditional enforcement of the subpoenas. Of course, we need not decide that question now [672 F.2d at 1273–76; footnotes omitted].

In an earlier case, *Richards of Rockford, Inc. v. Pacific Gas and Electric Co.*, 71 F.R.D. 388 (N.D. Cal. 1976), a federal district court judge reached a similar conclusion in an opinion that identified and balanced the various competing interests at stake. But in *Wright v. Jeep Corp.*, 547 F. Supp. 871 (E.D. Mich. 1982), decided seven months after *Allen*, a federal district court rejected a privilege claim and enforced a subpoena requiring a University of Michigan professor to produce research data from a study that was apparently completed (unlike the study in *Allen*).[44]

Products liability cases involving research by scientists working for federal agencies have also relied on *Allen* and its progeny. In *Farnsworth v. The Proctor & Gamble Co.*, 758 F.2d 1545 (11th Cir. 1985), the company sought the names and addresses of women who participated in a study of Toxic Shock Syndrome, a disease linked to the company's products. The study was conducted by scientists working for the Center for Disease Control, a federal agency. The court, citing *Allen, Richards of Rockford,* and *Wright,* ruled that the agency's interests in protecting the research subjects' identity outweighed the company's interest in contacting the women individually to confirm their medical histories. The court noted that the agency's purpose is the protection of public health, and that forced disclosure of confidential information could damage the agency's ability to conduct other studies that were important to the protection of public health.

Allen was again cited by a scholar attempting to protect the confidentiality of his data, but without success this time. In *Deitchman v. E. R. Squibb & Sons, Inc.*, 740 F.2d 556 (9th Cir. 1984), the drug company was a defendant in a products liability lawsuit by women whose mothers had taken diethylstilbestrol (DES) and who had contracted cancer, allegedly as a result of their prenatal exposure to DES. Herbst, a professor at the University of Chicago medical school, maintained a registry of individuals suffering from certain forms of cancer. Herbst had promised confidentiality to all patients whose records had been submitted to the registry, and also conducted research using information from the registry.

---

[44]In a second case involving the same University of Michigan professor and the same research data, *Buchanan v. American Motors Corp.*, 697 F.2d 151 (6th Cir. 1983), the appellate court refused to decide the privilege issue, instead holding that to compel an "expert who has no direct connection with the litigation" to testify was "unreasonably burdensome." The court therefore quashed a subpoena seeking the professor's appearance.

Squibb asked Herbst to produce the entire registry, and Herbst, citing both the confidentiality issue and his "academic freedom" not to release research results before they had undergone peer review, refused. Although a trial judge quashed the subpoena, the appellate court required the parties to negotiate about the scope of discovery and the methods to be used to protect the patients' confidentiality. The court stated that, although Squibb's discovery demand was far too broad, the company had a legitimate need for some of the information contained in the registry. The court suggested that the parties consider redaction, a protective order, and other measures calculated to minimize the burden on Herbst and to protect the confidentiality of the patients.

Another federal appellate court enforced a subpoena for unpublished data in *In re Mt. Sinai School of Medicine v. American Tobacco Co.*, 880 F.2d 1520 (2d Cir. 1989). The tobacco company was a defendant in a products liability lawsuit. The company had asked a researcher at the medical school to produce research data on the effects of smoking on asbestos workers. The researcher was not a party to the lawsuit and refused to produce the data, saying that he had promised the subjects confidentiality and that redacting the data would be very expensive and would take thousands of hours of his time. A motion to compel production of the evidence, filed in state court, was quashed.

The tobacco company filed a second motion in federal court, this time seeking only the data from already published scientific papers, covering two years of the study, and offering to pay the costs of deleting the confidential information. The court agreed to enforce the subpoena and issued a protective order to guard the identities of the research subjects.

The Second Circuit denied that there was an "absolute privilege for scholars," noting that the researcher's interest in avoiding disruption of his ongoing research is only one factor that the court considers in applying a balancing test; another factor would be the public's interest in accurate information. The court concluded that it was not unreasonable for the tobacco company to wish to examine the data that formed the basis for the articles, upon which expert witnesses (but not the researcher) were expected to testify on the plaintiffs' behalf. No qualified privilege was used in this case; instead, the court used the usual criteria for determining whether a discovery request is appropriate: relevance, burdensomeness, and the party's need for the information.

This case differs from *Allen* in that the data sought had already been published, so the researcher could not make the premature disclosure argument that the court considered so important in *Allen*. Also, the tobacco company was not seeking to compel the researcher to testify, so the privilege against compelled testimony was not an issue in this case. The interest in *Mt. Sinai* was primarily the researcher's time, the effect on his ongoing research program, and the potential for disclosure of the names of research subjects. The court applied a balancing test, weighing the tobacco company's need for the information against the adverse effect on the researcher and the research subjects. The court apparently concluded that these interests did not outweigh the tobacco company's need for the information, primarily because redaction would preserve the subjects' confidentiality.

Federal courts have been particularly unsympathetic to researchers when their data are required for criminal, rather than civil, proceedings. In *In re Grand Jury Subpoena,* 583 F. Supp. 991 (E.D.N.Y. 1984), *reversed,* 750 F.2d 223 (2d Cir. 1984), a doctoral student was conducting "participant observation" research for his dissertation at a restaurant on Long Island. When a suspicious fire and explosion destroyed the restaurant, the student's observations and notes on his conversations at the restaurant were subpoenaed by a grand jury. The student moved to quash the subpoena, claiming a "scholar's privilege" because he had promised confidentiality to his research subjects. The federal trial judge quashed the subpoena, comparing the student's interest in confidentiality to that of a news reporter's, as recognized in *Branzburg v. Hayes,* 408 U.S. 665 (1972). A federal appellate court reversed the trial judge's ruling and sent the case back to the trial judge for further analysis in light of the criteria specified by the appellate court.

The appellate court was not convinced that a "scholar's privilege" exists or that one should be applied under these circumstances. First the court discussed the showing that an individual claiming a scholar's privilege would need to make:

> Surely the application of a scholar's privilege, if it exists, requires a threshold showing consisting of a detailed description of the nature and seriousness of the scholarly study in question, of the methodology employed, of the need for assurances of confidentiality to various sources to conduct the study, and of the fact that the disclosure requested by the subpoena will seriously impinge upon that confidentiality [750 F.2d at 225].

The court explained further that no evidence had been presented about

> the nature of the work or of its role in the scholarly literature of sociology. One need not quip that "You can't tell a dissertation by its title" to conclude that the words "The Sociology of the American Restaurant" afford precious little information about the subject matter of [the student's] thesis [750 F.2d at 225].

The opinion suggests that the student would have been required to present testimony from recognized scholars justifying the seriousness of the subject and the appropriateness of the methodology. This requirement appears to be based upon the individual's status as a student rather than a holder of a Ph.D. The opinion describes the showing that must be made before a scholar's privilege could be considered:

> What exactly [the student's] role is, what kinds of material he hopes to collect, and how that role and that material relate to a need for confidentiality . . . , evidence of a considered research plan, conceived in light of scholarly requirements or standards, contemplating assurances of confidentiality for certain parts of the inquiry [750 F.2d at 225].

The court then discussed the limited nature of the scholar's privilege (if it exists), which would cover only those portions of the research material that required confidentiality. The court also noted that the scholar would be required to permit inspection of the material by a judge and redaction under the judge's supervision. The broad privilege claimed by the student, that all his research notes and journals were included, was roundly rejected by the court.

Another federal appeals court extended the trend against a "scholar's privilege" in *In re: Grand Jury Proceedings,* 5 F.3d 397 (9th Cir. 1993). Scarce, a doctoral student in sociology at Washington State University, had been asked to testify about conversations with some of his friends, animal rights activists who were accused of breaking into and damaging animal research facilities at the university. Scarce, who was conducting research on the animal rights movement and had written a book on the radical environmental movement, refused to testify and was jailed for six months. (For an account of this matter, see P. Monaghan, "Free After 6 Months: Sociologist Who Refused to Testify Is Released," *Chron. Higher Educ.,* November 3, 1993, A14–A15.) The court rejected the concept of a "scholar's privilege," stating that no cases had recognized the right of a scholar to withhold information from a grand jury where the information was relevant to a legitimate grand jury inquiry and was sought in good faith.

It appears that judges are increasingly hostile to claims of a researcher's or scholar's privilege, especially when the information is sought for a criminal, rather than a civil, proceeding. Absolute privileges appear to be unavailable to scholars, because judges have several strategies for protecting confidentiality and reducing the burden on the researcher. In light of these developments, faculty and administrators need to understand that promises of absolute confidentiality to research subjects may not be enforceable. Additional cases in which courts compelled discovery of research data include *Southwest Center for Biological Diversity v. U.S.D.A.,* 170 F. Supp. 2d 931 (D. Ariz. 2000); *Proctor & Gamble Co. v. Swilly,* 462 So. 2d 1188 (Ct. App. Fla. 1985); and *Burka v. U.S. Dept. of Health and Human Services,* 87 F.3d 508 (D.C. Cir. 1996). Courts refused to compel production of research data on the grounds that the requests were unduly burdensome in *Anker v. G. D. Searle & Co.,* 126 F.R.D. 515 (M.D.N.C. 1989), and *In re Snyder,* 115 F.R.D. 211 (D. Ariz. 1987).

Given judicial hostility to a "researcher's privilege," faculty or institutions facing compelled disclosure of research may fare better using the First Amendment argument that was successful in the *Dow Chemical* case. For example, in *In re Cusumano and Yoffie [U.S. v. Microsoft],* 162 F.3d 708 (1st Cir. 1998), Microsoft, which was facing antitrust litigation brought by the U.S. Department of Justice, sought confidential research notes from two professors who were not parties to the litigation. Professors Cusumano and Yoffie had interviewed executives of Netscape, a Microsoft competitor whose allegations of unfair competitive practices had led to the antitrust litigation. Those interviews, with additional data, had formed the basis for a book about Netscape. Microsoft sought to compel the two professors to produce the notes from their interviews, asserting that the notes were significant for Microsoft's defense against the antitrust litigation. The professors had interviewed more than forty current and former Netscape employees, promising that they would disclose no proprietary information and would verify with the informant all interview information that would be used in the book. The professors turned over some correspondence, but they refused to provide tapes or transcripts of the interviews and moved to quash Microsoft's subpoena.

A federal trial judge held a hearing and denied Microsoft's motion to compel production of the research. Using a balancing test, the court determined that Microsoft could have obtained the information it sought directly from the individuals whom the researchers had interviewed, and that its primary use of the information would be for impeachment of witnesses. The court also found that the researchers had a substantial interest in keeping the subpoenaed information confidential, and that significant First Amendment values favored its protection. The trial court retained jurisdiction to review individual items *in camera* (in chambers) to determine whether they were material to Microsoft's defense and stated that, should Microsoft be able to show particularized need for a particular item of information, the judge would order it to be produced. Microsoft appealed.

The U.S. Court of Appeals for the First Circuit affirmed the reasoning and the ruling of the trial court. Given the assurances made by the researchers, and the fact that, at the time the interviews were conducted, the antitrust case against Microsoft had not been filed, the interest of the researchers in maintaining the confidentiality of the interviews deserved "significant protection." The balancing test used by the trial court—Microsoft's need for the information versus the researchers' interest in confidentiality—was the proper standard, according to the court, citing an earlier First Circuit case, *Bruno & Stillman, Inc. v. Globe Newspaper Co.*, 633 F.2d 583 (1st Cir. 1980). (The court rejected Microsoft's argument that this case was irrelevant because it involved journalists rather than academic researchers.) Microsoft had access to a prepublication copy of the manuscript, which identified quoted individuals by name. Therefore, said the court, Microsoft could accomplish its purpose through deposing these individuals. With respect to the interests of the researchers:

> The opposite pan of the scale is brim-full. Scholars studying management practices depend upon the voluntary revelations of industry insiders to develop the factual infrastructure upon which theoretical conclusions and practical predictions may rest. These insiders often lack enthusiasm for divulging their management styles and business strategies to academics, who may in turn reveal that information to the public. Yet, pathbreaking work in management science requires gathering data from those companies and individuals operating in the most highly competitive fields of industry, and it is in these cutting-edge areas that the respondents concentrate their efforts. Their time-tested interview protocol, including the execution of a nondisclosure agreement with the corporate entity being studied and the furnishing of personal assurances of confidentiality to the persons being interviewed, gives chary corporate executives a sense of security that greatly facilitates the achievement of agreements to cooperate. Thus . . . the interviews are "carefully-bargained for" communications which deserve significant protection [162 F.3d at 717].

Allowing Microsoft access to the notes, tapes, and transcripts would "hamstring not only the respondents' future research efforts but also those of other similarly situated scholars" (162 F.3d at 717). "Even more important, compelling the disclosure of such research materials would [chill] the free flow of information to the public, thus denigrating a fundamental First Amendment value" (162 F.3d at 717). The trial court's decision to retain jurisdiction to review materials *in camera* protected Microsoft's interests adequately, according to the appellate court.

This case is interesting and important because both the trial and appellate courts were willing to extend First Amendment protection to confidential research findings. The case appears to have been decided solely on First Amendment grounds. The trial and appellate courts applied precedent from cases involving journalists without discussion of whether academicians deserve greater or lesser protection than their colleagues in the media; in fact, the appellate court appeared to equate the confidentiality concerns of academics and journalists. No claim was made that the material was protected by an "academic freedom" privilege; hence, that concept was not discussed; and there was no reference to the earlier cases involving confidentiality of research data.

Close attention should be paid to the particular context in which potential issues arise. Especially important are (1) the procedural and evidentiary rules of the court or administrative agency that would entertain the litigation and (2) the impact that disclosure of the requested information would have on academic freedom. (Suggestions for ways in which administrators and researchers can limit access to or interest in their research findings are found in N. Miller, "Subpoenas in Academe: Controlling Disclosure," 17 *J. Coll. & Univ. Law* 1 (1990); and in Diane E. Lopez, "The Compelled Disclosure of Research Data," National Association of College and University Attorneys Annual Conference Outline, June 26, 2002 (available at http://www.nacua.org).)

A second major issue involving confidentiality of research results is the requirement of some funding sources, both governmental and private, that research results be kept secret. Although this requirement presents the opposite dilemma of compelled disclosure, it is no less troubling from an academic freedom perspective.

When it is the government imposing the secrecy restrictions, the Constitution is asserted as the source of protection for the researcher's academic freedom right to publish research results. The regulations of several federal agencies authorize officials to prohibit release of certain findings without the funding agency's permission (see, for example, 48 C.F.R. §§ 324.70, 352.224–70 (1991), which authorize contract officers from the Department of Health and Human Services to place restrictions on disclosure of preliminary findings). At least one court has rejected the attempt of a government agency to prevent the publication of federally funded research without its permission. In *Board of Trustees of Leland Stanford Junior University v. Sullivan,* 773 F. Supp. 472 (D.D.C. 1991), the university argued that this restriction violated the First Amendment. Applying strict scrutiny to the federal regulation, the trial judge rejected as noncompelling the National Institutes of Health's argument that secrecy was required in order to protect prospective patients from "unwarranted hope" that could be raised by the release of preliminary findings (773 F. Supp. at 477, n.16).

But constitutional protections would typically not apply to funding restrictions imposed by private funding sources, such as corporations or foundations. Such restrictions, if incorporated into the contract, could be removed only if the funding source agreed. And unless certain state constitutions or cases decided under their authority included free speech guarantees that applied to private entities as well as the government (see, for example, *State v. Schmid,* discussed in Sections 1.5.2 and 11.6.3), it is not clear that a faculty member or an institution would have a cause of action against a private funding source that withdrew funding after the faculty member refused to agree to secrecy requirements.

(For an extended discussion of secrecy and university research in the context of government restrictions on disclosure, see "Focus on Secrecy and University Research," 19 *J. Coll. & Univ. Law* 199 (1993). This special issue of the journal includes four articles devoted to this subject.)

Sec. 7.8. Academic Freedom in Religious Colleges and Universities

In general, academic freedom disputes in religious institutions[45] are governed by the same contract law principles that govern such disputes in other private institutions (see Section 7.1.3 above). (These principles, as applied to academic freedom in teaching, are discussed in Section 7.2.5 above.) But the religious missions of religious institutions, and their affiliations with churches or religious denominations, may give rise to contract law issues that are unique to religious institutions. In addition, religious institutions may have First Amendment defenses to litigation that secular institutions do not have. Both of these matters are discussed in Section 6.2.5, and a more general discussion of First Amendment defenses is in Section 1.6.2. The *McEnroy* case below, and the case of *Curran v. Catholic University of America,* discussed in Section 6.2.5, illustrate how these matters may play out in academic freedom disputes between faculty members and religious institutions.

Academic freedom customs or professional norms in religious institutions may also vary from those in secular private institutions—particularly in situations where a faculty member takes positions or engages in activities that are contrary to the institution's religious mission or the religious principles of a sponsoring religious denomination. This type of problem, and the potential for clashes between *faculty* academic freedom and *institutional* academic freedom, are illustrated by the debate concerning *Ex Corde Ecclesiae,* issued by Pope John Paul II in 1990, and *Ex Corde Ecclesiae: The Application to the United States* (http://www.nccbuscc.org/bishops/excorde.htm), subsequently adopted by the U.S. Conference of Catholic Bishops. (For commentary on this debate, see James Gordon III, "Individual and Institutional Academic Freedom at Religious Colleges and Universities," 30 *J. Coll. & Univ. Law* 1, 20–25 (2003).)

---

[45]"Religious," when used in this section to refer to a college or university, covers institutions that are sponsored by or otherwise related to a particular church or denomination, as well as institutions that are nondenominational and independent of any particular church body.

To account for possible differences in academic freedom norms at religious institutions, the "1940 Statement of Principles on Academic Freedom and Tenure" includes a "limitations clause" specifying that "[l]imitations on academic freedom because of religious or other aims of the institution should be clearly stated in writing at the time of [a faculty member's] appointment" (*AAUP Policy Documents and Reports* (9th ed., 2001), 3). The meaning of this clause, its implementation, and its wisdom have been debated over the years (see, for example, the "1970 Interpretive Comments," comment no. 3, in *AAUP Policy Documents and Reports,* 6; and see generally Gordon, above, at 16–20). In 1999, the AAUP issued "operating guidelines" for applying the clause ("The 'Limitations' Clause in the 1940 Statement of Principles on Academic Freedom and Tenure: Some Operating Guidelines," in *AAUP Policy Documents and Reports,* 96).

When a religious institution invokes the limitations clause and imposes limits on the scope of academic freedom, contract law issues may arise concerning the interpretation of these limits as expressed in faculty appointment documents, the faculty handbook, or other institutional regulations; in addition, issues may arise concerning the extent of the religious institution's prerogative, under AAUP policies, to limit its faculty's academic freedom. When a religious institution adopts AAUP policies but does not invoke the limitations clause, issues may still arise concerning whether religious law governing the institution can justify limits on academic freedom or affect the analysis of contract law issues. In either situation, if an institution's personnel action appears to conflict with AAUP policy or to breach a faculty member's contract, the aggrieved faculty member may seek the protection of the AAUP in lieu of or in addition to resorting to the courts. The case of Carmel McEnroy, then a professor at the Saint Meinrad School of Theology in Saint Meinrad, Indiana, is illustrative. (See "Report: Academic Freedom and Tenure: Saint Meinrad School of Theology (Indiana)," in *Academe,* July–August 1996, 51–60.)

The school's administration had dismissed Professor McEnroy after it learned, and she admitted, that she had "signed an open letter to Pope John Paul II asking that continued discussion be permitted concerning the question of ordaining women to the priesthood" (*Id.* at 51). McEnroy, a "member of the Congregation of Sisters of Mercy of Ireland and South Africa," signed the letter "without citing her academic or religious affiliations" (*Id.* at 52). She was one of more than fifteen hundred signatories. At the time of the dismissal, the "*1940 Statement of Principles on Academic Freedom and Tenure* was adopted as institutional policy [and] printed in full in the Faculty Handbook, without specification of any limitations on academic freedom . . ." (*Id.* at 51). McEnroy contended that, in signing the letter, "she was exercising her right as a citizen as outlined in the *1940 Statement of Principles*" (*Id.* at 55). Church and school officials, in contrast, contended "that she had publicly dissented from the teaching of the church and was therefore disqualified from continuing in her faculty position" (*Id.*)—thus, in effect, asserting that McEnroy was dismissed on "ecclesial grounds" rather than "academic grounds" (*Id.* at 60), and that the 1940 Statement therefore did not apply (*Id.* at 56). The AAUP's investigating committee concluded that the 1940 Statement did apply and that Saint Meinrad's administration had "failed to meet its obligation to demonstrate that

[Professor McEnroy's] signing of the letter to Pope John Paul II rendered her unfit to retain her faculty position," as required by the 1940 Statement, thereby "violat[ing] her academic freedom" (*Id.* at 58, 59). (The committee also concluded that Saint Meinrad's administration had violated the due process principles in the 1940 Statement when it dismissed McEnroy.)

The AAUP's Committee A on Academic Freedom and Tenure accepted the investigating committee's report and recommended that the university be placed on the AAUP's list of censured administrations. At the AAUP's eighty-third annual meeting, the membership approved Committee A's recommendation (available at http://www.aaup.org/com-a/devcen.htm). (For a discussion of the AAUP censuring process, see Section 14.5 of this book.)

McEnroy subsequently filed suit against Saint Meinrad's and two of its administrators, claiming breach of contract. The trial court dismissed the case, and the Indiana appellate court affirmed (*McEnroy v. Saint Meinrad School of Theology,* 713 N.E.2d 334 (Ind. 1997)). Resolving an ambiguity in the professor's contract, the appellate court reasoned that, in addition to its academic freedom and due process terms, the contract also included terms regarding the Roman Catholic Church's jurisdiction over the school. Thus "resolution of Dr. McEnroy's claims would require the trial court to interpret and apply religious doctrine and ecclesiastical law," which would "clearly and excessively" entangle the trial court "in religious affairs in violation of the First Amendment."

A different type of academic freedom problem arises when a government agency seeks to investigate or penalize a religious college or university or one of its faculty members. Such disputes are "extramural" rather than "intramural" (see Section 7.1.5 above). The institution may claim, in defense, that the government's planned action would violate its institutional academic freedom; or the faculty member may claim, in defense, that the action would violate faculty academic freedom. Since the dispute concerns government action, both the religious institution and the faculty member may assert constitutional rights against the government. Sometimes the rights will be the same as secular private institutions and their faculty members would assert—for example, the free speech and press rights asserted in the "academic freedom privilege" cases in Section 7.7 above. At other times the rights will belong only to religious institutions and their faculty members; these are the rights protected by the establishment and free exercise clauses of the First Amendment (see generally Section 1.6.2).[46] Examples would include the cases in which an institution argues that federal or state court review of its religious practices would violate the establishment clause (see the *McEnroy* case above; and see also Section 6.2.5 of this book); and the cases in which the institution challenges the authority of a government agency, such as the EEOC, to investigate or regulate its religiously based practices (see Section 5.5).

---

[46]Faculty members at private secular institutions could also invoke free exercise and establishment clause rights if the challenged government action interfered with their personal religious beliefs or practices. A private secular institution itself could also invoke these clauses if government were to require that the institution involve itself in religious matters or prohibit it from doing so.

Selected Annotated Bibliography
Sec. 7.1 (General Concepts and Principles)

"Academic Freedom and Responsibility Symposium," 27 *J. Coll. & Univ. Law* 565–707 (2001). The first part of this symposium focuses on a proposed "Academic Freedom Policy and Procedures" document drafted by Martin Michaelson (567–71). There are three commentaries on this document, by Robert O'Neil, J. Peter Byrne, and Richard De George, followed by a response from Mr. Michaelson. The second part of the symposium contains two additional articles: "Academic Tradition and the Principles of Professional Conduct" by Neil Hamilton, and "Matters of Public Concern and the Public University Professor" by Chris Hoofnagle.

"Academic Freedom Symposium," 22 *Wm. Mitchell L. Rev.* 333–576 (1996). Contains twelve commentaries preceded by a foreword by Neil Hamilton. Commentaries are (1) Irving Louis Horowitz, "Contrasts and Comparisons Among McCarthyism, 1960s Student Activism, and 1990s Faculty Fundamentalism: Culture Politics and McCarthyism a Retrospective from the Trenches"; (2) Lionel Lewis, "McCarthyism and Academic Freedom: The 1950s and 1990s: Similarities and Noteworthy Differences"; (3) Wagner Thielens, "McCarthyism and Academic Freedom: Why Wasn't the Damage Worse? Some Answers from the Academic Mind"; (4) Seymour Martin Lipset, "1960s Student Activism and Academic Freedom: From the Sixties to the Nineties: A Double Edged Sword at Work"; (5) Todd Gitlin, "1960s Student Activism and Academic Freedom: Evolution of the Student Movement of the Sixties and Its Effect"; (6) David Horowitz, "1960s Student Activism and Academic Freedom: Leftwing Fascism and the American Dream"; (7) Nathan Glazer, "1990s Faculty Fundamentalism and Academic Freedom: Academic Freedom in the 1990s"; (8) Daphne Patai, "1990s Faculty Fundamentalism and Academic Freedom: There Ought to Be a Law"; (9) John Wilson, "1990s Faculty Fundamentalism and Academic Freedom: Myths and Facts: How Real Is Political Correctness?"; (10) Jordan Kurland, "1990s Faculty Fundamentalism and Academic Freedom: Commentary on Buttressing the Defense of Academic Freedom"; (11) Neil Hamilton, "Buttressing the Defense of Academic Freedom: Buttressing the Neglected Traditions of Academic Freedom"; and (12) Rita Simon, "Buttressing the Defense of Academic Freedom: What Should Professors Do?"

"The Academy in the Courts: A Symposium on Academic Freedom," 16 *U. Cal. Davis L. Rev.* 831 (1983). A two-part symposium. (The second part, "Discrimination in the Academy," is described in the "Academy in the Courts" entry for Section 6.4.) The first part, "The First Amendment in the Academy," contains three articles: Robert O'Neil, "Scientific Research and the First Amendment: An Academic Privilege"; Katheryn Katz, "The First Amendment's Protection of Expressive Activity in the University Classroom: A Constitutional Myth"; and Martin Malin & Robert Ladenson, "University Faculty Members' Right to Dissent: Toward a Unified Theory of Contractual and Constitutional Protection." Symposium also includes a foreword by John Poulos, which briefly recounts the history of institutional academic autonomy and reviews each article's critique of this concept.

Byrne, J. Peter. "Academic Freedom: A 'Special Concern of the First Amendment,'" 99 *Yale L.J.* 251 (1989). Develops a framework and foundation for the academic freedom that is protected by the First Amendment. Traces the development of academic freedom as construed by both academics and the courts and then espouses a new theory of "academic freedom based on the traditional legal status of academic institutions and on the appropriate role of the judiciary in academic affairs."

Byrne, J. Peter. *Academic Freedom Without Tenure?* (American Association for Higher Education, 1997). Part of AAHE's New Pathways Working Paper Series. Discusses the relationship between academic freedom and tenure, and suggests alternative methods of protecting academic freedom. Considers the "elements" that would be needed to protect academic freedom without a tenure system and whether such "elements" can protect academic freedom more efficiently than a tenure system does.

Byrne, J. Peter, "The Threat to Constitutional Academic Freedom," 31 *J. Coll. & Univ. Law* 79 (2004). Reviews the development of academic freedom as an academic norm; analyzes post-1990 judicial decisions that "threaten the demise of academic freedom as a constitutional right"; considers the counterbalance that may be provided by the Court's reliance on institutional academic freedom in *Grutter v. Bollinger*; and reviews "intellectual and demographic changes [that] argue for continuing judicial protection of colleges and universities from outside interference."

De George, Richard T. *Academic Freedom and Tenure: Ethical Issues* (Rowman & Littlefield, 1997). This book focuses on the question of whether academic tenure, as it commonly exists today, is an appropriate and efficient method for protecting academic freedom. Defends the existing tenure system while at the same time noting concerns and ethical issues about the system and suggesting improvements. Includes a section that reproduces pertinent documents and readings. A review of this book by John Cary Sims may be found at 25 *J. Coll. & Univ. Law* 443 (1998).

Doumani, Beshara (ed.). *Academic Freedom After September 11* (MIT Press/Zone Books, 2006). A diverse collection of essays by seven scholars. Against the backdrop of post–World War II developments, examines post 9-11 political interventions, their affects on academic freedom, and the conflicts that have arisen concerning the meaning of academic freedom.

Hamilton, Neil. *Zealotry and Academic Freedom: A Legal and Historical Perspective* (Transaction, 1996). Covers 125 years of the ongoing struggle for academic freedom, including discussion of new issues such as political correctness, racism, and gender discrimination. Also provides a frank look at the politics of higher education. Contains a comprehensive bibliography and a list of relevant cases.

Menand, Louis (ed.). *The Future of Academic Freedom* (University of Chicago Press, 1996). A collection of lectures by noted scholars from various disciplines, who debate the cutting-edge issues of academic freedom. This collection is the product of a lecture series sponsored by the AAUP.

O'Neil, Robert. *Is Academic Freedom a Constitutional Right?* Monograph 84-7 (Institute for Higher Education Law and Governance, University of Houston, 1984), reprinted (under title "Academic Freedom and the Constitution") in 11 *J. Coll. & Univ. Law* 275 (1984). An argument on behalf of the continued vitality of constitutionally based claims of academic freedom. Examines the current status of and conceptual difficulties regarding such claims and makes suggestions for faculty members and other academics to consider before submitting such claims to the courts for vindication.

Symposium, "Academic Freedom and Tenure Symposium," 15 *Pace L. Rev.* 1 (1994). Contains five articles that explore the foundations of academic tenure, contemporary criticisms of the system of academic tenure, and contemporary threats to the system. Articles are by Ernest van den Haag, Burton Leiser, Deborah Post, Robert Spitzer, and Irwin Polishook.

"Symposium on Academic Freedom," 66 *Tex. L. Rev.,* issue no. 7 (1988). Contains eighteen commentaries and responses preceded by a lengthy foreword by Julius Getman and Jacqueline Mintz. Commentaries include, among others, (1) Walter P. Metzger, "Profession and Constitution: Two Definitions of Academic Freedom in America"; (2) Matthew W. Finkin, "Intramural Speech, Academic Freedom, and the First Amendment"; (3) Charles E. Curran, "Academic Freedom and Catholic Universities"; (4) Lonnie D. Kliever, "Academic Freedom and Church-Affiliated Universities"; (5) Phoebe A. Haddon, "Academic Freedom and Governance: A Call for Increased Dialogue and Diversity"; (6) Rebecca S. Eisenberg, "Academic Freedom and Academic Values in Sponsored Research"; (7) David M. Rabban, "Does Academic Freedom Limit Faculty Autonomy?"; and (8) Douglas Laycock & Susan E. Waelbroeck, "Academic Freedom and the Free Exercise of Religion."

Van Alstyne, William W. (special ed.). "Freedom and Tenure in the Academy: The Fiftieth Anniversary of the 1940 Statement of Principles," 53 *Law & Contemp. Probs.,* issue no. 3 (1990); also published as a separate book, *Freedom and Tenure in the Academy* (Duke University Press, 1993). A symposium containing nine articles: (1) Walter P. Metzger, "The 1940 Statement of Principles on Academic Freedom and Tenure"; (2) William W. Van Alstyne, "Academic Freedom and the First Amendment in the Supreme Court of the United States: An Unhurried Historical Review"; (3) Judith Jarvis Thomson, "Ideology and Faculty Selection"; (4) Robert M. O'Neil, "Artistic Freedom and Academic Freedom"; (5) Rodney A. Smolla, "Academic Freedom, Hate Speech, and the Idea of a University"; (6) David M. Rabban, "A Functional Analysis of 'Individual' and 'Institutional' Academic Freedom Under the First Amendment"; (7) Michael W. McConnell, "Academic Freedom in Religious Colleges and Universities"; (8) Ralph S. Brown & Jordan E. Kurland, "Academic Tenure and Academic Freedom"; and (9) Matthew W. Finkin, "A Higher Order of Liberty in the Workplace: Academic Freedom and Tenure in the Vortex of Employment Practices and Law." Also includes a helpful bibliography of sources: Janet Sinder, "Academic Freedom: A Bibliography," listing 174 journal articles, books, and reports; and three appendices containing the 1915 AAUP "General Report," the "1940 Statement of Principles," and the 1967 "Joint Statement on Rights and Freedoms of Students."

See entry for Finkin in Selected Annotated Bibliography for Chapter 1, Section 1.2.

Sec. 7.2 (Academic Freedom in Teaching)

Braxton, John, & Bayer, Alan. *Faculty Misconduct in Collegiate Teaching* (Johns Hopkins University Press, 1999). Against a backdrop of survey data, the authors examine professional norms regarding teaching and conduct in the classroom, factors that influence teaching behavior and the development of professional norms, and the mechanisms by which institutions address faculty misconduct and by which professional norms are enforced. The authors recommend adoption of codes of ethics for college teaching.

Olivas, Michael. "Reflections on Professorial Academic Freedom: Second Thoughts on the Third 'Essential Freedom,'" 45 *Stan. L. Rev.* 1835 (1993). Presents the author's perspective on faculty academic freedom, with particular emphasis on conflicts that arise in the classroom. Considers and interrelates professional norms, First Amendment case law, and recent scholarly commentary.

O'Neil, Robert M. *Free Speech in the College Community* (Indiana University Press, 1997). Presents an array of free speech problems and their implications for the campus. Chapter 2, "The Outspoken University Professor," discusses dilemmas involving academic freedom in the classroom; and Chapter 8, "Academic Research and Academic Freedom," discusses dilemmas involving faculty research and publication. Leading cases are highlighted.

Smith, Sonya G. "*Cohen v. San Bernadino Valley College:* The Scope of Academic Freedom Within the Context of Sexual Harassment Claims and In-Class Speech," 25 *J. Coll. & Univ. Law* 1 (1998). Reviews the potential clash between a professor's First Amendment claims to academic freedom and students' claims to an academic setting devoid of sexual harassment. Article presents the issue through a discussion of the *Cohen* case, a 1996 Ninth Circuit case. Also presents a history and analysis of the *Connick/Pickering* test as it has been applied in other cases. Title VII and Title IX concepts of sexual harassment are compared along with supporting case law.

Sec. 7.3 *(Academic Freedom in Research and Publication)*

See entry for O'Neil in the Selected Annotated Bibliography for Section 7.2 above.

See O'Neil article listed under entry for Van Alstyne, "Freedom and Tenure in the Academy," in Selected Annotated Bibliography for Section 7.1 above.

See Eisenberg article listed under entry for "Symposium on Academic Freedom" in Selected Annotated Bibliography for Section 7.1 above.

Sec. 7.4 *(Academic Freedom in Institutional Affairs)*

See entry for Hamilton in Selected Annotated Bibliography for Section 7.1 above.

See Finkin article listed under entry for "Symposium on Academic Freedom" in Selected Annotated Bibliography for Section 7.1 above.

Sec. 7.5 *(Academic Freedom in Private Life)*

O'Neil, Robert. "The Private Lives of Public Employees," 51 *Or. L. Rev.* 70 (1971). Discusses the types of problems that can arise in the interaction of lifestyle and public employment. Symbolic expression, hair length, homosexual and heterosexual association, extracurricular writing, and other questions are examined. Although written primarily for the lawyer, the article is also useful for administrators of public postsecondary institutions.

See entry for DeChiara in Selected Annotated Bibliography for Section 7.6 below.

Sec. 7.6 *(Administrators' Authority Regarding Faculty Academic Freedom and Freedom of Expression)*

DeChiara, Peter. "The Need for Universities to Have Rules on Consensual Sexual Relationships Between Faculty Members and Students," 21 *Columbia J.L. & Soc. Probs.* 137 (1988). Reviews the issue of faculty-student sexual relationships and possible responses by universities. Reports on the author's survey of thirty-eight institutions. Discusses constitutional right-to-privacy implications of regulation. Author asserts that regulation is needed because consensual sexual relationships between faculty and students can create problems of pressured decisions, sexual harassment, and favoritism.

Sec. 7.7 (Protection of Confidential Academic Information: The "Academic Freedom Privilege")

Baez, Benjamin. "Confidentiality and Peer Review: The Paradox of Secrecy in Academe," 25 *Rev. Higher Educ.* 163 (2002). An essay that criticizes confidentiality in the peer review process, arguing that confidentiality benefits only the reviewer, and how it may inhibit a reviewer's critical analysis.

Cecil, Joe S., & Wetherington, Gerald T. (eds.). "Court-Ordered Disclosure of Academic Research: A Clash of Values of Science and Law," 59 *Law & Contemp. Probs.* 1 (1996). A Symposium issue on this topic, including articles by Barbara B. Crabb, "Judicially Compelled Disclosure of Researchers' Data: A Judge's View"; Robert M. O'Neil, "A Researcher's Privilege: Does Any Hope Remain?"; Elizabeth C. Wiggins & Judith A McKenna, "Researchers' Reactions to Compelled Disclosure of Scientific Information"; Sheila Jasanoff, "Research Subpoenas and the Sociology of Knowledge"; Michael Traynor, "Countering the Excessive Supboena for Scholarly Research"; and Bert Black, "Research and Its Revelation: When Should Courts Compel Disclosure?"; among others.

Rap, Rebecca E. "*In re Cusumano* and the Undue Burden of Using the Journalist Privilege as a Model for Protecting Researchers from Discovery," 29 *J. Law & Educ.* 285 (2000). Reviews the *Cusumano* case, and concludes that the researcher's privilege should be based upon academic freedom rather than modeled after the journalist's privilege.

Sec. 7.8 (Academic Freedom in Religious Colleges and Universities)

Bramhall, Eugene H., & Ahrens, Ronald Z. "Academic Freedom and the Status of the Religiously Affiliated University," 37 *Gonzaga L. Rev.* 227 (2001–02). Authors argue that religious institutions may reasonably limit academic freedom and still be considered legitimate universities to the same extent that secular universities with full academic freedom are considered legitimate. Article evaluates the philosophical justifications for academic freedom, acceptable limits on academic freedom based on these justifications, and factors other than academic freedom that characterize a legitimate university.

Curran, Charles E. "Academic Freedom and Catholic Universities," 66 *Texas L. Rev.* 1441 (1998). Author discusses academic freedom's history and importance at Catholic universities, and considers the impact of the 1979 Vatican document, *Sapientia Christiana*, canon 812 of the 1985 Code of Canon Law, and the 1985 Proposed Schema for a Pontifical Document on Catholic Universities. Author concludes that academic freedom for Catholic universities benefits the Roman Catholic Church. In response, see Lonnie D. Kliever, "Academic Freedom and Church-Affiliated Universities," 66 *Texas L. Rev.* 1477 (1988), which critiques Curran's articulation of academic freedom and advocates a broader concept of academic freedom than that which Curran sets out; see also the Laycock & Waelbroeck article below.

Laycock, Douglas. "The Rights of Religious Academic Communities," 20 *J. Coll. & Univ. Law* 15 (1993). Author evaluates the role of religious universities and law schools and endorses religious universities' right to limit academic freedom in cases of supreme importance to the school. Addresses constitutional protections for religious institutions, and the difficulties religious universities face in communicating the justifications for their limits on academic freedom.

Laycock, Douglas, & Waelbroeck, Susan E. "Academic Freedom and the Free Exercise of Religion," 66 *Texas L. Rev.* 1455 (1988). Authors utilize the dispute between Father Curran and the Catholic University of America to illustrate the right of churches to settle their own disputes, as well as to highlight the delicate balance between academic freedom and the tenets of faith at religious universities. Article also considers the civil contract law aspects of professors' relationships to religious universities.

McConnell, Michael W. "Academic Freedom in Religious Colleges and Universities," 53 *Law & Contemp. Probs.* 303 (1990; also reprinted in William W. Van Alstyne (ed.), *Freedom and Tenure in the Academy* (Duke University Press, 1993)). Argues that secular concepts of academic freedom should not be applied to faculty employment decisions at religious institutions. Addresses academic freedom in seminaries and theological schools, behavioral restrictions on faculty in religious colleges and universities, and the applicability of laws against discrimination on religious grounds. In response, see Judith Jarvis Thomson & Matthew W. Finkin, "Academic Freedom and Church-Related Higher Education: A Reply to Professor McConnell," in William W. Van Alstyne (ed.), *Freedom and Tenure in the Academy* (Duke University Press, 1993).

"A Symposium on the Implementation of *Ex Corde Ecclesiae*," 25 *J. Coll. & Univ. Law* 645 (1999) (Introduction by John H. Robinson). A collection of articles offering various interpretations and examples of the legal consequences of adopting *Ex Corde Ecclesiae*, the papal constitution on Catholic higher education. Article topics include the political context from which *Ex Corde Ecclesiae* emerged, a comparative study of Catholic Universities under *Ex Corde Ecclesiae* and Brigham Young University under the Church of Jesus Christ of Latter-Day Saints; an evaluation of whether it is prudent to subject American educational institutions to oversight such as that provided for in *Ex Corde Ecclesiae*; and the tension between academic freedom and religious oversight, including the theological "mandate" to which Catholic theologians are subject.

PART FOUR

THE COLLEGE AND ITS STUDENTS

8

The Student-Institution Relationship

Sec. 8.1. The Legal Status of Students

8.1.1. Overview. The legal status of students in postsecondary institutions changed dramatically in the 1960s, changed further near the end of the twentieth century, and is still evolving. For most purposes, students are no longer second-class citizens under the law. They are recognized under the federal Constitution as "persons" with their own enforceable constitutional rights. They are recognized as adults, with the rights and responsibilities of adults, under many state laws. And they are accorded their own legal rights under various federal statutes. The background of this evolution is traced in Section 1.2; the legal status that emerges from these developments, and its impact on postsecondary administration, is explored throughout this chapter.

Perhaps the key case in forging this shift in student status was *Dixon v. Alabama State Board of Education* (1961), discussed further in Section 9.4.2. The court in this case rejected the notion that education in state schools is a "privilege" to be dispensed on whatever conditions the state in its sole discretion deems advisable; it also implicitly rejected the *in loco parentis* concept, under which the law had bestowed on schools all the powers over students that parents had over minor children. The *Dixon* approach became a part of U.S. Supreme Court jurisprudence in cases such as *Tinker v. Des Moines School District* (see Section 9.5.1), *Healy v. James* (Sections 9.5.1 & 10.1.1), and *Goss v. Lopez* (Section 9.4.2). The impact of these public institution cases spilled over onto private institutions, as courts increasingly viewed students as contracting parties having rights under express and implied contractual relationships with the institution. Thus, at both public and private institutions, the failure to follow institutional policies, rules, and regulations has led to successful litigation by students who claimed that their rights were violated by this noncompliance (see subsection 8.1.3 below and Sections 9.2 & 9.4).

Congress gave students at both public and private schools rights under various civil rights acts and, in the Family Educational Rights and Privacy Act (FERPA; Section 9.7.1 of this book), gave postsecondary students certain rights that were expressly independent of and in lieu of parental rights. State statutes lowering the age of majority also enhanced the independence of students from their parents and brought the bulk of postsecondary students, even undergraduates, into the category of adults.

Now another stage in the evolution of students' legal status has been emerging. Developments at this new stage suggest a renewed emphasis on the *academic freedom* of students. In classical thought on academic freedom, the student's freedom to learn is clearly recognized and considered to be at least as important as the faculty member's freedom to teach. In more modern legal developments, courts have occasionally recognized the concept of student academic freedom; in *Piarowski v. Illinois Community College,* 759 F.2d 625, 629 (7th Cir. 1985), for instance, the court noted that the term "academic freedom" is "used to denote" not only "the freedom of the individual teacher" but also "the [freedom of] the student." But most academic freedom cases have been brought by faculty members, and most academic freedom rights that courts have protected have belonged to faculty members (see especially Section 7.2). Student academic freedom issues are discussed in subsection 8.1.4 below.

8.1.2. The age of majority.
The age of majority is established by state law in all states. There may be a general statute prescribing an age of majority for all or most business and personal dealings in the state, or there may be specific statutes or regulations establishing varying ages of majority for specific purposes. Until the 1970s, twenty-one was typically the age of majority in most states. But since the 1971 ratification of the Twenty-Sixth Amendment, lowering the voting age to eighteen, most states have lowered the age of majority to eighteen or nineteen for many other purposes as well. Some statutes, such as those in Michigan (Mich. Comp. Laws Ann. § 722.52), set age eighteen as the age of majority for all purposes; other states have adopted more limited or more piecemeal legislation, sometimes using different minimum ages for different purposes. Given the lack of uniformity, administrators and counsel should carefully check state law in their own states.

The age-of-majority laws can affect many postsecondary regulations and policies. For example, students at age eighteen may be permitted to enter binding contracts without the need for a cosigner, give consent to medical treatment, declare financial independence, or establish a legal residence apart from the parents. But although students' legal capacity enables institutions to deal with them as adults at age eighteen, it does not necessarily require that institutions do so. Particularly in private institutions, administrators may still be able as a policy matter to require a cosigner on contracts with students, for instance, or to consider the resources of parents in awarding financial aid, even though the parents have no legal obligations to support the student. An institution's legal capacity to adopt such policy positions depends on the interpretation of the applicable age-of-majority law and the possible existence of special state law provisions for postsecondary institutions. A state loan program, for instance, may have special definitions of dependency or residency that may not conform to general age-of-majority laws.

Administrators will thus confront two questions: What do the age-of-majority laws require that I do in particular areas? And should I, where I am under no legal obligation, establish age requirements higher than the legal age in particular areas, or should I instead pattern institutional policies on the general legal standard?

8.1.3. The contractual rights of students. Both public and private institutions often have express contractual relationships with students. The most common examples are probably the housing contract or lease, the food service contract, and the loan agreement. In addition, courts are increasingly inclined to view the student handbook or college catalog as a contract. When problems arise in these areas, the written contract, including institutional regulations incorporated by reference in the contract, is usually the first source of legal guidance.

The contractual relationship between student and institution, however, extends beyond the terms of express contracts. There also exists the more amorphous contractual relationship recognized in *Carr v. St. John's University, New York,* 187 N.E.2d 18 (N.Y. 1962), the modern root of the contract theory of student status. In reviewing the institution's dismissal of students for having participated in a civil marriage ceremony, the court based its reasoning on the principle that "when a student is duly admitted by a private university, secular or religious, there is an implied contract between the student and the university that, if he complies with the terms prescribed by the university, he will obtain the degree which he sought." Construing a harsh and vague regulation in the university's favor, the court upheld the dismissal because the students had failed to comply with the university's prescribed terms.

Although *Carr* dealt only with a private institution, a subsequent New York case, *Healy v. Larsson,* 323 N.Y.S.2d 625, *affirmed,* 318 N.E.2d 608 (N.Y. 1974) (discussed below in this Section), indicated that "there is no reason why . . . the *Carr* principle should not apply to a public university or community college."

Other courts have increasingly utilized the contract theory for both public and private institutions, as well as for both academic and disciplinary disputes. The theory, however, does not necessarily apply identically to all such situations. A public institution may have more defenses against a contract action. *Eden v. Board of Trustees of State University,* 374 N.Y.S.2d 686 (N.Y. App. Div. 1975), for instance, recognizes both an *ultra vires* defense and the state's power to terminate a contract when necessary in the public interest. (*Ultra vires* means "beyond authority," and the defense is essentially "You can't enforce this contract against us because we didn't have authority to make it in the first place.") And courts may accord both public and private institutions more flexibility in drafting and interpreting contract terms involving academics than they do contract terms involving discipline. In holding that Georgia State University had not breached its contract with a student by withholding a master's degree, for example, the court in *Mahavongsanan v. Hall,* 529 F.2d 448 (5th Cir. 1976), recognized the "wide latitude and discretion afforded by the courts to educational institutions in framing their academic requirements."[1]

In general, courts have applied the contract theory to postsecondary institutions in a deferential manner. Courts have accorded institutions considerable latitude to select and interpret their own contract terms and to change the terms to which students are subjected as they progress through the institution. In *Mahavongsanan*, for instance, the court rejected the plaintiff student's contract claim in part because an institution "clearly is entitled to modify [its regulations] so as to properly exercise its educational responsibility." Nor have institutions been subjected to the rigors of contract law as it applies in the commercial world (see, for example, *Slaughter v. Brigham Young University*, discussed in Sections 9.2.3 and 9.4.4).

In some instances, courts have preferred to use quasi-contract theory to examine the relationship between an institution and its students, and may hold the institution to a good-faith standard. In *Beukas v. Fairleigh Dickinson University*, 605 A.2d 776 (N.J. Super. Ct. Law Div. 1991), *affirmed*, 605 A.2d 708 (N.J. Super. Ct. App. Div. 1992), former dental students sued the university for closing its dental school when the state withdrew its subsidy. The university pointed to language in the catalog reserving the right to eliminate programs and schools, arguing that the language was binding on the students. But instead of applying a contract theory, the trial court preferred to analyze the issue using quasi-contract theory, and applied an arbitrariness standard:

> [T]his court rejects classic contract doctrine to resolve this dispute. . . . [T]he "true" university-student "contract" is one of mutual obligations implied, not in fact, but by law; it is a quasi-contract which is "created by law, for reasons of justice without regard to expressions of assent by either words or acts" [citing *Borough of West Caldwell v. Borough of Caldwell*, 26 N.J. 9 (1958)]. . . . This theory is the most efficient and legally-consistent theory to resolve a university-student conflict resulting from an administrative decision to terminate an academic or professional program. The inquiry should be: "did the university act in good faith and, if so, did it deal fairly with its students?" [605 A.2d at 783, 784].

Citing *AAUP v. Bloomfield College* (Section 6.8.2), the court explained its reasoning for using a good-faith standard rather than contract law:

> This approach will give courts broader authority for examining university decisionmaking in the administrative area than would a modified standard of judicial deference and will produce a more legally cohesive body of law than will application of classic contract doctrine with its many judicially created exceptions, varying as they must from jurisdiction to jurisdiction [605 A.2d at 784–85].

---

[1]Courts have also reviewed student challenges to academic or disciplinary decisions by colleges under the law of private associations. (See, for example, *Boehm v. University of Pennsylvania School of Veterinary Medicine*, 573 A.2d 575 (Pa. Super. 1990); *Clayton v. Trustees of Princeton University*, 519 F. Supp. 802 (D.N.J. 1981); and *Tedeschi v. Wagner College*, 404 N.E.2d 1302 (N.Y. 1980); and see generally Section 14.2 of this book.) But most of the cases continue to focus on breach of contract claims and other claims of a contractual nature.

The state's appellate court upheld the result and the reasoning, but stated that if the catalog was a contract (a question that this court did not attempt to answer), the reservation of rights language would have permitted the university to close the dental school.

Similarly, another New Jersey appellate court refused to characterize the student-institution relationship as contractual in a student's challenge to his dismissal on academic (as opposed to disciplinary) grounds. In *Mittra v. University of Medicine and Dentistry of New Jersey*, 719 A.2d 693 (N.J. Ct. App. 1998), the court stated that when the institution's action was taken for academic reasons,

> the relationship between the university and its students should not be analyzed in purely contractual terms. As long as the student is afforded reasonable notice and a fair hearing in general conformity with the institution's rules and regulations, we defer to the university's broad discretion in its evaluation of academic performance. . . . Rigid application of contract principles to controversies concerning student academic performance would tend to intrude upon academic freedom and to generate precisely the kind of disputes that the courts should be hesitant to resolve [719 A.2d at 695, 697].

Since the student had not identified any specific rule or regulation alleged to have been violated, the appellate court affirmed the trial court's award of summary judgment to the university.

In addition to challenging the application of curricular or other requirements, students have also asserted contract claims when challenging dismissals or other sanctions. Traditionally, courts have typically been more deferential to institutional decisions in dismissals for academic rather than for disciplinary reasons. For example, in a misconduct case, *Fellheimer v. Middlebury College*, 869 F. Supp. 238 (D. Vt. 1994), a federal court ruled that the student handbook of a private institution was contractually binding on the college and provided the basis for a breach of contract claim. In *Fellheimer*, a student challenged the fairness of the college's disciplinary process because he was not informed of all of the charges against him. (This case is discussed more fully in Section 9.4.4.) The court rejected the college's claim that the handbook was not a contract: "While [prior cases caution courts to] keep the unique educational setting in mind when interpreting university-student contracts, they do not alter the general proposition that a College is nonetheless contractually bound to provide students with the procedural safeguards that it has promised" (869 F. Supp. 243). The court ruled that Middlebury had breached its contract with the student because the disciplinary hearing had been flawed.

The existence of a contractual relationship between student and institution is significant if the student wishes to assert constitutional claims based on a property interest. In *Unger v. National Residents Matching Program*, 928 F.2d 1392 (3d Cir. 1991), the plaintiff, admitted to Temple University's residency program in dermatology, challenged the university's decision to terminate the program five months before she was to enroll. Unger claimed constitutional violations of both liberty and property interests. The court rejected the liberty interest claim, stating that Unger was inconvenienced by Temple's actions but was not precluded from seeking other training.

To Unger's claim that Temple's decision deprived her of a property interest, based on her contract with the university, the court replied that the claim failed for two reasons. First, Unger had no legitimate expectation that she would continue her graduate medical training; second, she had no entitlement to the training provided by the program. The court did find that Temple's offer of admission was a contract; but it was not the type of contract that created a property interest enforceable under federal civil rights law (see Section 3.5).

Although various courts have applied contract law principles when an institution's written materials make certain representations, they may be more hesitant to do so if the promise relied upon is oral. In *Ottgen v. Clover Park Technical College*, 928 P.2d 1119 (Wash. Ct. App. 1996), a state appellate court affirmed the trial court's dismissal of contract and state consumer fraud claims against the college. Five students who had enrolled in the college's Professional Residential Real Estate Appraiser program sued the college when a promise made by a course instructor, who was subsequently dismissed by the college, did not materialize. Although the instructor had promised the students that they would receive appraisal experience as well as classroom instruction, the opportunity for on-the-job experience did not occur. The court ruled that there was no contract between the college and the students to offer them anything but classroom education. College documents discussed only the classroom component and made no representations about the eligibility for licensure of individuals who had completed the program.

Despite the generally deferential judicial attitude, the contract theory has become a source of meaningful rights for students as well as for institutions, particularly when faculty or administrators either fail to follow institutional policies or apply those policies in an arbitrary way. Students have claimed, and courts have agreed, that student handbooks, college catalogs, and other policy documents are implied-in-fact contracts, and that an institution's failure to follow these guidelines is a breach of an implied-in-fact contract (see, for example, *Zumbrun v. University of Southern California*, 101 Cal. Rptr. 499, 502 (Ct. App. Cal. 1972)). Other cases have involved student claims that the totality of the institution's policies and oral representations by faculty and administrators create an implied contract that, if the student pays tuition and demonstrates satisfactory academic performance, he or she will receive a degree.[2] And although some public institutions have escaped liability in contract claims under the sovereign immunity doctrine (see Section 3.4), not all states apply this doctrine to public colleges (see, for example, *Stratton v. Kent State University*, 2003 Ohio App. LEXIS 1206 (Ct. App. Ohio, March 18, 2003) (unpublished)).

The U.S. Court of Appeals for the First Circuit, applying Rhode Island law, provided an explicit recognition of the contractual relationship between a

---

[2]Students have also sought to state claims of educational malpractice against colleges and their administrators and faculty. Courts have rejected these tort claims, but some have agreed to entertain breach of contract claims based upon institutional representations regarding licensure or accreditation that were alleged to be false. These cases are discussed in Section 3.3.3.

student and a college. In *Mangla v. Brown University,* 135 F.3d 80 (1st Cir. 1998), the court stated:

> The student-college relationship is essentially contractual in nature. The terms of the contract may include statements provided in student manuals and registration materials. The proper standard for interpreting the contractual terms is that of "reasonable expectation—what meaning the party making the manifestation, the university, should reasonably expect the other party to give it" [135 F.3d at 83].

And in *Goodman v. President and Trustees of Bowdoin College,* 135 F. Supp. 2d 40 (D. Maine 2001), a federal district court, applying Maine law, ruled that even though the college had reserved the right to change the student handbook unilaterally and without notice, this reservation of rights did not defeat the contractual nature of the student handbook.

Nevertheless, a reservation of rights clause or disclaimer in the college catalog or other policy document can provide protection against breach of contract claims when curricular or other changes are made. For example, in *Doherty v. Southern College of Optometry,* 862 F.2d 570 (6th Cir. 1988), the court rejected a student's claim that deviations from the stated curriculum breached his contractual rights. The college's handbook had specifically reserved the right to change degree requirements, and the college had uniformly applied curricular changes to current students in the past. Therefore, the court ruled that the changes were neither arbitrary nor capricious, and dismissed the student's contract claim.

Similarly, an express disclaimer in a state university's catalog defeated a student's contract claim in *Eiland v. Wolf,* 764 S.W.2d 827 (Tex. Ct. App. 1989). Although the catalog stated that the student would be entitled to a diploma if he successfully completed required courses and met other requirements, the express disclaimer that the catalog was not an enforceable contract and was subject to change without notice convinced the court to dismiss the student's challenge to his academic dismissal.

A reservation of rights clause was also present, but less important, in *Beukas v. Fairleigh Dickinson University,* discussed above. The court ruled that no express contract existed between the dental students and the university and that, under principles of "quasi-contract," the university could close the dental school as long as it acted in good faith.

In *Coddington v. Adelphi University,* 45 F. Supp. 2d 211 (E.D.N.Y. 1999), a student claimed that the private university and several individual administrators had violated the Americans With Disabilities Act (ADA; see Section 9.3.5) and breached his contract with the university by failing to accommodate his learning disabilities. Although the court dismissed the student's ADA claim and the contract claims against individual administrators, the court rejected the university's motion to dismiss the contract claim against the university itself. Noting that the student had paid the required tuition and had claimed to have relied upon "admission bulletins and other materials regarding Adelphi's programs and policies regarding students with learning disabilities" and the representations of certain administrators of his right to untimed tests and note takers, the court ruled that the student had sufficiently pleaded "the existence of a contractual agreement" with the university (but not with the individual administrators).

A case brought by a student against Yale University and his faculty advisors provides an interesting example of the use of contract law to challenge alleged professional misconduct by a graduate student's faculty mentors. In *Johnson v. Schmitz*, 119 F. Supp. 2d 90 (D. Conn. 2000), the student claimed that several professors had appropriated his ideas and used them in publications without his consent and without acknowledgment. The court refused to dismiss the student's breach of contract claims because the plaintiff stated that he had relied upon specific promises contained in university catalogs and documents, including "express and implied contractual duties to safeguard students from academic misconduct, to investigate and deal with charges of academic misconduct, and to address charges of academic misconduct in accordance with its own procedures" (119 F. Supp. 2d at 96). Although the university argued that judicial review of the student's claims involved inappropriate involvement in academic decisions, the court disagreed. Explaining that Johnson's claims did not allege that he was provided a poor-quality education, but that the university breached express and implied contractual duties that it had assumed, the court said that its review would be limited to "whether or not Yale had a contractual duty to safeguard its students from faculty misconduct, and, if so, whether that duty was breached in Johnson's case" (119 F. Supp. 2d at 96).

The court also allowed the plaintiff's negligence claim to be heard, ruling that he should be allowed to attempt to demonstrate that Yale had a duty to protect its students against faculty misconduct. This is an unusual ruling, given the typical rejection by courts of students' attempts to state claims of negligence in cases involving academic issues rather than personal injury claims (see Section 3.3.3).

The case of *Harwood v. Johns Hopkins*, 747 A.2d 205 (Ct. App. Md. 2000) provides an interesting example of an institution's successful use of a contract theory as a defense to a student lawsuit. Harwood, a student at Johns Hopkins University, had completed all of his degree requirements, but the degree had not yet been conferred when Harwood murdered a fellow student on the university's campus. The university notified Harwood that it would withhold his diploma pending the resolution of the criminal charges. Harwood pleaded guilty to the murder and was incarcerated. He then brought a declaratory judgment action against the university, seeking the conferral of his degree. The university argued that its written policies required students not only to complete the requirements for their degree, but to adhere to the university's code of conduct. The court ruled that, because the murder violated the university's code of conduct, the university had a contractual right to withhold the diploma.

Although courts are increasingly holding institutions of higher education to their promises and representations in catalogs and policy documents, they have rejected students' attempts to claim that only the material in the written documents is binding on the *student*. For example, the Supreme Court of Alaska ruled in favor of a nursing professor at the University of Alaska who required a student who had failed a required course to take a course in "critical thinking." When the student complained to the dean of the School of Nursing and Health

Sciences, the dean backed the professor, stating that because the requirement of this additional course was a condition of the plaintiff's remaining in the nursing program rather than removal from the program, her decision was final and could not be appealed within the university. The student then filed a breach of contract claim in state court, asserting that the student handbook did not list the course in critical thinking as required for the nursing degree.

In *Bruner v. Petersen,* 944 P.2d 43 (Alaska 1997), the state's highest court affirmed a trial court's ruling that there was no breach of contract, and also affirmed that court's award of attorney's fees to the university. Explicit language in the student handbook stated that it was not a contract, and allowed for the possibility of establishing conditions for reenrollment in any required course that a student had failed. Furthermore, said the court, the student had received all of the appeal rights provided by the catalog.

The nature of damages in a successful breach of contract claim was addressed in a case brought under Florida law. In *Sharick v. Southeastern University of the Health Sciences, Inc.,* 780 So. 2d 136 (Ct. App. Fla. 2000), a fourth-year medical student was dismissed for failing his last course in medical school. He sued the university for breach of contract, and a jury found that the university's decision to dismiss Sharick was arbitrary, capricious, and "lacking any discernable rational basis." Sharick had sought damages for future lost earning capacity as well as reimbursement of the tuition he had paid, but the trial judge would allow the jury only to consider damages related to the tuition payments. Sharick appealed the trial court's ruling on the issue of future lost earnings. The university did not appeal the jury verdict.

The appellate court reversed the trial court's limitation of damages to tuition reimbursement. Since previous cases had established that other contractual remedies, such as specific performance and *mandamus* to grant a degree were unavailable to plaintiffs suing colleges, the court stated that damages could properly include the value of the lost degree with respect to Sharick's future earnings. The Supreme Court of Florida first agreed to review the appellate court's ruling, then changed its mind, leaving the appellate decision in force (*Southeastern University of the Health Sciences, Inc. v. Sharick,* 822 So. 2d 1290 (Fla. 2002)). (For an analysis of the "lessons" of *Sharick,* see Scott D. Makar, "Litigious Students and Academic Disputes," *Chron. Higher Educ.,* November 8, 2002, B20.)

The contract theory is still developing. Debate continues on issues such as the means for identifying the terms and conditions of the student-institution contract, the extent to which the school catalog constitutes part of the contract, and the extent to which the institution retains implied or inherent authority (see Section 3.1) not expressed in any written regulation or policy. For example, in *Prusack v. State,* 498 N.Y.S.2d 455 (N.Y. App. Div. 1986), the court rejected the student's claim that a letter of admission from the university that had quoted a particular tuition rate was an enforceable contract, since other university publications expressly stated that tuition was subject to change. In *Eiland v. Wolf,* 764 S.W.2d 827 (Tex. Ct. App. 1989), reservation of rights language in a catalog for the University of Texas Medical School at Galveston absolved the institution of contractual liability. The catalog stated: "The provisions of this catalogue are subject to change without notice and do not constitute an irrevocable contract between any student . . . and the University." Furthermore, the catalog gave the faculty the right to determine whether a student's performance was satisfactory, and stated that "the Faculty of the School of Medicine has the authority to drop any student from the rolls . . . if circumstances of a legal, moral, health, social, or academic nature justify such a request" (764 S.W.2d at 838). The court said: "Given the express disclaimers in the document alleged to be a contract here, it is clear that no enforceable 'contract' existed" (764 S.W.2d at 838).

Also still debatable is the extent to which courts will rely on certain contract law concepts, such as "unconscionable" contracts and "contracts of adhesion." An unconscionable contract is one that is so harsh and unfair to one of the parties that a reasonable person would not freely and knowingly agree to it. Unconscionable contracts are not enforceable in the courts. In *Albert Merrill School v. Godoy*, 357 N.Y.S.2d 378 (Civ. Ct. N.Y. City 1974), the school sought to recover money due on a contract to provide data-processing training. Finding that the student did not speak English well and that the bargaining power of the parties was uneven, the court held the contract unconscionable and refused to enforce it.

A "contract of adhesion" is one offered by one party (usually the party in the stronger bargaining position) to the other party on a "take it or leave it" basis, with no opportunity to negotiate the terms. Ambiguities in contracts of adhesion will be construed against the drafting party (in these cases, the institution) because there was no opportunity for the parties to bargain over the terms of the contract (see, for example, *Corso v. Creighton University*, 731 F.2d 529 (8th Cir. 1984)). See also *K.D. v. Educational Testing Service*, 386 N.Y.S.2d 747 (N.Y. Sup. Ct. 1976), where the court viewed the plaintiff's agreement with Educational Testing Service (ETS) to take the Law School Admissions Test (LSAT) as a contract of adhesion, but ruled it valid because it was not "so unfair and unreasonable" that it should be disregarded by use of the available "pretexts," such as a declaration that it violated public policy.

The case of *Kyriazis v. University of West Virginia*, discussed in Section 2.5.5, is an example of a contract of adhesion that a court invalidated as contrary to public policy. In particular, the court's opinion suggests factors relevant to determining whether the bargaining powers of the parties are substantially uneven. In *Kyriazis*, the court found that the university had a "decisive bargaining advantage" over the student because (1) the student had to sign the release as a condition of sports participation and thus had no real choice; (2) the release was prepared by counsel for the university, but the student had no benefit of counsel when he signed the release; and (3) the university's student code required students to follow the directions of university representatives.

Since these contract principles depend on the weak position of one of the parties, and on overall determinations of "fairness," courts are unlikely to apply them against institutions that deal openly with their students—for instance, by following a good-practice code, operating grievance mechanisms for student complaints (see Sections 9.1.2–9.1.4), and affording students significant opportunity to participate in institutional governance.

Although a promise to treat the other party to the contract fairly and in good faith is part of every contract (*Restatement (Second) of Contracts* 205 (1981)), most claims by students using this theory have been unsuccessful. For example, in *Napolitano v. Trustees of Princeton University* (discussed in section 9.4.4), the court rejected a student's claim that withholding her degree for one year as punishment for plagiarism was a breach of the covenant of good faith and fair dealing. Said the court: "To upset Princeton's decision here, this court would have to find that Princeton could not in good faith have assessed the penalties it did against the plaintiff" (453 A.2d at 284). Other examples of judicial rejection of these claims are *Coveney v. President and Trustees of the College of the Holy Cross*, 445 N.E.2d 136 (Mass. 1983), and *Seare v. University of Utah School of Medicine*, 882 P.2d 673 (Utah Ct. App. 1994).

Although student attempts to argue that the institution has a fiduciary duty toward its students have typically been unsuccessful (Hazel Glenn Beh, "Student Versus University: The University's Implied Obligations of Good Faith and Fair Dealing," 59 *Maryland L. Rev.* 183, 202 (2000)), at least one court has ruled that a university and several of its faculty may have assumed a fiduciary duty to its graduate students. In *Johnson v. Schmitz,* discussed earlier in this Section, a federal trial court refused to dismiss a doctoral student's claim that the university breached its fiduciary duty toward the student by not protecting him from alleged academic misconduct by his faculty advisors. Said the court: "Given the collaborative nature of the relationship between a graduate student and a dissertation advisor who necessarily shares the same academic interests, the Court can envision a situation in which a graduate school, knowing the nature of this relationship, may assume a fiduciary duty to the student" (119 F. Supp. 2d at 97–98). The court also ruled that the plaintiff might be able to demonstrate that a fiduciary relationship existed between himself and his dissertation committee, and that the dissertation committee would need to demonstrate "fair dealing by clear and convincing evidence" because "the dissertation committee was created for no other purpose than to assist Johnson" (119 F. Supp. 2d at 98). The court ruled that the case should proceed to trial. (For more on fiduciary theories, see generally A. L. Goldman, "The University and the Liberty of Its Students—A Fiduciary Theory," 54 *Kentucky L.J.* 643 (1966).)

Other contractual issues may arise as a result of the action of institutional or state-level actors. For example, in *Arriaga v. Members of Board of Regents,* 825 F. Supp. 1 (D. Mass. 1992), students challenged the constitutionality of retroactive tuition increases ordered by the state board of regents after the state legislature, responding to a fiscal crisis, passed a law increasing tuition for nonresident students. Claiming that the institution's statements about the amount of tuition for nonresident students was a contract, the students argued that the regents' action impaired their contractual rights in violation of the U.S. Constitution's contracts clause, Article I, Section 10 (see Section 6.2.2).

The regents filed a motion to dismiss the lawsuit, arguing that they had the unilateral power to impose tuition increases, and thus it was not the legislature's action that was dispositive of the constitutional claim. The court was required to determine whether it was the action of the legislature or the regents that resulted in the tuition increase, for the contracts clause would apply only to the acts of the legislature unless it had delegated its power to the executive branch (here, the regents). The court concluded that, although the regents determined that tuition increases were necessary before the legislature formally passed the law, their action was in anticipation of the law and thus was controlled by the provisions of the contracts clause.

Students enrolled in programs that are terminated or changed prior to the students' graduation have found some state courts to be receptive to their claims that promotional materials, catalogs, and policy statements are contractually binding on the institution. An illustrative case is *Craig v. Forest Institute of Professional Psychology*, 713 So. 2d 967 (Ala. Ct. App. 1997), in which four students filed state law breach of contract and fraud claims against Forest. Forest, whose main campus was located in Wheeling, Illinois, opened a satellite campus in Huntsville, Alabama, and offered a doctoral degree program in psychology. Although the Huntsville campus was not accredited by the American Psychological Association (APA), a regional accrediting association, or the state, Forest's written materials allegedly implied that its graduates were eligible to sit for licensing examinations and to be licensed in Alabama. The Alabama Board of Examiners would not allow Forest graduates to sit for a licensing examination because its regulations provided that only graduates of accredited institutions were eligible to take the examination.

The Alabama campus proved to be a financial drain on Forest, and it closed the campus before the students had completed their doctorates. Because the college was not accredited, the students were unable to transfer credits earned at Forest to other doctoral programs.

The students' claims were based on the college's alleged promises that they could obtain a doctorate at the Huntsville campus and be eligible for licensure in Alabama. The trial court granted summary judgment to the college, but the appellate court reversed. Disagreeing with a ruling by the South Dakota Supreme Court in an earlier case, *Aase v. State*, 400 N.W.2d 269 (S.D. 1987), the court ruled that "it is not clear that Forest fulfilled all of its contractual obligations to the students merely by providing them with instruction for which they had paid tuition on a semester-by-semester basis" (713 So. 2d at 973). The scope of the contract could not be determined without a trial, said the court; although Forest had pointed to language in one publication that reserved its right to modify or discontinue programs, the court stated that this language was not "dispositive" and that all relevant documents needed to be considered. The court also ruled that a trial was necessary on the plaintiffs' fraud claims.

Contract law has become an important source of legal rights for students. Postsecondary administrators should be sensitive to the language used in all institutional rules and policies affecting students. Language suggestive of a commitment (or promise) to students should be used only when the institution is prepared to live up to the commitment. Limitations on the institution's commitments should be clearly noted where possible, and reservation of rights language should be used wherever appropriate. Administrators should consider the adoption of an official policy, perhaps even a "code of good practice," on fair dealing with students, and provide avenues for internal appeal of both academic and disciplinary decisions.

8.1.4. Student academic freedom. Student academic freedom is not as well developed as faculty academic freedom (the focus of Chapter Seven), either in terms of custom or in terms of law. Nevertheless, like faculty academic freedom, student academic freedom has important historical antecedents and is widely recognized in the academic community. Moreover, since the early 1990s, developments in academia and in the courts have focused attention on the academic freedom of students and raised new questions about its status and role.

The concept of student academic freedom was imported into the United States from Europe, where, in German universities, it was known as *Lernfreiheit,* the freedom to learn. (See H. S. Commanger, "The University and Freedom: 'Lehrfreiheit' and 'Lernfreiheit,'" 34 *J. Higher Educ.* 361 (1963); Richard Hofstadter & Walter Metzger, *The Development of Academic Freedom in the United States* (Columbia University Press, 1955), 386–91.) In 1915, in its foundational "General Declaration of Principles," the American Association of University Professors (AAUP) recognized *Lernfreiheit,* the student's freedom to learn, as one of the two components of academic freedom—the other being *Lehrfreiheit,* the teacher's freedom to teach. (*AAUP Policy Documents and Reports* (the "Redbook") (9th ed., 2001), 291–301). In the classic "1940 Statement of Principles on Academic Freedom and Tenure," the AAUP and the Association of American Colleges and Universities, eventually joined by more than 150 other higher education and professional associations as endorsers, specifically acknowledged "the rights of the . . . student to freedom in learning" (*AAUP Policy Documents and Reports,* 3). Subsequently, in its "Statement on Professional Ethics" (promulgated in 1966 and revised in 1987), the AAUP emphasized professors' responsibility to "encourage the free pursuit of learning in their students" and to "protect their academic freedom" (*AAUP Policy Documents and Reports,* 133).

In 1967, representatives of the AAUP, the Association of American Colleges and Universities, the U.S. Student Association, the National Association of Student Personnel Administrators, and the National Association for Women in Education promulgated a "Joint Statement on Rights and Freedoms of Students" that was endorsed by all five organizations and various other higher education and professional associations. The Joint Statement recognizes the "freedom to learn" and the freedom to teach as "inseparable facets of academic freedom" and emphasizes that "students should be encouraged to develop the capacity for critical judgment and to engage in a sustained and independent search for truth" (*AAUP Policy Documents and Reports,* 261). The Statement then elucidates "the minimal standards of academic freedom of students" that apply "in the classroom, on the campus, and in the larger community" (*Id.* at 264). This very helpful listing and exposition includes the freedom of "discussion, inquiry, and expression" in the classroom and in conferences with the instructor (*Id.* at 262); the freedom "to organize and join associations" of students, "to examine and discuss" issues and "express opinions publicly and privately" on campus, and "to invite and to hear" guest speakers (*Id.* at 263–64); the freedom "individually and collectively [to] . . . express views on issues of institutional policy" and "to participate in the formulation and application of institutional policy affecting academic and student affairs" (*Id.* at 264); the "editorial freedom of student publications," that is, "sufficient editorial freedom and financial autonomy . . . to maintain their integrity of purpose as vehicles for free inquiry . . . in an academic community" (*Id.*); and the freedom, "[a]s citizens," to "exercise the rights of citizenship," such as "freedom of speech, peaceful assembly, and right of petition," both on and off campus (*Id.* at 265). In 1992, the Joint Statement was reviewed, updated (with interpretive footnotes), and reaffirmed by an interassociation task force.

Beginning in the 1950s, the U.S. Supreme Court has gradually, but increasingly, recognized student academic freedom. In one of the earliest and most influential academic freedom cases, *Sweezy v. New Hampshire,* Chief Justice Warren's plurality opinion declared that "*[t]eachers and students* must always remain free to inquire, to study and to evaluate, to gain new maturity and understanding; otherwise our civilization will stagnate and die" (354 U.S. 234, 250 (1957) (emphasis added)). In subsequent years, the Court decided various cases in which it protected students' rights to freedom of speech, press, and association on campus (see, for example, *Widmar v. Vincent,* 454 U.S. 263 (1981), discussed in Section 10.1.5, and *Papish v. Board of Curators of the University of Missouri,* 410 U.S. 667 (1973), discussed in Section 10.3.5). These cases typically were based on generic First Amendment principles that apply both outside and within the context of academia (for example, the "public forum" principles used in *Widmar*) and did not specifically rely on or develop the concept of student academic freedom. In one of these cases, however, *Healy v. James,* 408 U.S. 169 (1972) (Section 9.5.1 & 10.1.1 of this book), the Court did emphasize that, in upholding the students' right to freedom of association, it was "reaffirming this Nation's dedication to safe-guarding academic freedom" (408 U.S. at 180–81, citing *Sweezy*). Then, in *Rosenberger v. Rector and Visitors of the University of Virginia,* 515 U.S. 819 (1995), the Court, citing both *Sweezy* and *Healy,* further linked student free expression rights with student academic freedom and provided historical context for the linkage.

Rosenberger involved a university's refusal to provide student activities funds to a student organization that published a Christian magazine. The Court determined that the refusal was "viewpoint discrimination" that violated the students' right to freedom of expression. (For discussion of this aspect of *Rosenberger,* see Section 10.1.5.) In supporting its conclusion, the Court reasoned that:

> [t]he danger [of chilling expression] is especially real in the University setting, where the State acts against a background and tradition of thought and experiment that is at the center of our intellectual and philosophic tradition. See *Healy v. James,* 408 U.S. 169, 180–181 (1972); *Keyishian v. Board of Regents of Univ. of State of N.Y.,* 385 U.S. 589, 603 (1967); *Sweezy v. New Hampshire,* 354 U.S. 234, 250 (1957). In ancient Athens, and, as Europe entered into a new period of intellectual awakening, in places like Bologna, Oxford, and Paris, universities began as voluntary and spontaneous assemblages or concourses *for students to speak and to write and to learn.* See generally R. Palmer & J. Colton, *A History of the Modern World* 39 (7th ed. 1992). The quality and creative power of *student intellectual life* to this day remains a vital measure of a school's influence and

attainment. For the University, by regulation, to cast disapproval on particular viewpoints of its students risks the suppression of free speech *and creative inquiry* in one of the vital centers for the Nation's *intellectual life,* its college and university campuses [515 U.S. at 835–36 (emphasis added)].

Thus, although *Rosenberger* is based on free speech and press principles like those the Court used in the earlier students' rights cases, it goes further than these cases in stressing the academic freedom context of the dispute and in emphasizing the student's freedom to learn as well as the student's more generic right to speak.

The case of *Board of Regents of University of Wisconsin System v. Southworth,* 529 U.S. 217 (2000), a mandatory student fees case coming five years after *Rosenberger,* can also be seen as a student academic freedom case. (*Southworth* is discussed in Section 10.1.2.) Justice Kennedy's majority opinion in *Southworth* did not specifically invoke academic freedom, as did his previous majority opinion in *Rosenberger,* and the students did not prevail in *Southworth* to the extent that they had in *Rosenberger.* Nevertheless, the Court made clear that the justification for subsidizing student organizations through mandatory fee allocations is to provide students "the means to engage in dynamic discussions of philosophical, religious, scientific, social, and political subjects in their extracurricular campus life outside the lecture hall" (529 U.S. at 233). A university that subsidizes student speech for this purpose, however, has a "corresponding duty" to avoid infringing "the speech and beliefs" of students who object to this use of their student fees—a duty that may be fulfilled by assuring that the mandatory fee system is "viewpoint-neutral" (*Id.* at 231–33). Thus, the overall justification for the viewpoint-neutral mandatory fee system is, in effect, the promotion of student academic freedom; the university's "duty" to protect objecting students is, in effect, a duty to protect their academic freedom; and the students' right to insist on such protection is, in effect, a First Amendment academic freedom right.

The three concurring Justices in *Southworth,* unlike the majority, did specifically invoke First Amendment academic freedom (*Id.* at 236–39). In an opinion by Justice Souter, these three Justices argued that the Court's prior opinions on academic freedom (see generally Section 7.1.4 of this book) provide the legal principles that the Court should have considered in resolving the case, even though these prior precedents would not "control the result in this [case]." While the concurring Justices emphasized the "academic freedom and . . . autonomy" of the institution more than student academic freedom, they did make clear that institutional academic freedom or autonomy does not obliterate student academic freedom. From the concurring Justices' perspective, then, the objecting students' claims could be cast as student academic freedom claims, and the university's defense could be considered an institutional academic freedom or autonomy defense. (Institutional academic freedom is discussed in Section 7.1.6 of this book.)

Before *Rosenberger* and *Southworth,* as suggested above, most student academic freedom claims were based on generic free expression principles. If academic freedom was mentioned by advocates or by the courts, it was as an add-on that gave nuance and additional weight to the traditional free expression claim. *Rosenberger* itself is perhaps the best example of this use of academic freedom arguments. The interests at stake in the earlier cases (and in *Rosenberger* itself), moreover, were traditional First Amendment interests in the right to speak rather than specific interests in the freedom to learn. Some of the cases after *Rosenberger* and *Southworth*, however, can be viewed differently; they are cast as (or are subject to being recast as) freedom to learn cases, that is, true student academic freedom cases. The *Southworth* case, as explained above, provides a kind of transitional example, combining elements of traditional free speech claims and elements of contemporary freedom to learn arguments.

Two post-*Southworth* cases, *Brown v. Li* in 2002 and the *Axson-Flynn* case in 2004, provide instructive examples of the "newer" type of student academic freedom claim.[3] Each of these novel U.S. Court of Appeals cases is discussed immediately below.

In *Brown v. Li,* 308 F.3d 939 (9th Cir. 2002), a master's degree candidate at the University of California at Santa Barbara added a "Disacknowledgments" section in his master's thesis in which he crudely criticized the graduate school's dean, university library personnel, a former governor of the state, and others. Because the thesis contained this section, the student's thesis committee did not approve it, resulting in the student exceeding the time limit for completing his degree requirements and being placed on academic probation. Although the university did award the degree several months later, it declined to place the thesis in the university library's thesis archive. When the student (now a graduate) sued the dean, the chancellor, the professors on his thesis committee, and the library director in federal court, claiming that their actions violated his First Amendment free speech rights, both the trial court and the appellate court rejected his claim. The appellate court resolved the case by identifying and considering the academic and curricular interests at stake, taking into account the "university's interest in academic freedom," the "First Amendment rights" of the faculty members, and the "First Amendment rights" of the student. To guide its decision making, the court relied on *Hazelwood School District v. Kuhlmeier,* 484 U.S. 260 (1988), a U.S. Supreme Court precedent granting elementary/secondary school teachers and administrators extensive discretion to make curricular decisions, and expressly adopted the case's reasoning for use in higher education. (See 308 F.3d at 947–52; and see Section 1.4.3 of this book for discussion of transferring lower education precedents to higher education.) Under *Hazelwood,* the appellate court explained, the defendants would prevail if their rejection of the plaintiff's thesis "was reasonably related to a legitimate pedagogical objective" (as the court ruled it was); and in applying this standard, the court would generally "defer[ ] to the university's expertise in defining academic standards and teaching students to meet them" (which the court did).

To supplement this mode of analysis, the court also briefly considered the relationship between the faculty members' academic freedom under the First

---

[3]For another example from the post-*Southworth* era, see the *Hayut* case discussed in Section 9.3.4; and for two interesting and quite different pre-*Southworth* examples, see *Salehpour v. University of Tennessee,* discussed in Section 9.5.3, and *Levin v. Harleston,* discussed in Section 7.3.

Amendment and that of the student. Describing a faculty member's right as "a right to . . . evaluate students as determined by his or her independent professional judgment" (see generally Section 7.2.3), the court determined that "the committee members had an affirmative First Amendment right not to approve Plaintiff's thesis." "The presence of [the faculty members'] affirmative right," the court emphasized, "underscores [the student's] lack of a First Amendment right to have his nonconforming thesis approved."

While one may question the court's willingness to apply *Hazelwood* with full force to higher education, as well as the court's stark manner of according faculty academic rights supremacy over student academic rights, *Brown v. Li* nevertheless provides a good description of basic limits on student academic freedom. As a general rule, said the court, faculty members and institutions, consistent with the First Amendment, may "require that a student comply with the terms of an academic assignment"; may refuse to "approve the work of a student that, in [the educator's] judgment, fails to meet a legitimate academic standard"; may limit a "student's speech to that which is germane to a particular academic assignment"; and may "require a student to write a paper from a particular viewpoint, even if it is a viewpoint with which the student disagrees, so long as the requirement serves a legitimate pedagogical purpose" (308 F.3d at 949, 951, 953). The court provided this example of the latter point:

> For example, a college history teacher may demand a paper defending Prohibition, and a law-school professor may assign students to write "opinions" showing how Justices Ginsburg and Scalia would analyze a particular Fourth Amendment question. . . . Such requirements are part of the teachers' curricular mission to encourage critical thinking . . . and to conform to professional norms . . . [308 F.3d at 953].

Axson-Flynn v. Johnson, 356 F.3d 1277 (10th Cir. 2004), concerned a former student in the University of Utah's Actor in Training Program (ATP) who had objected to reciting certain language that appeared in the scripts she was assigned to perform in her classes. The student's involvement with the ATP had begun with an audition for acceptance into the program. At the audition, she stated that "she would not remove her clothing, 'take the name of God in vain,' 'take the name of Christ in vain' or 'say the four-letter expletive beginning with the letter F.'" Despite her stipulations, she was admitted to the ATP and began attending classes. The student maintained that she informed her instructors that her stipulations were grounded in her Mormon faith.

When the student performed her first monologue, she omitted two instances of the word "goddamn" but still received an A for her performance. Later in the fall semester, she again sought to omit words that were offensive to her, but her instructor, Barbara Smith, advised her that she "would have to 'get over' her language concerns" and that she could "'still be a good Mormon and say these words.'" Smith delivered an ultimatum that either the student perform the scene as written or receive a zero on the assignment. The instructor eventually relented, however, and the student omitted the offensive words and received a high grade on the assignment. For the rest of the semester, the student continued to omit language that she found offensive from the scripts that she performed.

At the student's end-of-semester review, Smith and two other instructors addressed her omission of profane language from her performances. They advised her that "her request for an accommodation was 'unacceptable behavior'" and "recommended that she 'talk to some other Mormon girls who are good Mormons, who don't have a problem with this.'" The instructors then left the student with this choice: "'You can choose to continue in the program if you modify your values. If you don't, you can leave.'" When the student appealed to the ATP coordinator, he supported the instructors' position. Soon thereafter, the student withdrew from the program (and from the university) because she believed that she would be asked to leave.

Subsequently, the student filed suit against the ATP instructors and the ATP coordinator, alleging violations of her First Amendment rights. She claimed that (1) "forcing her to say the offensive words constitutes an effort to compel her to speak in violation of the First Amendment's free speech clause," and (2) "forcing her to say the offensive words, the utterance of which she considers a sin, violates the First Amendment's free exercise clause." Although the student did not explicitly base her claims on academic freedom principles, it is clear that she considered the defendants' actions to be a restriction on her freedom to learn. The defendants, on the other hand, did rely on academic freedom principles, and claimed that "requiring students to perform offensive scripts advances the school's pedagogical interest in teaching acting . . ." (356 F.3d at 1291). In response to the defendants' academic freedom arguments, the appellate court decided to apply the "principle of judicial restraint in reviewing academic decisions" but explained that it did not "view [academic freedom] as constituting a separate right apart from the operation of the First Amendment within the university setting" (356 F.3d at 1293, n.14).[4]

For her free speech claim, the student relied both on the public forum doctrine (see Section 9.5.2) and on U.S. Supreme Court precedents on "compelled speech" (see *Wooley v. Maynard*, 430 U.S. 705 (1977); and *West Virginia State Board of Education v. Barnette*, 319 U.S. 624 (1943)). The appellate court considered her argument to be that the ATP classrooms were a "public forum" in which the student had a right to be free from content restrictions on her speech, and that the state defendants had compelled her to speak (that is, to recite the profane words in the scripts), which government may not do. The public forum argument could not itself carry the day for the plaintiff, according to the court, since "[n]othing in the record leads us to conclude that . . . the ATP's classrooms could reasonably be considered a traditional public forum [or a] designated public forum" (356 F.3d at 1284–85). The classrooms were therefore a "nonpublic forum" in which instructors and administrators can regulate student speech "in

[4]For more extensive judicial comment on the relationship between academic freedom principles and the First Amendment, see, for example, *Martin v. Parrish* and *Hardy v. Jefferson Community College*, Section 7.2.2 of this book; and see generally Peter Byrne, "Academic Freedom: A 'Special Concern' of the First Amendment," 99 *Yale L.J.* 251 (1989).

any reasonable manner." Neither could the compelled speech argument necessarily carry the day for the plaintiff because students' First Amendment rights, in the school environment, "'are not automatically coextensive with the rights of adults in other settings,'" especially "in the context of a school's right to determine what to teach and how to teach it in its classrooms" (356 F.3d at 1284, quoting *Hazelwood v. Kuhlmeier* (below)). In establishing these baselines for the analysis, the appellate court, like the court in the earlier *Brown v. Li* case, relied expressly on the U.S. Supreme Court's decision in *Hazelwood School District v. Kuhlmeier,* the elementary/secondary education case.

The *Axson-Flynn* court's analysis did not end there, however, nor should it have. Following *Hazelwood,* the court determined that the student's speech was "school-sponsored speech." This is speech that a school "affirmatively promote[s]" as opposed to speech that it merely "tolerate[s]" and that may fairly be characterized as a part of the school curriculum (whether or not it occurs in a traditional classroom setting) because the speech activities are supervised by faculty members and "designed to impart particular knowledge or skills to student participants and audiences" (356 F.3d at 1286, quoting *Hazelwood* at 271). Regarding such speech, the "school may exercise editorial control 'so long as its actions are reasonably related to legitimate pedagogical concerns'" (*Id.* at 1286, quoting *Hazelwood* at 273). Under this standard, the school's restriction of student speech need not be "necessary to the achievement of its [pedagogical] goals," or "the most effective means" or "the most reasonable" means for fulfilling its goals; it need only be a reasonable means (or one among a range of reasonable means) for accomplishing a pedagogical objective.

In determining whether the defendants' compulsion of the student's classroom speech was "reasonably related to legitimate pedagogical concerns," the court gave "substantial deference to [the defendants'] stated pedagogical concern" (356 F.3d at 1290) and declined to "second-guess the pedagogical wisdom or efficacy of [their] goal." In extending this deference, the court noted the generally accepted propositions that "schools must be empowered at times to restrict the speech of their students for pedagogical purposes" and that "schools also routinely require students to express a viewpoint that is not their own in order to teach the students to think critically." As support for these propositions, the court cited *Brown v. Li* (above) and the example from that case (quoted above).

The *Axson-Flynn* court emphasized, however, that the judicial deference accorded to educators' pedagogical choices is not limitless. In particular, courts may and must inquire "whether the educational goal or pedagogical concern was *pretextual*" (emphasis added). The court may "override an educator's judgment where the proffered goal or methodology was a sham pretext for an impermissible ulterior motive" (356 F.3d at 1292).[5] Thus courts will not interfere

---

[5]The court in *Brown v. Li,* above, also made a brief reference to the problem of pretext, suggesting that it too would engraft a "no-pretext" requirement onto the basic *Hazelwood* analysis. Specifically, the court left open the possibility that a student might have a claim if the reasons for the rejection of the thesis were not "pedagogical"—as, for instance, if the committee had rejected the thesis because its members were offended by the opinions or ideas expressed in the "Disacknowledgments" section (*Brown v. Li,* 308 F.3d at 953–54).

"[s]o long as the teacher limits speech or grades speech in the classroom in the name of learning," but they may intervene when the limitation on speech is "a pretext for punishing the student for her race, gender, economic class, religion or political persuasion" (356 F.3d at 1287, quoting *Settle v. Dickson County School Bd.*, 53 F.3d 152, 155–56 (6th Cir. 1995)). Using these principles, the student argued that her instructors' insistence that she speak the words of the script exactly as written was motivated by an "anti-Mormon sentiment" and that their pedagogical justification for their action was merely a pretext. The court was sympathetic to this argument, pointing to the instructors' statements that the student should speak to other "good Mormon" girls who would not omit words from the script, and indicating that these statements "raise[ ] concern that hostility to her faith rather than a pedagogical interest in her growth as an actress was at stake in Defendants' behavior." The appellate court therefore remanded the case to the district court for further examination of the pretext issue.

On the student's second claim, based on the free exercise of religion, the appellate court framed the issue as whether adherence to the script was a "neutral rule of general applicability" and therefore would not raise "free exercise concerns," or a "rule that is discriminatorily motivated and applied" and therefore would raise free exercise concerns (see generally Section 1.6.2 of this book). The possibility of pretext based on anti-Mormon sentiment, which the court relied on in remanding the free speech claim, also led it to remand the free exercise issue to the district court for a determination of "whether the script adherence requirement was discriminatorily applied" to the student based on her religion.

Alternatively, regarding free exercise, the student argued and the court considered whether the ATP had a system of "individual exemptions" from the script adherence requirement. In circumstances "in which individualized exemptions from a general requirement are available, the government may not refuse to extend that system to cases of religious hardship without compelling reason" (356 F.3d at 1297, quoting *Employment Division v. Smith*, 494 U.S. 872, 884 (1990)). If the ATP instructors or the coordinator could make exceptions to class assignment requirements "on a case-by-case basis" by examining the "specific, personal circumstances" of individual students, said the court, this would be "a system of individualized exemptions." If ATP personnel furthermore granted exemptions for nonreligious but not for religious hardships, or discriminated among religions in granting or refusing exceptions, substantial free exercise issues would arise even if the class assignment requirements themselves were neutral and nondiscriminatory as to religion. Since there was evidence that one other ATP student, a Jewish student, had received an exception due to a religious holiday, and there was no other clarifying information in the record concerning individualized exemptions, the appellate court remanded the case for further proceedings on this issue as well.[6]

---

[6]The district court did not get the opportunity to develop the issues that the court of appeals had framed in this unusual case. After the appellate court's decision, the parties settled the case. As part of the settlement, the university agreed to implement a policy on religious accommodations for students. See Elizabeth Neff, "Script v. Scripture: U. Settles Case Over Student's Rights on Stage," *Salt Lake Tribune*, July 7, 2004.

The *Axson-Flynn* case therefore provides no definitive dispositions of the various issues raised, but it does provide an extended and instructive look at a contemporary "freedom to learn" problem. The court's analysis, once parsed as suggested above, contains numerous legal guidelines regarding the freedom to learn. These guidelines, combined with the more general guidelines found in the *Brown v. Li* case (above), will provide substantial assistance for administrators and counsel, and for future courts.

In addition to the judicial developments in *Brown v. Li* and *Axson-Flynn v. Johnson,* and *Rosenberger* and *Southworth* before them, there have been various other developments in academia that have reflected or stimulated greater emphasis on student academic freedom and what it entails. One major example is the concern about "hostile (learning) environments" (see Section 9.3.4). Most of the cases thus far have been brought by faculty members asserting violations of their own academic freedom.[7] These cases have made clear that, although faculty members' academic freedom may be "paramount in the academic setting," the faculty members' rights "are not absolute to the point of compromising a student's right to learn in a hostile-free environment" (*Bonnell v. Lorenzo,* 241 F.3d 800, 823–24 (6th Cir. 2001)). Thus the faculty cases have had an important impact on the academic freedom of students, and students have had an increasingly important stake in the disputes between faculty members and their institutions. Indeed, students have lodged some of the complaints that have precipitated such disputes. (See, for example, the *Cohen* case, the *Silva* case, the *Bonnell* case, and the *Hardy* case in Section 7.2.2.) A faculty member's actions may have hindered the students' freedom to learn, for instance, by demeaning certain groups of students, ridiculing certain students' answers, or using the classroom to indoctrinate or proselytize. If the faculty member prevails in such a dispute, student academic freedom may be diminished, and if the institution prevails it may be enhanced (see, for example, the *Bonnell* case and the *Bishop* case in Section 7.2.2). Or a faculty member may have used methods or materials that intrude upon other student interests in learning—for example, their interests in fair grading practices or in freedom from harassment. If the faculty member prevails, such student interests may receive less protection, and if the institution prevails they may receive more (see, for example, the *Bonnell* case in Section 7.2.2). Conversely, a faculty member may have acted in a way that guarded the students' freedom to learn or promoted related student interests; if the faculty member prevails in this situation, the students win too, and if the institution prevails they lose (see, for example, the *Hardy* case in Section 7.2.2). Such faculty cases thus have the potential to focus attention on student academic freedom and to influence the protection of student academic freedom through judicial acceptance or rejection of particular claims of faculty members.

---

[7]The leading exceptions are *Hayut v. State University of New York,* discussed in Section 9.3.4, which was brought by a student against the institution and a classroom instructor; and *Kelly v. Yale University,* 2003 WL 1563424 (D. Conn.), discussed in subsection 8.1.5 below, which was brought by a student at the Yale Divinity School who claimed that she was sexually assaulted by another student.

Another contemporary development implicating the freedom to learn is the continuing concern about "speech codes" and their effects on students (see Section 9.6), along with related concerns about the "political correctness" phenomenon on campus (see, for example, P. Berman (ed.), *Debating P.C.: The Controversy over Political Correctness on College Campuses* (Dell, 1992)). Required readings and exercises for student orientation programs have also raised concerns (see, for example, Erin O'Connor, "Misreading What Reading Is For," *Chron. Higher Educ.*, September 5, 2003),[8] as have diversity training programs for students (see, for example, Gary Pavela, "Thinking About the UVA 'Diversity Exercise,'" *Synfax Weekly Report*, September 23, 2003, 3179). In addition, there have been various claims (from within and outside the campus) about politicization and liberal bias in faculty hiring, selection of outside speakers for campus events, development of curriculum, selection of course materials, and the teaching methods, classroom remarks, and grading practices of instructors. (See Sara Hebel, "Patrolling Professors' Politics," *Chron. Higher Educ.*, February 13, 2004, A18.)

In the first years of the twenty-first century, such allegations and concerns led interested parties to draft and sponsor an "Academic Bill of Rights" for consideration by colleges and universities, and state boards and legislatures. The text of the Academic Bill of Rights (ABOR), commentary on the document, information on the author (David Horowitz), and background information on the matters addressed in the document can all be found on the Web site of Students for Academic Freedom, a primary sponsor of ABOR (http://www.studentsforacademicfreedom.org). For information on this organization, see Sara Hebel, "Students for Academic Freedom: A New Campus Movement," *Chron. Higher Educ.*, February 9, 2004, A18.

Bills or resolutions supporting ABOR principles have been introduced in a number of state legislatures, including those of California, Colorado, Florida, Georgia, Indiana, Ohio, and Pennsylvania. Two resolutions have been adopted, one in Georgia and one in Pennsylvania. (See, for example, General Assembly of Pennsylvania, House Resolution No. 177, Session of 2005, which establishes a "select committee" to investigate "academic freedom and intellectual diversity" in Pennsylvania state colleges and universities and community colleges.) A resolution supporting ABOR was also introduced in Congress (House Congressional Resolution 318, October 2003), and a similar provision was added to a House bill (H.R. 4283, May 2004). Legislative developments concerning ABOR are tracked on the Students for Academic Freedom Web site, above.

---

[8]At least one controversy regarding a student orientation reading assignment has resulted in litigation. In *Yacovelli v. Moeser*, Case No. 02-CV-596 (M.D.N.C. 2002), *affirmed*, Case No. 02-1889 (4th Cir. 2002), a case concerning the University of North Carolina/Chapel Hill, both the U.S. district court and the U.S. Court of Appeals rejected an establishment clause challenge to the reading program brought by various students and state taxpayers. The case is discussed in Donna Euben, "Curriculum Matters," *Academe*, November–December 2002, 86. In a later ruling, 324 F. Supp. 2d 760 (2004), the district court also rejected the plaintiffs' free exercise clause challenge to the reading program. The case is discussed in Section 7.1.5 of this book.

Higher education associations and commentators in and out of academia have also vigorously debated the Academic Bill of Rights and its underlying ideas. The debate has focused on the empirical basis for some of the expressed concerns, the nature and extent of the problems that such concerns may present, the extent to which student academic freedom (or faculty academic freedom) may be endangered by the alleged developments addressed by ABOR, and the extent to which ABOR and other suggested solutions for the perceived problems may themselves endanger student, faculty, or "institutional" academic freedom. (See, for example, AAUP, "For the Record: Academic Bill of Rights," in *Academe,* January–February 2004, 79–81); David Horowitz, "In Defense of Intellectual Diversity," *Chron. Higher Educ.,* February 13, 2004, B12; and Stanley Fish, "Intellectual Diversity: The Trojan Horse of a Dark Design," *Chron. Higher Educ.,* February 13, 2004, B13.) Subsequently, in June 2005, the American Council on Education and other higher educational organizations released a statement titled "Academic Rights and Responsibilities" that served as a response to much of the debate surrounding the Academic Bill of Rights (see Sara Hebel, "Higher Education Groups Issue Statement on Academic Rights and Intellectual Diversity on Campuses," *Chron. Higher Educ.,* July 1, 2005, A16). The statement, containing "five central or overarching principles" concerning "intellectual pluralism and academic freedom" on campus, is available at http://www.acenet.edu, under News Room/Press Releases.

This continuing debate on the Academic Bill of Rights and intellectual diversity, and the legislative developments and lobbying efforts that fuel the debate, are serving to raise new policy and legal issues concerning the customary and legal protections that academic freedom affords students as well as faculty. (For related discussion of faculty academic freedom, see Sections 7.1.5 and 7.2 through 7.4 of this book.) In addition, the legislative and lobbying developments regarding ABOR are raising new issues concerning so-called institutional academic freedom. (For further discussion of the latter, see Section 7.1.6 of this book.)

8.1.5. Students' legal relationships with other students.
Students have a legal relationship not only with the institution, as discussed in many Sections of this book, but also with other students, with faculty members, and with staff members. These legal relationships are framed both by external law (see Section 1.4.2), especially tort law and criminal law (which impose duties on all individuals in their relationships with other individuals), and by the internal law of the campus (see Section 1.4.3). For students' peer relationships, the most pertinent internal law is likely to be found in student conduct codes, housing rules, and rules regarding student organizations. Since such rules are created and enforced by and in the name of the institution, colleges and universities (as legal entities) are also typically implicated in student-student relationships, and in the resolution of disputes between and among students. In addition, institutions may become implicated in student-student relationships because aggrieved students may sometimes claim that their institution is liable for particular acts of other students. Although students generally do not act as

agents of their institutions in their relationships with other students (see generally Sections 2.1.3 & 3.2.3), there are nevertheless various circumstances in which institutions may become liable for acts of students that injure other students.

In *Foster v. Board of Trustees of Butler County Community College*, 771 F. Supp. 1122 (D. Kan. 1991), for example, the institution was held liable for the acts of a student whom the court considered to be a "gratuitous employee" of the institution. In *Morse v. Regents of the University of Colorado*, 154 F.3d 1124 (10th Cir. 1998), the court ruled that the institution would be responsible, under Title IX (see Section 13.5.3 of this book), for the acts of a Reserve Officer Training Corps (ROTC) cadet who allegedly sexually harassed another cadet *if* the first cadet was "acting with authority bestowed by" the university's ROTC program. And in *Brueckner v. Norwich University*, 730 A.2d 1086 (Vt. 1999), the institution was held liable for certain hazing actions of its upper-class cadets because the university had authorized the cadets to orient and indoctrinate the first-year students and was thus vicariously liable for the damage the cadets caused by hazing even though written university policy forbade hazing activity.

Students themselves can also become liable for harm caused to other students. In some of the fraternity hazing cases, for instance, fraternity members have been held negligent and thus liable for harm to fraternity pledges (see Section 10.2.4). In defamation cases, students—especially student newspaper editors—could become liable for defamation of other students. *Mazart v. State* (discussed in Sections 3.3.1 & 10.3.6) illustrates the type of dispute that could give rise to such liability. In other cases, relationships between students may occasion criminal liability. In *State v. Allen*, 905 S.W.2d 874 (Mo. 1995), for example, a student was prosecuted for hazing activities resulting in the death of a fraternity pledge, and the highest court of Missouri upheld the constitutionality of the state's anti-hazing criminal statute. Another possibility for student liability could arise under Section 1983, which creates individual liability for violation of persons' constitutional rights (see Section 4.7.4 of this book). This possibility is more theoretical than practical, however, since students, unlike faculty members, usually do not act under "color of law" or engage themselves in state action, as Section 1983 requires. (See *Mentavlos v. Anderson*, 249 F.3d 301 (4th Cir. 2001) (students), and compare *Hayut v. State Univ. of New York*, 352 F.3d 733, 743–45 (2d. Cir. 2003) (faculty members), both discussed in Section 1.5.2.)

One of the most serious contemporary problems concerning student relationships is the problem of peer harassment, that is, one student's (or a group of students') harassment of another student (or group of students). The harassment may be on grounds of race, national origin, ethnicity, sex, sexual orientation, religion, disability, or other factors that happen to catch the attention of students at particular times on particular campuses. Such behavior may create disciplinary problems that result in student code of conduct proceedings; and more generally it may compromise the sense of community to which most institutions aspire. (See generally *Peer Harassment: Hassles for Women on Campus* (Center for Women's Policy Studies, 1992); Thomas Mayes,

"Confronting Same-Sex, Student-to-Student Sexual Harassment: Recommendations for Educators and Policy Makers," 29 *Fordham Urban L.J.* 641 (2001).)

In addition, peer harassment may sometimes result in legal liabilities: the harasser may become liable to the victim of the harassment, or the institution may become liable to the victim. Tort law—for instance, assault, battery, and intentional infliction of emotional distress—usually forms the basis for such liability. In more severe cases, the student perpetrator may also become subject to criminal liability—for instance, under a stalking law, a sexual assault law, a rape law, a hate crime law, or a criminal anti-hazing law. Some laws, especially federal and state civil rights laws, may also make the institution liable to the student victim in some circumstances in which the institution has supported, condoned, or ignored the harassment. Under the federal Title VI statute (see Section 13.5.2), for example, the Tenth Circuit held that a victim of peer racial harassment has a private cause of action against the school if the school "intentionally allowed and nurtured a racially hostile educational environment" by being deliberately indifferent to incidents of peer harassment of which it was aware (*Bryant v. Independent School District No. I-38 of Gavin County,* 334 F.3d 928 (10th Cir. 2003)). And under the federal Title IX statute (see Section 13.5.3 of this book), another court held that a peer harassment victim had a cause of action against the institution where she was raped by another student if she remained "vulnerable" to possible future harassment by the perpetrator due to the institution's unwillingness to provide "academic and residential accommodations" pending the perpetrator's disciplinary hearing (*Kelly v. Yale University,* 2003 WL 1563424, 2003 U.S. Dist. LEXIS 4543 (D. Conn. 2003)).

The rest of this subsection focuses on peer sexual harassment under Title IX, the statute under which most of the litigation regarding peer harassment has occurred. This material should be read in conjunction with the material in Section 9.3.4 on faculty harassment of students. The definitions, examples, legal standards, and types of challenges addressed in that Section apply, for the most part, to peer harassment as well. As Section 9.3.4 indicates, *Franklin v. Gwinnett County Public Schools,* 503 U.S. 60 (1992), was the U.S. Supreme Court's first look at student sexual harassment claims under Title IX. But since *Franklin* concerned a faculty member's harassment of a student, it did not address or resolve issues concerning peer sexual harassment or an educational institution's liability to victims of such harassment. These questions were extensively discussed in the lower courts after *Franklin,* however; and as with questions about an institution's liability for faculty harassment, the courts took varying approaches to the problem, ranging from no liability at all (see *Davis v. Monroe County Board of Education,* 120 F.3d 1390 (11th Cir. 1997) (*en banc*)) to liability whenever the institution "knew or should have known" of the harassment (see *Doe v. Petaluma City School District,* 949 F. Supp. 1415 (N.D. Cal. 1996)). The U.S. Department of Education (ED) also addressed peer harassment and related liability issues in its document, *Sexual Harassment Guidance: Harassment of Students by School Employees, Other Students, or Third Parties,* 62 Fed. Reg. 12034 (March 13, 1997). Regarding peer sexual harassment, this Guidance stated that an institution would be liable under Title IX for a student's sexual harassment of another student if: "(i) a hostile environment exists in the school's programs or activities, (ii) the school knows or should have known of the harassment, and (iii) the school fails to take immediate and appropriate corrective action" (62 Fed. Reg. at 12039). The Guidance also addressed how a school or college may avoid Title IX liability for peer harassment:

> [I]f, upon notice of hostile environment harassment, a school takes immediate and appropriate steps to remedy the hostile environment, the school has avoided violating Title IX. . . . Title IX does not make a school responsible for the actions of harassing students, but rather for its own discrimination in failing to remedy it once the school has notice [62 Fed. Reg. at 12039–40].

In *Gebser v. Lago Vista Independent School District,* 524 U.S. 274 (1998), in a hotly contested 5-to-4 decision, the U.S. Supreme Court established an "actual knowledge" and "deliberate indifference" standard of liability for faculty harassment of a student. (For further discussion of this case, see Section 9.3.4.) It was not clear whether this standard would also apply to an institution's liability for peer harassment. One year later, in *Davis v. Monroe County Board of Education,* 526 U.S. 629 (1999), the Court relieved the uncertainty. In another 5-to-4 decision, the Court majority held that an educational institution's Title IX damages liability for peer harassment is based upon the same standard that the Court had established in *Gebser* to govern liability for faculty harassment:

> We consider here whether the misconduct identified in *Gebser*—deliberate indifference to known acts of harassment—amounts to an intentional violation of Title IX, capable of supporting a private damages action, when the harasser is a student rather than a teacher. We conclude that, in certain limited circumstances, it does [526 U.S. at 643].

The Court took considerable pains to develop the "limited circumstances" that must exist before a school will be liable for peer sexual harassment. First, the school must have "substantial control over both the harasser and the context in which the known harassment occurs" (526 U.S. at 645). Second, the sexual harassment must be "severe, pervasive, and objectively offensive":

> [A] plaintiff must establish sexual harassment of students that is so severe, pervasive, and objectively offensive, and that so undermines and detracts from the victims' educational experience, that the victim-students are effectively denied equal access to an institution's resources and opportunities. Cf. *Meritor Savings Bank, FSB v. Vinson,* 477 U.S. at 57, 67 (1986).

* * * *

> Moreover, the [Title IX requirement] that the discrimination occur "under any education program or activity" suggests that the behavior be serious enough to have the systemic effect of denying the victim equal access to an educational program or activity. Although, in theory, a single instance of sufficiently severe

one-on-one peer harassment could be said to have such an effect, we think it unlikely that Congress would have thought such behavior sufficient to rise to this level in light of the inevitability of student misconduct and the amount of litigation that would be invited by entertaining claims of official indifference to a single instance of one-on-one peer harassment. By limiting private damages actions to cases having a systemic effect on educational programs or activities, we reconcile the general principle that Title IX prohibits official indifference to known peer sexual harassment with the practical realities of responding to student behavior, realities that Congress could not have meant to be ignored [526 U.S. at 651, 652–53].

Speaking for the four dissenters, Justice Kennedy issued a sharply worded and lengthy dissent. In somewhat overblown language, he asserted:

I can conceive of few interventions more intrusive upon the delicate and vital relations between teacher and student, between student and student, and between the State and its citizens than the one the Court creates today by its own hand. Trusted principles of federalism are superseded by a more contemporary imperative. . . .

Today's decision mandates to teachers instructing and supervising their students the dubious assistance of federal court plaintiffs and their lawyers and makes the federal courts the final arbiters of school policy and of almost every disagreement between students. [526 U.S. at 685, 686 (Kennedy, J., dissenting)].

By highlighting the "limiting circumstances" that confine a school's liability, and adding them to those already articulated in *Gebser,* the Court in *Davis* appears to create a four-part standard for determining when an educational institution would be liable in damages for peer sexual harassment. The four elements are:

1. The institution must have "actual knowledge" of the harassment;
2. The institution must have responded (or failed to respond) to the harassment with "deliberate indifference," which the *Davis* Court defines as a response that is "clearly unreasonable in light of the known circumstances" (526 U.S. at 648);
3. The institution must have had "substantial control" over the student harasser and the context of the harassment; and
4. The harassment must have been "severe, pervasive, and objectively offensive" to an extent that the victim of the harassment was in effect deprived of educational opportunities or services.

The Court in *Davis* did not address the question of who within the institution must have received notice of the harassment or whether this individual must have authority to initiate corrective action—both factors emphasized in *Gebser.* Presumably, however, these factors would transfer over from *Gebser* to the peer harassment context and become part of the actual knowledge element—the first part of the four-part *Davis* standard.

The *Davis* standard of liability, therefore, is based upon but is not identical to the *Gebser* standard. The Court has added additional considerations into the *Davis* analysis that tend to make it even more difficult for a victim to establish a claim of peer harassment than to establish a claim of faculty harassment. As the Court noted near the end of its opinion in *Davis*:

> The fact that it was a teacher who engaged in harassment in . . . *Gebser* is relevant. The relationship between the harasser and the victim necessarily affects the extent to which the misconduct can be said to breach Title IX's guarantee of equal access to educational benefits and to have a systemic effect on a program or activity. Peer harassment, in particular, is less likely to satisfy these requirements than is teacher-student harassment [526 U.S. at 653].

The *Davis* Court's emphasis on *control* also suggests that peer harassment claims will be even more difficult to establish in higher education litigation than they are in elementary/secondary litigation. The majority opinion indicates that institutional control over the harasser and the context of the harassment is a key to liability, that the control element of the liability standard "is sufficiently flexible to account . . . for the level of disciplinary authority available to the school," and that "[a] university [would not] . . . be expected to exercise the same degree of control over its students" as would elementary schools (526 U.S. at 649). It should follow that colleges and universities, in general, have less risk of money damages liability under Title IX for peer harassment than do elementary and secondary schools because they exert less control over students and over the educational environment.

Davis and the lower court litigation that has followed, however, is not the last or only word for institutions regarding peer sexual harassment under Title IX. Subsequent to *Davis* (and *Gebser*), the U.S. Department of Education reconsidered and reaffirmed the Title IX guidelines on sexual harassment that it had originally promulgated in 1997. (See *Revised Sexual Harassment Guidance: Harassment of Students by School Employers, Other Students, or Third Parties,* 66 Fed. Reg. 5512 (January, 19, 2001), also available at http://www.wd.gov/offices/OCR/archives/shguide/index.html.) This Revised Guidance, which applies to all the department's Title IX enforcement activities involving sexual harassment, was accompanied by substantial commentary (including commentary on the case law) prepared by the department. The Guidance and commentary provide colleges and universities with a detailed blueprint for complying with their Title IX responsibilities regarding peer sexual harassment.

Sec. 8.2. Admissions

8.2.1. Basic legal requirements.
Postsecondary institutions have traditionally been accorded wide discretion in formulating admissions standards. The law's deference to institutional decision making stems from the notion that tampering with admissions criteria is tampering with the expertise of educators. In the latter part of the twentieth century, however, some doorways were

opened in the wall of deference, as dissatisfied applicants successfully pressed the courts for relief, and legislatures and administrative agencies sought to regulate certain aspects of the admissions process.

Institutions are subject to three main constraints in formulating and applying admissions policies: (1) the selection process must not be arbitrary or capricious; (2) the institution may be bound, under a contract theory, to adhere to its published admissions standards and to honor its admissions decisions; and (3) the institution may not have admissions policies that unjustifiably discriminate on the basis of characteristics such as race, sex, disability, age, residence, or citizenship. These constraints are discussed in subsections 8.2.2 to 8.2.4 below.

Although institutions are also constrained in the admissions process by the Family Education and Privacy Rights Act (FERPA) regulations on education records (Section 9.7.1), the regulations have only limited applicability to admissions records. The regulations do not apply to the records of persons who are not or have not been students at the institution; thus, admissions records are not covered until the applicant has been accepted and is in attendance at the institution (34 C.F.R. §§ 99.1(d), 99.3 ("student")). The institution may also maintain the confidentiality of letters of recommendation if the student has waived the right of access; such a waiver may be sought during the application process (34 C.F.R. § 99.12). Moreover, when a student from one component unit of an institution applies for admission to another unit of the same institution, the student is treated as an applicant rather than as a student with respect to the second unit's admissions records; those records are therefore not subject to FERPA until the student is in attendance in the second unit (34 C.F.R. § 99.5).

Students applying to public institutions may also assert constitutional claims based on the due process clause of the Fourteenth Amendment. In *Phelps v. Washburn University of Topeka,* 634 F. Supp. 556 (D. Kan. 1986), for example, the plaintiffs asserted procedural due process claims regarding a grievance process available to rejected applicants. The court ruled that the plaintiffs had no property interest in being admitted to the university, thus defeating their due process claims. And in *Martin v. Helstad,* 578 F. Supp. 1473 (W.D. Wis. 1983), the plaintiff sued a law school that had revoked its acceptance of his application when it learned that he had neglected to include on his application that he had been convicted of a felony and incarcerated. The court held that, although the applicant was entitled to minimal procedural due process to respond to the school's charge that he had falsified information on his application, the school had provided him sufficient due process in allowing him to explain his nondisclosure. (For a more recent example of the withdrawal of admission for an otherwise qualified applicant for failure to report a criminal offense, see Fox Butterfield, "Woman Who Killed Mother Denied Harvard Admission," *New York Times,* April 8, 1995, p. 1.)

Falsification of information on an application may also be grounds for later discipline or expulsion. In *North v. West Virginia Board of Regents,* 332 S.E.2d 141 (W. Va. 1985), a medical student provided false information on his application concerning his grade point average, courses taken, degrees, birth date, and marital status. The court upheld the expulsion on two theories: that the student had breached the university's disciplinary code (even though he was not a student at the time) and that the student had committed fraud.

8.2.2. Arbitrariness.
The "arbitrariness" standard of review is the one most protective of the institution's prerogatives. The cases reflect a judicial hands-off attitude toward any admissions decision arguably based on academic qualifications. Under the arbitrariness standard, the court will overturn an institution's decision only if there is no reasonable explanation for its actions. *Lesser v. Board of Education of New York*, 239 N.Y.S.2d 776 (N.Y. App. Div. 1963), provides a classic example. Lesser sued Brooklyn College after being rejected because his grade point average was below the cut-off. He argued that the college acted arbitrarily and unreasonably in not considering that he had been enrolled in a demanding high school honors program. The court declined to overturn the judgment of the college, stating that discretionary decisions of educational institutions, particularly those related to determining the eligibility of applicants, should be left to the institutions.

The court in *Arizona Board of Regents v. Wilson*, 539 P.2d 943 (Ariz. Ct. App. 1975), expressed similar sentiments. In that case a woman was refused admission to the graduate school of art at the University of Arizona because the faculty did not consider her art work to be of sufficiently high quality. She challenged the admissions process on the basis that it was a rolling admissions system with no written guidelines. The court entered judgment in favor of the university:

> This case represents a prime example of when a court should not interfere in the academic program of a university. It was incumbent upon appellee to show that her rejection was in bad faith, or arbitrary, capricious, or unreasonable. The court may not substitute its own opinions as to the merits of appellee's work for that of the members of the faculty committee who were selected to make a determination as to the quality of her work [539 P.2d at 946].

Another court, in considering whether a public university's refusal to admit a student to veterinary school involved constitutional protections, rejected arbitrariness claims based on the due process and equal protection clauses. In *Grove v. Ohio State University*, 424 F. Supp. 377 (S.D. Ohio 1976), the plaintiff, denied admission to veterinary school three times, argued that the use of a score from a personal interview introduced subjective factors into the admissions decision process that were arbitrary and capricious, thus depriving him of due process. Second, he claimed that the admission of students less well qualified than he deprived him of equal protection. And third, he claimed that a professor had told him he would be admitted if he took additional courses.

Citing *Roth* (Section 6.7.2), the court determined that the plaintiff had a liberty interest in pursuing veterinary medicine. The court then examined the admissions procedure and concluded that, despite its subjective element, it provided sufficient due process protections. The court deferred to the academic judgment of the admissions committee with regard to the weight that should be given to the interview score. The court also found no property interest, since the plaintiff had no legitimate entitlement to a space in a class of 130 when more than 900 individuals had applied.

The court rejected the plaintiff's second and third claims as well. The plaintiff had not raised discrimination claims, but had asserted that the admission of students with lower grades was a denial of equal protection. The court stated: "This Court is reluctant to find that failure to adhere exactly to an admissions formula constitutes a denial of equal protection" (424 F. Supp. at 387), citing *Bakke* (see Section 8.2.5). Nor did the professor's statement that the plaintiff would be reconsidered for admission if he took additional courses constitute a promise to admit him once he completed the courses.

The review standards in these cases establish a formidable barrier for disappointed applicants to cross. But occasionally someone succeeds. *State ex rel. Bartlett v. Pantzer*, 489 P.2d 375 (Mont. 1971), arose after the admissions committee of the University of Montana Law School had advised an applicant that he would be accepted if he completed a course in financial accounting. He took such a course and received a D. The law school refused to admit him, claiming that a D was an "acceptable" but not a "satisfactory" grade. The student argued that it was unreasonable for the law school to inject a requirement of receiving a "satisfactory grade" after he had completed the course. The court agreed, saying that the applicant was otherwise qualified for admission and that to make a distinction between "acceptable" and "satisfactory" was an abuse of institutional discretion.

All these cases involve public institutions; whether their principles would apply to private institutions is unclear. The "arbitrary and capricious" standard apparently arises from concepts of due process and administrative law that are applicable only to public institutions. Courts may be even less receptive to arbitrariness arguments lodged against private schools, although common law may provide some relief even here. In *Levine v. George Washington University* and *Paulsen v. Golden Gate University* (Section 8.2.6), for example, common law principles protected students at private institutions against arbitrary interpretation of institutional policy.

The cases discussed in this Section demonstrate that, if the individuals and groups who make admissions decisions adhere carefully to their published (or unwritten) criteria,[9] give individual consideration to every applicant, and provide reasonable explanations for the criteria they use, judicial review will be deferential.

8.2.3. The contract theory.
Students who are accepted for admission, but whose admission is reversed by the institution through no fault of the student,

---

[9]A case from the Alaska Supreme Court suggests that an institution may use additional admissions criteria if they are supported by an appropriate academic rationale. In *Hunt v. University of Alaska at Fairbanks*, 52 P.3d 739 (Alaska 2002), the court rejected a student's claim that requiring him to take a standardized test (which he did not pass) in addition to fulfilling all published admission requirements was arbitrary and capricious. The court disagreed, stating that, because the student could not meet the published criteria, the university had given him an additional mechanism to demonstrate that he was qualified for admission.

have met with some success in stating breach of contract claims. For example, the plaintiffs in *Eden v. Board of Trustees of the State University*, 374 N.Y.S.2d 686 (N.Y. App. Div. 1975), had been accepted for admission to a new school of podiatry being established at the State University of New York (SUNY) at Stony Brook. Shortly before the scheduled opening, the state suspended its plans for the school, citing fiscal pressures in state government. The students argued that they had a contract with SUNY entitling them to instruction in the podiatry school. The court agreed that SUNY's "acceptance of the petitioners' applications satisfies the classic requirements of a contract." Though the state could legally abrogate its contracts when necessary in the public interest to alleviate a fiscal crisis, and though "the judicial branch . . . must exercise restraint in questioning executive prerogative," the court nevertheless ordered the state to enroll the students for the ensuing academic year. The court found that a large federal grant as well as tuition money would be lost if the school did not open, that the school's personnel were already under contract and would have to be paid anyway, and that postponement of the opening therefore would not save money. Since the fiscal crisis would not be alleviated, the state's decision was deemed "arbitrary and capricious" and a breach of contract.

An Illinois appellate court ruled that a combination of oral promises, past practice, written promises, and a lack of notice about a change in admission standards constituted an implied promise to admit ten students to the Chicago Medical School. In *Brody v. Finch University of Health Sciences/Chicago Medical School*, 698 N.E.2d 257 (Ill. App. 1998), the plaintiffs had enrolled in a master's degree program in applied physiology because they had been promised, both orally and in the college's written documents, that they would be admitted to the medical school if they earned a 3.0 average or better. They had also been told that the college had followed this practice for several years. The year that the plaintiffs applied to the medical school, however, the school changed its practice of accepting all qualified graduates from the applied physiology program, and instead admitted only the top fifty. Six of the plaintiffs had received letters stating that they had been admitted, while the remaining plaintiffs had been told orally that they would be admitted. But the plaintiffs were not admitted and were not advised of this until shortly before the program was to begin. Some of the plaintiffs had resigned from their jobs and moved to Chicago; many had signed housing leases; and several had given up opportunities for study at other medical colleges.

The trial court ruled that the combination of the written statements, the oral promises, and the college's past practice created an implied contract, and that the college's determination two weeks prior to the beginning of the program to admit only fifty students from the applied physiology program was arbitrary and capricious. The college had made no effort to contact the students who were not admitted, and they had reasonably relied on the representations of college employees, written documents from previous years, and the college's past practice of admitting all applicants with a 3.0 or better grade point average. The appellate court affirmed, endorsing the trial court's analysis. (The applicants' state law consumer fraud cause of action had been rejected by the trial court because they had not addressed consumer protection issues in their complaint; the appellate court affirmed on this claim as well.)

But students relying on alleged promises by a faculty member that their admission is assured have been less successful. In *Keles v. Yale University*, 889 F. Supp. 729 (S.D.N.Y. 1995), *affirmed without opinion*, 101 F.3d 108 (2d Cir. 1996), the plaintiff sought admission to the graduate program in mechanical engineering at Yale University. He was rejected twice. He then contacted a professor in the department, seeking his assistance. The professor agreed to give the plaintiff a position as a research assistant and, "if things worked out," to write a letter of support for his third attempt to be admitted to the program. At the time of this agreement, the professor advised the student, who had been admitted to a graduate program at another university, to accept that offer rather than to take his chances on an uncertain outcome at Yale.

The plaintiff worked as a research assistant for the professor, who became dissatisfied with the plaintiff's work and refused to write the letter of support. He did, however, continue the plaintiff's appointment as a research assistant and paid the tuition for a course the plaintiff enrolled in, although he again recommended that the plaintiff seek admission to programs at other institutions. In the interim, the plaintiff applied to the Yale program and was rejected two more times. He filed claims for breach of contract and fraudulent inducement, claiming that the promises made by the professor were an oral contract promising to admit him to the graduate program.

The court noted that the professor had twice recommended that the plaintiff apply to other graduate programs and ruled that the breach of contract claims were clearly refuted by documentary evidence. Given the clarity of the professor's written agreements with the plaintiff, the court ruled that it was unreasonable for the plaintiff to believe that he had been admitted to the program. Determining that the professor and other Yale representatives had acted reasonably, the court rejected the plaintiff's claim that their actions had been arbitrary or in bad faith. The court granted summary judgment on all but one of the claims, and dismissed the remaining claim because the damages sought were less than $50,000, which is the jurisdictional threshold for diversity jurisdiction. The court also sanctioned the plaintiff's attorney for bringing frivolous claims. The appellate court affirmed without comment.

Despite the positive outcome for the university, this case serves as a warning to faculty and administrators concerning offers of assistance with admission, or representations about admission, that are made to students or potential students. It is important that admissions materials and student catalogs make clear who has the authority to admit students to a program, and the criteria that will be used to make admissions decisions. Offers to write letters of support or provide other assistance with admission should be carefully stated and limited as the Yale professor did. The temporary nature of an employment relationship with a potential student, such as the plaintiff in this case, should be made clear in a letter or similar document that specifies the terms of the individual's appointment; and in states where oral promises are contractually binding, faculty and administrators should specify that the written agreement is the entire

758 The Student-Institution Relationship

agreement between the parties. A statement in the college catalog or other official policy document that offers of admission are only official when made in
writing by the institution will help prevent claims by disappointed applicants
that oral representations by faculty or staff should be binding on the institution.

Thus, the contract theory clearly applies to both public and private schools,
although, as *Eden* suggests, public institutions may have defenses not available to private schools. While the contract theory does not require administrators to adopt or to forgo any particular admissions standard, it does require that
administrators honor their acceptance decisions once made and honor their
published policies in deciding whom to accept and to reject. Administrators
should thus carefully review their published admissions policies and any new
policies to be published. The institution may wish to omit standards and
criteria from its policies in order to avoid being pinned down under the contract theory. Conversely, the institution may decide that full disclosure is the
best policy. In either case, administrators should make sure that published
admissions policies state only what the institution is willing to abide by. If the
institution needs to reserve the right to depart from or supplement its published
policies, such reservation should be clearly inserted, with counsel's assistance,
into all such policies.

8.2.4. The principle of nondiscrimination

8.2.4.1. Race. It is clear under the Fourteenth Amendment's equal protection
clause that, in the absence of a "compelling state interest" (see Section 8.2.5),
no public institution may discriminate in admissions on the basis of race. The
leading case is *Brown v. Board of Education,* 347 U.S. 483 (1954), which,
although it concerned elementary and secondary schools, clearly applies to postsecondary education as well. The Supreme Court affirmed its relevance to higher
education in *Florida ex rel. Hawkins v. Board of Control,* 350 U.S. 413 (1956).
Cases involving postsecondary education have generally considered racial segregation within a state postsecondary system rather than within a single institution, and suits have been brought under Title VI of the Civil Rights Act of 1964
as well as the Constitution. These cases are discussed in Section 13.5.2.

Although most of the racial segregation cases focus on a broad array of
issues, a decision by the U.S. Supreme Court addressed admissions issues,
among others. In *United States v. Fordice,* 505 U.S. 717 (1992), private plaintiffs
and the U.S. Department of Justice asserted that the Mississippi public higher
education system was segregated, in violation of both the U.S. Constitution and
Title VI of the Civil Rights Act of 1964. Although a federal trial judge had found
the state system to be in compliance with both Title VI and the Constitution, a
federal appellate court and the U.S. Supreme Court disagreed. (This case is discussed in Section 13.5.2.)

Justice White, writing for a unanimous Court, found that the state's higher
education system retained vestiges of its prior *de jure* segregation. With regard
to admissions, Justice White cited the state's practice (initiated in 1963, just
prior to Title VI's taking effect) of requiring all applicants for admission to the
three flagship universities (which were predominantly white) to have a

minimum composite score of 15 on the American College Testing (ACT) Program. Testimony had demonstrated that the average ACT score for white students was 18, and the average ACT score for African American students was 7. Justice White wrote: "Without doubt, these requirements restrict the range of choices of entering students as to which institution they may attend in a way that perpetuates segregation" (505 U.S. at 734).

These admissions standards were particularly revealing of continued segregation, according to Justice White, when one considered that institutions given the same mission within the state (regional universities) had different admissions standards, depending on the race of the predominant student group. For example, predominantly white regional universities had ACT requirements of 18 or 15, compared to minimum requirements of 13 at the predominantly black universities. Because the differential admissions standards were "remnants of the dual system with a continuing discriminatory effect" (505 U.S. at 736), the state was required to articulate an educational reason for those disparities, and it had not done so.

Furthermore, the institutions looked only at ACT scores and did not consider high school grades as a mitigating factor for applicants who could not meet the minimum ACT score. The gap between the grades of African American and white applicants was narrower than the gap between their ACT scores, "suggesting that an admissions formula which included grades would increase the number of black students eligible for automatic admission to all of Mississippi's public universities" (505 U.S. at 737). Although the state had argued that grade inflation and the lack of comparability among high schools' course offerings and grading practices made grades an unreliable indicator, the Court dismissed that argument:

> In our view, such justification is inadequate because the ACT was originally adopted for discriminatory purposes, the current requirement is traceable to that decision and seemingly continues to have segregative effects, and the State has so far failed to show that the "ACT-only" admission standard is not susceptible to elimination without eroding sound educational policy [505 U.S. at 737–38].

The use of high school grades as well as scores on standardized tests is common in higher education admissions decisions, and the state's attempt to rely solely on ACT scores was an important element of the Court's finding of continued segregation.

Although most challenges to allegedly discriminatory admissions requirements have come from African American students, Asian and Latino students have filed challenges as well. In *United States v. League of United Latin American Citizens*, 793 F.2d 636 (5th Cir. 1986), African American and Latino college students raised Title VI and constitutional challenges to the state's requirement that college students pass a reading and mathematics skills test before enrolling in more than six hours of professional education courses at Texas public institutions. Passing rates on these tests were substantially lower for minority students than for white, non-Latino students.

Although the trial court had enjoined the practice, the appellate court vacated the injunction, noting that the state had validated the tests and that they were appropriate: "The State's duty . . . to eliminate the vestiges of past discrimination would indeed be violated were it to thrust upon minority students, both as role models and as pedagogues, teachers whose basic knowledge and skills were inferior to those required of majority race teachers" (793 F.2d at 643).

In response to the students' equal protection claim, the court found that the state had demonstrated a compelling interest in teacher competency and that the test was a valid predictor of success in the courses. Because the students could retake the test until they passed it, their admission was only delayed, not denied. In response to the students' liberty interest claim, the court found a valid liberty interest in pursuing a chosen profession, but also found that the state could require a reasonable examination for entry into that profession.

Latino students and civil rights groups also challenged the state's funding for public colleges and universities located near the Mexican border, arguing that they were more poorly funded because of their high proportion of Latino students. A jury, applying the state constitution's requirement of equal access to education, found that the state higher education system did not provide equal access to citizens in southern Texas, although it also found that state officials had not discriminated against these persons (K. Mangan, "Texas Jury Faults State on Equal Access to Top Universities," *Chron. Higher Educ.*, November 27, 1991, A25). A state court judge later ordered the state to eliminate the funding inequities among state institutions (K. Mangan, "9 State Colleges in South Texas to Get Massive Budget Increase," *Chron. Higher Educ.*, June 23, 1993, A23). But in *Richards v. League of United Latin American Citizens*, 868 S.W.2d 306 (Tex. 1993), the Texas Supreme Court ruled later that year that allegedly inequitable resource allocation to predominantly Hispanic public colleges did not violate students' equal protection rights.

Asian students have challenged the admissions practices of several institutions, alleging that the institutions either have "quotas" limiting the number of Asians who may be admitted or that they exclude Asians from minority admissions programs. Complaints filed with the Education Department's Office for Civil Rights (OCR), which enforces Title VI (see Section 13.5.2), have resulted in changes in admissions practices at both public and private colleges and universities. (For a discussion of this issue, see Note, "Assuring Equal Access of Asian Americans to Highly Selective Universities," 90 *Yale L.J.* 659 (1989).)

In addition to the Constitution's equal protection clause and the desegregation criteria developed under Title VI, there are two other major legal bases for attacking racial discrimination in higher education. The first is the civil rights statute called "Section 1981" (42 U.S.C. § 1981) (discussed in Section 5.2.4 of this book). A post–Civil War statute guaranteeing the freedom to contract, Section 1981 has particular significance because (like Title VI) it applies to private as well as public institutions. In the leading case of *Runyon v. McCrary*, 427 U.S. 160 (1976), the U.S. Supreme Court used Section 1981 to prohibit two private, white elementary schools from discriminating against blacks in their admissions policies. Since the Court has applied Section 1981 to discrimination against white persons as well as blacks (*McDonald v. Santa Fe Trail Transportation Co.*, 427 U.S. 273 (1976)), this statute would also apparently prohibit predominantly minority private institutions from discriminating in admissions against white students. (For an example of a challenge to a denial of admission to graduate school brought under both Title VI and Section 1981, see *Woods v. The Wright Institute,* 1998 U.S. App. LEXIS 6012 (9th Cir., March 24, 1998) (using subjective judgments as one of several criteria for admissions is not racially discriminatory).)

Section 1981 was used in a successful challenge to the racially exclusive policy of the Kamehameha Schools in Hawaii. The schools had been established under the will of Princess Bernice Pauahi Bishop, the last direct descendant of King Kamehameha I. Her will directed that private, nonsectarian schools be established, and three such schools now exist, none of which receives federal funds. Although the will did not direct that applicants of Hawaiian descent be preferred, the trustees of the trust created by her will directed that native Hawaiians be preferred, which meant that, unless there were space available, only individuals of Hawaiian descent would be admitted to the schools. In *Doe v. Kamehameha Schools,* 416 F.3d 1025 (9th Cir. 2005), a white student challenged the admissions policy of the schools under Section 1981, suing the schools, the estate, and the trustees. Using the burden-shifting theory of the *McDonnell-Douglas* case (discussed in Section 5.2.1), the court ruled that the schools' policy acted as an absolute bar to admission on the basis of race, and thus violated Section 1981. Because the will had not specified racial criteria for admissions, the court upheld the lower court's award of summary judgment for the estate and the trustees.

Another mechanism for attacking race discrimination in admissions is federal income tax law. In Revenue Ruling 71-447, 1971-2 C.B. 230 (*Cumulative Bulletin,* an annual multivolume compilation of various tax documents published by the Internal Revenue Service (IRS)), the IRS revised its former policy and ruled that schools practicing racial discrimination were violating public policy and should be denied tax-exempt status. Other IRS rulings enlarged on this basic rule. Revenue Procedure 72-54, 1972-2 C.B. 834, requires schools to publicize their nondiscrimination policies. Revenue Procedure 75-50, 1975-2 C.B. 587, requires that a school carry the burden of "show[ing] affirmatively . . . that it has adopted a racially nondiscriminatory policy as to students" and also establishes record-keeping and other guidelines through which a school can demonstrate its compliance. And Revenue Ruling 75-231, 1975-1 C.B. 158, furnishes a series of hypothetical cases to illustrate when a church-affiliated school would be considered to be discriminating and in danger of losing tax-exempt status. The U.S. Supreme Court upheld the basic policy of Revenue Ruling 71-447 in *Bob Jones University v. United States,* 461 U.S. 574 (1983), discussed in Section 13.3.2, footnote 38 of this book.[10] A private institution must certify that it has adopted and is following a policy of nondiscrimination in order for contributions to that institution to be tax deductible. However, the Internal Revenue Service has exempted organizations that provide instruction in a skilled trade to American Indians from the nondiscrimination requirement, ruling that limiting

---

[10]Cases and materials are collected in Jean F. Rydstrom, Annot., "Allowability of Federal Tax Benefits to a Private, Racially Segregated School or College," 7 A.L.R. Fed. 548.

access to the training to American Indians was not the type of discrimination that federal law intended to prevent (Revenue Ruling 77-272, 1977-2 CB 191).

The combined impact of these various legal sources—the equal protection clause, Title VI, Section 1981, and IRS tax rulings—is clear: neither public nor private postsecondary institutions may maintain admissions policies (with a possible exception for affirmative action policies, as discussed in Section 8.2.5) that discriminate against students on the basis of race, nor may states maintain plans or practices that perpetuate racial segregation in a statewide system of postsecondary education.

8.2.4.2. Sex. Title IX of the Education Amendments of 1972 (20 U.S.C. § 1681 *et seq.*) (see Section 13.5.3 of this book) is the primary law governing sex discrimination in admissions policies. While Title IX and its implementing regulations, 34 C.F.R. Part 106, apply nondiscrimination principles to both public and private institutions receiving federal funds, there are special exemptions concerning admissions. For the purposes of applying these admissions exemptions, each "administratively separate unit" of an institution is considered a separate institution (34 C.F.R. § 106.15(b)). An "administratively separate unit" is "a school, department, or college . . . admission to which is independent of admission to any other component of such institution" (34 C.F.R. § 106.2(p)). Private undergraduate institutions are not prohibited from discriminating in admissions on the basis of sex (20 U.S.C. § 1681(a)(1); 34 C.F.R. § 106.15(d)). Nor are public undergraduate institutions that have always been single-sex institutions (20 U.S.C. § 1681(a)(5); 34 C.F.R. § 106.15(e)); but compare the *Hogan* case, discussed later in this Section). In addition, religious institutions, including all or any of their administratively separate units, may be exempted from nondiscrimination. The remaining institutions, which are prohibited from discriminating in admissions, are (1) graduate schools; (2) professional schools, unless they are part of an undergraduate institution exempted from Title IX's admissions requirements (see 34 C.F.R. § 106.2(n)); (3) vocational schools, unless they are part of an undergraduate institution exempted from Title IX's admissions requirements (see 34 C.F.R. § 106.2(o)); and (4) public undergraduate institutions that are not, or have not always been, single-sex schools.[11]

Institutions subject to Title IX admissions requirements are prohibited from treating persons differently on the basis of sex in any phase of admissions and recruitment (34 C.F.R. §§ 106.21–106.23). Specifically, Section 106.21(b) of the regulations provides that a covered institution, in its admissions process, shall not

(i) Give preference to one person over another on the basis of sex, by ranking applicants separately on such basis, or otherwise;

---

[11]The admissions exemption for private undergraduate institutions in the regulations may be broader than that authorized by the Title IX statute. For an argument that "administratively separate" professional and vocational components of private undergraduate institutions should not be exempt and that private undergraduate schools that are primarily professional and vocational in character should not be exempt, see W. Kaplin & M. McGillicuddy, "Scope of Exemption for Private Undergraduate Institutions from Admissions Requirements of Title IX," memorandum printed in 121 *Cong. Rec.* 1091 (94th Cong., 1st Sess., 1975).

(ii) Apply numerical limitations upon the number or proportion of persons
of either sex who may be admitted; or

(iii) Otherwise treat one individual differently from another on the basis of sex.

Section 106.21(c) prohibits covered institutions from treating the sexes differently in regard to "actual or potential parental, family, or marital status"; from
discriminating against applicants because of pregnancy or conditions relating
to childbirth; and from making preadmission inquiries concerning marital status.
Sections 106.22 and 106.23(b) prohibit institutions from favoring single-sex or
predominantly single-sex schools in their admissions or recruitment practices if
such practices have "the effect of discriminating on the basis of sex."

Institutions that are exempt from Title IX admissions requirements are not
necessarily free to discriminate at will on the basis of sex. Some will be caught
in the net of other statutes or of constitutional equal protection principles. A
state statute such as the Massachusetts statute prohibiting sex discrimination
in vocational training institutions may catch other exempted undergraduate programs (Mass. Gen. Laws Ann. ch. 151C, § 2A(a)). More important, the Fourteenth Amendment's equal protection clause places restrictions on public
undergraduate schools even if they are single-sex schools exempt from Title IX.

After a period of uncertainty concerning the extent to which equal protection
principles would restrict a public institution's admissions policies, the U.S.
Supreme Court considered the question in *Mississippi University for Women v.
Hogan,* 458 U.S. 718 (1982). In this case, the plaintiff challenged an admissions
policy that excluded males from a professional nursing school. Ignoring the dissenting Justices' protestations that Mississippi provided baccalaureate nursing
programs at other state coeducational institutions, the majority of five struck
down the institution's policy as unconstitutional sex discrimination. In the
process, the Court developed an important synthesis of constitutional principles
applicable to sex discrimination claims. These principles would apply not only
to admissions but also to all other aspects of a public institution's operations:

> Because the challenged policy expressly discriminates among applicants on
> the basis of gender, it is subject to scrutiny under the equal protection clause of
> the Fourteenth Amendment. . . . That this statute discriminates against males
> rather than against females does not exempt it from scrutiny or reduce the stan-
> dard of review. . . . Our decisions also establish that the party seeking to uphold
> a statute that classifies individuals on the basis of their gender must carry the
> burden of showing an "exceedingly persuasive justification" for the classifica-
> tion. . . . The burden is met only by showing at least that the classification
> serves "important governmental objectives and that the discriminatory means
> employed" are "substantially related to the achievement of those objectives"
> [citations omitted].

> Although the test for determining the validity of a gender-based classification
> is straightforward, it must be applied free of fixed notions concerning the roles
> and abilities of males and females. Care must be taken in ascertaining whether
> the statutory objective itself reflects archaic and stereotypic notions. Thus, if the
> statutory objective is to exclude or "protect" members of one gender because

they are presumed to suffer from an inherent handicap or to be innately inferior, the objective itself is illegitimate. . . .

If the state's objective is legitimate and important, we next determine whether the requisite direct, substantial relationship between objective and means is present. The purpose of requiring that close relationship is to assure that the validity of a classification is determined through reasoned analysis rather than through the mechanical application of traditional, often inaccurate, assumptions about the proper roles of men and women [458 U.S. at 723–24].

Applying the principles regarding the legitimacy and importance of the state's objective, the Court noted that the state's justification for prohibiting men from enrolling in the nursing program was to compensate for discrimination against women. On the contrary, the Court pointed out, women had never been denied entry to the nursing profession, and limiting admission to women actually per-petuated the stereotype that nursing is "women's work." The state had made no showing that women needed preferential treatment in being admitted to nursing programs, and the Court did not believe that that was the state's pur-pose in discriminating against men. And even if the state had a valid compen-satory objective, said the Court, the university's practice of allowing men to audit the classes and to take part in continuing education courses offered by the school contradicted its position that its degree programs should only be avail-able to women.

The Court's opinion on its face invalidated single-sex admissions policies only at the School of Nursing at Mississippi University for Women (MUW) and, by extension, other public postsecondary nursing schools. It is likely, however, that this reasoning would also invalidate single-sex policies in programs other than nursing and in entire institutions. The most arguable exception to this broad reading would be a single-sex policy that redresses the effects of past discrimi-nation on a professional program in which one sex is substantially underrepre-sented. But even such a compensatory policy would be a form of explicit sexual quota, which could be questioned by analogy to the racial affirmative action cases (this book, Section 8.2.5).

Whatever the remaining ambiguity about the scope of the *Hogan* decision, it will not be resolved by further litigation at the Mississippi University for Women. After the Supreme Court decision, MUW's board of trustees—perhaps anticipating a broad application of the Court's reasoning—voted to admit men to all divisions of the university.

The *Hogan* opinion provided important guidance in a challenge to the law-fulness of male-only public military colleges. In *United States v. Commonwealth of Virginia*, 766 F. Supp. 1407, *vacated*, 976 F.2d 890 (4th Cir. 1992), the U.S. Department of Justice challenged the admissions policies of the Virginia Mili-tary Institute (VMI), which admitted only men. The government claimed that those policies violated the equal protection clause (it did not include a Title IX claim, since military academies and historically single-sex institutions are exempt from Title IX). Equal protection challenges to sex discrimination require the state to demonstrate "an exceedingly persuasive justification" for the clas-sification (*Hogan*, 458 U.S. at 739). In this case the state argued that enhancing diversity by offering a distinctive single-sex military education to men was an important state interest. The district court found that the single-sex policy was justified because of the benefits of a single-sex education, and that requiring VMI to admit women would "fundamentally alter" the "distinctive ends" of the educational system (766 F. Supp. at 1411).

The appellate court vacated the district court's opinion, stating that Virginia had not articulated an important objective sufficient to overcome the burden on equal protection. While the appellate court agreed with the trial court's finding that the admission of women would materially affect several key elements of VMI's program—physical training, lack of privacy, and the adversative approach to character development—it was homogeneity of gender, not maleness, that justified the program (976 F.2d at 897). The appellate court also accepted the trial court's findings that single-sex education has important benefits. But these findings did not support the trial court's conclusion that VMI's male-only policy passed constitutional muster. Although VMI's single-gender education and "citizen-soldier" philosophy were permissible, the state's exclusion of women from such a program was not, and no other public postsecondary education institution in Virginia was devoted to educating only one gender.

The appellate court did not order VMI to admit women, but remanded the case to the district court to give Virginia the option to (1) admit women to VMI, (2) establish parallel institutions or programs for women, or (3) terminate state support for VMI. On appeal, the U.S. Supreme Court refused to hear the case (508 U.S. 946 (1993)). Following that action, the trustees of VMI voted to underwrite a military program at a neighboring private women's college, Mary Baldwin College ("Virginia Military Institute to Establish Courses at Women's College," *New York Times,* September 26, 1993, p. A26).

The U.S. Department of Justice challenged the plan, saying that it is "based on gender stereotypes," and asked the trial court to order VMI to admit women and to integrate them into its full program. After the trial judge approved the parallel program at Mary Baldwin College, a divided panel of the U.S. Court of Appeals for the Fourth Circuit affirmed, finding that providing single-gender education was a legitimate objective of the state, and that the leadership program at Mary Baldwin College was "sufficiently comparable" to the VMI program to satisfy the demands of the equal protection clause (44 F.3d 1229 (4th Cir. 1995)). The dissenting judge argued that the state's justification for excluding women from VMI was not "exceedingly persuasive," and that the women's leadership program at Mary Baldwin College did not provide substantially equal tangible and intangible educational benefits; he thus concluded that maintaining VMI as a single-sex public institution violated the equal protection clause. A petition for rehearing *en banc* was denied.

The United States again asked the Supreme Court to review the appellate court's ruling, and this time the Court agreed. In a 7-to-1 decision (Justice Thomas did not participate), the Court ruled that VMI's exclusion of women violated the equal protection clause (518 U.S. 515 (1996)). Since strict scrutiny is reserved for classifications based on race or national origin, the Court used intermediate scrutiny—which Justice Ginsburg, the author of the majority opinion, termed "skeptical scrutiny"—to analyze Virginia's claim that single-sex education provides important educational benefits. Reviewing the state's history of providing higher education for women, the Court concluded that women had first been excluded from public higher education, and then admitted to once all-male public universities, but that no public single-sex institution had been established for women, and thus the state had not provided equal benefits for women. With regard to the state's argument that VMI's adversative training method provided important educational benefits that could not be made available to women and thus their admission would "destroy" VMI's unique approach to education, the Court noted that both parties had agreed that some women could meet all of the physical standards imposed upon VMI cadets. Moreover, the experience with women cadets in the military academies suggested that the state's fear that the presence of women would force change upon VMI was based on overbroad generalizations about women as a group, rather than on an analysis of how individual women could perform.

The Court then turned to the issue of the remedy for VMI's constitutional violation. Characterizing the women's leadership program at Mary Baldwin College as "unequal in tangible and intangible facilities" and offering no opportunity for the type of military training for which VMI is famous, the Court stressed the differences between the two programs and institutions in terms of the quality of the faculty, the range of degrees offered, athletic and sports facilities, endowments, and the status of the degree earned by students. Criticizing the Fourth Circuit for applying an overly deferential standard of review that the Court characterized as one "of its own invention," the Court reversed the Fourth Circuit's decision and held that the separate program did not cure the constitutional violation.

Chief Justice Rehnquist voted with the majority but wrote a separate concurring opinion because he disagreed with Justice Ginsburg's analysis of the remedy. The "parallel program" at Mary Baldwin College was "distinctly inferior" to VMI, said Justice Rehnquist, but the state could cure the constitutional violation by providing a public institution for women that offered the "same quality of education and [was] of the same overall calibre" as VMI. Justice Rehnquist's opinion thus differs sharply from that of Justice Ginsburg, who characterized the exclusion of women as the constitutional violation, while Justice Rehnquist characterized the violation as the maintenance of an all-male institution without providing a comparable institution for women.

Justice Scalia, the sole dissenter, attacked the Court's interpretation of equal protection jurisprudence, saying that the Court had used a higher standard than the intermediate scrutiny that is typically used to analyze categories based on gender. Furthermore, stated Justice Scalia, since the Constitution does not specifically forbid distinctions based upon gender, the political process, not the courts, should be used to change state behavior. Finding that the maintenance of single-sex education is an important educational objective, Justice Scalia would have upheld the continued exclusion of women from VMI.

The only other all-male public college, the Citadel, was ordered by a panel of the U.S. Court of Appeals for the Fourth Circuit to admit a female applicant whom that college had admitted on the mistaken belief that she was male (*Faulkner v. Jones*, 10 F.3d 226 (4th Cir. 1993)). The court ordered that she be admitted as a day student, and remanded to the district court the issue of whether she could become a full member of the college's corps of cadets. On remand the trial judge ordered that she become a member of the corps of cadets. The college appealed this ruling.

The U.S. Court of Appeals for the Fourth Circuit ruled that the Citadel's refusal to admit women violated the equal protection clause, and despite the state's promise to create a military-type college for women students, the court ordered the Citadel to admit women as students (51 F.3d 440 (4th Cir. 1995), affirming the order of the trial court in 858 F. Supp. 552 (D.S.C. 1994)). Ms. Faulkner began attending classes at the Citadel, but withdrew after a few days; other women students are attending the college.

Important as *Hogan* and the VMI cases may be to the law regarding sex discrimination in admissions, they are only part of the bigger picture, which already includes Title IX. Thus, to view the law in its current state, one must look both to *Hogan/Virginia* and to Title IX. *Hogan, Virginia,* and their progeny have at least limited, and apparently undermined, the Title IX exemption for public undergraduate institutions that have always had single-sex admissions policies (20 U.S.C. § 1681(a)(5); 34 C.F.R. § 106.15(e)). Thus, the only programs and institutions that are still legally free to have single-sex admissions policies are (1) private undergraduate institutions and their constituent programs and (2) religious institutions, including their graduate, professional, and vocational programs, if they have obtained a waiver of Title IX admission requirements on religious grounds (20 U.S.C. § 1681(a)(3); 34 C.F.R. § 106.12).

The use of standardized tests in admissions decisions has been attacked as a form of sex discrimination. Some of the standardized tests used to make admission decisions—the Scholastic Aptitude Test (SAT), for example—have been challenged because of the systematic gender differences in scores. When these test scores are used as the sole criterion for decisions about admissions or awarding scholarships, they may be especially vulnerable to legal challenge. In *Sharif v. New York State Education Department* (discussed in Section 8.3.3), a federal district court ruled that this practice violated Title IX and the Fourteenth Amendment's equal protection clause. If, however, the test score is one of several criteria that are considered in admissions decisions, the courts have upheld their use, despite the gender differences in scores (see, for example, *El-Attar v. Mississippi State University,* 1994 U.S. Dist. LEXIS 21182 (N.D. Miss., September 13, 1994)). (For analysis of the potential discriminatory effects of standardized testing, see K. Connor & E. Vargyas, "The Legal Implications of Gender Bias in Standardized Testing," *Berkeley Women's L.J.* 13 (1992). See also L. Silverman, "Unnatural Selection: A Legal Analysis of the Impact of Standardized Test Use on Higher Education Resource Allocation," 23 *Loyola L.A. L. Rev.* 1433 (1990).)

In addition to Title IX, other laws include prohibitions on sex discrimination in admissions. For example, one section of the Public Health Service Act's provisions on nurse education (42 U.S.C. § 296g) prohibits the Secretary of Health and Human Services from making grants, loan guarantees, or interest subsidy payments to schools of nursing unless the schools provide "assurances satis-factory to the Secretary that the school will not discriminate on the basis of sex in the admission of individuals to its training programs."

Recent trends in student enrollment suggest that rates of undergraduate enrollment for women have bypassed those of men among low-income and sev-eral minority groups. A report published in 2003 by the American Council on Education, *Gender Equity in Higher Education*, concluded that, although men were the majority in doctoral and professional programs, and also outnumbered women in master's programs in business and engineering, white women under-graduates outnumbered white men in the 1999–2000 academic year, as did women from African American, Hispanic, and Native American ethnicities with respect to their male counterparts.

8.2.4.3. Disability. Two federal laws—Section 504 of the Rehabilitation Act of 1973 (29 U.S.C. § 794) and the Americans With Disabilities Act (ADA) (42 U.S.C. § 12101 *et seq.*)—prohibit discrimination against individuals with dis-abilities (see Section 5.2.5 of this book). Before those laws were passed, these individuals had been the subject of a few scattered federal provisions (such as 20 U.S.C. § 1684, which prohibits discrimination against blind persons by insti-tutions receiving federal funds) and a few constitutional equal protection cases (such as *PARC v. Pennsylvania*, 334 F. Supp. 1257 (E.D. Pa. 1971), which chal-lenged discrimination against disabled students by public elementary and sec-ondary schools). But none of these developments have had nearly the impact on postsecondary admissions that Section 504 and the ADA have.

As applied to postsecondary education, Section 504 generally prohibits discrimination on the basis of disability in federally funded programs and activities (see this book, Section 13.5.4). Section 104.42 of the implementing regulations, 34 C.F.R. Part 104, prohibits discrimination on the basis of disability in admissions and recruitment. This section contains several specific provisions similar to those prohibiting sex discrimination in admissions under Title IX (see this book, Section 8.2.4.2). These provisions prohibit (1) the imposition of limitations on "the number or proportion of individuals with disabilities who may be admitted" (§ 104.42(b)(1)); (2) the use of any admissions criterion or test "that has a disproportionate, adverse effect" on individuals with disabilities, unless the criterion or test, as used, is shown to predict success validly and no alternative, nondiscriminatory criterion or test is available (§ 104.42(b)(2)); and (3) any preadmission inquiry about whether the applicant has a disability, unless the recipient needs the information in order to correct the effects of past discrimination or to overcome past conditions that resulted in limited participation by people with disabilities (§§ 104.42(b)(4) & 104.42(c)).

These prohibitions apply to discrimination directed against "qualified" indi-viduals with disabilities. A disabled person is qualified, with respect to post-secondary and vocational services, if he or she "meets the academic and technical standards requisite to admission or participation in the recipient's edu-cation program or activity" (§ 104.3(l)(3)). Thus, while the regulations do not prohibit an institution from denying admission to a person with a disability who does not meet the institution's "academic and technical" admissions standards, they do prohibit an institution from denying admission on the basis of the disability as such. (After a student is admitted, however, the institution can make confidential inquiry concerning the disability (34 C.F.R. § 104.42(b)(4)); in this way the institution can obtain advance information about disabilities that may require accommodation.)

In addition to these prohibitions, the institution has an affirmative duty to ascertain that its admissions tests are structured to accommodate applicants with disabilities that impair sensory, manual, or speaking skills, unless the test is intended to measure these skills. Such adapted tests must be offered as often and in as timely a way as other admissions tests and must be "administered in facilities that, on the whole, are accessible" to people with disabilities (§ 104.42(b)(3)).

In *Southeastern Community College v. Davis,* 442 U.S. 397 (1979), the U.S. Supreme Court issued its first interpretation of Section 504. The case concerned a nursing school applicant who had been denied admission because she is deaf. The Supreme Court ruled that an "otherwise qualified handicapped individual" is one who is qualified *in spite of* (rather than except for) his disability. Since an applicant's disability is therefore relevant to his or her qualification for a specific program, Section 504 does not preclude a college or university from imposing "reasonable physical qualifications" on applicants for admission, where such qualifications are necessary for participation in the school's program. The Department of Education's regulations implementing Section 504 provide that a disabled applicant is "qualified" if he or she meets "the academic and technical standards" for admission; the Supreme Court has made it clear, however, that "technical standards" may sometimes encompass reasonable physical requirements. Under *Davis,* an applicant's failure to meet such requirements can be a legitimate ground for rejection.

The impact of *Davis* is limited, however, by the rather narrow and specific factual context in which the case arose. The plaintiff, who was severely hearing impaired, sought admission to a nursing program. It is important to emphasize that *Davis* involved admission to a professional, clinical training program. The demands of such a program, designed to train students in the practice of a profession, raise far different considerations from those involved in admission to an undergraduate or a graduate academic program, or even a nonclinically oriented professional school. The college denied her admission, believing that she would not be able to perform nursing duties in a safe manner and could not participate fully in the clinical portion of the program.

While the Court approved the imposition of "reasonable physical qualifications," it did so only for requirements that the institution can justify as necessary to the applicant's successful participation in the particular program involved. In *Davis,* the college had shown that an applicant's ability to understand speech without reliance on lip reading was necessary to ensure patient safety and to enable the student to realize the full benefit of its nursing program. For programs without clinical components, or without professional training goals, it would be much more difficult for the institution to justify such physical requirements. Even for other professional programs, the justification might be much more difficult than in *Davis*. In a law school program, for example, the safety factor would be lacking. Moreover, in most law schools, clinical training is offered as an elective rather than a required course. By enrolling only in the nonclinical courses, a deaf student would be able to complete the required program with the help of an interpreter.

Furthermore, the Court did not say that affirmative action is never required to accommodate the needs of disabled applicants. Although the Court asserted that Section 504 does not require institutions "to lower or to effect substantial modifications of standards" or to make "fundamental alteration[s] in the nature of a program," the Court did suggest that less substantial and burdensome program adjustments may sometimes be required. The Court also discussed, and did not question, the regulation requiring institutions to provide certain "auxiliary aids," such as interpreters for students with hearing impairments, to qualified students with disabilities (see Sections 8.7.3 & 13.5.4). This issue was addressed in *United States v. Board of Trustees for the University of Alabama*, 908 F.2d 740 (11th Cir. 1990), in which the court ordered the university to provide additional transportation for students with disabilities. Moreover, the Court said nothing that in any way precludes institutions from voluntarily making major program modifications for applicants who are disabled.

Several appellate court cases have applied the teachings of *Davis* to other admissions problems. The courts in these cases have refined the *Davis* analysis, especially in clarifying the burdens of proof in a discrimination suit under Section 504. In *Pushkin v. Regents of the University of Colorado*, 658 F.2d 1372 (10th Cir. 1981), the court affirmed the district court's decision that the plaintiff, a medical doctor suffering from multiple sclerosis, had been wrongfully denied admission to the university's psychiatric residency program. Agreeing that *Davis* permitted consideration of disabilities in determining whether an applicant is "otherwise qualified" for admission, the court outlined what the plaintiff had to prove in order to establish his case of discrimination:

1. The plaintiff must establish a prima facie case by showing that he was an otherwise qualified handicapped person *apart from* his handicap, and was rejected under circumstances which gave rise to the inference that his rejection was based solely on his handicap.
2. Once plaintiff establishes his prima facie case, defendants have the burden of going forward and proving that plaintiff was not an otherwise qualified handicapped person—that is, one who is able to meet all of the program's requirements *in spite of* his handicap—or that his rejection from the program was for reasons other than his handicap.
3. The plaintiff then has the burden of going forward with rebuttal evidence showing that the defendants' reasons for rejecting the plaintiff are based on misconceptions or unfounded factual conclusions, and that reasons articulated for the rejection other than the handicap encompass unjustified consideration of the handicap itself [658 F.2d at 1387].

In another post-*Davis* case, *Doe v. New York University,* 666 F.2d 761 (2d Cir. 1981), the court held that the university had not violated Section 504 when it denied readmission to a woman with a long history of "borderline personality" disorders. This court also set out the elements of the case a plaintiff must make to comply with the *Davis* reading of Section 504:

> Accordingly, we hold that in a suit under Section 504 the plaintiff may make out a prima facie case by showing that he is a handicapped person under the Act and that, although he is qualified apart from his handicap, he was denied admission or employment because of his handicap. The burden then shifts to the institution or employer to rebut the inference that the handicap was improperly taken into account by going forward with evidence that the handicap is relevant to qualifications for the position sought (cf. *Dothard v. Rawlinson,* 433 U.S. 321 . . . (1977)). The plaintiff must then bear the ultimate burden of showing by a preponderance of the evidence that in spite of the handicap he is qualified and, where the defendant claims and comes forward with some evidence that the plaintiff's handicap renders him less qualified than other successful applicants, that he is at least as well qualified as other applicants who were accepted [666 F.2d at 776–77].

The *Doe* summary of burdens of proof is articulated differently from the *Pushkin* summary, and the *Doe* court disavowed any reliance on *Pushkin.* In contrast to the *Pushkin* court, the *Doe* court determined that a defendant institution in a Section 504 case "does not have the burden, once it shows that the handicap is relevant to reasonable qualifications for readmission (or admission), of proving that . . . [the plaintiff is not an otherwise qualified handicapped person]" (666 F.2d at 777, n.7).

The *Doe* case is also noteworthy because, in deciding whether the plaintiff was "otherwise qualified," the court considered the fact that she had a recurring illness, even though it was not present at the time of the readmission decision. This was an appropriate factor to consider because the illness could reappear and affect her performance after readmission. *Doe* is thus the first major case to deal directly with the special problem of disabling conditions that are recurring or degenerative. The question posed by such a case is this: To what extent must the university assume the risk that an applicant capable of meeting program requirements at the time of admission may be incapable of fulfilling these requirements at a later date because of changes in his or her disabling conditions?

Doe makes clear that universities may weigh such risks in making admission or readmission decisions and may consider an applicant unqualified if there is "significant risk" of recurrence (or degeneration) that would incapacitate the applicant from fulfilling program requirements. This risk factor thus becomes a relevant consideration for both parties in carrying their respective burdens of proof in Section 504 litigation. In appropriate cases, where there is medical evidence for doing so, universities may respond to the plaintiff's *prima facie* case by substantiating the risk of recurrence or degeneration that would render the applicant unqualified. The plaintiff would then have to demonstrate that his condition is sufficiently stable or, if it is not, that any change during his enrollment as a student would not render him unable to complete program requirements.

In *Doherty v. Southern College of Optometry*, 862 F.2d 570 (6th Cir. 1988), a federal appellate court considered the relationship between Section 504's "otherwise qualified" requirement and the institution's duty to provide a "reasonable accommodation" for a student with a disability. The plaintiff—a student with retinitis pigmentosa (RP), which restricted his field of vision, and a neurological condition that affected his motor skills—asserted that the college should exempt him from recently introduced proficiency requirements related to the operation of optometric instruments. The student could not meet these requirements and claimed that they were a pretext for discrimination on the basis of disability, since he was "otherwise qualified" and therefore had the right to be accommodated.

In ruling for the school, the district court considered the "reasonable accommodation" inquiry to be separate from the "otherwise qualified" requirement; thus, in its view, the institution was obligated to accommodate only a student with a disability who has already been determined to be "otherwise qualified." The appeals court disagreed, indicating that the "inquiry into reasonable accommodation is one aspect of the 'otherwise qualified' analysis" (862 F.2d at 577). To explain the relationship, the court quoted from *Brennan v. Stewart*, 834 F.2d 1248, 1261–62 (5th Cir. 1988):

> "[I]t is clear that the phrase 'otherwise qualified' has a paradoxical quality; on the one hand, it refers to a person who has the abilities or characteristics sought by the [institution]: but on the other, it cannot refer only to those already capable of meeting all the requirements—or else no reasonable requirement could ever violate Section 504, no matter how easy it would be to accommodate handicapped individuals who cannot fulfill it. This means that we can no longer take literally the assertion of *Davis* that 'an otherwise qualified person is one who is able to meet all of a program's requirements in spite of his handicap.' The question . . . is the rather mushy one of whether some 'reasonable accommodation' is available to satisfy the legitimate interests of both the [institution] and the handicapped person" [862 F.2d at 575].

The appellate court's interpretation did not change the result in the case; since the proficiency requirements were reasonably necessary to the practice of optometry, waiver of these requirements would not have been a "reasonable accommodation." But the court's emphasis on the proper relationship between the "otherwise qualified" and "reasonable accommodation" inquiries does serve to clarify and strengthen the institution's obligation to accommodate the particular needs of students with disabilities.

Students alleging discrimination on the basis of disability may file a complaint with the Education Department's Office for Civil Rights, or they may file a private lawsuit and receive compensatory damages (*Tanberg v. Weld County Sheriff*, 787 F. Supp. 970 (D. Colo. 1992)). Section 504 does not, however, provide a private right of action against the Secretary of Education, who enforces Section 504 (*Salvador v. Bennett*, 800 F.2d 97 (7th Cir. 1986)).

The provisions of the ADA are similar in many respects to those of Section 504, upon which, in large part, it was based. In addition to employment (see this book, Section 5.2.5), Title II of the ADA prohibits discrimination in access to services or programs of a public entity (such as a public college or university), and Title III prohibits discrimination in access to places of public accommodation (such as private and public colleges and universities). A rejected applicant could file an ADA claim under either Title II (against a public college) or Title III (against both public and private colleges).

The ADA specifies ten areas in which colleges and universities may not discriminate against a qualified individual with a disability: eligibility criteria; modifications of policies, practices, and procedures; auxiliary aids and services; examinations and courses; removal of barriers in existing facilities; alternatives to barriers in existing facilities; personal devices and services; assistive technology; seating in assembly areas; and transportation services (28 C.F.R. §§ 36.301–10). The law also addresses accessibility issues for new construction or renovation of existing facilities (28 C.F.R. §§ 36.401–6). The law is discussed more fully in Section 13.5.4 of this book.

The law's language regarding "eligibility criteria" means that in their admissions or placement tests or other admission-related activities, colleges and universities must accommodate the needs of applicants or students with disabilities. For example, one court held that, under Section 504, the defendant medical school must provide a dyslexic student with alternate exams unless it could demonstrate that its rejection of all other testing methods was based on rational reasons (*Wynne v. Tufts University School of Medicine,* 932 F.2d 19 (1st Cir. 1991), discussed in Section 9.3.5).

Students with learning disabilities are protected by both Section 504 and the ADA, and legal challenges by such students are on the rise. For example, in *Fruth v. New York University,* 2 A.D. Cases 1197 (S.D.N.Y. 1993), a student with learning disabilities challenged the university's decision to rescind his acceptance because he had failed to attend a required summer orientation session for students with learning disabilities. Relying heavily on *Doe v. New York University* (discussed above), the court ruled that, since the student's grades were lower than the university's required grade point average, the university's insistence that the student attend the summer program was reasonable and not in violation of the ADA.

State courts have looked to ADA jurisprudence in interpreting state law prohibitions against disability discrimination. An illustrative case is *Ohio Civil Rights Commission v. Case Western Reserve University,* 666 N.E.2d 1376 (Ohio 1996). The plaintiff, Cheryl Fischer, an applicant to the Case Western Reserve (CWR) medical school, had become totally blind during her junior year at CWR. CWR had provided Fischer with several accommodations as an undergraduate, including lab assistants and readers, oral examinations instead of written ones, extended exam periods, and books on tape. Fischer graduated *cum laude* from CWR.

All U.S. medical schools belong to the Association of American Medical Colleges (AAMC), which requires candidates for a medical degree to be able to "observe" both laboratory demonstrations and patient appearance and behavior. Despite Fischer's excellent academic record, CWR's medical school admissions committee determined that she did not meet the AAMC requirements because she was unable to see, and that she would be unable to complete the requirements of the medical school curriculum. Fischer reapplied the following year and again was denied admission. She filed a complaint under the Ohio nondiscrimination law with the Ohio Civil Rights Commission (OCRC), which found probable cause to believe that CWR had discriminated against Fischer. A county court affirmed the OCRC, but a state appellate court reversed, holding that CWR would be required to modify its program in order to accommodate Fischer's disability, which the law did not require. The Supreme Court of Ohio affirmed.

The Ohio Civil Rights Commission, which had found for Fischer, had placed great weight on the experience of a blind doctor who had received his training at Temple University Medical School. The court noted that he had been trained twenty years earlier, and that the faculty and students at the Temple medical school had devoted a substantial amount of time to working individually with that student. Furthermore, the court rejected the findings of the commission and trial court that, because Fischer could have completed the first two years of medical school training with minimal modifications of the program, the more substantial modifications of the rest of the medical school program (such as having others read X-rays and patient charts, and waiving the requirement that she learn how to draw blood or insert an intravenous tube) would not be an undue hardship for CWR. A number of medical educators had testified that it would be impossible to modify the methods of training a medical student to accommodate a blind individual. In addition, said the court, requiring CWR to admit Fischer would impose an undue burden upon the faculty because of the extensive individual attention she would require from them.

Furthermore, the court indicated that the design of curriculum and teaching methods are matters of academic judgment and are deserving of deference "unless it is shown that the standards serve no purpose other than to deny an education to the handicapped." It was irrelevant that Fischer intended to practice psychiatry rather than general medicine; the purpose of a medical school education was to produce general practitioners, not specialists.

In sum, postsecondary administrators should still proceed very sensitively in making admission decisions concerning disabled persons. *Davis* can be expected to have the greatest impact on professional and paraprofessional health care programs; beyond that, the circumstances in which physical requirements for admission may be used are less clear. Furthermore, while *Davis* relieves colleges and universities of any obligation to make substantial modifications in their program requirements, a refusal to make lesser modifications may in some instances constitute discrimination. Furthermore, interpretation of Section 504's requirements has evolved since *Davis,* as evidenced by the *Doherty* case; and in some cases the ADA provides additional protections for students.

A federal appellate court has ruled that "flagging" scores on standardized tests that have been taken with accommodations does not violate the ADA. In *Doe v. National Board of Medical Examiners*, 199 F.3d 146 (3d Cir. 1999), a medical student with multiple sclerosis requested, and obtained, additional time to take the U.S. Medical Licensing Examination, a standardized examination developed and administered by the National Board of Medical Examiners (NBME). The NBME's practice when reporting scores was to indicate that the examination had been taken with accommodations. The student asked the NBME to omit the "flagging" from his score report, but the organization refused. The student then sought a preliminary injunction, claiming that the practice of flagging test scores violated Title III of the ADA.

Although the trial court granted Doe a preliminary injunction, the appellate panel reversed. The NBME only flagged those scores when the test taker had been granted an accommodation that the board's psychometric experts believed could affect the validity of the test score. Additional time, which was the accommodation that Doe received, could affect the validity of his score; the score of another test taker who only received a large-print version of the exam would not be flagged because this accommodation would not affect the validity of the score. The court ruled that, in order to be entitled to an injunction, Doe would have to demonstrate that the validity of his test score as a predictor of success in further medical training was comparable to the validity of the scores of test takers who had not been accommodated. Because the ADA does not bar the flagging of test scores, and because Doe had not demonstrated that the additional time had no effect on the validity of his score, the court vacated the preliminary injunction. To Doe's claim that he would be discriminated against by residency and internship programs to which he would apply, the court responded that such potential discrimination could not be attributed to the NBME, and that such a claim was speculative.

Subsequent to the ruling in *Doe*, the College Board announced that, effective October 2003, it would no longer "flag" the test scores for individuals who were given extra time or other accommodations when taking the SAT. The Educational Testing Service has also halted the practice of flagging scores on the Graduate Management Admission Test (GMAT) and the Graduate Record Examination (GRE) (Eric Hoover, "Removing the 'Scarlet Letter': The College Board Will No Longer Flag the SAT-Score Reports of Students Granted Extra Time Because of Disabilities," *Chron. Higher Educ.*, July 26, 2002, A41).

8.2.4.4. Age. In *Massachusetts Board of Retirement v. Murgia*, 427 U.S. 307 (1976), the U.S. Supreme Court held that age discrimination is not subject to the high standard of justification that the equal protection clause of the Constitution requires, for instance, for race discrimination. Rather, age classifications are permissible if they "rationally further" some legitimate governmental objective. The Court confirmed the use of the "rational basis" standard for age discrimination cases in *City of Dallas v. Stanglin*, 490 U.S. 19 (1989), saying that this standard is "the most relaxed and tolerant form of judicial scrutiny under the Equal Protection Clause" (490 U.S. at 26).

In *Miller v. Sonoma County Junior College District,* No. C-74-0222 (N.D. Cal. 1974) (an unpublished opinion decided before *Murgia),* two sixteen-year-old students won the right to attend a California junior college. The court held that the college's minimum age requirement of eighteen was an arbitrary and irrational basis for exclusion because it was not related to the state's interest in providing education to qualified students.

In *Purdie v. University of Utah,* 584 P.2d 831 (Utah 1978), a case that can usefully be compared with *Miller,* the court considered the constitutional claim of a fifty-one-year-old woman who had been denied admission to the university's department of educational psychology. Whereas the *Miller* plaintiffs were allegedly too young for admission, Purdie was allegedly too old. But in both cases the courts used the equal protection clause to limit the institution's discretion to base admission decisions on age. In *Purdie* the plaintiff alleged, and the university did not deny, that she exceeded the normal admissions requirements and was rejected solely because of her age. The trial court held that her complaint did not state a viable legal claim and dismissed the suit. On appeal, the Utah Supreme Court reversed, holding that rejection of a qualified fifty-one-year-old would violate equal protection unless the university could show that its action bore a "rational relationship to legitimate state purposes." Since the abbreviated trial record contained no evidence of the department's admissions standards or its policy regarding age, the court remanded the case to the trial court for further proceedings.

In *Tobin v. University of Maine System,* 62 F. Supp. 2d 162 (D. Maine 1999), a sixty-five-year-old law school applicant who was denied admission sued under Section 1983, claiming a denial of equal protection. After examining the law school's admissions criteria (LSAT scores and grade point averages for the applicant's baccalaureate degree), the court concluded that the plaintiff had not established that his rejection was motivated by age discrimination, and awarded summary judgment to the university. The same court had earlier dismissed Tobin's claims of emotional distress, breach of contract, and breach of an implied covenant of good faith and fair dealing (59 F. Supp. 2d 87).

Both public and private institutions that receive federal funds are subject to the federal Age Discrimination Act of 1975 (42 U.S.C. § 6101 *et seq.*). Section 6101 of the Act, with certain exceptions listed in Sections 6103(b) and 6103(c), originally prohibited "unreasonable discrimination on the basis of age in programs or activities receiving federal financial assistance." In 1978, Congress deleted the word "unreasonable" from the Act (see this book, Section 13.5.5), thus lowering the statute's tolerance for discrimination and presumably making its standards more stringent than the Constitution's "rationality" standard used in *Purdie.* As amended and interpreted in the implementing regulations (45 C.F.R. Part 90), the Age Discrimination Act clearly applies to the admissions policies of postsecondary institutions.

The age discrimination regulations, however, do not prohibit all age distinctions. Section 90.14 of the regulations permits age distinctions that are necessary to the "normal operation" of, or to the achievement of a "statutory objective" of, a program or activity receiving federal financial assistance (see Section 13.5.5

of this book). Moreover, Section 90.15 of the regulations permits recipients to take an action based on a factor other than age—"even though that action may have a disproportionate effect on persons of different ages"—if the factor has a "direct and substantial relationship" to the program's operation or goals. The explanatory commentary accompanying the regulations provides examples of how the Office of Civil Rights would evaluate selection criteria that may bear a relationship to age (44 Fed. Reg. 33773–74 (June 12, 1979)).

State law also occasionally prohibits age discrimination against students. In its Fair Educational Practices statute, for example, Massachusetts prohibits age discrimination in admissions to graduate programs and vocational training institutions (Mass. Gen. Laws Ann. ch. 151C, §§ 2(d), 2A(a)).

Taken together, the Constitution, the federal law and regulations, and occasional state laws now appear to create a substantial legal barrier to the use of either maximum- or minimum-age policies in admissions. The federal Age Discrimination Act, applicable to both public and private institutions regardless of whether they receive federal funds, is the most important of these developments; administrators should watch for further implementation of this statute.

8.2.4.5. Residence. Public colleges and universities may provide preferences for state residents because of the high cost (subsidized by state taxpayers) of education and because it is more likely that in-state students will remain in the state after graduation and use their education to benefit the state and its residents (see generally *Rosenstock v. Board of Governors of the University of North Carolina,* 423 F. Supp. 1321, 1326–27 (M.D.N.C. 1976)). This is particularly true for professional training. In *Buchwald v. University of New Mexico School of Medicine,* 159 F.3d 487 (10th Cir. 1998), the court considered an equal protection challenge to a medical school admissions policy that favored long-term residents of the state over short-term residents. The district court had invalidated this preference as a burden on the fundamental right to travel (see Section 8.3.5 of this book). In remanding the case to the district court, the appellate court determined that the preference in favor of longer-term state residents served an interest in public health that "is not only legitimate but also compelling." This interest, as characterized by the court, is an interest in "selecting those candidates [for admission] likely to return to the state of New Mexico and supply needed medical care to underserved areas of the state" (159 F.3d at 498).

The plaintiff in the *Buchwald* case also presented a second type of challenge to residency preferences in admissions: that they burden the interstate movement of people and thus burden interstate commerce in violation of the federal Constitution's commerce clause (see generally Section 12.4). The appellate court quickly dispatched this argument by invoking the so-called market participant exception to the commerce clause:

> [P]laintiff argues that defendant's actions violate the dormant Commerce Clause. This claim fails to state a constitutional violation that could abrogate qualified immunity. The University of New Mexico's educational activities constitute participation in the market for educational services, not regulation of that

market. Thus the policies in question fall under the "market participant" exception to the dormant Commerce Clause. See *Reeves, Inc. v. Stake*, 447 U.S. 429, 436–39 (1980) [159 F.3d at 496].

The U.S. Supreme Court's decision in *Saenz v. Roe*, 526 U.S. 489 (1999), discussed in Section 8.3.5, suggests that state residency preferences and requirements for admission, when used by a public institution, could be challenged not only under the equal protection clause of the Fourteenth Amendment, but also under that amendment's "privileges or immunities" clause and its "citizenship" clauses. The case also suggests, however, that such admissions preferences or requirements could withstand challenge when there is a "danger" that "citizens of other states" will "establish residency for just long enough to acquire . . . [their] college education," the benefit of which "will be enjoyed after they return to their original domicile" (526 U.S. 505).

8.2.4.6. Immigration status. The eligibility of aliens for admission to U.S. colleges and universities has received heightened attention since the terrorist attacks of September 11, 2001. Although the Supreme Court ruled on equal protection grounds in 1982 that states could not deny free public education to undocumented alien children (*Plyler v. Doe*, 457 U.S. 202 (1982)), litigation related to alien postsecondary students has more often involved their eligibility for in-state tuition in state institutions than their eligibility for admission as such. The in-state tuition cases are discussed in Section 8.3.6 below.

As discussed in the Supreme Court's *Nyquist* case (Section 8.3.6.1 below), alienage is a suspect classification for purposes of postsecondary education benefits. A public institution's refusal to admit permanent resident aliens would therefore likely violate the federal equal protection clause. Private institutions are not bound by the equal protection clause, but could face liability for refusing to admit qualified resident aliens if the institution was engaged in some cooperative education program with the federal or state government that would be considered "state action" (see Section 1.5.2).

Temporary or nonimmigrant aliens have less protection under the federal Constitution. For example, in *Ahmed v. University of Toledo*, discussed in Section 8.3.6.1, the court distinguished between permanent resident aliens and temporary nonresident (nonimmigrant) aliens, refusing to subject a university policy that affected only nonresident aliens to strict scrutiny review under the equal protection clause. Under the lower "rational relationship" standard used by the court in *Ahmed*, a university policy that singled out nonresident aliens in order to meet a reasonable goal of the university would be constitutionally permissible. If a public institution were to deny admission only to aliens from a particular country, however, courts could view such a policy as national origin discrimination subject to strict scrutiny (see *Tayyari v. New Mexico State University*, 495 F. Supp. 1365 (D.N.M. 1980)).

More complicated are the legal issues that arise with respect to undocumented aliens. In 1996, Congress enacted the Illegal Immigration Reform and Immigrant Responsibility Act (IIRIRA, Pub. L. No. 104-208, 110 Stat. 3009, codified in scattered Sections of 8 and 18 U.S.C.). One IIRIRA provision

(8 U.S.C. § 1621(c)) declares that aliens who are not "qualified aliens"[12] are ineligible for certain public benefits, including public postsecondary education. However, the same section of the law also allows a state, after August 22, 1996, to enact laws that specifically confer a public benefit on aliens.

It is not yet clear whether admission to a public college or university is a "public benefit," and thus whether the IIRIRA applies to admissions policies. Although the court in the *Merton* case, discussed below, concluded that the IIRIRA was not intended to apply to college admissions, there have been no definitive rulings on whether college admission is a "benefit," and the views of commentators differ. (For a discussion of the application of the IIRIRA to admission to public colleges and universities, see Michael A. Olivas, "IIRIRA, the DREAM Act, and Undocumented College Student Residency," 30 *J. Coll. & Univ. Law* 435 (2004).)

In 2002, the Attorney General of Virginia sent a memo to all public postsecondary institutions in the state stating that they should not admit undocumented aliens. The memo also encouraged officials of the institutions to report the presence of any undocumented students on campus to the federal authorities. When the public colleges and universities in Virginia followed the dictates of the memorandum with respect to admissions policies, an association that advocates for undocumented workers, as well as several undocumented individuals, filed a lawsuit against the boards of visitors of these colleges and universities, asserting that their refusal to admit undocumented alien applicants violated the U.S. Constitution's supremacy, foreign commerce, and due process clauses. (For a discussion of supremacy clause principles, see Section 8.3.6 of this book.) The supremacy clause claim was based on the plaintiffs' assertion that the restrictive admissions policies of the institutions regulated immigration and thus interfered with federal immigration law. The plaintiffs' foreign commerce clause claim was based on the assertion that state policies denying admission to undocumented aliens burdened interstate commerce by precluding potential applicants from earning higher wages and sending funds to relatives living outside the United States. The due process claim was based on the plaintiffs' assertion that the policy of denying admission to undocumented aliens deprived them of a property interest in receiving a public education in Virginia community colleges, as well as a property interest in receiving fair and impartial admissions decisions based on review of their applications. The defendants moved for dismissal of all claims.

In *Equal Access Education v. Merton*, 305 F. Supp. 2d 585 (E.D. Va. 2004) (*Merton I*), the court first addressed the issue of standing. Several of the named plaintiffs were high school students whose academic achievement would have made them competitive for admission to Virginia universities, except for the fact that they were not citizens or lawful permanent residents. One plaintiff was a high school student who had temporary legal status, but who had been denied

---

[12]Section 1641 of the IIRIRA provides seven categories of aliens who are considered to be "qualified" and thus eligible for public benefits. In addition to documented aliens, the category includes political refugees, aliens granted asylum, and Cuban and Haitian refugees (8 U.S.C. § 1641(b)).

admission to a public university; he alleged that the denial was based on an inaccurate assumption that he did not have a lawful immigration status. The court found that the individual plaintiffs had standing to bring the suit, as did the association that had been formed to further the interests of undocumented high school students in attending public colleges and universities in Virginia.

In addressing the plaintiffs' supremacy clause claim, the court looked to *DeCanas v. Bica,* 424 U.S. 351 (1976), in which the U.S. Supreme Court upheld a California statute forbidding employers to hire undocumented aliens if such employment would have an adverse effect on lawful resident workers. The Supreme Court rejected a claim that the state law was preempted by federal law and set forth a three-part test for determining whether a state statute, action, or policy related to immigration was preempted by federal law. Under this test, federal law will preempt the state when: (1) the state statute, action, or policy is an attempt to regulate immigration; (2) the subject matter of the state law, action, or policy is one that Congress intended to prevent states from regulating, even if the state law does not conflict with federal law; or (3) the state statute, action, or policy poses an obstacle to the execution of congressional objectives, or conflicts with federal law, making compliance with both federal and state law impossible.

Applying the *DeCanas* tests, the court determined, with one exception noted below, that the Virginia policy to deny admission to undocumented applicants did not meet any of the conditions under which federal law would preempt the policy. Specifically, the court determined that, in passing the IIRIRA, Congress did not intend to regulate the admission of undocumented aliens to college, leaving that issue to the states. The IIRIRA merely dictated that, if undocumented aliens were admitted to public colleges and universities, they would have to be charged the same out-of-state tuition paid by U.S. citizens (8 U.S.C. § 1623(a)). As long as the college officials used "federal immigration status standards" rather than creating different state standards for determining whether an applicant was undocumented or not a lawful resident, there was no violation of the supremacy clause. But because no trial had been held to determine whether the colleges had created an alternate set of "state standards" to evaluate applicants' citizenship status, the court declined to dismiss that part of the plaintiffs' supremacy clause claim.

The court then turned to the plaintiffs' foreign commerce clause claim, which asserted that the admissions policies relegated the plaintiffs to low-wage jobs by denying them access to postsecondary education, thus limiting their ability to send funds to relatives living outside the United States. The court rejected this claim, noting that there was no allegation that the plaintiffs made or intended to make such payments and that, since undocumented aliens are not eligible under federal law to work in the United States, it was unlikely that they would be able to earn the type of salaries that would result in significant payments to foreign nationals.

The court rejected the plaintiffs' due process claim, stating that they did not have a property right in admission to Virginia community colleges because admission was discretionary on the part of the colleges. And because public

colleges and universities may deny admission to any applicant for any constitutionally permissible reason, said the court, there is no entitlement to any
particular procedures or criteria for admission. In *Merton I*, therefore, the court
dismissed all of the plaintiffs' claims except for the one portion of the supremacy
clause claim.

In *Equal Access Education v. Merton*, 325 F. Supp. 2d 655 (E.D. Va. 2004)
(*Merton II*), the court granted the defendant universities' motion for summary
judgment on that claim. The court did not rule on the merits of the claim,
however; instead it reconsidered the plaintiffs' standing in light of its rulings in
Merton I and determined that the plaintiffs no longer had standing to continue
the action.

During 2003 and 2004, bills were introduced in both houses of Congress that
would allow certain undocumented students to attend college in the United
States and to begin the process of legalization of the student's immigration status. The bills, S. 1545 (the DREAM Act) and H.R. 1684 in the 108th Congress,
had not been voted upon as of late 2005 (see S. 2075 (109th Cong.)). (For a discussion of these bills and their potential impact on the postsecondary education opportunities of undocumented students, see the Olivas article cited
above.)

8.2.5. Affirmative action programs.

Designed to increase the number
of minority persons admitted to academic programs, affirmative action policies
pose delicate social, pedagogical, and legal questions. Educators and public policy makers have agonized over the extent to which the goal of greater minority
representation, or diversity in general, justifies the admission of less or differently qualified applicants, particularly in professional programs. Courts have
grappled with the complaints of qualified but rejected nonminority applicants
who claim to be victims of "reverse discrimination" because minority applicants
were admitted in preference to them. Four cases have reached the U.S. Supreme
Court: *DeFunis* in 1973, *Bakke* in 1978, and *Grutter* and *Gratz* in 2003, all of
which are discussed below.

There are two types of affirmative action plans: "remedial" or "mandatory"
plans and "voluntary" plans.[13] The former are ordered by a court or government agency. There is only one justification that the courts have accepted for
this type of affirmative action plan: remedying or dismantling the present effects
of past discrimination that the institution has engaged in or supported.
"Voluntary" affirmative action plans, on the other hand, are adopted by the
conscious choice of the institution. As the law has developed, there are two justifications for this type of plan. The first parallels the justification for remedial or
mandatory affirmative action: alleviating the present effects of the institution's
own past discrimination. The second—newer and more controversial—
justification is achieving and maintaining the diversity of the student body.

---

[13]An affirmative action plan embodied in a consent decree, voluntarily accepted by the parties as a
basis for settling a case, would apparently be considered a voluntary rather than a mandatory
plan. See *Local No. 93, Int'l. Ass'n. of Firefighters v. City of Cleveland*, 478 U.S. 501, 516–17 (1986).

Just as there is a basic dichotomy between remedial and voluntary plans, there is also a basic distinction—developed in cases concerning race and ethnicity—between "race-conscious" voluntary affirmative action plans and "race-neutral" voluntary affirmative action plans. The former take race into account in decision making by providing some type of preference or advantage for members of identified minority groups. Race-neutral plans, on the other hand, do *not* use race as a factor in making decisions about particular individuals. Some allegedly race-neutral plans may have the foreseeable *effect* of benefiting certain racial or ethnic minorities, but this characteristic alone does not convert the neutral plan into a race-conscious plan, so long as the race of particular individuals is not itself considered in making decisions about them. Genuinely race-neutral plans raise fewer legal issues than race-conscious plans and are less amenable to challenge. If the plan is adopted for the purpose of benefiting some minorities over some nonminorities, however, and does have this intended effect, the plan could be subject to challenge as reverse discrimination and could be treated as a race-conscious plan. (See, for example, *Gomillion v. Lightfoot,* 364 U.S. 339 (1960); *Rogers v. Lodge,* 458 U.S. 613 (1982); and see generally Section 13.5.7.2 of this book.)

The legal issues concerning affirmative action can be cast in both constitutional and statutory terms and apply to both public and private institutions. The constitutional issues arise under the Fourteenth Amendment's equal protection clause, which generally prohibits discriminatory treatment on the basis of race, ethnicity, or sex, including "reverse discrimination," but applies only to *public* institutions (see Section 1.5.2 of this book). The statutory issues arise under Title VI of the Civil Rights Act of 1964 (prohibiting "race," "color," and "national origin" discrimination), and Title IX of the Education Amendments of 1972 (prohibiting sex discrimination), which apply to discrimination by both public and private institutions receiving federal financial assistance (see generally Sections 13.5.2 & 13.5.3 of this book); and under 42 U.S.C. § 1981, which has been construed to prohibit race discrimination in admissions by private schools whether or not they receive federal assistance (see Section 8.2.4.1 of this book).[14] In the *Bakke* case, a majority of the Justices agreed that Title VI uses constitutional equal protection standards for determining the validity of affirmative action programs (438 U.S. 265 at 284–87 (Powell, J.), 328–41 (Brennan, J., concurring in judgment), 412–18 (Stevens, J., concurring in judgment)). Standards

---

[14]The cases discussed below, and all of the major cases on affirmative action in admissions, involved race and/or ethnicity discrimination. Sex discrimination claims, however, are also a realistic possibility. A Georgia case provides a concrete example. Several rejected female applicants filed a lawsuit against the University of Georgia, challenging its practice of using gender preferences to make admission decisions in borderline cases. The U.S. district court ruled in the plaintiffs' favor. See *Johnson v. University System of Georgia,* 106 F. Supp. 2d 1362, 1375–76 (S.D. Ga. 2000). Because far more female than male students would have been admitted if gender had not been considered, the university had applied a lower standard to male applicants in an attempt to narrow the gap between the proportions of female and male students. The university then eliminated consideration of gender in making admissions decisions. See Dan Carnevale, "Lawsuit Prompts U. of Georgia to End Admissions Preferences for Male Applicants," *Chron. Higher Educ.,* September 3, 1999, A68.

comparable to those of the equal protection clause would also apparently be used for affirmative action issues arising under 42 U.S.C. § 1981, as suggested by the *Grutter* and *Gratz* cases, at least for public institutions and private institutions that receive federal financial assistance.[15] For Title IX affirmative action issues, equal protection standards would also apply; but it is not clear whether it would be the "intermediate scrutiny" standard that courts use when reviewing equal protection claims of sex discrimination (see *United States v Virginia,* 518 U.S. 515 (1996), discussed in subsection 8.2.4.2 above) or the "strict scrutiny" standard applicable to race claims under Title VI. (See *Jeldness v. Pearce,* 30 F.3d 1220 (9th Cir. 1994); *Johnson v. University System. of Ga.,* 106 F. Supp. 2d 1362 (S.D. Ga. 2000).) Thus, *Bakke, Grutter,* and *Gratz,* taken together, establish a core of comparable legal parameters for affirmative action, applicable to public and private institutions alike.

Both the Title VI and the Title IX administrative regulations also address the subject of affirmative action. These regulations preceded *Bakke* and are brief and somewhat ambiguous. After *Bakke,* the U.S. Department of Health, Education, and Welfare (HEW, now the U.S. Department of Education) issued a "policy interpretation" of Title VI, indicating that the department had reviewed its regulations in light of *Bakke* and "concluded that no changes . . . are required or desirable" (44 Fed. Reg. 58509, at 58510 (October 10, 1979)). This policy interpretation, however, did set forth guidelines for applying the Title VI affirmative action regulations consistent with *Bakke.*

When an institution has discriminated in the past, the Title VI and Title IX regulations require it to implement affirmative action programs to overcome the effects of that discrimination—a kind of remedial or mandatory affirmative action (34 C.F.R. §§ 100.3(b)(6)(i) & 100.5(i); 34 C.F.R. § 106.3(a)).[16] When the institution has not discriminated, the regulations nevertheless permit affirmative action to overcome the present effects of past societal discrimination— a type of voluntary affirmative action (34 C.F.R. §§ 100.3(b)(6)(ii) & 100.5(i); 34 C.F.R. § 106.3(b)). Under more recent judicial interpretations, however, these regulations and the 1997 Policy Interpretation could not validly extend to voluntary race-conscious or gender-conscious plans designed to remedy societal discrimination apart from the institution's own prior discrimination. (See the discussion in guideline 1 below in this subsection.)

---

[15]One appellate court has held, in a post-*Grutter* and *Gratz* case involving Section 1981, that Title VII standards (see Section 5.2.1 of this book), rather than equal protection standards, would apply with respect to "the order and nature of the proof" of intentional discrimination for a Section 1981 claim against a private school that does not receive federal funds; see *Doe v. Kamehameha Schools/Bernice Pauahi Bishop Estate,* 416 F.3d 1025 (9th Cir. 2005).

[16]The department, however, cannot require the institution to use admissions quotas as part of an affirmative action plan. Section 408 of the Education Amendments of 1976 (20 U.S.C. § 1232i(c)) provides that:

It shall be unlawful for the Secretary [of Education] to defer or limit any federal assistance on the basis of any failure to comply with the imposition of quotas (or any other numerical requirements which have the effect of imposing quotas) on the student admission practices of an institution of higher education or community college receiving Federal financial assistance.

The first case to confront the constitutionality of affirmative action admissions programs in postsecondary education was *DeFunis v. Odegaard*, 507 P.2d 1169 (Wash. 1973), *dismissed as moot*, 416 U.S. 312 (1974), *on remand*, 529 P.2d 438 (Wash. 1974). After DeFunis, a white male, was denied admission to the University of Washington's law school, he filed suit alleging that less-qualified minority applicants had been accepted and that, but for the affirmative action program, he would have been admitted. The law school admissions committee had calculated each applicant's predicted first-year average (PFYA) through a formula that considered the applicant's LSAT scores and junior-senior undergraduate average. The committee had attached less importance to a minority applicant's PFYA and had considered minority applications separately from other applications. DeFunis's PFYA was higher than those of all but one of the minority applicants admitted in the year he was rejected.

The state trial court ordered that DeFunis be admitted, and he entered the law school. The Washington State Supreme Court reversed the lower court and upheld the law school's affirmative action program under the equal protection clause as a constitutionally acceptable admissions tool justified by several "compelling" state interests. Among them were the "interest in promoting integration in public education," the "educational interest . . . in producing a racially balanced student body at the law school," and the interest in alleviating "the shortage of minority attorneys—and, consequently, minority prosecutors, judges, and public officials." When DeFunis sought review in the U.S. Supreme Court, he was permitted to remain in school pending the Court's final disposition of the case. Subsequently, in a *per curiam* opinion with four Justices dissenting, the Court declared the case moot because, by then, DeFunis was in his final quarter of law school, and the university had asserted that his registration would remain effective regardless of the case's final outcome. The Court vacated the Washington State Supreme Court's judgment and remanded the case to that court for appropriate disposition.

Though the *per curiam* opinion in *DeFunis* does not discuss the merits of the case, Justice Douglas's dissent presents a thought-provoking analysis of affirmative action in admissions. He discussed both "uniform" (or "race-neutral") plans) and "differential" (or "compensatory") plans (both further discussed below in this subsection) and then gave this assessment of the University of Washington law school's plan:

> [Under the] policy . . . presented by this case the [admissions] committee would be making decisions on the basis of individual attributes, rather than according a preference solely on the basis of race. To be sure, the racial preference here was not absolute—the committee did not admit all applicants from the four favored groups. But it did accord all such applicants a preference by applying, to an extent not precisely ascertainable from the record, different standards by which to judge their applications, with the result that the committee admitted minority applicants who, in the school's own judgment, were less promising than other applicants who were rejected. Furthermore, it is apparent that because the admissions committee compared minority applicants only with one another, it was necessary to reserve some proportion of the class for them,

even if at the outset a precise number of places were not set aside. That proportion, apparently 15% to 20%, was chosen because the school determined it to be "reasonable," although no explanation is provided as to how that number rather than some other was found appropriate. Without becoming embroiled in a semantic debate over whether this practice constitutes a "quota," it is clear that given the limitation on the total number of applicants who could be accepted, this policy did reduce the total number of places for which DeFunis could compete—solely on account of his race [416 U.S. at 332–33].

Justice Douglas did not conclude that the university's policy was therefore unconstitutional but, rather, that it would be unconstitutional unless, after a new trial, the court found that it took account of "cultural standards of a diverse rather than a homogeneous society" in a "racially neutral" way.

Five years after it had avoided the issue in *DeFunis,* the Supreme Court considered the legality of affirmative action in the now-famous *Bakke* case, *Regents of the University of California v. Bakke,* 438 U.S. 265 (1978). The plaintiff, a white male twice rejected from the medical school of the University of California at Davis, had challenged the school's affirmative action plan under which it had set aside 16 places out of 100 for minority applicants whose applications were considered separately from other applicants. According to Justice Powell's description of the plan, with which a majority of the Justices agreed:

> [T]he faculty devised a special admissions program to increase the representation of "disadvantaged" students in each medical school class. The special program consisted of a separate admissions system operating in coordination with the regular admissions process. . . .
> [C]andidates were asked to indicate whether they wished to be considered as . . . members of a "minority group," which the Medical School apparently viewed as "Blacks," "Chicanos," "Asians," and "American Indians." [If so], the application was forwarded to the special admissions committee. . . . [T]he applications then were rated by the special committee in a fashion similar to that used by the general admissions committee, except that special candidates did not have to meet the 2.5 grade point average cutoff applied to regular applicant. . . .
> From [1971] through 1974, the special program resulted in the admission of twenty-one black students, thirty Mexican-Americans, and twelve Asians, for a total of sixty-three minority students. Over the same period, the regular admissions program produced one black, six Mexican-Americans, and thirty-seven Asians, for a total of forty-four minority students. Although disadvantaged whites applied to the special program in large numbers, none received an offer of admission through that process [438 U.S. at 272–76].

The university sought to justify its program by citing the great need for doctors to work in underserved minority communities, the need to compensate for the effects of societal discrimination against minorities, the need to reduce the historical deficit of minorities in the medical profession, and the need to diversify the student body. In analyzing these justifications, the California Supreme Court had applied a "compelling state interest" test, such as that used by the state court in *DeFunis,* along with a "less objectionable alternative test." Although it assumed that the university's interests were compelling, this court determined that the university had not demonstrated that the program was the least burdensome alternative available for achieving its goals. (This analysis of possible alternatives is comparable to the "narrow tailoring" test that appeared in later litigation and was used by the Court in *Grutter* and *Gratz*.) The California court therefore held that the program operated unconstitutionally to exclude Bakke on account of his race and ordered that Bakke be admitted to medical school. It further held that the Constitution prohibited the university from giving any consideration to race in its admissions process and enjoined the university from doing so (*Bakke v. Regents of the University of California*, 553 P.2d 1152 (Cal. 1976)).

The U.S. Supreme Court affirmed the first part of this decision and reversed the second part. The Justices wrote six opinions (totaling 157 pages), none of which commanded a majority of the Court. Three of these opinions deserve particular consideration: (1) Justice Powell's opinion—in some parts of which various of the other Justices joined; (2) Justice Brennan's opinion—in which three other Justices joined (referred to below as the "Brennan group"); and (3) Justice Stevens's opinion—in which three other Justices joined (referred to below as the "Stevens group").

A bare majority of the Justices—four (the "Stevens group") relying on Title VI and one (Justice Powell) relying on the Fourteenth Amendment's equal protection clause—agreed that the University of California at Davis program unlawfully discriminated against Bakke, thus affirming the first part of the California court's judgment (ordering Bakke's admission). A different majority of five Justices—Justice Powell and the "Brennan group"—agreed that "the state has a substantial interest that legitimately may be served by a properly devised admissions program involving the competitive consideration of race and ethnic origin" (438 U.S. 265, 320 (1978)), thus reversing the second part of the California court's judgment (prohibiting the consideration of race in admissions). In summary, then, the Court invalidated the medical school's affirmative action plan by a 5-to-4 vote; but by a different 5-to-4 vote, the Court ruled that some consideration of race is nevertheless permissible in affirmative action admissions plans. Justice Powell was the only Justice in the majority for both votes.

In their various opinions in *Bakke*, the Justices debated the issues of what standard of review applies under the equal protection clause, what the valid justifications for affirmative action programs are, and the extent to which such programs can be race conscious, and whether the Title VI requirements for affirmative action are the same as those under the equal protection clause. No majority agreed fully on any of these issues, and they continued to be debated in the years following *Bakke*. Nevertheless, a review and comparison of opinions reveals three basic principles established by *Bakke* that were followed by later courts.

First, racial preferences that partake of quotas—rigid numerical or percentage goals defined specifically by race—are impermissible. *Second*, separate systems for reviewing minority applications—with procedures and criteria different from those used for nonminority applications—are impermissible. *Third*, Title VI embodies Fourteenth Amendment principles of equal protection and applies to race discrimination in the same way as the equal protection clause.

In addition to these principles that a majority of the Court adhered to in their various opinions, the Powell opinion in *Bakke* also includes important additional guidance for affirmative action plans. This guidance focuses primarily on the concept of student body diversity, and on the importance of individualized comparisons of all applicants. In addition, the Powell opinion (picking up on the Douglas opinion in *DeFunis*) addresses the concept of *differential* or compensatory affirmative action plans.

The core of Justice Powell's guidance on student body diversity is that:

> the state interest that would justify consideration of race or ethnic background . . . is not an interest in simple ethnic diversity, in which a specified percentage of the student body is in effect guaranteed to be members of selected ethnic groups, with the remaining percentage an undifferentiated aggregation of students. The diversity that furthers a compelling state interest encompasses a far broader array of qualifications and characteristics of which racial or ethnic origin is but a single though important element [438 U.S. at 315 (Powell, J.).]

The crux of Justice Powell's guidance on individualized comparisons of applicants is that:

> race or ethnic background may be deemed a "plus" in a particular applicant's file, yet it [may] not insulate the individual from *comparison with all other candidates for the available seats.* The file of a particular black applicant may be examined for his potential contribution to diversity *without the factor of race being decisive* when compared, for example, with that of an applicant identified as an Italian-American if the latter is thought to exhibit qualities more likely to promote beneficial education pluralism. . . . In short, an admissions program operated in this way is flexible enough to *consider all pertinent elements of diversity in light of the particular qualifications of each applicant,* and to place them on the same footing for consideration, although not necessarily according to them the same weight. Indeed, the weight attributed to a particular quality may vary from year to year depending upon the "mix" both of the student body and the applicants for the incoming class [438 U.S. at 317–18 (Powell, J.) (emphasis added)].

And regarding differential admissions plans, Powell stated:

> Racial classifications in admissions conceivably could serve a . . . purpose . . . which petitioner does not articulate: fair appraisal of each individual's academic promise in light of some bias in grading or testing procedures. To the extent that race and ethnic background were considered only to the extent of curing established inaccuracies in predicting academic performance, it might be argued that there is no "preference" at all [438 U.S. at 306 (Powell, J.)].

In completing his analysis in *Bakke,* Justice Powell used a "strict scrutiny" standard of review. The Brennan group, in contrast, used an "intermediate scrutiny" standard; and the Stevens group, relying on Title VI, did not directly confront the standard-of-review issue. Cases after *Bakke* but before *Grutter* and *Gratz* did resolve this issue, however—in particular *City of Richmond v. J. A. Croson Co.,*

488 U.S. 469 (1989), and *Adarand Constructors, Inc., v. Pena*, 515 U.S. 200, 220–21 (1995), both discussed in Section 5.4.2 of this book. Under these cases, a race-conscious affirmative action plan will be constitutional only if the institution can prove that its use of race is: (1) "narrowly tailored" to (2) further "compelling governmental interest." This "strict scrutiny" standard of review had previously been used in equal protection race discrimination cases that did not involve reverse discrimination; it is also the standard that was used by Justice Powell in *Bakke* (see 438 U.S. at 290–91) and by the state supreme courts in *DeFunis* and *Bakke.*

After the *Bakke* case, absent any consensus on the Court, most colleges and universities with affirmative action admissions plans followed the Powell guidelines. As the Court later explained in *Grutter*: "Since this Court's splintered decision in *Bakke,* Justice Powell's opinion . . . has served as the touchstone for constitutional analysis of race-conscious admissions policies. Public and private universities across the Nation have modeled their own admissions programs on Justice Powell's views . . ." (539 U.S. at 307). In early challenges to the Powell type of race-conscious plan, the institutions usually prevailed. Two important state court decisions upholding affirmative action programs of state professional schools provide examples. In *McDonald v. Hogness*, 598 P.2d 707 (Wash. 1979), the court relied heavily on the Powell opinion as well as the Brennan opinion in *Bakke* in upholding the University of Washington medical school's race-conscious admissions policy. And in *DeRonde v. Regents of the University of California*, 625 P.2d 220 (Cal. 1981), another state court relied heavily on the Powell and Brennan opinions, and on the Washington court's ruling in *McDonald*, to uphold the University of California at Davis law school's affirmative action policy. Both courts accepted student body diversity as a constitutionally sufficient justification for race-conscious admissions policies. A federal district court in New York did so as well in *Davis v. Halpern*, 768 F. Supp. 968 (E.D.N.Y. 1991).

After a period of relative quiet, however, a new round of court challenges to race-conscious admissions plans began in the 1990s, with several leading cases using reasoning and reaching results different from the earlier post-*Bakke* cases. In *Hopwood v. Texas*, 78 F.3d 932 (5th Cir. 1996), for instance, four rejected applicants sued the state and the University of Texas (UT) under the equal protection clause and Title VI, claiming that they were denied admission to the UT law school on the basis of their race. The plaintiffs challenged the continuing vitality of Justice Powell's opinion in the *Bakke* case and more generally challenged the authority of colleges and universities to use "diversity" as a rationale for considering race, gender, or other such characteristics as a "plus" factor in admissions. The law school's affirmative action admissions program gave preferences to African American and Mexican American applicants only and used a separate committee to evaluate their applications. "Cut-off scores" used to allocate applicants to various categories in the admissions process were lower for blacks and Mexican Americans than for other applicants, resulting in the admission of students in the "minority" category whose college grades and LSAT scores were lower than those of some white applicants who had been rejected.

The trial and appellate courts used the strict scrutiny standard of review, requiring the defendant to establish that it had a "compelling interest" in using racial preferences and that its use of racial preferences was "narrowly tailored" to achieve its compelling interest. The law school had presented five justifications for its affirmative action admissions program, each of which, it argued, met the compelling state interest test: (1) to achieve the law school's mission of providing a first-class legal education to members of the two largest minority groups in Texas; (2) to achieve a diverse student body; (3) to remedy the present effects of past discrimination in the Texas public school system; (4) to comply with the 1983 consent decree with the Office of Civil Rights, U.S. Department of Education, regarding recruitment of African American and Mexican American students; and (5) to comply with the standards of the American Bar Association and American Association of Law Schools regarding diversity. The federal district court ruled that the portions of the law school's admissions program that gave "minority" applicants a separate review process violated the Fourteenth Amendment—following Justice Powell's reasoning on this point in his *Bakke* opinion. The district court also held, however, that the affirmative action plan furthered the compelling interest of attaining diversity in the student body (the law school's second justification) and that it served to remedy prior discrimination by the State of Texas in its entire public school system, including elementary and secondary schools (the law school's third justification). A three-judge panel of the appellate court rejected these justifications and invalidated the law school's program. Addressing the diversity rationale first, the Fifth Circuit panel specifically rejected Justice Powell's reasoning about diversity and ruled that "achieving a diverse student body is not a compelling interest under the Fourteenth Amendment" (78 F.3d at 944). The appellate court then addressed the rationale of remedying prior discrimination. Although the court recognized that the state of Texas had discriminated on the basis of race and ethnicity in its public education system, the law school's admission program was not designed to remedy that prior unlawful conduct because the program gave preferences to minorities from outside Texas and to minorities who had attended private schools. Furthermore, said the court, in order for the admissions program to comply with constitutional requirements, the law school would have had to present evidence of a history of its own prior unlawful segregation. "A broad program that sweeps in all minorities with a remedy that is in no way related to past harms cannot survive constitutional scrutiny" (78 F.3d at 951). Once prior discrimination had been established, the law school would then have to trace present effects from the prior discrimination, to establish the size of those effects, and to develop a limited plan to remedy the harm. The "present effects" cited by both the law school and the district court—a bad reputation in the minority community and a perceived hostile environment in the law school for minority students—were insufficient, said the court, citing the Fourth Circuit's earlier opinion in *Podberesky v. Kirwan*, 38 F.3d at 147 (4th Cir. 1994) (discussed in Section 8.3.4).[17] One appellate judge, although concurring

---

[17]Another federal circuit court used reasoning similar to *Hopwood*'s to invalidate the University of Georgia's undergraduate admissions policy (*Johnson v. Board of Regents of the University of Georgia*, 263 F. 3d 1234 (11th Cir. 2001)).

in the result reached by the panel, disagreed with the majority's statement that diversity could never be a compelling state interest and—foreshadowing *Grutter*—asserted that it was an open question whether diversity could provide a compelling interest for a public graduate school's use of racial preferences in its admissions program.[18]

After *Hopwood*, but before *Grutter* and *Gratz*, various important developments took place outside the courts. In Texas, the state legislature passed a statute providing alternative means by which to foster diversity in the undergraduate programs of public colleges and universities in the state. The statute reads:

> (a) Each general academic teaching institution shall admit an applicant for admission to the institution as an undergraduate student if the applicant graduated with a grade point average in the top 10 percent of the student's high school graduating class in one of the two school years preceding the academic year for which the applicant is applying for admission and the applicant graduated from a public or private high school in this state accredited by a generally recognized accrediting organization or from a high school operated by the United States Department of Defense. . . .
>
> (b) After admitting an applicant under this section, the institution shall review the applicant's record, and any other factor the institution considers appropriate, to determine whether the applicant may require additional preparation for college-level work or would benefit from inclusion in a retention program . . . [Tex. Educ. Code Title 3, Ch. 51, § 51.803].

Florida and California also adopted "percentage plans." (For analysis of these plans, see Michelle Adams, "Isn't It Ironic? The Central Paradox at the Heart of

---

[18]In another Texas case challenging racial preferences—decided after *Hopwood* but before the U.S. Supreme Court's decisions in *Grutter* and *Gratz*—the Court provided guidance on how to resolve an institution's claims that the plaintiff would not have been admitted even if no racial preferences had been used. In *Lesage v. State of Texas*, 158 F.3d 213 (5th Cir. 1998), a three-judge appellate panel reversed the district court's summary judgment for the plaintiff because the decision to reject Lesage had been made prior to consideration of the applicants' race, and Lesage would not have been admitted irrespective of any racial considerations that might later have been used. Even if Lesage would not have been admitted absent racial preferences, said the appellate court, that issue was relevant only to the amount of damages, not to the determination of whether the university acted unlawfully by considering race and ethnicity in the preliminary application review process. If the university did employ racial preferences in the application screening process, then all applicants were not competing on an "equal footing," and this fact itself, whether or not any particular applicant would ultimately have been admitted, constituted an injury to nonminority applicants. The U.S. Supreme Court then disagreed with the reasoning of the appellate court (*Texas v. Lesage*, 528 U.S. 18 (1999)). Relying on the *Mt. Healthy* case (Section 7.6), the Court's *per curiam* opinion reasoned that, if a public institution could establish that it would have made the same decision without using the "forbidden consideration" (here, the applicants' race), then it could not be liable for that particular decision. The Court credited the university's argument that Lesage would not have been admitted even if the admissions process had been completely race neutral because seventy-three rejected applicants had higher grade point averages and higher Graduate Record Examination scores. On the other hand, said the Court, if a plaintiff challenged an ongoing program of race-conscious admissions, rather than a particular admissions decision, and sought "forward-looking" relief, there was no need to establish that he or she would have been admitted. Cases and authorities on these issues are collected in Annot., "Standing to Challenge College or Professional School Admissions Program Which Gives Preference to Minority or Disadvantaged Applicants," 60 A.L.R. Fed. 612.

'Percentage Plans,'" 62 *Ohio St. L.J.* 1729 (2001).) In the state of Washington, voters passed Initiative Measure 200 (I-200) (codified as Wash. Rev. Code § 49.60.400(1)), which prohibited discrimination or preferential treatment on the basis of race (and other suspect classes) in the state's "operation of public employment, public education or public contracting."[19] Similarly, the voters of California approved Proposition 209, an amendment to their state constitution that outlawed voluntary affirmative action. The California measure, passed in 1996, states that "the state shall not discriminate against, or grant preferential treatment to, any individual or group on the basis of race, sex, color, ethnicity, or national origin in the operation of public employment, public education, or public contracting" (Cal. Const., Art. I, § 31(a)). Several civil rights groups challenged the measure on constitutional grounds, arguing that the provision violated the equal protection clause of the Fourteenth Amendment. The trial court entered a preliminary injunction and temporary restraining order to stop the state from enforcing the law. In *Coalition for Economic Equity v. Wilson,* 122 F.3d 692 (9th Cir. 1997), the U.S. Court of Appeals overturned the ruling of the trial court. According to the appellate court, Proposition 209 imposed no burden on racial or gender minorities, since it forbade discrimination against them. Since there is no constitutional right to preferential treatment, said the court, forbidding preferential treatment on the basis of race or gender did not injure these groups. Characterizing the law as "neutral," and concluding that the plaintiffs had "no likelihood of success on the merits," the court vacated the preliminary injunction and remanded the case to the trial court. (For further discussion of the appellate court's opinion, see Jill Bodensteiner, "Discrimination Against Students in Higher Education: A Review of the 1997 Judicial Decisions," 25 *J. Coll. & Univ. Law* 331, 342–46 (1998).)

In 2003, the U.S. Supreme Court heard and decided the two University of Michigan cases together as "companion cases." In *Grutter v. Bollinger,* 539 U.S. 306 (2003), rejected white applicants challenged the law school's plan for affirmative action in admissions; in *Gratz v. Bollinger,* 539 U.S. 244 (2003), rejected white applicants challenged a plan of the university's undergraduate College of Literature, Science, and the Arts (LSA). Both plans were voluntary, race-conscious plans, but they were quite different in their particulars, as explained below. In each case, the plaintiffs alleged that the affirmative action plan violated not only the equal protection clause but also Title VI (42 U.S.C. § 2000d) and Section 1981 (42 U.S.C. § 1981). In *Grutter,* the Court upheld the law school plan by a 5-to-4 vote; in *Gratz,* the Court invalidated the undergraduate plan by a 6-to-3 vote. Justice O'Connor, who authored the majority opinion in *Grutter,* was the only Justice

---

[19]The passage of I-200 resulted in the dismissal of the prospective relief claims in a major lawsuit challenging the University of Washington law school's race-conscious affirmative action plan. See *Smith v. University of Washington Law School,* 233 F.3d 1188 (9th Cir. 2000). Since the new state law prohibited the law school from continuing to use its admissions policy, the plaintiff's claim was moot. The court allowed the case to continue, however, with regard to plaintiff's claims for damages for having been denied admission under the law school's pre–I-200 policy. In 2004, subsequent to the U.S. Supreme Court's rulings in *Grutter* and *Gratz* (below, this subsection), the appellate court decided this part of the case in the university's favor (*Smith v. University of Washington,* 392 F.3d 367 (9th Cir. 2004)).

in the majority in both cases. All together, the Justices issued thirteen opinions in the two cases. (See generally *Reaffirming Diversity: A Legal Analysis of the University of Michigan Affirmative Action Cases* (2003), a report by the Harvard Civil Rights Project, available at http://www.civilrightsproject.harvard.edu.) The *Grutter* majority reaffirmed the two basic points upon which a majority of the Justices in *Bakke* agreed: that rigid racial quotas are impermissible, and that other, more flexible forms of racial preferences are permissible. Further, the *Grutter* majority explicitly approved and adopted Justice Powell's reasoning in the *Bakke* case (539 U.S. at 323–25) and for the most part the *Gratz* majority did so as well (539 U.S. at 270–74). Justice Powell's principles regarding affirmative action in admissions, adhered to only by Justice Powell in *Bakke,* thus have now become the principles of the Court.

Like Justice Powell, both the *Grutter* and *Gratz* majorities applied a strict scrutiny standard of review. As explained by the *Gratz* majority, "strict scrutiny" review means that "'any person, of whatever race, has the right to demand that any governmental actor subject to the Constitution justify any racial classification subjecting that person to unequal treatment under the strictest of judicial scrutiny'" (*Gratz,* 539 U.S. at 270, quoting *Adarand,* 515 U.S. at 224). The *Grutter* majority used the same strict scrutiny standard but tempered its application to race-conscious admissions policies by emphasizing that courts should defer to the institution's own judgments about its educational mission. Both the law school policy (*Grutter*) and the undergraduate college policy (*Gratz)* met the "compelling interest" component of strict scrutiny (see below), but only the law school plan met the second, "narrow tailoring" prong.[20] Analytically, that is the difference between the two cases and the reason for the differing results.

In *Grutter,* the lead plaintiff, a white Michigan resident, sued university president Lee Bollinger and others, seeking damages, an order requiring her admission to the law school, and an injunction prohibiting continued racial discrimination by the law school. The plaintiff alleged that the law school used race "as a 'predominant' factor, giving applicants who belong to certain minority groups 'a significantly greater chance of admission than students with similar credentials from disfavored racial groups'" (539 U.S. at 306). The law school's admissions policy, drafted and adopted by a faculty committee in 1992, expresses the law school's interest in "achiev[ing] that diversity which has the potential to enrich everyone's education. . . ." The policy recognizes "many possible bases for diversity admissions" and provides that all such "diversity contributions are eligible for 'substantial weight' in the admissions process." While diversity therefore is not defined "solely in terms of racial and ethnic status," the policy does reaffirm a commitment to "racial and ethnic diversity with special reference to the inclusion of students from groups that have been historically discriminated against, like African-Americans, Hispanics and Native

---

[20]"Narrow tailoring" is a technical term, and its meaning is not immediately obvious. To enhance clarity, it is important to note that the term applies to the *means* by which an institution seeks to achieve the *end* of student body diversity—and in particular to the *race-conscious means* by which the institution seeks to achieve the *end* of racial and ethnic diversity.

Americans." (See 539 U.S. at 315–16, quoting from the trial court record.) The significance of race in admissions decisions "varies from one applicant to another;" while race may play no role in the decision to admit some students, for others "it may be a 'determinative' factor." The law school's goal is to include a "critical mass of under-represented minority students" in each class. "Meaningful numbers" rising to the level of a "critical mass" do not indicate a particular "number, percentage, or range of numbers or percentages," but only "numbers such that the under-represented minority students do not feel isolated or like spokespersons for their race." (See 539 U.S. at 314–16, quoting and paraphrasing testimony of the university's witnesses.)

The Court majority in *Grutter* (Justice O'Connor, joined by Justices Stevens, Souter, Ginsburg, and Breyer), adopting the reasoning of Justice Powell's *Bakke* opinion, rejected the plaintiffs' arguments. First, the *Grutter* majority held that "student body diversity is a compelling state interest that can justify the use of race in University admissions" (539 U.S. at 325). This is because "it is necessary that the path to leadership be visibly open to talented and qualified individuals of every race and ethnicity. All members of our heterogeneous society must have confidence in the openness and integrity of the educational institutions that provide . . . the training and education necessary to succeed in America" (539 U.S. at 332–33). Race and ethnicity, however, are not the only factors pertinent to student body diversity. Rather, student body diversity, as a compelling interest, entails a "broad range of qualities and experiences that may be considered valuable contributions" and "a wide variety of characteristics besides race and ethnicity . . ." (*Grutter*, 539 U.S. at 338–39). Moreover, the majority indicated that courts should "defer" to universities' judgments about "the educational benefits that diversity is designed to produce." "The institution's educational judgment that [student body] diversity is essential to its educational mission," said the Court, "is one to which we defer" (539 U.S. at 328).

Next, the majority in *Grutter* held that the law school's admissions policy was "narrowly tailored" to the interest in student body diversity. The policy's stated goal of "attaining a critical mass of underrepresented minority students" did not constitute a prohibited quota (539 U.S. at 335–36). Instead, the admissions process was "flexible enough" to ensure individual treatment for each applicant without "race or ethnicity" becoming "the defining feature" of the application (539 U.S. at 337). It was particularly important to the Court, regarding narrow tailoring, that "the Law School engages in a highly individualized, holistic review of each applicant's file, giving serious consideration to all the ways an applicant might contribute to a diverse educational environment"; that "the Law School awards no mechanical, predetermined diversity 'bonuses' based on race or ethnicity" (as had occurred in the program at issue in *Gratz*); that the law school "adequately ensures that all factors that may contribute to student body diversity are meaningfully considered alongside race in admissions decisions" (as the Harvard plan approved by Justice Powell in *Bakke* had done); that the "Law School does not . . . limit in any way the broad range of qualities and experiences that may be considered valuable contributions to student body diversity" and "seriously considers each 'applicant's promise of making a notable contribution to the class by way of a particular strength, attainment, or characteristic'"; that all "applicants have the opportunity to highlight their own potential diversity contributions through the submission of a personal statement, letters of recommendation, and an essay describing the ways in which the applicant will contribute to the life and diversity of the Law School"; and that, in practice, "the Law School actually gives substantial weight to diversity factors besides race, . . . frequently accept[ing] nonminority applicants with grades and test scores lower than underrepresented minority applicants (and other nonminority applicants) who are rejected . . ." (539 U.S. at 337–39).

Completing its narrow tailoring analysis, the Court in *Grutter* determined that the "holistic review" provided for by the policy does not "unduly" burden individuals who are not members of the favored racial and ethnic groups. The law school, moreover, had "sufficiently considered workable race-neutral alternatives" before adopting any racial preferences. Since the law school's policy therefore met both components of strict scrutiny review, the Court upheld the policy.

In *Gratz v. Bollinger*, the case involving the University of Michigan's undergraduate College of Literature, Science, and the Arts, the plaintiffs sought damages, declaratory relief, and an injunction prohibiting continued discrimination by the university. They argued that "'diversity as a basis for employing racial preferences is simply too open-ended, ill-defined, and indefinite to constitute a compelling interest capable of supporting narrowly tailored means'" (539 U.S. at 268, quoting Brief for Petitioners) and, further, that the university's admissions policy was not narrowly tailored to achieve the end of student body diversity.

According to the Court, the university's "Office of Undergraduate Admissions [oversaw] the . . . admissions process" and promulgated "written guidelines for each academic year." Under its admissions policy, the undergraduate college considered African Americans, Hispanics, and Native Americans to be "underrepresented minorities." The admissions policy employed a "selection index" under which each applicant could score up to a maximum of 150 points. Applicants received points in consideration of their "high school grade point average, standardized text scores, academic quality and curriculum strength of applicant's high school, in-state residency, alumni relationship, personal essay, and personal achievement or leadership" (539 U.S. at 254–55). Under an additional "miscellaneous" category, "an applicant was entitled to 20 points based upon . . . membership in an under-represented racial or ethnic minority group." An Admissions Review Committee provided an additional level of review for certain applicants flagged by admissions counselors. To be flagged, the applicant must have achieved "a minimum selection index score" and "possess a quality or characteristic important to the University's composition of its freshman class," examples of which included "socioeconomic disadvantage" and "underrepresented race, ethnicity or geography." While the evidence did not reveal "precisely how many applications [were] flagged for this individualized consideration . . . , it [was] undisputed that such consideration [was] the exception and not the rule . . ." (539 U.S. at 274).

The *Gratz* majority (Chief Justice Rehnquist, joined by Justices Scalia, O'Connor, Kennedy, and Thomas) held that "the admissions policy violates the

Equal Protection Clause of the Fourteenth Amendment" (as well as Title VI and
Section 1981) because it fails to provide "individualized consideration" of each
applicant and therefore is not "narrowly tailored" to achieve the compelling
interest in student body diversity. Specifically:

> The LSA's policy automatically distributes 20 points to every single applicant
> from an "underrepresented minority" group, as defined by the University. The
> only consideration that accompanies this distribution of points is a factual
> review of an application to determine whether an individual is a member of one
> of these minority groups. Moreover, unlike Justice Powell's example, where the
> race of a "particular black applicant" could be considered without being deci-
> sive, see *Bakke*, 438 U.S., at 317, 98 S. Ct. 2733, the LSA's automatic distribution
> of 20 points has the effect of making "the factor of race . . . decisive" for virtu-
> ally every minimally qualified underrepresented minority applicant [539 U.S.
> at 271–72].

The undergraduate plan, therefore, was "not narrowly tailored to achieve the
LSA's compelling interest in student body diversity" and therefore failed strict
scrutiny review.

Because Title VI and the equal protection clause embody the same legal standards, the *Grutter* and *Gratz* principles are applicable to both public institutions
and private institutions that receive federal financial assistance. These principles are also likely to apply, in general, to institutions' race-conscious decision
making in areas beyond admissions (for example, financial aid (as discussed in
Section 8.3.4), student orientation programs, or student housing). The principles of Justice Powell's opinion in *Bakke* also apply, since the Court approved
and adopted them in *Grutter* and *Gratz*. These various principles, according to
the Court, must be followed "in practice as well as in theory" (*Grutter*, 539 U.S.
at 338).

Read against the backdrop of *Bakke*, the *Grutter* and *Gratz* cases have brought
some clarity to the law of affirmative action in admissions. The legal and policy issues remain sensitive, however, and administrators should involve legal
counsel fully when considering the adoption or revision of any affirmative
action admissions policy. The following seventeen guidelines—the last twelve
of which apply specifically to race-conscious plans—can assist institutions in
their deliberations.[21]

1. As a threshold matter, an institution may wish to consider whether it has
ever discriminated against minorities or women in its admissions policies. If any
such unlawful discrimination has occurred in the past, and its existence could be
demonstrated with evidence sufficient to support a judicial finding of unlawful
discrimination, the law requires that the institution use affirmative action to the
extent necessary to overcome any present effects of the past discrimination.

---

[21]As for the other parts of this book that set out guidelines or suggestions for institutions or
others, the seventeen guidelines here are not intended as legal advice. For legal advice on the
matters covered in these guidelines or elsewhere in this Section, institutional administrators
should consult their institution's legal counsel.

(See the discussion in the *Bakke* opinions, 438 U.S. at 284, 328, & 414; see also the *Hopwood* case (above); and *Podberesky v. Kirwan,* discussed in Section 8.3.4.) The limits that *Grutter, Gratz,* and *Bakke* place on the voluntary use of racial preferences for diversity purposes do not apply to situations in which the institution itself has engaged in prior unlawful discrimination whose effects continue to the present. At least since *Bakke,* it has been clear that, when "an institution has been found, by a court, legislature, or administrative agency, to have discriminated on the basis of race, color, or national origin[,] [r]ace-conscious procedures that are impermissible in voluntary affirmative action programs may be required [in order] to correct specific acts of past discrimination committed by an institution or other entity to which the institution is directly related" (U.S. Dept. HEW, Policy Interpretation of Title VI, 44 Fed. Reg. 58509 at 58510 (October 10, 1979)). (For an example of a case applying this principle, see *Geier v. Alexander,* 801 F.2d 799 (6th Cir. 1986).) If a court or administrative agency makes such a finding and orders the institution to remedy the present effects of the past discrimination, the institution's plan will be a *mandatory* (or remedial) affirmative action plan (see discussion at the beginning of this subsection). Absent any such finding and order by a government body, the institution may nevertheless implement a *voluntary* affirmative action plan designed to remedy the present effects of past discrimination, if it makes its own findings on past discrimination and its present effects, and these findings are supportable with evidence of discrimination of the type and extent used by courts in affirmative action cases.

With respect to voluntary affirmative action, it is clear that institutions have a "compelling interest in remedying past and present discrimination" (*United States v. Paradise,* 480 U.S. 149, 167 (1987)). But this rationale may be used only when the institution seeks to remedy its own prior discrimination or that of other entities whose discrimination the institution has supported (or perhaps, for a public institution, the discrimination of the higher education system of which it is a constituent part). Remedying prior *societal* discrimination does not provide justification for the use of racial preferences—at least not unless the institution has been a participant or "passive participant" in such discrimination (see *City of Richmond v. Croson Co.,* 488 U.S. 469, 485–86, 492 (1989)). *Croson* and *Adarand Constructors, Inc., v. Pena,* 515 U.S. 200 (1995), taken together, make this point in cases that are not about education but whose reasoning would extend to education admissions. (For an education case that makes the same point, see *Wygant v. Jackson,* 476 U.S. 267, 274 (1986) (plurality opinion of Powell, J.).)

2. In considering whether to adopt or revise an affirmative action policy for admissions, an institution should rely demonstrably on the educational expertise of its faculty and academic administrators and involve policy makers at the highest levels of authority within the institution. These planners and decision makers should exercise special care in determining the institution's purposes and objectives in light of its educational mission, making their decisions in the context of these purposes and objectives. A lower court made these points clearly in a case decided two years before *Bakke* and more than twenty-five years before

Grutter and *Gratz*. In this case, *Hupart v. Board of Higher Education of the City of New York,* 420 F. Supp. 1087 (S.D.N.Y. 1976), the court warned:

> [E]very distinction made on a racial basis . . . must be justified. . . . It cannot be accomplished thoughtlessly or covertly, then justified after the fact. The defendants cannot sustain their burden of justification by coming to court with an array of hypothetical and *post facto* justifications for discrimination that has occurred either without their approval or without their conscious and formal choice to discriminate as a matter of official policy. It is not for the court to supply a . . . compelling basis . . . to sustain the questioned state action
> [420 F. Supp. at 1106].

3. An institution may consider one or a combination of two basic approaches to voluntary affirmative action: the *race-neutral* or *uniform* approach, and the *race-conscious* or *preferential* approach (see guidelines 4 and 6 below). An institution might also consider a third possible approach, falling between the other two, which may be called a *differential,* or *compensatory,* approach (see guideline 5 below). While all three approaches can be implemented lawfully, the potential for legal challenge increases as the institution proceeds from a race-neutral to a differential to a race-conscious approach. The potential for substantially increasing minority enrollment also increases, however, so that an institution that is deterred by the possibility of legal action may also be forsaking part of the means to achieve its educational and societal goals.

4. A *race-neutral* or *uniform* affirmative action policy involves revising or supplementing the institution's general admissions standards or procedures so that they are more sensitively attuned to the varying qualifications and potential contributions of all applicants, including minority and disadvantaged applicants. These changes are then applied uniformly to all applicants. For example, all applicants might be eligible for credit for working to help put themselves through school, for demonstrated commitment to living and working in a blighted geographical area, for being the first in one's family to attend college, for residing in an inner-city area from which the institution typically draws very few students, or for overcoming handicaps or disadvantages. Or institutions might cease using preferences for "legacies," or for members of a particular religious denomination whose membership includes relatively few minorities. Or institutions may use test scores from additional tests that supplement traditional standardized tests and test abilities beyond what the standardized test measures (for an example, see Robert Sternberg, "Accomplishing the Goals of Affirmative Action—With or Without Affirmative Action," *Change,* January–February 2005, 6, 10–13). Such changes would allow all candidates—regardless of race, ethnicity, or sex—to demonstrate particular pertinent qualities that may not be reflected in grades or scores on traditional tests. Numerical cutoffs could still be used if the institution determines that applicants with grades or test scores above or below a certain number should be automatically accepted or rejected.

In the *DeFunis* case in the U.S. Supreme Court (discussed above), Justice Douglas described aspects of such a policy (416 U.S. at 331–32), as did the

California Supreme Court in *Bakke* (553 P.2d at 1165–66). Justice Douglas gave this explanation of a uniform plan:

> The Equal Protection Clause did not enact a requirement that law schools employ as the sole criterion for admissions a formula based upon the LSAT and undergraduate grades, nor does it prohibit law schools from evaluating an applicant's prior achievements in light of the barriers that he had to overcome. A black applicant who pulled himself out of the ghetto into a junior college may thereby demonstrate a level of motivation, perseverance, and ability that would lead a fair-minded admissions committee to conclude that he shows more promise for law study than the son of a rich alumnus who achieved better grades at Harvard. That applicant would be offered admission not because he is black but because as an individual he has shown he has the potential, while the Harvard man may have taken less advantage of the vastly superior opportunities offered him. Because of the weight of the prior handicaps, that black applicant may not realize his full potential in the first year of law school, or even in the full three years, but in the long pull of a legal career his achievements may far outstrip those of his classmates whose earlier records appeared superior by conventional criteria. There is currently no test available to the admissions committee that can predict such possibilities with assurance, but the committee may nevertheless seek to gauge it as best it can and weigh this factor in its decisions. Such a policy would not be limited to blacks, or Chicanos, or Filipinos, or American Indians, although undoubtedly groups such as these may in practice be the principal beneficiaries of it. But a poor Appalachian white, or a second-generation Chinese in San Francisco, or some other American whose lineage is so diverse as to defy ethnic labels, may demonstrate similar potential and thus be accorded favorable consideration by the Committee [416 U.S. at 331–32].

(For an example of a more recent case in which the court upheld such "uniform" criteria for admissions as well as a related recruitment process, see *Weser v. Glen*, 190 F. Supp. 2d 384, 387–88, 395–406 (E.D.N.Y. 2000), *affirmed summarily without published opinion*, 168 *West's Educ. Law. Rptr.* 132 (2d Cir. 2002).)

5. A *differential* or *compensatory* affirmative action policy would be based on the concept that equal treatment of differently situated individuals may itself create inequality. Different or supplementary standards for such individuals would become appropriate when use of uniform standards would in effect discriminate against them. In *Bakke*, Justice Powell referred to a differential system by noting:

> Racial classifications in admissions conceivably could serve a . . . purpose . . . which petitioner does not articulate: fair appraisal of each individual's academic promise in light of some bias in grading or testing procedures. To the extent that race and ethnic background were considered only to the extent of curing established inaccuracies in predicting academic performance, it might be argued that there is no "preference" at all [438 U.S. at 306 n.43].

(See also the California Supreme Court's discussion of this point in *Bakke*; 553 P.2d at 1166–67.) Justice Douglas's *DeFunis* opinion also referred extensively to differential standards and procedures:

> The Indian who walks to the beat of Chief Seattle of the Muckleshoot tribe in Washington has a different culture than examiners at law schools. . . .

[Minority applicants may] have cultural backgrounds that are vastly different from the dominant Caucasian. Many Eskimos, American Indians, Filipinos, Chicanos, Asian Indians, Burmese, and Africans come from such disparate backgrounds that a test sensitively tuned for most applicants would be wide of the mark for many minorities . . . [416 U.S. at 334].

Justice Douglas went on to assert that the goal of a differential system is to assure that race is not "a subtle force in eliminating minority members because of cultural differences" and "to make certain that racial factors do not militate *against an applicant or on his behalf*" (416 U.S. at 335–36).

Using such a rationale, the institution might, for example, apply psychometric measures to determine whether a standardized admissions test that it uses is less valid or reliable as applied to its minority or disadvantaged applicants. If it is, the institution might consider using another supplementary test or some other criterion in lieu of or in addition to the standardized test (see Sternberg, above). Or if an institution provided preferences for "legacies," or for adherents of a particular religion or graduates of schools affiliated with a particular denomination, the institution may consider whether such a criterion discriminated in effect against applicants from particular minority groups; if it does, the institution may consider using other compensating criteria for the minority applicants who are disadvantaged by the institution's use of the discriminatory criterion. Since the institution would be revising its policies in order to advantage minority applicants, having determined that they are disadvantaged by the current policy, it is unlikely that such a revision would be considered race neutral, as a uniform system would be.

To remain true to the theory of a differential system, an institution can modify standards or procedures only to the extent necessary to counteract the discriminatory effect of applying a particular uniform standard or standards; and the substituted or supplementary standards or procedures must be designed to select only candidates whose qualifications and potential contributions are comparable to those of other candidates who are selected for admission. The goal, in other words, would be to avoid a disadvantage to minority applicants rather than to create a preference for them.[22]

6. A *race-conscious* or *preferential* affirmative action policy explicitly provides some form of advantage or preference available only to minority applicants. The admissions policies at issue in the cases discussed above, for the most part, fit within this category. It is the advantage available only to minorities that creates the reverse discrimination claim. For some institutions, especially highly selective institutions and large institutions with graduate and professional programs, some form of racial preference may indeed be necessary for the institution (or a particular school within the institution) to achieve

---

[22]Separate standards or procedures for minority applicants are generally impermissible when used in a way that provides a preference for such applicants (see guideline 8 below). Since a true differential plan does not provide any preference, it should follow that some separate treatment would be permissible when it serves the purposes of such a plan.

its educational and societal objectives. In *Bakke,* the four Justices in the Brennan group agreed that:

> [t]here are no practical means by which . . . [the university] could achieve its ends in the foreseeable future without the use of race-conscious measures. With respect to any factor (such as poverty or family educational background) that may be used as a substitute for race as an indicator of past discrimination, whites greatly outnumber racial minorities simply because whites make up a far larger percentage of the total population and therefore far outnumber minorities in absolute terms at every socioeconomic level. . . . Moreover, while race is positively correlated with differences in . . . [grades and standardized test] scores, economic disadvantage is not [438 U.S. at 376–77].

Race-conscious policies may thus fulfill objectives broader than those of differential policies. As the discussion in this subsection indicates, there are two leading objectives for which race-conscious policies may be used: alleviating the effects of past institutional discrimination (see guideline 1 above) and diversifying the student body (see guidelines 11 and 12 below).

7. An institution opting for a voluntary, race-conscious policy must assure that its racial preferences do not constitute a "quota." In *Bakke,* the Court ruled, by a 5-to-4 vote, that explicit racial or ethnic quotas constitute unlawful reverse discrimination. The Court in *Grutter* and *Gratz* affirmed this basic point. As the majority in *Grutter* explained, a quota "is a program in which a certain fixed number or proportion of opportunities are 'reserved exclusively for certain minority groups'" (539 U.S. at 335, quoting *Croson,* 488 U.S. at 496). Quotas "'impose a fixed number or percentage, which must be attained, or which cannot be exceeded'" and thus "'insulate the individual from comparison with all other candidates for the available seats'" (539 U.S. at 335, quoting *Sheet Metal Workers v. EEOC,* 478 U.S. 421, 495 (1986) (O'Connor, J., concurring and dissenting), and *Bakke,* 438 U.S. at 317 (Powell, J.)). Such a policy would violate the equal protection clause as well as Title VI. A goal, on the other hand, "'require[s] only a good-faith effort . . . to come within a range demarcated by the goal itself,' and permits consideration of race as a 'plus' factor in any given case while still ensuring that each candidate 'compete[s] with all other qualified applicants'" (539 U.S. at 335, citing and quoting *Sheet Metal Workers v. EEOC,* 478 U.S. at 495, and *Johnson v. Transportation Agency,* 480 U.S. 616, 638 (1987)). "[A] court would not assume that a university [employing such a policy] would operate it as a cover for the functional equivalent of a quota system" (*Bakke,* 438 U.S. at 317–18) (Powell, J.).

8. An institution using race-conscious policies should avoid using separate admissions committees, criteria, or cutoff scores for minority applicants. Such mechanisms are vulnerable to legal challenge, as the Court suggested in *Bakke* and directly held in *Grutter.* "[U]niversities cannot . . . put members of [certain racial] groups on separate admissions tracks. . . . Nor can universities insulate applicants who belong to certain racial or ethnic groups from the competition for admission" (*Grutter,* 539 U.S. at 334, citing *Bakke,* 438 U.S. at 315–16) (Powell, J.). The district court in *Hopwood* (above) invalidated part of the

University of Texas law school's plan on this basis (861 F. Supp. at 577–79). This does not necessarily mean, however, that any difference in treatment is always impermissible. In *Smith v. University of Washington*, 392 F.3d 367 (9th Cir. 2004), for instance, the court upheld a law school's use of a letter of inquiry that went only to some minority applicants, as well as a procedure for expedited review of certain minority applications done for recruitment purposes (392 F.3d at 376–78, 380–81).

9. Institutions may wish to clarify exactly why and how they use racial and ethnic preferences, distinguishing between the remedying-past-discrimination rationale and the student body diversity rationale. If employing the remedial rationale, the institution should identify and document the particular present effects of past institutional discrimination that the institution seeks to remedy. For the diversity rationale, the institution should define its diversity objectives and identify the particular values of diversity for its academic environment (see guideline 11 below). The institution may also wish to justify its choices of which minority groups it covers. (For discussion of the use of preferences for Asian American applicants, see *Smith v. University of Washington* in guideline 8 above, 392 F.3d at 378–79 (upholding a "slight plus" for Asian American applicants); and for discussion of possible pitfalls in limiting affirmative action programs to selected minority groups, see Gabriel Chin, "*Bakke* to the Wall: The Crisis of Bakkean Diversity," 4 *Wm. & Mary Bill Rts. J.* 881 (1996)).

10. An institution that has, or is considering, a voluntary, race-conscious admissions plan should be familiar with *state* law in its state regarding such plans. Some states have amended their state statutes or state constitutions to prohibit state institutions from using such plans. California and Washington, as discussed above, are leading examples. Other states may reach the same result through administrative regulations or through state court interpretations of the state constitution. Florida is a leading example (Fla. Admin. Code Ann. R. 6C-6.002(7)).

11. An institution relying on student body diversity as the justification for a voluntary, race-conscious admissions plan should consider clearly elucidating the importance of such diversity to the institution or to particular schools within the institutions and connecting student body diversity to the institution's or school's educational mission. The institution will likely want to make these judgments at a high level of authority and with substantial faculty participation (see guideline 2 above).

12. A race-conscious admissions policy should broadly define student body diversity to include numerous factors beyond race and ethnicity, and the policy in operation should result in substantial weight being given to such additional factors. "[A]n admissions program must be flexible enough to consider all pertinent elements of diversity in light of the particular qualifications of each applicant . . ." (*Grutter*, 539 U.S. at 334). The policy must take into account "a wide variety of characteristics besides race and ethnicity that contribute to a diverse student body" (*Grutter*, 539 U.S. at 339) and must "ensure that all factors that

may contribute to student body diversity are . . . fully considered alongside race in admissions decisions" (*Grutter,* 539 U.S. at 337). The admissions staff and committee must "giv[e] serious consideration to all the ways an applicant might contribute to a diverse educational environment" (*Grutter,* 539 U.S. at 337), so that these factors are taken into account and weighted appropriately "in practice as well as in theory" (*Grutter,* 539 U.S. at 338).

13. Race-conscious admissions policies must provide for "individualized consideration" of applicants. According to Justice Powell, the key to a permissible racial preference is "a policy of individual comparisons" that "assures a measure of competition among all applicants" (438 U.S. at 319, n.53) and that uses "race or ethnic background only as a 'plus' in a particular applicant's file" (438 U.S. at 317). Following Justice Powell, the *Grutter* majority specified that "race [must] be used in a flexible, nonmechanical way . . . as a 'plus' factor in the context of individualized consideration of each . . . applicant" (539 U.S. at 334, citing *Bakke,* 438 U.S. at 315–18) (Powell, J.). The institution's policy must "ensure that each applicant is evaluated as an individual and not in a way that makes an applicant's race or ethnicity the defining feature of his or her application. The importance of this individualized consideration in the context of a race-conscious admissions program is paramount . . ." (*Grutter,* 539 U.S. at 337).

14. Consistent with guideline 13, an institution should avoid using "automatic" points or bonuses that are awarded to all applicants from specified minority groups. There may be no "mechanical, predetermined diversity 'bonuses' based on race or ethnicity" (*Grutter,* 539 U.S. at 337). Such mechanisms are prohibited whenever the "automatic distribution of . . . points has the effect of making 'the factor of race . . . decisive' for . . . qualified minority applicants" (*Gratz,* 539 U.S. at 272, citing *Bakke,* 438 U.S. at 317) (Powell, J.).

15. When devising, revising, or reviewing a race-conscious affirmative action policy, an institution should give serious, good faith consideration to "race-neutral alternatives" for attaining racial diversity.[23] Race-conscious provisions may be utilized only if no "workable" race-neutral alternatives are available. Institutions have no obligation, however, to exhaust "every conceivable race-neutral alternative," or to adopt race-neutral alternatives that "would require a dramatic sacrifice of [other types of] diversity, the academic quality of all admitted students, or both" (*Grutter,* 539 U.S. at 340).

16. An institution with a race-conscious affirmative action policy should monitor the results it obtains under its policy. In particular, the institution should determine whether its policy in practice is in fact achieving the goal of student body diversity, broadly defined. In addition, the institution should periodically

---

[23]The Office for Civil Rights of the U.S. Department of Education has issued two sets of suggestions on possible race-neutral alternatives: "Achieving Diversity: Race-Neutral Alternatives in American Education" (2004), and "Race-Neutral Approaches in Postsecondary Education: Innovative Approaches to Diversity" (2003). Both documents are available on OCR's Web site at http://www.ed.gov/OCR.

determine whether consideration of race and ethnicity remains necessary to the achievement of racial and ethnic diversity. In doing so, institutions should monitor new developments regarding race-neutral alternatives and seriously consider any new alternatives that could prove "workable." Universities "can and should draw on the most promising aspects of . . . race-neutral alternatives as they develop" in other institutions and other states (*Grutter*, 539 U.S. at 342).

17. Institutions may not use race-conscious admissions policies as a *permanent* means for achieving racial and ethnic diversity. The Court in *Grutter* stated its belief that, in time (perhaps in twenty-five years, the Court predicted), societal conditions will progress to the point where such policies will no longer be needed. Thus, "race-conscious admissions policies must be limited in time" and must provide for "a logical end point" for the use of such policies. This limitation may be implemented "by sunset provisions . . . and periodic reviews to determine whether racial preferences are still necessary to achieve student body diversity" (*Grutter*, 539 U.S. at 342; see also guideline 16 above).

These seventeen guidelines can help postsecondary institutions, working with the active involvement of legal counsel, to expand the legal space they have to make their own policy choices about affirmative action in admissions. By carefully considering, justifying, documenting, and periodically reviewing their choices, especially choices involving racial and ethnic preferences, as suggested in these guidelines, institutions may increase the likelihood that their policies will meet constitutional and statutory requirements.

8.2.6. Readmission. The readmission of previously excluded students can pose additional legal problems for postsecondary institutions. Although the legal principles in Section 8.2 apply generally to readmissions, the contract theory (Section 8.2.3) may assume added prominence, because the student-institution contract (see Section 8.1.3) may include provisions concerning exclusion and readmission. The principles in Sections 9.2 through 9.4 may also apply generally to readmissions where the student challenges the validity of the original exclusion. And the nondiscrimination laws provide additional theories for challenges to institutional refusals to readmit students.

Institutions should have an explicit policy on readmission, even if that policy is simply "Excluded students will never be considered for readmission." An explicit readmission policy can give students advance notice of their rights, or lack of rights, concerning readmission and, where readmission is permitted, can provide standards and procedures to promote fair and evenhanded decision making. If the institution has an explicit readmissions policy, administrators should take pains to follow it, especially since its violation could be considered a breach of contract. Similarly, if administrators make an agreement with a student concerning readmission, they should firmly adhere to it. *Levine v. George Washington University*, C.A. (Civil Action) 8230-76 (D.C. Super. Ct. 1976), for instance, concerned a medical student who had done poorly in his first year but was allowed to repeat the year, with the stipulation that he would be excluded for a "repeated performance of marginal quality." On the second try, he passed all his courses but ranked low in each. The school excluded him. The court used contract principles to overturn the exclusion, finding that the school's subjective and arbitrary interpretation of "marginal quality," without prior notice to the student, breached the agreement between student and school. In contrast, the court in *Giles v. Howard University,* 428 F. Supp. 603 (D.D.C. 1977), held that the university's refusal to readmit a former medical student was not a breach of contract, because the refusal was consistent with the "reasonable expectations" of the parties.

Although institutions must follow their written readmission policies, the burden of demonstrating that readmission is warranted is on the student. In *Organiscak v. Cleveland State University,* 762 N.E.2d 1078 (Ohio 2001), a student dismissed from a master's program in speech-language pathology sued the university when it rejected her petition for readmission. The court rejected the student's claim that it was the university's responsibility to collect evidence of an improvement in her clinical skills; the burden was on the student to convince the university that her prior academic performance was an inappropriate indicator of her present ability to complete the program.

Another case illustrates the importance of carefully considering the procedures to be used in making readmission decisions. In *Evans v. West Virginia Board of Regents,* 271 S.E.2d 778 (W. Va. 1980), a student in good standing at a state school of osteopathic medicine had been granted a one-year leave of absence because of illness. When he sought reinstatement two months after termination of the leave, he was informed that because of his lateness he would have to reapply for admission. He did so but was rejected without explanation. The West Virginia Supreme Court of Appeals found that the student was "not in the same class as an original applicant to a professional school." Nor was he in the same position as a student who had been excluded for academic reasons, since "nothing appears of record even remotely suggesting his unfitness or inability to complete the remainder of his education." Rather, since he had voluntarily withdrawn after successfully completing two and a half years of his medical education, the student had a "reasonable expectation that he would be permitted to complete his education." He thus had "a sufficient property interest in the continuation and completion of his medical education to warrant the imposition of minimal due process protections."

The court prescribed that the following procedures be accorded the student if the school again sought to deny him readmission:

> (1) a formal written notice of the reasons should he not be permitted to continue his medical education; (2) a sufficient opportunity to prepare a defense to the charges; (3) an opportunity to have retained counsel at any hearings on the charges; (4) a right to confront his accusers and present evidence on his own behalf; (5) an unbiased hearing tribunal; and (6) an adequate record of the proceedings [271 S.E.2d at 781].

Given the fact that a readmission decision is an academic judgment, the extent of the procedural protections required by the court are especially rigorous.

The appellate court in *Evans* did not indicate the full terms of the school's policies regarding leave of absence and readmission or the extent to which these policies were put in writing. Other schools in the defendant's position may avoid legal hot water by having a clear statement of their policies, including any procedural protections that apply and the consequences of allowing a leave of absence to expire.

Although private institutions would not be subject to the Fourteenth Amendment due process reasoning in *Evans,* they should nevertheless note the court's assertion that readmission decisions encompass different considerations and consequences than original admission decisions. Even private institutions may therefore choose to clothe readmission decisions with greater procedural safeguards than they apply to admission decisions. Moreover, private institutions, like public institutions, should clearly state their readmission policies in writing and coordinate them with their policies on exclusion and leaves of absence.

Once such policies are stated in writing, or if the institution has a relatively consistent practice of readmitting former students, contract claims may ensue if the institution does not follow its policies. (For discussion of an unsuccessful contract claim by a student seeking readmission to medical school, see *North v. State of Iowa,* discussed in Section 8.2.1.)

Students may also allege that denials of readmission are grounded in discrimination. In *Anderson v. University of Wisconsin,* 841 F.2d 737 (7th Cir. 1988), a black former law student sued the university when it refused to readmit him for a third time because of his low grade point average. To the student's race discrimination claim, the court replied that the law school had consistently readmitted black students with lower grades than those of whites it had readmitted; thus, no systemic race discrimination could be shown against black students. With regard to the plaintiff's claim that the law school had refused to readmit him, in part, because of his alcoholism, the court determined that Section 504 requires a plaintiff to demonstrate that he is "otherwise qualified" before relief can be granted. Given the plaintiff's inability to maintain the minimum grade point average required for retention, the court determined that the plaintiff was not "otherwise qualified" and ruled that "[l]aw schools may consider academic prospects and sobriety when deciding whether an applicant is entitled to a scarce opportunity for education" (841 F.2d at 742). (For analysis of this case, see Comment, "*Anderson v. University of Wisconsin:* Handicap and Race Discrimination in Readmission Procedures," 15 *J. Coll. & Univ. Law* 431 (1989).)

A federal appellate court allowed a challenge to a denial of readmission to go to trial on a gender discrimination theory. In *Gossett v. State of Oklahoma ex rel. Board of Regents,* 245 F.3d 1172 (10th Cir. 2001), a male nursing student was required to withdraw from the program after receiving a D grade in a course. The student had presented evidence to the trial court that female students were treated more leniently than their male counterparts when they encountered academic difficulty. Although the trial court had rejected the evidence and had entered a summary judgment in favor of the university, the appellate court reversed, ruling that the student's evidence had raised material issues of fact that needed to be resolved at trial.

In *Carlin v. Trustees of Boston University*, 907 F. Supp. 509 (D. Mass. 1995), a student enrolled in a graduate program in pastoral psychology had requested a one-year leave of absence (later extended to two years) so that she could obtain treatment for a psychiatric disorder. Her academic performance prior to the leave had been satisfactory. The university denied her application for readmission, stating that she lacked the "psychodynamic orientation" for pastoral psychology. The student filed a Section 504 (Rehabilitation Act) claim against the university. Determining that the student was academically qualified and possessed the required clinical skills, and that the university's action was closely related to its knowledge that the student had been hospitalized, the court denied the university's summary judgment motion.

In contrast, in *Gill v. Franklin Pierce Law Center*, 899 F. Supp. 850 (D.N.H. 1995), the court denied the student's Section 504 claim. Gill was dismissed from the law school at the end of his first year for failure to maintain satisfactory academic performance. He applied for readmission, but a faculty committee denied his request. In his lawsuit, he asserted that, in the personal statement that accompanied his application, he had stated that he was the child of an alcoholic parent. The court rejected Gill's argument that this statement put the law school on notice that he suffered from posttraumatic stress disorder, ruling that schools need accommodate only those disabilities of which they are aware.

The U.S. Court of Appeals for the Sixth Circuit rejected the claim of a former student that a decision not to readmit him was motivated by disability discrimination. In *Doe v. Vanderbilt University*, 1997 U.S. App. LEXIS 34104 (6th Cir. 1997) (unpublished), the plaintiff had been placed on academic probation after his first year at Vanderbilt's school of medicine because of a combination of poor academic performance and "behavioral and attitudinal problems." At the end of his second year of medical school, a faculty committee recommended that the student be dismissed. At that point he disclosed to his advisor that he had bipolar disorder, a condition that caused severe mood swings. The committee reconsidered the student's case in light of the new information and gave the student an opportunity to address them. The committee voted a second time to recommend dismissal, and the student withdrew voluntarily before the faculty as a whole acted on the recommendation.

After obtaining medication for his disorder, the plaintiff sought readmission on two occasions. He was rejected twice. The first time, the one position open in the second-year class was awarded to a transfer student with better qualifications. The second time he applied, the school replied that there were no spaces remaining in the second-year class. The student filed claims under the ADA and the Rehabilitation Act, alleging that the denial of readmission was based on his disability. A trial court granted the university's motion for summary judgment, and the plaintiff appealed.

The appellate court affirmed, stating that the plaintiff had not demonstrated that he was qualified to be readmitted, nor that the reason he was denied readmission was his disability. The court said that the plaintiff had not shown that the medical school had excluded him even though it would have readmitted a student "whose academic performance and prospects were as poor but whose difficulties did not stem from a 'handicap'" (1997 U.S. App. LEXIS 34104 at *6). Furthermore, said the court, courts should respect the academic judgment of university faculties (citing *Ewing;* see Section 9.3.1).

At the time an institution suspends or expels a student either for problematic academic performance or behavior, the institution may specify conditions that a student must meet in order to be considered for readmission. In *Rosenthal v. Webster University,* 2000 U.S. App. LEXIS 23733 (8th Cir. 2000) (unpublished), a federal appellate court backed a private university's refusal to readmit a former student with bipolar disorder after it expelled him for carrying a gun and threatening to use it. A condition of Rosenthal's readmission was that he conduct himself appropriately during the period of suspension. Because the plaintiff had been charged with harassment after his suspension, he had failed to meet the conditions of his readmission, and the court ruled that the university was justified in refusing to readmit him.

Since the U.S. Supreme Court's *Garrett* decision (see Section 5.2.5), federal courts have struggled with the question of whether public universities can be sued under Title II of the ADA (see Section 13.2.11) for money damages (*Garrett* involved Title I of the ADA). In *Garcia v. S.U.N.Y. Health Sciences Center of Brooklyn,* 280 F.3d 98 (2d Cir. 2001), the U.S. Court of Appeals for the Second Circuit ruled that the teachings of *Garrett* applied to cases brought under Title II, and that a student's attempt to challenge a denial of readmission under the ADA failed because he had not asserted that the readmission was motivated by discriminatory animus or ill will due to disability, but simply because the institution had refused to accommodate him by readmitting him. With respect to Garcia's Section 504 claim, the court ruled that the state had not waived sovereign immunity against suit under Section 504 by accepting federal funds, because at the time it did so, it was believed that Congress had abrogated sovereign immunity through enactment of the ADA. Federal courts in other jurisdictions do not agree with this interpretation of Section 504, and thus this issue awaits resolution by the U.S. Supreme Court. Students seeking readmission under disability discrimination theories, however, could still maintain claims against public institutions if they merely seek injunctive relief and do not seek money damages.

Other special problems may arise in the readmission process if a student seeking readmission claims that he or she withdrew to avoid sexual (or other) harassment by a faculty or staff member, or that the student was excluded due to low evaluations or grades from a faculty member whose sexual advances the student had rejected. In *Bilut v. Northwestern University,* 645 N.E.2d 536 (Ill. Ct. App. 1994) (also discussed in Section 9.3.1), for example, a graduate student who had been denied an extension of time to complete her dissertation claimed that she had rejected the advances of her dissertation director. The court rejected her claims because her "testimony is inconclusive evidence of quid pro quo sexual harassment" and because other professors reviewing the student's work had "made his or her own independent scholarly and academic judgments" (645 N.E.2d at 543). In other cases, however, where the evidence of harassment is stronger and there is evidence that the harasser's evaluations infected the institution's academic judgments, the institution could be in jeopardy of both viable breach of contract claims (see *Bilut*) and Title IX claims (see Section 9.3.4).

Students may also raise tort claims in challenging denials of readmission. For example, in *Mason v. State of Oklahoma*, 23 P.3d 964 (Ct. Civil Apps. Okla. 2000), a law student, Perry Mason, was expelled for dishonesty in applying for financial aid. Mason claimed negligent and intentional infliction of emotional distress, denial of due process, violation of public policy, and breach of an implied contract. The court rejected all of the claims, affirming the trial court's dismissal of Mason's lawsuit.

The readmission cases demonstrate that colleges that specify the procedures for readmission (and follow them), use reasonable and relevant criteria for making readmission decisions, and can link those criteria to programmatic needs should prevail in challenges to negative readmission decisions.

Sec. 8.3. Financial Aid

8.3.1. General principles.
The legal principles affecting financial aid have a wide variety of sources. Some principles apply generally to all financial aid, whether awarded as scholarships, assistantships, loans, fellowships, preferential tuition rates, or in some other form. Other principles depend on the particular source of funds being used and thus may vary with the aid program or the type of award. Sections 8.3.2 through 8.3.8 discuss the principles, and specific legal requirements resulting from them, that present the most difficult problems for financial aid administrators. This Section discusses more general principles affecting financial aid.

The principles of contract law may apply to financial aid awards, since an award once made may create a contract between the institution and the aid recipient. Typically, the institution's obligation is to provide a particular type of aid at certain times and in certain amounts. The student recipient's obligation depends on the type of aid. With loans, the typical obligation is to repay the principal and a prescribed rate of interest at certain times and in certain amounts. With other aid, the obligation may be only to spend the funds for specified academic expenses or to achieve a specified level of academic performance in order to maintain aid eligibility. Sometimes, however, the student recipient may have more extensive obligations—for instance, to perform instructional or laboratory duties, play on a varsity athletic team, or provide particular services after graduation. The defendant student in *State of New York v. Coury*, 359 N.Y.S.2d 486 (N.Y. Sup. Ct. 1974), for instance, had accepted a scholarship and agreed, as a condition of the award, to perform internship duties in a welfare agency for one year after graduation. When the student did not perform the duties, the state sought a refund of the scholarship money. The court held for the state because the student had "agreed to accept the terms of the contract" and had not performed as the contract required.[24]

Students may also rely on contract law to challenge the withdrawal or reduction in amount of a scholarship. For example, in *Aronson v. University of Mississippi,* 828 So. 2d 752 (Miss. 2002), a student sued the university when it reduced the amount of a scholarship awarded to the student from $4,000 to $2,000. The university defended its decision by saying that the catalog, in which the scholarship amount had been listed as $4,000, was incorrect. Aronson filed a breach of contract claim against the university. The trial court dismissed the claim at the conclusion of the plaintiff's case, and the appellate court reversed, ruling for the student. The state supreme court reversed and remanded the case, saying that the university was entitled to present a defense. The university had argued that disclaimers in its student catalog and other information should have put the student on notice that the scholarship amount had been changed.

The law regarding gifts, grants, wills, and trusts may also apply to financial aid awards. These legal principles would generally require aid administrators to adhere to any conditions that the donor, grantor, testator, or settlor placed on use of the funds. But the conditions must be explicit at the time of the gift. For example, in *Hawes v. Emory University,* 374 S.E.2d 328 (Ga. Ct. App. 1988), a scholarship donor demanded that the university return the gift, asserting that the funds had not been disbursed as agreed upon. The court found the contribution to be a valid gift without any indication that its use was restricted in the way the donor later alleged.

Funds provided by government agencies or private foundations must be used in accordance with conditions in the program regulations, grant instrument, or other legal document formalizing the transaction. Section 8.3.2 illustrates such conditions in the context of federal aid programs. Similarly, funds made available to the institution under wills or trusts must be used in accordance with conditions in the will or trust instrument, unless those conditions are themselves illegal. Conditions that discriminate by race, sex, or religion have posed the greatest problems in this respect. If a public agency or entity has compelled or affirmatively supported the imposition of such conditions, they will usually be considered to violate the federal Constitution's equal protection clause (see, for example, *In Re Certain Scholarship Funds,* 575 A.2d 1325 (N.H. 1990)).[25] But if such conditions appear in a privately established and administered trust, they will usually be considered constitutional, because no state action is present. In

---

[24]Illustrative cases are collected in David B. Harrison, Annot., "Construction and Application of Agreement by Medical or Social Work Student to Work in Particular Position or at Particular Location in Exchange for Financial Aid in Meeting Costs of Education," 83 A.L.R.3d 1273. State age-of-majority laws (regarding a parent's obligation to support a child) are an important supplement to general contract law principles. These laws help the institution determine whether it should contract with the parent or the child in awarding aid and whether it should take parental resources into account in computing the amount of aid.

[25]Cases analyzing gender restrictions in charitable gifts or trusts are collected in Tracey A. Bateman, Annot., "Validity of Charitable Gift or Trust Containing Gender Restrictions on Beneficiaries," 90 A.L.R.4th 836. See also Phillip E. Hassman, Annot., "Construction and Application of State Equal Rights Amendments Forbidding Determination of Rights Based on Sex," 90 A.L.R.3d 158.

Shapiro v. Columbia Union National Bank and Trust Co. (discussed in Section 1.5.2), for instance, the Supreme Court of Missouri refused to find state action to support a claim of sex discrimination lodged against a university's involvement in a private trust established to provide scholarships exclusively for male students. Even in the absence of state action, however, a discriminatory condition in a private trust may still be declared invalid if it violates one of the federal nondiscrimination requirements applicable to federal fund recipients (see Sections 8.3.3 & 8.3.4).[26]

Conditions in testamentary or *inter vivos* trusts can sometimes be modified by a court under the *cy pres* doctrine. In *Howard Savings Institution v. Peep,* 170 A.2d 39 (N.J. 1961), Amherst College was unable to accept a trust establishing a scholarship loan fund because one of the trust's provisions violated the college's charter. The provision, stipulating that recipients of the funds had to be "Protestant" and "Gentile," was deleted by the court. Similarly, in *Wilbur v. University of Vermont,* 270 A.2d 889 (Vt. 1970), the court deleted a provision in a financial aid trust that had placed numerical restrictions on the size of the student body at the university's college of arts and sciences. In each case the court found that the dominant purpose of the person establishing the trust could still be achieved with the restriction removed. As the court in the *Peep* case explained:

> The doctrine of *cy pres* is a judicial mechanism for the preservation of a charitable trust when accomplishment of the particular purpose of the trust becomes impossible, impracticable, or illegal. In such a situation, if the settlor manifested an intent to devote the trust to a charitable purpose more general than the frustrated purpose, a court, instead of allowing the trust to fail, will apply the trust funds to a charitable purpose as nearly as possible to the particular purpose of the settlor [170 A.2d at 42].

However, if the court finds that a trust's purposes can still be realized, it will not permit changes. For example, in *In re R. B. Plummer Memorial Loan Fund Trust,* 661 N.W.2d 307 (Neb. 2003), an alumnus had created a trust to provide loans to students. Because very few students applied for loans from the trust, the university petitioned the court to permit it to make grants from the trust rather than loans. The court refused, finding that Plummer had believed that students should pay for college, and that the university was not promoting the loan opportunities sufficiently to make them attractive to students.

Given the numerous legal and public relations issues involved in institutional fund-raising and gift acceptance, administrators should develop a clear policy on the acceptance of gifts.

A third relevant body of legal principles is that of constitutional due process. These principles apply generally to public institutions; they also apply to

---

[26]The relevant cases are collected in A. S. Klein, Annot., "Validity and Effect of Gift for Charitable Purposes Which Excludes Otherwise Qualified Beneficiaries Because of Their Race or Religion," 25 A.L.R.3d 736.

private institutions when those institutions make awards from public funds (see Section 1.5.2). Since termination of aid may affect both "property" and "liberty" interests (see Section 6.7.2.1) of the student recipients, courts may sometimes require that termination be accompanied by some form of procedural safeguard. *Corr v. Mattheis,* 407 F. Supp. 847 (D.R.I. 1976), for instance, involved students who had had their federal aid terminated in midyear, under a federal "student unrest" statute, after they had participated in a campus protest against the Vietnam War. The court found that the students had been denied a property interest in continued receipt of funds awarded to them, as well as a liberty interest in being free from stigmas foreclosing further educational or employment opportunities. Termination thus had to be preceded by notice and a meaningful opportunity to contest the decision. In other cases, if the harm or stigma to students is less, the required procedural safeguards may be less stringent. Moreover, if aid is terminated for academic rather than disciplinary reasons, procedural safeguards may be almost nonexistent, as courts follow the distinction between academic deficiency problems and misconduct problems drawn in Section 9.4.3.

In *Conard v. University of Washington,* 834 P.2d 17 (Wash. 1992), the Washington Supreme Court ruled that student athletes do not have a constitutionally protected property interest in the renewal of their athletic scholarships. The court reversed a lower court's finding that the students, who had been dropped from the football team after several instances of misconduct, had a property interest in renewal of their scholarships. The financial aid agreements that the students had signed were for one academic year only, and did not contain promises of renewal. The supreme court interpreted the financial aid agreements as contracts that afforded the students the right to *consideration* for scholarship renewal and—citing *Board of Regents v. Roth* (see Sections 6.7.2.1 & 6.7.2.2)— refused to find a "common understanding" that athletic scholarships were given for a four-year period. Furthermore, the court said, the fact that both the university and the National Collegiate Athletic Association (NCAA) provided minimal due process guarantees did not create a property interest. Special considerations involving athletics scholarships and NCAA rules are discussed in Section 10.4.5.

Federal and state laws regulating lending and extensions of credit provide a fourth body of applicable legal constraints. At the federal level, for example, the Truth-in-Lending Act (15 U.S.C. § 1601 *et seq.*) establishes various disclosure requirements for loans and credit sales. Such provisions are of concern not only to institutions with typical loan programs but also to institutions with credit plans allowing students or parents to defer payment of tuition for extended periods of time. The federal Truth-in-Lending Act, however, exempts National Direct Student Loans (NDSLs; now Perkins Loans), Federal Stafford Loans, and Federal Family Education Loans) (see Section 8.3.2) from its coverage (15 U.S.C. § 1603(7)).

As a result of congressional action in 1996 to amend the Internal Revenue Code, all states have adopted college savings plans. Congress added Section 529 to the Internal Revenue Code (26 U.S.C. § 529), which allows a "state agency or instrumentality" to establish a program under which a person "may purchase tuition credits or certificates on behalf of a designated beneficiary which entitle the beneficiary to the waiver or payment of qualified higher education expenses of the beneficiary" (26 U.S.C. § 529(b)(1)). States may establish either prepaid tuition plans or savings plans; educational institutions may establish only prepaid tuition plans. Contributions to the plans are excluded from the contributor's gross income for federal income tax purposes. An amendment to Section 529 in 2002 allows a beneficiary to make a "qualified withdrawal" from a 529 plan that is free of federal income tax. There are penalties for withdrawals from the fund for noneducational purposes, and prepaid tuition plans differ from savings plans in significant ways. Basic information on these plans is available at http://www.savingforcollege.com. (For an assessment of these savings and prepaid tuition plans, see Michael A. Olivas, "State College Savings and Prepaid Tuition Plans: A Reappraisal and Review," 32 *J. Law & Educ.* 475 (2003).)

Given the multitude of tax (see Section 13.3.1), contract, and other legal complications of prepaid tuition plans, institutions should consult with counsel knowledgeable in these areas of the law before implementing such plans.

8.3.2. Federal programs.

The federal government provides or guarantees many millions of dollars per year in student aid for postsecondary education through a multitude of programs. To protect its investment and ensure the fulfillment of national priorities and goals, the federal government imposes many requirements on the way institutions manage and spend funds under federal programs. Some are general requirements applicable to student aid and all other federal assistance programs. Others are specific programmatic requirements applicable to one student aid program or to a related group of such programs. These requirements constitute the most prominent—and, critics would add, most prolific and burdensome—source of specific restrictions on an institution's administration of financial aid.

The most prominent general requirements are the nondiscrimination requirements discussed in Section 8.3.3, which apply to all financial aid, whether or not it is provided under federal programs. In addition, the Family Educational Rights and Privacy Act (FERPA) (discussed in Section 9.7.1) imposes various requirements on the institution's record-keeping practices for all the financial aid that it disburses. The FERPA regulations, however, do partially exempt financial aid records from nondisclosure requirements. They provide that an institution may disclose personally identifiable information from a student's records, without the student's consent, to the extent "necessary for such purposes as" determining the student's eligibility for financial aid, determining the amount of aid and the conditions that will be imposed regarding it, or enforcing the terms or conditions of the aid (34 C.F.R. § 99.31(a)(4)).

The Student Assistance General Provisions, 34 C.F.R. Part 668, lay out eligibility criteria for institutions wishing to participate in federal student assistance programs, and for students wishing to obtain aid under these programs. Institutional eligibility criteria are addressed at 34 C.F.R. § 668.8. Generally, an educational program that provides at least an associate's degree or the equivalent may participate in these programs if it meets federal requirements for program length, leads to at least an associate's degree, and meets other regulatory criteria. Proprietary institutions may also participate in federal student aid programs if they provide at least fifteen weeks of instruction that prepares students for "gainful employment in a recognized occupation," and meet other regulatory criteria. Proprietary institutions must also meet specific student completion rates and placement rates (34 C.F.R. § 668.8(e)).

The Student Assistance General Provisions require institutions to enter into a written "program participation agreement" with the Secretary of Education. The program participation agreement applies to all of the branch campuses and other locations of the institution. In the agreement, the institution must agree to a variety of requirements, including a promise that it will comply with all provisions of Title IV of the Higher Education Act (HEA) (the portion of the HEA that authorizes the federal student assistance programs), all regulations promulgated under the authority of the HEA, and all special provisions allowed by the statute. The institution must also certify that it will not charge students a fee for processing applications for federal student aid and that it will maintain records and procedures that will allow it to report regularly to state and federal agencies. The institution must also certify that it complies with a variety of laws requiring the disclosure of information, including the Student Right-to-Know and Campus Security Act (discussed in Section 8.6.3). Specific requirements of program participation agreements are found at 20 U.S.C. § 1994; regulations concerning these agreements are codified at 34 C.F.R. § 668.14.

Advances in technology have resulted in changes to definitions of terms in the General Provisions such as the term "week." Because of the increasing numbers of institutions offering courses to students via distance learning, previous definitions of "week" and "academic year" had excluded otherwise eligible students from receiving federal financial assistance. The Department of Education amended the General Provisions on November 1, 2002 (67 Fed. Reg. 67048, 67061), removing an earlier "twelve-hour rule" in the definition of "academic year" and permitting institutions that offer instruction at least one day per week to participate in the federal student assistance programs (34 C.F.R. § 668.3). In determining a student's eligibility for federal assistance, for instance, an institution must ascertain whether the student is in default on any federally subsidized or guaranteed loan or owes a refund on a federal grant, and must obtain the student's "financial aid transcript(s)" from other institutions to assist in this task (34 C.F.R. § 668.19).

The 2002 amendments of the General Provisions also provide several forms of "safe harbor" for providing incentives to individuals who recruit students for distance learning programs (67 Fed. Reg. 67048, 67072 (November 1, 2002)). The amendments to 34 C.F.R. § 668.14 allow institutions to hire individuals specifically to recruit students for employer-sponsored courses, provide token gifts to alumni or students in return for their assistance in recruiting students, with an annual limit per individual of $100, and payments to individuals who refer prospective students to the institution via the Internet.

Another provision of the Higher Education Act requires an institution participating in the federal student aid program to certify "that it has in operation a drug abuse prevention program that is determined by the institution to be accessible to any officer, employee, or student at the institution" (20 U.S.C. § 1094(a)(10)). Similar provisions in other laws that place obligations on institutions receiving federal funds are discussed in Section 13.4.4 of this book.

Students convicted of drug offenses are excluded from eligibility for federal student financial aid (20 U.S.C. § 1091(r)). The same section of the law provides that students who have satisfactorily completed a drug rehabilitation program that complies with criteria in federal regulations, and who have either had the conviction reversed or expunged or have passed two unannounced drug tests, may be restored to eligibility for federal student financial aid. Regulations for this provision are found at 34 C.F.R. § 668.40.

Most of the federal student aid programs were created by the Higher Education Act of 1965 (20 U.S.C. §§ 1070 *et seq.*), which has been reauthorized and amended regularly since that year. The most recent changes are contained in the Higher Education Amendments of 1998 (Pub. L. No. 105-244, 112 Stat. 1581). Financial aid programs for veterans and military personnel are in various acts (see Section 13.4.2).

The specific programmatic restrictions on federal student aid depend on the particular program. There are various types of programs, with different structures, by which the government makes funds available:

1. Programs in which the federal government provides funds to institutions to establish revolving loan funds—as in the Perkins Loan program (20 U.S.C. §§ 1087aa–1087ii; 34 C.F.R. Parts 673 & 674).

2. Programs in which the government grants funds to institutions, which in turn provide grants to students—as in the Federal Supplemental Educational Opportunity Grant (SEOG) program (20 U.S.C. § 1070b *et seq.*; 34 C.F.R. Parts 673 & 676) and the Federal Work-Study (FWS) program (42 U.S.C. § 2751 *et seq.*; 34 C.F.R. Parts 673 and 675).

3. Programs in which students receive grants directly from the federal government—as in the "New GI Bill" program (38 U.S.C. § 3001 *et seq.*; 38 C.F.R. Part 21) and the Pell Grant program (20 U.S.C. § 1070a *et seq.*; 34 C.F.R. Part 690).

4. Programs in which students receive funds from the federal government through the states—as in the Leveraging Educational Assistance Partnership Program (20 U.S.C. § 1070c *et seq.*; 34 C.F.R. Part 692) and the Robert C. Byrd Honors Scholarship Program (20 U.S.C. §§ 1070d-31, 1070d-33; 34 C.F.R. § 654.1).

5. Programs in which students or their parents receive funds from third-party lenders—as in the Federal Stafford Loan Program. In the Federal Family Educational Loan program, private lenders provide federally guaranteed loans. This program includes Stafford Loans made to students (20 U.S.C. § 1071 *et seq.*; 34 C.F.R. Part 682), Parent Loans for

Undergraduate Students (PLUS) made to parents (20 U.S.C. § 1078-2; 34 C.F.R. Part 682), and Consolidation Loans (20 U.S.C. § 1078-3; 34 C.F.R. Part 682).[27]

6. Programs in which students and parents borrow directly from the federal government at participating schools. The William D. Ford Direct Loan Program (20 U.S.C. § 1087a *et seq.;* 34 C.F.R. Part 685) includes Direct Stafford Loans, Direct PLUS Loans, and Direct Consolidation Loans. These programs allow institutions authorized by the Department of Education to lend money directly to students through loan capital provided by the federal government.

In order to receive aid, students required to register with Selective Service must file statements with the institutions they attend, certifying that they have complied with the Selective Service law and regulations. The validity of this requirement was upheld by the U.S. Supreme Court in *Selective Service System v. Minnesota Public Interest Research Group,* 468 U.S. 841 (1984). Regulations implementing the certification requirement are published in 34 C.F.R. § 668.37.

The U.S. Department of Education has posted on the World Wide Web a guide to the federal student assistance programs that provides information on applying for grants, loans, and work-study assistance. It is available at http://www.studentaid.ed.gov. The department also has a Web site on Information for Financial Assistance Professionals (IFAP), available at http://ifap.ed.gov, that provides information on the requirements for the various financial aid programs, lists available publications, and provides updates on recent changes in laws and regulations governing these programs. The Education Department publishes annually the *Federal Student Aid Handbook,* which is mailed to every institution participating in the federal student aid programs, and which also may be downloaded free from the IFAP Web site.

A law passed by Congress in 1999, the Gramm-Leach-Bliley Act (Pub. L. 106-102, November 12, 1999, codified in part at 15 U.S.C. §§ 6801(b), 6805(b)), and intended to reform the banking industry by broadening the scope of permissible business activities for banks, has been interpreted by the Federal Trade Commission (FTC) to apply to institutions of higher education that administer federal financial aid programs. The law's "Standards for Safeguarding Customer Information" (16 C.F.R. Part 314) requires covered entities, including colleges and universities, to restrict their disclosure of information about recipients of federal student aid and to develop a "comprehensive information security program" that protects the privacy of participants in financial transactions with the institution. A brief description of the requirements of the Safeguards Rule and relevant Web-based reference materials are available on the National Association of College and University Attorneys (NACUA) Web site in NACUALERT

---

[27]The Secretary of Education has the authority to cause guarantors of federal student loans to cease operations, a power that was recognized in *Student Loan Fund of Idaho, Inc. v. U.S. Department of Education,* 272 F.3d 1155 (9th Cir. 2001), *amended* by 2001 U.S. App. LEXIS 29338, *rehearing en banc denied,* 289 F.3d 599 (2002).

Vol. 1, No. 4 (May 16, 2003), available at http://www.nacua.org. The FTC has issued guidance for complying with the Safeguards Rule, which is available on the FTC's Web site at http://www.ftc.gov.

The receipt of Title IV funds is conditioned on compliance with a number of verification measures affecting both educational institutions and alien students. In order to participate in grants, loans, or work assistance under Title IV programs, all students must declare in writing that they are U.S. citizens or in an immigrant status that does not preclude their eligibility. Alien students are required to provide the institution with documentation that clearly establishes their immigration status, and further requires the institution to verify the status of such students with the Bureau of Citizenship and Immigration Services. Regulations related to the verification of a student's eligibility to receive federal student aid with respect to citizenship or lawful residence in the United States are found at 34 C.F.R. § 668.133. Institutions are prohibited from denying, delaying, reducing, or terminating Title IV funds without providing students with a reasonable opportunity to establish eligibility. If, after complying with these requirements, an institution determines that a student is ineligible, it is required to deny or terminate Title IV aid and provide the student with an opportunity for a hearing concerning his or her eligibility (34 C.F.R. § 668.136(c)).

Much of the controversy surrounding the federal student aid programs has concerned the sizable default rates on student loans, particularly at institutions that enroll large proportions of low-income students. Several reports issued by the General Accounting Office have been sharply critical of the practices of colleges, loan guarantee agencies, and the Department of Education in implementing the federally guaranteed student loan programs. As a result, substantial changes have been made in the laws and regulations related to eligibility, repayment, and collection practices. Collection requirements of federal student loan programs are discussed in Section 8.3.8.3.

Institutions that participate in federal student aid programs must have their program records audited annually by an independent auditor. Regulations regarding the conduct of the audit and reporting requirements appear at 34 C.F.R. § 668.24.

Federal courts have refused to authorize a private right of action against colleges or universities under the Higher Education Act for students to enforce the financial assistance laws and regulations (see, for example, *L'ggrke v. Benkula*, 966 F.2d 1346 (10th Cir. 1992); *Slovinec v. DePaul University*, 332 F.3d 1068 (7th Cir. 2003)). The courts have reached this result because the Higher Education Act vests enforcement of the financial aid program laws and regulations in the Secretary of Education (20 U.S.C. § 1082(a)(2)). Should the Secretary decline to act in a case in which an institution is violating the federal student aid requirements, a plaintiff with standing may bring an action against the Secretary of Education, but not against the college.

A few courts, however, have permitted students to use state common law fraud or statutory consumer protection theories against the Education Department, colleges, or lenders when the college either ceased operations or provided a poor-quality education (see, for example, *Tipton v. Alexander*, 768

F. Supp. 540 (S.D. W. Va. 1991)). (See Section 13.4.5 for a discussion of private rights of action under federal funding laws.) One court has permitted students to file a RICO (Racketeer Influenced Corrupt Organization) claim against a trade school, alleging mail fraud. In *Gonzalez v. North American College of Louisiana,* 700 F. Supp. 362 (S.D. Tex. 1988), the students charged that the school induced them to enroll and to obtain federal student loans, which they were required to repay. The school was unaccredited; and, after it had obtained the federal funds in the students' name, it closed and did not refund the loan proceeds.

Federal student aid programs bring substantial benefits to students and the colleges they attend. Their administrative and legal requirements, however, are complex and change constantly. It is imperative that administrators and counsel become conversant with these requirements and monitor legislative, regulatory, and judicial developments closely.

8.3.3. Nondiscrimination. The legal principles of nondiscrimination apply to the financial aid process in much the same way they apply to the admissions process (see Sections 8.2.4 & 8.2.5). The same constitutional principles of equal protection apply to financial aid. The relevant statutes and regulations on nondiscrimination—Title VI, Title IX, Section 504, the Americans With Disabilities Act, and the Age Discrimination Act—all apply to financial aid, although Title IX's and Section 504's coverage and specific requirements for financial aid are different from those for admissions. And affirmative action poses difficulties for financial aid programs similar to those it poses for admissions programs. Challenges brought under Title VI and the equal protection clause against institutions that reserve certain scholarships for minority students are discussed in Section 8.3.4.

Of the federal statutes, Title IX has the most substantial impact on the financial aid programs and policies of postsecondary institutions. The regulations (34 C.F.R. § 106.37), with four important exceptions, prohibit the use of sex-restricted scholarships and virtually every other sex-based distinction in the financial aid program. Section 106.37(a)(1) prohibits the institution from providing "different amount[s] or types" of aid, "limit[ing] eligibility" for "any particular type or source" of aid, "apply[ing] different criteria," or otherwise discriminating "on the basis of sex" in awarding financial aid. Section 106.37(a)(2) prohibits the institution from giving any assistance, "through solicitation, listing, approval, provision of facilities, or other services," to any "foundation, trust, agency, organization, or person" that discriminates on the basis of sex in providing financial aid to the institution's students. Section 106.37(a)(3) also prohibits aid eligibility rules that treat the sexes differently "with regard to marital or parental status."

The four exceptions to this broad nondiscrimination policy permit sex-restricted financial aid under certain circumstances. Section 106.37(b) permits an institution to "administer or assist in the administration of" sex-restricted financial assistance that is "established pursuant to domestic or foreign wills, trusts, bequests, or similar legal instruments or by acts of a foreign government." Institutions must administer such awards, however, in such a way that their "overall effect" is "nondiscriminatory" according to standards set out in Section 106.37(b)(2). Section 106.31(c) creates the same kind of exception for sex-restricted foreign-study scholarships awarded to the institution's students or graduates. Such awards must be established through the same legal channels specified for the first exception, and the institution must make available "reasonable opportunities for similar [foreign] studies for members of the other sex." The third exception, for athletics scholarships, is discussed in Section 10.4.6. A fourth exception was added by an amendment to Title IX included in the Education Amendments of 1976. Section 412(a)(4) of the amendments (20 U.S.C. § 1681(a)(9)) permits institutions to award financial assistance to winners of pageants based on "personal appearance, poise, and talent," even though the pageant is restricted to members of one sex.

Section 504 of the Rehabilitation Act of 1973 (see Section 13.5.4), as implemented by the Department of Education's regulations, restricts postsecondary institutions' financial aid processes as they relate to disabled persons. Section 104.46(a) of the regulations (34 C.F.R. Part 104) prohibits the institution from providing "less assistance" to qualified disabled students, from placing a "limit [on] eligibility for assistance," and from otherwise discriminating or assisting any other entity to discriminate on the basis of disability in providing financial aid. The major exception to this nondiscrimination requirement is that the institution may still administer financial assistance provided under a particular discriminatory will or trust, as long as "the overall effect of the award of scholarships, fellowships, and other forms of financial assistance is not discriminatory on the basis of handicap" (34 C.F.R. § 104.46(a)(2)).

A lawsuit challenging the denial of financial aid as alleged disability discrimination has had a tortured history, and is yet to be resolved. In *Johnson v. Louisiana Department of Education,* 2002 U.S. Dist. LEXIS 1284 (E.D. La. 2002), Johnson, a student at the University of New Orleans, had received financial aid from the university. Johnson experienced a "medical emergency" and withdrew from the university. Several months later, the university notified Johnson that he was no longer eligible for financial aid. Johnson was ready to resume his studies and appealed this decision. The appeals committee approved a continuation of financial aid, but imposed several academic conditions on continued eligibility for the aid. Because Johnson was not notified of the committee's decision until after the fall semester began, he missed several classes and was unable to attain the grade point average specified by the committee. He was denied further financial aid, and sued the university under Section 504.

Although the university claimed that it was immune from litigation for money damages under Section 504 on the grounds of sovereign immunity, the trial court disagreed. Citing an earlier ruling by the U.S. Court of Appeals for the Fifth Circuit in *Pederson v. Louisiana State University,* 213 F.3d 858 (5th Cir. 2000), which determined that the university had waived its sovereign immunity from Title IX claims (discussed in Section 13.1.6), the trial court ruled that the university had waived sovereign immunity by accepting funds under federal spending programs (here, federal financial aid funds).

The U.S. Court of Appeals for the Fifth Circuit vacated the trial court's opinion, 330 F.3d 362 (5th Cir. 2003), and remanded the case with instructions to dismiss Johnson's claims for lack of jurisdiction. Relying on a Fifth Circuit opinion issued after the trial court's opinion in *Johnson* (*Pace v. Bogalusa City School Board,* 325 F.3d 609 (5th Cir. 2003)), the appellate court ruled that the university had not waived sovereign immunity. *Pace* had also involved a Section 504 claim. The court in *Pace* had ruled that, until the decision of the U.S. Supreme Court in *Board of Trustees of the University of Alabama v. Garrett,* 531 U.S. 356 (2001), university officials were bound by earlier judicial precedent that the acceptance of federal funds did not constitute a waiver of sovereign immunity. After *Garrett,* said the court, any institution's decision to accept federal funds would constitute an express waiver under those statutes, such as Section 504, that expressly condition the receipt of federal funds on a state's waiver of sovereign immunity. However, Johnson's claims arose prior to the *Garrett* decision, and thus the university did not knowingly waive sovereign immunity.

The U.S. Court of Appeals for the Fifth Circuit granted a motion to rehear both *Johnson* and *Pace en banc* (*Johnson v. Louisiana Department of Education,* 343 F.3d 732 (5th Cir. 2003); *Pace v. Bogalusa City School Board,* 339 F.3d 348 (5th Cir. 2003)). The *en banc* court in *Pace* agreed with the panel's ruling that the state had waived Eleventh Amendment immunity (403 F.3d 272 (5th Cir. 2005)). There have been no further proceedings in *Johnson.*

The Americans With Disabilities Act also prohibits discrimination on the basis of disability in allocating financial aid. Title II, which covers state and local government agencies, applies to public colleges and universities that meet the definition of a state or local government agency. The regulations prohibit institutions from providing a benefit (here, financial aid) "that is not as effective in affording equal opportunity . . . to reach the same level of achievement as that provided to others" (28 C.F.R. § 35.130(b)(1)(iii)). Both public and private colleges and universities are covered by Title III as "places of public accommodation" (28 C.F.R. § 36.104), and are prohibited from limiting the access of individuals with disabilities to the benefits enjoyed by other individuals (28 C.F.R. § 36.202(b)).

Regulations interpreting the Age Discrimination Act of 1975 (42 U.S.C. §§ 6101–6103) (see Section 13.5.5 of this book) include the general regulations applicable to all government agencies dispensing federal aid as well as regulations governing the federal financial assistance programs for education. These regulations are found at 34 C.F.R. Part 110.

The regulations set forth a general prohibition against age discrimination in "any program or activity receiving Federal financial assistance" (34 C.F.R. § 110.10(a)), but permit funding recipients to use age as a criterion if the recipient "reasonably takes into account age as a factor necessary to the normal operation or the achievement of any statutory objective of a program or activity" (34 C.F.R. § 110.12) or if the action is based on "reasonable factors other than age," even though the action may have a disproportionate effect on a particular age group (34 C.F.R. § 110.13). With respect to the administration of federal financial aid, the regulations would generally prohibit age criteria for the receipt of student financial assistance.

Criteria used to make scholarship awards may have discriminatory effects even if they appear facially neutral. For example, research conducted in the 1980s demonstrated that women students tended to score approximately 60 points lower on the Scholastic Aptitude Test (SAT) than male students did, although women's high school and college grades tended to be higher than men's. In *Sharif by Salahuddin v. New York State Education Department*, 709 F. Supp. 345 (S.D.N.Y. 1989), a class of female high school students filed an equal protection claim, seeking to halt New York's practice of awarding Regents and Empire State Scholarships exclusively on the basis of SAT scores. The plaintiffs alleged that the practice discriminated against female students. The judge issued a preliminary injunction, ruling that the state should not use SAT scores as the sole criterion for awarding scholarships. (For a thorough analysis of legal and policy issues related to this issue, see K. Connor & E. J. Vargyas, "The Legal Implications of Gender Bias in Standardized Testing," 7 *Berkeley Women's L.J.* 13 (1992).)

8.3.4. Affirmative action in financial aid programs. Just as colleges and universities may adopt voluntary affirmative action policies for admissions in certain circumstances (see Section 8.2.5 above), they may do so for their financial aid programs. As with admissions, when the institution takes race, ethnicity, or gender into account in allocating financial aid among its aid programs or in awarding aid to particular applicants, issues may arise under the equal protection clause (for public institutions), Title VI, Title IX, or Section 1981 (42 U.S.C. § 1981). When the issues arise under Title VI, the "1994 Policy Guidance" on financial aid, issued by the U.S. Department of Education (ED), 59 Fed. Reg. 8756–64 (February 23, 1994), provides an important supplement to the statute and regulations.

The case of *Flanagan v. President and Directors of Georgetown College*, 417 F. Supp. 377 (D.D.C. 1976), provides an early example of affirmative action issues regarding financial aid. The law school at Georgetown had allocated 60 percent of its financial aid for the first-year class to minority students, who constituted 11 percent of the class. The remaining 40 percent of the aid was reserved for nonminorities, the other 89 percent of the class. Within each category, funds were allocated on the basis of need; but, because of Georgetown's allocation policy, the plaintiff, a white law student, received less financial aid than some minority students, even though his financial need was greater. The school's threshold argument was that this program did not discriminate by race because disadvantaged white students were also included within the definition of minority. The court quickly rejected this argument:

> Certain ethnic and racial groups are automatically accorded "minority" status, while whites or Caucasians must make a particular showing in order to qualify. . . . Access to the "favored" category is made more difficult for one racial group than another. This in itself is discrimination as prohibited by Title VI as well as the Constitution [417 F. Supp. at 382].

The school then defended its policy as part of an affirmative action program to increase minority enrollment. The student argued that the policy discriminated against nonminorities in violation of Title VI of the Civil Rights Act (see this volume, Section 13.5.2). The court sided with the student:

> Where an administrative procedure is permeated with social and cultural factors (as in a law school's *admission* process), separate treatment for "minorities" may be justified in order to insure that all persons are judged in a racially neutral fashion.
>
> But in the instant case, we are concerned with the question of financial need, which, in the final analysis, cuts across racial, cultural, and social lines. There is no justification for saying that a "minority" student with a demonstrated financial need of $2,000 requires more scholarship aid than a "nonminority" student with a demonstrated financial need of $3,000. To take such a position, which the defendants have, is reverse discrimination on the basis of race, which cannot be justified by a claim of affirmative action [417 F. Supp. at 384].

Although *Flanagan* broadly concludes that allotment of financial aid on an explicit racial basis is impermissible, at least for needs-based aid, the U.S. Supreme Court's subsequent decision in *Bakke* (see Section 8.2.5) appeared to leave some room for the explicit consideration of race in financial aid programs. ED's 1994 Policy Guidance, above, confirmed the view that race-conscious financial aid policies are permissible in some circumstances. And more recently, the Supreme Court's 2003 decisions in *Grutter v. Bollinger*, 539 U.S. 306 (2003), and *Gratz v. Bollinger*, 539 U.S. 244 (2003) (see Section 8.2.5), although concerned with admissions rather than financial aid, have given further support for the position that some consideration of race in allocating and awarding financial aid is permissible.

Since the U.S. Supreme Court has not yet decided a case on affirmative action in financial aid programs, the admission cases, *Grutter* and *Gratz*, are therefore the precedents most nearly on point. It is likely that the general principles from these cases will apply to financial aid programs as well, and that courts will use these principles to resolve equal protection, Title VI, and Section 1981 challenges to financial aid policies of public institutions, and Title VI and Section 1981 challenges to such policies of private institutions.[28] This assessment does not necessarily mean, however, that race-conscious financial aid policies will always be valid or invalid under the law in the same circumstances and to the same extent as race-conscious admissions policies. The Court made clear in *Grutter* and *Gratz* that "[n]ot every decision influenced by race is equally objectionable," and that courts therefore must carefully consider the "context" in which a racial or ethic preference is used. Since the "context" for financial aid policies typically has some differences from the "context" for admissions, as discussed

---

[28]One appellate court has suggested, however, in a post-*Grutter* and *Gratz* case, that somewhat different principles may apply under Section 1981 with respect to the "order and nature of the proof" of intentional discrimination (*Doe v. Kamehameha Schools/Bernice Pauahi Bishop Estate*, 416 F.3d 1025 (9th Cir. 2005)).

below, these differences may lead to some differences in legal reasoning, and perhaps results, in cases challenging affirmative action in financial aid.

The basic principles guiding a court's analysis, however, probably would not change from one context to the other. The threshold questions would likely still include whether the policy on its face or in its operation takes race into account in allocating or awarding financial aid, and if so, whether the policy uses racial quotas for either the dollar amount of aid available to minority applicants or the number of scholarships, loans, or other aid awards for minority applicants. There would still most probably be a need to determine the institution's justi-fication for taking race into account, and the documentation supporting this jus-tification. The permissible justifications for financial aid policies are likely to be the same as for admissions policies—student body diversity and remedying the present effects of the institution's past discrimination; and just as these inter-ests are "compelling interests" for purposes of admissions, they will likely be considered compelling for financial aid as well. The "narrow tailoring" test will also likely continue to apply as the basis for judging whether the consideration of race is designed, and carefully limited, to accomplish whichever compelling interest the institution has attributed to its race-conscious financial aid policies. Thus the strict scrutiny standard of review, as articulated and applied to admis-sions in *Grutter* and *Gratz,* also can guide analysis of race-conscious financial aid and "provide a framework for carefully examining the importance and the sincerity of the reasons advanced by the governmental decision-maker for the use of race *in that particular context*" (539 U.S. at 327; emphasis added).

There appear to be three particularly pertinent ways in which the context of financial aid differs from the context of admissions. *First,* institutions dispense financial aid through a variety of scholarship, loan, and work-study programs that may have differing eligibility requirements and types of aid packages. It may therefore be questionable, in particular cases, whether each "part" of the aid program that takes race into account may be analyzed independent of the other parts of the institution's overall aid program, or whether courts may or must consider how other parts of the program may work together with the challenged part in accomplishing the institution's interest in student body diversity or rem-edying past discrimination. *Second,* some of the institution's financial aid resources may come from private donors who have established their own eligi-bility requirements for the aid, and the institution may have various degrees of involvement in and control over the award of this aid from private sources. (The U.S. Department of Education's 1994 Policy Guidance, for example, distinguishes between private donors' awards of race-conscious aid directly to students, which aid is not covered by Title VI, and private donors' provision of funds to a col-lege or university that in turn distributes them to students, which funds are cov-ered by Title VI (see 59 Fed. Reg. at 8757–58, Principle 5).) Questions may therefore arise concerning whether and when such financial aid is fully subject to the requirements of the equal protection clause, or Title VI or Title IX, and whether such aid may or must be considered to be part of the institution's over-all aid program if a court considers how all the parts work together to accom-plish the institution's interests (see first point immediately above). *Third,* "the use of race in financial aid programs may have less impact on individuals who are not members of the favored group than the use of race in admissions. If individuals are not admitted to an institution, then they cannot attend it," but "individuals who do not receive a particular race-conscious scholarship may still be able to obtain loans, work-study funds, or other scholarships in order to attend." (See Elizabeth Meers & William Thro, *Race Conscious Admissions and Financial Aid Programs* (National Association of College and University Attorneys, 2004), 28; and see generally Meers & Thro at 24–30.)

The most vulnerable type of race-conscious aid is "race-exclusive" scholarships available only to persons of a particular race or ethnicity. Under the 1994 Policy Guidance, above, the U.S. Department of Education permits the use of race-exclusive scholarships in certain narrow circumstances (59 Fed. Reg. at 8757–58 (Principles 3, 4, & 5)). But under the *Grutter* and *Gratz* principles, as applied to financial aid policies, such scholarships may be viewed as employing racial quotas as well as a separate process or separate consideration for minority aid applicants—both of which are prohibited for admissions policies.

In a major case decided prior to *Grutter* and *Gratz, Podberesky v. Kirwan,* 38 F.3d 147 (4th Cir. 1994), a U.S. Court of Appeals invalidated a race-exclusive scholarship program of the University of Maryland. In *Podberesky,* a Hispanic student claimed that the university's Banneker Scholarship program violated Title VI and the equal protection clause. The district court and the appellate court applied strict scrutiny analysis. Defending its program, the university argued that it served the compelling state interest of remedying prior *de jure* discrimination, given the fact that the state was then still under order of the Office for Civil Rights, U.S. Department of Education, to remedy its formerly segregated system of public higher education. The university also argued that the goal of the student body diversity was served by the scholarship program.

The district court found that the university had provided "overwhelming" evidence of the present effects of prior discrimination and upheld the program without considering the university's diversity argument (764 F. Supp. 364 (D. Md. 1991)). The federal appeals court, however, reversed the district court (956 F.2d 52 (4th Cir. 1992). Although the appellate court agreed that the university had provided sufficient evidence of prior discrimination, it found the Office for Civil Rights' observations about the present effects of that discrimination unconvincing because they had been made too long ago (between 1969 and 1985); and it ordered the district court to make new findings on the present effects of prior discrimination. The appellate court also noted that race-exclusive scholarship programs violate *Bakke* if their purpose is to increase student body diversity rather than to remedy prior discrimination.

On remand to the district court, the university presented voluminous evidence of the present effects of prior discrimination, including surveys of black high school students and their parents, information on the racial climate at the university, research on the economic status of black citizens in Maryland and the effects of unequal educational opportunity, and other studies. The district court found that the university had demonstrated a "strong basis in evidence" for four present effects of past discrimination: the university's poor reputation in the black community, underrepresentation of blacks in the student body, the low retention and graduation rates of black students at the university, and a racially hostile campus climate (838 F. Supp. 1075 (D. Md. 1993)).

With regard to the university's evidence of the present effects of past discrimination, the court also commented: "It is worthy of note that the University is (to put it mildly) in a somewhat unusual situation. It is not often that a litigant is required to engage in extended self-criticism in order to justify its pursuit of a goal that it deems worthy" (838 F. Supp. at 1082, n.47). The court also held that the Banneker Scholarship program was narrowly tailored to remedy the present effects of past discrimination because it demonstrated the university's commitment to black students, increased the number of peer mentors and role models available to black students, increased the enrollment of high-achieving black students, and improved the recipients' academic performance and persistence. Less restrictive alternatives did not produce these results. The court did not address the university's diversity argument.

On appeal, the U.S. Court of Appeals for the Fourth Circuit again overruled the district court (38 F.3d 147 (4th Cir. 1994)). Despite the university's voluminous evidence of present effects of prior racial discrimination, the appellate court held that there was insufficient proof of present effects to establish a compelling interest for the race-exclusive scholarships. Furthermore, said the court, the scholarship program was not narrowly tailored to accomplishing the university's interest. The program thus failed both prongs of the strict scrutiny test.

The appellate court was sharply critical of the findings made by the district court on the present effects of prior discrimination. With respect to the district court's findings on the university's poor reputation in the minority community and the hostile racial environment on campus, the appellate court ruled that those then-present conditions were not closely related to the university's prior discrimination but were more directly a result of present societal discrimination that cannot form the basis for a race-conscious remedy. Regarding the findings of low retention and graduation rates of minority students, the appellate court held that this condition was not directly linked to the university's prior discrimination but was a result of economic and other unrelated factors. Similarly, regarding the underrepresentation of black students at the university, the appellate court held that this condition could not be traced directly to the university's prior discrimination; other factors, such as student preferences for predominantly minority public colleges in Maryland, decisions to apply only to out-of-state colleges, and decisions not to attend college at all could explain all or part of the underrepresentation.

The appellate court also rejected the district court's finding that the program provided role models and mentors to other black students, noting that the "Supreme Court has expressly rejected the role-model theory as a basis for implementing a race-conscious remedy" (38 F.3d at 159, citing *Wygant v. Jackson Board of Educ.*, 476 U.S. 267, 276 (1986) (plurality opinion)). In addition, the appellate court also criticized the university for asserting that its program was narrowly tailored to increase the number of black Maryland residents at the university, since the Banneker program was open to out-of-state students.

Thus, the court concluded: "[T]he program more resembles outright racial balancing than a tailored remedial program" (38 F.3d at 160).

Although the university had originally used two rationales for its race-conscious scholarship program—remediation of its own prior discrimination and enhancement of student diversity—the district court had addressed only the remediation rationale in its first decision. In the appellate court's first reversal of the district court, it rejected diversity as a rationale for race-exclusive programs. The university therefore did not argue that rationale in the second round of litigation, not did the district or appellate courts address it.

Podberesky thus signals the legal vulnerabilities of race- or gender-exclusive scholarship programs. At the least, *Podberesky* illustrates how difficult it may be to justify a race-based scholarship program using the remedying-prior-discrimination rationale. The other, less developed, part of *Podberesky,* rejecting the student diversity rationale, is inconsistent with the Supreme Court's decisions in *Grutter* and *Gratz,* and *Podberesky* therefore cannot be used to foreclose diversity rationales for race-conscious student aid programs. But, as suggested earlier in this subsection, *Grutter* and *Gratz* present institutions with other problems in demonstrating that a race-exclusive scholarship program is not the equivalent of a racial quota and does not employ a separate process insulating minority applicants from competition with nonminorities who seek financial aid. On the other hand, some room is apparently left open, by *Grutter* and *Gratz,* for an institution to argue that there are no race-neutral alternatives, or alternatives that do not involve exclusivity, for accomplishing the diversity objectives that it accomplishes with race-exclusive aid; or to argue that nonminority students are not unduly burdened by the race-exclusive program because their financial aid needs are met in other comparable ways with other funds under other programs. The U.S. Department of Education's 1994 Policy Guidance (above) appears to adopt a similar position (59 Fed. Reg. at 8757) and thus provides further support for the validity of some race-exclusive scholarships, at least under Title VI.[29]

Both public and private institutions that have race-conscious or gender-conscious financial aid programs may wish to review them in light of these various considerations, and institutions considering the adoption or modification of any such program will want to do the same. In addition, careful monitoring of further developments in the courts, the U.S. Department of Education, and in the states (including proposed amendments to the state constitution) is obviously warranted.

8.3.5. Discrimination against nonresidents.
State institutions have often imposed significantly higher tuition fees on out-of-state students, and courts have generally permitted such discrimination in favor of the state's own

---

[29]Similar issues could arise with sex-restricted scholarships, and similar arguments would be available to institutions. In addition, institutions may sometimes rely on a Title IX regulation that expressly permits sex-restricted scholarships awarded under wills, trusts, and other legal instruments if the "overall effect" of such awards is not discriminatory (34 C.F.R. § 106.37(b); see subsection 8.3.3 of this book, above).

residents. The U.S. Supreme Court, in the context of a related issue, said: "We fully recognize that a state has a legitimate interest in protecting and preserving the quality of its colleges and universities and the right of its own bona fide residents to attend such institutions on a preferential tuition basis" (*Vlandis v. Kline*, 412 U.S. 441, 452–53 (1973)). Not all preferential tuition systems, however, are beyond constitutional challenge.

In a variety of cases, students have questioned the constitutionality of the particular criteria used by states to determine who is a resident for purposes of the lower tuition rate.[30] In *Starns v. Malkerson*, 326 F. Supp. 234 (D. Minn. 1970), students challenged a regulation that stipulated: "No student is eligible for resident classification in the university, in any college thereof, unless he has been a bona fide domiciliary of the state for at least a year immediately prior thereto." The students argued, as have the plaintiffs in similar cases, that discrimination against nonresidents affects "fundamental" rights to travel interstate and to obtain an education and that such discrimination is impermissible under the Fourteenth Amendment's equal protection clause unless necessary to the accomplishment of some "compelling state interest." The court dismissed the students' arguments, concluding that "the one-year waiting period does not deter any appreciable number of persons from moving into the state. There is no basis in the record to conclude, therefore, that the one-year waiting period has an unconstitutional 'chilling effect' on the assertion of the constitutional right to travel." The U.S. Supreme Court affirmed the decision without opinion (401 U.S. 985 (1971)).

Other cases are consistent with *Starns* in upholding durational residency requirements of up to one year for public institutions. Courts have agreed that equal protection law requires a high standard of justification when discrimination infringes fundamental rights. But, as in *Starns,* courts have not agreed that the fundamental right to travel is infringed by durational residency requirements. Since courts have also rejected the notion that access to education is a fundamental right (see *San Antonio Independent School District v. Rodriguez,* 411 U.S. 1 (1973)), courts have not applied the "compelling interest" test to durational residency requirements of a year or less. In *Sturgis v. Washington,* 414 U.S. 1057 (1973), *affirming* 368 F. Supp. 38 (W.D. Wash. 1973), the Supreme Court again recognized these precedents by affirming, without opinion, the lower court's approval of Washington's one-year durational residency statute.

However, in *Vlandis v. Kline* (cited earlier in this Section), the Supreme Court held another kind of residency requirement to be unconstitutional. A Connecticut statute provided that a student's residency at the time of application

---

[30]The cases are collected in Kenneth Rampino, Annot., "Validity and Application of Provisions Governing Determination of Residency for Purpose of Fixing Fee Differential for Out-of-State Students in Public College," 56 A.L.R.3d 641. For citations to state statutes and regulations on residency determinations, and an analysis of the governance structure by which each state implements its requirements, see Michael A. Olivas, et al., "State Residency Requirements: Postsecondary Authorization and Regulations," 13 *Coll. L. Dig.* 157, printed in *West's Educ. Law. Rptr.* (NACUA Special Pamphlet, February 1983).

for admission would remain her residency for the entire time she was a student. The Supreme Court noted that, under such a statute, a person who had been a lifelong state resident, except for a brief period in another state just prior to admission, could not reestablish Connecticut residency as long as she remained a student. But a lifelong out-of-state resident who moved to Connecticut before applying could receive in-state tuition benefits even if she had lived in the state for only one day. Because such unreasonable results could flow from Connecticut's "permanent irrebuttable presumption" of residency, the Court held that the statute violated due process. At the same time, the Court reaffirmed the state's broad discretion to use more flexible and individualized criteria for determining residency, such as "year-round residence, voter registration, place of filing tax returns, property ownership, driver's license, car registration, marital status, vacation employment," and so on. In subsequent cases the Court has explained that *Vlandis* applies only to "those situations in which a state 'purports to be concerned with [domicile but] at the same time den[ies] to one seeking to meet its test of [domicile] the opportunity to show factors clearly bearing on that issue'" (*Elkins v. Moreno*, 435 U.S. 647 (1978), quoting *Weinberger v. Salfi*, 422 U.S. 749, 771 (1975)).

Lower courts have considered other types of residency criteria, sometimes (like the Supreme Court in *Vlandis*) finding them unconstitutional. In *Kelm v. Carlson*, 473 F.2d 1267 (6th Cir. 1973), for instance, a U.S. Court of Appeals invalidated a University of Toledo requirement that a law student show proof of postgraduation employment in Ohio before being granted resident status. This requirement created a type of irrebuttable presumption that "can act as an impossible barrier to many students who in utter good faith intend to and, for all other purposes, have succeeded in establishing residency in Ohio"; the regulation arbitrarily discriminated against such students, thus violating the equal protection clause. In *Samuel v. University of Pittsburgh*, 375 F. Supp. 1119 (W.D. Pa. 1974), a class action brought by female married students, a federal district court invalidated a residency determination rule that made a wife's residency status dependent on her husband's residency. While the state defended the rule by arguing the factual validity of the common law presumption that a woman has the domicile of her husband, the court held that the rule discriminated on the basis of sex and thus violated equal protection principles. And in *Eastman v. University of Michigan* 30 F.3d 670 (6th Cir. 1994), the court identified equal protection problems raised by a university durational residency requirement that did not clearly distinguish between *residency* and *domicile*. Remanding the case to the federal district court for further proceedings, the court reasoned:

> A durational requirement imposed on a domiciliary or bona fide resident . . .
> would run afoul of the Equal Protection Clause. Because domicile can be
> obtained without the passage of any particular period of time, such a require-
> ment imposed on one who has true domicile or bona fide residence in the state
> would not advance the legitimate state interest served by such a requirement—
> restricting preferential tuition rates only to domiciliaries. The requirement there-
> fore would lack a rational basis and violate the Equal Protection Clause.

Although the passage of a certain period of time, such as a year, may be relevant as evidence on the question of domicile, it cannot be dispositive. Thus, if the University's registrar requires some individuals to have a physical residence in Michigan for one year before considering evidence on their domicile or bona fide residence status, and also refuses to give them retroactive credit for residence at the time that his investigation, whenever conducted, shows that domicile or bona fide residence began, then the policy would be unconstitutional as an impermissible durational requirement imposed on domiciliaries. If, on the other hand, the registrar determines, based on all the evidence, whether the student is a domiciliary or bona fide resident at the time of admission, then the policy would not be unconstitutional . . . [30 F.3d at 673–74].

Other courts (like the U.S. Supreme Court in *Starns* and in *Sturgis*) have upheld particular residency criteria against constitutional objections. In *Peck v. University Residence Committee of Kansas State University,* 807 P.2d 652 (Kan. 1991), for instance, the court rejected students' arguments that the state residency requirements violated equal protection and procedural due process (807 P.2d at 663–64). And in *Smith v. Board of Regents of the University of Houston,* 874 S.W.2d 706 (Ct. App. Tex. 1994), the plaintiff applied for the in-state tuition rate after living in Texas and attending the University of Houston for one year. He had moved to Texas in 1987 to commence study at the university's law center. The plaintiff was a full-time student who had declared his intent "to attend law school and live and work [in Texas] after graduation." During the school year he worked part time for a law firm in Houston; during the summers he worked full time for the same firm. In addition, he was registered to vote in Texas, held a Texas driver's license, registered his car in Texas, and rented an apartment in Texas. The university denied his initial request for reclassification as an in-state student and every subsequent request he made before each of his remaining semesters at the university.

The Texas statute defines a nonresident student as "an individual who is 18 years of age or over who resides out of state or who has come from outside Texas and who registers in an educational institution before having resided in Texas for a 12-month period" (Tex. Educ. Code Ann. § 54.052(f)). There is a presumption in favor of this nonresident student classification "as long as the residence of the individual in the state is primarily for the purpose of attending an educational institution" (§ 54.054). The regulations of the Coordinating Board, Texas College and University System, provide for a reclassification if the individual withdraws from school and resides in the state while gainfully employed for twelve months, but does not provide for this reclassification if the nonresident maintains his status as a full-time student.

The plaintiff argued that the Texas statute governing residency created an unconstitutional, irrebuttable presumption of nonresidency. Citing *Vlandis v. Kline* (above), the court rejected this argument:

Unlike the Connecticut statute [at issue in *Vlandis*], the reclassification rules in Texas do not permanently "freeze" a student in a nonresident status based on the student's classification at the time of application to the university. A student may obtain reclassification in any number of ways. First, according to the policy on reclassification, a student will be entitled to reclassification if he or she withdraws from the University for a period of twelve months, and resides in Texas while gainfully employed. Secondly, the statute lists several factors that may result in reclassification. For example, a student may work full time in Texas, while enrolled as a student, or may purchase a homestead in Texas. Dependency on a parent or guardian who has resided in Texas for at least 12 months is also a factor that may result in reclassification. However, the factors listed in the statute are nonexclusive; therefore, presumably there are other circumstances that would result in reclassification. The rule in question also indicates that the "presumption of 'nonresident' is not a conclusive presumption," and may be overcome by showing "facts or actions unequivocally indicative of a fixed intention to reside permanently in the state" [874 S.W.2d at 709].

The court had no difficulty with the university's position that the plaintiff's statement of intent to remain in Texas was not sufficient proof of that intent: "to accept the plaintiff's argument would require the University to reclassify as a resident every student who, after attending the University for a year, makes a self-serving declaration that he intends to reside [in the state]."

The plaintiff also argued that the one-year waiting period infringed on his fundamental right to travel. Relying again on *Vlandis* as well as on *Starns v. Malkerson* (above), the court also rejected this equal protection claim:

> We find the reclassification statute distinguishable from either of the two situations in which a statute has been invalidated because it impinged upon the fundamental right to travel. The reclassification statute, and its one-year waiting period, does not involve a basic right or necessity. . . . The right to receive a lower tuition rate at a state university cannot be equated to the right to receive welfare benefits, medical care, or the right to vote. Neither does the reclassification statute, on its face, seek to apportion or limit the benefits accorded to the citizens of Texas based on the length or timing of their residence. Instead, the reclassification policy seeks to establish which students are in fact bona fide residents of the state of Texas [874 S.W.2d at 711].

Because it found that the Texas statute and the regulations promulgated by the coordinating board do not create an irrebuttable presumption of nonresidency or an impingement on the right to travel, but instead create a test of bona fide residency for purposes of tuition, the court rejected the student's claims and upheld the statute's constitutionality. Subsequently, in *Teitel v. University of Houston Board of Regents*, 285 F. Supp. 2d. 865 (S.D. Tex. 2002), a federal court also upheld the constitutionality of the Texas residency statute and regulations, rejecting arguments similar to those in *Smith* (as well as contract and negligence claims that were summarily dismissed).

The court's opinion in *Eastman v. University of Michigan*, 30 F.3d 670 (6th Cir. 1994), contains a useful discussion of the distinction between residency and domicile (30 F.3d at 672–73), as well as an implicit warning to drafters of residency regulations to exercise care in using these terms. The court also clarified that, while durational residency requirements are valid under *Starns, Sturgis,* and *Vlandis,* such a requirement would be unconstitutional if applied to a student *who has already established a bona fide domicile* (as opposed to a resident status) within the state (30 F.3d at 673–74).

In addition to establishing acceptable criteria, institutions must ensure that the procedures they follow in making residency determinations will not be vulnerable to challenges. For instance, they will be expected to follow any procedures established by state statutes or administrative regulations. Their procedures also must comply with the procedural requirements of the federal due process clause. In *Lister v. Hoover,* 706 F.2d 796 (7th Cir. 1983), however, the court held that the due process clause did not obligate the University of Wisconsin to provide students denied resident status with a written statement of reasons for the denial; see also *Michaelson v. Cox,* 476 F. Supp. 1315 (S.D. Iowa 1979). And in *Ward v. Temple University,* 2003 WL 21281768 (E.D. Pa. 2003), the court, citing *Lister,* asserted that "a public university such as Temple does not have to provide a full panoply of procedural protections to individuals claiming in-state residency status for tuition purposes" (2003 WL 21281768 at *4).

In most of the tuition residency cases discussed above, the courts analyzed the issues under the Fourteenth Amendment's equal protection and due process clauses. In *Saenz v. Roe,* 526 U.S. 489(1999), however, the U.S. Supreme Court determined that durational residency requirements for state services are also subject to analysis under the Fourteenth Amendment's "privileges or immunities" and "citizenship" clauses (14th Amend., § 1, sentences 1 & 2). (See Erika Nelson, Comment, "Unanswered Questions: The Implications of *Saenz v. Roe* for Durational Residency Requirements, 49 *U. Kan. L. Rev.* 193 (2000).) Relying on these two clauses, the Court by a 7-to-2 vote invalidated a California one-year durational residency requirement for welfare benefits. While this case thus identifies two additional bases upon which new arrivals may attack residency requirements for state benefits and services, these new arguments are not likely to be applied successfully to state residency requirements—particularly durational residency requirements—for tuition benefits. In its opinion, the Court distinguished state tuition benefits from state welfare benefits:

> [B]ecause whatever benefits [the plaintiffs] receive will be consumed while they remain in California, there is no danger that recognition of their claim will encourage citizens of other States to establish residency for just long enough to acquire some readily portable benefit, such as a divorce or a college education, that will be enjoyed after they return to their original domicile. See, e.g., *Sosna v. Iowa,* 419 U.S. 393 (1975); *Vlandis v. Kline,* 412 U.S. 441 (1973) [526 U.S. at 505].

Moreover, the Court said it was "undisputed" that the *Saenz* plaintiffs were citizens and thus residents of the state, and that it was not a case in which "the bona fides of [their] claim to state citizenship were questioned." Since issues about the bona fides of residency are the focus of most of the cases in this Section, these cases are apparently still good law after the *Saenz* decision.

Residency cases have increasingly focused on issues of state administrative law. Typically, these issues concern the authority of state higher education institutions to promulgate administrative rules and criteria for residency determinations, the legal interpretation of these rules and criteria, the burden of proof that petitioning students must meet to demonstrate residency, or the standard of review that courts must apply in reviewing administrative denials of residency petitions. In *Peck v. University Residence Committee* (above), for example, the student plaintiff had applied to the defendant residence committee for approval to pay the lower tuition charge for Kansas resident students. The committee denied his request despite the fact that he "(1) registered to vote and voted in Kansas; (2) registered an automobile in Kansas and paid personal property tax in Kansas; (3) insured his automobile in Kansas; (4) acquired a Kansas driver's license; (5) had a checking and savings account in Kansas; and (6) registered with the selective service in Kansas" (807 P.2d at 656). The state district court overruled the committee's decision, stating that its "action in denying Peck resident status is not supported by substantial evidence." Reversing the district court, the Supreme Court of Kansas held that, although the student had established physical residence in Kansas, he had not established the requisite intent to remain permanently in Kansas after graduation. Reviewing the committee's application of eight primary and nine secondary factors set out in state regulations for use in determining intent, the court concluded that most of the student's evidence related to secondary factors, which, standing alone, were "not probative for an intent determination because many are capable of being fulfilled within a few days of arriving in Kansas." The court also rejected the student's arguments that the residency regulations were inconsistent with the authorizing state statute (Kan. Stat. Ann. § 76-729(c)(4)). The court therefore reinstated the findings and decision of the residence committee.

In a Vermont case, *Huddleston v. University of Vermont,* 719 A.2d 415 (Vt. 1998), the Supreme Court of Vermont upheld a university regulation requiring students to prove their in-state residency status by "clear and convincing" evidence. Pursuant to the Vermont legislature's "broad delegation of authority" to the university's trustees to define eligibility for in-state tuition, the university had adopted procedures, rules, and documentation requirements for determining a student's tuition classification. The enabling statute (16 Vt. Stat. Ann. § 2282) did not mention burdens of proof, but the university nevertheless included the "clear and convincing" requirement in its regulations. The court upheld this provision because the university trustees had "implicit authority" to adopt a burden of proof requirement "in furtherance of this legislative charge to implement state policy on reduced tuition rates for in-state students."

A case from Oregon, *Polaski v. Clark,* 973 P. 2d 381 (Or. App. 1999), concerned the legal interpretation of residency rules. The plaintiff-student had served in the U.S. Air Force at various locations in the United States. He petitioned to be classified an Oregon resident for tuition purposes beginning with the 1996 winter term. In his application, he explained that "[f]rom October 1994, when I decided to become an Oregon resident upon my discharge, I did all I could to become an Oregon resident. I registered to vote, registered my vehicle, got an Oregon driver's license and changed my tax status to Oregon. I have recently even purchased my first home in Portland, and I intend to make Oregon my residence both now and in the future." The Interinstitutional Residency

Committee, and then the vice chancellor for academic affairs, of the Oregon higher education system denied the student's request on the basis that he had not maintained a "continuous presence" in Oregon for the twelve months prior to his request for resident classification, as required by the system's regulation which provides:

> (2) An Oregon resident is a financially independent person who, immediately prior to the term for which Oregon resident classification is requested:
>
> (a) Has established and maintained a domicile in Oregon of not less than 12 consecutive months; and
>
> (b) Is primarily engaged in activities other than those of being a college student [Or. Admin. Reg. 580–010–0030].

The student sought judicial review of the vice chancellor's decision. Applying the Oregon Administrative Procedure Act, the appellate court explained that, on a petition for judicial review, the court "reviews [only] for substantial evidence and errors of law" (973 P.2d at 383, citing Or. Admin. Reg. 183.484 (4)). The student claimed that the vice chancellor's interpretations of the residency regulations were incorrect (that is, were errors of law). The court determined, however, that the vice chancellor correctly interpreted the rules in denying petitioner resident status. In particular, while the twelve-month rule "does not demand an uninterrupted physical presence" in the state, "it does demand an uninterrupted 'presence,'" in the sense of domicile, "even though the person is physically absent."

In comparison, the court's decision in *Ravindranathan v. Virginia Commonwealth University,* 519 S.E.2d 618 (Va. 1999), concerned issues of the adequacy of evidence rather than issues of legal interpretation (or errors of law). The student had moved to Virginia from Illinois to attend Virginia Commonwealth University (VCU) for her undergraduate education and had stayed on to attend medical school at VCU. She sought residency status for medical school, claiming that her boyfriend lived in Virginia, she paid taxes in Virginia, she registered to vote in Virginia, her father had secured a license to practice medicine in Virginia, and her parents were preparing to move to Virginia. After a residency officer denied her in-state tuition status, the student appealed to the Residency Appeals Committee; when her petition was again denied, she filed suit asking the court to review and reverse these administrative decisions. A state statute provided that the court's function in such a case "shall be only to determine whether the decision reached by the institution could reasonably be said, on the basis of the record, not to be arbitrary, capricious or otherwise contrary to law" (519 S.E.2d at 670, citing Va. Code § 23-7.4:3(A)). The circuit court upheld the Residency Appeals Committee decision, and the Supreme Court of Virginia affirmed. The student had been a nonresident when she came to Virginia for undergraduate school, said the court, and a "presumption" arose that the student continued in the state "for the purpose of attending school and not as a bona fide domiciliary." The student had the evidentiary burden of rebutting this presumption "by clear and convincing evidence." The appeals committee decided she had not met this burden. Moreover:

The circuit court correctly refused to reweigh the evidence considered by the Residency Appeals Committee and, as required by Code § 23-7.4:3, the circuit court limited its review to "whether the decision reached by the institution could reasonably be said, on the basis of the record, not to be arbitrary, capricious or otherwise contrary to law."

* * * *

On appeal, the sole issue that we may consider is whether the circuit court was plainly wrong when it held that the Residency Appeals Committee's decision was not arbitrary, capricious, or otherwise contrary to the law. Our review of the record reveals that the facts upon which [the student] relies to support her purported Virginia domicile could also be deemed auxiliary to fulfilling her educational objectives or are routinely performed by temporary residents of this Commonwealth. Thus, the Residency Appeals Committee's decision was not arbitrary or capricious, and the circuit court's judgment upon review of that decision was not plainly wrong [519 S.E.2d at 620-21].

As these administrative law cases illustrate, institutions that act responsibly and consistently will usually be able to prevail when students assert state administrative law challenges to residency determinations. The evidentiary burdens on students may be high; the state statutes may accord considerable discretion to institutions to promulgate rules and make determinations; and the scope of judicial review may be quite narrow. Generally students, to be successful in court, will need to show that the institution has violated its own procedures for processing residency requests, ignored its own residency criteria, or committed a clear error of law in interpreting state law or its own rules.

Similarly, the constitutional cases earlier in this Section indicate that institutions should usually be able to prevail against constitutional challenges to residency regulations. Durational residency requirements of up to one year, and other requirements directly related to the establishment of domicile, will be constitutional so long as they are implemented with clear and specific criteria and basic due process procedures. The two fatal flaws that drafters need to assiduously avoid are (1) the creation of irrebuttable presumptions of nonresidency (see *Vlandis* and *Kelm* above), and (2) creating confusion between the concepts of domicile and residency (see *Eastman* above, and see also *Martinez v. Bynum*, 461 U.S. 321, 327–31 (1983)).

8.3.6. *Discrimination against aliens*

8.3.6.1. *Documented (immigrant and nonimmigrant) aliens.* In *Nyquist v. Jean-Marie Mauclet*, 432 U.S. 1 (1977), the U.S. Supreme Court set forth constitutional principles applicable to discrimination against resident aliens in student financial aid programs. The case involved a New York State statute that barred permanent resident aliens from eligibility for Regents' college scholarships, tuition assistance awards, and state-guaranteed student loans. Resident aliens denied financial aid argued that the New York law unconstitutionally discriminated against them in violation of the equal protection clause of the Fourteenth Amendment. The Supreme Court agreed.

The Court's opinion makes clear that alienage, somewhat like race, can be a "suspect classification." Discrimination against resident aliens in awarding financial aid can thus be justified only if the discrimination is necessary in order to achieve some compelling governmental interest.[31] The *Nyquist* opinion indicates that the state's interests in offering an incentive for aliens to become naturalized, and in enhancing the educational level of the electorate, are not sufficiently strong to justify discrimination against resident aliens with regard to financial aid.

Since the case was brought against the state rather than against individual postsecondary institutions, *Nyquist*'s most direct effect is to prohibit states from discriminating against resident aliens in state financial aid programs. It does not matter whether the state programs are for students in public institutions, in private institutions, or both, since in any case the state would have created the discrimination. In addition, the case clearly would prohibit public institutions from discriminating against resident aliens in operating their own separate financial aid programs. Private institutions are affected by these constitutional principles only to the extent that they are participating in government-sponsored financial aid programs or are otherwise engaging in "state action" (see Section 1.5.2) in their aid programs.

It does not necessarily follow from *Nyquist* that all aliens must be considered eligible for financial aid. *Nyquist* concerned permanent resident aliens and determined that such aliens as a class do not differ sufficiently from U.S. citizens to permit different treatment. Courts might not reach the same conclusion about nonresident aliens whose permission to be in the United States is temporary. In *Ahmed v. University of Toledo*, 664 F. Supp. 282 (N.D. Ohio 1986), for example, the court considered a challenge to the University of Toledo's requirement that all international students purchase health insurance. Those students not able to show proof of coverage were deregistered, and their financial aid was discontinued. The trial court ruled that the affected international students were not a suspect class for equal protection purposes, because only nonresident aliens were required to purchase the insurance; resident aliens were not. Since the situation was thus unlike *Nyquist*, where the challenged policy had affected resident rather than nonresident aliens, the court used the more relaxed "rational relationship" standard of review for equal protection claims rather than

---

[31]There are exceptions to this suspect class/strict scrutiny treatment of alienage classifications. One exception, directly pertinent to the financial aid issues, concerns the federal government's use of alienage classifications. When the federal government treats aliens differently from citizens, courts will presume that it has a legitimate reason for doing so—since the federal government (unlike state and local governments) has constitutional powers over matters of immigration and citizenship. Federal government alienage classifications are therefore not considered "suspect" and are not subject to the strict scrutiny standard the Court used in *Nyquist* (see, for example, *Mathews v. Diaz*, 426 U.S. 67 (1976)). A second possible exception may apply to classifications of nonresident (nonimmigrant) aliens—a class not involved in *Nyquist*. This possible exception is addressed in the *Ahmed* and *Tayyari* cases discussed below in this Section. An apparent third exception concerns classification of undocumented aliens; this exception is discussed in subsection 8.3.6.2 below. (Another exception, generally not relevant to financial aid issues, is discussed in Section 5.3.2 of this book with respect to state and local government employment.)

Nyquist's strict scrutiny standard (see generally, regarding strict scrutiny, Section 8.2.5), holding that the university's policy was rational and therefore constitutional. The U.S. Court of Appeals dismissed the students' appeal as moot (822 F.2d 26 (6th Cir. 1987)). In *Tayyari v. New Mexico State University,* 495 F. Supp. 1365 (D.N.M. 1980), however, the court did invalidate a university policy denying reenrollment (during the Iranian hostage crisis) to Iranian students who were nonimmigrant aliens in this country on student visas. The court considered the Iranian students to be members of a suspect class and determined that the university's reasons for treating them differently could not pass strict scrutiny.

Despite the *Tayyari* reasoning, public colleges and universities subject to the *Nyquist* principles can probably comply by making sure that they do not require students to be U.S. citizens or to show evidence of intent to become citizens in order to be eligible for financial aid administered by the institution. (The U.S. Department of Education has similar eligibility requirements for its student aid programs; see the Department's *Student Guide to Financial Aid,* available at http://studentaid.ed.gov/students/publications/student_guide/index.html; go to "who gets federal student aid" and then click on "eligible noncitizen." Institutions thus may decline to provide institutional aid to aliens who have F, M, or J visas (see Section 8.7.4 of this book) and other temporary nonresident aliens. Such a distinction between permanent resident and temporary nonresident aliens may be justifiable on grounds that institutions (and states) need not spend their financial aid resources on individuals who have no intention to remain in and contribute to the state or the United States. Whether institutions may also make undocumented resident aliens ineligible for financial assistance is a separate question not controlled by *Nyquist* and is discussed in subsection 8.3.6.2 below.

Moreover, since *Nyquist* does not affect state residency requirements, institutions may deny financial aid or in-state tuition status to aliens who are not state residents when the principles discussed in subsection 8.3.5 above permit it. Aid thus would not be denied because the students are aliens but because they are nonresidents of the state. Although state residency for aliens may be determined in part by their particular status under federal immigration law (see especially 8 U.S.C. § 1101(a)(15)), it is well to be cautious in relying on federal law. In *Elkins v. Moreno,* 435 U.S. 647 (1978), the University of Maryland had denied "in-state" status, for purposes of tuition and fees, to aliens holding federal G-4 nonimmigrant visas (for employees of international treaty organizations and their immediate families). The university argued the G-4 aliens' federal status precluded them from demonstrating an intent to become permanent Maryland residents. The U.S. Supreme Court rejected this argument, holding that G-4 aliens (unlike some other categories of nonimmigrant aliens) are not incapable under federal law of becoming permanent residents and thus are not precluded from forming an intent to reside permanently in Maryland. The Court then certified to the Maryland Court of Appeals the question whether G-4 aliens or their dependents are incapable of establishing Maryland residency under the state's common law.

In "Act 2" of this litigation drama, *Toll v. Moreno*, 397 A.2d 1009 (Md. 1979), *judgment vacated*, 441 U.S. 458 (1979), the Maryland court answered "No" to the Supreme Court's question. In the interim, however, the university had adopted a new in-state policy, which no longer used state residency as the paramount factor in determining in-state status for tuition and fees. Because the changed policy raised new constitutional issues, the Supreme Court ended Act 2 by vacating the Maryland court's judgment and remanding the case to the federal district court where the *Elkins* case had begun.

After the district court invalidated Maryland's new policy and the U.S. Court of Appeals affirmed, the case returned to the U.S. Supreme Court (*Toll v. Moreno*, 458 U.S. 1 (1982)) for Act 3. The Court held that the university's new policy, insofar as it barred G-4 aliens and their dependents from acquiring in-state status, violated the supremacy clause (Art. VI, para. 2) of the U.S. Constitution. The supremacy clause recognizes the primacy of federal regulatory authority over subjects within the scope of federal constitutional power and prevents state law from interfering with federal law regarding such subjects. Since the federal government's broad constitutional authority over immigration has long been recognized, federal law on immigration preempts any state or local law inconsistent with the federal law. Applying these principles in *Toll*, the Court reasoned:

> [Our cases] stand for the broad principle that "state regulation not congressionally sanctioned that discriminates against aliens lawfully admitted to the country is impermissible if it imposes additional burdens not contemplated by Congress." *De Canas v. Bica*, 424 U.S. 351, 358 n.6 (1976). . . .
>
> The Immigration and Nationality Act of 1952, 66 Stat. 163, as amended, 8 U.S.C. § 1101 et seq., . . . recognizes two basic classes of aliens, immigrant and nonimmigrant. With respect to the nonimmigrant class, the Act establishes various categories, the G-4 category among them. For many of these nonimmigrant categories, Congress has precluded the covered alien from establishing domicile in the United States. . . . But significantly, Congress has allowed G-4 aliens— employees of various international organizations, and their immediate families— to enter the country on terms permitting the establishment of domicile in the United States. . . . In light of Congress' explicit decision not to bar G-4 aliens from acquiring domicile, the State's decision to deny "in-state" status to G-4 aliens, *solely* on account of the G-4 alien's federal immigration status, surely amounts to an ancillary "burden not contemplated by Congress" in admitting these aliens to the United States [458 U.S. at 12–14; citations and footnotes omitted].[32]

As a result of the *Elkins/Toll* litigation, it is now clear that postsecondary institutions may not use G-4 aliens' nonimmigrant status as a basis for denying in-state status for tuition and fees purposes. It does not follow, however, that institutions are similarly limited with respect to other categories of

---

[32]The Court's opinion also includes alternative grounds for invalidating the university's policy— namely, that it interferes with federal tax policies under which G-4 visa holders are relieved of federal and some state and local taxes on their incomes. See 458 U.S. at 14–16.

nonimmigrant aliens. The nonimmigrant categories are comprised of aliens who enter the United States temporarily for a specific purpose and who usually must maintain their domicile in a foreign country (see, for example, 8 U.S.C. § 1101(a)(15)(B) (temporary visitors for pleasure or business); § 1101(a)(15)(F) (temporary academic students); § 1101(a)(15)(M) (temporary vocational students); and see generally Section 13.2.2 of this book). Such restrictions preclude most nonimmigrant aliens from forming an intent to establish permanent residency (or domicile), which is required under the residency laws of most states. Thus, federal and state law would apparently still allow public institutions to deny in-state status to nonimmigrant aliens, other than G-4s and other narrow categories that are not required to maintain domicile in their home countries.

It also remains important, after *Elkins/Toll,* to distinguish between nonimmigrant (nonresident) and immigrant (resident) aliens. Because immigrant aliens are permitted under federal law to establish U.S. and state residency, denial of in-state status because of their alienage would violate the federal supremacy principles relied on in *Toll* (Act 3). Moreover, such discrimination against immigrant aliens would violate the equal protection clause of the Fourteenth Amendment, as established in *Nyquist v. Mauclet,* discussed earlier in this subsection.

8.3.6.2. Undocumented aliens. Since the *Elkins/Toll* litigation, yet another critical distinction has emerged: the distinction between aliens with federal immigrant or nonimmigrant status on the one hand and undocumented aliens on the other. In some circumstances, the equal protection clause will also protect undocumented aliens from state discrimination in the delivery of educational services. In *Plyler v. Doe,* 457 U.S. 202 (1982), for instance, the U.S. Supreme Court used equal protection principles to invalidate a Texas statute that "den[ied] to undocumented school-age children the free public education that [the state] provides to children who are citizens of the United States or legally admitted aliens." Reasoning that the Texas law was "directed against children [who] . . . can have little control" over their undocumented status, and that the law "den[ied] these children a basic education," thereby saddling them with the "enduring disability" of illiteracy, the Court held that the state's interests in protecting its education system and resources could not justify this discriminatory burden on the affected children. *Plyler* dealt with elementary education; the key question, then, is whether the case's reasoning and the equal protection principles that support it would apply to higher education as well—in particular to state policies that deny to undocumented aliens financial aid or in-state tuition status that is available to U.S. citizens and documented aliens.

This question attracted a great deal of attention in California, where courts wrestled with it in a complex chain of litigation. In 1983, the California legislature passed a statute providing that "[a]n alien, including an unmarried minor alien, may establish his or her residence, unless precluded by the Immigration and Nationality Act (8 U.S.C. § 1101 et seq.) from establishing domicile in the United States" (Cal. Educ. Code § 68062(h)). It was not clear how this statute would apply to undocumented aliens who had been living in California and sought to establish residency for in-state tuition purposes. At the request of the chancellor of the California State University, the Attorney General of California issued an interpretation of the statute, indicating that an undocumented alien's incapacity to establish residence in the United States under federal immigration law precluded that same alien from establishing residency in California for in-state tuition purposes (67 *Opinions of Cal. Attorney General* 241 (Opinion No. 84-101 (1984)). Subsequently, the University of California and the California State University and College System formulated identical policies charging all undocumented aliens out-of-state tuition.

In *Leticia A. v. Regents of the University of California,* No. 588-982-4 (Cal. Super. Ct., Alameda County, orders of April 3, 1985, May 7, 1985, and May 30, 1985 ("*Statement of Decision*"), four undocumented alien students challenged the constitutionality of these policies on equal protection grounds. The plaintiffs had been brought into this country during their minority and had graduated from California high schools. Relying on the Supreme Court's reasoning in *Plyler,* and on the equal protection clause of the *state* constitution, the *Leticia A.* court determined that "higher education is an 'important' interest in California" and that the defendants' policies can survive equal protection scrutiny only if "there is a 'substantial' state interest served by the [blanket] classification" of undocumented aliens as nonresidents. The court then compared the rationales supporting this classification and those supporting the federal immigration laws:

> The policies underlying the immigration laws and regulations are vastly different from those relating to residency for student fee purposes. The two systems are totally unrelated for purposes of administration, enforcement and legal analysis. The use of unrelated policies, statutes, regulations or case law from one system to govern portions of the other is irrational. The incorporation of policies governing adjustment of status for undocumented aliens into regulations and administration of a system for determining residence for student fee purposes is neither logical nor rational [*Leticia A.* at 9–10].

The court therefore declared the defendants' policies unconstitutional (without rendering any judgment on the validity of Section 68062(h), on which the policies were based) and ordered the defendants to determine the state residence status of undocumented students and applicants for purposes of in-state tuition in the same way as it would make that determination for U.S. citizens.

Neither defendant appealed the *Leticia A.* decision. In 1990, however, a former employee of the University of California sued that institution to require it to reinstate its pre-*Leticia* policy. The employee, Bradford, had been terminated by the University of California for his "unwillingness to comply with the ruling of the [*Leticia A.*] court." The trial court granted summary judgment in favor of the employee. On appeal, in *Regents of the University of California v. Superior Court,* 276 Cal. Rptr. 197 (Ct. App. 2d Dist. 1990) (known as the *Bradford* case), the court reviewed the purpose and constitutionality of the defendant's pre-*Leticia A.* residency policy, as well as of Section 68062(h) itself. The court held that, as originally argued by the defendants in the *Leticia A.* litigation, Section 68062(h) "precludes undocumented alien students from qualifying as residents of California for tuition purposes." Then the court examined whether such an interpretation denied undocumented alien students the equal protection of the laws. Reasoning that undocumented aliens are commonly and legitimately denied basic rights and privileges under both state and federal law, that the university also denies the lower tuition rate to residents of other states and to aliens holding student visas, and that the state had "manifest and important" interests in extending this denial to undocumented aliens, the appellate court upheld the trial court's ruling.

Unlike the *Leticia A.* court, the appellate court in the *Bradford* case did not rely on the Supreme Court's *Plyler* decision but distinguished it on the basis of the "significant difference between an elementary education and a university education." Thus, the *Bradford* court's decision was in direct conflict with *Leticia A.* and served to uphold the constitutionality of Section 68062(h) as well as the University of California's pre-*Leticia A.* policy. After *Bradford*, litigation continued in the California superior courts to work out the implementation of that decision and its application to the California State University and College System, which was not a defendant in *Bradford* (see, for example, L. Gordon, "Immigrants Face Cal. State Fee Hike," *Los Angeles Times,* September 9, 1992, p. A3). Then, in a taxpayer action, *American Association of Women v. Board of Trustees of the California State University,* 38 Cal. Rptr. 2d 15 (Ct. App. 2d Dist. 1995), the court expressly disagreed with the reasoning of *Leticia A.,* affirmed that the *Bradford* decision "was correctly decided," and held that *Bradford* is "binding upon the California State University System." (For a review and critique of this line of cases, which concludes that *Leticia A.* represents the correct approach, see Michael A. Olivas, "Storytelling out of School: Undocumented College Residency, Race, and Reaction," 22 *Hastings Const. L.Q.* 1019, 1051–63 (1995).)

The practical significance of the California cases has been diminished, however, by later developments in California and nationwide. In late 1994, the California electorate approved Proposition 187, which, among other things, denied public services to undocumented aliens. Section 8 of the proposition, which was codified as Cal. Educ. Code § 66010.8, included public postsecondary education among the public services denied to undocumented aliens. In *League of United Latin American Citizens v. Wilson,* 908 F. Supp. 755 (C.D. Cal. 1995), the court invalidated most of the provisions of Proposition 187 and the implementing statutes on federal preemption grounds (see Section 13.1.1 of this book), but left intact the provision on denial of postsecondary education benefits in Cal. Educ. Code § 66010.8(a). Then, in 1996, Congress passed two new laws, the Personal Responsibility and Work Opportunity Reconciliation Act (PRWORA) and the Illegal Immigration Reform and Immigrant Responsibility Act (IIRIRA), to create uniform national rules regulating and restricting aliens' eligibility for public benefits. One provision of the IIRIRA, codified as 8 U.S.C. § 1621, makes undocumented aliens ineligible for "any state or local public benefit" (8 U.S.C. § 1621(a)) and defines such benefits to include "any . . . postsecondary education . . . benefit . . . for which payments or assistance are provided to an individual . . . by an agency of a state or local government"

(8 U.S.C. § 1621(c)(1)(B)). Relying on this provision, the district court that had issued the 1995 opinion reconsidered and revised its earlier disposition, concluding that the IIRIRA preempted Section 66010.8(a) and rendered it inoperative (*League of United Latin American Citizens v. Wilson*, 997 F. Supp. 1244 (C.D. Cal. 1997); see also *League of United Latin American Citizens v. Wilson*, 1998 WL 141325 (C.D. Cal. 1998)).

The end result appears to be that denial of state postsecondary education benefits to undocumented aliens—in California and in other states—is now governed primarily by federal law (the IIRIRA) rather than state law.[33] (Other provisions in 8 U.S.C. § 1611 govern undocumented aliens' eligibility for "Federal public benefit(s)," including "any . . . postsecondary education . . . benefit," and impose restrictions similar to those for state and local benefits in 8 U.S.C. § 1621.) The IIRIRA does, however, permit states to make undocumented aliens eligible for postsecondary benefits (and other state and local benefits) for which they are otherwise ineligible under Section 1621(a), but only if states do so "through the enactment of a state law after August 22, 1996, which affirmatively provides for such eligibility" (8 U.S.C. § 1621(d)). Another provision of the IIRIRA limits this state authority, specifically with respect to "postsecondary education benefit(s)," by providing that states may not provide greater benefits to undocumented aliens than it provides to United States citizens who are not residents of the state (8 U.S.C. § 1623). (For a review critique of these IIRIRA provisions and their impact on postsecondary education benefits for undocumented aliens, see Michael A. Olivas, "IIRIRA, The Dream Act, and Undocumented College Student Residency," 30 *J. Coll. & Univ. Law* 435, 449–57 (2004).)

IIRIRA is not likely to be the last word on these sensitive issues concerning financial aid for undocumented alien applicants and students. As of early 2005, eight states had passed legislation allowing undocumented students to qualify for in-state tuition rates (see, for example, Kan. Stat. Ann. 76-731(a)(2004)). In some other states, state universities have taken the same step without the support of post–IIRIRA state legislation. And the U.S. Congress itself is reconsidering the matter of education benefits and other protections for undocumented aliens. (See Olivas, above, 30 *J. Coll. & Univ. Law* at 455–63.)

The primary legislation, called the DREAM Act in the Senate, was introduced in the 108th Congress (S. 1545) and reintroduced in the 109th Congress (S. 2075), and was still pending as this book went to press (see also H.R. 1684 (108th Cong.) and H.R. 251 (109th Cong.)).

8.3.7. *Using government student aid funds at religious institutions.* Many states have student scholarship programs and other financial aid programs for students attending higher educational institutions within the state, and many of these programs cover students attending private (as well

---

[33]There is dispute, however, concerning whether the IIRIRA does, or should, apply in this way to benefits that are a function of state residency determinations, such as the in-state tuition rate; see Olivas, 30 *J. Coll. & Univ. Law* at 452–55 (cited in text below).

as public) institutions. The federal government, of course, also has financial aid programs for students in both private and public institutions (see Section 8.3.2 above). Legal problems may arise under such programs concerning the use of funds by students pursuing theological studies, studies to prepare them for religious vocations, or other religious instruction. More generally, problems may arise concerning the use of student aid funds by students attending religiously affiliated institutions, even when the students are pursuing secular or "nonreligious" studies. The issues that may surface are likely to be constitutional issues implicating the establishment and free exercise clauses in the federal Constitution's First Amendment and the parallel provisions in state constitutions. Section 1.6.3 of this book addresses the leading cases on such issues.

If a state or the federal government decides to *permit* use of its funds by students pursuing religious studies or attending religious institutions, the resulting issues are likely to be establishment (or "antiestablishment") issues. If a state or the federal government decides to *prohibit* use of its funds by students pursuing religious studies or attending religious institutions, the resulting issues are likely to be free exercise of religion issues. Under the federal Constitution, the leading establishment clause precedent is *Witters v. Department of Services for the Blind,* 474 U.S. 481 (1986) (see Section 1.6.3). The leading free exercise clause precedent is *Locke v. Davey,* 540 U.S. 712 (2004) (see Section 1.6.3).

Witters generally permits the inclusion of students pursuing religious studies in government aid programs, so long as the program is a "neutral" program serving students in both public and private institutions, and so long as a student's use of the funds at a religious institution results from the free and independent choice of the student. The establishment clause reasoning of *Witters* was solidified and extended by the U.S. Supreme Court's more recent decision in *Zelman v. Simmons-Harris,* 536 U.S. 639 (2002), which upheld an elementary/secondary school voucher program that included religious schools, even though most of the voucher recipients in the program used their vouchers to attend religiously affiliated schools. In some states, however, the state constitution is more restrictive than the federal Constitution, in which case there is less leeway for the state to include students pursuing religious studies or attending religious institutions in its aid programs. (See, for example, *Witters II,* discussed in Section 1.6.3.)

The more restrictive a state is regarding eligibility of students who pursue religious studies or enroll at religious institutions, the more likely it will be that excluded students will claim that the state has violated their federal free exercise rights. *Locke v. Davey* would then become the applicable precedent. In *Davey,* the Court narrowly construed the free exercise rights of students excluded from government aid programs and left considerable room for states to exclude students pursuing religious studies (particularly studies preparing one to enter the clergy) from state aid programs. It would be a different question, however, if a state were to exclude students attending a religious institution to pursue secular or "nonreligious" studies; it is unclear from *Davey* whether or not a student's free exercise claim would prevail in this situation. Moreover, some state constitutions may have freedom-of-religion clauses that the state courts interpret more broadly than the U.S. Supreme Court interpreted the federal free exercise clause in *Davey*. In this circumstance, the state would have less room to restrict the use of student aid funds.

When individual higher educational institutions award aid to their own students, the issues above typically do not arise. If the institution is public, it is generally prohibited—by the federal establishment clause, the state constitution, and other state law—from offering religious instruction; there would therefore not be any basis for questions of whether to award aid for this purpose. If the institution is private, on the other hand, the federal establishment and free exercise clauses do not apply (see Section 1.5.2), and similar state constitutional provisions usually do not apply; the private institution is therefore generally free to offer religious instruction, or not, and to award its own private financial aid funds to students pursuing such studies, or not, as it sees fit.[34]

8.3.8. Collection of student debts

8.3.8.1. Federal bankruptcy law. Student borrowers have often sought to extinguish their loan obligations to their institutions by filing for bankruptcy under the federal Bankruptcy Code contained in Title 11 of the *United States Code*.[35] The Bankruptcy Code supersedes all state law inconsistent with its provisions or with its purpose of allowing the honest bankrupt a "fresh start," free from the burden of indebtedness. A debtor may institute bankruptcy proceedings by petitioning the appropriate federal court for discharge of all his provable debts. Following receipt of the bankruptcy petition, the court issues an order fixing times for the filing and hearing of objections to the petition before a bankruptcy judge. Notice of this order is given to all potential creditors, usually by mail.

Debtors may petition for bankruptcy under either Chapter 7 or Chapter 13 of the Bankruptcy Code. Under a Chapter 7 "straight" bankruptcy, debts are routinely and completely discharged unless the creditors can show reasons why no discharge should be ordered (11 U.S.C. § 727) or unless a creditor can demonstrate why its particular claim should be "excepted" from the discharge order as a "nondischargeable debt" (11 U.S.C. § 523). Chapter 13, on the other hand, provides for the adjustment of debts for debtors with regular income. After filing a Chapter 13 petition, the debtor must submit a plan providing for full or partial repayment of debts (11 U.S.C. §§ 1321–1323), and the bankruptcy court must hold a hearing and decide whether to confirm the plan (11 U.S.C. §§ 1324–1325, 1327). Prior to the hearing, the bankruptcy court must notify all creditors whom the debtor has included in the plan; these creditors may then object to the plan's

---

[34]If the private institution is religiously affiliated, it would be protected by the federal establishment and free exercise clauses from governmental attempts to interfere with its choices on these matters. (See Section 1.6.2.)

[35]Because of the complexity of the law of bankruptcy, and its particular implications for the collection of student loans, a summary of the major issues is provided in this section. The discussion relies in part on Robert B. Milligan, Comment, "Putting an End to Judicial Lawmaking: Abolishing the Undue Hardship Exception for Student Loans in Bankruptcy," 34 *U.C. Davis L. Rev.* 221 (2000).

confirmation (11 U.S.C. § 1324). If the plan is confirmed and the debtor makes the payments according to the plan's terms, the bankruptcy court will issue a discharge of those debts included in the plan (11 U.S.C. § 1328(a)).

Bankruptcy law relevant to the collection of student debts has changed several times over the past forty years. Currently, the only exception to nondischarge is the "undue hardship" provision.[36] The provision is contained in 11 U.S.C. § 523(a)(8):

> **Section 523. Exceptions to discharge:**
> (a) A discharge under Section 727, 1141, 1228(a), 1228(b), or 1328(b) of this title does not discharge an individual debtor from any debt . . .
>
> (8) for an educational benefit overpayment or loan made, insured, or guaranteed by a governmental unit, or made under any program funded in whole or in part by a governmental unit or nonprofit institution of higher education, or for an obligation to repay funds received as an educational benefit, scholarship or stipend, unless excepting such debt from discharge under this paragraph will impose an undue hardship on the debtor and the debtor's dependents.

Student loans are nondischargeable under Chapter 13 (11 U.S.C. § 1328(a)). (For analysis of the prior versions of the bankruptcy law and the problems it posed for student loan collection, see Note, "Forging a Middle Ground: Revision of Student Loan Debts in Bankruptcy as an Impetus to Amend 11 U.S.C. § 523(a)(8)," 75 *Iowa L. Rev.* 733 (1990).)

Section 523(a)(8) covers loans made under any Department of Education student loan program as well as student loans made, insured, guaranteed, or funded by other "governmental units," such as state and local governments, and by nonprofit higher education institutions. Loans made by profit-making postsecondary institutions or privately owned banks (and not guaranteed or insured under a government program) are not covered by the provision and thus continue to be dischargeable. Moreover, Section 523(a)(8) applies to bankruptcies under both Chapter 7 and Chapter 13.

When a debtor files a petition under either Chapter 7 or Chapter 13 of the Bankruptcy Act, such filing creates an automatic "stay" against the attempts of creditors to collect from the debtor (11 U.S.C. § 362). Even if a student loan is nondischargeable under Chapter 7, the filing of a bankruptcy petition may nevertheless affect the institution's efforts to collect the debt. The bankruptcy judge may modify or cancel this prohibition during the proceedings, however, if the institution can show cause why such action should be taken (11 U.S.C. § 362(d)(1)).

In order for a borrower to request that a federal student loan be discharged in bankruptcy through the "undue hardship" exception, the debtor must file a

---

[36]Cases and authorities are collected at Andrew M. Campbell, Annot., "Bankruptcy Discharge of Student Loan on Ground of Undue Hardship Under § 523(a)(8)(B) of Bankruptcy Code of 1978 (11 U.S.C.A. § 523(a)(8)(B))," 63 A.L.R. Fed 570. See also Ana Kellia Ramares, Annot., "Validity, Construction, and Application of Statutes, Regulations, or Policies Allowing Denial of Student Loans, Student Loan Guarantees, or Educational Services to Debtors Who Have Had Student Loans Scheduled in Bankruptcy," 107 A.L.R. Fed. 192.

separate lawsuit in federal bankruptcy court against the agency or institution holding the loan. Several public colleges have challenged such suits, claiming that Eleventh Amendment immunity prevents them from being sued in federal court. If sovereign immunity protects state colleges (or other state agencies) in such cases, federal student loans made by these entities would effectively be nondischargeable under current law.

In *Tennessee Student Assistance Corporation v. Hood*, 319 F.3d 755 (6th Cir. 2003), *affirmed on other grounds and remanded*, 541 U.S. 440 (2004), the appellate court sided with the bankruptcy court's ruling that Congress had abrogated states' sovereign immunity for bankruptcy claims when it enacted Article I, Section 8 of the U.S. Constitution, thus requiring the state (or, in this case, the state student assistance agency) to be involved in the bankruptcy proceeding for purposes of determining whether the loan should be discharged on the grounds of undue hardship.

The U.S. Supreme Court, in a 7-to-2 opinion written by Justice Rehnquist, affirmed the outcome below, but refused to address the issue of the abrogation of sovereign immunity, stating that discharge of a student loan does not implicate sovereign immunity. Although the Court conceded that being served with process was an "indignity" to the state, the bankruptcy court did not have *in personam* jurisdiction over the state; its jurisdiction was *in rem*, and was limited to the debtor's property and estate. Even if Congress had not abrogated sovereign immunity under the bankruptcy clause (a finding that the Court did not make), said the Court, the bankruptcy court would still have the authority to make the undue hardship determination that the debtor was seeking in this case, and the state would be bound by that ruling, just as any other creditor would be bound.

There has been considerable litigation on the scope of the "undue hardship" exception to nondischargeability in Section 523(a)(8). In general, bankruptcy courts have interpreted this exception narrowly, looking to the particular facts of each case (see Scott Pashman, Note, "Discharge of Student Loan Debt Under 11 U.S.C. § 523(a)(8): Reassessing 'Undue Hardship' After the Elimination of the Seven-Year Exception," 44 *N.Y.L. Sch. L. Rev.* 605 (2001)). Primary importance has been attached to whether the student debtor's economic straits were foreseeable and within his control. Federal courts have established several tests for undue hardship.

The test created in *Brunner v. New York State Higher Education Services Corp.*, 831 F.2d 395 (2d Cir. 1987), has been used by the majority of federal appellate courts. The three-part test requires the court to determine

1. that the debtor cannot maintain, based on current income and expenses, a "minimal" standard of living for [himself or] herself and [his or] her dependents if forced to repay the loans; and

2. that additional circumstances exist indicating that this state of affairs is likely to persist for a significant portion of the repayment period of the student loans; and

3. that the debtor has made good faith efforts to repay the loans [831 F.2d at 396].

Because the *Brunner* standard is fact sensitive and requires a court to determine whether an individual has acted in "good faith," results across circuits, and even within the same circuit, are difficult to predict. For example, in *In re: Peel*, 240 B.R. 387 (N.D. Cal. 1999), a student loan debtor who graduated from chiropractic college filed for Chapter 7 bankruptcy. He had made some payments on the loan when he was financially able to. The court found that the debt was an undue hardship for the plaintiff and discharged his loan because his income was, and was projected to be, insufficient to repay the loan. On the other hand, the court in *In re Roberson*, 999 F.2d 1132 (7th Cir. 1993) rejected the plaintiff's request to discharge his loan, despite the fact that the debtor was unemployed, owed child support, and had twice been convicted of driving while intoxicated.

Another approach to determining whether the plaintiff's debt should be discharged under the "undue hardship" criterion is the test created in *In re Bryant*, 72 B.R. 913 (E.D. Pa. 1987). Rejecting the typically subjective standards used in the *Brunner* test, the court ruled that, if the plaintiff's income exceeded the federal poverty rate, the debt would be ruled nondischargeable. Other issues that courts may take into consideration in determining whether undue hardship exists are the debtor's mental illness (*In re Meling*, 263 B.R. 275 (N.D. Iowa 2001)), but not the disability of a debtor's spouse (*In re Naranjo*, 261 B.R. 248 (E.D. Cal. 2001)), or the number and health of dependents (*Educational Credit Management Corp. v. Ross*, 262 B.R. 460 (W.D. Wis. 2000) (no discharge where debtor has no dependents)). In other cases, courts have approved a partial discharge, reducing the amount of debt that the debtor must repay (see, for example, *In re Yapuncich*, 266 B.R. 882 (D. Mont. 2001)).

Cosigners and nonstudents (such as parents) who take out federally guaranteed student loans also appear to be covered by the nondischargeability provisions of the bankruptcy law.[37] In *Webb v. Student Loan Funding Corp.*, 151 Bankr. Rptr. 804 (N.D. Ohio 1992), the parent, the obligor on a federal Parent Loans for Undergraduate Students (PLUS) loan taken out for her daughter's college education, argued that she had not received a direct benefit from the loan (her daughter, not she, had received the education). The court disagreed, stating that the parent did receive at least an indirect benefit, and that this reason was insufficient to exempt PLUS loans from the clear intent of the bankruptcy law's statutory language. Similarly, in *In re Hammarstrom*, 95 Bankr. Rptr. 160 (N.D. Cal. 1989), the court held that the exception to dischargeability in Section 523(a)(8) unambiguously applied to the debtor, whether or not the debtor received a direct benefit from the loan. And in *In re Pelkowski*, 990 F.2d 737 (3d Cir. 1993), the court overturned a lower court ruling that the loan was not an "educational" loan if the debtor was a cosigner or guarantor of the loan for the student borrower. After analyzing the legislative history of the amendments to the Bankruptcy Code related to federal student loans, the court concluded that

---

[37]Cases and authorities are collected at Lora C. Siegler, Annot., "Applicability to Obligations of Nonstudent Co-obligors of Exception to Discharge in Bankruptcy for Educational Loans Under 11 U.S.C. § 523(a)(8)," 120 A.L.R. Fed. 609.

Congress had acted for the purpose of reducing debtor abuse of the federal student loan program; extending the nondischargeability provisions to nonstudent debtors would further the intent of Congress in this regard. (For analysis of this issue, see Note, "Non-Student Co-Signers and Sec. 523(a)(8) of the Bankruptcy Code," 1991 *U. Chicago Legal Forum* 357 (1991).)

Students may be precluded from further borrowing under the federal student loan program if they have had earlier loans discharged in bankruptcy. In *Elter v. Great Lakes Higher Education Corp.*, 95 Bankr. Rptr. 618 (E.D. Wis. 1989), a bankruptcy court allowed a state guarantee agency to deny a new educational loan to such students. (For analysis of this issue, see Comment, "*Elter v. Great Lakes Higher Education Corporation:* State Agencies That Grant Educational Loans May Discriminate Against Student Bankrupts Who Default on Prior Educational Loans," 17 *J. Coll. & Univ. Law* 261 (1990).)

The provisions of Section 523(a)(8) of the Bankruptcy Code apply to "educational loans," not to student debt incurred by failing to pay tuition or fees. Such indebtedness is dischargeable in bankruptcy, according to several court opinions. (See, for example, *In re Renshaw*, 222 F.3d 82 (2d Cir. 2000), in which Cazenovia College and the College of St. Rose intervened in bankruptcy proceedings brought by students who had been permitted to enroll and take classes despite their failure to pay tuition. Because the college's forbearance with respect to collecting the tuition was not a formal "loan," the debt was dischargeable in bankruptcy, according to the court. See also *In re Mehta*, 262 B.R. 35 (D.N.J. 2001).)

(For suggestions regarding appropriate institutional actions in collecting student loans from debtors in bankruptcy, see Julia R. Hoke, *The Campus as Creditor: A Bankruptcy Primer on Educational Debts* (National Association of College and University Attorneys, 2006).)

8.3.8.2. Withholding certified transcripts. The Bankruptcy Code generally forbids creditors from resorting to the courts or other legal process to collect debts discharged in bankruptcy (11 U.S.C. § 524(a)(2)). Under the former Bankruptcy Act, however, there was considerable debate on whether informal means of collection, such as withholding certified grade transcripts from a student bankrupt, were permissible. In *Girardier v. Webster College*, 563 F.2d 1267 (8th Cir. 1977), decided under the old Act, the court held that the Act did not prohibit private institutions from withholding certified transcripts. Besides reducing the scope of this problem by limiting the dischargeability of student loans, the 1978 Bankruptcy Act appears to have legislatively overruled the result in the *Girardier* case.

The provision of the old Act that was applied in *Girardier* prohibited formal attempts, by "action" or "process," to collect discharged debts. In the 1978 Act, this provision was amended to read (with further amendments in 1984):

> A discharge in a case under this title . . . operates as an injunction against the commencement or continuation of an action, the employment of process, or an act, to collect, recover or offset any such debt as a personal liability of the debtor, whether or not discharge of such debt is waived [11 U.S.C. § 524(a)(2)].

The language, especially the phrase "or an act," serves to extend the provision's coverage to informal, nonjudicial means of collection, thus "insur[ing] that once a debt is discharged, the debtor will not be pressured in any way to repay it" (S. Rep. No. 95989, 95th Cong., 2d Sess., reprinted in 1978 *U.S. Code Cong. Admin. News* 5866).

The 1978 Act also added the words "any act" to a related provision, Section 362(a)(6), which prohibits creditors from attempting to collect debts during the pendency of a bankruptcy proceeding. Bankruptcy courts have construed this language to apply to attempts to withhold certified transcripts (see *In re Lanford*, 10 Bankr. Rptr. 132 (D. Minn. 1981)). This legislative change, together with the change in Section 524(a)(2), apparently prevents postsecondary institutions from withholding transcripts both during the pendency of a bankruptcy proceeding and after the discharge of debts, under either Chapter 7 or Chapter 13.[38]

The charge typically made when a college refuses to provide a transcript for a student who has filed a bankruptcy petition is that the college has violated the "automatic stay" provisions of the Bankruptcy Code (11 U.S.C. § 362) (*In re Parham*, 56 Bankr. Rptr. 531 (E.D. Va. 1986); *Parraway v. Andrews University*, 50 Bankr. Rptr. 316 (W.D. Mich. 1986)). Even though the debt is nondischargeable, courts in most federal circuits have ruled that the college may not withhold the transcript during the automatic stay period (*In re: Gustafson*, 934 F.2d 216 (9th Cir. 1990); *In re: Weiner Merchant, Debtor*, 958 F.2d 738 (6th Cir. 1992)). However, federal courts in the Third Circuit have ruled for the colleges, reasoning that the colleges were entitled to withhold the transcript for nonpayment of a student loan prior to the filing in bankruptcy, and thus continuing to withhold the transcript maintains the status quo, which is the purpose of the automatic stay. (See, for example, *Johnson v. Edinboro State College*, 728 F.2d 163 (3d Cir. 1984); and *In re: Billingsley*, 276 B.R. 48 (D.N.J. 2002). For analysis of the limitations that the bankruptcy law places on colleges with regard to withholding transcripts, see P. Tanaka, *The Permissibility of Withholding Transcripts Under the Bankruptcy Law* (2d ed., National Association of College and University Attorneys, 1995).)

The situation is different if, as in the majority of situations, the student has not filed a bankruptcy petition. Nothing in the Bankruptcy Code would prohibit postsecondary institutions from withholding transcripts from such student debtors. Moreover, the code does not prevent institutions from withholding transcripts if the bankruptcy court has refused to discharge the student loan debts. In *Johnson v. Edinboro State College* (discussed above), for example, the bankruptcy court had declared a former student to be bankrupt but did not discharge his student loans because he had failed to prove that a hardship existed. Nevertheless, the bankruptcy court had held that the college was obligated to issue the student a transcript because of the Bankruptcy Code's policy to guarantee debtors "fresh starts." When the college appealed, the Court of Appeals

---

[38]Public institutions may also be restrained by Section 525 of the Bankruptcy Code, which forbids "governmental units" from discriminating against bankrupts in various ways—apparently including denial of transcripts (see *In re Howren*, 10 Bankr. Rptr. 303 (D. Kan. 1980)).

overruled the bankruptcy court, holding that when a bankrupt's student loans are nondischargeable under Section 523(a)(8), the policy of that section overrides the code's general fresh-start policy. The college therefore remained free to withhold transcripts from the student.

Entities that seek to collect federal student loans are subject to the Fair Debt Collection Practices Act (15 U.S.C. §§1692 *et seq.*). This law provides for civil penalties for using false, deceptive, unfair, or "unconscionable" methods of collecting debts. *Kort v. Diversified Collection Services,* 394 F.3d 530 (7th Cir. 2005) illustrates the application of this law and its "bona fide error" defense. In *Crockett v. Edinboro University,* 811 A.2d 1094 (Pa. Commw. Ct. 2002), a former student sued the college under the Pennsylvania Unfair Trade Practices and Consumer Protection Law (73 P.S. §§ 201-1–201-9.3) and the Fair Debt Collection Practices Act. The student had not completed his degree and his student loans became due before he graduated. The college refused to issue a transcript because the student had not made arrangements to repay the loan. The court ruled that the student's claims were barred by sovereign immunity.

Although private colleges do not have the protection of sovereign immunity, plaintiffs have similarly had difficulty persuading courts that withholding a transcript in situations not involving bankruptcy violated some legal right. In *Sheridan v. Trustees of Columbia University,* 745 N.Y.S.2d 18 (N.Y. App. Div. 2002), a student denied his transcript for failure to pay an outstanding tuition bill sued the university for breach of contract, fraud, negligent misrepresentation, and intentional infliction of emotional distress. The court dismissed all claims, finding that the university's behavior was reasonable and that the university had no obligation to forward the transcript to graduate schools in light of the unpaid debt.

Similarly, nothing in the federal Family Educational Rights and Privacy Act (FERPA) concerning student records (see this book, Section 9.7.1) prohibits institutions from withholding certified transcripts from student debtors. If an institution enters grades in a student's records, FERPA would give the student a right to see and copy the grade records. But FERPA would not give the student any right to a *certified* transcript of grades, nor would it obligate the institution to issue a certified transcript or other record of grades to third parties. Nor does FERPA prevent a college to which a former student owes student loan repayment from refusing to provide letters of recommendation as long as the loan is in default (*Slovinec v. DePaul University,* 332 F.3d 1068 (7th Cir. 2003)).

The most likely legal difficulty *would* arise under the federal Constitution's due process clause, whose requirements limit only public institutions (see Section 1.5.2). The basic question is whether withholding a certified transcript deprives the student of a "liberty" or "property" interest protected by the due process clause (see generally Sections 9.4.2–9.4.3). If so, the student would have the right to be notified of the withholding and the reason for it, and to be afforded some kind of hearing on the sufficiency of the grounds for withholding. Courts have not yet defined liberty or property interests in this context. But under precedents in other areas, if the institution has regulations or policies entitling students to certified transcripts, these regulations or policies could create a property interest that would be infringed if the institution withholds a transcript without notice or hearing. And withholding certified transcripts from a student applying to professional or graduate school, or for professional employment, may so foreclose the student's freedom to pursue educational or employment opportunities as to be a deprivation of liberty. Thus, despite the lack of cases on point, administrators at public institutions should consult counsel before implementing a policy of withholding transcripts for failure to pay loans, or for any other reason.[39]

8.3.8.3. Debt collection requirements in federal student loan programs.[40] During the late 1980s and 1990s, the default rate on federal student loans increased sharply. In 1990, the default rate was 22.4 percent, or nearly one in four borrowers. Funding required for these defaulted federal student loans was the fourth largest expenditure in the U.S. Education Department's budget (Roger Roots, "The Student Loan Debt Crisis: A Lesson in Unintended Consequences," 29 *Sw. U. L. Rev.* 501 (2000)). The federal government stepped up its debt collection activities, putting pressure on borrowers and institutions alike to increase repayment of the loans.

The Perkins Loan (formerly National Direct Student Loan) program's statute and regulations contain several provisions affecting the institution's debt collection practices. The statute provides (in 20 U.S.C. § 1087cc(4)), that where a note or written agreement evidencing such a loan has been in default despite the institution's due diligence in attempting to collect the debt, the institution, under certain circumstances, may assign its rights under the note or agreement to the United States. If the debt is thereafter collected by the United States, the amount, less 30 percent, is returned to the institution as an additional capital contribution. The Perkins Loan regulations (34 C.F.R. § 674.41 *et seq.*) provide that each institution maintaining a Perkins Loan fund must accept responsibility for, and use due diligence in effecting, collection of all amounts due and payable to the fund. Due diligence includes the following elements: (1) providing borrowers with information about changes in the program that affect their rights and responsibilities (34 C.F.R. § 674.41(a)); (2) conducting exit interviews with borrowers when they leave the institution and providing them with copies of repayment schedules that indicate the total amount of the loans and the dates and amounts of installments as they come due (34 C.F.R. § 674.42(b)); (3) keeping a written record of interviews and retaining signed copies of borrowers' repayment schedules (34 C.F.R. § 674.42(b)(4)); and (4) staying in contact with borrowers both before and during the repayment period, in order to facilitate billing and keep the borrowers informed of changes in the program that may affect rights and obligations (34 C.F.R. § 674.42(c)).

---

[39]Cases and authorities are collected in Ana Kellia Ramares, Annot., "Validity, Construction, and Application of Statutes, Regulations, or Policies Allowing Denial of Student Loans, Student Loan Guarantees, or Educational Services to Debtors Who Have Had Student Loans Scheduled in Bankruptcy," 107 A.L.R. Fed. 192; and Lewis J. Heisman, Annot., "Violation of Automatic Stay Provisions of 1978 Bankruptcy Code (11 U.S.C.A. § 362) as Contempt of Court," 57 A.L.R. Fed. 927.

[40]See generally, Annot., "Rights and Obligations of Federal Government, Under 20 U.S.C.S. § 1080, When Student Borrower Defaults on Federally Insured Loan," 73 A.L.R. Fed. 303.

The institution must also use specified "billing procedures" (set forth at 34 C.F.R. § 674.43), including statements of notice and account and demands for payment on accounts that are more than fifteen days overdue. If an institution is unable to locate a borrower, it must conduct an address search (34 C.F.R. § 674.4). If the billing procedures are unsuccessful, the institution must either obtain the services of a collection agency or utilize its own resources to compel repayment (34 C.F.R. § 675(a)).

The Federal Family Education Loan (FFEL, formerly Guaranteed Student Loan (GSL)) program includes fewer provisions related to debt collection, since postsecondary institutions are not usually the lenders under the program. The regulations require (at 34 C.F.R. § 682.610(a)), that participating institutions establish and maintain such administrative and fiscal procedures and records as may be necessary to protect the United States from unreasonable risk of loss due to defaults. Another approach to debt collection, with more specifics than FFEL but fewer than Perkins, is illustrated by the Health Professions Student Loan program (42 C.F.R. Part 57, subpart C). Participating institutions must exercise "due diligence" in collecting loan payments (42 C.F.R. § 57.210(b)) and must maintain complete repayment records for each student borrower, including the "date, nature, and result of each contact with the borrower or proper endorser in the collection of an overdue loan" (42 C.F.R. § 57.215(c)).

In order to step up collection activities under the Health Education Assistance Loan (HEAL) program (42 U.S.C. § 292 et seq.; 42 C.F.R. Part 60), the Public Health Service of the Department of Health and Human Services issued regulations authorizing institutions to withhold transcripts of HEAL defaulters (42 C.F.R. § 60.61). The regulations also require schools to note student loan defaults on *academic* transcripts. (For a discussion of the lawfulness of withholding student transcripts, see Section 8.3.8.2.)

Prior to 1991, the statute of limitations for defaulted student loans was six years. However, the Higher Education Technical Amendments of 1991 (Pub. L. No. 102-26, 105 Stat. 123, codified as amended at 20 U.S.C. § 1091(a)) deleted the six-year statute of limitations temporarily. The Higher Education Amendments of 1992 made the deletion permanent. Following passage of the amendments, the question before the courts was whether student loans in default for more than six years prior to the amendments' enactment were now subject to collection. The courts have ruled that they are (see, for example, *United States v. Glockson,* 998 F.2d 896 (11th Cir. 1993); see also *United States v. Mastronito,* 830 F. Supp. 1281 (D. Ariz. 1993)).

A law passed by Congress in October 1990, the Student Loan Default Prevention Initiative Act of 1990 (Pub. L. No. 101-508, 104 Stat. 1388, codified at various sections of 20 U.S.C.), is aimed at reducing the number of defaulted loans by rendering institutions with high default rates ineligible to participate in certain student loan programs. Section 1085 provides that any institution whose "cohort default rate" exceeds a certain threshold percentage for three consecutive years loses its eligibility for participation in the FFEL program for the fiscal year in which the determination is made and for the two succeeding years. The regulations specifying how default rates are calculated appear at

34 C.F.R. § 668.15. The process for calculating the cohort default rate was described in *Canterbury Career School, Inc. v. Riley*, 833 F. Supp. 1097 (D.N.J. 1993). In this case the threshold beyond which termination would occur was 30 percent. The court also discussed the due process protections (particularly the opportunity for a hearing) available to schools threatened with termination of their eligibility to participate in federal student aid programs.

In another case, a chain of cosmetology schools challenged the Secretary of Education's decision to terminate the schools' eligibility to participate in the FFEL program. The plaintiffs charged that a "paper" appeal process, rather than a full-blown adversary hearing on the record, violated their rights of due process on both procedural and substantive grounds. The schools also charged that the Secretary had miscalculated the default rate. In *Pro Schools, Inc. v. Riley*, 824 F. Supp. 1314 (E.D. Wis. 1993), the trial court disagreed, noting that the Secretary was permitted to use default data from years prior to the enactment of the Student Loan Default Prevention Initiative Act, and that the use of these data did not make the Act itself retroactive because the issue was the schools' present eligibility, not their past eligibility (citing *Association of Accredited Cosmetology Schools v. Alexander*, 979 F.2d 859 (D.C. Cir. 1992)). Although the court accepted the plaintiffs' argument that continued eligibility for participation in the federal programs was both a property and a liberty interest (citing *Continental Training Services, Inc. v. Cavazos*, 893 F.2d 877 (7th Cir. 1990)), it viewed the written appeal process as sufficient to protect the schools' due process rights.

In *Ross Learning, Inc. v. Riley*, 960 F. Supp. 1238 (E.D. Mich. 1997), three technical schools whose eligibility to participate in the Federal Family Education Loan Programs had been terminated because their cohort default rates were equal to or greater than 25 percent challenged the Secretary's decision. The court determined that no due process violations had occurred, and that the Secretary had complied with the Higher Education Act.

Institutions have several weapons in their fight to collect Perkins Loans from defaulting student borrowers. The Student Loan Default Prevention Initiative Act permits colleges to use collection agencies to recover defaulted loans, and also permits judges to award attorney's fees to institutions that must litigate to recover the unpaid loans. In *Trustees of Tufts College v. Ramsdell*, 554 N.E.2d 34 (Mass. 1990), the court noted these provisions, but limited the attorney's fees to the state law standard, rather than the more generous ceiling that the university argued was permitted by federal regulations. The regulations interpreting the Act are found at 34 C.F.R. §§ 674.46 and 674.47.

For those loans that have been assigned to the federal government for collection, federal agency heads may seek a tax offset against the debtor's tax refunds by request to the Internal Revenue Service (as provided in 26 U.S.C. § 6402(d)). According to *Thomas v. Bennett*, 856 F.2d 1165 (8th Cir. 1988), the six-year statute of limitations on actions for money damages brought by the United States (28 U.S.C. § 2415(a)) does not bar the tax offset, because the statute of limitations does not negate the debt but only bars a court suit as a means of collection; the debt is still collectible by other means. By regulation, however, the Internal Revenue Service has provided that it will not use the offset procedure for any debt that has been delinquent for more than ten years at the time offset is requested (26 C.F.R. § 301.6402-6(c)(1)). This regulation was upheld in *Grider v. Cavazos,* 911 F.2d 1158 (5th Cir. 1990). The appellate court refused to permit the Secretary of Education to intercept the tax refunds of two individuals who had defaulted on their loans fifteen and eleven years earlier. Although the Secretary had argued that the loans became delinquent when the banks assigned the loans to the Secretary for collection, the court sided with the debtors' argument that the loans went into default when the required payments to the bank (the lender) were not made. The court commented:

> [We] take no pleasure in giving aid and comfort to those former students who shirk their loan repayment obligations by hiding behind statutes of limitation. We can only ask in rhetorical wonderment why the Secretary continues quixotically to pursue judicial construction of the Regulation instead of simply asking his counterpart in the Department of the Treasury to close the loophole in the Regulation with a proverbial stroke of his pen [911 F.2d at 1164].

A similar result occurred in *Lee v. Paige,* 276 F. Supp. 2d 980 (W.D. Mo. 2003), *affirmed,* 376 F.3d 1179 (8th Cir. 2004), in which the court rejected the Secretary of Education's attempt to offset the Social Security benefits of an individual who defaulted on student loans more than twenty years earlier. Interpreting the Debt Collection Improvement Act, which authorizes federal agencies to recover outstanding student loans by offsetting the debtor's Social Security benefits (31 U.S.C. § 3716(c)(3)(A)(i)), the court noted that the new law had left unchanged the original Debt Collection Act's provision that claims that had been outstanding for more than ten years could not be offset. However, in *Lockhart v. U.S.,* 376 F.3d 1027 (9th Cir. 2004), a case decided just two weeks before *Lee,* the U.S. Court of Appeals for the Ninth Circuit ruled that the Debt Collection Act's ten-year limit did not preclude the offsetting of Social Security benefits to obtain repayment of educational loans because the Higher Education Assistance Act, amended in 1991, provided that "notwithstanding any other provision of statute . . . no limitation shall terminate the period within which . . . an offset, garnishment, or other action initiated by . . . the Secretary [of Education] . . . for the repayment of [a student loan shall be made]" (20 U.S.C. §§ 1091a(a)(1)–(2)). The court in *Lee* had rejected that argument, ruling that when the 1991 amendments were enacted, Social Security benefits were not subject to offset, and thus Congress could not have intended that the abolition of the ten-year limitations period would apply to the offset of Social Security benefits.

Lockhart appealed, and the U.S. Supreme Court unanimously affirmed the appellate court's ruling in *Lockhart v. U.S.,* 126 S. Ct. 699 (2005). Rejecting the reasoning of *Lee,* the Court ruled that the Debt Collection Improvement Act "clearly makes Social Security benefits subject to offset, [providing] exactly the sort of express reference that the Social Security Act says is necessary to supersede the anti-attachment provision."

Students challenging their obligation to repay federal student loans have found some creative solutions in situations where the college involved either has closed or did not provide the promised educational services. In some cases students have argued that the lending banks or the state agency guarantors of their federal student loans must be subject to state law regarding secured transactions. (For a case in which students successfully argued this theory, see *Tipton v. Alexander*, 768 F. Supp. 540 (S.D. W. Va. 1991).) And in *Keams v. Tempe Technical Institute, Inc.*, 39 F.3d 222 (9th Cir. 1994), the court ruled that the Higher Education Act did not preempt state tort law regarding the circumstances under which a loan obligation is enforceable. Although the court dismissed the students' claims under the Higher Education Act (finding no private right of action), it allowed the state tort law claim to proceed.

Students arguing under other state law theories, however, have been less successful. In *Bogart v. Nebraska Student Loan Program*, 858 S.W.2d 78 (Ark. 1993), the Supreme Court of Arkansas rejected a group of students' claim that the guarantee agency and the banks who actually loaned the money to the students were agents of the stenographic school, against which the students had obtained a judgment for fraud, which they were then unable to collect. The court ruled that the Higher Education Act preempted the students' claims under agency law. A similar result occurred in *Veal v. First American Savings Bank*, 914 F.2d 909 (7th Cir. 1990).

In *Jackson v. Culinary School of Washington*, 811 F. Supp. 714 (D.D.C. 1993), the court rejected the claims of students seeking to have their loan obligations declared null and void because of the Secretary of Education's allegedly negligent supervision of the school's default rate and the quality of its curriculum. After appeals to the federal appellate courts and the U.S. Supreme Court, the U.S. Court of Appeals for the District of Columbia Circuit vacated the trial court's earlier opinion and ordered it to exercise its discretion in determining which defendants could be subject to District of Columbia consumer protection laws (59 F.3d 254 (D.C. Cir. 1995)). No further opinions in this case have been published.

In *Armstrong v. Accrediting Council for Continuing Education and Training, Inc.*, 168 F.3d 1362 (D.C. Cir. 1999), a student loan debtor filed a claim for declaratory and injunctive relief against an agency that had previously accredited the National Business School, a for-profit vocational school in Washington, D.C., that went bankrupt after the plaintiff students had obtained Guaranteed Student Loans and paid tuition. The plaintiff filed claims under the FTC Holder Rule (see Section 13.2.9), the Higher Education Act, and the District of Columbia Consumer Credit Protection Act. The appellate court ruled that such misconduct by schools and lenders could not be attacked through state consumer fraud laws, but noted that the 1992 amendments to the Higher Education Act helped to reduce the likelihood that students enrolling in proprietary schools would face the same kinds of problems that this plaintiff encountered.

Collection of student loans is a critical issue for colleges and universities, for legal reasons and because of the implications of student default rates for continued eligibility to participate in the federal student aid program. College and university officials should use experienced counsel and student aid professionals to develop and enforce student financial aid policies that fully comply with state and federal requirements.

Sec. 8.4. Student Housing

8.4.1. Housing regulations. Postsecondary institutions with residential campuses usually have policies specifying which students may, and which students must, live in campus housing. Such regulations sometimes apply only to certain groups of students, using classifications based on the student's age, sex, class, or marital status. Institutions also typically have policies regulating living conditions in campus housing. Students in public institutions have sought to use the federal Constitution to challenge such housing policies, while students at private colleges have used landlord-tenant law or nondiscrimination law to challenge housing regulations.[41]

Challenges to housing regulations typically fall into two categories: challenges by students required to live on campus who do not wish to, and challenges by students (or, occasionally, nonstudents) who wish to live in campus housing (or housing affiliated with a college), but who are ineligible under the college's regulations. An example of the first type of challenge is *Prostrollo v. University of South Dakota,* 507 F.2d 775 (8th Cir. 1974).

In *Prostrollo,* students claimed that the university's regulation requiring all single freshmen and sophomores to live in university housing was unconstitutional because it denied them equal protection under the Fourteenth Amendment and infringed their constitutional rights of privacy and freedom of association. The university admitted that one purpose of the regulation was to maintain a certain level of dormitory occupancy to secure revenue to repay dormitory construction costs. But the university also offered testimony that the regulation was instituted to ensure that younger students would educationally benefit from the experience in self-government, community living, and group discipline and the opportunities for relationships with staff members that dormitory life provides. In addition, university officials contended that the dormitories provided easy access to study facilities and to films and discussion groups.

Although the lower court ruled that the regulation violated the equal protection clause, the appellate court reversed the lower court's decision. It reasoned that, even if the regulation's primary purpose was financial, there was no denial of equal protection because there was another rational basis for differentiating freshmen and sophomores from upper-division students: the university officials' belief that the regulation contributed to the younger students' adjustment to college life. The appellate court also rejected the students' right-to-privacy and freedom-of-association challenges. The court gave deference to school authorities' traditionally broad powers in formulating educational policy.

---

[41]The cases are collected in Donald M. Zupanec, Annot., "Validity, Under Federal Constitution, of Policy or Regulation of College or University Requiring Students to Live in Dormitories or Residence Halls," 31 A.L.R. Fed. 813. See also Jeffrey F. Ghent, Annot., "Validity and Construction of Statute or Ordinance Forbidding Unauthorized Persons to Enter upon or Remain in School Building or Premises," 50 A.L.R.3d 340.

A similar housing regulation that used an age classification to prohibit certain students from living off campus was at issue in *Cooper v. Nix,* 496 F.2d 1285 (5th Cir. 1974). The regulation required all unmarried full-time undergraduate students, regardless of age and whether or not emancipated, to live on campus. The regulation contained an exemption for certain older students, which in practice the school enforced by simply exempting all undergraduates twenty-three years old and over. Neither the lower court nor the appeals court found any justification in the record for a distinction between twenty-one-year-old students and twenty-three-year-old students. Though the lower court had enjoined the school from requiring students twenty-one and older to live on campus, the appeals court narrowed the remedy to require only that the school not automatically exempt all twenty-three-year-olds. Thus, the school could continue to enforce the regulation if it exempted students over twenty-three only on a case-by-case basis.

A regulation that allowed male students but not female students to live off campus was challenged in *Texas Woman's University v. Chayklintaste,* 521 S.W.2d 949 (Tex. Civ. App. 1975), and found unconstitutional. Though the university convinced the court that it did not have the space or the money to provide on-campus male housing, the court held that mere financial reasons could not justify the discrimination. The court concluded that the university was unconstitutionally discriminating against its male students by not providing them with any housing facilities and also was unconstitutionally discriminating against its female students by not permitting them to live off campus.

The university subsequently made housing available to males and changed its regulations to require both male and female undergraduates under twenty-three to live on campus. Although the regulation was now like the one found unconstitutional in *Cooper,* above, the Texas Supreme Court upheld its constitutionality in a later appeal of *Texas Woman's University v. Chayklintaste,* 530 S.W.2d 927 (Tex. 1975). In this case the university justified the age classification with reasons similar to those used in *Prostrollo,* above. The university argued that on-campus dormitory life added to the intellectual and emotional development of its students and supported this argument with evidence from published research and experts in student affairs.

In *Bynes v. Toll,* 512 F.2d 252 (2d Cir. 1975), another university housing regulation was challenged—in this case a regulation that permitted married students to live on campus but barred their children from living on campus. The court found that there was no denial of equal protection, since the university had several very sound safety reasons for not allowing children to reside in the dormitories. The court also found that the regulation did not interfere with the marital privacy of the students or their natural right to bring up their children.

Housing regulations limiting dormitory visitors have also been constitutionally challenged.[42] In *Futrell v. Ahrens,* 540 P.2d 214 (N.M. 1975), students claimed that a regulation prohibiting visits by members of the opposite sex in

---

[42]Cases and authorities are collected in Donald M. Zupanec, Annot., "Validity of Regulation of College or University Denying or Restricting Right of Student to Receive Visitors in Dormitory," 78 A.L.R.3d 1109.

dormitory bedrooms violated their rights of privacy and free association. The regulation did not apply to the lounges or lobbies of the dorms. The court held for the institution, reasoning that even if the regulation affected rights of privacy and association, it was a reasonable time-and-place restriction on exercise of those rights, since it served legitimate educational interests and conformed with accepted standards of conduct.

Taken together, these cases indicate that the courts afford colleges broad leeway in regulating on-campus student housing. An institution may require some students to live on campus; may regulate living conditions to fulfill legitimate health, safety, or educational goals; and may apply its housing policies differently to different student groups. If students are treated differently, however, the basis for classifying them should be reasonable. The cases above suggest that classification based solely on financial considerations may not meet that test. Administrators should thus be prepared to offer sound nonfinancial justifications for classifications in their residence rules—such as the promotion of educational goals, the protection of the health and safety of students, or the protection of other students' privacy interests.

Besides these limits on administrators' authority over student housing, the Constitution also limits public administrators' authority to enter student rooms (see Section 8.4.2) and to regulate solicitation, canvassing, and voter registration in student residences (see Sections 11.4.3 & 11.6.4).

For private as well as public institutions, federal civil rights regulations limit administrators' authority to treat students differently on grounds of race, sex, age, or disability. The Title VI regulations (see Section 13.5.2) apparently prohibit any and all different treatment of students by race (34 C.F.R. §§ 100.3(b)(1)–(b)(5) & 100.4(d)). The Title IX regulations (see Section 13.5.3 of this book) require that the institution provide amounts of housing for female and male students proportionate to the number of housing applicants of each sex, that such housing be comparable in quality and in cost to the student, and that the institution not have different housing policies for each sex (34 C.F.R. §§ 106.32 & 106.33). Furthermore, a provision of Title IX (20 U.S.C. § 1686) states that institutions may maintain single-sex living facilities.

The Section 504 regulations on discrimination against people with disabilities (see Section 13.5.4) require institutions to provide "comparable, convenient, and accessible" housing for students with disabilities at the same cost as for nondisabled students (34 C.F.R. § 104.45). The regulations also require colleges to provide a variety of housing and that students with disabilities be given a choice among several types of housing (34 C.F.R. § 104.45(a)).

A federal court's analysis of a student's religious discrimination challenge to mandatory on-campus residency is instructive. In *Rader v. Johnston,* 924 F. Supp. 1540 (D. Neb. 1996), an eighteen-year-old first-year student at the University of Nebraska-Kearney challenged the university's policy requiring first-year students to live on campus. Students who were nineteen, married, or living with their parents or legal guardians were expressly excepted from the policy. The rationale for the policy, according to the university, was that it "fosters diversity, promotes tolerance, increases the level of academic achievement, and improves the graduation rate of its students, [while] ensur[ing] full occupancy of . . . residence halls" (924 F. Supp. at 1543). The student contended that living in the campus residence halls would hinder the free exercise of his religion. Since he did not qualify for exception under any of the enumerated exceptions to the residency policy, he petitioned the university for an ad hoc exception "on the ground that his religious convictions exhort him to live in an environment that encourages moral excellence during [his] college career," and, to this end, he requested that the university "allow him to live with other students of similar faith in the Christian Student Fellowship facility, across the street from the . . . campus." The university denied the student's request, citing its rationale for the residency requirement and finding that nothing in the residence hall environment would hinder the student's practice of religion.

The court, relying on a U.S. Supreme Court decision in *Church of the Lukumi Babalu Aye v. City of Hialeah,* 508 U.S. 520 (1993) (Section 1.6.2 of this book), found in favor of the student. It cited the fact that "over one-third of freshman students are excused" from the residency requirement under the enumerated exceptions or under ad hoc exceptions that the university "routinely granted" for other students. The university had, according to the court, created "a system of 'individualized government assessment' of the students' requests for exemptions" from the residency requirement, and had granted numerous exceptions for nonreligious reasons, but had "refused to extend exceptions to freshmen who wish to live at CSF [Christian Student Fellowship] for religious reasons" (924 F. Supp. at 1553). Under *Lukumi Babalu Aye,* therefore, the university's on-campus residency policy for first-year students was not "generally applicable" or "neutrally applied" to all students and could withstand judicial scrutiny, as applied to Rader, only if the denial of his request for an exception "serves a compelling state interest."

Although the court agreed that the interests enumerated in the university's housing policy could be legitimate and important to the state, it found that the university's implementation of the policy, which allowed more than one-third of the students to be granted exceptions, "undercuts any contention that its interest is compelling." These interests therefore could not justify the resulting infringement on Rader's free exercise rights.

Students lodged a claim against Yale University that was similar to the *Rader* claim. This suit was dismissed by a federal district court in *Hack v. The President and Fellows of Yale College,* 16 F. Supp. 2d 183 (D. Conn. 1998), *affirmed,* 237 F.3d 81 (2d Cir. 2000). Yale requires all unmarried freshman and sophomore students under twenty-two years old to live in campus housing. Four Orthodox Jewish undergraduate students requested exemptions from the housing requirement because all of Yale's residence halls are coeducational, and the students stated that their religion forbade them to live in a coeducational environment. When the university refused to exempt the students from the housing requirement, they filed a lawsuit claiming that the housing policy violated the U.S. Constitution by interfering with their free exercise of religion, that it also violated the Fair Housing Act (FHA) and the Sherman Antitrust Act, and that it constituted a breach of contract.

The court dismissed the students' constitutional claims, ruling that Yale was a private university and not subject to constitutional restrictions. The students had claimed that, because the governor and lieutenant governor of Connecticut were *ex officio* members of Yale's governing body, the university was a state actor. Citing *Lebron v. National Passenger R.R. Corp.*, 513 U.S. 374 (1995) (Section 1.5.2 of this book), the court ruled that having two public officials on a governing board of nineteen was insufficient under the test articulated in *Lebron* to constitute state action. The court then ruled that the plaintiffs did not have standing to sue under the Fair Housing Act because Yale had not refused to provide housing to the students on the basis of their religion; it had provided them housing that they had paid for, but in which they refused to live.

With respect to the antitrust claim, the court ruled that the students' complaint had not specifically stated whether the tying market (see Section 13.2.8) that Yale was alleged to be attempting to monopolize was "a general university education or an Ivy League education" (16 F. Supp. 2d at 195). Furthermore, said the court, the plaintiffs had not identified the relevant market at issue; substitutes for Yale's campus housing could be obtained by attending a different university. Despite the plaintiffs' attempt to argue that the outcome in the Hamilton College antitrust case (Section 10.2.2) protected their claim against dismissal, the court responded that the Hamilton College case merely established that a private college affected interstate commerce, and that the plaintiff's failure to define the relevant market alleged to be monopolized by Yale doomed their complaint to failure.

In *Fleming v. New York University*, 865 F.2d 478 (2d Cir. 1989), a graduate student who used a wheelchair claimed that the university overcharged him for his room, in violation of Section 504 of the Rehabilitation Act. The trial court dismissed his claim, and the appellate court affirmed. The student had requested single occupancy of a double room as an undergraduate; the university charged him twice the rate that a student sharing a double room paid. After intervention by the U.S. Office for Civil Rights, the university modified its room charge to 75 percent of the rate for two students in a room.

When the student decided to enroll in graduate school at the university, he asked to remain in the undergraduate residence hall. The university agreed, and charged him the 75 percent fee. However, because of low occupancy levels in the graduate residence halls, graduate students occupying double rooms there were charged a single-room rate. When the student refused to pay his room bills, the university withheld his master's degree. The court ruled that the student's claim for his undergraduate years was time barred. The claim for disability discrimination based on the room charges during his graduate program was denied because the student had never applied for graduate housing; he had requested undergraduate housing. There was no discriminatory denial of cheaper graduate housing, the court said, because the student never requested it.

The Age Discrimination Act regulations (see Section 13.5.5) apparently apply to discrimination by age in campus housing. As implemented in the general regulations, the law apparently limits administrators' authority to use explicit age distinctions (such as those used in *Cooper v. Nix* and *Texas Woman's University v. Chayklintaste*) in formulating housing policies. Policies that distinguish among students according to their class (such as those used in *Prostrollo v. University of South Dakota*) may also be prohibited by the Age Discrimination Act, since they may have the effect of distinguishing by age. Such age distinctions will be prohibited (under § 90.12 of the general regulations) unless they fit within one of the narrow exceptions specified in the regulations (in §§ 90.14 & 90.15) or constitute affirmative action (under § 90.49) (see generally Sections 13.5.5 & 13.5.6 of this book). The best bet for fitting within an exception may be the regulation that permits age distinctions "necessary to the normal operation . . . of a program or activity" (§ 90.14). But administrators should note that the four-part test set out in the regulation carefully circumscribes this exception. For policies based on the class of students, administrators may also be helped by the regulation that permits the use of a nonage factor with an age-discriminatory effect "if the factor bears a direct and substantial relationship to the normal operation of the program or activity" (§ 90.15).

The Fair Housing Act prohibits discrimination in housing on the basis of "familial status" (42 U.S.C. § 3604 (1989)). This statute may create rights for married students greater than they are afforded under the Constitution in cases such as *Bynes v. Toll* above. A case brought under both the Fair Housing Act and Title IX of the Education Amendments of 1972 (Section 13.5.3), although subsequently vacated for lack of jurisdiction, suggests a potential source of liability for colleges and landlords of off-campus housing. In *Wilson v. Glenwood Intermountain Properties, Inc.,* 876 F. Supp. 1231 (D. Utah 1995), *vacated,* 98 F.3d 590 (10th Cir. 1996), the trial court rejected claims by two nonstudent plaintiffs that the housing regulations of Brigham Young University (BYU) violated these laws and that the actions of landlords, who had entered into agreements with BYU to segregate their housing by gender and to rent only to BYU students, also violated the Fair Housing Act. The litigation involved claims of discrimination on the basis of gender, religion, and familial status. Regarding gender, the plaintiffs claimed that the landlords' segregation of tenants by gender violated the FHA requirement that landlords offer nondiscriminatory "terms, conditions, and privileges" in the rental of housing; and that the landlords' advertisements, which noted that they rented only to male, or only to female, BYU students, discriminated against them on the basis of gender.

The trial court dismissed the claims involving religious discrimination and discrimination with respect to advertising on jurisdictional grounds, but ruled on the plaintiffs' other gender discrimination claim on the merits, awarding summary judgment to the defendants. The appellate court vacated the lower court's judgment and remanded the case with instructions to dismiss, ruling that the plaintiffs lacked standing to challenge the landlords' practices as a form of gender discrimination. Preliminarily, the court stated, renting only to students does not violate the Fair Housing Act, so the plaintiffs lacked standing because, as nonstudents, they would not be eligible to rent from these landlords even if they could meet the gender requirements. But the court carefully examined the claim of discriminatory advertising (which the trial court had dismissed with very little analysis), stating that, had the plaintiffs alleged that they had been injured by the gender-exclusive advertising, they may have been able to state a claim. Because no such injury had been shown, the existence of the "discriminatory" advertising, by itself, was insufficient to confer standing on the plaintiffs to challenge the landlords' actions under the Fair Housing Act.

Another group protesting discrimination in housing policies are same-sex couples. These couples have claimed that because they are not allowed to marry, they are unfairly excluded from a benefit extended to married students. Furthermore, since many colleges and universities prohibit discrimination on the basis of sexual orientation, gay couples have argued that denying them housing violates the institution's nondiscrimination regulations. Several universities, including the University of Pennsylvania and Stanford University, have provided university housing to unmarried couples, including those of the same sex.

In *Levin v. Yeshiva University,* 691 N.Y.S.2d 280 (Sup. Ct. N.Y. 1999), *affirmed,* 709 N.Y.S.2d 392 (N.Y. App. Div. 2000), *affirmed in part and modified in part,* 96 N.Y.2d 484 (N.Y. 2001), a same-sex couple who were medical students at the university wished to live in university housing that was reserved for married students, their spouses, and dependent children. The medical school requires proof of marriage in order for spouses to live with students in campus apartments. The plaintiffs had been offered student housing, but were not permitted to live together. They argued that they were in a long-term committed relationship and that the medical school's housing regulations violated the New York State Roommate Law (Real Property Law § 235-f); the New York State and New York City Human Rights Laws (Exec. L. §§ 296(2-a), 296(4), & 296(5); and the N.Y.C. Admin. Code § 8–197(5)) because the regulations discriminated against the plaintiffs on the basis of their marital status. They also argued that the housing regulations had a discriminatory impact upon them because they were homosexuals.

The trial court rejected all the plaintiffs' claims. Regarding marital status discrimination, the court cited New York case law that permitted landlords to "recogniz[e] the institution of marriage and distinguish[ ] between married and unmarried couples" [691 N.Y.S.2d at 282]. The plaintiffs were not denied housing by the medical school, said the court—they were provided the same type of housing for which other single students were eligible. Furthermore, New York appellate courts had ruled that a domestic partnership was not a marriage for purposes of health benefits for public school teachers. Regarding the disparate impact claim, the court repeated that the plaintiffs had been given housing by the medical school, and that Yeshiva University was not responsible for the fact that they could not marry.

Finally, the court rejected the claim under New York's roommate law that allows tenants to live with their spouses and children, or with friends of their own choosing. This law was not intended to cover college housing, according to the court, because college housing is short term, available only as long as the tenants are students, provided as a benefit and a convenience to students, and offered at below-market rates.

The students appealed, and although the appellate court affirmed the trial court's ruling in all respects, the students' subsequent appeal to New York's highest court was somewhat more successful. Although the high court affirmed the lower courts' rulings on the marital status discrimination, they reinstated the plaintiffs' cause of action claiming that the housing policy had a disparately disproportionate impact on homosexuals, a potential violation of New York City's Human Rights Law.

Many colleges have established "theme" housing linked to linguistic or cultural groups. Questions have arisen as to whether these residences, which may not be, or may be perceived not to be, open to all students, violate civil rights laws. The U.S. Department of Education has determined that Cornell University did not violate Title VI of the Civil Rights Act of 1964 (Section 13.5.2) by creating "ethnic program houses," which are residence halls whose residents are predominantly members of a particular race or ethnic group. The positive ruling was premised on the understanding that admission to the residences was not restricted to a particular race or ethnic group (Karla Haworth, "Education Department Finds No Civil-Rights Violations at Cornell's Ethnic Houses," *Chron. Higher Educ.*, October 4, 1996, A45).

Regarding tort liability, residential colleges and universities may wish to consider that requiring students to live in student housing may create a duty to protect them from foreseeable harm, even if the housing is not owned by the university (see generally Section 8.6.2). For an example, see *Knoll v. Board of Regents of the University of Nebraska* (Section 8.6.2.), which discusses institutional liability for an off-campus injury that occurred in a fraternity house subject to the college's student housing policies.

8.4.2. Searches and seizures.

8.4.2. Searches and seizures. The Fourth Amendment secures an individual's expectation of privacy against government encroachment by providing that:

> the right of the people to be secure in their persons, houses, papers, and effects, against unreasonable searches and seizures, shall not be violated, and no warrants shall issue, but upon probable cause, supported by oath or affirmation, and particularly describing the place to be searched, and the persons or things to be seized.

Searches or seizures conducted pursuant to a warrant meeting the requirements of this provision are deemed reasonable. Warrantless searches may also be found reasonable if they are conducted with the consent of the individual involved, if they are incidental to a lawful arrest, or if they come within a few narrow judicial exceptions, such as an emergency situation.

The applicability of these Fourth Amendment mandates to postsecondary institutions has not always been clear. In the past, when administrators' efforts to provide a "proper" educational atmosphere resulted in noncompliance with the Fourth Amendment, the deviations were defended by administrators and often upheld by courts under a variety of theories. While the previously common justification of *in loco parentis* is no longer appropriate (see Section 8.1.1), several remaining theories retain vitality. The leading case of *Piazzola v. Watkins*, 442 F.2d 284 (5th Cir. 1971), provides a good overview of these theories and their validity.

In *Piazzola*, the dean of men at a state university, at the request of the police, pledged the cooperation of university officials in searching the rooms of two students suspected of concealing marijuana there. At the time of the search, the university had the following regulation in effect: "The college reserves the right to enter rooms for inspection purposes. If the administration deems it necessary, the room may be searched and the occupant required to open his personal baggage and any other personal material which is sealed." The students' rooms were searched without their consent and without a warrant by police officers and university officials. When police found marijuana in each room, the students were arrested, tried, convicted, and sentenced to five years in prison. The U.S. Court of Appeals for the Fifth Circuit reversed the convictions, holding that "a student who occupies a college dormitory room enjoys the protection of the Fourth Amendment" and that the warrantless searches were unreasonable and therefore unconstitutional under that amendment.

Piazzola and similar cases establish that administrators of public institutions cannot avoid the Fourth Amendment simply by asserting that a student has no reasonable expectation of privacy in institution-sponsored housing. (Compare *State v. Dalton*, 716 P.2d 940 (Wash. Ct. App. 1986).) Similarly, administrators can no longer be confident of avoiding the Fourth Amendment by asserting the *in loco parentis* concept or by arguing that the institution's landlord status, standing alone, authorizes it to search to protect its property interests. Nor does the landlord status, by itself, permit the institution to consent to a search by police, since it has been held that a landlord has no authority to consent to a police search of a tenant's premises (see, for example, *Chapman v. United States*, 365 U.S. 610 (1961)).

However, two limited bases remain on which administrators of public institutions or their delegates can enter a student's premises uninvited and without the authority of a warrant.[43] Under the first approach, the institution can obtain the student's general consent to entry by including an authorization to enter in a written housing agreement or in housing regulations incorporated in the housing agreement. But, according to *Piazzola*, the institution cannot require the student to waive his or her Fourth Amendment protections as a condition of occupying a residence hall room.

Thus, housing agreements or regulations must be narrowly construed to permit only such entry and search as is expressly provided, and in any case

---

[43]In *New Jersey v. T.L.O.*, 469 U.S. 325 (1985), the U.S. Supreme Court created a judicial exception to the warrant requirement for certain searches of public school students. However, the Court's opinion directly applies only to public elementary and secondary schools. Moreover, the opinion applies (1) only to searches of the person or property (such as a purse) carried on the person, as opposed to searches of dormitory rooms, lockers, desks, or other such locations (469 U.S. at 337, n.5), and (2) only to "searches carried out by school authorities acting alone and on their own authority," as opposed to "searches conducted by school officials in conjunction with or at the behest of law enforcement agencies" (469 U.S. at 341, n.7).

to permit only entries undertaken in pursuit of an educational purpose rather than a criminal enforcement function. *State v. Hunter,* 831 P.2d 1033 (Utah App. 1992), illustrates the type of search that may come within the *Piazzola* guidelines. The director of housing at Utah State University had instigated and conducted a room-to-room inspection to investigate reports of vandalism on the second floor of a dormitory. Upon challenge by a student in whose room the director discovered stolen university property in plain view, the court upheld the search because the housing regulations expressly authorized the room-to-room inspection and because the inspection served the university's interest in protecting university property and maintaining a sound educational environment.

Under the second approach to securing entry to a student's premises, the public institution can sometimes conduct searches (often called "administrative searches") whose purpose is to protect health and safety—for instance, to enforce health regulations or fire and safety codes. Although such searches, if conducted without a student's consent, usually require a warrant, it may be obtained under less stringent standards than those for obtaining a criminal search warrant. The leading case is *Camara v. Municipal Court,* 387 U.S. 523 (1967), where the U.S. Supreme Court held that a person cannot be prosecuted for refusing to permit city officials to conduct a warrantless code-enforcement inspection of his residence. The Court held that such a search required a warrant, which could be obtained "if reasonable legislative or administrative standards for conducting an area inspection are satisfied"; such standards need "not necessarily depend upon specific knowledge of the condition of the particular dwelling."

In emergency situations where there is insufficient time to obtain a warrant, health and safety searches may be conducted without one. The U.S. Supreme Court emphasized in the *Camara* case (387 U.S. at 539) that "nothing we say today is intended to foreclose prompt inspections, even without a warrant, that the law has traditionally upheld in emergency situations." Although a warrantless search based upon the possibility of a health or safety problem may be permissible under the Fourth Amendment, this exception is a narrow one. The Supreme Judicial Court of Massachusetts determined that a warrantless search of a residence hall room by campus police at Fitchburg State College violated the Fourth Amendment to the U.S. Constitution. In *Commonwealth v. Neilson,* 666 N.E.2d 984 (Mass. 1996), a student challenged his arrest for illegal possession of marijuana, asserting that the search of his room was unconstitutional. Neilson had signed a residence hall contract providing that student life staff members could enter student rooms to inspect for health or safety hazards. A maintenance worker believed he heard a cat inside a four-bedroom suite; one of the bedrooms was occupied by Neilson. The maintenance worker reported the sound to college officials, who visited the suite and informed the occupants that no cats were permitted in university housing. The official posted notices on the bedroom doors of the suite, stating that a "door-to-door check" would be held that night to ensure that no cat was present. When the officials returned, Neilson was not present. They searched his bedroom, and noticed that the closet light was on. Because they were concerned that there might be a fire hazard, they opened the door and discovered two 4-foot marijuana plants growing under the light. At that point, the campus police were called; they arrived, took pictures of the marijuana, and removed it from the room. No search warrant was obtained at any time.

The court stated that the initial search (to locate the cat) was reasonable, as was the decision to open the closet door, since it was based upon a concern for the students' safety. The constitutional violation occurred, according to the court, when the campus police arrived and seized the evidence without a warrant or the consent of Neilson. Neilson, in the residence hall contract, had consented to student life officials entering his room, but had not consented to campus police doing so. Furthermore, the "plain view" doctrine did not apply in this case because the campus police were not lawfully present in Neilson's room. The plain view doctrine allows a law enforcement officer to seize property that is clearly incriminating evidence or contraband when that property is in "plain view" in a place where the officer has a right to be. The court therefore concluded that all evidence seized by the campus police was properly suppressed by the trial judge.

Before entering a room pursuant to the housing agreement or an administrative (health and safety) search, administrators should usually seek to notify and obtain the specific consent of the affected students when it is feasible to do so. Such a policy not only evidences courtesy and respect for privacy but would also augment the validity of the entry in circumstances where there may be some doubt about the scope of the administrator's authority under the housing agreement or the judicial precedents on administrative searches.

A state appellate court ruled that a "dormitory sweep policy" is *prima facie* unconstitutional. In *Devers v. Southern University*, 712 So. 2d 199 (La. Ct. App. 1998), the court addressed the legality of the university's policy, which stated: "The University reserves all rights in connection with assignments of rooms, inspection of rooms with police, and the termination of room occupancy." The plaintiff, Devers, was arrested when twelve bags of marijuana were discovered in his dormitory room. The drugs were found by university administrators and police officers during a "dormitory sweep" that the university stated was authorized by its housing policy. Devers was expelled from the university after a hearing in which the student judicial board found him guilty of violating the student code of conduct. Devers sued the university, claiming that the search violated the Fourth Amendment. Although the university reached a settlement with Devers with respect to his expulsion (it was reduced to a one-term suspension), his constitutional claim was not settled.

The trial court held that the housing regulation was *prima facie* unconstitutional, and the appellate court affirmed. The court distinguished *State v. Hunter* because the wording of the housing regulation in *Hunter* differed from the language adopted by Southern University. The regulation in *Hunter* authorized entry into students' dormitory rooms for maintaining students' health and safety, for maintaining university property, and for maintaining discipline. Southern's regulation was broader, and would allow unauthorized entry into a student's room for any purpose. The court also distinguished *Piazzola v. Watkins* because its regulation did not authorize searches by police, as did Southern's. The court noted that Southern "has many ways to promote the safety interests of students, faculty and staff" without using warrantless police searches.

In addition to these two limited approaches (housing agreements and administrative searches) to securing entry, other even narrower exceptions to Fourth Amendment warrant requirements may be available to security officers of public institutions who have arrest powers. Such exceptions involve the intricacies of Fourth Amendment law on arrests and searches (see generally *Welsh v. Wisconsin*, 466 U.S. 740 (1984)). The case of *State of Washington v. Chrisman*, 455 U.S. 1 (1982), is illustrative. A campus security guard at Washington State University had arrested a student, Overdahl, for illegally possessing alcoholic beverages. The officer accompanied Overdahl to his dormitory room when Overdahl offered to retrieve his identification. Overdahl's roommate, Chrisman, was in the room. While waiting at the doorway for Overdahl to find his identification, the officer observed marijuana seeds and a pipe lying on a desk in the room. The officer then entered, confirmed the identity of the seeds, and seized them. Chrisman was later convicted of possession of marijuana and LSD, which security officers also found in the room.

By a 6-to-3 vote, the U.S. Supreme Court applied the "plain view" exception to the Fourth Amendment and upheld the conviction. The Court determined that, since an arresting officer has a right to maintain custody of a subject under arrest, this officer lawfully could have entered the room with Overdahl and remained at Overdahl's side for the entire time Overdahl was in the room. Thus, the officer not only had the right to be where he could observe the drugs; he also had the right to be where he could seize the drugs. According to the Court,

> It is of no legal significance whether the officer was in the room, on the threshold, or in the hallway, since he had a right to be in any of these places as an incident of a valid arrest. . . . This is a classic instance of incriminating evidence found in plain view when a police officer, for unrelated but entirely legitimate reasons, obtains lawful access to an individual's area of privacy.

Chrisman thus recognizes that a security officer may enter a student's room "as an incident of a valid arrest" of either that student or his roommate. The case also indicates that an important exception to search warrant requirements—the plain view doctrine—retains its full vitality in the college dormitory setting. The Court accorded no greater or lesser constitutional protection from search and seizure to student dormitory residents than to the population at large. Clearly, under *Chrisman*, students do enjoy Fourth Amendment protections on campus; but, just as clearly, the Fourth Amendment does not accord dormitory students special status or subject campus security officials to additional restrictions that are not applicable to the nonacademic world.

The Supreme Court placed an important restriction on the plain view doctrine in *Arizona v. Hicks*, 480 U.S. 321 (1987). A police officer, who had entered an apartment lawfully for Fourth Amendment purposes, noticed some stereo equipment that he believed might be stolen. He moved the equipment slightly to locate the serial numbers and later ascertained that the equipment was, in fact, stolen. The Court ruled that the search and seizure were unlawful because the police officer did not have probable cause to believe the equipment was stolen—only a reasonable suspicion, which is insufficient for Fourth Amendment purposes.

Administrators at private institutions are generally not subject to Fourth Amendment restraints, since their actions are usually not state action (Section 1.5.2). But if local, state, or federal law enforcement officials are in any way involved in a search at a private institution, such involvement may be sufficient to make the search state action and therefore subject to the Fourth Amendment. In *People v. Boettner*, 362 N.Y.S.2d 365 (N.Y. Sup. Ct. 1974), *affirmed*, 376 N.Y.S.2d 59 (N.Y. App. Div. 1975), for instance, the question was whether a dormitory room search by officials at the Rochester Institute of Technology, a private institution, was state action. The court answered in the negative only after establishing that the police had not expressly or implicitly requested the search; that the police were not aware of the search; and that there was no evidence of any implied participation of the police by virtue of a continuing cooperative relationship between university officials and the police. A similar analysis, and similar result, occurred in *State v. Nemser*, 807 A.2d 1289 (N.H. 2002), when the court refused to suppress evidence of drugs seized by a Dartmouth College security officer because the college's residence hall search policy had not been approved or suggested by the local police. A Virginia appellate court reached a similar conclusion in *Duarte v. Commonwealth*, 407 S.E.2d 41 (Va. Ct. App. 1991), because the dean of students at a private college had told college staff to search the plaintiff's room, and police were not involved in the search. And in *State v. Burroughs*, 926 S.W.2d 243 (Tenn. 1996), the Tennessee Supreme Court ruled that a warrantless search of a dormitory room by a director of residence life at Knoxville College, a private institution, did not involve state action, and thus his removal of drug paraphernalia and other evidence did not violate the student's Fourth Amendment rights. The court noted that the student handbook and housing contract both forbid the possession or use of alcohol and drugs, and gave the residence hall director authority to search student rooms. Moreover, noted the court, the search was conducted by a college official, not a police officer, to further the educational objectives of the college, not to enforce the criminal law.

(For a comprehensive analysis of the application of search and seizure law to colleges, see Jan Alan Neiger, "An Overview of Search and Seizure Law on Campus," *Synthesis: Law and Policy in Higher Education*, Vol. 12, no. 4 (Spring 2001). See also Kristal Otto Stanley, "The Fourth Amendment and Dormitory Searches—A New Truce," 65 *U. Chicago L. Rev.* 1403 (1998).)

Sec. 8.5. Campus Computer Networks

8.5.1. Freedom of speech. Increasingly, free speech on campus is enhanced, and free speech issues are compounded, by the growth of technology. Cable and satellite transmission technologies, for instance, have had such effects on many campuses. But the clearest and most important example—now and for the foreseeable future—is computer communications technology. Computer labs, laptops, campus local area networks (LANs), servers, and Internet gateways have assumed a pervasive presence on most campuses, and are used increasingly by the campus community for e-mail communications, discussion groups, Web pages, research, access to information on campus programs and services, and entertainment. Students—the focus of this Section—may be both senders (speakers) and receivers (readers); their purposes may be related to coursework or extracurricular activities, or may be purely personal; and their communications may be local (within the institution) or may extend around the world.

As the amount, variety, and distance of computer communications have increased, so have the development of institutional computer use policies and other institutional responses to perceived problems. The problems may be of the "traffic cop" variety, occasioning a need for the institution to allocate its limited computer resources by directing traffic to prevent traffic jams. Or the problems may be more controversial, raising computer misuse issues such as defamation, harassment, threats, hate speech, copyright infringement, and academic dishonesty. The latter types of problems may present more difficult legal issues, since institutional regulations attempting to alleviate these problems may be viewed as content-based restrictions on speech.

Public institutions, therefore, must keep a watchful eye on the First Amendment when drafting and enforcing computer use policies. Just as federal and state legislation regulating computer communications may be invalidated under the free speech and press clauses (see Section 13.2.12), particular provisions of campus regulations can be struck down as well if they contravene these clauses. Private institutions are not similarly bound (see *CompuServe, Inc. v. Cyber Promotions, Inc.,* 962 F. Supp. 1015, 1025–27 (S.D. Ohio 1997); and see generally Section 1.5.2). Yet private institutions may voluntarily protect student free expression through student codes or bills of rights, or computer use policies themselves, or through campus custom—and may occasionally be bound to protect free expression by state constitutions, statutes, or regulations; thus administrators at private institutions will also want to be keenly aware of First Amendment developments regarding computer speech.[44]

---

[44]In addition to freedom of expression concerns, computer communications also present personal privacy concerns to which colleges and universities should be attentive. See, for example, Constance Hawk, *Computer and Internet Use on Campus* (Jossey-Bass, 2001), Ch. 3 ("Privacy Issues in Electronic Communications"), 81–117. Public institutions, for instance, should be aware of the Fourth Amendment implications of searching students' personal computer files (see generally Sections 7.1.1 & 7.1.4), and both public and private institutions should be aware of privacy rights concerning computerized records that students may have under FERPA (see generally Section 9.7.1 of this book) and privacy rights concerning computer communications that students may have under the Electronic Communications Privacy Act (ECPA) (see generally Section 13.2.12.2 of this book). In addition, state statutes (many similar to the federal ECPA) and state common law principles may protect the privacy of students' computer communications in certain circumstances.

Under existing First Amendment principles (see generally Sections 9.5.1, 9.5.2, & 9.6.2), administrators should ask four main questions when devising new computer use policies, or when reviewing or applying existing policies:

1. Are we seeking to regulate, or do we regulate, the *content* of computer speech ("cyberspace speech")?

2. If any of our regulations are content based, do they fit into any First Amendment exceptions that permit content-based regulations—such as the exceptions for obscenity and "true threats"?

3. (a) Does our institution own or lease the computer hardware or software being used for the computer speech; and (b) if so, has our institution created "forums" for discussion on its computer servers and networks?

4. Are our regulations or proposed regulations clear, specific, and narrow?

For *question 1,* if a computer use policy regulates the content of speech—that is, the ideas, opinions, or viewpoints expressed—and does not fall into any of the exceptions set out below under question 2, the courts will usually subject the regulation to a two-part standard of "strict scrutiny": (1) Does the content regulation further a "compelling" governmental interest, and (2) is the regulation "narrowly tailored" and "necessary" to achieve this interest? (See, for example, *Mainstream Loudoun v. Board of Trustees of the Loudoun County Library,* 24 F. Supp. 2d 552, 563–68 (E.D. Va. 1998), discussed below in this subsection.) The need to act in cases of copyright infringement, bribery, fraud, blackmail, stalking, or other violations of federal and state law may often be considered compelling interests, as may the need to protect the institution's academic integrity when computers are used for "cheating." In *Mainstream Loudoun* (above) the court also assumed "that minimizing access to illegal pornography and avoidance of creation of a sexually hostile environment are compelling government interests" (24 F. Supp. 2d at 565). Regulations furthering such interests may therefore meet the strict scrutiny standard if they are very carefully drawn.[45] But otherwise this standard is extremely difficult to meet. In contrast, if a computer regulation serves "neutral" government interests not based on the content of speech (for example, routine "traffic cop" regulations), a less stringent and easier to meet standard would apply.

In *American Civil Liberties Union of Georgia v. Miller,* 977 F. Supp 1228 (N.D. Ga. 1997), for instance, a federal district court in Georgia considered the validity of a state statute prohibiting data transmitters from falsely identifying themselves in Internet transmissions (Georgia Code Ann. § 16-9-93.1). In invalidating the Georgia statute, the court emphasized that a "prohibition of

---

[45]As an adjunct to strict scrutiny analysis, courts may also apply the prior restraint doctrine to some content-based restrictions. In *Mainstream Loudoun* (discussed below in the text of this subsection), for instance, the court determined that the blocking of Internet sites was an unconstitutional prior restraint because the blocking policy included neither sufficient standards nor adequate procedural safeguards (24 F. Supp. 2d at 568–70).

Internet transmissions which 'falsely identify' the sender constitutes a presumptively invalid content-based restriction" on First Amendment rights. Recognizing that there is a "right to communicate anonymously and pseudonymously over the Internet" (977 F. Supp. at 1230), the court held that the state may not blanketly prohibit all Internet transmissions in which speakers do not identify themselves or use some pseudonym in place of an accurate identification. The court in *Miller* also held, however, that "fraud prevention . . . is a compelling state interest." Thus, if speakers were to use anonymity or misidentification in order to defraud the receivers of their Internet messages, then prohibition of false identification would be appropriate so long as the regulation is narrowly tailored to meet the fraud prevention objective. The court suggested that, in order to be narrowly tailored, a regulation must, at a minimum, include a requirement that the speaker has intended to deceive or that deception has in fact occurred (977 F. Supp. at 1232). Thus, for instance, if a public institution were to promulgate narrowly tailored regulations that prohibit speakers from intentionally "misappropriat[ing] the identity of another specific entity or person" (977 F. Supp. at 1232), such regulations would apparently be a valid content-based restriction on speech.

Regarding *question 2*, if a restriction on computer speech is content based, and thus presumptively invalid under the strict scrutiny standard of review, it would still be able to survive if it falls into one of the exceptions to the First Amendment prohibition against content-based restrictions on expression. All these exceptions are technical and narrow, and collectively would cover only a portion of the computer speech institutions may wish to regulate, but in certain cases these exceptions can become very important. One pertinent example is obscenity, which is recognized in numerous cases, including computer cases, as a First Amendment exception (see Sections 10.3.4 & 13.2.12). Another related exception is child pornography, which need not fall within the U.S. Supreme Court's definition of obscenity to be prohibited, but instead is subject to the requirements that the Court established in *New York v. Ferber*, 458 U.S. 747 (1982). The exception for false or deceptive commercial speech, and commercial speech that proposes unlawful activities, is also pertinent to computer speech (see *Central Hudson Gas and Electric Corp. v. Public Service Commission*, 447 U.S. 557, 563–64 (1980)), as is the exception for "true threats" that was established in *Watts v. United States*, 394 U.S. 705 (1969), and further developed in *Virginia v. Black* (see Section 9.6.2 of this book).[46]

It is the exception for "true threats" that has received the greatest amount of attention in contemporary cyberspeech cases. In *United States v. Alkhabaz aka Jake Baker*, 104 F.3d 1492 (6th Cir. 1997) (*affirming on other grounds,*

[46]There is also an exception for "fighting words," but since this exception is narrowly defined to include only face-to-face communications, it has no apparent application to cyberspeech. Defamatory speech and speech that constitutes incitement may also be regulated, but the analysis is different than for the "exceptions" or "categorical exceptions" just discussed. See generally William Kaplin, *American Constitutional Law* (Carolina Academic Press, 2004), Ch. 12, Secs. C.2(1), D.1, & D.2. Incitement analysis, and the difference between incitement and advocacy, are addressed in the *American Coalition of Life Advocates* case discussed below in this subsection.

890 F. Supp. 1375 (E.D. Mich. 1995)), for example, and again in *United States v. Morales,* 272 F.3d 284 (5th Cir. 2001), courts struggled with whether particular computer communications were threats for the purposes of 18 U.S.C. § 875(c) (see Section 13.2.12.3 of this book). Ultimately, using a combination of statutory and constitutional analysis, the courts concluded that Baker's e-mail messages in the first case were not threats for purposes of the federal statute, but Morales's chat room postings in the second case were threats for purposes of the statute. Another instructive example, providing more fully developed First Amendment analysis, is the case of *Planned Parenthood of Columbia/ Willamette, Inc., et al. v. American Coalition of Life Advocates, et al.,* 290 F.3d 1058 (9th Cir. 2002).

The defendants in the *American Coalition of Life Advocates* (ACLA) case were organizations and individuals engaged in anti-abortion activities, and the plaintiffs included physicians claiming that they had been threatened and intimidated by these activities. On a Web site operated by a third party, the ACLA had posted the names and addresses of numerous doctors that the posting identified as abortionists. Those doctors on the list who had been murdered, allegedly by anti-abortionists, were particularly noted, as were those doctors who had been wounded. These listings in the "score card" of murders and woundings were labeled as the "Nuremberg Files." Before posting these materials on the Web site, the ACLA had also circulated "wanted posters" containing similar information, and, in fact, three physicians had been murdered after being featured on a wanted poster. The court emphasized the importance of understanding the defendants' messages in the context in which they were made, and that the relevant context included both the wanted posters and the Web site postings, as well as the pattern of murders of physicians whose names had been featured in these communications. Analyzing the speech in context, the court determined that the First Amendment's free speech clause did not protect the defendants because the speech could be considered to be a "death threat message" and therefore a "true threat" within the meaning of *Watts v. United States.* "If ACLA had merely endorsed or encouraged violent reactions of others, its speech would be protected. However, while advocating violence is protected, threatening a person with violence is not" (290 F.3d at 1072).

The court articulated this useful guideline for determining when speech constitutes a true threat and is therefore unprotected by the First Amendment: "Whether a particular statement may properly be considered to be a threat is governed by an objective standard—whether a reasonable person would foresee that the statement would be interpreted by those to whom the maker communicates the statement as a serious expression of intent to harm or assault" (290 F.3d at 1074, citing *United States v. Orozco-Santillan,* 903 F.2d 1262, 1265 (9th Cir. 1990)). Applying this test, the court emphasized that physicians on the lists of abortionists "wore bullet-proof vests and took other extraordinary security measures to protect themselves and their families." ACLA "had every reason to foresee that its expression of intent to harm" through the wanted posters and the Web site "would elicit this reaction." The physicians' fears "did not simply happen; ACLA intended to intimidate them from doing what they do. This . . . is conduct that we are satisfied lacks any protection under the First Amendment. . . . ACLA was not staking out a position of debate but of threatened demise" (290 F.3d at 1086).

Regarding *question 3*, institutions may put themselves in a stronger regulatory position regarding student cyberspeech if they only restrict communications on *the institutions'* computers, servers, or networks; and if they structure student use in a way that does not create a "public forum" (see generally Section 9.5.2 of this book). The First Amendment standards would be lower and would generally permit content-based restrictions (regardless of whether they fall into one of the exceptions discussed above) other than those based on the particular viewpoint of the speaker. But if the institution, for policy reasons, chooses to use some portion of its computers, servers, or networks as an open "forum" for expression by students or by the campus community, then the normal First Amendment standards would apply, including the presumption that content-based restrictions on speech are unconstitutional. (See Joseph Beckham & William Schmid, "Forum Analysis in Cyberspace: The Case of Public Sector Higher Education," 98 *West's Educ. Law Rptr.* 11 (May 18, 1995).) The public forum concept is no longer limited to physical spaces or locations and apparently extends to "virtual" locations as well. In *Rosenberger v. Rector and Visitors of University of Virginia* (Section 10.1.5), for instance, the U.S. Supreme Court declared a student activities fund to be a public forum, subject to the same legal principles as other public forums, even though it was "a forum more in a metaphysical than a spatial or geographic sense . . ." (515 U.S. at 830).

Loving v. Boren, 956 F. Supp. 953 (W.D. Okla. 1997), provided the first illustration of public forum analysis being applied to a university computer system. The University of Oklahoma was concerned that some of the Internet news groups on the university news server were carrying obscene material. Consequently, the university adopted an access policy under which the university operated two news servers, A and B. The A server's content was limited to those news groups that had not been "blocked" or disapproved by the university; the B server's news group content was not limited. The A server was generally accessible to the university community for recreational as well as academic purposes; the B server could be used only for academic and research purposes, and then only by persons over age eighteen. Although the court rejected a free speech clause challenge to this policy, it did so on the basis of conclusory reasoning that reflects an incomplete understanding of the public forum doctrine. One conclusion the court reached, however, does appear to be valid and important: the restriction of the B server to academic and research purposes does not violate the First Amendment because "[a] university is by its nature dedicated to research and academic purposes" and "those purposes are the very ones for which the [computer] system was purchased" (956 F. Supp. at 955). The court apparently reached this conclusion because it did not view any part of the university's computer services as a public forum. The better view, however, is probably that the B server is a "limited forum" that the university has dedicated to academic use by restricting the purposes of use rather than the content as such. On this reasoning, the court should have proceeded to give separate consideration to the question of whether the A server was a public forum and, if so, whether its content could be limited as provided in the university's policy.[47]

A later case, *Mainstream Loudoun v. Board of Trustees of Loudoun County Library*, 24 F. Supp. 2d 552 (E.D. Va. 1998), provides better guidelines for determining whether a computer system's server or network is a public forum. The defendant library system had installed site-blocking software on its computers to prevent patrons from using these computers to view sexually explicit material on the Internet. The issue was whether the library's restrictions were subject to the strict scrutiny standards applicable to a "limited public forum," or to the lesser standards applicable to a "non-public forum." The court indicated that there are three "crucial factors" to consider in making such a determination: (1) whether the government, by its words and actions, displayed an intent to create a forum; (2) whether the government has permitted broad use of the forum it has created and "significantly limited its own discretion to restrict access"; and (3) "whether the nature of the forum is compatible with the expressive activity at issue" (24 F. Supp. 2d at 562–62). Using these factors, the court determined that the public library system was a limited public forum, that is, a public forum "for the limited purposes of the expressive activities [it] provide[s], including the receipt and communication of information through the Internet." Being a public forum, the library system's restriction on computer communications was subject to strict scrutiny analysis (see above in this subsection), which it could not survive; the restriction was therefore invalid under the First Amendment.

Under *question 4* in the list above, the focus is on the actual wording of each regulatory provision in the computer use policy. Even if a particular provision has been devised in conformance with the First Amendment principles addressed in questions 1, 2, and 3, it must in addition be drafted with a precision sufficient to meet constitutional standards of narrowness and clarity. If it does not, it will be subject to invalidation under either the "overbreadth" doctrine or the "vagueness" doctrine (see generally Sections 9.5.1, 9.5.3., & 9.5.6 of this book).

In *American Civil Liberties Union v. Miller* (above), for instance, the court determined that the language of the Georgia statute presented both overbreadth problems and vagueness problems. Regarding overbreadth, the court remarked that "the statute was not drafted with the precision necessary for laws regulating speech" because it "prohibits . . . the use of false identification to avoid social ostracism, to prevent discrimination and harassment, and to protect privacy," all of which are protected speech activities. The statute was thus "overbroad because it operates unconstitutionally for a substantial category of the speakers it covers" (977 F. Supp. at 1233). Similarly, regarding vagueness,

---

[47]There were also other potential issues that the court did not address separately: whether the B server could be restricted to persons over age eighteen (see generally *Reno v. American Civil Liberties Union*, 521 U.S. 844 (1997), in Section 13.2.12.2); and whether the standards and procedures for blocking materials from the A server were constitutionally sufficient (see the *Mainstream Loudoun* case, footnote 39, above in this subsection; and see generally Section 10.3.4).

the court determined that the statute's language did not "give fair notice of proscribed conduct to computer network users," thus encouraging "self-censorship"; and did not give adequate guidance to those enforcing the statute, thus allowing "substantial room for selective [enforcement against] persons who express minority viewpoints" (977 F. Supp. at 1234).

One may fairly ask whether all the preexisting First Amendment principles referenced in questions 1 through 4 should apply to the vast new world of cyberspace. Indeed, scholars and judges have been debating whether free speech and press law should apply in full to computer technology. (See, for example, Lawrence Lessig, "The Path of Cyberlaw," 104 *Yale L.J.* 1743 (1995); Timothy Wu, "Application-Centered Internet Analysis," 85 *Va. L. Rev.* 1163 (1999).) Although courts are committed to taking account of the unique aspects of each new communications technology, and allowing First Amendment law to grow and adapt in the process, thus far none of the basic principles discussed above have been discarded or substantially transformed when applied to cyber-speech. In fact, in the leading case to date, *Reno v. American Civil Liberties Union* (Section 13.2.12.2), the U.S. Supreme Court opinion relied explicitly on the principles referenced in the discussion above. Thus, although counsel and administrators will need to follow both legal and technological developments closely in this fast-moving area, they should work from the premise that established First Amendment principles remain their authoritative guides.

8.5.2. Liability issues. Colleges and universities may become liable *to students* for violating students' legal rights regarding computer communications and computer files; and they may become liable *to others* for certain computer communications of their students effectuated through a campus network or Internet service. The following discussion surveys the major areas of liability concern.

To help minimize First Amendment liability arising from institutional regulation of campus computer speech, administrators at public institutions may follow the guidelines suggested by the four questions set out in subsection 8.5.1 above. In addition, administrators might adopt an analogy to student newspapers to limit institutional liability for their students' uses of cyberspace. To adopt this analogy, the institution would consider students' own Web sites, bulletin boards, or discussion lists to be like student newspapers (see generally Section 10.3) and would provide them a freedom from regulation and oversight sufficient to assure that the students are not viewed as agents of the institution (see Section 10.3.6). Institutions might also create alternatives to regulation that would either diminish the likelihood of computer abuse or enhance the likelihood that disputes that do arise can be resolved without litigation. For instance, institutions could encourage, formally and informally, the development of cyberspace ethics codes for their campus communities. (For a foundation for such a code, see Marjorie Hodges & Gary Pavela, "Ten Principles of Civility in Cyberspace," and "Civility in Cyberspace," in *Synthesis: Law and Policy in Higher Education,* Vol. 8, no. 4 (Spring 1997), 624, 631.) To a large extent, the success of such codes would depend on widespread consensus about the norms established and the willingness to enforce them by peer pressure and cyberspace "counterspeech."

Another helpful initiative might be for institutions to provide a mediation or arbitration process adapted to the context of cyberspace. (See generally M. Katsh, "Dispute Resolution in Cyberspace," 28 *Conn. L. Rev.* 953 (1996).) Such a process could be conducted using outside assistance, perhaps even online assistance. Two Web sites to consult regarding cyberspace dispute resolution are The Virtual Magistrate Project, available at http://www.vmag.org and The Online Ombuds Office at http://www.ombuds.org.

In two other leading areas of concern—tort law and copyright law—federal law now provides institutions some protection from liability for students' online statements and their unauthorized transmission of copyrighted materials. (See generally Jonathan Bond & Matthew Schruers, "Safe Harbors Against the Liability Hurricane: The Communications Decency Act and the Digital Millennium Copyright Act," 20 *Cardozo Arts & Ent. L.J.* 295 (2002).)

Regarding tort law, the Communications Decency Act (CDA), discussed in Section 13.2.12.2 of this book, contains a Section 509, codified as 47 U.S.C. § 230, that protects "interactive computer service" providers (which include colleges and universities) from defamation liability and other liability based on the content of information posted by others. Section 230(c)(1) applies when a third-party "information content provider" has posted or otherwise transmitted information through a provider's service, and protects the provider from the liabilities that a "publisher or speaker" might incur in such circumstances (47 U.S.C. §§ 230(c)(1), (f)(2) & (3)).[48] As one court has explained:

> By its plain language, § 230 creates a federal immunity to any cause of action that would make service providers liable for information originating with a third-party user of the service. Specifically, § 230 precludes courts from entertaining claims that would place a computer service provider in a publisher's role. Thus, lawsuits seeking to hold a service provider liable for its exercise of a publisher's traditional editorial function—such as deciding whether to publish, withdraw, postpone or alter content—are barred [*Zeran v. America Online, Inc.,* 129 F.3d 327, 330 (4th Cir. 1997)].

The Section 230(c)(1) immunity apparently extends beyond state tort law claims to protect interactive computer service providers from other state and federal law claims that could be brought against publishers or speakers. For example, in *Noah v. AOL Time Warner, Inc.,* 261 F. Supp. 2d 532, 537–39 (E.D. Va. 2003), *affirmed* per curiam *in an unpublished opinion,* 2004 WL 602711 (4th Cir.), the court held that Section 230(c)(1) protected an Internet service provider from liability under a federal civil rights statute, Title II of the Civil Rights Act of 1964 (42 U.S.C. § 2000a(b)). In addition, Section 230(c)(2) protects service providers from civil liability for actions that they take "in good faith to restrict

---

[48]For case law, see Annot., "Liability of Internet Service Provider for Internet or E-Mail Defamation," 84 A.L.R.5th 169.

access to or availability of material" that they consider "to be obscene, lewd, lascivious, filthy, excessively violent, harassing, or otherwise objectionable . . ." (47 U.S.C. § 230(c)(2)(A); and see, for example, *Mainstream Loudoun v. Board of Trustees of Loudoun County Library*, 2 F. Supp. 2d 783 (E.D. Va. 1998)). Section 230 does not provide any immunity, however, from prosecution under federal criminal laws or from claims under intellectual property laws (47 U.S.C. §§ 230(e)(1) & (2)).

By its express language, Section 230 also protects "user(s)" of interactive computer services, such as persons operating Web sites or listservs on a provider's service. In *Batzel v. Smith*, 333 F.3d 1018 (9th Cir. 2003), for example, the court held that an operator of a listserv was a "user" who would be immune under Section 230(c)(1) from a defamation claim if another "information content provider" had provided the information to him and he reasonably believed that the material was provided for purposes of publication. Users are protected under Section 230 to the same extent as providers. Litigation continues, however, on the scope of the user provisions and the extent of the immunity that Section 230 provides for users and providers. (See, for example, *Barrett v. Rosenthal*, 9 Cal. Rptr. 3d 142 (Cal. App. 2004), *opinion superceded and review granted*, 87 P. 3d 797 (Cal. 2004).)

Regarding copyright law, the Digital Millennium Copyright Act (DMCA), discussed in Section 13.2.5 of this book, contains a provision, 17 U.S.C. § 512, that protects Internet "service provider(s)," including colleges and universities, from certain liability for copyright infringement. Specifically, the DMCA establishes "safe harbor" protections for Internet service providers against copyright infringement liability attributable to the postings of third-party users (including students and faculty members) in certain circumstances and under certain conditions (see §§ 512(a)–(d)). The safe harbor provisions also provide some protection for Internet service providers against liability to alleged infringers (including faculty members and students) for erroneously removing material that did not infringe a copyright (17 U.S.C. § 512(g)), and some protection against persons who file false copyright infringement claims (17 U.S.C. § 512(f)). In addition, the DMCA contains a provision that, under certain circumstances, specifically protects colleges and universities, as Internet service providers, from vicarious liability for the acts of their faculty members and graduate students (17 U.S.C. § 512(e)).

Individual students (and faculty members) also have some protections under the DMCA. If a student operates a Web site that is maintained on the institution's servers, he or she will have some protection against false copyright infringement claims (17 U.S.C. § 512(c)). In *Online Policy Group v. Diebold, Inc.*, 337 F. Supp. 2d 1195 (N.D. Cal. 2004), the plaintiff students sought monetary damages from the defendant, a copyright holder who had claimed that the students' posting violated its copyright. The university had removed the posting on the Web site after it had received the defendant's notice of an alleged copyright infringement. The court ruled in favor of the students and ordered the defendant to pay them money damages because "no reasonable copyright holder could have believed" that the postings in question "were protected by copyright."

Taken together, Section 230 of the CDA and Section 512 and related provisions of the DMCA provide some leeway for institutions to regulate and monitor their computer systems as their institutional missions and campus cultures may require, and also serve to encourage institutions to create alternatives to regulation as well as dispute-resolution processes (see subsection 8.5.1 above).

One further, emerging, area of liability concern for institutions involves disabled students. Under Section 504 of the Rehabilitation Act (see Section 13.5.4 of this book) and Titles II and III of the Americans With Disabilities Act (see Section 13.2.11 of this book), institutions could become liable for discriminating against disabled students with respect to access to computer communications, or for failing to provide disabled students with computer-based auxiliary aids or services that would be considered reasonable accommodations. (See generally Sections 8.7.3 & 9.3.5.4 of this book; and see also Constance Hawke & Anne Jannarone, "Emerging Issues in Web Accessibility: Implications for Higher Education," West's Educ. Law Reporter (March 14, 2002), 715–27.)

Sec. 8.6. Campus Security

8.6.1. Security officers. Crime is an unfortunate fact of life on many college campuses. Consequently, campus security and the role of security officers have become high-visibility issues. Although contemporary jurisprudence rejects the concept that colleges are responsible for the safety of students (see Section 3.3.2), institutions of higher education have, in some cases, been found liable for injury to students when the injury was foreseeable or when there was a history of criminal activity on campus.[49] Federal and state statutes, discussed in Section 8.6.3, also impose certain requirements on colleges and their staffs to notify students of danger and to work collaboratively with state and local law enforcement to prevent and respond to crime on campus.

The powers and responsibilities of campus security officers should be carefully delineated. Administrators must determine whether such officers should be permitted to carry weapons and under what conditions. They must determine the security officers' authority to investigate crime on campus or to investigate violations of student codes of conduct. Record-keeping practices also must be devised.[50] The relationship that security officers will have with local and state police must be cooperatively worked out with local and state police forces. Because campus security officers may play dual roles, partly enforcing public criminal laws and partly enforcing the institution's codes of conduct, administrators should carefully delineate the officers' relative responsibilities in each role.

---

[49]Cases and authorities are collected in Joel E. Smith, Annot., "Liability of University, College, or Other School for Failure to Protect Student From Crime," 1 A.L.R.4th 1099.

[50]For a general discussion of the legal restrictions on record keeping, see Sections 9.7.1 and 9.7.2. The Family Educational Rights and Privacy Act, discussed in Section 9.7.1, has a specific provision on law enforcement records (20 U.S.C. § 1232g(a)(4)(B)(ii)). Regulations implementing this provision are in 34 C.F.R. §§ 99.3 (definitions of "disciplinary action or proceeding" and "education records") and 99.8.

Administrators must also determine whether their campus security guards have, or should have, arrest powers under state or local law. For public institutions, state law may grant full arrest powers to certain campus security guards. In *People v. Wesley*, 365 N.Y.S.2d 593 (City Ct. Buffalo 1975), for instance, the court determined that security officers at a particular state campus were "peace officers" under the terms of Section 355(2)(m) of the New York Education Law. But a state law that grants such powers to campus police at a religiously controlled college was found unconstitutional as applied because its application violated the establishment clause (*State of North Carolina v. Pendleton*, 451 S.E.2d 274 (N.C. 1994)). For public institutions not subject to such statutes, and for private institutions, deputization under city or county law (see *People of the State of Michigan v. VanTubbergen*, 642 N.W.2d 368 (Mich. Ct. App. 2002)) or the use of "citizen's arrest" powers may be options (see *Hall v. Virginia*, 389 S.E.2d 921 (Va. Ct. App. 1990)).

If campus police have not specifically been granted arrest powers for off-campus law enforcement actions, the resulting arrests may not be lawful. Decisions from two state courts suggest that campus police authority may not extend beyond the borders of the campus if the alleged crime did not occur on campus. For example, in *Marshall v. State ex rel. Dept. of Transportation*, 941 P.2d 42 (Wyo. 1997), the Wyoming Supreme Court invalidated the suspension of the plaintiff's driver's license, stating that his arrest was unlawful and thus the license suspension was tainted as well. Marshall, the plaintiff, had been driving by (but not on) the campus, and a security officer employed by Sheridan College believed that Marshall was driving a stolen car. The security officer followed Marshall and pulled him over. Although Marshall was able to demonstrate that the car was not stolen, the security officer believed that Marshall was driving while intoxicated. Marshall refused to be tested for sobriety, and his license was suspended. Because this was not a situation where a campus police officer was pursuing a suspect, the court ruled that the campus police officer had no authority to stop or to arrest Marshall, and thus the license suspension was reversed.

Some states, however, have passed laws giving campus police at public colleges and universities powers similar to those of municipal police. See, for example, 71 Pa. Stat. § 646.1 (2003), which provides that campus police may "exercise the same powers as are now or may hereafter be exercised under authority of law or ordinance by the police of the municipalities wherein the college or university is located. . . ." This statute overrules two Pennsylvania cases, *Horton v. Commonwealth of Pennsylvania*, 694 A.2d 1 (Pa. Commw. 1997), and *Commonwealth of Pennsylvania v. Croushore*, 703 A.2d 546 (Pa. Super. 1997), in which state appellate courts had ruled that campus police had no authority to effect arrests beyond the borders of the campus. State laws vary considerably regarding the off-campus authority of campus police officers, and the particular facts of each incident may also have an effect on the court's determination. (For additional cases addressing this issue, see *People v. Smith*, 514 N.E.2d 1158 (Ill. App. Ct. 1987); and *Councill v. Commonwealth*, 560 S.E.2d 472 (Va. Ct. App. 2002).)

Police work is subject to a variety of constitutional restraints concerning such matters as investigations, arrests, and searches and seizures of persons or private property. Security officers for public institutions are subject to all these restraints. In private institutions, security officers who are operating in conjunction with local or state police forces (see Section 8.4.2) or who have arrest powers may also be subject to constitutional restraints under the state action doctrine (see Section 1.5.2). In devising the responsibilities of such officers, therefore, administrators should be sensitive to the constitutional requirements regarding police work.

Campus police or security guards responding to student protests and demonstrations must walk a fine line between protecting human and property interests and respecting students' constitutional rights of speech and assembly. In *Orin v. Barclay*, 272 F.3d 1207 (9th Cir. 2001), the federal appellate court rejected most of a student's constitutional challenges to limitations on a campus protest ordered by the dean and the campus security chief at a public community college, with the exception of the requirement that the protesters "not mention religion." The court ruled that the security officers had qualified immunity for their arrest of the plaintiff for trespassing, but that his claim of First Amendment violations for the prohibition of religious speech could proceed.

Administrators should also be sensitive to the tort law principles applicable to security work (see generally Sections 3.3.2 & 4.7.2). Like athletic activities (Section 10.4.9), campus security actions are likely to expose the institution to a substantial risk of tort liability. Using physical force or weapons, detaining or arresting persons, and entering or searching private property can all occasion tort liability if they are undertaken without justification or accomplished carelessly. Police or security officers employed by public colleges may be protected by qualified immunity if, at the time of the alleged tort by the officer, he or she reasonably believes in light of clearly established law that his or her conduct is lawful (*Saucier v. Katz*, 533 U.S. 194 (2001)). Private security officers who are not deputized and who do not have arrest powers, however, may not be protected by qualified immunity (*Richardson v. McKnight*, 521 U.S. 399 (1997)).

Jones v. Wittenberg University, 534 F.2d 1203 (6th Cir. 1976), for example, dealt with a university security guard who had fired a warning shot at a fleeing student. The shot pierced the student's chest and killed him. The guard and the university were held liable for the student's death, even though the guard did not intend to hit the student and may have had justification for firing a shot to frighten a fleeing suspect. The appellate court reasoned that the shooting could nevertheless constitute negligence "if it was done so carelessly as to result in foreseeable injury."

Institutions may also incur liability for malicious prosecution if an arrest or search is made in bad faith. In *Wright v. Schreffler*, 618 A.2d 412 (Pa. Super. Ct. 1992), a former college student's conviction for possession and delivery of marijuana was reversed because the court found that the defendant had been entrapped by campus police at Pennsylvania State University. The former student then sued the arresting officer for malicious prosecution, stating that the officer had no probable cause to arrest him, since the arrest was a result of the entrapment. The court agreed, and denied the officer's motion for dismissal. See also *Penn v. Harris,* 296 F.3d 573 (7th Cir. 2002) (no liability for malicious prosecution because the police had probable cause to arrest him for disorderly conduct).

Campus police may also be held liable under tort law for their treatment of individuals suspected of criminal activity. In *Hickey v. Zezulka,* 443 N.W.2d 180 (Mich. Ct. App. 1989), a university public safety officer had placed a Michigan State University student in a holding cell at the university's department of public safety. The officer had stopped the student for erratic driving, and a breathalyzer test had shown that the student had blood alcohol levels of between 0.15 and 0.16 percent. While in the holding cell, the student hanged himself by a noose made from his belt and socks that he connected to a bracket on a heating unit attached to the ceiling of the cell.

The student's estate brought separate negligence actions against the officer and the university, and both were found liable after trial. Although an intermediate appellate court upheld the trial verdict against both the university and the officer, the state's supreme court, in *Hickey v. Zezulka,* 487 N.W.2d 106 (Mich. 1992), reversed the finding of liability against the university, applying Michigan's sovereign immunity law. The court upheld the negligence verdict against the officer, however, noting that the officer had violated university policies about removing harmful objects from persons before placing them in holding cells and about checking on them periodically. The court characterized the officer's actions as "ministerial" rather than discretionary, which, under Michigan law, eliminated her governmental immunity defense.

In light of *Hickey,* universities with local holding cells should make sure that campus police regulations are clear about the proper procedures to be used, particularly in handling individuals who are impaired by alcohol and drugs, and should ensure that the procedures are followed to reduce both the potential for harm to individuals and liability to the institution or its employees.

In *Baughman v. State,* 45 Cal. Rptr. 2d 82 (Cal. App. 1995), university police were sued for invasion of privacy, emotional distress, and conversion pursuant to the destruction of computer disks during a search undertaken in connection with a lawfully issued warrant. The court found that the officers had acted within their official capacity, that they were therefore immune from damages resulting from the investigation, and that the investigation justified an invasion of privacy.

Overlapping jurisdiction and responsibilities may complicate the relationship between campus and local police. California has attempted to address this potential for overlap in a law, Section 67381 of the Education Code. This law, passed by the state legislature in 1998, requires the governing board of every public institution of higher education in the state to "adopt rules requiring each of their respective campuses to enter into written agreements with local law enforcement agencies that clarify operational responsibilities for investigations" of certain violent crimes that occur on campus (homicide, rape, robbery, and aggravated assault). These agreements are to designate which law enforcement agency will do the investigation of such crimes, and they must "delineate the specific geographical boundaries" of each agency's "operational responsibility."

8.6.2. Protecting students against violent crime. The extent of the
institution's obligation to protect students from crime on campus—particularly,
violent crimes committed by outsiders from the surrounding community—has
become a sensitive issue for higher education. The number of such crimes
reported, especially sexual attacks on women, has increased steadily over the
years. As a result, postsecondary institutions now face substantial tactical and
legal problems concerning the planning and operation of their campus security
systems, as well as a federal law requiring them to report campus crime
statistics.

Institutional liability may depend, in part, on where the attack took place and
whether the assailant was a student or an intruder. When students have
encountered violence in residence halls from intruders, the courts have found
a duty to protect the students similar to that of a landlord. For example, in
Mullins v. Pine Manor College, 449 N.E.2d 331 (Mass. 1983), the court approved
several legal theories for establishing institutional liability in residence hall security cases. The student in *Mullins* had been abducted from her dormitory room
and raped on the campus of Pine Manor College, a women's college located in
a suburban area. Although the college was located in a low-crime area and there
was relatively little crime on campus, the court nevertheless held the college
liable.

Developing its first theory, the court determined that residential colleges have
a general legal duty to exercise due care in providing campus security. The court
said that, because students living in campus residence halls cannot provide their
own security, the college's duty is to take reasonable steps "to ensure the safety
of its students" (449 N.E.2d at 335). Developing its second theory, the court
determined "that a duty voluntarily assumed must be performed with due care."
Quoting from Section 323 of the *Restatement (Second) of Torts,* a scholarly work
of the American Law Institute, the court held that when a college has taken
responsibility for security, it is "subject to liability . . . for physical harm resulting
from [the] failure to exercise reasonable care to perform [the] undertaking." An
institution may be held liable under this theory, however, only if the plaintiff can
establish that its "failure to exercise due care increased the risk of harm, or . . .
the harm is suffered because of the student's reliance on the undertaking."

Analyzing the facts of the case under these two broad theories, the appellate
court affirmed the trial court's judgment in favor of the student. The facts relevant to establishing the college's liability included the ease of scaling or opening
the gates that led to the dormitories, the small number of security guards on
night shift, the lack of a system for supervising the guards' performance of their
duties, and the lack of deadbolts or chains for dormitory room doors.

Courts have ruled in two cases that universities provided inadequate residence hall security and that lax security was the proximate cause of a rape in
one case and a death in a second. In *Miller v. State,* 478 N.Y.S.2d 829 (N.Y. App.
Div. 1984), a student was abducted from the laundry room of a residence hall
and taken through two unlocked doors to another residence hall where she was
raped. The court noted that the university was on notice that nonresidents
frequented the residence hall, and it criticized the university for failing to take

"the rather minimal security measure of keeping the dormitory doors locked when it had notice of the likelihood of criminal intrusions" (478 N.Y.S.2d at 833). "Notice" consisted of knowledge by university agents that nonresidents had been loitering in the lounge of the residence hall, and the occurrence of numerous robberies, burglaries, criminal trespass, and a rape. The court applied traditional landlord-tenant law and increased the trial court's damage award of $25,000 to $400,000.

In the second case, *Nieswand v. Cornell University*, 692 F. Supp. 1464 (N.D.N.Y. 1988), a federal trial court refused to grant summary judgment to Cornell University when it denied that its residence hall security was inadequate and thus the proximate cause of a student's death. A rejected suitor (not a student) had entered the residence hall without detection and shot the student and her roommate. The roommate's parents filed both tort and contract claims (see Sections 3.3 & 3.4 of this book) against the university. The court, citing *Miller*, ruled that whether or not the attack was foreseeable was a question of material fact, which would have to be determined by a jury. Furthermore, the representations made by Cornell in written documents, such as residence hall security policies and brochures, regarding the locking of doors and the presence of security personnel could have constituted an implied contract to provide appropriate security. Whether a contract existed and, if so, whether it was breached was again a matter for the jury.

In another case involving Cornell, the university was found not liable for an assault in a residence hall by an intruder. The intruder had scaled a two-story exterior metal grate and then kicked open the victim's door, which had been locked and dead-bolted. In *Vangeli v. Schneider*, 598 N.Y.S.2d 837 (N.Y. App. Div. 1993), the court ruled that Cornell had met its duty to provide "minimal security" as a landlord.

Even if the college provides residence hall security systems, courts have ruled that the institution has a duty to warn students living in the residence hall about the use of these systems and how to enhance their personal safety. In *Stanton v. University of Maine System*, 773 A.2d 1045 (Maine 2001), the Supreme Court of Maine vacated a lower court's award of summary judgment for the university, ruling that a sexual assault in a college residence hall room was foreseeable, and that the college should have instructed the student, a seventeen-year-old girl attending a preseason soccer program, on how to protect herself from potential assault. Citing *Mullins*, discussed above, the court ruled that the plaintiff's complaint raised sufficient issues of material fact to warrant a trial. The court rejected, however, the plaintiff's implied contract claim because no written or oral contract had been entered by the parties.

Institutions that take extra precautions with respect to instructing students about safety may limit their liability for assaults on students, as in *Murrell v. Mount St. Clare College*, 2001 U.S. Dist. LEXIS 21144 (S.D. Iowa, September 10, 2001). A second-year student was sexually assaulted by the guest of a fellow student whom she had allowed to spend the evening in her residence hall room. Earlier that day, the student asked the guests to leave, left her door unlocked, and prepared to take a shower. The guest entered the room and raped her. The court, in granting the college's motion for summary judgment, noted that the college had provided a working lock, which the plaintiff had not used, had provided the students with a security handbook with guidelines that, if ignored, could lead to fines, and had held a mandatory meeting at the beginning of the school year to discuss residence hall safety and to warn students against leaving doors unlocked or propped open.

An opinion of the Supreme Court of Nebraska linked a university's oversight of fraternal organizations with its duty as a landlord to find the institution liable for a student's injuries. Although *Knoll v. Board of Regents of the University of Nebraska*, 601 N.W.2d 757 (1999), ostensibly involves alleged institutional liability for fraternity hazing, the court rested its legal analysis, and its finding of duty, on the landowner's responsibility for foreseeable harm to invitees. The student, a nineteen-year-old pledge of Phi Gamma Delta fraternity, was abducted from a building on university property and taken to the fraternity house, which was not owned by the university. University policy, however, considered fraternity houses to be student housing units subject to the university's student code of conduct, which prohibited the use of alcoholic beverages and conduct that was dangerous to others. Knoll was forced to consume a large quantity of alcohol and then was handcuffed to a toilet pipe. He broke free of the handcuffs and attempted to escape through a third floor window, from which he fell and sustained serious injuries.

Knoll argued that, because he was abducted on university property, the university had a duty to protect him because the abduction was foreseeable. Although the university argued that the actions were not criminal, but merely "horseplay," the court stated that the actions need not be criminal in nature in order to create a duty. And although the university did not own the fraternity house or the land upon which it was built, the court noted that the code of conduct appeared to apply with equal force to all student housing units, irrespective of whether they were located on university property. Therefore, the university's knowledge of prior code violations and criminal misconduct by fraternity members was relevant to the determination of whether the university owed the plaintiff a duty.

Unforeseeable "pranks" or more serious acts by students or nonstudents do not typically result in institutional liability. For example, in *Rabel v. Illinois Wesleyan University*, 514 N.E.2d 552 (Ill. App. Ct. 1987), the court ruled that the university had no duty to protect a student against a "prank" by fellow students that involved her abduction from a residence hall, despite the fact that the assailant had violated the college's policy against underage drinking. (See also *L.W. v. Western Golf Association*, 712 N.E.2d 983 (Ind. 1999).) A similar result was reached in *Tanja H. v. Regents of the University of California*, 278 Cal. Rptr. 918 (Cal. Ct. App. 1991); the court stated that the university had no duty to supervise student parties in residence halls or to prevent underage consumption of alcohol. Even in *Eiseman v. State*, 518 N.Y.S.2d 608 (N.Y. 1987), the highest court of New York State refused to find that the university had a legal duty to screen applicants who were ex-convicts for violent tendencies before admitting them. (For analysis of this case, see D. M. Kobasic, E. R. Smith, & L. S. Barmore

Zucker, *"Eiseman v. State of New York:* The Duty of a College to Protect Its Students From Harm by Other Students Admitted Under Special Programs," 14 *J. Coll. & Univ. Law* 591 (1988).)

The difference in outcomes of these cases appears to rest on whether the particular harm that ensued was foreseeable. This was the rationale for the court's ruling in *Nero v. Kansas State University,* 861 P.2d 768 (Kan. 1993). In *Nero,* the Supreme Court of Kansas considered whether the university could be found negligent for permitting a student who had earlier been charged with sexual assault on campus to live in a coeducational residence hall, where he sexually assaulted the plaintiff, a fellow student. The court reversed a summary judgment for the university, declaring that a jury would have to determine whether the attack was foreseeable, given that, although the university knew that the student had been accused of the prior sexual assault, he not yet been convicted. If the jury found that the second assault was foreseeable, then it would address the issue of whether the university had breached a duty to take reasonable steps to prevent the second attack.

Foreseeability was again the issue in a pair of cases involving violent crimes against students in academic facilities. In *Jesik v. Maricopa County Community College District,* 611 P.2d 547 (Ariz. 1980), a student, during registration at the college, reported to a security guard employed by the college that, following an argument, another individual had threatened to kill him. The security guard took no steps to protect the student. About an hour after the report, the assailant returned to campus carrying a briefcase. The student pointed out the assailant to the same security guard, and the guard assured him that he would be protected. The guard then questioned the assailant, turned to walk away, and the assailant shot and killed the student.

The plaintiff, the father of the murdered student, sued the president and the individual members of the governing board of the community college district, the executive dean and dean of students at Phoenix College, the security guard (Hilton), and the community college district. The trial court summarily dismissed the case against all defendants except the security guard. The plaintiff appealed this dismissal to the Arizona Supreme Court, which first considered the potential liability of the officials and administrators. The plaintiff argued that "[the individual] defendants controlled an inadequate and incompetent security force [and thus should be] liable for any breach of duty by that security force." To establish the "duty" that had been breached, the plaintiff relied on a series of Arizona statutes that required the community college district's governing board, where necessary, to appoint security officers (Ariz. Rev. Stat. Ann. §§ 15-679(A)(3) and (9)); "to adopt rules and regulations for the maintenance of public order" (§ 13-1093); and to prevent "trespass upon the property of educational institutions [or] interference with its lawful use" (§ 13-1982). The court rejected this argument, finding that the statutes in question did not establish any specific standard of care but "only set forth a general duty to provide security to members of the public on school property."

Having discovered no specific legal duty chargeable to the individual defendants (excluding the security officer, whose potential liability the trial court had not rejected), the Arizona court next considered the liability of the community college district itself. Rejecting the plaintiff's request to adopt two liability principles from the *Restatement (Second) of Torts*,[51] the court found this principle controlling in Arizona:

> A public school district in Arizona is liable for negligence when it fails to exercise ordinary care under the circumstances. [Arizona cases have] established that students are invitees and that schools have a duty to make the premises reasonably safe for their use. If a dangerous condition exists, the invitee must show that the employees of the school knew of or created the condition at issue [611 P.2d at 550].

The court then determined that the *respondeat superior* doctrine applies to governmental defendants under Arizona law, so that the community college district could be held liable for the negligence of its employees. Therefore, if the plaintiff could show at trial that the district's security guard had breached the duty set out above, while acting within the scope of employment, the district would be liable (along with the employee) for the death of the plaintiff's son.

The *Jesik* court also discussed an Arizona statute (Ariz. Rev. Stat. Ann. § 15442(A)(16)) that imposes a standard of care on public school districts and community college districts (see 611 P.2d at 550 (original opinion) and 551 (supplemental opinion)). The court did not base its decision on this statute, since the statute was not yet in effect at the time the crime was committed. But the court's discussions provide a useful illustration of how state statutes may affect liability questions about campus security. In a later case, *Peterson v. San Francisco Community College District*, 205 Cal. Rptr. 842 (Cal. 1984), the court did rely on a statutory provision to impose liability on the defendant. The plaintiff was a student who had been assaulted while leaving the campus parking lot. Her assailant had concealed himself behind "unreasonably thick and untrimmed foliage and trees." Several other assaults had occurred at the same location and in the same manner. Community college officials had known of these assaults but did not publicize them. The court held that the plaintiff could recover damages under Section 835 of the California Tort Claims Act (Cal. Govt. Code § 810 *et seq.*), which provides that "a public entity is liable for injury caused by a dangerous condition of its property" if the dangerous condition was caused by a public employee acting in the scope of his employment or if the entity "had actual or constructive notice of the dangerous condition" and failed to correct it. The court concluded that the failure to trim the foliage or to warn students of the earlier assaults constituted the creation of such a dangerous condition.

If the crime victim has engaged in misconduct that could have contributed to the injury, at least in part, the institution may escape liability. In *Laura O. v. State*,

---

[51]Section 318 of the Restatement deals with the duty of a possessor of land to control the conduct of persons permitted to use the land. Section 344 deals with the duty of a possessor of land held open to the public for business purposes to protect members of the public from physical harm caused by third persons.

610 N.Y.S.2d 826 (N.Y. App. Div. 1994), the court held that a university in New York was not liable to a student who was raped in a campus music building after hours. She had been practicing the piano at a time when students were not allowed in the building. Although the student claimed that university officials knew that students used non-dormitory buildings after closing hours, the court stated that the university's security procedures were appropriate. Since the building was not a residence hall and the student was not a campus resident, the university did not owe the student a special duty of protection.

(For further analysis of institutional liability with regard to rapes that occur on campus, see R. Fossey & M. C. Smith, "Institutional Liability for Campus Rapes: The Emerging Law," 24 *J. Law & Educ.* 377 (1995).)

The cases in this Section illustrate a variety of campus security problems and a variety of legal theories for analyzing them. Each court's choice of theories depended on the common and statutory law of the particular jurisdiction and the specific factual setting of the case. The theories used in *Nero,* where the security problem occurred in campus housing and the institution's role was comparable to a landlord's, differ from the theories used in *Jesik,* where the security problems occurred elsewhere and the student was considered the institution's "invitee." Similarly, the first theory used in *Mullins,* establishing a standard of care specifically for postsecondary institutions, differs from theories in the other cases, which apply standards of care for landlords or landowners generally. Despite the differences, however, a common denominator can be extracted from these cases that can serve as a guideline for postsecondary administrators: when an institution has foreseen or ought to have foreseen that criminal activity will likely occur on campus, it must take reasonable, appropriate steps to safeguard its students and other persons whom it has expressly or implicitly invited onto its premises. In determining whether this duty has been met in a specific case, courts will consider the foreseeability of violent criminal activity on the particular campus, the student victim's own behavior, and the reasonableness and appropriateness of the institution's response to that particular threat.

8.6.3. Federal statutes and campus security. Following what appears to be an increase in violent crime on campus, the legislatures of several states and the U.S. Congress passed laws requiring colleges and universities to provide information on the numbers and types of crimes on and near campus. The federal legislation, known as the "Crime Awareness and Campus Security Act" (Title II of Pub. L. No. 101-542 (1990)), amends the Higher Education Act of 1965 (this book, Section 8.3.2) at 20 U.S.C. § 1092(f). The Campus Security Act, in turn, was amended by the Higher Education Amendments of 1992 (Pub. L. No. 102-325) and imposes requirements on colleges and universities for preventing, reporting, and investigating sex offenses that occur on campus. The Campus Security Act, passed in response to activism by parents of a student murdered in her college residence hall room and others with similar concerns, is also known as the "Clery Act," named after the young woman who was murdered.

The Campus Security Act, as amended by the Higher Education Amendments of 1992, requires colleges to report, on an annual basis,

> statistics concerning the occurrence on campus, during the most recent calendar year, and during the 2 preceding calendar years for which data are available, of the following criminal offenses reported to campus security authorities or local police agencies—
>   (i) criminal homicide;
>   (ii) sex offenses, forcible or nonforcible;
>   (iii) robbery;
>   (iv) aggravated assault;
>   (v) burglary;
>   (vi) motor vehicle theft;
>   (vii) arson;
>   (viii) arrests or persons referred for campus disciplinary action for liquor law violations, drug-related violations, and illegal weapons possession.

The law also requires colleges to develop and distribute to students, prospective students and their parents, and the Secretary of Education,

> (1) a statement of policy regarding—
>   (i) such institution's campus sexual assault programs, which shall be aimed at prevention of sex offenses; and
>   (ii) the procedures followed once a sex offense has occurred.

The law also requires colleges to include in their policy (1) educational programs to promote the awareness of rape and acquaintance rape, (2) sanctions that will follow a disciplinary board's determination that a sexual offense has occurred, (3) procedures students should follow if a sex offense occurs, and (4) procedures for on-campus disciplinary action in cases of alleged sexual assault.

The Campus Security Act also requires colleges to provide information on their policies regarding the reporting of other criminal actions and regarding campus security and campus law enforcement. They must also provide a description of the type and frequency of programs designed to inform students and employees about campus security.

In one of its most controversial provisions, the law defines "campus" as

> (i) any building or property owned or controlled by the institution of higher education within the same reasonably contiguous geographic area and used by the institution in direct support of, or related to its educational purposes; or
> (ii) any building or property owned or controlled by student organizations recognized by the institution.

The second part of the definition would, arguably, make fraternity and sorority houses part of the "campus," even if they are not owned by the college and are not on land owned by the college.

Regulations implementing the Campus Security Act appear at 34 C.F.R. § 668.46. These regulations require that crimes reported to counselors be included in the college's year-end report, but they do not require counselors to report crimes to the campus community at the time that they learn of them if the student victim requests that no report be made. The regulations require other college officials, however, to make timely reports to the campus community about crimes that could pose a threat to other students.

Colleges must report on their security policies and crime statistics annually, and must distribute these reports to all enrolled students and current employees, to prospective students upon request, to prospective employees upon request, and to the U.S. Department of Education. Additional information about reporting requirements and other provisions of the Campus Security Act can be found at http://ifap.ed.gov. Another helpful Web site is at http://www.securityoncampus.org/schools/cleryact.

In September 1996, the U.S. Department of Education issued its first charge against a college for violating the Campus Security Act. The department released a report citing Moorhead State University for violating the Act by compiling inaccurate crime statistics and not making annual crime reports public. The department did not impose any sanctions but threatened possible penalties if the university did not comply with the law within thirty days (Karla Haworth, "Education Department Finds a College Violated U.S. Crime-Reporting Law," *Chron. Higher Educ.*, September 27, 1996, A44). In 2000, the department levied a $25,000 fine against Mount St. Clare College (Iowa) for failing to comply with the reporting requirements of the Campus Security Act ("Education Dept. Fines College on Crime Law," *Chron. Higher Educ.*, July 14, 2000, A33).

Several states have promulgated laws requiring colleges and universities either to report campus crime statistics or to open their law enforcement logs to the public. For example, a Massachusetts law (Mass. Ann. Laws ch. 41 § 98F (1993)) has the following requirement:

> Each police department and each college or university to which officers have been appointed pursuant to the provisions of [state law] shall make, keep and maintain a daily log, written in a form that can be easily understood[, of] . . . all responses to valid complaints received [and] crimes reported. . . . All entries in said daily logs shall, unless otherwise provided by law, be public records available without charge to the public.

Pennsylvania law requires colleges to provide students and employees, as well as prospective students, with information about crime statistics and security measures on campus. It also requires colleges to report to the Pennsylvania State Police all crime statistics for a three-year period (24 Pa. Cons. Stat. Ann. § 2502 (1992)).

These federal and state requirements to give "timely warning" may be interpreted as creating a legal duty for colleges to warn students, staff, and others about persons on campus who have been accused of criminal behavior. If the college does not provide such a warning, its failure to do so could result in successful negligence claims against it in the event that a student or staff member is injured by someone who one or more administrators know has engaged in allegedly criminal behavior in the past. (For analysis of institutional liability and potential defenses, see Section 3.3.2.1.)

In 2000, Congress enacted the Campus Sex Crimes Prevention Act (CSCPA), Pub. L. 106-386, 114 Stat. 1464, which became effective on October 28, 2002. The CSCPA adds subsection (j) to the Jacob Wetterling Crimes Against Children and Sexually Violent Offender Registration Act, 42 U.S.C. § 14071, which requires individuals who have been convicted of criminal sexually violent offenses against minors, and who have been determined by a court to be "sexually violent predators," to register with law enforcement agencies. The CSCPA requires individuals subject to the Wetterling Act to provide the notice required in the statute if he or she is an employee, "carries on a vocation," or is a student at any institution of higher education in the state, as well as providing notice of any change in status. The law enforcement agency that receives the information then notifies the college or university. The CSCPA also amends the Campus Security Act at 20 U.S.C. § 1092(f)(1), requiring colleges to include in their annual security report a statement as to where information about registered sex offenders who are employees or students may be found (see 34 C.F.R. § 668.46 (b)(12)). It also amends FERPA (Section 9.7.1 of this book) to provide that FERPA does not prohibit the release of information about registered sex offenders on campus. Guidelines implementing the CSCPA may be found at 67 Fed. Reg. 10758 (2002).

Sec. 8.7. Other Support Services

8.7.1. Overview. In addition to financial aid services (Section 8.3), housing (Section 8.4), information technology services (Section 8.5), and security services (Section 8.6), institutions provide various other support services to students. Health services, auxiliary services for students with disabilities, services for foreign (international) students, child care services, and legal services are prominent examples that are discussed in this Section. Other examples include academic and career counseling services, placement services, resident life programming, entertainment and recreational services, parking, food services, and various other student convenience services (see generally Section 15.3.1). An institution may provide many of these services directly through its own staff members; other services may be performed by outside third parties under contract with the institution (see Sections 15.2.2 & 15.3.1) or by student groups subsidized by the institution (see Section 10.1.3). Funding may come from the institution's regular budget, from mandatory student fees, from revenues generated by charging for the service, from government or private grants, or from donated and earmarked funds. In all of these contexts, the provision of support services may give rise to a variety of legal issues concerning institutional authority and students' rights, as well as legal liability (see generally Section 2.1), some of which are illustrated in subsections 8.7.2 through 8.7.5 below.

8.7.2. Health services. Health services provided by colleges and universities continually expanded during the latter half of the twentieth century. There were many contributors to these developments—for example, an increased demand for mental health services; the need to respond to public health emergencies such as AIDS; the expanding presence of women on campus, which stimulated the need for women's health services; the expanding presence of students with disabilities having special health needs; increased emphasis on preventive medicine and wellness programs; the increased visibility of alcohol abuse, drug abuse, and other risky student behaviors with medical implications; and pressures in the nation's health care system leading to increasing numbers of students without health insurance or other means of access to health care. Paralleling the expansion (and the diversification) of campus health care services has been an expansion of the legal requirements applicable to student health services offices and practitioners.

Traditionally, the primary body of law applicable to health care providers was negligence law (see Sections 3.3.2 & 4.7.2.2 of this book, and especially Section 3.3.2.5 on student suicide), including malpractice (see Sections 4.7.2.2 & 12.5.5 of this book), along with state statutes and regulations regarding licensure of practitioners and facilities (see Section 12.5.5). Adding to that base, health services facilities and health care practitioners are now also subject to a variety of other bodies of law, including various laws prohibiting discrimination in access to campus health services (discussed below); occupational health and safety laws (see Section 4.6.1 of this book); environmental protection laws (see Section 13.2.10 of this book); various record-keeping laws, including FERPA (see Section 9.7.1 of this book), and also including HIPAA (Section 13.2.14) *if* the medical clinic also serves patients other than students and qualifies as a "covered provider"; and laws governing research (see Sections 12.5.5 & 13.2.3) for health services offices that participate in research projects. In addition, health services offices may be subject to the accreditation requirements of the Accreditation Association for Ambulatory Health Care (AAAHC).

The federal civil rights spending statutes (see Section 13.5 of this book) prohibit postsecondary institutions that are federal fund recipients from discriminating by race, national origin, sex, disability, or age in the provision of health services and benefits. The Title IX regulations, for example, provide that institutions must not exclude students from, or deny students the benefits of, health services on grounds of sex, and must not discriminate by sex in the provision of any "medical, hospital, accident, or life insurance benefit, service, policy, or plan to any of its students" (34 C.F.R. § 106.39). Likewise, the Title IX regulations prohibit discrimination in health services on the basis of pregnancy or childbirth, or, in some situations, on the basis of "parental, family, or marital status" (34 C.F.R. § 106.40). And the regulations for Section 504 of the Rehabilitation Act provide that institutions may not exclude disabled students from participation in health insurance programs or deny them the benefits of such programs (34 C.F.R. § 104.43), and that institutions must provide disabled students "an equal opportunity for participation in" health services and personal counseling services (34 C.F.R. § 104.37).

The numerous day-to-day applications of these civil rights statutes, and of the various other laws noted above, have seldom resulted in noteworthy litigation. Rather, the legal issues that have resulted in court battles and appellate court opinions, or have attracted the attention of Congress, usually involve special applications of these laws (for example, the Title IX sex discrimination law's application to abortion services, as discussed below), or the invocation of other laws (for example, federal antitrust law as in one of the cases below), or constitutional challenges to health services policies (as in several cases below).

Health services and health insurance involving birth control—that is, abortion, sterilization, or the distribution of contraceptive devices—provide a primary example of issues that have attracted Congress's attention and have also resulted in litigation. The problem may be compounded when the contested service is funded by a student activities fee or other mandatory fee. Students who oppose abortion on grounds of conscience, for instance, may object to the mandatory fees and the use of their own money to fund such services. The sparse law on this point suggests that such challenges will not often succeed. In *Erzinger v. Regents of the University of California,* 187 Cal. Rptr. 164 (Cal. Ct. App. 1982), for instance, students objected to the defendants' use of mandatory fees to provide abortion and pregnancy counseling through campus student health services. The court rejected the students' claim that such use infringed their free exercise of religion. (See generally Thomas Antonini, Note, "First Amendment Challenges to the Use of Mandatory Student Fees to Help Fund Student Abortions," 15 *J. Coll. & Univ. Law* 61 (1988).)

Similarly, in another case about birth control services, *Goehring v. Brophy,* 94 F.3d 1294 (9th Cir. 1996), the court relied in part on the *Erzinger* decision to uphold a University of California at Davis mandatory student registration fee used to subsidize a university health insurance program that covered the cost of abortion services. The university required that all its graduate and professional students have health insurance. Students could acquire this insurance through the Graduate Student Health Insurance Program, which provided a subsidy of $18.50 per insured student, per quarter, to reduce the cost of the premiums; funds generated by the mandatory student fees covered the cost of the subsidy. Students could opt out of this program by proving that they have health insurance from another provider. The plaintiffs claimed that the university's use of their mandatory fees to subsidize health insurance that covered abortion services violated their free exercise of religion. Their sincerely held religious beliefs, they argued, prevented them financially contributing in any way to abortion services.

In analyzing this claim, the appellate court looked to the Religious Freedom Restoration Act (RFRA), 42 U.S.C. § 2000bb. Although RFRA has since been invalidated by the U.S. Supreme Court (see Section 1.6.2), the *Goehring* court's reasoning would still be useful in free exercise cases under the First Amendment or state constitutions.[52] The court held that the plaintiffs had failed to

---

[52]A college or university's first line of defense against a free exercise claim, however, would usually be to argue that the student health insurance or health services requirements are "neutral" and "generally applicable" under *Employment Division, Dept. of Human Resources of Oregon v. Smith,* 494 U.S. 872 (1990) (Section 1.6.2 of this book), and thus subject only to minimal scrutiny by the courts.

"establish that the university's subsidized health insurance program imposes a substantial burden on a central tenet of their religion." Several factors were critical to the court's conclusion:

> The plaintiffs are not required to purchase the University's subsidized health insurance—undergraduate students are not required to have health insurance and graduate students may purchase insurance from any provider. Moreover, the student health insurance subsidy is not a substantial sum of money and the subsidy, taken from registration fees, is distributed only for those students who elect to purchase University insurance. Furthermore, the plaintiffs are not required to accept, participate in, or advocate in any manner for the provision of abortion services. Abortions are not provided on the University campus. Students who request abortion services are referred to outside providers [94 F.3d at 1299–1300].

The court also concluded that "even if the plaintiffs were able to satisfy the substantial burden requirement, the University's health insurance system nonetheless survives constitutional attack because it . . . is the least restrictive means of furthering a compelling government interest."[53] Three "compelling" university interests supported the health insurance program: (1) providing students with affordable health insurance that many would be unable to obtain if it was not available through the university; (2) helping prevent the spread of communicable disease among students who must eat, sleep, and study in close quarters; and (3) protecting students from the distractions of undiagnosed illnesses and unpaid medical bills that could interfere with their studies. Relying on cases that rejected free exercise challenges to the federal government's collection and expenditure of tax dollars, the court determined that exempting students from paying the portion of the mandatory fee that subsidized the insurance program would not be a viable alternative:

> [T]he fiscal vitality of the University's fee system would be undermined if the plaintiffs in the present case were exempted from paying a portion of their student registration fee on free exercise grounds. Mandatory uniform participation by every student is essential to the insurance system's survival. . . . [T]here are few, if any, governmental activities to which one person or another would not object [94 F.3d at 1301].

Other questions concerning campus abortion services have arisen under federal statutes and regulations. During Congress's consideration of the Civil Rights Restoration Act of 1987 (see Section 13.5.7.4 of this book), an issue arose concerning whether an institution's decision to exclude abortions from its campus medical services or its student health insurance coverage could be considered

---

[53]This is a classical strict scrutiny standard. Under the federal free exercise clause, this standard would not apply if the insurance program is "neutral" and "generally applicable" within the meaning of the *Employment Division v. Smith* case (see footnote 51 above, and see generally Section 1.6.2 of this book.)

sex discrimination under the Title IX regulations (see 34 C.F.R. §§ 106.39 & 106.40). Congress responded by including two "abortion neutrality" provisions in the 1987 Act: Section 3(a), which adds a new Section 909 (20 U.S.C. § 1688) to Title IX, and Section 8 (20 U.S.C. § 1688 note). Under these provisions, neither Title IX nor the Civil Rights Restoration Act may be construed (1) to require an institution to provide abortion services, (2) to prohibit an institution from providing abortion services, or (3) to permit an institution to penalize a person for seeking or receiving abortion services related to a legal abortion.

Another development concerning abortion services arose from the 1988 amendments to the Department of Health and Human Services' (HHS) regulations for Title X of the Public Health Service Act (42 U.S.C. §§ 300–300a-6), which provides federal funds for family planning clinics. These amendments (53 Fed. Reg. 2922 (February 2, 1988)), an initiative of the Reagan administration, prohibited fund recipients (some of whom were campus health clinics or university-affiliated hospitals) from providing counseling or referrals regarding abortion. In *Rust v. Sullivan,* 500 U.S. 173 (1991), the U.S. Supreme Court upheld these regulations, popularly known as the "Gag Rule," against a challenge that they violated the free speech rights of physicians and the privacy rights of pregnant women. After President Clinton took office, however, he directed the Secretary of HHS to suspend the regulations (58 Fed. Reg. 7455 (1993)) and initiate a new rule-making process aimed at reinstituting regulations similar to those in effect prior to the 1988 amendments. The regulations, subsequently adopted, and codified at 42 C.F.R. §§ 59.1–59.12, repeal the Gag Rule. Under these regulations, hospitals and health clinics operating a Title X funded family planning project may provide clients with information on pregnancy termination, upon request, if done in a neutral, nondirective manner and presented as an option along with prenatal care and delivery, infant care, foster care, and adoption. Project staff, however, may not perform abortions for project patients (42 C.F.R. § 59.5).

Other issues concerning health services and health insurance are illustrated by *Lee v. Life Insurance Co. of North America,* 23 F.3d 14 (1st Cir. 1994). Three University of Rhode Island (URI) students challenged a URI requirement that all undergraduate students pay a fixed fee for the use of the university's on-campus medical clinic, and that they also carry supplementary health insurance. Students had the option of obtaining the additional insurance from the Life Insurance Company of North America (LINA) or from another insurance provider, except that URI would not accept coverage by either Rhode Island Blue Cross or health maintenance organizations based in Rhode Island. Students who did not purchase supplementary coverage were billed for LINA coverage and were not permitted to register for the following semester until the LINA bill had been paid. The students claimed that URI's practice of conditioning matriculation on payment of the student health fee and the LINA insurance premium was an illegal "tying arrangement" under the Sherman Antitrust Act (see generally Section 13.2.8 of this book). They also claimed that the practice violated the Fourteenth Amendment's due process clause (because it infringed their right to select their own physicians) and equal protection clause (because the fee and premiums paid by male and female students were equal, despite the fact that male students did not use gynecological services).

The district court dismissed all of the students' claims, and the appellate court affirmed. Because URI lacked "appreciable economic power" in either the higher education "market" or the health care "market," the students could not claim that the university had created a monopoly. Despite the fact that, in some ways, an education at URI is "unique," said the court, the students had a wide selection of other colleges that would provide a similar type and quality of education. Furthermore, the students could transfer courses from URI to other colleges, and so had not been injured by the alleged tying arrangement should they decide not to return to URI. Because the students knew before they enrolled at URI that this policy existed, they could not use antitrust jurisprudence to argue that they were "locked in" to an economic situation that they did not desire. Moreover, since the students knew about the health clinic fee and health insurance requirement before they enrolled, there was no due process violation; and since the students could not demonstrate that the university had intended to burden male students in a discriminatory fashion, there was no equal protection violation.

Institutions with health services offices will find useful guidance in the American College Health Association (ACHA) publication, *Guidelines for a College Health Program* (1999) (for availability, see http://www.acha.org); in the "College Health Programs" section of the *CAS Professional Standards for Higher Education* issued by the Council for the Advancement of Standards in Higher Education (for availability, see http://www.cas.edu); and in the most recent edition of the *Accreditation Handbook for Ambulatory Health Care* published by the Accreditation Association for Ambulatory Health Care (AAAHC), available at http://www.aaahc.org.

8.7.3. Services for students with disabilities. When students need support services in order to remove practical impediments to their full participation in the institution's educational program, provocative questions arise concerning the extent of the institution's legal obligation to provide such services. Courts have considered such questions most frequently in the context of auxiliary aids for students with disabilities—for example, interpreter services for hearing-impaired students. *University of Texas v. Camenisch*, 451 U.S. 390 (1981), is an early, and highly publicized, case regarding this type of problem. A deaf graduate student at the University of Texas alleged that the university had violated Section 504 of the Rehabilitation Act of 1973 by refusing to provide him with sign-language interpreter services, which he claimed were necessary to the completion of his master's degree. The university had denied the plaintiff's request for such services on the grounds that he did not meet the university's established criteria for financial assistance to graduate students and should therefore pay for his own interpreter. The district court had issued a preliminary injunction ordering the university to provide the interpreter services, irrespective of the student's ability to pay for them, and the U.S. Court of Appeals affirmed the district court (616 F.2d 127 (5th Cir. 1980)). The U.S.

Supreme Court vacated the judgment in favor of the plaintiff, however, holding that the issue concerning the propriety of the preliminary injunction had become moot because the plaintiff had graduated. Thus, the *Camenisch* case did not furnish definitive answers to questions concerning institutional responsibilities to provide interpreter services and other auxiliary aids to disabled students. A regulation promulgated under Section 504 (34 C.F.R. § 104.44(d)) however, does obligate institutions to provide such services, and this obligation apparently is not negated by the student's ability to pay. But the courts have not ruled definitively on whether this regulation, so interpreted, is consistent with the Section 504 statute. That is the issue raised but not answered in *Camenisch.*

A related issue concerns the obligations of federally funded state vocational rehabilitation (VR) agencies to provide auxiliary services for eligible college students. The plaintiff in *Camenisch* argued that the Section 504 regulation (now § 104.44(d)) does not place undue financial burdens on the universities because "a variety of outside funding sources," including the VR agencies, "are available to aid universities" in fulfilling their obligation. This line of argument suggests two further questions: whether the state VR agencies are legally obligated to provide auxiliary services to disabled college students and, if so, whether their obligation diminishes the obligation of universities to pay the costs (see J. Orleans & M. A. Smith, "Who Should Provide Interpreters Under Section 504 of the Rehabilitation Act?" 9 *J. Coll. & Univ. Law* 177 (1982–83)).

Two cases decided shortly after *Camenisch* provide answers to these questions. In *Schornstein v. New Jersey Division of Vocational Rehabilitation Services,* 519 F. Supp. 773 (D.N.J. 1981), *affirmed,* 688 F.2d 824 (3d Cir. 1982), the court held that Title I of the Rehabilitation Act of 1973 (29 U.S.C. § 100 *et seq.*) requires state VR agencies to provide eligible college students with interpreter services they require to meet their vocational goals. In *Jones v. Illinois Department of Rehabilitation Services,* 504 F. Supp. 1244 (N.D. Ill. 1981), *affirmed,* 689 F.2d 724 (7th Cir. 1982), the court agreed that state VR agencies have this legal obligation. But it also held that colleges have a similar obligation under Section 104.44(d) and asked whose responsibility is primary. The court concluded that the state VR agencies have primary financial responsibility, thus diminishing universities' responsibility in situations in which the student is eligible for state VR services. There is a catch, however, in the application of these cases to the *Camenisch* problem. As the district court in *Schornstein* noted, state VR agencies may consider the financial need of disabled individuals in determining the extent to which the agency will pay the costs of rehabilitation services (see 34 C.F.R. § 361.47). Thus, if a VR agency employs a financial need test and finds that a particular disabled student does not meet it, the primary obligation would again fall on the university, and the issue raised in *Camenisch* would again predominate.

Disputes have continued, however, over whether state vocational rehabilitation agencies must pay for support services, as well as tuition and books, for disabled students. New York courts resolved two cases in which student clients of the state Office of Vocational and Educational Services for Individuals with Disabilities demanded that the agency pay their tuition and fees for law school. In *Murphy v. Office of Vocational and Educational Services for Individuals with*

Disabilities, 705 N.E.2d 1180 (N.Y. 1998), and in *Tourville v. Office of Vocational and Educational Services for Individuals with Disabilities*, 663 N.Y.S.2d 368 (N.Y. App. Div. 1997), the courts rejected the claims of students that, despite the fact that the agency had paid for their undergraduate education, it was legally bound to pay for their law school expenses as well. Although *Tourville* was decided on procedural grounds (the plaintiff had not entered an individualized written rehabilitation program (IWRP) plan with the agency), the *Murphy* court decided that the plaintiff had been prepared for the career that she agreed to in her IWRP, and the agency was not required to pay for additional education that was not contemplated by her plan.

In *Murdy v. Bureau of Blindness and Visual Services*, 677 A.2d 1280 (Pa. Commw. Ct. 1996), a blind student (Murdy) had entered an agreement with the bureau under which it agreed to pay for eight semesters of undergraduate education and to provide support services, assuming that Murdy maintained satisfactory academic progress. Murdy needed a ninth semester to complete his undergraduate degree, and the bureau refused to pay his tuition or to pay for support services. The court upheld the bureau's determination because it found that the student was aware that the bureau would cover only eight semesters, and the reasons that the student needed the ninth semester did not fit the agency's criteria for extending support beyond the standard time limit.

These cases suggest that, although state vocational rehabilitation or similar agencies may have the primary responsibility to provide funding for their student clients, colleges and universities will be asked to provide additional support services, or will be asked to provide more extensive services when a student's eligibility for state-funded services expires. State vocational rehabilitation agencies are attempting to shift the funding responsibility for student support services to colleges and universities, a trend that, if it continues, may dissuade colleges from recruiting students with disabilities. (For a discussion of the state agency–higher education conflict, see Jeffrey Selingo, "States and Colleges Wrangle over Paying for Services to Disabled Students," *Chron. Higher Educ.*, June 19, 1998, A37. For a discussion of the effects of this dispute on students, see Debra Hamilton, "Deaf College Students and Sign Language Costs: Why Postsecondary Education Must Confront the VR System," 28 *Coll. L. Dig.* 9 (April 16, 1998), 230–39.)

Public colleges and universities that have established offices serving students with disabilities may now be required to provide additional services to disabled students in compliance with the National Voter Registration Act (NVRA), known as the "motor voter law" (42 U.S.C. § 1973gg-5(a)(2)(B)). This law requires states to designate as voter registration agencies "all offices in the State that provide State-funded programs primarily engaged in providing services to persons with disabilities" (42 U.S.C. § 1973gg-5(a)(2)(B)). In *National Coalition for Students with Disabilities Education and Legal Defense Fund v. Gilmore*, 152 F.3d 283 (4th Cir. 1998), the National Coalition sued the state of Virginia under the NVRA after a student with disabilities had been rebuffed in her attempt to register to vote at the Office of Disability Support Services at George Mason University, a public college in Virginia.

The primary dispute between the parties concerned the meaning of the word "office" in the NVRA. The coalition argued that any subdivision of a government department providing services to individuals with disabilities was obligated to comply with the NVRA. The state responded that the NVRA only required a state to provide voter registration assistance at agencies created by the state legislature and funded by appropriations specifically earmarked for services to individuals with disabilities. The appellate court ruled that the plain meaning of the statutory language, the type of "offices" suggested by the statute as additional sites for providing voter registration services (public libraries, fishing and hunting license bureaus, unemployment compensation offices), and with the dictionary definition of "office," supported the coalition's position. Since the trial court record demonstrated that the offices providing services to students with disabilities at Virginia Polytechnic Institute and the University of Virginia were within this broader definition of "office," the appellate court held that they are subject to the NVRA. Since the record did not contain sufficient facts about the Office of Disability Support Services office at George Mason University, the court remanded this matter to the trial court to determine the sources, nature, and handling of funding for that office.

8.7.4. Services for international students.

International students, as noncitizens, have various needs that are typically not concerns for students who are U.S. citizens. Postsecondary institutions with significant numbers of foreign students face policy issues concerning the nature and extent of the services they will provide for foreign students, and the structures and staffing through which they will provide these services (for example, a network of foreign student advisers or an international services office). Simultaneously, institutions will face legal issues concerning their legal obligations regarding foreign students enrolled in their academic programs. This section focuses primarily on the status of foreign students under federal immigration laws—a critical matter that institutions must consider both in determining how they will assist foreign students and prospective students with their immigration status, and in fulfilling the reporting requirements and other legal requirements imposed on them by the laws and regulations. Other matters concerning employment of foreign nationals, which is pertinent when institutions provide part-time employment for international students, is addressed in Section 4.6.5. Matters concerning admissions and in-state tuition, primarily of interest to state institutions, are addressed in Sections 8.2.4.6 and 8.3.6 above. Matters concerning federal taxation of foreign nationals, and the institution's tax withholding obligations, are briefly addressed in Section 13.3.1.

The immigration status of international students has been of increasing concern to higher education as the proportion of applicants and students from foreign countries has grown. In 1980 there were approximately 312,000 nonresident alien students on American campuses. Over the decade this figure grew steadily, reaching 407,000 nonresident alien students in 1990 and 548,000 in 2000, at which time international students comprised approximately 3.5 percent of all students enrolled in U.S. colleges (*Digest of Education Statistics* (National

Center for Education Statistics, 2002), 483). This escalating growth slowed, however, after the federal government adopted new visa restrictions in the aftermath of the 9/11 tragedy, and by 2004 the numbers had declined more than 2 percent from the previous year (Burton Bollag, "Enrollment of Foreign Students Drops in U.S.," *Chron. Higher Educ.,* November 19, 2004, A1).

Foreign nationals may qualify for admission to the United States as students under one of three categories: bona fide academic students (8 U.S.C. § 1101(a)(15)(F)), students who plan to study at a vocational or "nonacademic" institution (8 U.S.C. § 1101(a)(15)(M)), or "exchange visitors" (8 U.S.C. § 1101(a)(15)(J)). In each category the statute provides that the "alien spouse and minor children" of the student may also qualify for admission "if accompanying him or following to join him."

The first of these three student categories is for aliens in the United States "temporarily and solely for the purpose of pursuing [a full] course of study . . . at an established college, university, seminary, conservatory, . . . or other academic institution or in a language training program" (8 U.S.C. § 1101(a)(15)(F)(i)). This category is called "F-1," and the included students are "F-1's." There is also a more recently created "F-3" subcategory for citizens of Canada and Mexico who live near the U.S. border and wish to commute to a U.S. institution for part-time study. The second of the three student categories is for aliens in the United States "temporarily and solely for the purpose of pursuing a full course of study at an established vocational or other recognized nonacademic institution (other than a language training program)" (8 U.S.C. § 1101(a)(15)(M)(i)). This category is called "M-1," and the included students are "M-1's." The spouses and children of students in these first two categories are called "F-2's" and "M-2's," respectively. The third of the student categories, exchange visitor, is known as the "J" category. It includes, among others, any alien (and the family of any alien) "who is a bona fide student, scholar, [or] trainee, . . . who is coming temporarily to the United States as a participant in a program designated by the Director of the United States Information Agency, for the purpose of . . . studying, observing, conducting research . . . or receiving training" (8 U.S.C. § 1101(a)(15)(J)). Exchange visitors who will attend medical school, and the institutions they will attend, are subject to additional requirements under 8 U.S.C. § 1182(j).

Visa holders in other nonimmigrant categories not based on student status may also be able to attend higher educational institutions during their stay in the United States. G-4 visa holders are one such example (see Section 8.3.6.1 of this book); H-1 visa holders (temporary workers) are another. The rules for these visa holders who become students may be different from those described below with respect to students on F-1, M-1, and J-1 visas.

The Department of State's role in regulating international students is shaped by its power to grant or deny visas to persons applying to enter the United States. Consular officials verify whether an applicant alien has met the requirements under one of the pertinent statutory categories and the corresponding requirements established by State Department regulations. The State Department's regulations for academic student visas and nonacademic or vocational student visas are in 22 C.F.R. § 41.61. Requirements for exchange visitor status are in 22 C.F.R. § 41.62.

The Department of Homeland Security's Bureau of Citizenship and Immigration Services (CIS) has authority to approve the schools that international students may attend and for which they may obtain visas from the State Department (8 C.F.R. § 214.3). The CIS is also responsible for ensuring that foreign students do not violate the conditions of their visas once they enter the United States. In particular, the CIS must determine that holders of F-1 and M-1 student visas are making satisfactory progress toward the degree or other academic objective they are pursuing. The regulations under which the CIS fulfills this responsibility are now located in 8 C.F.R. § 214.2(f) for academic students and 8 C.F.R. § 214.2(m) for vocational students.

The Department of Homeland Security's Bureau of Immigration and Custom Enforcement (ICE) operates the Student and Exchange Visitors Information System (SEVIS) that colleges must use to enter and update information on every student with a student or exchange visitor visa.[54] The SEVIS regulations, 8 C.F.R. Parts 103 and 214, require each college or university to have a "Designated School Official" (DSO) who is responsible for maintaining and updating the information on F-1, F-3, and M-1 students (8 C.F.R. § 214.3) and a "Responsible Officer" for J-1 (exchange visitor) students (8 C.F.R. § 214.2).

In order to obtain an F-1 visa, the student must demonstrate that he or she has an "unabandoned" residence outside the United States and will be entering the United States in order to enroll in a full-time program of study. The student must present a SEVIS Form I-20 issued in his or her own name by a school approved by the CIS for attendance by F-1 foreign students. The student must have documentary evidence of financial support in the amount indicated on the SEVIS Form I-20. And, for students seeking initial admission only, the student must attend the school specified in the student's visa.

The regulations specify the periods of time for which foreign students may be admitted into the country and the circumstances that will constitute a "full course of study." In addition, the regulations establish the ground rules for on-campus employment of foreign students, off-campus employment (much more restricted than on-campus employment), transfers to another school, temporary absences from the country, and extensions of stay beyond the period of initial admission.

Given the complexity of the immigration legislation and regulations, and the substantial consequences of noncompliance (including the real possibility that international students may be required to return to their home countries before they have completed their studies), there is no substitute for experienced, informed staff and for expert legal advice. Training for new staff and professional development programming for established staff are also critically important, as is information technology support sufficient to implement the SEVIS requirements and other reporting and record-keeping requirements.

---

[54]SEVIS is authorized by Section 641 of IIRIRA, 8 U.S.C. § 1372(a), as amended by Section 416 of the U.S.A. PATRIOT Act, 8 U.S.C. § 1227(a), and supplemented by the Enhanced Border Security and Visa Entry Reform Act, Section 501, 116 Stat. 543, 8 U.S.C. § 1701.

Helpful guidance on legal requirements is available on the Citizenship and Information Services Web site (http://www.uscis.gov) and the Immigration and Customs Enforcement Web site (http://www.ice.gov). In addition, the Association of International Educators maintains a Web site (http://nafsa.org) with much useful information, including the organization's *NAFSA Adviser's Manual of Federal Regulations Affecting Foreign Students and Scholars,* a comprehensive and frequently updated reference on federal requirements for students and visitors; and the NAFSA report on "Internationalizing the Campus 2003: Profiles of Success at Colleges and Universities," which will be helpful with broader strategies for international student services.

Due to SEVIS and the expanded reporting requirements for institutions, as well as the increased access of federal investigators to information concerning international students, their privacy has been a growing concern. While the Family Educational Rights and Privacy Act (FERPA) (Section 9.7.1 of this book) continues to protect the privacy of international students' student records, the federal government may now waive some FERPA requirements as needed to operate SEVIS (see Illegal Immigration Reform and Immigrant Responsibility Act (IIRIRA), § 641(c)(2), 8 U.S.C. § 1372 (c)(2)), and to fight terrorism (see USA PATRIOT Act, § 507, 20 U.S.C. § 1232g(j)). (For guidance on the interplay between FERPA and immigration statutes and regulations, see Laura W. Khatcheressian, "FERPA and the Immigration and Naturalization Service: A Guide for University Counsel on Federal Rules for Collecting, Maintaining and Releasing Information about Foreign Students," 29 *J. Coll. & Univ. Law* 457 (2003).)

8.7.5. Child care services. Child care is another context in which a court has addressed a claim for support services needed to overcome some practical impediment to education. In *De La Cruz v. Tormey,* 582 F.2d 45 (9th Cir. 1978), several low-income women brought suit challenging the lack of child care facilities on the campuses of the San Mateo Community College District. The plaintiffs alleged that the impact of the district's decision not to provide child care facilities fell overwhelmingly on women, effectively barring them from the benefits of higher education and thus denying them equal educational opportunity. The women claimed that the policy constituted sex discrimination in violation of the federal Constitution's equal protection clause and Title IX of the Education Amendments of 1972, 20 U.S.C. § 1681 *et seq.* The district court dismissed the case for failure to state any claim on which relief could be granted, and the plaintiffs appealed. The appellate court, reversing the district court, ruled that the complaint could not be summarily dismissed on the pleadings and remanded the case for a trial on the plaintiffs' allegations.

Although the district's policy did not rest on an explicit gender classification, the appellate court acknowledged that a facially neutral policy could still violate equal protection if it affected women disproportionately and was adopted or enforced with discriminatory intent. And while Title IX would similarly require proof of disproportionate impact, "a standard less stringent than intentional discrimination" may be appropriate when a court is considering a claim under that statute. Regarding disproportionate impact, the court explained:

> There can be little doubt that a discriminatory effect, as that term is properly understood and has been used by the Supreme Court, has been adequately alleged. The concrete human consequences flowing from the lack of sufficient child care facilities, very practical impediments to beneficial participation in the District's educational programs, are asserted to fall overwhelmingly upon women students and would-be students.
>
> [T]he essence of the plaintiffs' grievance is that the absence of child care facilities renders the *included* benefits less valuable and less available to women; in other words, that the effect of the District's child care policy is to render the entire "package" of its programs of lesser worth to women than to men. . . . Were the object of their challenge simply a refusal to initiate or support a program or course of particular interest and value to women—women's studies, for instance—the case might be a much easier one [582 F.2d at 53, 56–57].

After remand, the parties in *De La Cruz* agreed to an out-of-court settlement that provided for the establishment of child care centers on the defendant's campuses. A trial was never held. It is therefore still not known whether the novel claim raised in *De La Cruz,* or similar claims regarding discrimination regarding child care services, would be recognized by the courts. It is now clear, however, that a plaintiff must allege and prove discriminatory intent in order to prevail on any such claim in court, not only under the equal protection clause, but also under Title IX (see Sections 13.5.7.2 & 13.5.9 of this book). In contrast, in the administrative enforcement process, when relying on the Title IX regulations, proof of discriminatory intent may not be necessary to make out a showing of noncompliance (see Sections 13.5.7.2 & 13.5.8 of this book).

As with other services such as health care (subsection 8.7.2 above) and campus security (Section 8.6 above), the legal risks associated with providing child care are considerable. (For a checklist of matters to address to minimize legal risk, and a process for determining whether to contract out or "self-operate" child care services, see Goldstein, Kempner, Rush, & Bookman, *Contract Management or Self-Operation: A Decision-Making Guide for Higher Education* (Council of Higher Education Management Associations, 1993), 49–53).

8.7.6. Legal services. In the context of student legal services, the case of *Student Government Ass'n. v. Board of Trustees of the University of Massachusetts,* 868 F.2d 473 (1st Cir. 1989), illustrates complex questions concerning the provision of student legal services. The university had terminated its existing campus legal services office (LSO), which represented students in criminal matters and in suits against the university. Students challenged the termination as a violation of their First Amendment free speech rights. In order for students' access to legal services to be protected under the First Amendment, the legal services office must be considered a "public forum" (see Section 9.5.2) that provides a "channel of communication" between students and other persons (868 F.2d at 476). Here the students sought to communicate with two groups through the LSO: persons with whom they have disagreements, and the attorneys staffing the LSO. Since the court system, rather than the LSO itself, was the actual channel of communication with the first group, the only channel of communication the LSO provided was with the LSO attorneys in their official capacities. The court did not extend First Amendment public forum protection to this channel because the university was not *regulating* communication in the marketplace of ideas, but only determining whether to *subsidize* communication. Having only extended a subsidy to the LSO, the university could terminate this subsidy unless the plaintiffs could prove that the university was doing so for a reason that itself violated the First Amendment—for instance, to penalize students who had brought suits against the university, or to suppress the assertion (in legal proceedings) of ideas the university considered dangerous or offensive. The court determined that the termination was "nonselective," applying to all litigation rather than only to litigation that reflected a "particular viewpoint," and thus did not serve to penalize individual students or suppress particular ideas. The termination therefore did not violate the free speech clause of the First Amendment. (See Patricia Shearer, Jon A. Ward, & Mark A. Wattley, Comment, "*Student Government Association v. Board of Trustees of the University of Massachusetts*: Forum and Subsidy Analysis Applied to University Funding Decisions," 17 *J. Coll. & Univ. Law* 65 (1990).)

Since the appellate court's decision in the *University of Massachusetts* case, the U.S. Supreme Court has decided two cases that bear importantly on issues concerning student legal services at public institutions: *Rosenberger v. Rector and Visitors of University of Virginia,* 515 U.S. 819 (1995) (discussed in Sections 10.1.5 & 10.3.2 of this book), and more particularly, *Legal Services Corporation v. Velazquez,* 531 U.S. 533 (2001). Both cases support the application of First Amendment viewpoint discrimination principles to cases like the *University of Massachusetts* case. *Velazquez* specifically establishes that "advice from the attorney to the client and the advocacy by the attorney to the courts" is private speech protected by the First Amendment. *Velazquez* also illustrates how viewpoint discrimination principles would apply to cases in which a public institution has limited the types of problems or cases covered by a student legal services program, rather than terminating an entire program.

Selected Annotated Bibliography

General

"Joint Statement on Rights and Freedoms for Students," 52 *AAUP Bulletin* 365 (1967). A set of model guidelines for implementing students' rights on campus, drafted by the Association of American Colleges, the American Association of University Professors, the National Student Association, the National Association of Student Personnel Administrators, and the National Association of Women Deans and Counselors, and endorsed by a number of other professional organizations. (See discussion of the Joint Statement by William Van Alstyne in Grace W. Holmes (ed.), *Student Protest and the Law* (Institute of Continuing Legal Education, 1969), 181–86.) In the early 1990s, a larger group of associations affirmed the Joint Statement and updated it with a set of interpretive notes (see "Report: Joint Statement on Rights and Freedoms of Students," *Academe* (July–August 1993), 47).

Young, D. Parker, & Gehring, Donald D. *The College Student and the Courts* (College Administration Publications, 1973, and periodic supp.). Briefs and supporting comments on court cases concerning students, with new cases added in quarterly supplements.

Sec. 8.1 *(The Legal Status of Students)*

Beh, Hazel G. "Downsizing Higher Education and Derailing Student Educational Objectives: When Should Student Claims for Program Closures Succeed?" 33 *Ga. L. Rev.* 155 (1998). Discusses several theories of the student-institution relationship in the context of program and institution closure. Suggests that the implied-in-law contract theory is the most likely to balance the legitimate interests of both students and the institution when dealing with program closure.

Cherry, Robert L., Jr. "The College Catalog as a Contract," 21 *J. Law & Educ.* 1 (1992). A review of litigation regarding the contractual status of college catalogs. Discusses disclaimers, reservation of rights clauses, and other significant drafting issues.

LaTourette, Audrey Wolfson, & King, Robert D. "Judicial Intervention in the Student-University Relationship: Due Process and Contract Theories," 65 *U. Detroit L. Rev.* 199 (1988). Reviews constitutional and contract law disputes between students and colleges. Authors conclude that heightened judicial scrutiny of institutional due process has strengthened students' procedural rights, but that courts remain deferential to substantive academic judgments. Includes a comprehensive analysis of due process in academic and disciplinary decisions, as well as an overview of the application of contract law to student-institution relationships.

Meleaer, K. B., & Beckham, Joseph C. *Collegiate Consumerism: Contract Law and the Student-University Relationship* (College Administration Publications, 2003). Discusses a variety of contractual issues related to admission, grading, academic dismissal, and educational malpractice.

Olswang, Steven G., Cole, Elsa Kircher, & Wilson, James B. "Program Elimination, Financial Emergency, and Student Rights," 9 *J. Coll. & Univ. Law* 163 (1982–83). Analyzes one particular aspect of the contract relationship between institution and student: the obligations the institution may have to the student when the institution has slated an academic program for elimination.

See also, regarding sexual harassment, the Cole entry, the Cole & Hustoles entry, the Dziech & Hawkings entry, and the Sandler & Shoop entry in the Selected Annotated Bibliography for Chapter 5, Section 5.3; and the Fitzgerald entry and the Paludi entry in the Selected Annotated Bibliography for Chapter 6, Section 6.4.

Sec. 8.2 *(Admissions)*

Bowen, William, Kurzweil, Martin, & Tobin, Eugene. *Equity and Excellence in American Higher Education* (University of Virginia, 2005). Chapter 6, "Race in American Higher Education: The Future of Affirmative Action," addresses the role and effects of race-conscious admissions programs, the *Grutter* case and its aftermath, and suggestions for the future. Chapter 7, "Broadening the Quest for Equity at the Institutional Level," compares race preferences in admissions with other preferences now in use (for example, preferences for legacies) and advocates use in some circumstances of preferences based on low socioeconomic status.

Coleman, Arthur & Palmer, Scott. *Diversity in Higher Education: A Strategic Planning and Policy Manual Regarding Federal Law in Admission, Financial Aid, and Outreach* (2d ed., College Entrance Examination Board, 2004). This report, updated after the Supreme Court's decisions in *Grutter* and *Gratz,* distills the basic principles from these cases and applies them to race-conscious decision making in admissions, financial aid, and outreach programs. Also provides guidelines for institutional self-assessments in these areas and provides suggestions on the consideration of race-neutral alternatives.

Hurley, Brigid. Note, "Accommodating Learning Disabled Students in Higher Education: Schools' Legal Obligations Under Section 504 of the Rehabilitation Act," 32 *B.C. L. Rev.* 1051 (1991). Reviews statutory and regulatory provisions of Section 504 of the Rehabilitation Act of 1973, as well as judicial interpretations of Section 504 for higher education. Examines the reasonable accommodation requirement, the feasibility of the "undue financial burden" defense on behalf of the college, and the practice of "flagging" disabled students in institutional records.

Johnson, Alex M., Jr. "Bid Whist, Tonk and *United States v. Fordice:* Why Integrationism Fails African-Americans Again," 81 *Cal. L. Rev.* 1401 (1993). Criticizes the Supreme Court's *Fordice* opinion regarding the present effects of former *de jure* segregation in public colleges and universities, particularly the potential effect of the opinion on traditionally black colleges.

Justiz, Manuel J., Wilson, Reginald, & Bjork, Lars G. *Minorities in Higher Education* (ACE-Oryx, 1994). Includes nineteen articles written by higher education leaders, which discuss how minority enrollment can be increased, financial aid policies that encourage minority enrollment, the effect of new technology on minority students, achievement of minority students, racial/ethnic implications of assessing students, minorities in graduate education, and faculty diversity.

Leonard, James. "Judicial Deference to Academic Standards Under Section 504 of the Rehabilitation Act and Titles II and III of the Americans With Disabilities Act," 75 *Neb. L. Rev.* 27 (1996). Provides an overview of Section 504 of the Rehabilitation Act and Titles II and III of the ADA, analyzing judicial interpretations of the "otherwise qualified" requirement in the laws. Summarizes constitutional and common law principles used by courts when asked to review academic judgments, and examines the standards used by lower courts to evaluate student requests for program modifications. Concludes that deference to academic judgment is warranted.

Loewe, Eugene Y. (ed). *Promise and Dilemma: Perspectives on Racial Diversity and Higher Education* (Princeton University Press, 1999). Contains essays concerning minority student achievement and affirmative action policy by Randall Kennedy, Richard J. Light, L. Scott Miller, Mamphela Ramphele, Neil J. Smelser, Claude M. Steele, Chang-Lin Tien, and Philip Uri Treisman. The Steele essay on "stereotype threat" discusses research on the causes of the "test gap" between minority and nonminority students.

Loewy, Arnold. "Taking *Bakke* Seriously: Distinguishing Diversity from Affirmative Action in the Law School Admissions Process," 77 *N. Carolina L. Rev.* 1479 (1999). Argues that diversity and affirmative action are different concepts, and that diversity is broader than the racial or ethnic categories used for many campus affirmative action programs. Argues that decisions based on diversity rationales are sounder than those based upon affirmative action rationales.

Meers, Elizabeth, & Thro, William. *Race-Conscious Admissions and Financial Aid Programs* (National Association of College and University Attorneys, 2004). Reviews the U.S. Supreme Court's decisions in the *Grutter* and *Gratz* affirmative action cases, and analyzes the validity of race-conscious admissions and financial aid policies in light of principles from these two cases and other legal sources. Discusses enforcement of the limits on affirmative action through private lawsuits and through the Office of Civil Rights, U.S. Department of Education. Also contains guidelines and suggestions for institutions.

Mumper, Michael. "Higher Education in the Twenty-First Century: The Future of College Access: The Declining Role of Public Higher Education in Promoting Equal Opportunity," 585 *Annals Am. Acad. Pol. & Soc. Sci.* 97 (2003). Argues that higher education opportunity for low-income individuals has declined because of declining state support for higher education, increases in tuition, and federal student aid policies. Asserts that these trends are undermining the role of public higher education in promoting equal opportunity.

O'Neil, Robert M. "Preferential Admissions Revisited: Some Reflections on *DeFunis* and *Bakke*," 14 *J. Coll. & Univ. Law* 423 (1987). Presents an analysis of the state of the law after *DeFunis* and *Bakke*, and the first round of subsequent lower court cases, and includes perceptive reflections on the current and future prospects of race-preferential admissions policies. See also *Discriminating Against Discrimination: Preferential Admissions and the DeFunis Case* (Indiana University Press, 1976), a detailed examination of the *DeFunis* case and the continuing issues emerging from it. Author argues in favor of special admissions programs for minorities, considering and rejecting various nonracial alternatives in the process.

Sindler, Allan P. *Bakke, DeFunis, and Minority Admissions: The Quest for Equal Opportunity* (Longman, 1978). A thought-provoking analysis of the various issues raised by affirmative admissions policies. Traces the issues and their implications through the U.S. Supreme Court's pronouncement in *Bakke*.

Stokes, Jerome W. D., & Groves, Allen W. "Rescinding Offers of Admission When Prior Criminality Is Revealed," 105 *Educ. Law Rptr.* 855 (February 22, 1996). Reviews two high-profile cases in which institutions withdrew admission offers after applicants' prior criminal behavior was revealed. Discusses theories of potential liability if a fellow student is injured by a student who has committed violence in the past.

Sullivan, Kathleen M. "After Affirmative Action," 59 *Ohio St. L.J.* 1039 (1998). Examines the issue of class-based, rather than race-based, affirmative action and discusses how legal challenges to such programs might be defended. Concludes that race-neutral proxies for increasing racial diversity are constitutional.

"Symposium: *Regents of the University of California v. Bakke*," 67 *Cal. L. Rev.* 1 (1979). Contains articles, comments, and a book review on issues relating to *Bakke*. Lead articles, all by noted legal scholars, are Derrick A. Bell, Jr., "*Bakke*, Minority Admissions, and the Usual Price of Racial Remedies"; Vincent Blasi, "*Bakke* as Precedent: Does Mr. Justice Powell Have a Theory?"; Robert G. Dixon, Jr., "*Bakke*: A Constitutional Analysis"; R. Kent Greenawalt, "The Unresolved Problems of Reverse Discrimination"; Louis Henkin, "What of a Right to Practice a Profession?"; Robert M. O'Neil, "*Bakke* in Balance: Some Preliminary Thoughts"; and Richard A. Posner, "The *Bakke* Case and the Future of Affirmative Action."

Tribe, Lawrence. "Perspectives on *Bakke*: Equal Protection, Procedural Fairness, or Structured Justice?" 92 *Harvard L. Rev.* 864 (1978). A theoretical discussion of *Bakke*'s ramifications. Draws on broad themes of constitutional law of particular interest to lawyers.

Williams, Wendy M. (ed.). "Special Theme: Ranking Ourselves: Perspectives on Intelligence Testing, Affirmative Action, and Educational Policy," 6 *Psychol. Pub. Pol'y. & L.* 5 (2000). A special journal issue devoted to the relationship between intelligence testing and college admissions. Includes twenty-one articles from legal, psychometric, historical, economic, and sociological perspectives.

Sec. 8.3 (Financial Aid)

Butler, Blaine B., & Rigney, David P. *Managing Federal Student Aid Programs* (National Association of College and University Attorneys, 1993). An overview of the federal student aid programs. Discusses institutional eligibility for participation in these programs, federal oversight of institutional participation, and the audit process. A primer for attorneys unfamiliar with federal student aid programs and their complexity.

Douvanis, Gus. "Is There a Future for Race-Based Scholarships?" *Coll. Board Rev.*, no. 186 (Fall 1998), 18–23, 29. Recommends that institutions review their use of racial preferences in awarding financial aid. Reviews federal and state legislation, regulations, and litigation. Suggests ways that institutions may be able to justify continued use of race-based financial aid.

Fossey, Richard, & Bateman, Mark (eds.). *Condemning Students to Debt* (Teachers College Press, 1998). Examines the shift in federal policy from student grants to student loans, and the implications for lower- and middle-class students and their families. Warns that women and minorities are disadvantaged by this shift, and discusses the risk involved in accumulating large student loan debts.

Hoke, Julia R. *The Campus as Creditor: A Bankruptcy Primer for Administrators and Counsel* (National Association of College and University Attorneys, 2005). Reviews bankruptcies filed under Chapter 7 and Chapter 13, provides recommendations for dealing with student loan debtors who have filed bankruptcy, and provides guidance on the matter of withholding transcripts of students or former students who have defaulted on loans.

Jennings, Barbara M., & Olivas, Michael A. *Prepaying and Saving for College: Opportunities and Issues* (The College Board, 2000). Discusses the history of and later developments in state prepaid tuition plans. Raises issues of enhancing student choice, the implications of a financial downturn, and suggests the need for closer evaluation of the outcomes of these programs.

King, Jacqueline E. (ed.). *Financing a College Education: How It Works, How It's Changing* (ACE-Oryx, 1999). Includes essays on how families pay for college, how the federal needs analysis system works, the implications of student loan borrowing for undergraduates, student aid after tax reform, and the debate between merit- and need-based aid policies, among other topics.

McDaniel, Diane L., & Tanaka, Paul. *The Permissibility of Withholding Transcripts Under the Bankruptcy Law* (2d ed., National Association of College and University Attorneys, 1995). Discusses provisions of the bankruptcy law relevant to an institution's right to withhold a transcript during or following a bankruptcy action.

National Association of College and University Business Officers. *Student Loan Programs: Management and Collection* (2d ed., NACUBO, 1997). Discusses regulatory requirements regarding student loan programs, default standards, requirements for audits, and student loan consolidation issues. Includes sample forms, federal regulations, and a glossary of terms.

Olivas, Michael A. *"Plyler v. Doe, Toll v. Moreno,* and Postsecondary Admissions: Undocumented Adults and 'Enduring Disability,'" 15 *J. Coll. & Univ. Law* 19 (1986). Examines the impact of two important U.S. Supreme Court cases on the rights of undocumented aliens to attend and receive resident status at public higher education institutions. Proposes that the Court's treatment of undocumented alien elementary school students in Texas (in *Plyler v. Doe*) may be extended to other jurisdictions as well as to the higher education arena. Includes a table, with accompanying explanatory text, of the regulatory or policy-making entities that formulate higher education residency requirements in each of the states.

Olivas, Michael A. "Administering Intentions: Law, Theory, and Practice of Postsecondary Residency Requirements," 59 *J. Higher Educ.* 263 (1988). Traces the legal basis for resident and nonresident tuition charges through examination of the statutes, regulations, and administrative practices governing the fifty state systems and the District of Columbia. Explores seven types of alternative models for making residency determinations and sets out suggestions for reform. Includes four helpful tables organizing and summarizing data.

Roots, Roger. "The Student Loan Debt Crisis: A Lesson in Unintended Consequences," 29 *Sw. U. L. Rev.* 501 (2000). Analyzes federal student aid policy and describes its effect on student indebtedness. Argues that the availability of federal student loans have contributed to increases in college tuition.

St. John, Edward P. *Refinancing the College Dream: Access, Equal Opportunity, and Justice for Taxpayers* (Johns Hopkins University Press, 2003). Argues that changes in federal student aid policy have reduced higher education opportunity for low-income students, and that moderate changes to these policies could result in enhanced access without unduly burdening taxpayers.

Somers, Patricia, & Hollis, James M. "Student Loan Discharge Through Bankruptcy," 4 *Am. Bankr. Inst. L. Rev.* 457 (1996). Reviews the major issues raised in bankruptcy cases involving law and their implications for the discharge of student loans. Does not include changes to federal student loan programs resulting from the Higher Education Amendments of 1998.

Wellmann, Jane. *Accounting for State Student Aid: How State Policy and Student Aid Connect* (Institute for Higher Education Policy, December 2002). Available at http://www.ihep.org. Reviews student aid policy in eleven states; provides profiles of individual states complied from published and unpublished documents and interviews with state-level policy makers.

Williams, Rosemary E. *Bankruptcy Practice Handbook* (2d ed., Clark, Boardman, Callaghan, 1995). "Takes you through a sample case from initial contact and interview through conclusion under each chapter of the Code." Written for attorneys on both sides of a bankruptcy case. Includes forms, sample letters, and checklists as well as discussion of the roles of trustees, examiners, and attorneys representing creditors.

Woodcock, Raymond L. "Burden of Proof, Undue Hardships, and Other Arguments for the Student Debtor Under 11 U.S.C. § 523(a)(8)(B)," 24 *J. Coll. & Univ. Law* 377 (1998). Discusses theories that favor student debtors seeking discharge of federal student loans, reviews litigation in which courts have accepted or rejected these theories, and suggests approaches for courts and financial institutions that would support the social policy undergirding the federal student loan program.

See also Meers & Thro entry in Selected Annotated Bibliography for Section 8.2 above.

Sec. 8.4 (Student Housing)

Christman, Dana E. "Change and Continuity: A Historical Perspective of Campus Search and Seizure Issues," 2002 *BYU Educ. & L.J.* 141 (2002). Discusses constitutional issues related to residence hall searches, with particular emphasis on public institutions of higher education.

Delgado, Richard. "College Searches and Seizures: Students, Privacy and the Fourth Amendment," 26 *Hastings L.J.* 57 (1975). Discusses the legal issues involved in dormitory searches and analyzes the validity of the various legal theories used to justify such searches.

Gehring, Donald D. (ed.). *Administering College and University Housing: A Legal Perspective* (rev. ed., College Administration Publications, 1992). An overview of legal issues that can arise in the administration of campus housing. Written in layperson's language and directed to all staff involved with campus housing. Contains chapters by Gehring, Pavela, and others, covering the application of constitutional law, statutory and regulatory law, contract law, and tort law to the residence hall setting, and provides suggestions for legal planning. Includes an appendix with a "Checklist of Housing Legal Issues" for use in legal audits of housing programs.

Sec. 8.5 (Campus Computer Networks)

EDUCAUSE/Cornell Institute for Computer Policy and Law. Web site, available at http://www.educause.edu/icpl/, provides a collection of computer use policies from institutions throughout the country, information on computer policy development, and links to other sites on topics such as computer privacy, First Amendment issues, and service providers' liability. To access these materials, click on "library resources."

Kaplin, William, & Pavela, Gary. "Sexual Harassment and Cyberspace Speech on Campus," available at http://law.edu/Fac_Staff/KaplinW/rick.cfm, or at http://www.collegepubs.com/ref/sfxcsestdyricksrevenge.shtml. Contains a case study ("Rick's Revenge") on cyberspace sexual harassment effectuated by campus Web sites and e-mail, along with commentary on the case study and on recent cases delineating Title IX's applicability to sexual harassment. A fuller version of the case study, including a mediation exercise complete with role instructions, is available from the Center for Dispute Resolution at Willamette University College of Law.

Office of Information Technology, University of Maryland. "NEThics," available at http://www.inform.umd.edu/CompRes/NEThics/. Collects information—including suggestions, resources, and links to other sites—on law, policy, and ethics issues regarding computer use on campus.

O'Neil, Robert M. "The Internet in the College Community," 17 *N. Ill. U. L. Rev.* 191 (1997). Using three real-life case studies as a base, this article explores the application of First Amendment principles to cyberspace and, especially, to campus problems regarding the Internet. Takes the position that, in general, "[s]peech in cyberspace should be as free from government restraint as is the printed or spoken word."

Symposium, "Emerging Media Technology and the First Amendment," *104 Yale L.J.* 1613 (1994), provides various perspectives on the role of freedom of expression in the technological revolution. Contains a foreword by Owen Fiss, "In Search of a New Paradigm," followed by seven commentaries: (1) Jerry Berman & Daniel J.

Weitzner, "Abundance and User Control: Renewing the Democratic Heart of the First Amendment in the Age of Interactive Media"; (2) Anne Wells Branscomb, "Anonymity, Autonomy, and Accountability: Challenges to the First Amendment in Cyberspace"; (3) M. Ethan Katsh, "Rights, Camera, Action: Cyberspatial Settings and the First Amendment"; (4) Thomas G. Krattenmaker & L. A. Powe, Jr., "Converging First Amendment Principles for Converging Communications Media"; (5) Lawrence Lessig, "The Path of Cyberlaw"; (6) Cass R. Sunstein, "The First Amendment in Cyberspace"; and (7) Eugene Volokh, "Cheap Speech and What It Will Do."

Sermersheim, Michael. *Computer Access: Selected Legal Issues Affecting Colleges and Universities* (2d ed., National Association of College and University Attorneys, 2003). A monograph addressing issues regarding students' and faculty members' access to computers and the Internet. Provides suggestions and guidelines for institutions developing or revising computer access policies. Also includes discussion of the USA PATRIOT Act's impact on computer access.

Sec. 8.6 *(Campus Security)*

Burling, Philip. *Crime on Campus: Analyzing and Managing the Increasing Risk of Institutional Liability* (2d ed., National Association of College and University Attorneys, 2003). Discusses theories of legal liability when crime occurs on campus, discusses legislation requiring colleges to report crime statistics and other information, and suggests steps that institutions can take to reduce the impact of crime on campus. Discusses event management, campus disciplinary procedures that involve violations of both the student code of conduct and criminal law.

Fisher, Bonnie S., Hartman, Jennifer L., Cullen, Francis T., & Turner, Michael G. "Making Campuses Safer for Students: The Clery Act as a Symbolic Legal Reform," 32 *Stetson L. Rev.* 61 (2002). Reviews the history of the Clery Act and assesses whether it has met its goal of providing accurate information on campus crime. Concludes that the achievements of the Clery Act have been more symbolic than substantive.

Giles, Molly. Comment, "Obscuring the Issue: The inappropriate Application of in *loco parentis* to the Campus Crime Victim Duty Question," 39 *Wayne L. Rev.* 1335 (1993). Reviews the propensity for crime victims and/or their parents to attempt to hold the university liable for the acts of third parties of the negligence of the students themselves.

Gregory, Dennis E., & Janosik, Steven M. "The Clery Act: How Effective Is It? Perceptions from the Field—The Current State of the Research and Recommendations for Improvement," 32 *Stetson L. Rev.* 7 (2002). Reviews media and scholarly commentary on the effectiveness of the Clery Act and its contribution to reducing crime on campus. Provides recommendations for increasing safety on campuses.

Jacobson, Jeffrey S. *Campus Police Authority: Understanding Your Officers' Territorial Jurisdiction* (National Association of College and University Attorneys, 2006). Discusses variations in state laws regarding the authority of campus police to effect off-campus arrests or other police actions. Provides suggestions for expanding campus officers' territorial authority and for minimizing institutional liability for officers' actions. Includes court cases and links to state statutes.

National Association of College and University Business Officers. *Campus Crime Reporting: A Guide to Clery Act Compliance* (ACE-NACUBO Advisory Report

2002-02). Reviews requirements of the federal laws requiring that campus crime statistics be reported to all enrolled students and current employees, as well as to the U.S. Department of Education. Includes definitions of terms. Forms, helpful Web pages, and other resources are included.

Smith, Michael Clay. *Crime and Campus Police: A Handbook for Campus Police Officers and Administrators* (College Administration Publications, 1989). Discusses risk management, the proper procedure for searches and seizures and arrests on campus, campus judicial procedures, frequent problems encountered by campus police and administrators, white-collar crime on campus, and alcohol issues.

Smith, Michael Clay, & Fossey, Richard. *Crime on Campus: Legal Issues and Campus Administration* (ACE-Oryx, 1995). Includes discussion of college liability issues, response to crimes, buildings and crime, and strategies for coping with alcohol abuse on campus. Provides suggestions for complying with the Student Right-to-Know and Campus Security Acts.

Sec. 8.7 (Other Support Services)

National Association of College and University Business Officers. *Child Care Services: A Guide for Colleges and Universities* (NACUBO, 1993). A monograph providing advice to administrators on establishing and operating child care programs for the benefit of students and others. Includes discussion of licensing and accreditation.

See Hurley entry in Selected Annotated Bibliography for Section 8.2.